Oracle Press™

Oracle JDeveloper 11*g* Handbook

A Guide to Oracle Fusion Web Development

About the Authors

Duncan Mills is senior director of product management for Oracle's Application Development Tools, including Oracle JDeveloper, Oracle Enterprise Pack for Eclipse, Forms, and the ADF Framework. Duncan is currently responsible for product direction, evangelism, and courseware development around the development tools products. He has been working with Oracle in a variety of application development and DBA roles since 1988. For the past fourteen years he has been working at Oracle in both support and product development, spending the last eight years in product management. Duncan is the co-author of the Oracle Press book *Oracle JDeveloper 10*g *for Forms and PL/SQL Developers: A Guide to Web Development with Oracle ADF* (McGraw-Hill Professional, 2006).

For nearly three decades, Oracle, the world's largest enterprise software company, has provided the software and services that enable organizations to get the most up-to-date and accurate information from their business systems. With over 275,000 customers—including 98 of the Fortune 100—Oracle supports customers in more than 145 countries. For more information about Oracle, visit www.oracle.com.

Peter Koletzke is a technical director and principal instructor for the Enterprise e-Commerce Solutions practice at Quovera, in Mountain View, California, and has worked in the database industry since 1984. Peter has presented at various Oracle users group conferences more than 250 times and has won awards such as Pinnacle Publishing's Technical Achievement, Oracle Development Tools Users Group (ODTUG) Editor's Choice (twice), ODTUG Best Speaker, ECO/SEOUC Oracle Designer Award, the ODTUG Volunteer of the Year, and NYOUG Editor's Choice (twice). He is an Oracle ACE Director and an Oracle Certified Master. Peter has co-authored seven other Oracle Press books (variously with Dr. Paul Dorsey, Avrom, and Duncan) about Oracle JDeveloper, Oracle Forms and Reports, and Oracle Designer.

Quovera (www.quovera.com) is a business consulting and technology integration firm that specializes in delivering solutions to the high technology, telecommunications, semiconductor, manufacturing, software and services, public sector, and financial services industries. Quovera deploys solutions that deliver optimized business processes quickly and economically, driving increased productivity and improved operational efficiency. Founded in 1995, the company has a track record of delivering hundreds of strategy, design, and implementation projects to over 250 Fortune 2000 and high-growth middle market companies. Quovera's client list includes notable organizations such as Cisco Systems, ON Semiconductor, New York State, Sun Microsystems, Lawrence Livermore National Laboratory, Seagate, Toyota, Fujitsu, Visa, and Cendant.

Avrom Roy-Faderman works for Quovera as a Java EE consultant, architect, developer, and instructor, specializing in the Oracle Application Development Framework, as well as an Oracle ACE Director. He is a Sun Certified Programmer for the Java Platform and has acted as lead developer on diverse application projects ranging from e-business and online order systems to health-care provisioning for governmental and private organizations. He's also a regular speaker at Oracle user group conferences and is the co-author, with Paul Dorsey and Peter Koletzke, of two books: the *Oracle9*i *JDeveloper Handbook and the Oracle JDeveloper 10*g *Handbook*, both from McGraw-Hill and Oracle Press.

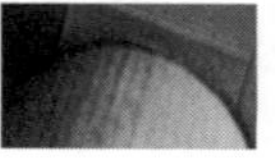

NOTE

Sample code for the hands-on practices in this book as well as errata are available from the websites mentioned in the Introduction's section "Websites for Sample Files."

Oracle JDeveloper 11*g* Handbook

A Guide to Oracle Fusion Web Development

Duncan Mills
Peter Koletzke
Avrom Roy-Faderman

New York Chicago San Francisco
Lisbon London Madrid Mexico City Milan
New Delhi San Juan Seoul Singapore Sydney Toronto

The McGraw-Hill Companies

Library of Congress Cataloging-in-Publication Data

Mills, Duncan.
Oracle JDeveloper 11g handbook : a guide to Oracle fusion web development / Duncan Mills, Peter Koletzke, Avrom Roy-Faderman.
p. cm.
Includes bibliographical references and index.
ISBN 978-0-07-160238-9 (alk. paper)
1. Internet programming. 2. Oracle JDeveloper. 3. Web sites—Design.
I. Koletzke, Peter. II. Faderman, Avrom. III. Title.
QA76.625.M55 2010
006.7—dc22 2009034497

McGraw-Hill books are available at special quantity discounts to use as premiums and sales promotions, or for use in corporate training programs. To contact a representative, please e-mail us at bulksales@mcgraw-hill.com.

Oracle JDeveloper 11*g* Handbook: A Guide to Oracle Fusion Web Development

1234567890 DOC DOC 019

ISBN 978-0-07-160238-9
MHID 0-07-160238-0

Sponsoring Editor
Lisa McClain

Editorial Supervisor
Janet Walden

Project Manager
Smita Rajan, Glyph International

Acquisitions Coordinator
Meghan Riley

Technical Editors
Ann Horton
Eric Marcoux

Technical Reviewers
Rich Bruno
Patrice Daux
Susan Duncan
Kate Heap
Pam Gamer
Jeff Gallus
Steve Muench
Lynn Munsinger
Frank Nimphius
Shaun O'Brien
Blaise Ribet
Grant Ronald
Dave Schneider

Technical Review Coordinator
Glen Maslen

Copy Editor
Bob Campbell

Proofreader
Christine Andreasen

Indexer
Jack Lewis

Production Supervisor
Jean Bodeaux

Composition
Glyph International

Illustration
Glyph International

Art Director, Cover
Jeff Weeks

Cover Designer
Pattie Lee

For Amanda, Josh, Sam, and Hissy.
—Duncan Mills

For my folks, Jan and Max.
—Peter Koletzke

For Nilakash, a sudden blue sky on a rainy day.
—Avrom Roy-Faderman

Contents at a Glance

PART IV
ADF Model

PART V
Developing the Sample Application

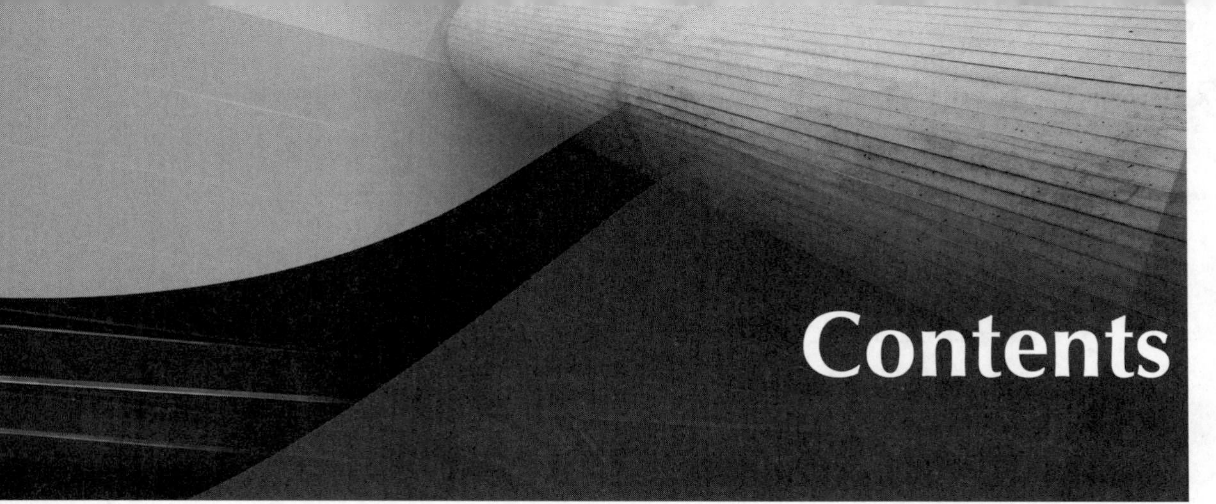

Contents

PART III
ADF View and Controller

PART IV
ADF Model

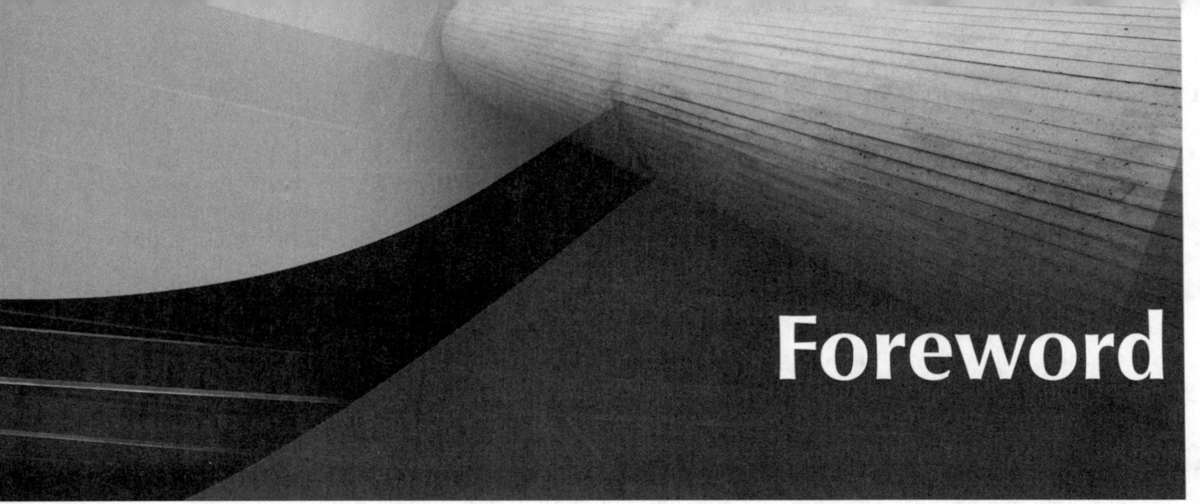

Foreword

I have worked as the architect in the tools group at Oracle for the past seven years, with the last three of those years also spent leading the development team. In all that time, we have been driving toward a single vision. Our goal is to create a tightly integrated, highly productive environment for a diverse set of developers building Java-, Java EE–, and SOA-based applications. I think what we have delivered with JDeveloper and ADF 11*g* is the realization of that vision.

As we have been working on building JDeveloper and ADF 11*g* over the past few years, the rest of the company was getting behind us as well. JDeveloper and ADF 11*g* are not only a best-of-breed development environment and runtime to build your custom applications, but they are also the basis for all of the new products coming out of Oracle. Oracle WebCenter 11*g*, Oracle SOA Suite 11*g*, and the next-generation Fusion packaged applications are all built using the ADF technology using JDeveloper.

What this means is that the contents of this book will not only get you productive and up to speed on building custom Java and J2EE applications using JDeveloper and ADF, but they will also provide you the necessary skills to build applications with Oracle WebCenter and Oracle SOA Suite 11*g*, as well as customize and extend Fusion packaged applications. When considering the vast market of Oracle middleware and packaged applications customers, there is a lot of opportunity for anyone with this skillset.

When thinking about a group of people qualified to write a book on this subject, I can't think of a better balanced team than Duncan, Peter, and Avrom. Duncan has been with Oracle since well before our shift to Java technology and has been a key contributor in helping us build a tool and framework that appeal to developers from a wide variety of backgrounds. Duncan and his product management team have been on the front lines with customers helping them adopt the 11*g* technology for the past two years.

Complementing Duncan's internal perspective is Peter, who works as an external consultant in the market. Peter has written four previous books on JDeveloper and is a long-time guru and presenter on the topic. He is widely known as an expert on the Oracle tools and offers a wealth of information and experience from the view of a customer.

Rounding things off is Avrom. Avrom was previously a documentation writer in the JDeveloper team at Oracle, and one of the most hands-on doc writers I have worked with. Avrom is able to get deep into the technology, and then use his skills as a writer to clearly articulate to the reader on how things work.

We are very proud of the Oracle JDeveloper and ADF 11*g* release and are eager for more and more people to get their hands on it and try it out. Whether you are coming from a background of Java, Oracle Forms, PeopleTools, C/C++, or the scripting world, I think you will find this book and the technology it describes very approachable and powerful in helping you build applications.

—Ted Farrell
Chief Architect & SVP, Tools & Middleware
Oracle Corporation

Acknowledgments

Books are magical and powerful things. There is something about the handling of the medium and the absoluteness of that old business card or ticket stub that you use as a bookmark that defines your progress and understanding of the subject matter. Although we all have so much information at our fingertips through online documentation and the ubiquitous Google, the presence of a well-constructed and linear source of data in the form of a thick wodge of paper adds some undefined quality to the learning process of any technical subject.

When Peter and I collaborated on our last book back in 2006, we created, I think, a unique resource for the Oracle Development community, and certainly everyone we ever spoke to echoed that sentiment. But times move on, technology changes, and like some kind of primeval migration instinct, the urge to write arose again and here we are. Much has changed in that time, and much has remained the same. I still work for Oracle, although my role and circumstances changed considerably as I uprooted my family five and a half thousand miles from ancient Winchester in England to California. In the course of all this upheaval, I also took on much more management responsibility for the product management and curriculum development teams within the Oracle Tools division. None of which is actually very conducive to freeing up time for writing, but there you go.

So why do it? Frankly, strange as it may sound, I find this stuff just too exciting. I've been working with database development tools and Java frameworks for many, many years, and I have to say that JDeveloper 11*g* and the Application Development Framework have reached a level of maturity and functionality that just blows me away. Already, when I look at the business applications that both Oracle and its customers are creating with the Fusion tools, I see something that sets a standard that the rest of the industry is going to have a hard job catching up with. I just want to rush out and physically shake developers out of their love affair with the 1990s. So this book is, I suppose, a more polite way of doing that.

For this book Peter and I are joined by Avrom, a long-time colleague of us both over the years and a hugely valuable addition to the team. Avrom brings a wealth of technical knowledge and possibly more important, practical experience of applying it. One of the roles of the technical book writer is to be an advocate on the readers' behalf and to ask the questions that you've not thought of yet, and keep asking them until they get the answer. In this respect Avrom is tenacious, a veritable Canadian Mountie of the technical whys and hows. This book is so much the better for that.

Peter, as my partner in crime for the last book, and so many joint technical presentations over the years, gets the less dashing comparison with epoxy. If you want to thank any one person for actually getting the book done and holding us together as a team, then Peter's your man. He's organized and herded us through the process, always riding the deadlines and managing the unglamorous tasks of styling and page count. All of this, and still one of the best people I know at expressing deeply technical subjects in a totally accessible manner.

In an attempt to spread the blame I'll say that a book is only as good as its reviewers, but of course we've had a fantastic review and editing team for the *Handbook*. Ann Horton took on the monumental task of technical editor at short notice and has done so well. All of these chapter reviewers have donated their own time to make this the book it is: (in no particular order) Dave Schneider, Eric Marcoux, Lynn Munsinger, Frank Nimphius, Shaun O'Brien, Grant Ronald, Blaise Ribet. And a special mention must go to Glenn Maslen, who managed the review process for us, and to the review "Dream Team" of Pam Gamer, Kate Heap, and Patrice Daux, who did such a great job of reviewing Part V of the book in particular—a daunting task with preproduction software. Steve Muench, the godfather of ADF Business Components, deserves a big thanks for his help with the sample application where he helped us out of some sticky situations with advice and much patience.

Thanks to all at Oracle Press, Lisa McClain in particular, who patiently steered us through the whole process yet again and whose understanding of the realities of writing against preproduction software has been invaluable.

Of course, every book needs a good foreword, and I have to thank Ted Farrell, my boss and the real moving force behind JDeveloper and ADF, for his contribution, vision, and patience over the last two years or so.

The last word has to be for my family: Amanda, my perfect and understanding wife (did I mention that she is perfect?), Josh and Sam, who gave me the excuse for many hours of writing whilst sitting in the corner at Golden State Taekwondo in San Carlos—somewhat different from the traditional coffee shop writing environment, believe me!—and finally, of course, little Zoë, who kept me company for so many of those early morning writing sessions. Without all of their support this simply would not have happened. Guys, I owe you one.

—Duncan Mills
Foster City, CA, USA
October 2009

If you compare our signature lines in this acknowledgments section and know our area or do some quick digging, you'll find that the California communities in which we authors live form a small triangle, in the center of which is Redwood Shores, the location of Oracle HQ. It would have been nice if this serendipity of geographic proximity had somehow made the collaborative process required for a multi-author book such as this much quicker and easier than any of the other seven Oracle Press books, which I've co-authored variously with Duncan and Avrom and also with Dr. Paul Dorsey (who, although he was originally signed up for this book, had to bow out early in the process due to work pressures). However, due to a long product incubation slowed somewhat by various corporate acquisitions "relatively quick and easy" did not happen this time.

Throughout that long (and sometimes hard) process, we had many contributors to this rather large volume without whom you would not be reading this and whom, therefore, I'd like to thank. First, I'd like to extend my great appreciation to my co-authors, Duncan and Avrom. I'm constantly in awe of how they successfully juggle the full-time demands of parenting with full-time IT work and book work. Despite my earlier claims to a "long and hard" process, I did learned a lot from reading, reviewing, and questioning their material.

Duncan, thanks again for hosting our FTP server as well as for your insightful and patient mentoring and for inventing and implementing an application that shows off the great new aspects of ADF and JDeveloper in a practical way. Sidebar to Duncan: if you are ever looking for additional employment opportunities as a senior developer/architect . . . well, you know how to get in touch with me.

I have the pleasure not only of working in the same company as Avrom but also of collaborating with him on client projects. Avrom, thanks for sharing in writing your deep knowledge of ADF internals as well as for sticking with this really long-running project. I'd like to take this opportunity to publicly extend my apologies for all my e-nagging about the various deadlines (but you *are* now two days overdue on your last time report!).

A large group of others contributed in many ways and now that their work is complete, it's a real pleasure to be able to thank them for their effort. Ann Horton, who worked as technical editor for the last book Duncan and I wrote, just happens to be on a team in Oracle that was using JDeveloper 11*g* (in its pre-production releases) to create applications. We couldn't have asked for a better fit for a technical editor. Thanks, Ann, for your expert insight and patience! Merci beaucoup to Eric Marcoux, our other technical editor and fellow Oracle ACE Director. Eric is also one of the Fusion Middleware 11*g* early adopters, and his project (outside Oracle) is using the entire technology stack, including JDeveloper 11*g*. Eric, your comments as a non-Oracle employee working with a real application (also using pre-production software) were very, very helpful.

My appreciation for additional technical reviews also goes to Rich Bruno, an Oracle consultant whom I work with on a client project at NY State Office of Alcoholism and Substance Abuse Services (OASAS). Rich brought into his reviews a longtime, in-the-trenches knowledge of JDeveloper 9*i* and 10*g* and the Oracle database. Rich worked through many of the hands-on practices in their early stages (no small accomplishment there) and gave helpful suggestions for many of the chapters in the book. Our other technical reviewers on the Oracle Product Management side also provided crucial comments and corrections, including information about features I hadn't figured out or known on my own. For those reviews, thanks Patrice Daux, Susan Duncan, Kate Heap, Pam Gamer, Jeff Gallus, Steve Muench, Lynn Munsinger, Frank Nimphius, Shaun O'Brien, Blaise Ribet, Grant Ronald, and Dave Schneider for all your valuable input. Also thanks to Glen Maslen for keeping our chapters flowing among the Oracle group. Another thanks to the Oracle JDeveloper documentation team. The early documentation was amazingly complete and helped greatly in learning new features.

Thanks also go to my boss, Austin Erlich, CEO of Quovera, for the flexibility in scheduling required to balance book work with client work. I'd also like to recognize the stellar IT staff at OASAS with whom I have worked for many years for their patience with my erratic work schedule and for helping me stay aware that not everyone in the Oracle development community is fully in tune with all the new aspects of Java (yet). My gratitude also goes to Karen Cannell, Editor-in-Chief of the *Oracle Development Tools User Group (ODTUG) Technical Journal,* for reviewing an early version of the book for an article in that excellent journal.

I also appreciate the professionalism and friendliness of the McGraw-Hill staff who helped this book project manifest, especially Lisa McClain, Smita Rajan, Robert Campbell, Janet Walden, Jean Bodeaux, and Jack Lewis with whom we worked directly.

As always, Mom, Dad, and Marilyn, thank you for sympathizing with and showing a constant interest in the struggles of the book process.

Most importantly, thanks to my wife, Anne, for her understanding and support. Anne, I foresee a vacation in the near future without the laptop.

—Peter Koletzke
San Carlos, CA, USA
October 2009

Five years is a long time.

It's hard for me to believe, but that's how long it's been since the last time I wrote an acknowledgment page, for the *Oracle JDeveloper 10*g *Handbook*. A lot has happened in that time, for me personally, for JDeveloper, and for the world of web applications.

Everyone knows how the web has changed. What was once a vehicle for reading news and making purchases has become a major part of our lives, and the static sequence of web pages and forms of the old Web have turned to a proliferation of sites as interactive and dynamic as any desktop application. And JDeveloper has changed apace: An application developed with JDeveloper 11*g* bears almost as little resemblance to one developed with JDeveloper 10*g* as does Facebook to `trn`. That's what has made writing this book so exciting: the feeling of being involved with a true technological revolution. So first, I must send a big "thank you" to the JDeveloper team, just for making this possible by producing such a cool piece of software.

My life has changed pretty dramatically too, both professionally and personally. Since the *Oracle JDeveloper 10g Handbook*, I've gone from being a member of the JDeveloper team to a very enthusiastic partner. I'd like to thank my current (no longer new—I'm writing this close to my fifth anniversary with them) employers, Quovera, Inc., for taking what must have seemed like a real chance by hiring a technical writer with no proven production development experience and helping me become the consultant and developer that I am today. In particular, I'd like to thank both my manager of record, Austin Erlich, and my mentor and the project manager of most of my projects, Peter Koletzke, for the understanding and flexibility they've shown when I've had to balance the demands of paying work and the brick of paper you're holding in your hands.

But of course, my thanks to Peter only barely *begin* with such abstracta as "understanding" and "flexibility." This is our third book together, and I've worked with him on any number of development projects, as well. This man is a *genius* of project planning and implementation. Peter plans it, It Gets Done, and unless you've actually spent a year or so in the wilds of bookland, you probably can't guess just how important that is. (Yes, I know you can guess it's absolutely vital. It's more important than *that*.)

This is only my first book with Duncan Mills (although, of course, I worked with him during my years at Oracle), but I hope it won't be my last. In addition to balancing the sometimes tricky load of official Oracle responsibilities and two highly opinionated co-authors (an experience I remember well from books past), Duncan has been a consistent voice of moderation and reason throughout the process. The massive sample application presented in this book, which Duncan created, certainly would not have existed at all if the rest of us had gone charging off with our wild-eyed sample application ideas, without his patient advice and guidance on what scope would and would not prove useful in an introductory text.

I owe a special debt of gratitude to both my co-authors for this book in particular. In the early months of this year, I contracted a case of pneumonia that simply would not go away. I lost over two months of productivity to the bug, which would have damaged or even killed this book's prospects if they hadn't stepped in and taken tons of editing—far, far more than their fair share—off of my plate. Both even took over part of my share of the manuscript.

The primary work of a consultant, of course, is not writing books but, well, consulting. A project as large as this perforce takes time away from the software development projects that form my bread and butter. I'd like to thank all my clients over the last two years for their support and understanding when book deadlines loomed, most especially the people at the New York State Office of Alcoholism and Substance Abuse Services. I'd also like to give special thanks to my Quovera colleague, Igor Gorbunov, who stepped in when book deadlines and software deadlines seemed headed for unavoidable collision.

Our technical editor, Ann Horton, has done truly heroic work turning a gigantic amount of text by three people, each with our own idiosyncratic style, into a unified whole. Eric Marcoux, another technical editor, also assisted greatly in the early stages of the process. And our technical readers, Patrice Daux, Pam Gamer, Kate Heap, Steve Muench, Lynn Munsinger, Frank Nimphius, Shaun O'Brien, Grant Ronald, Blaise Ribet, and Dave Schneider, have caught what must be thousands of errors in the initial drafts. Particular thanks go to Steve Muench, who tirelessly and patiently answered my questions, follow-up questions, follow-up follow-ups, and, more than once, follow-ups to those. Many thanks are also due to our editor, Lisa McClain, and her entire team at McGraw-Hill.

Love and thanks to my parents, Lillian Faderman and Phyllis Irwin, who, as always, have been immovable rocks of support, and congratulations to their finally sanctioned marriage in the summer of 2008. Thanks to my friends, especially Jonathan Kaplan and Mark Barry, for well-timed distractions. Thanks to everybody at the Ralston Peets in Belmont, who have provided probably half the calories, and 95 percent of the caffeine, that I converted into words for the book. Thanks to my cats, especially Nixie, who despite chewing through two baby monitor cords, two telephone cords, a camera cord, and the power cord to Ina's computer (three times!) has entirely refrained from chewing through the cords to the computers on which I write.

Probably the biggest change for me in the past five years is the entry into my life of my son Nilakash. It's a very different experience, writing a book as a family man, from writing one as a young single guy or newlywed. My wife, Ina, deserves an entire uniform's worth of medals for her help, love, support, and patience, which stood up even when I all but disappeared into my work for weeks on end. And thanks too to Nilakash for his understanding, which must have been hard at times; thanks and a promise of more Daddy time in the future. And thanks to both of them for making each day brighter.

—Avrom Roy-Faderman
Belmont, CA, USA
October 2009

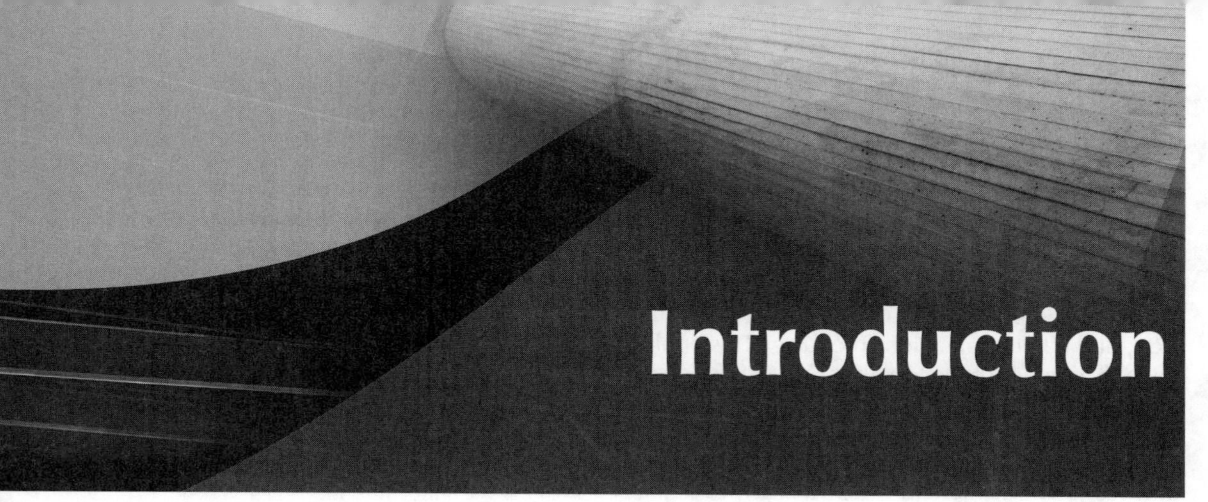

Introduction

This is not a novel to be tossed aside lightly.
It should be thrown with great force.

—Dorothy Parker (1893–1967)

Here's the problem: developing an application using Java tools is very different from developing an application in other environments. As with any modern problem in virtually any realm, you can tap into a wealth of material on the Internet and obtain excellent tools to help with the solution. However, sifting through all of that material and finding the best way to use the tools could take more time than you have. Moreover, the information and tools you discover on your own may not be the best for your situation. For success with your first application, you need to know which subjects are important, which techniques are proven to work best, and which details are crucial to productivity. Briefly, the problem boils down to, "What is the best way to work in this environment?"

This is problem at which we are throwing this book.

The motivation for writing this introduction was to expand upon our vision of the book's objectives, purpose, and contents so you can decide whether it will be useful for you and, if the answer is "Yes" or "Maybe," how best to use the book. This introduction includes details about the book's intended audience, objectives, contents, and scope. It also provides tips and advice about how best to follow the *hands-on practices* (practical step-by-step examples) in several parts of the book.

Who Is This Book For?

As the title and subtitle of the book states, we address the material in this book to those who wish or need to use Oracle JDeveloper 11*g* to create web applications with the Fusion technologies—the technologies Oracle uses to create Oracle Fusion Applications—the next generation of Oracle's packaged applications (which now includes Oracle E-Business Suite, PeopleSoft, Siebel CRM, and other applications products). This book is a "handbook," not in the sense of a complete guide to all areas of the tool (because that function is well handled in the online JDeveloper Help Center) but in the sense that it is a guide for creating Java-enterprise standard, web applications using JDeveloper 11*g*.

Although it may be erring on the conservative side, we assume that non-Java readers have no knowledge of or experience in *Java Enterprise Edition* ("Java EE" or Java standards-based) web development. We do assume that you have some experience at least with browsing web applications and are familiar with the tasks required to develop a database application. Although not a prerequisite, if you have worked on a Java EE web development project, you will be more quickly able to absorb the concepts needed to understand web application work. You will gain knowledge of best practices and solid techniques for JDeveloper work.

Java-aware readers will find chapters that dive into low-level techniques for interacting with data using Oracle's business services layer. In addition, we sneak some more advanced techniques into the hands-on practices in Part V. Java folks will also become aware of the robust and highly productive declarative techniques offered for writing applications in JDeveloper.

The 11*g* release of JDeveloper is quite a bit different from earlier releases, and even developers, who have a head start to learning this version of the tool due to experience with previous versions, will benefit from the discussion of the additional features in this version.

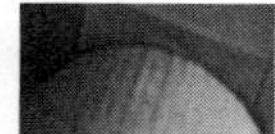

NOTE

*All of the material in this book has been verified with the first Oracle JDeveloper 11*g *production release (version 11.1.1.1.0, build 5407). Earlier builds of JDeveloper 11*g *may not work the same way or at all with the hands-on practices. For later builds, you may need to adapt to slightly different names and features. Although many of the concepts for building applications are the same with JDeveloper 10*g*, we do not recommend trying to follow the overviews or hands-on practices closely using a release of JDeveloper before 11*g *(build 5407).*

Do I Need to Know Java?

Since JDeveloper generates code, including some written in the Java language, it is important that you have a basic understanding of Java before beginning serious development work. This book does not explain the Java language in any detail, because the pages are filled with specific information about JDeveloper. Chapter 4 provides an overview of some of the necessary Java concepts (as well as concepts for other languages) in case you need a review or a bit of background before taking your first formal training class in Java. However, at some point in your learning process, you will also want to obtain some training or to study one or more Java books. The Sun Microsystems Java website (java.sun.com) contains a wealth of free introductory and advanced information, including self-directed tutorials that you can use to become familiar with Java.

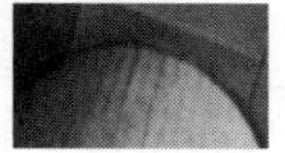

NOTE
As this is being written, the effects of Oracle Corporation's acquisition of Sun Microsystems (the owner of Java) are unknown. Therefore, we refer to Sun Microsystems throughout the book as an autonomous entity.

The JDeveloper wizards create a lot of code for you. This code is completely functional, well formatted, and built to follow best practices. You can learn a lot by examining and analyzing the code that the wizards create. If you are new to Java web development, after reading through Chapter 4's language concepts, you can look at the generated code and test your understanding of the various languages in which the files are written, for example, Java and XML.

Part II is considerably more Java-intensive than the rest of the book. Some sections of Part II describe features of JDeveloper that require some understanding of object-oriented programming to grasp and some hand-coding in Java to use. We expect that the brief Java background provided in Chapter 4 will be enough to make the chapters in Part II useful, but some further training in Java will make some of the subtleties expressed in those chapters clearer. Developing the sample application in Part V does not require deep knowledge of Java. However, although we supply all Java (as well as other language) code fragments needed to complete the tasks, we strongly encourage you to study and understand them so that you can effectively solve similar programming challenges in the future.

Objectives

No book can teach you all possible techniques that you will need when you face a real application development task. If it could, this would take away much of the challenge, excitement, and demand for creativity that application developers face and often take pride in handling every day. However, a book can empower you with knowledge about the underlying principles; this knowledge will help you face future application challenges presented to you.

Therefore, the book's objectives are as follows:

- **To explain in some detail the technology** behind the code you create in JDeveloper 11*g*, Release 1 (JDeveloper 11.1.1.1.0) with Application Development Framework (ADF) Business Components, ADF Faces Rich Client, ADF Task Flow, the ADF Model, and JavaServer Faces (JSF). This background information will give you a context for understanding what you are doing in the tool and how to address development requirements and any problems that may occur.
- **To demonstrate development** of a somewhat real-world application that uses the same technology stack as the Oracle Fusion Applications.
- **To show you some of the basic techniques** required to develop a typical application. We provide gentle introductions and explanations of some techniques so that you can fully understand why you are performing certain actions in JDeveloper.
- **To prove the productivity you can gain** using JDeveloper's declarative and visual tools to create and edit application code.
- **To present some best practices** for approaching requirements in a web application. There are always many paths to a goal, and this is very true of Java EE development. We provide opinions about some paths we recommend with reasons for those opinions.

- **To guide you toward additional sources of information** for more details. These sources include those that have helped us, as well as others, understand aspects of Java web development. These references are scattered throughout the body of the book in context of the applicable subjects.

The Java EE Knowledge Problem

You likely have read or heard material about Java EE web development and JDeveloper, but you still may not be comfortable with the concepts. In fact, so-called introductions to Java EE often leave you with more questions than understanding. This is a natural effect of learning new material, but it seems to be particularly true with this environment, which already has a well-established and expert-level user community. That user community is highly qualified to present the concepts and examples to others and is quite generous in doing so. However, as is true with any instructor, Java EE writers many times assume that readers have understood more than they actually have mastered. This assumption means that new content is not properly assimilated because the reader has an incomplete understanding of that content's foundation.

You can obtain any information about the technologies behind Java EE web development from the Internet. The wealth of available information actually contributes to the steep learning curve for non-Java developers. When trying to learn a technology, you need to search for the right source, decide which sources are reliable and correct, read and understand multiple explanations (because one explanation is rarely complete for your purpose), and integrate them into a comprehensive picture. However, you are not sure whether all the knowledge you gain in this way is essential and true. You would like to reduce the knowledge to only that which is true and essential. Providing you with the true essentials is one of the goals of this book.

The JDeveloper 11*g* Solution

When you run JDeveloper, you will see the splash screen motto—"Productivity with Choice," as shown in the following illustration.

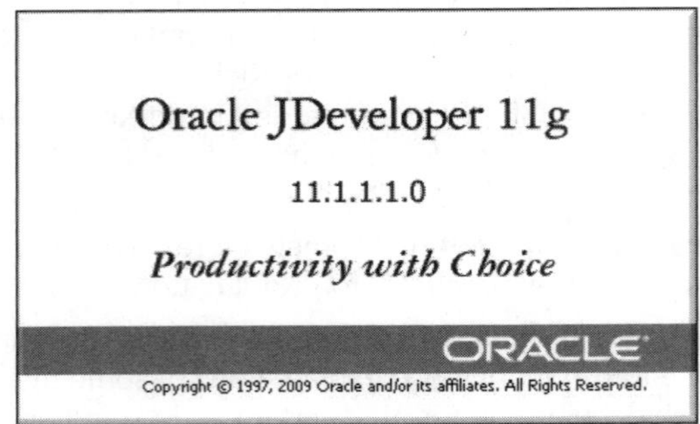

This motto means that JDeveloper supports different ways of creating code, for example, typing code text, declaring property values, and performing visual layout. It also correctly implies that JDeveloper supports development work using any Java EE technology. You will not need more than one tool—JDeveloper handles it all. However, before JDeveloper 11*g*, this same motto frustrated some non-Java developers because it meant that they needed to be aware of the ins and outs of various technologies, and they needed to make technology choices with little direction from Oracle.

Older application-building technologies often provide a single technology suite for deploying web applications and a defined path for development. However, when working in a Java environment and, therefore, in JDeveloper, you need to string together various Java EE technologies for a final solution. The danger of a wrong selection exists unless you study carefully and obtain some help from those with experience.

With JDeveloper 11*g*, you can still select from any Java EE technology, and JDeveloper will support your development work. However, Oracle has provided a defined path that it uses to create Oracle Fusion Applications: ADF Business Components with JSF and ADF Faces Rich Client—the technologies we explain in this book.

Information in This Book vs. Information from Other Sources

A small number of readers may worry that a book in the Oracle Press series might repeat material found elsewhere. Therefore, it is necessary to assure this group that the material in this book is original and unique, although it is thankfully not the only information available about JDeveloper. JDeveloper has an active user community and wide support within the Oracle development world. Much material has been written about JDeveloper 11*g* already and will be written about JDeveloper 11*g* in the future, including several books mentioned in the later section "Oracle Press Books." Most of this material is available from the following sources:

Oracle Technology Network (OTN) This website (www.oracle.com/technology) contains many pages devoted to work with JDeveloper, ADF Business Components, and ADF Faces. Most OTN articles focus on a specific application-development feature and provide examples with little or no Java technology background explanation. This type of material is a critical source of practical information about techniques. It can save you much time in researching how to solve a particular programming problem. Start browsing for information from the JDeveloper home page (www.oracle.com/technology/products/jdev/).

Oracle ADF Learning Center As of this writing, an OTN website page called "Oracle ADF Learning Center" (www.oracle.com/technology/products/adf/learnadf.html) provides useful information, including demos, tutorials, developer's guides, and sample applications to experienced Java developers as well as traditional tools developers.

ADF Developer's Guide The *Fusion Developer's Guide* online book is available in the Oracle ADF Learning Center as well as in the JDeveloper Help Center. It targets the same audience as this book and contains some similar techniques. However, it provides many more examples of different types of code you may need to write. We think that this developer's guide is a perfect follow-on book to our book. Once you come to an understanding about the Java EE web technologies and basic development techniques here, you can use the developer's guide to round out your understanding or to provide you with specific techniques not discussed here.

JDeveloper Help Center In addition to detailed (and some overview) information on OTN, the JDeveloper *Help Center* (online help system) provides more tool-oriented information about accomplishing specific tasks. For example, JDeveloper contains several useful features, such as *Cue Cards* that provide step-by-step instructions for performing a certain task or for developing a certain type of page, *Favorites* that allow you to create a list of help topics of interest, and *Dynamic Links* that display a list of help topics relevant to the task at hand. The entry point for the Help Center is the Help menu in the JDeveloper IDE or the Help Center window (**Help | Table of Contents**).

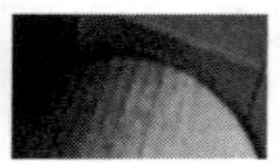

NOTE
Menu selections from right-click (context) menus or the JDeveloper main menu are marked in boldface throughout the book with "|" symbols separating menu, submenu, and menu item selections.

What's Different about This Book?

Although a wealth of material about web development using JDeveloper is available from various sources, much of it assumes you have some background in the basics of Java and Java EE. This book helps you better assimilate that material by providing the necessary background information for your web development work.

In addition, although many techniques and white papers you will find on the Web provide clear steps for creation of all types of web application code, this book has the luxury of spending many pages on a technique as well as on the background material and practical hands-on steps you need to know to understand the technique more fully.

Coming up with best practices from the many information sources available to you can be daunting. This book guides you down a development path using Fusion technologies and, at the same time, states and demonstrates best practices for this path at appropriate moments in the discussion.

Contents of the Chapters

To provide you with a better idea of the subjects we think you need to know about Java EE web development using JDeveloper, it is useful to briefly examine the contents of each chapter. In addition, although we've designed the chapters to be read in order, you may find some of the overview chapters review material that you can skip over until later.

The chapters are organized into five parts: Overviews, ADF Business Components, ADF View and Controller, ADF Model, and Developing the Sample Application.

Part I: Overviews

Developing Java EE web applications using JDeveloper and ADF requires familiarity with concepts that will be new to you if you have previously worked in other environments. You may have heard about and learned about some of these concepts before. However, so many Java EE technologies are available that you may be at a loss to know which technologies you need to learn most thoroughly. Part I of this book introduces you to the concepts you will run into when developing Java EE web applications with ADF in JDeveloper 11*g*.

Most of the chapters in this part (as well as Parts II, III, and IV) are structured around questions listed at the beginning of each chapter. This should make finding an answer for a particular question easier later on, but the chapters are also intended to be read from start to finish. Although Part V is dedicated to hands-on practices that provide step-by-step instructions about how to complete tasks, some of the chapters in Part I provide general instructions for JDeveloper work that illustrate the concepts discussed in later chapters. While understanding those concepts is not dependent upon working in JDeveloper while you are reading, you might find that following along using JDeveloper helps you understand these concepts better.

Chapter 1 leads the overviews by defining and relating JDeveloper, ADF, Fusion, and Fusion development. All of these topics are foundations upon which everything in this book is built.

Chapters 2 and 3 introduce and provide a tour of the main areas of JDeveloper, which you will use for working with Fusion technologies.

Chapter 4 explains *Java EE*—a set of specifications and best practices for developing and deploying a Java-oriented application—as well as the technologies it specifies; it also describes how web communications work to fill in the picture of how Java EE web technologies work at runtime. Chapter 4 finishes by briefly defining the various languages you will use when developing a Java EE web application.

Part II: ADF Business Components

Part II focuses on *ADF Business Components (ADF BC),* the framework that your application will use to communicate with the database. Chapter 5 introduces this framework and explains how it fits into ADF. Chapter 6 explains how to create business components that directly represent your database objects and the relationships between them, and that encapsulate and enforce business logic. Chapter 7 shows how to create components that query data from the database or provide static data, and how to aggregate this data for use by your user interface. Chapter 8 demonstrates how to encapsulate complex data operations.

Part III: ADF View and Controller

The theme of Part III is the *View* and *Controller layers* of a Java EE application, which are responsible for rendering the user interface and for handling user interactions and data flow, respectively. The View layer technology of choice for Fusion Applications is the Java EE technology, JavaServer Faces (JSF). Chapters 9 and 10 introduce JSF and provide hands-on practices that allow you to dig a bit into JSF internals.

Chapter 11 explains how ADF supplies a Controller layer, ADF Controller, which manages user interactions such as button clicks and defines the logic for which page or part of a page will be displayed.

Chapter 12 closes out Part III by describing (and demonstrating in hands-on practices) an Oracle component library, *ADF Faces Rich Client,* which supplies a large range of JSF components that offer highly interactive functionality.

Part IV: ADF Model

Part IV discusses *ADF Model (ADFm),* which performs the previously daunting task of *data binding*—connecting user interface and controller code to data supplied by the business services layer. Chapter 13 introduces the ADF Model layer and the files it uses for binding data on the page and in controller activities. Chapter 14 explores the ADF Model bindings topic in more depth and explains how to edit and implement bindings beyond the defaults. Chapter 15 explains *executables,* ADFm components that perform actions during the page or activity life cycle, and explains how to work with ADFm from within managed beans.

Part V: Developing the Sample Application

There is absolutely nothing like the practical application of concepts to help them sink in; in addition to helping you absorb concepts, it is often easier to explain a technical concept with real code that implements a real-life requirement. Therefore, we dedicate roughly a third of the book to walking you through hands-on practices, most of which develop a sample application called *The Ultimate Human Resources Application (TUHRA),* version 2 (version 1 was used as an example in our previous book, *Oracle JDeveloper 10*g *for Forms & PL/SQL Developers*). After an explanation of design principles and best practices for working with JDeveloper and ADF in Chapter 16, we spend the rest of Part V guiding you though development of application pages using JDeveloper, ADF Business Components, ADF Faces Rich Client, and JSF.

NOTE
Although Part V develops the TUHRA2 application, we use screenshots and examples from the application in earlier chapters as well.

The main application you create in this part of the book contains elements you would usually build into a real-world system. The application demonstrates data search and edit capabilities as well as the display of hierarchical data. Chapters 17 through 20 set up the application and complete these pages. Chapter 21 walks you through adding users, groups, and code to handle security in the application. Chapter 22 shows how to *deploy the application*—copy the application files to the server so the application can be run in a web environment.

The practices in this part of the book contain discussion material that provides more detail about the tasks you are completing. Sidebars and paragraphs headed "Additional Information" anticipate questions you might have while completing the development steps.

All hands-on practices are divided into major phases of work (numbered with Roman numerals), and these phases are divided into sections, each of which contains a logical unit of work. At the end of each major phase of development, the practice contains a section called "What Did You Just Do?" which explains again the result of the steps you followed. Some phases end with an additional section called "What Could You Do Next?" which provides guidance about variations or possible enhancements you could make to the code you just wrote.

It is important to the learning process not only to complete a series of steps by following the instructions, but also to comprehend exactly what occurred in those steps. The detailed explanations and summaries at the end of each phase are intended to help with that comprehension.

NOTE
As mentioned throughout the book, completed code for each chapter of the sample application, as well as some additional features, is provided on the websites mentioned in the "Websites for Sample Files" section later in this introduction. You can use this code to check your work or to view additional techniques not detailed in the book.

It is not our intention in these chapters to provide you with all techniques you will ever need to build web applications. Rather, the intention is to guide you through some basic techniques that go far beyond the defaults provided by the JDeveloper wizards. This type of work should make you think about and grasp how ADF and the other frameworks work, and this will help you solve programming problems in future projects.

Subjects Not Discussed in This Book

As just mentioned, in this book we do not intend to provide you with every technique you will ever need when developing an application. We do discuss most of the technology concepts and basic techniques you will require in a real project. However, you will need to refer to other sources for information on other essential topics, such as:

Integration with Service-Oriented Architecture (SOA) Oracle bases Fusion Applications around SOA principles. Although Chapter 1 explains SOA strategies, due to space limitations, this book chooses to focus on core JDeveloper techniques that you will use to build applications in a SOA environment, rather than explain or demonstrate SOA development. We would strongly encourage you to investigate SOA integration further in other Oracle Press titles.

How ADF Compares with Application Express *Application Express* (APEX, formerly HTML DB) is an Oracle product that provides a rapid application development environment for creating web applications. The development environment, runtime engine, and application code reside as PL/SQL in an Oracle database. Although you can develop the same type of web application using either ADF or APEX, their architectures are completely different. APEX is not used to build Fusion Applications and does not fit into the Fusion technology stack. Therefore, we do not spend time in this book comparing the ADF and APEX environments or explaining APEX other than in this paragraph.

Reports Development Although application development is not complete without a reporting system, we do not devote space in this book to discussing reports development. Some reporting needs can easily be handled by read-only JSF screens that are formatted in a printer-friendly way. ADF Faces provides container components that can assist in the layout, but for more flexibility in report building, Oracle is building reports for Fusion Applications using BI Publisher (previously XML Publisher). The Oracle BI Publisher home page on OTN is currently www.oracle.com/technology/products/xml-publisher. Development shops that use other reporting tools such as Oracle Reports, Oracle Application Express, or the PL/SQL Web Toolkit, can continue to use those tools with applications built in JDeveloper 11*g*.

NOTE
In Part V, we show how you can generate an Excel spreadsheet containing data displayed in the browser. This technique may fulfill some users' reporting requirements.

Additional Development Tools—Ant and JUnit Development efforts with JDeveloper often employ other tools, such as Ant (ant.apache.org) for building deployment files or running scripts; and JUnit (www.junit.org) for testing Java code. These (and many other) useful tools integrate well with JDeveloper and complement its features.

A Complete Sample Application Although the hands-on practices in Part V take you through development and deployment techniques for some of the most common types of screens—query, browse, add, delete, and edit, with security features—you will need many more techniques to complete a real enterprise-level application.

Web Application System Development Life Cycle (SDLC) This book focuses on the Development phase of a full SDLC. Along the way, it provides tips and best practices for work you would perform in the Design phase, and many of the techniques you learn in the book will guide how you design your application. However, other than this implied support, the selection and design of an SDLC for a web application project is beyond the scope of this book.

Getting the Most Out of This Book

The chapters in this book are intended to be read in sequential order. We have included material that we think will help you when developing Java EE web applications and think you will gain something from each chapter.

However, we realize that you may need information about a certain subject before reviewing the entire book. You can find subjects in the book using the following features:

- Contents and Contents at a Glance
- Index
- Questions in the beginning of the chapters (Part I through Part IV)
- Lists of phases and sections in the hands-on practice chapters (Parts III and V)

You may be able to skim through a chapter that addresses a subject already within your comfort zone. For example, if you have a working knowledge of Java EE basics, scan through that material in Chapter 4 and pay attention only to information about any unfamiliar technologies or technologies that you need to review.

Following the Hands-On Practices

Although you can gain useful knowledge by just reading the text in this book, we highly recommend that you perform the steps in the hands-on practices. Although these hands-on practices contain some standalone explanations, merely reading them will provide minimal benefit. The hands-on practices provide experience with concepts introduced throughout the book, and new and more detailed concepts are provided in the practices. Therefore, it is useful to stop while working in a hands-on practice and read these concepts embedded inside the hands-on practices so that you can have a context for the task at hand.

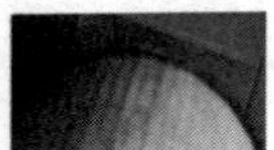

CAUTION
*As mentioned before, the material in this book has been tested with JDeveloper 11g build 5407 (the first production version of JDeveloper released with Fusion Middleware 11*g *R1). The practices will not work with any version of JDeveloper before that. If you are using a later version of JDeveloper 11g, you may need to adjust some of the instructions, although the principles and best practices should remain accurate.*

Preparing for the Hands-On Practices

You will need JDeveloper 11*g* and access to sample HR database schema, as described next.

Installing JDeveloper

You will need to install JDeveloper 11*g* (production build 5407 or later), which is available as a free download from the Oracle website. For computers running Windows or Linux, navigate to the JDeveloper home page at www.oracle.com/technology/products/jdev and look for the download link (currently in the top-right corner of the page). Download the Studio Edition, complete installation version for your operating system; this version includes the Java Development Kit that is compatible with this release of JDeveloper.

After you have downloaded the install file, run the installer executable. The install wizard will start up. This installer will create a local instance of Oracle Fusion Middleware, including JDeveloper 11*g* and Oracle WebLogic Server. Follow the install wizard and accept all of its defaults.

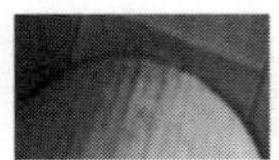

CAUTION
*Be sure to select an install directory that does not already contain Oracle 11*g *Fusion Middleware.*

When the installer completes, your Start menu will contain a new program group for Oracle Fusion Middleware 11.1.1.1.0. This group will contain JDeveloper as well as WebLogic Server utilities.

TIP
After installing JDeveloper, copy the JDeveloper shortcut in the Start menu to your desktop or taskbar toolbar. This will allow you to start up JDeveloper more quickly.

Browser Requirements

You work with JavaServer Faces (ADF Faces Rich Client) components in JDeveloper 11*g*. At this writing, these components require one of the following web browsers:

- Internet Explorer, version 7.0 or later
- Mozilla Firefox, version 2.0 or later
- Safari, version 3.0

The JDeveloper Install Guide documents certified browser versions. Follow links from the Release Notes (**Help | Release Notes**) to access the Install Guide.

JDeveloper System Requirements

The JDeveloper 11*g* Install Guide describes system requirements. Oracle recommends running JDeveloper in one of the following operating systems: Windows XP (SP 2), Server 2003 (R2), or 2000 (SP 4); Red Hat Enterprise Linux 3.0 or 4.0; or Mac OS X 10.4.*x* (dual CPU). As with most software, the more memory you have, the better, but at least 2GB is recommended. Including all middleware in the installation file, JDeveloper Studio Edition requires about 1.4GB of hard disk space. If you are running a database on the same computer as JDeveloper, add the database's requirements to those numbers.

It is always useful to review the Release Notes for any Oracle product for known limitations and issues. JDeveloper is no exception.

NOTE
This book was prepared with and provides examples in the Microsoft Windows operating system. If you run JDeveloper on another operating system, you will need to translate any instructions that require work outside of JDeveloper into techniques using that other operating system. In addition, we tested the code with the latest versions of the Microsoft Internet Explorer and Mozilla Firefox browsers.

Accessing the Sample Database Schema

Although JDeveloper supports connecting to any database with a JDBC driver, we focus on some specific features of the Oracle database. This book builds examples using database objects installed in the HR schema of an Oracle9*i*, 10*g*, or 11*g* database. Oracle8*i* also offers the HR schema, but its tables are slightly different. Should you not have access to the HR schema, you can download an installation script from the sample code websites. In later versions of the database, the HR schema is locked and you (or a DBA) will need to unlock it ("ALTER USER hr ACCOUNT UNLOCK;").

If you do not have access to an Oracle database and would like to install one on a desktop or other computer for nonproduction, development purposes, we highly recommend Oracle Express Edition (Oracle Database XE). Oracle Database XE is another free download available at OTN (oracle.com/technology/xe). This database is currently limited to 4GB of data (1GB for database memory), and the HR schema is preinstalled with the database. As mentioned before, be sure your computer hardware contains enough memory for both the database and for JDeveloper to run at the same time.

Ensuring Success with the Hands-On Practices

Your experience with development in the hands-on practices should be trouble-free. However, it is possible that you will run into problems that are not easy to debug. Although problems are a natural part of any development effort, and the process of solving problems that arise is an excellent learning tool, we want you to ultimately be successful in completing the practices. Therefore, we offer the following tips:

Do Not Type Ending Periods and Commas into Values Many steps in the practices direct you to type in or select a value for a field. To clearly designate the value you are supplying, we enclose it in double quotation marks (for example, "true"). We comply with standard American punctuation conventions in these situations. For example, if a sentence in the text requires a period or comma after the value, we enclose the period or comma inside the quotes. However, unless instructed, you should not add the period or comma to the value. For example, a sentence might be written as follows:

Fill in *Rendered* as "#{bindings.DepartmentId.inputValue}."

In this example, you would only type in the value from "#" to "}" without the sentence-ending period (".").

Test the Application When the Instructions Indicate If you run into a problem, backtrack through the steps you followed after the last successful run, and look for typos or missed techniques.

Slow Down We have found ourselves, at times, wanting to quickly complete an exercise. However, in this haste, we miss (or misread) a critical step or part of a step.

Debug the Code Although code that JDeveloper creates is not likely to cause problems, you should check any code you have typed into JDeveloper, whether it be in an editor or a property field, especially snippets of code and property values containing expressions. In addition, double-check the order and contents of the nodes in the Structure window for the files you are working with. You can compare these with the sample solutions visually in the Structure window or using the comparison utility mentioned later on.

Read Error Statements Carefully Error reporting in Java-oriented code has become much more sophisticated lately. Java stack trace messages often look overwhelming, but reading the clues carefully (particularly at the top of the stack of any detail exception) should give you a direction for finding the problem. In addition, don't forget to look in the Structure window (explained in Chapter 3) for errors and allow it to help you find the problem code and the solution.

Compare Your Code with the Sample Application Files The sample code websites contain an ending application file set for each phase of the hands-on practices in each chapter. You can download the working code and compare it with your code using the file comparison utilities available from the right-click menu on a file in the navigator, as shown here:

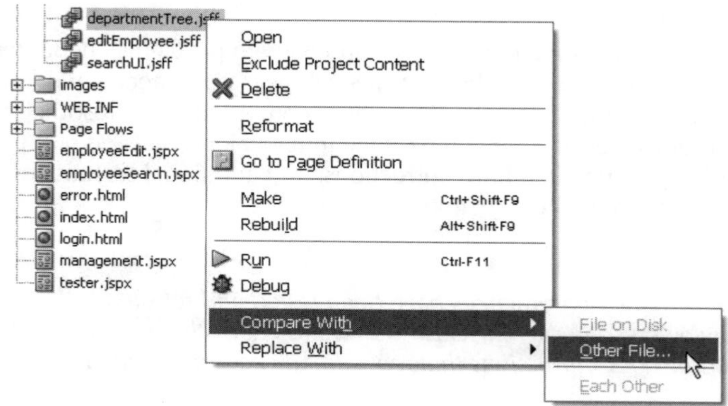

Frequently Back Up the Application Directory We (and our reviewers) advise that you back up the application directory after a successful test for application functionality (at least at the end of each chapter in Part V, or even after each phase or section that concludes with a test). That way, if you experience problems in a later stage, you can restore the backup and reapply the changes you made after the backup. Use a file manager, such as Microsoft Windows Explorer, to copy the top-level directory (containing the application workspace .jws file and the project subdirectories), and paste it to another location (optionally renaming it to indicate the save point).

Although the practices in Part V are intended to be run sequentially, you can use the sample end-of-phase application files available on the book's website to skip chapters. For example, if you wanted to start with the hands-on practice in Chapter 19, you could install the Chapter 18 ending application and use it to work through the steps in Chapter 19.

Stop, Restart, Undeploy If you experience unexplained errors such as files that worked before are no longer accessible, it may be that running the application many times in JDeveloper has caused an inconsistent memory state. You can usually clear this problem by stopping the application and the default server or by restarting JDeveloper, which will stop the server.

Running an application in JDeveloper deploys it. (Chapter 22 provides details about deployment.) If JDeveloper cannot restart an application because it is already deployed, you can manually undeploy the application using the Application Server Navigator (**View** | **Application Server Navigator**) and expanding the IntegratedWLSServer node. Select **Undeploy** from the right-click menu on the application node.

Google Is Your Friend In addition to assistance you may gain from the OTN website, you can also broaden your search to the World Wide Web using a search engine like google.com. The truth is out there.

Check the Look and Feel Over time, we anticipate a slight change in the look and feel of the ADF Faces components used in the sample application. The chapters currently show screenshots using the 11.1.1.1.0 production version of JDeveloper 11*g*, Release 1 (build 5407). The hands-on practices chapters contain steps you can follow to switch the skin (look and feel) if your version is later and the components do not match the screenshots. You can follow those steps if you wish to match the screenshots exactly, or you can leave the default look and feel intact.

Authors' Availability

Unfortunately, the authors are not able to help you with problems encountered in the hands-on practices. However, you can use the OTN JDeveloper forum (accessible from the JDeveloper home page) to post questions for the JDeveloper community. This resource is also useful for answering questions that occur when working in JDeveloper outside of the book's practices.

We intend to post updated files, corrections, and additional techniques on the sample code websites mentioned in the next section.

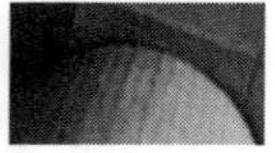

NOTE
Although the hands-on practices have been tested and retested by several reviewers, defects may exist. Be sure to check the websites mentioned next for corrections that may already be documented.

Websites for Sample Files

Links to sample files and errata for this book may be found through links at www.tuhra.com—named after the sample application you develop in Part V of this book. In addition, the authors' websites contain information about this book and other topics of interest to Oracle developers—www.avromroyfaderman.com for Avrom Roy-Faderman and www.groundside.com/blog/content/DuncanMills for Duncan Mills.

The Downloads page of the McGraw-Hill Professional website also hosts links to the sample files for this book—www.oraclepressbooks.com.

Further Study

You will need more information than this book contains to learn the subject of application development in JDeveloper fully. Most developers agree that the best learning experience is gained from focusing efforts on a real development project. Books can help you get started learning about a technology and can serve as one source of reference material for when you get stuck in development. For this extra information, we again point you toward all the sources mentioned before in this Introduction as well as in references throughout the book. Several other resources are worth mentioning at this point.

Oracle Press Books

We are pleased to state that the franchise this author group (with the addition of Dr. Paul Dorsey) has long held on the JDeveloper topic within the Oracle Press series is expanding to other authors and additional titles. At this writing, the following related books are in process:

- *Oracle Fusion Developer Guide: Build Rich Internet Applications with Oracle ADF Business Components & ADF Faces,* by Lynn Munsinger and Frank Nimphius
- *Oracle WebCenter 11*g *Handbook: Build Rich, Customizable Enterprise 2.0 Applications,* by Frédéric Desbiens, Peter Moskovits, and Philipp Weckerle
- *Oracle SOA Suite 11*g *Handbook,* by Lonneke Dikmans and Lucas Jellema

Check www.oraclepressbooks.com or with your favorite bookseller for future availability details.

Oracle User Groups

In addition to these resources, we strongly urge you to take advantage of information available from independent Oracle user groups. These groups meet at local, regional, national, and international levels. Some offer newsletters or journals in addition to online forums. For example, the Oracle Development Tools User Group (ODTUG, www.odtug.com) offers conferences, free electronic mailing lists, and white papers, all geared toward sharing information gained by experience in business environments. The Independent Oracle Users Group (IOUG, www.ioug.org) also provides a technical tips repository and information about many local Oracle user groups in the Americas. A web search engine will also assist you in finding an independent Oracle user group near you.

PART I

Overviews

There is nothing more difficult to take in hand, more perilous to conduct, or more uncertain in its success, than to take the lead in the introduction of a new order of things.

—Niccolò Machiavelli (1469–1527), *The Prince*

CHAPTER 1

Overview of Fusion Development and ADF

When you innovate, you've got to be prepared for everyone telling you you're nuts.

—Larry Ellison (1944–)

ver the last few years we've heard an ever-increasing buzz around the term Fusion within the Oracle community as Oracle pushes forward with its next generation of business applications. Fusion means different things to different people, something that we will discuss shortly, but its use as a term to define an architecture and development methodology is the focus of this book.

This first part of the book provides an essential overview of some of the key technologies and tools that you will encounter as a developer working in this space. This chapter introduces some of the key architectural issues and concepts, Chapters 2 and 3 provide an introduction to the JDeveloper IDE and Chapter 4 discusses the key technologies that define the web platform as a whole. Subsequent parts of the book drill into some of the fundamental framework pieces and provide a guided tutorial to help you to build your first Fusion application. We start, though, with this chapter, which provides an introduction to Fusion architecture and technology from the point of view of the developer. In the course of this introduction, it also touches on the Oracle Application Development Framework (ADF), which eases development chores when working with the Fusion platform. The chapter discusses answers to the following questions:

- **What is Fusion?**
- **What is a framework?**
- **What is Oracle ADF?**
- **Why should I use JDeveloper?**

What Is Fusion?

We have deliberately used the term "Fusion" in this book's title rather than listing specific technologies or frameworks. Fusion as a term is used in multiple places as a brand by Oracle, and of course it's a popular brand name for many other, nonsoftware products, ranging from razors to cars. Oracle refers to Fusion in two distinct branding contexts:

- **Oracle Fusion Middleware** This is the entire suite of middleware used to run modern, standards-based applications. It provides a runtime environment for applications written to the Java Platform, Enterprise Edition (Java EE) APIs, Service-Oriented Applications, and much more. We'll be explaining what this infrastructure supplies a little later on in this chapter.
- **Oracle Fusion Applications** This is a project undertaken by Oracle to both unify and modernize its entire suite of packaged business applications. The term Fusion Applications covers packaged applications for financial management, human capital management, customer relationship management, and much more. This is a huge undertaking in software terms involving thousands of programmers working for several years, but it is important to note that the techniques and software used for that project are exactly what we describe in this book.

Oracle Fusion Middleware provides a runtime and development environment for Oracle Fusion Applications, so there is a natural usage of a common branding there. However, when we refer to Fusion in this book, we're really employing a third use of the word: Fusion Architecture. The common link here is that the *Oracle Fusion Architecture* defines the core architecture and technologies used to build the Oracle Fusion Applications products, which in turn will be deployed on Oracle Fusion Middleware (or indeed, in principle, to any other standards-based application server). As continually writing the phrase "an application based on the principles of Fusion Architecture" is a bit of a mouthful, we will tend to use the shorthand form "Fusion application" when referring to such an application. Understand from this that we mean any application architected on these principles, rather than specifically meaning one of Oracle's packaged applications.

The Origins of Oracle Fusion Architecture

Before looking more closely at the details of the Fusion Architecture, let's take a step back and consider what the traditional database-driven application looks like. Note that we will make no apology for concentrating on applications that connect to databases here; the majority of our business applications do so, and since you are reading a book with "Oracle" in the title, we might expect at least a degree of interest in where the data is stored. In addition, although we do not focus specifically on Service Oriented Architecture (SOA) in later chapters, we need to spend a bit of time in this chapter explaining it so you can understand where Fusion fits with SOA.

Taken as a group, the authors of this book have over 50 years of experience working with and writing applications for the Oracle relational database. For most of that time the development pattern has largely been static, although the technologies and platforms have certainly changed. Throughout this period the core development paradigm has been one of a very close match between the user interface and the relational tables in the database. In this model, business logic for an application is either encoded into the application tier in the relevant language—Java, C, or PL/SQL—or into the database in the form of PL/SQL (or occasionally Java). What is more, a lot of key functions within this model are implemented as batch processes, as they are too expensive or complex to run inline. Such batch programs may be responsible for reporting functions, data transformation, communication with other systems, and so on, but every system has them, as shown in Figure 1-1.

Figure 1-1, represents several generations of Oracle tooling, from Oracle Forms with over 20 years of service all the way through to some of the newer Java-based frameworks. This traditional model is obviously very successful; otherwise, it would not have persisted for so long and in so many forms. All of these frameworks and development methodologies share a common bond with the database as the hub of all things. However, the development landscape is rapidly changing, and standards compliance is now a key business driver rather than a nice-to-have. The watchword nowadays is "integration."

The Rise of SOA

When you think of integration today, you think of *Service-Oriented Architecture (SOA)*. *SOA* is not really anything new; it is a re-expression of an old idea: reusable components that are distributed throughout the network. The attractive propositions behind such a component-based model are that they encourage reuse of functionality and that the components or services themselves can be located in the most suitable place for that function, rather than being embedded within your program. As a simple example, imagine a business process that attempts to audit transactions to look for patterns that might indicate fraudulent activity. A process like this has needs that illustrate

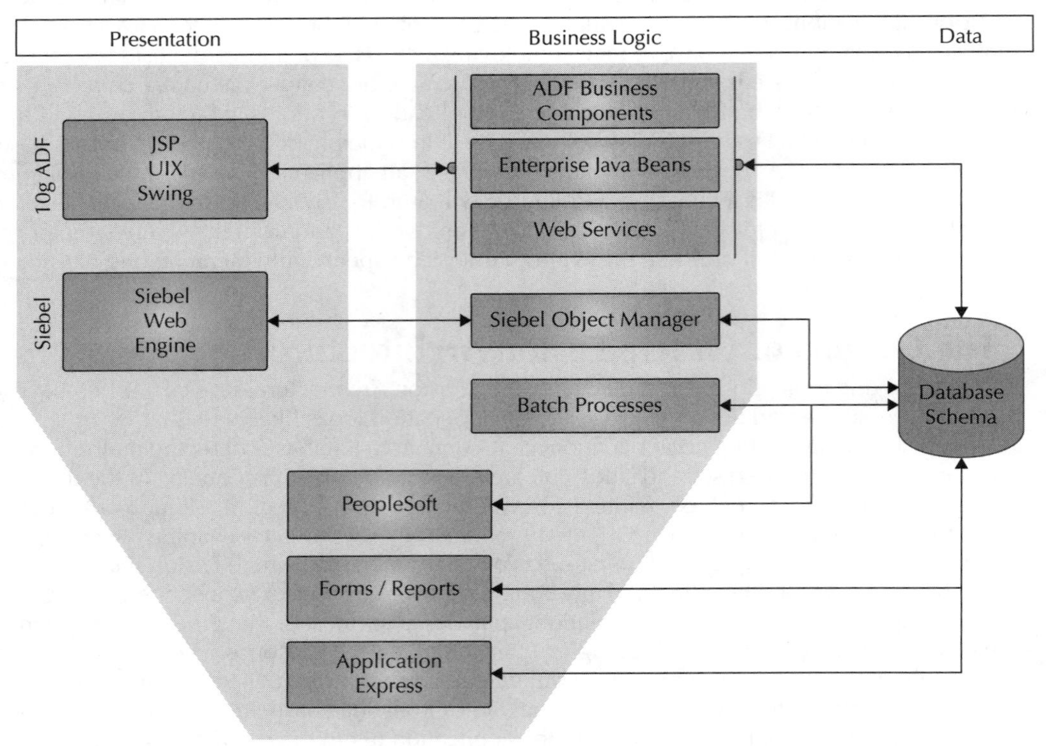

FIGURE 1-1. *The traditional Oracle application architecture*

both location importance and reusability. On the factor of location, such a process will probably crunch through a lot of database information to look for warning signs, so running it on or near to the database will be important. On the factor of reusability, aspects of the process, such as alerting the correct staff, need access to the corporate escalation map. This escalation processing is likely to be reusable throughout the enterprise, so it should not be programmed into the core audit function.

SOA is all about using and assembling these services without compromising their functionality in the process. For example, if you wanted to include this higher-level audit function into your data entry system, you can do so, but without having to worry about the performance aspects of pattern matching or how to establish whom to alert. All of this is encapsulated within the high-level audit service, which in turn might be consuming multiple subservices to achieve its goals.

The idea of remote reusable services itself is well established; it has surfaced before in various forms such as Microsoft's DCOM (Distributed Common Object Model) and CORBA (Common Object Request Broker Architecture). Both of these attempts at a distributed service model failed to become pervasive for a variety of reasons such as complexity and cost; however, the most significant factor in the failure of both platforms was the transport mechanisms that they use. Both DCOM and CORBA use low-level TCP/IP protocols to communicate between remote servers and as a result have a real problem when the application needs to cross firewall boundaries or pass between proxy servers. This factor constrained these architectures to use within the enterprise and prevented their use as a transport mechanism between partners or trading groups. In fact, even within a single enterprise, firewalls will exist to create demilitarized zones (DMZs) for sensitive applications and databases. These firewalls experience the same communications issues when DCOM and CORBA are used.

How Is SOA Different?

There is no doubt that the SOA concept has evolved from and aims to solve the same reuse problems as the earlier attempts at distributed computing such as DCOM and CORBA. However, it has been much more successful for the following reasons:

- **Communication is based on hypertext transfer protocols** SOA primarily uses web services protocols for communication. *Web services* (centrally stored application functions available through the Web) use the Hypertext Transfer Protocol (HTTP) or HTTP Secure (HTTPS) as a transport layer and have already solved the problem of how to traverse firewalls and proxy servers. Additionally the web services community has already solved many of the secondary problems associated with third-party communication, including how to standardize security, encrypt the data, and define levels of service for remote service use.

NOTE
Chapter 4 discusses web communications and HTTP protocols.

- **Through web services, SOA has a common lexicon** These include a service description format in the *Web Services Description Language (WSDL)* and a common discovery and publishing mechanism through the Universal Description, Discovery, and Integration (UDDI) standard, which acts as a yellow pages for services.
- **SOA emphasizes orchestration, not just communication** Protocols like CORBA and DCOM allow programmers to write code that utilizes both local and remote function calls; however, all of that code was at a functional code level. SOA concentrates on the more abstract task of integrating at the service level rather than the function level. Using orchestration languages such as the Business Process Execution Language (BPEL), this task is something that can be achieved, to a certain level, by a suitably trained business analyst rather than requiring a programmer at every step. Generally the process of orchestration itself will involve the use of a diagram to map the outputs of one service to the inputs of another.

Unlike a standard such as CORBA, SOA has not been built top-down by committee. Instead it is much more of an accepted usage model for these existing standard pieces such as web services, BPEL, and UDDI; all of these standards are well served by the Oracle tooling and, of course, provided as runtime implementations by Fusion Middleware or any other standards-based application server.

What Are the Key SOA Technologies to Understand?

In a large enterprise development, core SOA tasks such as service orchestration and creation are likely to be managed by an entirely different team from the team building the UIs for an application. This approach makes a lot of sense; the skill sets are very different, and teams building SOA services need to take the broader view across the enterprise so as to identify areas of common functionality and reuse.

The reality is of course that many developments are conducted on a smaller scale and may not have the luxury of dedicated teams devoted to architecture and shared service development, so even if you will be concentrating on building core Online Transaction Processing (OLTP) screens, you may have to venture into the world of SOA. So, let's look at the key terms and technologies of SOA in Fusion Middleware:

- **Business Process Execution Language (BPEL)** *BPEL* is an Extensible Markup Language (XML)–based language used to orchestrate multiple services together. BPEL processes look a little like flow charts with inputs, outputs, branches, and so forth. Fortunately the diagram-based editors provided by JDeveloper make it easy to pick up and use. Oracle also provides another similar modeling tool, called the Business Process Modeler, which is discussed in the sidebar "About BPM."
- **Enterprise Service Bus (ESB)** The *ESB* acts as a central clearing house for SOA-based transactions. It offers three key functions. First, the ESB acts as an event broker where clients can simply post a message to the ESB and then interested services can subscribe to that event and be triggered on demand. Second, the ESB acts as a service abstraction layer, allowing services to be moved without disrupting any clients that consume them. Third, the ESB provides transformation services to facilitate message translation between different services. Most Fusion applications integrate with the *Mediator,* a lightweight implementation of the ESB (explained further in the section "Business Logic" later in this chapter).
- **Rules Engine** This component provides a standardized way of defining sets of rules for expert systems and complex processes. The rules engine is driven by sets of rules that can be altered at runtime rather than being coded into the application.
- **Human Workflow** This part describes a business process that is not specifically computational but rather concentrates on tasks such as approvals. Workflow systems are driven by an understanding of approval chains, permissions, and hierarchies. As the name suggests, Human Workflow processes involve interaction with a person, which is what distinguishes them from the fully automated processes implemented in BPEL.
- **Composite** A composite is a term used for a complex or multi-part application that combines many of these technologies into one logical unit that is easier to deploy and monitor than its component parts.

About BPM

At the time of writing, BPM was a separate tool from the JDeveloper IDE, which is the focus of this book (although it will be merged into JDeveloper in the future). Rather than being focused at developers, it is more of a tool and notation for business analysts, providing them with a very visual approach to defining processes and workflows. As a higher-level abstraction of a process, it allows the analyst to both define the flow of a process and, to a certain extent, generate user interfaces that it will require. It also provides the infrastructure parts to actually execute those processed.

BPM generates out a mix of artifacts, including a process flow in the form of Business Process Modeling Notation (BPMN). In some ways, BPMN is a competing notation to BPEL; however, Oracle Fusion Middleware uses the same core engine to support both notations at runtime.

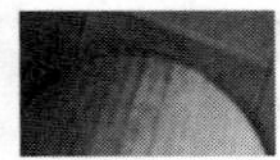

TIP

More complete coverage of the mechanics and usage of SOA technologies in Oracle Fusion Middleware is available in the sister volume for this book mentioned in the Introduction: Oracle SOA Suite 11g Handbook (McGraw-Hill Professional/Oracle Press, 2010).

How to Get It Wrong with SOA

As you have seen, many technologies sit under the SOA umbrella, not just web services. Taken as a whole, the platform is very attractive; services and processes can be mixed and matched at will without having to be explicitly designed to work with each other. Likewise, integration with external systems becomes much easier if both sides utilize SOA principles. However, those that adopt SOA have a tendency to make the following two fundamental mistakes, particularly when using SOA in database-backed systems.

Everything Is a Service? Architects unseasoned in SOA have a tendency to take the SOA message too literally and assume that absolutely every data access or process should be defined using SOA architecture and protocols. With a typical database application, such as an OLTP system, this is almost always the wrong thing to do. Relational databases already have a universal standardized and abstract protocol for interacting with the database—SQL. In a typical data entry form there is nothing to be gained by hiding data access behind a web service interface; doing so will reduce performance because of the additional cost of marshaling and un-marshaling data between Java and XML at either end of the service interface in addition to the extra overhead in shipping messages through different layers. Hiding data access behind a web service will also hide useful capabilities of the SQL interface from the client, for example, features such as array fetching, transactions, and key relationships. When data is needed for remote access as part of a genuine process orchestration, then it is reasonable to expose just that required data through web service protocols; however, the remaining 98 percent of your data access should not pay the penalty just to satisfy this corner case. The mantra for SOA designers needs to be "everything can be a service" as opposed to "everything is a service."

Service Granularity One of the hardest jobs for a service architect is that of defining the correct level of granularity for a service. Many beginners who fall at the "everything must be a service" hurdle will often also end up defining those services at too fine a level. As an example, consider an HR-related function—promote an employee. This function represents a single, expressible use case with a basic set of inputs, for example, employee ID, new job grade, and new salary. However, encapsulated within that larger process may be multiple steps, including approving, updating the employee record with the new grade information, and integrating with the payroll system. So this is a great example of a use-case-driven service that is hiding complexity from the consumer and can react to changes in the business process if required. An overly granular approach to building in the same functionality might define separate services for updating the EMPLOYEES table and notifying the payroll system. Architecting the application in this way would force the developer to carry out the service orchestration in the calling program, thus hard-coding parts of the high-level use case into the application rather than encapsulating it behind the service façade.

The rules of thumb for service granularity are to ask the questions: "Does this service make any sense when used on its own?" "Could this whole service be relocated?" and "Is this service reusable in a variety of situations?" If there are dependencies and other steps in a process that must be invoked for this service to be valid, it may be defined at too low a level.

There may well be functions that operate at a finer level of functionality as part of a larger process orchestration, but these would be for internal consumption only.

Is Thick Database the Way Forward?

The so-called thick database architecture is occasionally held up as an alternative to SOA and Fusion development for the Oracle community. The idea behind *thick database architecture* is that everything from validation to workflow to complex business processes and even user interface should be defined in the database using a combination of PL/SQL code, views, and metadata. Thick database architecture is defined as having the following advantages:

- **Code is colocated with data** Code that works with data is colocated with that data and there is no network overhead used to transport data and SQL statements.
- **Business rules can be highly dynamic** Every system encodes a series of rules or validations for the data and processing. Some of these will be simple, hard-coded validations, but many are more complex, contain variable data, or change over time. If the metadata that configures those rules is held in the database, then the system becomes very agile, as that metadata can be easily changed on the running system.
- **UI independence is achieved** Using thick database architecture, you can simplify your user interface development and become independent of the technology that you are using. User interface technologies change more rapidly than core database technologies, and this architecture allows you to switch between technologies much more cheaply. You can also bridge between older UI technologies such as Oracle Forms and newer technologies such as JSF using this common layer.
- **Familiarity with PL/SQL is rewarded** Coding is done in a language that Oracle developers understand—PL/SQL.

On the surface, thick database architecture does seem like an attractive proposition for incumbent PL/SQL developers, as it provides a coexistence model that does not require them to venture too far out of their comfort zone. However, as with SOA, taken to extremes, the thick database architecture can be misused in each of those categories and does not necessarily offer more than the SOA and Fusion technology stack can:

- **Code is colocated with data** This is certainly a very good thing when that particular piece of code has to crunch through thousands of records to perform some calculation. For any such requirement, the database is certainly the place to put the code. However, most data access for an OLTP system is not of this nature, and in most modern systems it is not going to be acceptable for the user to have to post a transaction to the database just to perform a simple validation check. Among other problems this also introduces a long running stateful transaction into the database context which can seriously affect the scalability of the system. Users also want much richer UIs than the block-mode solution of a thick database can provide. Therefore, regardless of your use of thick database principles, you will inevitably end up duplicating code in the middle tier and the database tier. (This may not be a bad thing in any case.)

  It is also a fallacy to assume that a core validation such as checking for a value in a list is always going to be more efficient when conducted in the database. When performing this kind of work in the middle tier, the frameworks will be caching data for later reuse and the caches can be explicitly shared among the entire user population. (This is something we'll look at in Chapter 7.) As with all received wisdom, there is no substitute for prototyping and proving to yourself one way or another that the performance you receive using your preferred method falls within acceptable parameters.

- **Business rules can be highly dynamic** This is indeed a key requirement of modern systems, and although you can take the decision to build your own metadata-based infrastructure in the database to provide such flexibility, you can also just use off-the-shelf capabilities. Features used by Fusion applications such as Business Logic Units (covered in Chapter 6) and the Rules Engine provide much of the desired flexibility. Also note that the SOA-based architecture is designed to make business processes as a whole more dynamic, not just the micro-rules within them. SOA-based systems also can have the advantage that processes can be easily versioned at runtime. This increases the safety factor as new processes are brought on-stream, as only new transactions will pick up the changes and existing transactions can continue under the old rules. Although runtime versioning is possible with database-based business rules systems, it requires a less standard, homegrown solution.
- **UI independence is achieved** Fusion Architecture is based on a Model-View-Controller design pattern (discussed in Chapter 4) where the coupling between the business service (Model) layer and the UI (View) layer is already a loose one. The thick database architecture proposes a second layer of abstraction through database views and PL/SQL packages, allowing the reuse of a common table API between legacy and Java applications. In this case, the abstraction pattern within the database can be a very useful tool even when exposing that data through a Fusion middle tier. Since the Fusion Architecture already factors UI code away from business services code, the difference between the way Fusion Architecture and the thick database approach provide separate UI and business services layers is minimal.
- **Familiarity with PL/SQL is rewarded** You cannot argue against PL/SQL; it is a great language and is actively evolving. However, to a large extent, learning a new language is not a big barrier to overcome. Any programmer should be familiar with the basics of writing procedural code; for example, the exact semantics of writing a loop are of secondary importance. This is particularly true when you are using an advanced code editor such as JDeveloper, which will almost write the code for you if you take advantage of its templating and auto-completion features. In addition, as we describe in Chapter 4 in the section "Level of Knowledge", developers do not need a high level of mastery with a new language to be immediately productive.

Let's preview some of the key features of the Fusion Architecture that provide support for putting more of an application infrastructure in the middle tier.

- **Declarative Development** One of the prime objectives of Fusion Architecture for the development team that created the underlying frameworks and tools was to enable application creation with as little coding as possible. Less code to write means less code to go wrong and less code to maintain. So most of a Fusion application, like an iceberg, exists below the surface in the form of declarative metadata. If you just concentrate on validation and basic business logic as areas of overlap with a thick database approach, the contrast becomes evident. From a declarative perspective, the database can implement simple check constraints and validate the relationships between tables, but pretty much everything else requires custom code.

Using the ADF Business Components framework within JDeveloper, the declarative palette is much richer than before, in terms of both the types of declarative check style validations and of advanced features like Business Logic Groups, which allow multiple sets of business rules to apply conditionally to a row, depending on some deciding factor such as the value of a particular column. The semantics of the declarative coding within ADF Business Components are also richer, allowing the developer to traverse relationships as part of validations and so forth.

- **Agility** In the subset of applications that have significant integration with other services, the loose coupling within a SOA composite provides a great deal of flexibility for making changes to the processes quickly and safely; for example, as mentioned earlier, multiple versions of a process can be in flight at any one time.
- **Customization** This is a key part of the Fusion Architecture feature set. Runtime metadata such as business logic, process flow and screen UI designs is managed through a service called Metadata Services (MDS). *MDS* provides an engine for running customizations on top of a core application that can provide multiple versions of the application, implementing different business logic, processes or UI. These versions may be differentiated by job function, department, or company. We will discuss MDS in more detail later in the chapter.
- **Caching** As mentioned earlier, the middleware engine and the frameworks that run on it provide caching by default. The Fusion Architecture frameworks allow developers to define the caches rather than caching being a DBA tuning exercise.
- **Security** Although the database effectively manages its own security, the scope is constrained to the database. When dealing with a modern SOA-based application, security needs to extend beyond the boundaries of the local process; for example, although a user executing a business function is locally authenticated and authorized, what happens if that process has to call out to some remote service to perform some work? The SOA infrastructure already has the protocols in place to manage the trust and service-level agreements between systems.
- **Scalability** This is a feature part of n-tier systems; connections are managed and the database is only used when it is needed. For example, a few hundred concurrent database connections may be required to support a concurrent user population of tens of thousands. This contrasts with a model that involves storing user state within the database session, which implies either a one-to-one client to database connection relationship (as is true in Oracle Forms), or at the very least, programming work by the PL/SQL programmer to manage the persistence and reconstitution of state from the session.

  Of course, the success of scalability depends on how you write the application. It is perfectly possible to write a bad application that uses middleware and consumes more resources than the equivalent two-tier application. Fortunately, JDeveloper helps the developer in this area; for example, it provides auditing to warn the developer when something that they have done will prevent the application from migrating or failing over between nodes on a middleware cluster.

In summary, when it comes to how much work and logic you put into the database tier, it is a matter of being pragmatic. As you have seen, Fusion Middleware provides many capabilities out of the box that would be a lot of work to implement manually in PL/SQL database code. On the other hand, the database is highly capable and is there to be utilized. Also remember that the database should be a gatekeeper of the data that is stored within it, so relational integrity and basic validation such as check constraints should always be implemented no matter where the bulk of the business logic ends up, even if this seems like an apparent duplication of effort.

The Fusion Architecture

We've established that taking either SOA or the thick database architecture to the extreme is probably the wrong idea. The fact remains that in most applications, the core task is to move data in and out of the database. This use case remains unchanged from the traditional model that Figure 1-1 illustrates. Fusion Architecture as shown in Figure 1-2 reflects this reality; it is really an evolution of the traditional model that does not ignore direct database access for OLTP but adds in extra dimensions.

The top half of Figure 1-2 is similar to the mode used in the tradition model, although as you will see in later chapters, there has been a significant shift in the capabilities of the user interface and in the way that information is presented. Where things change is the area below the dashed line where parts of the Fusion Middleware suite are used. In this next section, we'll examine how these new components are used.

Assuming that the basic business problems have not changed, why is there suddenly a need to involve much more technology? One of the key factors is that, although the basic functions of our systems have not changed, the technology allows them to be implemented in a much better way. A traditional OLTP system includes an inline portion, the basic data entry and reporting functions; it also almost always includes more code in the form of batch jobs and integration code. In the traditional model of Oracle development you would often see logical transactions, which are invoked by some action in the UI, but not completed until some overnight job has run. Once you break down the functionality of these batch systems, you will find that their existence is largely explained by integration needs, whether it is in the form of generating some data file to transfer to a partner—for example payroll information—or to generate emails in some kind of workflow.

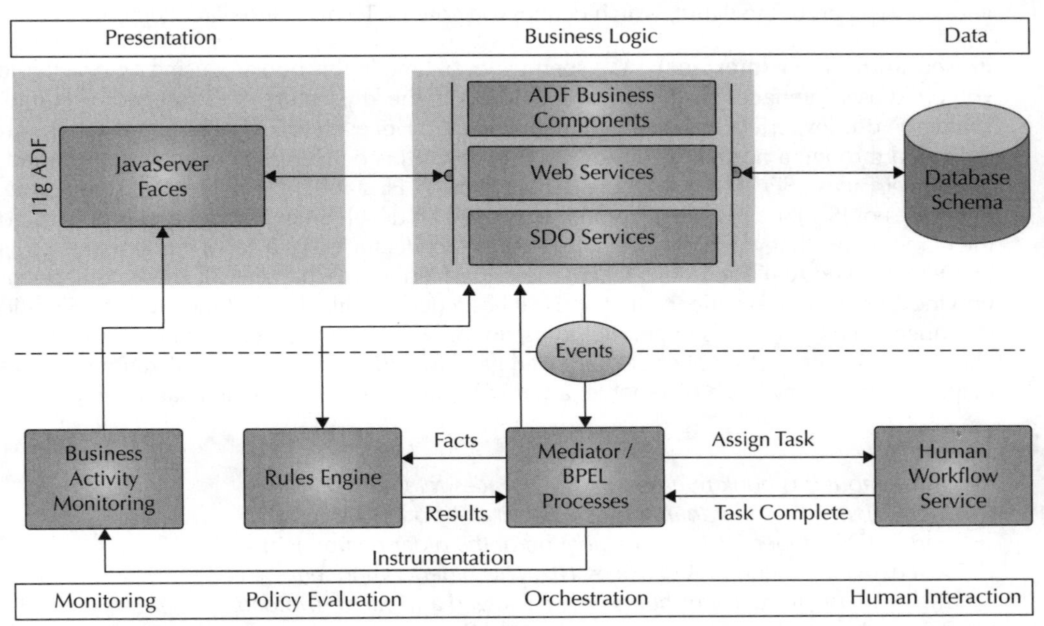

FIGURE 1-2. *Fusion architecture as an evolution of the traditional model*

The change is that the underlying infrastructure now provides all of the standards-based engines to manage these conversations with external systems in-line, rather than as batch, and there is no need for the build-your-own infrastructure approach of the past.

Another use case for batch processing, apart from integration and human workflow, is complexity. Often you would be unable to run a function or calculation inline because it would take too long. Thankfully SOA principles can also help out here as well—you can invoke asynchronous processes as easily as synchronous ones. Of significance here is the fact that BPEL has the concept of compensation.

Compensation

Compensation is the process of recovering from errors, similar in concept to a rollback for the database, but potentially much more complex. Imagine a simple process for increasing an employee's salary. From the database perspective this is a simple update to a column in a row in the table. From perspective of the larger process, it would include a series of approvals and communication between the HR system and the payroll system (which might have been outsourced). So, if there is some downstream failure such as the departmental budget being exceeded, the transaction as a whole will need to be undone and the implications of this will extend beyond the core database that the UI is working with. "Compensation" is the name given to this recovery process, and it allows the developer to design the remediation process in just as much detail as the original process. An implication for the designers of SOA services is that they must think not only about the service design for carrying out a particular action, but also about the corresponding interfaces for use by compensating transactions.

Breaking Down the Architecture

Let's look at each of the components in Figure 1-2 and examine what they are used for, starting with the top part of the figure, which defines the core OLTP part of the architecture.

Presentation (User Interface) We spend a lot of time in this book focusing on exactly how you build user interfaces for this platform. However, the key feature of the view or user interface is that the user experience is very rich (highly interactive) even though these applications are delivered through a normal web browser. The core UI is delivered by a technology called JavaServer Faces (JSF), which is a core part of the Java EE standard. Chapter 9 discusses the basic principles of JSF. JSF provides a component-based UI development model and is only as good as the components that you have available. Fusion Architecture uses a set of components provided by Oracle called ADF Faces Rich Client (described further in Chapter 12). These components provide an end-user experience that approaches a desktop-like level of interactivity. Significantly, the range of components is huge, including not only the core data entry widgets that you would expect, but also a vast number of charts and gauges, and more exotic visualizations such as maps, hierarchy viewers, a pivot table, a Calendar, and even a full Gantt chart component.

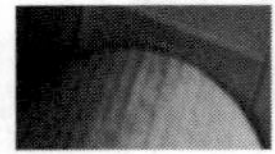

NOTE

Throughout this book references to ADF Faces refer to ADF Faces Rich Client 11g rather than the ADF Faces components shipped as part of JDeveloper 10.1.3. Any mention of the older component set will explicitly mention ADF Faces 10g. This older component set is still available in ADF 11g but is now packaged as Apache Trinidad. Trinidad is an Open Source project created from the donation of ADF Faces 10g to the Apache Foundation.

If there is one feature that you will immediately notice from the applications that Oracle produces using this technology, it is the way that these components are used to provide a visually attractive and engaging user interface. Another aspect of the user interfaces is the inclusion of features that would seem more at home on a social networking site such as Facebook. You can think of these social features as adding a dimensional context to data within an application. For example, you look at a record, and you can see who last changed it. This is not new, but you might now also be able to see that that person is currently online; in addition, you might actually be able to establish an instant messenger session with them, or click to call them over Voice over IP. Again, these are part of the middleware capabilities, which can add significant value to the users of your application.

A significant part of this social instrumentation requires infrastructure to back it up in terms of services and storage. Oracle's WebCenter product adds this value on top of the ADF core UI capabilities.

TIP
The Oracle WebCenter product is described in depth in another Oracle Press book (mentioned in the Introduction): Oracle WebCenter 11g Handbook: Build Rich, Customizable Enterprise 2.0 Applications *(McGraw-Hill Professional/Oracle Press, 2010).*

Business Logic We have already discussed the placement of business logic to a certain degree, and we describe the actual technology in some detail in later chapters. However, at this stage it is important to grasp the following key Fusion Architecture concepts:

- All data access to the business service layer from the user interface flows through an intermediate data binding abstraction layer. As you will see, interacting with this binding layer is one of the key skills of a Fusion developer.
- Most database access is still directly to the database rather than via some proxy such as a web service and is defined declaratively or in SQL.
- The core business service provider (ADF Business Components) is used to service SOA processes as well as user interfaces.
- A strong direct linkage exists between ADF Business Components and the Mediator for invoking SOA processes as part of a normal business transaction. This linkage utilizes a capability called *Service Data Objects (SDO),* which is used to efficiently pass state between the business service and any associated BPEL process. The why and the how of this capability are beyond the scope of this book but are discussed in the online documentation and the *Oracle SOA Suite 11*g *Handbook.*

Data Let us not forget the database. At the core of all of these applications is still the requirement for solid relational design.

SOA Tier The bottom half of Figure 1-2 is getting into newer territory, working right to left:

- **Human Interaction** The reality of many systems is that they have the concept of approvals at some stage. In simple applications, approvals could just be part of the functional user interfaces, provided that all of the approvers in the system actually have access to and use the user interfaces. In more complex cases, something a bit more robust is needed.

Capabilities such as approval by email, approval chains, approval delegation and escalation, and so forth are all baked into the Human Workflow Service. Additionally, the work lists that are used within the service are all built using the same technology as the user interfaces you will be building for the rest of the application, so customization and integration of those interfaces is no great challenge.

- **Orchestration** The orchestration space largely belongs to two technologies: the Mediator (or its bigger brother the Enterprise Service Bus) and the Business Process Execution Language Process Manager (BPEL PM or just BPEL for short). The *Mediator,* as its name suggests, is basically a routing engine to take events and distribute them to the relevant orchestration engine, which is usually BPEL. In the process, the Mediator may transform or map the payload of the event, although this will be less common within an application, where you own all of the interfaces and can dictate the required data structures. The key task of the Mediator then is to abstract away the details of the location and nature of the process that will be processing the event.

  BPEL PM itself is the main SOA engine. It is driven by the BPEL language, an XML syntax that provides a way of describing the process flows that are required. In the context of the JDeveloper IDE, this flow language is written through the medium of a BPEL diagram. This diagram allows the developer to draw the flow that will integrate the various services, which need to be coordinated as part of a transaction.

- **Policy Evaluation** Much like Human Interaction, many applications have the need for this capability and in the past have largely implemented it as custom code. The major focus in this space is the Rules Engine, although you can also consider policy evaluation in terms of governance of the running application—key performance indicators, and so forth. (This then overlaps with Monitoring.) Sticking to the Rules Engine, we are concentrating on the types of rules defined within an expert system, rather than the fixed business logic that would be defined with a simple validation on the business entity.

  A good example would be an insurance application. When an application for insurance coverage is made, you will need to consider many logical factors to calculate the level of risk associated with the request. What's more, those rules may change between deployments (if this application is being re-sold) or even depend on factors such as time. The Rules Engine is driven by rule sets that can be defined dynamically by expert business users, rather than developers, and can be easily customized after deployment when the application is live. Many Oracle customer systems today have hand-created exactly this kind of functionality in custom PL/SQL code and fact tables. Now the capability is available, out of the box, in Oracle Fusion Middleware.

- **Monitoring** Knowing exactly what is going on is one of the bigger problems of managing composite SOA applications. Multiple services may be consumed by an application, so visibility into how those services are performing is needed to measure the health of the application as a whole. If you cast your mind back to the traditional approach with batch engines, generally the batch job succeeds or it fails. If it fails, you find out in the morning, try and fix the issue, and just re-run the job. A batch job is asynchronous anyway, so that is a workable solution. In the more modern architecture things are much more fluid and it is much more important to have a real-time view of how the various moving parts are performing, in terms of being alerted both when things are not working at all, for example when losing connectivity to a partner's service, and when things are simply slowing down at some link in the chain.

Oracle Fusion Middleware provides an engine for managing all of this information in the Business Activity Monitoring (BAM) service. *BAM* allows applications to be instrumented to output key performance data and correlates that information for presentation in the relevant management dashboards. Detailed discussion of BAM is out of scope for this book, but it is important to the Fusion Architecture overview to know that the data the BAM server makes available is just viewed as another service by the ADF framework that Fusion uses. Therefore, with an application instrumented with BAM the developer can easily expose performance metrics within the application. Information that was previously only available to administrators through specialized dashboards or through output logs can now be exposed within the core application user interface. In addition, BAM provides a data push capability referred to as *active data*. When a Fusion application user interface is bound to an active data service, its display will update dynamically as the underlying data changes without the user having to refresh the screen. This allows for the creation of real-time dashboards.

Now that we've discussed the high-level view of what moving parts may go into a Fusion application, it is time to drill down into an overview of the framework that makes much of this possible, the Oracle Application Development Framework (ADF).

What Is a Framework?

ADF is the development framework used by Fusion applications that we have already alluded to. Let us start out, however, by examining exactly what we mean by a framework before moving on to the technical pieces of ADF specifically.

When confronted with a set of low-level APIs, such as the Java EE APIs, programmers naturally start to develop common patterns and convenience methods for fulfilling requirements that come up again and again. After a while, most developers will build up their own personal toolkit of handy code and techniques that they can reuse whenever they encounter a familiar use case. Sometimes, problems are so common across the industry that formal recipes or design patterns are recognized for handling with the scenario.

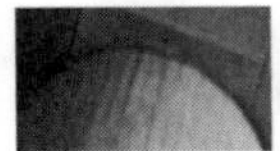

TIP
There are many sources for more information about design patterns. The seminal treatment is the classic Design Patterns: Elements of Reusable Object-Oriented Software *(Addison-Wesley Professional, 1994), also referred to as the "Gang of Four book" after the four authors. This treatment of the subject is not lightweight, so we'd also recommend* Head First Design Patterns *(O'Reilly Media, Inc., 2004) as a more approachable treatment of the subject that focuses on Java in its examples and* Design Patterns in Java *(Addison-Wesley Professional, 2006).*

Frameworks evolve as concrete implementations of such patterns, factoring out the repeated portion of the task, and leaving programmers with a more limited exercise of configuring the parameters of the framework to their needs and much less coding overall although coding is never completely eliminated. The scope of a framework can vary. Some frameworks address specific parts of the application development process. For example, *object-relational mapping* (O/R mapping), used to convert between object-oriented and relational structures (such as class instances and database tables), is an important but constrained task. Many O/R mapping frameworks have evolved and compete; some, such as Hibernate, are from the open-source community; others, such as ADF Business Components or Oracle TopLink (EclipseLink), are from the commercial world. As you will see, using one of these existing frameworks for O/R mapping is a sensible thing; the skill comes in choosing a framework that will be best for implementing a particular project profile.

Frameworks are not confined to point solutions (addressing one and only one task), such as O/R mapping. Some have evolved to supply a much larger range of the functionality needed to provide the infrastructure for a complete application. For instance, the Apache Struts framework handles user interface creation, page flow control, and a certain amount of security. Inevitably, this has led to the development of larger frameworks, such as the Oracle Application Development Framework (ADF), JBoss Seam, and Spring, which directly provide infrastructure for some tasks as well as inheriting functionally by aggregating and integrating smaller frameworks, such as the O/R mapping solutions or JavaServer Faces. These conglomerates are referred to as meta-frameworks, described further in the sidebar "Meta-Frameworks."

The Anatomy of a Framework

We explained how frameworks evolve out of standardized solutions to common tasks, in the process implementing the best practice for solving that particular problem. However, what transforms a programmer's toolkit of simple APIs into a framework? Part of this, of course, is determined by the scope of the problem; beyond that, the following attributes imply framework status:

- **Configured, not coded** By definition, a framework performs most boilerplate and plumbing tasks for you. In order for that to happen, the framework must offer a way to define configuration data that provides the information it needs. This configuration data, or *metadata,* is sometimes injected through code or code annotations, but more often through some sort of configuration file. XML is typically used for such metadata files in modern frameworks, although this does not have to be the case.

Meta-Frameworks

We've just started to define a framework, and already we've introduced a twist in the form of meta-frameworks. What's this all about? A *meta-framework* is an end-to-end application development framework that encompasses a wide range of functionality. The meta-framework not only provides functionality, but it may also encapsulate or subsume multiple single-solution frameworks. If a single-solution framework is a screwdriver, a meta-framework is the whole toolbox.

Furthermore, the definition of meta-frameworks includes the idea that they offer choice and pluggability for particular tasks. For the O/R mapping example, meta-frameworks, such as Oracle ADF or Spring, allow the developer to choose one out of a whole range of O/R mapping solutions to implement the data access function. The important distinction is that the actual choice of implementation will not have an effect on the rest of the application. The user interface, for instance, will be unaware of the actual O/R mapping mechanism being used. This allows for much more flexibility in the development of the application as well as ease in changing the underlying technologies later should the need arise.

- **Runtime component** Applications written using frameworks rely on the framework infrastructure code being available at runtime. This infrastructure code may be deployed with the application as libraries, or it may exist as some kind of runtime engine that the application runs on.
- **Design-time component** Since frameworks need to be configured with your business domain's profile, they need to have some way of helping you create that configuration. This facility may take the form of complete IDE support, including graphical editors and syntax checkers; or it may be a more manual process, for instance, a *Document Type Definition (DTD)* containing XML element and attribute names used to verify that an XML configuration file is valid.

If you review the many frameworks available within the Java EE universe, you'll see a vast spectrum of pretenders to the framework title. Many open-source frameworks, for instance, are weak on the design-time support or concentrate too much on coded configuration rather than on metadata-driven configuration. (See the sidebar "The Importance of Metadata" for details.) So let's look at what turns "just another framework" into something that you might actually want to use.

The Importance of Metadata

Although you can usually configure frameworks using both code and metadata, metadata has some advantages. First, you achieve a clean separation of framework configuration from application logic; second, you have the potential for customization without recompiling.

The first point is perhaps obvious. It is easy to understand the sense in keeping code that configures the basic framework operation separate from the code that implements the business logic so that updates are easier in case either layer changes. The second point, however, has implications that are more profound. The ability to customize an application through metadata can make the initial installation and setup of an application easier. For example, you can develop code while pointing the application database connection to a development database. Then, when you need to install the application in a production situation, you change a configuration file that points to the production database. The change is small and contained, and requires minimal testing.

Further, the metadata may be manipulated at runtime to customize an application. For example, your code can change metadata for security rules at runtime if the application has to adapt based on the credentials of the connected user.

The management and storage of such complex metadata is a problem. To this end, Oracle ADF has a complete set of services for managing and storing metadata called *Metadata Services (MDS)*. The presence of MDS is largely transparent to a developer using ADF, but its services underlie all of the framework metadata handling in the JDeveloper IDE and the WebCenter runtime environment. MDS is of particular importance to organizations building applications for resale, although it can also have a place in applications used by multiple user communities within an organization. It allows a core application to be developed and then customized in a nondestructive way by its consumers. Such customizations are recorded as differences to the core application and do not physically change the base source code. This process simplifies the entire upgrade and patch process for the product using MDS technology.

What Characterizes a Good Framework?

Although we've defined a framework as a best-practice implementation that includes runtime, design time, and a little configuration, there is much more to a framework than that. Let's consider the factors that make a framework truly useful:

- **Functional depth** The framework must provide all features needed for a particular functional area. This is the one area when a well-thought-out commercial or open source framework can outshine an in-house toolkit. The framework must be able to handle every eventuality in the problem domain. Take, for example, an O/R mapping framework that handles basic query syntax but cannot map outer joins. Such a limitation may not have mattered to the original developer, but if you suddenly need that capability in your application, what do you do? You certainly don't want to employ a second framework just to fulfill that niche requirement.
- **Functional scope** The functional depth argument works the other way, too. A framework can be too specialized to a particular domain. An O/R mapping framework that specializes in only the query of data and that does not manage updates is of limited use in most applications, no matter how deep its query functionality. Learning to use a framework well takes time; you don't want to have to repeat that exercise for every piece of point functionality in a system.
- **Being as declarative as possible** You would expect that a framework will relieve you of the burden of coding, and this implies that most of the interaction with the framework will be in configuring it with the relevant metadata, rather than writing lower-level code.
- **Clean APIs** Frameworks must provide a clean separation between the underlying code and the programming interface that the framework exposes to the developer. The framework's authors should be able to change its implementation without affecting the code in existing business applications. This problem is particularly difficult in the Java EE world, as the frameworks and code written using them are generally both written in Java. In Java, it is fairly simple for a developer to inadvertently call an internal function by mistake or to override an internal-only class accidentally (or even deliberately to obtain some extra functionality). An update to the framework can break that type of code.
- **Extensible APIs** It is a fact of life that you can't please 100 percent of the people 100 percent of the time. Frameworks have a similar problem here. By necessity a framework has to be a compromise and has to dictate certain ways of carrying out a task; after all, it's doing most of the work for you. A good framework will, however, give the programmer the hooks to extend or add functionality at the ground level to the framework, to customize it in a nondestructive way to more closely meet the needs of a particular task. It is often through the provision of such mechanisms that frameworks evolve: as one particular extension becomes more and more popular, it becomes a candidate for rolling into the core framework itself.
- **Tooling** Many frameworks attempt to make your life easier by allowing you to configure them using metadata. However, if this involves having to manually write XML files, for example, you may well lose many of the productivity gains that the framework promises, because XML coding is prone to syntax errors that are difficult to debug. A framework does not need associated IDE support to make it successful, but such support will certainly boost adoption by flattening the learning curve. A good example of this is the Apache Struts framework. The Struts framework was popular before any kind of visual

Struts tool was available, but with the introduction of diagrammatic representations of Struts page flows in IDEs, such as JDeveloper and Eclipse, Struts use grew immensely. Developers using Struts in such graphical environments need never learn the syntax of the Struts XML configuration file or, indeed, the in-depth mechanics of how Struts works.

- **Scalability** There is a world of difference in writing an application to track membership of a local soccer club and building out an enterprise HR system. One of the key abstractions that a good framework makes is to prevent the programmer from having to design and code the application around the need for scalability. The framework should take care of this as part of the plumbing and make those optimizations for scalability, such as supporting clusters of servers, transparent to the application developer if at all possible.
- **Community and Acceptance** Frameworks evolve in a Darwinian environment; that is, widespread adoption is more a key to survival than technical brilliance. Particularly with open-source frameworks, the framework will survive and evolve only as long as people feel that it's worthwhile and are prepared to give their time to both using and maintaining it. Successful frameworks tend to have a snowball effect: they are discussed more on the Web; more books are written about them; and because more information is available, the framework becomes even more popular. An active user community is another natural result of wide acceptance. An active user community can offer support and experience in real solutions that are not available from the framework's author. Therefore, a user community adds to the snowball.
- **Support** The most expensive part of using a framework is never the purchase price (if there is one); it's the investment in time to learn and use the framework and the maintenance of the system you create with that framework down the line. With open-source frameworks, you have access to the source code, but in many cases, you may not have the expertise or desire to understand that code well enough to fix bugs yourself.
  As soon as you make a change, you need to either contribute that change back to the community (assuming that there still is a community at that point), with the possible legal issues that this may cause in many organizations, so that the change can become part of the framework. Alternatively, you can keep the change to yourself, but then you're stuck with a custom implementation of the framework, and if and when the framework evolves to the next level, your change may not be relevant or supported.
  The fashionable business models in the open-source world recognize this issue. Much open-source software is now directly funded by companies looking to profit from support or consulting services in those frameworks. This is the ultimate loss-leader. Of course, this provides a loose coupling in terms of support, because those vendors can just walk away if something better comes along. Frameworks from stable companies like Oracle Forms and ADF at least offer a degree of service level, with commitments to error correction and so on. This is what gives them such tremendous longevity (for example, more than 20 years and counting for the Oracle Forms framework) and makes them a surer bet for typically long-lived commercial applications.

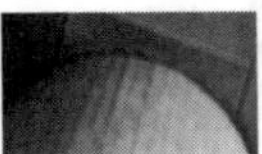

TIP
The source code for the ADF framework is available to supported Oracle customers on request. If you have an Oracle Support contract, contact Oracle Support Services to ask for a copy.

- **Documentation** The learning curve for a framework is greatly reduced if it offers complete documentation in several categories: a reference for the APIs and framework classes, development guides with examples, and IDE documentation with task-oriented explanations. The more documentation the framework offers, the better the perception of its ease of use. This adds to its popularity as well as to its usefulness.

What Is Oracle ADF?

The *Oracle Application Development Framework* (Oracle ADF or just ADF) is a meta-framework that fulfills the core requirements for a framework as outlined in the preceding section. ADF integrates a mix of subframeworks to provide the key functions for object-relational mapping and other forms of service access, data bindings, and user interface, along with the functional glue to hold it all together. Nearly everything that a core OLTP application needs is already encapsulated within ADF. However, if something is not available, you can add external packages and libraries to extend the meta-framework or push the work into the SOA layer using the available hooks.

Figure 1-3 shows the core technologies available within the overall Model-View-Controller (MVC) design pattern used by ADF.

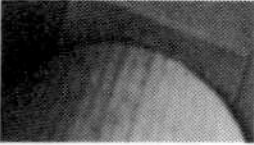

NOTE
Chapter 4 discusses the MVC pattern along with much of the core technology that is used by ADF.

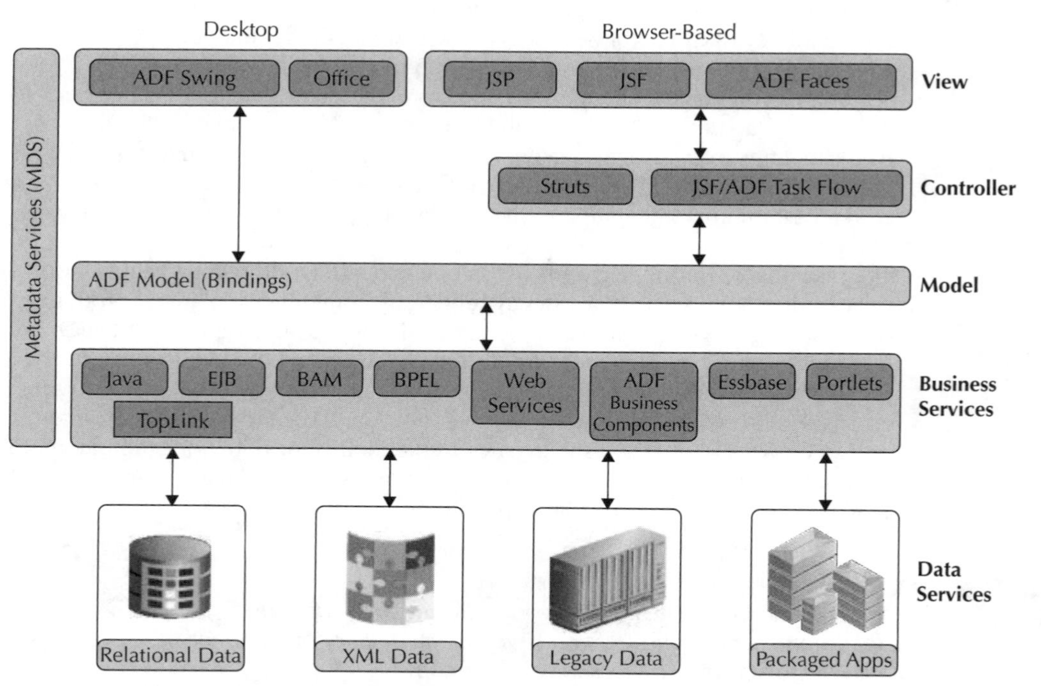

FIGURE 1-3. *The Oracle ADF technologies*

Since this book focuses on the key ADF technologies used by Fusion (ADF Faces, ADF Controller, and ADF Business Components), we will not discuss all of the possible technologies in the ADF architecture. However, Figure 1-3 highlights the pluggability of ADF as a meta-framework. ADF coordinates your selections from a range of technologies that fulfill various logical functions, such as interacting with the database and generating user interfaces. The key component is a layer provided by the ADF framework: ADF Model (or ADFm). The *ADF Model* layer (depicted as the Model section of Figure 1-3) acts as the glue between the various business service providers, such as Enterprise JavaBeans (EJBs) or web services, and the consumers of those services, generally the user interface that you are building. We discuss the ADF Model layer in detail in Chapter 13.

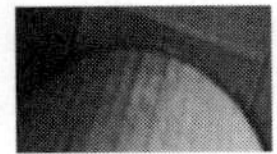

NOTE
The ADF Model binding layer is being considered in the Java Community Process (JCP) as an extension to the J2EE standard. The proposal is covered in the Java Specification Request (JSR) 227, which you can find using the JSR search feature at www.jcp.org.

How Do I Choose Technologies?

ADF is a great offering, but the capability to plug in several different solutions into each functional area gives rise to a problem—there is almost too much choice. If the technologies to be used for an application have not been predefined for you, what slice through the available technology stack should you use?

When starting out on your first Java EE project using ADF, you are going to come up against this technology question right away. The first step when creating an application presents the Create Application dialog, which asks you to select an application template, as shown next. Each template consists of a different combination of technologies.

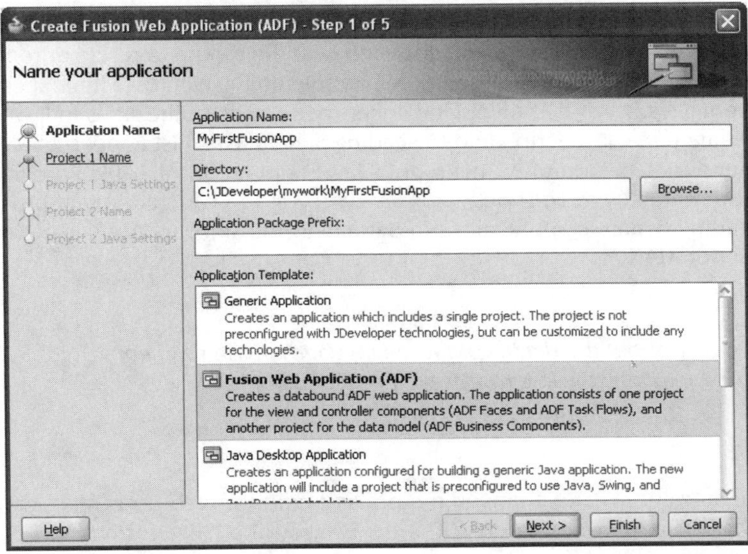

If you make a wrong choice, you can always change your mind later on, but it's better to get it right from the start. Reading the descriptions will help you make the decision.

When building a traditional data entry–style application of the type you would build with Oracle Forms, PeopleTools, or the PL/SQL Web Toolkit, you need to make a technology choice for two main functional areas: user interface and database integration.

User Interface Technology

This book concentrates on building web applications for delivery through a standard web browser, without the use of plug-ins or Java applets. This means we concentrate on UI technologies that can generate standard HTML, and maybe some JavaScript to create the screens. A large number of technologies available in the Java EE world address this task, for example, JavaServer Pages (JSP), servlets, Velocity, Tapestry, Wicket, and JavaServer Faces (JSF). However, JDeveloper best supports JSP and JSF.

Before the advent of JSF, the user interface was a difficult area in which to make a decision; JSP technology has the benefits of being widely used, but it provides a rather low level of UI capabilities and is hugely fragmented in terms of the libraries and techniques to use even within that single technology stack.

JSF has changed this picture considerably, and because of the way it is architected, it brings some key capabilities to the table; we discuss some of these later in the chapter.

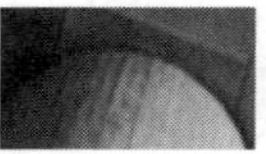

NOTE
Chapter 9 describes JSF in more detail.

But What Is a Modern User Interface?

Over the last two or three years there has been a fundamental shift in user expectation when it comes to web-delivered user interfaces. Public applications such as Yahoo Mail and Google Maps have reset expectations of what a web user interface can do, and in the process the bar has been raised considerably for the average web developer.

Examples of the kinds of interactivity that users have come to expect are drag and drop, instant validation, screens, which can be manipulated with the mouse to resize or reorder, and so on.

The sad reality is that these modern, highly interactive web user interfaces are really hard to build without a framework to help. Developers need to combine skills in Java, or some other server-side language, JavaScript, and Cascading Style Sheets just to get started. Then they have to enter the mysterious world of Asynchronous JavaScript and XML (AJAX) programming, and finally they are confronted by the distinctly nonstandard ways in which different browsers behave in the area of building dynamic applications in particular. The sidebar "AJAX in a Nutshell" explains a bit more about AJAX.

NOTE
Don't worry about the details of these languages at the moment. Chapter 4 explains these terms in a bit more detail.

Why JSF?

JavaServer Faces has really changed the playing field for web user interface development. Published as a standard in March 2004, JSF is now, like JSP, a formal part of the new Java platform specification (Java EE 5), and Java enterprise container engines, such as Oracle's WebLogic, implement a JSF service in order to conform to this standard.

Ajax in a Nutshell

AJAX (or "Ajax," described in Chapter 4) stands for Asynchronous JavaScript and XML, and describes a series of techniques for allowing components on the page to communicate with the server in the background. Fortunately, you don't have to worry about the mechanics of all of this when using ADF; it's all taken care of. So when you see the term "AJAX," just think "rich user interface."

JSF technology is attractive because of the following characteristics:

- **Component-based architecture** All UI elements within JSF are components and are written to a standard specification. These components can be complex and can consist of many sub-elements. For example, a tree control consists of images to connect the nodes, hyperlinks for the nodes, buttons to expand and collapse all, and a lot of dedicated JavaScript. Because components are standardized, you can pick and choose from multiple open-source or commercial sets of widgets and create your own, if required. The components will (in theory) all work together and be consistent to use.
- **Programming model** Each JSF component is able to register action handlers and listeners for events. Put simply, for something such as carrying out an action in reaction to a button press, the programmer just has to write a piece of what we'll call "trigger" code that is associated with the button definition in the UI and automatically executed by JSF when that button is pressed. Contrast this to JSP or servlet development, where the programmer needs to decode the request object to determine if a button was pressed and, if so, which one was pressed. Therefore, JSF makes the whole process of wiring up code to UI events much simpler for the programmer.
- **Page layout** In the same way that each UI element in JSF is a component, screens collect and organize those components within specialized layout components. This removes the requirement from the developer to code low-level screen layout tasks using HTML tables and style sheets. It also requires much less code to define a single screen, since the boilerplate HTML elements used to generate a particular layout are created only at runtime. Some JSF component sets, such as *ADF Face Rich Client* and *Apache Trinidad,* also support the concept of multiple look and feel—custom skins, templates, and other definition files that enforce a common look and feel within an application. These capabilities allow the whole graphical aspect of an application to be changed after creation without having to change each and every page.
- **Component pool** The Fusion developer is fortunate in having around 150 different components available for use from within the ADF Faces Rich Client component set. This pool of components includes the usual elements for creating data entry forms. However, also included are components such as the following:
  - Charts and graphs
  - Gauges and dials for status display
  - Geographical maps
  - Pivot tables
  - Hierarchy viewer

In addition, ADF Faces offers some specialized nonvisual components to perform tasks such as file download, accessibility support, data export, dialog windows, and so on. Therefore, the JSF developer immediately has a much richer palette to work from, and what is most important, each component works with every other component in the same way. This blurs many of the old lines between specialized developer categories such as Graphical Information Systems specialists and Business Intelligence specialists. With a JSF application using an advanced component set such as ADF Faces, you can see all of these categories blended into one.

- **Device-independent rendering** Through the use of components and layout containers, the programmer is actually coding an abstracted definition of a page rather than hard-coding the actual HTML tags that the web browser displays. JSF includes a mechanism called *render kits*—code that can enable a single page definition to be rendered in a device-specific way at runtime. For example, render kits allow a JSF page to run unchanged in a normal browser or on a handheld device. The JSF component and its render kit, rather than the developer, is responsible for creating the correct markup tags for the target device. This point is key when developing really rich user interfaces. Components that need a lot of scripting support to create client-side interactivity can take care of rendering the correct scripting for the particular browser that the end user is using. This saves the developer a huge headache. (Also see the sidebar "JSF and AJAX—A Rocky Road.")
- **Security** One of the secret problems of a modern AJAX (interactive) web application is that because there is a backchannel continually transmitting information between the browser and the server, the so-called attack surface for hackers is greatly increased. Because JSF enables the components to encapsulate the client-side scripting, they can be fully tested and hardened to remove any risk. If you hand-build the equivalent code for this kind of client-side interactivity, then that code becomes a security problem for you rather than one for Oracle.

Therefore, with the advent of JSF, the problem of choosing the correct UI technology has been greatly simplified. There is no doubt that with the framework, and the component sets provided by ADF, applications that have a similar level of interactivity to thick-client desktop applications are a possibility. What's more, you can write them without the in-depth knowledge of browser nuances or JavaScript.

JSF and AJAX—A Rocky Road

Although the component-based model of JSF promises seamless interactivity from components from different places, the reality does not quite match the vision. The problem here is how those components manage AJAX transactions. The techniques now used for these very rich web user interfaces were popularized only after the core JSF component specification was laid down. The JSF component vendors such as Oracle all wanted to enable their components with this rich functionality. However, because the JSF standards do not define how this should be done, the industry now has several competing implementations, which are not interoperable. As a result you are unlikely to be able to mix components from different component libraries on the same page. Fortunately, the ADF Faces Rich Client and Data Visualization Tools (DVT) component sets provide a pretty wide palette to choose from.

This entire AJAX compatibility issue is currently being addressed as part of the JCP's JSF Expert Group's discussion for the next release of the JSF specification. So, with luck, this will cease to be an issue in the future.

Database Integration

In a database-centric language such as PL/SQL, you may take it for granted that you can just embed a SQL statement without thinking about how it will actually be issued or how the data will be handled. However, in the Java EE world, things are different. You cannot just embed SQL within the code; you need to use specific APIs to handle the SQL. Low-level Java Database Connectivity (JDBC) APIs (explained a bit more in Chapter 4) are available for accessing the database. However, by taking this approach, you are continually repeating code and introducing more places for bugs to creep in, not something you really want to be doing. Therefore, with Java, you need to use one of the higher-level O/R mapping frameworks supported by ADF.

Your Choices for Database Integration

ADF offers two primary choices for directly mapping database objects to Java code. Each choice exhibits a slightly different focus and suits different communities of developers. The choices follow:

- ADF Business Components
- Enterprise JavaBeans (EJBs) using the Java Persistence API (JPA)

ADF Business Components ADF Business Components (ADF BC) is a powerful and rich framework for mapping database objects into Java. It forms one of the core frameworks of the ADF stack of technologies (as shown in Figure 1-3). It is widely used in the Oracle community and is the key object-relational mapping tool for Fusion Applications. Consequently it's the technology that we concentrate on in the rest of this book (for reasons further discussed later, in the section "Selecting the O/R Mapping Tool"). It is well suited to what we call the *relational viewpoint,* where you approach the design process after creating a well-formed relational database design. This, after all, is the way that most database developments are run—with the database designer, DBA, and coders working closely together.

Enterprise JavaBeans (EJB) and JPA The Enterprise JavaBeans standard defines a server-side component architecture for Java Platform, Enterprise Edition (Java EE) loosely based (conceptually, at least) on the JavaBeans standard used for Java GUI components. The EJB standard defines a series of services for handling database persistence and transactions using an EJB container, which is usually, although not always, provided by the application server's Java EE container. EJBs have had such bad press in the past that they've become somewhat of a cliché. However, things have changed in the EJB world with the latest revision of the specification—EJB 3.0. The Java Community Process expert group driving this latest revision of the standard (JSR 220) received the message that EJB was unnecessarily complex, so EJB 3.0 is focused on simplification. EJB 3.0 also defines entity beans as *Plain Old Java Objects (POJOs)*—standard Java class files—without having to implement all of the interfaces and artifacts required by earlier standards. The EJB standard learned from its past mistakes and is turning into a usable way to handle data. As part of this revamp of EJB, the *Java Persistence API* was introduced as a core part of the implementation. Unlike traditional EJB, JPA is not exclusively tied to a full Java EE container and can be used to access databases from within Java SE as well as Java EE.

NOTE
For more information about the JPA in particular, you can refer to the FAQ at java.sun.com/javaee/overview/faq/persistence.jsp.

On the positive side, using EJB does have some advantages: all of the major development IDEs can help you build them, and every vendor's EJB container provides all of the EJB services required for persistence and transactional support at runtime.

However, to a traditional Oracle developer, EJBs are still going to be a less attractive option for the following reasons:

- **You do not write "normal" SQL** Instead, you write in a slightly different dialect using the EJB Query Language.
- **The EJB container generally handles persistence and querying** Embedded hints in the form of code annotations define the management of data and relationships in data, such as sequence-number generation and master-detail queries. None of this is a bad thing but traditional Oracle developers may find this a little hard to adapt to and feel that EJBs lack the degree of control that they require.
- **EJB is a bare-bones framework** You need to write your own code to add capabilities, such as validation in the EJB layer, although the Java standards are being enhanced as this book is being written to add a declarative data capability to JavaBeans generally. Note also that ADF actually provides a way to decorate bindings to EJBs with some basic metadata based validation as well. Neither of these techniques provides the same power or flexibility as the built-in validation capabilities of ADF BC.
- **It is not based on metadata** With an EJB application there is much more Java code to write, and every line of that code is one more line to debug and maintain, and one line less that can be customized at runtime.

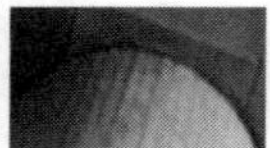

NOTE
Oracle's implementation of EJB 3.0 within Fusion Middleware uses Oracle TopLink (an O/R mapping framework) under the covers. This foundation opens the way for users of Oracle's particular implementation to use native SQL, and to gain all of the benefits in performance and resource usage that TopLink provides. TopLink also adds additional features above being an implementation of the JPA, providing, among other things, Object-to-XML mapping and database web services.

Selecting the O/R Mapping Tool

This book is biased to approaching Java Enterprise Edition development from a relational perspective, which is the normal perspective for existing users of the Oracle database. Accordingly, we don't hesitate to recommend that you use ADF Business Components. This recommendation is not intended to minimize the effectiveness of other options, but experience has shown that traditional Oracle developers, in particular, adapt to ADF Business Components fairly quickly.

We'll look at some of the reasons for that next. However, one of the benefits of using the ADF framework is that, should you choose to use any of the other options, such a decision will not really affect the user interface of the project; it will just affect the mechanics of the model or database integration layer and the amount of code that you have to write.

ADF Business Components is attractive for the following reasons:

- **It emphasizes declarative definition** It's possible to build a relatively sophisticated database integration layer without a single line of handwritten code. You can generate default mappings to database tables using a wizard. JDeveloper will *introspect* (automatically examine properties of) the database schema and not only generate the table mappings but also put in place all of the artifacts and rules required to enforce referential integrity. It is worth noting that declarative definition also provides a cleaner upgrade path for the future and opens up the possibility of customization using the metadata customization capabilities of the framework.
- **It provides the ability to define basic validation rules** It does so in a declarative fashion, just as with declarative O/R mapping. This type of declaration includes validating an attribute based on a database lookup—something that is relatively easy in PL/SQL and tools like Oracle Forms but that is generally not an off-the-shelf function in O/R mapping frameworks.
- **It exploits the power of the database** ADF Business Components will run against non-Oracle databases, but Oracle is its core competency; this focus allows it to support functionality such as *inter*Media (now known as Oracle Multimedia) types and bulk (array) operations.
- **It provides a rich event model** This allows developer much more control over the internal processing order and other features.

We'll spend a lot more time with ADF Business Components in detail in Part II of this book.

Why Should I Use JDeveloper?

We've been making oblique references to the JDeveloper IDE throughout this chapter without really touching on what it is. JDeveloper is a free tool that Oracle supplies to help developers build applications for deployment onto both the middleware platform and the database. It provides a wide range of capabilities as we will show, but most important, it is the tool that is used to build the Fusion Applications within Oracle itself.

At its heart, JDeveloper is a development environment engineered to make the end user developer (you) as productive as possible. It manages the delicate balancing act of providing very visual abstractions for tasks such as page flow design or page layout, without preventing access to the underlying source. Thus, developers are able to work in a mode that suits them for the task on hand. This is really important as developers cycle through the learning process with a new API or framework. The visual editors help them to get up to speed quickly and produce working code, even when they are not entirely sure how it works and what it is doing. However, once the developer's use of the technology matures, that same visual editor does not have to get in the way. There is always the option to drop down into the underlying source code and make the changes there—an approach which is often quicker. The following illustration shows the multiple views available to the developer for editing a page flow. We can see (from top to bottom) the diagram view, the structured overview view, and of course the XML source code.

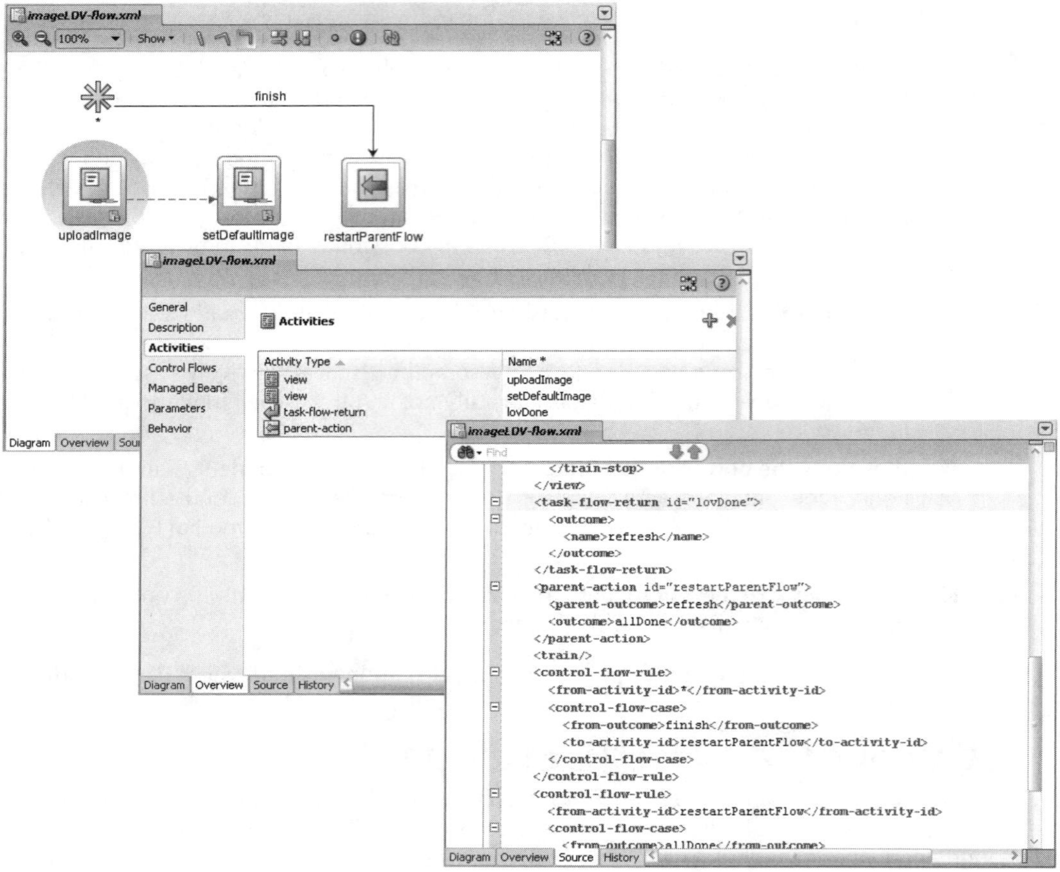

Any of these views, in combination with the Structure Window and the Property Inspector, can be used to manipulate the object. JDeveloper takes care of keeping everything in sync. This approach of the IDE is also crucial when teams of developers are working together on the same artifacts. They can all use their favored views (or even a different IDE all together), and everything will be kept synchronized.

NOTE

Chapter 2 discusses the key structural features of the IDE such as the Structure window and the Property Inspector.

Of key importance is the range of technologies available to the developer. JDeveloper is a *platform IDE*; that is, it serves the development needs of the entire Oracle platform, from working with SQL and PL/SQL in the database, to creating Java EE web UIs, to SOA orchestration, to customizing Oracle's packaged applications. It is literally the Swiss Army Knife of IDEs and is best of its breed in many of those core tasks. One area of particular focus, of course, is the support for the ADF development framework. To use ADF in another IDE such as Eclipse would mean a lot of editing of raw XML files. In JDeveloper, the developer uses a drag-and-drop environment instead; all in all, it is a lot more attractive for building Fusion-style applications.

JDeveloper is also a very adaptable IDE that can be both customized and extended to meet your requirements. Some of the aspects of customization such as the basic environment, layout, keyboard shortcuts, code templates, and so forth can be altered from within the tool. Other customizations require the creation of plug-ins for the product. We don't have space to discuss that topic in this book, but it's a really interesting process to get into and really not as difficult as you might expect. Head over to OTN (www.oracle.com/technology) if you have an interest in that.

Of course, there is much, much more to talk about in relation to JDeveloper, so much so in fact that we devote the next two chapters to it.

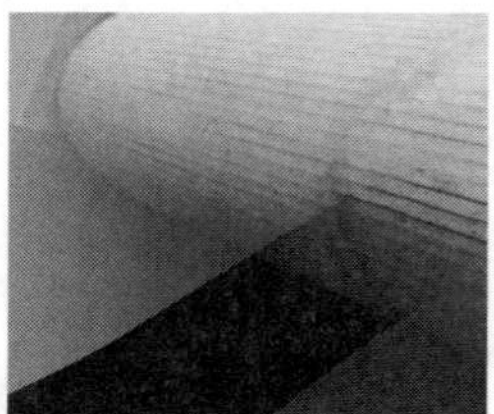

CHAPTER 2

Introduction to the JDeveloper Integrated Development Environment

Beware the ides of March.

—William Shakespeare (1564–1616), *Julius Caesar* (I, ii, 18)

Java *integrated development environments (IDEs)* have come a long way since the early days of Java programming when the development tool of choice was vi or Notepad. As the Java language has evolved and introduced new technologies, tools vendors such as Oracle have kept up by creating IDEs that make the tasks required in designing, creating, testing, and deploying Java-related applications easier.

Since its initial 1.0 release as AppBuilder for Java, JDeveloper has followed the industry trends and has included features that match or exceed the more mainstream Java IDEs. Although JDeveloper has won the favor of many reviewers in the Java industry, it has been most popular with development shops centered around Oracle products. One example of such a shop, albeit an extremely large one consisting of several thousand developers, is Oracle Corporation. Oracle uses JDeveloper to create the Fusion Applications suite (the follow-on version for Oracle applications or E-Business Suite mentioned in Chapter 1). Therefore, the Oracle applications developers are solid proof that JDeveloper can support large teams and a large application development effort. Moreover, that Fusion Applications relies on JDeveloper means that we are assured that Oracle will continue to support and enhance JDeveloper, as it did with Oracle Forms, which was used to create its E-Business Suite.

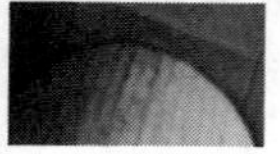

NOTE

The JDeveloper IDE is written in Java. The choice of Java means that JDeveloper may be run in the Java Virtual Machines (JVMs) of different operating systems with few, if any, changes. This makes JDeveloper portable between operating systems.

Creating an application in the Java environment requires creating and organizing hundreds of files. Whether you are an experienced or a novice Java programmer, the number of files and detailed file requirements of each technology can be daunting. As with any good IDE such as Oracle Forms or Visual Studio .NET, JDeveloper assists your development efforts by taking care of the following two development functions that can be time consuming and tedious:

- **Code creation** When you use JDeveloper to create files, the IDE uses its internal templates to preload the files with the code that all files of that type require. For example, when you create a JavaServer Faces (JSF) file, JDeveloper adds all standard code that sets up aliases for the tag libraries that this type of file needs. It also adds standard tags required for all JSF files. This feature can speed up development significantly and make developers much more productive. JDeveloper also automatically creates supporting files for the files you create, like the faces-config.xml file needed for JSF work.
- **Code organization** The large number of files needed for a Java project must work together and be located in standard directories or packages. JDeveloper automates the tedious tasks of keeping the files for an application in the proper locations and assembling them into deployment packages for the production server.

JDeveloper contains an enormous number of features for editing files as well as for code generation and code organization. Although the methods for accomplishing normal development tasks are easy to learn on your own, it will help to have an overview of the basic JDeveloper tools you will use for major development tasks. In addition, it will help to know some tips for best use of these areas. This chapter provides an overview of the IDE basics and offers some tips for how to best use them. The material in this chapter addresses the following questions:

- **What are the important features of the JDeveloper IDE?**
- **How can I best use the Help Center?**
- **How does source code version control work in JDeveloper?**

The main objective of this chapter is to provide an overview of the main features of the JDeveloper IDE. Chapter 3 delves into details about specific IDE tools, which you will use for Fusion web development. This chapter approaches the IDE explanation differently than the JDeveloper help system (called "*Help Center*"), which is focused mostly on explaining one feature at a time. Also, this chapter abbreviates the discussions of many subjects in order to provide a coherent overview. Therefore, you will want to refer to the online JDeveloper help system for further details about the features mentioned in this chapter as well as features not explained in this chapter.

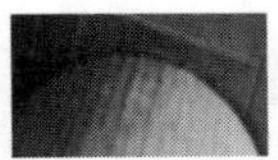

NOTE
You will obtain practice with the IDE windows mentioned in this chapter and many of the tools mentioned in Chapter 3 when following the hands-on practices later in the book. Although this chapter does not contain hands-on practices, if you want to explore the IDE as you read, you can open an application in JDeveloper (or create one using the New Application option).

What Are the Important Features of the JDeveloper IDE?

The JDeveloper IDE offers features that allow you to create and maintain applications using many different styles of code. For example, the JDeveloper code editors assist in editing plain text files. In addition, JDeveloper excels in its support for the declarative and visual style of development. You will find yourself most effective when you use both styles of development although you may spend more time in one than the other. The IDE offers common methods to access the tools you need, regardless of the development style you choose for work at any given moment. The main aspects to know about early on are how to select a role, how to manipulate IDE window, where to find functions in the main toolbar, and what type of functions are found in the main menu bar.

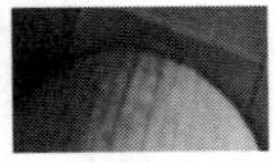

NOTE
An "application" in JDeveloper is a collection of projects, which you are working on (previously called "application workspace" or "workspace"). A "project" in JDeveloper is a collection of files, usually with related functionality, such as files that access the database. Usually, all projects in an application are deployed (distributed to the server) together. You will see these terms used throughout this chapter. Chapter 3 explains these concepts a bit more.

JDeveloper Roles

The first time you open JDeveloper, you will receive a dialog such as that shown next, requesting a role selection. Selecting anything other than "Default Role" will reduce the options available in that JDeveloper session. This can assist in reducing the complexity of the IDE and tailoring it for the type of work you need to perform.

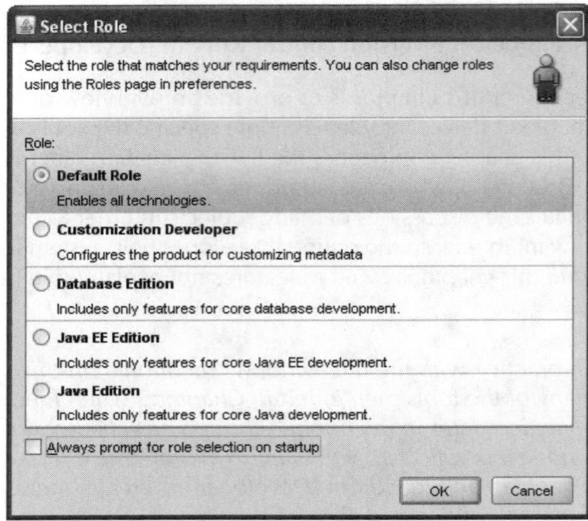

By selecting the "Always prompt for role selection on startup" checkbox, you will see this dialog each time you start JDeveloper. If you most often work with JDeveloper in a single way, you can turn off this dialog to facilitate JDeveloper startup. You can change the role or this checkbox selection at any time by selecting **Tools** | **Preferences** and navigating to the Roles node in the Preferences dialog.

For the purposes of following examples in the book, we recommend using the Default Role option because it does not limit the menus and other selections in the IDE.

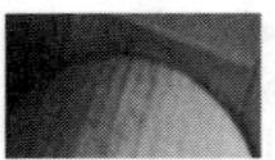

NOTE
When starting JDeveloper after installing or upgrading the IDE, you will also receive a dialog prompting for migrating settings. For the initial installation, choose to not migrate settings (because you have none to migrate). If you are upgrading JDeveloper 10g or 11g, migrating settings can help by setting IDE preference and connections to their state in the preceding version.

The Main IDE Window

You can start JDeveloper from a desktop icon (mentioned in the Introduction) or directly from the executable file, jdeveloper.exe, in the JDEV_HOME directory, where JDEV_HOME is the JDeveloper directory under the directory in which you installed Fusion Middleware, for example in MS Windows, C:\Oracle11g\Middleware\JDeveloper. Alternatively (in an MS Windows operating system) select **Start** | **Programs** | **Oracle Fusion Middleware 11.1.1.1.0** | **JDeveloper Studio 11.1.1.1.0**.

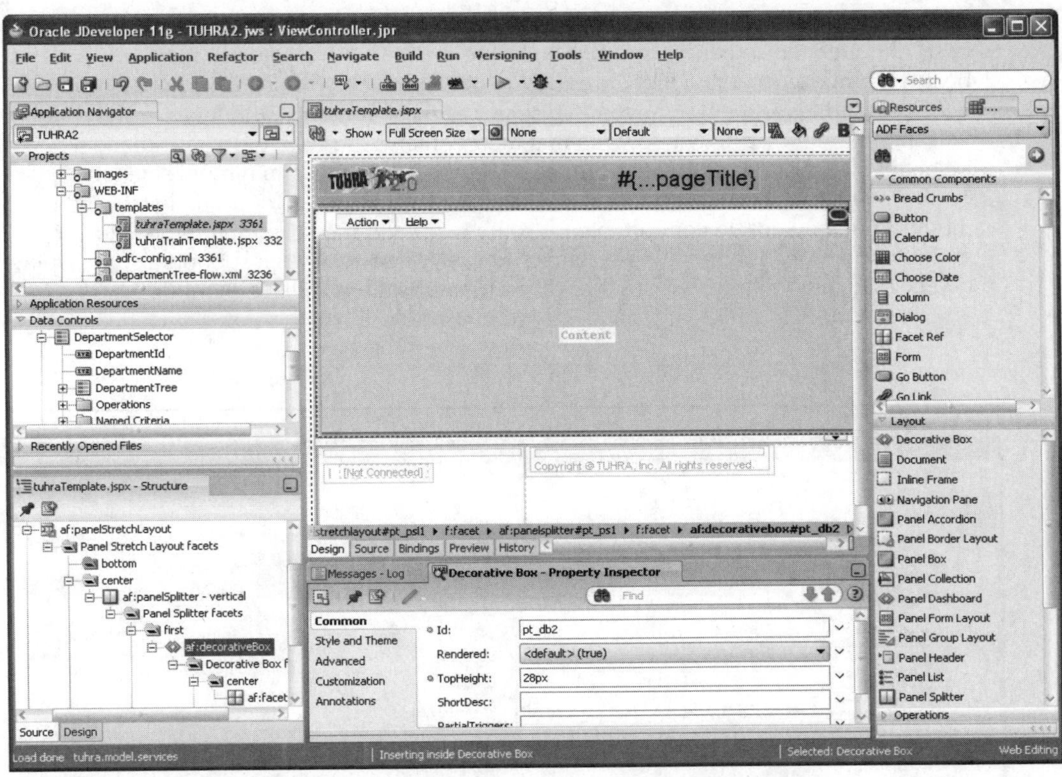

FIGURE 2-1. *The JDeveloper IDE window, displayed in 1024×768 resolution*

When you start JDeveloper, an IDE window such as the one shown in Figure 2-1 appears. (See the sidebar "About Monitor Resolution" for recommendations about display hardware. The introduction to this book provides recommendations about other hardware.) As this figure shows, the IDE window contains a number of tools. These tools appear inside the IDE in locations called *windows*. Although these windows are docked to and are part of the main IDE window by default, you can drag most of them out as separate windows if needed. There are two types of windows, which exhibit different behaviors in the IDE — the editor window and dockable windows. These windows are described next in general terms.

About Monitor Resolution

JDeveloper contains many work areas, and you usually need to have several of them open at the same time. Therefore, you need as much screen real estate as possible. The first rule of thumb for JDeveloper windows is to maximize the size of the IDE window. The next rule of thumb is to maximize screen real estate by using a monitor set to a high resolution such as 1280×1024 (or higher). Figure 2-2 shows JDeveloper running in a 1280×1024 resolution. Compare that with Figure 2-1, where the screen is running a 1024×768 resolution.

(continued)

As in most modern GUI development tools, a large monitor and high resolution are best. Although the screenshots in this book use a 1024×768 resolution for clarity, you will be more productive with a higher resolution, because you will be able to open more windows and leave them arranged to display the most content. With lower resolutions, you will spend time resizing windows so that their contents are visible. This is time that could be better spent on other tasks. As a rule, a 19-inch monitor is a minimum size for 1280×1024 resolution. A resolution of 1600×1200 works on a good-quality, 21-inch monitor but may not be comfortable for some people. A more optimal setup is to use multiple monitors (for operating systems such as Windows XP that support a split display) and display different IDE windows or different applications in each monitor.

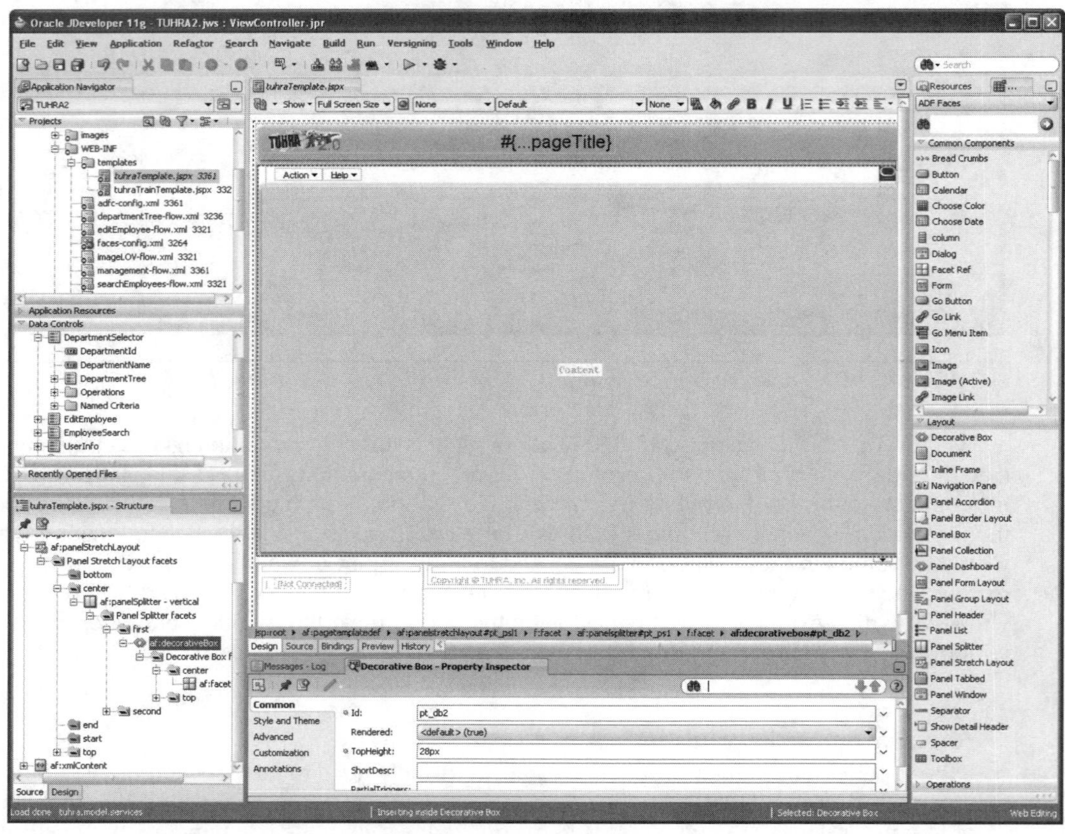

FIGURE 2-2. *The JDeveloper IDE displayed in 1280×1024 resolution*

Editor Window

The *editor window* is an editing container in the center of the IDE window. It is the main window for most development and is normally used to display or edit a single file at a time. The name of the file that is active in the editor will be displayed in the IDE window title. Although the editor window normally shows only one file, it can be split to show multiple views of the same file or multiple files at the same time (as described later).

TIP

You can resize any window inside the IDE frame by dragging an edge. Other windows will be resized, if needed, to accommodate the new window size. The IDE window will remain the same size.

You can view and edit files in different ways. For example, you use the Java Source Editor to directly modify the source code for a Java application that displays Swing controls; you use the Java UI Visual Editor to modify the same file by modifying a visual representation of the file. Both editors appear in the same editor window area. Chapter 3 discusses details about the editors and viewers that can be displayed inside the editor window, but it is useful first to examine some of the features and operations available in this window.

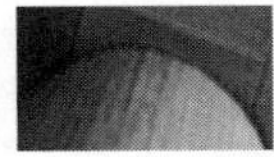

NOTE

The type of file you are editing determines the type of editor that appears by default. For example, when you open a JSF file, the visual editor will appear; when you open a Java class file, the source code editor will appear.

Displaying the Editor Window You display the editor window for a file either by selecting **Open** from the right-click menu and clicking on the file name in the navigator, or by double clicking the file name in the navigator. The default arrangement of JDeveloper windows places the editor window in the large center area of the IDE, with the dockable windows containing support features around it.

Editor Tabs You can display different editors for a single file using the *editor tabs* at the bottom of the editor window. For example, for a JSF document file, the tab area at the bottom of the window contains a Design tab that displays the JSP/HTML Visual Editor and a Source tab that displays the XML Editor, as shown here:

You will also notice a Bindings editor tab that displays an XML Editor window for the binding file, and a History editor tab that displays a list of changes made to the file in the current session, and if you are using a version control system such as Subversion, in that source control system as well.

Document Tabs The editor window can also hold more than one file. You switch back and forth between files using the *document tabs* at the top of the editor window as shown here:

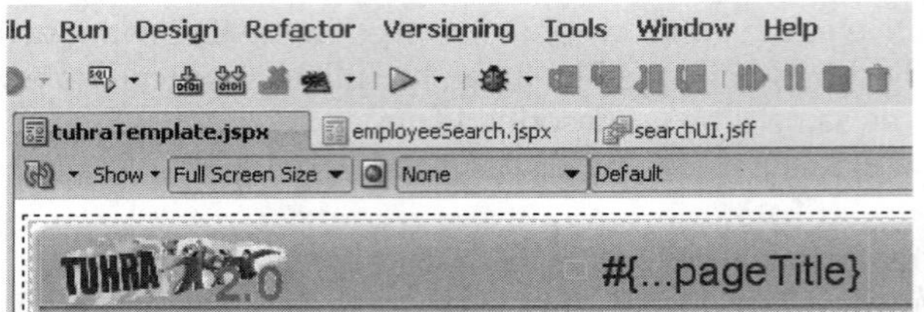

Document tabs contain the name of the file (in this example, tuhraTemplate.jspx, employeeSearch.jspx, and searchUI.jsff) and an icon indicating the type of file within the editor. If the number of document tabs exceeds the room in the editor window, a pulldown in the top-right corner of the window will allow you to navigate to any open document.

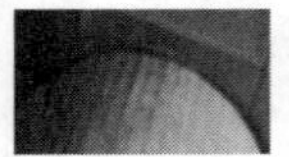

TIP
Double clicking any editor tab will maximize the editor window to fill the IDE window. This technique is handy in many situations, for example, when you are laying out UI pages or when you need to split the editor window. Double clicking a maximized document tab will restore the size and position. You can use this technique for dockable windows as well.

Splitting and Unsplitting the Editor Window You can combine the use of document tabs and document tabs to display more than one file at a time and to display more than one view of the same file. Figure 2-3 shows an example of an editor window containing the JSP/HTML Visual Editor view of tuhraTemplate.jspx in the top left. The same file is displayed in the XML (code) Editor in the top right. In addition, the editor window shows the employeeSearch.jspx file in split windows for the XML Editor (lower left) and the Page Data Binding Definition editor (or "Bindings Editor") (lower right).

You can accomplish this type of arrangement using a combination of several techniques (after clicking in the editor window):

- **Window | Split Document** This menu selection automatically splits the active file in the editor window so that you can look at two views of the same file. Split Document is also available from the right-click menu on a document tab.
- **The splitter bars** The *splitter bars* allow you to divide or merge views of a file and are located above the vertical scrollbar and to the right of the horizontal scrollbar in an editor window (as shown in Figure 2-3). Dragging the horizontal splitter bar down or the vertical splitter bar to the left will create another view of the same file. This technique is an alternative to the **Split Document** menu selection.
- **Window | New Tab Group** This menu selection will open the file in a separate pane in the editor window. Alternatively, you can grab a document tab and drag and drop it inside another open file in the editor window. As you drag, a window outline will move over the area where the window will end up when you drop it.

Horizontal splitter bar

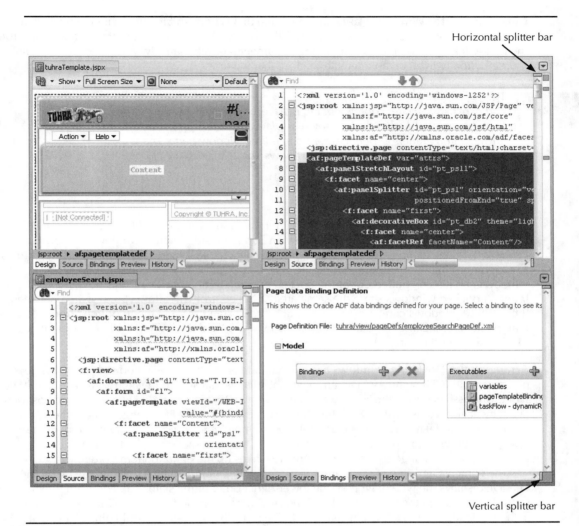

Vertical splitter bar

FIGURE 2-3. *Split editor window*

Unsplitting a window is just a matter of using the techniques in reverse—**Window** | **Unsplit Document** (which will remove all split windows for the selected file), dragging a splitter bar, or dragging and dropping. Use **Window** | **Collapse Tab Groups** to combine two document panes into one window.

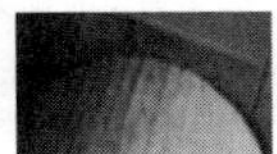

NOTE

As with all operations in JDeveloper, if you have more than one editor window open for a single file, changes in one editor will be immediately reflected in all other editors.

Closing an Editor Window You can close a file that is open in an editor window by clicking the document tab's close ("x") icon (as with all windows in JDeveloper) or by selecting **Close** from the right-click menu on the corresponding document tab. Alternatively, you can click the center mouse button (wheel) on an open tab to close that window.

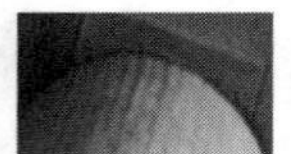

TIP
You can also activate a document tab by selecting it from the Window menu, or from the pulldown displayed by clicking the down arrow button at the top-right corner of an editor window pane. The Window option in this pulldown also allows you to activate or close a document.

Dockable Windows

Dockable windows may be anchored (docked) to the top, bottom, or sides of the outer IDE window. The Application Navigator window embedded inside the IDE window, as shown in Figure 2-2, is one example of a dockable window. Dockable windows typically contain features to support editing code files; therefore, they are arranged around the editor window. These windows can also be pulled out of the docked position to float inside or outside of the IDE frame. If docked windows share the same area, a tab control will allow you to switch between them. These windows can be displayed or activated using the View menu options. You manipulate the docking or floating operations by dragging the window title bar as described later in "Docking and Floating a Window."

Arranging the Dockable Windows By default, areas for dockable windows line the inside perimeter of the IDE window in an arrangement such as that shown in Figure 2-1. (By default, no window is assigned to the inside top perimeter of the IDE window.) You can change the positions taken by each area using the Dockable Windows page of **Tools | Preferences** (under the Environment node) as shown in Figure 2-4. For example, if you click the curved arrow in the lower-left corner of this page, then click the curved arrow in the lower-right corner, the arrangement will change so that the bottom area takes up the entire bottom border.

The contents and size of these areas vary, depending upon the type of work you are doing. The IDE displays the type of work in the lower-right corner of the status bar. For example, the status bar will show the phrase "Web Editing" if you have opened the JSP/HTML Visual Editor for a JSP application file as shown in Figure 2-1. The status bar will show "Xml Editing" if you are viewing and interacting with the Source tab of the same file. The windows will be arranged in the same way as they were the last time the arrangement was active. You can select alternative arrangements using the right-click menu on that corner of the status bar.

Docking and Floating a Window Floating (undocking) a dockable window only requires dragging the title bar or tab of the window away from the docking edge to the center of the IDE window. When the window outline is over the center of the IDE window, releasing the mouse button will undock the window and make it float over the other windows.

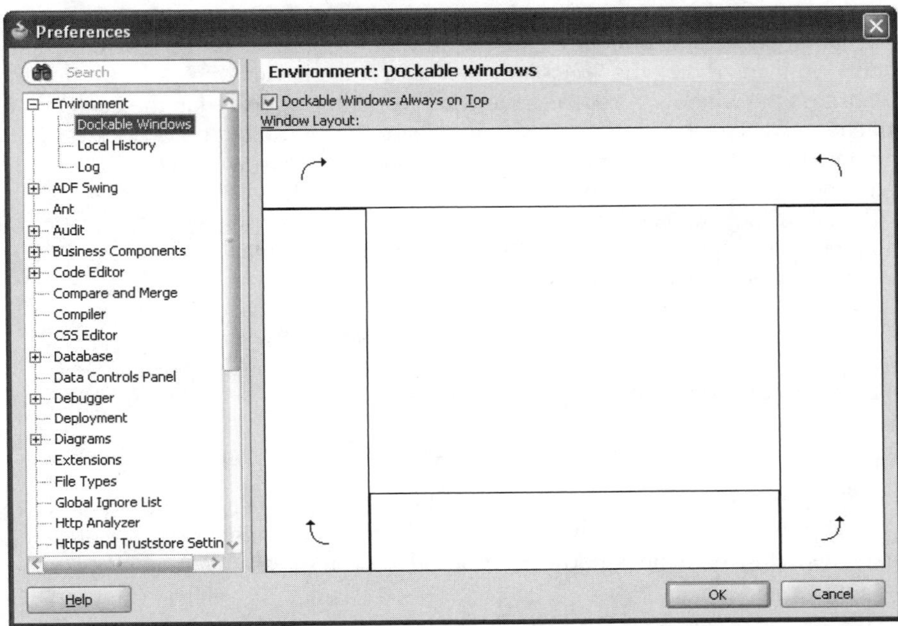

FIGURE 2-4. *Dockable windows page of the Preferences dialog*

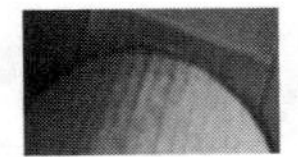

TIP
Floating the Component Palette or Data Controls panel windows will allow you to maximize the visual editor window and still drop components into the editor. Maximizing the visual editor while the palette windows are docked will hide these windows.

Docking a dockable window requires grabbing the window's title bar and dragging the window until the mouse cursor reaches the border of the outer window. You will see the window outline snap into place on that side of the outer IDE window. Releasing the mouse button window will then dock the window. The drag (and snap to border) is shown on the right.

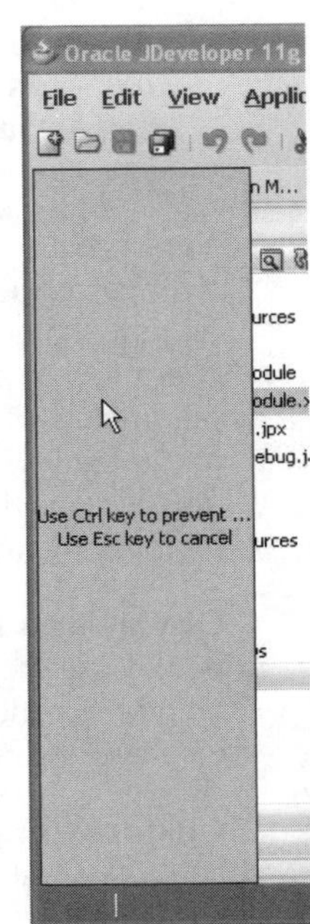

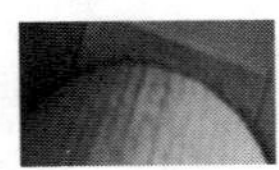

TIP
*You can alternatively select the **Float** option from the right-click menu on a docked window tab to undock the window. Selecting **Dock** from a floating window tab will dock the window again, although you may need to move it to the desired area after docking it.*

Merging Dockable Windows into the Same Space You can move a dockable window into the same space as another dockable window so that both windows share the same area. For example, if you had undocked the Structure window and wanted to dock it over the Application Navigator window, you would drag the Structure window over the navigator area and watch the outline as you position the window. As soon as the window outline appeared in the center of the Application Navigator window, you would release the mouse button to dock the Structure window on top of the Application Navigator window; the two windows will share the same space, and each will have a tab you can click to activate it.

The tab will contain an icon and a title that indicates its contents. If the space within the window is insufficient for titles, only the tab icon will be displayed. For example, the following shows tabs in the navigator window area:

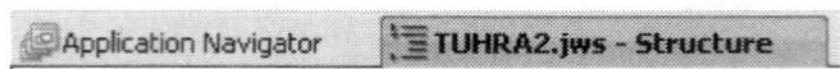

If this area is narrowed, one or more titles will not be displayed, as shown here:

With some experimentation, you can see how a window can be docked under, over, to the left of, or to the right of another window. The outline of the window you are dragging provides a visual clue as to where the window will dock when you release the mouse button.

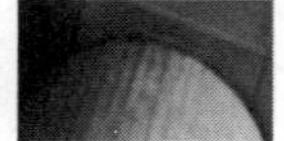

TIP
If you haven't mastered the dockable windows feature in other tools, working with it in JDeveloper can be frustrating at best. Before you start any serious work, dedicate five minutes or so to experimenting with the techniques for docking, floating, merging, minimizing, and restoring dockable windows. This will help your productivity (and sanity) later on. To restore the default, exit JDeveloper and delete windowinglayout.xml in the JDEV_HOME\system11.1.1.1.x\o.ide directory.

Minimizing When a window is docked, a Minimize (dash) icon appears in the window's upper-right corner. Clicking the Minimize icon causes the window to collapse and a tab with the window name to appear in the nearest margin. Clicking that tab (or just holding the mouse cursor over the tab) opens the window. Moving the mouse cursor over another window hides the minimized window. Clicking the Restore button; which replaces the Minimize button in a minimized window, will cause the window to be displayed regardless of the window in focus. Since the navigator area is used infrequently, you may find it useful to minimize it; doing so will increase the available space for other windows.

Displaying a Dockable Window Dockable windows open automatically when they are needed for a particular task. If a window you want to see is not displayed, you can select it from the View menu (for example, **View | Log** to display the Log window). If the window is already displayed, it will be activated when you select it from the View menu.

Customizing the Main IDE Window

You can employ several methods to modify how the IDE looks and works. You can resize and reposition the windows inside the IDE. You can also create JDeveloper extensions that present your own wizards, property editors, and file creation dialogs using the Extension SDK documented in the JDeveloper Help Center. You can also change key mapping and default code formatting. However, the main way to change the most commonly customized features is contained in the Preferences dialog.

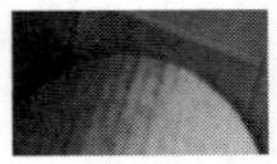

NOTE
*You can modify the key assignment scheme by loading another scheme such as the key assignments for Visual C++. To reassign the keyboard shortcuts, select **Tools | Preferences** and click the Load Preset button on the Accelerators page. This page contains a number of preset selections.*

Preferences Dialog The Preferences dialog (**Tools | Preferences** shown in Figure 2-4) is the main location for modifying the behavior of the tools (and many other IDE features). This dialog contains a navigator for different categories of settings. Changing a setting in this dialog changes the behavior in the tool. Most changes are immediate, although some require exiting and reloading JDeveloper. Examples of some of these preferences are mentioned throughout this chapter and Chapter 3.

TIP
As with many windows in JDeveloper, the Preferences dialog offers a search field (on top of the navigator) that you can use to search for text in preferences or preference navigator nodes. This is quite handy if you cannot immediately find a preference you need to set.

The IDE Look and Feel The ability to change the look and feel (aspects such as colors, fonts, and the treatment of window edges) of an application is a feature of the Swing (Java UI components) used to build JDeveloper. You can define the look and feel for your JDeveloper session using the Environment page of the Preferences dialog (**Tools | Preferences**). The *Look and Feel* property specifies the general category, and the *Theme* field specifies color schemes within that category. After setting this option, you will see a dialog to restart JDeveloper so that the new setting will take effect.

NOTE
All screenshots in this book were captured with the IDE environment set to the default "Oracle" look and feel and "Fusion Blue" theme current with the first release of JDeveloper 11g. Subsequent releases may look slightly different.

TIP
JDeveloper will load faster if a reduced set of features is enabled. You can reduce the number of features loaded when JDeveloper is started by using the Extensions page of the Preferences dialog. This page allows you to deselect features that you do not use or use infrequently.

Main Toolbar

The IDE main toolbar contains frequently accessed commands for file creating, saving, compiling, and debugging, as well as standard edit commands (cut, copy, past, undo, and redo). All toolbar buttons provide tooltip hints that appear when the mouse cursor is held over the button. All functions performed by the toolbar icons also appear in the main menu and some appear in the right-click menus.

NOTE
The editor window and dockable windows also offer toolbars for frequently used operations.

Main Menu Bar

The IDE main menu bar offers access to a large number of operations. You should be able to find the option you need by browsing the menus, but some features are worthy of special mention. Therefore, this section explains some of functionality in the main menu bar that you might otherwise miss.

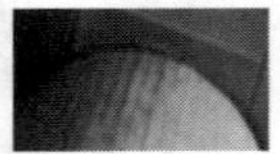

TIP
Items in JDeveloper's menus are context sensitive. That is, they will be disabled or hidden if they are not appropriate to the type of file. If you do not see or cannot select a menu option that you need, change the focus to the relevant file type or window. Sometimes this technique requires some experimentation to discover the focus that is required for menu items.

In addition to the main menu bar, JDeveloper uses right-click (context) menus extensively. Almost everything in the IDE offers right-click menu options for frequently used operations. Many of these options are also contained in the main IDE menu. Therefore, instead of listing and explaining all of the right-click menu selections here, it will be more useful to provide the following tip.

TIP
Always be aware that an operation you may want to perform on a particular object in the IDE may be more easily accessible in a right-click menu than in a main menu option. In addition, some accelerator key presses (such as CTRL-N *to display the New Gallery) will help you access common operations quickly. For a listing navigate to the Shortcut Keys node in the Preferences dialog.*

File Menu

This menu contains common operations such as opening files (**Open**), closing files (**Close**), saving a file (**Save**), and saving all changed files (**Save All**). It also allows you to delete a file (**Delete**). The **New** option (discussed in Chapter 3's "New Gallery" section) creates a file or other element such as a connection. A **Rename** option changes the name of a file. If you want to rename a class file that is used by other class files, use the Refactor menu items (discussed in the section "Refactor Menu" later).

NOTE
When you change a file, JDeveloper will italicize its name in the Application Navigator and document tab to signal that the file needs to be saved. If you close the IDE with an unsaved file, JDeveloper will display a prompt where you indicate whether you would like to save the changes.

The **Reopen** menu item shows a list of all files recently opened. You can select from that list and load projects into the IDE more quickly because you do not have to browse the file system.

You can load an existing file into an editor or viewer by selecting the **Open** item in this menu. This will open the file but not add it to the active project, in case you just want to edit, copy, or view the file's contents. To add a copy of (not just a reference to) an existing file into your project directory, use the **Import** menu option. You can include a file inside a WAR or EAR (types of Java archive files formatted like Zip files) as well as to an existing file. The **Import** item can also just include the file without copying it.

TIP
*To copy a file, select it in the navigator and select **File | Save As**. You can then specify the new name and directory in the dialog that appears.*

File Comparisons The **Compare With** submenu of the File menu (also available from the right-click menu on a file in the Application Navigator) allows you to perform a file "diff" (comparison) between the selected file and another file as shown here:

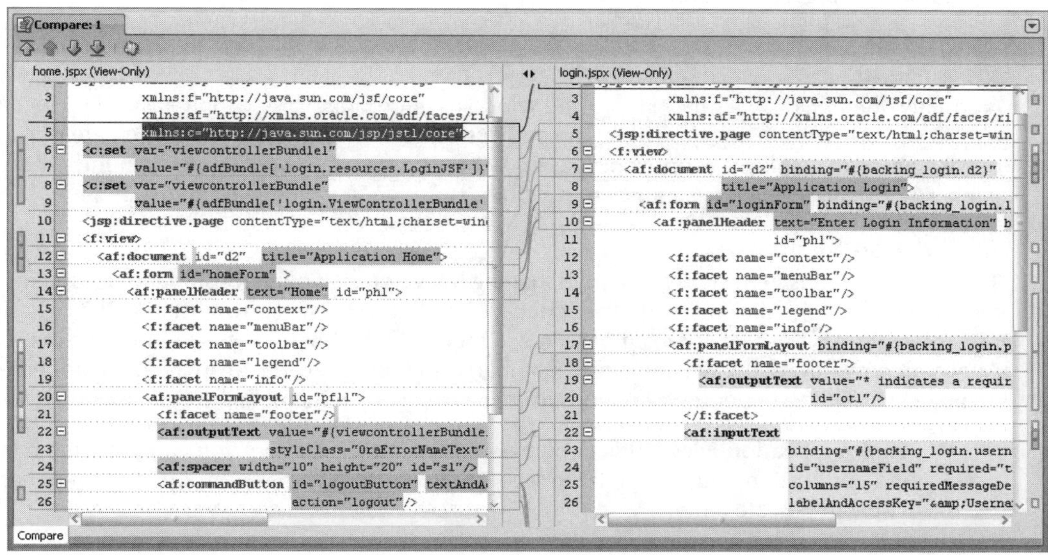

This dialog allows you to edit the current version of the file (displayed in the right side of the window). You can compare files from the version control system using the Compare With submenu of a file's right-click menu. In addition, if you group together files in the same application (using CTRL click), you can select **Each Other** from this submenu to compare the files. If you compare project nodes, the file comparison is performed on the XML code in the project files. This is also the case with other objects you create in JDeveloper such as diagram objects.

NOTE
The Compare dialog only shows differences between files. You cannot edit the files in the results dialog. However, the History tab allows you to edit files; for example, you can revert a change from a previous version in source control or from a previous state in the editor session.

Edit Menu

The Edit menu provides the standard cut, copy, paste, redo, and undo editing features. Many items here have keyboard shortcuts (such as CTRL-Z for **Undo**) that are faster to use than the menu selections. The **Properties** item allows you to view and modify the definitions of some objects such as database connections in the Database Navigator. Other objects make properties available in the right-click menu of the Application Navigator. For example, project properties are available using the Properties right-click menu option (and also from a menu item in the Tools menu). Editor objects such as JSF components display properties in the Property Inspector.

NOTE
*The keyboard shortcuts mentioned in this book are based upon the default key assignments. You can modify the key assignment scheme by loading another scheme such as the key assignments for Eclipse. To reassign the keyboard shortcuts, select **Tools | Preferences** and click the Load Preset button on the Shortcut Keys page. This page contains a number of preset selections.*

View Menu

Normally, the IDE displays the editors and windows appropriate to a certain task. The View menu allows you to override or supplement the choices that the IDE makes about which areas to display. You can display a window or make a window active by selecting items in this menu. You can also display or hide the status bar and toolbars using View menu selections.

Application Menu

This menu contains items that assist in managing JDeveloper applications. Many of its items are repeated in the right-click menu on the application pulldown (down-arrow icon) in the right side of the Application Navigator, for example, **New**, **Open**, **Close**, **Delete**, **Rename**, and **Version**. Both Application menus (pulldown and main menubar) also provide access to application properties and deployment utilities. Other useful options from the Application menu in the main menubar follow.

- **Find Application Files** This option displays a window where you can enter file names in the application. Other search items locate text within files, so this option is very handy if you can't locate a file.

- **Manage Templates** This Application menu selection opens the Manage Templates dialog (shown next) where you can view, add, and remove the technology templates that you can apply to new application workspaces.

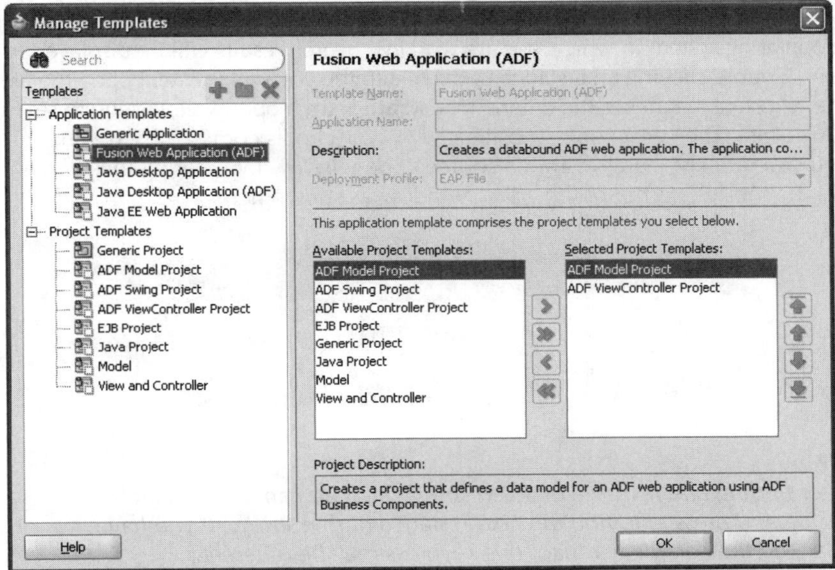

- **Edit Resource Bundle** This option allows you to define and change resource bundles that provide messages and values to your application. Chapter 10 contains information and hands-on practice work with resource bundles.
- **Default Project Properties** Use this item to set characteristics for new project files. This is useful if you need to change a particular setting for all subsequent projects.

Refactor Menu

This menu contains options for *refactoring* code, renaming or moving a file, and cascading the change to all dependent files. Refactoring to rename Java class files also changes the class declaration code (for example, `public class TestClass`) and the constructor code so that they properly match the new file name. Renaming a file using the File menu will not automatically change the class declaration, constructors, or other files that reference it. These refactoring options allow you to safely reorganize code at any time. Developers often find this type of reorganization necessary, despite the best design efforts.

The Refactor menu also offers options to move to another file or to rename parts of a file, such as methods and fields. Refactoring to reorganize your code is a common task and you will use Refactor menu options in the hands-on practices throughout this book.

Search Menu

The Search menu contains standard find features. Selecting text to search for in the current editor window will load it into the *Text to Search For* field in the Find Text dialog (**Find** menu option). This dialog allows you to find (and optionally replace) text within the file in the editor window.

It contains handy search features such as *Wrap Around* to search from the top if the text is not located below the cursor, as well as *Scope* options for defining how to replace text.

The Search menu also offers a **Find in Files** option that allows you to search for files containing text that you specify, even if the text is within a .zip or .jar archive file. This is similar to the Windows Explorer file search feature. However, it is platform independent, so you can use this dialog regardless of the operating system in which you are working. Search results will be displayed in the Log window. Double clicking an instance of the text in the Log window will open the file and navigate to the line whose text matches the criteria. The **XPath Search** option allows you to search for information in an XML file. (The W3Schools website at www.w3schools.com/Xpath explains XPath in detail.)

You can quickly search within a source code window by entering the search text inside the field in the top-left corner of the editor window as shown here:

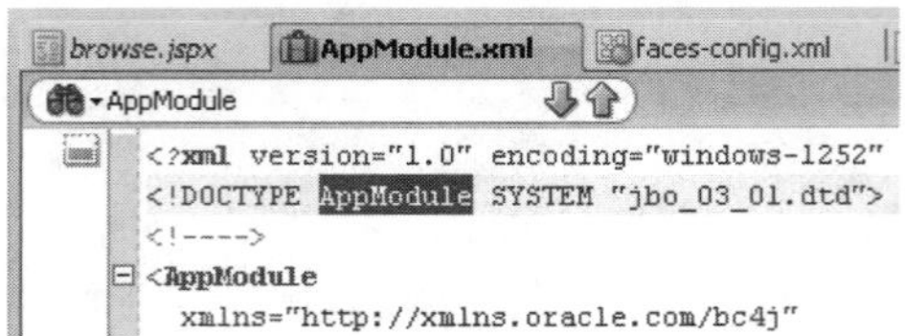

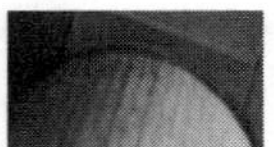

TIP

After finding one instance of a text string, you can cancel the search dialog and press F3 *to find the next instance of that string. (If you have changed the default key map, this keypress may be different.)*

Navigate Menu

This menu contains items to set, clear, and find *bookmarks* (lines of code to which you can easily navigate) in a source code file. This is handy if you are frequently navigating back to the same lines of code. Setting a bookmark places a "bookmark" icon in the left margin of the Code Editor. The editor *gutter* (left margin) also includes options to manage bookmarks. **Go to Recent Files** shows a list of files you have recently opened in JDeveloper.

This menu also contains selections for navigating through messages in the Log window (**Go to Next Message** and **Go to Previous Message**). You can jump to a specific line number using **Go to Line**. The following are other items in this menu:

- **Select in Navigator** This selection will find the file node in the navigator that corresponds to a file that is open in an editor window.
- **Select in Structure** This item selects the node in the Structure window that corresponds to an object selected in an editor such as the JSP/HTML Visual Editor.
- **Go to Java Type** This selection (CTRL- –) displays a dialog where you enter or find a class name. When you click OK in that dialog, the source code file for that class is loaded into a Code Editor window (but not into the navigator). You can view the code and comments. The Structure window shows the contents of the source code file.
- **Go to Javadoc** allows you to find *Javadoc* (standard Java documentation generated in a special format) documentation for a class instead of the source code.

The **Go to Declaration** option in the Code Editor's right-click menu has a effect similar to the **Go to Java Type** option but the former option loads the source file of the item at the cursor location.

If the cursor item is a class name, this option loads the source file for the class; if the cursor item is a primitive variable or object, this option displays the declaration of that variable or object; if the cursor item is a method, this option displays the method declaration.

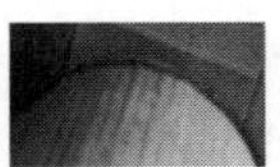

NOTE
When JDeveloper navigates to a class file, it creates code stubs if the class has no available source code. If it is not able to determine the code, it will display a message in the status bar of the IDE.

Build Menu

This menu contains various **Make** and **Rebuild** commands. It also offers items for running Ant—a popular script-language interpreter (ant.apache.org) most often used to process scripts that build (make) projects and create deployment files. Using the **Deploy** submenu of this menu, you can *deploy* (create a standard archive file containing application files and copy it to the server) based on a deployment profile you define. **Javadoc <filename>** creates Javadoc files for the selected file. **Audit <filename>** analyzes the code according to defined standards. **Clean <project_name>** removes compiled files from the project directory.

NOTE
The Make commands compile only modified files. Rebuild compiles all files.

Run Menu

The Run menu contains items for running the project or file that is selected. This menu offers selections to run the *Profiler,* which provides details about runtime memory and CPU usage. **Terminate** in this menu stops a running program.

NOTE
When you run a file in JDeveloper, all changed files in the project will be recompiled automatically. If you prefer to control compilation more closely, you can turn off this behavior in the Run/Debug/Profile page of the Property Properties dialog (accessed by double clicking the project in the navigator).

Debug Options JDeveloper contains a full-featured debugger. It is accessible from items on the Run menu. **Debug <project>** starts a debugging session and executes the code until the first breakpoint. In the debugging session, many of the items in this menu will become enabled. Clicking the Debug toolbar icon or pressing SHIFT-F9 will also run the project in debug mode.

NOTE
Chapter 3 contains an introduction to the main features of the debugger. In addition, the JDeveloper Help Center contains more information about the debugger in the topics, starting with the Table of Contents node "Designing and Developing Applications\Developing Java Applications\Programming in Java\Debugging Java Programs."

Source Menu

The Source menu appears when the Source tab is active in the editor window. It contains items that access the features of a code editor; as usual, many of these items are also available in the right-click menu in the source code editor. Although the contents of this menu vary, depending on the type of file you are editing, you will find items such as the following (for a Java class file):

- **Completion Insight** and **Parameter Insight** activate code assistance features described in the section "Code Insight and Tag Insight" in Chapter 3.
- **Expand Template** automatically inserts a code snippet defined for a code abbreviation. (Code templates are described in Chapter 3.)
- **Quick Javadoc** displays a small box containing Javadoc text for a single method or class referenced in the code.
- **Override Methods** allows you to select from a list of methods available (from the class file hierarchy) to the Java class file you are editing. Selecting one or more methods from this list will create code stubs in your file as a starting point for overriding the selected methods.
- **Implement Interface** displays a dialog where you can browse and select an interface file that your Java class will implement. After you select one or more interfaces and click OK, JDeveloper will add the `implements` clause to your class definition and will add method stubs for which you will need to write code.
- **Generate** options provide stubs for commonly required code units such as *accessors* (Java methods used to set and retrieve values from variables in a Java class) and *constructors* (code units in a Java file used to create objects).
- **Add Javadoc Comments** creates a Javadoc block that you can use as a starting point for your comments on a method or class.
- **Surround With** embeds the selected code inside a code structure, such as `if..else`.
- **Toggle Line Comments** modifies the source code by commenting or uncommenting a number of lines.
- **Indent Block** and **Unindent Block** move blocks of code to the right or left, respectively.
- **Widen Imports** changes imports for a specific class so that they reference the package that is the parent of the specific class. This option allows you to write code that refers to any Java class in that package without separate import statements for each class.
- **Reformat** rearranges the white space in the file so that it complies with default standards or standards you have set in the Preferences dialog (Code Editor\Code Style page). This utility works on both Java and XML code.

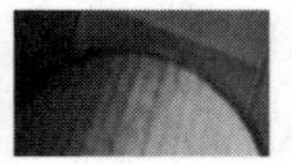

TIP

As mentioned, some menu options may be activated using key press combinations. For example, you can also access Toggle Line Comments by pressing CTRL-/.

Compare Menu

The Compare menu appears when a file comparison window is active. The menu options in this menu repeat the functions of the buttons in the comparison window toolbar, such as **Go to Next**

Difference and **Go to Previous Difference**. **Generate Patch** allows you to create a file containing the differences between files; you can apply this file to another file checked out of a source control system so that file can be updated in the source control system (**Versioning | Apply Patch**).

History Menu

The History menu appears when the History tab of a source code editor window is open. Like the Compare menu, it contains items for navigation buttons that appear in the History window. It also offers a **Restore from Revision** option that allows you to revert changes made to a file.

TIP
Using buttons in the middle splitter bar of the History window, you can revert changes made to a file on a one-by-one basis. Although the Compare window looks similar, it does not allow modifications to the files.

Diagram Menu

The Diagram menu appears when a diagram is active in the editor window. This menu contains utility functions that assist the layout tasks in the UML modelers (class diagram, activity diagram, sequence diagram, and use case diagram) and various class model variations (Java classes, business components, database objects, EJBs, and web services). The **Publish Diagram** item allows you to save the diagram as a .svg, .svgz, .jpg, or .png file.

Versioning Menu

The Versioning menu offers items for a source control system (also called "version control system" or "software configuration management") so that you can track changes made to source code and keep backup copies of different versions of your code. A later section in this chapter—"How does Source Code Version Control Work in JDeveloper?"—explains the operations you will use from this menu.

Tools Menu

The Tools menu contains a number of functions not found anywhere else, such as the **Preferences** option already mentioned. Other functions available in the Tools menu include wizards for setting up ADF Security and items such as the following:

- **Configure Palette** This item displays the Configure Component Palette dialog that allows you to add to or modify the contents of the Component Palette window (discussed in the section "Component Palette" in Chapter 3).
- **Manage Libraries** This item opens the Manage Libraries dialog, where you can create, modify, and remove groups of files that are organized into libraries. This option is used often by developers who are in charge of setting up libraries for use by other developers.
- **Plug-in HTML Converter** This item calls a standard Java utility (Java Plug-in HTML Converter) that converts an HTML file containing applet tags to a file that supports a plugin (for Swing classes, for example). Since this is an external utility, it includes its own help text, which is not incorporated into the JDeveloper Help Center.
- **SQL Worksheet** This option opens a utility in the editor window that allows you to enter SQL commands in much the same way as in SQL*Plus, but this utility is part of JDeveloper, so you do not need to install SQL*Plus. This feature is described in the section "SQL Worksheet" in Chapter 3.

- **SQL*Plus** This option starts the SQL*Plus command-line SQL tool, which is distributed with other Oracle software such as the database. When you select this option, a dialog will appear where you select (or create) a database connection. The first time you use this option, another dialog will then prompt you for the name and location of SQL*Plus before opening a SQL*Plus window. You can also define the SQL*Plus executable on the SQL*Plus page of the Preferences dialog.

TIP
*You can also open SQL*Plus from the right-click menu on a specific Connections node.*

- **External Tools** This item allows you to add programs outside of JDeveloper into the JDeveloper Tools menu, right-click menu, and IDE toolbar. You can configure the external program to load a file selected in JDeveloper. Explore this dialog and utilize the Help buttons if you want to learn more about this feature.

A number of other Tools menu options manage access to the database: **Database Copy**—to create objects in one account that are the same as objects in another account; **Database Diff**—to compare and synchronize the objects in different database accounts; and **Database Export**—to create Data Definition Language (DDL) scripts for objects and data in the database.

Window Menu

The Window menu contains items for splitting and unsplitting document windows and for creating and collapsing tab groups. Other items switch focus to one of the open windows so that you can activate a window that does not have focus. The **Go to** submenu contains options to navigate among the open windows or to open a list of files from which you can select. Use the **Assign File Accelerator** submenu to associate a shortcut (such as ALT-2) with the active window.

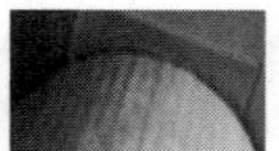

NOTE
As mentioned, you can navigate between document windows using the pulldown in the top-right corner of the editor window.

Help Menu

Some items in the Help menu correspond to the tab pages in the Help window: **Table of Contents**, **Help Favorites**, and **Dynamic Help**. The menu also contains several items that link to content on the Oracle Technology Network (OTN) website. Other items display the **Start Page**, **Release Notes**, and **About** dialog (for version information), as well as **Cue Cards** (step-by-step instructions) and **Tip of the Day** (quick tips that can also appear when you start JDeveloper). The **Check for Updates** item accesses the OTN website (or local file system) and displays a dialog that allows you to view available JDeveloper patches and add-ins from the Oracle or the JDeveloper community.

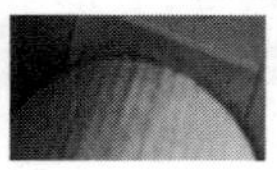

NOTE
*The **Check for Updates**, **JDeveloper Forum**, and **Oracle Technology Network** menu options require an Internet connection.*

How Can I Best Use the Help Center?

You start the JDeveloper Help Center (help system) by selecting **Table of Contents** (or **Search**, **Cue Cards**, **Help Favorites,** or **Dynamic Help**) from the Help menu (or by pressing F1). The main help system interface appears in the Help Center window. Finding a topic in the Help Center is relatively easy for anyone who has used a modern help system or Internet search engine, but a brief description of its features should help you find topics more quickly.

Finding the Help Topic

The Help button in various wizards and dialogs in JDeveloper opens a context-sensitive help page in a separate nonmodal window as shown in Figure 2-5. You can open this window by pressing the help key (F1 in Windows). You can either close the help window or just move it to the side and continue to interact with the wizard or dialog.

Other than this context-specific help, you can find help topics by selecting **Help | Search** and entering keywords in the search field displayed in the top-right corner of the window as shown here:

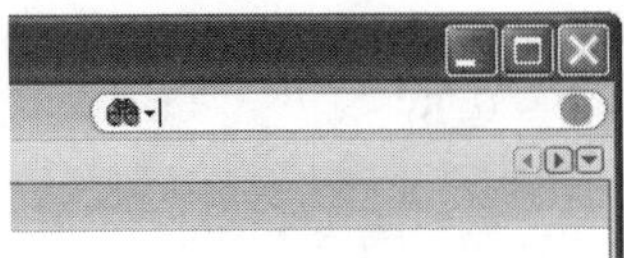

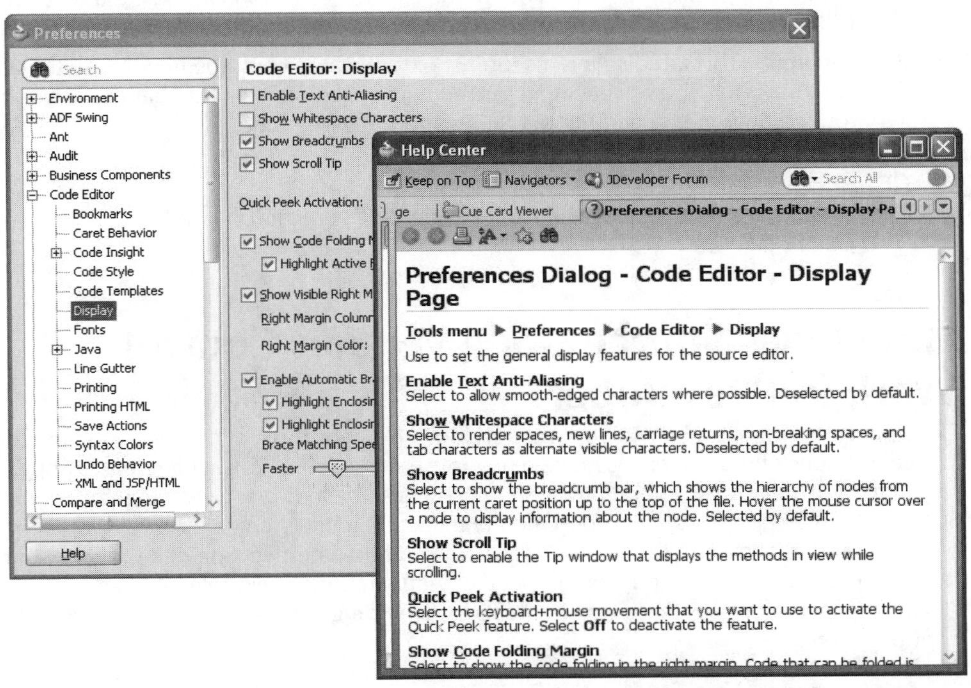

FIGURE 2-5. *Context-sensitive help for the Preferences dialog*

Pressing ENTER or clicking the arrow button next to the search field will initiate the search. A list of topic matches will then appear in the Help Center editor window. You can click a link for one of these matches to open another tab containing that topic. All topics stay open in separate tabs until you close them. A list of open topics is available in the pulldown directly under the search field in the top-right corner of the screen.

TIP
Fast access to help topics is also available by entering keywords in the search field in the top-right corner of the JDeveloper IDE window. This field performs the same type of search as its clone in the Help Center window, but the IDE search field displays results in a popup list under the field. Selecting a topic will open the Help Center window with that topic displayed.

Other than the tabs for each open help topic, the Help Center window displays the following tabs:

- **Contents** This tab displays a list of topics arranged hierarchically in folders and in leaf nodes that represent topic pages.
- **Favorites** This tab displays a list of topics you have marked as *favorites*, content that you would like to view again. You mark a topic as a favorite using the Add to Favorites toolbar (star) button that is displayed when a help topic appears in the Help Center window. When you save a topic as a favorite, you can place it in folders that you create. The topic will then appear under that folder in the Favorites tab. You can delete the favorite topic using the right-click menu on the topic node in the Favorites tab.
- **Dynamic** This tab displays a short list of topics that could be needed for the type of work in which you are engaged. As the name suggests, this list changes as you move from editing one type of file to editing another type of file.

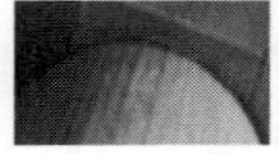

TIP
Display or hide a help system tab using the right-click menu on any Help Center tab.

How Does Source Code Version Control Work in JDeveloper?

Developing software rarely involves one developer, a single application, or a one-time release. Typically, teams of developers produce many integrated applications with releases appearing regularly over time. A *version control system* (VCS, also called *software configuration management*, SCM, or *source control system*) is designed to track and identify changes to development objects over time and to allow the developers to not only edit the latest version of a program, but also to return to previous releases and work in parallel with a more current release.

JDeveloper addresses these requirements by providing extensions to the following version control systems:

- Concurrent Versions System (CVS, www.nongnu.org/cvs/)
- Subversion (subversion.tigris.org)

- IBM Rational ClearCase (www.ibm.com/software/awdtools/clearcase)
- Serena Dimensions (www.serena.com/products/dimensions/)
- Perforce (www.perforce.com)
- MS Team System (msdn.microsoft.com/en-us/teamsystem)

If your version control system is not listed or if it is not available by default, select **Help | Check for Updates** to look for the relevant extension.

TIP
Details about setting up and using your own or natively supported version control systems are provided in the JDeveloper online help. Start your research in the "Designing and Developing Applications\ Using Versioning" node in the Contents tab.

If you have a choice in version control systems, it is worth considering Subversion, which many in the industry consider to be an improvement on CVS. Concepts for using Subversion (abbreviated as *SVN*) and CVS in JDeveloper are very similar. The rest of this section explains how to work with version control systems in JDeveloper using Subversion as an example.

TIP
*Consult the JDeveloper Help Center for the Subversion version number you need for your version of JDeveloper 11*g.

Working with Subversion

Subversion support is active by default in JDeveloper. Two setup steps are required.

1. Set Up or Locate the Repository If Subversion is set up in your development environment already, select **Versioning | Version Application**; then select Subversion and click OK. A Create Subversion Connection dialog will appear where you specify details about the Subversion *repository*—the container for files you wish to manage with version control. (Click the Help button if you need details about the fields in this dialog.)

If you would like to create a small, local repository for testing purposes (or because you are a sole developer for a project and want to keep the best practice of using version control), select **Versioning | Subversion | Create Repository** and enter a directory to hold the repository files and a repository name. Otherwise, for a multiple developer team, an administrator will set up a repository on a central server by downloading the Subversion server (from subversion.tigris.org), installing it, and setting up a repository using command-line commands appropriate to the server.

TIP
If you only use one version control system, you can save some overhead in JDeveloper if you turn the other extensions off using ***Versioning | Configure****. This will eliminate the need to select the version control system from a submenu for each versioning operation. (If you decide to set up a single version control system, you will not need to select the Subversion submenu for all versioning options mentioned in the rest of this chapter.)*

2. Import a Module If your application has not been saved yet to the repository, you or an administrator will need to store the application by importing it into the repository. This action creates a Subversion *module,* a named group of files. The repository can hold many modules.

An Import Module dialog will automatically appear after creating a connection. Alternatively, after you create the connection, you can summon the Import Module dialog using **Versioning** | **Version Application**; then selecting Subversion and clicking OK. The Import to Subversion Wizard will appear. Follow the wizard to import the application that is open in JDeveloper.

TIP
A how-to white paper on OTN, "Team Development Using Subversion," describes best practices for Subversion work in JDeveloper.

Using Repository Files

Once an application is imported into a Subversion repository, any developer can access files within it. The developer will issue a *check out* command (**Versioning** | **Subversion** | **Check Out**) to download all files from the repository and create a *working copy,* a set of all files in the application, on the local developer's desktop computer. The developer can also add files to the application in the repository at any time. The repository stores all copies of the file throughout its life cycle. These copies are called *versions* or *revisions* and are assigned an internal number.

When you request an update of a file (**Versioning** | **Subversion** | **Update**), by default Subversion returns the most recent version from the repository, but all versions of a file are available.

TIP
If the application is under Subversion control, all relevant Subversion commands are available from the right-click menu on file nodes in the Application Navigator.

Committing Files

Once developers check out local working copies of the files, they can make changes to the files and *commit* (save) them back to the Subversion repository using JDeveloper (**Versioning** | **Subversion** | **Commit Working Copy**). Committing a working copy creates a new version in the Subversion repository.

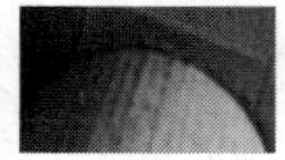

NOTE
Versioning menus and submenus in JDeveloper contain both "Commit" and "Commit Working Copy" selections. The former runs the standard SVN commit command for a single file. The latter commits all files within the selected node in the Application Navigator. This command makes committing a number of files much easier.

Subversion and JDeveloper handle file concurrency. For example, two developers check out (or update) the same file at the same time and make changes to it. The first developer commits the file, which increments the version number for that file in the repository. When the next developer changes and commits the file, Subversion notices the difference between the repository version and the version the developer made changes to. It then attempts to merge the changes into the master copy for the second developer. If merging is not possible, it issues a notice that the file has *conflicts* (inconsistencies between file versions). The second developer will then need to resolve these conflicts by merging the changes using JDeveloper's merge utility. Once the conflicts are resolved and the second developer's changes are merged, the second developer can commit those changes.

You can also lock files so that another developer cannot commit a changed working copy of that file while you hold the lock. However, since this mechanism can tie up development work for a file, it is best used only for a binary file that cannot be merged by normal means.

TIP
It makes good sense to be sure that files you commit to source control work with other files in the application. Otherwise, if developers refresh their copies of the application with your faulty code, they may not be able to run the application. Also, adding a comment (about the change you made) in the Commit dialog is a recognized best practice.

Adding Files

If you add a file to the application in JDeveloper, you need to select **Versioning | Subversion | Add** from the right-click menu to add it to the repository. When that operation completes, you then commit the file as usual.

Refreshing a Working Copy

If you need to refresh your working copy of a file because someone has committed a change to that file, select **Update Working Copy** from the right-click menu on the file (or node to refresh all files under that node).

Pending Changes Window

The best way to keep track of files you and others have changed in the repository is the Pending Changes window (**Versioning | Subversion | Pending Changes**) shown here:

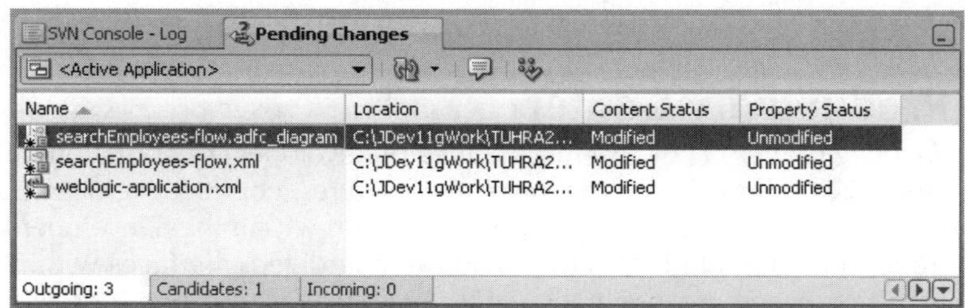

This window displays changed files in three tabs: Outgoing (for changes you need to commit), Candidates (for files you have added to the application but not to the repository), and Incoming (for files that others have committed since you updated your copy). You can interact with the repository using the right-click menu on files listed in these three tabs.

Version History and Version Compare

When you have source control enabled, the History editor tab allows you to view the version numbers, dates, and comments added to the versions of the file in the repository. Double clicking any version file will open it in read-only mode in a new editor window. As mentioned, local history (changes made in JDeveloper but not committed) is visible in this window as well.

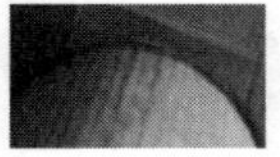

TIP
*You can change the size of the local history buffer in the Preferences dialog (**Tools | Preferences**), Environment\Local History page. Preferences that control the behavior of comparison and merge utilities appear on the Compare and Merge page.*

Version Navigator

The Version Navigator (**View | Versioning Navigator**) window allows you to see all the connections you have made to version control repositories (regardless of the type). You can use this window to create directories, check out files, and delete files in the repository.

State Overlay Icons

By default, JDeveloper displays *state overlay icons* that indicate the status of the file or directory; the overlay icons appear in the navigator next to each file that is associated with Subversion. The following illustration shows some of these icons.

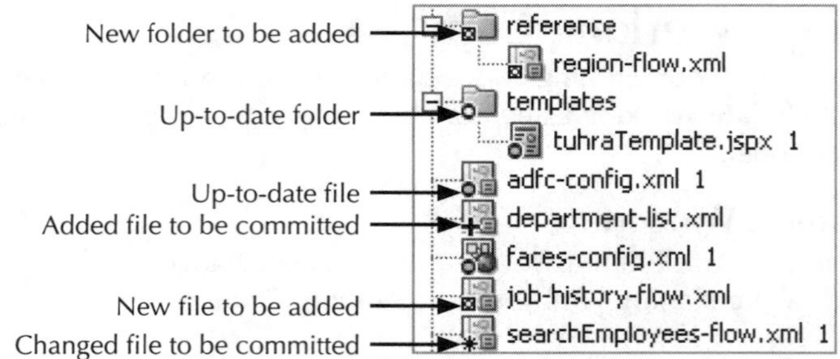

Team Productivity Center

Team Productivity Center (TPC) extends the idea of developer collaboration built into version control systems. TPC allows you to define team structures, conduct live developer-to-developer chats, and connect to various external repositories from within the JDeveloper IDE.

A key function of Oracle TPC is to provide standardized interfaces within JDeveloper into common defect management (bug tracking) systems such as the open source JIRA (www.atlassian .com) or Bugzilla (www.bugzilla.org) packages. This interface allows the developer to work with defect reports within JDeveloper as well as to link code elements to defects or other documents. TPC is available as an extension to JDeveloper 11*g* that you load using **Help | Check for Updates**.

CHAPTER 3

JDeveloper Tools

Intelligence . . . is the faculty of making artificial objects, especially tools to make tools.

—Henri Bergson (1859–1941), *L'Evolution Créatrice (Creative Evolution)*

he JDeveloper IDE introduced in the preceding chapter offers a myriad of tools to assist in creating web application code. The main tools you will probably use within the IDE to develop Fusion web applications follow:

- **Application Navigator** to create, edit, and find files for your application (Project panel), to interact with the database and other connections (Application Resources panel), to select data-bound components to drop into a UI page (Data Controls panel), and to view a list of files you have worked with (Recently Opened Files panel)
- **Resource Palette** to manage database and application server connections as well as to provide access to other items such as ADF libraries
- **New Gallery** to create any type of file
- **Application Overview** to view a summary of the application's state
- **Structure window** to examine and change the order and the arrangement of source code using drag-and-drop operations
- **Component Palette** to select and then drop objects onto a user interface page
- **Property Inspector** to explore and set attribute values for elements in the user interface and other code
- **Log window** to view messages from JDeveloper operations such as the outcome of a compilation or runtime process
- **Code Editor** to interact with plain text files in various forms such as JSP, XML, or Java
- **Debugger** to find and help you fix problems in the code
- **JSP/HTML Visual Editor** to design the user interface of a web page
- **Modelers and diagrammers** to performing Unified Modeling Language (UML) design tasks
- **Database Navigator** to access and change database objects

This chapter introduces these tools to complete the discussion of the IDE begun in Chapter 2. This chapter also offers tips that will help you be more productive when using them. The hands-on practices throughout the book will give you experience with most of these tools.

Application Navigator

The *navigator*—a hierarchical view consisting of a series of indented nodes—is a familiar interface style and needs little explanation because it is used by many other nondevelopment tools, such as Windows Explorer. JDeveloper uses this interface style in a number of tools, one of which is the Application Navigator, shown in the following illustration. This window is divided into collapsible panels for Projects—described in the next section; Application Resources—for connections such as database connections and for *descriptors,* application-specific configuration files;

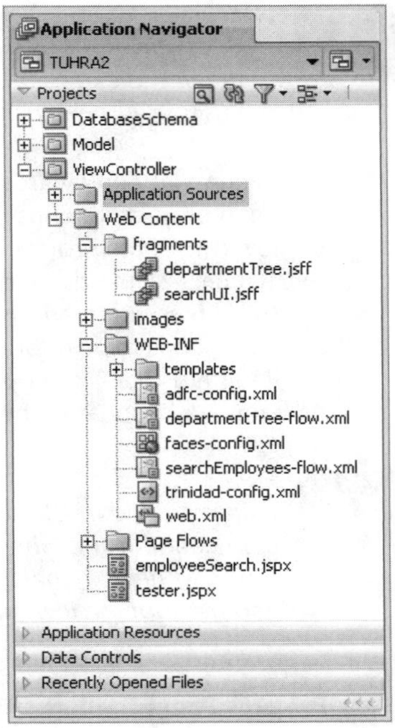

Data Controls—for data-bound components that you can drag into the UI files, and Recently Opened Files—for a list of files you have just opened.

TIP
Clicking the split bar at the top of a panel will collapse or expand the panel.

Projects Panel

The Projects panel allows you to create, view, and edit applications, projects, files, and other components. This navigator shows a view of the files you are working on grouped into projects.

Applications

The top organizational level in the navigator is the *application,* which contains all files related to a specific development effort. You can *open* (load from the file system) many applications in a JDeveloper session, but only one is visible in the Application Navigator at any given time. The files from more than one application can be open at the same time in various editors.

You can select, open, switch between, and create applications using the pulldown in the top of the navigator. For example, the TUHRA2 application is shown in the preceding illustration. You can open many applications at once in JDeveloper. When you close and reopen JDeveloper, the applications previously open will reopen. You can close an application (by selecting **Close Application** from the right-click menu on the application name) so that it is no longer displayed.

NOTE
When you switch between applications, open files within the applications remain open. Closing the application will close all open files in that application. When you close an application, JDeveloper will present a dialog to ask if you just want to close the open files in the application or to close the open files and remove the application from the IDE.

Projects

An application is a logical container for *projects,* which contain the files needed for the system you are creating. The application nodes in the preceding screenshot are DatabaseSchema, Model, and ViewController (the top-level nodes in the Projects panel). Although you can divide the files in your application into any number of projects, each project usually contains related files used for a specific purpose. For example, in the sample application, the DatabaseSchema project contains files used to create the database structures used in the application; Model contains the ADF Business Components files used to access the database; and ViewController contains files used to render the user interface and to process user events.

NOTE
Both applications and projects represent XML files in the file system, but their file extensions are not displayed in the IDE. The application file uses a .jws extension, and the project file uses a .jpr extension.

When you deploy an application, you deploy all code required for the application regardless of which project contains the files. Deployment also ensures that all required libraries are deployed with the project code. You will learn more about and work with deployment techniques in Chapter 22's hands-on practice.

Code files you work on for the application are displayed in nodes under each project node. Different icons appear for different types of files. When you select a file, the file name appears in the IDE status bar. When you double click a file, the file will open in the relevant editor. The filename will appear in the JDeveloper IDE title bar as well as in the document tab.

TIP
As mentioned in Chapter 2, you can open files that are not part of any application using ***File | Open****. This is useful if you just want to quickly look at a file external to the application but do not want to open another tool to view that file.*

Projects Panel Toolbar The Projects panel displays the following toolbar.

This toolbar contains buttons for: *Project Properties* to display the dialog where you can change project settings; *Refresh* to redraw the display in case it is not current; *Working Sets* to define and select sets of files (described more in the next section); and *Navigator Display Options*. The last of these buttons displays a menu containing options you can use to set preferences for displaying the list of files. For example, you can select **Sort by Type** to group files of the same kind together instead of displaying the files alphabetically.

NOTE
Selecting options from the Navigator Display Options menu will affect the display of all open applications.

Working Sets The Working Sets button in the Projects toolbar displays a menu containing options for creating and selecting *working sets,* named groups of files within an application. This feature is handy when working with an application that contains a large number of files and you only need to look at a small set of those files. The default working set is all files in the application, but you can reduce this to a specific list of files by selecting the files or by applying a file name filter using the **Manage Working Sets** option from the Working Sets toolbar button. If you select this option, a dialog such as the following will appear:

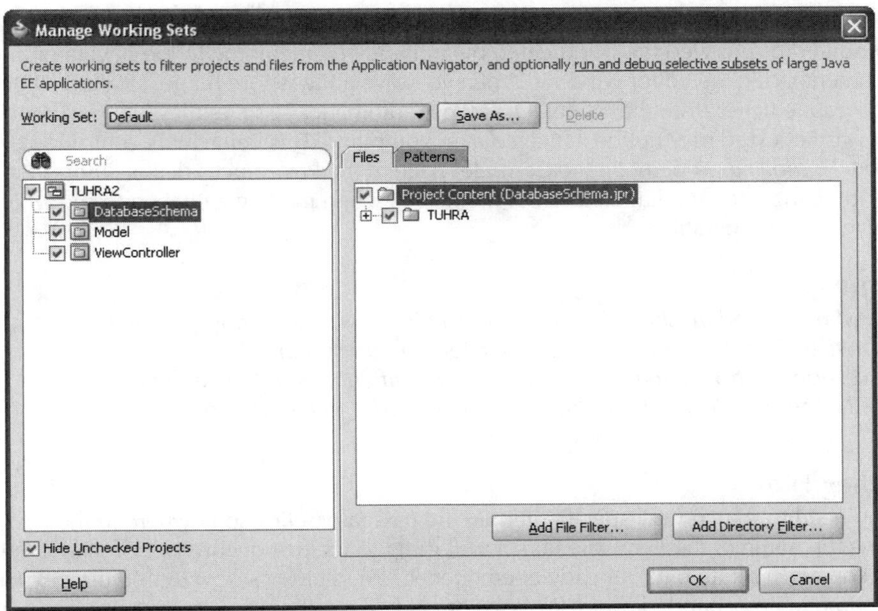

You can then select or deselect files for the working set (for example, to hide all projects except the DatabaseSchema project). Then you click Save As to save the list as a name, for example, "DB Design Only." When you return to the navigator display, the new working set will appear in the list displayed by the Working Set button. You can tell which working set is active from the checkmark in the pulldown on the Working Sets button as shown here:

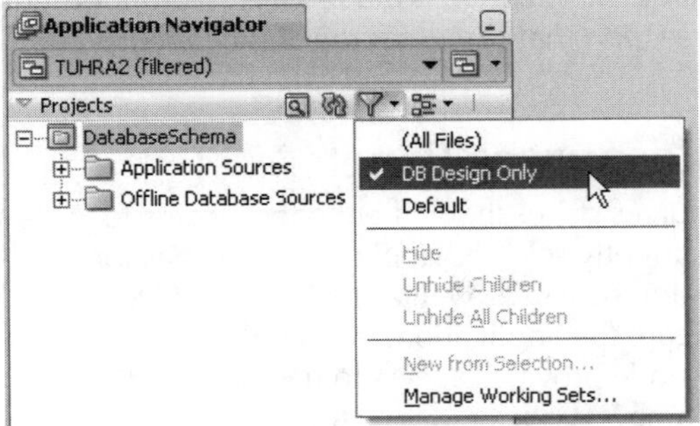

In addition, notice that "filtered" appears next to the application name to indicate that a working set is active. This working set applies only to the application for which it was created.

TIP

If your application contains projects that you do not always need to compile, run, or debug (for example, you are working on only a small number of a large list of projects), you can set up a working set to hide those projects. Then you can choose to compile, run, or debug only the working set of projects rather than the entire application.

Changed File Indicator

A modified or unsaved file is indicated by an italicized file name in the navigator and on the document tab in the editor window. When you save a file whose name is italicized, JDeveloper removes the italics from the name. JDeveloper automatically saves files before compiling, so a name that was italicized may not be italicized after compiling. This behavior is controlled by the *Save All Before Compiling* property on the Compiler page of the Preferences dialog (**Tools | Preferences**).

You can watch the italicization of file names when making a change to see which files are affected by an operation.

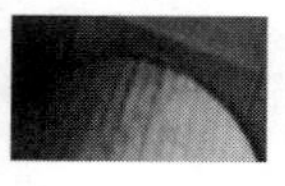

TIP
As mentioned in Chapter 2, state overlay icons will also show changes to files if you are connected to a version control system. With a version control system, you can see all modified files in the Pending Changes window without having to open nodes in a navigator.

Finding Files

If you need to search for a specific item in the navigator, click somewhere in the navigator and start typing the name of the item. The cursor will jump to the first occurrence of that name if the node that contains that item has already been opened. Press DOWN ARROW to find the next occurrence of the name in an expanded node. Press ESC or click in another window to exit search mode.

JDeveloper offers a more sophisticated file search in the File List window accessed by selecting **Application | Find Application Files**. Results will include all files regardless of the working set you have selected.

NOTE
*You can also search anywhere in the file system for files containing a text string by using the "**Search | Find in Files**" feature described in Chapter 2 in the section that discusses the Search menu.*

Application Resources Panel

The Application Resources panel shown here offers access to connections for the currently selected application (such as for a database or application server) as well as to descriptor files that are used to configure the application.

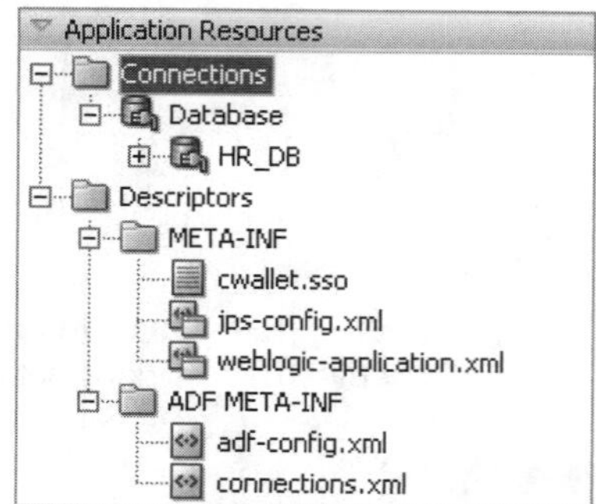

The Connections node provides access to database and other connections you have associated with the selected application. The Descriptors node provides access to files that contain settings for the application, such as adf-config.xml, where you specify ADF metadata settings, or deployment descriptor files, where you specify details about a deployment (collecting files to move to an application server).

You can create resources in this panel using the right-click menu on either node. You can alternatively copy resources by dragging and dropping from the Resource Palette described earlier.

Data Controls Panel

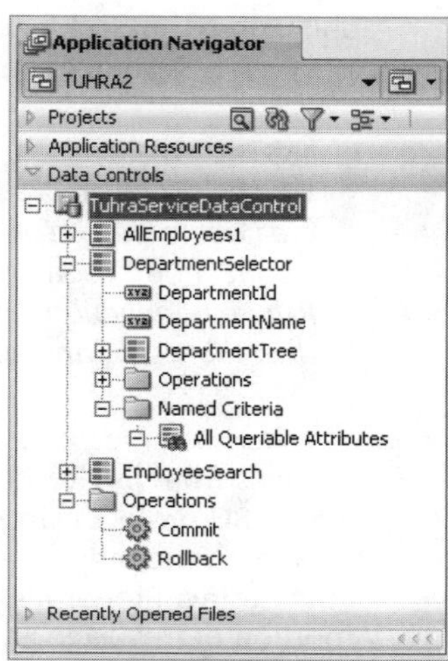

The Data Controls panel of the Application Navigator offers data controls (described in the "Data Controls" section of Chapter 13) that allow you to automatically bind UI components to data sources in the business services layer. This window, shown on the right, contains a view of the data elements, such as ADF business components, that are available in the application.

In this example, the DepartmentSelector node is a *collection* of data elements (rows) that is available in the application. Attributes, such as DepartmentId and DepartmentName, under the collection node represent the individual column values within a row. When you drag a node such as a collection (rows and columns) from this palette onto a UI page, such as a JavaServer Faces (JSF) file, a menu of options will appear. The following shows the menu that would appear when a collection is dropped with an expansion of the Forms menu.

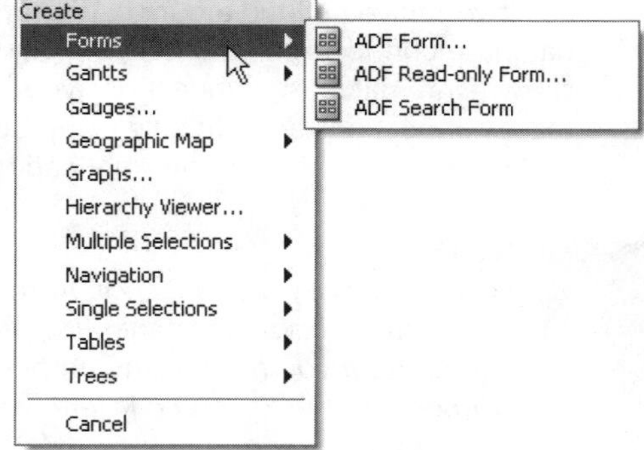

When you select an option from this menu, JDeveloper will add components to the page and connect (bind) them to data elements represented in the Data Controls panel. The hands-on practices later in this book will demonstrate several variations of this technique.

Recently Opened Files Panel

The Recently Opened Files panel of the Application Navigator displays a list of files or other objects (such as PL/SQL code units) that you have worked with in the editors. This list is retained when you exit JDeveloper.

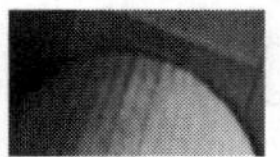

NOTE

*You can access files you have recently accessed in the JDeveloper session using **Navigate | Go to Recent Files**. This list of files is cleared when you exit JDeveloper. In addition, **File | Reopen** displays a list of files that you have opened.*

Resource Palette

The Resource Palette window (accessed using **View | Resource Palette**) allows you to share components and libraries (resources) as well as connections to databases and application servers. It is similar to the Application Resources panel, but the Resource Palette items are available to all applications, not just the application active in the Application Navigator, as is the case with the Application Resources panel.

NOTE
When you create a database connection, you receive an option to create it in the Resource Palette (IDE Connections panel) or in the Application Resources panel (of the current application). The Resource Palette connections are available outside any application, and you can drag them into any application to make application-specific copies.

When you create or assign resources in an application, you have the option of copying resources from the Resource Palette. For example, you can assign a database connection to an ADF BC project using the Business Components page of the Project Properties dialog. A portion of this page is shown here.

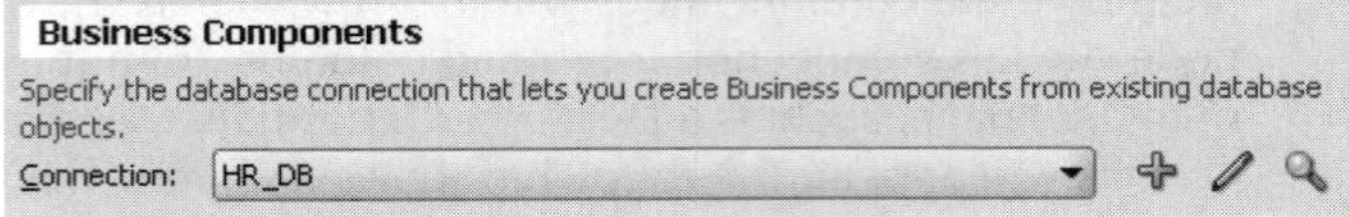
Business Components
Specify the database connection that lets you create Business Components from existing database objects.
Connection:
HR_DB

If you have defined a connection in the Resource Palette, you would click the "Browse IDE database connections" (magnifying glass) button on the right side. This would display a dialog showing all database connections you have created outside of any application. Selecting one of these connections and clicking Copy Connection will copy the connection to the application. It will then be displayed in the Application Resources panel.

NOTE
When you copy a connection from the Resource Palette to the Application Resources panel, the properties of the copy are separate. Therefore, if you modify any property of the application-specific connection, the Resource Palette version of that same connection will remain unchanged.

New Gallery

The New Gallery offers dialogs that build starting code for a specific kind of new file. Wizards and creation dialogs are all started from the New Gallery. You access the New Gallery, shown in Figure 3-1, by using **File** | **New** or by selecting **New** from the right-click menu on various nodes in the navigator.

NOTE
Figure 3-1 shows the New Gallery category nodes that appear with the first production version of JDeveloper 11g, Release 1 (11.1.1.1.0), build 5407.

This window is divided into a categories navigator on the left and a list of items within that category on the right. The main nodes in the navigator roughly parallel the Java EE tiers (Business, Client, Database, Web) with an additional node for General. Enabling different JDeveloper *extensions* (features added to the IDE as shipped, also called "add-ins" or "add-ons") will also change the categories and items available in this navigator. Figure 3-1 shows the New Gallery tab

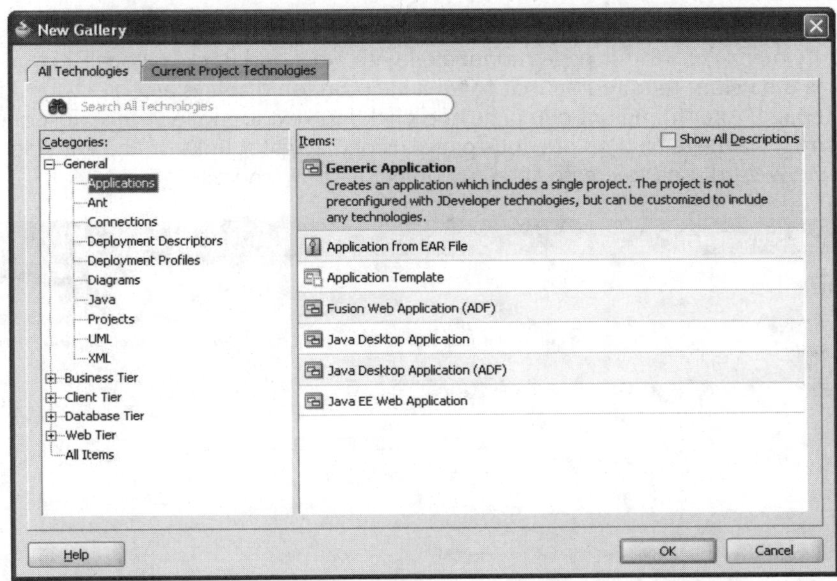

FIGURE 3-1. *The New Gallery*

"All Technologies," which displays all categories of items. Normally, the New Gallery displays the Current Project Technologies tab first.

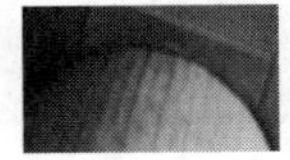

TIP
The New Gallery category "All Items" at the bottom of the navigator is useful if you are unclear in which category an option is displayed. After viewing the list of all items, you can search for an item using the search field at the top of the window.

If you need to create a project, you can start up the New Gallery from the New Project right-click menu item on the application pulldown at the top of the Application Navigator. The New Gallery will then initially display the General\Projects category. You can alternatively navigate to that category if you start the New Gallery using another method.

After you select an object from one of the categories and click OK, the file node will be created in the Application Navigator under the project that you selected. Depending on the object, the appropriate wizard or dialog will appear and prompt you for properties. JDeveloper uses these property values to create starting code.

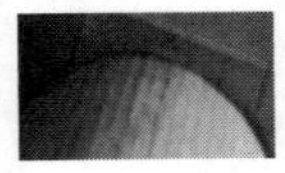

TIP
Instead of selecting ***New*** *from the right-click menu to display the New Gallery, you can press* CTRL-N*. Also, the selected node will often determine where the file will be located in the file system by default, although the dialog or wizard usually allows you to change that location.*

Wizards

A *wizard* is a dialog (modal window) that leads you through the steps of creating a file or other object by means of various pages connected with Next and Back buttons. Text on each page explains the values required on that page; a Help button displays a context-sensitive help topic for that page. After filling out one page and clicking Next to move to the subsequent page, you can usually navigate back to previous pages using navigator links on the left side of the dialog. A sample wizard used to create an entity object is shown here:

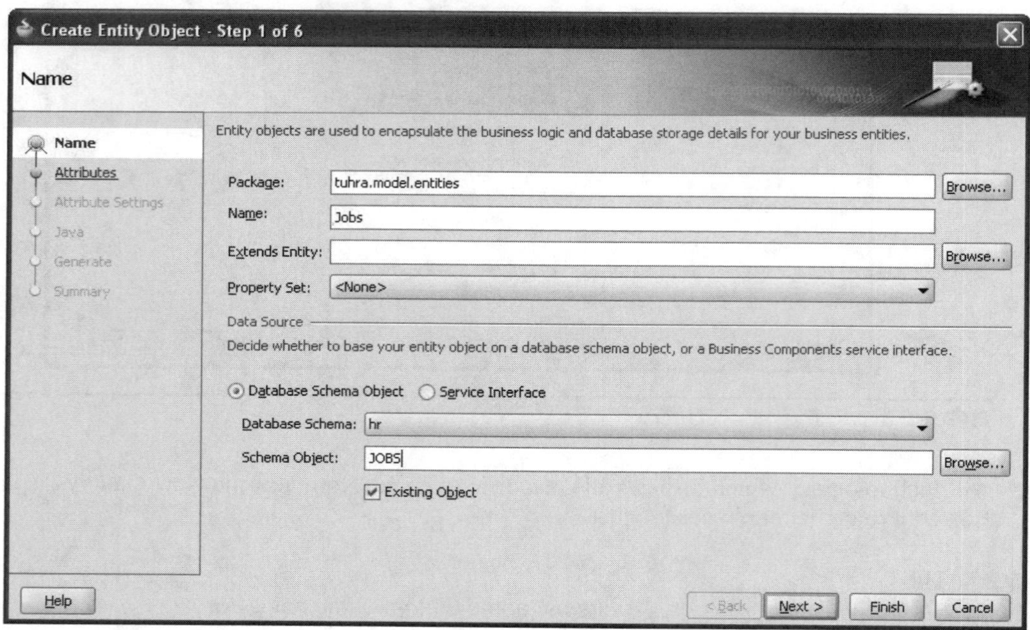

Once you create the file using a wizard, you will use an editor or other dialog to modify it. For example, the entity object editor used to modify the entity created by the Create Entity Object wizard appears in the editor window as shown here:

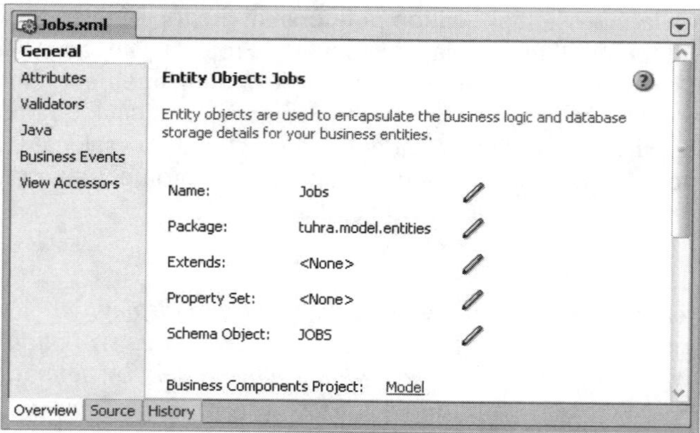

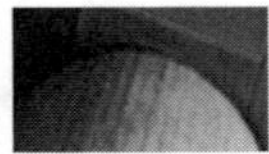

NOTE
You can define your own wizards and add them to the New Gallery. Start at the help system table of contents node "Developing JDeveloper Extensions\Writing JDeveloper Extensions\Developing a New Gallery Wizard" for technical information about adding a wizard.

Creation Dialogs

For some New Gallery items, JDeveloper offers creation dialogs, which allow you to specify characteristics of files or objects you are creating. For example, the following illustration shows the Create Database Connection dialog, where you can define the name and other properties of a database connection. As with the wizards, settings in the dialog affect the code that is generated.

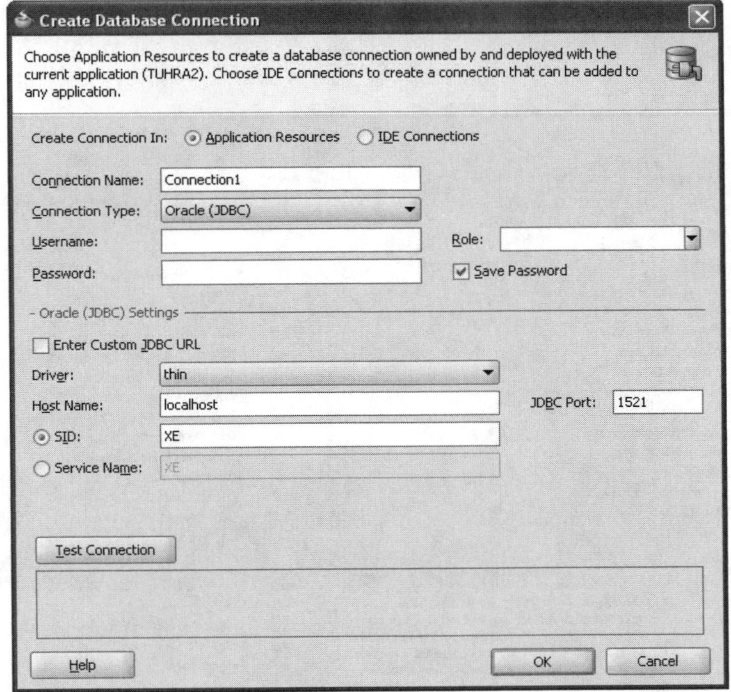

TIP
You can resize most wizards, dialogs, and user interface windows. In addition, some dialogs and wizards have multi-pane areas, which you can resize if something that you need to see is not visible.

Application Overview Window

The Application Overview window (**Application | Show Overview**) shown in Figure 3-2 provides a summary of the application. It contains separate panels for each category of *components* (in this context, files or objects) in the application. For example, Figure 3-2 displays panels for Java Files, XML Files, Offline Databases, and Page Flows. You can also define which projects to represent using the *Show* pulldown in the top-left corner of the window. The sample shown in Figure 3-2 displays all projects. The top of the window also contains a File Summary area that shows how many files are available in the projects you've selected. The File Summary area also displays file status links. Clicking one of these links will open a page, listing all files in the selected projects that match the status you clicked.

NOTE

This section shows and describes the version of the Application Overview window as of the first production release of JDeveloper 11g, 11.1.1.1.0. The format of this window may change slightly in future releases.

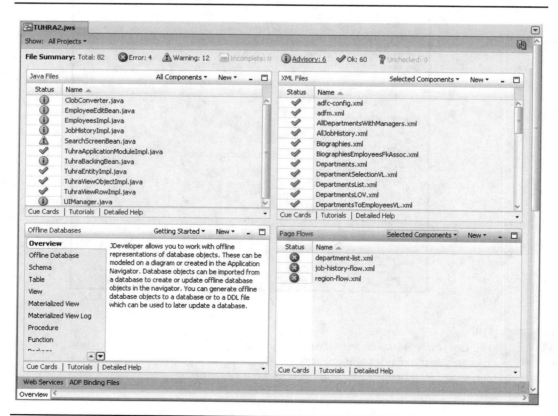

FIGURE 3-2. *Application Overview window*

Application Overview Panel Techniques

You can drag and drop panels on top of other panels to rearrange them. Alternatively, you can use right-click menu options on the title bar of a panel to move it.

The title bar of each panel contains controls for minimizing (or restoring) and maximizing the panel. When you minimize a panel, its title will appear in the bottom margin of the window. For example, in Figure 3-2, the Web Services and ADF Binding Files panels are minimized. Clicking a minimized title will restore the panel into the Application Overview window. Maximizing a panel will cause it to fill the window in the same way that double clicking an editor tab will cause it to fill the IDE window.

The title bar of each panel also contains a pulldown menu (shown below) where you can change which components to display in the panel.

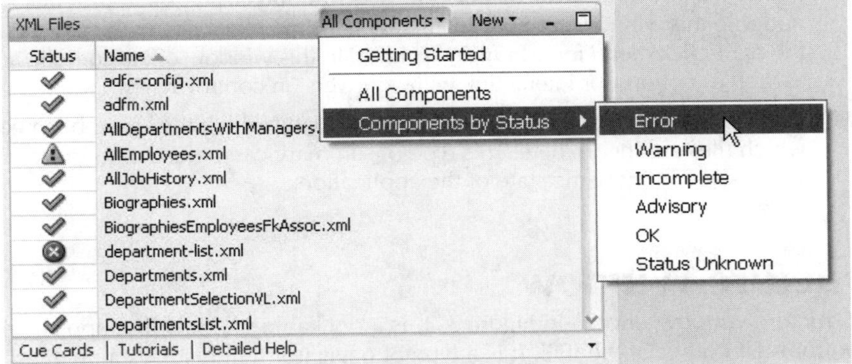

NOTE
Changing the way components are displayed in the Application Overview window panels does not affect the contents of the projects in the application.

For example, if you select "All Components," the panel will display all components of that category in the project or projects. You can filter files by file status, display all components, or show overview information (by selecting "Getting Started") that you can use to learn about the component files. In Figure 3-2, the Java Files panel shows all components; the XML Files panel shows only selected components with a status of "OK"; the Offline Databases panel shows Getting Started information; and the Page Flows panel shows files with an error status.

In addition, the title bar contains a *New* pulldown that you can use to create files of the category represented in the panel. For example, the Java Files' *New* pulldown offers menu items for Java Class and Java Interface. The bottom margin of each panel contains links for Cue Cards, Tutorials, and Detailed Help that will open the relevant topic in the Help Center.

TIP
You can resize the panels within the window using the splitter bars between panels.

How Can the Application Overview Window Help?

In general, the Application Overview provides quicker access to information about the application than any other tool. It also offers easy ways to perform the following tasks:

- **Read brief information snippets** about the component using the Getting Started selection. As the name suggests, this feature is particular useful when you need a quick introduction to the component type. If you need more information, you can use the Help Center links at the bottom of the panels.
- **Create files or objects** of the relevant type using the *New* pulldown. This method can be faster than opening the New Gallery and finding the file type from a much larger list. The options in the *New* pulldown trigger the same wizards and dialogs as the New Gallery.
- **Load files into the editor or perform other actions** using the right-click menu. The file nodes in this window are as fully functional as the file nodes in the navigator. For example, the right-click menu for Java files displayed in this window offers compile and run options as well as options for interacting with your version control system.
- **View a summary of the application** by reviewing which files have been completed and which files are incomplete. This type of summary can be useful to managers or anyone who needs to know the state of the application.

Structure Window

The Structure window, shown in Figure 3-3, is a dockable window that appears by default in the bottom-left corner of the IDE. It is a type of navigator that displays a detailed view of the objects within the properties of the file or node selected in the Application Navigator. If an editor window has *focus* (the window where the cursor is active), the Structure window displays the objects within the file in the active editor. Figure 3-3 shows the structure of a JSF JSP file; the nodes in this window represent the XML elements that compose the file, including a visual display of the hierarchy in which they are arranged. The form that this view takes depends upon the selected file type and the editor that has focus. For example, when a Java class file is open in the Code Editor, the Structure window displays details of the class, such as the imports, methods, superclass, and properties.

NOTE
The Structure window displays icons identifying type of object. In addition, hint text (tooltips) with more information about the file will appear when you rest the mouse on a node in the Structure window.

Structure Window Operations

You can open additional Structure windows by clicking the New View icon in the Structure window toolbar (or by selecting **View** | **Options** | **New View** after selecting a node in the Structure window). This feature is handy if you need to freeze one structure view (using the Freeze View button in the Structure window toolbar) and visually compare it with the structure view for a different object.

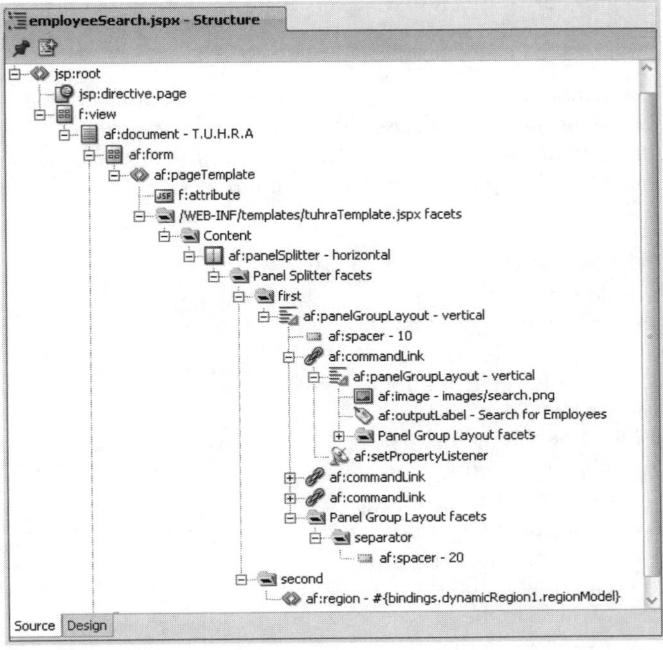

FIGURE 3-3. *Structure window*

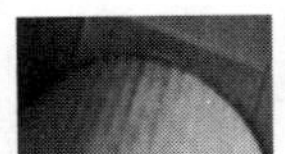

TIP
Normally, the Structure window displays details about the object selected in an editor or navigator. If you want to edit or navigate to other files but keep the view in the Structure window unchanged, click the Freeze View (red pin) icon in the Structure window toolbar. Click the button again to unfreeze the view.

The right-click menu in the Structure window offers sophisticated file editing. For example, the right-click menu in the Structure window for a JSF JSP file allows you to cut, copy, paste, delete, and insert tags or components. When you double click a node in the Structure window, the applicable editor will open if it is not already open, and the focus will be placed on the selected object or section of code. For example, double clicking an import node in the Structure window for a Java application file will open the Code Editor for that file and select the import statement. You can use the Structure window in this way as a table of contents to navigate through a large file.

If you are editing a file in the Code Editor or if you have selected a file in the Application Navigator, the Structure window will also show syntax errors such as mismatched tags and mismatched curly brackets. If you are typing code into the editor, the errors are displayed as you move the cursor. The following example shows how errors made while editing a Java class file will be displayed in the Structure window:

Errors
Unexpected token string literal.
Field declaration: Expecting ;.

Double clicking an error opens the editor to the problem code line. After you correct the error and move the mouse cursor to a different line, the error listing will disappear.

TIP
The Structure window toolbar for a Java file contains buttons to help sort or filter the display. You can use the "Sort by Type" button for ordering the contents. Other buttons allow you to hide or display methods, fields, static members, and public members.

Drag-and-Drop Support

The Structure window allows you to reorder the source code using drag-and-drop operations. For example, you want to move a LastName column item above a FirstName column item in a JSF page fragment file. Instead of editing the source code and selecting, cutting, and pasting the text for the LastName column tag and its child tags (or dragging and dropping or by cutting and pasting it in the editor), you could drag it and drop it above the FirstName item in the Structure window as shown in this illustration.

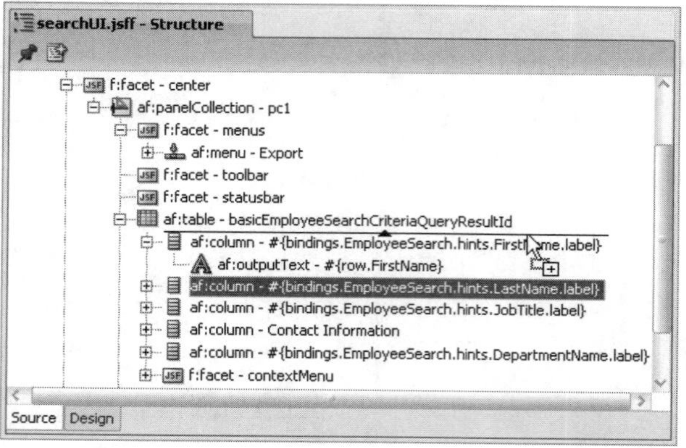

After you select the object, arrowed lines will appear to indicate where the object would be located if you dropped it at that point. Once you drop the object, the source code will be rearranged. If you drop a child object on top of a master object, the child object will be nested inside the master (as the last child node).

Structure Window Views

For some file types, the Structure window displays different views of the same file. For example, the following illustration shows the Overview tab and Source tab for a faces-config.xml file (the main configuration file for the JSF controller). Both views represent the same items but organize them differently.

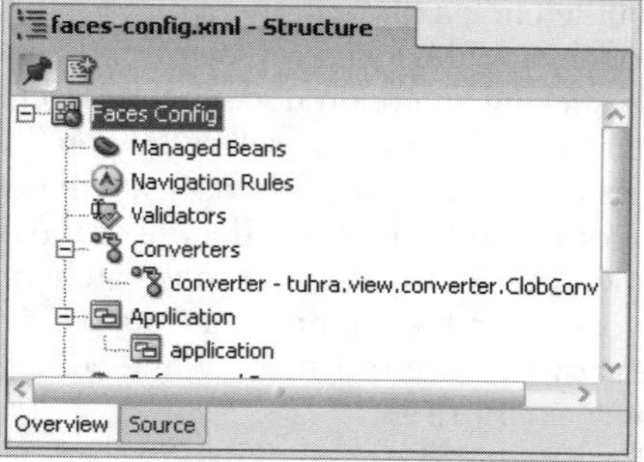

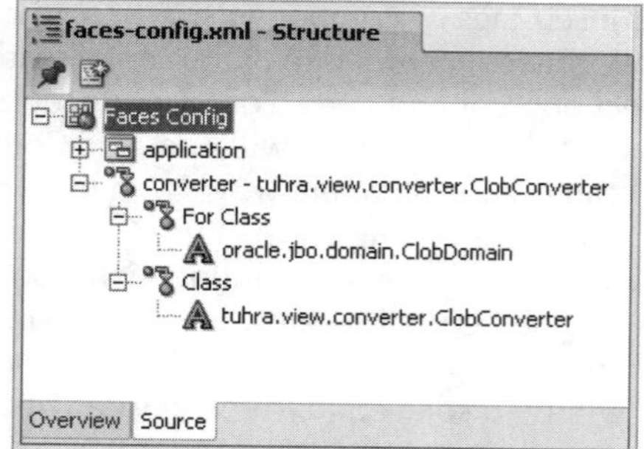

Component Palette

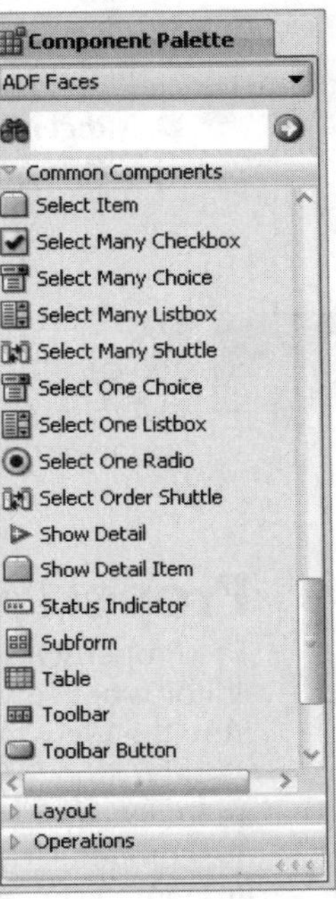

The Component Palette window (shown in the illustration on the right) contains pages of components you use in the visual editors for various styles of code such as Java client, JSF JSP files, or HTML files. (If the Component Palette window is not displayed, press CTRL-SHIFT-P or select **View | Component Palette**.) You can switch between pages by selecting the page from a pulldown at the top of the Component Palette window. The pages that are available at any given time are based on the file that is active in the editor window.

The Component Palette contents change depending upon the file that is being edited. For example, if the cursor is in the Java Visual Editor for a Java application, the Component Palette contains applicable components from the Swing and AWT libraries. If the cursor is in the JSP/HTML Visual Editor for a JSF JSP file, the Component Palette contains applicable controls from the various JSP tag libraries supplied with JDeveloper. If a modeler is active, the Component Palette contains diagram components. As shown in the illustration, the Component Palette page may contain collapsible panels similar to the panels in the Application Navigator.

Although you would typically drop components from the Component Palette onto a visual editor, you can also drop them into the Source tab of an editor window.

TIP

Sometimes dropping a component to the correct nested container component on a JSF JSP page is a bit difficult. You may find that you have more control by dropping components into the relevant nodes in the Structure window. Alternatively, you can select a master node in the Structure window and click the component in the palette to add that component as a child component.

The tooltips for the icons in the Component Palette contain brief explanations of the component. The right-click menu option **Help** displays the full online help page for a selected component. By default, the palette shows an icon and a text label for each control, but you can hide the text label for each icon by selecting **Icon View** from the right-click menu on the Component Palette.

Normally, JDeveloper determines which components are required for the type of file you are editing, but you can add pages for other libraries by selecting **Edit Tag Libraries** from the right-click menu in a Component Palette page.

You can create Component Palette pages for certain types of components using the Configure Component Palette dialog (**Tools | Configure Palette**).

My Components

The Component Palette contains a page called "My Components," which you can use to hold components you access often. This page contains the following panels:

- **Favorites** When you select **Add to Favorites** from the right-click menu on a component in any page, that component will appear in the Favorites panel.

- **Code Snippets** You can drag and drop frequently used code blocks into this panel from any editor. You then provide a name that will appear in this panel. Clicking the snippet name will add the code to the code editor. This panel only appears when the Source editor tab is active.
- **Recently Used** JDeveloper automatically adds components you have used to this panel. You can use the components in this panel in the same way as the components in any other page.

TIP
You can also use Code Templates to quickly add frequently used code to the file you are editing. This feature is described in the section "Code Templates" later in this chapter.

Property Inspector

The Property Inspector window, shown in Figure 3-4, automatically displays when a visual editor is active; as is true of any window, if the Property Inspector does not appear, select it from the View menu. This window displays properties relevant to the component selected in a visual editor, Structure window, or code editor. For example, Figure 3-4 shows the properties for an image component selected in the JSP/HTML Visual Editor. The Property Inspector tab shows the component type. The properties are divided into sections, which appear as tabs when the Property Inspector is wide enough to accommodate tabs, as in Figure 3-4.

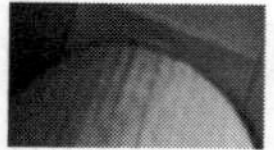

NOTE
Selecting a property in the Property Inspector will display help text in a panel under the properties.

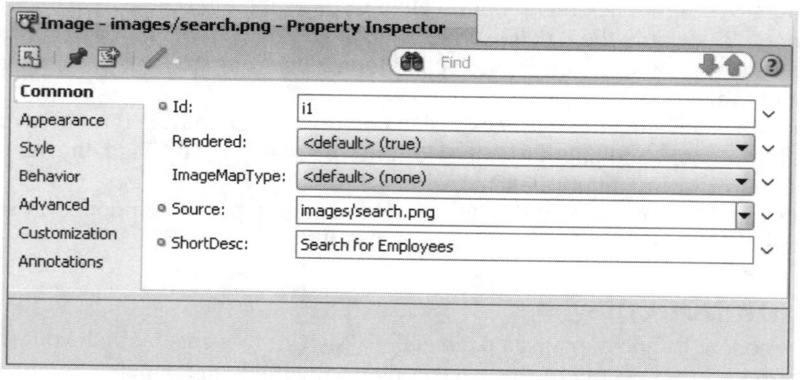

FIGURE 3-4. *Property Inspector*

If the Property Inspector window is not wide enough to display tabs (such as when the window is docked on a side of the JDeveloper IDE) or is high enough to show all sections, the sections will appear as collapsible headings in the window as shown here:

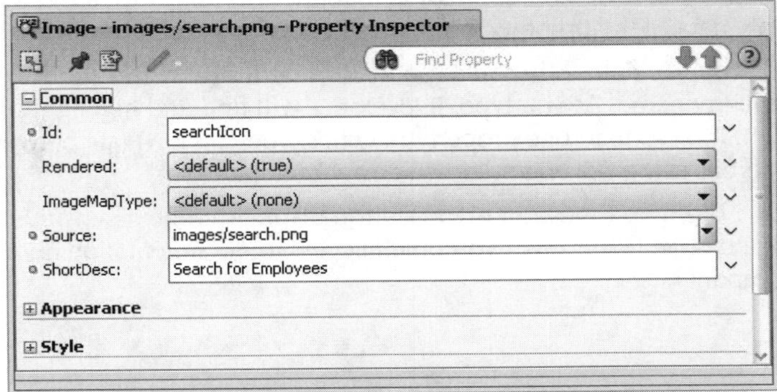

Modifying property values in this window modifies text in the source code file. If the property value is blank or marked as "default" in the Property Inspector, that property will not appear in the source code file.

TIP
Press ENTER *or click another property to make the change on a property permanent. Clicking in another window may not record the change.*

Property Inspector Operations

The toolbar at the top of the Property Inspector window (shown in Figure 3-4) offers the following features:

- **Enable/disable Auto-Extend** If this toggle button is depressed, the Property Inspector window will expand to show all properties when the mouse cursor passes over the Property Inspector window. If the button is toggled in the up position (level with the background), the Property Inspector window will not expand automatically. The automatic expansion of this window is handy because it allows you to quickly look at or change any property value, although it might take some time to become accustomed to this behavior.
- **Freeze View** Normally the Property Inspector will display the properties for the component you have selected in the visual editor or code editor. Clicking the red pin button will stop the Property Inspector from updating when you click the next component. This feature is useful in combination with the next one for comparing property values between components.
- **New View** Clicking this button opens another Property Inspector window, which is usually helpful for comparing properties between components. You can set up this comparison by clicking the Freeze View button when the cursor is on the first component; clicking New View to open another Property Inspector window; and then selecting another component.

- **Edit Component Definition** If this button is active for a component, it will display an editor for that component.
- **Bind to ADF Control** This button appears for certain components. It helps you to create an Expression Language expression that refers to (binds to) a Model layer object that will supply data to the property. Chapter 13 explains bindings in detail.
- **Find property field** This field (on the top-right side of the window) allows you to type a property name. As you type, JDeveloper will find and highlight property names that match. If more than one property matches, you can navigate between the matching properties using the up and down arrow buttons.
- **Help** The help (question mark) button displays context-sensitive help text for the selected object. This gives you quick access to documentation about the properties for a component.

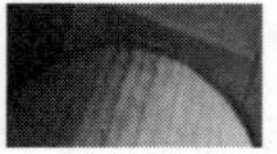

TIP
You can group together components in the visual or source editor (using CTRL*-click) and apply values to the group. This action will assign the same value to all selected components.*

Log Window

The Log window shows messages from various operations such as running, debugging, or compiling code. If the message is an error, you can double click the error text, and the problem code will be highlighted in the editor. This gives you a quick way to navigate to the problem area. The right-click menu in the Log window allows you to select and save the text into a file for later use. The messages are color-coded for easier reading.

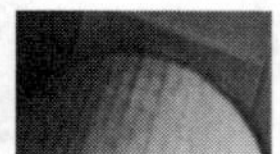

TIP
Using the Preferences dialog (Environment\Log node), you can modify settings for the number of lines displayed, for colors assigned to various text types, and for optionally storing the log window output in a file.

The Log window area opens new windows for different types of activities; you can navigate between them using the tabs. For example, running a JSF page in JDeveloper will display messages from the WebLogic Server inside the Log window; another Log window will display messages from compiling the project before running the file.

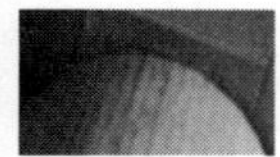

TIP
Right-click menu options in the Log window allow you to clear, copy, save, and find text in the window. Finding text (using the search field accessed using CTRL-F*) will highlight the matching text in the Log window. This feature is especially useful for finding debug messages.*

Code Editor

Various code editors allow you to create and modify plain text files such as JSF page files, other XML files, properties files, Java class files, JavaScript files, and Cascading Style Sheets (CSS). You open a file for editing in a code editor by double clicking the file name in the Application Navigator or by selecting **Open** from the right-click menu for a file node. The Source tab of the code editor displays the code editor.

Many characteristics such as fonts, syntax colors, undo behavior, and tab size are customizable using selections from the Code Editor node of the Preferences dialog (**Tools** | **Preferences**), as shown in Figure 3-5.

The Code Editor uses standard Windows shortcut keys such as CTRL-C for Copy and CTRL-V for Paste (on Windows operating systems). Search for "keymaps, list of available" in the Index Search tab of the help system to find the supplied key mappings. You can customize these keymaps if needed using the Shortcut Keys page of the preferences dialog (**Tools** | **Preferences**).

TIP
*Extended paste (CTRL-SHIFT-V or **Edit** | **Extended Paste**) enables you to select text to paste into the editor from clipboard history.*

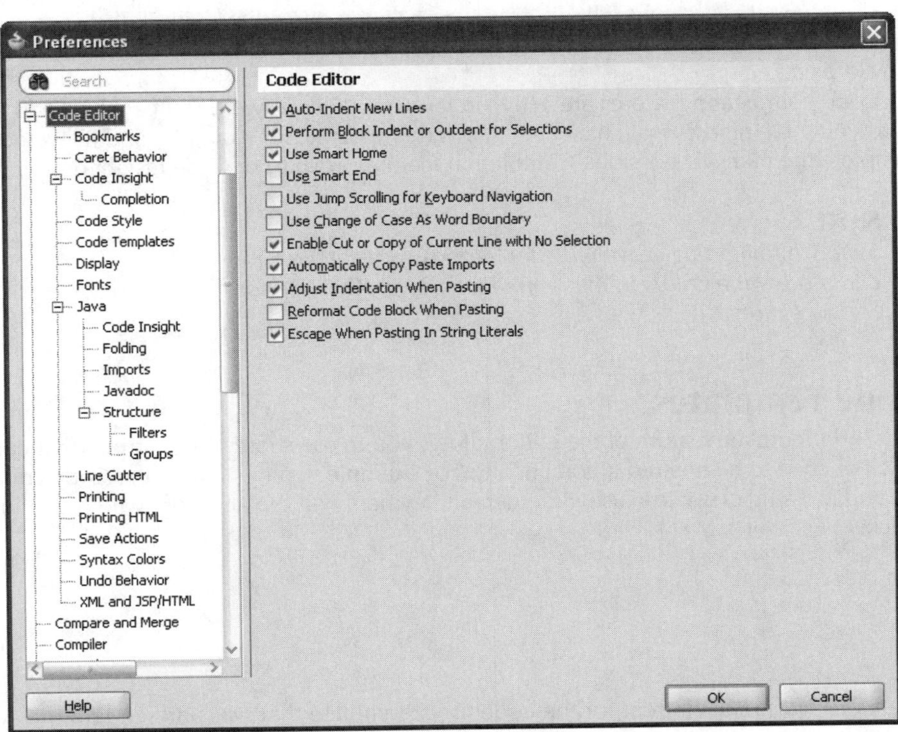

FIGURE 3-5. *Code Editor preferences*

You can drag and drop selected text in the editor by highlighting it with the mouse and dragging and dropping it into the new location. The right-click menu contains actions that you would use frequently (for example, Cut, Copy, Paste, and Undo). Many of the Source menu items discussed in Chapter 2 are also available from the right-click menu in the code editor.

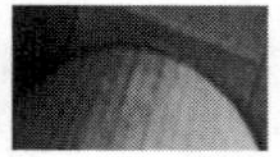

TIP
*The file name and path of the file open in the editor are shown in the IDE window title bar. You will also see the file name and path in the IDE status bar when you click the file node in a navigator. In addition, a tooltip containing the file name will appear when you hold the mouse above a file node in a navigator or above a document tab. Select **Edit | Copy Path** to copy the file name, including its path, into the clipboard.*

End Tag Completion and Code Completion

The *End Tag Completion* feature adds an ending tag for tag language files such as HTML, JSF JSP page, and XML. The editor determines the file type (by the file extension) and applies this behavior. For example, when you edit an HTML or JSP file in the editor, the editor fills in ending tags (for a starting tag such as "<af:table>") as you type the start of the ending tags. For example, after you type the "</" that follows an `af:table` tag, the editor will fill the ending tag in as "</af:table>." This behavior is defined on the Preferences dialog's "Code Editor\XML and JSP/HTML" page.

Code completion features are active in Java class files as well. You can press CTRL-SHIFT-SPACEBAR after typing the first several characters in a variable name, for example, and JDeveloper will complete the name, if possible. Completion features are part of Code Insight described later.

NOTE
Syntax highlighting is available for various types of files. You can modify the colors in the Preferences page "Code Editor\Syntax Colors."

Code Templates

The Code Template feature of the editor allows you to use shortcut text strings that can trigger a block of code to be entered automatically. For example, typing "for" in the Code Editor for a Java file and pressing CTRL-ENTER (using the default keymap) will replace "for" with the following code block:

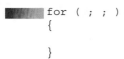

```
for ( ; ; )
{

}
```

The word "for" is a shortcut for the code block template that was entered into the editor. The keypress CTRL-ENTER activates the shortcut and transforms it into the code template text.

You can view, define, and modify these templates in the Preferences dialog (**Tools** | **Preferences**) Code Editor\Code Templates page as shown next.

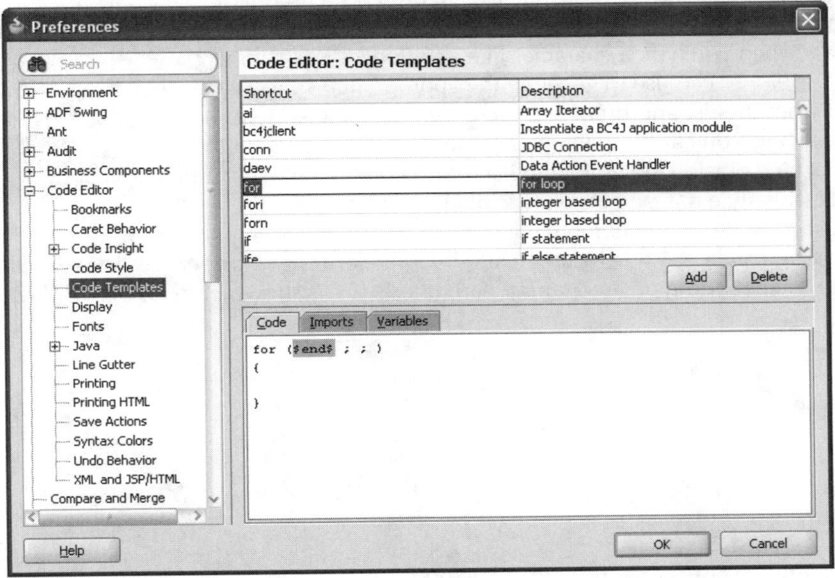

TIP

*To view line numbers in the code editor, select **Toggle Line Numbers** from the right-click menu in the left margin (gutter) of the editor window. This is faster than setting the preference in the Preferences dialog Code Editor\Line Gutter page.*

Java class files require import statements to support references to class names. In addition to defining text blocks that will be inserted into the code, you can define import statements that will appear in the imports section. The Imports tab in the Preferences dialog's Code Editor\Code Templates page allows you to specify the import statements that will be inserted with the code. If your code already contains import statements for the parent package, the import code will not be inserted.

TIP

*As mentioned in Chapter 2, you can add an external editor (or any other software) to the Tools menu and other locations in JDeveloper by using the **Tools** | **External Tools** dialog. If you use another editor to save a file that is open in JDeveloper, you can reload that file automatically (with or without a confirmation dialog) according to reload settings on the Environment page of the Preferences dialog.*

Code Insight and Tag Insight

JDeveloper offers another feature to help you write code for Java, JSP, PL/SQL, HTML, and XML source files. This feature, called *Code Insight* (for Java and PL/SQL) or *Tag Insight* (for tag languages), pops up context-sensitive lists of elements that are appropriate to the type of file you are editing in the context of the code you are typing. For example, for Java class files, Code Insight presents lists of methods, constants, imports, and method parameters. For a JSP, Code Insight presents a list of component tags as shown in this illustration. This type of list appears when you type a character like a period (".") or colon (":") that JDeveloper can use to generate the appropriate list. You can select from the list and press ENTER to enter the selected text. Alternatively, you can keep typing and navigate to a match in the list. Clicking outside the pulldown list (or pressing ESC) will dismiss the list. This style of Code Insight is called *completion insight* because it assists you in completing code that you are writing.

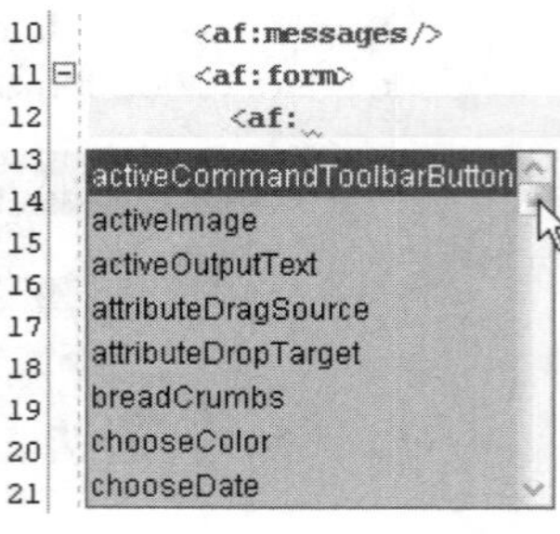

Another style of Code Insight, called *parameter insight,* presents a list of valid arguments for a method after you type an opening parenthesis "(" as shown here for a Java class file:

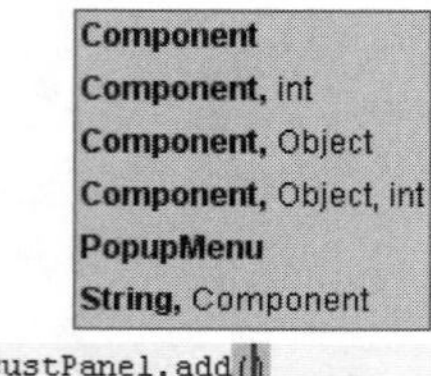

This example shows that the `add()` method is overloaded with different parameter lists. You do not select from this list but use it as a reminder of the types of objects or variables that can act as parameters to the method. This list will automatically appear when you type an opening parenthesis. Code Insight for tag languages works in a similar way.

Use the Code Editor\Code Insight page of the Preferences dialog to modify the time delay before Code Insight appears or to turn the feature off and on. Regardless of the settings in this dialog, Code Insight will appear if you press the appropriate key combinations (CTRL-SPACEBAR by default for code insight or CTRL-SHIFT-SPACEBAR for parameter insight).

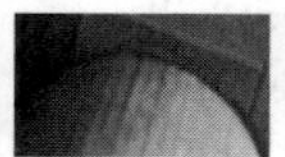

CAUTION
Java classes for which you want to obtain insight must be defined in the CLASSPATH of the project's settings (Libraries and Classpath page). You also need to compile your code if you want Code Insight to find its members. In addition, this feature may not work if the file has compile errors. If Code Insight is not available, an appropriate message will appear in the editor's status bar.

Other Text Editing Features

The code editor offers a multitude of features some of which apply to specific types of files.

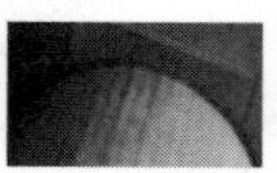

TIP
If the code editor does not work the way you think it should, be sure to explore the Preferences dialog to see if you can adjust it.

Quick Javadoc

You can display the main Javadoc for a Java class, method, or member by selecting **Quick Javadoc** from the right-click menu (or from the Source menu) on an element in the code editor as shown here for the JRegionPanel interface:

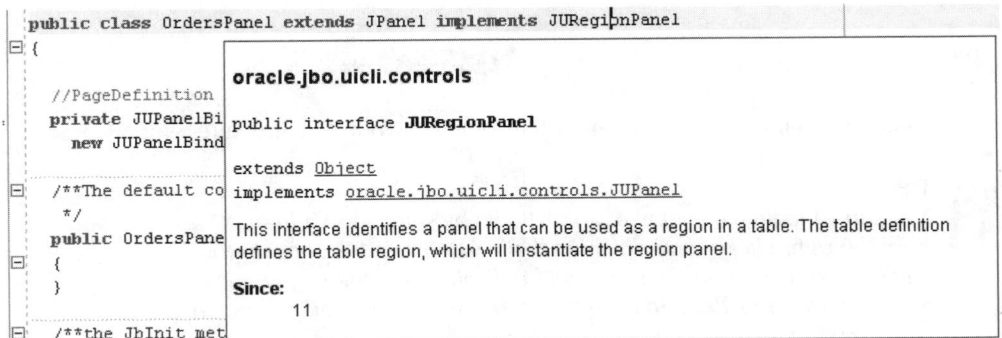
public class OrdersPanel extends JPanel implements JURegionPanel
oracle.jbo.uicli.controls
public interface JURegionPanel
extends Object
implements oracle.jbo.uicli.controls.JUPanel
This interface identifies a panel that can be used as a region in a table. The table definition defines the table region, which will instantiate the region panel.
Since:
11

Breadcrumbs

The bottom margin of many editors displays a *breadcrumb* (flat navigation hierarchy) list as shown in the bottom part of the editor window for a JSF file here:

This breadcrumb area (directly above the editor tabs) allows you to view the structure of the file in a single line instead of in a hierarchy as in the Structure window. As with the Structure window, clicking a code element listed in the breadcrumb will select the code in the code editor. Holding the mouse cursor over one of the arrows at the start or end of the visible breadcrumbs will automatically scroll through the display if additional elements exist. Clicking an arrow to the right of an element's breadcrumb will display a pulldown list of the child elements for that element. This feature is extremely useful when working with code that contains a deeply nested hierarchy such as a JSF page.

Import Assistance

If a class you use in your Java source code is missing an import statement, a wavy line will appear under the class name. After a short time, a hint will pop up somewhere above the line of code. This hint explains that you can press ALT-ENTER to create an import statement for that class. If the hint does not appear, press ALT-ENTER to see the hint, and ALT-ENTER again to add the import. In addition to the wavy line, a light bulb icon will appear in the editor gutter. Clicking that icon will display a menu of techniques you can use to resolve the import problem.

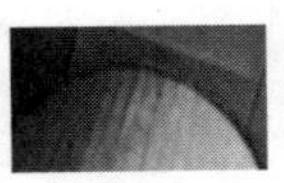

NOTE
JDeveloper can automatically add imports as you type code based on settings on the Code Editor\Java\Imports page of the Preferences dialog.

Syntax Error Highlighting

After you move the cursor off a line of code, the Code Editor will display any relevant syntax or semantic error by placing a wavy line under the problem code. If you hold the mouse over that line of code, a hint will appear containing the error text, as shown here:

As mentioned before, errors like this will also be shown in the Structure window.

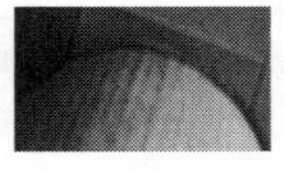

TIP
*You can validate the syntax of an XML file by selecting **Validate XML** from the right-click menu on an XML file (such as a JSF page) in the navigator or code editor. Errors will be displayed in the Log window. Selecting **Make** or **Rebuild** from that menu will also display errors in the Log window.*

Working with PL/SQL

You can also use JDeveloper to edit PL/SQL database code either from scripts or opened from the Database Navigator. This section explains how to work with PL/SQL code you have opened or want to compile in a database. All work with PL/SQL in the database starts with the Database Navigator.

After opening the Database Navigator (**View | Database Navigator**, described in the section "Database Navigator" later in this chapter), find the database code object (function, procedure, package, or package body) by expanding either the application node or the IDE Connections node. Then select **Edit** from the right-click menu on that object. An edit dialog will appear with some properties. Clicking OK in that dialog will open the file for editing. If you want to make a copy of the object, change the default name in the interim dialog; the editor will load the code with the new name.

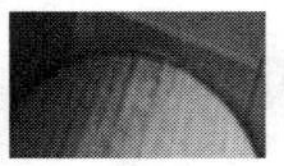

CAUTION
*If you just double click the code unit to open it (or select **Open** from the right-click menu), the editor will open in read-only mode.*

You can create database code (and any other database object) with the **New <object>** option from the right-click menu on a node such as Package. A create dialog will then appear where you name the object and specify its details; after clicking OK, an editor window will open so that you can define the details of the code.

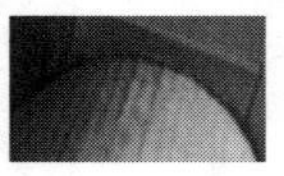

TIP
You can alternatively create database objects such as PL/SQL code using the New Gallery category Database Tier\Database Objects.

Compiling PL/SQL Code To compile the code and save it to the database, select **Make** from the right-click menu of the editor or click Save (or click the editor toolbar Compile button). Compile errors will be displayed in the Log window.

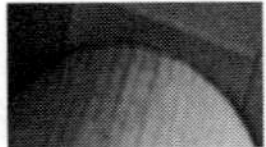

CAUTION

Although database objects appear in the Resource Palette and in the Application Resources panel of the Application Navigator, you cannot open them from those tools. However, the Resource Palette allows you to perform a database object search for using the search field at the top of the panel. The Database Navigator and Application Resources panel only allow navigator searches for names within nodes that have been opened.

Running PL/SQL Code After creating and compiling PL/SQL subprograms, you can test them in standalone mode. Select the program unit in the Database Navigator and click the Run button (or select **Run** from the right-click menu on the program's node or in the editor window). A window such as the following will appear:

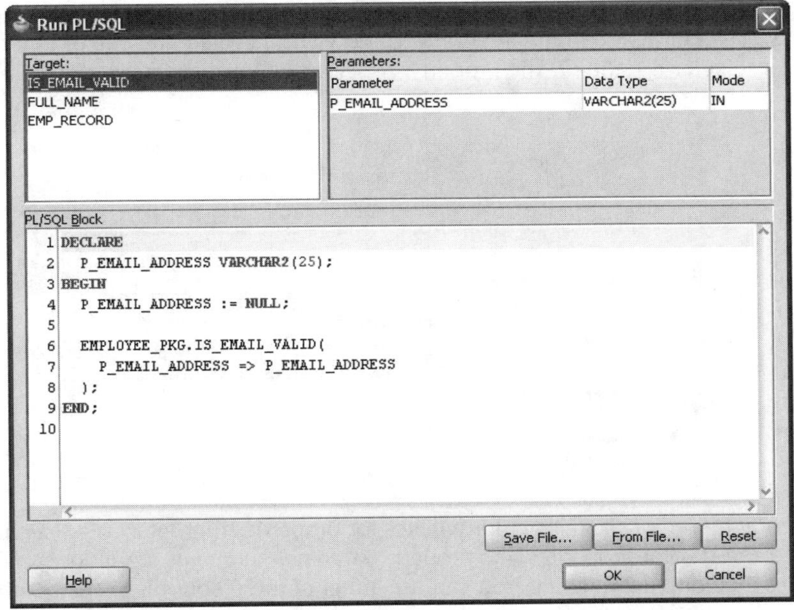

If you are running a PL/SQL package as shown in the preceding illustration (although this package is not included in the sample HR schema), you then select a subprogram in the Target panel. A PL/SQL block that runs the subprogram will appear in the PL/SQL Block panel. You then assign values to the variables declared in this block for the subprogram's parameters. When you click OK, the subprogram will be run with the parameter values passed to it in the variables. If the subprogram is a function, the output value from the function will be displayed in the Log window by a call to DBMS_OUTPUT.PUT_LINE. You can add any other PL/SQL code needed to this test block. You can also save the block to a file and reload a file before running the code.

Debugging PL/SQL Code Selecting **Debug** from the right-click menu in the editor while a PL/SQL code unit is open will run the code in debug mode. The debugger is described further in the "Debugger" section later in this chapter.

Cascading Style Sheets Editing

The ADF Faces components you use to create Fusion web applications contain extensive support for *skins,* named definitions that provide a common look and feel to your application using Cascading Style Sheets (CSS) files. JDeveloper provides editor support for defining these CSS files or any other CSS file your application requires.

To use these features, open the CSS file in the editor window. The Structure window will display the list of selectors (styles), as shown here:

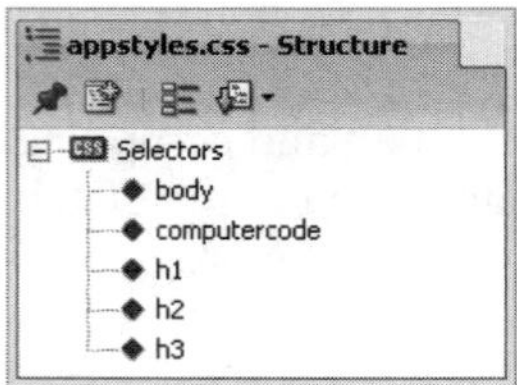

Selecting a selector name in the Structure window will navigate the cursor to the line of code where the selector is defined. The Property Inspector will display all properties and values for that selector, as shown next:

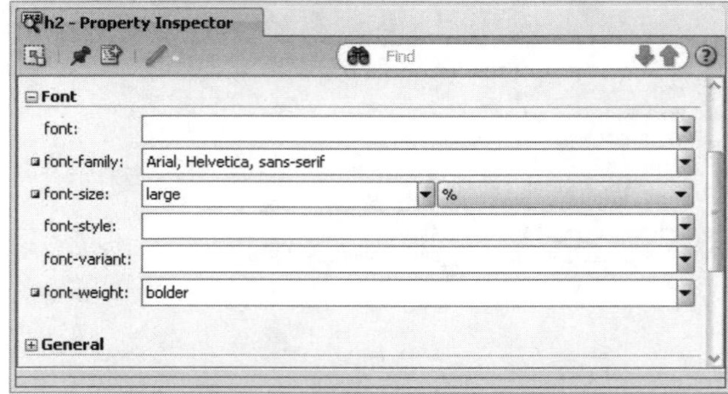

The Property Inspector contains color palettes for properties that set a color (such as *background-color*). For these color properties, the property value field contains a pulldown palette and a button that opens a color palette dialog. You can use either of these controls to set a color. You can make changes to properties in the Property Inspector or in the editor. The editor provides Code Insight for style attributes and values. For example, on a blank line inside a selector definition, you can press CTRL-SPACEBAR to show a list of properties that you can set for that selector. After entering the property name and a colon, you can press CTRL-SPACEBAR again to show a list of valid property values, such as the following list for a border property:

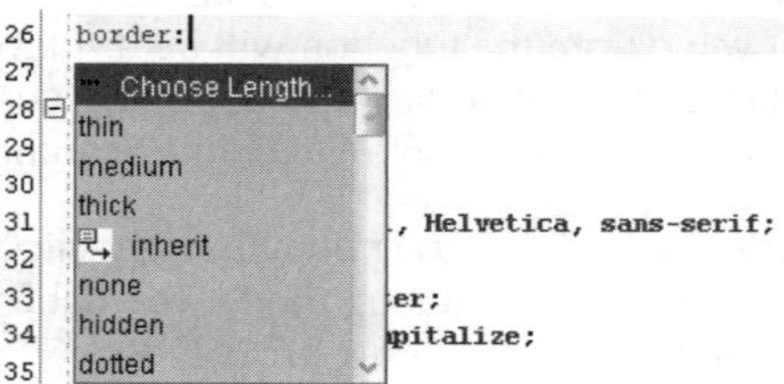

Notice that the first entry in the list is "Choose Length," which will display another dialog where you can enter a value with units. The other property values are styles and colors that you can select.

Viewing CSS Selectors The Preview tab for a CSS file displays class selectors for standard HTML tags in the way they will appear in the browser. If you define custom selectors, create a preview file with an HTML extension that includes sample text inside the <body> tag. Surround sample text with each custom selector. For example, you create a global selector "computer code" using the following CSS definition:

```
.computercode
{
  font-family: 'Courier New';
}
```

You then create a preview file called customCSS.html with the following code:

```
<html>
  <body>
    <p class="computercode">This is computer code.</p>
  </body>
</html>
```

The last step to viewing this style in the previewer is to define the Style Sheet Preview Page property on the CSS Editor page of the Preferences dialog so that it points to customCSS.html. When you click Preview in the CSS file, you will see the previewCSS.html file with the custom selector. If you do not see the new preview file, close the CSS file and reopen it.

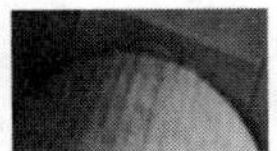

NOTE
If you define a custom preview file, you need to include samples for all selectors you wish to preview, even standard HTML selectors.

JavaScript Editing

JDeveloper provides support for editing JavaScript files. As with CSS files, the ADF Faces components you use for building applications contain built-in JavaScript behavior. However, you may need to create JavaScript to provide functionality outside the normal component set's capabilities. You can create JavaScript files using the JavaScript File item in the New Gallery Web Tier\HTML category.

While you edit the JavaScript file, Code Insight can help you type code for built-in JavaScript functions and parameters. Code templates (activated with CTRL-ENTER) can help you enter standard constructs like if else ("ife" and CTRL-ENTER) or for loops ("for" and CTRL-ENTER).

You can debug JavaScript using a Mozilla Firefox browser in the same way you debug any Java or JSP code. The following setup steps need to be completed in preparation for a JavaScript debugging session:

1. **Set up a run configuration.** In the Project Properties dialog (double click the ViewController project node), select the Run/Debug/Profile node and click New. Name the configuration **JSDebug**, for example, and leave the default setting to copy the default profile. Click OK.

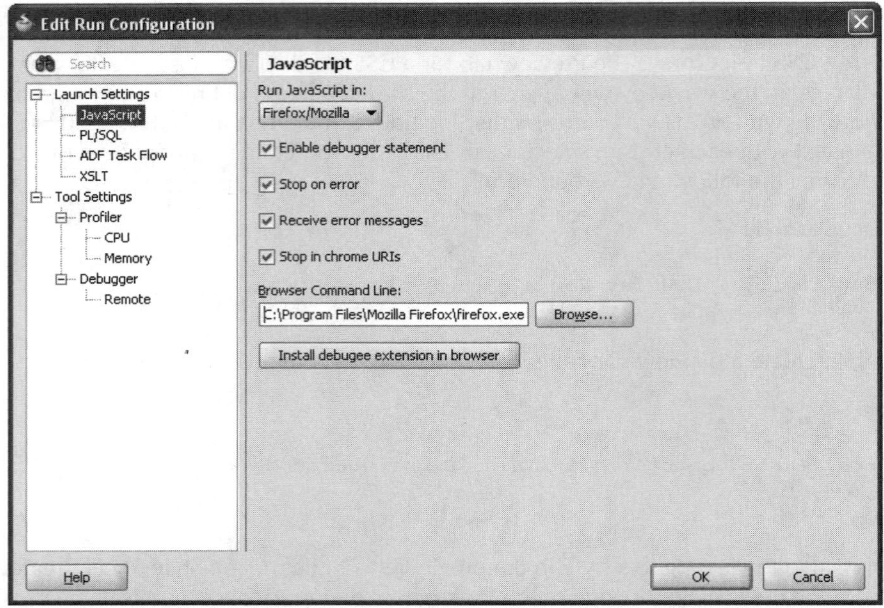

FIGURE 3-6. *Run configuration for JavaScript debugging*

2. **Customize the run configuration,** as shown in Figure 3-6. Select the new configuration and click Edit. On the Launch Settings\JavaScript page, select "Firefox/Mozilla" in the *Run JavaScript in* pulldown. In the *Browser Command Line* field, enter the location and name of the Mozilla Firefox command line (for example, "C:\Program Files\Mozilla Firefox\firefox.exe"). Use the Browse button to find the file if needed.
3. **Install an extension.** If you have not done so before, click the "Install debugee extension in browser" button to install the Oracle JavaScript Debug Agent extension. Firefox will restart. You only need to install the extension once.
4. **Set up remote debugging.** On the Tool Settings\Debugger\Remote page, select "Attach to Mozilla/Firefox" in the *Protocol* pulldown. Click OK.

Once you have set up the project in this way, you can set breakpoints (by clicking the gutter of any line in the JavaScript file) and select **JSDebug** from the right-click menu on the debug (red bug) icon. The application will run and stop for debugging when it reaches a JavaScript line where you have defined a breakpoint. You can then browse the execution path and view and set variable values as described in the next section, "Debugger."

Debugger

JDeveloper offers a full-featured debugger that you can use to examine the execution path and data values for files written in various languages such as Java, JSP tags, ADF Faces and JSF, and JavaScript.

The debugger helps you find points where the code is in error by *tracing* (stepping through and stopping at) individual lines of code. It includes the ability to handle many JDK versions (version 1.2 and later), and to debug code on remote machines. To run a file in debug mode, you need to be sure the *Full Debug Info* checkbox is selected (the default value) on the Compiler page of the Project Properties dialog (**Application** | **Project Properties**). The file compiles with special debugging information. After you set breakpoints to pause the runtime process, the file will run in a modified JDeveloper window such as that shown for a JSP file in Figure 3-7.

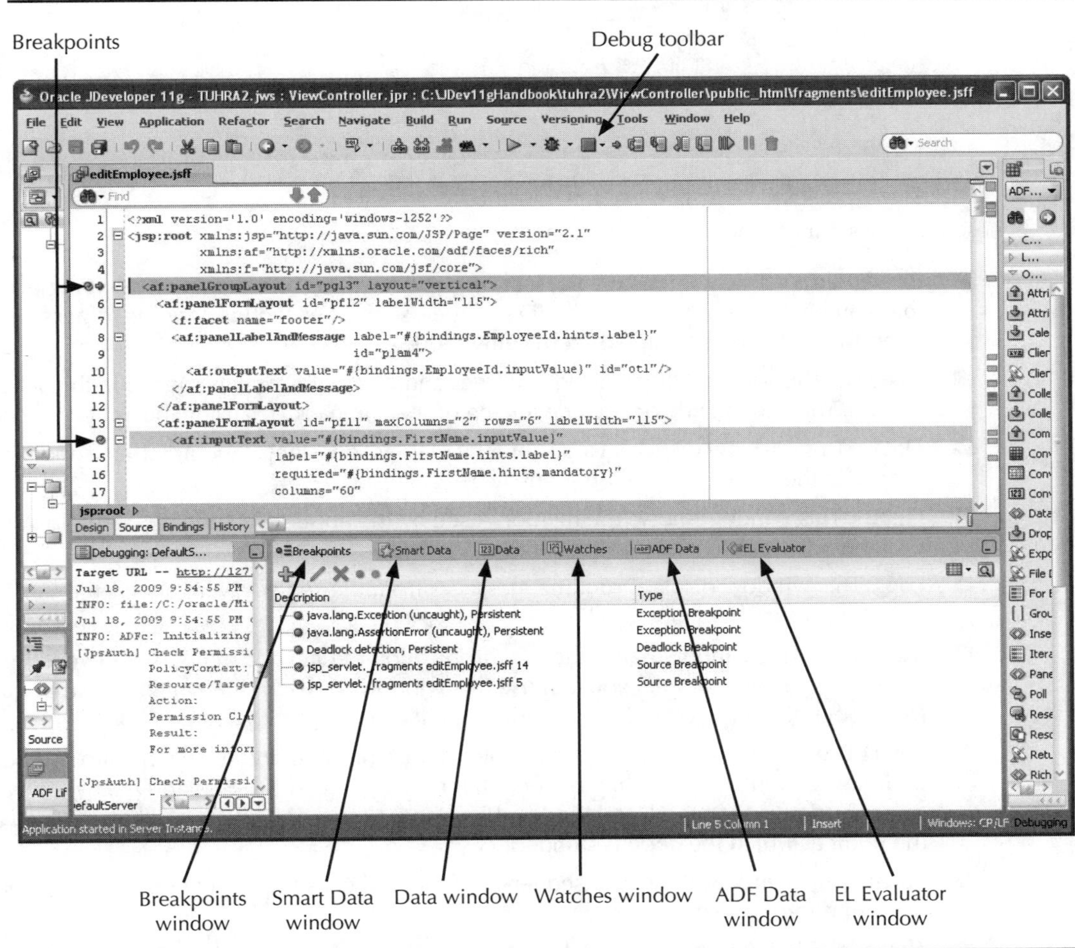

FIGURE 3-7. *JDeveloper running a JSF JSP in debug mode*

Debugger Windows

Various windows appear by default in debug mode, but you can display or hide the windows using the **View** | **Debugger** submenu items shown here:

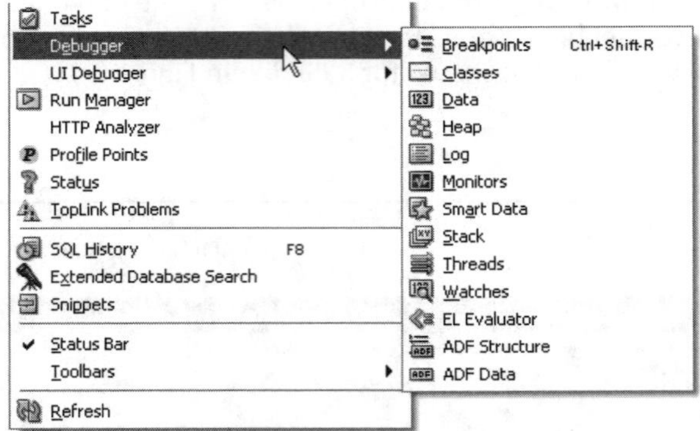

These windows offer the following functionality:

- **Breakpoints** This window displays all *breakpoints* (program execution stopping points) that you have set or that are set by JDeveloper (such as exceptions and deadlocks). This window is viewable outside of debugging mode.
- **Classes** This window displays the packages and classes that will be traced in the debug session. You can include or exclude tracing of specific packages using the right-click menu.
- **Data** This window displays values of all variables, constants, and arguments that are in scope for the current execution point.
- **Heap** This window shows the memory used by the application, which can help you find memory leaks in the application.
- **Log** This window displays runtime messages from the server. It also shows the same set of buttons as in the debug toolbar.
- **Monitors** This window tracks the synchronization of data and activities between threads of execution. For example, you can use this window to determine which thread is waiting for another thread to complete. This kind of check is helpful in detecting deadlocks.
- **Smart Data** This window shows variables, constants, and arguments that are used close to the execution point (the line of code that is being traced). The Smart Data window is more restrictive than the Data window because it shows only elements that are used near the point at which the code is stopped.
- **Stack** This window shows the sequence of method calls that preceded the execution point (the *stack*).
- **Threads** This window shows all program execution lines. Since you can write multi-threaded programs in Java, you may need to examine the state of the current simultaneously executing threads.
- **Watches** You use this window to display the current values of the expressions for which you have set *watches* (expressions that contain program variables or other data elements and their operators).

- **EL Evaluator** This window allows you to track and change values inside Expression Language expressions, for example, for EL property values in an ADF Faces application.
- **ADF Structure** This window displays the hierarchical arrangement of the component tree created in memory on the server for an ADF Faces JSF JSP file. Chapter 9 discusses the JSF component tree.
- **ADF Data** This window displays the memory area on the server for an ADF Faces JSF JSP file or task flow and allows you to watch binding values.
- **Inspector** This window is not available in the View menu but is available as the **Inspect** option from the right-click menu after selecting a variable or expression in the Code Editor, Watches window, Data window, or Smart Data window. You can open many Inspector windows and use each one to track a single variable or expression.

Running the Debugger

You can set breakpoints at lines of code where you wish the program to stop by clicking the left margin of the editor window. The line of code will be highlighted in pink and a red dot will appear in the left margin.

You can start a debugging session from the IDE by clicking the Debug button, pressing SHIFT-F9, or selecting **Debug** from the right-click menu on the file in the editor or Application Navigator. When debug mode is in effect, you can use the Debug menu items or toolbar buttons to *step over* (execute the next method), *step into* (execute the program or go to the next line), *step out* (return to the calling method without stopping), *step to end of method* (execute the program to the end of the current method or to the next breakpoint), or terminate the debug session. More information on debugging operations is available in help topics in the JDeveloper online help system (search for "debugger").

Debugging PL/SQL

You can debug PL/SQL code in an Oracle database that is version 8*i* or beyond. For Oracle 9.2 (9*i,* release 2) or later, the connection user must be granted the DEBUG CONNECT SESSION and the DEBUG ANY PROCEDURE system privileges. Before Oracle 9.2, no special privileges are required. You can set breakpoints by clicking in the left margin next to a line of code. When you run the subprogram using the **Debug** menu item, the runtime session will stop at the breakpoint and you can examine variables, view the execution thread, and step through the code. You can start your search for more information by searching the help system for "About Debugging" to find the topic "About Debugging PL/SQL Programs and Stored Java Programs."

Other Tools for Improving Code

In addition to the debugger, you can apply the following tools to assist in making your code more consistent and more efficient:

- **CPU Profiler** This tool, accessed from the Run menu, provides detailed information about the processor resource time used by your code as it is running.
- **Memory Profiler** This tool, also accessed from the Run menu, provides detailed information about memory used by the code as it is running.

- **UI Debugger** This debugger, accessed from the Run menu, allows you debug the user interface objects for a Swing or AWT Java file.
- **Auditing** This tool (in the Build menu) analyzes your code according to standards that you can tune. You would run this tool before compiling the code.

JSP/HTML Visual Editor

Visual editors provide a display of the user interface components that is similar to the runtime display. You can modify the components by dragging and dropping and using other familiar drawing operations. Changes you make in the visual editor, such as adding components or containers, will be reflected immediately in the source code. The JSP/HTML Visual Editor shown in Figure 3-8 provides these features for JSP (including JSF JSP files) and HTML files. The hands-on practices later in this book provide many examples of how best to work with this editor.

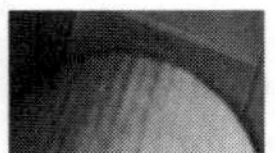

NOTE

If you are using JDeveloper to create "Java applications" (Java running on the desktop), you can use the Java Visual Editor to display layouts of Swing and AWT control. This editor also contains a Menu Editor to work with pulldown menus. You access the Menu Editor by double clicking an item under the Menu node in the Structure window UI Structure tab.

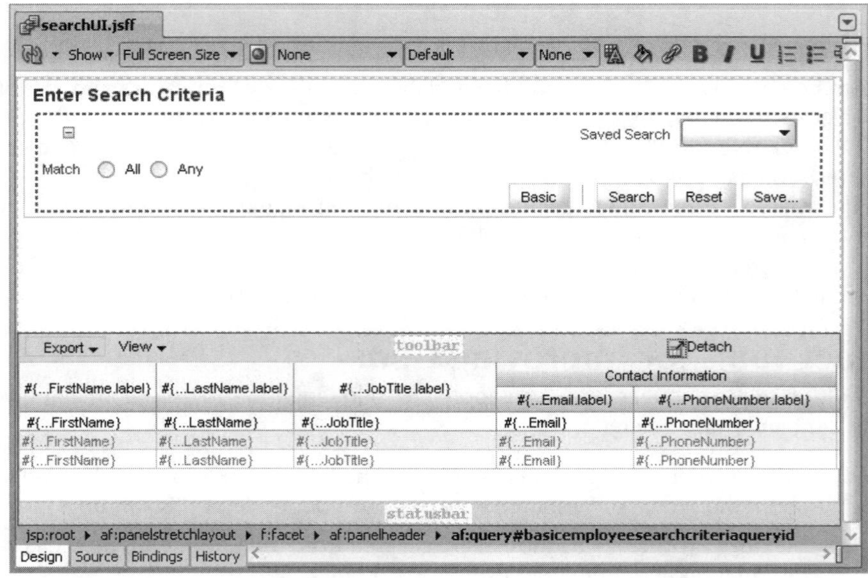

FIGURE 3-8. *JSP/HTML Visual Editor*

The JSP/HTML Visual Editor interacts primarily with tag language code that you open from the Application Navigator. If the file is open, clicking the Design tab will display the visual editor. The toolbar contains a "Select reference device" pulldown that you can use to change the view size to emulate the display in a particular monitor resolution such as 800×600.

The toolbar also contains a *Show* pulldown that allows you to display icons, which indicate various aspects of the components. For example, selecting **Data Control Bindings | Bound Components** from the *Show* pulldown will display an icon at the top-right corner of components, which components have been attached to data through data bindings. Similarly, selecting **Data Control Bindings | Unbound Components** from the *Show* pulldown will display a different icon indicating that the component does not have a value derived from a binding. The illustration here shows icons for the Unbound Item (unbound) and Employee ID (bound) components:

NOTE
Your icons may appear differently if you are using an early production release of JDeveloper 11g.

Modelers and Diagrammers

Although a detailed discussion about modelers (diagrammers) is out of scope for this book, it is useful to briefly examine the types of diagrams you can create in JDeveloper and to explain some of their common operations.

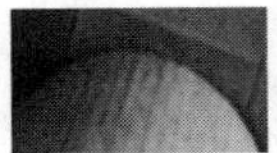

NOTE
The help system table of contents nodes "Development Tools Overview\Modelers and Diagrammers" and "Modeling with Diagrams" provide the starting points for help about the modelers and diagrammers.

Types of Diagrams

JDeveloper 11*g* includes the following Unified Modeling Language (UML) modelers:

- Class diagram
- Activity diagram
- Use case diagram
- Sequence diagram

In addition, you can represent one or more of the following types of objects on a UML class diagram or use case diagram:

- Java classes
- ADF business components
- Database objects
- EJBs

JDeveloper also offers the following non-UML modelers:

- XML Schema Editor
- JSF Navigation Diagrammer
- Struts Page Flow Modeler

These diagrammers are not UML, but they use many of the same diagramming techniques. These diagrams are discussed later in this section.

TIP
To learn more about UML, start at the source: www.uml.org.

Creating a UML Diagram

Each of the UML diagrams and each type of object just listed has a dedicated item in the General\ Diagrams category of the New Gallery, as shown in the following illustration. (You may need to select the All Technologies tab to see all items.)

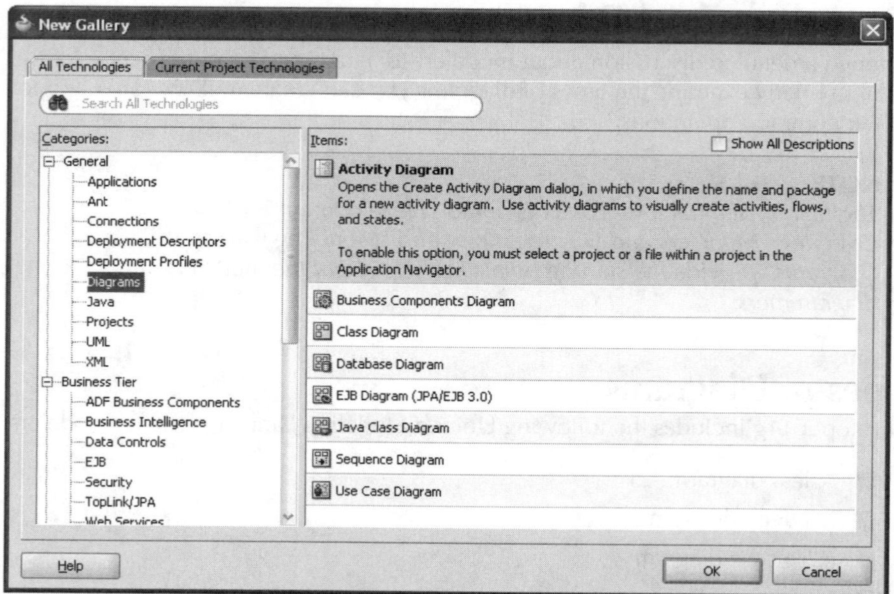

After you select a type of diagram and click OK, a dialog appears where you can name the diagram and indicate a package name where the diagram will be stored. Clicking OK on this dialog opens a new diagram window in the editor window. The selected page in the Component Palette contains elements specific to the item you selected in the New Gallery. However, component pages containing other symbol types will also be available, as shown on the right for a database diagram.

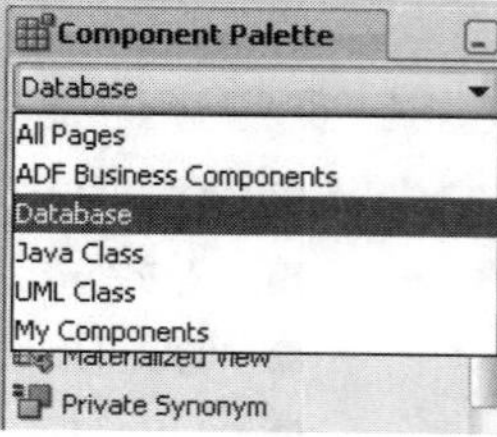

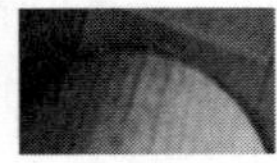

TIP

Except for Activity Diagram symbols, all diagram symbols of similar type (for example, Java classes for a Business Components diagram) should be available as pages in the Component Palette for a UML diagram. If a Component Palette page for a particular symbol set does not appear, create a blank diagram of the missing type and then close it without saving.

Some Diagramming Operations

The top-left corner of the diagram window contains a toolbar with Zoom In and Zoom Out buttons as well as a pulldown to select the zoom percentage. The toolbar also contains a tool for automatically changing the arrangement of diagrammed objects. This is useful to provide a starting place for modifying the layout after dropping a number of objects into the diagram. The toolbar also offers tools for changing the color, font, and font size of selected objects.

Another feature provided for changing the view is the Thumbnail window (**View** | **Thumbnail**). This window contains a small representation of the page with a rectangle indicating the current viewport of the page in the diagram window. For example, the following shows the Thumbnail window on the left displaying the location of the view in a database diagram:

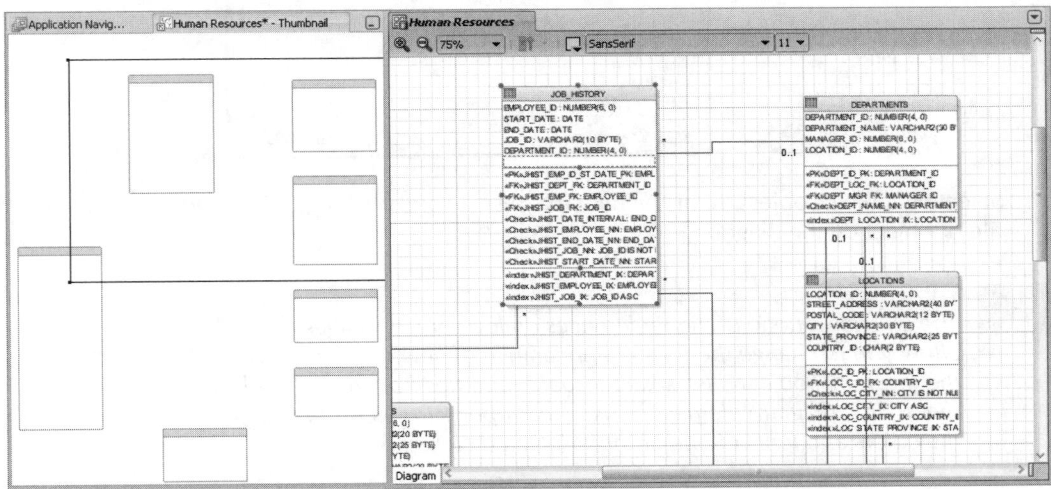

The diagrams provide the drag-and-drop features you would expect for resizing and moving diagram elements. In addition, the right-click menu on diagram elements contains an item for **Visual Properties** where you can modify the subelements displayed as well as the colors and fonts for a single or a selected group of elements. This set of properties also appears in the Property Inspector. The **Properties** right-click menu item (alternatively activated by double clicking the object) opens the appropriate properties dialog or editor for that element; for example, selecting **Properties** from the right-click menu on a database table symbol, shows the Edit Table dialog. (You will practice these techniques with a database diagram in Chapter 17.)

Some diagram elements allow you to generate code or database objects. For example, an ADF BC entity object contains a right-click **Generate Business Objects** submenu containing items for **Default Data Model Components** (for ADF business component objects) and **Database Objects** (to create a table in the database).

The right-click menu on the diagram surface contains a **Publish Diagram** option that you can use to save the diagram image to a file as mentioned in the Chapter 2 section "Diagram Menu." It also contains an **Add to Diagram** item that displays the Add to Diagram dialog (shown next).

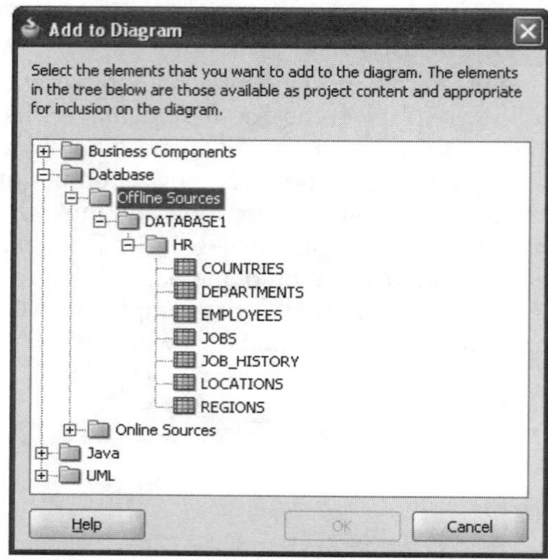

Selecting a file or object in this hierarchical display and clicking OK will add an element for that file or object on the diagram.

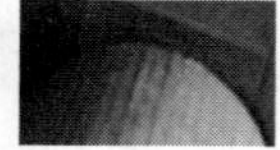

TIP

The Diagrams node of the Preferences dialog contains pages that allow you to change the default appearance of new objects drawn on the diagram. You can also select Visual Properties from the right-click menu on a diagram element or use the Property Inspector to change the colors and fonts of one or more selected elements.

Activity Diagram

The Activity Diagram offers the same type of operations as the other diagrammers except that you cannot use symbols other than Activity Diagram symbols. You use this tool to create a standard UML activity diagram for business processes (like the more traditional Data Flow Diagram or flow chart). As with most process modeling tools, you can define activities (processes) and transitions (flows) and drill into an activity to represent detailed activities and transitions within the main activity. As with flow charts, you can model decision points for conditional transitions. You can optionally model activities within *swim lanes*—horizontal regions on the diagram that represent ownership or location of the activities within.

XML Schema Editor

JDeveloper 11*g* offers the XML Schema Editor for creating, viewing, and modifying XML schemas. An *XML schema* is an .xsd file that defines the structure, content, and language elements used in a set of XML files. (It is a replacement for the older concept of Document Type Definition files.) You associate XML files with the schema file so that the tags within the XML file can be validated and interpreted. You can display this editor by creating (using the General\XML category, XML Schema item of the New Gallery) or editing an XML schema file.

The Design tab of the XML Schema Editor is shown in Figure 3-9 for thepermissionshook.xsd file in the oracle.adfm.jar file (located in JDEV_HOME\jdev\extensions). The Source tab displays a text version of the code in the file. Using the Component Palette, you can drop elements into the design area and set their properties using the Property Inspector. You can also use the right-click menu on an object in the XML Schema Editor to add elements and modify the file. The Structure window will track the object hierarchy as you edit the file.

More information about the XML Schema Editor is available starting at the help system Table of Contents node "Working with Application Design Tools\Working with Source Files\About Source Files\About Source Files\About the XML Schema Editor."

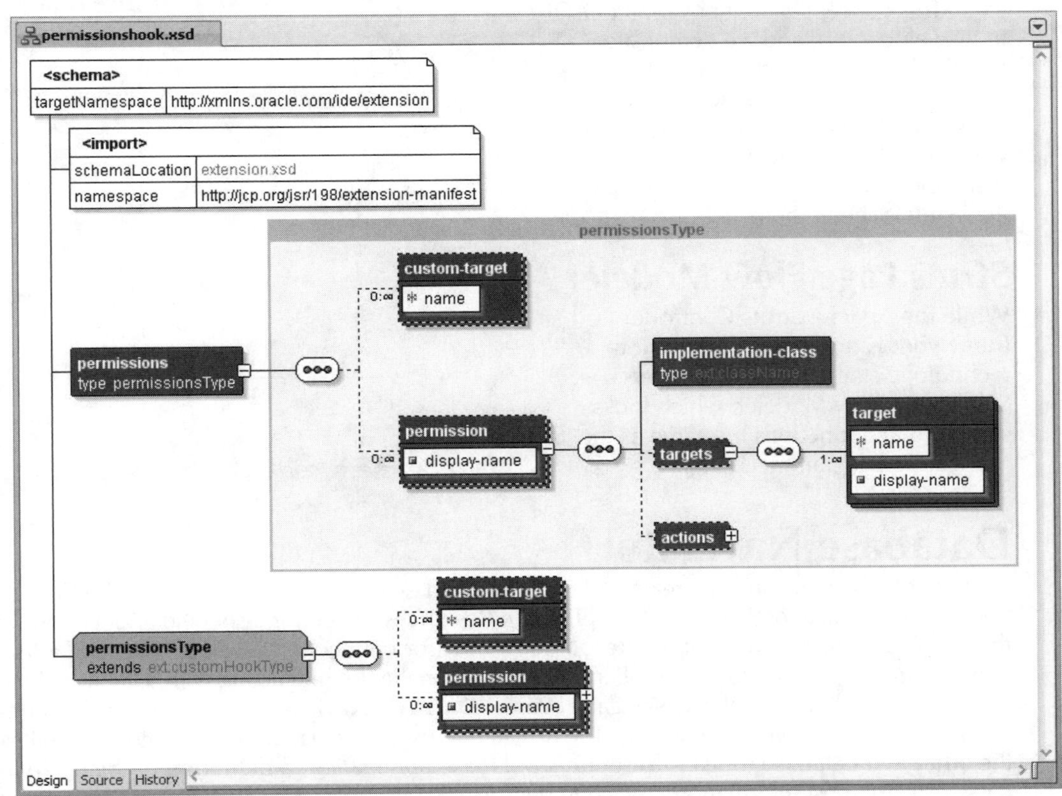

FIGURE 3-9. *XML Schema Editor*

JSF Navigation Diagrammer

The JSF Navigation Diagrammer (shown here) is another diagrammer that does not use UML symbols. It is primarily a visual representation of the JSF controller configuration files, such as faces-config.xml. You use this diagram to visually define pages and navigation cases that are written into the configuration file. Several chapters in this book (such as Chapter 10) provide hands-on practices that use this diagrammer.

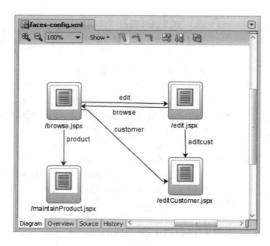

You can display a JSF Navigation Diagrammer session by opening the configuration file (such as faces-config.xml) in a JSF project. Click the Diagram tab if the diagrammer is not visible.

ADF Task Flow Diagrammer

The ADF Task Flow Diagrammer allows you to model task flows that manage parts of the page. This concept is an innovation of ADF in JDeveloper 11g and we demonstrate it in the hands-on practices in Part V of this book. You use the same techniques to work with this diagrammer as you do to work with the JSF Navigation Diagrammer. A sample task flow diagram (editEmployee-flow.xml) is shown here.

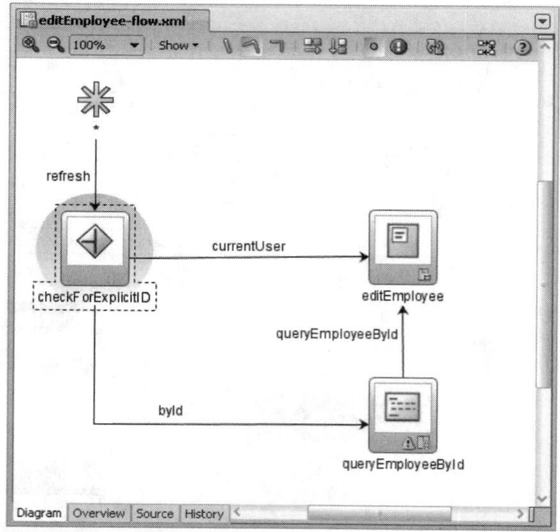

Struts Page Flow Modeler

While the Apache Struts Controller framework is not used in the Fusion technology stack, JDeveloper offers a Struts Page Flow Modeler, which looks similar to and functions the same as the JSF Navigation Diagrammer.

Database Navigator

As described before, you can create and manage database connections using either the Connections node in the Application Navigator's Application Resources panel (for a specific application) or in the IDE Connections panel of the Resource Palette (for connections available to copy into any application). However, these tools offer limited functionality for interacting with database objects.

Another tool, the Database Navigator (**View | Database Navigator**), provides the capability to edit as well as view database objects. The first step in using the Database Navigator (as well as the other two database tools) is to set up a *database connection,* a definition of the username, password, and host information needed to define a Java Database Connectivity (JDBC) connection.

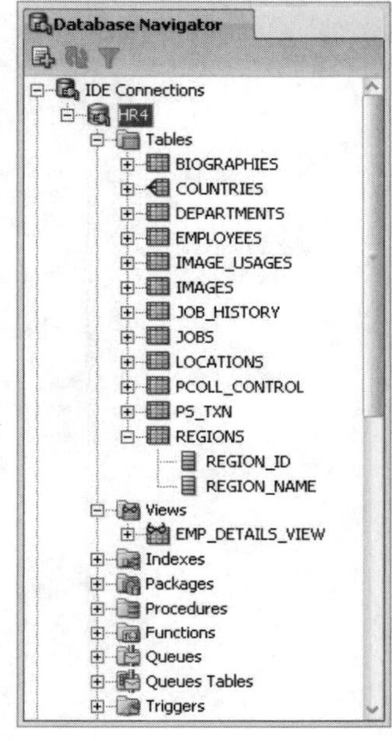

(The creation dialog for database connections is shown in the section "Creation Dialogs" earlier in this chapter.) Once you set up a database connection, double clicking that name will open the connection and display the database object nodes as shown on the right.

TIP
You can import database connections from Oracle SQL Developer or any version of JDeveloper and import them into JDeveloper 11g. Use appropriate right-click menu options on the connections nodes of the Database Navigator to create and import the connections. In addition, the Resource Palette and Application Navigator also allow you to create database connections.

This navigator displays database objects owned by the schema defined in the database connection properties. You can also navigate to database objects owned by other schemas if the connection user has been granted access to those objects using the Other Users node at the bottom of the navigator. This navigator displays connections set up in the Resources Palette (in the Database Navigator's IDE Connections node) or in the Application Resources panel (under the specific application name) of all open applications.

Double clicking a database object in this navigator displays relevant information in the editor window. For example, double clicking a table name will open the table viewer, which contains the editor tabs such as Columns, Data, Constraints, Grants, Statistics, Triggers, Dependencies, Details, Indexes, and SQL. These tabs allow you to view and modify details of the database objects.

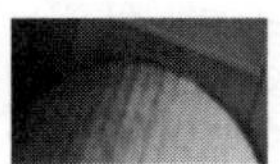

TIP
The Data tab for a table object allows you to change data and commit that change to the database.

Selecting Edit from a database code node (for example, a PL/SQL trigger) opens an editor you can use to modify the code as described in the section "Working with PL/SQL" earlier in this chapter.

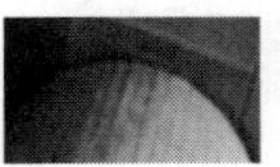

NOTE
If you have used Oracle SQL Developer, the database development tool, the JDeveloper Database Navigator and its associated editors will look very familiar because both tools share the same code base.

SQL Worksheet

The right-click menu of a Database Navigator connection node offers an option for **Open SQL Worksheet**. Selecting this item opens the SQL Worksheet tool in an editor window, as shown in Figure 3-10.

The top pane of the window allows you to enter and execute SQL statements or run PL/SQL blocks using a database connection selected in the top-right corner pulldown. When you click the

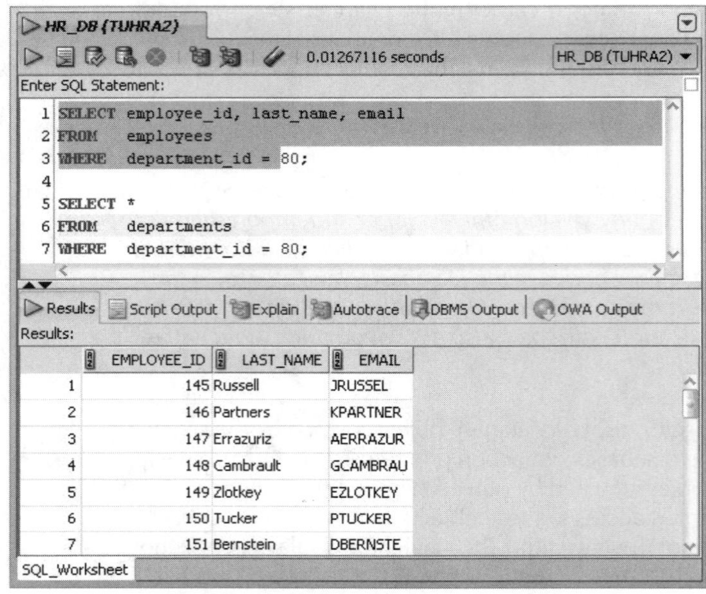

FIGURE 3-10. *SQL Worksheet*

"Execute Statement" arrow button (or press F9), the statement is issued to the database and the results are displayed in the Results panel (for queries) or status bar at the status bar at the bottom-left corner of the JDeveloper IDE window (for statements other than queries). If the result is data (such as for a SELECT statement), the Results panel will display the rows of data in a scrollable table.

You can enter more than one command in the SQL Worksheet and execute them one at a time by placing the cursor somewhere in the statement and by clicking the "Execute Statement" button (or by pressing F9). Clicking Run Script (F5) will run all statements in the window and will display results in the Results window's Script Output page.

TIP

*You can alternatively run SQL*Plus from the* ***SQL*Plus*** *right-click menu option on the connection node in the Database Navigator. SQL*Plus is not shipped with JDeveloper, so you need to have it installed before this menu option will work.*

The right-click menu of the editor pane contains a **SQL History** selection that displays a window (alternatively activated by pressing F8) showing a list of statements you have entered in SQL Worksheet. Double clicking a statement in that window will load it into the editor window.

The right-click menu in the editor pane also contains options for the toolbar actions as well as for using Query Builder to create SELECT statements from graphical representations of database objects. The results pane contains tab areas for viewing a query result grid, script output, Explain Plan results, Autotrace results, DBMS output, and Oracle Web Agent (OWA) output (if you are using the PL/SQL Web Toolkit htp and htf packages to generate HTML from a PL/SQL block).

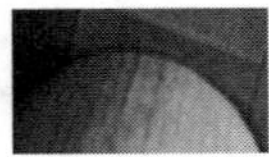

TIP
*The View menu includes several utility options for database work such as **Database Reports**—prebuilt queries that display output in the editor window—and **Find DB Object**—to search for various types of database structures.*

Database Documentation

An option on the right-click menu of the database connection name node, **Generate DB Doc**, creates an HTML front-end application, shown in Figure 3-11, which you can use to browse database objects without connecting to a database. After selecting this option, specify a disk location into which the documentation will be generated. JDeveloper will generate the documentation files and open the browser to the index.html file in the directory you specify. The generated interface allows selecting database object types in the top-left panel and searching those objects in the bottom-left panel. Selecting an object will fill the right-side panel with a set of tabs containing details about the object.

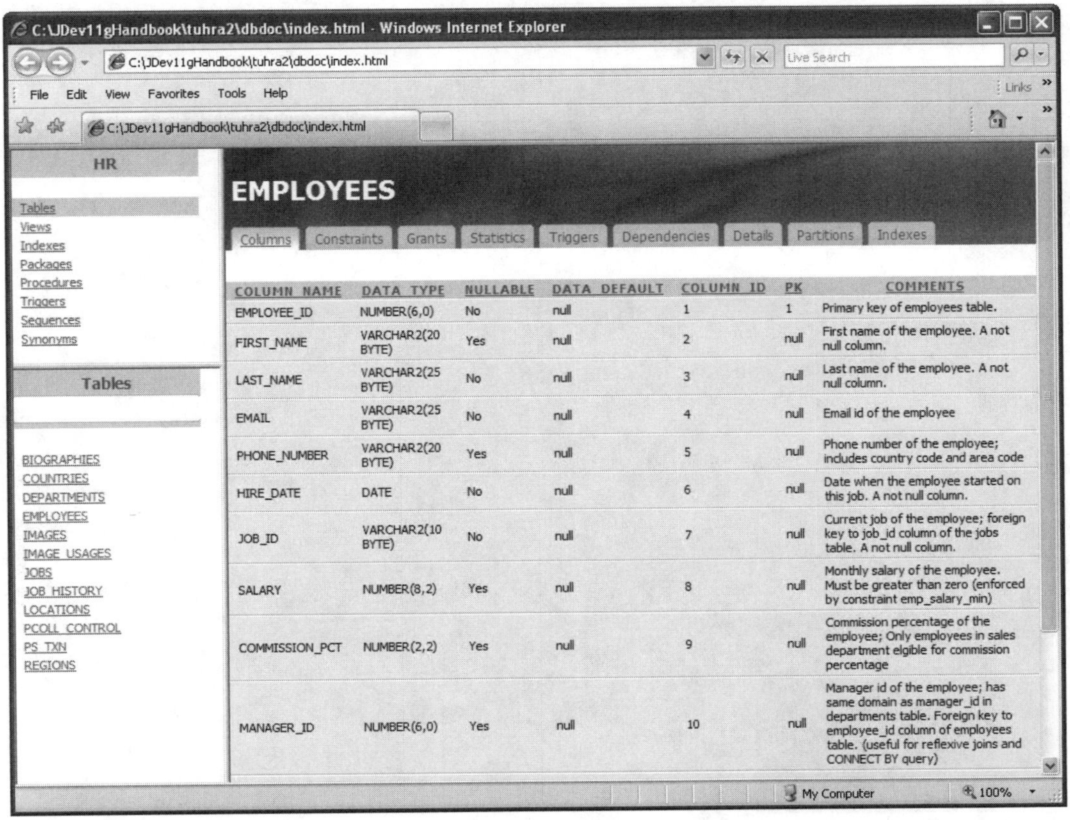

C:\JDev11gHandbook\tuhra2\dbdoc\index.html - Windows Internet Explorer

HR: Tables, Views, Indexes, Packages, Procedures, Triggers, Sequences, Synonyms

Tables: BIOGRAPHIES, COUNTRIES, DEPARTMENTS, EMPLOYEES, IMAGES, IMAGE_USAGES, JOBS, JOB_HISTORY, LOCATIONS, PCOLL_CONTROL, PS_TXN, REGIONS

EMPLOYEES

Columns | Constraints | Grants | Statistics | Triggers | Dependencies | Details | Partitions | Indexes

COLUMN_NAME	DATA_TYPE	NULLABLE	DATA_DEFAULT	COLUMN_ID	PK	COMMENTS
EMPLOYEE_ID	NUMBER(6,0)	No	null	1	1	Primary key of employees table.
FIRST_NAME	VARCHAR2(20 BYTE)	Yes	null	2	null	First name of the employee. A not null column.
LAST_NAME	VARCHAR2(25 BYTE)	No	null	3	null	Last name of the employee. A not null column.
EMAIL	VARCHAR2(25 BYTE)	No	null	4	null	Email id of the employee
PHONE_NUMBER	VARCHAR2(20 BYTE)	Yes	null	5	null	Phone number of the employee; includes country code and area code
HIRE_DATE	DATE	No	null	6	null	Date when the employee started on this job. A not null column.
JOB_ID	VARCHAR2(10 BYTE)	No	null	7	null	Current job of the employee; foreign key to job_id column of the jobs table. A not null column.
SALARY	NUMBER(8,2)	Yes	null	8	null	Monthly salary of the employee. Must be greater than zero (enforced by constraint emp_salary_min)
COMMISSION_PCT	NUMBER(2,2)	Yes	null	9	null	Commission percentage of the employee; Only employees in sales department elgible for commission percentage
MANAGER_ID	NUMBER(6,0)	Yes	null	10	null	Manager id of the employee; has same domain as manager_id in departments table. Foreign key to employee_id column of employees table. (useful for reflexive joins and CONNECT BY query)

FIGURE 3-11. *Database documentation*

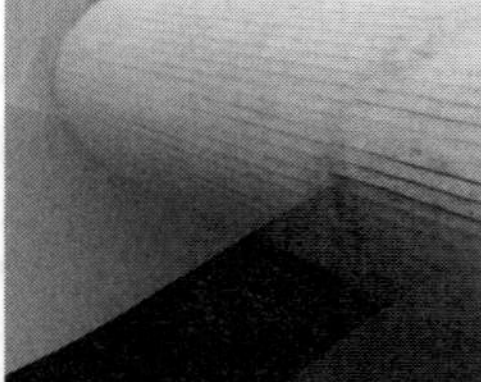

CHAPTER 4

Technology Background

One pill makes you larger
And one pill makes you small
And the ones that mother gives you
Don't do anything at all.
Go ask Alice
When she's ten feet tall.

—Grace Slick (1939–), *White Rabbit* (1967)

n recent times, IT organizations have been tasked more and more with charting a course for writing new applications in and migrating existing applications to a Java environment. On the surface, this task might seem to be a matter of using predetermined methods and technologies. However, one major aspect of Java is its enormous variety and breadth. There is no one way to create a system; in fact, there are probably hundreds of combinations of Java technologies that could serve any one purpose. This makes the decision of selecting the proper technology combination daunting, especially if the Java environment is new to the organization.

When making a decision, you need to collect as much information about the choices as possible. Information about Java technologies is certainly prominent in the Oracle world, as it is across the IT industry. However, general introductory information about the world of Java is rare. Literature available in trade publications and on the Web often assumes that the reader is familiar with at least some of the basics and buzzwords. Grasping these basics is essential to assimilating and understanding any specific technology. In turn, understanding the technologies will help in making the decisions needed to collect these technologies into the proper environment for a particular application, as well as in the work performed during development of the application.

This chapter provides overviews of the technology concepts you will need to know when developing Java-based web applications such as those in the Fusion stack introduced in Chapter 1. These overviews will prepare you for the details of these technologies discussed in the rest of this book. The chapter starts with an explanation of the basics of the Java platform and the main technologies that it offers for implementing database applications. It then explains how the Hypertext Transfer Protocol (HTTP) communication process works in a web application and which languages you will need to learn to be effective in the Fusion development environment.

The discussions in this chapter focus around these questions:

- **What is Java Platform, Enterprise Edition?**
- **What are the main styles of Java EE code?**
- **How do web communications work?**
- **What languages do I need to know for web development?**

What Is Java Platform, Enterprise Edition?

Java Platform, Enterprise Edition (Java EE) is a set of standards and specifications (called a *platform*) that defines the environment for running software written using the Java language. Java EE (formerly called "J2EE") is created and maintained by Sun Microsystems, but anyone may suggest and work on enhancements using the Java Community Process (explained further in the sidebar "About the Java Community Process").

About the Java Community Process
Java Community Process (JCP) is the means by which new and enhanced features and technologies are added to the Java standards (www.jcp.org). The JCP Executive Committee examines a proposal for viability; if it is approved, the committee assigns it a Java Specification Request (JSR) number. Then, a committee of experts works on the enhancement and presents it to the community for comments and suggestions. After several approval steps, the enhancement is ratified or rejected. Ratified JSRs may then become part of a platform's standards. This process occurs for new versions of the platforms (such as Java EE) as well as for parts of the platform (such as the Java language).

Java EE is not a product. Instead, vendors create Java EE–compliant products by implementing the Java EE specifications. As the *enterprise platform,* Java EE describes components for software applications intended to serve an entire organization. Two other platforms describe architectures and technologies used for applications running in different environments:

- *Java Platform, Standard Edition (Java SE)* describes components used for applications running on a desktop computer. This platform also includes the Java language distributed as the *Java SE Development Kit (JDK),* which includes libraries and executables needed to run code written in Java.
- *Java Platform, Micro Edition (Java ME)* describes a runtime environment used for applications that run on small, portable devices that have minimal memory, small displays, and power limitations, such as cell phones or personal digital assistants (PDAs).

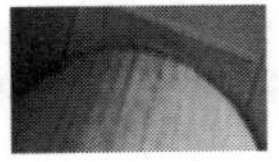

NOTE
At this writing, the current version of Java EE is 5.0, which includes Java SE 5. The current version of Java SE is 6. Java EE 6.0 is in the JCP as JSR 316.

Java EE contains all components in Java SE, such as the Java language. The additional functionality that Java EE adds to Java SE is in the realm of multi-tier deployment and web technology. This makes Java EE popular with organizations that need to build applications that will be run on the Web.

Online References

The Java EE specifications are available at the java.sun.com website (navigate through the Java EE links and look for "specifications"). You will find much overview information on the Sun website, but as a first reference, we highly recommend the *Java EE Tutorial,* an extensive online introduction, also available at java.sun.com (most easily found by searching for "Java EE Tutorial" on www.google.com). This online guide introduces Java EE in terms of an architecture model.

TIP
Although it is not a prerequisite for working through the Java EE Tutorial, you can also access the "Java Tutorial" at java.sun.com. The "Java Tutorial" provides an excellent overview of the Java language.

Java EE Architecture Model

Java EE defines *components*—technologies such as JavaServer Pages (JSP) code—which you assemble with other components to create an application. The *Java EE architecture model* divides these components into logical runtime *tiers,* or layers. Figure 4-1 shows these tiers (represented by rounded boxes) with some of their components. Java runtime processes (described in detail in the sidebar "About the JRE and JVM") run code in one or more of these tiers.

About the JRE and JVM

The Java runtime, called the *Java Runtime Environment (JRE)* consists of an executable file (such as java.exe on MS Windows) and a number of library files, which interpret and run the code in an application. A *Java Virtual Machine (JVM)* refers to both the executable file and to an instance of this executable running as an operating system process. Sometimes, the terms "JRE" and "JVM" are used interchangeably to refer to a Java runtime process. JVMs can also run other types of code such as that written in Groovy (discussed in the section "Groovy" later in this chapter).

Client Tier

User interface code runs on this tier (usually a desktop computer or mobile client device). A web browser displays a Hypertext Markup Language user interface, or a JVM presents the interface (in the case of a Java application or applet). These interfaces interact with the user. Code running in the client JVM is described later in this chapter, in the section "Application Client."

Web Tier

The Web Tier runs user interface code on a *Java EE server*—a server computer located outside of the user's desktop computer. This server is often referred to as a *web server* or *application server,* although those terms are less precise in terms of Java EE architecture. The Web Tier is responsible

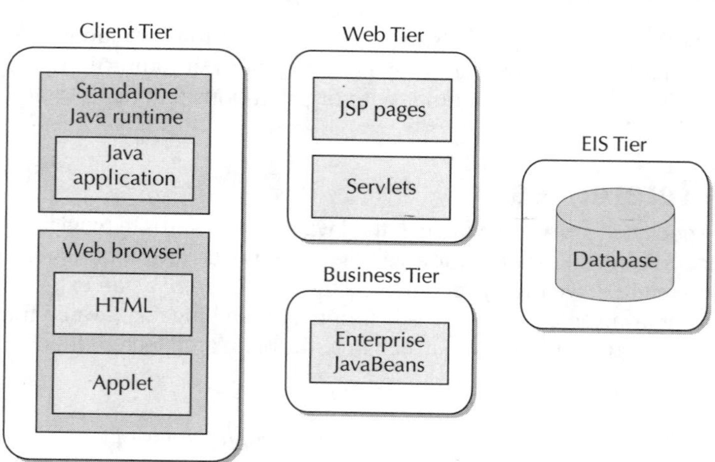

FIGURE 4-1. *Java EE architecture model*

for running application code (for example, JSP or servlet code) inside a JVM and sending user interface code such as Hypertext Markup Language (HTML) to the Client Tier device. Code running in the Web Tier JVM (the *Web container*) is described in this chapter's section "Web Client."

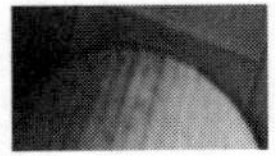

NOTE
HTML was created so that plain text files displayed in a web browser could be formatted with colors, fonts, graphics, and links to other pages. HTML also contains a set of user interface controls, such as fields and forms, so that information can be sent to the application server for processing.

Business Tier

The Business Tier runs validation and business logic code, as well as code such as Enterprise JavaBeans (EJBs) or ADF Business Components (ADF BC) that accesses a data source like a database. It connects the Web Tier or Client Tier to the Enterprise Information System (EIS) Tier. The JVM on this tier is called the "EJB container."

EIS Tier

The EIS Tier represents the database (or other data source) for business data. The EIS Tier also represents preexisting database applications that are out of Java EE's scope. This book assumes that you are using a single Oracle database, but that database could be distributed across a grid or a series of servers. The sidebar "Accessing the Database with JDBC" describes briefly how this kind of database access is accomplished.

Accessing the Database with JDBC

Java Database Connectivity (JDBC) is a library of Java classes included with the JDK that allows you to easily access a relational database from a Java program in the same way that SQL*Net allows easy access to the database from an Oracle Forms (or other client) application. You do not use SQL*Net on the client if you are using JDBC, although the Oracle database uses the TNS Listener (SQL*Net) process to support JDBC connections.

Typically, application code constructs SQL statements and issues them to the database through calls to methods in the JDBC library. Technologies such as ADF Business Components and EJBs (introduced in Chapter 1) use JDBC in this way but shield you from having to call JDBC directly in your code.

JDBC is the most frequently used database access method because it is implemented in Java class files and, therefore, allows you to embed standard SQL inside Java code. The JDBC API is included in the Java SE Development Kit and is mentioned in the Java EE specifications. However, many frameworks (such as EJBs and ADF Business Components) have been built on top of JDBC to make it easier to use. (Frameworks are described in Chapter 1.) You can create connections in JDeveloper to access any database that offers a JDBC driver.

Java EE Tiers and Server Hardware

Java EE tiers do not necessarily correspond on a one-to-one basis with computer server hardware. More than one tier can be located on a single computer server, but a single tier can alternatively span servers. This flexibility allows you to scale application easily; if more processing power is needed for a particular tier, you can add servers to that tier. It also provides robustness—if a server fails, other servers in the same group can handle its requests.

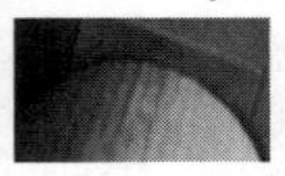

NOTE
The Client Tier and EIS Tier components often run on separate computers, a client desktop and a database server, respectively. On the other hand, the Web Tier and Business Tier components often run on the same computer or set of computers—the "Java EE server."

Java EE Containers

Java EE services called *containers* provide the ability for the code in a component to run on a Java EE server. The Web Tier and Business Tier code runs inside JVMs located on a remote computer. Thus, the *Web container* is basically a JVM on a server that is customized to run Web Tier components as well as some Business Tier components such as ADF BC. Similarly, the *EJB container* is also a JVM on an application server that runs EJBs. Java EE–compliant application server programs, such as Oracle Application Server 11*g,* must supply these container processes as standard features. In addition to runtime services, these containers offer services such as connection pooling so that many clients can share the same database connection; and transaction support so that database commit and rollback operations can be associated with a particular user session.

WebLogic Server *Oracle WebLogic Server* (*WLS,* formerly from BEA Systems) supplies Java EE–compatible container services to Oracle Application Server 11*g*. WLS runs within the Oracle Application Server environment but can also be run as a standalone server. JDeveloper includes a copy of WLS with which you can run web client applications inside of JDeveloper.

NOTE
*The Java container in Oracle Application Server and JDeveloper versions 9*i *and 10*g *was called "Oracle Containers for Java EE" (OC4J).*

BluePrints and Design Patterns

Java developers rely on a resource called BluePrints (java.sun.com/reference/blueprints) for information about best practices and proven application architectures. BluePrints also offers *design patterns,* low-level code solutions for solving common problems. Model-View-Controller (MVC) is a popular design pattern that is used extensively in Oracle Application Development Framework (ADF) and in JDeveloper.

Model-View-Controller

Model-View-Controller is a frequently used design pattern (originally developed for Smalltalk, another object-oriented programming language) that defines a separation of application code into three layers, as shown here.

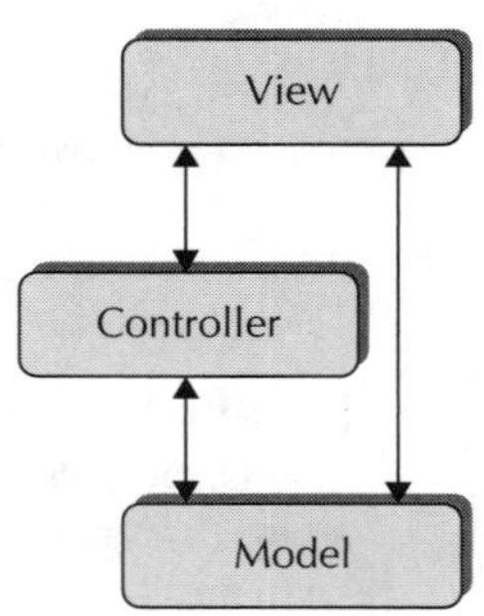

- **Model** The Model layer defines and validates the data used by the application. It includes code to validate business rules and to communicate data to and from the database. It interacts with the View layer to notify it of changes in the data. It interacts with the Controller layer by receiving and processing requests to update data in the application.

- **View** The View layer provides the user interface that displays data from the Model layer. It interacts with the Controller layer by receiving requests to update the user interface and by sending it user events (for example, a button press).
- **Controller** Code in the Controller layer determines what happens after a user event occurs in the View layer. It interacts with the View layer to request user interface updates; it sends requests to the Model layer when data needs to be updated. The Controller layer is responsible for *task flow*—the determination of what the View layer will render, and what changes to data the Model layer will make, after a certain data or user event.

The intention of MVC is to allow the code that implements a particular area of the application to be reused by many implementations of another area. For example, you could use the same Model code to supply data to a desktop web browser application, as well as to an application displayed on a cell phone. These two display devices might not be able to share the Controller layer, but reusing the Model layer code can save a great deal of work and many maintenance worries. Regardless of how much reuse is actually possible, MVC is still a valid guide.

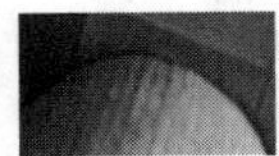

NOTE
As mentioned in Chapter 1, ADF architecture is based on the MVC design pattern.

Other than the MVC design pattern, technologies within the Java EE component architecture are the most important, most frequently used, and most referenced part of Java EE. When you start a Java EE project, you need to make decisions about which technologies to use in each tier of the Java EE architecture.

What Are the Main Styles of Java EE Code?

Instead of offering a laundry list of the components of the Java EE component architecture, it is more useful to examine the components in the context of how they are assembled into the following styles of code named in the Java EE specifications:

- **Application client** The application runs in a JVM on the client computer (also called *desktop applications* or *thick client applications*).
- **Web client** The application runs in a JVM on a Java EE server (also called *web browser applications, thin-client applications,* or *light-client applications*).

We will discuss the technology components you would use in each of these two styles. We will assume that you are using an Oracle database as a data source, and therefore will not mention other options in the EIS tier. Each of these code styles works differently only in the other three tiers.

NOTE
All examples in this section show Enterprise JavaBeans in the Business Tier, since it is defined in the Java EE specifications, although this book and Fusion architecture focus on ADF Business Components.

Application Client

The *application client* coding style runs Java application code in the Client Tier. Java EE defines two types of clients that run solely in the Client Tier: Java applications and applets.

Java Applications

A *Java application* (known in the Java world as an *application*) consists of compiled Java code that runs in a JVM on the client computer. In the early days of Java, the Java application was the only way to deploy Java code. The Java runtime code and the compiled Java application files must be installed on the client computer (or on a network computer accessible by the client computer). Figure 4-2 shows this component in the Java EE tiers.

In this application client example, the application program running in the JVM on the Client Tier communicates with Enterprise JavaBeans on the Business Tier. The EJBs supply business rules logic and the JDBC connection to the EIS Tier database.

EJBs are shown on the Business Tier, which is often on an application server computer; locating the EJBs on a separate server allows multiple client applications (and multiple users) to access the same code. Alternatively, this code could be placed on the client computer. In this situation, Java EE Client Tier and Business Tier code would reside on the client computer and the computer architecture would be two-tier (client/server).

Windowed Java applications are often written using code objects derived from the JDK *Swing* library such as panels, text fields, labels, pulldown menus, and buttons that result in a standard GUI look and feel, as shown in the following illustration.

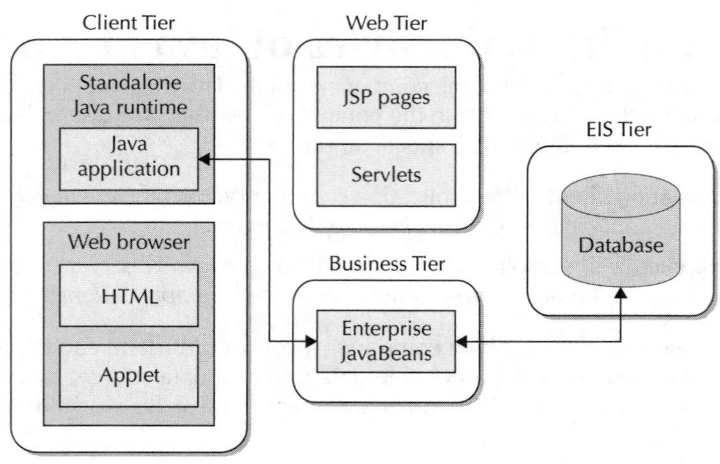

FIGURE 4-2. *Java EE application client architecture*

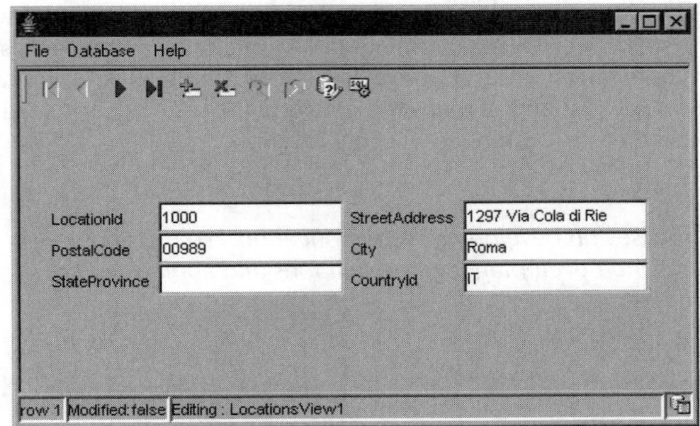

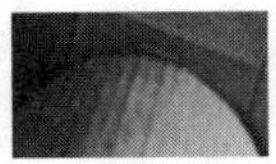

NOTE
JDeveloper is an example of a full-featured Java application that uses Swing (and other similar) libraries to present the IDE.

Traditionally, Java applications were chosen when the system required highly interactive and controllable user-interface components that offered immediate event processing and design-time support. Swing is a standard Java SE UI component library, but other third-party libraries also offer this type of control set.

NOTE
As you will see in later chapters, JSF components such as ADF Faces offer interactive features that rival those of Java applications and previous GUI technologies.

Applets

An *applet* is a Java program running on the Client Tier within the JVM of a web browser. Applets were the first method created for making Java applications available through the Web. An applet can be displayed as a window embedded inside the browser's window; it can alternatively be displayed as a separate window that is part of the browser session. Applets use the same highly interactive controls (for example, those from the Swing library) as Java applications, and their appearance and behavior is the same as Java applications written using those controls.

An applet and its supporting libraries need to be installed on the client computer. It is started when the user issues a Hypertext Transfer Protocol (HTTP) request using a web browser HTML control, such as a link or button. The request is for the web server to return an HTML page to the browser. The HTML page contains an `<APPLET>` tag that signals the browser to open a JVM session. The `<APPLET>` tag also includes a reference to the Java applet file that the session will run. If the Java applet file does not exist on the client computer, it is downloaded from the application server. Then, the JVM takes control and runs the applet.

Both Java applications and applets access compiled Java files on the client and run them in a JVM on the client. The main difference between Java applications and applets is that an applet runs in a web browser session. If the web browser session is closed, the applet closes.

Applets run in the browser session, which normally cannot read and write to the client computer file system. Security signature files allow client file system access to occur, but this is viewed by some organizations as a potential security risk because a program distributed from the web can access the local, and perhaps the network, file systems. Applications that use applet technology are, therefore, prohibited in some locations.

NOTE
This book focuses on developing web applications, so methods for designing and developing Java applications and applets are not discussed further.

Web Client

A Java EE *web client* presents an interface on the Client Tier and runs application code in the Web Tier. For example, an application can execute Java code on an application server; this application code queries or otherwise interacts with the Business Tier for data needs; it then typically assembles an HTML page and returns it to a web browser. The user interacts with the page and sends data access and update requests to the application running on the application server. As another example of Java EE multi-tier server architecture (shown in Figure 4-3): the Client Tier runs a web browser on the client's desktop (or mobile) computer, the Web Tier runs the application (for example JSP) code, and EJBs in the Business Tier interface between the UI code and the database.

Running application code on a centralized server offers ease of maintenance because the application can be updated or patched in one location. Clients access a single installation; as mentioned before, applets also offer this advantage. In addition, you can deploy and maintain client installations of Java applications using a Sun Microsystems technology *Java Web Start,* which users access with a web browser.

The web client adds another strong benefit to the central server strategy—it requires no client-side installations other than the web browser. This benefit—that only a browser, not a special runtime, is needed to run a web application—was the main improvement on the

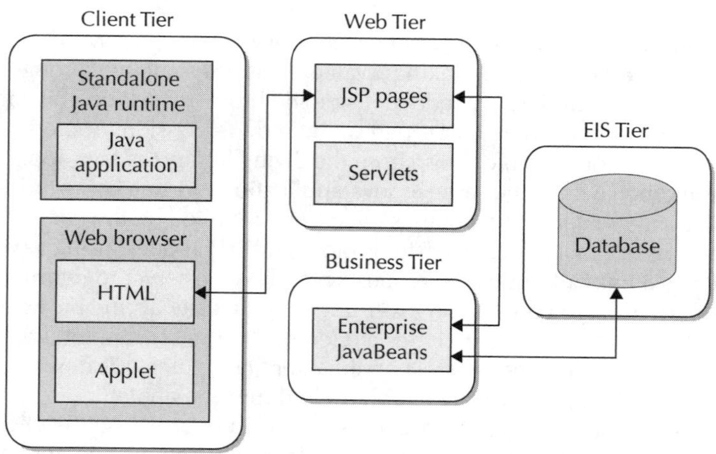

FIGURE 4-3. *Java EE web client architecture*

applet style of web application. This architectural style places the burden of processing on the application server, but as the number of application users grows, servers can be added or upgraded to handle the increased load.

One traditional limitation to web client architecture is that the controls offered by HTML are very basic. Although HTML offers user interface controls, such as text fields, buttons, checkboxes, pulldown lists, and radio button groups, the range of controls and their embedded functionality does not match those offered by the application client. With new web components such as those offered in the ADF Faces library, this limitation has been virtually eliminated. Using code written in JavaScript and CSS languages and techniques such as Asynchronous JavaScript and XML (AJAX)—all described further later in this chapter—web client interactivity (and the corresponding user productivity) can rival that of application client functionality.

As is true of the Java EE application client, a number of web client technologies offer alternatives for coding and functionality. The main Java EE web client alternatives are servlets, JavaServer Pages (JSP), and JavaServer Faces (JSF).

Servlet

Servlets were the first style of Java code used for the web client architecture. In general, a *servlet* is a program that extends the capabilities of a server. In the case of Java EE code, the term "servlet" usually refers to an *HTTP servlet* that extends the capabilities of an HTTP server. (HTTP is described in more detail in the section "How Do Web Communications Work?" later in this chapter.)

You can use *back-end servlets* to perform server-level operations that do not interact with or display to the user. However, the examples in this book are servlets used for user interfaces. Although writing user-interface servlet code is a rare occurrence these days, web client code written using JSPs and JSF runs in an environment based on servlets, so it is useful to understand a bit about servlets.

The following shows how the servlet process works:

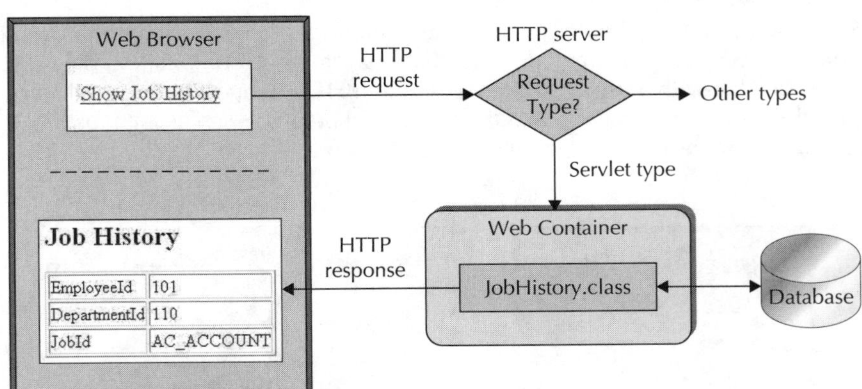

An HTTP server receives a request for content or processing, the *HTTP request,* from a client, such as a web browser. The request is transmitted from the client through the network using the HTTP protocol. A standard HTTP request causes the server to find a resource such as an HTML page in the file system and return it to the web browser (as an *HTTP response*). If the request is not for an HTML page or other standard resource, the server interprets the HTTP request and determines (by the directory or file name) what type of file it should process. If the request is for a servlet, the Web container on the server runs a Java program (the servlet, JobHistory.class in this example) that assembles the page dynamically based on parameters sent in the request.

The Java program can then query and send data to the database and format the resulting data or message into the HTTP response—in this case, an HTML page.

The servlet is coded in pure Java. That is, all code is contained in a Java class file that is compiled and available in the file system of the server. Java class files use a .java extension for the source code and a .class extension for the compiled, runtime code. The Java class file can contain database access code as well as print statements that will be output to the HTTP stream (and that eventually will be rendered in the web browser). For example, the following code snippet might appear in a servlet:

```
out.println("<html><body>");
out.println("  <h2>Job History</h2>");
out.println("  <table border='1'>");
out.println("    <tr><td>");
out.println("      EmployeeId");
out.println("    </td><td>");
out.println(getJobHistoryEmployeeId());
out.println("    </td></tr>");
```

This code would send each print statement to the HTTP response stream. Since Java is a full-featured programming language, the Java file can contain any kind of logic to manipulate the data and the page. This sample contains mostly HTML and display values, but it also contains a sample call to a Java method `getJobHistoryEmployeeId()`, which could retrieve data from the database. The print statements would construct an HTTP response containing HTML and values from the database. The response would be sent to the client's browser, and the browser would render the HTML.

In summary, UI servlets are written in Java, run in a container (JVM) on the server, and output HTML to the browser.

JavaServer Pages

JavaServer Pages (JSP) technology is a variation (and most consider it an improvement) on servlet technology. A *JSP page* is a web client file that is written in a combination of HTML and JSP tags. It is saved in a file with a .jsp or .jspx extension; an HTTP request to the application server that contains this extension indicates that the file should be processed as a JSP page. JSP page processing is demonstrated in the following illustration:

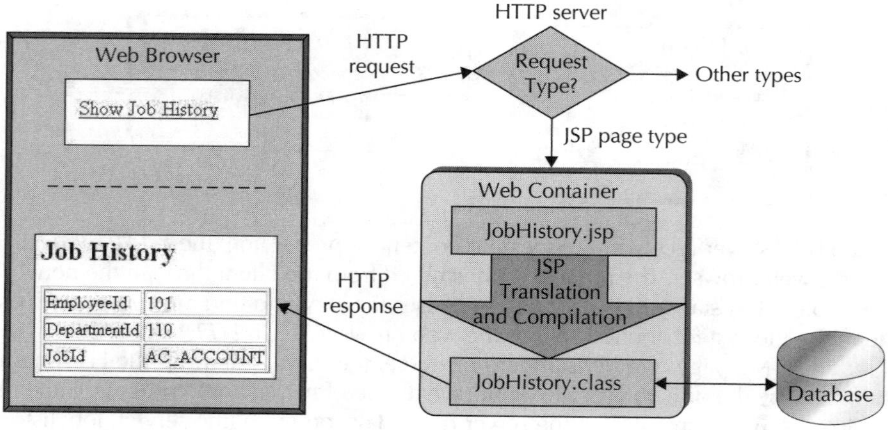

The communication flows are similar to those of a servlet. As with the servlet, the web server runs the JSP file in the Web container. The first time a JSP page is run on a server, the Web container converts it to a servlet file (.java) in a process called *JSP translation*. It then compiles the servlet file into a .class file. Once the .class file is available on the server, it can be run for future requests from any client without the translation and compilation processes. If the .jsp file is changed and copied to the server, the server will sense that the .jsp file is out of sync with the .class file and will translate and compile it into a new .class file.

Then, the .class file is run in the same way as a normal servlet, because it is a normal servlet at that point in the process. The only difference between servlets and JSP pages is the additional JSP translation process and the style of code. JSP source code contains a mixture of HTML tags and JSP tags. For example, you could create a JSP source file to create the same HTML code as the example servlet shown before by substituting standard HTML tags for the `println()` statements that contain HTML and by using the following instead of the method call in the servlet example:

```
<%= getJobHistoryEmployeeId() %>
```

HTML elements are coded directly in the JSP file without print statements. The JSP translator wraps the HTML tags in print statements when it creates the servlet file. JSP coding style is different from the servlet use of pure Java because of these raw HTML tags. It is also different from a static HTML page because it contains dynamic, Java-like elements, such as the example method call just shown.

You can also write Java class files to implement the custom functionality that you need to call from a JSP page. You then declare the files as a *tag library,* a set of files that is cataloged in an XML file called a *tag library descriptor* (.tld file). After including in the JSP code a reference to the tag library descriptor, you can then use these custom tags.

JSPs allow you to embed scripting elements (*scriptlets,* small pieces of Java code that run procedural logic to construct the page) as well as expressions as shown in the last code listing. Java EE experts agree that overuse of scripting elements in the JSP page can make the code less reusable and harder to maintain. Therefore, the preference is to use libraries or custom action tags when complex logic is required. In fact, this is one of the conditions that led the Java community to develop a follow-on technology called JavaServer Faces.

JavaServer Faces

JavaServer Faces (JSF) technology is another Java EE component that provides user interface and control functionality to Java EE applications. The JSF tag libraries offer user interface components (also just called "components") that contain a rich set of properties and events that manage user interactions and the state of the data inside the component. JSF components also include the capability to easily bind the data in the elements to database objects and other data sources.

Since JSF tags are often embedded inside a JSP page, the runtime architecture for JSF is the same as for JSP pages. The difference between JSP pages and JSP pages with JSF is the additional functionality and built-in UI components, events, and controller code that JSF provides.

NOTE
The JSF code demonstrated throughout this book is contained in JSP files, but few or no JSP or HTML tags appear in those file. Usually, JSF tags will suffice and are more flexible than JSP or HTML tags, so we recommend sticking with JSF tags as much as possible.

JSF evolved from the need to make JavaServer Pages development easier and more reusable. As mentioned, JSP code contains a mixture of standard HTML markup tags and JSP-specific tags that can include embedded scriptlets (Java snippets) for processing logic and *action tags* (references to Java class files) for performing operations such as database queries and for generating additional HTML tags. JSP developers found themselves creating reusable libraries to perform high-level operations such as displaying the results of a query in a multi-row, multi-column HTML table. This required the use of frameworks not included in the Java standards or customized libraries, which were even more nonstandard.

In addition, JSP technology is only a solution for the View layer. It requires a separate framework for Controller functions. A popular framework used as a JSP Controller layer is Apache Struts, but this framework is not supported by the Java EE standards, so seamless integration with JSP (which is a Java standard) is the responsibility of the developer.

JSF evolved from the need for a standard Controller framework as well as for high-level components (for example, the table for query results). Since JSF is an integral member of the Fusion technology stack, we need to describe it in much more detail than we have room for in this chapter. Therefore, we'll stop the JSF introduction at this point and pick it up again in Chapters 9 and 10.

How Do Web Communications Work?

This book focuses on Java EE development for web applications using JSF code inside JSP files. When you run application code on the Web, communication occurs between the web browser on the user's desktop and the web server. Most of the details of this communication are hidden from users. In most situations, these details are also hidden from developers. However, knowing the capabilities and mechanics of the communications to and from the browser will serve you well as you develop and debug web applications.

The most important *communications protocol* (message formatting guideline) for all web applications, including those built using Java EE architectures, is *Hypertext Transfer Protocol (HTTP)*. In fact, web servers are HTTP servers, so HTTP is at the heart of the World Wide Web.

HTTP Overview

Web applications use HTTP for communications between the client's web browser and the application code running on an application server. As with all communication protocols, a round-trip communication process consists of a request and a response. The *request* (also called an *"HTTP request"*) is a message asking for resources (such as an HTML page or image file) or an action from another computer. A *response* (also called an *"HTTP response"*) is a return message from the computer to which a request was sent. These messages often include browser content, such as HTML text or images. Figure 4-4 shows these two messages with some of their contents. Descriptions of the contents of the request and response messages follow.

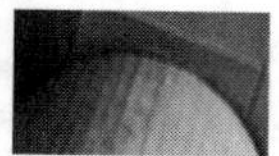

NOTE

HTTP uses TCP/IP (Transmission Control Protocol/Internet Protocol). TCP/IP is a lower-level protocol that defines how the hardware communicates. When you develop web applications, you interface with HTTP, not directly with TCP/IP.

HTTP Request

Request line

```
POST /jspapp/forum_query.jsp HTTP/1.1
```

Headers

```
User-Agent: Mozilla/4.0 (compatible; MSIE 6.0)
Host: www.oracle.com
Accept-Language: en-us
```

Message body

```
<!-- for POST: query parameter-value pairs -->
forumName=jdev
searchFor=11g new features
startDate=Jan-01-2009
```

Web Browser

Web Server

HTTP Response

Status line

```
HTTP/1.1 200 OK
```

Headers

```
User-Agent: Mozilla/4.0 (compatible; MSIE 6.0)
Server: www.oracle.com
Date: Sat, 23 May 2009 14:23:01 GMT
Content-Type: text/html; charset=utf-8
```

Message body

```
<html>
  <head><title>Forum Search Results</title>
  </head>
  <body>
  <!-- rest of page -->
```

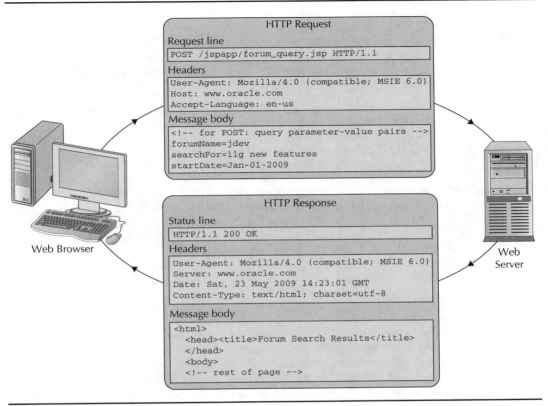

FIGURE 4-4. *An HTTP communication session*

HTTP Request

The browser sends an HTTP request message when the user clicks a link or button on the page or enters an address in the browser's address (location) field. As shown in Figure 4-4, the request consists of a request line, headers, and a message body.

NOTE
A detailed explanation of HTTP appears on the TCP/IP Guide website, www.tcpipguide.com.

Request Line

The request line contains the *method*—a command to the server (described in the section "Methods" later); *a Uniform Resource Identifier (URI)*—a unique identifier for a resource on the Web (see the sidebar "About URIs and URLs" for more information); and the HTTP version—1.1 is the most recent version of HTTP.

About URIs and URLs

As mentioned, URIs uniquely identify resources such as files. The Web uses the Uniform *Resource Locator (URL)* format, a subset of the URI standard, to uniquely locate a web resource (such as a file) in HTTP communications. Here is an example using the Oracle website's domain and some fictitious details:

```
http://www.oracle.com:8080/jspapp/forum_query.jsp?forum_name=jdev&
   searchFor=11g%20new%20features&startDate=Jan-01-2009
```

This URL identifies the *host* (www.oracle.com) using dot separators between hierarchical components; the *web server listener port* (8080), which is omitted if the default port assigned to the server, usually 80, will be used; the *context root* (/jspapp), also called the *application directory* (or *virtual directory*), which is the top-level directory for a web application and may be mapped to a physical directory on the application server; the *path* (in this case a file, forum_query.jsp); and *query parameters* consisting of name-value pairs: *forum_name* with a value of "jdev," *searchFor* with a value of "11g new features" ("%20" represents the space character), and *startDate* with a value of "Jan-01-2009."

Headers

Headers identify the requestor and indicate how the content will be obtained. Headers consist of a series of header fields. Each header field consists of the name of the header entry followed by either a value or a directive. For example, an "Accept" header indicates the media types that the client will receive; and a "Host" header defines the computer to which the request is sent—in this example, www.oracle.com. The Host header is the only required header field for a request.

NOTE

Standard headers are documented in the HTTP specifications on the World Wide Web Consortium (W3C) website: www.w3.org/Protocols/rfc2616/rfc2616.html. W3C is the owner and maintainer of standards for various web application languages such as HTML.

Message Body

The request can also send a message body to the server. The message body is typically used in a POST method request (described later) to supply parameter values to the server application. It is not usually used with a GET method request, because the information in the URL provides parameter values to the server application.

HTTP Response

When the web server receives the HTTP request, it gathers content and sends it back to the browser as an HTTP response. As shown in Figure 4-4, the response consists of the status line, headers, and message body.

Status Line

The status line contains values that indicate success or failure of the request: the HTTP version—such as HTTP/1.1; the status code—for example, 100s indicate that the server is still processing the request, and 400s indicate an error with the client request such as authorization failure; and the reason phrase—which repeats the information of the code in a friendlier format.

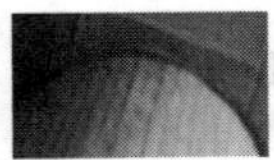

NOTE
You can find a listing of all status codes at www.w3.org/Protocols/rfc2616/rfc2616-sec10.html.

Headers

The response header fields are formatted in the same way as the request headers, although some different headers are used. For example, a "Content-Length" header designates the length in bytes of the message body sent after the headers; "Content-Type" defines the format of the content.

Message Body

After the headers, the HTTP response includes the actual content (message body) requested by the client. This is usually the file (also called an *entity*) requested by the client.

State Management and Cookies

HTTP defines a *stateless connection* consisting of a standalone request and a standalone response. A stateless connection is one where the server does not know that a particular request was issued by the client that issued a previous request. This interaction works for a situation that only requires requesting and returning a file, but it is unsuited for e-commerce and database transaction situations, where the server needs to tie a number of requests together.

HTTP was not originally designed to retain state information on the server to tie one request to another. However, a feature called *cookies* allows the server to store information about the client session in the browser session's memory; optionally, the response can specify a *persistent cookie,* which stores cookie information in a file on the client's computer (in a directory such as C:\Documents and Settings\<username>\Local Settings\Temporary Internet Files). Then, when another request is issued to the same server, this information will be sent in the request header. The cookie contains the host name and path, a cookie name, value, and expiration date, as shown here in the cookie information after a request from the Sun Microsystems' website.

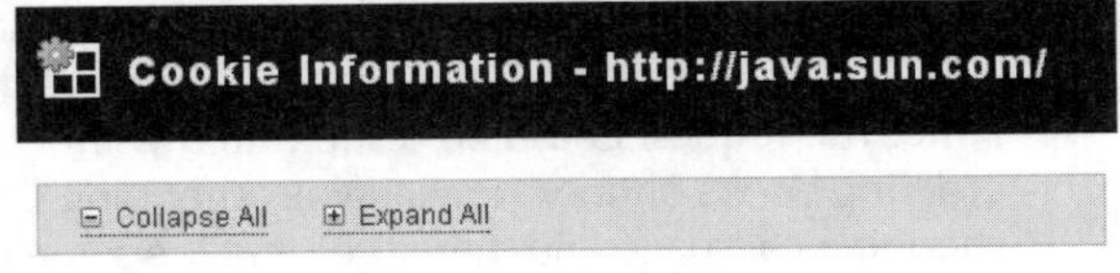

NAME	JSESSIONID
VALUE	2C05650DB667E2AF3DF981794831B127
HOST	java.sun.com
PATH	/
SECURE	No
EXPIRES	At End Of Session

NOTE
This illustration shows cookie information using the Firefox Web Developer toolbar available at addons.mozilla.org/firefox. This toolbar also allows you to view the response headers and other useful information about a browser session.

An example of cookie usage is the session ID. The session ID ties one request from a particular browser to a subsequent request. This is useful for many database transactions whose life cycle spans multiple HTTP requests, for example, if the user issued one request to update a record, another to insert a record, and yet another to commit the update and insert. The application can write a cookie (in a persistent file or in client memory) that stores the session ID retrieved from the application server, and this information can be sent with each request so that the application server can tie the requests to a particular database session.

However, users can disable cookies and break the mechanism that stores the session ID. If this could be a problem in an application, the application can use a technique called *URL rewriting* to circumvent this problem. URL rewriting consists of writing the session ID directly into the HTTP response message body. Then, the browser can send this session ID back to the application server in subsequent requests. URL rewriting is a service of most modern controller frameworks, such as the JSF controller.

The Java EE environment has added to HTTP communications an API called the *HTTP Session* that allows developers to maintain state. HTTP Session consists of a Java class containing methods that can be used to create and read information about the application user session.

Methods

An HTTP method specified in the HTTP request commands the server to perform a particular task. The most frequently used methods are GET and POST.

GET

The *GET method* retrieves content from the server based on the URL. It can only supply parameters coded into the URL (the query parameters mentioned before); the URL is usually specified using a link or entered using the URL field of the browser. Large amounts of data cannot be passed to the server this way because the *URL size limitation* is 2083 characters for most browsers.

Another limitation of the GET method is that the query parameters are easily visible to the user in the URL (address or location) field of the browser. Users could potentially figure out the calling syntax for a server action and make an unintended request by sending different parameter values.

GET is used for requests that can be repeated safely without side effects—usually, just retrieving a file. The request could be resubmitted without causing a change in data. For example, when ordering books online, viewing your shopping cart has no effect on your order. If you refresh the shopping cart page and therefore send the same request to the server to display the shopping cart, your order will not change.

POST

POST sends information to the server. The parameter values are coded into the request's message body, as depicted in Figure 4-4; this hides the calling mechanism from the casual user although savy users can still hack into parameters and values. A POST request is most often sent from a button or image click after filling out fields in a form.

POST is best for requests that cannot be repeated safely (such as submitting data input from a form). For example, in the book website example, you would navigate to the description page for a book, fill in the quantity of "1," and click the submit button. This adds one book to your order. If that page were to use a GET request and then that page were refreshed, the quantity of books would increase. This is an undesirable side effect.

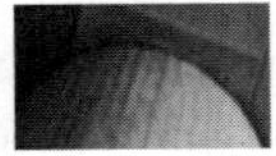

NOTE
"HTTP Secure (HTTPS)" is used in an encrypted Secure Sockets Layer (SSL) session. The request and response messages are encrypted and considered secure, because only a key shared between client and server will allow the messages to be read. Otherwise, it works the same way as HTTP.

The Steps in a Web Application Round-Trip

Using the concepts from the preceding overview of how HTTP works, we can now examine the steps an application goes through in a request-response communication round-trip, as in the example shown in Figure 4-5. This discussion assumes that the host computer domain has been assigned a domain name on the client computer or on a server, as described in the sidebar "About Domain Name System and Domains." It also assumes that the HTTP request is sent through the Internet instead of being handled by the client or a local network.

About Domain Name System and Domains

HTTP supports locating a web server by using an IP address such as 141.146.9.91 (currently assigned to www.oracle.com). Numbers, such as those that compose an IP address, are not very user-friendly. In addition, they are subject to change based on hardware and network architectures. Therefore, an important part of a typical round-trip is resolution of the domain name.

The client computer may contain a list of domains and IP addresses; on a computer running MS Windows, it is usually in the C:\Windows\drivers\system32\drivers\etc\hosts file. If this file does not contain the IP address, the address must be supplied by a *Domain Name System (DNS) server*—a network server that translates a domain name (such as www.oracle.com) to the Internet Protocol (IP) address that represents an actual host computer. This DNS (sometimes expanded to *Domain Name Service*) server could be located on the local network or on the Web. The name resolution process is not part of HTTP, although it plays an integral part in the HTTP round-trip. A domain name on the Web is assigned a unique IP address by a *domain registration service*, which has access to the means to copy a domain/IP pair to DNS servers on the Internet.

1. A process on the HTTP web server—called the *listener* or *HTTP daemon (HTTPD),* listens for a request from the network on a specific port (by default, port 80).
2. The user clicks a link on an HTML page that contains the following reference:

```
http://www.oracle.com/jspapp/jsp/forum_query.jsp?forum_name=jdev&
   searchFor=11g%20new%20features&startDate=Jan-01-2009
```

3. The browser assembles an HTTP request (specifying a GET method in this case) and sends it to the network (the Internet, in this example).
4. A DNS server on the network translates the domain name to an IP address and sends the message to the web server.

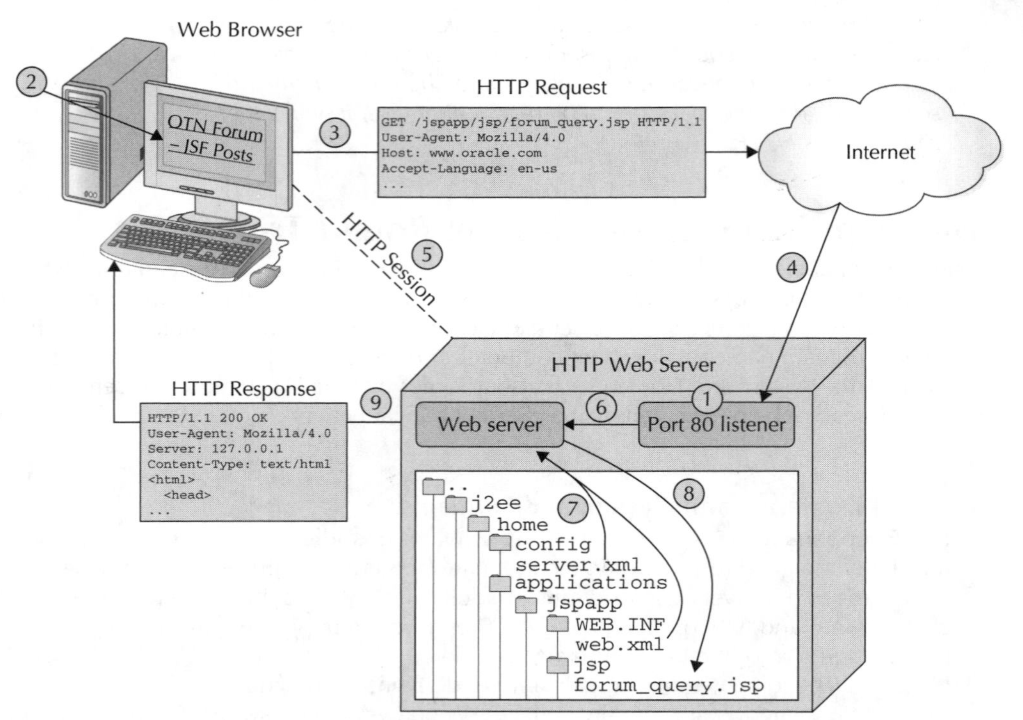

FIGURE 4-5. *HTTP request-response round-trip*

5. The port 80 listener accepts the request and allows the client to set up a connection session so that data communication can occur.
6. The listener passes control to the web server program.
7. The web server parses the request and determines if the request is for static content that can be retrieved from the file system or for dynamic content, which requires another process to build the content. If the request is for dynamic content, the web server uses values in the server.xml and web.xml files (described in the sidebar "About server.xml and web.xml") to determine the location of the application files. The context root (in this example, "jspapp") is associated either with the location of the static content or with the process that will supply the content.
8. The web server runs the code associated with the file (if it is a Java EE program, such as a servlet or the JSP page in this example) or opens the file (if it is an HTML or other type of nonprogram file).
9. The web server constructs a response containing the requested content and then sends that response to the browser. The browser then renders the content and closes the connection.

About server.xml and web.xml

Java EE specifies the standards for the descriptor files the web server uses for fulfilling requests. When the web server needs to find a Java EE web application file to satisfy an HTTP request, it parses the context root from the URL. It then looks for an entry such as the following in *server.xml* (a file containing configuration information, which, in the case of WebLogic Server is spread across config.xml, weblogic.xml, and application.xml files):

```
<application name="jspapp" path="../applications/jspapp" />
```

This entry identifies the application (the *name* attribute) and associates it with the physical directory (the *path* attribute). The file mentioned in the URL will be located in a subdirectory (for example, /jsp) of the context root directory. Therefore, the URL http://www.oracle.com/jspapp/jsp/forum_query.jsp may point to the forum_query.jsp file a specific Oracle Application Server 11*g* (web server) directory, for example C:\oracle\middleware\user_projects\applications\forum\jspapp\jsp (in an MS Windows operating system).

If the URL contains no file name, the application server determines which file to open based on an entry in *web.xml*—the *web module deployment descriptor.* web.xml is another XML file, which is located in the context root's WEB-INF directory. Web.xml contains information such as information about servlets that will be used to process files in the application (for example, the Faces Servlet used to process JSF JSPs).

NOTE

Tim Berners-Lee, the inventor of the World Wide Web, tells the story of how web communications work to "kids of various ages (6–96)" at his W3C website page, www.w3.org/People/Berners-Lee/Kids.html.

Asynchronous JavaScript and XML (AJAX)

The recent movement to make web applications more interactive has led to acceptance and wide use of *Asynchronous JavaScript and XML (AJAX)*. AJAX (sometimes spelled as "Ajax" as explained in the sidebar "'AJAX' or 'Ajax?'") consists of a number of technologies that have existed for some time (such as JavaScript and XML); it allows you to write code that refreshes only part of the page instead of the entire page. This enhances the user experience because the user does not need to wait for the entire page to redraw after clicking a button or link, changing a data value, or interacting with the page in some other way.

This high interactivity has been the domain of applications running on the desktop from the start. However, until AJAX, no generally accepted solution existed to provide high interactivity to web applications. In addition to the benefit of faster page interactions, AJAX saves bandwidth because the request and response messages described in the preceding section are smaller. However, AJAX usually increases the frequency of communications with the server.

"AJAX" or "Ajax?"

Jesse James Garner is credited with coining the term "AJAX" in a 2005 essay, "Ajax: A New Approach to Web Applications" (www.adaptivepath.com/ideas/essays/archives/000385.php). He states, "The name is shorthand for Asynchronous JavaScript + XML . . . ," indicating to us that "AJAX" is an acronym (although Garner spelled it as "Ajax"). Later discussions in the user community forwarded the idea that AJAX techniques could be implemented using other technologies, indicating to us that a new term ("Ajax") not an acronym ("AJAX") might be appropriate. We feel that this latter distinction is very subtle; moreover, ADF Faces uses JavaScript and XML to implement AJAX functionality (described in the section "How Does Partial Page Rendering Work?" of Chapter 12). Therefore, we standardize on the "AJAX" form of the term throughout the book.

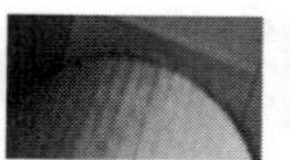

NOTE

The higher interactivity that the AJAX technique offers web user interfaces is part of a general concept—"Web 2.0"—that defines using the Web in a different, more productive way. Web 2.0 concepts include much more than web user interfaces, although web content interactivity is a key element.

ADF Faces components include native AJAX functionality, so you automatically include AJAX in your application when you use ADF Faces. ADF Faces also allows you to supplement this functionality of the ADF Faces components using declarative methods. Even though you will write little if any AJAX code, it is useful to have a general understanding of how AJAX works.

The Steps in an AJAX Process

AJAX adds these parts to the standard web communications:

- **A JavaScript function** to process a user event, send a request to the Web container, and set up a callback to wait for the server's return message. Another JavaScript (callback) function handles the server's return message.
- **An `XMLHttpRequest` object** created by the JavaScript function to send an XML message to the server. This object is supported by the JavaScript engine in the web browser.
- **A custom servlet** running in the Web container to processes data from the request from the JavaScript function on the page and to send a message back to the page.

For example, the user enters a value in a *Postal Code* field and you would like the page to look up the postal code in the database and fill in the *City* field automatically without requiring a page submit and refresh. The steps in this process are shown in Figure 4-6 and listed next:

1. The user enters the postal code and moves the cursor out of the field.
2. A JavaScript event (`onChange`) calls a `codeToCity()` function written in the HTML page.

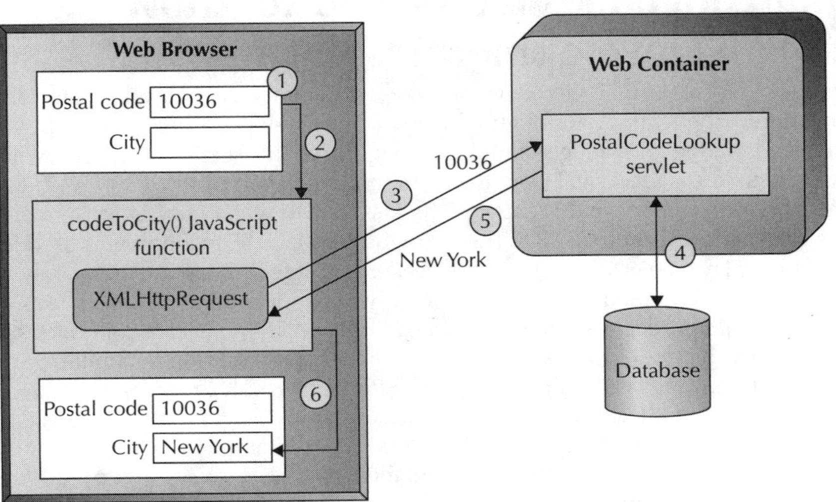

FIGURE 4-6. *Example AJAX process*

3. The function creates an XMLHttpRequest object and calls its `open()` method with arguments of the HTTP method, the URL of the server (including a virtual directory that points to the servlet), and an indicator to declare whether the request will be made asynchronously. Values (in this case, the postal code) appear as query parameters in the URL. The request is issued to the Web container. The JavaScript function sets up the callback function to wait for the server's response.
4. The container routes the information to the PostalCodeLookup custom servlet. The servlet processes the values passed to it—in this case, it queries the database with the postal code to look up the city.
5. The servlet sends an XML document containing the results to the web browser.
6. The callback JavaScript function receives this XML, determines whether the request was a success, and, if it was successful, updates only the City field.

Resources for AJAX

If you would like to learn more about AJAX, start by visiting these websites:

- **AJAX Tutorial** This website describes AJAX mechanisms and code (www.learn-ajax-tutorial.com).
- **Ajaxian** This website is a very active storehouse of all aspects of AJAX (ajaxian.com).
- **Asynchronous JavaScript Technology and XML (Ajax) With the Java Platform** This article by Greg Murray contains a more detailed version of the steps described in this section (java.sun.com/developer/technicalArticles/J2EE/AJAX).

What Languages Do I Need to Know for Web Development?

For better or worse, Java EE web development work these days relies on many languages to create a full-featured application. Although tools such as JDeveloper 11*g* help greatly, web developers still need a working knowledge of multiple languages. This section discusses which languages you really need to know for Java EE web development in JDeveloper.

As mentioned earlier in this chapter, the first style of web client code (servlets) required source code written purely in Java. The more modern Java EE technologies used for web client development, JavaServer Pages (JSP) and JavaServer Faces (JSF) applications, rely less on code written purely in Java than servlets do. Naturally, the more you know about Java, the better, but you can be quite productive with a knowledge of Java on the level required for *scripting* (code snippets rather than full systems of Java classes); at this level, you are familiar with the basic Java concepts and language constructs, and can write logic to solve problems. The reason that Java is used less in JSP and JSF applications is that you program using JSP and XML tags rather than Java. The tags point to a tag library that lists Java class files that implement the tag functionality, but you do not usually work directly with these class files.

In some cases, when creating a Java EE web user interface, you need to write Java code to implement custom business logic or page navigation. In this case, the IDEs, such as JDeveloper, handle much of the mechanics of creating and maintaining these files. In addition, frameworks such as ADF handle the *plumbing* (infrastructure that connects all parts of the application) for you; you do not need to write Java code specifically for that purpose. Your main time is spent in writing the business-specific application logic that defines data validation and transformation and user interaction (page flow and events).

CAUTION

Although it is possible to be productive developing a web application by using Java for scripting purposes, a web project cannot easily succeed using developers who only know this level of Java. An enterprise-class application will also require at least one expert-level Java EE architect who can set directions and standards, and who can either code or guide the coding of framework extensions.

The Web Development Experience

Modern IDEs and technologies such as JDeveloper 11*g* and ADF reduce the need to write as much code as with previous Java web technologies. Since HTML is used for displaying content in the browser, a working understanding of HTML is important, even though the tools generate most of the HTML that you will need. Dragging and dropping components into a visual editor creates JSP tags that you can view and modify in the source code editor. At runtime, the Web container assembles an HTML file with output from the tags and sends the file in an HTTP response message.

For example, you can use a single component from the ADF Faces library (`af:table`) and its child column component (`af:column`) to display an HTML table containing rows and columns of data (in addition to some user interface features, such as navigation buttons and sort buttons). You code this component by dropping it into the visual editor from the Data Controls panel (or Component Palette) and setting its properties using the Property Inspector. Setting properties, especially properties that bind the component to data sources, may require Expression Language (explained in the section "Expression Language" later in this chapter). The internal workings of the Java, JavaScript, and XML code (used for the look and feel) that make up the component are not usually important; you are just using prewritten library code when you include its tag. However, should you need to modify the component's behavior in a way that the property interface does not provide, you will need to write some Java code.

More details about ADF Faces and JDeveloper 11*g* appear throughout this book. The important point for this discussion of languages is that the style of coding using ADF Faces and JDeveloper 11*g* is different from the style of coding in earlier versions of JDeveloper. Development with ADF Faces and JDeveloper 11*g* consists more of declarative programming (dragging and dropping components and setting their properties) than it does of writing lines of code. This means that the burden of mastering the many languages used in a Java EE web application is lessened.

The Level of Knowledge Needed

This book concentrates on explaining how to develop JSF-based applications, since these applications are easiest for a non-Java programmer and they meet the needs of most modern applications. The language skills required for JSF development in JDeveloper 11*g* are listed, with corresponding levels and uses, in Table 4-1. In this table, the Level Needed column designates one of the following skill levels:

- **Basic** This level refers to an understanding of all language fundamentals, such as syntax, logic constructs, datatypes, code assembly, compilation, and library usage. A developer at a basic level will need to refer to code examples frequently but knows how to code the solution to a programming problem using the language. A developer will need to spend some time studying the language formally or informally to achieve this level. Novice developers without this level will not be as useful for project work.
- **Intermediate** This level includes all the basic skills plus the ability to quickly write basic code without having to refer to samples or reference material. Developers will quickly progress to this level from the Basic level during the first project in which they use the language.
- **Expert** This level includes all the intermediate skills plus a good understanding of how to modify framework functionality. This level requires a high level of experience and facility with the particular language. A developer will progress to this level after assisting another expert developer with this type of code or after spending time coding a framework extension.

A prerequisite with all skill levels is the ability to find examples of code usages for the particular level; these reference sources are usually available on the Web or in books. The following discussion about languages mentions websites available at the time of writing.

Although it is out of scope for this book to explain details of these languages, it can discuss some of their basics and advise you about where to look for further information.

Java

Java (the language) is defined by Java SE specifications and available as part of the *Java SE Development Kit (JDK),* previously called Software Development Kit (SDK). Java was released in May 1995 and is considered to be an evolution of C++. Compiled C++ code is specific to an

Language (Use)	Level Needed	Primary Use
Java (using frameworks such as ADF Faces)	Basic	Writing specific business components code for validation and special handling of model objects, as well as coding conditional page flow.
Java (extending and overriding framework features)	Expert	Supplementing or replacing functionality supplied by the framework. This requires research into the framework's capabilities and architecture, as well as writing framework-level code.
Hypertext Markup Language (HTML)	Basic/None	Modifying code generated with component drag-and-drop operations; infrequently constructing new pages from scratch with no IDE support. You can (and should) code JSF pages without any HTML. The JSF tags and the HTML renderer take care of the HTML for you, but knowledge of HTML helps you understand the HTML they generate.
Extensible Markup Language (XML)	Basic/ Intermediate	The property editors and visual editors in JDeveloper generate XML code for you, but it is helpful to know the structure of XML so that you can read (and modify) the generated code.
JavaScript	Basic/None	Providing customized user interaction functionality, for example, special handling of a checkbox selection. With ADF Faces, you can often define special functionality declaratively without writing JavaScript code.
Cascading Style Sheets (CSS)	Intermediate/ None	Defining, modifying, or using cascading style sheets for making the appearance of application pages consistent. If you use prebuilt look-and-feel templates, no CSS coding is needed. If you need to create an ADF Faces *skin* to change the application's look and feel, a good understanding of CSS.
Expression Language (EL)	Basic/None	Supplying data to components from properties or methods in the application. JDeveloper's Expression Builder dialog can help you create correct EL expressions for many binding needs.
Groovy	Basic	This language is used for scripting tasks such as validation, error messages, and bind variable values in ADF Business Components work.

TABLE 4-1. *Languages Needed for JSF Web Development in JDeveloper 11g*

operating system and requires the developer to manage the memory used by the program, for example, by allocating and de-allocating memory and by addressing data using memory locations. Compiled Java code is portable, which means that the same compiled code will work in any operating system that can run a Java interpreter. Also, Java handles memory management automatically, without pointers and addressing.

Code Organization

Java code is located in class files, which appear inside packages. The class path and import statements ensure that code is accessible. Libraries store collections of classes oriented toward a common function.

Java class files that have some functionality in common are assigned to a *package,* which usually represents a file system directory. Class files and their packages can be placed in *archive* files that use a .jar or .zip extension (also called *JAR files*). The Java runtime can find and run class files inside these archive files. Archive files facilitate the handling of the many files that make up an application.

The Java runtime looks for files by navigating the directory list stored in an operating system (environment or shell) variable, *CLASSPATH.* This variable holds the *class path,* a list of the JAR files used for an application. The class path can also include physical file system directories if the Java files are not archived, that is, if they are separate files in the file system. For example, the class path in a Windows environment could mix JAR file and directory names, as shown here:

```
CLASSPATH=C:\JDev\jdk\jre\lib\rt.jar;C:\app\project;C:\app\project\lib\app.zip
```

In this example, the Java interpreter will look for class files inside the JAR file, the C:\app\project directory, and the Zip file.

JAR files such as the ADF Business Components core classes can be collected into *libraries,* which usually provide a certain function such as database access. JDeveloper assigns libraries to projects automatically when you select an application workspace template to create an application workspace. At runtime, JDeveloper constructs a class path containing all the JAR files that make up the libraries assigned to the project.

Object Orientation

Java incorporates the three basic principles of *object orientation (OO)*: inheritance, encapsulation, and polymorphism. The most important of these to understand is, fortunately, the most familiar concept—inheritance.

Inheritance The inheritance principle means that a class can be designated as a child of another class using the keyword `extends`. A *subclass* (child class) is considered a *specialization* of the parent class (the *generalization*), because it refines or adds something to the parent.

You can only specify one parent for each Java class, but that parent can have a parent, and so on, up to an unlimited number of steps. Therefore, the functionality available to a particular class from its *class hierarchy* (the line of classes from the parent up to the `Object` class) can be substantial.

Inheritance is the most important of the three OO principles for Java work at the basic level, because you need to understand that a class file takes many of its characteristics from its parent.

Encapsulation The encapsulation principle means that the details of the program being called are hidden from the caller. A good example of encapsulation is a set of methods called *getters and setters* (or *accessors*) that you write to retrieve values from and write values to a variable that is private to the class. Callers may not access the variable directly; they must go through the approved interface—the getters and setters. Encapsulation is a frequently used design principle in Java work.

Polymorphism The polymorphism principle means that a class can modify or override aspects of any class from which it inherits. A program that calls a method may not know which class from the class hierarchy is servicing the call. This principle is applied most frequently at the advanced

Java level when subclassing framework classes for specialized requirements. It is also used when creating template classes that will serve as a basis for other classes.

Classes and Objects In object-orientated thinking, the *class* is a blueprint or pattern from which you will build something. The "something" you build from a class is an *object*. The preceding discussion has presented the Java class as the container for code units; the class also acts as the pattern on which code objects are built. In Java, an object looks much like a variable in other languages.

Resources for Java

When learning and using Java, you will need to rely on websites as well as books. The following list contains resources we have found useful:

- *Java Tutorial,* mentioned before, is available at java.sun.com (Sun Microsystems), which is the online source of all things Java. This online guide explains Java basics using many examples. You can also purchase a print version of this tutorial.
- *Thinking in Java,* by Bruce Eckel, is a well-established, popular, complete guide to Java that is available online at www.mindview.net/Books/TIJ (for the free third edition) or www.mindview.net/Books/TIJ4 (for the fourth edition). You can also purchase hard-copy versions of *Thinking in Java* from links on that website.
- *Java: The Complete Reference, Seventh Edition* by Herb Schildt (McGraw-Hill Professional, 2006)
- *Head First Java, 2nd Edition* by Kathy Sierra and Bert Bates (O'Reilly Media, Inc., 2005)

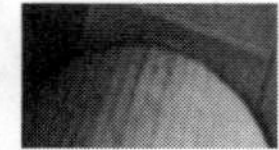

TIP
Chapter 5 from the Oracle JDeveloper 10g Handbook (by Roy-Faderman, Koletzke, and Dorsey, McGraw-Hill Professional 2004) contains more introductory information about Java, including longer code examples and hands-on practices; this chapter is available with the downloadable files for this book on the authors' websites mentioned in the section "Websites for Sample Files" in the Introduction to this book.

Hypertext Markup Language (HTML)

Using JSF and ADF Faces components requires virtually no Hypertext Markup Language (HTML). However, all JSF and ADF Faces code generates HTML code at runtime if the intended client is a web browser, because it passes through the HTML *render kit,* a layer that translates JSF components into HTML, before being sent to the web browser. Therefore, it is useful to have a grasp of basic HTML concepts.

HTML is a display language that does not support processing on the client side. All processing for values sent from an HTML form to the server must be performed on the server. However, a popular add-on to HTML—JavaScript—provides a programmatic way to handle user interactions without requiring server round-trips. (JavaScript is described further in the section "JavaScript.")

HTML was developed primarily to display formatted text and graphics inside a web browser and to allow navigation to other web pages using text, graphics links, or submit buttons. HTML has evolved, and its capabilities have been extended beyond the initial purposes, but it remains focused on displaying content sent from a web server.

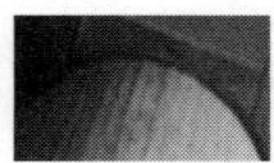

NOTE
Variations on HTML include DHTML (Dynamic HTML) that combines HTML with JavaScript and CSS for interactivity, and XHTML (Extensible HTML) that adds strict enforcement of tag matching and case sensitivity.

Tags, Attributes, and the Tag Hierarchy

HTML surrounds text to be formatted with *tags,* keywords inside less-than and greater-than symbols, for example, "`<html>`." The tag that ends a format or structure begins with a slash; for example, to boldface text, you can surround it with the "strong" tag: "`The next word is <strong>bold</strong>`." The browser will display the text with the word "bold" in boldface.

HTML tags offer *attributes,* which refine their actions. For example, the anchor tag "`a`" is used to link to another web resource using an attribute, `href`, that defines the linked page, for example, `<a href="http://www.oracle.com">Oracle Corporation</a>`. In this example, the words "Oracle Corporation" would appear specially formatted (underlined by default) in the browser. When the user clicked "Oracle Corporation," the browser would load the requested page, in this case, the Oracle home page defined by the `href` attribute.

NOTE
HTML code is not case sensitive. Also, the browser ignores multiple spaces and blank lines embedded in the body. If you want to add a blank line, use the "`<p>`" (paragraph) or "`<br>`" (line break) tags. If you want to add multiple spaces, add the entity *(code representation of a special character) for the non-breaking space, "` `" (without quotation marks but including the semicolon).*

HTML tags are arranged hierarchically on the page with the `html` tag appearing as the root tag that surrounds all other tags. The following HTML shows some of these principles and, through the code indentation, suggests how the HTML tags appear in a hierarchy.

```
<html>
  <head>
    <title>Sample HTML File</title>
  </head>
  <body>
    <h1>Sample Body Text</h1>
    The next word is <strong>bold</strong>.
    <p />
    <a href="http://www.oracle.com">Oracle Corporation</a>
  </body>
</html>
```

This file would display in the browser as follows:

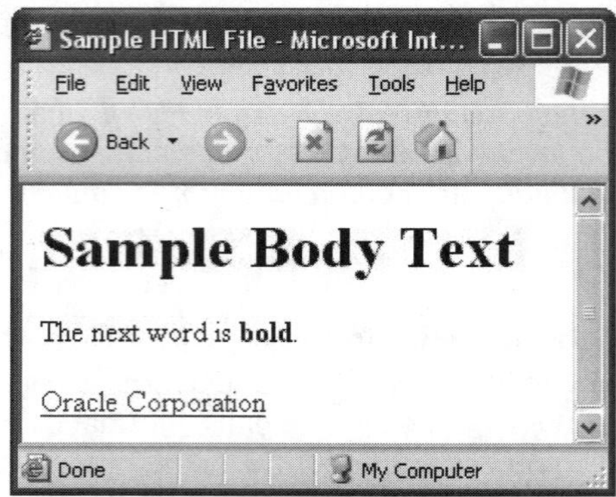

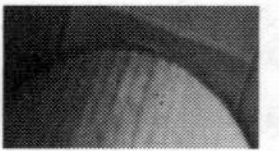

NOTE
Notice that the paragraph ("<p />") tag is formatted as a combination of a start tag and an end tag (including the slash). This is a shortcut for coding the start and end tags—"<p></p>." Browsers may interpret some tags, such as the paragraph tag, correctly even if the end tag is not present, but it is good practice to include both start and end tags (or the shortcut) for each tag.

The JDeveloper Structure window representation of this page is as follows:

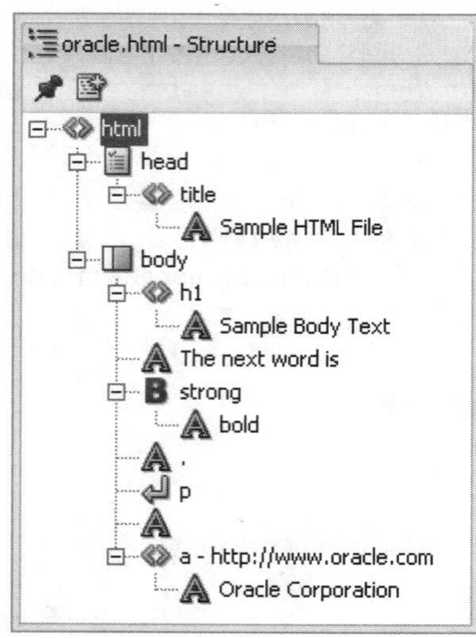

NOTE
Since browsers ignore blank spaces in HTML, as is true of most programming languages, indenting source code is useful only for those who need to read the source code. As with all programming languages, indenting code is considered a good practice because it makes the code easier to read.

The HTML Form

The HTML form, or `form` tag, is another child element of the `body` tag. It is the primary communication tool the browser offers for the user to communicate with the server.

The form holds all user interaction tags, such as input fields (`input type="text"`) and buttons (`input type="button"`). An HTML page may contain more than one form. Each form is named, for example:

```
<form name="deptdata">
```

The form is also associated with an *action,* such as a JSP file, that is run when the form is submitted to the server, as in this example:

```
<form name="deptdata" action="deptmodify.jsp">
```

The form tag can also specify which HTTP method will be used to send data to the server, for example, GET or POST, as shown here:

```
<form name="deptdata" action="deptmodify.jsp" method="get">
```

The processing for a form begins when the user fills in values for fields and clicks a submit button. The browser assembles the values and names of all fields inside the HTML form containing the submit button and forms an HTTP request containing the field name-value pairs in the URL (for a GET method) or in the message body (for the POST method). The browser adds to the end of the URL the name of the file referenced by the *action* attribute of the form tag. The browser sends the HTTP request; the server finds the target file referenced in the URL and passes the name-value pairs to it as parameters. The target file processes the parameters and sends an HTTP response message to the browser, which displays the response content.

Resources for HTML

The source for all HTML standards, and a good starting point for reference material and examples, is the custodian and owner of HTML standards—the World Wide Web Consortium (www.w3c.org). This website contains links to tutorials and specifications you can use for more information.

In addition, examining source code for any web page (in Internet Explorer, select **View | Source** from the menu or **View Source** from the right-click menu on the page) can give you ideas for your HTML code.

JavaScript

As mentioned, HTML is a text-and-graphics display language that has no capability for processing on the client side. Processing a request from an HTML page occurs on a server after the page is submitted. However, HTML supports embedding *JavaScript,* a scripting language (that has no relationship with Java) that provides procedural processing when the page is loaded or when the user interacts with elements on the page. JavaScript, developed by Netscape Communications

Corporation, is the most popular HTML embedded scripting language as well as a core language of AJAX, described earlier in this chapter.

CAUTION
JavaScript is interpreted by browsers in a relatively standard way, but it is a good idea to test the application with each browser you intend to support to be sure the JavaScript you use is supported by those browsers.

Events

JavaScript executes in response to user events, and you can write code in the HTML page (usually in the head section or in a separate file accessed from the head section) that is called from event attributes on form objects. For example, you can code *JavaScript functions* (the JavaScript code unit) and call this code from input fields using the attributes `onMouseOver` (when the mouse cursor hovers over an object), `onChange` (when the user selects a value from a pulldown), `onLoad` (when the page is first rendered), and `onClick` (when the user clicks an object). You have probably seen websites that display a pulldown menu as the mouse cursor hovers over an image or word. JavaScript can supply this kind of functionality.

The following shows a single-field HTML form (actionForm) with an embedded call to a JavaScript function in an `onChange` event attribute:

```
<form name="actionForm">
  Last Name: <input type="text" name="lastName"
    onChange="return validUpperAlpha('Last Name', this.value);" />
</form>
```

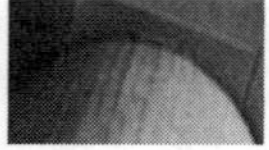

NOTE
The symbol "this.value" in the preceding code is a reference to the value of the lastName *field. If you needed to reference the* lastName *field from a script called from another field or button, you would use the fully qualified name of the field, including the document reference and form name, for example, "document.actionForm.lastName."*

This example calls a function, `validUpperAlpha()`, that is written in a file referenced in the HTML head section. This function runs when the `onChange` event fires (the user clicks TAB or clicks out of the input field). The function might be written as follows:

```
function validUpperAlpha(fieldLabel, fieldValue) {
  var validChars = "ABCDEFGHIJKLMNOPQRSTUVWXYZ";
  var isValid = true;
  var oneChar;
  for (i = 0; i < fieldValue.length && isValid == true; i++)  {
    oneChar = fieldValue.charAt(i);
    if (validChars.indexOf(oneChar) == -1)  {
      isValid = false;
      alert (fieldLabel + " may only contain uppercase letters.");
    }
  }
  return isValid;
}
```

The code checks if the text passed to it (represented by `this.value` in the input tag) contains only uppercase letters. If it contains something other than uppercase letters, the function displays an alert dialog containing the field label and returns "false" to the `onChange` event. The `onChange` event failure will cause the cursor to stay in the field. If the validation succeeds, the function returns "true" and the `onChange` event allows the cursor to leave the field.

Before coding a JavaScript validation such as this, check the built-in validators for the JSF or ADF Faces component you need to validate because they may provide the functionality you need. For example, JSF offers standard validation for a required value.

Page Objects and Attributes

JavaScript uses a *Document Object Model (DOM)* to address objects on the page. In the preceding HTML example, the symbol "this" referred to the object (the input field). The *value* attribute for that object represented the contents of the field. A fully qualified object name in JavaScript includes the name of the form (much like addressing an item in Oracle Forms using "block.item" syntax). For example, a field called "empName" in a form called "empForm" would be referenced as `document.empForm.empName` in JavaScript. Other object attributes, such as `style`, can supply other information—for example, whether the object is displayed. You can also set these attributes; the following JavaScript will hide the userName field in the actionForm form:

```
document.actionForm.userName.style.display = "none";
```

Although JavaScript shares main keywords with Java, JavaScript uses loosely defined datatypes and is not always arranged in classes, so even if you know Java, you will still need to understand JavaScript-specific coding rules.

Resources for JavaScript

Many examples of JavaScript are available from various websites. You can start your research about JavaScript at javascript.internet.com. As with most languages, the best way to learn this language is to find examples for a particular need using web searches. In addition, you may find a JavaScript reference book (such as *Head First JavaScript* by Michael Morrison) useful.

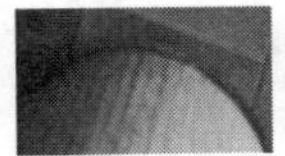

NOTE
As mentioned, ADF Faces requires little or no JavaScript coding so you will not use JavaScript frequently in ADF work.

Cascading Style Sheets (CSS)

HTML relies on the browser to specify the fonts, sizes, and colors used to display text. You can add a `font` tag and its attributes to specify a font, but this tag is *deprecated*—supported now but targeted to be removed from future releases of HTML. Cascading style sheets are preferred over the `font` tag for specifying fonts, sizes, and colors for text on an HTML page.

CSS Files

Cascading Style Sheets (CSS) is a language that specifies how an HTML component or area will be displayed. CSS definitions can be assigned directly to the *style* attribute of many HTML tags. CSS definitions also may be stored as named selectors in the head section of an HTML file, the same as with JavaScript. However, CSS selectors are more often stored in a file that is referenced in the HTML page head section so that the file can be accessed by many HTML pages.

Selectors (Styles)

The CSS file contains *selectors* (named definitions of style-oriented attributes, such as font, color, and size) that act much in the same way as a style in a word processing program like Microsoft Word. For example, you can apply a heading level 1 tag to a paragraph on your page and specify that this tag use a CSS selector that presents the text in red, Arial, 24 point. You can apply the same selector to many objects on your page, and those objects will all take the characteristics of the selector.

You can use CSS to achieve a common look and feel for your application's pages. Each page can refer to the same selectors in a common CSS file.

A selector definition contains a selector name followed by an attribute-value pair separated by a colon. Attributes are delimited by semicolons, and the list of attributes is surrounded with curly brackets.

CSS selectors are coded in a number of varieties, the most important of which are listed here:

- **Universal selector** This type of selector can be applied to any HTML tag using the `class` attribute of the HTML element. For example, a universal selector named BlueBold can be applied to any tag, such as `p`, using `<p class="BlueBold" />`.
- **Class selector** This variety of selector is written for a specific HTML tag, such as `td`. You name the selector with `<tag_name>.<selector_name>`. For example, a style called "td.highlight" can only be applied to `td` (table cell) tags using `<td class="highlight">`
- **Type selector** This variety of selector is written for a specific tag and redefines the default way in which the browser displays this tag throughout the document. For example, a selector called "p" will be applied to all `p` (paragraph) tags without the need for a class attribute on each tag. The `p` tag would appear as only "`<p>`" with no class attribute. The `p` type selector style will be applied automatically to any `p` tags.

The following example of a simple CSS demonstrates the syntax for the universal, class, and type specifiers in the `tinytext`, `p.warning`, and `H1` selectors, respectively:

```
*.tinytext {
      font-size:70%;
}
p.warning {
    display: block;
    font-family: Arial, Helvetica, Geneva, sans-serif;
    font-size: 95%;
H1 {
    font-family: Arial, Helvetica, sans-serif;
    font-size:170%;
    color:#336699;
}
```

Applying a Selector

HTML tags contain an attribute, `class`, that you use to specify a universal or class selector from a style sheet attached to the HTML file. For example, the following will specify that the `p` tag use the selector "warning":

```
<p class="warning">
```

If more than one warning selector is available to a page (for example, from multiple CSS files attached to the page and from selectors defined in the page head area), the styles will *cascade,* or add to each other. If the selectors conflict for any given attribute, a single value is selected using the *CSS precedence order* based on location (from low to high precedence: browser default, external style sheet, style inside the `head` tag, and style inside the element tag).

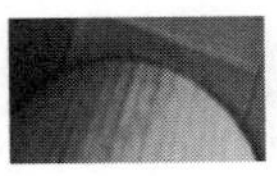

CAUTION
The type selector that replaces a tag style is not intended for use with the class attribute. The browser will ignore any type selector names coded as class attribute values (such as H2, P, or BODY).

Resources for CSS

As with HTML, the custodian of CSS specifications and the first stop to make when learning the language is the World Wide Web Consortium, www.w3c.org. You can open and edit CSS files in JDeveloper as described in the "Cascading Style Sheets Editing" section of Chapter 3. JDeveloper shows styles in the Structure window and Property Inspector.

NOTE
JSF and ADF Faces components have default style assignments but you can override them by assigning visual property-value pairs to the inlineStyle *property (like the HTML* style *attribute) or by assigning a CSS selector name to the* styleClass *property (like the HTML* class *attribute).*

Extensible Markup Language (XML)

Extensible Markup Language (XML) is an omnipresent language in Java EE web applications. It is used whenever a hierarchical description is needed, for example, to store property values or to define the structure of a web page. The main aspects of XML that you need to know when developing web applications follow.

XML Is a Tag Language XML uses the same syntax elements and structure as other tag languages, such as HTML. Like HTML, XML uses tag elements expressed with opening ("< tag >") and closing ("</tag>") tags; each tag element can have multiple properties (attributes) to make its behavior explicit and customized; some tag elements can be embedded within the opening and closing tags of other tag elements. Therefore, if you understand how to read and write HTML, you understand how to read and write XML.

NOTE
XML requires "well-formed code," whereas in some cases, HTML does not. Well-formed code means that each start tag has a corresponding end tag. In addition, XML, unlike HTML, is case sensitive.

XML Has No Standard Tags The primary purpose and characteristic of XML is extensibility—that is, anyone can define an *XML schema,* which defines the *elements* (tags) available for a particular use and the properties for those elements. The XML schema declares the name of the elements, the properties each element offers, and how the elements are nested hierarchically.

An XML schema is stored in an XML file; an older type of tag definition file, called *Document Type Definition (DTD),* used a different syntax to store the allowable tags and attributes, but its use is rare these days. To prevent conflicts between XML schemas that define the same tag names but use them for different purposes, an XML schema is assigned a *namespace,* a general name for XML schemas. An XML document can reference tags from more than one namespace. You often see XML tags prefixed with a letter or two, for example, "`af:column`"; these prefixes specify the XML namespace (abbreviated as "xmlns") to which they belong.

Since the schema designer defines tags for a specific purpose, unlike HTML, there is no single set of XML tags that you can learn. Each XML schema has its own set of tags and rules for using them. Once you understand the concepts of opening and closing a tag element, of tag elements having properties, and of the hierarchical arrangements of tag elements, you have enough background in XML for the purposes of XML development.

NOTE
An example of hierarchical tags in HTML is the "title" tag, which can only be used between the "head" beginning and end tags, which, in turn, can only be used inside the "html" start and end tags. The "html" tag is the top of the HTML tag hierarchy.

JDeveloper Wizards and Editors Write and Maintain the XML for You In JDeveloper, XML needed by some frameworks, such as ADF BC, is created and modified by interaction with property editors and wizards. All properties set in these declarative tools for ADF BC (and some other frameworks) are written into an XML file. Instead of editing the XML file using the Code Editor, you edit the XML file by reopening its property editor and interacting with the editor's pages.

JDeveloper offers property editors for some other XML files, such as the *faces-config.xml* file (which defines page flow and file locations for a JSF-based application), although you can also edit its source code in the Code Editor. Using the Code Editor to modify an XML file requires knowledge of the framework service the file defines. The Code Editor and Structure window in JDeveloper assist with syntax checking, but XML code is not compiled, so you need to be careful when using the Code Editor. Since XML files are used for core definitions in many frameworks, making an error when editing an XML file in the Code Editor could cause an entire system to fail.

NOTE
This book focuses on development of JSF files for the user interface layer. JSF is an XML-style tag language that, combined the HTML render kit, outputs HTML tags for a web application. To make JSF files most generic, you should not use HTML (or other markup language) tags in conjunction with JSF tags.

Resources for XML You can find more information about XML at the w3c.org website and also in tutorials at www.w3schools.com.

Expression Language

In an effort to reduce the amount of scriptlet and nontag Java language in JSP files, Sun Microsystems introduced *JavaServer Pages Standard Tag Language (JSTL)* with the JSP 1.2 specification. This language includes JSP tags for procedural processing operations, such as conditional statements and iterative structures. In addition, it contains *Expression Language (EL),* which defines syntax for accessing dynamic values.

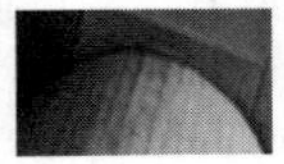

NOTE
EL is also known as "Variable Binding Language (VBL)" because EL allows you to bind component attributes to variable values. However, EL also allows you to bind to methods, so it is technically more inclusive than VBL.

JSF adopted and adapted EL. You use EL in JDeveloper to define data binding and other dynamic values for attributes of various JSF elements. The standard syntax for an EL expression is as follows:

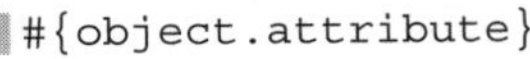

```
#{object.attribute}
```

JSF prefixes the expression with "#," whereas JSTL expressions use the "$" prefix. Unlike JSTL expressions, JSF expressions can define both bindings to method calls and read-write data.

For example, the expression "#{backing_login.usernameField}" represents an object instantiated from the backing bean for the login.jsp file ("backing_login" is defined as the name of the `Login` class file in the faces-config.xml file). The expression accesses the *usernameField* attribute of that object. You can build expressions most easily using the Expression Builder dialog, as described in the hands-on practices later in this book. In addition to attributes, you can express methods for the object. EL also allows you to build more complex expressions using mathematical and logical operators.

Resources for Expression Language

More information about EL used for JSF is available in *The Java EE 5 Tutorial* (Chapter 5) (currently at java.sun.com/javaee/5/docs/tutorial/doc/). Look for the topic "Unified Expression Language."

Groovy

Groovy was developed by the Java community (currently in the JCP as JSR 241) as a scripting language designed for situations where the full power of Java and associated overhead is unnecessary for the job at hand. Although the specification has not completed all steps in the JSR process, a fully functional version of the language is in broad use. Groovy is an object-oriented language that not surprisingly looks much like very basic Java. However, Groovy is compiled at runtime, so you can embed Groovy snippets in XML in the same way you can embed JavaScript inside HTML. When the Java runtime engine reaches a Groovy expression, it will compile and run it.

JDeveloper uses Groovy version 1.0 as a scripting language for ADF BC to accomplish several tasks such as validation, validation error messages, bind variables, attributes, and attribute default values. You will see examples of Groovy in action in later chapters. At this stage, it is useful to look at the basics.

Groovy Basics

Groovy code is contained in Java classes; therefore, you can call Groovy from Java. You run Groovy code in a Groovy runtime that parses and processes the source code (remember that there is no compilation needed). The Groovy toolkit also contains a shell in which you can test Groovy statements interactively. For work in JDeveloper, we are interested in the third way to run Groovy code: by embedding it in another language, which can execute Groovy statements through the Groovy runtime.

Groovy code is much simpler than Java due to differences like the following:

- **Dynamic typing** As with JavaScript, you do not declare datatypes for Groovy variables. This means that you do not need to match variable types or use casting or methods to convert one type to another.
- **No statement-end character** Groovy does not use the semicolon to end its statements.
- **Public everything** Groovy classes and methods are public (accessible from all locations) by default, although you can restrict access using access modifiers.
- **No return statements** This is a requirement in Java for methods that are declared with a return type.
- **No inheritance** You cannot subclass a Groovy class, but dynamic typing provides many of the same features as subclassing.
- **No primitive datatypes** Groovy only uses classes to declare objects. This means all Groovy objects can have data and can call the methods on the class from which they are declared.

An example of a Groovy class used to create an object that represents a database view follows:

```
class DatabaseView
{
  name
  columnList
  tableList
  // this method returns the Data Definition Language statement
  viewDDL {
    "CREATE VIEW " + name + " AS SELECT " + columnList + " FROM " + tableList
}
```

You can then issue the following Groovy statements to use the features of this class.

```
empView = new DatabaseView()
empView.name = "EMPLOYEE_VW"
empView.tableList = "EMPLOYEE"
empView.columnList = "EMPLOYEE_ID, FIRST_NAME, LAST_NAME, EMAIL"
println "The DDL for the " + empView.name + " is: " + empView.viewDDL
```

Other Groovy Features

Groovy allows you to create standalone functions (methods outside of a class) using the keyword `def`. You can also create methods called *closures* that can be called from outside objects or for variables from the class in which they are defined.

Groovy is a standard procedural language with conditional and iterative control statements—using the same keywords as in Java. It also offers collection datatypes to store more than one object in the same structure.

Resources for Groovy

You can start learning more about Groovy at the following websites:

- **Groovy home** The groovy.codehaus.org website is the main source for all things Groovy.
- **Sun developers' website** Search on java.sun.com for articles and introductions such as "Getting to Know Groovy" (currently at java.sun.com/developer/technicalArticles/JavaLP/groovy/index.html).
- **JSR website** You can track the scope and progress of JSR-241 here: jcp.org/en/jsr/detail?id=241.
- **Steve Muench's *Dive into Oracle ADF* blog** This website addresses Groovy's use for ADF BC in the article "Groovy Scripting Tips for ADF Business Components" located here: radio.weblogs.com/0118231/2007/05/22.html.
- **alt.lang.jre: Feeling Groovy** This article on the IBM website provides a good introduction to Groovy: www-128.ibm.com/developerworks/java/library/j-alj08034.html. Search google.com for the article name (in quotes) if that URL does not work.

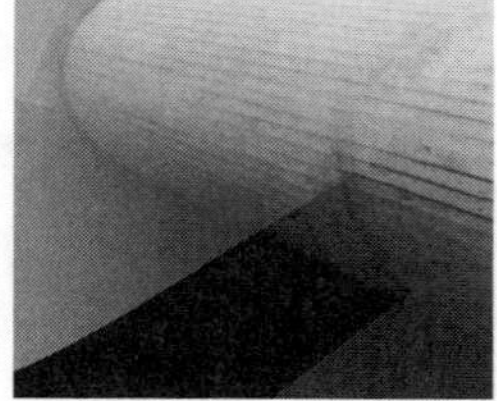

PART II

ADF Business Components

The real problem is not whether machines think but whether men do.

—Burrhus Frederic Skinner (1904–1990),
Contingencies of Reinforcement (1969)

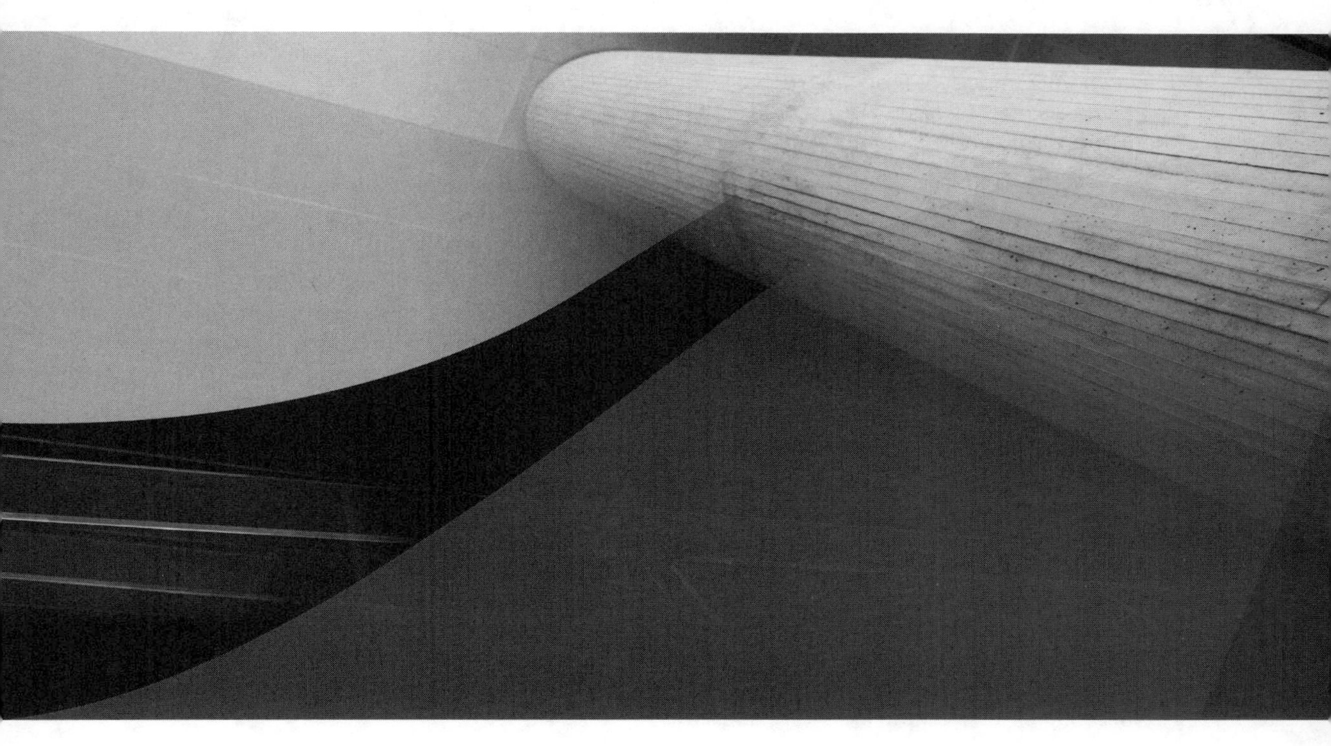

CHAPTER 5

Introducing ADF Business Components

"If everybody minded their own business,"
the Duchess said, in a hoarse growl,
"the world would go round a great deal faster than it does."

—Lewis Carroll [Charles Lutwidge Dodgson] (1832–1898),
Alice's Adventures in Wonderland

racle ADF Business Components (ADF BC) is the Oracle Fusion Java EE technology for creating business services. Business services provide object/relational (O/R) mappings, business logic, queries, transaction handling, and data access for an application. They do not provide a user interface or control flow. The view and controller layers of an ADF application communicate with business services through the model layer and provide the user interface and control flow.

Chapters 1, 2, and 3 provided an overview of the capabilities of JDeveloper, ADF, and Fusion, and Chapter 4 offers an overview of other technologies you will need to develop Fusion applications. Part II discusses ADF BC, a central part of ADF, in depth. This chapter builds on the description of ADF BC in Chapter 1. It provides an overview of ADF BC, describing its components and how it fits into the ADF framework. Chapter 6 explains how to create business components that provide O/R mappings and encapsulate business logic. Chapter 7 shows how to create components that query data from the database or provide static data, and how to assemble these components into a data model for your application. Chapter 8 demonstrates how to encapsulate complex data operations.

This chapter answers the following questions:

- **Why use ADF BC?**
- **How do business components use Java and XML?**
- **What are the major business components?**
- **Which components support the major business components?**
- **How can I visualize my business components?**

Why Use ADF BC?

In earlier releases of JDeveloper, ADF BC (then called "BC4J") provided two major benefits over the available alternative business service technologies (hand-coded JDBC and Enterprise JavaBeans–EJB). It provided declarative O/R mapping and query functionality, as well as easy hooks for binding user interface components. Now, these two advantages are mitigated somewhat. The Java Persistence Architecture (JPA), Oracle TopLink, and frameworks such as Hibernate offer powerful and simple O/R mapping and query functionality; also, the ADF Model provides declarative binding of user interface components to many business services out of the box, and to any business service with the development of a custom data control. However, there are still reasons why ADF BC is an ideal way to develop business services for applications, particularly for developers with more relational database background than object orientation background. If you are concerned about using a vendor-specific framework for business services, see the sidebar, "How Safe Is a Vendor-Specific Framework?"

Java Enterprise Design Patterns

The components that make up ADF BC already implement many of Sun's Java Enterprise design patterns (introduced in Chapter 4), which are part of the Java EE BluePrints documentation (java.sun.com/reference/blueprints). These patterns make Java EE applications much more efficient, by reducing round-trips and the amount of data that must be included in each round-trip and by utilizing the cache more efficiently. JPA and JavaBeans developers who want to create high-performance, scalable applications need to implement these design patterns—or something like them—themselves. If you use ADF BC, you do not need to worry about these design patterns; since ADF BC is architected using these design patterns, any system that uses ADF BC automatically is based on these design patterns.

Business Logic Framework

ADF BC, unlike most other available business service technologies, provides an extensive declarative framework for implementing business rules. As discussed in Chapter 1, you need to make a decision whether to implement business rules in the database or the application. Moreover, even if you do decide to place business rules in your application, you need to decide whether to place them in the application's business services layer, in the model layer, in the controller layer, or as JavaScript generated by the view layer and running on the client machine.

However, if you decide to place business rules in the business services layer, the declarative framework for business rules makes ADF BC an even stronger choice for your business services technology. The remainder of this section is devoted to considerations that may help you decide if the business services layer is the right choice for the location of your business rules, once you have decided to implement rules in the application rather than the database.

Rules in Business Services Business rules in the business services provide easy reuse between multiple Java EE applications and are enforced in all Java EE applications in which they are included. They require a round-trip from client to application server before they are enforced, but not a round-trip to the database. ADF BC has a very powerful and flexible declarative validation framework, meaning that you will only occasionally need to write procedural code for validation. Moreover, exceptions thrown by ADF BC components are automatically integrated into ADF Faces' message framework.

Rules in the ADF Model The ADF Model allows you to attach declarative validation to particular UI control bindings. This allows for declarative validation in applications that do not use ADF BC as their business services layer. Like validation in the business services, validation in the model applies whenever data is sent to the application server. However, the ADF Model validation framework is not as powerful as the ADF BC validation framework. Moreover, because control bindings are associated with particular pages or regions in an application, validation placed in the model has limited reusability. Data processing considerations are the same as those for the business services. The ADF Model layer is discussed in Part IV of this book.

Rules in the Controller JSF and ADF provide a few simple server-side validators that can be set to fire when a particular field's value is submitted. Moreover, you can create additional JSF validators that perform more complex operations. These validators are easy to reuse across Java EE applications, but except for the few pre-built validators, they must be developed in Java; while their use is declarative, their definition is not.

The ADF Controller also allows you to create actions that route based on conditions, and ADF Faces RC allows you to call server-side listener methods. These can all be used to enforce business rules, but with the exception of routing based on conditions (which is declarative but can be limited), all require Java coding to define. The ADF Controller layer is discussed in Chapter 11.

JavaScript You can enforce business rules in JavaScript code, which, while it is stored on the server, is downloaded to the client and interpreted and run directly in the user's browser. As such, this is the most interactive form of business logic—it can be fired immediately, with no network round-trip. However, data required in business rules implemented here must be downloaded to the client machine; for rules involving more than a few hundred kilobytes of data, this is rarely advisable (and the limit is far lower if you expect some users to connect over non-broadband connections). Still more importantly, rules that are more than a convenience to the user should never be enforced in JavaScript alone; since the code is downloaded onto the user's machine and interpreted there, it is quite easy for a user with malicious intent to circumvent such rules. When maximum interactivity is desired, it is advisable to redundantly implement business rules here and in another layer.

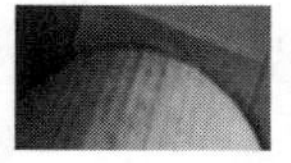

CAUTION

Users can disable JavaScript on the client, so you need to repeat rules enforced by JavaScript validation in other layers such as the application server or database.

Deployment Flexibility

ADF Business Components can be deployed in the following ways:

- **To a Java EE web container** as part of a web application
- **To a Java EE EJB container** as an EJB Session Bean available to other Java EE applications
- **As a web service,** for example, to an Enterprise Service Bus (ESB) or for use in a Business Process Execution Language (BPEL) system. This makes the ADF BC service available to applications using any technology, inside or (if you make it available) outside your organization
- **To a library** ready to be included, with design-time support for the model layer, in other applications developed in JDeveloper

Switching between these deployment modes is a purely declarative change, requiring no re-coding.

Database Orientation

Many, though not all, developers who use Oracle ADF have a background that is more oriented toward database technologies than it is toward object-oriented languages. For these developers, ADF BC has an additional advantage as mentioned in Chapter 1: its concepts are likely to be familiar. Tables, queries, database transactions, and object types all have close correlates in ADF BC. While these concepts appear in any business service technology that can access the database, other technologies are not fundamentally organized around such concepts but rather around concepts that are likely to be familiar to developers with a background in object-oriented design.

How Safe Is a Vendor-Specific Framework?

Some technical managers and developers are concerned about using a vendor-specific, rather than open-source, framework. While ADF BC is compatible with any Java EE-compliant application server and any SQL-92-compliant database, the source is not open, so users are reliant on Oracle for any support or bug fixes. A desire to use open-source technologies is very understandable, but there are factors that should ameliorate these worries about ADF BC.

NOTE
Chapter 1 contains additional discussion about the benefits of ADF.

Oracle Is Heavily Invested in ADF BC In addition to being a central piece of Fusion, ADF is used both internally in Oracle to develop the Oracle Fusion Applications suite and by customers who need to customize their applications.

ADF BC Is Highly Evolved As a result of Oracle's heavy investment in ADF BC, the framework is fully evolved and proven in many production application suite and custom applications. It has been used and has evolved since the early JDeveloper releases (JDeveloper 3.0, November 1999).

NOTE
You can find a list of JDeveloper releases and their release dates on Steve Muench's blog: radio.weblogs.com/0118231/stories/2005/02/25/historyOfJdeveloperReleases.html.

You Can Take Advantage of Oracle Support While using a vendor's technology requires that you rely on the vendor for support, it also allows you to rely on that vendor. Open-source technologies often have vibrant communities surrounding them, with many people happy to provide support, but it is nobody's job to support an open-source technology. Unless your organization is confident that it can internally fix bugs in your underlying technology, open source can actually be riskier than using a vendor's product such as ADF BC (as mentioned in Chapter 1).

How Do Business Components Use Java and XML?

As explained in Chapter 1, the technologies that constitute the Fusion technology stack are frameworks that manifest as a set of Java class libraries that use XML metadata to provide most customization but are also extensible in Java. Therefore, creating a Fusion application often does not require writing much procedural code; instead, you can use visual tools to declaratively develop XML files that represent your application components. The classes in the libraries contain code that handles the XML files to produce application behavior. However, if you want your XML files handled in a way other than the default, you can extend many of these classes to provide further customization. ADF BC technology follows this general model. Each ADF BC component definition is primarily implemented as an XML file, which you can edit using wizards and visual tools. Classes in the ADF BC library read the information stored in these files and use it to provide application behavior. However, many business component definitions can also have their own custom classes, which extend the classes in the ADF BC library to further customize application behavior. These custom classes are further described in Chapters 6 and 7.

What Are the Major Business Components?

This section will discuss the central business component definitions that you will define in almost any ADF BC project: entity object definitions, associations, view object definitions, view link definitions, and application module definitions. The relationships between these objects are depicted in Figure 5-1. We will explain more about the relationships and objects in this diagram throughout the rest of the chapter.

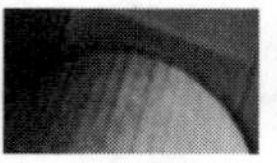

NOTE

The terminology we use in this book is somewhat different than what you may occasionally see in the IDE. For more information, see the sidebar, "Business Components, Definitions, and Instances."

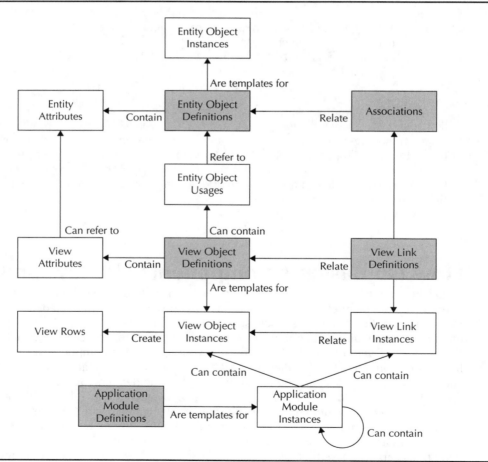

FIGURE 5-1. *ADF BC object relationships*

Business Components, Definitions, and Instances

The JDeveloper IDE often refers simply to components such as "entity objects," "view objects," "view links," and "application modules," but these terms are ambiguous. An important distinction exists between the *definitions* of these objects, which are analogous to Java classes, and specific *instances* of the objects, which are analogous to Java objects. Just as with the Java class/object distinction, you can think of this as a distinction between design time and runtime: you create definitions in the JDeveloper IDE; at runtime, these definitions are used as a template for instances.

Entity Object Definitions

An *entity object definition* generally corresponds to a single database table, view, or synonym (in rare cases, it can correspond to a database package API, or a table-like structure in a nonrelational data source). For simplicity, the remainder of this section will discuss database tables only; database views (with or without INSTEAD OF triggers) and synonyms are handled very similarly.

One of the primary functions of ADF BC (or any other business services technology) is to provide object/relational mappings between Java objects that an application can use and entities in the database. A relational database consists of, among other objects, a set of tables, each of which contains columns. For example, the table DEPARTMENTS contains the following columns and their corresponding datatypes:

Column Name	SQL Datatype
DEPARTMENT_ID	NUMBER
DEPARTMENT_NAME	VARCHAR2
MANAGER_ID	NUMBER
LOCATION_ID	NUMBER

ADF BC represents the database table as an entity object definition. An entity object definition contains *entity attributes,* which typically represent the table columns, although the mapping is not always exactly one-to-one. (For more information about the mapping between table columns and entity attributes, see Chapter 6.)

The types of the attributes are Java classes that correspond to the SQL types of the columns. Departments, the entity object definition for DEPARTMENTS, includes the following entity attributes:

Attribute Name	Java Type
DepartmentId	`oracle.jbo.domain.Number`
DepartmentName	`java.lang.String`
ManagerId	`oracle.jbo.domain.Number`
LocationId	`oracle.jbo.domain.Number`

Java does not directly support SQL datatypes. However, each SQL datatype can be mapped to a Java type. Some of these Java types are classes in `java.lang` (such as `java.lang.String`), and others are in the package `oracle.jbo.domain` (which is discussed later, in the section "Domains").

As shown in the illustration on the right, an extract from Figure 5-1, an entity object definition is the template for *entity object instances,* which are single Java objects representing individual rows in a database table.

For example, the entity object definition Departments provides a template for entity object instances that represent individual rows of the DEPARTMENTS table, such as the one with the following attribute values:

Attribute Name	**Attribute Value**
DepartmentId	A `Number` holding the value 10
DepartmentName	A `String` holding the value "Administration"
ManagerId	A `Number` holding the value 200
LocationId	A `Number` holding the value 1700

Each entity object instance is responsible for storing, validating, and performing INSERT, UPDATE, and DELETE operations for its corresponding database row. It is not responsible for querying the data from the database; this responsibility belongs to view object instances, as described in the later section "View Object Definitions."

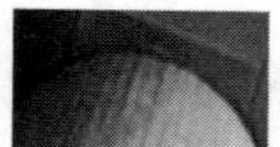

NOTE
In its traditional definition, the term "Data Manipulation Language" (DML) refers to the SQL statements INSERT, UPDATE, DELETE, and SELECT. Oracle and others shorten the meaning of DML to INSERT, UPDATE, and DELETE only and, therefore, separate those statements from SELECT, which technically does not modify data. We use Oracle's definition in this book but recognize the traditional definition as well.

An entity object definition consists of an XML file, which provides metadata, and between zero and three custom Java classes, which can extend classes in the ADF BC library to modify their behavior. For example, the entity object definition XML file Departments.xml would contain the following lines of code among others to describe the DEPARTMENTS table and a DEPARTMENT_ID column. You will notice the database object references and the corresponding names used in the ADF BC entity object.

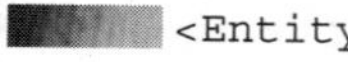

```
<Entity
  xmlns="http://xmlns.oracle.com/bc4j"
  Name="Departments"
```

```
Version="11.1.1.53.3"
DBObjectType="table"
DBObjectName="DEPARTMENTS"
AliasName="Departments"
BindingStyle="OracleName"
UseGlueCode="false">
<DesignTime>
  <AttrArray Name="_publishEvents"/>
</DesignTime>
<Attribute
  Name="DepartmentId"
  IsNotNull="true"
  Precision="4"
  Scale="0"
  ColumnName="DEPARTMENT_ID"
  SQLType="NUMERIC"
  Type="oracle.jbo.domain.Number"
  ColumnType="NUMBER"
  TableName="DEPARTMENTS"
  PrimaryKey="true">
  <DesignTime>
    <Attr Name="_DisplaySize" Value="22"/>
  </DesignTime>
</Attribute>
```

As mentioned, JDeveloper maintains ADF BC XML files for you based on properties you set in property editors and wizards such as the Create Entity Object Wizard, the first page of which is shown here:

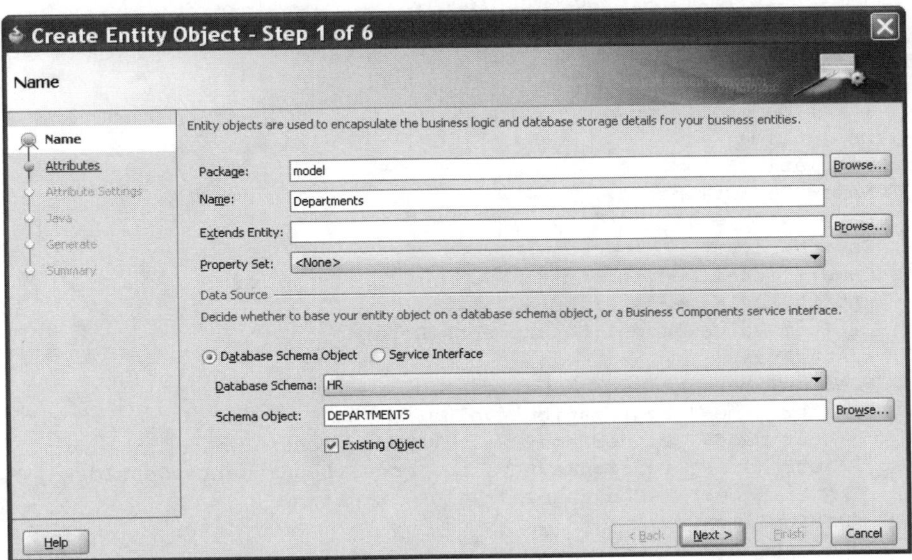

You can modify most of the values you enter in the create wizards, using editor windows. Chapter 6 explains how to create entity object definitions.

Associations

Just as tables are often related to one another, entity object definitions are often related to one another. Relationships between entity object definitions are represented by *associations,* as shown in the illustration on the right, an excerpt from Figure 5-1.

You can think of an association as the representation of a relationship such as a foreign key relationship. In the most common case, an association matches one or more attributes of a "source" (or master) entity object definition with one or more attributes of a "destination" (or detail) entity object definition, just as a foreign key constraint matches one or more columns of a parent table with one or more columns of a child table. If you are creating associations like this, you can (but do not need to) base them on foreign key constraints in the database.

Associations, however, can also represent more complex relationships, such as many-to-many relationships. For example, there is a many-to-many relationship between the tables EMPLOYEES and JOBS, relating a row of EMPLOYEES to a row of JOBS if, and only if, the employee has held the job in the past. Since one employee may have held many past jobs, and one job may have been held by many employees in the past, this is a relationship that cannot be represented as a single foreign key relationship. The analogous relationship between the entity object definitions Employees and Jobs, however, could be represented by an association.

An association is implemented as an XML file, which provides metadata about the specific table relationship. The following shows an example of the XML code, EmpDeptFkAssoc.xml, for an association that represents the relationship between the DEPARTMENTS (master) table and the EMPLOYEES (detail) table. Notice the definition of the association name, EmpDeptFKAssoc, and an attribute at one end of the association (Departments.DepartmentId).

```
<Association
  xmlns="http://xmlns.oracle.com/bc4j"
  Name="EmpDeptFkAssoc"
  Version="11.1.1.53.3">
  <DesignTime>
    <Attr Name="_isCodegen" Value="true"/>
  </DesignTime>
  <AssociationEnd
    Name="Departments1"
    Cardinality="1"
    Source="true"
    Owner="model.Departments">
    <AttrArray Name="Attributes">
      <Item Value="model.Departments.DepartmentId"/>
    </AttrArray>
    <DesignTime>
      <Attr Name="_aggregation" Value="0"/>
      <Attr Name="_finderName" Value="Departments1"/>
      <Attr Name="_foreignKey" Value="model.Departments.DeptIdPk"/>
      <Attr Name="_isUpdateable" Value="true"/>
    </DesignTime>
  </AssociationEnd>
```

Chapter 6 explains how to define associations.

View Object Definitions

An entity object definition usually represents a table, view, or synonym in the database. But you generally do not present all of the information stored in a database object in one application interface. Also, you may want data taken from more than one database object. SQL allows you to select exactly the data that you need from one or more tables, views, or synonyms. This is also the primary reason why ADF BC offers *view object definitions,* most (though not all) of which correspond to SQL queries. Most view object definitions actually store a SQL SELECT statement. In this respect, a view object definition is much like a database view, which is really only a stored query.

Just as an entity object definition contains entity attributes, a view object definition contains *view attributes,* which correspond to columns of the query result. For example, the view object definition AllEmployees stores the following query (some query columns have been removed for brevity):

```
SELECT Employee.EMPLOYEE_ID,
       Employee.FIRST_NAME,
       Employee.LAST_NAME,
       Employee.MANAGER_ID,
       Employee.DEPARTMENT_ID,
       EmployeeDepartment.DEPARTMENT_NAME,
       EmployeeDepartment.DEPARTMENT_ID AS DEPARTMENT_DEPARTMENT_ID,
       EmployeeManager.FIRST_NAME AS MANAGER_FIRST_NAME,
       EmployeeManager.LAST_NAME AS MANAGER_LAST_NAME,
       EmployeeManager.EMPLOYEE_ID AS MANAGER_EMPLOYEE_ID,
       EmployeeManager.FIRST_NAME || ' ' || EmployeeManager.LAST_NAME
                                   AS MANAGER_FULL_NAME
FROM   EMPLOYEES Employee,
       DEPARTMENTS EmployeeDepartment,
       EMPLOYEES EmployeeManager
WHERE  (Employee.DEPARTMENT_ID = EmployeeDepartment.DEPARTMENT_ID (+)) AND
       (Employee.MANAGER_ID = EmployeeManager.EMPLOYEE_ID (+))
```

This view object definition contains the following view attributes:

Attribute Name	Java Type
EmployeeId	oracle.jbo.domain.Number
FirstName	java.lang.String
LastName	java.lang.String
ManagerId	oracle.jbo.domain.Number
DepartmentId	oracle.jbo.domain.Number
DepartmentName	java.lang.String
DepartmentDepartmentId	oracle.jbo.domain.Number
ManagerFirstName	java.lang.String
ManagerLastName	java.lang.String
ManagerEmployeeId	oracle.jbo.domain.Number
ManagerFullName	java.lang.String

As shown in the following excerpt from Figure 5-1, view object definitions may (but need not) be based on one or more *entity object usages,* which are references to entity object definitions that correspond to single tables or aliases in the view object definition's FROM clause.

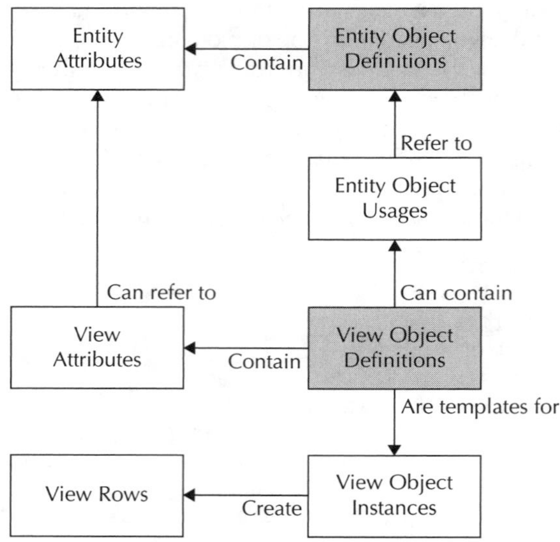

View attributes can then map to entity attributes within the entity usages. For example, AllEmployees contains two usages of the entity object definition Employees, corresponding to the two aliases in the query (Employee and EmployeeManager) and one usage of the entity object definition Departments (corresponding to the alias EmployeeDepartment). Most of AllEmployee's view attributes are mapped to entity attributes within these three entity object usages. The exception is the attribute ManagerFullName, which is not mapped to any underlying entity attribute.

As shown in the preceding illustration, a view object definition is the template for *view object instances,* which are particular caches of retrieved data. A view object instance is responsible for executing the query specified in its definition (possibly modified in some way) and creating *view rows,* which represent individual rows of the query's result set, much as entity object instances represent individual table rows. View rows can store the column values directly, or, for view attributes mapped to entity attributes, can request that the entity object definition store the values in an entity object instance corresponding to the correct table row. Chapter 7 explains view rows in much greater detail.

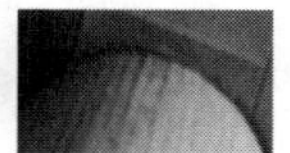

TIP
One helpful way to remember the roles of view object instances and entity object instances is to remember that a view object instance is responsible for being a data source (executing a query), and each entity object instance is responsible for being a data target (performing DML operations for one row of a table).

Though most view object definitions contain SQL queries, other types of view object definitions are possible, such as the following:

- View object definitions based on static lists of data defined within JDeveloper
- View object definitions based on PL/SQL functions
- View object definitions based on requests to nonrelational data sources

A view object definition consists of an XML file, which provides metadata, between zero and seven custom Java classes, which can extend classes in the ADF BC library to modify their behavior, and between zero and two Java interfaces, which can specify functionality accessible through the ADF Model layer. The following code listing shows part of a view object definition XML file, AllDepartments.xml, representing an unfiltered list of departments and based on the Departments entity object. Notice the reference to the Departments entity object and the SelectList attribute containing the SELECT portion of the query. You will also see the definition for a view attribute, DepartmentId, based on the Departments entity attribute DepartmentId.

```
<ViewObject
  xmlns="http://xmlns.oracle.com/bc4j"
  Name="AllDepartments"
  Version="11.1.1.53.3"
  SelectList="Departments.DEPARTMENT_ID,
       Departments.DEPARTMENT_NAME,
       Departments.MANAGER_ID,
       Departments.LOCATION_ID"
  FromList="DEPARTMENTS Departments"
  BindingStyle="OracleName"
  CustomQuery="false"
  PageIterMode="Full"
  UseGlueCode="false">
  <DesignTime>
    <Attr Name="_codeGenFlag2" Value="VarAccess"/>
  </DesignTime>
  <EntityUsage
    Name="Departments"
    Entity="model.Departments"/>
  <ViewAttribute
    Name="DepartmentId"
    IsNotNull="true"
    PrecisionRule="true"
    EntityAttrName="DepartmentId"
    EntityUsage="Departments"
    AliasName="DEPARTMENT_ID"/>
```

Chapter 7 explains how to create view object definitions.

View Link Definitions

As shown in the following excerpt from Figure 5-1, a *view link definition* represents a relationship, such as a master-detail relationship, between the query result sets of two view object definitions.

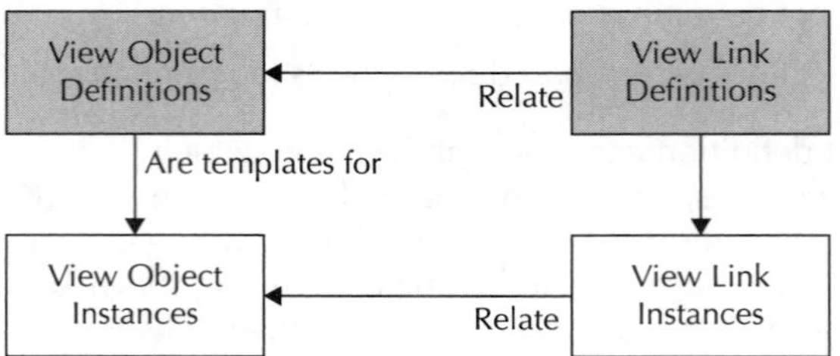

A view link definition consists of two parts:

- A list of attributes from one view object definition (the *source* of the view link definition)
- A parameterized fragment of a WHERE clause that can be appended to the query contained by the other view object definition (the *destination* of the view link definition)

A view link definition is a template for *view link instances,* which relate two view object instances. By plugging attributes from a particular view row of the instance of the source into the parameters of the WHERE clause fragment, the rows of the instance of the destination can be limited so that the two instances stand in a master-detail relationship.

For example, the view object definition AllEmployees contains the following SQL query:

```
SELECT Employees.EMPLOYEE_ID,
       Employees.FIRST_NAME,
       Employees.LAST_NAME,
       Employees.EMAIL,
       Employees.DEPARTMENT_ID,
       Employees.HIRE_DATE,
       Employees.JOB_ID,
       Employees.MANAGER_ID,
       Employees.SALARY
FROM EMPLOYEES Employees
```

The view object definition AllJobHistory contains the following SQL query:

```
SELECT JobHistory.EMPLOYEE_ID,
       JobHistory.START_DATE,
       JobHistory.END_DATE,
       JobHistory.JOB_ID,
       JobHistory.DEPARTMENT_ID
FROM JOB_HISTORY JobHistory
```

These view object definitions are related by the view link definition EmployeeJobHistoryVL. This view link definition identifies a single view attribute, EmployeeId, from AllEmployees, and a parameterized fragment of a WHERE clause to append to the query contained in AllJobHistory:

```
:Bind_EmployeeId = JobHistory.EMPLOYEE_ID
```

If EditEmployee is an instance of AllEmployees, and EmployeeJobHistory is an instance of AllJobHistory, an instance of EmployeeJobHistoryVL, EmployeeJobHistoryVL1, can relate these view object instances. EmployeeJobHistoryVL1 will change the query for EmployeeJobHistory (and only that one instance) so that it reads as follows:

```
SELECT JobHistory.EMPLOYEE_ID,
       JobHistory.START_DATE,
       JobHistory.END_DATE,
       JobHistory.JOB_ID,
       JobHistory.DEPARTMENT_ID
FROM JOB_HISTORY JobHistory
WHERE :Bind_EmployeeId = JobHistory.EMPLOYEE_ID
```

When a particular view row from EditEmployee (for example, one where the EmployeeId attribute is "101") is selected, the EmployeeId attribute from that row is plugged in to the parameter Bind_EmployeeId in the query just listed, causing EmployeeJobHistory to return only rows where JobHistory.EMPLOYEE_ID matches that value (for example, only rows where EmployeeId is "101").

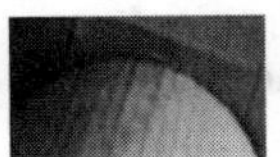

NOTE
For convenience in defining the ends of a view link definition, you can base a view link definition on an association. The attributes at each end of the association become the attributes at each end of the view link definition.

A view link definition is implemented as an XML file, which provides metadata, primarily the source and destination view object definitions, the source attributes, and the WHERE clause fragment. The following code listing shows part of the XML file for a view link definition showing the view link name and a definition of the attribute at one end.

```
<ViewLink
  xmlns="http://xmlns.oracle.com/bc4j"
  Name="EmployeeJobHistoryVL"
  Version="11.1.1.53.3">
  <DesignTime>
    <Attr Name="_isCodegen" Value="true"/>
  </DesignTime>
  <ViewLinkDefEnd
    Name="AllEmployees"
    Cardinality="1"
    Owner="tuhra.model.queries.main.AllEmployees"
    Source="true">
    <DesignTime>
      <Attr Name="_finderName" Value="Employee"/>
      <Attr Name="_isUpdateable" Value="true"/>
    </DesignTime>
    <AttrArray Name="Attributes">
      <Item Value="tuhra.model.queries.main.AllEmployees.EmployeeId"/>
    </AttrArray>
  </ViewLinkDefEnd>
```

Chapter 7 explains how to create view link definitions.

Application Module Definitions

An *application module definition* is an encapsulation of a single business task. It defines which data will be required for the task, is responsible for ensuring that that data is queried and updated when needed, and provides other data services that might be required during the performance of that task. A task can be defined broadly or narrowly—a single application module definition might correspond to a task as broad as "allow customers to browse, search, and buy items" or as narrow as "handle customer checkout."

An application module definition provides a template for *application module instances,* which perform the relevant task for, in general, a single user (although it is possible for users to share application module instances in certain cases; for more information, see the sidebar "Sharing and Reusing Application Module Instances").

NOTE
The application module instance provides database transaction processing. In other words, COMMIT and ROLLBACK statements are issued at the level of the application module instance.

As shown in the following excerpt from Figure 5-1, application module instances can contain view object instances, view link instances that relate the view object instances, and other application module instances (which perform subtasks of the primary task).

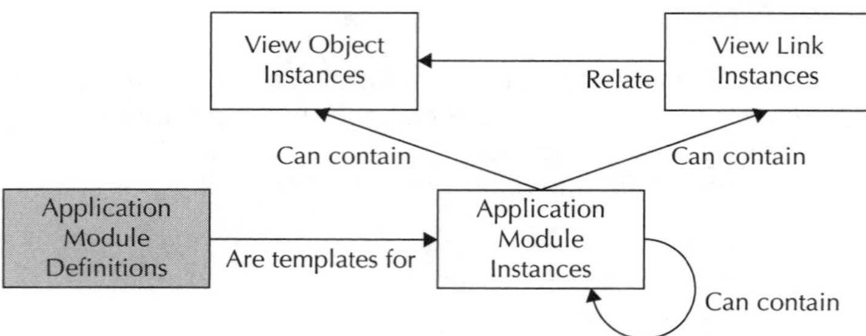

The application module definition contains a tree, called the *data model,* which specifies which of these instances the application module instance must contain.

For example, the data model for the application module definition TuhraService specifies that its instances will require a number of view object instances, including an instance of AllEmployees named EditEmployee, and an instance of AllJobHistory named EmployeeJobHistory. These instances will need to be joined by an instance of EmployeeJobHistoryVL named EmployeeJobHistoryVL1. This data model is shown here:

Each instance of TuhraService will contain view object and view link instances as specified by the data model (and would contain other application module instances as well, if the data model specified any).

Sharing and Reusing Application Module Instances

There are two ways in which application module instances can be used by more than one user: through sharing and through reuse. A *shared application module instance* contains data that is identical at all times for all application users, such as static lists and data from lookup tables. Using a shared application module instance can save considerable memory—only one copy of the data is needed for all users—but it can only be used for data that all users have access to, and for which no transactional distinctions between users are required.

Application module instances can be reused as well. The ADF BC framework maintains a pool of application module instances for each application module definition. These can be used, at different times, by different users. The pool is responsible for ensuring data consistency, so that each user sees the appropriate data for him or her, even if another user previously used the application module instance.

Chapter 7 contains more information about shared application module instances and application module pools.

An application module instance that is not contained by any other application module instance is called a *top-level* application module instance. At any particular time, a top-level application module instance corresponds to a single database transaction. Its view object instances query data from within that transaction, creating view rows (and entity object instances, if the view attributes are mapped to entity attributes) that are stored in caches maintained by the application module instance. When entity object instances from within an application module instance's cache perform DML, the DML takes place within the transaction. Lower-level application module instances share the top-level instance's transaction. Application module instances survive past transaction boundaries, maintaining their caches if the transaction is committed and rolling back their caches if the transaction is rolled back.

CAUTION
Embedding application modules too deeply can cause performance issues. Oracle Fusion Applications are developed with the guideline of a single non-nested application module to represent a unit of work.

An application module definition consists of an XML file, which provides metadata, between zero and three custom Java classes, which can extend classes in the ADF BC library to modify their behavior, and optionally one Java interface, which can specify operations available through the ADF Model layer. The following shows part of the XML code definition for the TuhraService application module. You will notice the application module name and a definition of two view object instances (the `ViewUsage` element), EditEmployee and EmployeeJobHistory, as well as the view link instance (the `ViewLinkUsage` element) EmployeeJobHistoryVL1.

```
<AppModule
  xmlns="http://xmlns.oracle.com/bc4j"
  Name="TuhraService"
  Version="11.1.1.52.34"
  ComponentClass="tuhra.model.framework.TuhraApplicationModuleImpl"
  ClearCacheOnRollback="true">
```

```
<DesignTime>
  <Attr Name="_deployType" Value="0"/>
</DesignTime>
<ViewUsage
  Name="EditEmployee"
  ViewObjectName="tuhra.model.queries.main.AllEmployees"/>
<ViewUsage
  Name="EmployeeJobHistory"
  ViewObjectName="tuhra.model.queries.main.AllJobHistory"/>
<ViewLinkUsage
  Name="EmployeeJobHistoryVL1"
  Version="11.1.1.52.34"
  ViewLinkObjectName="tuhra.model.queries.main.EmployeeJobHistoryVL"
  SrcViewUsageName="tuhra.model.services.TuhraService.EditEmployee"
  DstViewUsageName="tuhra.model.services.TuhraService.EmployeeJobHistory"
  Reversed="false"/>
```

Chapter 7 explains how to create application module definitions.

Which Components Support the Major Business Components?

Some business components have a smaller but definite part to play in ADF BC technology: domains, validation rules, business logic units, and property sets. You do not need to create these components in every application, either because you can use pre-built components or because you do not need them at all. However, an understanding of these supporting components will help you create better applications.

Domains

As discussed in the sections "Entity Object Definitions" and "View Object Definitions," the types of entity attributes and view attributes are classes, instances of which hold attribute values. Some of these classes are standard Java classes from the package `java.lang`, such as `java.lang.String` and `java.lang.Boolean`, but many are specialized classes called *domains*.

Domains hold both a value (for example, the domain `oracle.jbo.domain.Number` can hold an integer, long, double, float, or even an object of type `java.math.BigInteger` or `java.math.BigDecimal`) and some database mapping information (for example, `oracle.jbo.domain.Number` contains information about precision and scale).

However, it is also possible to create customized domains. For example, if you create an entity object definition containing an attribute based on a column with an Oracle object type, JDeveloper will automatically generate a custom domain. This domain represents the Oracle object type, containing Java wrappers for the object type's fields and methods. You can also create domains for your own complex types.

Finally, you can create domains that encapsulate business logic. Suppose you have many database columns, possibly in different tables that are all very similar. Not only are they of the same SQL type (for instance, VARCHAR2), but they all contain information in exactly the same form, such as a URL. You may need business logic that is simultaneously associated with multiple columns; for example, any and all URLs must begin with a protocol type, a colon, and two slashes. Rather than putting this logic in every entity object definition that contains one of these columns, you can create a URL domain that contains the validation code. Then you just need to ensure that the appropriate entity attributes are all instances of that domain rather than of type `java.lang.String`.

Most domains are implemented as Java classes, but domains that represent complex types use an XML file to store metadata information about the underlying type. Chapter 6 discusses domains further.

Validation Rules

As stated in the section "Why Use ADF BC?," ADF BC provides an extensive validation framework. At the heart of this framework are *validation rules,* Java classes that can be declaratively configured to provide validation for individual entity attributes or cross-attribute validation for entity object instances.

ADF BC provides a large number of powerful validation rules for you to use, from simple rules that ensure a value is within a static range to rules that allow you to write very complex requirements in the expression language Groovy (introduced in Chapter 4).

If these validation rules are not sufficient for your needs, you can write Java code to perform your validation. There are a number of ways to do this, including using custom domains as described in the preceding section, but one option is to create your own custom validation rules. Creating a custom validation rule requires creating a Java class that implements the `oracle.jbo.rules.JboValidatorInterface` interface, but once you have created the rule, you can apply it declaratively anywhere you could apply a built-in validation rule.

A validation rule is a Java class, although for built-in validation rules, you will never need to understand the details of the class. Chapter 6 explains how to use and create validation rules.

Business Logic Units

Sometimes different business logic applies to different entity object instances from the same definition.

For example, instances of the Employees entity object definition might have different business logic, depending on the job title of the employee. *Business logic units* allow you to provide multiple combinations of business rules for the same entity object definition. Each business logic unit you create for an entity object definition provides one possible set of business rules. You can add validation rules to business logic units just as you would add them to entity object definitions.

Business logic units related to one entity object definition are members of a *business logic group,* which is part of the entity object definition. The business logic group specifies a particular entity attribute to act as a discriminator. The correct business logic unit will be determined for each entity object instance at runtime based on the value of the discriminator attribute.

A business logic unit is implemented as an XML file that contains metadata about the business rules that apply to appropriate entity object instances and about the attributes (if any) they apply to. Chapter 6 explains how to create business logic units and provides examples.

Property Sets

ADF BC is a business services technology, not a view technology. However, sometimes formatting information for a particular attribute (such as a date) is consistent over a wide range of occurrences in the user interface; in that case, for maximum reusability, it is useful to store some UI information with the attribute itself.

Both entity attributes and view attributes allow you to create *UI hints* (also called *control hints*), formatting information that is accessible to the view layer through the ADF Model. UI hint information is stored in a localizable resource bundle (file), one for each entity or view object definition that uses UI hints. Setting UI hints individually on each attribute that requires them is simple and may be sufficient for your purposes.

However, UI hints often go together. For example, the TUHRA application contains a number of attributes, across multiple entity and view object definitions that all represent various names (employee name and manager name, for example). You might want similar formatting for all of these, such as the same text field width and CSS style. Setting appropriate UI hints on each employee name attribute may be cumbersome.

Instead of setting UI hints individually on attributes, you can define a *property set,* which is a collection of UI hints. Property sets can be applied to entity attributes and view attributes, which, by default, automatically inherit all their UI hints. You can still override particular UI hints from a property set at the attribute level.

A property set is implemented as an XML file. Chapter 13 explains how to create and use UI hints and property sets.

How Can I Visualize My Business Components?

It's helpful when you are designing business components to work with them in a visual way. As mentioned in the section "Models and Diagrammers" of Chapter 3, you can use the JDeveloper UML diagrammer to depict ADF Business Components. Figure 5-2 shows a small set of business components. Chapter 6 explains how to create diagrams of business components.

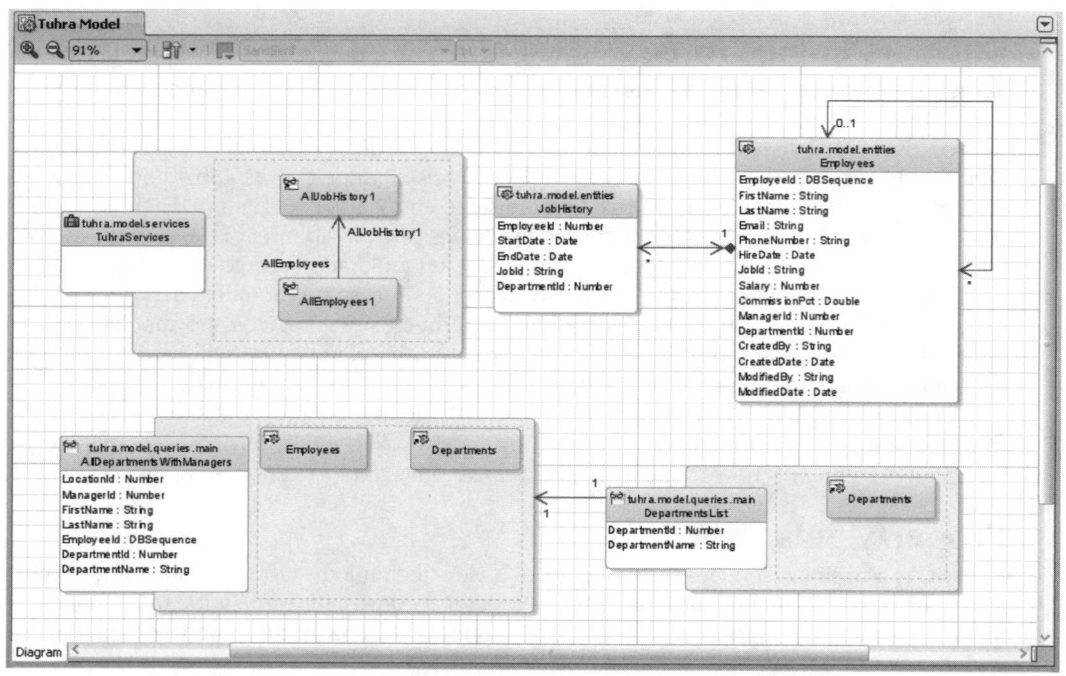

FIGURE 5-2. *ADF Business Components diagram*

Notice the TuhraServices application module definition that contains the view object instance AllEmployees1 and its detail view object instance, AllJobHistory (the arrow represents the view link instance that implements the master/detail relationship). To the right of the application module are the JobHistory and Employees entity object definitions, which are related by an association. The Employees entity object is also related to itself (ManagerId to EmployeeId) by a second association. Below the application module definition is the AllDepartmentsWithManagers view object definition, which is based on entity object usages called "Employees" and "Departments" (usages of the Employees and Departments entity object definitions, respectively). Below the entity object definitions is the DepartmentsList view object definition, which is based on the Departments entity object usage (of the Departments entity object definition) and is related to AllDepartmentsWithManagers with a view link definition.

Chapters 6 and 7 contain further examples of using this diagrammer to visually represent an ADF Business Components design.

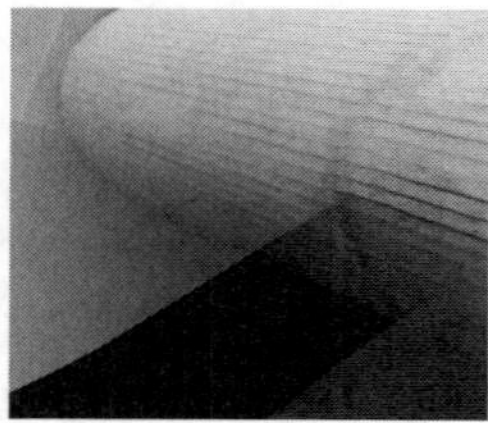

CHAPTER 6

Specifying a Business Domain

. . . any thing so o'erdone is from the purpose of playing, whose end, both at the first and now, was and is, to hold as 'twere the mirror up to nature: to show virtue her feature, scorn her own image, and the very age and body of the time his form and pressure.

—William Shakespeare (1564–1616), *Hamlet*, Act III, Scene 2

he first step in creating a business services layer for a data-aware application is to create a *business domain*: components that correspond to your database tables, views, and synonyms, and that specify the business rules that your data follows. As we explained in Chapter 5, ADF BC models database tables, views, and synonyms as entity object definitions; it models relationships between them (such as those specified by foreign key constraints) as associations.

Entity object definitions can provide enforcement of your business rules, whether alone or redundantly with another layer.

This chapter answers the following questions:

- **What are entity object definitions and entity object instances?**
- **What is an association?**
- **How do entity attributes work?**
- **How do you create and edit entity object definitions and associations?**
- **How do you implement attribute-level validation?**
- **How do you implement entity-level validation?**
- **How does the ADF BC validation cycle work?**
- **How do you implement attribute defaulting and calculation?**
- **How do you synchronize with database defaulting and calculation?**
- **How do you implement polymorphic business rules?**

What Are Entity Object Definitions and Entity Object Instances?

As described in Chapter 5, an entity object definition corresponds to a database table, view, or synonym. You can create it using several techniques described in the section "Creating Entity Object Definitions" later in this chapter. It has entity attributes corresponding to columns of Java types corresponding to the SQL types. It acts as a template for entity object instances, which represent single rows of data and are responsible for validating and performing DML operations for those single rows.

Chapter 5 also stated that an entity object definition comprises an XML metadata file and between zero and three Java classes. This section explains how these elements can work together to constitute an entity object definition and to provide a template for entity object instances.

Entity Object XML Metadata

All entity object definitions involve an XML file. This file contains the metadata that describes the entity object, including the following:

- **The database object** to which the entity object definition maps
- **The attributes of the entity object definition** including their Java types, the columns to which they map, and the SQL datatypes of those columns
- **References to associations** in which the entity object definition participates and how it participates in them
- **Declaratively specified business rules** applying to the individual attributes or to the entity object definition as a whole
- **Other declarative features** of the entity object definition, such as control hints, property sets, business logic groups, and tuning information

You will never need to directly edit the entity object XML file, except in the rare situation where the XML file has become corrupt (such as through a file system problem or uncontrolled shutdown while JDeveloper is writing to the XML). Almost always, you will modify the XML file using JDeveloper's visual editors. We explain various components of the editors throughout this chapter.

Entity Object Classes

When the ADF BC framework needs to create an entity object instance (for example, to be the basis of a view row created to hold queried data), it instantiates the class `oracle.jbo.server.EntityImpl` and configures it based on the entity object definition's XML metadata. The object created by this process is an entity object instance.

`EntityImpl` has all the methods required to initialize a newly created entity object instance, to prepare an entity object instance for deletion, to perform DML operations, and to retrieve and change attribute values. However, you can create an *entity object class,* a subclass of `EntityImpl` that is customized to a particular entity object definition. If you create an entity object class, the corresponding entity object instances will be instances of that class, rather than direct instances of `EntityImpl`.

By default, an entity object class is named after its entity object definition, with the suffix "Impl" added. For example, the entity object class for the Employees entity object definition, by default, would be named `EmployeesImpl`. For information about changing naming conventions for ADF BC classes, see the sidebar, "Changing Class Naming Conventions."

Entity Attribute Accessors

The class `EntityImpl` implements the interface `oracle.jbo.Row`, which contains methods, `getAttribute()` and `setAttribute()`, that allow access to attribute values using generic parameters and return values. If you generate an entity object class, you can also generate accessors (getters and setters) for each attribute. For example, if you generate accessors for `EmployeesImpl`, the class will contain `getSalary()` and `setSalary()` methods, which retrieve and change the value of the Salary attribute, respectively. There are two substantial advantages to generating these accessors, as opposed to relying on the `getAttribute()` and `setAttribute()` methods.

Entity Attribute Accessors Are Typesafe Entity attribute accessors are typesafe, which means that they take fully typed objects as parameters and have fully typed return values. For example, `getSalary()` has a return type of `Number` and no parameters, and `setSalary()` has a return type of `void` and takes a `Number` as a parameter. This can be very helpful in eliminating coding errors. If you make a mistake with an attribute's Java type, JDeveloper's syntax highlighting will show the error as you code, and the compiler will also show the error at compile time.

Changing Class Naming Conventions

We recommend using the default naming conventions ADF BC uses for custom classes; they are intuitive and useful. However, you can change all of the naming conventions ADF BC uses for custom classes in the Preferences dialog (select **Tools | Preferences**), on the Entity Object tab of the "Business Components \ Class Naming" page, as shown here:

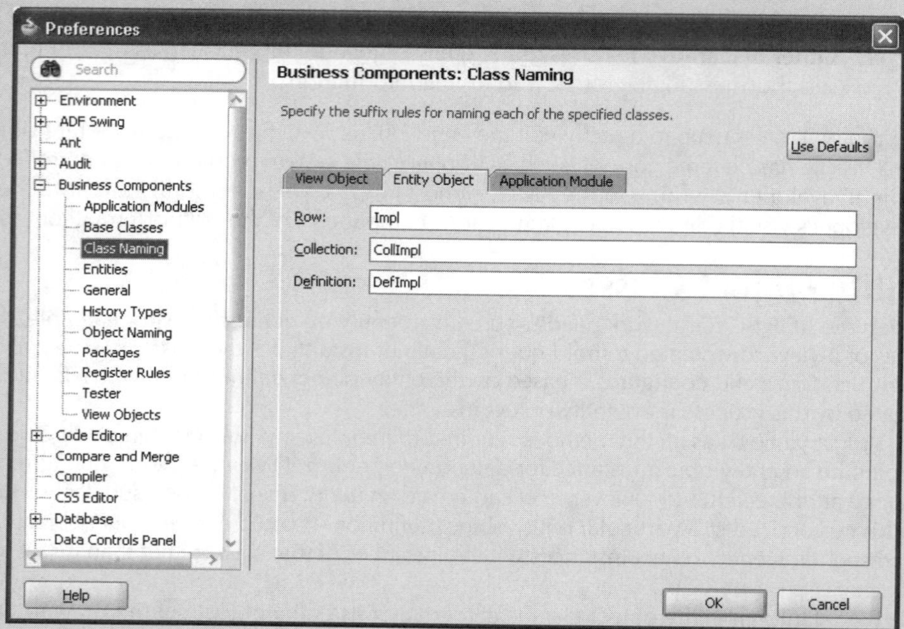

This tab contains the suffixes for the entity object class (Row), entity collection class (Collection), and entity definition class (Definition). For example, if you enter "Object" in the *Row* field, the entity object class for Employees will be `EmployeesObject`. If you make the *Row* field blank, the entity object class for Employees will be `Employees`. The other portions of the dialog deal with naming conventions for view object and application module classes and interfaces.

The following lines of code will be flagged in the code editor and cause compile-time errors because they assume the Salary attribute has the wrong type (`String`, as opposed to `Number`).

```
String salary = myEmployeesImpl.getSalary();
myEmployeesImpl.setSalary("$2000");
```

In contrast, `getAttribute()` and `setAttribute()` are not typesafe: `getAttribute()` takes a `String` (the attribute name) as an argument and has a return type of `java.lang.Object`; `setAttribute()` takes a `String` (the attribute name) and an `Object` as arguments. If you make a mistake regarding the Java type of your attributes, you will not get a compile-time error.

Instead, your application will throw an exception at runtime, requiring substantially more work to debug. Neither of the following lines of code will cause compile-time errors or be flagged in the JDeveloper code editor (even though they make mistakes about the type of the attribute); instead, they will throw exceptions when called at runtime, making it possible to miss the errors before production if they are not adequately covered by test cases:

```
String salary = (String)myEntityImpl.getAttribute("Salary");
myEntityImpl.setAttribute("Salary", "$2000");
```

Using the entity attribute accessors can also make it easier to debug typos in attribute names. For example, the first of the following lines of code will be flagged in the code editor and will yield a compile-time error (because the method name should be spelled `getSalary()`); the second will throw an exception when called at runtime:

```
Number salary=myDepartmentsImpl.getSallery();
Number salary=myEntityImpl.getAttribute("Sallery");
```

Entity Attribute Accessors Provide Hooks for Business Rules If you want to place business rules in the business logic tier (some advantages and disadvantages of doing so are explained in Chapter 1), you can edit the implementation of entity attribute setter methods to add business rules that need to fire when that attribute is changed. If you want to validate changes to data, you can add custom Java code to the body of these methods to enforce your requirements. If you want to trigger events whenever an attribute is changed, you can write Java code to do that as well. There are several other options for implementing attribute-level business rules, such as attribute validation and calculation, which are explained in the sections "How Do You Implement Attribute-Level Validation?" and "How Do You Implement Attribute Defaulting and Calculation?" However, writing attribute-level business rules directly in the setter methods is often the quickest way to implement validation code and matches standard practice for JavaBean technology. Additionally, some attribute-level business rules, such as events that trigger when an attribute is changed, must be implemented in setter methods.

Overriding Methods in EntityImpl

In addition to the accessor methods, entity object classes also allow you to override various methods in the `EntityImpl` class to implement other sorts of business rules. For example, by overriding `EntityImpl.create()` in an entity object class, you can implement defaulting rules or trigger events whenever a row is created. This is explained in greater detail in the section "How Do You Implement Attribute Defaulting and Calculation?"

Entity Definition Classes

An entity object definition's XML file holds metadata that describes the entity object. However, in order to properly use this metadata, the ADF BC framework must create a Java class to represent this XML metadata. This Java class is an instance of `oracle.jbo.server.EntityDefImpl`. There is only one `EntityDefImpl` instance for each entity definition in a Java EE application; the framework will access the same object across entity object instances and even users.

`EntityDefImpl` contains all the methods required to discover information about an entity object definition's name, O/R mappings, attribute properties, validation rules, or anything else specified in the entity object definition's XML file. It even contains methods that allow you to change these properties dynamically.

CAUTION
Be careful when changing an entity object definition's properties at runtime. Remember that you are doing so not just for a single user, but for all users of the entity object definition.

You can also create an entity definition class, a subclass of `EntityDefImpl` that is customized to a particular entity object definition. If you create an entity definition class, ADF BC will use an instance of that class to represent the XML, rather than a direct instance of `EntityDefImpl`.

Unlike entity object classes, which many applications require, entity definition classes are required by relatively few applications. However, there are two reasons you might want to extend `EntityDefImpl`: to create convenience methods that you can use to retrieve specific metadata about an entity object definition, and in the situation when you need to override one of `EntityDefImpl`'s methods. An example of creating and overriding methods for an entity definition class is provided in the section "How Do You Synchronize with Database Defaulting and Calculation?"

Entity Collection Classes

The top-level application module instances for a particular user's session maintain caches of all entity object instances and view rows in memory for that single user. The cache of entity object instances for a particular entity object definition, as used by a single top-level application module instance (or any of its nested application module instances), is an instance of the class `oracle.jbo.server.EntityCache`.

`EntityCache` contains all the methods required to add and remove entity object instances from the cache, iterate through all entity object instances in the cache, or find a particular entity object instance in the cache based on its primary key attributes. However, you will rarely use these methods, or in any way manipulate the cache of entity object instances, directly. Instead, you will manipulate a cache of view rows, which will automatically find and make appropriate changes to underlying entity caches. Chapter 7 explains this process.

It is even less likely that you will need to create a custom subclass of `EntityCache` for a particular entity object definition, but you can do so. This subclass is called an *entity collection class,* and it allows you to override methods on `EntityCache`.

TIP
The Javadoc for `EntityCache` contains details that you will need when overriding or calling its methods.

Custom Framework Classes

Sometimes you need to extend the normal behavior of business components throughout a project, rather than on a component-by-component basis; for example, you may want all entity object instances in a project to share some behavior that is not provided for by the framework itself. Rather than implementing this behavior in a custom entity object class for each entity object definition, you can create custom framework classes that implement this behavior. *Custom framework classes* extend the ADF BC base classes (for example, a custom framework entity object class would extend `EntityImpl`), and all entity object definitions use them (or extensions of them) to represent their entity object instances, XML wrappers, or caches.

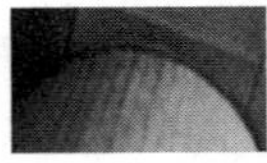

TIP

In addition to creating custom framework classes within your application, you may wish to create higher-level custom framework classes in a separate application. You can then deploy them as a library and import them into various applications as needed (for more information about deployment, see Chapter 22). Deploying as a library allows you to create enterprise-wide functionality. Your enterprise-level framework classes should extend the framework base classes directly; your application-level framework classes should extend the enterprise-level framework classes.

For example, if you created a custom framework entity object class, `TuhraEntityImpl`, and registered it with a project, and then created an entity object class for a particular entity object definition in the project, the entity object class would extend `TuhraEntityImpl` rather than extending `EntityImpl` directly. If you do not create an entity object class for the entity object definition, its entity object instances would be direct instances of `TuhraEntityImpl`.

After you create custom framework classes (which you do as you would create any Java class), you can specify that a project should use them on the "Business Components\Base Classes" page of the Project Properties dialog, as shown in Figure 6-1. You can also make particular entity object definitions use custom framework classes (rather than making all entity object definitions in a project use them) by clicking the Extends button on the Java page of those entity object definitions' editors. Editors for entity object definitions are explained in the section "How Do You Create and Edit Entity Object Definitions and Associations?"

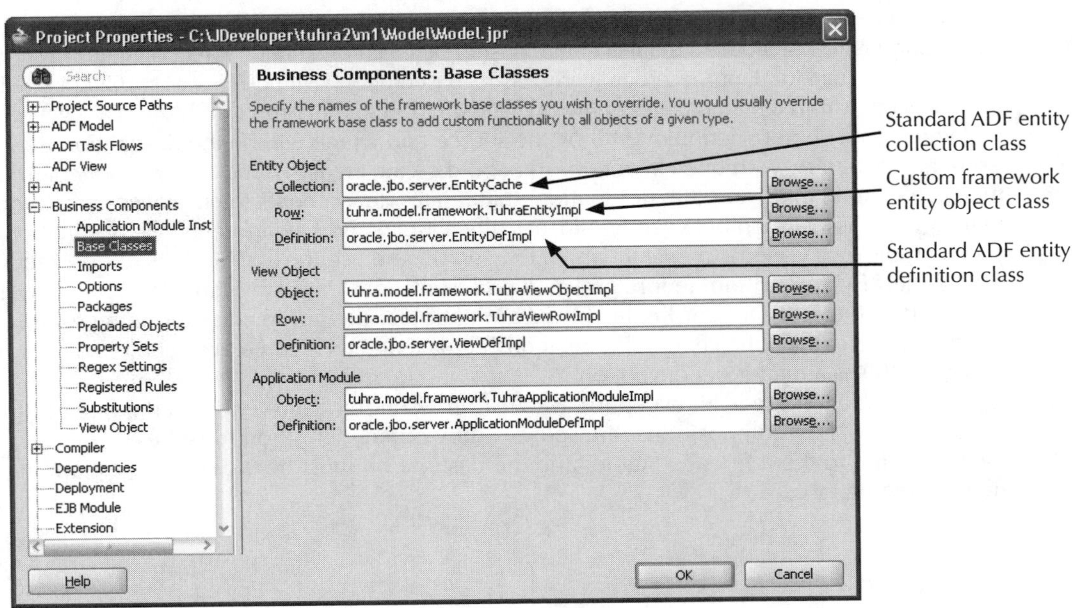

FIGURE 6-1. *Specifying custom framework classes*

You will create and specify custom framework classes in Chapter 19; a specific use for custom framework classes is explained in the section "How Do You Synchronize with Database Defaulting and Calculation?"

TIP

We suggest creating custom framework classes and registering them with your projects whether you think you need them or not; you can leave any class you do not yet have a use for as an empty stub. If you register a custom framework class with a project after you have already created business components in the project, you must open each business component in an editor and then save it to change the component to use the custom framework class. Registering custom framework classes before creating business components will keep you from needing to do this, should you discover you need enterprise-level or application-level customizations later. This practice is discussed further in Chapter 16.

What Is an Association?

An *association* connects two entity object definitions. It specifies a relationship between entity object instances from the first entity object definition and entity object instances from the second entity object definition. An association has no Java classes—it is specified entirely by an XML file and, in some cases, by methods in the relevant entity object classes.

The entity object definitions on either end of an association are called its "source" and "destination" entity object definitions. The source and destination need not be distinct; the association could instead be a recursive relationship between one entity object definition and itself, such as the association EmployeeManagerFkAssoc, based upon EMPLOYEE_MANAGER_FK, which associates rows from the Employees entity object definition to other rows from the same definition.

Which entity object definition will be the source and which will be the destination is, essentially, arbitrary, with one exception. You could create an association between Departments (the source) and Employees (the destination) that relates departments to employees who work there, and an association between Employees (the source) and Departments (the destination) that relates employees to departments in which they work, and use the associations to do exactly the same things. By convention, in foreign-key-type associations ("one-to-many" associations, as described in the section "Cardinality"), the entity object definition corresponding to the referenced table (the "one" end of the relationship) is made the source entity object definition; but again, this is a matter of convention.

As just stated, there is an exception to this rule—compositions (explained in the section "Compositions"). In compositions, the source entity object definition must be the one corresponding to the referenced table, and the destination must be the one corresponding to the referencing table.

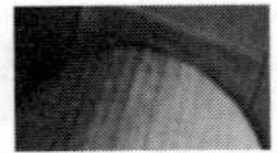

CAUTION
An association can be reverse-engineered from a foreign key constraint, but it does not enforce a foreign key constraint. At runtime, it is possible to create destination entity object instances with "foreign key" values that do not match the referenced key value of any source entity object instance. The exception, again, is compositions—referential integrity is enforced for containees. The section "How Do You Implement Entity-Level Validation?" explains how to enforce referential integrity for entity object instances that are not containees in composition relationships.

Cardinality

Any binary relationship has a *cardinality*—an indication of the number of instances that can occur on either side of a relationship. If you have worked with Unified Modeling Language (UML) or Entity Relationship Diagram (ERD) diagrams, you are already familiar with relationship cardinality.

Cardinality Concepts

The most common relationship shown on an ERD is a foreign key relationship between tables, where a row from the referenced table corresponds to any number of rows from the referencing table. Each detail row is linked to, at most, one master row, but a master row can be linked to any number of detail rows. This kind of relationship has a cardinality of one-to-many. For example, the relationship between departments and their employees is one-to-many, as shown here:

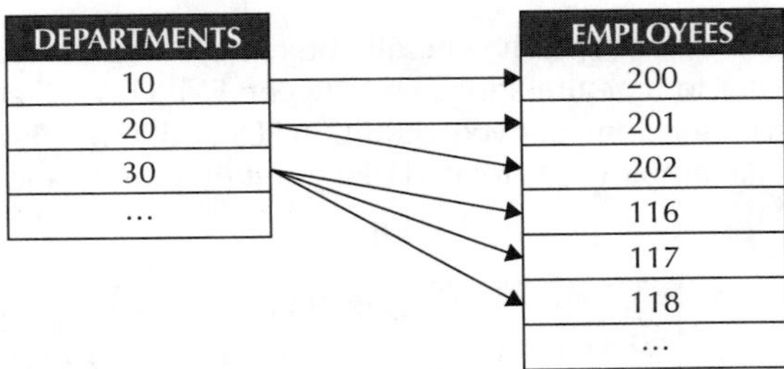

There is a more specific way to categorize foreign key relationships. Some foreign key constraints apply to required attributes, meaning that each detail row must correspond to exactly one master row. Some foreign key constraints apply to nullable attributes, meaning that each detail row must correspond to at most one row. You can distinguish between these relationships by using a formal notation for cardinality. For example, the cardinality "1-*" applies to foreign keys based on required detail attributes. The "1" means that each detail row must correspond to exactly 1 master row; the "*" means that each master row can correspond to any number of detail rows. The cardinality "0..1-*" applies to foreign keys based on nullable detail attributes. The "0..1" means that each detail row can correspond to 0 master rows or 1 master row.

Some relationships have one-to-one cardinalities. These are rare in relationships between tables, because they represent the use of two tables to store data that could be stored in one. These are relationships that can be represented by foreign key constraints with a UNIQUE constraint on the detail attributes. For example, in the TUHRA application, each employee can, optionally, have a biography. This would lead to a one-to-one relationship (specifically, a "1-0..1" relationship) between the EMPLOYEES table and the BIOGRAPHIES table, as shown here:

EMPLOYEES
100
101
102
103
104
105
...

BIOGRAPHIES
Bio for 100
Bio for 101
Bio for 103
Bio for 105
...

Finally, some relationships have many-to-many cardinalities, although these cannot be represented by a single foreign key relationship. An employee may have held any number of past jobs, and any number of employees may have held one job, so this relationship between EMPLOYEES and JOBS is many-to-many (that is, *-*), as shown here:

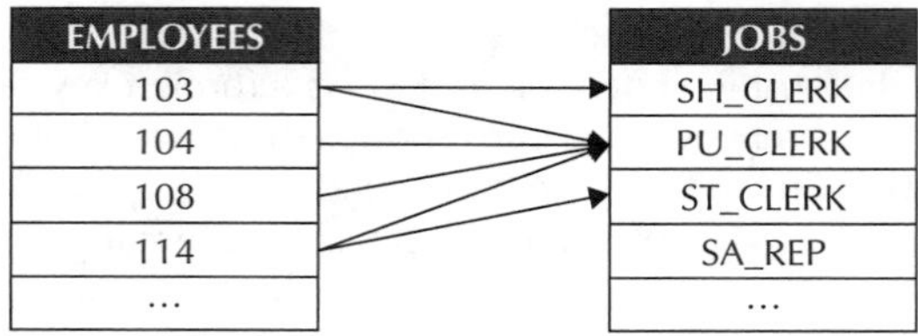

A many-to-many association can generally be represented by two one-to-many associations. For example, the many-to-many relationship between EMPLOYEES and JOBS is represented by two foreign key constraints, one between EMPLOYEES and JOB_HISTORY, and one between JOBS and JOB_HISTORY. An employee is related to a job if they share a job history entry as a detail, as shown here:

EMPLOYEES
EMPLOYEE_ID
103
104
108
114

JOB_HISTORY		
EMPLOYEE_ID	START_DATE	JOB_ID
103	1993-01-04	SH_CLERK
103	1989-09-21	PU_CLERK
104	1996-02-17	PU_CLERK
108	1998-03-24	PU_CLERK
114	1999-01-01	ST_CLERK
114	1999-12-17	PU_CLERK

JOBS
JOB_ID
SH_CLERK
PU_CLERK
ST_CLERK
SA_REP

In this many-to-many relationship, the table JOB_HISTORY is called an "intersection table."

Associations and Cardinality

Just as relationships between tables have a cardinality, associations between entity object definitions have a cardinality. ADF BC associations can be one-to-many ("0..1-*" or "1-*"), one-to-one ("0..1-1" or "1-1"), many-to-many (*-*), or the inverse of any of these. For example, in a "0..1-*" association, an entity object instance from the destination can be related to at most one entity object instance from the source, and an entity object definition from the source can be related to any number of entity object instances from the destination.

In addition to source and destination entity object definitions, many-to-many associations require a third entity object definition, the *intersection entity object definition,* based on an intersection table.

Source and Destination Attributes

One-to-one, one-to-many, and many-to-one associations work on essentially the same principles. Attributes from the source entity object definition are selected as the source attributes of the association. For each source attribute, there is a (not necessarily distinct) corresponding attribute in the destination entity object definition, called a destination attribute of the association. The association relates entity object instances if every source attribute value from the source entity object instance is equal, as defined by the method `Object.equals()`, to its corresponding destination attribute value in the destination entity object instance.

For example, the association EmpDeptFkAssoc has the entity object definition Departments as its source, and the entity object definition Employees as its destination. It has one source attribute, DepartmentId (an attribute of Departments), and one destination attribute, also called DepartmentId (but this is an attribute of Employees). Both of these attributes are of type `Number`. If the DepartmentId value of a particular entity object instance of Departments matches the DepartmentId value of a particular entity object instance of Employees, the association will relate those instances, as shown here:

Departments entity object instance

DepartmentId	DepartmentName	ManagerId	...
90	"Executive"	100	...

Employees entity object instance

EmployeeId	LastName	DepartmentId	...
100	"King"	90	...

JDeveloper can automatically generate one-to-one or one-to-many associations based on foreign key relationships (with or without UNIQUE constraints on the foreign key columns, respectively). In these automatically generated associations, the source attributes are based on the referenced columns from the referenced table, and the destination attributes are based on the corresponding foreign key columns from the constrained table.

Many-to-many associations work slightly differently. While attributes from the source entity object definition still makes up the source attributes of the association, there are no directly corresponding attributes in the destination entity object definition. Instead, each source attribute has a corresponding attribute in the intersection entity object definition. Separate attributes in the intersection entity object definition each have corresponding attributes in the destination entity object definition; these are the destination attributes of the association.

For example, you can create a many-to-many association EmployeesPastJobs, based on the many-to-many relationship between employees and the jobs that they have held in the past. The source entity object definition of this association is Employees, the destination entity object definition is Jobs, and the intersection entity object definition is JobHistory.

The attribute EmployeeId from Employees is the sole source attribute of the association. It corresponds to the attribute EmployeeId from JobHistory. A separate attribute from the intersection, JobId, corresponds to the sole destination attribute, JobId from Jobs. The relationship between an entity object instance from Employees and a corresponding entity object instance from Jobs is shown here:

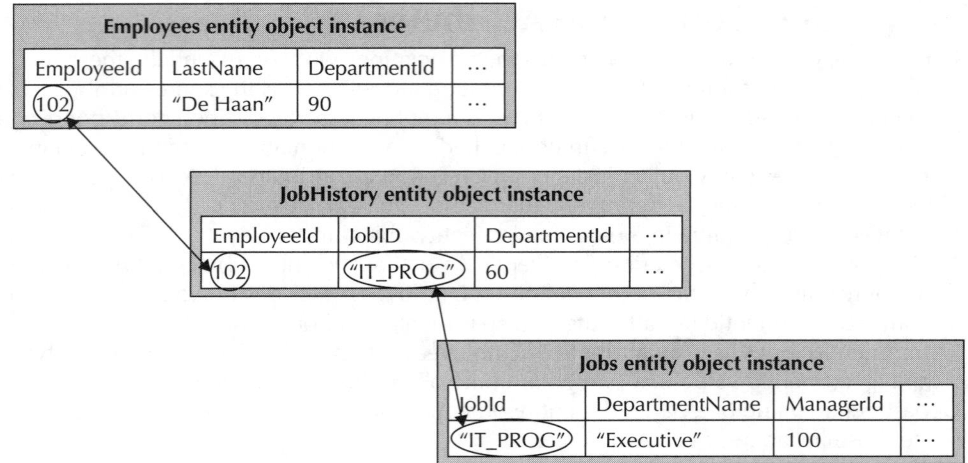

Association Accessors

An *association accessor* is an operation (sometimes implemented as a Java method) by which an entity object instance at one end of an association can access the related entity object instances at the other end of the association. By default, JDeveloper generates accessors at both ends of an association. You can change this behavior if you will only need to use the association in one direction (doing this may simplify your code slightly), but the default behavior is acceptable in the vast majority of applications. An accessor that travels from the destination to the source is called a *source accessor,* and an accessor that travels from the source to the destination is called a *destination accessor.*

Association accessors, which are described in the entity object definitions' XML files, can be used by view object and view link definitions to specify cross-entity relationships (Chapter 7 explains this in more detail). In addition, if you generate an entity object class for a file, JDeveloper will use the accessor's name to generate a getter method that returns the associated entity object instance or instances. For example, the association EmpJobFkAssoc has a source accessor named "Job" and a destination accessor called "EmployeesInJob." If you generate an entity object class for Jobs, it will contain a method `getEmployeesInJob()`, and if you generate an entity object class for Employees, it will contain a method `getJob()`.

The return type of the method differs depending on whether it is returning a "one" side or a "many" side of the association. If the method is returning a "one" side, its return type will be the entity object class of the associated entity object definition, or `EntityImpl` if the associated entity object definition has no entity object class. The returned object will be the associated entity object instance itself (or possibly `null`, if the side has cardinality "0..1" and there is no associated instance). For example, because `EmployeesImpl.getJob()` returns the "one" side of the association, it will have a return type of EntityImpl or (if the entity object class for Jobs has been generated) JobsImpl. You can use this method to retrieve the associated entity and then use methods (such as getter methods) on that entity object instance, such as in the following code, which could be placed in the EmployeesImpl class:

```
JobsImpl jobForThisEmployee = getJob();
String jobTitle = jobForThisEmployee.getJobTitle();
// do something with the job title
```

If the method is returning a "many" side, the return type of the method will be oracle.jbo.RowIterator, which Oracle recommends you cast to the class oracle.jbo.RowSet. This is a collection of entity object instances that supplies a default iterator. In other contexts, a RowSet instance can contain other types of objects, as long as those objects are of a class that implements the interface oracle.jbo.Row (this is explained further in Chapter 8, in the section "How Do You Implement Query-Level Methods?"), but the RowSet instances returned by getter methods for associations always contain entity object instances. Once you have retrieved a RowSet, you can cycle through it (via its default iterator) using its next() method, which returns the first Row in the RowSet when it is first called, and the next Row each subsequent time, and its hasNext() method, which returns true when the default iterator has another row. Since these rows are entity object instances, you can cast them to entity object classes or EntityImpl to use methods on those classes.

For example, because JobsImpl.getEmployeesInJob() returns the "many" side of the association, it will have a return type of RowIterator, which you can cast to RowSet. You can cycle through this RowSet instance, cast the Row instances to EntityImpl or (if you have generated the entity object class for Employees) EmployeesImpl, and then use methods (such as getter methods) on those entity object instances, as demonstrated in the following code (which could be added to a method in JobsImpl):

```
RowSet employeesForThisJob = (RowSet) getEmployeesInJob();
while (employeesForThisJob.hasNext()) {
  EmployeesImpl currentEmp =
    (EmployeesImpl) employeesForThisJob.next();
  String firstName = currentEmp.getFirstName();
  // Do something with the first name
}
```

Compositions

Consider two different sorts of foreign key relationships: relationships like the one between employees and the departments in which they work, and relationships like the one between job histories and the employees that they are histories for. Certainly, employees need to work in a department, but an employee is not, strictly speaking, just part of a department. Employees exist independently of their departments; you can eliminate a department and preserve the employees within it by just moving them to another department. By contrast, an employee's job history is just part of an employee, rather than an independently existing thing. It makes no sense to delete an employee without deleting his or her job history.

An association such as the one between employees and their job histories, where the detail is nothing but a part of the master, is called a *composition* or a *composite association*. When you create default business components, associations based on foreign keys with ON DELETE CASCADE are made compositions, but you can change this behavior, either to make other associations compositions or to remove the composition property from default compositions. Because of the close relationship between the *containees,* the details in a composition, and their *containers,* or masters, ADF BC will not allow users to delete a container without deleting the containees. You can also, optionally, add the following behaviors to a composition:

Optimize for Database Cascade Delete If an association is based on a foreign key with ON DELETE CASCADE, ADF will not issue DML to delete those instances when the changes are posted to the database, whether they've been automatically deleted (via "Implement Cascade Delete," as explained next) or explicitly deleted by the application. This considerably improves performance.

Implement Cascade Delete If you select this option and the application requests that a container be deleted, ADF will automatically delete all containees first.

Cascade Update Key Attributes If you select this option and the values of source attributes change for a particular master entity object instance, the values of the destination attributes of all detail instances will change with it, so as to preserve the association. For example, if you have a composition between an entity object definition called "Employees" and one called "JobHistory," and you select this option, when the EmployeeId value of an Employees entity object instance is changed, selecting this option will ensure that the EmployeeId values of all associated JobHistory instances will change as well. Usually, users are not allowed to change primary key attributes, but the framework may change them in some circumstances, as explained in the section, "The DBSequence Domain."

Update Top-Level History Columns Entity object attributes can be used to mark the history of each row—when and by whom each row was added or modified. If this option is selected, when a child in the composition is added or modified, the parent will be marked as modified as well. You will use history columns in the hands-on practice in Chapter 17.

Lock Level This option changes locking behavior. This is explained in the section "How Do Application Module Instances Manage Transactional State?" in Chapter 7.

How Do Entity Attributes Work?

As we explained in Chapter 5, in general, each database column (with its SQL datatype) is mapped to an entity attribute (with its Java type). However, there can be more or fewer attributes in an entity object definition than in the corresponding database table, and there is some flexibility in the mappings between SQL datatypes of columns and the Java types of attributes.

Persistent and Transient Attributes

Entity attributes that map to a database column are called *persistent* attributes. Although you usually define one persistent attribute for each database column, you can remove attributes for database columns that your application does not need.

In addition, you can add transient entity attributes to an entity object definition. *Transient attributes* are attributes that do not map to database columns. Because they do not map to a persistent data source, values of transient attributes do not last longer than a single session; but they can be useful places to store information within a single session. Most frequently, transient attributes hold calculated values. The section "How Do You Implement Attribute Defaulting and Calculation?" explains how to calculate values for transient attributes.

You can add or remove attributes from an entity object definition using an ADF Business Components diagram or using the Entity Object Wizard or Editor (as explained in the section "How Do You Create and Edit Entity Object Definitions and Associations?").

Attribute Types and Column Datatypes

Table 6-1 shows the default type mappings between column datatypes and entity object attribute Java types. Essentially, numeric types are mapped to a `Number`; character types are mapped to a `String`; date types are mapped to a `Date`, `Timestamp`, `TimestampTZ`, or `TimestampLTZ`; and LOB or structured types are mapped to specialized domains (domains were introduced in Chapter 5 and are covered more extensively in the current chapter in the sections "Working with Built-in Domains," "Object Type Domains," and "Validation Domains."

However, you can change the data type of entity object attributes from the default, although the types you select must always be classes, not primitive types. For example, you can map a BIT column, or a NUMBER column that you are certain contains only values of "1" and "0," to an attribute of column type `java.lang.Boolean` ("1" will be treated as true; "0" as false).

Column Datatype	Java Type
NUMBER, TINYINT, SMALLINT, INTEGER, BIGINT, INT, REAL, DOUBLE, FLOAT, DECIMAL, NUMERIC, BIT	`oracle.jbo.domain.Number`
VARCHAR2, NVARCHAR2, CHAR, VARCHAR, LONG	`java.lang.String`
DATE, TIME, DATETIME	`oracle.jbo.domain.Date`
TIMESTAMP	`oracle.jbo.domain.Timestamp`
TIMESTAMP WITH TIME ZONE	`oracle.jbo.domain.TimestampTZ`
TIMESTAMP WITH LOCAL TIME ZONE	`oracle.jbo.domain.TimestampLTZ`
RAW, LONG RAW	`oracle.jbo.domain.Raw`
CLOB	`oracle.jbo.domain.ClobDomain`
BLOB	`oracle.jbo.domain.BlobDomain`
BFILE	`oracle.jbo.domain.BFileDomain`
ARRAY, VARRAY	`oracle.jbo.domain.Array`
REF	`oracle.jbo.domain.Ref`

TABLE 6-1. *Default Type Mappings for Entity Object Attributes*

CAUTION

Be careful when changing the type of an entity attribute from the default. If, for example, you map a column of type NUMBER to an attribute of type `java.lang.Integer`, and the column contains nonintegral values, those values will be truncated to integers when they are loaded into entity object instances. This can corrupt the data when it is posted to the database.

You can change entity attribute types using an ADF Business Components diagram or using the Entity Object Wizard or Editor (as described in the section "How Do You Create and Edit Entity Object Definitions and Associations?").

*inter*Media Domains

If you create an entity object attribute based on a column with an *inter*Media datatype, JDeveloper, by default, maps it to one of a selection of specialized domains, the inter*Media domains*. Unlike most domains, which reside in the package `oracle.jbo.domain`, the *inter*Media domains are in the package `oracle.ord.im`. The default type mappings for *inter*Media datatypes are shown in Table 6-2. We do not recommend changing these type mappings.

Working with Built-in Domains

The domains in the `oracle.jbo.domain` package have a number of methods for working with their values without converting the values into more standard Java types, such as `Number.add()`. For more information on these methods, see the Javadoc for the individual domains. More commonly, however, you will want to do one of two tasks:

Create a Domain Instance Based on a Standard Java Type Most domains (all but the LOB, structured datatype, and *inter*Media domains) provide constructors that you can use to create new instances from standard Java types. For example, `Number` provides constructors that accept a single parameter of type `int`, `float`, `long`, or `double` (as well as some standard numeric object types, such as `java.math.BigInteger`). The following code will create a `Number` with a value of 5.2:

```
Number fivePointTwo = new Number(5.2);
```

***inter*Media Datatype**	**Java Type**
ORDSYS.ORDAudio	`oracle.ord.im.OrdAudioDomain`
ORDSYS.ORDDoc	`oracle.ord.im.OrdDocDomain`
ORDSYS.ORDImage	`oracle.ord.im.OrdImageDomain`
ORDSYS.OrdImageSignature	`oracle.ord.im.OrdImageSignatureDomain`
ORDSYS.OrdVideo	`oracle.ord.im.OrdVideoDomain`

TABLE 6-2. *Type Mappings for interMedia Datatypes*

Extract the Value of a Domain Instance as a Standard Java Type Most of the built-in domains (all but the LOB, structured datatype, and *inter*Media domains) provide methods you can use to extract their values as standard Java types. For example, `Number` contains the methods `intValue()`, `floatValue()`, `longValue()`, and `doubleValue()`, which extract the domain's value as an `int`, `float`, `long`, and `double`, respectively. If the `Number`'s value does not fit in the specified type, it will be truncated. For example, the following code returns a value of 5 (the value is truncated to an integer):

```
Number fivePointTwo = new Number(5.2);
return fivePointTwo.intValue();
```

NOTE

You only need to use these constructors and methods if you are working with domains inside Java code. ADF Faces (discussed in Part III) contains automatic converters that read text input values and create appropriate domains for them. The converters then read domains back out as strings for display. ADF Faces also offers the ability to display LOB and interMedia domains, and to allow users to upload files to create LOB and interMedia domains.

Object Type Domains

ADF BC automatically associates standard SQL datatypes with Java classes. However, some table columns are of custom Oracle object types. As mentioned in Chapter 5, Oracle object type columns are represented as custom *object type domains*. When you create an entity object definition based on a table with an Oracle object type column, JDeveloper automatically creates a custom domain for you and maps the column to an entity attribute with that domain as its Java type. If you have object types embedded in object types, JDeveloper recursively creates custom domains for all of them.

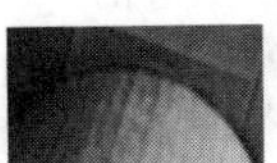

NOTE

ADF does not support object types for non-Oracle databases.

Like an entity object definition, an object type domain has a number of attributes (one for each attribute in the Oracle object type). All attributes have Java types, with default mappings just like entity attribute mappings. You can delete attributes from domains, add transient attributes to them, or change attribute types, just as you can for entity object definitions.

Domains are not used to represent Oracle object types that occur in object tables. If you create a table using CREATE TABLE <table> OF <object_type>, and you base an entity object definition on that table, JDeveloper will not create a domain to represent the object type; instead, it will just create entity attributes for each of the object type's attributes.

Object type domain classes have accessors for their attributes, just as entity object classes do.

Primary Key and Alternate Key Attributes

Every entity object definition must include one or more attributes defined as *primary key attributes*, which ADF uses to look up unique entity object instances. This is true even if the underlying database object is a view or otherwise does not have a primary key. When you create an entity object definition (as explained in the section "How Do You Create Entity Object Definitions and Associations?") from a database object with a primary key, the primary key column(s) are, by default, selected as primary key attributes. When you create an entity object definition from a table or synonym for a table with no primary key, either you must designate primary key attributes or JDeveloper will automatically create an attribute based on the pseudo-column ROWID and will mark that attribute as a primary key attribute. If you create an entity object definition from a view or synonym for a view, you must specify primary key attributes in order for the view to work properly.

The attribute (or combination of attributes) you select for your primary key attributes must be (jointly) unique; your application may throw an `oracle.jbo.TooManyObjectsException` if they are not.

In addition to a primary key, you can specify *alternate keys,* other jointly unique combinations of attributes that can be used to look up entity object instances. Using primary or alternate keys to perform lookups is explained in Chapter 8.

How Do You Create and Edit Entity Object Definitions and Associations?

The details of creating and editing the entity object definitions and associations that represent your business domain will be shown in Chapters 18 and 20. However, this section provides an overview of the options for creating and editing entity object definitions and associations.

Creating Entity Object Definitions and Associations

There are a number of ways to create the entity object definitions and associations that represent your business domain.

The Create Business Components from Tables Wizard

You can create an entire set of default business components using the Create Business Components from Tables Wizard, accessible from the New Gallery or by selecting **New Business Components from Tables** on a package's right-click menu. The first page of the wizard, shown in Figure 6-2, allows you to specify database tables, views, and synonyms for which to create default entity object definitions. The other pages allow you to specify other business components and, optionally, a location for a UML diagram of your business components. The attributes of default entity object definitions correspond one-to-one with columns in the corresponding database object. Moreover, the attributes are all defined with the ADF default Java types for the SQL datatypes of the columns. The section "How Do Entity Attributes Work?" explains these default types and other options for entity attribute types.

If the Create Business Components from Tables Wizard creates entity object definitions from database objects that have a foreign key relationship, it will also create one-to-many associations between those entity object definitions. The entity attributes corresponding to the referenced columns will be the source attributes of the association, and the attributes corresponding to the foreign key columns will be the destination attributes.

Dragging from the Application Navigator to a Business Components Diagram

If, in the Create Business Components from Tables Wizard, you opt to create a UML diagram, JDeveloper will automatically add your default business components to the diagram. However, you can create additional entity object definitions and associations on the generated diagram, or create entity object definitions and associations on a diagram you create directly from the New Gallery, by

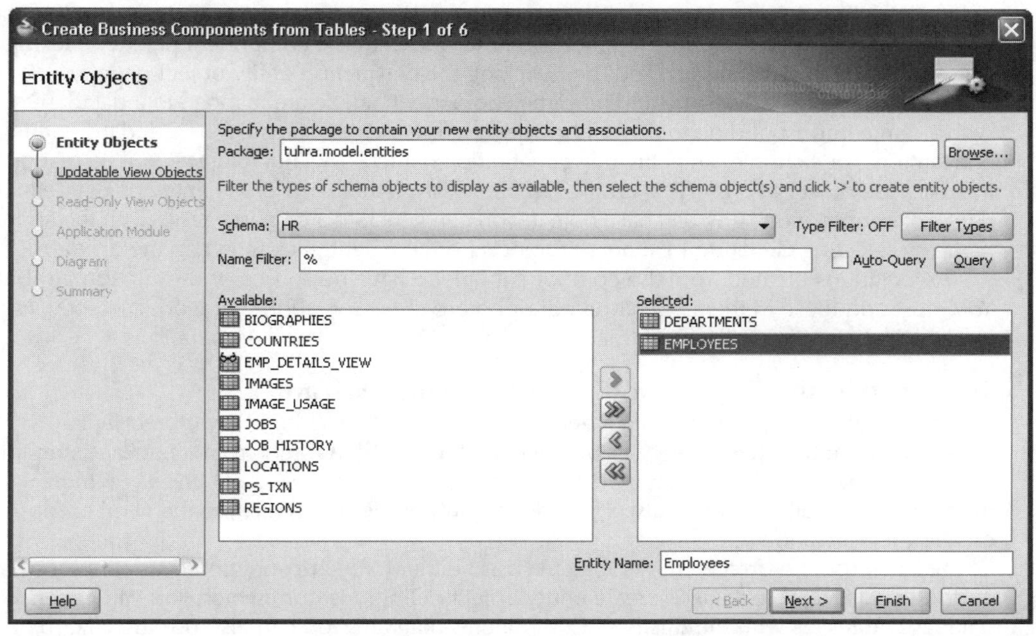

FIGURE 6-2. *The Entity Objects page of the Create Business Components from Tables Wizard*

dragging tables, views, or synonyms from under the "Connections\Database\<connection_name>" node in the Applications Navigator's Application Resources panel onto the diagram. This operation will generate default entity object definitions from the tables, views, or synonyms. It will also create associations based on foreign key relationships among those tables, views, or synonyms, or between the new objects and existing entity object definitions. Finally, it will add representations of the created business components to the diagram.

Dragging from the Component Palette to a Business Components Diagram

When an ADF BC diagram is open, the component palette displays various business components, as shown here:

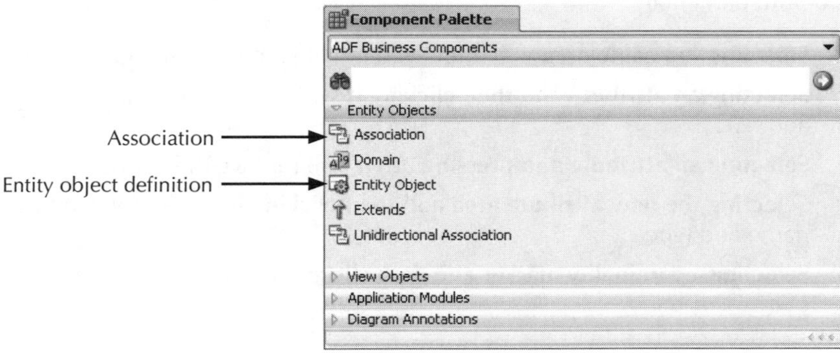

You can create entity object definitions by clicking the Entity Object icon in the component palette and then dragging to or clicking the diagram. You can create associations between these entity object definitions by clicking the Association icon in the component palette, clicking the source entity object definition, and then clicking the destination entity object definition.

Entity object definitions created from the component palette are mapped to a database object with a name corresponding to the entity object definition's name using the standard naming convention. For example, an entity object definition named "MyEntityObject" will be mapped to the database object MY_ENTITY_OBJECT, if one exists. If the name of the entity object definition does not correspond to any database object, you can generate a database table with the appropriate name by selecting **Generate | Database Objects** from the right-click menu on the diagram.

Associations created from the component palette have no source or destination attributes. You must add these in the association editor before the association will work correctly. For more information, see the section "Editing Entity Object Definitions and Associations."

The Create Entity Object and Create Association Wizards

You can create a single entity object definition by using the Create Entity Object Wizard, accessible from the New Gallery or by selecting **New Entity Object** from a package's right-click menu. This method takes longer than the other creation processes, but it gives you more immediate control over the entity object definition's properties, lessening the need for post-creation modifications.

You can use the Create Entity Object Wizard either to create entity object definitions based on existing database objects or to create entity object definitions from which you can generate database tables, as with the Business Components diagram. You can also use the wizard to remove attributes or add transient attributes, change attribute data types from the default, implement some simple business rules, and choose which custom entity classes to generate.

You can create a single association by using the Create Association Wizard. This wizard allows you to specify cardinality, source and destination entity object definitions and attributes, whether to generate association accessors, whether the association is a composition, and which optional composition properties to apply.

Editing Entity Object Definitions and Associations

There are several ways to edit entity object definitions and associations.

Editing Entity Object Definitions and Associations on the Diagram

You can rename entity object definitions, add or remove entity attributes, change the type of entity attributes, and change the cardinality of associations directly on the diagram, as shown in Figure 6-3. In particular:

- **Selecting the name area** will allow you to type a new entity object definition name.
- **Selecting an attribute and then clicking it** will allow you to change the attribute name and type.
- **Selecting an attribute and pressing DELETE** will remove the attribute.
- **Selecting the new attribute area and then clicking it** will allow you to add an attribute name and type.
- **Selecting a cardinality marker and then clicking it** will allow you to change the cardinality of an association.

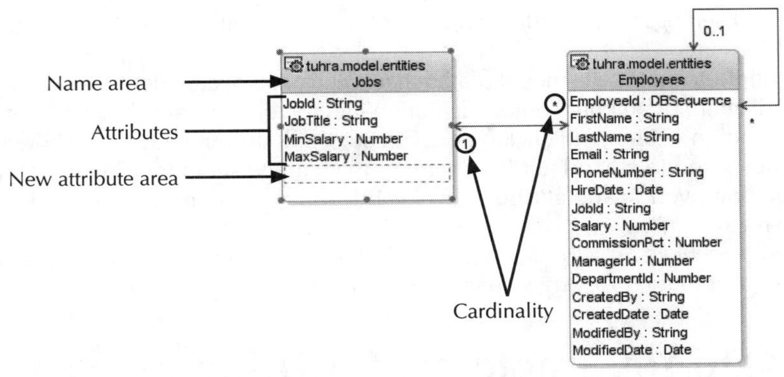

FIGURE 6-3. *A simple Business Components diagram*

Editors for Entity Object Definitions and Associations

By double-clicking an entity object definition in the Application Navigator or on a diagram, you can open it in an editor. Unlike the Create Entity Object Wizard, this is a nonmodal editor window rather than a modal dialog. It allows you to change any property of an entity object definition you can set in the Create Entity Object Wizard, plus a number of additional properties, such as more complex validation rules, tuning properties, and security properties.

By double-clicking an association in the Application Navigator or on a diagram, you can open it in an editor similar to the editor for entity object definition.

Editing Custom Entity Classes

If you have generated custom entity object classes, entity definition classes, or entity collection classes, you can find them in the Application Navigator by expanding the business components node in question, as shown in this illustration.

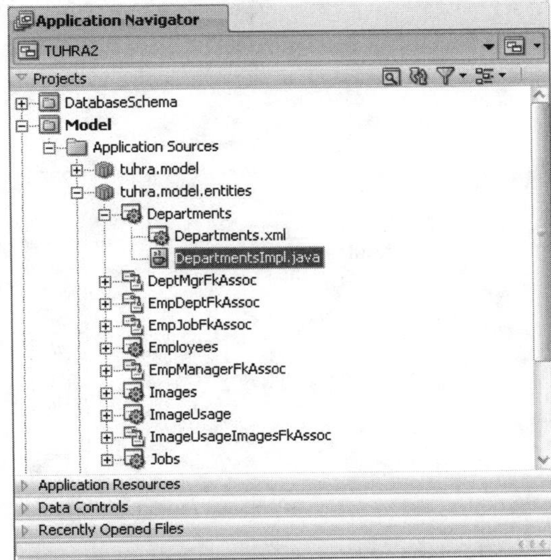

You can open a code editor for these classes by double-clicking them. In addition, most options available on any Java class are available on these classes from the right-click menu. The notable exceptions are **Refactor | Rename** and **Refactor | Move**, which are not available for these classes; custom entity classes must follow the naming conventions used by the project and must reside in the same package as the entity object XML.

Editing Individual Attribute Settings

You can edit settings for individual entity attributes using either the Attribute Editor or the Property Inspector.

The Attribute Editor is a modal dialog that you can invoke by double-clicking an attribute in an ADF BC diagram or an entity object definition's editor, or by selecting an attribute in an entity object definition's editor and clicking the Edit Selected Attribute button as shown in Figure 6-4. This dialog allows you to edit all attribute settings that can be set in the Create Entity Object Wizard, and also allows you to add attribute-level validation rules, control hints, and settings that affect attribute recalculation.

When you select an attribute in the Attributes page of an entity object definition's editor, its settings appear in the Property Inspector. You can also change the settings there.

How Do You Implement Attribute-Level Validation?

The simplest kind of business rule is one that needs to fire whenever an attribute value is changed, to make sure the new value passes some test. For example, the LastName attribute in Employees is mandatory (cannot be null) and can contain at most 25 characters. The UsageType attribute in ImageUsages is mandatory and must match either "E" or "L". Logic like this is called attribute-level validation because it is intended to check the value of a single attribute in a single row.

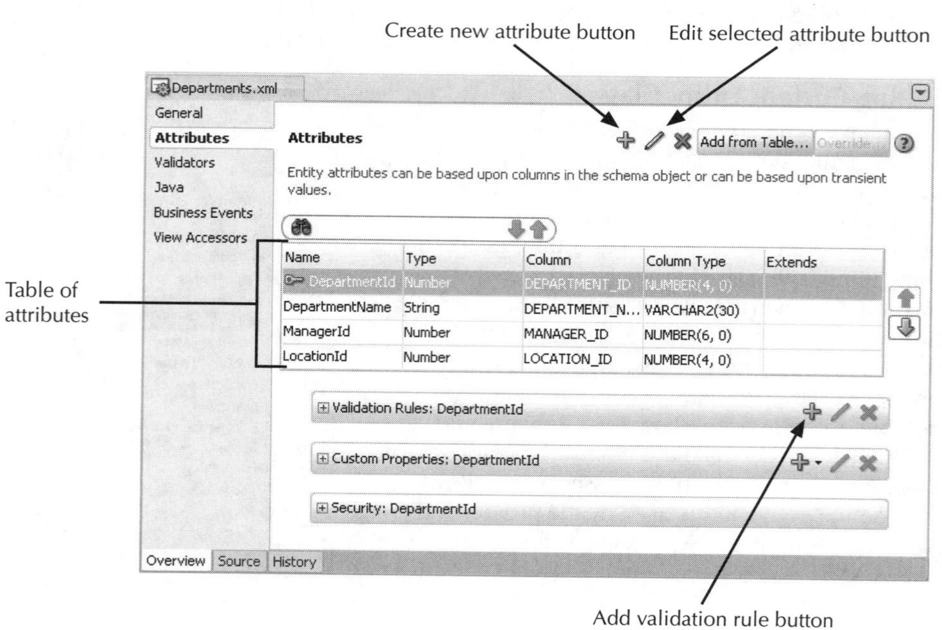

FIGURE 6-4. *The Attributes page of an entity object definition's editor*

Mandatory Value Type Updatable area Refresh After area

Database Column Type

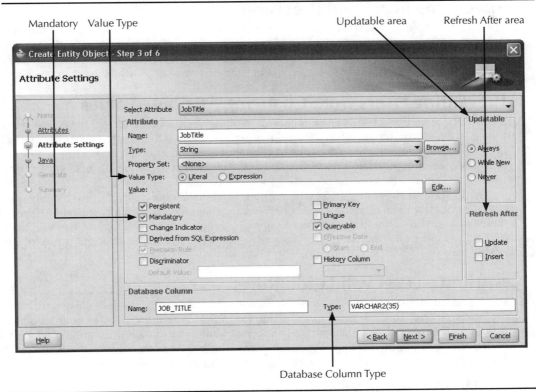

FIGURE 6-5. *The Attribute Settings page of the Create Entity Object Wizard*

Specifying Mandatory Attributes

You can mark an attribute as mandatory on the Attribute Settings page of the Create Entity Object Wizard (as shown in Figure 6-5), in the attribute Property Inspector, or in the Entity Attribute page of the Attribute Editor.

When you create an entity object definition from a table, JDeveloper determines whether any column in the table has a NOT NULL constraint. If this constraint has been defined, JDeveloper automatically marks the corresponding attribute as mandatory.

NOTE

Although you can mark attributes as unique, this setting is not enforced by Oracle ADF. It only affects tables generated from entity object definitions by adding a UNIQUE constraint on the database table. The section "Entity-Level Validation Rules" contains information on enforcing uniqueness in the Business Services layer.

Specifying Scale and Precision

The database column type that corresponds to an entity attribute is visible and editable in the Attribute Settings page of the Create Entity Object Wizard (as shown in Figure 6-5), in the attribute's Property Inspector, or on the Entity Attribute page of the Attribute Editor. If this type includes a scale and/or precision, the precision and scale will be enforced by ADF BC when the attribute is set.

Preventing Users from Changing Attribute Values

If you want to prevent users from changing an attribute value, you can select the *Never* radio button in the Updatable region of the Attribute Settings page of the Create Entity Object Wizard (as shown in Figure 6-5), or on the Entity Attribute page of the Attribute Editor. This setting prevents generation of a setter method, and causes an attempt to set the attribute via a call to `setAttribute()` to throw an `oracle.jbo.ReadOnlyAttrException`.

If you want to allow users to set an attribute value for a new (not yet posted) entity object instance, but not to change the value for an instance that already has a corresponding row in the database, you can select the *While New* radio button in the same region. This will throw a `ReadOnlyAttrException` if an attempt is made to change the attribute value for a posted row.

Attribute-Level Validation Rules

Validation rules (also called *validators*), as explained in Chapter 5, are Java classes that can be declaratively configured to provide validation for individual entity attributes or cross-attribute validation for entity object instances. A number of built-in validation rules are included in the ADF Business Components libraries, ranging from the simple to the almost infinitely flexible. This section explains the application of validation rules at the entity attribute level.

Considerations for Any Validation Rule

All validation rules can be applied on the Validators page of an entity object definition's editor (as shown in Figure 6-6) by selecting an attribute or an entire entity and clicking the Create New Validator button. In addition, you can add a validation rule to an attribute on the Attributes page of an entity object definition's editor (as shown in Figure 6-4) by selecting an attribute and clicking the Add Validation Rule button, or on the Validation page of the Attribute Editor. You can edit a validation rule by double-clicking it.

When you apply or edit a validation rule, a dialog appears. This dialog is called either "Add Validation Rule" or "Edit Validation Rule," but with one exception (the dropdown list that allows you to select a validation rule type is read-only in the "Edit Validation Rule" dialog), the dialogs are identical.

Each dialog contains three tabs.

The Rule Definition Tab This tab allows you to configure the content of the validation rule. As such, its appearance is different for different validation rule types. The appearance for each validation rule type is discussed in the sections on the various validation rules.

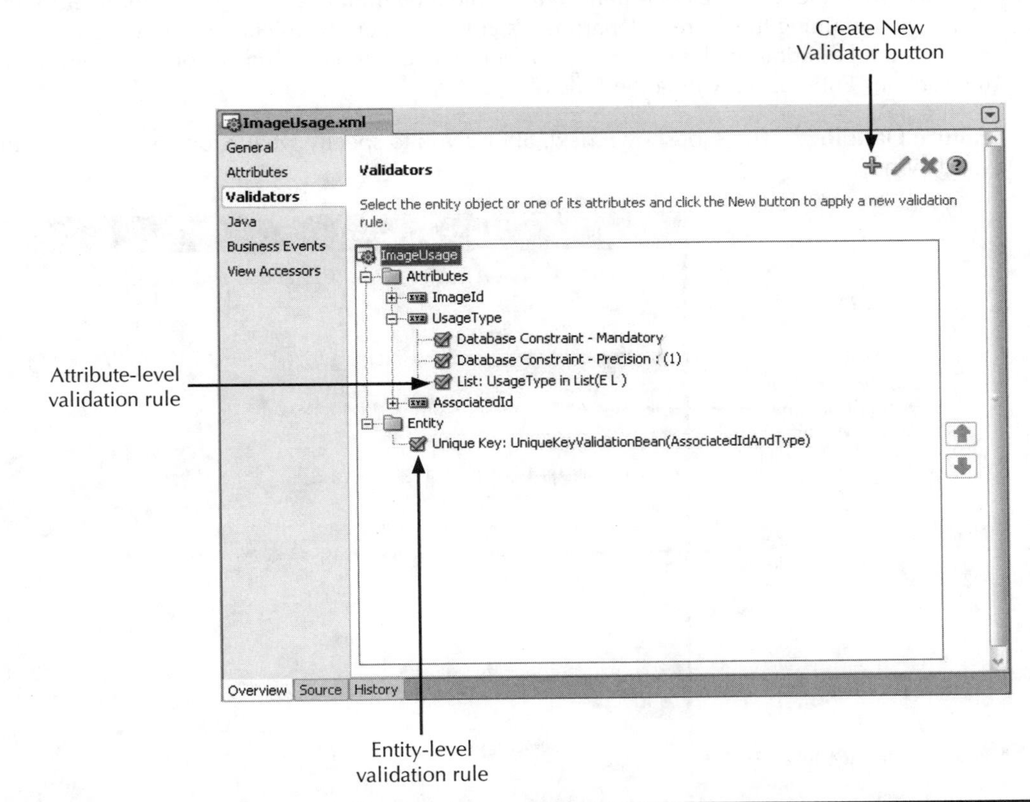

FIGURE 6-6. *The Validators page of an entity object definition's editor*

The Validation Execution Tab This tab allows you to specify a Groovy Boolean expression. If you do so, the validation rule will only be checked when the expression evaluates to "true." In addition to standard Groovy constructs, there are a number of variables that ADF will make available in the context of attribute-level validation.

You can use entity attribute names in the expression to refer to their values. For example, you can refer to the value of Salary with the variable `Salary`; if the validation rule is being fired because Salary is being changed, this will refer to the prechange value. If you want to refer to the new value that the attribute is being set to, you can do so with the variable `newValue`.

To refer to the entity object instance, you can use the variable `source`. This is helpful when, for example, you want to call methods on the entity object instance.

You can even access associated entity object instances in the Groovy expression by using the appropriate accessor attribute name. For example, in a rule for the Employees entity object definition, `Departments` will refer to the employees' corresponding Departments entity object instance; in a rule for the Departments entity object definition, `Employees` will refer to the `RowSet` containing the current department's Employees entity object instances.

This tab has additional functionality for entity-level validation rules. For more information, see the section "Entity-Level Validation Rules."

Failure Handling This tab, shown next, allows you to specify what happens when data fails validation.

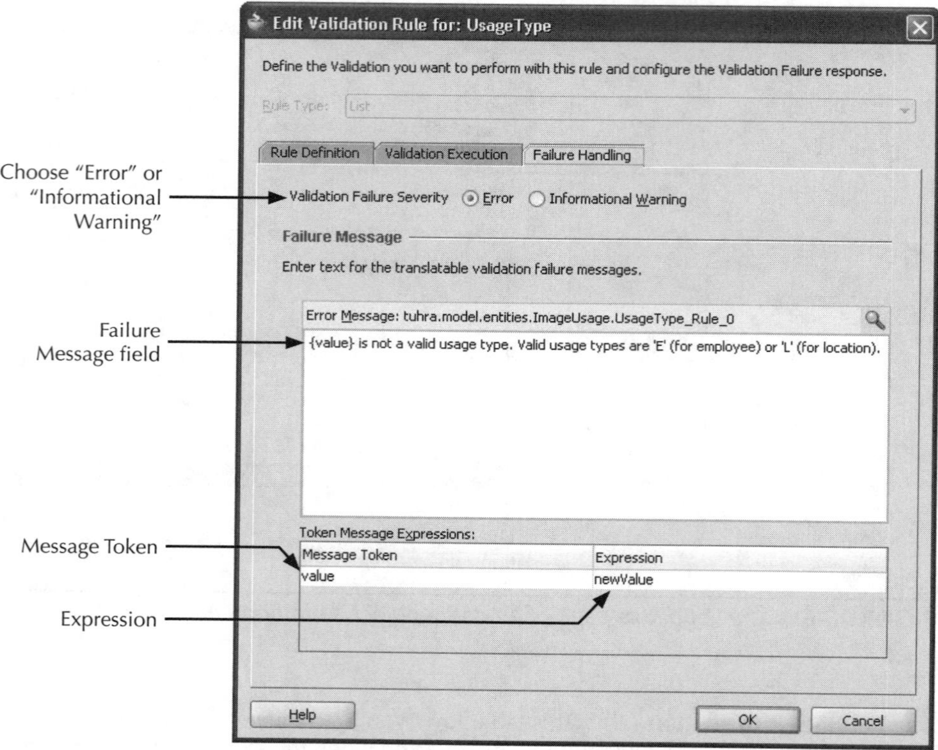

Errors cause the application's UI to flag the field and display an error message. They also prevent the attribute value from being changed. Informational warnings do not prevent the change of the attribute to the new value; they just cause the application's UI to flag the field and display a warning message.

You can enter a message in the *Failure Message* field. This field can contain identifiers in curly brackets for which Groovy expressions can be substituted. When you include an expression in curly brackets, the expression appears in the *Message Token* column of the *Token Message Expressions* table. You should enter the corresponding Groovy expression in the Expression column of that table. The same variables are available here as in the Validation Execution tab.

The Compare Validation Rule

The Compare validation rule allows you to specify that an attribute must stand in a relationship to a specified value. You can specify the value as a literal (such as "50" or "NAME"), as the first column of the first row of a SQL query, as a value of a view attribute in the first view row in a view object instance's cache, or as a value of a view attribute in the first view row of a view accessor (view attributes, view rows, view object instances, and view accessors are explained in Chapter 7). You can require that the attribute stand in any of the standard arithmetic relationships (such as equals or greater than) to the specified value. For example, the following image shows a validation rule requiring that the Salary attribute of Employees be less than or equal to 24000:

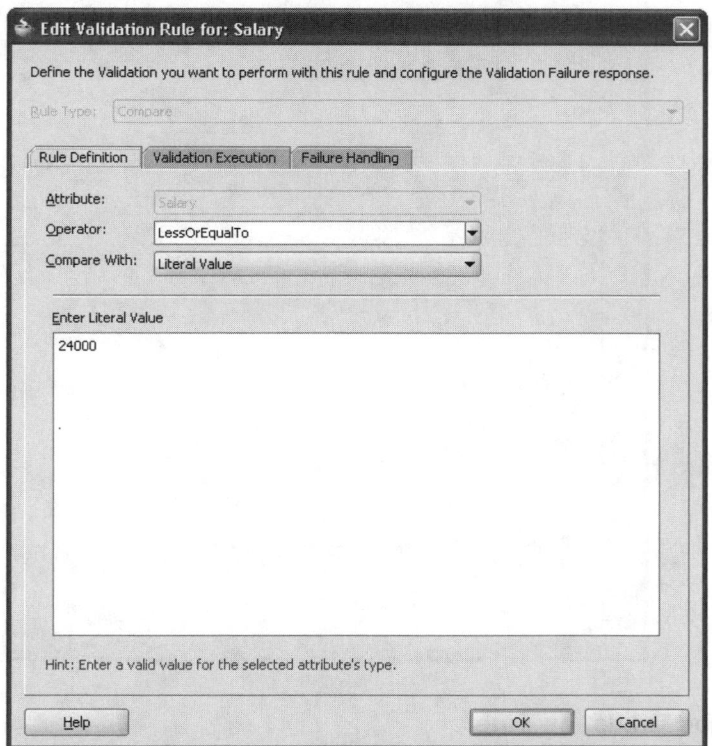

The Length Validation Rule

Some table columns specify a precision and/or scale, and these are enforced at the ADF BC level as explained in the section "Specifying Scale and Precision." However, for table columns that do not provide specifications that imply a maximum length, you can still enforce a maximum length using a Length validation rule. The rule allows you to specify a literal value, expressed in either bytes or characters. Validation will fail when an attempt is made to set the attribute to a value with length greater than that specified.

The List Validation Rule

The List validation rule allows you to provide a list of values, from which any value for the attribute must come. You can specify this list as a static list of literals, values from the first column returned by a SQL query, or values for a particular view attribute within a particular view object instance or view accessor's cache. For example, the following illustration shows a validation rule that requires the UsageType attribute of the ImageUsages entity object definition to match either "E" or "L":

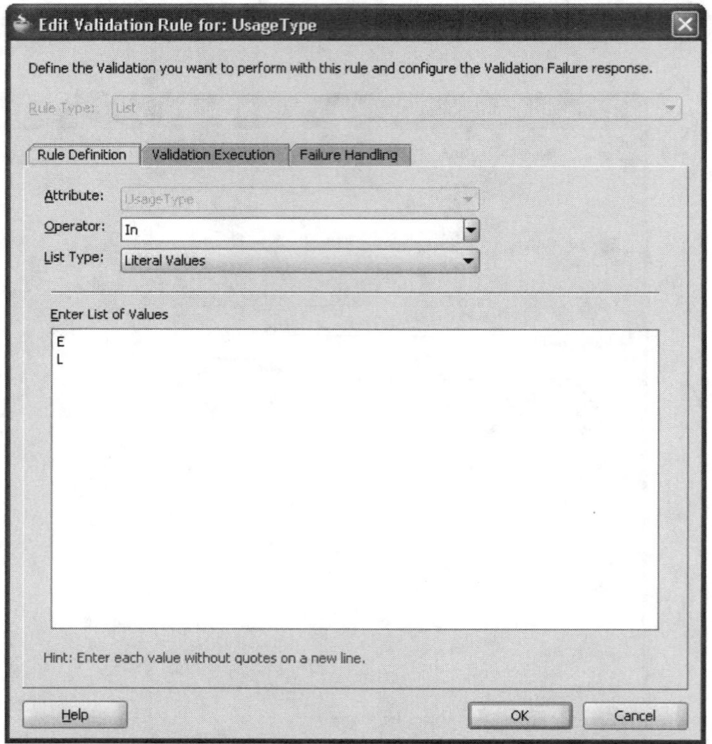

The Method Validation Rule

If you want to write a validation test in Java, you can do so with the Method validation rule. Adding a Method validation to an attribute automatically creates a public method with a return type of `boolean` and a single parameter with a type that matches the Java type of the attribute. You should then implement the method to return `true` if the parameter is an acceptable value for the attribute, and `false` if the parameter is not an acceptable value. For example, you could define a Method validation rule on the attribute Salary, generate a `validateSalary()` method stub in `EmployeesImpl`, and implement the method as follows (in `EmployeesImpl`) to require that an Employees instance's Salary be less than or equal to its manager's Salary:

```
public boolean validateSalary(Number value) {
  boolean isValid = true;
  EmployeesImpl mgr = getManager();
  if (mgr != null && getSalary() != null) {
    Number mgrSal = mgr.getSalary();
    if (mgrSal != null && mgrSal.intValue() < value.intValue()) {
      isValid = false;
  }
  return isValid;
}
```

When an attempt is made to change an attribute's value, the potential new value is passed in to the method, and validation fails if the method returns `false`.

The Range Validation Rule

The Range validation rule allows you to specify an inclusive range within which a value must or must not fall. Unlike the value used in a Compare validator, these values must be specified as literals.

The Regular Expression Validation Rule

The Regular Expression validation rule allows you to specify a Java-style regular expression that a potential attribute value must or must not match (for an explanation of Java-style regular expressions, which are very similar to Perl-style regular expressions, see the Javadoc for `java.util.regexp.Pattern`). When you add a Regular Expression validation rule to an attribute, you can enter your own regular expression or select from two predefined regular expressions:

- **Email Address** Uses the regular expression `[A-Z0-9._%+-]+@[A-Z0-9.-]+\.[A-Z]{2,4}`, which matches syntactically valid email addresses (except for case, but selecting Email Address also automatically marks the expression as case-insensitive, as explained later in this section)
- **Phone Number (US)** Uses the regular expression `[0-9]{3}-?[0-9]{3}-?[0-9]{4}`, which matches U.S. telephone numbers in the format xxx-xxx-xxxx

You can also select any of the following options:

- **Case Insensitive** Rules ignore mismatches due solely to the case of letters.
- **DotAll** Rules allow the dot character in their expressions to match any character, including line terminators (normally, dot characters do not match line terminators).
- **Multiline** Rules allow the `$` and `^` characters to match the beginning and end of lines (normally, those characters only match the beginning and end of the entire input).
- **Unicode Case** Rules support Unicode characters (normally, rules support only ASCII characters).
- **Canon Eq** Rules use canon equality, which allows you to use escaped formats for characters in the regular expression—for example, under canon equality, the expression `\u030A` matches the character `?`.

The following illustration shows a validation rule requiring that a Job instance's JobId be two capital letters, followed by an underscore, followed by 2–4 capital letters:

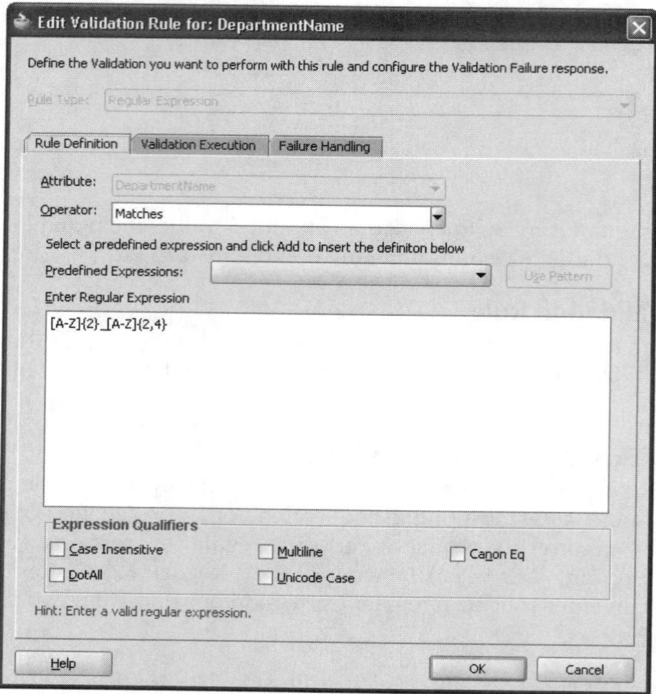

The Script Expression Validation Rule

The Script Expression validation rule allows you to specify a Groovy Boolean expression. The data is considered valid if the expression evaluates to `true`, and invalid if it evaluates to `false`. You can refer to the same contextual objects as in the Validation Execution tab. For example, the following expression would ensure that the Salary of an Employees instance is within the employee's Job's salary grade:

```
newValue == null || source.job == null ||
( ( source.job.minSalary == null ||
    newValue >= source.job.minSalary ) &&
  ( source.job.maxSalary == null ||
    newValue <= source.job.maxSalary )
)
```

Custom Validation Rules

With the preceding validation rules, especially the Method and Script Expression rules, you can implement any programmable requirement on an attribute's value. However, there are still reasons to create customized validation rules. You might have a type of requirement that cannot be implemented with one of the simpler validation rules (such as the Range rule), but wish to provide easier configuration for the rule than writing a method or Groovy expression.

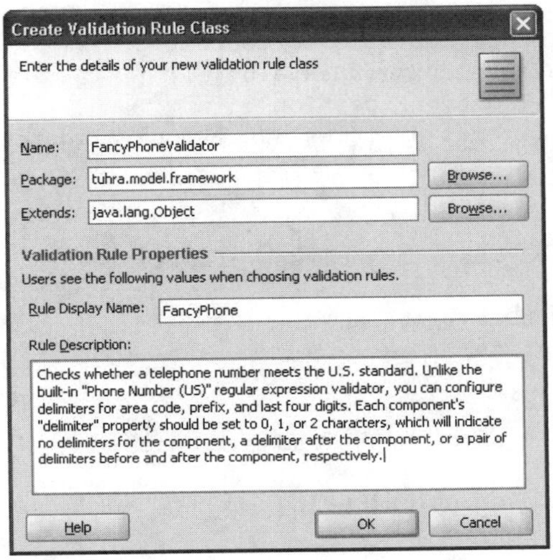

FIGURE 6-7. *The Create Validation Rule Class dialog*

Creating a custom validation rule requires some Java coding, but once it is created, it can be customized and used declaratively again and again.

A validation rule is any class that implements the interface `oracle.jbo.server.rules.JbiValidator` or `oracle.jbo.server.rules.JboValidatorInterface`. You can create your own validation rule by implementing this interface; JDeveloper will create a stub implementation of `JboValidatorInterface` for you if you select Validation Rule from the Business Components section of the New Gallery and complete a dialog like the one shown in Figure 6-7.

The stub contains simple implementations of all of the methods required by the `JboValidatorInterface` interface. For example, the stub created according to the dialog in Figure 6-7 is as follows:

```
package com.tuhra.model.entities;

import oracle.jbo.ValidationException;
import oracle.jbo.rules.JboValidatorContext;
import oracle.jbo.rules.JboValidatorInterface;

public class FancyPhoneValidator implements JboValidatorInterface {
  private String description = "Checks whether a telephone number " +
    "meets the U.S. standard.\n"         // Description continues

  public FancyPhoneValidator() {
  }

  /**Return true if value is valid.
   */
  public boolean validateValue(Object value) {
    return true;
  }
```

```
  /**Invoked by framework for validation.
   */
  public void validate(JboValidatorContext ctx) {
    if (!validateValue(ctx.getNewValue())) {
      throw new ValidationException(
        "com.tuhra.model.entities.FancyPhoneValidator validation failed");
    }
  }

  /**Description of what this class validates.
   */
  public String getDescription() {
    return description;
  }

  /**Description of what this class validates.
   */
  public void setDescription(String str) {
    description = str;
  }
}
```

Implementing validateValue() You should implement the `validateValue()` method to return true if the `value` parameter is an acceptable value, and false otherwise. You can also add fields (with getters and setters) that can be used to configure the validation rule; you can refer to these fields within your `validateValue()` method. For example, to implement this validation rule as described, you should create three additional `String` fields as shown next, and generate default accessors for them.

```
private String areaCodeDelimiter;
private String prefixDelimiter;
private String suffixDelimiter;
```

Then, you can refer to these fields inside your `validateValue()` method, as demonstrated here:

```
private static final String THREE_DIGIT_PATTERN = "[0-9]{3}";
private static final String FOUR_DIGIT_PATTERN = "[0-9]{4}";
private Pattern phonePattern = null;  // This field is initialized when first needed

/**Return true if value is valid.
 * This method uses the class java.util.regexp.Pattern to match a constructed
 * regular expression against the value's String representation.
 */
public boolean validateValue(Object value) {
  if (value == null) return true;
  if (phonePattern == null) {
    initPhonePattern();
  }
  return phonePattern.matcher(value.toString()).matches();
}

/**Configures the phone number Pattern based on the parameters
 * provided
```

```
 */
private void initPhonePattern() {
  String areaCodeRegexp = createRegexp(areaCodeDelimiter, THREE_DIGIT_PATTERN);
  String prefixRegexp = createRegexp(prefixDelimiter, THREE_DIGIT_PATTERN);
  String suffixRegexp = createRegexp(suffixDelimiter, FOUR_DIGIT_PATTERN);
  phonePattern = Pattern.compile(areaCodeRegexp+prefixRegexp+suffixRegexp);
}

/**Creates a regular expression by adding a delimiter to a base pattern
 * @return The new expression
 */
private String createRegexp(String delimiter,
                            String basePattern) {
  String regexp;
  switch (delimiter.length()) {
    case 0: regexp = basePattern;
            break;
    case 1: regexp = basePattern + delimiter;
            break;
    default: regexp = delimiter.charAt(0) + basePattern + delimiter.charAt(1);
  }
  return regexp;
}
```

Once you have created a validation rule, it will be available in the Add Validation Rule dialog's Validation Rule Type list. Your custom fields, as well as the `description` field, will be editable by the developer adding the rule to an attribute. For example, the following illustration shows the rule configured to accept phone numbers in the format (xxx)xxx-xxxx:

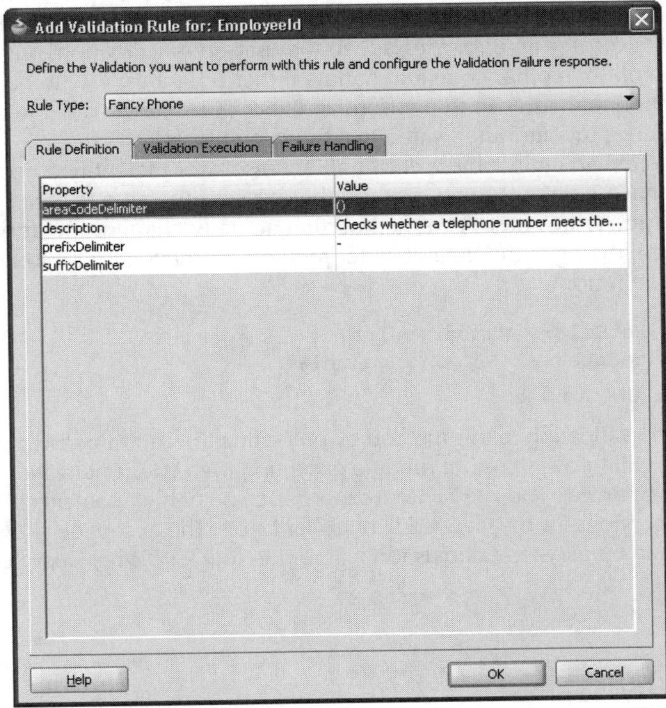

This could have been accomplished by configuring a Regular Expression validation rule for the phone number format appropriate to each use case, but applying the Fancy Phone validation rule does not require writing any regular expressions; once the rule is created, applying it to attributes is easy.

ADF allows you to define a custom Swing `JPanel`, which can act as a more user-friendly Rule Definition tab for custom validation rules. For example, you could create a Rule Definition tab that treats the Description as help text, has rollover help for each field, or limits the number of characters you can enter into each delimiter field to 2 (since characters past the second in a delimiter are ignored). However, creating these special customizers is beyond the scope of this book; for more information, see Section 37.9.2, "Adding a Design Time Bean Customizer for Your Rule," of the *Fusion ADF Developer's Guide*.

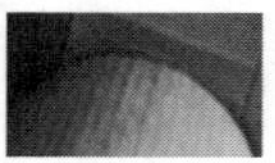

TIP
As with custom framework classes, we recommend implementing custom validation rules (and their customizers, if any) in a separate application that can be deployed as a JAR file and reused as a library across the enterprise.

Adding Validation to Setter Methods

The standard Java method for validating field values is to add logic to the methods that set those values. You can use a similar technique to add validation logic to entity object attributes. Because of the comparative flexibility of the 11*g* declarative validation framework, we do not suggest using setter validation nearly as often as in previous releases of JDeveloper. However, sometimes you may need greater control than even the new validation framework provides. For example, you may not want to display an error message to the user upon validation, but instead catch the validation exception in other code and handle it there. The best way to do this is to create a custom exception that you can throw from an entity object setter method, and wrap code that attempts to change the attribute's value in a try/catch block.

If you generate an entity object class and accessors for the entity object's attributes, each attribute will have a default setter method that passes the value to `EntityImpl.setAttributeInternal()`, a method that actually changes the attribute's value. For example, the following is the default setter method for the Salary attribute of the Employees entity object definition:

```
public void setSalary(Number value) {
  setAttributeInternal(SALARY, value);
}
```

You can add validation to this method by preceding the call to `setAttributeInternal()` with code that will throw a custom runtime exception if `value` is not valid. This runtime exception should extend `oracle.jbo.ValidationException`, which contains functionality to assist with marshaling exceptions for the view and controller layers. The exception shown next, which you might throw if an employee's salary is too high or too low for his/her salary grade, is an example:

```
package com.tuhra.model.framework.exceptions;

import oracle.jbo.ValidationException;

public class SalaryOutOfRangeException extends ValidationException {

  private final Number salary;
  private final Number violatedBoundary;
  private final boolean boundaryMin;

  /** Creates an exception for an employee salary with a range outside his/her
   * salary range
   * @param salary The the out-of-range salary value
   * @param violatedBoundary The value of the boundary the salary violates
   * @param boundaryMin Whether the violated boundary is the minimum
   * (false means the violated salary is the maximum)
   */
  public SalaryOutOfRangeException(Number salary,
                                   Number violatedBoundary,
                                   boolean boundaryMin) {
    super("Salary out of range for this employee's job");
    this.salary = salary;
    this.violatedBoundary = violatedBoundary;
    this.boundaryMin = boundaryMin;
  }

  /** Returns the problematic salary.
   */
  public Number getSalary() {
    return salary;
  }

  /** Returns the violated boundary salary.
   */
  public Number getViolatedBoundary() {
    return violatedBoundary;
  }

  /** Returns whether the violated salary is the minimum.
   *  @return true, if the violated salary is the minimum,
   *  false if it is the maximum
   */
  public boolean isBoundaryMin() {
    return boundaryMin;
  }
}
```

Once you have created a custom exception, you can use it in the entity attribute's setter method, as shown next:

```
public void setSalary(Number value) {
  EntityImpl job = getJob();          // Call an association accessor method
  if (value != null && job != null) {
    Number minSal = job.getAttribute("MinSalary");
    if (minSal != null && value.intValue() < minSal.intValue()) {
      throw new SalaryOutOfRangeException(value, minSal, true);
    }
    Number maxSal = job.getAttribute("MaxSalary");
    if (maxSal != null && value.intValue() > maxSal.intValue()) {
      throw new SalaryOutOfRangeException(value, maxSal, false);
    }
  }
  setAttributeInternal(DATAPRECISION, value);
}
```

This code throws the custom exception if a user tries to set the Salary attribute to a value outside the range for the employee's job.

You can wrap any block of code in your application that might change the Salary of an Employees entity object instance to a try/catch block that handles a `SalaryOutOfRangeException`, such as the following trivial code that prints an error message to the console:

```
try {
  methodThatMightChangeSalary();
} catch (SalaryOutOfBoundsException e) {
  System.err.println("Salary " + e.getSalary() +
                     " is out of range. Salary must be at " +
                     e.isBoundaryMin()?"least ":"most " +
                     e.getViolatedBoundary() + ".");
}
```

Alternatively, you can let ADF handle the error; the message the user will see will be the argument passed to `super()`: "Salary out of range for this employee's job."

Validation Domains

Custom domains can also be used to provide validation. These domains, called validation domains, wrap other domains or standard Java classes (such as String) that can be used as attribute types, but include validation code as well. These domains can be used for many attributes just by setting the attribute's type to the validation domain. For example, suppose (as in the section "The Regular Expression Validation Rule") that you want to require that various attributes follow the standard format for a job ID (two capital letters, followed by an underscore, followed by 2–4 capital letters), but that you do not want to attach a validation rule to every such attribute. You can instead create a validation domain that you can use as a datatype for each of the attributes.

Creating a Validation Domain

You can create a validation domain by selecting **New Domain** from the right-click menu of a Business Components package, or by selecting Domain from the "Business Tier\ADF Business Components" section of the New Gallery, and ensuring that "Domain for an Oracle Object Type" is not selected on the first page of the Create Domain Wizard that opens. On the second page of the wizard, you can select which existing Java type you want the domain to wrap, as well as several other settings, as shown here:

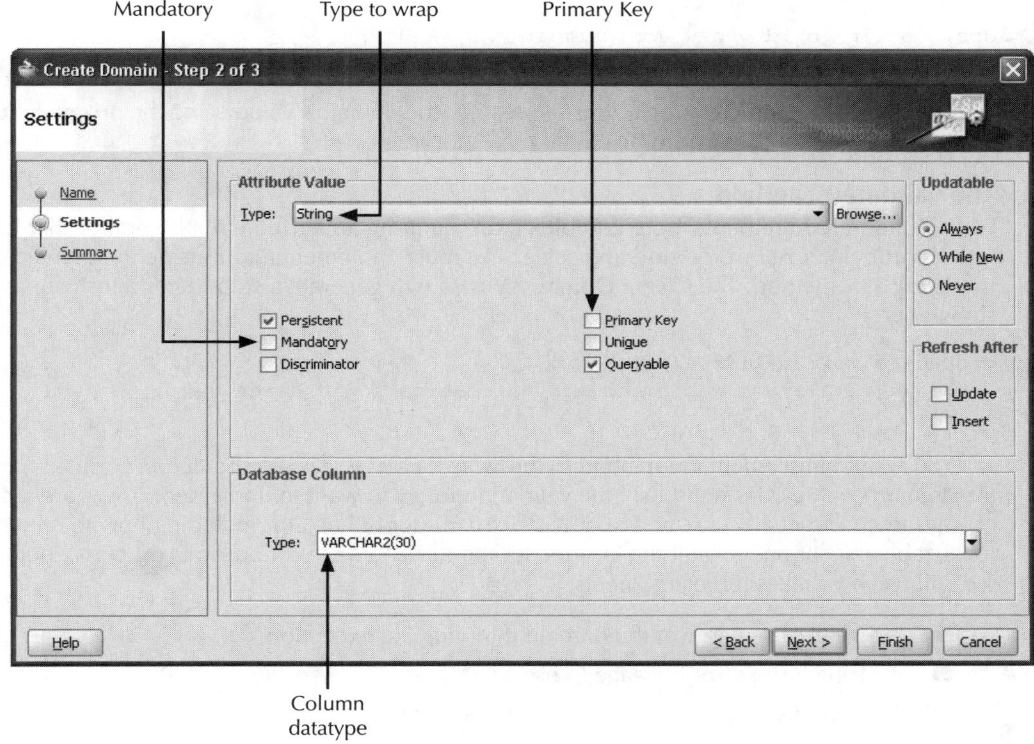

By selecting settings such as *Mandatory* or *Primary Key*, or by specifying a size, scale, or precision for the domain, you can require that all attributes with the domain as their datatype have those properties. For example, attributes with a mandatory domain as their type must always be mandatory; attributes with a primary key domain as their type are always parts of their entity object definition's primary key, and attributes that have a domain that maps to a VARCHAR(30) can only have 30 characters in their values.

Working with Validation Domain Values

The way to retrieve the value of a validation domain depends on the type of domain that the validation domain wraps. Domains that wrap other domains (such as a domain that wraps `Number`) actually extend those domains and have transparent constructors. So, for example, if `NumberValidationDomain` wraps `Number`, you can construct a `NumberValidationDomain` from an `int`, `float`, `long`, `double`, or any of a long list of numeric types, just as you would construct a `Number`, and you can extract a value using methods such as `intValue()`, `floatValue()`, `longValue()`, and `doubleValue()`, as shown here:

```
NumberValidationDomain five = new NumberValidationDomain(5);
int fiveInt = five.intValue();
```

Domains that wrap nondomain Java types (such as `String`) include constructors that take an argument of that type (and use it as the value of the domain), and a method, `getData()`, that returns the object. `getData()` has a return type of `Object`, so you must cast it to the appropriate type to work with it, as shown here, with a domain that wraps a `String`:

```
JobIdDomain jobId = new JobIdDomain("AD_PRES");
int jobIdLength = ((String) jobId.getData()).length();
```

Within the domain class itself, you can refer to the domain's value using the private field `mData`, which does not need to be cast.

The validate() Method

For validation requirements more complex than requiring an attribute not be null or that it fit into a particular size or precision and scale, you must implement a test inside the domain class' `validate()` method. The Create Domain Wizard will generate a stub method for you, as shown here:

```
protected void validate() {
  //  ### Implement custom domain validation logic here. ###
}
```

You should implement the method to throw an `oracle.jbo.DataCreationException` if the domain's value does not satisfy the validation rule you want to implement. There are a number of ways to construct a `DataCreationException` (for full details, including how to construct a localizable exception, consult the Javadoc for the `DataCreationException` class), but the one we will use here takes three arguments:

- **A String** The name of the domain throwing the exception
- **A String** The error message to use
- **An Exception** A root cause of the exception (which can be null in most cases)

The method does not need to do anything if the domain's value satisfies the validation rule you want to implement.

The following code implements the `validate()` method for a domain that requires its String value to be in standard Job ID format.

```
private static Pattern regex = Pattern.compile("[A-Z]{2}_[A-Z]{2,4}");

protected void validate() {
  if (mData != null && ! regex.matcher(mData).matches()) {
    throw new DataCreationException(getClass().getName(),
      mData + " is not a valid Job ID.",
      null);
  }
}
```

How Do You Implement Entity-Level Validation?

Some validation logic does not apply to a single attribute, but rather to multiple attributes in the same row. For example, you might want to require that an Employees instance's salary be over

15,000 if, and only if, the instance is an executive (with job ID "AD_VP" or "AD_PRES"). You cannot apply this logic as an attribute-level validation for the following reasons:

- **You cannot implement this validation on the Salary attribute alone** It has to be applied when a user enters or changes the value of JobId.
- **You cannot implement this validation on the JobId attribute alone** It has to be applied when users enter or change the value of Salary.
- **You cannot implement this validation twice** You can't implement it on both the Salary and JobId attributes, since it will then be impossible to change either—as soon as the first one is changed, validation will fail (since the second hasn't yet been changed to match) and the change will be rejected.

This kind of business rule requires entity-level validation, that is, value-checking logic that applies to an entire row, rather than to a single attribute. Entity-level validation is not invoked as soon as an attribute changes value. Rather, when an attribute value changes, the entity object will be marked as needing validation. This validation can be enforced when a user changes rows or tries to commit a row.

Entity-Level Validation Rules

In addition to applying a validation rule to an entity object attribute, you can apply a rule to an entire entity object definition; any such rule will be enforced at the entity level. You can apply an entity-level validation rule on the Validators tab of an entity object definition's editor by selecting the Entity node in the tree and clicking the "Create a New Validator" (green plus "+" button), shown in Figure 6-6. This opens the Add Validation Rule dialog, just as it does when you apply a validation rule to an entity attribute (as in the section "Attribute-Level Validation Rules"). Similarly, you can edit an entity-level validation rule by double-clicking it in the Validators tab; this action opens the Edit Validation Rule dialog.

The Validation Execution tab on these dialogs is more complex than that for attribute-level validation rules, and the list of rules available at the entity level is different.

The Validation Execution Tab for Entity-Level Validation Rules

The Validation Execution tab for entity-level rules is shown in Figure 6-8. As with the tab for attribute-level rules, it contains a Conditional Execution Expression field in which you can enter a Groovy Boolean expression; the validation rule will only be checked if the expression evaluates to true.

The tab contains other controls as well. One is a pair of radio buttons:

- **Execute at Entity Level** The default setting; this causes the validation rule to fire (assuming other conditions are met) whenever the user navigates away from a row or attempts to commit.
- **Defer Execution to Transaction Level** Only enabled for the Key Exists and Method validation rules; this causes the validation rule to fire only when the user attempts to commit data. This provides less regular user feedback but can be significantly more efficient.

Additionally, the tab allows you to select an "Execute Only if One of the Selected Values Has Been Changed" checkbox and then use a shuttle control to select one or more entity attributes.

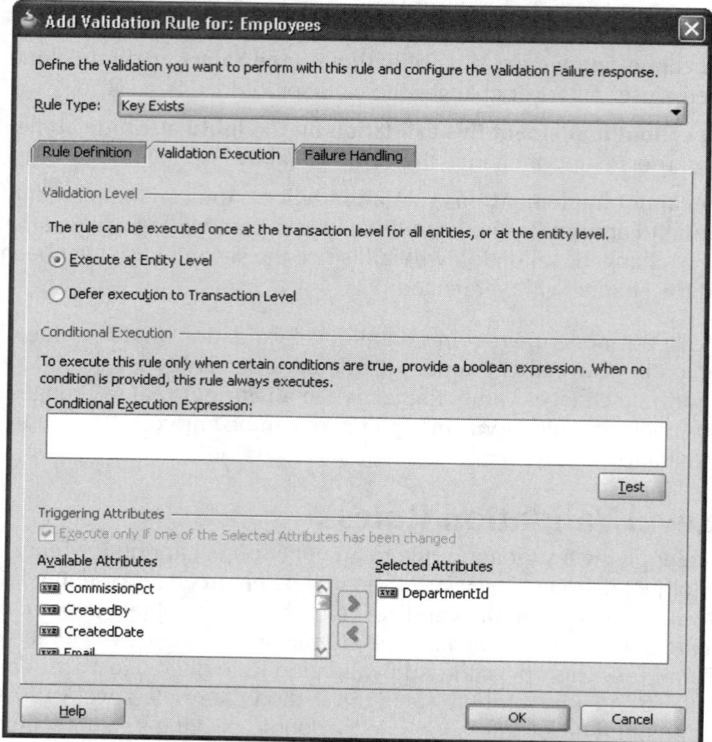

FIGURE 6-8. *The Validation Execution tab of the Add Validation Rule dialog for entity-level validation rules*

The rule will only fire (on navigation or commit) if it has not yet been fired since one of the selected attributes changed. For example, in the case of the rule, "Employees instance's salary must be over 15,000 if, and only if, the instance is an executive," you could select this option and the Salary and JobId entity attributes, and this would cause the rule to execute only if one or both of those attributes has changed.

Attribute-Level Rules at the Entity Object Level

All the rules covered in the section "Attribute-Level Validation Rules" are available for Entity-Level validation rules, and there are only a few differences in the way they work:

- **The rules will not execute when an attempt is made to set or change an attribute value** Rather, they will execute when you specify on the Validation Execution tab.
- **You must select an attribute on the Rule Definition tab** This is true for all of these rules, with the exception of the Method and Script Expression validation rules.
- **You cannot use the newValue Groovy Variable** This is true in the Script Expression validation rule or the Validation Execution tab for any of the rules; by the time the rules are executed, the value of the attribute will already have been set.

- **No parameters are generated** For methods generated for a Method validation rule, access entity attributes in this method using their getters.

The Collection Validation Rule

If the entity object definition contains an association accessor that retrieves the children of a composition, you can apply a Collection validation rule. This rule acts like the Compare attribute-level validation rule, except that instead of comparing an attribute with a value, the Collection rule performs a group function on an attribute of the child entity object instances and compares that with a value.

For example, suppose you wanted to require that no image be used in multiple usage types. You could implement this with a Collection validation rule, as shown here:

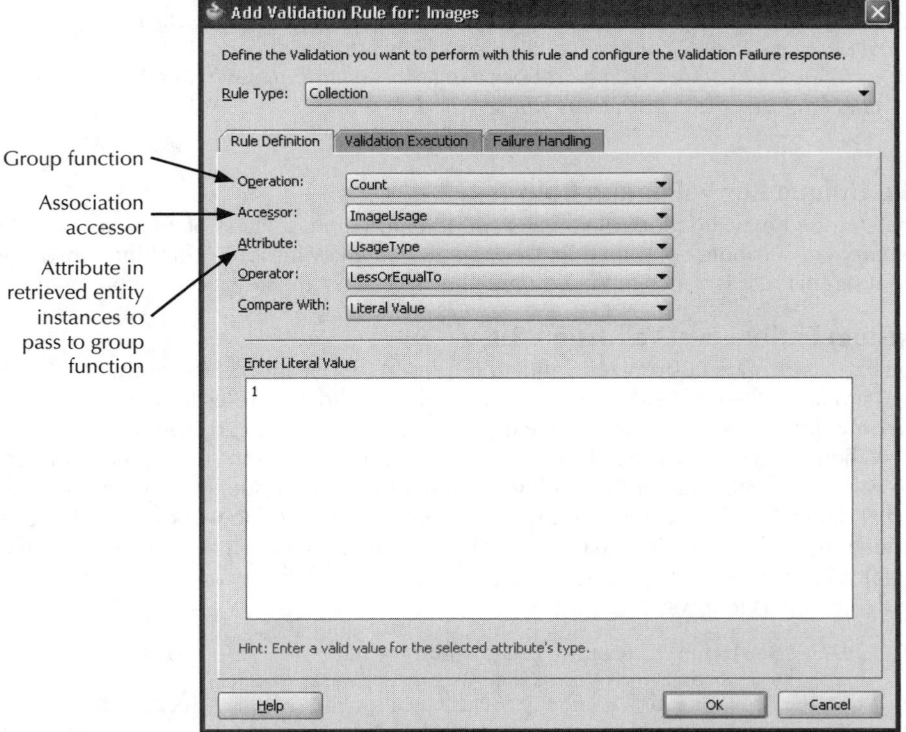

The Key Exists Validation Rule

As stated in the section "What Is an Association?"—associations, with the exception of compositions, do not enforce FOREIGN KEY constraints; they allow you to create entity object instances on the "many" side of a one-to-many (or many-to-one) association with no corresponding entity object instances on the "one" side. To actually enforce a FOREIGN KEY constraint on the destination of an association, you can use the Key Exists validation rule.

Creating this rule requires that you select an association for which the entity object definition represents the "many" side. Whenever the rule is fired for an instance of the entity object definition,

ADF BC will ensure that there is a corresponding entity object instance on the "one" side, and will throw an exception if there isn't.

NOTE

You will usually not need to specify a Key Exists validation rule, even if you must ensure that the key exists. As explained in the "What Are View Link Definitions and View Link Instances?" section of Chapter 7, it is possible to configure your data model so that foreign key attributes of detail rows are automatically configured to match the referenced attributes in the selected master row. If you do not provide the UI for your users to change these attributes from the automatic configuration, it will not be possible to use your application to create orphaned detail rows. You will only need to use the rule if it is not feasible to create your application this way (for example, if you must allow users to enter or change the foreign key attributes manually), or if you have code that may set or change these attributes without checking that the constraint is still satisfied.

The Unique Key Validation Rule

The Unique Key validation rule allows you to enforce uniqueness of an entity object definition's primary key attribute combination, or of an alternate key attribute combination, if one exists. Creating this rule is very simple; you only have to select the key from a dropdown list.

Custom Entity-Level Validation Rules

You can also create customized validation rules for application at the entity level. This process is very similar to the process for creating customized validation rules for attribute-level validation; the only difference is the way in which you implement the `validateValue()` method.

When `validateValue()` is called for a custom validation rule applied at the entity level, the value parameter, rather than being a potential attribute value, is the entity object instance to be validated. You can cast the value to `EntityImpl` in order to work with it. For example, a validation rule that required that one attribute of an entity object instance be a prefix (proper initial substring) of another attribute of that instance might have a `validateValue()` method implemented as follows:

```
public boolean validateValue(Object value) {
  EntityImpl entityToValidate = (EntityImpl) value;
  Object prefixObj = entityToValidate.getAttribute(prefixAttr);
  Object fullStringObj = entityToValidate.getAttribute(fullStringAttr);
  if (!(prefixObj instanceof String) || !(fullStringObj instanceof String)) {
    throw new NonStringPrefixValidatorException();
  }
  String prefix = (String) prefixObj;
  String fullString = (String) fullStringObj;
  return (prefix != null && fullString != null &&
    prefix.length() > 0 && prefix.length() < fullString.length() &&
    fullString.startsWith(prefix));
}
```

The preceding code executes the following steps:

- **Line 2** Cast the value parameter to `EntityImpl`.
- **Lines 3–4** Retrieve the value of two attributes from the entity to validate. `prefixAttr` and `fullStringAttr` would need to be added to the validation rule class as `String` fields with default getters and setters; they are the customizable entity attribute names for the prefix and the attribute of which it should be a prefix.
- **Lines 5–7** Throw an exception if either attribute value is not a `String`; this means that the validation rule has not been correctly applied. `NonStringPrefixValidatorException` would need to be created separately (as a subclass of `JboException`).
- **Lines 8–9** Cast the attribute values to `String` so that they can be compared.
- **Lines 10–13** Return true if neither attribute value is null and the attribute value that is supposed to be a prefix of the other attribute value is in fact a proper initial substring of that attribute value.

Validation in the Entity Object Class

As with attribute-level validation, the ADF BC validation framework is more powerful than in previous releases, and we recommend using validation outside that framework only in special cases, particularly in the case where you need to throw a custom exception on validation failure because you have written other code that can catch and handle that exception.

The validateEntity() Method

The method `EntityImpl.validateEntity()` is called whenever a user tries to navigate between rows or commit a transaction. You can override this method to throw an instance of `JboException` (generally, an instance of a custom subclass) if your validation requirements are not satisfied, just as you can for setter methods at the attribute level.

An overridden version of `validateEntity()` should always include, in a `finally` block, a call to the superclass method. The following example shows a possible `validateEntity()` method in `EmployeesImpl`; the method throws a `SalaryMismatchException` if either the Salary is greater than 15,000 for a nonexecutive or the Salary is less than 15,000 for an executive. (The exception is a subclass of `JboException` and not shown):

```
protected void validateEntity() {
  try {
    testSalaryForExec();
  } finally {
    super.validateEntity();
  }
}

private void testSalaryForExec() {
  Number salary = getSalary();
  String jobId = getJobId();
  if (salary != null && jobId != null) {
    if ( salary.intValue() > 15000 &&            // Salary too high for
         ! jobId.equals("AD_PRES") &&            // non-executive
         ! jobId.equals("AD_VP") ) {
```

```
        throw new SalaryMismatchException(salary, jobId,
                                          SalaryMismatchException.TOO_HIGH);
      } else if ( salary.intValue() < 15000 &&    // Salary too low for
                ( jobId.equals("AD_PRES") ||      // executive
                  jobId.equals("AD_VP") ) {
        throw new SalaryMismatchException(salary, jobId,
                                          SalaryMismatchException.TOO_LOW);
      }
    }
  }
```

The beforeCommit() Method

The method `EntityImpl.beforeCommit()` is called right before a transaction is committed to the database. You can override this method to throw an instance of `JboException` if your validation requirements are not satisfied. This is similar to an entity-level validation rule that has been deferred to the transaction level, as described in the section "The Validation Execution Tab for Entity-Level Validation Rules." `EntityImpl.beforeCommit()` takes a single argument of type `oracle.jbo.server.TransactionEvent`. For almost all purposes, you can ignore this parameter; just pass it to the superclass method in a `finally` block at the end of your overridden method.

The following code enforces the same validation requirements as the `validateEntity()` method in the section "The validateEntity() Method," except this code defers validation until the user tries to commit the row. It makes use of the method `testSalaryForExec()` from the code listing in that section.

```
public void beforeCommit(TransactionEvent transactionEvent) {
  try {
    testPctUsedPctFree();
  } finally {
    super.beforeCommit(transactionEvent);
  }
}
```

If you write validation logic in a beforeCommit() method, you must set the configuration property *jbo.txn.handleafterpostexc* to `true`. Setting configuration properties is explained in Chapter 7, in the section, "Editing or Creating Configurations for Application Module Definitions."

How Does the ADF BC Validation Cycle Work?

Not all implementations of validation logic are equivalent; they fire at different times. This can be important when some validation tests assume others have been passed, or rely on side effects of other validation code.

The Attribute-Level Validation Process

Figure 6-9 shows the flow of attribute-level validation. Validation code contained in validation domains fires first, when the new values for entity object attributes are first created. If the data passes that test, an attempt is made to set the entity object attribute to the new value. The framework invokes the attribute's setter method, and any tests that have been implemented in setter

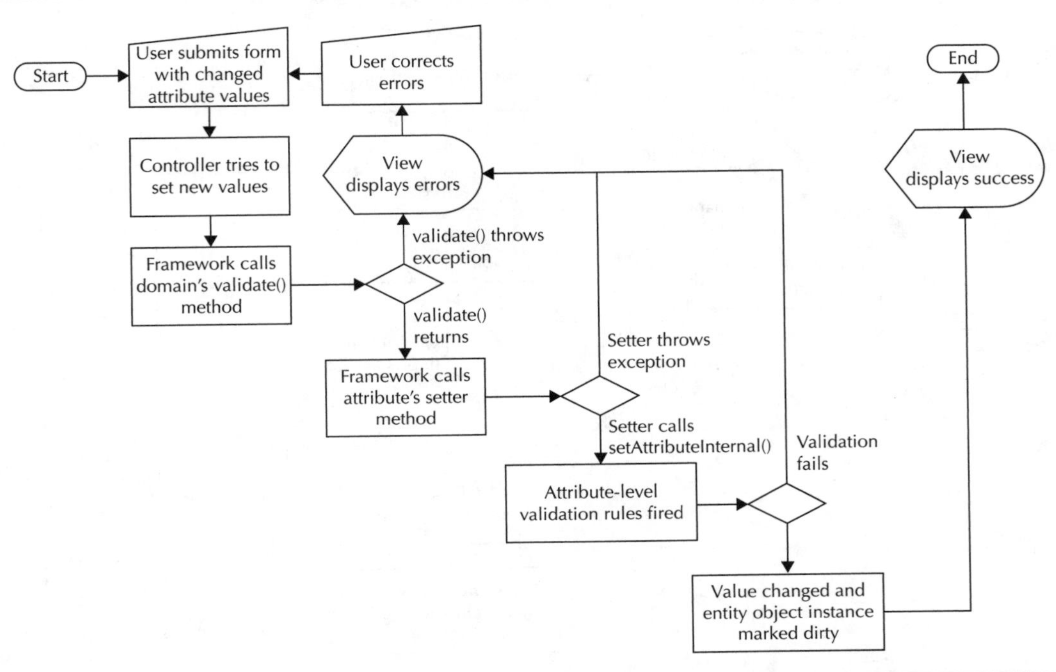

FIGURE 6-9. *Attribute-level validation*

code execute. If those tests do not throw an exception, the setter method reaches its last line, the call to `setAttributeInternal()`. It is during the execution of `setAttributeInternal()` that attribute-level validators fire. If the data passes this final test, the value of the attribute is actually changed, and the row is marked as "dirty," requiring entity-level validation.

The Nondeferred Entity-Level Validation Process

Figure 6-10 shows the flow of nondeferred entity-level validation, such as what occurs on the old row whenever a user navigates from one row to another. If the form submission (which occurs during any navigation event) also involves submission of new values for the attributes, these values must first undergo attribute-level validation as shown in Figure 6-9. In either case, the row checks to see whether it has been marked as "dirty" by an attribute change, and if so, nondeferred entity-level validation proceeds. First, the framework calls the `validateEntity()` method on the entity object instance, and any tests that have been implemented in an overridden version of the method execute. If those tests do not throw an exception, the method reaches its last line, the call to the superclass method. This method invokes any nondeferred entity-level validation rules that apply; if the entity object is successfully validated, it is marked as "clean" and navigation is allowed to proceed.

When an entity object instance is a container in a composition, it will perform entity-level validation on its containees whenever it undergoes entity-level validation (this occurs as the last step in the validation process).

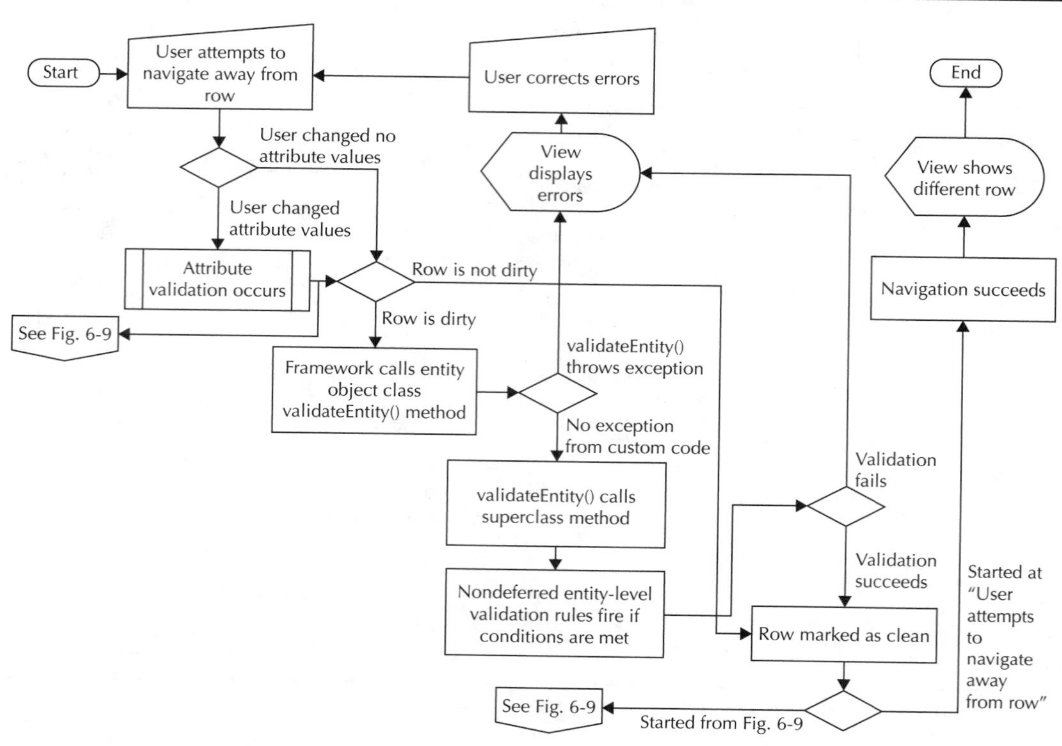

FIGURE 6-10. *Nondeferred entity-level validation*

The Deferred Entity-Level Validation Process

Figure 6-11 shows the flow of entity-level validation that has been deferred to an attempt to commit the transaction. As with row navigation, when a user submits a commit request, any new attribute values posted with the request must go through attribute-level validation. Then, the framework performs nondeferred entity-level validation, as shown in Figure 6-10, on any dirty entity object instances that remain in the cache. If the entity object instances are validated successfully, they are posted to the database, and the framework prepares for a `commit()` operation. Then, the framework invokes any deferred entity-level validation rules that apply, as shown in Figure 6-11. When this process has been performed on each entity object instance in the cache, the commit operation proceeds.

Validation Loops

Java code in setters, the `validateEntity()` or `beforeCommit()` method, or custom validation rules, and Groovy expressions used in Script Expression validators or other locations, can change attributes as side effects. For example, if the `validateEntity()` method in `EmployeesImpl` calls a setter method, it will have the effect of changing an attribute value during validation.

If this happens, ADF BC will start the validation cycle over as soon as it completes, since the entity object instance is now in a new state—possibly an invalid one. However, to avoid the risk

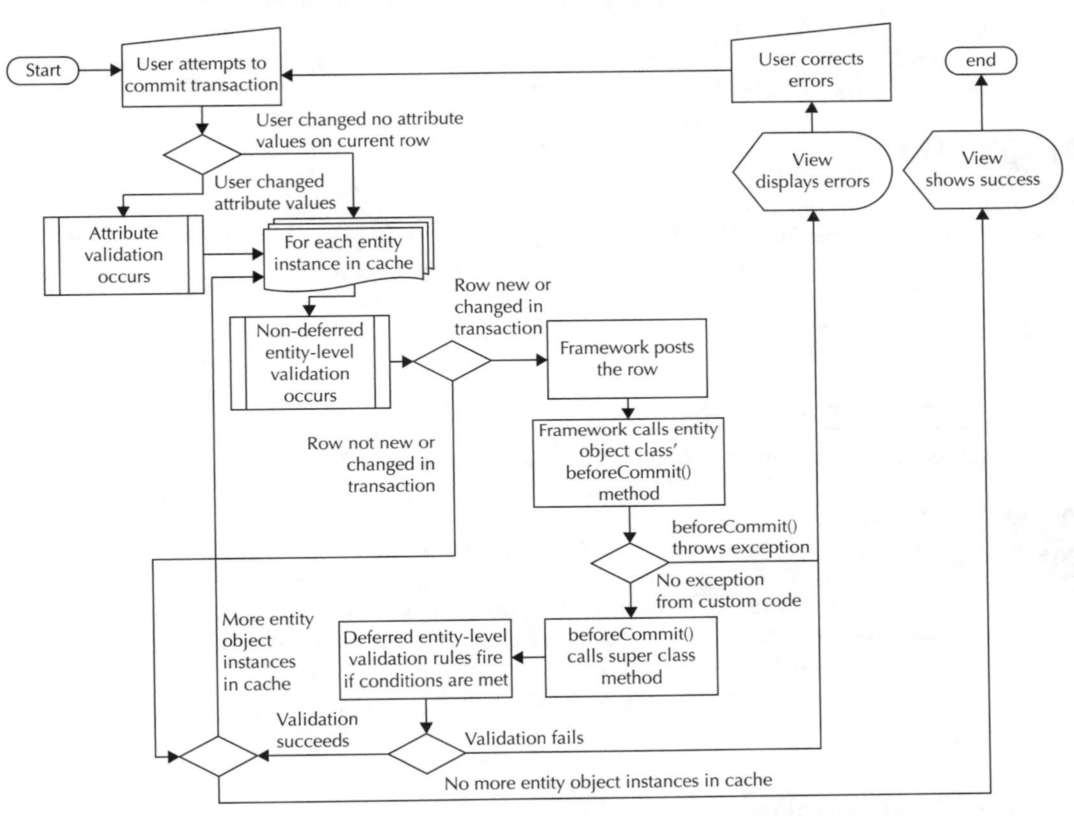

FIGURE 6-11. *Deferred entity-level validation*

of infinite loops, ADF BC imposes a limit on the number of times it will perform the validation cycle because of attribute changes that are side effects of validation. If the last pass through the cycle changes attribute values as a result of side effects, the validation process will throw a `JboException` with the message "JBO-28200: Validation threshold limit reached. Invalid Entities still in cache." To avoid this exception, you should be careful to ensure that any form of validation that might change attributes will eventually hit a base case where no attributes are changed, and that this will happen before the validation threshold is reached.

The validation threshold defaults to 10. You can change this by changing the *jbo.validation.threshold* property in an application module definition's configuration, as described in Chapter 7.

How Do You Implement Attribute Defaulting and Calculation?

Defaulting and calculation are two ways of automatically providing attribute values. *Defaulting* provides an initial value for an attribute when a new row is created. This value may change later, but an initial starting point is supplied by the system, not the user. This is analogous to a BEFORE

INSERT trigger in the database that calculates a value for one or more columns when none is supplied by the INSERT statement. *Calculation* applies to attributes that are not stored persistently, but rather are continuously maintained based on the value of other attributes. This is analogous to what is done by a database view with derived columns.

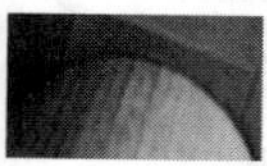

NOTE
The word "calculation" is used here in a very specific way. You can, of course, calculate values for persistent attributes by programmatically calling those attributes' setters. "Calculation," as we are using the term, applies to attributes whose values are always determined by an expression or formula rather than a value stored for them in a table field.

Attribute Defaulting

Persistent attributes can be defaulted for new entity object instances in a number of ways.

NOTE
In the large majority of cases, you do not need to default foreign key attributes, even if you want detail entity object instances to start out with master entity object instances. The framework will automatically default these values for you based on the way the application module instance's data model is set up; for more information, see the section "What Are View Link Definitions and View Link Instances?" in Chapter 7.

Literal Default Values

The simplest sort of defaulting is when you want each new row to share a common specific value. For example, you might want the CommissionPct attribute of all new Employees entity object instances to start out as `0`. You can implement this default by selecting "Literal" in the *Value Type* radio group on the Entity Attribute page of the Attribute Editor or the Attribute Settings page of the Create Entity Object Wizard, as shown in Figure 6-5, and then entering a value directly into the *Value* field.

Groovy-Calculated Default Values

In many cases, you need a default value for an attribute to vary depending on the circumstances in which the entity object instance is created, such as the initial value of other attributes, attribute values from an associated entity object instance, or the current system time. You can implement this dynamic defaulting of attributes using a Groovy expression. Select Expression in the *Value Type* radio group on the Entity Attribute page of the Attribute Editor or the Attribute Settings page of the Create Entity Object Wizard, as shown in Figure 6-5, and then click the Edit button beside the *Value* field to open the Edit Expression dialog, shown next:

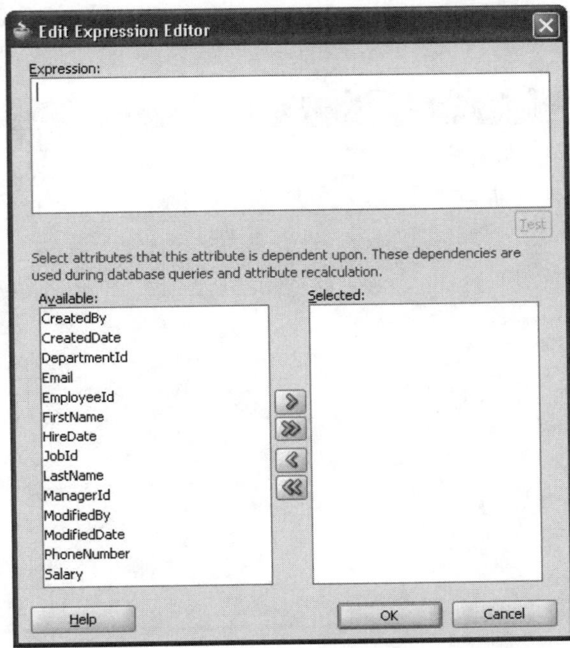

In the *Expression* field, you can enter any Groovy expression that evaluates to the correct datatype, using the same variables described in the section "How Do You Implement Attribute-Level Validation Rules?" The shuttle is ignored when you use this dialog to calculate default values.

Java-Calculated Default Values

If you do not want to use Groovy in your project, you can also calculate default values in Java code in an entity object class.

You can set attribute default values in Java by overriding the method `EntityImpl.create()` and setting attribute values there after a call to the superclass method, as shown here (this code could appear in the entity object class for the Employees entity object definition):

```
protected void create(AttributeList attrs) {
  super.create(attrs);
  setHiredate(new Date(Date.getCurrentDate()));
}
```

Other modes of attribute defaulting occur during the call to the superclass method, so in your custom code, you can assume that these values are already populated.

Attribute Calculation

The first step in providing a calculated attribute is to create a transient attribute. You can create a transient attribute by clicking the Create New Attribute (green plus "+") button on the Attributes page of an entity object definition's editor, as shown in Figure 6-4, or the New button on the

Attributes page of the Create Entity Object Wizard. This opens the New Entity Attribute dialog, shown next:

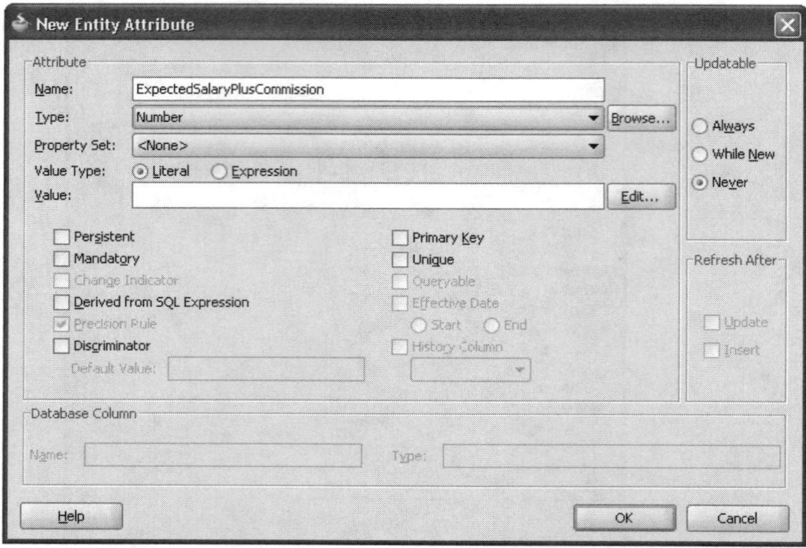

Specify a name and Java type for the attribute and deselect the Persistent checkbox to make the attribute transient. In addition, the user should not be able to change the value of most calculated attributes, which you can enforce by selecting the Never radio button in the Updatable area.

Once you have created a transient attribute, you can implement a calculation for it.

Calculating an Attribute Value Using Groovy

The process of calculating an attribute value with a Groovy expression is similar to the process of defaulting an attribute value with a Groovy expression. While editing a transient attribute, select "Expression" in the *Value Type* radio group and then click the Edit button beside the *Value* field to open the Edit Expression dialog, just as you would to implement defaulting for a persistent attribute. However, the version of the Edit Expression dialog for transient attributes (shown here) is different than that for persistent attributes.

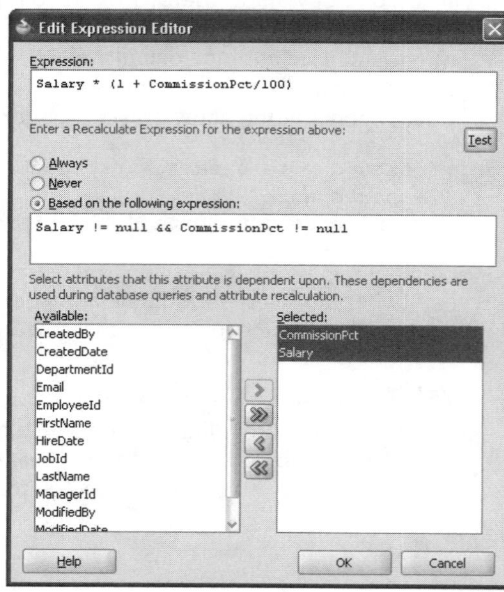

As in the persistent attribute version of the Edit Expression dialog, you can edit a Groovy expression that evaluates to the correct Java type in the *Expression* field. However, then you can select a radio button to determine whether the expression is considered for re-evaluation every time a change is made to an entity object instance, never (that is, if the expression is only evaluated when an entity object instance is first created or retrieved from the database), or according to a separate Boolean Groovy expression. You can further limit attribute recalculation by selecting attributes using the shuttle; the expression will only be re-evaluated if (in addition to the Boolean expression evaluating to true, if a Boolean expression is used) one of the selected attributes has changed.

Calculating an Attribute Value Using SQL

You can base an attribute value on a SQL expression by selecting the *Derived from SQL Expression* checkbox in the Entity Attribute page of the Attribute Editor or the Attribute Settings page of the Create Entity Object Wizard (as shown in Figure 6-5). This opens a checkbox in which you can enter a SQL expression that will calculate the attribute's value based on an initial SQL query. The SQL expression must be one that would be valid in the following query:

```
SELECT <expression>
FROM <table>
```

In this query, <expression> represents the SQL expression used for calculation, and <table> refers to the database object on which the entity object definition is based.

SQL-calculated attributes are only calculated when a row is first retrieved from the database (or if the attribute is set to refresh on update or insert as is described in the section "How Do You Synchronize with Database Defaulting and Calculation?"). To maintain these attributes at other times, use Java, as explained in the following section.

Calculating an Attribute Value Using Java

You can perform all attribute calculation using Java, or use Java code to maintain an attribute that was initially calculated using SQL. The code you will need is the same in both cases.

Implementing Attribute Calculation in a Getter Method First, you must add code to the calculated attribute's getter method that attempts to calculate the attribute whenever it is requested, if it still has a null value. This technique, called *lazy initialization,* is often used in Java applications to defer calculations until they are first required, without having to re-perform them every time a value is requested. For example, you could edit the getter method for a transient attribute, ExpectedSalaryPlusCommission, in the EmployeesImpl entity object class, so that it resembles the following code snippet:

```
public Number getExpectedSalaryPlusCommission() {
  Number expectedSalaryPlusCommission =
    (Number)getAttributeInternal(EXPECTEDSALARYPLUSCOMMISSION);
  if ( expectedSalaryPlusCommission == null &&
       getSalary() != null ) {
    if (getCommissionPct() == null) {
      expectedSalaryPlusCommission = getSalary();
    } else {
      expectedSalaryPlusCommission = new Number(
        getSalary().intValue * (1 + getCommissionPct.floatValue()));
    }
    populateAttribute(EXPECTEDSALARYPLUSCOMMISSION, expectedSalaryPlusCommission);
  }
  return expectedSalaryPlusCommission;
}
```

The preceding code performs the following actions:

- **Lines 2–3** Retrieve the value currently being stored for the transient attribute.
- **Lines 4–5** Perform tests to see whether the attribute value needs to be calculated; calculation should take place if the current attribute value is null and the current value of the Salary attribute is not null.
- **Lines 6–11** Calculate the new value for the transient attribute.
- **Line 12** Calls a method, `populateAttribute()`, to store the calculated value so that it does not need to be recalculated with each request. `populateAttribute()` sets an attribute value much as `setAttributeInternal()` does, but it is different in the following ways:
  - It can be used even on read-only attributes. (It is not directly callable from the controller layer, so users cannot call it themselves.)
  - It bypasses validation rules.
  - It does not mark the entity object instance as "dirty," requiring entity-level validation.
  - It does not mark the entity object instance as requiring posting to the database.
- **Line 12** Returns the (possibly newly calculated) attribute value.

Triggering Attribute Recalculation in Setter Methods Once an attribute has been calculated in a getter method, it will not be recalculated as long as its value is not null. If you want to maintain the calculation, you must set the calculated attribute's value to null whenever an attribute value on which it depends changes. You can do this in the setter methods for attributes on which the attribute value depends, as shown here:

```
public void setSalary(Number value) {
  setAttributeInternal(SALARY, value);
  populateAttribute(EXPECTEDSALARYPLUSCOMMISSION, null);
}

public void setCommissionPct(Number value) {
  setAttributeInternal(COMMISSION_PCT, value);
  populateAttribute(EXPECTEDSALARYPLUSCOMMISSION, null);
}
```

How Do You Synchronize with Database Defaulting and Calculation?

If database triggers create an initial value for a column or maintain a column based on other column values, you must integrate this into your entity object definitions. Otherwise, your entity object instances may become out of synch with the database after posting new or changed instances because, by default, ADF BC does not requery data after executing DML.

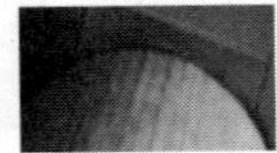

CAUTION
The information contained in this section applies only to entity object definitions based on tables. Using database sequences with entity object definitions based on database views with INSTEAD_OF triggers is explained in Section 37.6, "Basing an Entity Object on a Join View or Remote DBLink," in the Fusion Developer's Guide for Oracle ADF.

The DBSequence Domain

Many numeric primary key attributes are automatically populated or updated by database triggers that select new values from sequences. ADF BC provides a domain, `oracle.jbo.domain.DBSequence`, which can be used instead of `Number` for corresponding entity object attributes. `DBSequence` acts exactly like `Number` except for two important differences:

- **When a new entity object instance is created** ADF automatically populates attributes typed to `DBSequence` with unique, temporary negative values. This ensures that primary keys involving `DBSequence` attributes can be used to find unique instances in the entity object cache without making a database round-trip to select a new value from the database sequence.
- **When a newly created entity object instance is posted** ADF refreshes attributes typed to `DBSequence` with the value inserted by the database trigger.

The Importance of Posting Order

If you have a `DBSequence` attribute that is a source or destination attribute in an association, it is important to post the `DBSequence` attribute's entity object instance before posting the associated entity object instance. Otherwise, the following scenario may occur:

1. The user creates a new entity object instance, and ADF sets the value of its `DBSequence` attribute to –1.
2. The user creates a new associated entity object instance, which requires that its `Number` attribute be set to –1.
3. The user requests that data be posted.
4. Because posting order is not being controlled, the associated entity object instance may be posted first. A row will be inserted with –1 in its foreign key column.
5. The original entity object instance is posted. A row will be inserted and its primary key column will be populated from the database sequence. What should be the detail row will be orphaned, because the foreign key column no longer matches the primary key.

If the association is not a composition with "Cascade Update Key Attributes" selected, you will need to manually update the `Number` attribute once the permanent value of the `DBSequence` attribute is retrieved. Then the following successful process will replace the problematic one discussed previously:

1. The user creates a new entity object instance, and ADF sets the value of its `DBSequence` attribute to –1.
2. The user creates a new associated entity object instance, which requires that its `Number` attribute be set to –1.

3. The user requests that data be posted.
4. Because posting order is being controlled, the entity object instance with the `DBSequence` value will be posted first. A new row is inserted, with its primary key populated from the database sequence, which will be loaded into the `DBSequence` attribute.
5. Either because the association is a composition with Cascade Update Key Attributes selected, or because the application implements it, the `Number` attribute in the associated entity object instance is changed to match the newly retrieved sequence value.
6. The associated entity object instance is posted. The new row that is inserted has a foreign key that matches the primary key in the row inserted in Step 5; the relationship is maintained.

Creating a Custom Entity Definition Framework Class to Expose Appropriate Accessor Methods

To control posting order and manually cascade update key attributes, entity object instances need to discover what associations they participate in that require changes to posting order or cascade updates. You could do this in an entity object class, but the lists of relevant associations would need to be re-created for every entity object instance. It is more efficient to lazily create and store lists of such associations at the entity definition level. You can do this in a custom entity definition framework class.

Fields and Getter Methods The two lists of association accessors needed are as follows:

- A list of association accessors such that the other side of the association is based on one or more `DBSequence` attributes. For these associations, it is important to make sure the other side of the association posts first.
- A list of association accessors such that this side of the association is based on one or more `DBSequence` attributes. For these associations, it is important to cascade update key attributes when posting this side of the association.

You will need fields and public getter methods for them (the fields do not require public setters), as follows:

```
private List<AssociationDefImpl> mastersToPost = null;
private List<AssociationDefImpl> detailsToUpdate = null;

public List<AssociationDefImpl> getDetailsToUpdate() {
  if (detailsToUpdate == null) {
    detailsToUpdate = getDbSeqAssocs(true);
  }
  return detailsToUpdate;
}

public List<AssociationDefImpl> getMastersToPost() {
  if (mastersToPost == null) {
    mastersToPost = getDbSeqAssocs(false);
  }
  return mastersToPost;
}
```

An explanation of the preceding code follows:

- **Lines 1–2** Defines the two lists of accessors and initialize them to null (they will be lazily loaded by the getter methods). `oracle.jbo.server.AssociationDefImpl` is the class ADF uses to represent association accessors. `mastersToPost` will contain the association accessors such that the other side of the association is based on one or more `DBSequence` attributes, and `detailsToUpdate` will contain the association accessors such that this side of the association is based on one or more `DBSequence` attributes.
- **Line 4** Is the beginning of the getter method for `detailsToUpdate`.
- **Line 5** Checks whether `detailsToUpdate` still needs to be loaded.
- **Line 6** Calls a method, `getDbSeqAssocs()`, which is shown in the next section. This method retrieves the association accessors such that either this side or the other side of the association (depending on the Boolean attribute passed in) is based on `DBSequence` attributes.
- **Lines 11–16** Forms the getter method for `mastersToPost`. This uses a lazy initialization process identical to the one in `getDetailsToUpdate()` except for the value passed to `getDbSeqAssocs()`.

Implementing getDbSeqAssocs() The getter methods described in the preceding section both depend on the method `getDbSeqAssocs()`, shown here:

```
01: private List<AssociationDefImpl> getDbSeqAssocs(boolean thisSide) {
02:   List<AssociationDefImpl> selectedAssocs =
03:     new ArrayList<AssociationDefImpl>();
04:   AssociationDefImpl[] allAssocs = getAssociationDefImpls();
05:   for (AssociationDefImpl assoc:allAssocs) {
06:     AssociationEnd endToCheck = thisSide ?
07:       assoc.getAssociationEnd():
08:       assoc.getOtherAssociationEnd();
09:     if (hasDbSequenceAttr(endToCheck)) {
10:       selectedAssocs.add(assoc);
11:     }
12:   }
13:   return selectedAssocs;
14: }
```

The preceding code steps through the following process:

- **Lines 2–3** Creates a list to hold the association accessors as they are found.
- **Line 4** Calls the method `EntityDefImpl.getAssociationDefImpls()`, which returns an array containing all the association accessors for the entity object definition.
- **Lines 6–8** Chooses an association end (represented by `oracle.jbo.server.AssociationEnd`) to check for `DBSequence` attributes based on the parameter passed in to the method.

- **Line 9** Calls a method, `hasDbSequenceAttr()`, which is implemented in the following section. This method determines whether an association end is based on at least one `DBSequence` attribute.
- **Line 10** Adds the association (if the appropriate end is based on at least one `DBSequence` attribute) to the list.

Implementing hasDbSequenceAttr()

The `hasDbSequenceAttr()` method, shown next, determines whether one of the attributes an association end is based on is of type `DbSequence`.

```
01: private boolean hasDbSequenceAttr(AssociationEnd endToCheck) {
02:   boolean foundDbSequence = false;
03:   AttributeDefImpl[] attrs = endToCheck.getAttributeDefImpls();
04:   for (AttributeDefImpl attr:attrs) {
05:     if (DBSequence.class.isAssignableFrom(attr.getJavaType())) {
06:       foundDbSequence = true;
07:       break;
08:     }
09:   }
10:   return foundDbSequence;
11: }
```

The preceding code steps through the following process:

- **Line 2** Initializes a variable that starts out false but will become true if a `DBSequence` attribute is found in the association end.
- **Line 3** Calls the method `AssociationEnd.getAttributeDefImpls()` to retrieve an array of attributes (represented by the class `oracle.jbo.server.AttributeDefImpl`) that act as the defining attributes for the association end (source or destination attributes, depending on which end of the association is being examined).
- **Lines 5–7** These are executed for each attribute and test whether the attribute's Java type is `DBSequence` or a subclass thereof (the method `java.lang.Class.isAssignableFrom()` tests whether one class or interface is identical to or is an extension or implementation of another). If the attribute passes the test, `foundDbSequence` is assigned to be true and the attribute loop is broken.

Creating a Custom Entity Object Framework Class to Control Posting Order and Cascade Update Key Values

You can override the method `EntityImpl.postChanges()` in a custom framework entity object class to control posting order and manually cascade update key attributes. `postChanges()` is the method that performs DML operations.

Overriding EntityImpl.postChanges() The overridden method is shown here:

```
public void postChanges(TransactionEvent event) {
  Map<AssociationDefImpl, Object> detailsToUpdateMap = null;
  TuhraEntityDefImpl def = (TuhraEntityDefImpl) getEntityDef();
  if (STATUS_NEW == getPostState()) {
```

```
05:     postFirst(event, def.getMastersToPost());
06:     detailsToUpdateMap = prepareDetails(def.getDetailsToUpdate());
07:   }
08:   super.postChanges(event);
09:   if (detailsToUpdateMap != null) {
10:     adjustDetails(def.getDetailsToUpdate(), detailsToUpdateMap);
11:   }
12: }
```

The preceding code performs the following actions:

- **Line 2** initializes a variable, `detailsToUpdateMap`, that will map association accessors returning `EntityImpl` or `RowSet` instances requiring updating to the values they return for this entity object instance.
- **Line 3** retrieves this entity object instance's entity definition and casts it to the custom entity object class described in the preceding section. This code assumes that the entity definition class is named `TuhraEntityDefImpl`; you should change it to cast the entity definition to your organization's entity definition class.
- **Line 4** tests whether this entity is new in the current transaction. If the entity is not new, there will be no conversion from temporary `DBSequence` values to actual values from the database sequence, which means no special behavior is required.
- **Line 5** calls the method `postFirst()`, which is created later in this section to ensure that all entity object instances containing `DBSequence` attributes on which this instance depends are posted before this instance.
- **Line 6** populates `detailsToUpdateMap` using the method `prepareDetails()`, which is created later in this section. The method will discover every entity object instance or rowset containing attributes that depend on `DBSequence` attributes from this entity object instance. It is important to collect these before posting this entity object instance, since they will become disassociated with it as soon as the `DBSequence` attributes are refreshed from the database and will need to be readjusted to fit it.
- **Line 8** calls the superclass method to post this entity object instance.
- **Line 9** calls the method `adjustDetails()`, which adjusts attributes in the instances collected in Line 6 to re-associate those instances with the just-posted instance.

CAUTION
This code will lead to an infinite loop in the case of dependency loops between new entity object instances. For example, if a user attempts to create both a department and a manager of that department who is also a member of the department in a single transaction, the code will enter an infinite loop, as posting the department requires posting the manager first (to retrieve the department's correct ManagerId), and posting the manager requires posting the department first (to retrieve the manager's correct DepartmentId). You should not use the technique described in this section if you are going to allow simultaneous posting of new entity object instances that may have an association loop between them.

Implementing postFirst() The `postFirst()` method must ensure that all entity instances containing `DBSequence` attributes on which this instance depends are posted to the database. The code is as follows:

```
01: private void postFirst(TransactionEvent event,
02:                          List<AssociationDefImpl> accessorsToPostFirst) {
03:   for (AssociationDefImpl accessor:accessorsToPostFirst) {
04:     EntityImpl associatedEntity = (EntityImpl) getAttribute(accessor.getIndex());
05:     if (associatedEntity != null && STATUS_NEW == associatedEntity.getPostState()) {
06:       associatedEntity.postChanges(event);
07:     }
08:   }
09: }
```

The preceding code performs the following actions:

- **Line 3** Loops through all the accessors that return entity object instances that must be posted first.
- **Line 4** Calls the method `oracle.jbo.server.EntityImpl.getAttributeValue()` to retrieve the associated entity object instance for each accessor. `getAttributeValue()` is just the same as `getAttribute()`, except that instead of taking a `String` or `int` parameter representing the attribute's name or index, it takes an `AttributeDefImpl` representing the attribute itself as its parameter.
- **Lines 5–6** Tests whether the associated entity is itself new in this transaction, and if so, post the entity so that its `DBSequence` attributes are updated from the database and cascaded.

Implementing `prepareDetails()` The `prepareDetails()` method must collect all entity object instances and RowSets that may need to be adjusted to match `DBSequence` attributes from this entity object instance after it is posted. It collects these instances into a map indexed by the association accessors that return the instances. The method is implemented here:

```
private Map<AssociationDefImpl, Object> prepareDetails(
  List<AssociationDefImpl> accessorsToUpdate) {
  Map<AssociationDefImpl, Object> detailMap =
    new HashMap<AssociationDefImpl, Object>();
  for (AssociationDefImpl assoc:accessorsToUpdate) {
    detailMap.put(assoc, getAttributeValue(assoc));
  }
  return detailMap;
}
```

The preceding code cycles through the accessors, adding the object (`EntityImpl` or `RowSet` instance, depending on association cardinality) to the map indexed by its accessor.

Implementing adjustDetails() The `adjustDetails()` method must adjust the `EntityImpl` and `RowSet` instances collected by `prepareDetails()` to re-associate them with the current entity object after it posts. It is shown next:

```
01: private void adjustDetails(List<AssociationDefImpl> accessorsToUpdate,
02:                            Map<AssociationDefImpl, Object> detailsToUpdateMap)
03: {
04:   for (AssociationDefImpl assoc:accessorsToUpdate) {
05:     Object detail = detailsToUpdateMap.get(assoc);
06:     if (detail instanceof EntityImpl) {
07:       adjustDetailEntity((EntityImpl) detail, assoc);
08:     } else {
09:       RowSet detailRS = (RowSet) detail;
10:       while (detailRS.hasNext()) {
11:         adjustDetailEntity((EntityImpl) detailRS.next(), assoc);
12:       }
13:     }
14:   }
15: }
```

The preceding code steps through the following process:

- **Line 4** Loops through each accessor that requires a cascade update.
- **Line 5** Retrieves the object (`EntityImpl` or `RowSet` instance) that was associated with this entity by the accessor before the entity was posted. The method needs to adjust this object so that it is associated with this entity again.
- **Lines 6–7** If the object is an `EntityImpl` instance, these lines call the method `adjustDetailEntity()`, which is implemented in the next section to adjust a single entity instance to re-associate it with the current instance.
- **Lines 8–11** If the object is a `RowSet` instance, these lines loop through the `RowSet` and call `adjustDetailEntity()` for each entity object instance it contains.

Implementing adjustDetailEntity() The `adjustDetailEntity()` method must adjust a single entity object instance that contains attributes depending on `DBSequence` attributes from the currently posting entity object instance. Its code is shown here:

```
01: private void adjustDetailEntity(EntityImpl detail
02:                                 AssociationDefImpl accessorForDetail) {
03:   AttributeDefImpl[] thisSideAttrs =
04:     accessorForDetail.getAssociationEnd().getAttributeDefImpls();
05:   AttributeDefImpl[] otherSideAttrs =
06:     accessorForDetail.getOtherAssociationEnd().getAttributeDefImpls();
07:   for (int i=0; i < thisSideAttrs.length; i++) {
08:     DBSequence sequenceAttr = (DBSequence) getAttribute(thisSideAttrs[i].getIndex());
09:     detail.setAttribute(otherSideAttrs[i].getIndex(),
10:                         sequenceAttr.getSequenceNumber()
11:   }
12: }
```

The preceding code steps through the following operations:

- **Lines 3–4** Retrieves the definitions of attributes, in order, on the posting entity object instance's side of the association.

- **Lines 5–6** Retrieves the definitions of attributes, in order, on the `detail` parameter's side of the association.
- **Lines 7–11** Loop through the attributes retrieved in Lines 3–4 and, for each such attribute, adjust the value of the corresponding attribute in detail so that the association is restored.

Other Database Defaulting and Database Calculations

Triggers that default columns not from a sequence, and that maintain columns after updates, are easier to integrate with ADF BC than those that default columns from database sequences, although the integration is less complete.

ADF BC contains functionality that lets you retrieve new values from the database after an INSERT or UPDATE operation. Unlike `DbSequence`-typed attributes, the framework does not create temporary values for not-yet-posted entity object instances; you will have to do this yourself if an attribute corresponding to a database-defaulted column is marked Mandatory or is needed to make a primary key or alternate key unique.

You can request refreshes for attributes using the checkboxes in the Refresh After area of the Attribute Editor or of the Attribute Settings page of the Create Entity Object Wizard, as is shown in Figure 6-5.

How Do You Implement Polymorphic Business Rules?

Sometimes tables contain somewhat heterogeneous data, and different rows must obey different validation rules. For example, you might want to require that "E"-type image usages have an AssociatedId that matches an employee ID, and that "L"-type image usages have an AssociatedId that matches a location ID. Simple *polymorphic* business rules (rules that are different for different rows) can be implemented using business logic groups. A *business logic group*, as explained in Chapter 5, is a collection of business logic units—sets of business rules—that can be applied to different instances of an entity object. More complex polymorphism can be implemented using *polymorphic entity object definitions,* which are hierarchies of entity object definitions that inherit from one another.

Business Logic Groups

Which business logic unit is applied to a particular entity object instance depends on the value of one attribute, which is called the business logic group's "discriminator attribute," or simply its "discriminator." For example, if you want to define different sets of rules for instances of ImageUsages with a UsageType of "L" or "E", you would create a business logic group for ImageUsages using the UsageType attribute as its discriminator.

Creating Business Logic Groups and Business Logic Units

You can create a business logic group by clicking the Create New Business Logic Group button on the General page of an entity object definition's editor, as shown in Figure 6-12. This opens the Define Business Logic Group dialog, shown here:

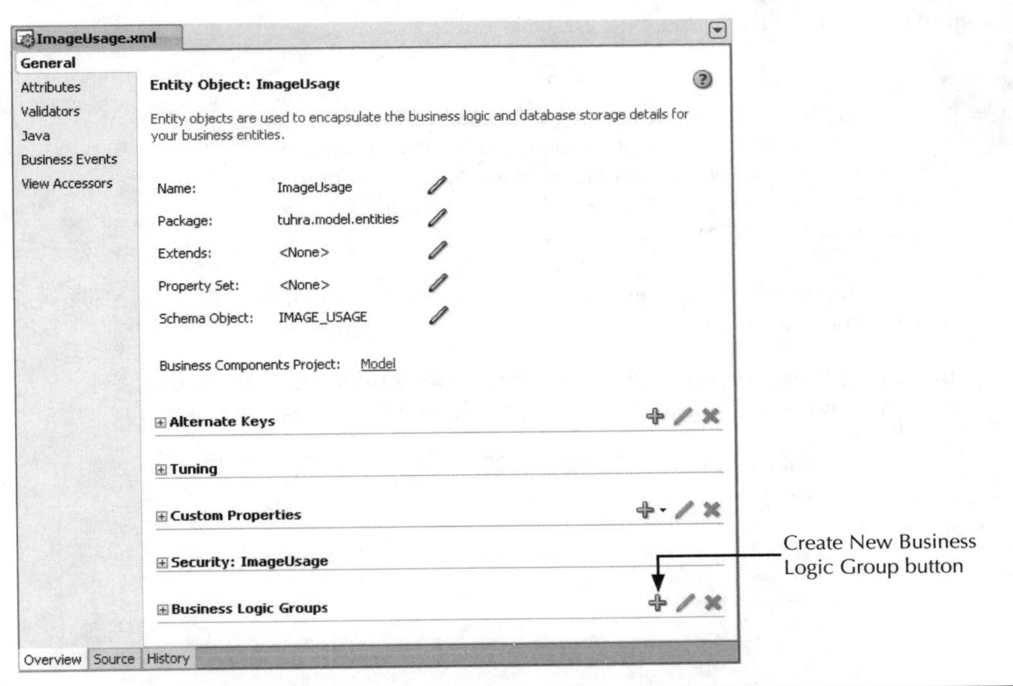

FIGURE 6-12. *The General page of an entity object definition's editor*

In this dialog, you name your business logic group and select a discriminator attribute for it, which can be any attribute of type `String`.

Once you have created a business logic group, you can create business logic units for various possible discriminator values by selecting the Entity Business Logic Unit item from the "Business Tier\ADF Business Components" category of the New Gallery. This opens the Create Business Logic Unit dialog, shown here:

Create Business Logic Unit
Enter the details of your new Business Logic Unit.
Base Entity Name: tuhra.model.entities.ImageUsage Browse...
Business Logic Group: ImageUsageTypeGroup
Unit Name: E
Package: tuhra.model.entities Browse...
Help OK Cancel

To create the business logic unit, first browse for the entity object definition containing the group this unit belongs to (*Base Entity Name*). Then, select the business logic group from the dropdown list. Finally, enter the value for the discriminator attribute that you want this business logic unit to handle in the *Unit Name* field, select a package (if you want to use a different one from what is displayed), and click OK.

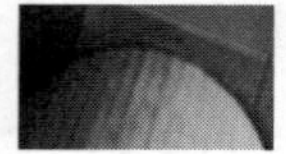

NOTE
The Unit Name field is misleadingly labeled, as the value you enter here will not be the name of the business logic unit. Business logic units are named <entity definition name>_<business logic group name>_<discriminator attribute value>, for example, ImageUsage_ImageUsageTypeGroup_E.

You can edit a business logic unit by double-clicking it in the Application Navigator; it will open in a specialized editor.

Specifying Polymorphic Attribute Properties and Validation Rules

The Attributes page of a business logic unit's editor is shown here:

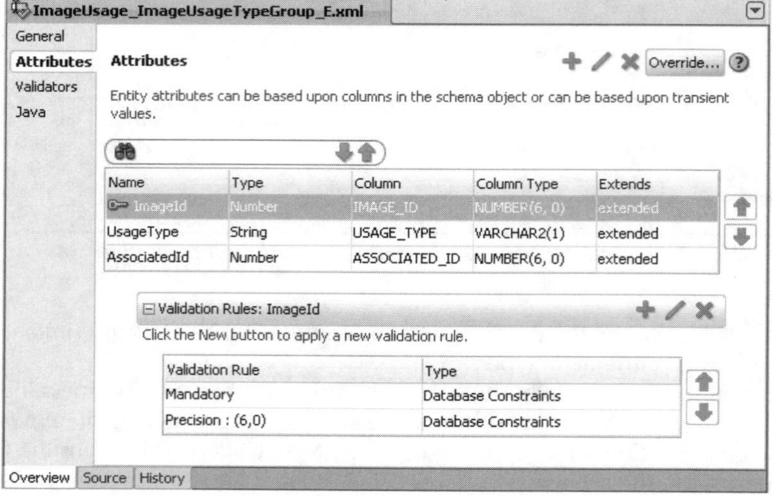

If you click the Override button, you can select attributes for which you want to specify polymorphic properties. For example, overriding an attribute allows you to: make a normally nonmandatory attribute mandatory within the unit, provide customized attribute calculations, make a normally editable attribute read-only, or to attach attribute-level validation rules that apply only within the business logic unit.

Once you have overridden an attribute, you can double-click it in the table to open it in the Attribute Editor, and change the attribute's properties. You can only change requirements on the attribute to make them more restrictive than normal. For example, you can make a normally nonmandatory attribute mandatory, or a normally editable attribute read-only, but not the reverse.

You can use the Validation page of the business logic unit's editor to apply validation rules that apply only to entity object instances that fall within the business logic unit. You can apply attribute-level validation rules to overridden attributes, as well as entity-level validation rules, just as you would apply them on the Validation page of an entity object definition's editor (as explained in the sections "Attribute-Level Validation Rules" and "Entity-Level Validation Rules ").

Polymorphic Entity Object Definitions

While business logic groups and business logic units provide a simple way to implement polymorphism, they have some considerable limitations. A business logic unit can add validation rules to an entity object and make attribute updatability more restrictive, but it cannot add new attributes or provide programmatic validation, calculation, or defaulting. If your application needs more complete polymorphism than is provided by business logic groups, you have the option of creating polymorphic hierarchies of entity object definitions.

Once you have created one entity object definition, you can create other entity object definitions that extend it. These other entity object definitions are based on the same database object as the original entity object definition, but their instances are only used to represent a portion of the database table's rows.

Setting Up an Entity Object Definition to Be Extended

The first step in creating a hierarchy of polymorphic entity object definitions is to create a base entity object definition. This is an ordinary entity object definition, based on a database table, view, or synonym. However, to enable polymorphism, you must select one or more attributes to be discriminator attributes. Which sub-entity object definition is used to create an entity object instance representing a particular database object row will depend on the values of the database object columns corresponding to discriminator attributes.

You can mark an entity attribute as a discriminator attribute on the Attribute Settings page of the Create Entity Object Wizard (shown in Figure 6-5) or in the Attribute Editor. You will do this in the hands-on practice in Chapter 20.

Creating an Extension of an Entity Object Definition

The best way to create an entity object definition that extends another is by using the Create Entity Object Wizard. The Name page of the wizard allows you to specify an entity object definition to extend; you will do this in Chapter 20. You can then select attributes to override (these must include the discriminator attributes), just as you can in a business logic unit; but in addition, you can also add new attributes, such as calculated attributes where the calculation only makes sense for particular row subtypes.

You must also fill in declarative "default values" (as explained in the section "How Do You Implement Attribute Defaulting and Calculation") for each of the discriminator attributes. These values are not really used as defaults; rather, they are used to determine when a particular sub-entity object definition is used to create an entity object instance to represent a row. For example, the ImageType attribute is a discriminator attribute for ImageUsages. EmployeeImageUsages, an extension of ImageUsages, overrides the ImageType attribute and gives it a "default value" of "E." This means that, when a row of IMAGE_USAGES has an IMAGE_TYPE value of "E," an instance of EmployeeImageUsages will be created to represent it.

Validation, Calculation, and Defaulting in Extended Entity Object Definitions

As with business logic groups, you can add entity-level validation rules to sub-entity object definitions, can add attribute-level validation rules to overridden attributes, and make the updatability of such attributes more restrictive. However, unlike in business logic groups, you can also add programmatic validation, calculation, and defaulting to overridden attributes in sub-entity object definitions.

You can set the same declarative calculation and defaulting properties on an overridden attribute (other than a discriminator attribute) in a sub-entity object definition that you can set on any other entity attribute. In addition, if you elect to create an entity object class for a sub-entity object definition, the class will extend the entity object class for the parent definition, and will automatically contain overridden accessor methods for all overridden attributes as well as getters and setters for attributes unique to the extension. You can also override the `validateEntity()` method in an entity object subclass to provide programmatic entity-level validation.

Polymorphic Entity Object Definitions and Associations

An association that has a sub-entity object definition on one end will only return instances of that sub-entity object definition. For example, EmployeesImageUsageAssoc is an association between the Employees and EmployeeImageUsages entity object definitions, with `EmployeeId` as its source attribute and `AssociatedId` as its image attribute. The destination accessor of this association will return a `RowSet` containing entity object instances satisfying two criteria:

- The instances' `AssociatedId` attribute values will all match the `EmployeeId` attribute of the Employees instance, as with all associations.
- The instances' `UsageType` attribute values will all be "E," so that they are instances of EmployeeImageUsages.

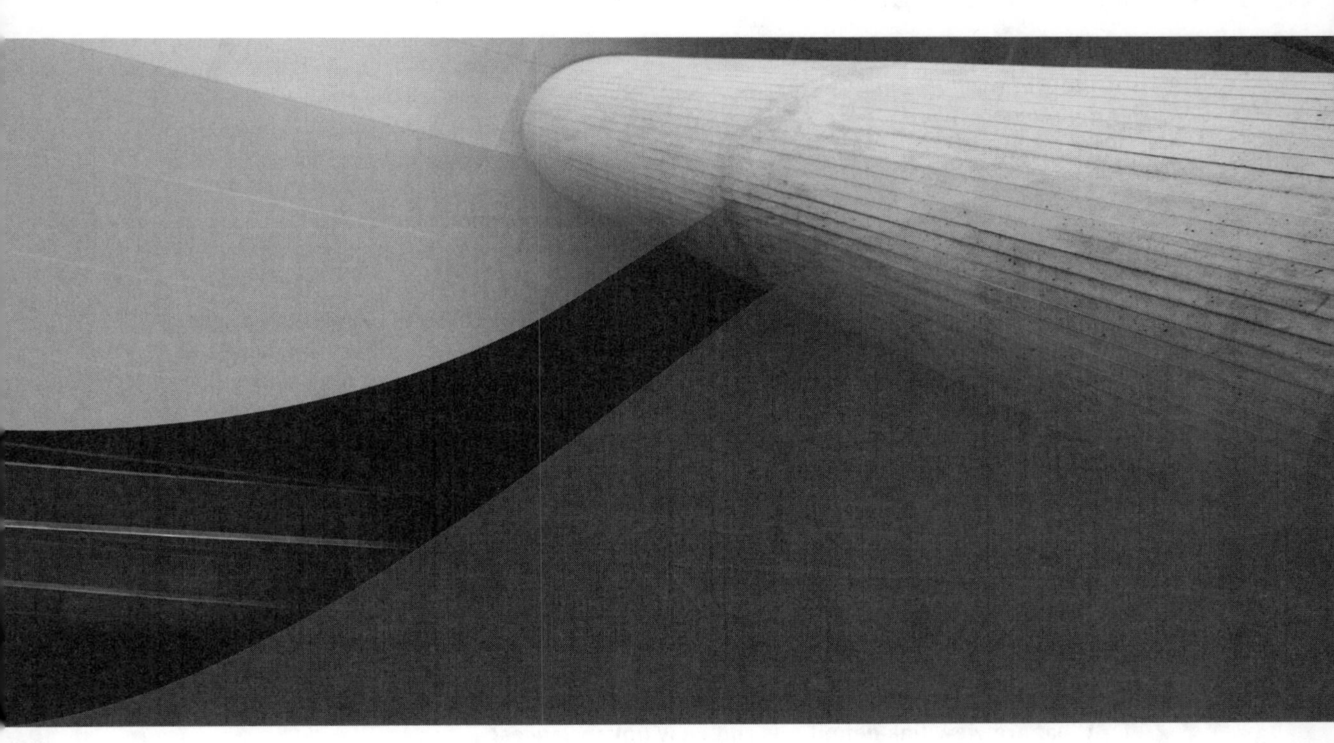

CHAPTER 7

Assembling a Data Model

All is waste and worthless, till
Arrives the selecting will,
And out of slime and chaos, Wit
Draws the threads of fair and fit.

—Ralph Waldo Emerson (1803–1882), *Wealth*

hapter 6 explained how to create entity object definitions and associations to represent features of the database and encapsulate business logic. This chapter discusses how to create view object definitions that query data from the database and view link definitions that specify relationships between query results. It also discusses application module definitions that specify a data model—a collection of view object and view link instances—for other parts of your application.

This chapter answers the following questions:

- **What are view object definitions, view object instances, and view rows?**
- **How do view attributes work?**
- **How do you create and edit view object definitions?**
- **How do you specify view object queries?**
- **How can view object instances handle row creation, row deletion, and association changes?**
- **What are view link definitions and view link instances?**
- **How do you create and edit view link definitions?**
- **What are application module definitions and application module instances?**
- **How do you use view object instances as LOVs?**
- **How do application module instances manage transactional state?**

What Are View Object Definitions, View Object Instances, and View Rows?

As described in Chapter 5, a view object definition is a source of data that normally corresponds to a SQL query. You can create it using several techniques described in the section "Creating View Object Definitions" later in this chapter. The view object definition contains view attributes corresponding to query columns. These attributes are defined using Java types that correspond to the SQL datatypes of the columns. The view object definition acts as a template for view object instances, which are responsible for executing the query. These view object instances contain view rows, which represent single rows returned by the query.

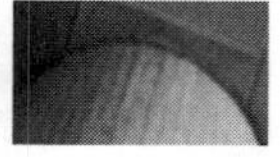

NOTE

The claim that a view object definition corresponds to a SQL query is an oversimplification. Most view object definitions correspond to SQL queries, but static view object definitions (described in the section "How Do You Use View Object Instances as LOVs?") and programmatic view object definitions create or retrieve data differently.

Chapter 5 also stated that a view object definition comprises an XML metadata file, between zero and seven Java classes, and between zero and two Java interfaces. This section explains how the XML file and three of the classes can work together to constitute a view object definition to provide a template for view object instances and their view rows.

NOTE
The remaining four Java classes and the interfaces are only used when you create custom service methods (discussed in Chapter 8) or web services.

View Object XML Metadata

All view object definitions involve an XML file. This file contains the metadata that describes details of the view object, including the following:

- **SQL Query** The SELECT statement that view object instances based on the definition should execute.
- **Entity usages in the view object definition** The entity usages include references to entity object definitions, how the entity usages relate to elements of the FROM clause in the SQL query, and how they relate to one another in the view object definition.
- **Attributes of the view object definition** The attribute properties include the database columns to which they map, the entity attributes on which they are based (if any), and their Java types (if they are not based on entity attributes).
- **References to view link definitions** This metadata refers to view link definitions in which the view object definition participates, and contains information about how it participates in them.
- **Other declarative features** Examples of other features are UI hints (control hints), property sets, and tuning information.

You will never need to directly edit a view object XML file, except in the rare situation where the XML file has become corrupt (as mentioned in Chapter 6). The vast majority of the time, you will modify the XML file using JDeveloper's visual editors. Various components of the editors are explained throughout this chapter.

View Object Classes

When the ADF BC framework needs to create a view object instance, it instantiates the class `oracle.jbo.server.ViewObjectImpl` and configures it according to the view object definition's XML metadata. The object created by this process is a view object instance.

`ViewObjectImpl` has all the methods required to set query bind variables, execute queries, and navigate through query result sets. However, you can create a *view object class,* a subclass of `ViewObjectImpl` that is customized to a particular view object definition. If you create a view object class, the corresponding view object instances will be instances of that class, rather than direct instances of `ViewObjectImpl`.

By default, a view object class is named after its view object definition, with the suffix "Impl" added. For example, the view object class for the AllEmployees view object definition, by default, would be named `AllEmployeesImpl`. (Chapter 6 contains information about changing naming conventions for ADF BC classes.)

Although for many purposes, you do not need to create view object classes for your view object definitions, in some cases it may be useful, since view object classes provide a number of features.

Query Bind Variable Accessors

`ViewObjectImpl` contains methods, `getNamedWhereClauseParam()` and `setNamedWhereClauseParam()`, which allow access to query bind variable values. However, if you generate a view object class, then you can also generate accessors (getters and setters) for each bind variable. For example, the EmployeesSearch view object definition contains a bind variable called QueryEmail; if you generate accessors for `EmployeesSearchImpl`, the class will contain `getQueryEmail()` and `setQueryEmail()` methods, which retrieve and change the value of the QueryEmail variable value, respectively. These accessors are typesafe (as described in Chapter 6), making errors more likely to appear at compile time, rather than runtime.

Overriding Methods in ViewObjectImpl

In addition to the accessor methods, view object classes also allow you to override various methods in the `ViewObjectImpl` class to change query execution behavior.

View Object–Level Service Methods

View object classes are the appropriate location to write *view object–level service methods,* methods that perform tasks based on a particular query or its results and can be called declaratively from the view or controller layer. Service methods are the focus of Chapter 8.

View Row Classes

When the ADF BC framework needs to create a view row (for example, to represent a row of queried data), it instantiates the class `oracle.jbo.server.ViewRowImpl` and configures it based on the view object definition's XML metadata. The object created by this process is a view row.

`ViewRowImpl` has all the methods required to initialize a newly created view row (including creating any underlying entity object instances), to prepare a view row for deletion (which involves marking any underlying entity object instances for deletion), and to retrieve and change attribute values. However, you can create a *view row class,* a subclass of `ViewRowImpl` that is customized to a particular view object definition. If you create a view row class, the corresponding view rows will be instances of that class, rather than direct instances of `ViewRowImpl`.

By default, a view row class is named after its view object definition, with the suffix "RowImpl" added. For example, the view row class for the AllEmployees view object definition, by default, would be named `AllEmployeesRowImpl`.

View Attribute Accessors

The `ViewRowImpl` class, like the `EntityImpl` class, implements the interface `oracle.jbo.Row`, which means it contains the methods `getAttribute()` and `setAttribute()`. Just as these methods on `EntityImpl` allow access to entity attribute values, on `ViewRowImpl` they allow access to view attribute values. Like entity object classes, view row classes (if generated) also contain typesafe accessors for the view attributes.

Overriding Methods in ViewRowImpl

Because `ViewRowImpl` and `EntityImpl` both implement `Row`, they contain many similar methods. For example, by overriding `ViewRowImpl.create()` in a view row class, you can trigger events whenever a new view row is created. In most cases, events like this are better implemented in an entity object class, because entity object definitions may be reusable across many view object definitions. However, in some cases (such as when the event you want to trigger involves multiple entity object usages, or doesn't involve any), it may make more sense to implement them in a view row class.

View Definition Classes

Just as an instance of `oracle.jbo.server.EntityDefImpl` is a Java class for representing metadata defined in an entity object definition's XML file, an instance of `oracle.jbo.server.ViewDefImpl` is a Java class for representing metadata in a view object definition's XML file. There is only one `ViewDefImpl` instance per view object definition in a running ADF application; the framework will access the same object across view object instances and even user sessions.

`ViewDefImpl` has all the methods required to discover information about a view object definition's name, query, attribute properties, or anything else specified in the view object definition's XML file. It even contains methods that allow you to change these properties dynamically.

CAUTION
Be careful about changing a view object definition's properties at runtime. Remember that you are doing so not just for a single user, but for all users of the view object definition.

You can also create a view definition class, which extends `ViewDefImpl` in the same way an entity definition class extends `EntityDefImpl`. Like entity definition classes, view definition classes are required by relatively few applications. The reasons for doing so are much the same as the reasons for creating an entity definition class (as described in Chapter 6).

Custom Framework Classes

As stated in Chapter 6, sometimes you need to extend the normal behavior of Business Components throughout a project, rather than on a component-by-component basis; for example, you may want all entity object instances in a project to share some behavior that is not provided for by the framework alone. Chapter 6 explains how to create custom framework classes for entity object definitions that implement this behavior.

You can also create custom framework classes for view object definitions. These classes extend the ADF BC base classes (for example, a custom framework view object class would extend `ViewObjectImpl`), and all view object definitions use them (or extensions of them) to represent their entity object instances, XML wrappers, or caches. Chapter 6 contains details on specifying custom framework view object classes.

NOTE
You will create various framework classes in the hands-on practices in Part V of this book.

How Do View Attributes Work?

As described in Chapter 5, view attributes are usually based on entity attributes from the view object definition's entity usage's and are usually mapped to columns from the view object definition's SQL query. However, there are a number of exceptions to this rule. Moreover, some view attributes play particular roles in a view object definition.

Persistent, SQL-Only, Entity-Derived, and Transient View Attributes

Because view attributes can, but do not need to, be based on entity attributes, and because they can, but do not need to, be mapped to columns in the SQL query, there are four possible view attribute types, as shown in Table 7-1. Population and caching behavior works differently for each of these view attribute types, so you need to understand all four of these types to make good choices during view object definition design.

Persistent View Attributes

A *persistent* view attribute is one that is both mapped to a query column and to an entity attribute. When a view object instance with entity-derived view attributes first executes its query, it sends the query to the database. The database returns a result, as shown in Figure 7-1.

The columns in the query result are mapped to view attributes and to the entity attributes they are based on, as shown in Figure 7-2.

Next, entity object instances are created, and the attributes are populated with the appropriate result column data and inserted into entity caches (one for each entity object definition the view object uses), as shown in Figure 7-3. There may not be as many instances in each entity cache as there are rows in the query result; the entity object usages' primary key attributes are used to determine how many rows are needed. For example, in Figure 7-3, there is one Departments entity object instance (with a DepartmentId of 80) and one Jobs entity object instance (with a JobId of "SA_REP") corresponding to two rows of the query result. Note that only some of the entity attributes (those corresponding to query columns) are populated; the rest remain null and will be queried when necessary. More information appears in the sidebar "Fault-in."

View Attribute Type	Mapped to Query Column?	Mapped to Entity Attribute?
Persistent	Yes	Yes
SQL-Only	Yes	No
Entity-Derived	No	Yes
Transient	No	No

TABLE 7-1. *View Attribute Types*

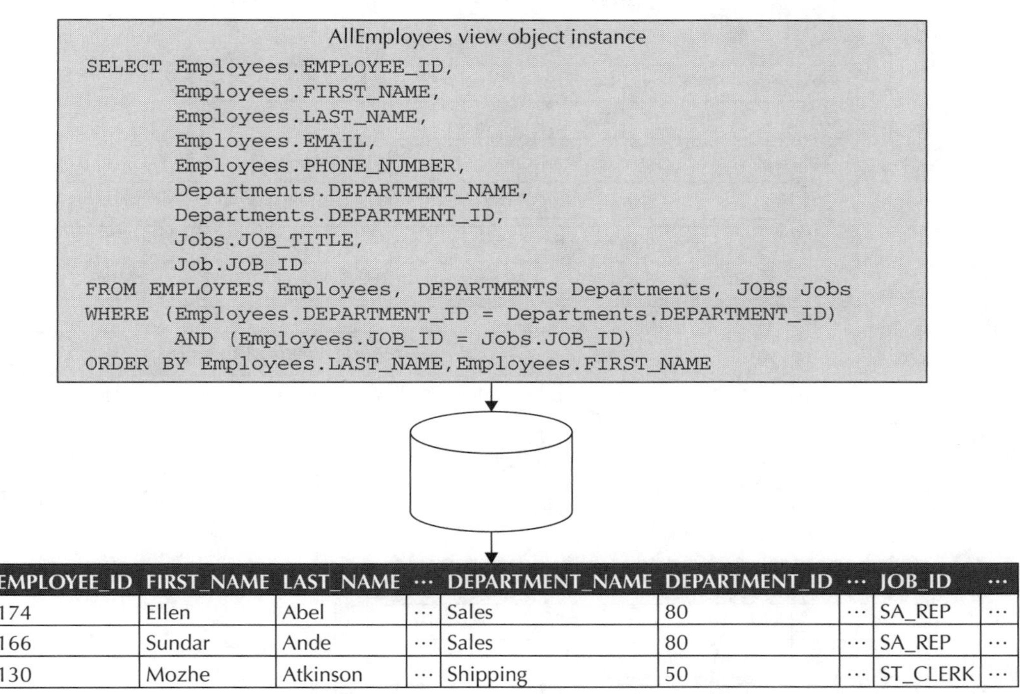

AllEmployees view object instance
SELECT Employees.EMPLOYEE_ID,
Employees.FIRST_NAME,
Employees.LAST_NAME,
Employees.EMAIL,
Employees.PHONE_NUMBER,
Departments.DEPARTMENT_NAME,
Departments.DEPARTMENT_ID,
Jobs.JOB_TITLE,
Job.JOB_ID
FROM EMPLOYEES Employees, DEPARTMENTS Departments, JOBS Jobs
WHERE (Employees.DEPARTMENT_ID = Departments.DEPARTMENT_ID)
AND (Employees.JOB_ID = Jobs.JOB_ID)
ORDER BY Employees.LAST_NAME,Employees.FIRST_NAME
EMPLOYEE_ID FIRST_NAME LAST_NAME ··· DEPARTMENT_NAME DEPARTMENT_ID ··· JOB_ID ···
174 Ellen Abel ··· Sales 80 ··· SA_REP ···
166 Sundar Ande ··· Sales 80 ··· SA_REP ···
130 Mozhe Atkinson ··· Shipping 50 ··· ST_CLERK ···

FIGURE 7-1. *Executing a query and returning a result*

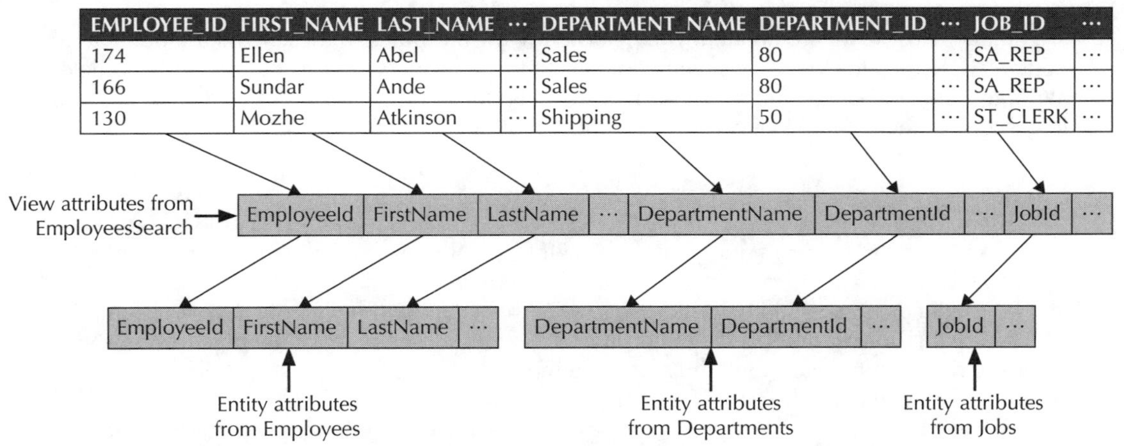

FIGURE 7-2. *Associating the query result columns with view and entity attributes*

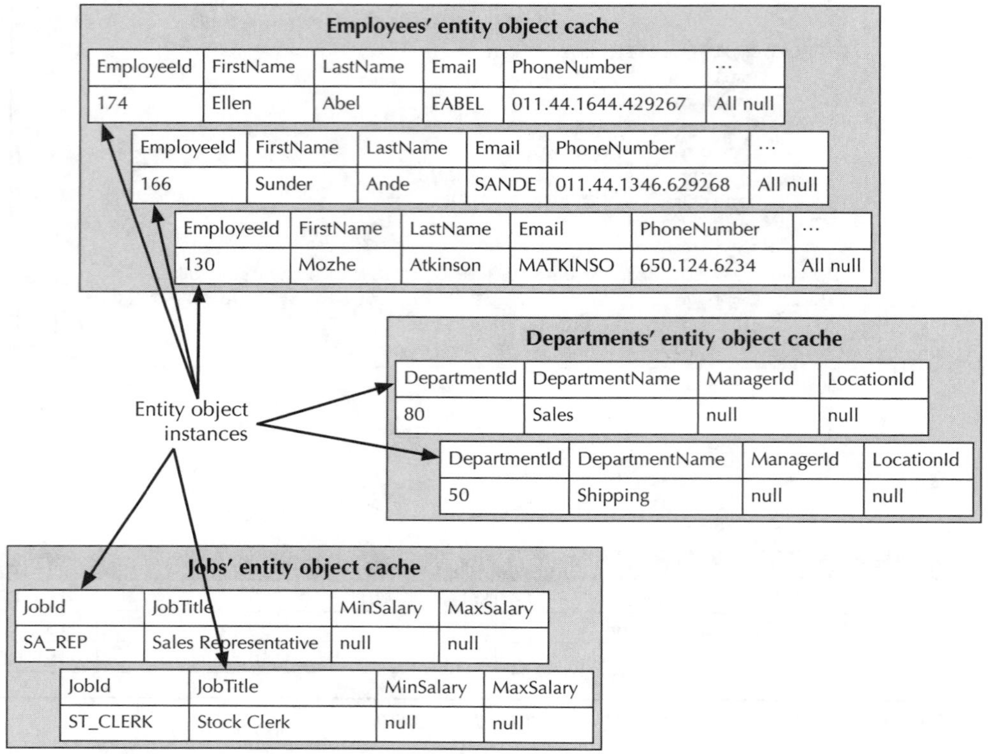

FIGURE 7-3. *Populating entity caches*

Finally, view rows are created. The persistent view attributes in these rows are not actually populated. Rather, the view rows retain pointers to the relevant entity object instances and delegate attribute storage, change, and retrieval to those entity object instances. These view rows are inserted into the view cache for the view object instance, as shown in Figure 7-4.

Fault-In

A view object definition's query rarely contains all columns from all tables; when tables have a large number of columns (especially if some of those columns have LOB or *inter*Media datatypes), this is critical to save both execution time and memory consumption. However, if, for example, a validation rule for a retrieved entity attribute depends on a nonretrieved entity attribute, and a user attempts to change the retrieved attribute, the framework will need the value for the nonretrieved attribute.

This triggers *fault-in,* a process whereby ADF retrieves all unpopulated attributes for a particular entity object instance (using a query by primary key) whenever a not-yet-retrieved attribute is requested. This prevents the framework from needing to make return trips to the database each time a new attribute value is needed.

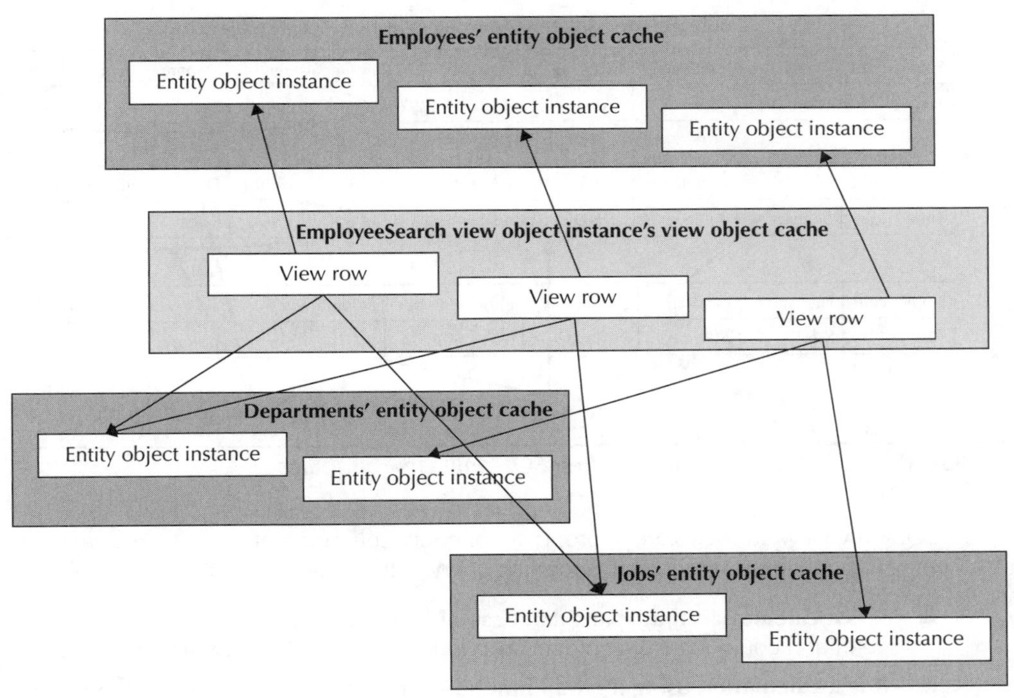

FIGURE 7-4. *Populating view caches: persistent view attributes*

NOTE

Strictly speaking, a persistent view attribute does not need to be mapped to a persistent entity attribute. You could map a persistent view attribute to a transient entity attribute; in that case, the view row will still take the initial value of the attribute from a column in a query result set row and then delegate storage, change, and retrieval to the entity object instance, although the attribute value will never be written to the database.

SQL-Only View Attributes

A *SQL-only* view attribute is one that is mapped to a column in the view object's SQL query but is not mapped to an underlying entity attribute. The values of SQL-only attributes are held in the view cache for the view object instance; view rows are responsible for handling SQL-only attribute storage, change, and retrieval themselves, rather than delegating to entity object instances, as shown in Figure 7-5 (which shows the cache of a view object instance based on a view definition that uses exclusively SQL-only attributes).

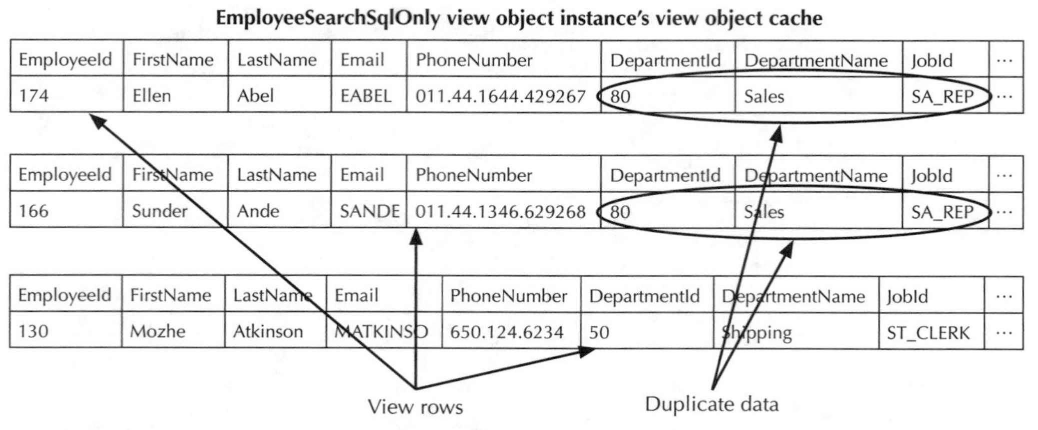

FIGURE 7-5. *Populating view caches: SQL-only view attributes*

SQL-only view attributes are appropriate for query columns that cannot logically be mapped to an entity attribute because the corresponding query column has one of the following properties:

- **It is a calculation that spans database objects** In this case, no single entity object definition could logically hold an appropriate entity attribute to map the view attribute to.
- **It is a calculation using a group function** In this case, entity object instances, which correspond to database object rows, would not be appropriate for storing the retrieved data.

While it is possible to use SQL-only view attributes to store data taken directly from database object columns or single-table calculations, we instead recommend using persistent view attributes (based on persistent or transient entity attributes), for the following reasons:

Using Persistent View Attributes Uses Less Memory for Data Retrieved by a View Object Instance For some join queries, using entity-derived attributes for attributes of the parent table can save memory. Contrast Figure 7-4 with Figure 7-5, which shows how an EmployeeSearch view object instance would cache data if all its attributes were SQL-only. In Figure 7-5, data from DEPARTMENTS and JOBS is stored twice—once for each row corresponding to the Sales department and the job SA_REP. In Figure 7-4, one entity object the containing the data is created for each table, and multiple view rows can point to it.

Using Persistent View Attributes Ensures Consistency Across View Object Instances EmployeeSearch and AllEmployees each have attributes that map to columns queried from EMPLOYEES. In particular, each has a persistent attribute, FirstName, which maps to the same data. Because this attribute is persistent, view rows delegate changes to and retrieval of its value to the underlying entity object instance, as shown in Figure 7-6. Because of this, when a view row (such as a row from an instance of AllEmployees) changes the value of FirstName, the changes are automatically visible in any rows of EmployeeSearch that use the same entity instance.

If the FirstName attribute were SQL-only, in either EmployeeSearch or AllEmployees, this automatic synchronization would not happen, because the in-memory value would not be

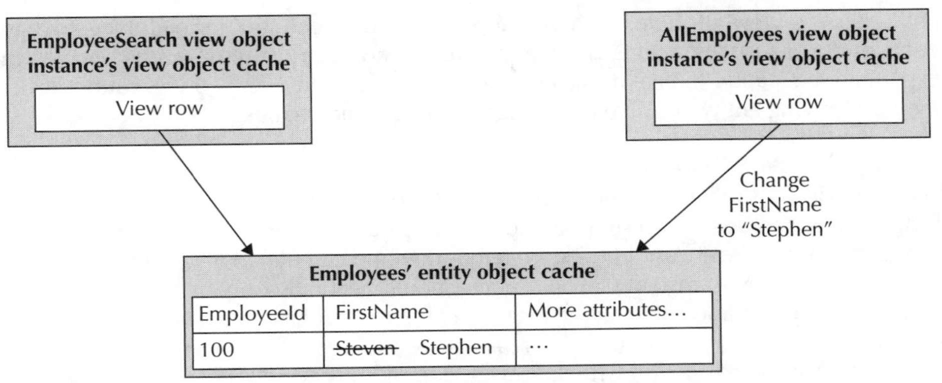

FIGURE 7-6. *Synchronization between view object instances*

shared by these view rows. To see the change in an EmployeeSearch instance, you would need to post any changes made by the AllEmployees view object instance to the database (only possible if at least that view object was using a persistent attribute) and re-execute the EmployeeSearch instance's query.

Only Persistent View Attributes Can Write Changes to the Database View rows cannot perform DML operations directly, but rather must delegate DML operations to entity object instances. Because of this, changes to SQL-only view attributes, which do not delegate storage and update to entity attributes, cannot be saved to the database. You need a persistent view attribute based on a persistent entity attribute to write data to the database.

Using Persistent View Attributes Uses Less Memory for Data Retrieved Across View Object Instances If your data model contains multiple view object instances based on the same view object definition, they will maintain separate caches of view rows, so that one cache can, for example, be limited by a different view link instance than the other. Any duplicate data between the queries will only be stored once (in the entity object cache) if it is placed in persistent attributes, but it will be stored twice (in each view object cache) if it is placed in SQL-only attributes.

The same consideration applies to view object instances based on separate view object definitions, so long as they need to retrieve data in common. For example, EmployeeSearch and AllEmployees both need to retrieve data from EMPLOYEES. Because they both contain persistent attributes from usages of Employees, the data in those attributes only needs to be stored once, in the entity object cache. If the attributes were SQL-only, their data would need to be stored twice, in each view object cache.

Using Persistent View Attributes Allows You to Use Intersection Tables Without Expert SQL Mode Many-to-many view link definitions that use intersection tables require the destination view object definition (and the source view object definition, under some circumstances) to use expert SQL mode, unless the source and destination attributes of the view link definition are persistent. More information is provided in the section "What Are View Link Definitions and View Link Instances?"

Entity-Derived View Attributes

Entity-derived view attributes are not mapped to a query column. Instead, they are based on an entity attribute (usually a transient one) that uses a nonquery method to calculate its values, as explained in Chapter 6. Like persistent view attributes, entity-derived view attributes delegate to their underlying entity attribute for storage, retrieval, and change.

Transient View Attributes

Transient view attributes are neither mapped to a query column nor based on entity attributes. Instead, they can be used to store temporary or calculated values in the view cache, much the way entity-derived view attributes store temporary and calculated values in an entity cache. Like SQL-only attributes, transient view attributes should generally only be used when an underlying entity attribute is inappropriate (because the calculation relies on more than one table, or is based on values of SQL-only attributes). The reasons are similar: entity-derived attributes perform essentially the same function while allowing data sharing within and between view caches and ensuring consistency across view caches.

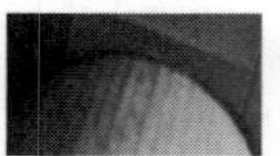

TIP
You can define attribute-level declarative validation rules on transient view attributes.

SQL-Only View Object Definitions

A *SQL-only view object definition* is a view object definition that is not based on entity object usages but that defines a SELECT statement. Because of this, SQL-only view object definitions can have only SQL-only and transient attributes, not attributes based on entity attributes. SQL-only view object definitions are indicated when you do not need the services of an entity object (INSERT, UPDATE, and DELETE capabilities), and when none of the attributes can be reasonably mapped to a database object column.

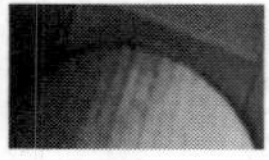

NOTE
We use the term "SQL-only" for this type of view object definition, whereas the JDeveloper help system and IDE sometimes refer to this type of view object definition as "read-only" to distinguish it from entity object–based view object definitions.

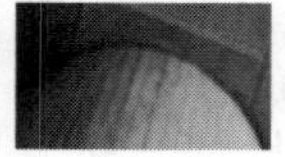

TIP
A PL/SQL function that returns a PL/SQL table can serve as the source of data in the FROM clause of a SELECT (FROM TABLE(CAST(<PL/SQL function>))). If you use this technique inside a SQL-only view object, you can pass view object bind variables to the PL/SQL function.

View Attribute Updatability and Read-Only Entity Object Usages

As noted, only persistent view attributes can actually write changes to the database, but it is possible to change the data in other types of view attributes in memory. This is especially useful for entity-derived and transient attributes, but it is possible with SQL-only attributes as well. To prevent this, an attribute must be marked as never updatable or only updatable while new.

Persistent or entity-derived view attributes that are based on never-updatable entity attributes are themselves automatically never updatable. Ones that are based on updatable-when-new entity attributes can be marked as never updatable or updatable when new. Ones that are based on always-editable entity attributes can be marked as never updatable, updatable when new, or always updatable.

Transient or SQL-only view attributes can be marked as never updatable, updatable when new, or always updatable.

You can mark an entire entity object usage as not updatable (read-only). All view attributes based on entity attributes from that usage will be considered never updatable. By default, JDeveloper marks every entity object usage in a view object definition other than the first as read-only (because they are frequently used to read lookup information that should not be edited), but you can change this.

By default, JDeveloper marks all attributes in a SQL-only view object definition as never updatable (because, in the most common case, developers do not want to allow edits that cannot be persisted), but you can change this.

View Attribute Types

Persistent and entity-derived view attributes inherit their datatypes from their underlying entity attribute, as should be expected given that they actually delegate their data storage to the underlying attribute. SQL-only and transient attributes allow you to specify a Java type; the types available are the same as those available to entity attributes, as described in Chapter 6. Because view attributes often use domains as their Java types, the information about working with domains in Chapter 6 applies at the view object level as well as the entity object level.

Key and Alternate Key Attributes

When a view object definition contains entity object usages, it must contain each entity object usage's primary key attributes. (JDeveloper adds these for you automatically when you add an entity object usage to a view object definition.) These attributes are required to maintain the pointers to underlying entity object instances to which each view row needs to delegate.

These attributes form a default key for the view object definition if the view attribute is based on an attribute from an updatable (not a read-only) entity object usage. A view object definition's key is similar to an entity object definition's primary key; it provides a unique way to identify or find a particular view row. For view object definitions with entity usages, you can optionally specify additional attributes to form part of the key (although you cannot remove entity usage primary key attributes from the key). For SQL-only view object definitions, you must specify key attributes (which should be jointly unique, like the components of a primary key) to enable row navigation.

View object definitions with at least one entity object usage can also specify *alternate keys,* other ways of identifying one or more view rows. These keys are unlike entity object definition alternate keys in that you cannot select an arbitrary set of jointly unique attributes. Instead, you create an alternate key for a view object definition by selecting alternate keys for some or all of the underlying entity object usages. A view row matches the alternate key if each of its underlying entity object instances matches the appropriate alternate key (if any).

Using keys or alternate keys to perform lookups is explained in Chapter 8.

How Do You Create and Edit View Object Definitions?

This section provides an overview of the options for creating and editing view object definitions. For specific details of the process of creating and editing view object definitions, see the examples provided in Chapters 18 and 20.

Creating View Object Definitions

There are a number of ways to create the view object definitions your application needs to retrieve data.

The Business Components from Tables Wizard

As explained in Chapter 6, you can create an entire set of default business components using the Create Business Components from Tables Wizard, accessible from the New Gallery or by selecting **New Business Components from Tables** on a package's right-click menu. As explained in Chapter 6, the first page of the wizard allows you to select database tables, views, and synonyms for default entity object definitions. The second page allows you to specify entity object definitions for entity-based view object definitions.

These defaults have a single entity usage, pointing to the selected entity object definition. The attributes of default entity-based view object definitions are persistent or entity-derived attributes based on each of the attributes from the entity object definition. The third page of the wizard allows you to specify database objects for default SQL-only (which the wizard calls "read-only") view object definitions.

The Default Data Model Components Wizard

You can create an entire set of default data model components (view object definitions, view link definitions, and an application module definition) using the Default Data Model Components Wizard, accessible from the New Gallery, or by selecting **New Default Data Model Components** on a package's right-click menu. The first page of the wizard allows you to select entity object definitions to use for default entity-based view object definitions.

Dragging from the Component Palette to a Business Components Diagram

As mentioned in Chapters 5 and 6, you can create a business components diagram from the New Gallery item (Diagrams or ADF Business Components categories). When an ADF BC diagram is open, the Component Palette shows various business components, as shown in Figure 7-7.

You can create view object definitions by clicking the View Object icon in the Component Palette and then dragging to or clicking a blank area of the diagram. You can add entity object usages to view object definitions by clicking the Entity Object Usage icon in the Component Palette and then dragging to or clicking a view object definition that is already on the diagram; you will be prompted to select an entity object definition for the usage to refer to, and to enter a name for the usage.

The Create View Object Wizard

You can create a single view object definition by using the Create View Object wizard, accessible from the New Gallery or by selecting **New View Object** from a package's right-click menu.

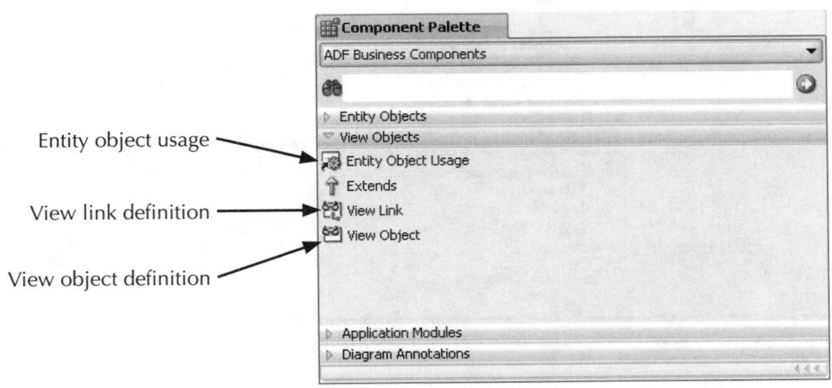

FIGURE 7-7. *The View panel*

This method requires more steps than the other creation processes but gives you more precise control over the view object definition's properties, lessening the need for later modifications.

You can use the Create View Object Wizard to create any of the following types of view object definitions:

- **Entity-based view object definitions**, which contain entity usages
- **SQL-only view object definitions**, called "read-only" by the wizard, with a query but no entity usages
- **Static view object definitions**, which let you specify rows and attribute values at design time rather than using a query to generate data (static view objects are explained in the section "How Do You Use View Object Instances as LOVs?")
- **Programmatic view object definitions** for which you must override `ViewObjectImpl` methods in a view object class to retrieve data in a custom manner.

Editing View Object Definitions

There are several ways to edit view object definitions.

Editing View Object Definitions on the Diagram

Using a Business Components diagram that contains view object definitions, you can rename those view object definitions, change the type of transient and SQL-only view attributes, add transient view attributes, remove any view attributes (except those based on the primary key attributes of entity object usages), and add or remove entity object usages, as shown in Figure 7-8. In particular:

- **Selecting the Name area** will allow you to type a new view object definition name.
- **Selecting an attribute and then clicking it** will allow you to type a new attribute name, as well as a type if the view attribute is transient or SQL-only.

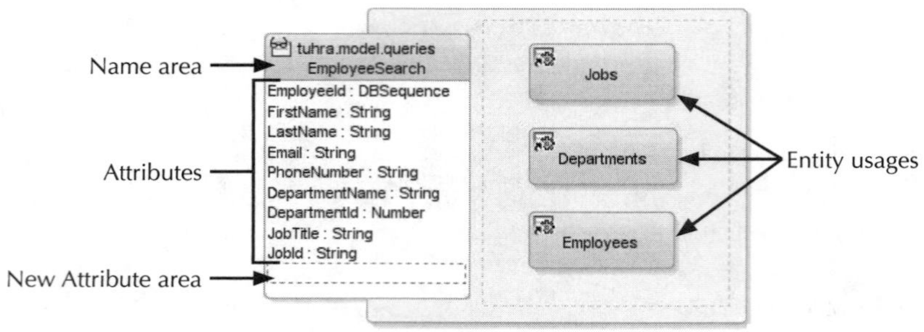

FIGURE 7-8. *A View object definition on a diagram*

- **Selecting an attribute and pressing** DELETE will delete the attribute, unless the attribute is based on a primary key attribute of an existing entity object usage.
- **Selecting the New Attribute area and then clicking it** will allow you to type a new attribute name and type; the attribute created will be transient.

Editors for View Object Definitions

By double-clicking a view object definition in the Application Navigator or on a diagram, you can open it in an editor window. Like the editors for entity object definitions and associations, this is a nonmodal editor window that allows you to change any property of a view object definition you can set in the Create View Object Wizard, except whether the view object definition uses a query (that is, is SQL-only or entity-based), a static list of values, or programmatic data retrieval. You can also specify a number of additional properties, such as named view criteria objects (explained in the section "How Can You Change Queries at Runtime?"), tuning properties, and security properties.

TIP
The Edit (pencil) button in all ADF BC editor windows will open a dialog with properties for the item selected in the editor.

Editing Custom View Classes

If you have generated custom view object, definition, or row classes, you can find them in the Application Navigator by expanding the view object definition's node, as shown to the right.

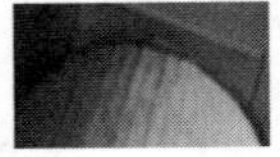

NOTE
If you or JDeveloper have created resource bundle classes (for example, to hold error message text) for a view object, that class will also appear in the same area.

You can open a code editor for these classes by double-clicking them. In addition, most options available on any Java class are available on these classes from the right-click menu—the notable exceptions are **Refactor | Rename** and **Refactor | Move**. This is because custom view classes must follow the naming conventions used by the project and must reside in the same package as the view object XML.

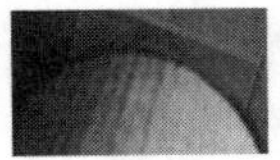

TIP
If you need to rename the Java classes and XML file used for any ADF BC object, select the object's node in the navigator. Refactor utilities will rename all files under that node.

Editing Individual Attribute Settings

You can edit settings for individual view attributes using either the Attribute Editor or the Property Inspector.

You can open the Attribute Editor by double-clicking a view attribute in an ADF BC diagram or a view object definition's editor, or by selecting an attribute in a view object definition's editor and clicking the Edit Selected Attribute button. This editor is very similar to the Attribute Editor for entity attributes, described in Chapter 6. The differences are as follows:

- The Entity Attribute page is read-only, and only displays the properties of underlying entity attributes for persistent or entity-derived view attributes.
- The View Attribute page allows you to change all attribute settings that can be set in the Create View Object Wizard, and it also allows you to add attribute-level validation rules (for transient attributes), UI hints, and settings that affect attribute recalculation.
- There is no "Validation Rules" page except for transient view attributes; you cannot add declarative validation to other view attributes.

When you select an attribute in the Attributes page of a view object definition's editor, the Property Inspector appears in the Log window. You can also use this window to change an attribute's settings.

How Do You Specify View Object Queries?

Most view object definitions are created based on one or more entity object usages. The view object definitions' persistent view attributes are based on entity attributes from those definitions. For example, the view object definition EmployeesSearch is based on usages of the entity object definitions Employees, Departments, and Jobs. In these cases, the view object definitions' default queries are constructed from the tables and columns represented by the entity object definitions.

You can specify a view object's query on the Query page of the Create View Object Wizard, or by clicking the Edit SQL Query icon on the Query page of a view object definition's editor, as shown in Figure 7-9, to open the Edit Query dialog, shown here:

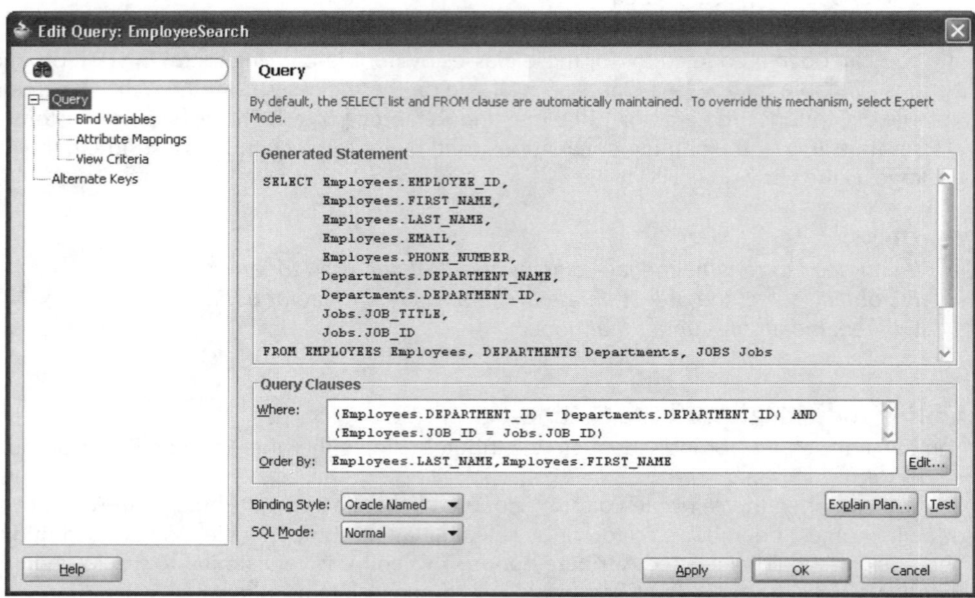

If you are creating or editing a view object definition with entity object usages, the page or dialog will allow you to select "Normal," "Declarative," or "Expert" SQL mode for the view object's query, and the rest of the page or dialog will change depending on your selection. If you are creating or editing a SQL-only view object definition, the page or dialog will always be in expert SQL mode. The modes are described in this section.

Normal SQL Mode

Normal SQL mode is a way of specifying a view object definition's query such that the query's SELECT and FROM clauses are maintained by JDeveloper. You optionally specify a WHERE clause, for which JDeveloper provides a default, and an ORDER BY clause that are appended to the query. Default view object definitions with entity usages use normal SQL mode, though you can change their SQL mode by editing them.

Normal Query FROM and SELECT Clauses

The FROM clause that JDeveloper generates contains the underlying database objects for each entity object usage's definition, aliased to the name of the entity object usage. Using another example, an EmployeeJobSearch view object definition could contain usages of the entity object definitions Employees, Jobs, and JobHistory. The usages would be called Employees, Jobs, and JobHistory, so the FROM clause of EmployeesJobSearch's query would be the following:

```
FROM EMPLOYEES Employees,
     JOBS Jobs,
     JOB_HISTORY JobHistory
```

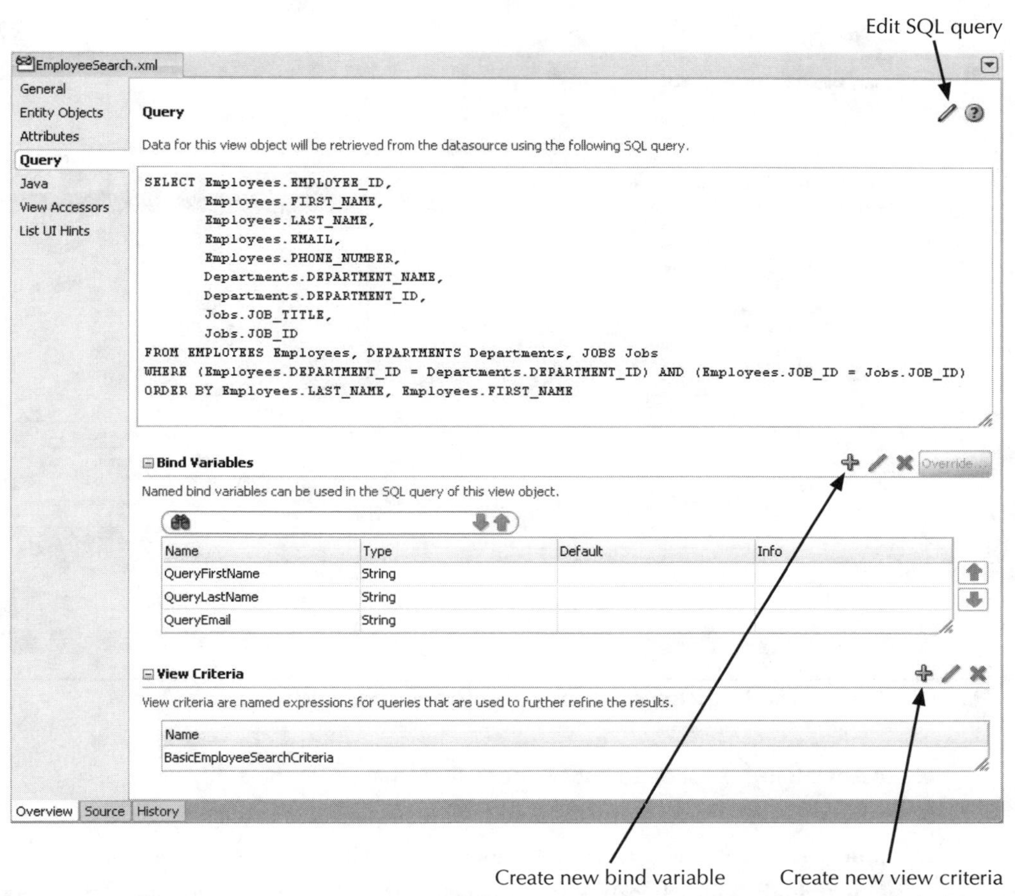

FIGURE 7-9. *The Query page of a view object definition editor*

The SELECT clause of the query contains one column for each view attribute, except for transient and entity-derived attributes (which are explained in the section "How Do View Attributes Work?").

Normal Query WHERE Clauses

In a view object definition with a single entity object usage, JDeveloper does not supply a default WHERE clause, although you can add one yourself. However, when you add a second or later entity object usage to a view object definition, you can choose ways in which it is related to existing entity object usages in that definition, as shown in Figure 7-10. This allows JDeveloper to generate a default WHERE clause for you, based on the following settings:

- **Selected** The entity object usage.
- **Alias** The usage's alias in the FROM clause (also the name of the usage).
- **Definition** The underlying entity object definition.

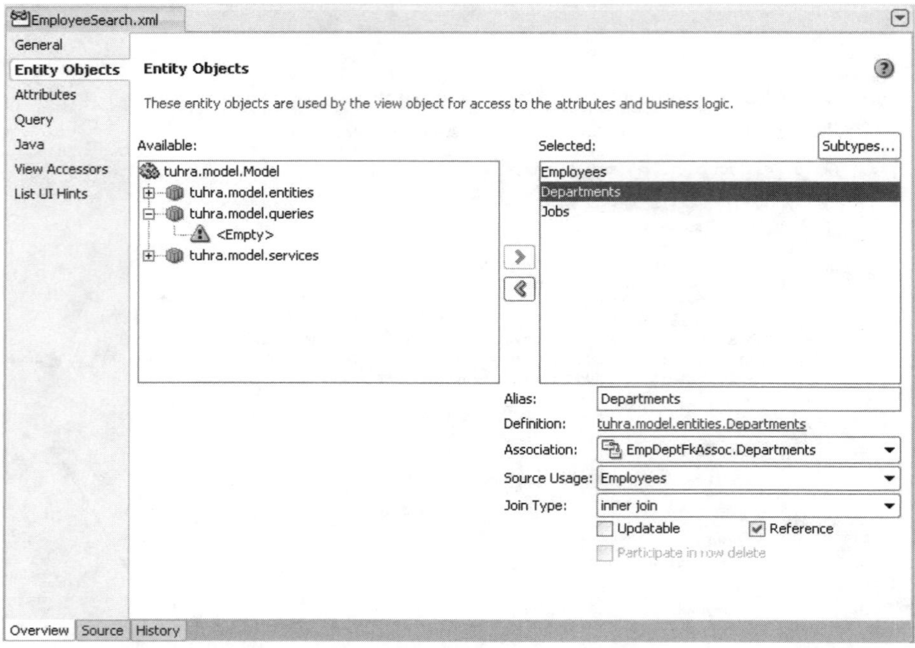

FIGURE 7-10. *The Entity Objects tab of a view object definition's editor*

- **Association** A list of potential associations that relate the entity objects.
- **Source Usage** Which previous entity object usage this is related to.
- **Join Type** Where to put (+) in the generated WHERE clause (if needed).
- **Updatable** If this checkbox is not selected, rows from this entity object are read-only.
- **Reference** If checked, the related row from the reference entity object data source will be queried when the master row changes (as described in the section "Reference Entity Usages").
- **Participate in row delete** Whether a delete of a view row will delete the corresponding entity object instance for this usage. This is used for updatable entity usages only.

The Association pulldown contains the following options:

No Association If you choose to give the new entity object usage no association (by choosing "None" in the Association dropdown list), JDeveloper does not create a WHERE clause component for it. Unless you edit the WHERE clause, the query will return a Cartesian product involving the entire table.

NOTE
Cartesian product queries are rare but necessary if outer joins are not sufficient to supply blank rows.

Default Association If you select "default" in the Association dropdown list JDeveloper will look for columns in the two entity object usages with common names. For example, since Employees and Departments both have an attribute called "DepartmentId," the component of the WHERE clause of EmployeesSearch generated for this association will be as follows:

```
Employees.DEPARTMENT_ID = Departments.DEPARTMENT_ID
```

NOTE
The default option is only available in the view object editor after creating the view object. It is not available in the Create View Object Wizard.

A Particular Association Accessor If there are any associations between the new entity object usage and any previously added entity object usages, you can choose an accessor that returns instances from the new entity object usage. (You usually only will be able to choose one accessor from an association, but you can choose either accessor from associations between an entity object definition and itself, such as EmpMgrFkAssoc.) This will generate a WHERE clause that requires source attributes of the source entity object usage to match destination attributes of the destination entity object usage.

For example, there are two associations between Employees and Departments: EmpDeptFkAssoc and DeptMgrFkAssoc. EmpDeptFkAssoc has a single source/destination attribute pair: DepartmentId from Employees is paired with DepartmentId from Departments. This generates the following WHERE clause fragment:

```
Employees.DEPARTMENT_ID = Departments.DEPARTMENT_ID
```

If, instead, EmployeeSearchView used DeptMgrFkAssoc (which pairs EmployeeId from Employees with ManagerId from Departments), the generated WHERE clause fragment would be as follows:

```
Employees.EMPLOYEE_ID = Departments.MANAGER_ID
```

For any of these options, you can select whether you want the generated portion of the WHERE clause to be an inner join, left outer join, or right outer join.

Normal Query ORDER BY Clauses

JDeveloper does not generate a default ORDER BY clause, but you can specify one. Stating the ORDER BY clause using the *Order By* property will sort the view rows.

Editing Queries in Normal SQL Mode

The Edit Query dialog for normal SQL mode shown before contains the *Generated Statement* field, which represents the entire SQL query, including JDeveloper-generated SELECT and FROM clauses. The *Where* field is, of course, the SELECT statement WHERE clause (in this case, the JDeveloper default) and any criteria predicates you type here will change the generated statement. You specify the *Order By* field to create the ORDER BY clause in the query.

Declarative SQL Mode

Declarative SQL Mode is a way of specifying a view object definition's query such that the query is generated at runtime from declarative properties you specify. The query is generated on the fly and can change based on the attributes on the page.

Declarative Query FROM and SELECT Clauses

The FROM clause of a declarative query works exactly like that of a normal query, except that it is generated at runtime rather than design time. However, the SELECT clause of a declarative query does not always contain a column for every persistent or SQL-only attribute in the view object definition. Instead, ADF automatically generates a SELECT clause at runtime that queries data for only the attributes actually used by the user interface. Only if other attributes are required by business logic is the entire view row faulted in (as explained in the sidebar "Fault-in" earlier in this chapter).

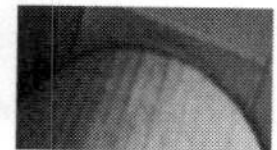

TIP

If you want to ensure that the SELECT clause of a declarative query always queries data for all attributes (for example, to avoid fault-in), you can select Include all attributes in runtime-generated query *in the Tuning section of the General page of the view object definition's editor.*

Declarative Query WHERE Clauses

ADF generates a basic WHERE clause at runtime based on the view object definition's entity object usages and the associations between them, much like the default WHERE clause generated by JDeveloper for normal queries. Unlike normal query WHERE clauses, however, declarative query WHERE clauses do not allow you to edit them. You can, however, specify additional conditions for the WHERE clause by adding one or more view criteria objects.

View Criteria Objects, Groups, and Items A *view criteria object* (sometimes called "a view criteria" in the JDeveloper user interface and online help) is a structured set of requirements that can be used to construct a SQL condition for use in a WHERE clause. A view criteria object consists of one or more *groups,* conditions that can be ANDed or ORed together. Each group is a conjunction of *items,* which are requirements (ANDed or ORed together) that a particular view attribute stands in a relation, or *operator,* to zero or more values, specified as literals or bind variables. A view criteria object, with its single group and that group's three items, is shown in Figure 7-11.

Selecting a criteria node and clicking Add Criteria will add a nested criteria node to which you can add groups.

View Criteria Operators The operators allowed depend on the SQL type of the attribute's underlying table column or expression. For example, attributes corresponding to a NUMBER column can be compared to a single literal value or a bind variable value for the following operators:

- Equal to
- Not equal to

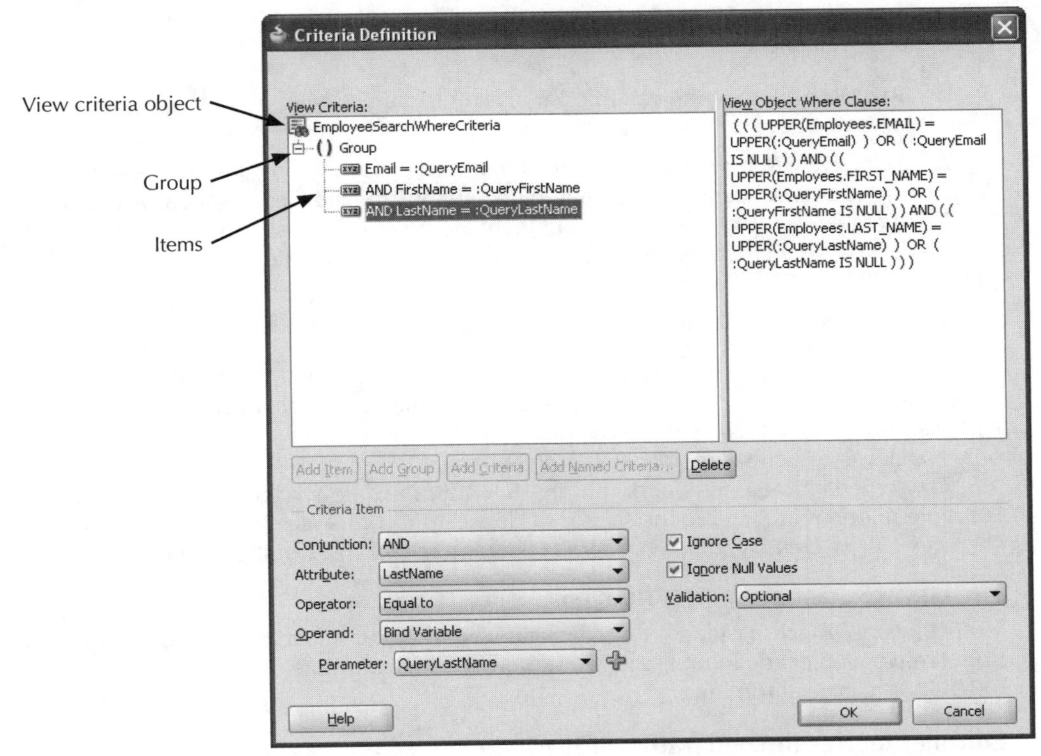

FIGURE 7-11. *The Criteria Definition dialog*

- Less than
- Less than or equal to

Attributes corresponding to a NUMBER column can be compared to two literal values or two bind variable values using these operators:

- Greater than
- Greater than or equal to

For example, the "AND Email = :QueryEmail" item shown in Figure 7-11 requires that the column underlying the Email attribute be equal to the bind variable :QueryEmail (subject to the item options discussed in the subsection "View Criteria Item Options". Using bind variables in a View Object query is explained further in the section "How Can You Change Queries at Runtime?"

View Criteria Item Options A view criteria item for an attribute that maps to a VARCHAR2 query column can be set to perform a case-insensitive search (by comparing uppercase versions of the attribute and literal/variable values), as shown in Figure 7-11.

In addition, you can choose a type of validation for a view criteria item that uses a bind parameter, as shown in Figure 7-11, which describes whether the bind variable value can be null. The options available are as follows:

- **Required** If the bind variable value is null, attempting to execute the query will throw an `oracle.jbo.AttrValException`.
- **Selectively Required** If the bind variable value is null, but at least one other item in the group uses a literal or a non-null bind variable, the view criteria item will be ignored. If the bind variable value is null but there are no other items in the group, or all of the other items in the group use bind variables that are also null, attempting to execute the query will throw an `oracle.jbo.AttrValException`.
- **Optional** A null value for the bind variable will be accepted.

If the view criteria item is marked "optional," which values will satisfy the view criteria item when the bind variable value is null depends on whether *Ignore Null Values* is selected. If *Ignore Null Values* is selected, every value (including NULL) will satisfy the view criteria item; otherwise, only NULL values will satisfy the view criteria item.

View criteria have a number of uses in ADF BC, in addition to their use in declarative queries. For more information, refer to the sections "How Can You Change Queries at Runtime?" and "What Are View Link Definitions and View Link Instances?" later in this chapter.

Declarative Query ORDER BY Clauses

To specify an ORDER BY clause for a declarative query, you select an ordered list of attributes from the view object definition, and a sort order for each attribute. ADF converts this list to an ORDER BY clause at runtime.

Editing Queries in Declarative SQL Mode

The Edit Query dialog for declarative normal SQL mode is shown here:

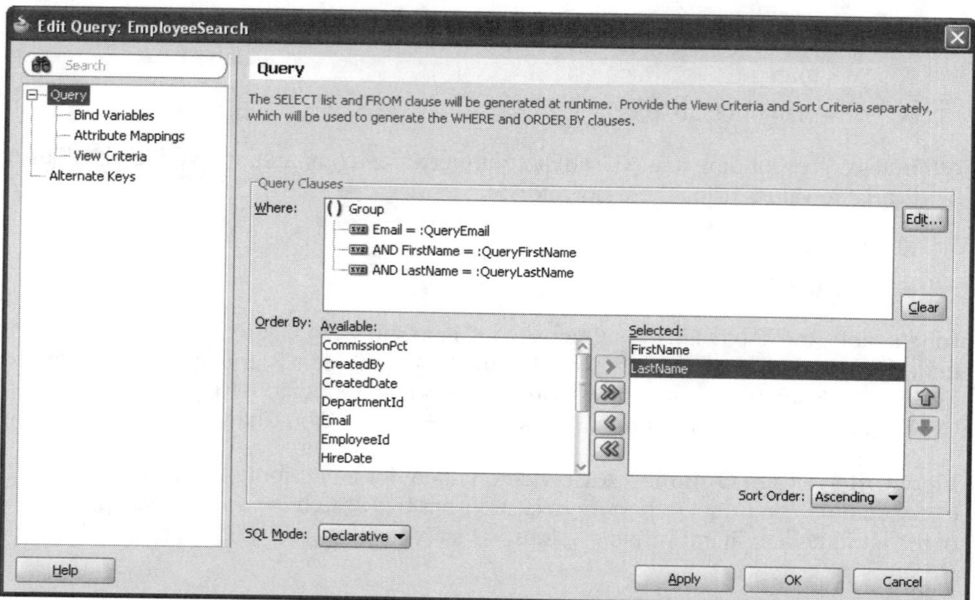

You can specify ascending or descending sort order using the *Sort Order* pulldown after selecting an attribute. Click Edit to open the Criteria Definition dialog (shown in Figure 7-11), which will build the WHERE clause criteria.

Expert SQL Mode

Expert SQL mode allows you to enter any query you require for a view object definition, but requires more maintenance than the other SQL modes. In an expert SQL mode query, you manually enter the query for the view object, plus an optional separate ORDER BY clause. At runtime, ADF executes the query "SELECT * FROM (<VO_QUERY>) ORDER BY <ORDER_BY_CLAUSE>," where <VO_QUERY> is the expert mode query you specify, and <ORDER_BY_CLAUSE> is the separate ORDER BY clause. JDeveloper assigns an alias to <VO_QUERY> of "QRSLT."

TIP
Although you usually do not need a table alias in the ORDER BY clause for an expert mode query, if you do need to include one, use "QRSLT" to represent the entire query.

As is explained in the sections "Dynamic Queries" and "What Are View Link Definitions and View Link Instances?" view object instances can append WHERE clauses to this larger query to modify it for execution.

The query can be any query that is valid for use as an inline view, and so it can contain not only SELECT, FROM, WHERE, and ORDER_BY clauses, but also GROUP BY clauses and UNION operations (though not the FOR UPDATE clause, or any other construct not allowed in an inline view).

NOTE
There is a difference between an ORDER BY clause entered as part of the expert query and the optional separate ORDER BY clause. Since the latter is appended to the statement that selects from the inner view, it should refer to query column aliases in the inner view (if they exist), not table column names. In addition, if the expert query is a UNION, the separate ORDER BY clause can mingle rows from the union.

Because JDeveloper and ADF cannot use entity object usages to create the FROM clause of their queries, SQL-only view object definitions must use expert SQL mode. However, you can use expert SQL mode in view object definitions with entity object usages, as well. If you use expert SQL mode with persistent view attributes, JDeveloper will try to match attributes to columns, but you need to cross-check this mapping of attributes' query columns and underlying entity attributes, as explained next.

Persistent View Attributes and Expert SQL Mode

If you use normal or declarative SQL mode in a view object definition, the definition's query's SELECT clause is created, in part, based on the persistent view attributes you select for the view object. Because of this, JDeveloper can automatically determine which entity attributes should be populated with which query columns, as shown in Figure 7-2.

If you use expert SQL mode in a view object definition, however, you specify the entire query, including its SELECT clause (or clauses, in the case of unions), independently of persistent attribute selection. Because of this, JDeveloper and ADF cannot automatically do the work of mappings shown in Figure 7-2. Instead, you must specify and maintain which query columns map to which persistent attributes of the view object on the Query\Attribute Mappings page of the Edit Query dialog, as shown here:

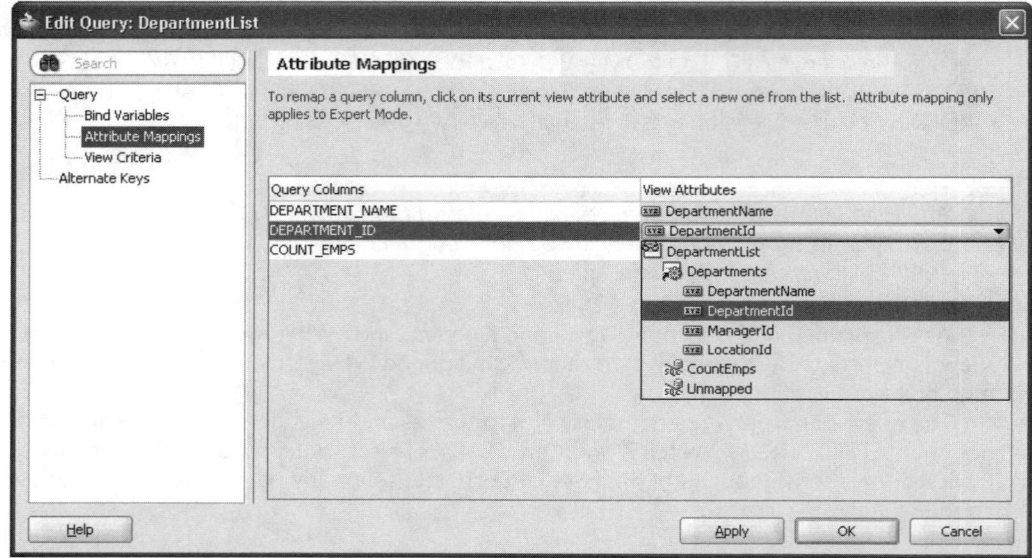

The DEPARTMENT_ID query column is mapped to the DepartmentId attribute from the entity object usage Departments. Notice the CountEmps SQL-only view attribute in the list of available attributes.

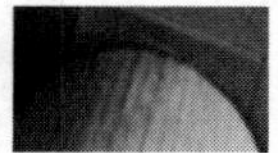

CAUTION

It is important to maintain these mappings correctly. Mapping incorrect query columns (especially calculated columns) to persistent entity attributes can result in application errors and even, in rare cases, data corruption when the entity object instance attempts to write data queried from one column or expression into a separate column.

Editing Queries in Expert SQL Mode

The Edit Query dialog for expert SQL mode is shown next:

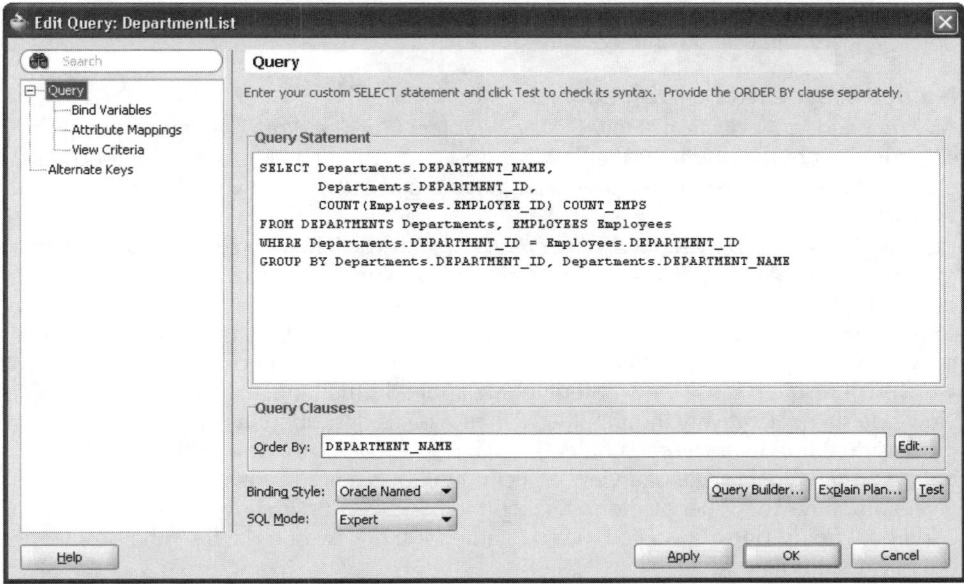

Notice that the *Order By* property is applied using a separate field rather than being embedded in the query. The *Query Statement* area consists of editable custom SQL.

Dynamic Queries

Sometimes, you need to allow a view object instance flexibility to modify its query (inherited from its view object definition) at runtime. For example, users may only be able to see restricted query results; if the restrictions differ from user to user, you need to allow particular view object instances in separate user's data model to change their copy of the query based on who the user is. Alternatively, you may need to temporarily restrict a view object instance's query to match query-by-example (QBE) parameters or to match a more complex search condition.

Bind Variables

There are a number of ways to include bind variables in a view object definition's query:

- Directly type them into a query in expert SQL mode.
- Include them in the WHERE clause of a query in normal SQL mode.
- Use them in the view criteria object of a query in declarative SQL mode, as described in the section "How Do View Object Queries Work?"

In addition to including bind variables in the view object's query, you must register them with the view object; click the "Create new bind variable" icon on the Query page of a view object definition's editor (shown in Figure 7-9), or use the Bind Variables page of the Create View Object Wizard. This requires specifying a Java type for each variable (such as `String` for VARCHAR2 variables or `Number` for NUMBER variables).

Once you have specified bind variables, you can access and change them from a view object instance, as explained in the section "What are View Object Definitions and View Object Instances?" The ADF model layer also contains declarative methods for accessing them declaratively, as described in Chapter 14. Once bind variable values are set, executing (or re-executing) the view object's query will use the entered values.

Named View Criteria Objects

As explained in the section "How Do View Object Queries Work?" a view criteria object is a structured set of requirements that can be used to construct a SQL condition for use in a WHERE clause. That section explained how declarative-mode queries use view criteria to construct their WHERE clause.

You can also specify *named view criteria objects,* which are view criteria that can be appended to the WHERE clause of individual view object instances at runtime. At runtime, you can switch between view criteria objects by passing a view criteria object's name to the method `ViewObjectImpl.setApplyViewCriteriaName()`, or by passing an array containing multiple view criteria objects' names to `ViewObjectImpl.setApplyViewCriteriaNames()`, which will result in those view criteria being applied simultaneously. You can also switch between view criteria declaratively through the ADF model, as described in Chapter 14.

To add named view criteria objects, click the "Create new view criteria" (green "+" plus) button on the Query page of a view object definition's editor, shown in Figure 7-9. This opens a version of the Edit Query Criteria Dialog (the basic version is shown in Figure 7-11) with two additional fields; one allows you to set a name for the view criteria, the other lets you specify a query execution mode.

Query Execution Modes The view criteria objects used in declarative queries always operate by adding a WHERE clause to the view object definition's query; that is, the filter is always applied (and only applied) when the query is executed. If a new view row is created, or the attribute values of an existing view row change in such a way that the row no longer satisfies the view criteria object, the view row will continue to appear as one of its instance's rows until changes are posted to the database and the query is re-executed. Named view criteria objects, by contrast, can specify one of three *query execution modes,* which affect how the view criteria object filters rows:

- **Database** mode works exactly like a view criteria object used in declarative queries; the view criteria object is applied as a WHERE clause to the view object definition's query.
- **In memory** mode filters view rows held in the cache, hiding nonmatching rows from the application.
- **Both** mode both adds a WHERE clause to the view object definition's query and filters view rows in the cache.

The Database mode is the fastest of these modes, and the one that uses the least memory in the application server; however, any changes to data must be posted and the query re-executed before the changed data is filtered appropriately. The In memory mode immediately filters rows according to changes, but because the query alone is not filtered, far more rows may be retrieved from the database, and far more view row instances created, than will actually be used. Moreover, filtering rows in memory is generally slower than allowing the database to filter them. Both mode has more overhead than the other two modes (since the database needs to process a WHERE clause and the in-memory filter needs to be maintained), but eliminates the disadvantages of the other methods: the filter is automatically maintained without a database round-trip, and no more rows will be retrieved from the database than will actually be displayed.

Changing a View Object Instance's Entire WHERE Clause or Entire Query

If you need to completely change a view object query's WHERE clause, you can pass a WHERE clause (without the word "WHERE") into the method `ViewObjectImpl.setWhereClause()`. You can also change a view object's entire query if you need to (for example, to change an expert SQL mode view object's HAVING clause, or the calculation of a SQL-only attribute) by passing the new query into `ViewObjectImpl.setQuery()`, although unpredictable behavior may result if you change the number, datatypes, or aliases of query columns, or the FROM clause of a query. These methods are substantially slower than the other techniques discussed in this section; they should be used only if the other techniques discussed are not an option.

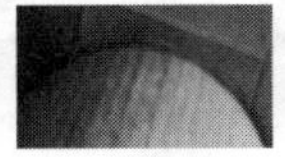

CAUTION
Never construct a WHERE clause or query using unfiltered data entered by the user; doing so opens you to attacks by SQL injection from malicious users. Instead, either filter user input to make sure it does not contain SQL code, or use bind variables and view criteria instead of setQuery().

How Can View Object Instances Handle Row Creation, Row Deletion, and Association Changes?

In addition to querying data from the database, view object instances are able to create and delete rows, and manage attribute changes that can affect the way in which they point to entity object instances.

Reference Entity Usages

Any entity usage you add to a view object instance other than the first is, by default, a reference entity usage (although you can change that as shown in Figure 7-10). A *reference entity usage* allows a view row to change which entity object instance it points to, depending on values of foreign key attributes from other entity usages.

Figure 7-12 shows how an entity usage's being a reference entity usage can make a difference in how it handles change in data from other usages. The view object definition AllDepartmentsWithManagers contains two entity object usages: one of Departments, and one of Employees. Because the Employees usage is a reference usage, when the value of ManagerId in a Departments instance (the source attribute of the association between the entity object usages) changes, the view row based on it automatically begins pointing to a different Employees instance in order to maintain the association.

In general, reference entity object usages should not be marked as "Updatable," (in the view object editor's Entity Object page) because it's usually not the developer's intent to allow editing of reference data through a view row. Even in exceptions to this, it is almost always wise to make

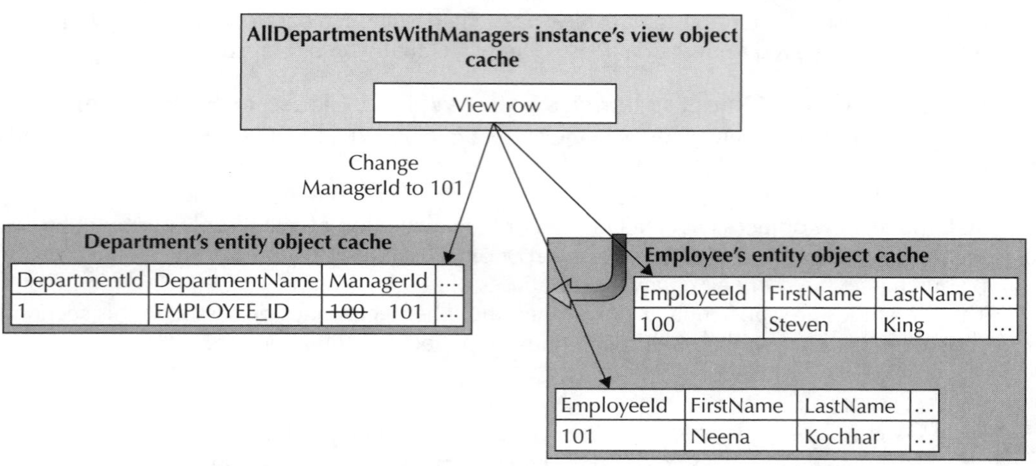

FIGURE 7-12. *Reference entity usages and data change*

the view attributes corresponding to the reference usage's primary key attributes read-only. Changing which entity object instance a reference entity object usage points to should be done by changing values of attributes associated with those primary key attributes in a different entity object usage, not changing the values of the primary key attributes themselves.

Creating View Rows

When the application creates a new view row, the following happens:

1. For each non–reference entity object usage in the view row's view object definition, a new entity object instance is created (no instances are created for view rows from SQL-only view object instances).
2. Any defaulting or creation logic specified by each entity object instance's entity object definition (as explained in Chapter 6) executes.
3. If no default value is supplied in the entity attribute, any defaulting or creation logic specified by the view row's view object definition executes. If the entity object declares a default value, the view object will use it.
4. If the view row's view object instance is a detail in a master-detail relationship (created by a view link instance), some of its attributes may be prepopulated to match the currently selected master view row. This is explained in the section "What Are View Link Definitions and View Link Instances?"
5. The attributes populated through steps 2–4 may be sufficient to determine existing instances of the reference entity object usages for the view row to point to. If so, the view row will point to those instances.
6. If no existing instance for a particular entity object usage is found, one will be created.

Deleting View Rows

When your application deletes a view row, the following happens:

1. The entity object instance corresponding to the first entity object usage is marked for deletion, as long as that entity object usage is updatable. (Deleting view rows from a SQL-only view object definition does not affect any entity object instances.)
2. If any other entity object usages are marked as "Updatable" and "Participate in row delete" (using options shown in Figure 7-10), the instances corresponding to those usages are marked for deletion as well. Note that this is not generally the desired behavior for reference entity object usages, so those should usually not be marked as participating in row deletion (read-only entity object usages cannot participate in row deletion).
3. The view row is removed from the view cache, together with any other view rows that rely on entity object instances that have been marked for deletion.

What Are View Link Definitions and View Link Instances?

A view link definition connects two view object definitions. It specifies a relationship between view rows from the first view object definition and view rows from the second view object definition. A view link definition includes no Java classes—it is specified entirely by an XML file and, in some cases, by methods in the relevant view row classes.

The view object definitions on the ends of a view link definition are called its *source* and *destination* view object definitions. The source and destination need not be distinct; the association could instead be a recursive relationship between one view object definition and itself. This is similar to the source and destination entity object definitions for an association.

As with associations, which view object definition will be the source and which will be the destination is essentially arbitrary, although if one view object definition will primarily be used to query details of the other, the source view object definition is conventionally the master, and the destination is conventionally the detail.

A view link instance is an instance of the class `oracle.jbo.server.ViewLinkImpl` that has been configured using a view link definition as a template. This instance also refers to master and detail view object instances, which must be instances of the source and destination view object definitions (respectively or vice versa; the master instance can be an instance of the source or destination view object definition).

Like associations, view link definitions have cardinality; the possible cardinalities are the same as those for associations as described in Chapter 6.

Source and Destination Attributes

Like associations, view link definitions specify source attributes from the source view object definition, and, for each source attribute, a corresponding destination attribute in the destination view object definition. You can choose these attributes directly, or you can select an association to base the view link on if all of the following are true:

- Each view object definition contains at least one entity object usage.
- At least one of the source view object definition's usages is connected via an association to at least one of the destination's usages.

- The source view object definition contains attributes mapped to the association's source attributes.
- The destination view object definition contains attributes mapped to the association's destination attributes.

In this case, the view attributes based on the association's source attributes will become the source attributes of the view link definition, and the view attributes based on the association's destination attributes will become the destination attributes of the view link definition.

View Link SQL

Each view link definition contains two parameterized SQL expressions, its *WHERE clause* and its *reverse WHERE clause*. These expressions allow for access of destination view rows from a source view row or access of source view rows from a destination view row, respectively. For the purposes of this section, we will concentrate of the view link definition's WHERE clause; the reverse WHERE clause works exactly the same way, except that source and destination are reversed.

A view link definition's WHERE clause is a bit of SQL specifying relationships between bind variables that correspond to the view link definition's source attributes and columns from the destination view object definition's query. For example, the view link definition DepartmentsToEmployeesVL connects the view object definitions AllDepartments and AllEmployees, and has the single source attribute DepartmentId (from AllDepartments). The definition has the following WHERE clause:

```
(:Bind_DepartmentId = Employees.DEPARTMENT_ID)
```

Bind_DepartmentId is a bind variable that corresponds to DepartmentId from AllDepartments, and Employees.DEPARTMENT_ID is a column from an AllEmployees' query.

Similarly, a view link definition's reverse WHERE clause is a bit of SQL specifying relationships between bind variables that correspond to the view link definition's destination attributes and columns from the source view object's query. DepartmentsToEmployeesVL has the following reverse WHERE clause:

```
(:Bind_DepartmentId = Departments.DEPARTMENT_ID)
```

Here, :Bind_DepartmentId is a bind variable that corresponds to DepartmentId from AllEmployees, and Departments.DEPARTMENT_ID is a column from an AllDepartments' query.

How the WHERE Clause Works at Runtime

ADF can use the WHERE clause to access a collection of destination view rows from a particular source view row. First, the WHERE clause is appended to the query SELECT * FROM <Q>, where <Q> is the destination view object definition's query. The source attribute values from the selected source view row are then set as the values of their corresponding bind variables. For example, consider the row from AllDepartments that has a DepartmentId attribute value of "90." ADF can retrieve related rows from AllEmployees using DepartmentEmployeesVL's WHERE clause. First, the WHERE clause is applied to the AllEmployee's query to yield the following:

```
SELECT * FROM (
  SELECT Employees.COMMISSION_PCT,
         Employees.CREATED_BY,
         Employees.CREATED_DATE,
         Employees.DEPARTMENT_ID,
```

```
        Employees.EMAIL,
        Employees.EMPLOYEE_ID,
        Employees.FIRST_NAME,
        Employees.HIRE_DATE,
        Employees.JOB_ID,
        -- other columns omitted to save space in this listing
        Jobs.JOB_ID AS JOB_ID1
  FROM EMPLOYEES Employees, IMAGE_USAGE ImageUsage, IMAGES Images, JOBS Jobs
  WHERE (ImageUsage.IMAGE_ID = Images.IMAGE_ID(+)) AND
        (Employees.JOB_ID = Jobs.JOB_ID) AND
        ImageUsage.ASSOCIATED_ID(+) = Employees.EMPLOYEE_ID AND
        ImageUsage.USAGE_TYPE(+) = 'E'
  ORDER BY Employees.LAST_NAME,Employees.FIRST_NAME
) WHERE (:Bind_DepartmentId = Employees.DEPARTMENT_ID)
```

Then, the value "90" is applied as a bind value for :Bind_DepartmentId.

A reverse WHERE clause is applied very similarly, reversing the roles of the source and destination view object instances.

How the WHERE Clause Is Created for Normal or Expert SQL Mode

If the destination view object definition uses normal or expert SQL mode, JDeveloper will automatically create a default view link WHERE clause, but you can change this WHERE clause yourself. For view links that are *not* based on a many-to-many association, the default WHERE clause requires any destination view row instance to have destination attributes that match the source view row instance's source attributes. For example, since AllEmployees uses normal query mode, JDeveloper generated the following default WHERE clause:

```
WHERE (:Bind_DepartmentId = Employees.DEPARTMENT_ID)
```

This requires retrieved destination rows to have DEPARTMENT_ID values that match the source attribute values from the currently selected source view row. Since the destination attribute DepartmentId is mapped to these columns, this will link the source view row to destination view rows having destination attributes that correspond to its source attributes.

The same applies to the default reverse WHERE clause if the source view object definition uses normal or expert SQL mode.

For many-to-many view links based on a many-to-many association, the default WHERE clause makes use of the intersection database object to return only rows that refer to associated entity object instances. For example, the many-to-many association EmployeesPastJobs, introduced as an example in Chapter 6, is based on the many-to-many relationship between employees and the jobs that they have held in the past. The source entity object definition of this association is Employees (corresponding to the EMPLOYEES table), the destination entity object definition is Jobs (corresponding to JOBS), and the intersection entity object definition is JobHistory (corresponding to JOB_HISTORY).

You could create a view link definition, EmployeesPastJobsVL, between the view object definitions AllEmployees (which contains a usage of Employees) and a view object instance AllJobs (which would contain a usage of Jobs), based on EmployeesPastJobs. Assuming AllJobs uses normal or declarative SQL, JDeveloper will generate the following default WHERE clause:

```
WHERE (:EmployeeId = JobHistory.EMPLOYEE_ID) AND
      (JobHistory.JOB_ID = Jobs.JOB_ID)
```

At runtime, ADF will append this WHERE clause to the query of a detail instance of AllJobs, and it will also append the following to that query's FROM clause:

```
JOB_HISTORY JobHistory
```

ADF can identify the intersection table to add because this view link definition was based on the many-to-many association containing it; if you create a many-to-many view link definition without an underlying association, you need to add the FROM clause fragment yourself using expert SQL mode; you will also need to edit the view link definition's WHERE clause to make use of the intersection table.

The preceding WHERE clause will cause the detail instance to retrieve rows from JOBS only if they are related (via the intersection JOB_HISTORY) to the currently selected master view row.

A many-to-many view link's reverse WHERE clause will work similarly if the source view object definition uses normal or expert SQL mode, with the roles of source and destination reversed.

How the WHERE Clause Is Created for Declarative SQL Mode

If the destination view object definition uses declarative SQL mode, JDeveloper will not generate a default WHERE clause at design time. Instead, ADF will generate the WHERE clause (which matches the default WHERE clauses for normal and expert SQL mode) at runtime. You cannot modify this clause (unlike the generated defaults for other query modes), but you can select a named view criteria object from the destination view object definition to restrict the query results further. You can do the same for the reverse WHERE clause if the source view object definition uses declarative SQL mode.

View Link Accessors

A *view link accessor* is an operation (sometimes implemented as a Java method) by which a view row at one end of a master-detail relationship specified by a view link definition can access the related view rows at the other end of the relationship. An accessor that extends from the destination to the source is called a *source accessor,* and an accessor that extends from the source to the destination is called a *destination accessor.* By default, JDeveloper generates only a destination accessor. You can change this behavior if you need to add a source accessor, but the default behavior is acceptable in a majority of applications.

If you generate a view object class for a view object definition, JDeveloper will use the accessor's name to generate a getter method that returns the associated view row instance or instances. For example, the view link DepartmentsToEmployeesVL has a source accessor named Department and a destination accessor called EmployeesInDepartment. If you generate a view row class for AllDepartments, it will contain a method `getEmployeesInDepartment()`, and if you generate a view row class for AllEmployees, it will contain a method `getDepartment()`.

The return type of the method differs depending on whether it is returning a "one" side or a "many" side of the view link definition. If the method is returning a "one" side, its return type will be the view row class of the associated view object definition, or `ViewRowImpl` if the associated view object definition has no view row class. The returned object will be the single row returned by the query (or possibly `null`, if the side has cardinality "0..1" and the query returns no rows).

If the method is returning a "many" side, the return type of the method will be `oracle.jbo.RowIterator` that you should cast to `RowSet`, just as with an association accessor method that returns a "many" side (as explained in Chapter 6). Unlike `RowIterator` instances returned by getter methods for associations, however, `RowIterator` instances returned by getter methods for view links always contain view row instances.

Calling these methods from the view row class does not require that there be a view link instance joining the current view object instance with a view object instance of the target type, or even that there be a view object instance of the target type in the data model. Calling the method just executes the appropriate view link–limited query, creates view rows based on its results, and returns either the view row or a `RowIterator` instance containing view rows.

This is different than when a view link instance is linking master and detail view object instances in the data model. That case is explained in the section "What Are Application Module Definitions and Application Module Instances?"

How Do You Create and Edit View Link Definitions?

This section provides an overview of the options for creating and editing view link definitions.

Creating View Link Definitions

There are a number of ways to create view link definitions.

The Create Business Components from Tables Wizard and the Create Default Data Model Components Wizard

When you create default view object definitions with entity usages by selecting entity object definitions on the second page of the Create Business Components from Tables Wizard or on the first page of the Create Default Data Model Components Wizard (as explained in the section "How Do You Create and Edit View Object Definitions?"), the wizard will automatically create view link definitions based on every association between selected entities.

When you create default SQL-only view object definitions by selecting tables on the third page of the Create Business Components from Tables Wizard, the wizard will automatically create a one-to-many view link definition for each foreign key relationship between your selected tables. The source view object definition will be the view object definition based on the referenced table, and the source view attributes will be the view attributes based on the referenced columns. The destination view object definition will be the view object definition based on the table with the foreign key constraint, and the destination view attributes will be those based on the foreign key columns. The view link definition will only contain one accessor, from source to destination.

Dragging from the Component Palette to a Business Components Diagram

When an ADF BC diagram is open, the Component Palette shows various business components, as shown in Figure 7-7. You can create view link definitions between diagrammed view definitions by clicking the View Link icon in the Component Palette, clicking the source view object definition, and then clicking the destination view object definition.

View link definitions created from the Component Palette have no source or destination attributes. You must add these in the view link definition editor before the view link definition will work correctly. The section "Editing View Link Definitions" contains more information.

The Create View Link Wizard

You can create a single view link definition by using the Create View Link Wizard. This wizard allows you to specify cardinality, source and destination view object definitions and attributes, WHERE and reverse WHERE clauses (or named view criteria objects, for use with the runtime-generated WHERE and/or reverse WHERE clauses that work with declarative SQL mode), and whether to generate view link accessors.

Editing View Link Definitions

There are several ways to edit view link definitions.

Editing View Link Definitions on a Diagram

Just as with associations, you can select and then click one of the cardinality markers on a view link definition to change it (as described in Chapter 6).

Editors for View Link Definitions

By double clicking a view link definition in the Application Navigator or on a diagram, you can open it in an editor. Like the editors for view object definitions, this is a nonmodal editor window. It allows you to change any property of a view link definition that you can change in the Create View Link Wizard.

What Are Application Module Definitions and Application Module Instances?

As described in Chapter 5, an application module definition defines which data will be required for a particular task (which can be defined as broadly or narrowly as the developer wants) and what services might be required during the performance of that task. It specifies a data model, which defines view object, view link, and nested application module instances that will be required for the performance of that task. In this way, it acts as a template for application module instances, which handle the data needs of the relevant task for a single user.

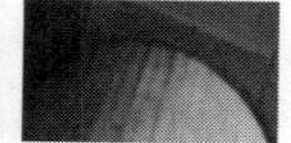

NOTE

It is an oversimplification to say that application module instances handle the data needs for only one user. This is true most of the time, but application module recycling (described in the section "How Do Application Module Instances Manage Transactional State?") and shared application module instances (described in the section "How Do You Use View Object Instances as LOVs?") may allow a single application module instance to handle the data needs of multiple users over its life cycle.

Chapter 5 also states that an application module definition comprises an XML metadata file, between zero and three Java classes, and optionally a Java interface. This section explains how the XML file and two of the classes can work together to constitute an application module definition and to provide a template for application module instances.

NOTE

The remaining Java class and the interface are only used when you create custom service methods. This topic, as well as the Java class and the interface, are discussed in Chapter 8.

Application Module XML Metadata

All application module definitions involve an XML file. This file contains the metadata that describes the application module definition, including the following:

- **Descriptions of view object instances** that the data model requires, including which definitions they should be based on and a unique name for each instance
- **Descriptions of view link instances**, including which definitions they should be based on, which view object instances they relate, which of those view object instances is the master and which the detail, and a unique name for each view link instance
- **Descriptions of nested application module instances**, including which definitions they should be based on and a unique name for each instance
- **Other declarative features** of the view object definition, such as which service methods its instances provide (as described in Chapter 8) and tuning information

Almost all of the time, you will modify the XML file using JDeveloper's visual editors. Various components of the editors are explained throughout the rest of this chapter.

Application Module Classes

When the ADF BC framework needs to create an application module instance, it instantiates the class `oracle.jbo.server.ApplicationModuleImpl` and configures it according to the application module definition's XML metadata. The object created by this process is an application module instance.

`ApplicationModuleImpl` has all the methods required to manage the current database transaction; retrieve view object, view link, and nested application module instances specified in the application module definition's data model; create new view object, view link, or nested application module instances dynamically; or dynamically remove one of these instances from its data model. However, you can create an *application module class,* a subclass of `ApplicationModuleImpl` that is customized to a particular application module definition. If you create an application module class, the corresponding application module instances will be instances of that class, rather than direct instances of `ApplicationModuleImpl`.

By default, an application module class is named after its application module definition, with the suffix "Impl" added. For example, the view object class for the TuhraService application module definition, by default, would be named `TuhraServiceImpl`. (Chapter 6 contains information about changing naming conventions for ADF BC classes.)

Creating an application module class is not required for all applications, but it can be useful, as explained next.

View Object, View Link, and Nested Application Module Instance Getter Methods

`ApplicationModuleImpl` contains the methods, `findViewObject()`, `findViewLink()`, and `findApplicationModule()`, which allow retrieval of view object instances, view link instances, and nested application module instances from the data model. If you generate an application module class, it will contain accessors for each view object instance, view link instance, and nested application module instance the application module definition specifies. For example, the TuhraService application module definition specifies that the data model should contain a view object instance called DepartmentSelector; if you generate a custom application module class, the class will contain a `getDepartmentSelector()` method, which retrieves the relevant view object instance. These accessors have the advantage of being typesafe, making errors more likely to appear at compile time, rather than runtime. In particular, if you've generated a view object class for an included view object instance, the getter method for that instance will have a return type of your view object class, rather than `ViewObjectImpl`; similarly, if you've generated an application module class for a nested application module instance, the getter method for that instance will have a return type of the application module class, rather than `ApplicationModuleImpl`.

Overriding Methods in ApplicationModuleImpl

In addition to the accessor methods, view object classes also allow you to override various methods in the `ApplicationModuleImpl` class to change transactional behavior, although doing so is beyond the scope of this book.

Application Module–Level Service Methods

Application module classes are the appropriate location to write *application module–level service methods,* methods that perform tasks that are inappropriate for view object–level or view row-level service methods and can be called declaratively from the view or controller layer. Service methods are the focus of Chapter 8.

Application Module Definition Classes

Just as an instance of `oracle.jbo.server.EntityDefImpl` is a Java class for representing metadata defined in an entity object definition's XML file, an instance of `oracle.jbo.server.ApplicationModuleDefImpl` is a Java class for representing metadata in an application module definition's XML file. There is only one `ApplicationModuleDefImpl` instance per application module definition in a running ADF application; the framework will access the same object across application module instances.

`ApplicationModuleDefImpl` contains all the methods required to discover and change information about an application module definition's specified data model (as distinct from the current data model of any particular application module instance, which can be accessed as explained in the section "Application Module Classes" and changed using techniques explained in Chapter 8), transactional behavior, state management mechanisms, and so on. You can find specifics of this class in its Javadoc.

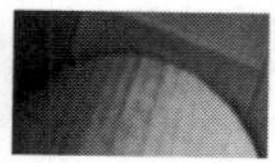

CAUTION

Be careful about changing an application module definition's properties at runtime. Remember that you are doing so not just for a single user, but for all users of the application module definition.

You can also create an application module definition class, which extends `ApplicationModuleDefImpl` in the same way an entity definition extends `EntityDefImpl`. Like entity definition classes, application module definition classes are required by relatively few applications. The reasons for doing so are much the same as the reasons for creating an entity definition class, as described in Chapter 6.

Custom Framework Classes

As explained in Chapter 6 and in the section "What Are View Object Definitions and View Object Instances," you can create custom framework classes that extend ADF's base Business Components classes and that your own business component definitions use or extend. This is true for application modules as well; you can create custom framework application module classes that extend `ApplicationModuleImpl` to provide common behavior as well as custom framework application module definition classes that extend `ApplicationModuleDefImpl`, and use these classes as base classes for multiple application module definitions.

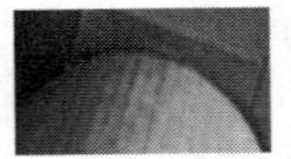

NOTE
As mentioned, the hands-on practices in Part V of this book provide examples of creating custom framework classes.

How Application Module Instances Implement Their Data Model

When an application module instance is created, it creates view object and view link instances as specified by the data model. Some of the view object instances are *top-level* in the data model, that is, not the detail of any other view object instance. Some of the view object instances are configured by view link instances to be details of other view object instances.

View link instances, unlike view link definitions, are always directional. While the decision of which view object definition should be the source of a view link definition, and which the destination, is essentially arbitrary, particular view link instances always have a master view object instance and a detail view object instance.

The first time (in any user's session) that a particular view row of the master view object instance is selected, the view-link limited query of the detail view object instance is executed and view rows are created, just as if you had called the view link accessor method on the master instance. However, instead of just returning a `RowIterator` containing all the rows, the detail view object definition places them in its cache and points to them with a *query collection,* a collection of pointers to cached view rows.

A view object instance only makes one query collection at a time visible to the view and controller layers of the application, so the user will only see rows from one query collection—the one that corresponds to the currently selected master row. However, these query collections are maintained when the current row in the master view object instance changes, so when the user returns to an old master row, the query does not need to be re-executed.

How Do You Create and Edit Application Module Definitions?

This section provides an overview of the options for creating and editing application module definitions.

Creating Application Module Definitions

There are a number of ways to create the application module definitions your application needs to support its tasks.

The Business Components from Tables Wizard and the Default Data Model Components Wizard

As explained in Chapter 6, you can create an entire set of default Business Components using the Create Business Components from Tables Wizard, accessible from the New Gallery or by selecting **New Business Components from Tables** on a package's right-click menu. As explained in Chapter 6 and in the sections "How Do You Create and Edit View Object Definitions" and "How Do You Create and Edit View Link Definitions," the first three pages of the wizard allow you to create default entity object definitions, associations, entity-based view object definitions, SQL-only view object definitions, and view link definitions.

Similarly, as explained in the sections "How Do You Create and Edit View Object Definitions" and "How Do You Create and Edit View Link Definitions," the first page of the Create Default Data Model Components Wizard allows you to create default entity-based view object definitions and view link definitions.

The fifth page of the Business Components from Tables Wizard and the second page of the Default Data Model Components Wizard each allow you to create a default application module definition, if you want to.

A default application module has a data model that contains the following:

- **A top-level view object instance** for each view object definition the wizard creates
- **A view link instance** for every view link definition the wizard creates, which will use the appropriate top-level view object instance as a master
- **A detail view object instance** for each of the view link instances

A default application module definition's data model will be at most two levels deep; no details of details will be created by default.

Dragging from the Component Palette to a Business Components Diagram

When an ADF BC diagram is open, the Component Palette shows various Business Components, as shown in Figure 7-13.

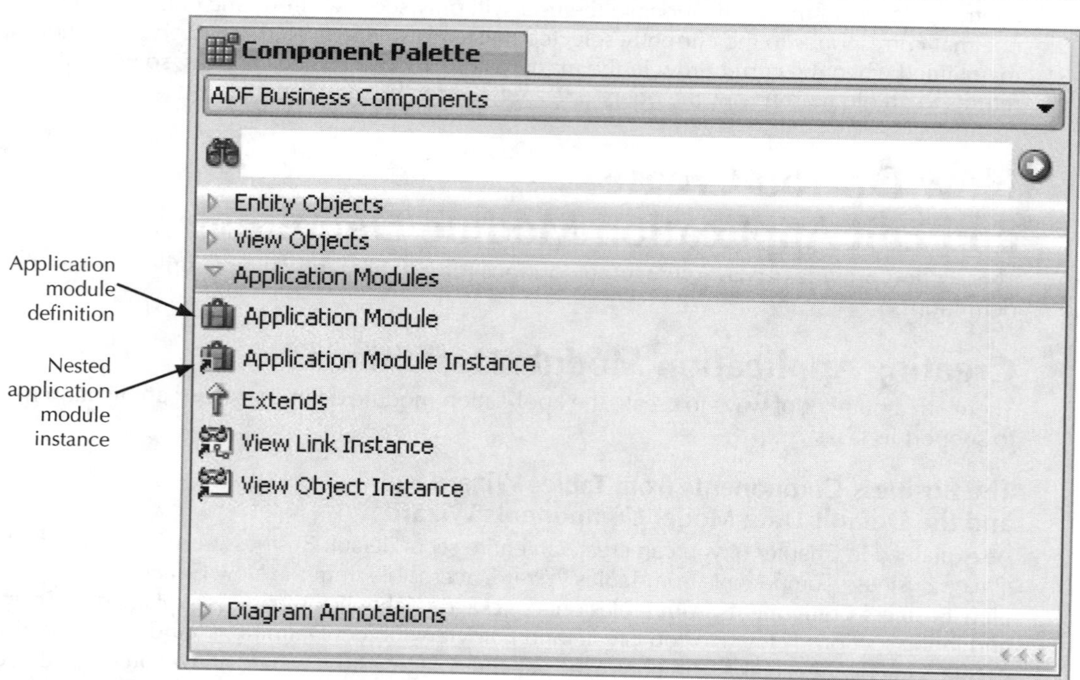

FIGURE 7-13. *The Application Module panel of the Diagram Component Palette*

You can create application module definitions by clicking the Application Module icon in the Component Palette and then dragging to or clicking the diagram. You can add nested application module instances and nested view object instances to an application module definition's data model by clicking the Application Module Instance icon or View Object Instance icon in the Component Palette and then dragging to or clicking an application module definition that is already on the diagram; you will be prompted to select another application module definition or view object definition to use as a template for the instance, and then to enter a unique name for the instance within the data model.

You can add view link instances to the application module definition's data model by clicking the View Link Instance icon in the Component Palette, clicking a view object instance already within the application module's data model, and then clicking another view object instance within the application module. The first view object instance will be the master in the relationship, the second the detail. JDeveloper will search for an appropriate view object definition on which to base the view object instance. If none are found, the operation will fail; if exactly one is found, it will be used to act as the template for the instance. If more than one are found, you will be prompted to select one.

Figure 7-14 shows a simple application module definition as it appears on a diagram. Notice the EmployeeSearch view object instance and the DepartmentSelector, DepartmentTree, and EmployeesInDepartment view object instances related by view link instances.

The Create Application Module Wizard

You can create a single application module definition by using the Create Application Module Wizard, accessible from the New Gallery or by selecting **New Application Module** from a package's right-click menu. This wizard allows you to specify a data model and which of the application module Java classes to generate. This method requires more steps than the other creation processes but gives you more detailed control over the application module definition's properties, lessening the need for later modifications.

Editing Application Module Definitions

There are several ways to edit application module definitions, once they are created.

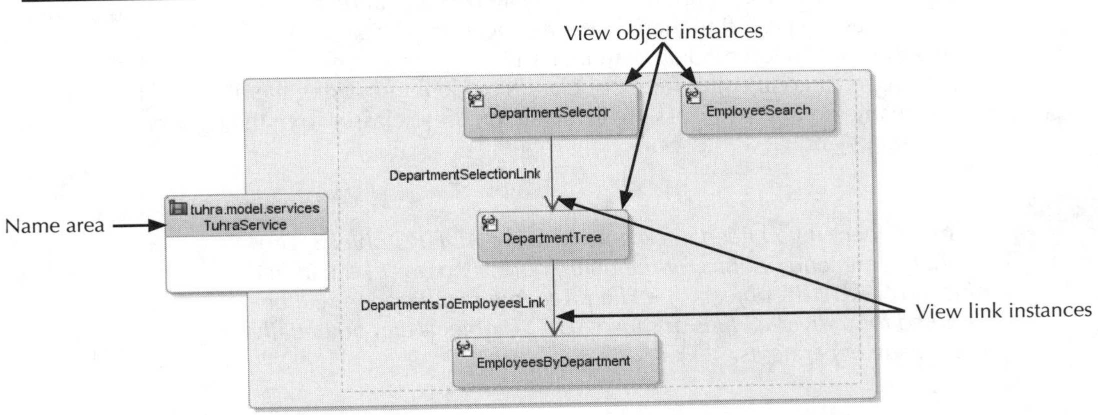

FIGURE 7-14. *A simple application module definition on a diagram*

Editing Application Module Definitions on the Diagram

You can rename application module definitions, add additional elements to their data model, rename existing data model elements, or delete data model elements as shown in Figure 7-14. In particular:

- **Selecting the Name area of the application module definition** will allow you to rename the definition.
- **Selecting the Name area of a view object or nested application module instance** will allow you to rename the instance.
- **Selecting the name of a view link instance** will allow you to rename the instance.
- **Selecting a nested application module instance or view link instance and pressing** DELETE will delete the instance.
- **Selecting a view object instance and pressing** DELETE will delete the instance and any view link instances for which it is the master or detail.

Editors for Application Module Definitions

By double-clicking an application module definition in the Application Navigator or on a diagram, you can open it in an editor. Like the editors for other Business Components, this is a nonmodal editor window, which allows you to change any property of an application module definition you can set in the Create Application Module Wizard (most saliently the data model). You can also specify a number of additional properties such as tuning properties.

Editing View Object Instances in an Application Module Definition On the Data Model page of an application module's editor, you can select a view object instance from the data model and click Edit to open the Edit View Instance dialog. This allows you to select named view criteria from the underlying view object definition. Selected named view criteria will be automatically applied to the view object instance. In addition, you can select bind variable values for any or all bind variables in the view object definition.

Editing Custom Classes

If you have generated custom application module or application module definition classes, you can find them in the Application Navigator by expanding the application module definition's node, as shown here.

You can open a code editor for these classes by double-clicking them. In addition, most options available on any Java class are available on these classes from the right-click menu, just as for custom entity and view classes.

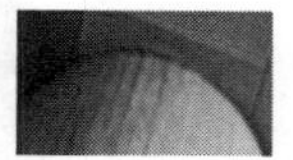

NOTE

*As mentioned, if you need to rename or move ADF BC objects, use the Refactor menu options for the entire object, not for files within the object. For ADF BC objects, the **File | Rename** menu option will be disabled for individual files because ADF BC objects can potentially have many dependents.*

Editing or Creating Configurations for Application Module Definitions

Each application module definition is created with two default configurations, or switchable sets of properties that affect runtime behavior. One, named `<ApplicationModuleDefName>Local` (where `<ApplicationModuleDefName>` is the name of the application module definition), is used by default to instantiate top-level application module instances, and one, named `<ApplicationModuleDefName>Shared`, is used by default to instantiate shared application module instances (described in the section, "How Do You Use View Object Instances as LOVs?"). You can edit these configurations or make additional configurations as alternatives to `<ApplicationModuleDefName>Local`.

You can edit these configurations by selecting **Configurations** from the right-click menu on an application module. This opens the Manage Configurations dialog, shown here:

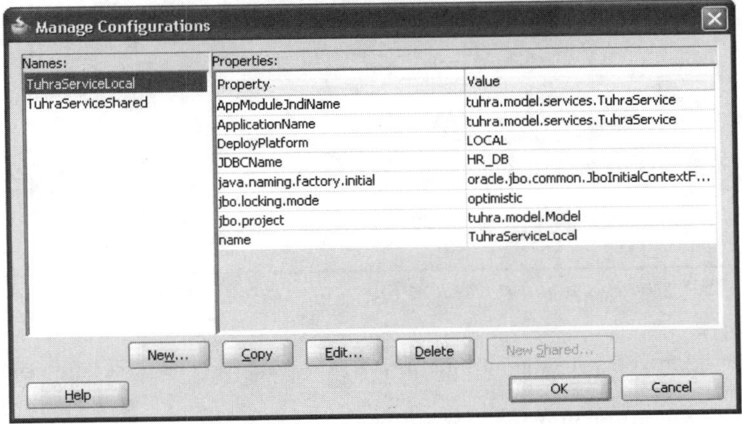

Clicking **New** or **Edit** in the Manage Configurations dialog opens the Edit Business Components Configuration dialog. This dialog has three tabs:

- **The Application Module tab** shown allows you to specify how the application module will connect to the database.
- **The Pooling and Scalability tab** configures the application module and connection pools. This is explained in the section "How do Application Module Instances Manage Transactional State?"
- **The Properties tab** provides a property inspector that allows you to specify a large number of properties governing the behavior of business components.

A complete discussion on using application module configurations is beyond the scope of this book. Most of the defaults provided are acceptable for most applications, but there are three properties that should be changed in the almost all Fusion web applications:

JDBC Connection Type As shown in Fig. 7-15, the Application Module tab of the Edit Business Components Configuration dialog contains a dropdown which allows you to specify the method the application module will use to connect to the database. The default value of the dropdown list is *JDBC URL*, which means that the application module will connect to the database using connection

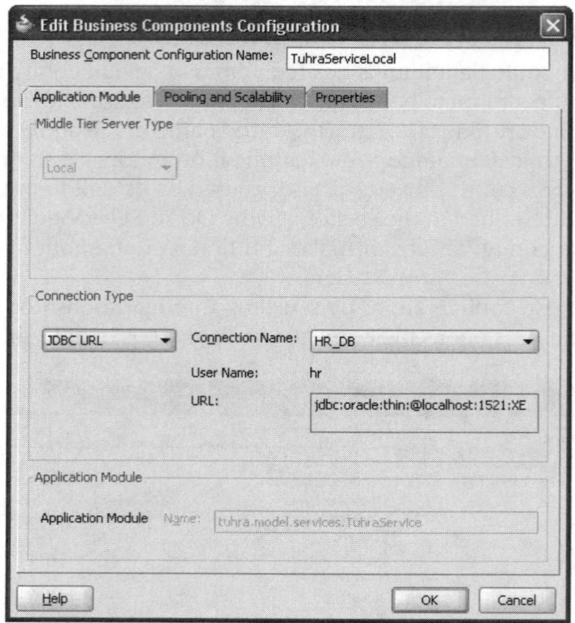

FIGURE 7-15. *The Application Module Tab of the Edit Business Components Configuration Dialog*

information deployed with the application. This is not a security risk; the connection password is encrypted.

However, for production applications, you should select the other option, *JDBC Datasource*. A *JDBC Datasource* is a connection to a database which is set up and configured on the server. Your application server administrator can create a JDBC datasource for all applications that share a database and user; when you select this option, all you need to supply is the datasource's name. Using JDBC datasources decouples applications from the connections they use; if database connection information for a set of applications changes, the application server administrator can update the JDBC datasource, and the applications need not be changed and redeployed.

Locking Mode By default, ADF Business Components acquires locks on database rows using a strategy called "pessimistic locking." However, this is not desirable for the large majority of web applications. Instead, web applications should use a locking strategy called "optimistic locking." You can change the locking strategy to optimistic on the Properties tab of the Edit Business Components Configuration dialog, by changing the value of the property *jbo.locking.mode* to "optimistic." The section "Locking" explains locking strategies in detail.

Referenced Pool Size A property called the "referenced pool size" controls how the application should handle large numbers of users. The default for this property's value is 10, but most applications will be optimized at a significantly higher value; you can do this on the Pooling and Scalability tab of the Edit Business Components Configuration dialog. The section "Application Module Pooling" explains the function of the referenced pool size and how you can determine the correct pool size for your application.

How Do You Use View Object Instances as LOVs?

Often database queries are intended to provide lists of values (LOVs) from which the user can select a value for a separate field in another table. View object instances can be used to provide LOV data for particular view and entity attributes.

View Accessors

A *view accessor* (not to be confused with a view object accessor or a view link accessor) is a pathway in a view object definition or entity object definition that allows it to access a particular view object instance for LOV data. Certain declarative validation rules can use entity object definition view accessors for validation against an LOV (as described in Chapter 6, in the section "Attribute-Level Validation Rules"). View object attributes can use view accessors in view object definitions to provide data for the dropdown lists and LOV windows that users use to edit them. You can add view accessors to an entity object or view object definition by clicking the "Create new view accessors" button on the View Accessors page of the definition's editor. This button opens the View Accessors dialog, shown here:

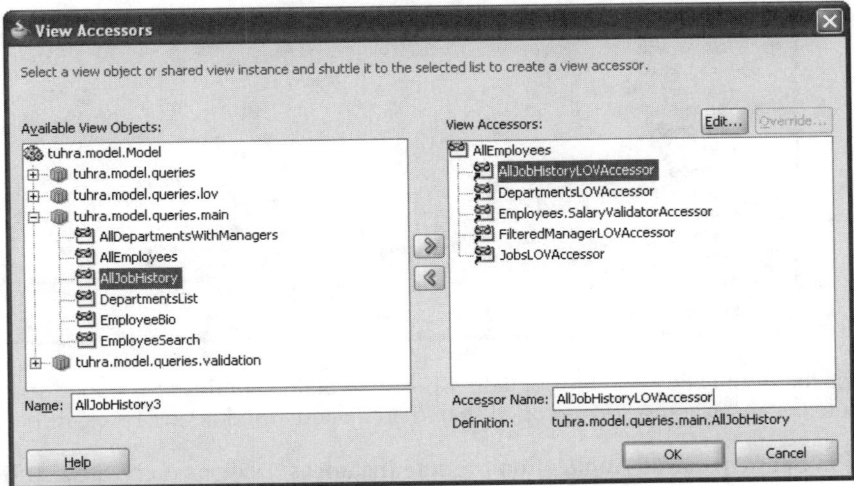

You create a view accessor by shuttling a view object definition or view object instance to the View Accessors list and clicking OK.

If you create a view accessor on an entity object definition, all view object definitions that use the entity object definition will inherit its view accessors.

View Accessors Based on View Object Definitions

The simplest way to create a view accessor is to base it directly on a view object definition. When the application traverses such an accessor, the framework creates an anonymous view object instance to query the appropriate rows and retrieve a row set.

Shared Application Module Instances

To create view accessors that access particular view object instances out of data models, you need to create shared application module instances for your project. A *shared application module instance* is a direction to ADF to create a particular application module instance that holds view object instances needed by view accessors. The definition for that instance must be in the same application as any entity or view object definitions that will use it, but it need not be in the same project. This is a more complex process than simply basing a view accessor directly on a view object definition, but it allows multiple applications to share queried LOV data, which may greatly increase efficiency.

There are two types of shared application module instances: session-scoped instances and application-scoped instances. You can create both of these on the "Business Components\ Application Module Instances" page of the Project Properties dialog, as shown here:

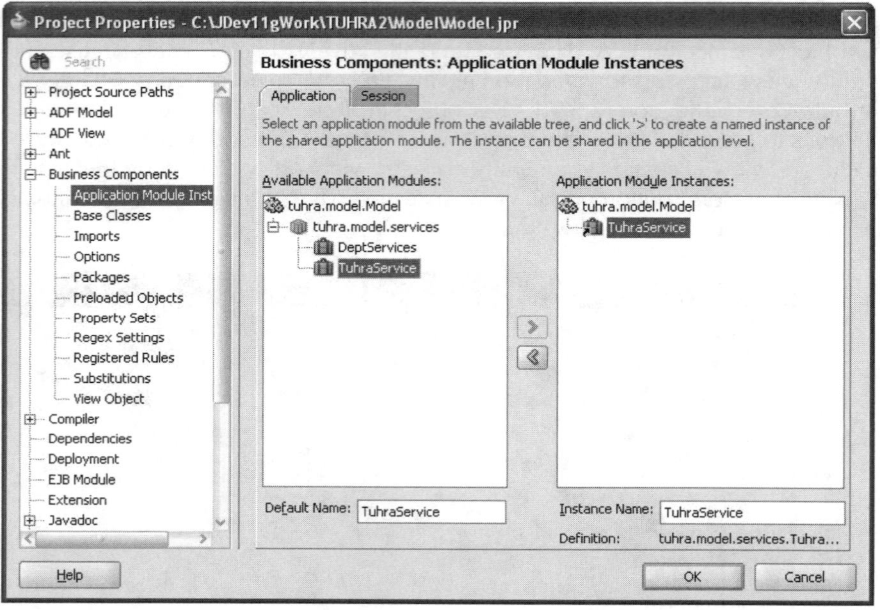

Notice the Application and Session tabs where you define application-scoped shared application module instances and session-scoped shared application module instances, respectively.

Session-Scoped Shared Application Module Instances When you create a session-scoped shared application module instance, this instructs ADF to create a single instance of the specified application module definition per application session—that is, per user. In that respect, session-scoped shared application module instances are much like ordinary application module instances: they provide separate access, for each user, to a unique set of view object instances and view link instances. The view object instances maintain different caches for each user. The only difference is that session-scoped shared application module instances provide their view object instances for the use of view accessors.

Application-Scoped Shared Application Module Instances Fairly frequently, LOV data can easily be shared across users. Data from a code table, for example, is generally not editable by users, so every user should be able to share a single cache of data. This saves both in-memory storage and database queries.

This is what happens when you create an application-scoped shared application module instance: you instruct ADF to create a single instance of the specified application module definition, to be shared across sessions and users.

Specifying View Criteria Objects and Bind Variables for View Accessors

You can edit a view accessor by selecting it and clicking Edit in the View Accessors dialog. This allows you to specify view criteria objects and/or bind variable values to customize the query that retrieves the view accessor row set.

You can specify bind parameter values as Groovy expressions, which allows you to plug in row-specifc values. For example, the entity object definition Employees contains a view accessor, SalaryValidatorAccessor, which returns rows from an anonymous instance of the view object definition SalaryValidator. SalaryValidator contains the bind variable JobIdToValidate. SalaryValidatorAccessor specifies the Groovy expression "JobId" as the value for this bind variable, so when the accessor is called from any instance of Employees, that instance's JobId will be set as the value of JobIdToValidate for the purposes of retrieving the row set.

You will create view accessors and specify view criteria and bind variable values for them in Chapter 19.

LOV View Attributes

Once you have added a view accessor to a view object definition, you can use that accessor to create an LOV for one of the view attributes. Select the attribute for the LOV (called the "base attribute" on the Attributes page of the view object editor, and click the "Add list of values" (green "+" plus) button in the List of Values region, as shown in Figure 7-16.

This opens the Create List of Values dialog, which contains two tabs: Configuration and UI Hints.

The Configuration Tab

In the Configuration tab of the list of values dialog, you specify a view object accessor and a view attribute (called the "list attribute") from its view object instance. This helps the client create a dropdown or LOV window based on the view object accessor such that, if the user selects a row, the base attribute will be populated by the value of the list attribute from the selected row.

You can also specify additional pairs of base and list attributes, allowing the user's selection to set more than one attribute simultaneously. The Configuration tab is shown here:

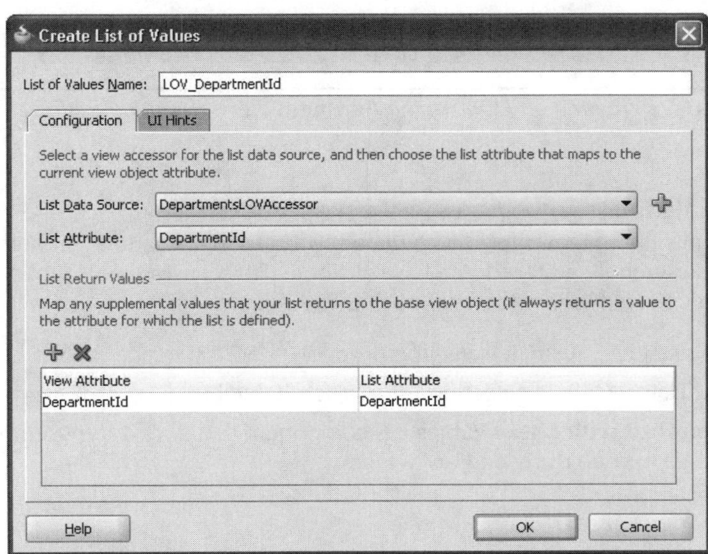

FIGURE 7-16. *Creating an LOV on the Attributes view object definition's editor*

The UI Hints Tab

In the UI Hints tab of the list of values dialog, you give information that helps your view layer present a user-friendly editor for the base attribute. For a Fusion web application, you can specify a default UI control type for the editor using any of following:

- **Choice List** A single-selection dropdown list
- **List Box** A single-selection list in a scrollable box
- **Input Text with List of Values** A component that allows the user to type in a value or search for one using an LOV window

- **Combo Box** A combination component that allows the user to type in a value or select from a dropdown list of the first few options
- **Combo Box with List of Values** A combination component that allows the user to type in a value, select from a dropdown list of the first few options, or open an LOV window
- **Radio Group** A group of radio buttons, one for each row returned by the view accessor

The tab also lets you select one or more attributes from the view accessor to display in the control. These need not include the list attributes; you can display an attribute containing a user-friendly description of each option while actually using a numeric code for a list attribute. If you specify multiple attributes here, they are shown as different columns in a table in LOV windows and separated by spaces in dropdown lists, scrollable list boxes, and radio button labels.

For control types that include LOV windows, you can optionally specify search functionality. For those that include dropdown lists, you can optionally request that the list display recently used selections at the top. For those that include dropdown lists or list boxes, you can optionally request a "No Selection" option. The UI Hints tab is shown here:

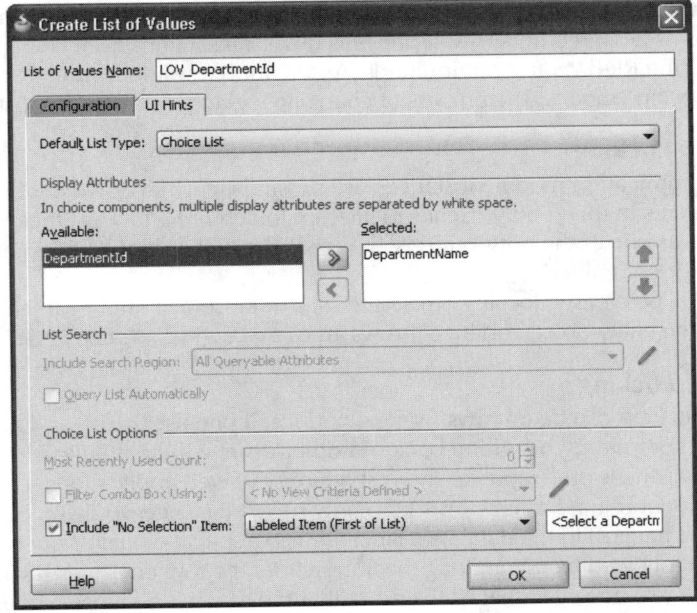

Static View Object Definitions

A *static view object definition* is a view object definition that, instead of getting data from a SQL query, uses a table of literal values provided by the developer at design time. Static view object definitions can be used anywhere in an application, but they are especially well suited to provide LOV data in application-scoped shared application module instances.

When you specify in the Create View Object Wizard that you want to create a static view object definition, instead of being asked to specify entity object usages or to enter a query, you are asked first to specify attribute names and then to enter rows of literal data, one row at a time. The attributes you create form the columns of the table of literal data.

Since changing the data held in a static view object definition requires recompiling and redeploying your application, rather than just updating the database, static view object definitions are best for small sets of data that are projected to change very rarely, if at all.

How Do Application Module Instances Manage Transactional State?

In an application, each shared application module instance and each top-level (non-nested) application module instance manages its own database transaction and maintains its own set of cached data in memory. Nested application module instances inherit their database transaction from their parent.

Dealing with multiple transactions and caches raises a number of issues, including how to prevent data conflicts and how to manage separate data caches for what may be a large number of users.

Locking

Locking is a RDBMS feature that prevents users in different transactions from causing data conflicts. When a lock is acquired on a row, it prevents other transactions from changing that row. Locks persist until the RDBMS transaction ends. Application module instances can use one of two automatic locking modes. The process of changing locking mode is demonstrated in Chapter 18.

Pessimistic Locking

By default, application module instances use pessimistic locking, which means they instruct entity object instances in their entity caches to attempt to acquire a lock on their corresponding table row as soon as one of their attributes is changed. The lock is maintained until the transaction is rolled back or committed.

Therefore, pessimistic locking blocks the second person attempting to change an attribute; when they do so, the entity object instance throws an `oracle.jbo.AlreadyLockedException`.

Optimistic Locking

Pessimistic locking can tie up rows for long periods. If one user changes data and then waits a long time before committing or rolling back, no other users will be able to change that data at all. Optimistic locking is preferable for the vast majority of web applications. Under *optimistic locking,* the application module instance instructs entity object instances to defer locking until they are posted (with changes) to the database. Since in web applications, post operations are usually immediately followed by committing the transaction, the row does not stay locked for long.

This requires, however, that ADF ensure that the following scenario does not occur:

1. User A and User B query data from the database.
2. User A and User B both change the data.
3. User A posts his/her changes to the data. The change is committed and the locks immediately released.
4. User B posts his/her changes to the data. The change is committed, silently overwriting or conflicting with user A's changes.

ADF prevents this by maintaining a snapshot of each entity object instance that is created to represent an existing table row. This snapshot of the queried row state is maintained even if the user changes the row. When the user attempts to acquire a lock (immediately before posting), ADF checks the snapshot against the current row's state in the database; a difference implies that there have been changes outside the application since the row was queried, and the entity object instance throws an `oracle.jbo.RowInconsistentException`.

As stated in the section, "Editing or Creating Configurations for Application Module Definitions," you can set the locking mode on the Properties tab of the Edit Business Components Configuration dialog.

Change Indicators If an entity object definition represents a table with large rows, the process of comparing the snapshot with the database row's current state may be resource-intensive. Many of these tables contain timestamps or other columns or sets of columns that are guaranteed to change whenever the row is updated. If you are working with a table like that, you may want to set one or more entity attributes as change indicators.

The *change indicators* of an entity object definition are attributes corresponding to table columns such that at least one of those columns is guaranteed to change in any row that is updated. If an entity object definition has change indicator attributes, only those attribute value snapshots will be compared to the values in the database for purposes of determining whether the row has changed since it was queried.

Application Module Pooling

The entity and view caches maintained by a top-level application module instance or session-scoped shared application module instance can be an expensive resource. When large numbers of users connect simultaneously (each receiving their own instance and their own cache), maintaining all of this data in memory could lead to performance or stability problems.

Moreover, establishing an initial JDBC connection (which a top-level application module instance or shared application module instance must do) is a time- and resource-consuming operation. Creating a new connection every time a user session begins can lead to performance and network congestion issues.

An *application module pool* is a resource manager that helps maintain scalability by determining which caches need to be maintained in memory, which can be temporarily swapped to the database (to a table called PS_TXN), and which can be safely discarded. There can be one application module pool for each application module definition.

Checking Application Module Instances into the Pool

When a user session is temporarily done using an application module instance (which occurs between each request/response cycle), it checks the application module instance back into the pool. It maintains an *application module cookie,* which is an object keyed to a session cookie downloaded to the user's browser, that points to that application module instance. While the session continues, the application module instance is marked as "managed"; when the user's session expires, the application module cookie disappears, the instance's caches are cleared, and the instance is marked as "stateless." Whether an instance is managed or stateless has an impact on what happens the next time an application tries to check the instance out of the pool.

Checking Application Module Instances out of the Pool for the First Time

When a particular session first requires an application module instance, it requests one from the pool. If there is already a stateless instance in the pool, the pool will return that instance.

If there is no stateless instance in the pool and the number of instances in the pool is below a threshold called the *referenced pool size*, or if there are no instances of any sort in the pool, the pool will create and return a new stateless instance. If, however, creating a new instance would exceed the referenced pool size and there is a managed application module instance in the pool, that application module instance will be passivated before being returned.

NOTE
In some earlier versions of JDeveloper, the referenced pool size was called the "recycle threshold."

Passivation is a process by which the transactional state of a managed application module instance (change logs, new row states, transient attribute values, bind variable values, current rows, and so on) is written to the database table PS_TXN, following which the application module's in-memory caches are then cleared so that they can be used again.

Re-Checking Application Module Instances out of the Pool

When a particular session requests an application module instance that it has previously released as managed, the pool checks whether it has been passivated and recycled. If not, it returns that instance to the application.

If the application module instance has already been passivated, the application module pool obtains a new application module instance (using the same strategy as for a first check-out request) and *activates* it, restoring its state from the database table PS_TXN. The activated application module instance is returned to the session, identical to the application module instance that the session released.

Determining a Referenced Pool Size

Determining the best referenced pool size for your application involves a tradeoff between two resources. A lower referenced pool size will result in a smaller number of caches being retained in application server memory; a higher referenced pool size will result in fewer database hits for activation and passivation. As stated in the section, "Editing or Creating Configurations for Application Module Definitions," you can set the referenced pool size on the Pooling and Scalability tab of the Edit Business Components Configuration dialog.

The default value of the referenced pool size is 10. This is a very safe value for testing, but most applications will be optimized at a considerably higher value. For most applications, we recommend starting with a referenced pool size of 20. Then, you should perform stress tests equivalent to both your expected average server hit rate and your expected peak server hit rate and analyze causes of poor performance. If performance is slow primarily because of many disk swaps on the application server, the application needs a lower referenced pool size. If performance is slow primarily because of a disproportionately high number of database hits (much more than a linear progression from a single user), performance will likely benefit from a higher referenced pool size. You should repeat this process until you find a referenced pool size that provides acceptable performance at the peak hit rate and the best performance possible (compatible with acceptable peak hit rate performance) at the average hit rate.

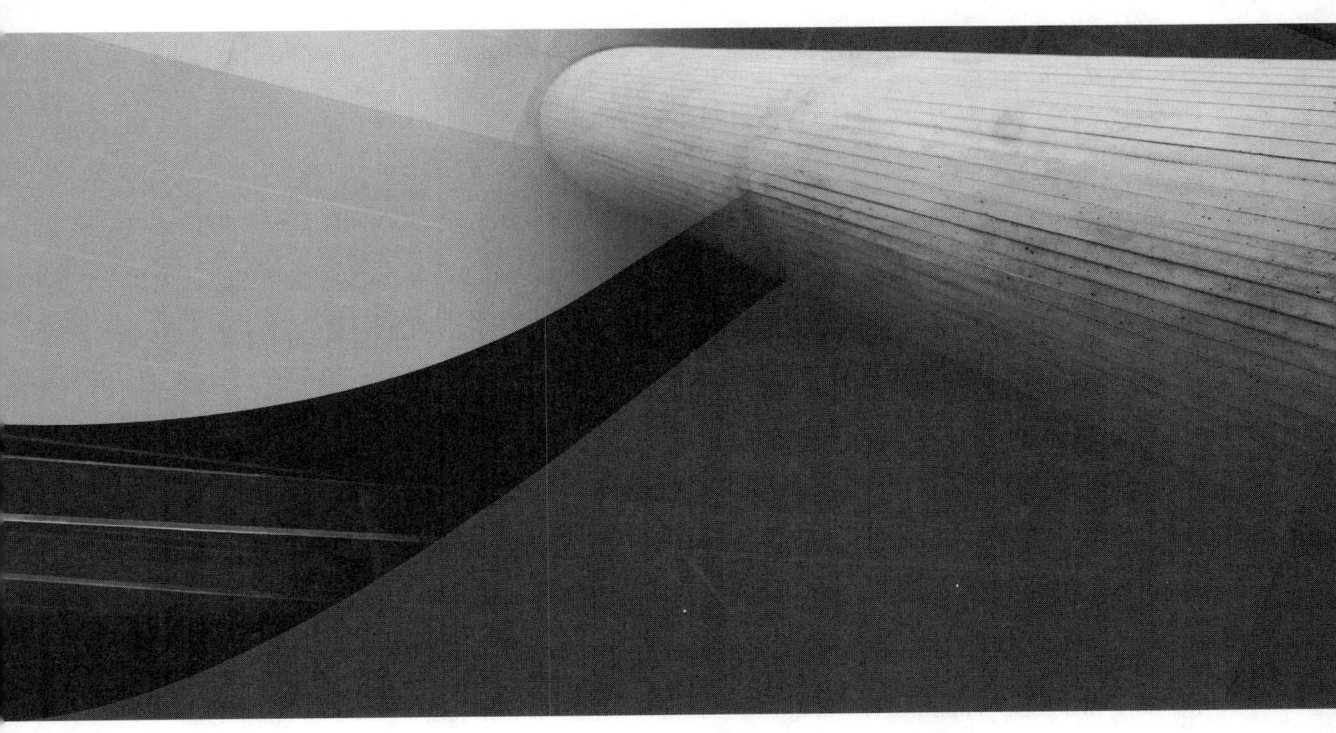

CHAPTER 8

Providing Custom Data Services

Sow good services; sweet remembrances will grow them.

—Mme. de Staël [Anne de Staël-Holstein] (1776–1817)

Chapter 7 explains how to assemble data for other parts of your application by creating appropriate view object, view link, and application module definitions and assembling instances of them into a data model. Top-level application module instances, containing view object, view link, and nested application module instances, expose their standard services to the application, for example, transactional commit and rollback, query-by-example (QBE) search, attribute retrieval and setting, and row navigation, paging, creation, and deletion. Data controls (explained in Chapter 13) expose these features to clients in a consistent way.

Sometimes, however, you want to provide custom data services that are not included in the standard set. Such services are often compositions of the previous services, for example, searching for rows matching a particular QBE condition, iterating through them, and performing a particular data change on each. However, the service must encapsulate what would be for the user, or even an automated task flow, a complex procedure into a single service call. In certain circumstances, you might want to allow a user or the controller to perform an operation (such as dynamic creation of a new view object instance) or retrieve information (such as table metadata) that is not normally accessible outside of ADF business components.

This chapter discusses mechanisms for creating and exposing *custom service methods,* methods in a custom application module, view object, or view row class that a data control can expose to the controller layer of an application, to be activated with a single user click or task flow activity. Note that not all encapsulations of complex procedures are service methods; procedures that should execute every time a particular piece of data changes, for example, are better implemented in a custom validation rule, validation domain, or the relevant entity attribute's setter method. Service methods are best for procedures that are initiated by a specific request from the user or task flow.

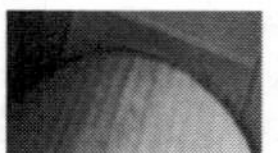

NOTE

You can create two fundamental types of service methods in your business components layer: client service methods, which are accessed locally (or via Remote Method Invocation [RMI], which is beyond the scope of this book) through the ADF Model layer, and web service methods, which are accessed via web service protocols. This chapter deals exclusively with client service methods.

This chapter answers the following questions:

- **What sort of method can be a service method?**
- **How do you expose methods as service methods?**
- **How do you implement single-row methods?**
- **How do you implement query-level methods?**
- **How do you implement cross-query or transaction-level methods?**

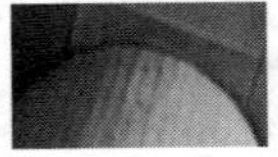

NOTE
This chapter digs deeply into ADF BC internals. However, the declarative features of ADF BC are powerful enough that you will probably need to dig in at this level only occasionally. When you do, in addition to the explanations in this chapter, you can also rely on the Fusion Developer's Guide (included in the JDeveloper Help Center and as a separate PDF file on otn.oracle.com) and Javadoc for each Java class mentioned.

What Sort of Method Can Be a Service Method?

Only certain methods on an application module, view object, or view row class can be exposed as service methods. For a method to be exposable as a service method, all its parameter types must come from the following list, and its return type must be `void` or from the following list:

- **Java primitives**
- **`java.lang.Serializable`** as well as any of its subinterfaces or any class that implements it (all Business Components domains implement `Serializable`)
- **`oracle.jbo.Row`** and subinterfaces, but not implementing classes except those that also implement `Serializable`
- **`oracle.jbo.RowSet`** and subinterfaces (which include `RowIterator`, `RowSetIterator`, and `ViewObject`, introduced later in this chapter), but not implementing classes except those that also implement `Serializable`
- **`java.util.Iterable`** or any of its subinterfaces (such as `java.util.List` or `java.util.Map`), so long as any specific objects passed to or returned by the method are instances of classes that implement `Serializable` and the containees of the `Iterable` will always be from this list
- **Arrays** of any type from this list

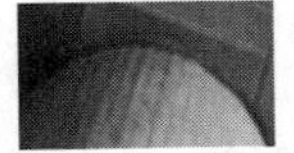

CAUTION
The JDeveloper design time will allow you to export methods with return or parameter types of `Iterable` or its subinterfaces even if the method may return non-`Serializable` implementations of these or instances of them containing objects of unacceptable types. However, this will cause an exception at runtime. The standard implementations of `Iterable`, which are in the `java.util` package, all implement `Serializable`, so this caution only applies if you are using a custom or unusual implementation of `Serializable` or cannot guarantee that the containees will all be from the preceding list.

How Do You Expose Methods as Service Methods?

Once you have created a method that satisfies the criteria laid out in the section "What Sort of Method Can Be a Service Method?" you can make it a service method by exposing it on a client interface.

Client Interfaces

A *client interface* is a Java interface exposing service methods written on an application module class, view object class, or view row class. You cannot access a business components method from your application's view or controller layer unless it is exposed on a client interface. These interfaces are automatically created for you when you declare the first appropriate method as a service method. They are automatically maintained for you when you change the list of exposed methods.

View Row Client Interfaces

A *view row client interface* is an interface extending the interface `oracle.jbo.Row` and exposing the service methods written on a view row class. When you expose a custom method on the view object definition, the view row client interface is automatically created and the definition's view row class will automatically be marked as implementing the interface.

By default, a view row client interface is named after its view object definition, with the suffix "Row" added. For example, the view row client interface for the AllDepartmentsWithManagers view object definition, by default, would be named `AllDepartmentsWithManagersRow`. For information about changing naming conventions for ADF BC classes, see Chapter 6.

View Object Client Interfaces

A *view object client interface* is an interface extending the interface `oracle.jbo.ViewObject` and exposing the service methods written on a view object class. When you expose a custom method on the view object definition, the view object client interface is automatically created and the definition's view object class will automatically be marked as implementing the interface.

By default, a view object client interface is named after its view object definition. For example, the client interface for the AllDepartmentsWithManagers view object definition, by default, would be named `AllDepartmentsWithManagers`.

Application Module Client Interfaces

An *application module client interface* is an interface extending the interface `oracle.jbo.ApplicationModule` and exposing the service methods written on an application module class. When you expose a custom method on the application module definition, the application module client interface is automatically created and the definition's application module class will automatically be marked as implementing the interface.

By default, an application module client interface is named after its application module definition. For example, the client interface for the TuhraService application module definition, by default, would be named `TuhraService`. The default package for the client interface is the "common" subpackage of the component (such as an application module).

Adding Methods to Client Interfaces

You can edit an application module client interface by clicking the "Edit Application Module Client Interface" (pencil) button on the Java tab of the application module definition's editor, as shown next.

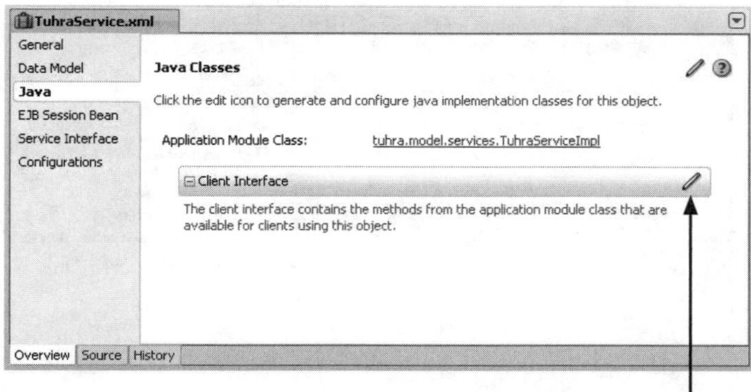

Edit application module client interface

This button will be enabled only if you have defined one or more service methods in the application module class. You can add or edit a view object client interface or view row client interface by clicking the same button on the Java tab of the view object definition's editor.

Clicking this button opens the Edit Client Interface dialog, shown next:

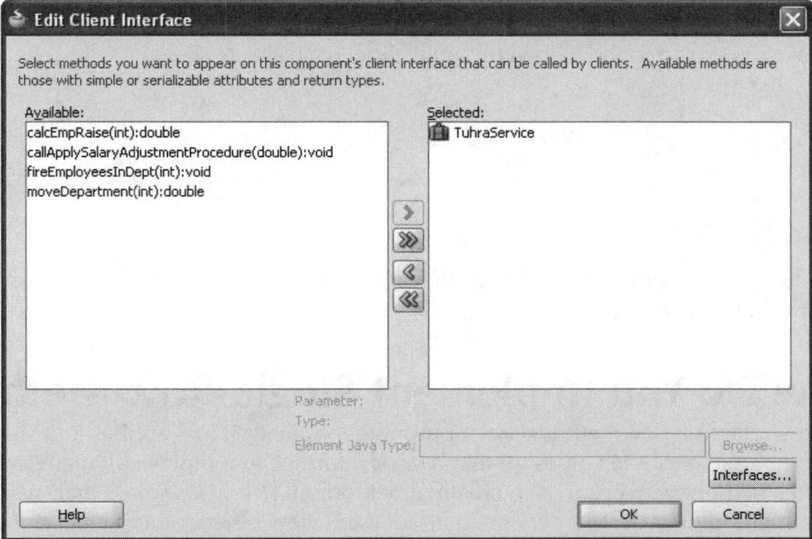

Methods that satisfy the requirements described in the section, "What Sort of Method Can Be a Service Method?" are shown in the *Available* list; you can add them to the client interface by shuttling them to the *Selected* list as shown here:

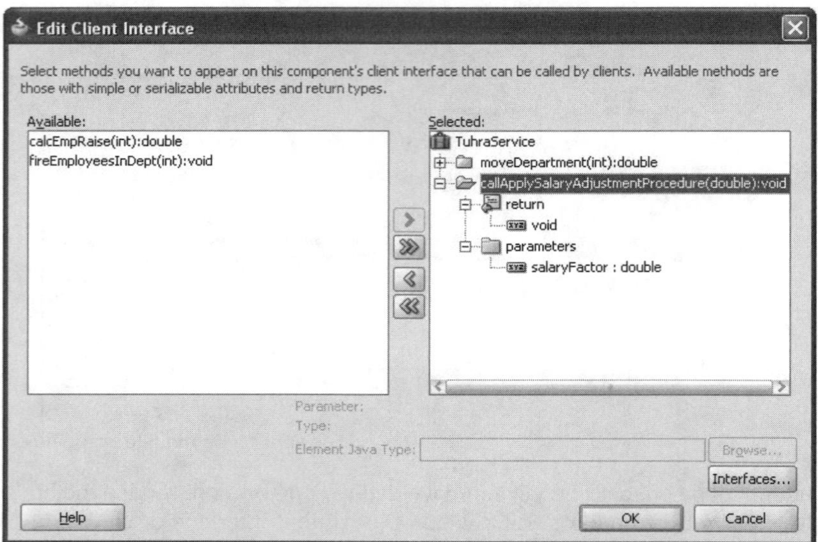

The first time you move one or more service methods to the client interface and click OK in the Edit Client Interface dialog, the client interface Java interface file (for example, TuhraService.java) and the file for a client-side Java class that implements it (for example, TuhraServiceClient.java) will be created as shown in the following Application Navigator nodes:

In addition, the editor will now display the names of the new Java classes and the exposed methods as shown in Figure 8-1.

How Do You Implement Single-Row Methods?

View row class service methods are appropriate for any task that applies to a specific row, such as setting multiple attribute values on that row or returning a complex calculated value based on attributes in the row. You can also create a method on a view row class that, while it is not a service method, is used by a service method at the view object or application module level.

View row–level methods will generally use some or all of the following:

- **Getter and/or setter methods** for view object attribute values
- **View link accessor methods** to return related view rows or `RowIterator` instances (which you should cast to `RowSet`) containing related view rows

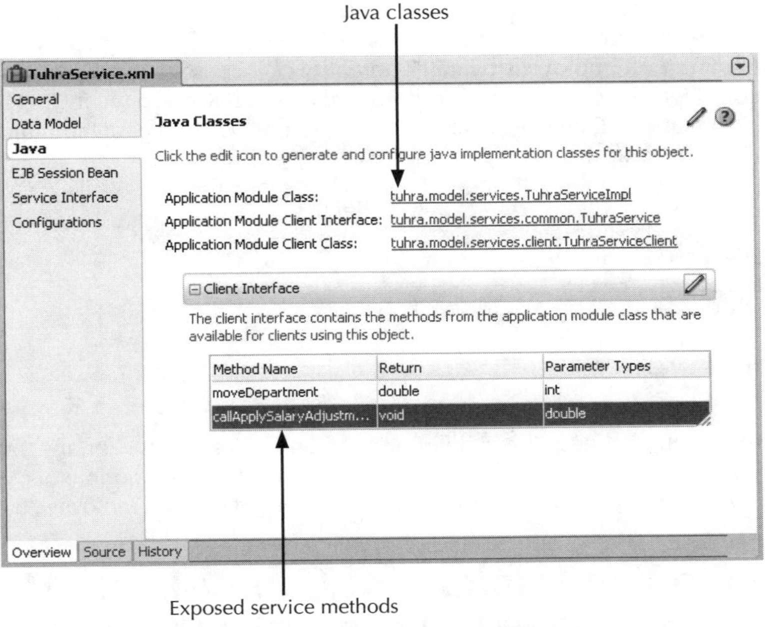

FIGURE 8-1. *Application module editor after exposing a service method*

- **View accessor methods** to return `RowIterator` instances (which you should cast to `RowSet`) of rows retrieved through a view row accessor
- **The `RowSet` methods `hasNext()` and `next()`** to cycle through those rows (for more information about these methods, see Chapter 6).

For example, you could implement a view row-level service method `payRaiseForAll()` in the view row class `AllDepartmentsWithManagersRowImpl` as follows:

```
public void payRaiseForAll(double pctAmount) {
  RowSet employees = (RowSet) getEmployeesInDepartment();
  while (employees.hasNext()) {
    AllEmployeesRowImpl employee = (AllEmployeesRowImpl) employees.next();
    int oldSalary = employee.getSalary().intValue();
    int newSalary = (int) (oldSalary * (1 + pctAmount/100));
    employee.setSalary(newSalary);
  }
}
```

The preceding code calls the view link accessor `getEmployeesInDepartment()` to retrieve a `RowSet` instance. Then, the method cycles through the `RowSet` instance, making changes to each row.

When you generate a view row class, it automatically contains getter methods for each entity object usage (the method returns the entity object instance that this view row refers to via the usage).

If a method applies to attributes from a single entity usage, you may be able to improve reusability by writing the method in the appropriate entity object class instead and creating a very simple method in the view row class that delegates to the entity object method. For example, the view object definition AllEmployees contains an entity object usage of Employees called Manager. So you could write a complex method, `entityLevelMethod()`, in `EmployeesImpl` (the entity object class for Employees), and write the following simple method in the class `AllEmployeesRowImpl`:

```
public Number delegateToEntityLevelMethod() {
  Number retVal = null;
  EmployeesImpl entity = getManager();
  if (entity != null) {
    retVal = entity.entityLevelMethod();
  }
  return retVal;
}
```

This way, you can reuse the code in `entityLevelMethod()` for any usage of Employees in any view object definition by calling a similar delegating method in other view row classes (or one in `AllEmployeesRowImpl` that calls the method on the Employees usage of Employees).

How Do You Implement Query-Level Methods?

View object class service methods are appropriate for any task that applies to a particular set of query results, such as making a multi-row calculation, deleting multiple rows, or changing the view object instance's query. You can also create a method in a view object class that, while not a service method, can be called by an application module–level service method.

Retrieving View Rows

In many cases, the purpose of methods written in a view object class is to process or manipulate particular view rows within its cache. This section explains a number of techniques for accessing view rows within a view object class.

Accessing the Current Row

Should you need to access the currently selected row in a view object instance's cache, you can do so by calling the method `ViewObjectImpl.getCurrentRow()`. The return type of this method is `oracle.jbo.Row`, so you should cast it to `ViewRowImpl` or a particular view row class to call any methods not provided by the `Row` interface, as shown here in code that could be written inside a method on the view object class `AllEmployeeImagesImpl`:

```
AllEmployeeImagesRowImpl currentRow =
  (AllEmployeeImagesRowImpl) getCurrentRow();
Number imageId = currentRow.getImageId();
```

Cycling Through Rows in the View Object Instance's Row Set

The current row in a view object instance is maintained by an iterator called the view object instance's *default row set iterator*. While you could use this iterator to cycle through the rows in the view object's query collection, doing so would lose the place of the view object instance's current row. If your method needs to cycle through view rows to process them, rather than to perform navigation, you should instead create a *secondary row set iterator,* an iterator that keeps track of an alternate "current row."

A row set iterator is an object of type `oracle.jbo.RowSetIterator`, which provides methods called `next()` and `hasNext()` for use in looping through rows.

The process of looping through rows using a secondary row set iterator is as follows:

1. Create the secondary row set iterator.
2. Use the `hasNext()` and `next()` methods to create a loop through the rows of the row set iterator.
3. Inside the loop, cast each row appropriately (if you need methods not exposed by `oracle.jbo.Row`) and manipulate it as desired.
4. Close the row set iterator.

An example of this process is provided in the following code, which could be written inside an `AllEmployeeImagesImpl` method:

```
01: RowSetIterator it = createRowSetIterator(null);
02: while (it.hasNext()) {
03:   AllEmployeeImagesRowImpl currentRow =
04:      (AllEmployeeImagesRowImpl) it.next();
05:   String id = currentRow.getImageId();
06:   // do something with id/currentRow here
06: }
07: it.closeRowSetIterator();
```

- **Line 01** creates the row set iterator by calling the method `ViewObjectImpl.createRowSetIterator()`. You can optionally pass a `String` into this method, which provides a name for the row set iterator. If multiple secondary row set iterators are open at the same time, each must have a distinct name.
- **Line 02** opens the loop through the rows in the view object instance's current row set.
- **Lines 03–04** retrieve the next row in the row set and cast it to the custom view row class. The cast is necessary because Line 5 calls a typesafe accessor method from that class, which is not exposed by `oracle.jbo.Row`.
- **Line 05** retrieves the value of the row's ImageId attribute, using the typesafe getter method.
- **Line 06** is a placeholder for code that uses the ImageId attribute and processes or manipulates the row in further ways, such as calling a view row-level method (as described in the section, "How Do You Implement a Method on a View Row Class?")
- **Line 07** closes the row set iterator by calling the method `RowSetIterator.closeRowSetIterator()`.

NOTE

This code listing is simplified for illustration purposes. Line 07 would more properly be placed inside the finally section of a try-finally block in case the while loop raises exceptions. It is important to close the iterator regardless of whether exceptions occur.

Finding a Particular Row by Key

The ADF Faces model layer provides a declarative way for the client to find a row by a key. However, ADF also provides a programmatic way to find a row by key so that you can do it within a service method.

Key Objects As explained in Chapter 6, a view object definition's key is a set of view attributes whose values uniquely identify a view row, and which includes all primary key attributes from any updatable underlying entity object usage. Within a custom service method, you can create a *key object,* a Java encapsulation of values for some or all of the attributes in the key. You can use this key object to retrieve a `RowSet` or array containing some or all of the rows that match the appropriate values.

A key object is an instance of the class `oracle.jbo.Key`, which you can construct by passing an array of values into its constructor. The array of values should satisfy these requirements:

- **It should have as many elements as the view object definition has key attributes**, in the order in which the attributes occur in the view object definition.
- **Some of the elements may be `null`**, but for each updatable entity object usage, either all the elements corresponding to the entity object usage's primary key attributes must be `null`, or none can be. Attributes added to the key beyond the primary key attributes from updateable entity object usages cannot be `null`.

Finding Rows by Key Once you have created a key object, you can use it to retrieve a `RowIterator` (which you can cast to a `RowSet`) containing matching rows by calling the method `ViewObjectImpl.findByAltKey()` (you can use this method, as explained next, even if you are finding a row by the view object definition's key rather than by an alternate key). This method takes the following parameters:

- **A value of `null`** to find rows by the view object's key; other possible values are explained in the section "Alternate Keys."
- **The key object** to match; if some of the key object's values are `null`, they will be treated as wildcards that match any value.
- **An `int`** indicating the maximum number of view rows to find; a value of –1 means to return every matching view row.
- **A `boolean`** that should usually be `false`; a value of `true` means to ignore the current WHERE clause of a normal or declarative SQL mode query, any WHERE clause applied via a view criteria object, any WHERE clause applied via a view link instance, and any WHERE clause applied via the `setWhereClause()` method.

For example, in the sample application, the view object definition AllEmployees has one key attribute: EmployeeId. You could use the following code in a method on the AllEmployees view object class to retrieve the first (and only) view row that has EmployeeId 101:

```
Key key = new Key(new Object[] {
  new Number(101);
});
RowSet foundRows = (RowSet) findByAltKey(null, key, 1, false);
```

You can also use another method, `findByKey()`, to search for view rows. `findByKey()` takes two parameters:

- **The key object** to match; if some of the key object's values are null, they will be treated as wildcards which match any value.
- **An `int`** indicating the maximum number of view rows to find; a value of `-1` means to return every matching view row.

Instead of a row iterator, `findByKey()` returns an array of type `Row[]`.

Alternate Keys As explained in Chapter 7, a view object definition's alternate key is a combination of alternate keys for some or all of its entity object usages.

Once you have created a key object for an alternate key, you can use it to retrieve a `RowIterator` (which you can cast to a `RowSet`) containing matching rows by calling the method `ViewObjectImpl.findByAltKey()`, just as you do to retrieve rows matching the view object definition's key. The only difference is in the first parameter you pass to `findByAltKey()`—instead of a value of null, you pass the name of the alternate key you want to use.

Navigating Through the Cache

The ADF Model layer allows you to declaratively navigate through a view object instance's cache, moving forward or backward one or multiple rows at a time, jumping to the beginning or end of the cache, or navigating based on key values. However, you may need to change the current row pointer programmatically, within a service method.

`ViewObjectImpl` provides methods `first()`, `previous()`, `next()`, and `last()`, which both return the appropriate row and change the current row pointer accordingly. It also contains the methods `hasPrevious()` and `hasNext()`, Boolean tests that allow you to call `previous()` and `next()` safely, as in the following code, which could be written inside any view object class' method as follows:

```
if (hasNext()) {
  Row r = next();
}
```

If you have retrieved a row (for example, using `findByAltKey()`) that is in the view object instance's cache, you can move the current row pointer to that row by passing the row into `setCurrentRow()`, as shown here:

```
Key key = new Key(new Object[] {
  new Number(101)
});
RowIterator foundRows = findByAltKey(null, key, 1, false);
if (foundRows.hasNext()) {
  setCurrentRow(foundRows.next());
}
```

Creating and Deleting Rows

`ViewObjectImpl` contains four methods that let you insert and delete rows from the view cache: `createRow()`, `createAndInitRow()`, `insertRow()`, and `removeCurrentRow()`.

If the view object definition contains entity object usages, the relevant entity object instances will be created or marked for deletion. When the transaction is committed, these rows will be added to or deleted from the database.

The `createRow()` method returns a new view row (its return type is `Row`), and `insertRow()` inserts that row into the view cache right before the current row, as in the following example:

```
Row newRow = createRow();
insertRow(newRow);
```

It is important to call both of these methods. Just creating a row will not make it visible in the application's user interface.

You can also create a row and set values for some or all of its attributes at the same time using the method `createAndInitRow()`. This method takes an argument of type `oracle.jbo.NameValuePairs`. You can populate a `NameValuePairs` instance by calling the method `NameValuePairs.setAttribute()`, which works very similarly to `Row.setAttribute()`, as shown next:

```
NameValuePairs nvp = new NameValuePairs();
nvp.setAttribute("FirstName", "Elwood");
nvp.setAttribute("LastName", "Fritchie");
nvp.setAttribute("DepartmentId", new Number(90));
Row newRow = createAndInitRow(nvp);
insertRow(newRow);
```

As with `create()`, you need to insert rows created with `createAndInitRow()`. The primary advantage of using `createAndInitRow()`, rather than using `create()` and setting the attribute values directly on the row, is for view object definitions based on polymorphic entity object definitions. For example, consider a view object definition (which does not exist in the sample application) called "ImagesView" that contains a usage of the ImageUsages entity object definition, which has a discriminator attribute UsageType. You can use `createAndInitRow()` to populate this attribute as the row is created, as shown here:

```
NameValuePairs nvp = new NameValuePairs;
nvp.setAttribute("UsageType", "E");
Row newRow = createAndInitRow(nvp);
insertRow(newRow);
```

When you do this, the new row will be based on an instance of EmployeesImageUsage, which corresponds to the discriminator value "E."

NOTE

createAndInitRow() is also useful when you have implemented polymorphism at the view object, rather than the entity object, level. For more information about polymorphism at the view object level, see the section "38.6.5 Working with Polymorphic View Rows" of the Fusion Developer's Guide for Oracle ADF.

The `removeCurrentRow()` method removes the current row. If there is a UI component bound to a view object instance which executes `removeCurrentRow()`, the ADF Model Layer (explained in Part IV) will move the current row pointer to point to the next row, or the previous row if there is no next row. Otherwise, the current row pointer will point to null until you move it by calling one of the row navigation methods.

You can also delete a view row by calling `remove()` directly on the row object. The row deleted in this way does not need to be current. The following example deletes the AllEmployees view row with EmployeeId 101:

```
Key key = new Key(new Object[] {
  new Number(101)
});
RowIterator foundRows = findByAltKey(null, key, 1, false);
if (foundRows.hasNext()) {
  foundRows.next().remove();
}
```

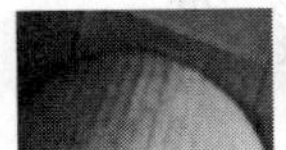

NOTE
Remember that if you have jbo.locking.mode set to "pessimistic," deleting rows in this way will acquire a row lock immediately. If jbo.locking.mode is set to "optimistic" (recommended for web applications), the database will not be affected until you issue a COMMIT or POST statement.

Modifying Queries and Filtering Rows

Chapter 7 explained a number of general techniques for allowing flexibility in view object instances' queries at runtime. This section explains how to modify these queries within view object–level methods.

Setting Named Bind Variables

When you generate a custom view object class, JDeveloper will automatically add typesafe accessors for its bind variables. These accessors do not follow standard naming conventions in that they do not automatically capitalize the first letter of the variable name. So, for example, if the view object definition AllEmployees had a bind variable named "queryFirstName," its view object class would contain methods with the following declarations:

```
public void setqueryFirstName(String value);
public String getqueryFirstName();
```

For the sake of clarity, we recommend naming bind variables with an initial capital letter. For example, the bind parameter is actually named "QueryFirstName," so the view object class contains the following methods with more standard-looking names:

```
public void setQueryFirstName(String value);
public String getQueryFirstName();
```

The ADF Model automatically exposes the ability to set bind parameters and re-execute the query, so that you can do so from a button or link on a page. However, you can also call these methods from within a service method.

After setting bind parameters, you will generally need to re-execute the view object instance's query; you can do this by calling the method `ViewObjectImpl.executeQuery()`, as shown here in this code that could be written inside an AllEmployees view object class method:

```
setQueryFirstName("Neena");
executeQuery();
```

Switching Named View Criteria

As explained in Chapter 7, you can apply a single named view criteria object by passing its name into `ViewObjectImpl.setApplyViewCriteriaName()`, or apply several named view criteria objects simultaneously by passing an array of their names into `ViewObjectImpl.setApplyViewCriteriaNames()`. If any of the new or old applied view criteria objects use database execution mode or both modes, you then need to re-execute the view object's query to make sure that all and only the appropriate rows are shown.

Filtering Rows in Memory

With the exception of named view criteria with in-memory execution mode or both execution modes, filtering rows via where clauses or the other mechanisms in this section is done at database query–execution time. This has two main consequences:

- **You must re-execute the query** after changing it using any of those mechanisms.
- **Rows added to an entity cache but not yet posted to the database** will appear in all view object instances that use the relevant entity definition, even if those view object definitions' WHERE clauses would exclude them.

To filter rows in memory, you can use named view criteria with in-memory execution mode or both execution modes, or you can apply row matches in memory. A *row match* is an object of type `oracle.jbo.RowMatch`, which encapsulates a WHERE-clause equivalent that can be used to filter rows in memory. `RowMatch` has a constructor which takes a `String`, which resembles a SQL WHERE clause (without the "WHERE" keyword), except that attribute names are used instead of column names, and only the following SQL operations and functions are supported:

- **The comparison operators** =, <, >, <=, >=, <>, `LIKE`, and `BETWEEN`
- **The boolean logical operators**
- **The row functions** `UPPER`, `TO_CHAR`, `TO_DATE`, and `TO_TIMESTAMP`

After applying a row match or making a change that interacts with view criteria with in-memory execution mode or both execution modes, you still need to call `executeQuery()` on the view object instance, but you can temporarily set up the view object so that it queries the entity cache rather than the database, or queries both, by calling the method `ViewObjectImpl.setQueryMode()`. This method accepts a `byte`, which is one of the following:

- **`QUERY_MODE_SCAN_DATABASE_TABLES`**, a constant representing the default mode, which executes the query against the database (using the query's WHERE clause but then applying the RowMatch or in-memory view criteria object if one has been specified)
- **`QUERY_MODE_SCAN_ENTITY_ROWS`**, a constant representing a mode that executes the query against the entity cache (using only the RowMatch or in-memory execution mode view criteria object)

- **QUERY_MODE_SCAN_UNPOSTED_ENTITY_ROWS,** a constant representing a mode that executes the query against the entity cache, but excludes any rows that already exist in the database
- **QUERY_MODE_SCAN_VIEW_ROWS**, a constant representing a mode that executes the query exclusively against rows already in the view cache (using only the RowMatch or in-memory execution mode view criteria object, but in general the WHERE clause was applied when the rows were originally queried)
- **Any number of the preceding**, bitwise-disjoined (using the "|" operator), to indicate multiple sources

For example, the following code, which could appear in a method in the view object class for the definition JobsLOV, applies an additional, in-memory filter to the rows in one of its instances:

```
01: RowMatch rowMatch=new RowMatch("JobId like AD%");
02: applyRowMatch(rowMatch);
03: setQueryMode(QUERY_MODE_SCAN_VIEW_ROWS);
04: executeQuery();
05: setQueryMode(QUERY_MODE_SCAN_DATABASE_TABLES);
```

This code performs the following actions:

- **Line 01** creates a row match.
- **Line 02** applies the row match.
- **Line 03** sets the query mode so that it exclusively filters existing view rows, without going to the database
- **Line 04** executes the query against the existing view rows.
- **Line 05** sets the query mode back to the default.

How Do You Implement Cross-Query or Transaction-Level Methods?

Application module class service methods are appropriate for any task that acts on the results of multiple queries, such as calling multiple view object service methods (possibly performing cross-view object instance calculations on the return values). They are also appropriate to tasks that apply to no particular set of query results but to the transaction or data model as a whole, such as the dynamic creation of view object instances.

Finding View Object and Nested Application Module Instances in the Data Model

In many cases, the purpose of methods written in an application module class is to process or manipulate data. This generally requires gaining access to the view object instances in the data model. Application module classes provide getter methods for each view object instance directly in the data model (that is, not inside a nested application module instance). These getter methods use the view object class as their return type, if a view object class has been generated. If no view object class has been generated, they use `ViewObjectImpl` as their return type. For example, the application module definition TuhraService contains (among others) view object instances in its data model called EmployeeSearch (an instance of the view object definition EmployeeSearch) and DepartmentTree (an instance of the view object definition AllDepartmentsWithManager).

If you generate a custom view object class for the EmployeeSearch view object definition, but not for the AllDepartmentsWithManager view object definition, the class `TuhraServiceImpl` will contain methods with the following declarations:

```
public EmployeeSearchImpl getEmployee()
public ViewObjectImpl getDepartmentTree()
```

If your primary application module definition contains nested application module instances, the application module class will also contain getter methods for the nested application module instances. These getter methods use the application module class for the nested instance as their return type, if it has been generated, and use `ApplicationModuleImpl` as their return type, if there is no nested application module class.

If an accessor returns a particular application module class, it can call that class' view object instance getters to retrieve view object instances from the nested application module. Otherwise, you can pass the name of a view object instance into the method `ApplicationModuleImpl.findViewObject()` to retrieve such an instance, as in the following code (which assumes the existence of a nested application module instance called OrgChartModule, which itself contains an instance of AllEmployees called EmpsForOrgChart):

```
public ApplicationModuleImpl orgChartModule = getOrgChartModule();
public AllEmployees empsForOrgChart = (AllEmployees)
  orgChartModule.findViewObject("EmpsForOrgChart");
```

The `findViewObject()` method is also useful to retrieve view object instances that were added at runtime (as described in the next section, "Creating and Removing View Object Instances Dynamically") and therefore do not have typesafe accessors.

Once you have retrieved view object instances, you can call methods on their custom implementation classes (if any) or manipulate them in other ways (such as by adding view link instances at runtime, as described later in this section).

Creating and Removing View Object Instances Dynamically

It is possible that the specific view object instances your application needs, or even the total number of instances, may vary based on user actions. In this case, you may need to add view object instances to the data model of a particular application module instance in a service method, rather than being able to rely entirely on the data model you define in the application module editor.

Adding a view object instance to an application module instance's data model always adds it as a top-level instance with no details, not as a participant in a master-detail relationship. If you want to create a master or detail instance, first create the instance at the top level and then add an appropriate view link instance, as described in the subsection "Creating and Removing Master-Detail Relationships Dynamically."

CAUTION

If you add a view object instance to the data model and do not remove it, ADF will throw an error if you attempt to add it again using the same name. This may happen if you add a view object instance to the data model in a service method that may be called multiple times. Because of this, you may want to test for the view object's existence before attempting to add it, as in the following code:

```
ViewObject voInstance=findViewObject("NewInstance");
if (voInstance == null) {
  /* code to create a view object instance named "NewInstance" */
}
```

Creating View Object Instances from Existing View Object Definitions

Creating only a view object definition does not require that an instance of that definition automatically appear in every application module definition's data model. You can create a number of view object definitions at design time, and add them to the application module's data model only when they are required. Similarly, you can add additional instances of a view object definition to a data model that already contains one or more instances.

To do this, you call the method `ApplicationModuleImpl.createViewObject()`, which takes the following parameters:

- A name for the new view object instance
- The package-qualified name of the view object definition to use

For example, if you want to create an instance of the EmployeesSearch view object definition (which is in the package `tuhra.model.queries.main`) called NewEmployees, you would use the following code from within a method inside the application module class:

```
createViewObject("NewEmployees", "tuhra.model.queries.main.EmployeesSearch");
```

Creating View Object Instances with a Single Entity Object Usage on the Fly

In addition to dynamically creating view object instances based on existing view object definitions, you can also create view object instances from definitions created on the fly, with no preexisting view object definition. Where reasonable, you should create these definitions with an entity object usage, for the reasons described in Chapter 7.

Creating on-the-fly view object definitions with multiple entity object usages is a complex process and beyond the scope of this book; here, we will only discuss creating on-the-fly view object definitions with a single entity object usage. Moreover, the definition you create must use a query form much like normal SQL mode: You can specify SELECT, FROM, WHERE, and ORDER BY clauses, but you cannot specify clauses such as GROUP BY. The view object will perform default attribute mappings for the SELECT clause based on column names; SELECT clause columns that do not match entity object attributes under the default conversion become SQL-only attributes.

You can create an instance of such an on-the-fly view object definition by calling the method `ApplicationModuleImpl.createViewObjectFromQueryClauses()`, which accepts the following `String` parameters:

- A name for the new view object instance
- The package-qualified name of the entity object definition to use
- The SELECT clause of the query (without the word "SELECT")
- The FROM clause of the query (without the word "FROM")
- The WHERE clause of the query (without the word "WHERE")
- The ORDER BY clause of the query (without the words "ORDER BY")

For example, suppose you wanted to create a view object instance using an on-the-fly definition with one usage of Departments and the following query:

```
SELECT DEPARTMENT_NO,
       DEPARTMENT_NAME,
       MANAGER_ID
FROM DEPARTMENTS
```

You could do this with the following code in a method in the application module class:

```
createViewObjectFromQueryClauses("NewDeptsByManagerInstance",
                                 "tuhra.model.entities.Departments",
                                 "DEPARTMENT_NO, DEPARTMENT_NAME, MANAGER_ID",
                                 "DEPARTMENTS",
                                 null, null);
```

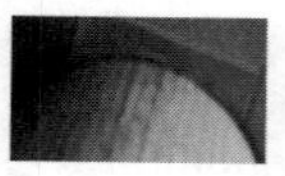

CAUTION
As always, never construct SQL statements directly from user input unless you filter the input to exclude SQL keywords and symbols first.

Creating SQL-Only View Object Instances on the Fly

If you want to create an instance of an on-the-fly view object definition with a more complex query, you need to use a SQL-only view object definition. You can do this by calling the method `ApplicationModuleImpl.createViewObjectFromQueryStmt()`, which takes two parameters:

- A name for the new view object instance
- A SQL query

Removing View Object Instances from the Data Model

Removing a view object instance, whether dynamically created or otherwise, from the data model is simple. `ViewObjectImpl` provides a method, `remove()`, that will remove the instance on which it is called from the application module's data model. For example, you could remove the view object instance "NewDeptsByManagerInstance" using the following code in an application module instance:

```
ViewObjectImpl deptsByMgr = (ViewObjectImpl)
  findViewObject("NewDeptsByManagerInstance");
if (deptsByMgr != null) {
  deptsByMgr.remove();
}
```

Creating and Removing Master-Detail Relationships Dynamically

Sometimes you must create a view link instance dynamically. In particular, since dynamically created view object instances are not in the data model at design time, the data model cannot contain view link instances that involve them (as masters, details, or both).

You can add view link instances to a particular application module instance at runtime in one of two ways, depending on whether you already have a view link definition to use.

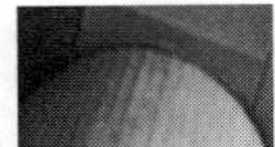

CAUTION
As with view object instances, if you add a view link instance to the data model and do not remove it, ADF will throw an error if you attempt to add it again using the same name. This may happen if you add a view link instance to the data model in a service method that may be called multiple times. Because of this, you may want to test for the view link's existence before attempting to add it, as in the following code:

```
ViewLink vlInstance = findViewLink("NewLink");
if (vlInstance == null) {
  /* code to create a view object instance named "NewLink" */
}
```

Creating View Link Instances from Existing View Link Definitions

If both view object instances that you want to join in a master-detail relationship are based on view object definitions you created at design time (either because the instances were added to the data model at design time or because they were added using the `createViewObject()` method), you can create a view link definition between those view object definitions, and then use it at runtime to create a view link instance by calling the method `ApplicationModuleImpl.createViewLink()`, which takes the following arguments:

- The name of the view link instance to be created
- The package-qualified name of the view link definition to use
- The view object instance to use as a master
- The view object instance to use as a detail

For example, suppose you have created a view link definition, EmployeesJobsFkLink (in the package `tuhra.model.queries`), between the view object definitions AllJobs and AllEmployees. You have an instance of AllEmployees called "EmployeeDisplay" in the data model, and at runtime, you want to make it a detail of an instance of AllJobs, NewJobsInstance, that you created using `createViewObject()`. You could do this with the following code:

```
createViewLink("NewEmpJobsLink",
               "tuhra.model.queries.EmployeesJobsFkLink",
               findViewObject("NewJobsInstance"),
               getEmployeeDisplay());
```

Creating Association-Based View Link Instances on the Fly

Suppose you do not have access to a view link definition created at design time (because, for example, one of the view object instances you want to join was created using `createViewObjectFromQueryClauses()`), but both view object definitions contain entity object usages that are known at design time. Then, you can predefine an association between the entity object definitions and use that association in an application module method to create a view link from an on-the-fly view link definition by calling the method `ApplicationModuleImpl.createViewLinkFromEntityAssocName()`, which takes the following arguments:

- A name for the view link instance to be created
- The package-qualified name of the association
- The view object instance to be used as the master
- The view object instance to be used as the detail

Creating View Link Instances from View Object Attributes on the Fly

You can also create a view link instance from an on-the-fly view link definition without using associations, by specifying source and destination attributes and, optionally, a custom view link WHERE clause. To do this, you first need to create arrays of source and destination attributes, represented by objects of the type `oracle.jbo.AttributeDef`. You can retrieve one of these objects by passing the attribute name into the method `ViewObject.findAttributeDef()`. For example, to create a view link instance on-the-fly between AllJobs and EmployeeDisplay (and you do not have any appropriate view link definition or association), you would first retrieve the view object instances and create arrays of the source and destination attributes, as shown in the following code:

```
ViewObject allJobs = getAllJobs();
ViewObject employeeDisplay = getEmployeeDisplay();
AttributeDef[] sourceAttrs = new AttributeDef() {
  allJobs.findAttributeDef("JobId")
};
AttributeDef[] destAttrs = new AttributeDef() {
  employeeDisplay.findAttributeDef("JobId");
}
```

Then, you could call the method `ApplicationModuleImpl.createViewLinkBetweenViewObjects()`, which takes the following arguments:

- The name of the view link instance to create.
- An optional accessor name, which can later be passed into the `getAttribute()` method on the master view object instance to retrieve a `RowSet` containing its details; this is much like calling an accessor method for an ordinary view link instance. You can use `null` if you do not need this functionality.
- The master view object instance.
- The array of source (master) attributes.
- The detail view object instance.
- The array of destination (detail) attributes.
- An optional view link WHERE clause; if you pass in `null` for this attribute, ADF will use the default view link WHERE clause. View link WHERE clauses are explained in Chapter 7.

An example of this method call is shown here:

```
createViewLinkBetweenViewObjects("NewViewLinkInstance",
                                 null,
                                 allJobs,
                                 sourceAttrs,
                                 employeeDisplay,
                                 destAttrs,
                                 null);
```

Removing View Link Instances

You can delete view link instances from the data model in much the same way you can remove view object instances: By locating them using the method `ApplicationModule.findViewLink()` and then calling their `remove()` method, as shown in the following code:

```
ViewLink linkToRemove = findViewLink("NewViewLinkInstance");
if (linkToRemove != null) {
  linkToRemove.remove();
}
```

Manipulating Transactions

As explained in Chapter 13, you can declaratively commit or roll back a transaction from the view or controller layer using the ADF Model. However, you may want to commit or roll back a transaction atomically, as part of a coarse-grained service method.

To commit or roll back a transaction, you must first acquire a *transaction object,* an object of type `oracle.jbo.Transaction`, which represents the database transaction used by an application module instance at any given time. Transaction objects do not map one-to-one to database transactions; a single transaction object will serve a top-level application module for (with certain exceptions that are beyond the scope of this book) its entire lifetime, surviving commit and rollback operations. However, at any particular time, a transaction object represents exactly one database transaction.

Every top-level or shared application module instance has its own transaction object. Nested application module instances inherit their transaction objects (and therefore their database transactions) from their top-level instances.

You can access a transaction object by calling the method `ApplicationModuleImpl.getTransaction()`. Then you can use the methods `Transaction.commit()` and `Transaction.rollback()` to either post and commit the transaction to the database or roll back the transaction and empty all caches (so that they can be queried anew).

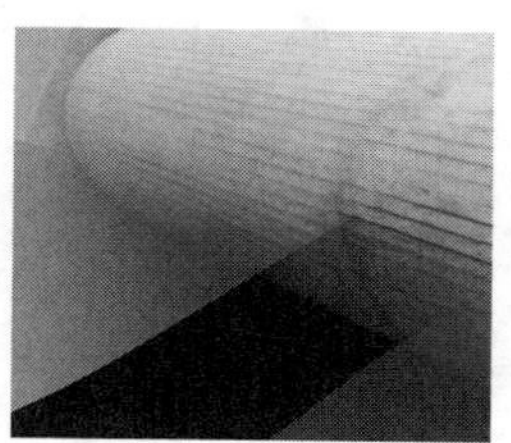

PART III

ADF View and Controller

Every day you may make progress. Every step may be fruitful.
Yet there will stretch out before you an ever-lengthening, ever-ascending, ever-improving path.
You know you will never get to the end of the journey.
But this, so far from discouraging, only adds to the joy and the glory of the climb.

—Sir Winston Churchill (1874–1965), *Strand Magazine* (Dec. 1921/Jan. 1922)

CHAPTER 9

JavaServer Faces Basics

There are three things I always forget.
Names, faces, and—the third I can't remember.

—Italo Svevo (1861–1928)

The purpose of frameworks (and of new development technologies in general) is to make development within a complex environment easier. Technologies evolve so that development can be faster, cheaper, and more accurate. It is one thing to develop a technology and create guidelines about how best to use it. It is another to actually apply that theory to a real-world application development project. The proof of the technology and its methods comes from applying it. Therefore, as a natural course in the evolution of a technology or framework, features and methods are added that improve development productivity. At some point, needs arise that require core changes to the original technology. At this point, the technology's authors must decide to evolve it with a rewrite or to replace it with another technology and end the life cycle of the original technology.

This kind of evolution has occurred with Java EE web technology. As mentioned in Chapter 4, Java EE web technology evolved from Java applets to HTTP servlet code written in pure Java. This evolution was a major shift in development and deployment environments. The next major shift was from servlets to JavaServer Pages technology, which mixes HTML and JSP tags. JSP pages are translated into and run as servlets, so they share the deployment environment, but the code is different and requires less hands-on work with Java. The next major evolution in Java EE web technology was from JSP pages to JavaServer Faces (JSF) pages. JSF technology was ratified as a standard in March 2004 through the *Java Community Process (JCP),* which Sun Microsystems uses to obtain the participation of Java experts when introducing new technologies and existing technology upgrades (jcp.org).

Since this book focuses on Fusion web development using JSF technology, we need to provide some more details about JSF concepts. This chapter explains the basics of JSF and provides a bit more information about ADF Faces to supplement the material in Chapter 1 and Chapter 4. Information about JSF architecture and design principles abounds on the Web. Therefore, this chapter will focus on what you, as a developer who may be new to this environment, need to know to be productive in creating JSF-based code. The chapter answers the following questions:

- **Why was JSF developed?**
- **What JSF concepts do I really need to know now?**
- **Where can I find additional information about JSF?**

Part III of this book provides details about the View and Controller layers to complement the material about the ADF Business Components (Business Services layer) in Part II. Part III contains some brief hands-on practices so that you can get a taste of development work using JSF technology. Chapter 10 consists of hands-on practices that introduce you to some of the JSF concepts this chapter discusses. Chapter 11 digs into details about task flows, which offer additional Controller-level features for the View layer. Chapter 12 discusses more details about the ADF Faces components used in the View layer.

NOTE

*ADF Faces in JDeveloper 11*g *is properly called "ADF Faces Rich Client" or "ADF Faces RC" to distinguish it from "ADF Faces" in JDeveloper 10*g*. Since this book focuses only on JDeveloper 11*g*, it usually shortens "ADF Faces RC" to just "ADF Faces."*

Although the chapters in this part of the book illustrate concepts from Part I, they also introduce new topics. As mentioned in the Introduction, merely reading the text in these chapters will not benefit you as much as reading the text and completing any steps we provide for working in JDeveloper.

NOTE
This chapter assumes that you have been exposed to the Java EE, JSP, JSF, and ADF Faces material in Chapter 1 and the brief JSF overview in Chapter 4.

Why Was JSF Developed?

The popularity of JSP technology grew rapidly because it was easier to use than the preceding technologies. Instead of building up an HTML page using print statements and coding low-level details of the HTTP communication in a servlet file, developers could concentrate on creating the HTML page using HTML tags and JSP (Java-oriented) tags. They could use HTML visual editors for the visual design and Java tools for the required Java logic. In the early days of JSP technology, developers used the core JSP tags with Java *scriptlets* (small bits of Java code embedded in tags within the JSP file) added for custom functionality. The scriptlets supplied logic to conditionally display items or to retrieve data. They would also supply logic that determined page navigation (page flow).

However, developers found themselves writing the same scriptlets in each application; this made the code difficult to maintain, so they started creating their own custom tags to perform the same function as those scriptlets (for example, drawing an HTML table containing rows and columns of data). They then stored the tags in tag libraries and referenced these tags in each application.

This served the Java community up to a point, but, even though frameworks supplied many of the custom tag libraries required for an application, the Java platform standards (Java EE) did not regulate the foundation on which these libraries were built. In addition to problems with design consistency, developers found JSP custom tag libraries lacking consistency in a number of other areas. JSF grew out of the need to address inconsistencies and inefficiencies in areas such as these:

Components The days of writing JSP files that included large amounts of JSP scriptlet tags and JSP expression tags came to an end when developers found that approach nonproductive for code modifications and framework usage. Wrapping complex functionality and display characteristics into a single tag—the *UI component* (or just *component*)—became a goal for most tag libraries. As mentioned before, a single component could query a database table and present an HTML table structure, with data from the query arranged into rows and columns in the table. JSF supplies similar, high-level controls and supports them with a standard. Developers spend little or no time coding HTML layout tags and spend more time on the arrangement of components and how they are used to solve business requirements. They define the functionality and display characteristics of the component by setting property (attribute) values and arranging them inside layout containers.

Layout Containers *Layout containers* (also called *layout components, container components,* or *containers*) are components that provide a structure for the components nested inside them (using the tag hierarchy). When you add components to a JSF page, you plug them into areas inside the layout container. The child components will maintain their relative position if the user resizes the window at runtime. For example, an ADF Faces layout container, `af:panelGroupLayout`, can display child objects in a vertical or horizontal arrangement.

Another benefit of using layout containers is that you do not need to worry about coding HTML tables or CSS selectors to position components in specific locations in the page. The HTML and CSS code is created for you based on the functionality and areas defined for the container. Another benefit of layout containers is that they abstract the component arrangements from the specific markup language. For example, you can stack components into an `af:panelFormLayout` layout container. If the JSF page appears in a web browser, the components will appear inside an HTML table. If the display is in a wireless device, the components will appear inside the corresponding table structure specific to the wireless markup language.

Support for Different Display Devices Before JSF, running an application on different display devices, such as a web browser or a PDA, usually required rewriting the View layer code to use a different technology. Tag libraries that supported multiple display devices were, again, not standard. JSF separates the View layer components from their display using a render kit that outputs a certain style of code.

NOTE
Enterprise applications target web browsers more frequently than any other style. Therefore, the examples in this book assume that the application will be running in a web browser.

Controller The MVC design pattern specifies that a separate code layer (the Controller) defines page flow and data communications. In addition, the Front Controller design pattern describes a single handler for all requests in an application. The patterns are clear, but in the past, the developer was responsible for implementing them. Open-source controller frameworks, the most popular being Apache Struts, removed the need for developers to implement custom controllers and provided the infrastructure needed to manipulate page flow. However, these controller frameworks did not tie the Controller layer to View layer tag libraries in a standard way. JSF includes a Controller layer that is integrated with the JSF View layer tag libraries and defined in the Java EE specifications.

Event Processing User events, such as a button press, had no standard handling mechanism in web technologies before JSF. JSF defines an event model for its tags using listeners and actions.

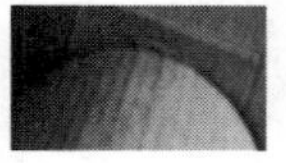

NOTE
JSF was a new addition to the Java EE specification in release 5, Java EE 5—now usually shortened to "Java EE."

What JSF Concepts Do I Really Need to Know Now?

Fortunately, just as with most other modern frameworks, you only need to know a subset of everything there is to know about JSF concepts to start creating JSF pages. However, as is true of any technology, the more you know, the more creative you can be when faced with a development challenge. The resources mentioned in the later section "Where Can I Find Additional Information About JSF?" will continue your JSF education.

What Is JSF?

JSF consists mainly of specifications that resulted from the JCP (jcp.org), focused on Java Specification Request (JSR) 127. The specification was revised as JSR 252 and is included in the current Java platform specifications, Java EE 5. In principle, JSF technology supports any type of client device and programming code markup language. However, Sun Microsystems offers a *Reference Implementation (RI)*—code libraries that prove that the standard supports real code—for servlets (as class libraries) and JSP technology (as tag libraries). These libraries contain classes and tags for the components and functionality described later in this section. Since RI libraries are tested and proven implementations of the standard, you can use them as a basis for your own code. The RI also includes a *render kit* (a code layer that translates JSF tags into a specific output format) for HTML output from JSP components.

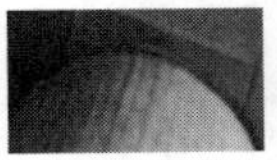

NOTE
MyFaces, an open-source, non-Sun JSF implementation is available at the open-source Apache website page myfaces.apache.org. An earlier version of ADF Faces (10.1.3) was donated to the public domain to kick off the Trinidad project of MyFaces.

Understanding JSF requires knowing a little about each of these concepts:

- Runtime architecture
- JSF-oriented files
- Components
- Designing cross-platform interfaces

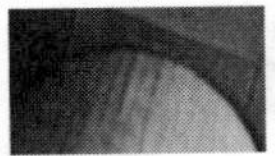

NOTE
Many of the principles discussed in this section are exemplified in the application you will develop in the hands-on practice in Chapter 10.

Runtime Architecture

JSF code runs in a Web Tier container (discussed in Chapter 4) in the same way as servlet code. Figure 9-1 shows the main actors in the request-response round-trip communication for a JSF file. JSP files are the standard view technology used for JSF components running on the Web; you usually code JSF inside a JSP file (although JSF, theoretically, supports multiple-view layer technologies). In this example, the JSF code is contained within a JSP file. The browser issues an HTTP request to the web server. The web server finds the URL's virtual directory name in the web.xml file and passes the request to the Faces Servlet that is running (or that will be started) on the web server. The Faces Servlet handles the request by passing control to an object created using the life cycle class (`javax.faces.lifecycle.Lifecycle`). This `Lifecycle` class processes the JSF file using a set of steps called the *JSF Life Cycle* (described later in this section).

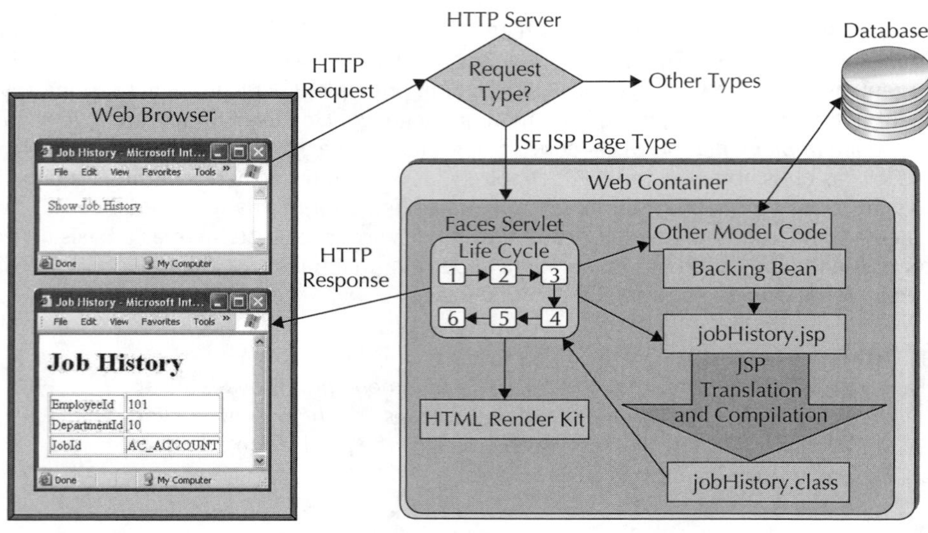

FIGURE 9-1. *JSF JSP runtime*

NOTE
The Faces Servlet initializes an object typed from the `FacesContext` class that stores state information and data pertaining to the user interface elements, as well as information about the request session. You can tap into the `FacesContext` object in your code, as shown in a practice in Chapter 10.

The servlet accesses any necessary Model layer code to obtain values from the data source (such as a database). The servlet instantiates the bean if a component property value refers to an element in a backing bean (described in the sidebar "About Managed Beans and Backing Beans"). The Faces Servlet then assembles the page (shown here with a .jsp extension identifying it as a JSP page). The file runs through the normal JSP translate and compile steps. The application then assembles an HTTP response using a render kit (in this case, the HTML render kit), which converts the display elements to an HTML page. It then sends the response to the web browser. The process for other display types, such as for a PDA or cell phone client, is similar, although their render kits are different.

JSF Life Cycle

The `FacesServlet` and `Lifecycle` objects work together to process the HTTP request and assemble an HTTP response using the six steps described in this section (represented in Figure 9-1). A JSF application can support requests to non-JSF components, but processing of a non-JSF request follows an abbreviated version of the life cycle. This description focuses on the process for requests that address JSF components.

About Managed Beans and Backing Beans

A *bean* in Java (also called a "*JavaBean*") is a class file that conforms to a standard format. A *managed bean (MBean)* is a Java object containing code used to handle operations and data for a resource (in this case, for components on the page). In JSF work, a managed bean is manipulated (created and destroyed) by the JSF controller. It can handle operations and data for one or more pages, or do so for many pages (for example, to support a logout action available on many pages). The JSF framework controls the instantiation and subsequent calling of this managed bean. The general convention is to use one managed bean for each JSF page or page fragment, although some prefer a single managed bean for more than one page in the application.

The term *backing bean* is used to denote a managed bean assigned to a single page or page fragment. A JSF page may not require special code for its components; in this case, you would not create a managed bean for that page.

The rough idea is that the steps proceed in the order indicated by their numbers. However, as the servlet processes events it may bypass one or more steps. For example, if there is an error in step 2, an error message would normally be queued for display later in the life cycle. However, the JSF code can be written to jump directly to step 6 (Render Response) and bypass the intermediate steps.

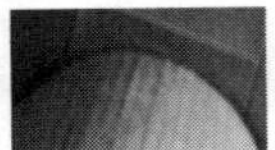

NOTE

Various sources, including some from Oracle, refer to the "JSF life cycle" as the "JSF lifecycle." Although this book adopts the classical form of this term ("life cycle"), the two forms are synonymous.

1. Restore the Component Tree The components used in a JSF application are arranged in the file in a hierarchical way. This hierarchy, the *component tree* (also called the *UI tree*), corresponds to the tag hierarchy you would see in an HTML file (plus any other files or components included on the page at runtime). For example, the following illustration shows the JDeveloper Structure window view of the JSF home page you will create in a hands-on practice in Chapter 10:

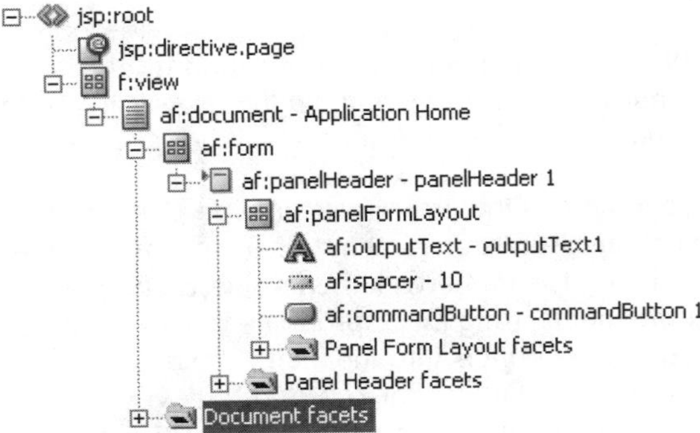

Two types of page requests affect JSF processing: the *initial request,* where the user requests the page for the first time; and a *postback,* where the user submits a page that was previously loaded into the browser. For a postback, the component tree is already created in the `FacesContext` object. It is stored there when the page is first rendered (in step 6). For an initial request, the component tree has not been created in the `FacesContext`, so processing passes from this step directly to step 6 to render the content.

NOTE
The root component in a JSF file is `f:view`. All other JSF tags will appear within this tag. A JSP file may have element tags outside the `f:view` tag (such as taglib directives), but these are used to assist in processing the JSP file.

2. Apply Request Values In this step, the `Lifecycle` instance populates the components in the component tree with data from the request parameters. These values are held in a buffer area and the process does not validate the assigned datatypes yet. Events that apply to this step are also processed.

3. Process Validations This step applies *conversions* (defined in *converter* components) that translate the plain-string value loaded into the buffer for each component in the preceding step to the datatype assigned to that component.

You can define *validation* (using validator components)—for a component to check the value assigned to it. For example, you can define a minimum and maximum value validator. This step applies these validations.

Validations and conversions are bypassed for a particular component if that component is assigned an *immediate* property value of "true." You would set this value for a component that you would not want to validate, such as a button.

If any validation or conversion fails, the error messages are queued and the process jumps to step 6 for rendering the response. In addition, event code written for this step is executed. Errors or messages from these events are also sent to the message queue.

4. Update Model Values Just as step 2 sets values for the components in the component tree from the request, this step sets the values for the corresponding components in the Model layer code. As before, if errors occur in validations or conversions, the messages are queued and the process jumps to step 6 for rendering the response. As with all phases, appropriate events are also processed or queued.

5. Invoke Application This step performs application-level tasks, such as page navigation, as appropriate to the request. Events are handled if the page being restored contains components that fired events. Therefore, this step runs any event code you have written.

6. Render Response If this is the first request to a page, control is passed from step 1. The `FacesServlet` object builds the component tree as specified in the JSF file and stores the tree in the `FacesContext` object. The framework then requests components in the tree to be rendered; this results in the components using the appropriate render kit to output markup text (such as HTML), which the JSF servlet buffers into the final page definition.

Messages that were queued from previous steps are written to the output as well. In addition, the state of the page (for example, the component data values) is stored so that subsequent requests can use it for the restore view step. This step ends with the Faces Servlet sending an HTTP response to the browser containing the buffered page output.

Working with the JSF Life Cycle During most JSF development work that you perform, the life cycle is transparent. However, knowing a bit about the life cycle steps should give you an idea about the richness of the environment. It can also assist when debugging or when you need to write specialized code to alter the normal runtime behavior. You can control the JSF runtime process with custom code. You can also customize the life cycle using additional ADF life cycle steps as explained in the section "How Can I Override and Add to the ADF Model Life Cycle?" in Chapter 15. JDeveloper provides the *ADF Declarative Debugger,* which can display details about the ADF life cycle runtime.

JSF-Oriented Files

When you set up a project for JSF work in JDeveloper by including the JSF technology scope in the project (or using a JSF application template), the web deployment descriptor file (web.xml) is automatically modified so that it contains a definition that the Faces Servlet will load when the application starts as shown here:

```
<servlet>
    <servlet-name>Faces Servlet</servlet-name>
    <servlet-class>javax.faces.webapp.FacesServlet</servlet-class>
    <load-on-startup>1</load-on-startup>
</servlet>
```

Additional code in web.xml sets up a pointer for requests that contain a designated virtual directory (such as "/faces/") as in the following code:

```
<servlet-mapping>
    <servlet-name>Faces Servlet</servlet-name>
    <url-pattern>/faces/*</url-pattern>
</servlet-mapping>
```

NOTE
For an ADF application, web.xml will contain references to additional servlets and filters.

You will interact with the following types of files when developing a JSF application: managed beans, faces-config.xml, and the JSF JSP file.

Managed Beans

As mentioned in the section "Runtime Architecture" previously, a managed bean may be associated with the JSF JSP page file. For example, a login.jsp page file would use a managed bean class file typically named "Login.java." The Java file contains the code needed to process events that are outside of the declarative framework. (You will write managed bean code to handle button-click events in Chapter 10.)

In addition, the managed bean class can contain accessors (getters and setters) for the objects on the page (for example, text fields), so you can manipulate the values of these objects programmatically. These accessors manipulate a private object for each component in the JSF file. This object and its accessors can be used to change the characteristics of the object as well as its behavior.

For example, if your JSF file contains a text input field, lastName, the managed bean class would contain a lastName `HtmlTextInput` variable as well as a `getLastName()` method to retrieve the value of the variable, and a `setLastName()` method to change the value of the variable. The following example shows how to use the `getLastName()` method to assign the object's properties.

```
getLastName().setRendered(false);
```

In this code, the getter, `getLastName()`, provides access to the component and `setRendered()` changes the *rendered* property value.

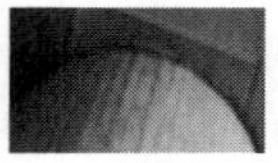

NOTE
Working with a managed bean is necessary only if you need to change the default behavior or provide special processing for the page. You do not need to create one otherwise.

Events and Action Listeners One of the strengths of the JSF framework is its rich model for event handling. Events occur due to some user interaction, such as a button click or list selection. You can write *action listener* methods in the managed bean to handle these events. For example, an OK button called "okButton" in a JSF page could have a corresponding action listener method called `okButton_action()` written in the managed bean. When the user clicks the OK button, the code in this method would be run. JSF action listener methods are, by convention, named with a prefix of the component they work for. A single action method can be reused to provide the event handler for many components.

The action listener name is associated with the component using a property, such as *Action* for a button component. Alternatively, you can code a separate listener class (that implements the `ActionListener` interface). You then associate that class with the component using a different property, such as *ActionListener* for a button component.

NOTE
If JSF components render as HTML controls in a web browser, you can set event properties, such as onClick, on JSF components to run JavaScript code you have written. With ADF Faces, use an `af:clientListener` component under an ADF Faces component to define the JavaScript event.

faces-config.xml

This XML file, called the *application configuration resource file,* contains definitions that specify the following:

- **Navigation rules** for defining flow from one page to another
- **Managed bean definitions** for making JavaBean code accessible in the application
- **Render kits** that are used to display the page in a certain encoding, such as HTML or WML
- **Converters**, mentioned before, which change the type of data from the plain-vanilla string supplied by the HTTP request parameter value to a specific datatype for a component value
- **Validators**, also mentioned earlier, which check the value of the data (for example, the range of the value or its length)

Although this file is coded in XML, JDeveloper offers a visual representation of the navigation rules in the JSF Navigation Diagram. You can code other entries in this file using the code editor (the Source tab) or a property editor available from the Overview tab. The practice in Chapter 10 demonstrates both methods.

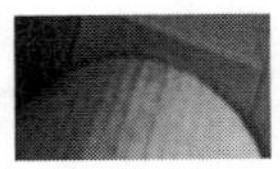

NOTE
The section "Creating a Task Flow Definition" in Chapter 11 discusses another configuration file, adfc-config.xml, used for controlling task flows in ADF applications.

A Note about Struts The open-source, highly evolved Struts framework has become popular for the Controller layer of a JSP or servlet application. Struts is not supported by the Java EE standards, but due to its widespread use, Struts was a very popular technology choice before JSF technology was released. The JSF controller serves the same purpose for JSF applications as Struts served for JSP applications. Therefore, you do not need to use Struts when creating a JSF application. However, JDeveloper supports working with Struts and provides a visual tool, the *Struts Page Flow Modeler,* which you can use to interact with Struts components defined in the struts-config.xml file.

JSF JSP file

The JSF JSP file (also just called the "JSF file") contains all user interface components arranged in the same kind of hierarchy as with any HTML or JSP file. When developing a JSF application, you write View layer code in the JSF JSP file, and you write Model and Controller code in the managed bean and faces-config.xml file. When working with the JSF JSP file in JDeveloper, you can use declarative and visual tools, such as the JSP/HTML Visual Editor, Property Inspector, and Structure window. You can also use the XML Code Editor to write or modify code outside of the declarative tools. You can create and run JSF JSP files in two different forms: a JSP page and a JSP document.

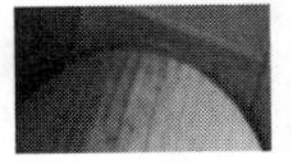

NOTE
As mentioned in Chapter 3, the Structure window sometimes allows you to position components more precisely than is possible in the JSP/HTML Visual Editor. You can also drag and drop components from any node to any applicable node. You can add components by dragging them from the Component Palette or from the right-click menu on the structure node.

JSP Page and JSP Document The *JSP page* is a file with a .jsp extension that contains both HTML tags and JSP-oriented tags. It is the traditional style used for JSP files. The benefit of this file type is that it allows you to use HTML tags, which you can display and design in an HTML editor such as Dreamweaver. JDeveloper also provides HTML editing and viewing capabilities, including a formatting toolbar that helps you enter HTML tags in a visual way.

The *JSP document* is a file with a .jspx extension that contains only well-formed XML code (mentioned in Chapter 4). In this case, *well-formed code* means that all start tags have corresponding end tags and all tag elements are named with lowercase names.

Although some browsers can interpret HTML tags without closing tags, XML parsers are stricter than browsers about requiring well-formed code. JDeveloper provides a way to view JSP document code in a visual way and to edit it using the Property Inspector and some drag-and-drop functions.

Should I Use a .jsp or a .jspx File? You can use either JSP pages or JSP documents for creating JSP code that contains JSF tags. However, since JSF architecture supports multiple display device types, you can choose to use a tag library such as ADF Faces that does not require any HTML. Therefore, the separation of HTML and JSP tags that a JSP page offers is not important. Page design consists more of selecting which tags to use and of setting their properties. Those tags will draw major areas of the page without the requirement for HTML design.

Using a format that is independent of the display device technology can make your application more flexible. Whether your application will support multiple display devices is still not a firm decision point for using either JSP pages or JSP documents because you can code both JSP pages and JSP documents without HTML. However, it is more difficult to write HTML within a JSP document, and selecting the JSP document as a standard may help enforce writing portable code. It is a natural choice for files you will be editing only in JDeveloper, because JDeveloper is built to help you lay out and maintain JSF tags and ADF Faces in a visual way. Other HTML editing tools support layout with JSP pages better, and if you will need to design the page using a tool other than JDeveloper, a JSP page might be a better choice.

Why Does This Book Use JSP Documents? As you may have gathered from the preceding discussion, the choice of whether to use JSP pages or JSP documents for JSF work is almost arbitrary. However, developing an application in a way that is less dependent upon a display device can have strategic advantages. For example, if another display device ever becomes more popular than the web browser, an application written using a portable language (such as ADF Faces inside a JSP document) will have a better chance of running on that new device without being rewritten.

Another strong advantage of developing JSP documents in JDeveloper is code validation. The IDE applies rules for validating syntax, and it shows some syntax errors immediately after navigating off the line of code. The stricter rules for validating XML tags will ensure that your file contains only well-formed code. In addition, and most important, some features of ADF Faces work only when using the XML style enforced by JSP documents. This book uses JSP documents in its examples because of their portability and better support for writing better code.

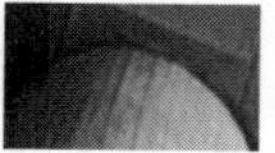

NOTE
Fusion applications are written using JSP documents.

Components

JSF components for JSP work are contained in two reference implementation (RI) libraries:

- **JSF Core** This tag library contains components, such as validators and converters, that are used in conjunction with other components. Components in this library use the "f" prefix, for example, `f:loadbundle`.
- **JSF HTML** This tag library contains HTML user interface components, such as text input, buttons, labels, and radio options. You refer to these components using the "h" prefix, for example, `h:datatable`, `h:column`, and `h:form`.

NOTE
As mentioned, the JSF standard supports multiple output device styles through the use of render kits, but the initial RI only offers an HTML render kit for JSP files. ADF Faces RC also provides render kits for HTML clients. Its underlying technology, ADF Faces 10g (technically called "Apache MyFaces Trinidad"), offers render kits for TELNET and wireless clients as well.

Facets

Some components may be placed inside of other components as a child object in the component hierarchy, for example, an `af:column` inside an `af:table`. In addition to nesting related components, you can nest components using the *facet,* a named subcomponent. It is up to the component to determine where to render the contents of a particular facet. For example, the ADF Faces `af:panelBorderLayout` component supports top, bottom, start, and end facets. Items in these facets will appear in specific positions within the page, as shown in Figure 9-2.

NOTE
A facet can only contain one component, but that one component can be a layout container (such as `af:panelForm`), which can contain more than one component.

The visual editor for JSPs provides special support for facets in a component by displaying *facet drop zones* into which you can place components. These drop zones are shown as gray dotted boxes in Figure 9-2. They reflect the relative layout of the components at runtime.

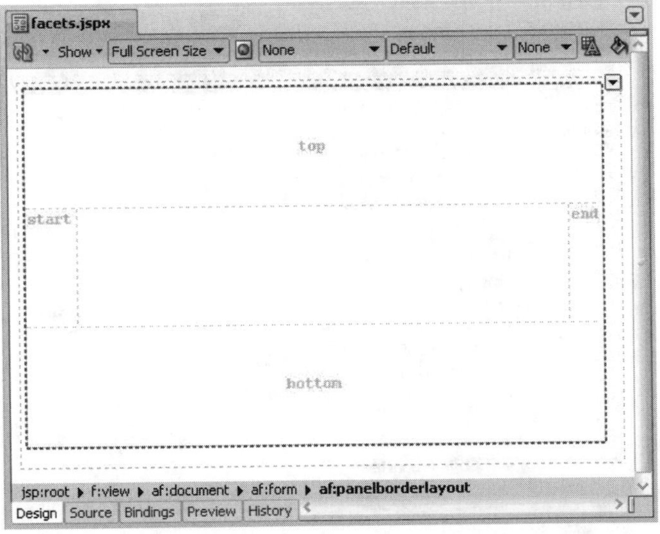

FIGURE 9-2. *af:panelBorderLayout with its facets*

NOTE
You do not need to use all facets for a component.

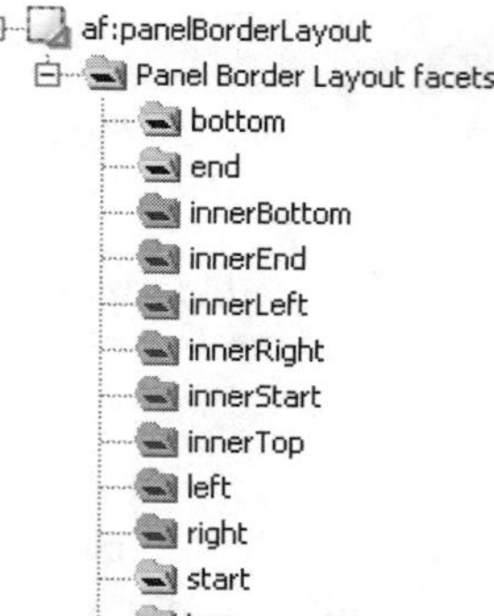

Facets are important in controlling and adapting standardized layouts (skins) within JSF applications, because they provide a type of named API for component children that can be changed without having to recode the page.

The bottom, end, start, and top facets for `af:panelBorderLayout` display drop zones by default, but you can drop components into the Structure window for other facets (or for the default facets), as shown here.

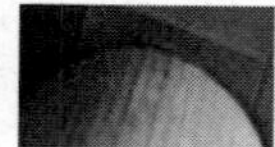

TIP
To quickly navigate to a component and expand the Structure window hierarchy to a particular component, select that component in a visual editor.

You can control the facets displayed in the visual editor by checking the relevant facet names in the right-click submenu selection, **Facets – <component>**, on the component in the Structure window, as shown in Figure 9-3.

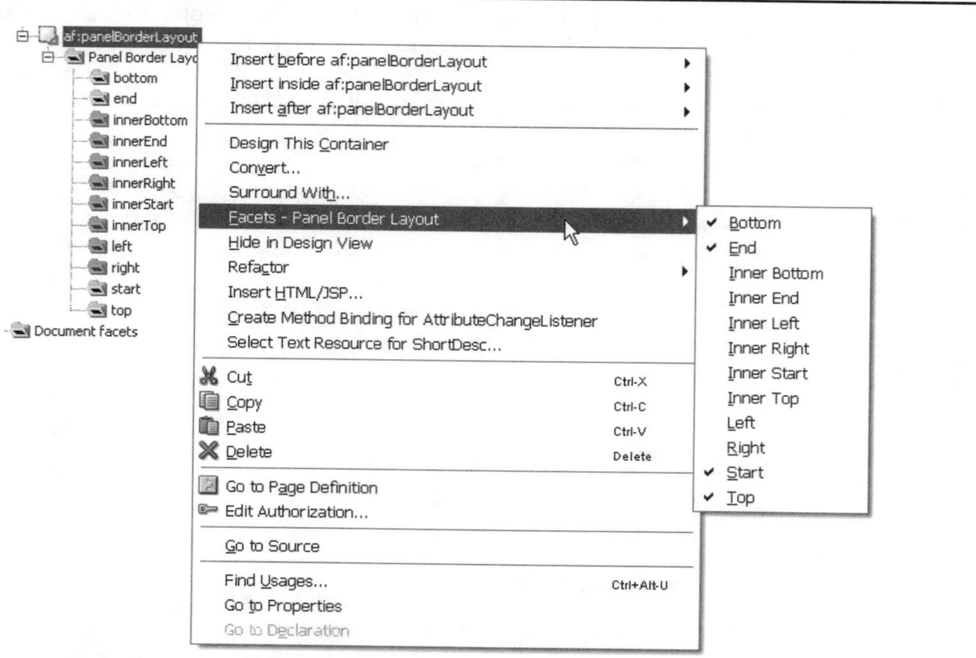

FIGURE 9-3. *Displaying or hiding facets in the Structure window*

ADF Faces Rich Client

As mentioned in Chapter 1, the ADF Faces Rich Client (referred to throughout the book as "ADF Faces") is a set of component tags contained in class libraries and tag libraries. ADF Faces 10*g* (in JDeveloper 10.1.3) evolved to allow access in JSF code to the enhanced component set offered previously as ADF UIX.

NOTE
Chapter 12 explains a bit more of the history and more about the main characteristics and features of ADF Faces.

The examples in the applications developed in Part V of this book focus on use of ADF Faces components. ADF Faces is designed to be displayed on different devices.

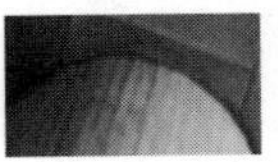

NOTE
ADF Faces RC require a Java EE container that is capable of running JSF 1.2 code such as Oracle WebLogic Server 10.3 or later. Oracle Application Server's OC4J 10.1.3 is not capable of running JSF 1.2 code. ADF Faces Rich Client also requires a client browser of Internet Explorer 7.0 or later, Mozilla Firefox 2.0 or later, or Safari, version 3.0.

HTML and ADF Faces When working with ADF Faces, you do not code HTML tags directly. Instead, you use ADF Faces components that will be rendered in a web browser using HTML tags. For example, ADF Faces offers a component, `af:inputText`, which renders an HTML form input item (a text field) when displayed in a web browser.

ADF Faces Layout Container As mentioned before, layout containers hold other components. The process of creating a file with ADF Faces consists of adding layout containers tags, and then inserting components within the containers. ADF Faces offers layout containers, such as `af:panelBorderLayout`, that contain a number of predefined areas, as shown in Figure 9-2. These predefined areas use JSF facets to provide default positions for objects on the page. After dragging this component onto the page, you can drag other components to each of the facet areas you need to use.

ADF Faces layout containers provide automatic layout capabilities that reposition or stretch child components when the container is resized.

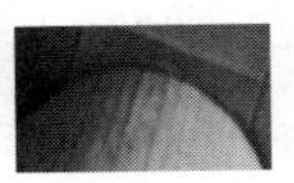

NOTE
Mastering the layout containers is a key skill needed to achieve the perfect UI layout. Chapter 12 discusses more about layout containers, and you use them to build a sample application in Part V of this book.

Tag Libraries

Just as JSF offers Core and HTML tag libraries, ADF Faces offers Core tag libraries (prefixed with "af"). It also offers *Data Visualization Tools (DVT)* tags for graphs and charts. This tag library is represented with a dvt prefix. Some of the ADF Faces components are parallel to JSF components.

For example, the JSF RI component `h:inputText` has an ADF Faces equivalent, `af:inputText`, used to present a text entry field. You can distinguish between these components in code, because of their prefixes ("h" for JSF RI and "af" for ADF Faces). Also, the ADF Faces tags offer many more properties than the RI tags.

These prefixes for components that you use on the page are defined in a `jsp:root` tag in the beginning of the JSF JSP file as follows:

```
<jsp:root
    xmlns:jsp="http://java.sun.com/JSP/Page" version="2.1"
    xmlns:af=http://xmlns.oracle.com/adf/faces/rich
    xmlns:f="http://java.sun.com/jsf/core"
    xmlns:dvt="http://xmlns.oracle.com/dss/adf/faces">
```

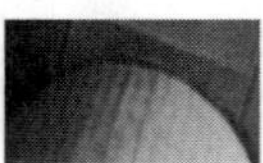

NOTE
JDeveloper automatically adds the appropriate `jsp:root` *prefix definitions the first time you drag a component from that library onto the page. Technically, you can change the prefix in this definition, but it is best to stick with the default prefixes that JDeveloper assigns.*

ADF Faces Properties

In general, ADF Faces components offer more properties and built-in functionality than the JSF RI components. For example, the ADF Faces `af:inputText` component includes a *label* property (for a prompt) that is not included with the comparable JSF RI component. Also, unlike the JSF RI component, the ADF Faces component validates items marked as required using JavaScript, which does not require a communications trip to the server.

Figure 9-4 shows the Property Inspector view (split into three columns) of the `af:inputText` component properties so that you can see the large range of properties available for a typical ADF Faces component.

Messages

As the application runtime proceeds, messages are written to the `FacesContext` object. They are placed into a queue until the last step of the life cycle renders a response. You can programmatically add messages to a component (`af:messages`) using managed bean code.

JSF messages support the idea of specific text for specific locales and languages. To implement this feature, you abstract the messages out of the JSF JSP file into *message bundle* files (also called *resource files*) that hold all text for the application (one message bundle for each location or language). The JSF controller matches the correct language file and uses it to supply messages for the application. Chapter 10 contains more information and hands-on practices for creating and using message bundles.

Designing Cross-Platform Interfaces

ADF Faces and JSF support the concept of displaying the user interface on different types of client devices. The render kit used to display the application is specific to each device's needs, but the same JSF code can display a user interface in a web browser or cell phone or other wireless device. If the application needs to support multiple client platforms, you would work this requirement in from the starting point. You would need to set a standard that code in the

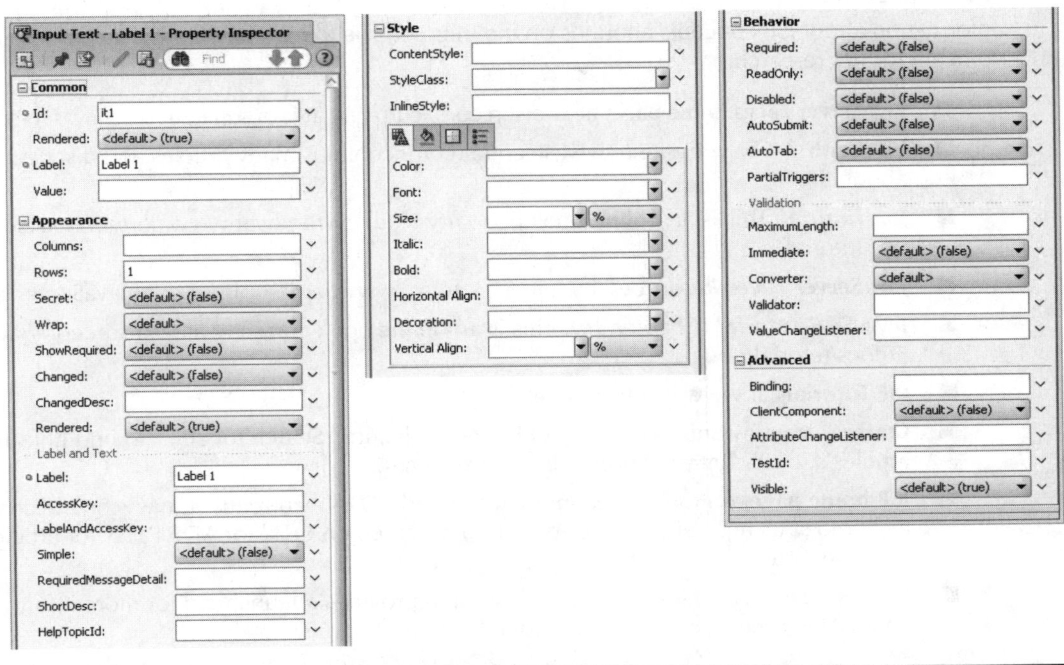

FIGURE 9-4. *Property list for the af:inputText ADF Faces component*

application avoids the use of HTML tags. In addition, you would create a standard to avoid use of JavaScript and CSS, both of which are add-ins to HTML browser code that may not work on other display devices.

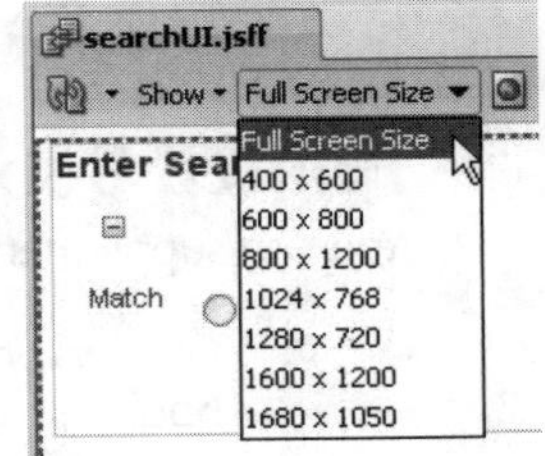

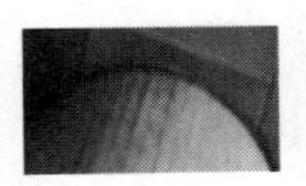

TIP

The JDeveloper visual editor offers a screen size pulldown (shown on the right) that you can use to see how the layout you have designed will appear in different screen resolutions.

Where Can I Find Additional Information about JSF?

This chapter describes most of the JSF basics you will need to know to start working with JSF technology. Although the hands-on practices in Part V will provide knowledge based on practical experience, you will likely need other resources for learning about JSF. The authors have found the following resources useful.

Websites

Information about JSF concepts abounds on the Internet. The following websites are good places to begin further research:

- **JavaServer Faces home page**, at java.sun.com, currently at java.sun.com/j2ee/javaserverfaces.
- **JSF Central**. This website (www.jsfcentral.com) contains many articles and discussions about JSF.
- ***JSF Tutorial***. This is an online book by Marty Hall, currently at www.coreservlets.com/JSF-Tutorial.
- ***JavaServer Faces Resources***, by James Holmes, www.jamesholmes.com/JavaServerFaces.
- ***Java EE 5 Tutorial (Chapter 10)***. This is an online book currently at java.sun.com/javaee/5/docs/tutorial/doc/.
- **JSF Tutorials** at www.jsftutorials.net.
- **OnJava**, at www.onjava.com, by O'Reilly Media, Inc. Search for "JSF" to find links for articles such as "Introduction to JavaServer Faces."
- **JSF home page**, on Oracle Technology Network (OTN), currently at www.oracle.com/technology/tech/java/jsf.html; also perform a search on OTN for ADF Faces for articles about that subject.
- **Rich Enterprise Applications**, showcases and provides a launchpad for more information about ADF Faces components (rea.oracle.com).

CAUTION
The website addresses presented are current as this chapter is being written. If your requests to these addresses fail, use a web search engine to look for their new locations.

Printed Books

You can supplement information about JSF from the Web using printed books, such as the following:

- *JavaServer Faces in Action,* by Kito D. Mann (Manning Publications, 2004). This is a good book for overall JSF learning and reference.
- *Core JavaServer Faces,* by David Geary and Cay Horstmann (Sun Microsystems Java Press, Prentice Hall PTR, 2004). Some chapters of this book are also available online at www.horstmann.com/corejsf/.
- *JSF: The Complete Reference,* by Chris Schalk and Ed Burns (McGraw-Hill/Professional, 2006). This book is an in-depth look at JSF technology.
- *JavaServer Faces Programming,* by Budi Kurniawan (McGraw-Hill/Professional, 2004). This is a good book about basic JSF concepts.
- *Pro JSF and Ajax: Building Rich Internet Components,* by Jonas Jacobi and John Fallows (APress, 2006). This is an advanced book, which is useful for those who need to know how to create their own JSF components that use Asynchronous JavaScript and XML (AJAX) technology for a highly interactive user interface.

CHAPTER 10

Your First JSF

By nature, men are nearly alike;
by practice, they get to be wide apart.

—Confucius (551–479 B.C.), *The Confucian Analects*

An ounce of practice is worth more than tons of preaching.

—Mahatma Gandhi (1869–1948)

The guiding principle for practices in this book is that you will absorb detailed concepts better if you use them right away in code that builds an application. Although we do not present all possible techniques you will ever need when creating a real-world application, the hands-on practices should make you think about how to perform basic web development tasks in JDeveloper 11*g*. The hands-on practices also point you toward external resources that can be useful when you are stuck on a specific programming problem.

This chapter provides three hands-on practices that build on the introductions to JavaServer Faces technology in Chapter 9. The first hands-on practice uses largely manual techniques for building a simple, two-page, non-data-aware JSF application. We stop at many points along the way to discuss what is going on in the background so that you can obtain a more detailed understanding of the files that are being created and manipulated when you use JDeveloper's declarative and visual operations. We feel that with this type of detailed introduction, you will be better able to understand and debug applications you create.

Please keep in mind throughout this practice that in normal JDeveloper work, you will not need to modify or even examine some of the files we show you during this practice. In Part V of this book, you will develop a sample application using a more standard development flow that concentrates on visual and declarative programming techniques.

The discussion about centralizing messages and the last two hands-on practices in this chapter explain message bundle files work and how to access them within the application.

TIP
The section "Ensuring Success with the Hands-on Practices" in the Introduction to this book provides some advice about how to handle errors and solve problems that may occur during this work.

Hands-on Practice: Create a JSF Login and JSF Home Page

A standard exercise when learning any new programming language is the "Hello World" application that demonstrates a user interface that receives input from the user, processes the input, and displays a message. This chapter's hands-on practice takes a similar, but more expanded approach and shows how you can create a pair of simple JSF pages that emulate login and home page screens.

To allow the example to focus on JSF concepts with less distraction, this application does not connect to a database or pay much attention to real-world security needs. You will build this application to implement the following features:

- **A login page** with user name and password fields marked as required.
- **Validation** of the user name and password fields. Both are required, and can be from one to 20 characters long. However, the only valid password is "JSF." This password is hard-coded in the application, although it would normally be authenticated using security services of the application server as discussed in Chapter 21. Error messages are displayed for invalid or missing entries.
- **Additional logic** on the login page to display the password after three unsuccessful attempts. Of course, real-world applications would not show the password but would instead take some action such as logging the repeated attempts or locking the user account.
- **A Login button** that submits the form to the server, which will validate the data and pass control to the Home page if validation succeeds.
- **A Home page** that displays the user name and a welcome message.
- **A Logout button** on the home page that returns to the login.

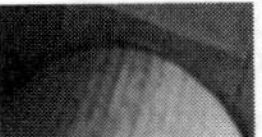

NOTE
*As we've mentioned several times before, be sure you are running a supported web browser (Internet Explorer 7.0 or later, Mozilla Firefox 2.0 or later, or Safari, version 3.0). If you want to set up a browser for JDeveloper work that is different from your default browser, open the Preferences dialog (**Tools | Preferences**) and navigate to the Web Browser and Proxy page. Set the path and name of the browser in the* Browser Command Line *property and click OK.*

Developing these pages consists of the following phases:

I. Create the application and a project

II. Diagram the page flow

III. Create the login and home pages

- Create the JSF pages

IV. Add components to the login page

- Add the layout containers
- Add the visual components
- Test the page

V. Add components to the home page

- Remove Automatic Backing Bean updates
- Add JSF components
- Set the `af:outputText` value as an expression
- Set component properties and test the page

VI. Add navigation and validation logic to the application

- Add the navigation and validation code
- Test the validation and navigation logic

As with all practices in this book, sample code and code snippets for long code examples are available on the websites mentioned in the section "Websites for Sample Files" of the Introduction.

NOTE
Although this section does not use database data, it assumes that you have read the installation notes and installed JDeveloper as mentioned in the Introduction section "Preparing for the Hands-on Practices."

I. Create the Application and a Project

In this phase of the practice, you create the JDeveloper code containers—an application and projects.

1. Open JDeveloper as described in the Introduction to this book.

   Additional Information: In Windows, look in the Programs menu for **Oracle Fusion Middleware 11.1.1.1.0 | JDeveloper Studio 11.1.1.1.0** or a shortcut on your desktop.

2. In the Application Navigator, click New Application (if the selection appears) or select **New Application** from the application name pulldown. The Create Generic Application dialog will appear, as shown here:

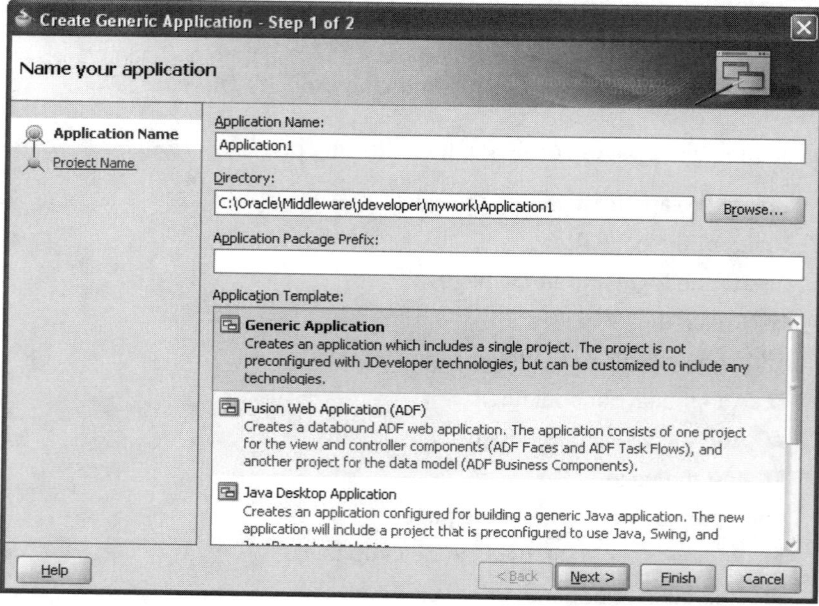

NOTE
As mentioned, throughout the book we comply with American typesetting standards, which place a sentence- or clause-ending punctuation mark inside the quotes. Do not type this punctuation mark into the value unless instructed to do so.

3. Fill in *Application Name* as "LoginJSF," and *Directory* as "<HANDBOOK_HOME>\LoginJSF" where "<HANDBOOK_HOME>" is a directory where you want to store your applications, for example, "C:\JDev11gHandbook\LoginJSF." Change the *Application Package Prefix* to "login" and select "Generic Application" in the *Application Template* pane if it is not already selected.

   Additional Information: The "Generic Application" option creates a project that is not assigned any specific *technology* (also called "*technology scope*")—a selection of libraries oriented to a specific type of development, such as ADF BC or JSF. Some technology scope selections create specific project names in specific directories. However, if you select "Generic Application," JDeveloper will prompt you for a project name and directory. You will add technologies in another step so that you can see how the process works. This selection is useful for demonstration purposes, such as this simple application, but for production applications, you would select a template (such as "Fusion Web Application (ADF)") that contains projects with specific technologies, such as ADF Business Components.

4. Click Next. On the project page, enter the project name as "ViewController." The directory name will be rewritten to include the new project name (for example, "C:\JDev11gHandbook\LoginJSF\ViewController"). Leave this directory name.

5. You will be using the ADF Faces components to build this JSF application so in the Project Technologies region, select ADF Faces and click ">" to move it to the *Selected* area.

   Additional Information: Notice that technologies for Java, JSF, and JSP and Servlets were automatically added when you added the ADF Faces technology because ADF Faces work requires those technologies as well. You can add technologies to a project later using the Project Properties dialog (a right-click menu option on the project node). However, adding technologies now will filter the selections available in the New Gallery. You can always view all choices, regardless of the selected technologies, by clicking the All Technologies tab of the New Gallery.

6. Click Finish. The application and project will appear in the navigator. Notice that several standard configuration files required for JSF projects will appear under the ViewController project as shown here.

   Additional Information: The WEB-INF node contains *faces-config .xml* (the *application configuration resource,* also called *application configuration file*), and *web.xml* (the web module deployment descriptor introduced in Chapter 4). The Page Flows node displays the same faces-config.xml file.

   ViewController
   Web Content
   WEB-INF
   faces-config.xml
   web.xml
   Page Flows
   faces-config.xml

NOTE
The faces-config.xml file appears under two nodes in the Application Navigator because it is applicable to both categories (WEB-INF and Page Flows). It is the same file.

What Did You Just Do? You just created the JDeveloper application that organizes the projects you are working on. You also created a project that is used to store the application files. For this example, you just needed a single project, so you used the "Generic Application" template when creating the application. You then created a project and configured it for the ADF Faces technology. To verify the technology selections, double click the ViewController project node to display the

Project Properties dialog. Select the Technology Scope node and notice that the Project Technologies tab contains ADF Faces, Java, JSF, and Java and Servlets in the *Selected* region. Click Cancel to close the dialog.

NOTE
Double clicking the project node is a shortcut for selecting ***Project Properties*** *from the right-click menu on the project node.*

It is worthwhile at this point to look at the files that have been created: web.xml and faces-config.xml.

faces-config.xml

Adding the JSF technology to the selected technologies created the application configuration resource, faces-config.xml. Open faces-config.xml (under the WEB-INF node) by double clicking its name in the navigator. Click the Source tab of the editor. Other than the XML definition tags at the beginning of the file, this file contains an empty root node, faces-config, as shown here (the line numbers do not appear by default in the Code Editor):

```
01: <?xml version="1.0" encoding="windows-1252"?>
02: <faces-config version="1.2" xmlns="http://java.sun.com/xml/ns/javaee">
03:
04: </faces-config>
```

- **Line 01** defines this file as an XML file.
- **Line 02** references the XML namespace (the xmlns attribute) that supplies the tag set available to the document. Although the value of the *xmlns* attribute appears to be a web address, the XML schema (tag definition) is actually located in a Java library file in the local file system—the web-facesconfig_1_2.xsd file in the jsf-ri.jar file. You can find this JAR file under JDEV_HOME\ modules\oracle.jsf_1.2.7.1.
- **Line 04** closes the root *element* (XML tag) for the file, faces-config. All other elements will be contained inside this root element.

NOTE
You can turn line numbers on or off in the Code Editor by selecting ***Toggle Line Numbers*** *from the right-click menu in the* line gutter *(left-hand margin).*

web.xml

JDeveloper generates the web.xml file automatically when you create a web project or associate the project with the web technology scope (such as JSF or ADF Faces). Open this file and view its Source tab. The entire web.xml file that is created by default is shown next.

```
<?xml version = '1.0' encoding = 'windows-1252'?>
<web-app xmlns:xsi="http://www.w3.org/2001/XMLSchema-instance"
     xsi:schemaLocation="http://java.sun.com/xml/ns/j2ee
     http://java.sun.com/xml/ns/j2ee/web-app_2_5.xsd" version="2.5"
     xmlns="http://java.sun.com/xml/ns/j2ee">
  <servlet>
```

```
04:     <servlet-name>Faces Servlet</servlet-name>
05:     <servlet-class>javax.faces.webapp.FacesServlet</servlet-class>
06:     <load-on-startup>1</load-on-startup>
07:   </servlet>
08:   <servlet-mapping>
09:     <servlet-name>Faces Servlet</servlet-name>
10:     <url-pattern>/faces/*</url-pattern>
11:   </servlet-mapping>
12: </web-app>
```

This code defines the following elements:

- **Lines 01 and 02** define this file as XML and start the root element (web-app) that encloses the other elements in this file.
- **Lines 03–07** associate a name, "Faces Servlet," with the `FacesServlet` class file. This file is provided by the JSF libraries and is used to process JSF files.
- **Lines 08–11** direct the web server to send requests containing the /faces/ virtual directory to the Faces servlet for processing.
- **Line 12** closes the file.

Normally, you do not need to modify this file, but if you need to add or change elements in this file, you use the XML Editor that is now open in the Source tab. You can alternatively interact with this file using the Overview tab, which displays the Web Application Deployment Descriptor Editor, shown here.

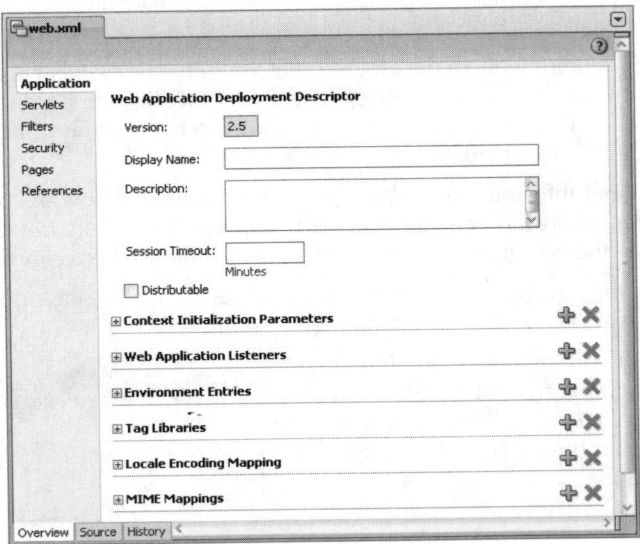

This editor organizes the XML elements into property fields that you can modify. You can expand or collapse the headings to view all elements as shown for the MIME Mappings region. Links on the left allow you to navigate to different categories of elements. Changes you make in this editor are written into the web.xml source code, and changes you make in the Source tab are reflected in this editor.

II. Diagram the Page Flow

Since this application will contain only two pages, you will define a very simple page flow. This phase will demonstrate how to design the page flow in the JSF Navigation Diagram before adding any code for the pages. The application you develop in Part V of this book will demonstrate a slightly more complex navigation using task flows, but for this example, you only need navigation from the login page to the home page, and from the home page back to the login page.

1. Open the faces-config.xml file, if it is not already open (double click faces-config.xml under WEB-INF in the Application Navigator). Click the Diagram tab to display the empty diagram page.

2. Drag a JSF Page component from the Components panel of the Component Palette to the diagram. (If the Component Palette is not visible, select it from the View menu.) After you drop the JSF Page component onto the page, the name will become editable. Change the name to "login" and press ENTER. JDeveloper will add a "/" prefix, so the page icon will appear as shown here.

   Additional Information: The icon contains a page symbol drawn partially with a dotted line to indicate that no file has been associated with this diagram element.

3. Click the Source tab to examine the code in faces-config.xml. Notice that nothing has been added since you looked before, because no file has been linked to the diagrammed page element. Up to this point, you have only interacted with the diagram in design mode. Click the Diagram tab again.

4. Drop another JSF Page from the Component Palette to the right of the login symbol. Enter the name as "home" and press ENTER. As before, JDeveloper will add a "/" prefix to the file name.

5. In the Diagram view of the faces-config.xml file, click JSF Navigation Case in the Component Palette, click the login symbol, and click the home symbol to draw the navigation case line. Click the navigation case name if it is not editable, and change it to "gohome." Press ENTER to complete the edit mode.

   Additional Information: *Navigation cases* define the flow of control from one page to another. Navigation cases are named "success" by default, but it is a best practice to rename them so that you can more easily distinguish between them within your code.

6. Under the navigation case line, draw another navigation case from home to login in the same way. Name the navigation case "logout."

7. Click the orthogonal button (the third button to the right of the Show pulldown) in the diagram toolbar and rearrange the objects to roughly match the adjacent illustration.

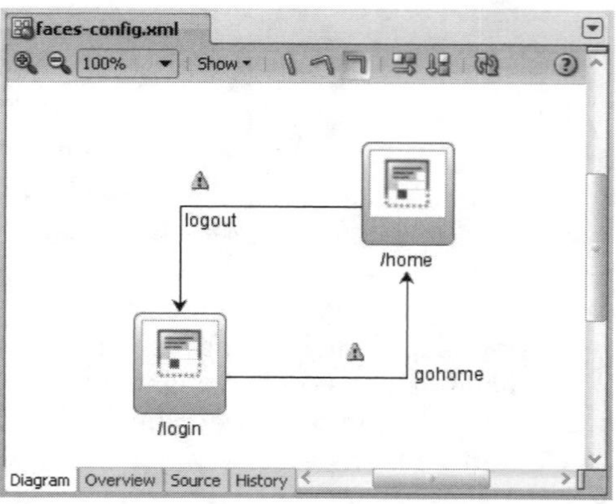

Additional Information: JDeveloper draws connecting lines in an orderly way using three line styles: *direct* (straight lines without angled bends or "doglegs"), *polyline* (angled bends that you define), and *orthogonal* (right-angle bends). Clicking the relevant button in the diagram toolbar (to the right of the Show pulldown displayed in the preceding illustration) sets the line style for that diagram.

TIP
After setting the line style, change the position of a page symbol so that you can see how JDeveloper redraws the lines using that line style.

8. Notice that the navigation cases are also displayed in the Structure window. The Structure window contains a hierarchical view of the diagrammed elements.

   Additional Information: Small diagrams like this do not need navigation assistance. For larger diagrams, you can use the Thumbnail window (**View | Thumbnail** if the window is not already visible) to display part of the diagram in the editor window. You can also use the zoom buttons or pulldown in the diagram toolbar to change the size of the diagram view.

NOTE
A yellow triangle information icon attached to the navigation case indicates that the page at the (arrow) end of the navigation has not yet been created.

9. Click Save All.

What Did You Just Do? You used the JSF Navigation Diagram to depict the two pages and the flows between them. This example application starts with page design. Alternatively, you could start by coding the page (.jspx) files and then work out the navigation diagram afterwards. The finished application will include a page design diagram, where each page symbol has an associated page file. It doesn't matter whether you create the page file code or diagram the pages first. In fact, since design and development are often performed iteratively, you will probably find yourself working in both ways to complete an application.

Some code was added to faces-config.xml, so in the interest of understanding a bit about this file, it is worthwhile taking a quick look at it.

Application Configuration Resource (faces-config.xml)

Click the Source tab of the faces-config.xml file. You will see the following listing inside the tags shown earlier (again, without the line numbers):

```
<navigation-rule>
  <from-view-id>/login</from-view-id>
  <navigation-case>
    <from-outcome>gohome</from-outcome>
    <to-view-id>/home</to-view-id>
  </navigation-case>
</navigation-rule>
<navigation-rule>
  <from-view-id>/home</from-view-id>
```

```
12:    <navigation-case>
13:      <from-outcome>logout</from-outcome>
14:      <to-view-id>/login</to-view-id>
15:    </navigation-case>
16: </navigation-rule>
```

The first navigation-rule element (lines 03–09) specifies that navigation flows from /login to /home if the outcome is "gohome" (the name you assigned to the navigation case in the diagram). You can define when you want the navigation to occur by setting the outcome string in backing bean code or in the *action* property of a command button or link.

The second navigation-rule element (lines 10–16) specifies flow from /home to /login if the backing bean or the action property indicates an outcome of "logout." The from-view-id and to-view-id elements identify the start and end of the navigation in both navigation-rule sections.

III. Create the Login and Home Pages

You are now ready to create the JSF files. You can start the Create JSF Page dialog from the New Gallery (Web Tier\JSF category) to create a file, and add that file to the JSF Navigation Diagram afterwards. Alternatively, you can start the Create JSF Page dialog from the JSF Navigation Diagram by double clicking a page symbol that has no page associated with it. As mentioned in Chapter 9, JSF code is usually contained in a JSP file and you can code JSP files in two styles: the JSP page and the JSP document. This hands-on practice, and the others in this book, uses the JSP document style (.jspx files).

Create the JSF Pages

The following steps create files corresponding to the symbols you dropped onto the diagram.

1. Click the Diagram tab of the JSF Navigation Diagram editor. Double click the /login page icon. The Create JSF Page dialog will appear.
2. Ensure that the *Create as XML Document (*.jspx)* checkbox is selected. This setting will add to the default page name (login) a ".jspx" extension. Leave the other defaults; for example, do not specify a page template.

NOTE
Notice (but do not select) the "Render in Mobile Device" checkbox. This setting allows you to configure the file to use libraries that support a wireless (PDA or cellphone) client in case the file needs to be displayed on such a device.

3. Click the plus ("+") symbol next to Page Implementation to expand the implementation region. Select "Automatically Expose UI Components in a New Managed Bean" and leave the default in *Name* as "backing_login" and *Class* as "Login." Change *Package* from its default (application package plus "backing" package) to "login.view.backing." This package assignment will allow you to place other files in the view package if needed but still keep the backing beans in a separate package (view.backing).

   Additional Information: The backing bean is created from this dialog selection, but you can alternatively create it later and associate it with the JSF file using the Overview tab (Managed Beans page) of the faces-config.xml file. The backing bean will also hold the event methods for buttons and other logic needed to process the page.

NOTE
You can write the code for more than one page inside a single managed bean. Some developers prefer this style because it provides a centralized point for all action code.

4. Click OK to create the JSF file. Click Save All.

   Additional Information: The JSP file will open in the visual editor. The nodes in the Application Navigator will display the new login.jspx file and its backing bean file, Login.java, as well as a trinidad-config.xml file (explained in the section "Working with Skins" in Chapter 12) as shown here.

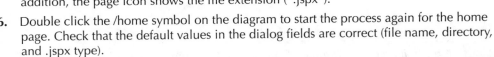

5. In the Diagram tab of the faces-config.xml file, notice that the page symbol within login.jspx is now made of solid lines, indicating that a real JSF page file is available for navigation. In addition, the page icon shows the file extension (".jspx").

6. Double click the /home symbol on the diagram to start the process again for the home page. Check that the default values in the dialog fields are correct (file name, directory, and .jspx type).

7. Expand the Page Implementation area. Notice that the managed bean option is preselected because you selected it for the login.jspx page. (JDeveloper remembers the previous preference.) Change *Package* to "login.view.backing" (you might be able to select it from the pulldown that appears when you click inside this field).

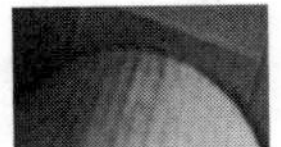

TIP
The Page Implementation region heading contains a hint that appears when the region is collapsed. This hint identifies the state of the managed bean radio group selection that is displayed when you expand the region.

8. Click OK. The file will be created and will be visible in the navigator as well as in the visual editor.

9. Click Save All.

What Did You Just Do? You used the JSF Navigation Diagram to create two JSF page files. The process of creating each file linked it to a separate backing bean, which will hold processing logic and data access logic for the page.

We will now take a brief look at the contents and style of code in one of the JSF document files (the other contains similar elements), the application configuration resource (faces-config.xml), and one of the backing bean files (Login.java).

JSF File

The home.jspx file should already be open in the JSP/HTML Visual Editor. If it is not, double click it in the Application Navigator and be sure the Design tab is selected. This view of the file shows the visual and some nonvisual elements on the page. At this point, you have not added anything to the page, but you will see a blue, dotted rectangle on the page. If you select one of those dotted lines the cursor focus will move to that object, and the status bar of the editor will show the name and location (tag hierarchy) of the component as follows:

jsp:root ▸ f:view ▸ af:document#d2 ▸ **af:form#f2**
Design | Source | Bindings | Preview | History

This status line indicates that the selected component is `af:form`, which is nested within the `jsp:root`, `f:view`, and `af:document` tags as shown in the Structure window snippet here:

NOTE
You can ignore any warnings shown in the Structure window for now. You will fix these warnings later.

Now click the Source tab to view the source code version of the elements you viewed in the Structure window. The code will appear as follows (although your component IDs may be different):

```
01: <?xml version='1.0' encoding='windows-1252'?>
02: <jsp:root xmlns:jsp="http://java.sun.com/JSP/Page" version="2.1"
03:           xmlns:f="http://java.sun.com/jsf/core"
04:           xmlns:h="http://java.sun.com/jsf/html"
05:           xmlns:af="http://xmlns.oracle.com/adf/faces/rich">
06:   <jsp:directive.page contentType="text/html;charset=windows-1252"/>
07:   <f:view>
08:     <af:document id="d2" binding="#{backing_home.d2}">
09:       af:form id="f2" binding="#{backing_home.f2}"></af:form>
10:     </af:document>
11:   </f:view>
12: <!--oracle-jdev-comment:auto-binding-backing-bean-name:backing_home-->
13: </jsp:root>
```

This JSF code contains the following elements:

- **Line 01** identifies the document as an XML file.
- **Lines 02–05** begin the file and specify the tag libraries—JSP, JSF Core, JSF HTML, and ADF Faces—used in the file and their namespace prefixes—jsp, f, h, and af respectively. Tag names will start with the prefix, for example, `f:view` in line 07 represents the view tag in the JSF core tag library.
- **Line 06** specifies that the content created will identify itself to the web browser as HTML text with a Windows character set.

- **Lines 07 and 11** define the JSF tag container (`f:view`) used for all the other elements in the page. This tag identifies the file as a JSF page. The `f:view` tag is a required component for all JSF files.
- **Lines 08 and 10** define the ADF Faces container. When passed to the HTML render kit (which will create HTML markup language code from the ADF faces component code), this tag generates the opening and closing `<html>`, `<head>`, and `<body>` tags. The binding property is assigned to an Expression Language expression (described in the "Expression Language" section of Chapter 4) representing the component in the backing bean (referenced by "backing_home" here and in the faces-config.xml file). It also specifies the ID of the component, "d2."
- **Line 09** defines an ADF Faces form tag, `af:form`, and assigns the binding property in the same way as with the `af:document` tag. It also specifies the ID of the component, "f2." The `af:form` tag works similarly to a standard HTML form (described in the section "The HTML Form" of Chapter 4); it submits values in its child controls (for example, input fields or pulldown lists) to the server.
- **Line 12** is a JSP comment line used at design time only. It identifies the backing bean name that is associated with this page in the faces-config.xml file. This line declares that JDeveloper should update the backing bean's members when the *Id* property for an element in the JSF file changes or when you add or delete components in the page. You will see this automatic renaming process in action later on.
- **Line 13** closes the JSF file.

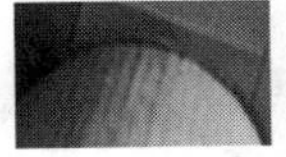

TIP
You can use several methods to view help for a code element in JDeveloper. For Java files, position the cursor in a class name or method name and select ***Go to Javadoc*** *from the right-click menu.* ***Go to Declaration*** *in that same menu shows you where the code element is defined (master class or variable declaration).* ***Quick Javadoc*** *in the right-click menu displays a popup window containing an excerpt from the class Javadoc. For non-Java sources (such as the JSF or faces-config.xml files), press* F1 *when the cursor is positioned in the element and the Help window will load with applicable reference material.*

Application Configuration Resource (faces-config.xml)

The faces-config.xml file was automatically modified when you created the JSF files so that it contains references to the backing beans. Adding a reference to an resource file is known as *registering* the file to the application. At this point in the development of the sample application, we have registered two backing beans with the application, Login.java and Home.java. Click the Source tab for the faces-config.xml file. You will see that JDeveloper added the following (without the line numbers):

```
<managed-bean>
  <managed-bean-name>backing_login</managed-bean-name>
  <managed-bean-class>login.view.backing.Login</managed-bean-class>
  <managed-bean-scope>request</managed-bean-scope>
```

```
24:     <!--oracle-jdev-comment:managed-bean-jsp-link:1login.jspx-->
25:   </managed-bean>
26:   <managed-bean>
27:     <managed-bean-name>backing_home</managed-bean-name>
28:     <managed-bean-class>login.view.backing.Home</managed-bean-class>
29:     <managed-bean-scope>request</managed-bean-scope>
30:     <!--oracle-jdev-comment:managed-bean-jsp-link:1home.jspx-->
31:   </managed-bean>
```

This code registers both managed beans in a similar way as explained here for the Login.java managed bean:

- **Lines 20 and 25** declare a managed (backing) bean. JDeveloper added this entry because you specified in the wizard that the login.jspx file would use a backing bean for its data and logic.
- **Line 21** defines the name of the bean (backing_login) that you specified in the JDeveloper Create JSF Page dialog. This name will be used as a prefix when you refer to the elements inside the backing bean. For example, to access the `f2` element in the backing bean for the login.jspx file, you would use the token `backing_login.f2`.
- **Line 22** specifies the fully qualified Java class name for this backing bean.
- **Line 23** declares the *scope*: that is, how long the bean will be retained in memory. The sidebar "About Scope" briefly describes the available scope values.
- **Line 24** is a comment JDeveloper uses to link this backing bean to the JSF file. When you change a name (*Id* property) of an element in the JSP document, JDeveloper rewrites the backing bean so that its variables and accessor methods use the new name. This comment corresponds to the special comment line (21) described earlier for the home.jspx file.
- **Lines 26–31** follow the same pattern to declare the backing bean for the home page.

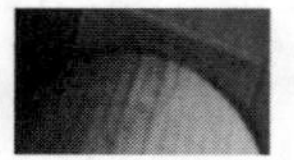

NOTE
If you open the JSF Navigation Diagram, you will see that it now shows the .jspx extension on both pages and that the yellow triangle information symbols on the navigation case lines have disappeared because the page files exist.

The Backing Bean (Login.java)

The faces-config.xml file registers the backing bean (managed bean), Login.java, that is used to hold code for the JSF file, login.jspx. The Home.java file is registered similarly for the home.jspx file. The contents of the Login.java file follow. As before, line numbers appear only in this listing and they may vary slightly from your line numbers. Expand the Application Sources\login.view .backing node in the navigator, and double click the Login.java file if you want to follow along in the Code Editor. (So that you can see all lines, you may need to expand any collapsed structures using the "+" signs in the editor's margin.)

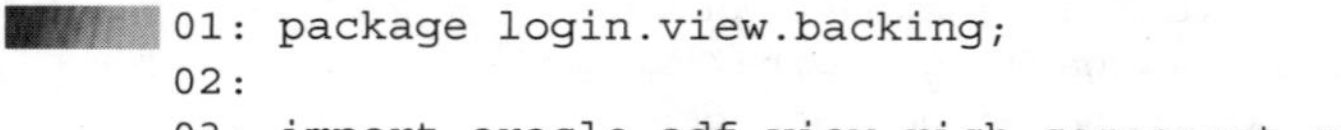

```
package login.view.backing;

import oracle.adf.view.rich.component.rich.RichDocument;
```

```
import oracle.adf.view.rich.component.rich.RichForm;

public class Login
{
  private RichForm f2;
  private RichDocument d2;
  public void setF2(RichForm f2)
  {
    this.f2 = f2;
  }

  public RichForm getF2()
  {
    return f2;
  }

  public void setD2(RichDocument d2)
  {
    this.d2 = d2;
  }

  public RichDocument getD2()
  {
    return d2;
  }
}
```

About Scope

The *scope setting* for a bean instance (or variable) determines how long that element will remain in memory. The JSF framework offers three scopes: request, session, and application. The *request scope* signifies that the bean will be retained in memory only for the HTTP request and response; the data held in the bean will not be available after that time. In the *session scope,* the bean will be retained across requests for the same client session. When the client disconnects (logs out) or times out, the bean will be destroyed. The *application scope* setting retains the bean across client sessions. This setting is useful for beans that need to hold globally available data.

In addition to the standard JSF scopes, ADF offers a *page flow scope* (formerly called "process scope"), which is retained across pages (for requests within the same browser window). It is a longer scope than request scope but shorter than session scope, because page flow scope ends when a new window is opened in the same session. ADF also adds a *view scope,* which is recreated for each new page, and a *backing bean scope,* which is active for a page fragment or declarative component on a page and, therefore, separates each page fragment or declarative component in a package. (Scope and the ADF and JSF life cycle phases are described further in the JDeveloper Help Center topic "Understanding the JSF and ADF Faces Lifecycles.")

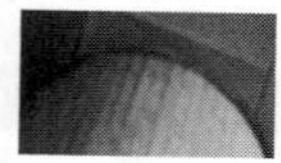

NOTE
JDeveloper will format curly brackets (end of line or new line) according to a preference you set. Select ***Tools | Preferences,*** *navigate to the Code Editor\Code Style node, and set the "Profile" to "JDeveloper Classic" to better match examples shown throughout this chapter (other parts of the book match the Java Code Conventions profile more closely).*

This file is a standard class file that contains the following elements:

- **Line 01** is a package instruction.
- **Lines 03–04** are imports for the ADF Faces document and form elements.
- **Line 06** is the class declaration.
- **Lines 07 and 29** are class block delimiters.
- **Line 08** defines a private variable, `f2`, declared as a `RichForm` type. This variable (object) represents the `af:form` tag.
- **Line 09** defines a private variable, `d2`, declared as a `RichDocument` type. This variable (object) represents the `af:document` tag.
- **Lines 10–28** are added by JDeveloper as accessor methods for each component in the JSP document. In this case, you have not yet added any components, but creating the JSP document automatically created the document and form components. The accessor methods `setF2()` and `getF2()` support the `af:form` component, and the accessor methods `setD2()` and `getD2()` support the `af:document` component.

A name such as "f2" is not very descriptive, although it might serve the purpose if you do not need to distinguish it from other similar form tags. In that situation, you would need to assign a more descriptive name. JDeveloper maintains the link between a JSF file element and its code in the backing bean. We will demonstrate this feature in later steps after showing how to handle warning messages:

1. Open the login.jspx file in the editor, and click the Design tab if it is not already active.
2. You will now resolve the warnings displayed in the Structure window. Select **View | Status** (not Status Bar) to display the Status window as shown here.

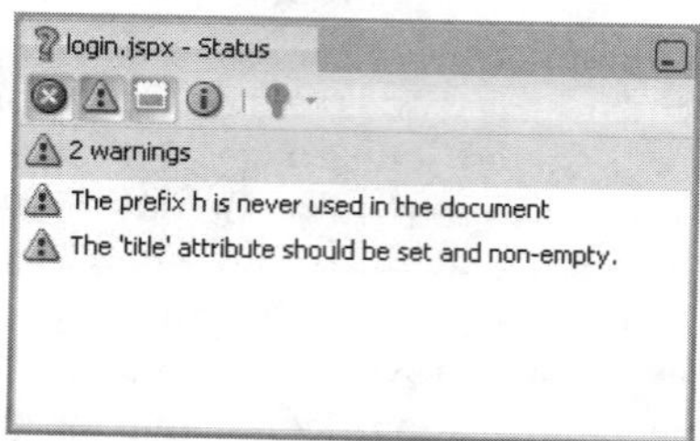

Additional Information: This window shows the same warnings as in the Structure window but allows you to filter the messages by types (for example, error, warning, incomplete, or advisory).

3. On the "The prefix h is never used . . ." message, select **Remove unused xmlns attribute** from the right-click menu. The source code will be updated and the error will disappear.

   Additional Information: This option is also available from the right-click menu on that message's node under the Warnings section of the Structure window.

4. Click the Source tab in the editor window. On the "The 'title' attribute should be set . . ." message in the Status window, select **Goto Source** from the right-click menu.

   Additional Information: This option is not available in the Structure window, but you can double click the message in the Structure window to navigate to the relevant source code.

5. The source code editor will open and the `af:document` tag should be selected.

6. In the Property Inspector, set *Title* as "Application Login." If the Property Inspector is not open, select it in the View menu. (If necessary, expand the Common section to display the *Title* property.) This text will display in the browser window title at runtime. Click ENTER to set the property value and the warning message in the Structure window and Status window should disappear.

7. Select the form object by clicking its node (`af:form`) in the Structure window (under the `af:document` node). This will display the form properties in the Property Inspector.

   Additional Information: You can also select an element by clicking it in the visual editor, but some components, such as `af:form`, are a bit easier to select in the Structure window. At this point you can close the Status window by clicking the "X" icon in its tab.

8. Change the *Id* property to "loginForm" and press ENTER to register the change. A dialog will appear, indicating that the rename operation is being propagated to other files (the backing bean in this case).

   Additional Information: Move the cursor to another property to trigger the renaming process, if you do not see this dialog after pressing ENTER.

CAUTION
Component names (the "Id" property) should start with lowercase, as is a convention for Java object names.

9. Click the Source tab if the code is not displayed and notice that the *id* attribute of the form element has been renamed.

10. Click the Login.java document tab in the window to display the code (or open the file from the navigator, if it is not already open).

    Additional Information: Notice that the private variable and accessor method names have been renamed to `loginForm`, `setLoginForm()`, and `getLoginForm()`, although the arguments used by the methods have not been renamed. As you add elements to the JSF file, you will be able to rename them so that you can distinguish the elements more easily and the backing bean code will automatically synchronize to the new names. You can use Refactor options to rename the arguments. If you want to try this, select the f2 argument by double clicking it. Then select **Refactor | Rename**. Fill in *Rename to* as "form" and click OK. Both instances of f2 will be replaced.

11. Open the Source tab for home.jspx. Repeat the steps to resolve the warnings using a *Title* property value of "Application Home."

12. In the Source tab, change the *Id* property of the form element (line 8) to "homeForm." Navigate off the line. Notice that no renaming dialog appears.
13. Open Home.java and click the Source tab. Notice that the form variable and accessors have not been renamed. The renaming feature is only available in the Property Inspector and JSP/HTML Visual Editor.
14. Return to the home.jspx window and press CTRL-Z multiple times to restore the *Id* property to "f2." Click the Design tab; select the `af:form` node in the Structure window; and in the Property Inspector change the *Id* property to "homeForm"; press ENTER to register the change. This time, the accessors in the backing bean will be renamed.
15. Click Save All.

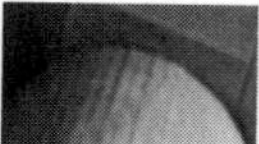

CAUTION
As just demonstrated, if you rename the form in the Source view of the file, the name change will not cascade to other elements.

IV. Add Components to the Login Page

This phase demonstrates how to add layout containers, messages, fields, and a button to the login page. Since this application is only concerned with showing how to develop a simple file that demonstrates JSF basics, it does not connect the pages to the database. Hands-on practices later in the book will explore that subject in some detail.

In this phase, you select components from the Component Palette. These components are not automatically bound to data sources, so you need to add mechanisms to load data into and read data from the components.

Applications that require database access normally contain one or more Model projects that represent tables. When this code is available, you will select components as data controls from the Data Controls panel instead of selecting components from the Component Palette. The Data Controls panel method adds ADF Faces components that are automatically bound to the Model layer objects. Other practices in this part of this book demonstrate adding components using the Data Controls panel.

When designing a screen layout, it is important to consider the arrangement of layout containers and their child components. When starting with ADF Faces, it is important to scan the documentation (such as the list of ADF Faces tags available in the JDeveloper Help Center's tag library reference pages) to find appropriate layout containers and other components. Drawing a layout arrangement with notes about the component types will be helpful when it comes time to add components to the file. For example, you could draw this layout as a hierarchy (as shown in Figure 10-1) to indicate how you will place components within containers. You could alternatively represent the hierarchy as nested boxes.

In this diagram, the `af:form` component is the parent for the other components. It corresponds to the HTML `form` tag and must enclose all components whose values are submitted to the server. The direct child component for `af:form` is `af:panelHeader`, which allows you to place a title on the page and place components under that title. Inside `af:panelHeader` is `af:panelFormLayout`, which lays out its child components in rows and columns. The user interacts with or uses these child components within `af:panelFormLayout`: `af:inputText` (for the two text fields), `af:commandButton` (the submit button for the page), and `af:outputText` (a read-only text message inside the footer facet that displays text about required fields).

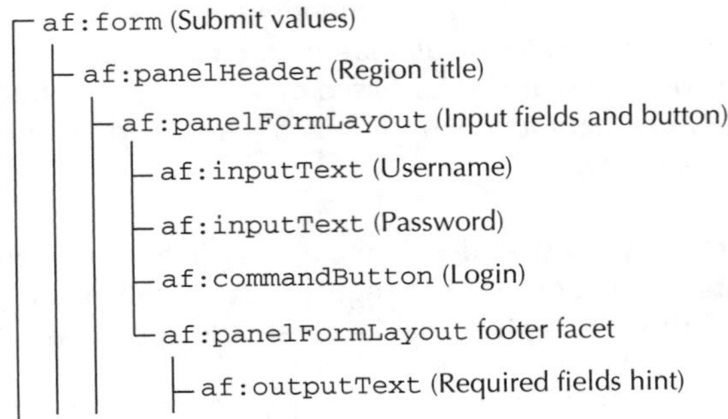

FIGURE 10-1. *A hierarchical design for an ADF Faces component layout*

Add the Layout Containers

One of the first steps when creating a JSF project is working out templates so that all pages can share a look and feel. Although this example ignores the template step, the hands-on practice in Chapter 17 demonstrates templating principles.

In this section, you add layout containers that will hold other objects. The steps in this example use the Structure window to position components. A JSF or ADF Faces file (and even a standard HTML file) is laid out hierarchically. Sometimes, it is easier to lay out a component in a specific position in this hierarchy using the visual representation of that hierarchy in the Structure window. Also, it is usually possible to perform a layout task by dragging and dropping directly into the visual editor, but you will still need to check the Structure window to be sure that the component lands in the correct place in the hierarchy.

1. Open the login.jspx file (by double clicking the login.jspx file in the navigator), or select its tab in the editor, if it is already open. Click the Design tab if it is not selected.
2. Be sure the Component Palette is accessible. It usually appears in the right-hand side of the JDeveloper window. If it is not displayed, select it using **View | Component Palette**.
3. Be sure the Structure window is displayed. This usually appears in the lower-left corner of the JDeveloper window, but you can display it using **View | Structure** if it is not visible.
4. Select the ADF Faces page from the Component Palette pulldown if it that page is not visible. Locate the Panel Header component in the Layout panel of the Component Palette. Drag and drop the Panel Header component on top of the `af:form` tag in the Structure window, as shown on the right.

   Additional Information: The Structure window should now appear as follows:

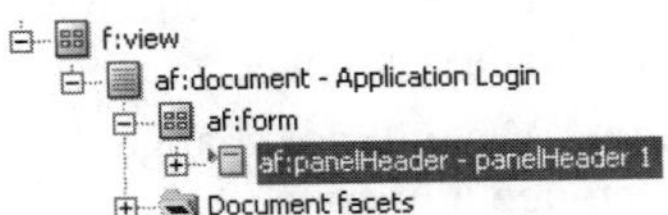

NOTE
The label for your `af:panelHeader` component may be slightly different. JDeveloper generates default labels and names for components you drop into the editor based on the component name and an index number that increments for each new component of the same type in the same file.

5. If your Structure window nodes do not appear in the same order as the illustration, use drag-and-drop operations to rearrange them until they match. Click the Design tab if it is not in focus. The JSP/HTML Visual Editor should appear as follows:

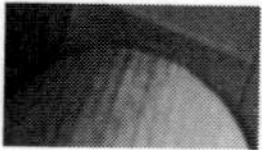

TIP
*You can correct a drag-and-drop operation by selecting **Edit | Undo** (CTRL-Z) or by dragging components around in the Structure window.*

Additional Information: The `af:panelHeader` component is an ADF Faces layout container that displays a heading and can contain stacked child components. It has no other inherent layout capabilities.

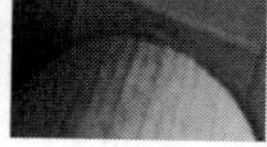

TIP
One way to reorder the components inside another component is to drag the child component on top of the parent component. Components nested in this way always appear below all other child components at the same level.

6. The `af:panelHeader` tag should now appear nested under an `af:form` tag. Be sure the `af:panelHeader` is selected. Be sure the Property Inspector is visible (select **View | Property Inspector** if it is not).
7. Change the *Text* property to "Enter Login Information" and press ENTER. This text will now appear as the main heading for the page.

   Additional Information: We will not change the *Id* property of this component because we do not need to reference it in code.

TIP
You can also type some text changes such as this directly in the JSP/HTML Visual Editor. However, you will probably find it faster and easier to use the Property Inspector.

8. You now need a layout container to hold the form's objects. ADF Faces offers an `af:panelFormLayout` component that stacks fields and keeps their prompts aligned. Drag a Panel Form Layout from the Layout panel of the Component Palette, and drop it on top of the `af:panelHeader` tag in the Structure window.

9. Expand the panel tags and you will see the arrangement shown here.

   af:panelFormLayout
   Panel Form Layout facets
   footer
   Panel Header facets
   context
   info
   legend
   menuBar
   toolbar

   Additional Information: As mentioned in Chapter 9, some ADF Faces containers, such as `af:panelFormLayout` in this example, offer *facets*—predefined areas into which you can place child objects. Usually, the child component appears in a specific location on the page within the parent component. In this case, a facet exists for footer elements. When you place a component inside this facet, it will automatically be placed at the bottom of all child components.

10. Click Save All.

Add the Visual Components

You are now ready to add the form fields, button, and a footer message. ADF Faces offers `af:inputText`, an improvement on the standard JSF input field, `h:inputText`. The ADF Faces component adds a prompt, a richer set of validators, and default messages to the JSF component. ADF Faces also supplies an `af:commandButton` component used to submit the form. All components use a default style defined in the ADF Faces libraries, and you do not need to apply styles manually.

TIP
As discussed in Chapter 12, you can change the default ADF Faces styles if the defaults are not suitable for your environment. Look for white papers about altering the look-and-feel definitions (skins) *of ADF Faces at otn.oracle.com. In addition, the help system contains a topic, "Customizing the Appearance Using Styles and Skins," that will assist (search for "skins" to find this topic).*

As mentioned in the explanation of the HTML form in Chapter 4, the form tag (`af:form`) must surround the fields and buttons it submits to the server.

1. Select the `af:panelFormLayout` tag in the Structure window. In the Common Components panel of the ADF Faces page in the Component Palette, click Input Text. (This is an alternative layout technique to the drag-and-drop operation you have used before.) A field and label will appear in the editor, and the tag will be nested under the `af:panelFormLayout` component in the Structure window.

   Additional Information: `af:inputText` allows the user to enter data that will be submitted when the form is submitted. This field will hold the user's name.

2. To demonstrate another technique for adding components, click the `af:inputText` node in the Structure window and press CTRL-C (to copy the component). Click the `af:panelFormLayout` node and press CTRL-V (to paste a copy of the component under this node). Another field and label will appear in the visual editor. This field will hold the login password.

TIP

Yet another way to create duplicate objects is to press CTRL while selecting the component to copy, then dropping the selection and releasing CTRL on the node or area where the copies should appear (such as the `af:panelFormLayout` component).

3. Drag and drop a Button (from the Common Components panel) on top of the `af:panelFormLayout` node of the Structure window. A command button will appear in the visual editor. This button will be used to submit the login values.

   Additional Information: The Structure window `af:panelHeader` node should now appear as shown on the right.

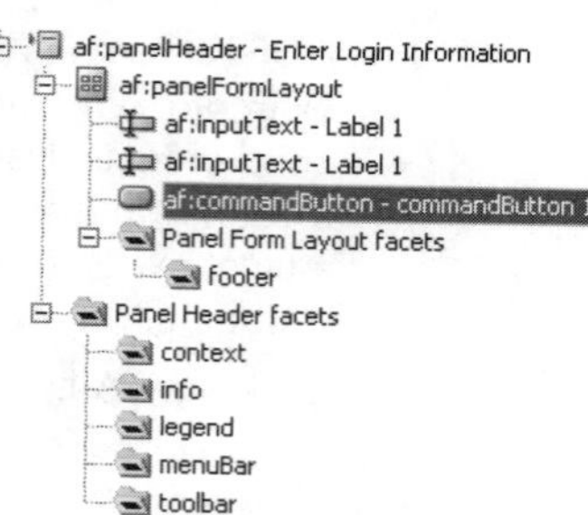

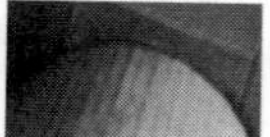

TIP

You can hold the mouse cursor above a Component Palette item, such as Button, to view a tooltip containing a description of the component as well as its ADF Faces name.

4. Both `af:inputText` fields will be required. You can make changes to both fields at the same time. Select the two fields by clicking one and CTRL clicking the other in the Structure window. (You may need to wait a couple of seconds for the Property Inspector to merge the properties.) In the Property Inspector, expand the Behavior region (or click the Behavior tab) and set the *Required* property to "true."

   Additional Information: Setting the *Required* property to "true" for an ADF Faces field causes an asterisk to display in the label. For example, the field label for the first field now appears as "* Label 1." This suggests to the user that this field requires input.

5. With both fields still selected, set the following properties. (Be sure to press ENTER after entering each value so JDeveloper can register the change.)
   - *MaximumLength* in the Behavior region as "20" (the limit of the number of characters a user can type in the field)
   - *Columns* in the Appearance region as "15" (the width on the page)
   - *RequiredMessageDetail* in the Appearance region as "is required" (this text will appear as an error message if the user submits the form without a value in this field)

6. In the Design tab, click the page outside of a field to deselect the two fields.

7. From the Common Components panel of the ADF Faces page in the Component Palette, drag an Output Text component and drop it on top of the footer tag in the JSP/HTML Visual Editor. (This is yet another way to add components to the page.) The object will replace the placeholder for the footer facet and the Structure window will appear as shown in Figure 10-2.

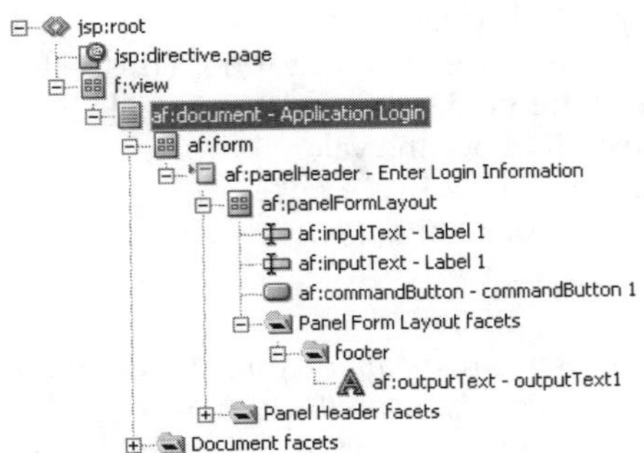

FIGURE 10-2. *Structure window excerpt after all components are in place*

8. Click Save All.
9. Click the Design tab if it is not already active. You can now fine-tune more properties on each component. Select the topmost `af:inputText` item in the Structure window. You have set some of its properties already. Now set the following properties (pressing ENTER after each setting):

   Id in the Common region as "usernameField"
   LabelAndAccessKey in the Appearance region as "&Username"
   Label in the Appearance region as blank. Remove the value so the preceding property will take effect.
   ShortDesc in the Appearance region as "Your name" (this appears as popup hint text)

   Additional Information: The *LabelAndAccessKey* property combines a field prompt with an access key assignment. (An *AccessKey* property just assigns the access key.) The *access key* allows the user to navigate to a field by pressing ALT-<LETTER>, where "ALT" is a browser-specific key ("ALT" in Internet Explorer or ALT-SHIFT in Firefox and Safari) and "<LETTER>" is the letter that appears in the label after an ampersand character. For example, the *LabelAndAccessKey* value "&Username" will be displayed as "* Username."

   The letter following the ampersand ("U") is underscored to signify that the user can press ALT-U (in Internet Explorer) to move the cursor to that field. The access key need not be the first letter in the label, but it does need to appear in the label.

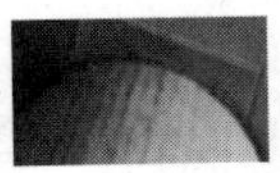

TIP
You can view reference information about a component and its properties by selecting the component in the visual editor, clicking the Source tab, and pressing F1. The reference page for the component will appear. This page should give you additional clues for the component's use. You can view help for properties by dragging the hint panel at the bottom of the window into view, then selecting the property in the Property Inspector, as shown on the right for ShortDesc.

10. Select the second field and set its properties as follows:
    Id as "passwordField" (press ENTER)
    Secret in the Appearance region as "true" (This setting will convert the characters the user enters in this field to dots so that an onlooker cannot see the password.)
    Label as no text. (Remove the value.)
    LabelAndAccessKey as "&Password"
    ShortDesc as "Just Something Fun"

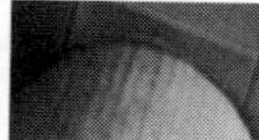

TIP
Get into the habit of pressing ENTER after typing a property so that the value will register before you navigate the cursor to a different place. This keypress is not required for values set using pulldown lists or popup dialogs.

11. Select the `af:commandButton` component and set its properties as follows. (Be sure to press ENTER after changing a value.)
    Id as "loginButton" (This change will be written into the backing bean.)
    Text as blank (Remove the value.)
    TextAndAccessKey as "&Login"

    Additional Information: The page should appear in the visual editor as follows:

12. Select the `af:outputText` item and set its Value property (Common region) as "* indicates a required field."
13. Click Save All.

Test the Page

Although the logic to process input and navigate to the home page is not in place, you can run this page in the Integrated WLS Server to view its appearance in the browser.

You can also look at the page in a web browser without running the server by using the right-click menu option **Preview in Browser** on any page. As a third alternative, the *Preview tab* of the editor window shows the page's components without running the server. Both of these previewers provide an approximation of the runtime appearance of the page but do not allow you to test any of the functionality. Running the page using the Integrated WLS Server is the only way to test functionality through JDeveloper.

1. Be sure the login.jspx file is active (click its document tab in the editor if you are not certain). Select **Run** from the right-click menu in the editor. You can alternatively press CTRL-F11 when the page is active.

2. The server will start, the application will be deployed, and the page will appear in your browser. Without entering data, click Login to submit the form. Since you did not fill in mandatory fields, the following dialog will appear:

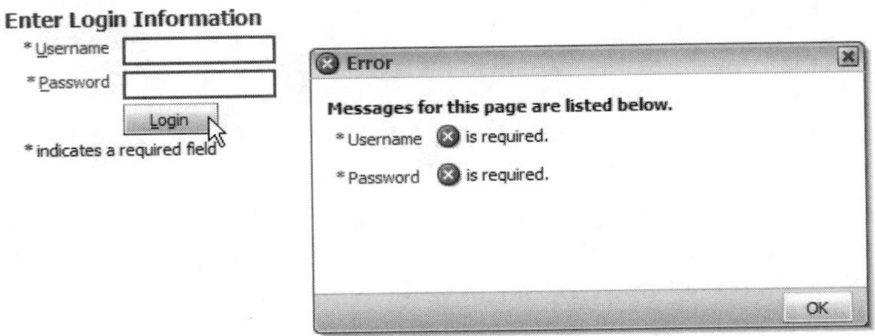

3. Notice that the dialog contains the field labels from the *LabelAndAccessKey* property and the text from the *RequiredMessageDetail* property.

   Additional Information: You may also notice that this dialog did not require a round-trip request to the server; you can usually tell if the page submits to the server because part or all of the page is redrawn. In this case, JavaScript on the page checked the values before submitting the page to the server. The dialog you are viewing is a JavaScript alert dialog. JSF reference implementation (RI) components allow you to set the *Required* property, but that setting requires a round-trip to the server.

4. Click OK to dismiss the validation error dialog.

5. Click in the *Username* field. (An error message callout containing the error text for this field will appear.) Type your name and press TAB to move the cursor to the *Password* field value; another error message callout will appear for this field. Click Login again; the second field's error message will reappear as shown here:

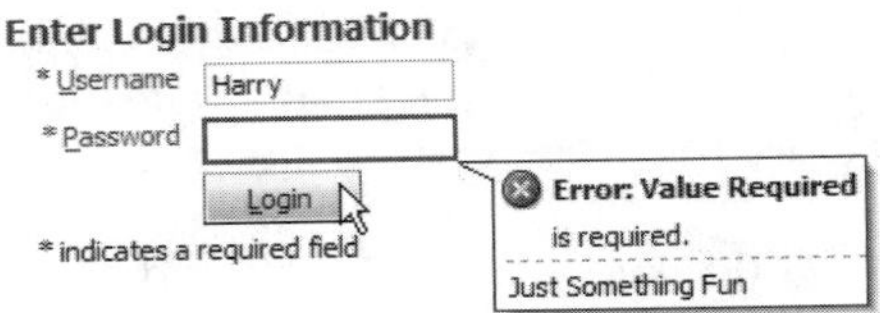

   Additional Information: You do not need to click anything to enter data in the field, although you can click the window background to hide the message.

6. Enter some text in the Password field. Notice that the *Secret* property setting changes the input to dots. Click Login. The error message does not appear. Nothing happens because you have not coded any action.

7. Press ALT-P and ALT-U (ALT-SHIFT-P and ALT-SHIFT-U for Firefox or Safari) to test the navigation to the fields based on the access key. You will see the *Short Desc* (hint) text appear as the cursor enters the fields. This navigation aid is helpful to assisting users who prefer or require keyboard navigation. ALT-L (ALT-SHIFT-L) navigates to the button and activates it as if you clicked it.

   Additional Information: Again, nothing will occur if you click this button, because you have not handled the submit action yet.

TIP
*To examine the HTML created by the JSF components, select **View | Source** (Internet Explorer) or **View | Page Source** (Firefox) when running a JSF page.*

8. Close the browser window. Click the red Terminate button in the IDE toolbar and select the application name (LoginJSF) from the button's pulldown as shown here.

Additional Information: This action undeploys the application but does not stop the default server. Selecting DefaultServer from this pulldown will stop the Integrated WLS Server. You do not need to undeploy the application or stop the server each time you test the application, but doing so ensures that no information or error states are held in server memory between test runs. Also, in the following chapters in this book, changes you make to database access code (using ADF Business Components) may not take effect until the application is undeployed and the server is restarted to clear out any objects cached in memory.

NOTE
Chapter 22 discusses and provides a hands-on practice for WebLogic Server deployment.

What Did You Just Do? In this phase, you added ADF Faces layout containers to the login JSF file. These layout containers abstract the HTML layout so that you do not need to worry about coding HTML structures such as tables and rows. Some ADF Faces containers also offer facets—prebuilt slots into which you can add components.

In addition, you added components to the login page and set their properties; then you tested the page. Many properties you set for the ADF Faces field items (such as *LabelAndAccessKey, Required, Columns, Secret,* and *MaximumLength*) may already be familiar if you have experience with other development tools. The property set offered by ADF Faces is richer than most other Java EE–oriented component sets, including the JSF RI components.

It is time to take another quick look at the JSP file and the backing bean. The faces-config.xml file has not changed since you last examined it.

Login JSF File Select the document tab for login.jspx. Click the Source tab and locate the tags for the ADF Faces containers—`af:panelHeader` and `af:panelFormLayout`. Find the `af:panelFormLayout`'s facet, as shown the following code:

```
<af:panelFormLayout binding="#{backing_login.pfl1}"
                   id="pfl1">
  <f:facet name="footer">
    <af:outputText value="* indicates a required field"
                   binding="#{backing_login.ot1}"
                   id="ot1"/>
  </f:facet>
     <!-- more components here -->
</af:panelFormLayout>
```

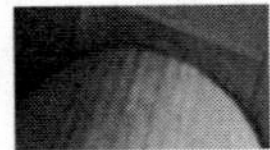

NOTE

Many of the components are still set to their default "Id" property value (for example, "ot1" for the `af:outputText` component). As mentioned, it is not necessary to reassign the "Id" property of all components you use in a JSF file. However, you will find descriptive names useful if you write backing bean code. In this code, you need to distinguish between multiple occurrences of text fields or other components in the same file, and descriptive names make this identification easier.

The `af:outputText` component is assigned to this facet, so it will appear in the footer area. Remember that all ADF Faces components will be sent as HTML to the web browser (or in another language to other display devices such as a PDA). For the HTML display, layout containers will create HTML tables with specific properties. Components such as `af:inputText` and `af:commandButton` will create HTML form elements such as fields and buttons, respectively.

If you run this file, view its HTML source in the browser, save the source to an HTML file in the file system, and open the file in JDeveloper, after reformatting the text, you will end up with 268 lines of code with HTML tables nested at least three levels deep as shown in the following Structure window snippet.

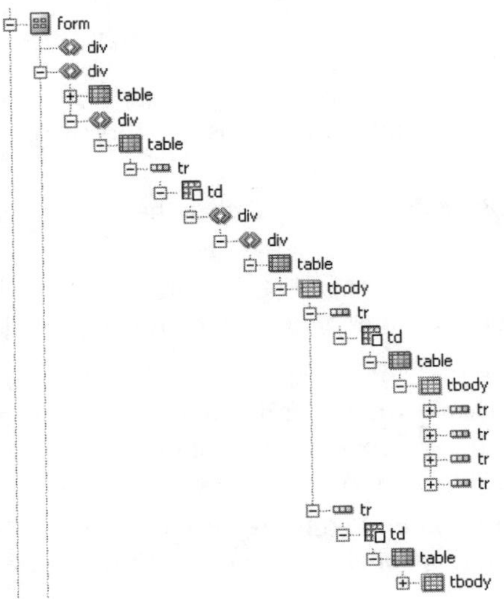

The JSF file contains around 43 lines of code, which has no HTML and fewer levels of nested containers. In other words, using JSF and ADF Faces tags supplies a large amount of HTML output, which provides sophisticated layouts. In addition, you do not code much, if any, HTML; the JSF code—or, more correctly, the HTML render kit—is responsible for generating HTML for the browser.

Spend a bit more time familiarizing yourself with the components in the source code for login.jspx. Identify the property values you set in the Property Inspector. Remember that you can always view the help page for a component by clicking inside the tag in the Code Editor and pressing F1.

The Backing Bean File The Login.java backing bean for this page has grown substantially since you last viewed it. Each time you drop a component onto the visual editor, JDeveloper creates accessor methods and a private variable for the object. When you change the *Id* property, JDeveloper sweeps through the backing bean and changes the accessors and private variable to match the new component name. Open the editor for the Login.java file, and scan through it to find the private variable and accessors for `usernameField`, for example. All other objects in the JSP file have similar code units. Browse the contents a bit further using the Structure window. You may need to click the Show Methods or Show Fields button in the Structure window toolbar to see these elements.

V. Add Components to the Home Page

The intent of the home page in this example is to demonstrate page navigation and value passing, and, therefore, it contains very few components.

Remove Automatic Backing Bean Updates

The auto-bind comments in faces-config.xml and the JSF file are handy when learning about backing beans. However, for production-level work, you would normally choose to turn off this feature because it creates variables and accessors that you will never use. In fact, you may not even need a backing bean file at all for many JSF files you create. This section disables the variable and method updates to the backing bean that are automatically triggered by changes in the JSF file.

1. Click the home.jspx file tab if the file is already open. (Double click the home.jspx node in the navigator if the home.jspx file is not already open.) Click the Design tab if it is not already selected.
2. Select **Design | Page Properties** and click the Component Binding tab. Unselect *Auto Bind*. Click OK.

   Additional Information: This action will remove the following line in the faces-config.xml file as well as a corresponding line in the home.jspx file:

   ```
   <!--oracle-jdev-comment:managed-bean-jsp-link:1home.jspx-->
   ```
3. Open the faces-config.xml file and confirm that the comment line for home.jspx has been removed. Open home.jspx file and confirm that the corresponding comment line has been removed. Click Save All.

   Additional Information: You have just removed support for automatic updates of the Home.java file that occur when you change properties or add items in home.jspx.

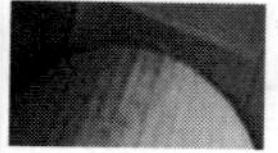

NOTE
Restoring the Auto Bind *selection will re-establish the automatic update support.*

Add JSF Components

This section adds a layout container and three child components to the Home page.

1. Return to the home.jspx page and click the Design tab. As with the login page, drag a Panel Header component from the Component Palette Layout panel, and drop it on top of the `af:form` tag in the Structure window.
2. As with the login page, drop a Panel Form Layout component on top of the `af:panelHeader` node in the Structure window. Although you will not use the footer facet, this container offers the appropriate component stacking behavior.

   Additional Information: As you saw when creating the Login page, you can add components in the correct location in the structure by selecting the parent object and then clicking the new child object type in the Component Palette. A child component will appear under the parent component with no drag-and-drop operation. The next step uses this technique again.
3. Select the new `af:panelFormLayout` node in the Structure window, and click Output Text in the Common Components panel of the Component Palette. An `af:outputText` node will appear under `af:panelFormLayout`.

   Additional Information: As you saw with the required message text in the login page, the `af:outputText` component will be rendered as plain text on the page.
4. Drop a Spacer component from the Component Palette (Layout panel) onto the `af:panelFormLayout` component in the Structure window. The new component will appear under the `af:outputText` component. The *Spacer* component provides vertical or horizontal space between components.
5. Select the `af:panelFormLayout` and click Button in the Component Palette to add an `af:commandButton` child component.

   Additional Information: This button will be used to send control back to the Controller layer so that the Login page can be redisplayed. This is an alternative to the browser's Back button, which can cause the problems mentioned in the sidebar "The Back Button and Refresh Button Problem."
6. Click Save All. The structure should appear something like this:

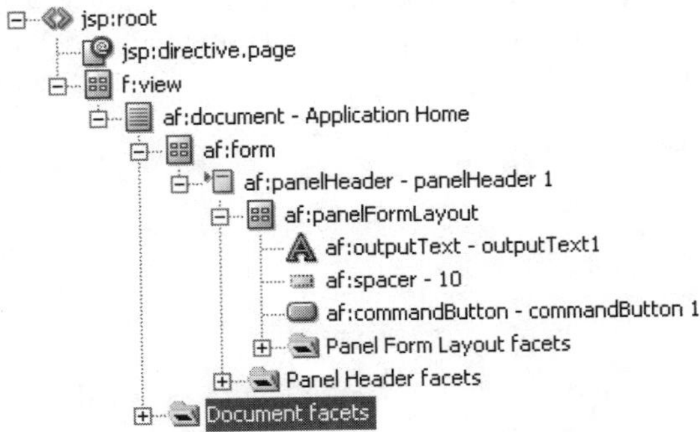

The Back Button and Refresh Button Problem

Users may be accustomed to clicking the browser's Back button to return to the preceding page or the Refresh button to reload the page. This can cause problems with web applications that use a Controller layer, like the JSF controller or Struts, because the browser Back button returns to the preceding page in the browser's page history without calling code in the Controller layer. The Controller will, therefore, not know the state of the application's data, and the preceding page will either not load properly or may place the application into an inconsistent or unstable state. The same problem occurs with the browser's Refresh button, which just reloads the same page, again without calling Controller layer code. This is a problem in all web applications, not only those using Java EE technology or ADF libraries.

Most frameworks do not offer programmatic solutions for this problem yet. At this point in web technologies, the solutions consist of user education (to warn them of incorrect results when using these buttons) and hiding the browser's buttons (using a JavaScript window call that specifies no toolbars), although users can still press keyboard shortcuts to perform the Back and Refresh functions. Other solutions consist of writing JavaScript that deletes the browser history, or checking a timestamp on the page and issuing a warning about an inconsistent state. In addition, the ADF controller offers some support for detecting a Back button click; to understand this support, start with a search in the JDeveloper Help Center for the topic "Creating Complex Task Flows." (Chapter 11 of this book discusses the ADF Task Flow Controller.)

Another partial solution is for the application to provide the equivalent of the Back button, as with the Logout button on this page, that performs standard Controller actions. This allows the user to perform the same function as the browser's Back button and also uses the standard Controller actions.

Set the af:outputText Value as an Expression

You can base the text that appears in the `af:outputText` component on an EL expression that refers to the username field on the Login page so that the username typed into the Login page will appear in the text. This section sets up this functionality.

1. In the home.jspx editor window, select the `af:outputText` component and find the *Value* property in the Property Inspector. From the pulldown on the right side of the *Value* property field, select "Expression Builder . . ." as shown here:

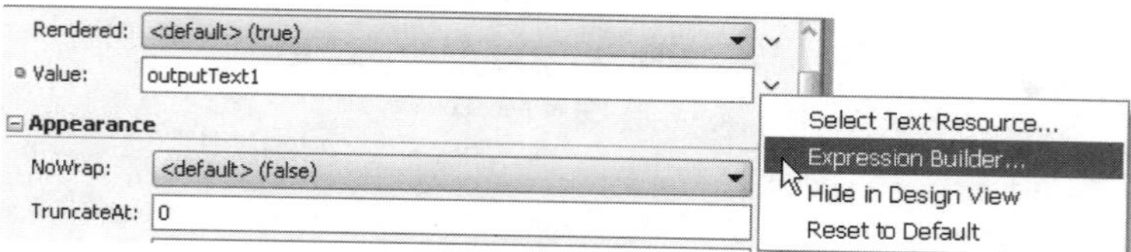

2. The Expression Builder dialog shown in Figure 10-3 will appear. This dialog assists in building an expression used to supply a value to this property. Delete the contents of the *Expression* field and type "Welcome " (including the trailing space). In the next step, you will fill in that phrase with an expression that contains the value of the Username field on the login page.

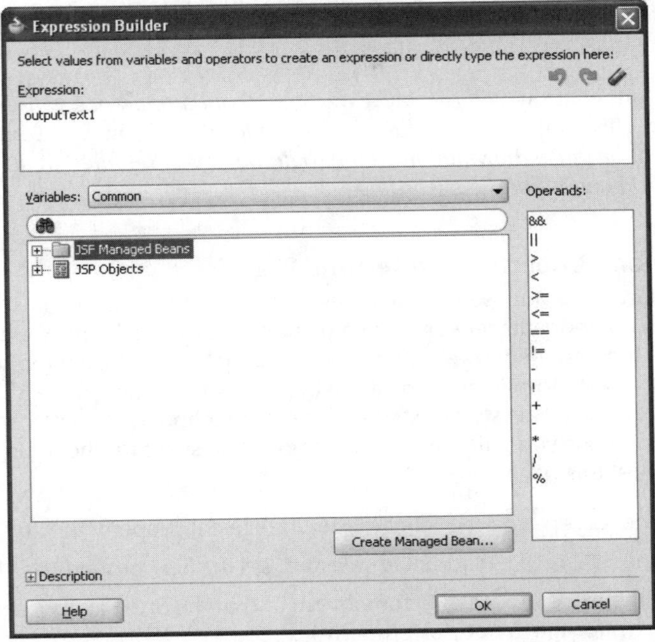

FIGURE 10-3. *The Expression Builder dialog for the* Value *property*

Additional Information: Since the username value is loaded into a field on the Login page and that field is controlled by a backing bean with accessors for the field's value, you can build an expression that will call the accessor for that field. You build this expression using Expression Language (EL), as introduced in the section "Expression Language" in Chapter 4. This dialog will help you build a proper expression, so you do not need to master EL syntax right away.

3. You need to select something that will represent the value of the Username field, which has an *Id* property of "usernameField" in login.jspx. Remember that the data for login.jspx is supplied by a managed bean, known to the controller as backing_login. These clues will lead you to the correct expression. Start the search by expanding the JSF Managed Beans node.

4. Find the backing_login node and expand it. You will see a node for the usernameField element. Expand that node and scroll down until you find the value node. Select the value node. The expression "`#{backing_login.usernameField.value}`" will load into the *Expression* field in the dialog.

   Additional Information: Reading backward in the object hierarchy, the *value* property is supplied for the usernameField element contained in the managed bean backing_login (as defined in faces-config.xml). If that backing bean contains a getter for the field (`getUsernameField()`), the expression will call that getter. If the getter does not exist, the expression will call a generic `get()` method in the managed bean class (or any class from which it inherits).

5. Click OK. The expression and literal text will appear in the *Value* property and also in the visual editor as Welcome #{...usernameField.value}.

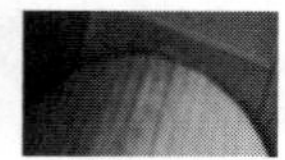

NOTE
The Structure window will display a warning about a reference value not found. This relates to the value expression for the `af:outputText` *component because the value from the login page will be filled in at runtime. You can ignore this warning.*

Set Component Properties and Test the Page

This section starts by setting some properties of the components you have added to the page.

ADF Faces components render using a default set of style sheets. You can override the default appearance of a component by applying visual characteristics (using the subtabs in the Style region of the Property Inspector) or by applying a new Cascading Style Sheets (CSS) selector that is available in the ADF Faces set of styles. This section chooses the latter strategy because applying a style selector means you will rely on a common style sheet for the interpretation of the selector. Then you will test this page.

1. With the `af:spacer` tag selected, set the *Height* property to "20."
2. With the `af:panelHeader` tag selected, set the *Text* property as "Home."
3. Select the `af:outputText` component and in the Style region, select Edit from the pulldown for the *StyleClass* property.

   Additional Information: Editing selections in the Property Inspector display additional editor windows that allow you to set property values in an easier way. In this case, a style selection dialog appears as shown here:

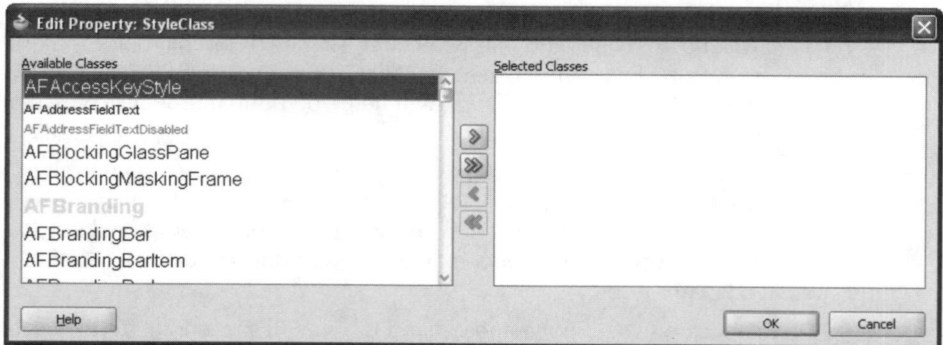

4. The *Available Classes* list shows all CSS selectors available to this ADF Faces component.
5. Type "orae" to scroll the list to names starting with those letters. Select "OraErrorNameText" and click ">"to move the selector name to the *Selected Classes* list. Click OK. The text will turn to a bold red font.

   Additional Information: Of course, if you are certain of the selector name and its spelling, you can just type it into the Property Inspector field and bypass the dialog.

6. Set the following properties for the `af:commandButton` component. Remember that you can search for property names using the search field in the top-right corner of the Property Inspector.
   Id as "logoutButton"
   Text as blank
   TextAndAccessKey as "&Logout"

   Additional Information: As you saw for the Login button on the Login page, the *TextAndAccessKey* property for the `af:commandButton` works similarly to the *LabelAndAccessKey* property for the `af:textInput` component. It underscores the letter following the "&" in the property, in this example "L." When the user presses ALT-L (ALT-SHIFT-L), the button will be activated as if the user had clicked it.

7. Click Save All.

8. Although you have not connected this page to the login page, you can now run this page to check its visual elements. Click the mouse cursor in the home.jspx editor window and select *Run* from the right-click menu in the editor.

   Additional Information: The home page will appear in your browser without the user name in the message. As before, the button will not work yet.

9. Close the browser. Stop the application and stop the Default Server using the Terminate button in the IDE toolbar.

What Did You Just Do? You added components to the home page show the user name, a page heading ("Home"), and a button to return to the login page. With the assistance of the Expression Builder for the *Value* property, you defined the `af:outputText` value using an EL expression. You also changed the default style for the output text component by selecting an existing ADF Faces CSS selector. Then you ran the JSP pages to check that they appear correctly. You will specify the navigation and logic to check and process values entered by the user in the next phase.

Examine the home.jspx file's code to identify its elements. Notice that the EL data bindings appear as property values, as you would expect, because you entered the expressions in the Property Inspector.

VI. Add Navigation and Validation Logic to the Application

This phase specifies the page navigation and adds logic in the backing bean for the validation and other required functionality.

Add the Navigation and Validation Code

Navigation, validation, and other logic are initiated by a user event, for example, a Login button click. Event logic is coded in a managed bean listener method named, by convention, "<component>_action," where "<component>" is the name (*Id* property value) of the JSF component, such as the command button. For example, you would use a method called "loginButton_action" to run code when the user clicks the `af:commandButton` component with an *Id* property of "loginButton." JDeveloper can add a method stub for this event, as you will see in this section. This method serves as a place to enter any code that applies to the navigation. You will use this technique to define the navigation from the login page to the home page, because you need to check the number of logins and to validate the password.

The event code validates the user name and password values and returns a value to the controller. If the login is successful, the event code will return "gohome" (the name of the navigation case in the faces-config.xml file) and the home.jspx page will load. If the login is unsuccessful, the event code will return null, a message will be added to the FacesContext message area, and control will remain on the login page.

If you have no code to run for a particular navigation, you can define navigation in the *action* property for an `af:commandButton` (or `af:commandLink`). We show how to use this technique for the navigation from the home page back to the login page. No additional logic in the backing bean code or elsewhere is required for this type of navigation.

As you saw earlier, error messages for required values are displayed in an ADF Faces dialog. The code you will add in this section issues error messages that will be shown on the page. Loading the messages component requires a small amount of Java code, as explained in the sidebar "About Messages in FacesContext."

1. Display the Design page of the home.jspx file. Click the Logout button. In the *Action* property in the Common region (Button Action section) of the Property Inspector, select "logout" from the pulldown.

   Additional Information: The *Action* pulldown contains a list of all navigation cases you have defined from this page. In this case, you only defined one navigation case called "logout," so that is the only value preloaded into the property's pulldown. (You can verify this name by looking in the faces-config.xml source code.) You do not need any conditional or validation logic for this navigation, because the framework performs the navigation based on the *Action* property setting.
2. Click Save All.

About Messages in FacesContext

The JSF life cycle adds messages to the FacesContext memory area. You can programmatically add messages to this area as well. To access the FacesContext area in the managed bean code, you create a `FacesContext` object that represents the current instance of the context using code similar to the following:

```
FacesContext messageContext = FacesContext.getCurrentInstance();
```

You can then load messages into the context area using the `addMessage()` method. The string passed to `addMessage()` must be inside a `FacesMessage` object. You can combine these requirements into a single line of code that calls `addMessage()` on the current context object and passes it a new `FacesMessage` object loaded with the desired text. The following shows an example of how you would place the "Hello JSF World" message into the FacesContext area so that it will be displayed in the standard ADF Faces message area (in this case, an error dialog):

```
messageContext.addMessage(null, new FacesMessage("Hello JSF World"));
```

3. Display the Design tab of the login.jspx file. Double click the Login button. A Bind Action Property dialog will appear; you use this dialog to identify the managed bean name and method name for this button. Select Method Binding, leave the defaults (backing_login and loginButton_action), and click OK. The Login.java file will appear in the editor, and the cursor will navigate to a newly added method, `loginButton_action()`.

4. Delete the following lines in this method stub:

```
// Add event code here...
return null;
```

5. In their place, enter the following code. As before, the line numbers are for reference purposes and should not appear in the code text. As you type in class names that are not yet available, JDeveloper will detect missing import statements and prompt you to press ALT-ENTER to resolve them.

   Additional Information: When you type in the FacesContext line, a popup message will appear to prompt you to enter an import. If you press ALT-ENTER, a selection list will appear. Select the FacesContext class from this list. Repeat this action for the line that contains FacesMessage and select the FacesMessage class from the list.

```
FacesContext messageContext = FacesContext.getCurrentInstance();

String returnResult = "gohome";
loginAttempts++;

if (!passwordField.getValue().toString().equals("JSF"))
{
  returnResult = null;
  if (loginAttempts >= 3)
  {
    // message displayed in the FacesContext dialog
    messageContext.addMessage(null, new FacesMessage("You seem " +
        " to have forgotten that the password is \"JSF.\""));
  }
  else
  {
     messageContext.addMessage(null,
        new FacesMessage("Incorrect login. Try again."));
  }
}
else
{
  loginAttempts = 0;
  passwordField.setValue(null);
}

return returnResult;
```

NOTE
Files containing code snippets for all source code in this book are available at the websites mentioned in the section "Websites for Sample Files" in the Introduction.

6. In addition, outside of this and any other method (at the top of the class where the private variables are declared), declare the variable to hold the number of login attempts as follows:

   ```
   int loginAttempts = 0;
   ```

   Additional Information: We will explain how this code works a little later.

7. Select **Make** from the right-click menu in the Code Editor to compile the class file. Fix any syntax errors that the compiler finds.
8. Click Save All.
9. The variable that stores the number of login attempts, `loginAttempts`, needs to be incremented across multiple requests (command button clicks). The scope for the backing bean is set to "request" by default, but this would reset the value each time the page is submitted. You need to change this scope to "session." Select the Overview tab of the faces-config.xml file.

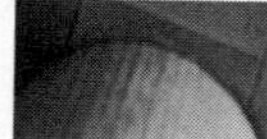

NOTE
Normally, backing beans are left at their default scope of "request." By convention, you would normally use a managed bean that is shared among pages to code functionality required across requests (application or session scopes). For simplicity in illustrating the concept of scope, this example sets the backing bean's scope directly and does not create a separate managed bean.

10. On the Managed Beans page, in the backing_login row, change the *Scope* pulldown to "session." This action resets the scope of the backing bean so that the login attempts counter will persist across requests.
11. Click Save All.
12. Select the Login.java backing bean file tab in the editor to examine the code you just entered. This block of code performs the following actions:
    - **Line 01** creates the context object that represents messages you will display.
    - **Line 03** declares and initializes a return object with the value "gohome." Returning this value will instruct the controller to forward to the Home page. The code reassigns this object to null if the validation fails. In that case, the controller will not forward to the home page.
    - **Line 04** increments the login counter variable, `loginAttempts`. This variable is retained throughout the user session but is reset to zero if a login attempt is successful (in line 23).
    - **Lines 06–15** run if the password is not "JSF." The `getValue()` method calls the getter method for the component's variable in the backing bean. For example, the value of the passwordField component is accessed in the Login.java backing bean using the `getPasswordField()` method, declared by the following method signature:

      ```
      public RichInputText getPasswordField()
      ```

      Notice that `getPasswordField()` returns a `RichInputText` type. However, the `getValue()` method that calls `getPasswordField()` returns an `Object` type.

To compare this `Object` type with a null string, you need to convert it to a string (using the `toString()` method available to all Objects). Finally, a null pointer exception can result from a comparison with a null string, so you need to use the `equals()` method to compare the value with the desired password. (If this Java expression seems complex, there is no need to worry; you will soon be able to construct expressions like this faster than you can explain them.)

- **Line 08** sets the return object to null if the password is not "JSF" so that the controller will not forward to the home page.
- **Lines 09–14** check if the user has attempted three or more logins. If so, a message is set into the context area in Lines 12–13 using `addMessage()`. This message shows the user the password (although you would never show a password in a real-world situation). The error message shows the user's correct password inside quotes; the backslash characters in the string escape the double quotes that follow, so they can appear as a literal inside the string delimited by double quotes. For example, "\"JSF.\"" will appear as "JSF." on the page.
- **Lines 15–19** are reached if the number of login attempts is fewer than three. This code sets a message indicating an unsuccessful login.
- **Lines 22–24** are reached if the password is correct ("JSF").
- **Line 23** resets the number of login attempts to zero in case the user returns to the login page to attempt another login.
- **Line 24** clears the password field in case the user returns to the login page. The password must be reentered each time the login page appears.
- **Line 27** returns the value that has been set in the logic before it. If all validation succeeds, the value will still be set to "gohome," which causes the controller to forward to the Home page. If any validation fails, the return value passed to the controller will be null and no page navigation will occur.

Test the Validation and Navigation Logic

This section tests the validation and navigation code you just created.

1. Before testing the login.jspx file again, be sure the faces-config.xml Diagram tab is active, and, on the login.jspx icon, select **Set as Default Run Target** from the right-click menu.

   Additional Information: This will set a property in web.xml that will cause the server to find login.jspx whenever a file other than a JSP file in the project is run. Notice that a green halo appears behind the login.jspx file symbol in the diagram, indicating that it is the default run target. Now, whenever you run any non-JSP file in the ViewController project, JDeveloper will automatically run login.jspx.

NOTE
The default run target adds or changes the value in a `welcome-file` tag in the web.xml file.

2. Press F11 to run the project or select **Run** from the right-click menu on the ViewController project node. (JDeveloper will automatically save all modified files when you run the application.) The login.jspx file will display. (If it does not, stop the application and server and try again.)

3. You have already tested the error alert that indicates whether either field is blank when you click Login, but you may test other combinations of null values if you wish.
4. Enter a user name. Enter a password other than "JSF." Click Login and the messages dialog will appear, indicating that the login is incorrect, as shown here:

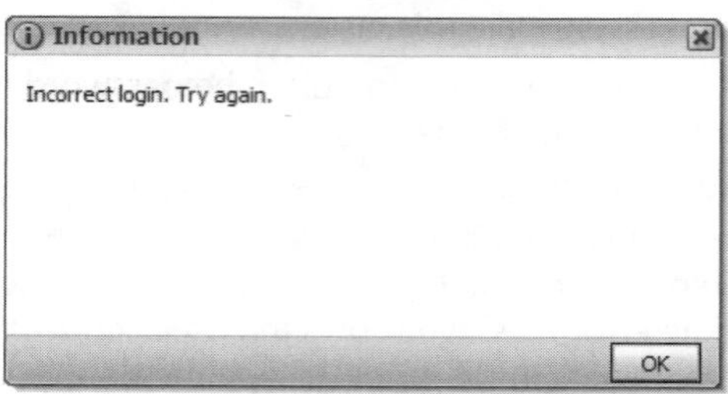

5. This dialog is not modal, but click OK to dismiss it. Then try logging in two more times without the correct password. The third unsuccessful login attempt will show a different message and display the required password. Dismiss the dialog.
6. Enter the password as "JSF" (using uppercase) and be sure the user name is still filled in. Click Login and the home page will load with a title containing the user's name.
7. Click Logout to return to the login page. The login page will reappear with no messages and no password (although the user name will be retained).
8. Close the browser. Stop the application.

What Did You Just Do? In this phase, you defined the page navigation from login to home and from home to login. Both navigation cases were triggered by button clicks. The former navigation case required validating the user name and password fields, and returning success if the values were valid; returning "gohome" caused the controller to follow the navigation case and forward to the home page. The logic returned null and displayed a message on the login page if the password was invalid.

The home page Logout button is connected to the navigation case "logout" through the *Action* property, and this navigation will occur regardless of data values. Therefore, clicking Logout will always redisplay the login page.

What Could You Do Next? Not all pages require backing bean code. You demonstrated this principle by disabling support for automatic backing bean updates from changes to home.jspx in the editor or Property Inspector. If you examine Home.java now, you will see the same code as before you started adding components to the page. You can prove the principle that backing beans are not always needed by deleting Home.java using the following steps:

1. Select the Home.java file in the Application Navigator and select **Refactor | Delete Safely**. You will see a dialog that indicates that file usages were found, which indicates this file is referenced by other files.
2. Click View Usages to display the dependent code in the Log window—faces-config.xml in this case. Double click the line of code in the Log window to navigate to that line in the file.

3. Remove the entire managed-bean section that references Home.java (five lines of code).
4. Select Home.java in the Application Navigator again and select **Refactor | Delete Safely** to delete the file. (Ignore any errors that do not point to another dependency.) Click Save All.
5. Run the ViewController project again.
6. You will find that the Login page runs. If the Home page also works, you can ignore the remaining steps except the last one to close everything.
7. If the Home page does not work, examine the server messages in the Log window; you may still see reference to "backing_home," so you will need to find that reference and remove it.
8. Select **Search | Find in Files** and specify a search within the ViewController project for "backing_home." You will see two references in the home.jspx file. Remove the *binding* attribute and its quoted value in both places referenced by the search results.
9. Run the project again. This time the application should work as designed.
10. Close the browser; stop the application; and stop the server.

A few more areas you can explore follow:

- **Support for wireless displays** You can build in support for other display devices, such as a wireless device. The Create JSF Page dialog contains a checkbox to include this support. You can then run the same application in the other devices. This demonstrates how specific render kits are activated to support special devices. To test this feature on your local computer, you need an emulator for the alternative device. Start your search for the required code and emulators on the www.oracle.com/technology JDeveloper home page.
- **Centralize messages** You can place messages shown to the user in all JSP pages inside a single text file instead of in the compiled code. The rest of this chapter explores this topic a bit more.

Centralize the Messages

JSF offers the ability to store *messages*—text such as prompts, errors and warnings, button labels, and tab labels as text strings inside a *message bundle* (also called a *resource bundle*), a Java file or properties file that contains key-value pairs defining the text displayed to users. You can access this file programmatically in the backing bean (or other Controller) code as well as declaratively within EL expressions. The benefits of message bundles are as follows:

- **They centralize messages** That way, you can change any message in the application by editing a single file.
- **They allow you to internationalize (localize) the application** You can create separate message bundle files for each language you need to support. Each message bundle would contain all messages used in the application translated into the local language. These language files share the same file name prefix and a suffix indicating the language. The JSF runtime engine retrieves the locale information from the browser's settings and uses the appropriate file to supply messages to the application.

- **They make it easy to replace default validation messages** The JSF framework allows you to code validators for each component by embedding a child tag—such as `<f:validateLength minimum="8" maximum="20">`—inside the opening and closing tags of the component (for example, `af:inputText`). This validator calls default functionality and displays a default error message under the component (such as a field). You can replace the default error message using message bundles. The sidebar "Using a Message Bundle for JSF Error Messages" describes this a bit more.

Hands-on Practice: Access a Message Bundle with EL

The simplest example of (and easiest way to work with) message bundle files uses Expression Language expressions in property values. This technique does not require writing Java code. You first register the message file with the project. Then you create expressions in EL that reference the text and, at the same time, create the message tokens in the message bundle file. The following steps demonstrate how this method works starting with the application you developed in the first hands-on practice of this chapter.

1. Double click ViewController in the Application Navigator and select the Resource Bundle page as shown in the following illustration. Be sure the *One Bundle Per Project* radio button is selected and change *Default Project Bundle Name* to "login.resources.LoginJSF."

   Additional Information: These settings indicate the location and name of the file you will use to contain messages.

Using a Message Bundle for JSF Error Messages

Default JSF messages are not completely user-friendly. For example, the standard JSF message for a required field (and InputText component with the *Required* property set to "true"), which the user has left blank, is "Validation Error: Value is required." This message does not indicate the problem field name, and the wording may not be as descriptive as you might like.

To replace messages such as these, you create entries with predefined names (keys) in the message bundle file. For example, naming the message "javax.faces.component.UIInput.REQUIRED" will cause the JSF runtime to replace the default error message for required text with whatever you have assigned to that message. You can find the JSF error message names in an article on java.sun.com; search for the tutorial "Customizing a Standard Validator Message" (with or without quotes). This technique will only redefine the default message that the framework provides. The hands-on practice at the end of this chapter shows how to programmatically insert messages into the `FacesContext` object so they can be displayed as part of the page processing.

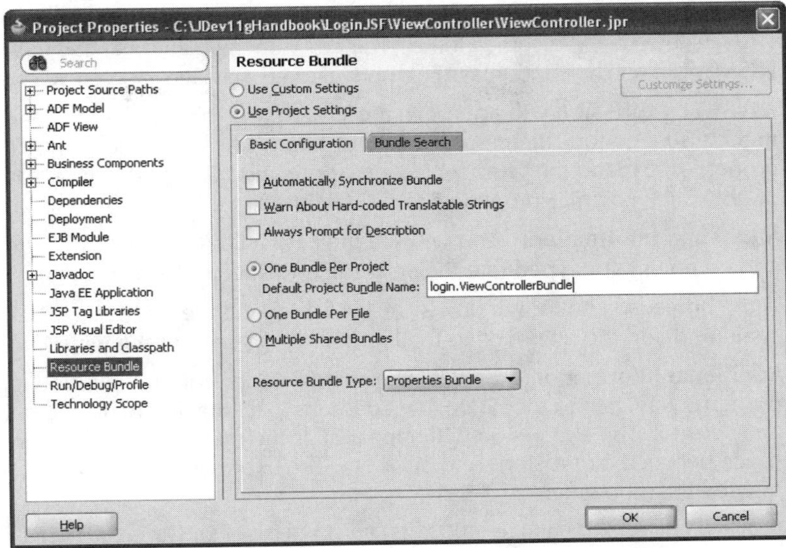

2. Be sure the *Resource Bundle Type* is "Properties Bundle" and click OK. If a confirmation dialog appears with a warning about renaming keys, click Yes.
3. In the Design tab of the home.jspx file, select the `af:outputText` component. In the Property Inspector, select Select Text Resource from the pulldown in the *Value* property. The following dialog will appear:

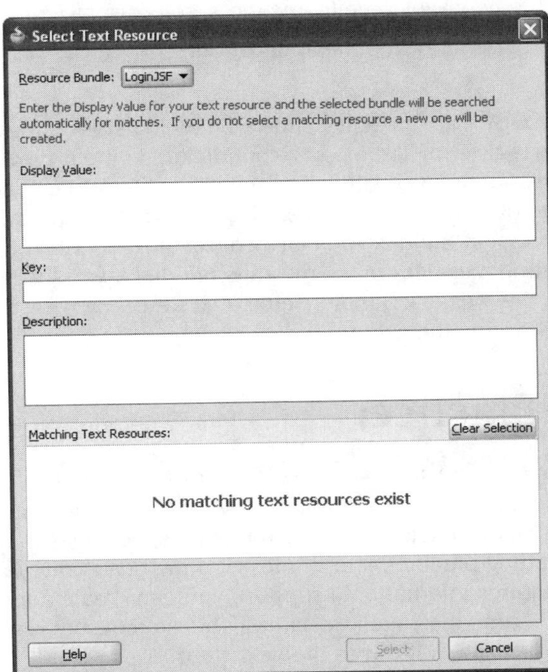

4. Notice that the LoginJSF resource bundle name appears in the top of this dialog. Enter *Display Value* as "Welcome Home." The *Key* value will automatically fill in as "WELCOME_HOME." Fill in Description as "English welcome message" and click Save and Select.
5. A new EL expression will appear in the *Value* property and the message will be displayed in the visual editor. The message you just set up was written to a new file, LoginJSF.properties. Expand the ViewController\Application Sources\login.resources nodes and double click LoginJSF.properties to display it in the editor.

   Additional Information: You will see the key, WELCOME_HOME, and the message text and comment you typed into the Select Text Resource dialog.
6. In the home.jspx editor window's Design tab, select the `af:outputText` component again and add the reference to the login name again after the welcome message.

   Additional Information: Select Expression Builder from the pulldown in the *Value* property. Navigate to the JSF Managed Beans\backing_login\usernameField\value node and select it. The expression will appear after the message bundle expression. Type a space between expressions and click OK. The expression in the *Value* property should now be the following:

   ```
   #{viewcontrollerBundle.WELCOME_HOME} #{backing_login.usernameField.value}
   ```
7. The message bundle message is available in the Expression Builder as well. To verify how this works, open the Expression Builder (from the pulldown next to the *Value* property) and navigate to JSP Objects. (It is not a managed bean and so it will not appear under the JSF Managed Beans node.) You will see a node for viewcontrollerBundle and under it, your message. Click Cancel.
8. Click Save All. Run the application. Test successful navigation to the Home page and verify that the new Welcome Home message is displayed correctly.
9. Close the browser and stop the application.

What Did You Just Do? This practice showed how to access a message bundle message using an EL expression by registering the message bundle file in the project properties and then composing an expression to access the message in the file. You can add messages directly to the message file (instead of using the Select Text Resource dialog) and those messages will be available in the Expression Builder. You can also use the Select Text Resource dialog to create expressions for existing messages in the message bundle. If you just want to construct EL for an existing message in the message bundle, Select Text Resource is easier because you don't need to navigate a hierarchy to find the value.

Hands-on Practice: Access a Message Bundle with Java

You can try out the concept of programmatically referring to message bundle messages by using the code in this hands-on practice. This example adds messages to the message bundle you created in the preceding practice. It also adds backing bean code to extract the messages. If your application requires international support, you can create additional message files in the same way, using the same message key names. The exercise of creating additional files is left to you, but it follows the same pattern as the next steps.

This example will demonstrate how to use the properties (text) file you just created containing key-value pairs for the message. Alternatively, you can create a Java file that loads key-value pairs into a collection object. The last option is to create an *XML Localization Interchange File Format (XLIFF)* file, which also contains key-value pairs and can also be localized, but which is formatted in XML.

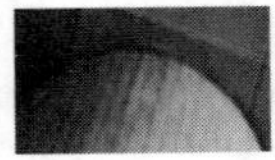

NOTE
The JDeveloper Help Center topic "Internationalizing and Localizing Pages" describes more about the options and techniques for changing messages based on the user's language.

1. In the Application Navigator, double click the LoginJSF.properties file under ViewController\Application Sources\login.resources. The file will open in the editor. Add the following lines of code at the end of the file:

```
# login attempt messages
incorrectLogin=Incorrect login. Try again.
loginHint=You seem to have forgotten that the password is "JSF."
```

2. Lines starting with "#" are comment lines. Click Save All.
3. You can now add code to read these messages. You need to add an object that represents the contents of the message bundle file. Then you can programmatically reference specific messages from that bundle. Open Login.java in the editor.
4. In the `loginButton_action()` method, in the blank line under the declaration of `messageContext` (Line 01 in the preceding listing), add the following code:

```
ResourceBundle messageBundle = ResourceBundle.getBundle(
          "login.resources.LoginJSF",
          messageContext.getViewRoot().getLocale());
```

   Additional Information: This statement declares a message bundle object of type `ResourceBundle`. It references the LoginJSF.properties file you just created in the login.resources directory and specifies that you need to obtain the locale from the context area. (Notice that you do not need to enter the file extension ".properties.") The context area stores information about the session, including the user's preferred language. *Locale* specifies a language and includes the concept that a language may be used in one way by a certain region and in another way by another region. For example, the English language can be used in UK or U.S. forms, and that form (the region) would be stored as a user preference available to the browser. Message bundle files can use a locale suffix of language (for example, LoginJSF_en.properties) or a locale suffix of both language and region (for example, LoginJSF_en_us.properties). If your application only offers one message file, that file will be used regardless of the user's locale preference.

5. A wavy red line will appear under `ResourceBundle`. Press ALT-ENTER and select the ResourceBundle class to add the proper import.

   Additional Information: JDeveloper will usually automatically insert imports to resolve the class names. This behavior is defined by selecting the Code Insight property, *Automatically Add Import When Completing a Fully-Qualified Class Name* in the Preferences dialog page Code Editor\Java\Code Insight (**Tools** | **Preferences**). If JDeveloper does not automatically resolve the class name imports, hold the cursor over the class name and press ALT-ENTER to add the import (for example, `java.util.ResourceBundle`).

6. Replace the `addMessage()` call for the message that displays the "JSF" password (Lines 12 and 13 in the preceding listing) with the following:

```
messageContext.addMessage(null, new FacesMessage(messageBundle.
  getString("loginHint")));
```

   Additional Information: This code refers to the loginHint key in the message bundle file (the file is now represented as the messageBundle object in the code).

7. Replace the `addMessage()` call that indicates to the user to try again (Lines 17 and 18 in the preceding listing) with this:

```
messageContext.addMessage(null, new FacesMessage(messageBundle.
  getString("incorrectLogin")));
```

8. Click Save All.

9. Run the application and login incorrectly to see the two login error messages stored in the message bundle file.

   Additional Information: If you would like more practice with this concept, work on replacing the "Home" and "Enter Login Information" strings with text in the LoginJSF .properties file.

10. Close the browser, stop the application, and stop the server process.

What Did You Just Do? This practice showed how to create a message bundle file and access its messages in a backing bean Java file. Programmatic access is a handy feature, but the EL method described in the preceding hands-on practice is much easier and quicker if you just need a message for a property value.

CHAPTER 11

The ADF Controller and Task Flows

We herd sheep, we drive cattle, we lead people.
Lead me, follow me, or get out of my way.

—George S. Patton (1885–1945)

The *ADF Controller (ADFc)* is one of the most important new features of the ADF Framework introduced with 11*g* and a key part of any Fusion technology based application. Unlike other major parts of the framework, such as ADF BC, the ADF Controller is a totally new feature, although it will have some familiar concepts and features for developers that have built applications in Apache Struts or JavaServer Faces in the past. The key artifact that the controller introduces into the framework is a *task flow*, which is the metadata that the developer creates to configure the controller's operation.

This chapter provides an overview of the key concepts and features of the ADF Controller that most developers will need for the creation of Fusion-style applications. In the course of this introduction to the feature, we'll cover the following questions:

- **What is the ADF Controller and why is it needed?**
- **Why are task flows needed?**
- **What are the different types of task flows?**
- **How can I reuse task flows?**
- **How can I debug a task flow?**

What Is the ADF Controller and Why Is It Needed?

The concept behind the ADF Controller and the task flows it uses is very simple: at its core, it is a page flow controller—it fulfills the controller function within the Model-View-Controller design pattern. Applications use the controller as a way to abstract navigation through the application, the programmer will cause the application to raise an event such as "NextPage," and the controller is in charge of working out what that actually means. The controller will map the event to a physical page and then perform the navigation to it, on the behalf of the calling page. The benefit of this controller mechanism is that pages do not have those hard-coded relationships, making them reusable and simplifying maintenance should a change be required in the navigation sequence or the name of a page.

Basic page flow is a core feature of ADFc, but it is nothing new. As we saw briefly in Chapter 9, JSF already has navigation metadata for basic page flow that can be defined within the faces-config.xml file, and JDeveloper even provides a diagram to make the creation of page flows as simple as possible. So why does ADF need something different for Fusion?

The Problem with JSF

In many ways, it seems like controller functionality was tacked onto the JSF standard as an afterthought. JSF is all about creating user interfaces for web pages and needed some way of stringing a sequence of pages together. The default controller functionality supplied within JSF only handles that basic task. The existing navigation functionality provided by JSF is sufficient for the needs of basic applications; however, it is severely challenged when faced with the requirements of modern rich UIs for a variety of reasons:

- **Core JSF Navigation is all about whole pages** Within a modern Ajax web application, much more activity is going to happen within a single page. To a user's perception, the experience of using an application changes from the function–per–page view of a traditional stateless web application to something much more like a desktop application. They will see the shell of the application staying as a static frame and content within different areas of the screen changing as they interact with it. For this to be possible, subsets of UI smaller than pages—*page fragments*—have to be used.
- **It's not just pages** Core JSF navigation only has two concepts; views (pages) and navigation cases that wire them together. In reality more than that is needed; for example, what if code must be called to set up some data context before navigating to a page? What if the page flow navigation needs to be conditionally branched? Both of these use cases are possible using JSF, but they have to be handled either by putting that logic into the page's code itself or by extending and overriding parts of JSF for your application. They are not handled as out-of-the-box capabilities of the controller.
- **Reuse of pages** Although one of the key features for a controller is to allow a page to be isolated from its peers by abstracting navigation, JSF does not really deliver true page reusability. The JSF navigation metadata does not provide any way of defining a page to be used in multiple contexts within the application. So, as in the flow control case, logic to handle reuse has to be coded into the page itself, rather than being expressed in a declarative fashion. As an example, if you wanted to use a page as a List of Values, that could be called from several other pages, you would be responsible for coding the logic required to work out, in each instance, which page called the LOV and how data should get passed back.
- **Reuse of flows** JSF has a monolithic controller model. You can actually define many faces-config.xml files for an application; however, at runtime, the navigation models for all of them are combined into one large flat, navigation map. There is no concept of being able to define page flows that can be reusable in different parts of the application or in multiple applications, or of being able to nest flows recursively. Much of the ADF Controller functionality is shaped by having to address this reuse problem.

Fortunately, one thing that the JSF standard specification does very well is to define a comprehensive set of extension points to allow the framework to be enhanced with extra functionality. ADF takes advantage of this and allows the users to (optionally) use ADFc as a replacement controller.

With ADFc in the picture, all of these reuse and navigation scenarios are easy to handle. Additionally, the integration with JSF, as a whole, is so seamless that switching between basic JSF navigation and task flow is a simple task even for experienced JSF programmers used to working with the existing controller. When building a Fusion application, you should always use the ADF Controller.

Creating a Task Flow Definition

If you have created an application using the *Fusion Web Application (ADF)* template from the New Gallery, JDeveloper will have already created a task flow definition file for you. A file called adfc-config.xml will have been pre-created in the ViewController project's /WEB-INF/ directory.

Notice that there is still a faces-config.xml file as well in the same directory, and recall from Chapter 9 that the faces-config.xml file configures a JSF application with its navigation rules and managed beans. Although JSF's default navigation mechanism is not used within a Fusion application, the faces-config.xml file may still be required for a limited set of other JSF-related functions such as defining global resource bundles and data type converters.

TIP
When a task flow is present in a project, the Application navigator will show an additional node labeled as "Page flows" under the Web Content node for that project. This folder in the navigator shows shortcuts to any task flow definition files in the project, so you can either edit the files from here or expand the WEB-INF directory to locate them.

If the Fusion Web Application template was not used to create the application, a project can still be enabled for task flows by adding the *ADF Page Flow* technology scope in the project properties.

The adfc-config.xml file is directly analogous to the JSF faces-config.xml file and defines the unbounded task flow for the application. We will discuss the different types of task flow, including unbounded task flows, later in the chapter. If you double click this configuration file in the Application Navigator, it will open into a diagram view by default. Like most of the editors in JDeveloper, the task flow editor has multiple pages or views, as shown in Figure 11-1, plus a Component Palette. As with the other diagrams in the IDE, a thumbnail view of the diagram is also available to help navigation around large page flows.

As you would expect, the available editor views for task flows are accessed using the tabs that are displayed at the bottom of the panel. The default view is the diagram editor, which, just like the diagram for the faces-config.xml file, provides a drag-and-drop surface to lay out the task flow. You can see, however, that unlike the diagram for JSF navigation flow, the Component Palette has a larger set of elements than just pages, as we explore in the next section.

In addition to the diagram view, the editor also exposes a Source view for editing the XML metadata directly, and an Overview view that provides a structured window onto that metadata and the history view.

About Task Flows and Managed Beans

Just as the faces-config.xml file encodes information in addition to the actual navigation rules, the same is true for task flow definitions. Each task flow can include managed bean definitions using exactly the same metadata format as the faces-config.xml definitions. What is interesting about the ADF Controller is that it brings three extra bean storage scopes to the table. Conventional JSF applications allow managed beans to be defined (stored at) Application, Session, None, or Request level/scope. The ADF Controller provides the following additional scopes:

- pageFlow
- view
- backingBean

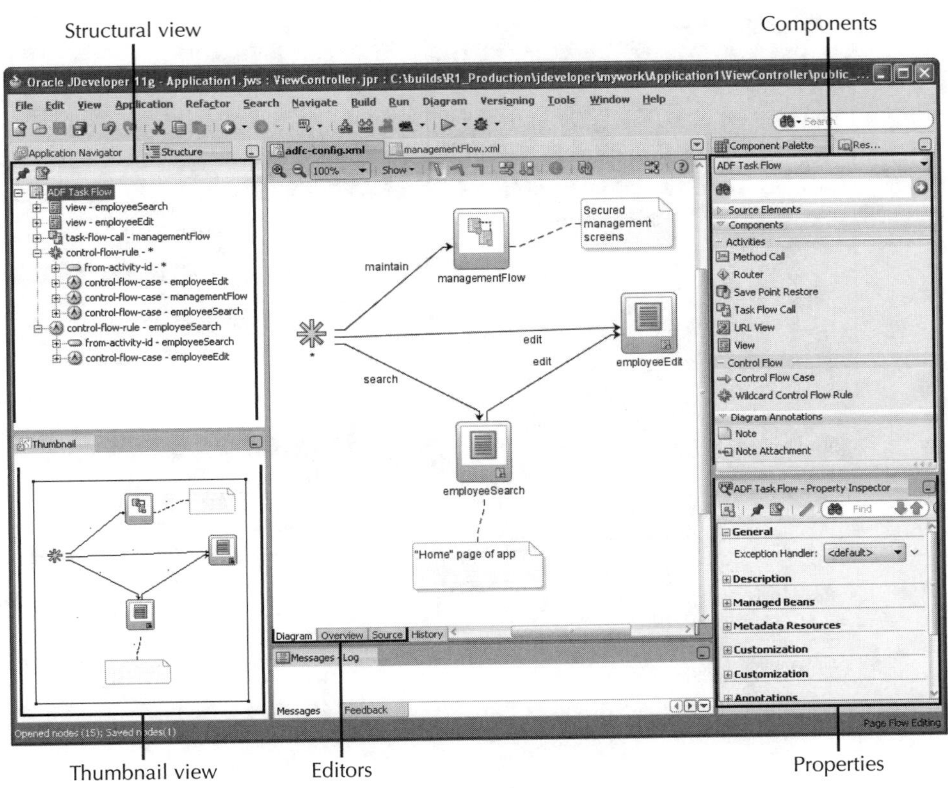

FIGURE 11-1. *Task flows in the JDeveloper IDE*

About pageFlow Scope The rather confusingly named *pageFlow scope* is the key memory scope used in task flows. The name here is somewhat historical, and although "taskFlow" might have been a more accurate name for the memory scope, we have to live with pageFlow instead. The memory area defined by this scope is private to each instance of a task flow and lives as long as that task flow, or one of its children, is active. What's more, if an application is running with more than one instance of the same task flow, each will have its own private version of pageFlow scope. This allows recursive calls to a task flow by ensuring that multiple copies of the flow do not corrupt each other's data. The pageFlow scope is one of the key enhancements provided by ADFc over the default JSF state management model, and it is one of the core elements needed to address the reusability constraints of JSF. Figure 11-2 shows the definition of a pageFlow scope managed bean through the overview panel of the task flow editor.

NOTE

In the overview editor for task flows shown in Figure 11-2 several other subtabs are available. Activities and control flows are covered next, and we'll get to the more advanced topics of Parameters and Behaviors a little later in the chapter.

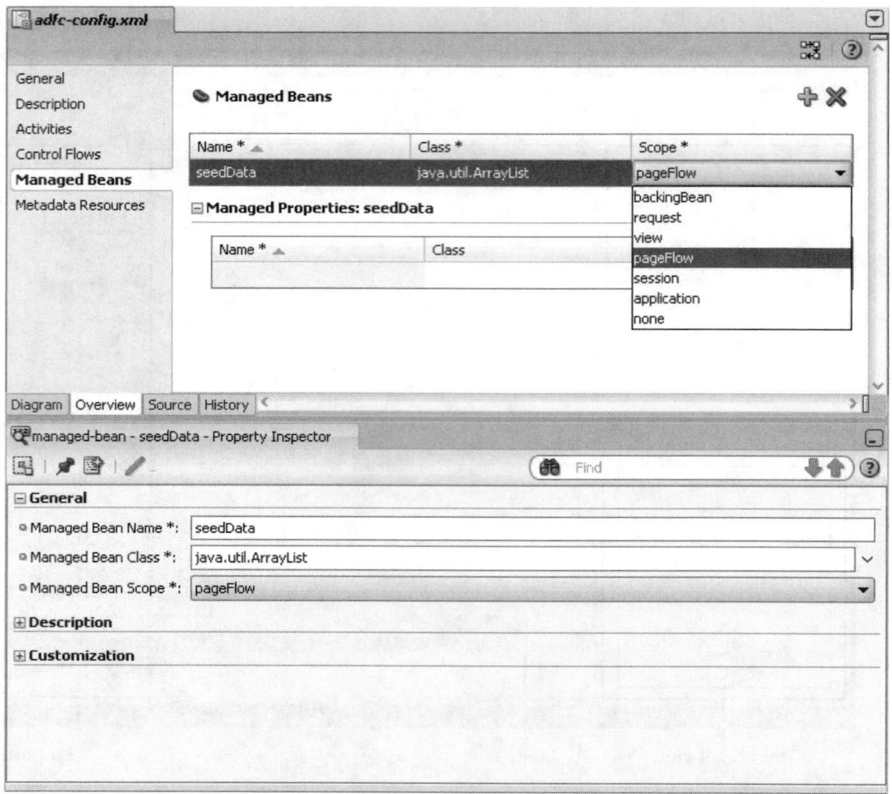

FIGURE 11-2. *Defining a managed bean*

When using pageFlow scope managed beans in expression language, you must use the `#{pageFlowScope...}` prefix. JSF will not automatically search in any of the custom ADFc scopes if only provided with the name of a managed bean, so always ensure that the scope qualifier is specified.

About View Scope Because ADFc allows the programmer to call the same task flow recursively and, as we will see later, combine multiple task flows onto the same page, even the addition of pageFlow scope is not enough. Many applications need to have a way of storing information just for use in the context of the current page. Conventionally, the JSF Request scope is used for this purpose. The required data hangs around for the duration of the current HTTP Request and is then discarded. However, this is limited in two respects: First, the request may end but the user is on the same page, and this can catch programmers out because the previous contents of the request scope are now gone. Second, with ADFc, as we will see, pages may be composed of many page fragments. The programmer may need to maintain state for the lifetime of each of these mini-pages, and each needs to be sandboxed and have different lifespan durations.

The new *view scope* provides exactly this functionality. Any state stored in the view scope of a particular task flow will persist from the moment it is first referenced until the view activity (page or page fragment) changes. This also means that if other tasks such as method calls take place between the user leaving the first page and entering the second page, the stored view scope state will still be available up until the moment that the second page is invoked.

When using view scope managed beans in expression language, you must use the `#{viewScope...}` prefix.

About backingBean Scope The final extra scope introduced by the controller is *backingBean* scope. Again, don't be fooled by the name. You might expect that backingBean scope is the scope that you would used to hold the so-called backing beans or page-specific managed beans; however, a programmer should generally use the viewScope for that specific task. The backingBean scope covers a very specific use case where two or more instances of a particular managed bean may be present in the same page. Usually, JSF will ensure that within a particular scope, if a managed bean is named, every consumer will share the same object. This is generally the desirable behavior. However, when you are building some types of reusable components (such as the ADF Faces Declarative Components), you will want each to have its own state rather than automatically picking up some shared data. Imagine, for example, a declarative component in a table column. Although at design time you only create one component on the screen, at runtime one instance will be created for every displayed row and you will not want them to get the data mixed up between rows!

When using backingBean scope managed beans in expression language, you must use the `#{backingBeanScope...}` prefix.

Task Flow Components

The Component Palette shown in Figure 11-1 shows some components listed under *Activities* and some under *Control Flow*. There are also facilities for attaching documentation to the task flow diagram in the form of annotations. The annotations and attachments are identical to those available in all of the other diagrams in JDeveloper.

Notice that the Component Palette also has an accordion (section) labeled as Source Elements. This sub-panel on the palette exposes all of the XML elements available for use in the task flow directly. You will only ever need to use this view of the components when interacting with the source code directly or building up the configuration file using the Structure window. Both of these approaches require some expertise to get right and should be avoided until the developer is comfortable with the underlying metadata of the configuration file. So, for now, keep that accordion pane collapsed to prevent confusion.

Looking at the available components classified as *activities* and *control flow* in the main Components accordion pane, you can see these components:

- **Method Call** Provides a way to execute code within the flow.
- **Router** Provides a way to branch the flow based on some declarative condition.
- **Save Point Restore** Part of an advanced feature that allows the developer to take a snapshot of, and then later restore, application state at a specific point in the flow.
- **Task Flow Call** Allows a task flow to be called from this task flow.
- **URL View** Provides a way to reach out of the flow and potentially out of the web application to some arbitrary URL such as http://www.oracle.com.
- **View** Is the most commonly used activity type and of course allows the display of a page or page fragment.

- **Control Flow Case** Defines the actual flow between two activities. This is similar to a navigation case exposed by the default JSF navigation engine.
- **Wildcard Control Flow Rule** Provides a way to define an origin for one or more global control flow cases that are shared by, and available from, multiple activities on the diagram.

Save point restore is discussed toward the end of the chapter, in the section "Advanced Task Flows." The other components are explained in more detail next in the order in which they will generally be encountered. In this section we will discuss the use of the components in conjunction with a task flow diagram. However, remember that alternatively, developers can use the source code view, the Structure window, the Overview pane of the task flow, or any combination of these to create activities for the task flow. We encourage you to explore these different views on the metadata as you go along so that you can become familiar with the relationship between the diagram's visualization and the underlying XML. Over time, you will probably find yourself spending more time in the XML source code view for certain tasks and it's perfectly okay to mix and match your development style in that way.

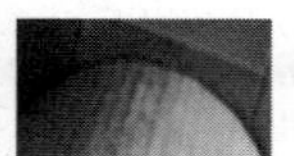

NOTE
There are two additional task flow activities not present in the preceding list: Task Flow Return *and* Parent Action. *These activities are specific to a subtype of task flow called a bounded task flow and are discussed in that section of the chapter.*

View

View activities correspond to pages (or as we will see later, fragments of pages) and, as such, are the most widely used of the activity types. When the flow transitions to a view activity, the requested UI is displayed and the flow will stop until the user carries out some action to cause the next navigation in the flow.

View activities can be created on the diagram in two ways, either by dragging the view activity onto the diagram from the Component Palette, or by dragging an existing JSF page, or page fragment, from the Application Navigator onto the diagram. In the former case the new activity will be given a default name, for example *view1,* and will be marked with a warning icon. This icon is there to remind the developer that although the activity is now in the flow, it is not fully defined because it has yet to be associated with an actual page to display.

The normal action for the developer at this point would be to double click the view activity in the diagram, which will take them through the process of creating a new JSF page associated with the activity. If the page already exists in the application, rather than double clicking the icon, the Property Inspector can be used to select the page that this view activity displays. This is one of the mechanisms for reusing the same physical page in multiple ways on the same task flow.

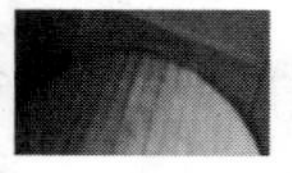

TIP
The name of the page pointed to by the view activity and the name of the view activity itself do not have to be the same. The purpose of the controller is to provide an abstraction between the physical page and its use, so that later on the page can be moved or renamed without the overall flow having to be changed. If you use JDeveloper to rename (refactor) a page, then it will take care of updating any task flow definitions with the new name for you.

If a view activity is created by dragging and dropping a page from the Application Navigator, then the resulting activity is already wired up to that page and will not show the warning icon. The name for the new view activity will be based on the name of the page that was dragged, although in all cases you can click the name in the diagram to change it, or use the Property Inspector to change the *id* property of the activity—which will in turn update the label on the diagram. A page can be dragged into the diagram several times to allow its reuse in different contexts; in each case a unique default name will be generated for the view activity.

Once a view activity is defined on the diagram, it is ready to run; just choose **Run** or **Debug** from the right-click menu.

TIP

Because a page can be reused in several different task flows throughout the application, it is a good idea always to run the page from the icon in the task flow that you are testing, rather than by using the right-click menu and choosing Run or Debug on the page JSP(X) file itself. This way, the context in which you want to run the page is unambiguous.

There is a bit more to view activities than simply pointing to a JSF file. View activities have additional metadata that can be defined to further refine their behavior. All of these capabilities are exposed through the Property Inspector as shown in Figure 11-3.

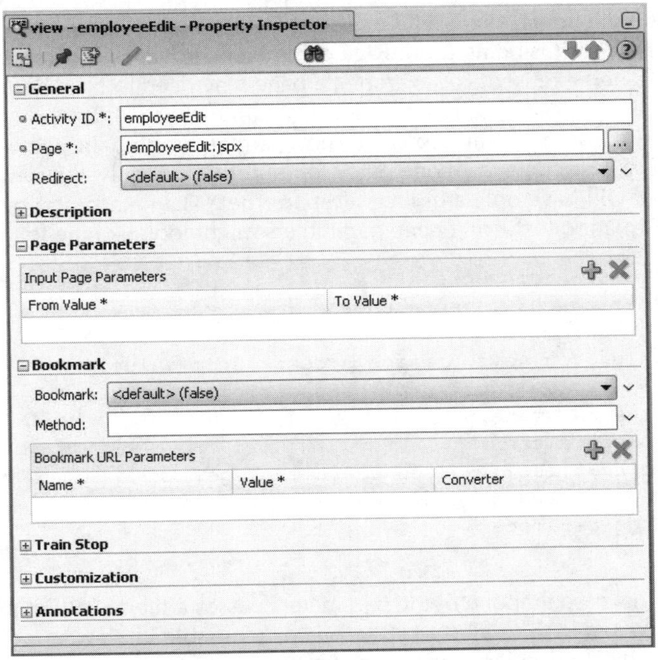

FIGURE 11-3. *The Property Inspector for a task flow view activity*

The Redirect Property By default, controllers such as Apache Struts, JSF, and ADFc use a mechanism called *forwarding* to display a new page to the user. When a controller forwards between pages, the one thing that the end user might notice is that the URL shown in the browser address bar does not change. Basically, the browser is unaware that a different physical page is being displayed. The behavior has some implications, both good and bad. On the positive side, this is the most efficient way for the application to operate, and this is why all of the controllers do it. On the negative side, users are sometimes confused by the content of the screen changing but the URL staying the same. This lack of a direct relationship between the URL and the page also has implications for both bookmarking and security (when the security mechanism is based on matching URL patterns, as is the case for basic Java EE security).

The view activity has a mechanism in the *redirect* property, which is exposed as a true/false dropdown list in the General section of the Property Inspector, as shown in Figure 11-3. The default value is false, but if set to true, then the controller will tell the browser to construct and GET a new URL for this view activity. Setting the property will meet user expectation and cause the URL to change as the user navigates to this page; however, there are two side effects to consider: First of all, an extra network round-trip will be required to manage the GET request from the browser, and second, the ADF Binding Context for the request (discussed in Chapter 14) will be destroyed and rebuilt for the new page. This could result in certain data being unavailable for mapping into page parameters.

We will see, later in the chapter, how ADF implements an alternative mechanism for bookmarking, and later, in Chapter 21, for security, so there is little reason to actually set this flag.

Page Parameters The next interesting section in the Property Inspector for view activities is the Page Parameters section. As task flow allows the developer to reuse a page in multiple places in a flow (or in multiple flows), it is useful to be able to configure that page in some way that reflects the context in which it is being used. Page parameters provide a basic API mechanism for the page when it is being reused. For example, a page may need to have different titles, depending upon the context in which it is being used. Page parameters can be used to pass in a value to be used for this. The *from-value* and *to-value* shown in the Property Inspector in Figure 11-3 both use EL expressions to map data from one place to another. Generally, the *to-value* will be a variable in viewScope that will have only a limited lifespan. The XML metadata to set a dynamic page title and some information text using page parameters might look like the following snippet:

```
<view id="accessWarningScreen">
  <page>/genericWarning.jspx</page>
  <input-page-parameter>
    <from-value>You Have Limited Access</from-value>
    <to-value>#{viewScope.infoPageHeaderText}</to-value>
  </input-page-parameter>
  <input-page-parameter>
    <from-value>#{res['reducedAccess.messageText']}</from-value>
    <to-value>#{viewScope.infoPageMsg}</to-value>
  </input-page-parameter>
</view>
```

Notice in this case that one of the parameters passes a literal value "You Have Limited Access" to be stored in the `infoPageHeaderText` variable in viewScope, and the second parameter uses expression language to read a string from a resource bundle to populate the `infoPageMsg` variable.

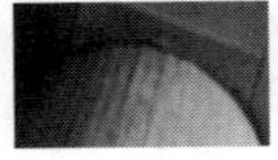

NOTE
Page Parameters provide a degree of limited flexibility to allow page reuse, but there is no provision for more complex activities such as running a variable piece of code before the page is displayed. Bounded task flows, which we discuss later, do provide that more sophisticated reuse capability and are the more common reuse mechanism.

Bookmarking In our discussion on the *redirect* property, bookmarking was mentioned as one of the reasons for wanting the URL to change in the browser. In reality, having a bookmarkable page will involve more than just the pointer to the correct page, which is the only capability provided by the redirect flag. In most cases you want to be able to bookmark a page "in context," that is, have a way to navigate to the page and restore the same set of data that you were viewing when you saved the reference to the page. This is also a requirement for systems that need to generate so called *deep links* to pages to include in an email message. We have all seen examples of this in online shopping and travel systems where details of your order or trip are mailed to you and a simple click on the hyperlink in the email takes you directly into a summary screen for it. For applications such as this, the URL that is presented to the user has to encode not only the correct page, but also enough information to identify the user and the topic.

The bookmarking-related properties of the view activity, as shown in Figure 11-3, are:

- **Bookmark** A Boolean value to indicate that the page should be bookmarkable.
- **Method** Will be set to an EL reference to a method that is used to process any data passed in from the bookmark URL to set up the correct context for the page. For example, this method property might be bound to the `executeWithParams()` method exposed by a View Object. This would allow the arguments passed on the URL to be mapped directly into bind variables used by the View Object query.
- **URL Parameters** A bookmarkable page will generally have one or more parameters that will encode the information required to reconstruct the page. Each parameter has a name that will be used on the URL, and a value. The value property of the parameter should be an EL expression that will be used in read-write mode. When the page is displayed and the URL constructed, the value expression will be evaluated into a string and encoded into the URL. Conversely, when a bookmark is used to restore a page, the value passed in the named parameter will be injected into the managed bean defined by the value expression.

  Finally, each of the parameters can have a converter defined. The converter is another EL value reference that points to a class that implements the ADFc `UrlParameterConverter` interface. All URL parameters are Strings, and so the converter can be used to manage the transformation from a string form to some other data type. For example, a parameter value such as "coords=10,25" might be transformed into a Coordinate object with separate attributes for x and y values (longitude=10, latitude=25). For a full example of the code required to do this, see the later section "URL View" in this chapter. A URL view activity uses the same encoding/decoding methodology.

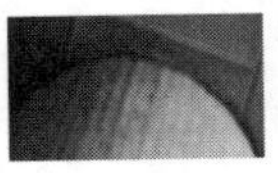

NOTE
The bookmark property and the redirect property are mutually exclusive. In addition, like redirect, the bookmark property only applies to view activities that display pages, not page fragments.

Train Stops View activities can be used in wizard-style user interfaces called *trains,* in which the user steps through a sequence of activities in a particular order. Trains are discussed in some detail later in the chapter, and the train-specific view activity properties are covered here.

Method Call

As a task flow encounters a method call activity, it will execute the code that the method call activity is linked to. Expression language is used to associate the activity with a method in a managed bean, or to a method exposed through the ADF Bindings mechanism that we will cover in detail in Chapter 14. For example, a very common use case within a task flow is to want to create a new empty record before navigating to a page to edit that record. The task flow to do this is shown here.

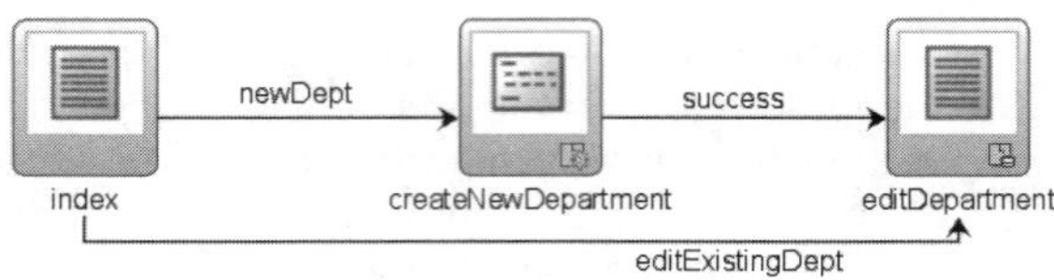

In this case, the method call activity createNewDepartment is bound to the Create operation of the view object instance in question. This is achieved by dropping an empty method call activity onto the diagram, and then dragging the CreateInsert operation from the Data Controls panel and dropping it on top of the new activity. This process will automatically wire up the activity, resulting in a set of properties for the activity as shown in Figure 11-4.

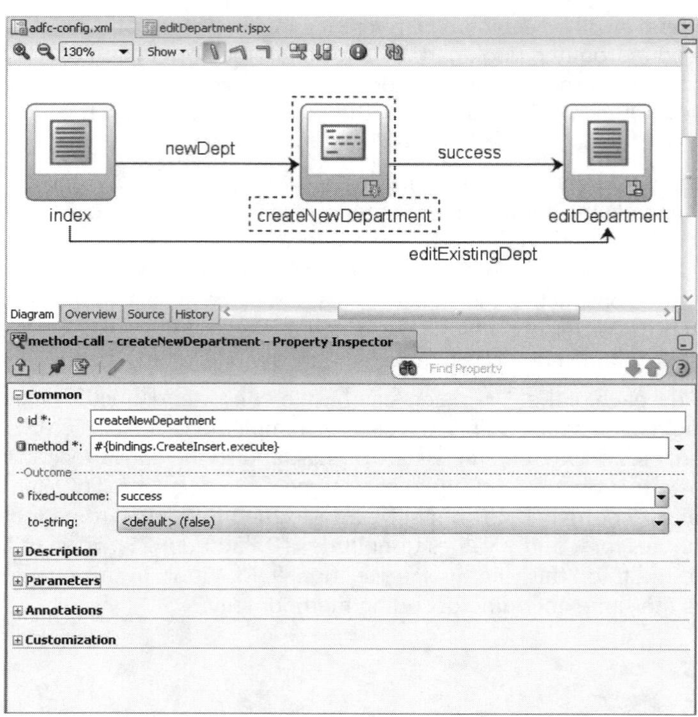

FIGURE 11-4. *Properties for a data-bound method call activity*

The methods that are invoked from a method call activity can have any signature, but the way in which parameters are passed to that method will differ, depending on if the method is just an arbitrary managed bean method, or if it is a data-bound method exposed through the data control.

Calling Managed Bean Methods With an ad hoc method defined within some managed bean, the method is associated with the activity by using the EL picker on the method property, or by entering the expression directly. Any arguments that the method requires are defined through the activity *Parameters* property in the overview editor.

Likewise, as is shown in the *return-value* property in Figure 11-5, any return value from the method call can also be stored for further use using an EL expression.

Calling Data Bound Methods As discussed earlier, methods exposed through data binding can be associated with a method call activity by dragging and dropping that method or operation onto the diagram. If the method concerned has one or more arguments, these are not set using the method call activity parameters. Instead, the arguments are passed via the method binding definition in binding metadata. This is consistent with the way that parameters will be passed when the same service method is bound to a UI widget in a page. This topic is covered in detail in Chapter 14.

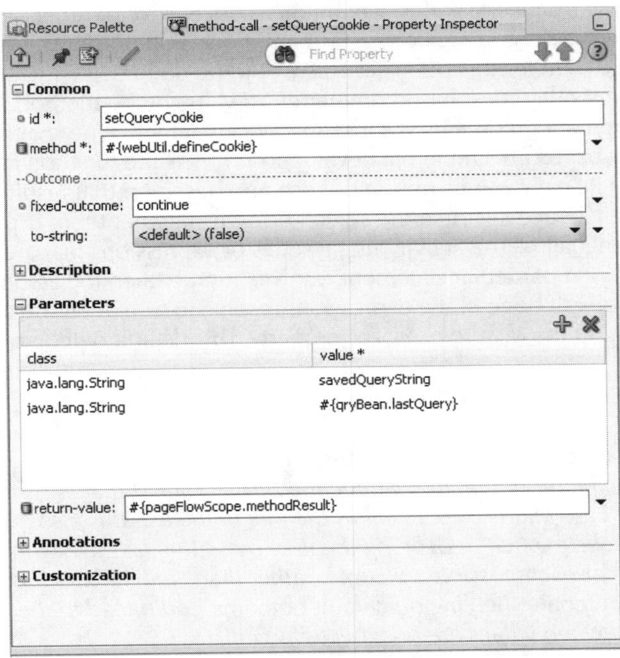

FIGURE 11-5. *Setting parameters for a method call activity*

Managing the Outcome of a Method Call Activity Methods that are called from a method call activity can, as shown in Figure 11-5, have a return value. There is no particular signature required, but if the value that is returned can be converted into a `String`, then that `String` result can be used as an outcome to control subsequent navigation. This behavior is controlled by the Boolean property *to-string* on the method call activity itself.

If the method does not return a value, or it does not return a value that can be converted to a string, or if you simply don't care about using that value to control the outcome, then the *fixed-outcome* property can be used instead of *to-string*. Using *fixed-outcome,* the navigation is essentially hard-coded. In the example used in Figure 11-5, such a fixed outcome of "continue" is used.

NOTE

As in the case of parameters to a method call activity, the return-value *property is only used for methods accessed out of managed beans. Data-bound service methods use the pageDef file to manage the storage of return values in the same way that the arguments to those same methods are handled.*

Router

It is not uncommon within a task flow to want to make portions of the flow conditional. This can be useful to allow a single task flow definition to cover several related use cases, or it may be that a single use case is complex enough to need decision points and branching. A method call activity could be used for this purpose. This would be done by taking advantage of the *to-string* property to switch outcomes, based on the return value of the method. However, this is such a common requirement that it makes sense to have an activity type specifically for this job of routing the flow based on simple data evaluation. This is the function of a router activity. It is able to evaluate EL expressions to true or false and based on that result direct the flow.

A router activity acts just like the switch or case statement that is present in many programming languages. The activity lists a series of expressions that are evaluated in the order that they appear. If a particular statement resolves to true, then the associated outcome is the one raised by the router. If none of the expressions resolve to true, then the activity will fall back to the outcome defined in the *default-outcome* property. This default outcome is a required property of this activity type.

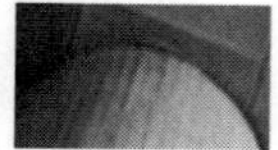

TIP

The cases (expression + associated outcome) listed for a router are evaluated in the order that they are defined. Therefore, it makes sense to place the case that is most likely as the first in the list. It is also a good idea to be explicit in defining the flow by setting up cases with expressions for each possible outcome, rather than "failing back" to the default-outcome. *Relying on* default-outcome *could lead to the wrong result when values are unexpectedly null.*

Taking the simple task flow illustrated next, the router called "createOrEditBranch" can be used to make the task flow able to either create new records or edit an existing record as shown here.

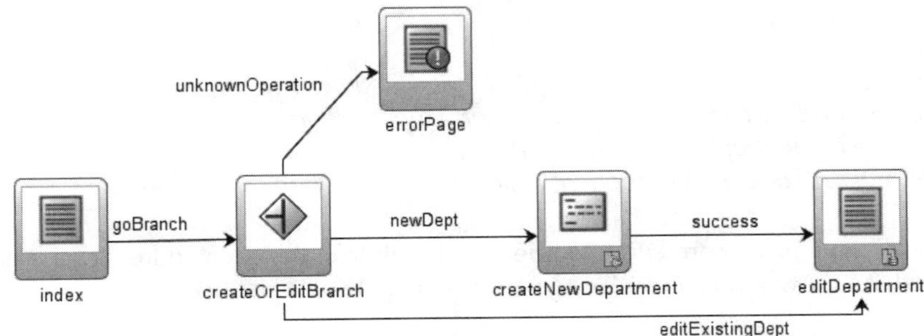

In this case, the router activity uses a value stored on the pageFlowScope to make a decision about following the *newDept* outcome or the *editExistingDept* outcome. The properties for the router are shown here.

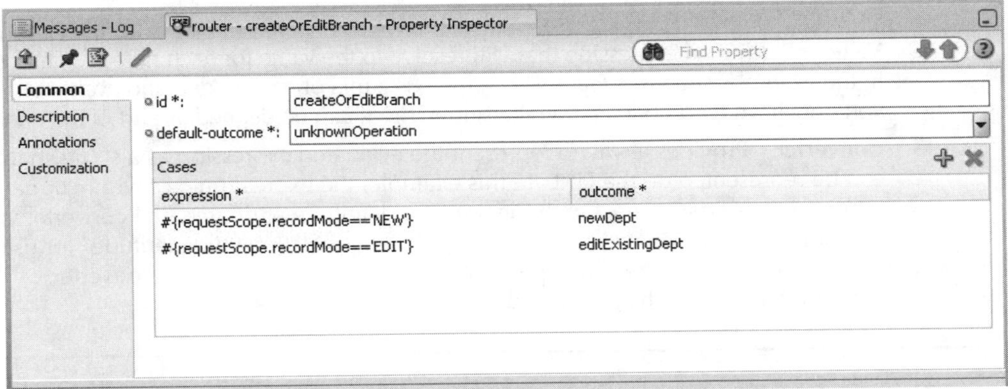

Notice that in this case an explicit *unknownOperation* outcome has also been created to act as the default fallback routing.

Task Flow Call

One of the key enhancements of the ADF Controller over basic JSF navigation is the ability to have encapsulated flows that can be reused in many places. How to create such flows and wire them in is discussed later on in the chapter, in the section "Bounded Task Flows." For now, all you need to understand is that the task flow call activity represents the transition of one task flow into a nested task flow, and that as part of this process, data can be passed both into and out of the nested flow. Only bounded task flows can be called from a task flow call activity, and the simplest way to create a task flow call activity is to drag an existing bounded task flow from the Application Navigator into the parent task flow diagram. Once a task flow call activity is set up, it can be treated just like a view activity and wired into the flow. We discuss how to pass data into a task flow later in the chapter.

URL View

A URL view activity represents an external resource, usually a web page outside of the scope of the application itself.

NOTE
There is a current restriction that a URL view activity will always open the required URL in the current browser window. If you want to just pop the content up in an extra window to the side, then consider using the ADF `af:goLink` component inside of the UI definition instead.

The activity has a core URL parameter that will take the base address of the page that is required. As shown in Figure 11-6, parameters can also be defined.

Parameters for a URL View Activity If the URL of a particular target page is fixed, then there is no need to be concerned with the parameter capabilities of a URL view activity; however, if the URL that you need to construct is in some way dynamic, then the parameters allow you to build up a standard query string without having to write code to concatenate the variable parts together. Notice from Figure 11-6 that three bits of information can be provided for each parameter.

- **Name** Defines the name for the parameter that will be appended on to the URL. In the example the parameters are *ll, z,* and *t,* respectively.
- **Value** Defines an expression that will resolve to the value for each named parameter. In the example, shown in Figure 11-6, there is a mix of hard-coded and evaluated values. If you only have hard-coded parameters, then these can be defined as part of the *url* property.
- **Converter** Provides a way to represent the evaluated expression as a string so that it can be represented on the URL. In this example, the expression `#{oracleLocation}` returns a coordinate object with longitude and latitude attributes. The converter will take that object and flatten it out into a String in the format "longitude,latitude" for use on the URL. Note that the z (zoom level) parameter does not require a converter, as it is a simple integer value that can be automatically encoded as a String.

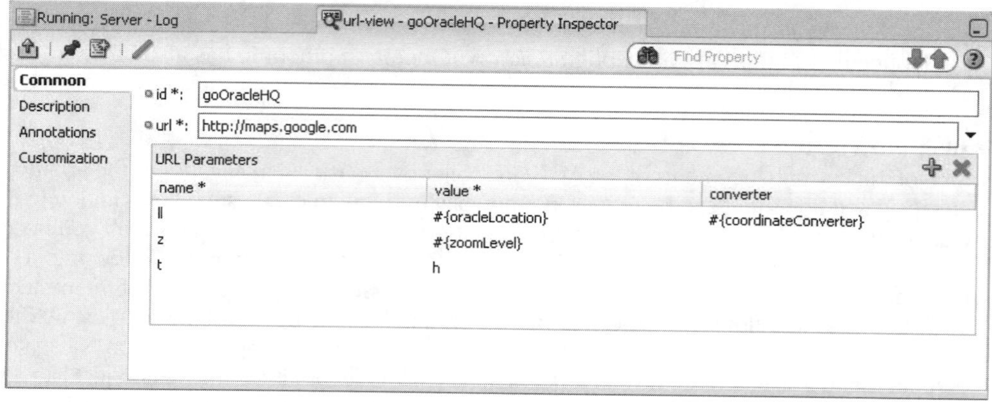

FIGURE 11-6. *Defining a URL view activity*

The complete xml for the URL view activity shown in Figure 11-6 is as follows:

```
<url-view id="goOracleHQ">
  <url>http://maps.google.com/</url>
  <url-parameter>
    <name>z</name>
    <value>#{zoomLevel}</value>
  </url-parameter>
  <url-parameter>
    <name>t</name>
    <value>#{'h'}</value>
  </url-parameter>
  <url-parameter>
    <name>ll</name>
    <value>#{oracleCoordinates}</value>
    <converter>#{coordinateConverter}</converter>
  </url-parameter>
</url-view>
```

Parameter Converters The converter used in the example from Figure 11-6 is a very simple piece of code that will take a complex `Coordinate` object (implementation not shown) and output a `String` (and vice versa). This is accomplished using a small Java class that implements the `oracle.adf.controller.UrlParameterConverter` interface. Here is the sample code:

```
package com.tuhra.view;
import java.util.StringTokenizer;
import oracle.adf.controller.UrlParameterConverter;

/**
 * This class implements the UrlParameterConverter to allow the expression of
 * coordinates as Strings that can be passed as a URL argument and the
 * reconstruction of a coordinate from a string passed in on a URL
 */
public class CoordinateURLConverter implements UrlParameterConverter {

  /**
   * The interface method defined for re-constructing an object from a string
   * passed on the URL
   * @param value Coordinate expressed as a string in the format
   * "longitude,latitude" e.g.?coord=10.223,-12.234
   * @return a Coordinate object
   */
  public Object getAsObject(String value) {
    //For simplicity assume that the string is in the correct format
    String[] longLat = value.split(",");
    Coordinate coord = new Coordinate();
    coord.setLongitude(Double.valueOf(longLat[0]));
    coord.setLatitude(Double.valueOf(longLat[1]));
    return coord;
  }
```

```
  /**
   * The interface method defined for expressing a Coordinate object as a
   * string in the format "longitude,latitude" for use as a URL parameter
   * @param value Coordinate object
   * @return String in the format "longitude,latitude"
   */
  public String getAsString(Object value) {
    Coordinate coord = (Coordinate)value;
    StringBuilder builder = new StringBuilder();
    builder.append(coord.getLongitude());
    builder.append(',');
    builder.append(coord.getLatitude());
    return builder.toString();
  }
}
```

This converter class is defined as a request scope managed bean called coordinateConverter, and the framework will call the `getAsString()` and `getAsObject()` methods as required.

Control Flow Case

Control flow cases provide the wiring between activities in the task flow. Each case is given a name and represents a specific event that can be raised as an outcome by UI elements on a page, or by another activity type such as a method call activity. Each control flow case can be further qualified with an action. This defines that only when a particular action binding raises a specific outcome will this case be matched. This extra qualifying *from-action* property is optional and rarely used.

Once control flow cases have been defined for a page, then the IDE will automatically list them in the Property Inspector for action items such as `af:commandButton` or `af:commandLink` on that page. This is shown by this illustration:

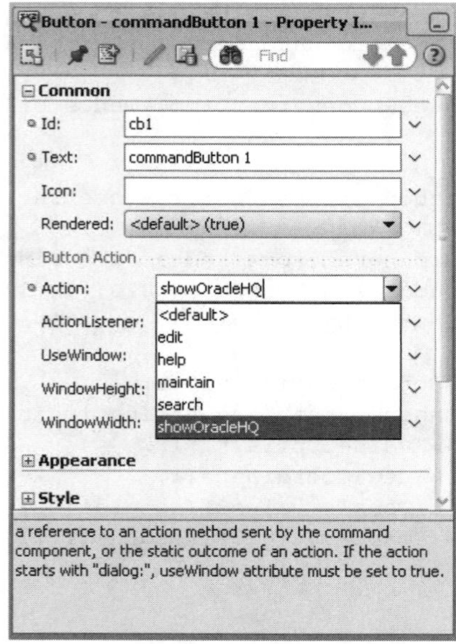

Wildcard Control Flow Rule

In many flows, certain activities may be called from more than one place. For example, a view activity called "aboutApplication" might be called from a link on the bottom of every page in the UI. The developer can, of course, draw in control flow cases from every other view activity to the "aboutApplication" view activity, but this would get a little tedious and could make the diagram harder to read. To handle this situation, ADFc, like JSF itself, supports the concept of wildcard or global control flow rules. These allow you to just define a rule once (for example a rule called "about") between a wildcard control flow rule and the destination. When an action is invoked from a particular activity and emits a particular outcome, ADFc will first of all look for explicit control flow cases in the task flow that have an origin in the current activity that match the outcome. If there is no matching control flow case, then the framework will look for rules emanating from a wildcard control flow rule that match.

Normally it is sufficient to have one single wildcard control flow rule to act as an origin for shared rules; however, the framework does allow a little more precision than that. The default name for the wildcard is simply "*"—which means that it will match any other activity as an alternative source of control flow cases. The name of a wildcard control flow rule can be refined with a prefix, but it must always have a trailing "*" character. If the name of the rule were "pr*," for example, then the control flow rules that it defines could be used from activities named "programming" or "prototype" but would not be used by activities named "editEmployee" or "poll," as they do not match the string pattern.

Types of Task Flows

Earlier on in the chapter, mention was made that more than one type of task flow exists. The two available types are bounded and unbounded task flows. The bounded task flow has a further subtype called a train. In this section of the chapter we look at how these types differ and how they can be used.

Unbounded Task Flows

When a project with the ADF Page Flow technology scope is created, it will contain a task flow definition file called adfc-config.xml by default. This is an unbounded task flow. Such task flows are called "unbounded" simply because they have no explicit start or end. With an unbounded flow, the user can start from any vew activity they like. Functionally, the flow is equivalent to the conventional page flow defined by a faces-config.xml. It is important to understand that for an application there is one, and only one, unbounded task flow. It is possible to have several separate definition files containing unbounded task flow definitions, but at runtime, these are all merged into a single logical flow.

Menu Model Generation

As all of the view activities within the unbounded task flow are accessible via the URL, the design time diagram for an unbounded task flow definition has a neat capability to automatically generate a menu model. This menu model can then be bound to the appropriate ADF Faces components that can be driven by such a model—for example, a set of tabs or a dropdown menu.

The menu is generated by the option **Create ADF Menu Model** on the right-click mouse menu on the diagram. When it is selected, four things will happen:

1. **The Create ADF Menu Model dialog appears** This allows the developer to specify a name and location for the menu model file.

2. **An XML file is generated** It uses the name defined for the menu in the dialog in the selected place (usually the /WEB-INF directory). It contains a summary of all the menu items (which will only be the available view activities in the configuration). You can alter the menu item labels by editing this file.
3. **A managed bean entry is created in the adfc-config.xml file** This bean is of the class `oracle.adf.view.rich.model.MDSMenuModel` and reads the XML file generated in step 2 to actually construct the menu at runtime. The bean is defined on the request scope and uses the same name that was selected for the menu when it was created (generally root_menu). Notice that the name of the menu XML file is passed in as the source managed property for the bean.
4. **Wildcard control flow cases are constructed** Each leads to the view activities defined in the menu that don't already have them. These auto-generated control flow cases are prefixed with "adfMenu_." If control flow cases have already been defined for a particular view activity, then these will be reused rather than a new one being created.

The menu model that is initially created from the view activities on the diagram can be refreshed from the right-click mouse menu if more view activities are added into the task flow later. The generated menu XML file can also be used as a starting point for a more complex menu structure with grouped menu items and multiple levels. This particular topic is well documented in the Web User Interface Developer's Guide for ADF in the JDeveloper online help, which explains all of the options for customizing the XML file, managing translations, combining multiple menu files into one logical structure, and so on.

The Developer's Guide also demonstrates the code technique for using this XML-defined menu to drive the UI using the `af:navigationPane` component.

When to Use Unbounded Task Flows

As we grow more experienced with Fusion technologies, it is becoming evident that most applications will have very little content in their unbounded task flow. The rule of thumb here is to consider which pages within the User Interface can be used as application entry points; these may be URLs entered directly by a user, emailed as hyperlinks, or stored as a bookmark in a browser. If your application contains pages that make no sense or cannot work if called in this way, then they probably belong in a bounded task flow instead.

Bounded Task Flows

Bounded task flows differ from the unbounded task flow in an application in several important respects:

- They have one entry point and zero or more exit points.
- They can be parameterized and maintain private state.
- They can be nested within other task flows using the task flow call activity, or nested in pages or page fragments using the ADF region component.
- They can be flows that use entire pages or just fragments of pages.

Bounded task flows are created by selecting the *Create as Bounded Task Flow* check box in the Create Task Flow dialog as shown in Figure 11-7. This option is exposed through the New Gallery in the **Web Tier | JSF** section:

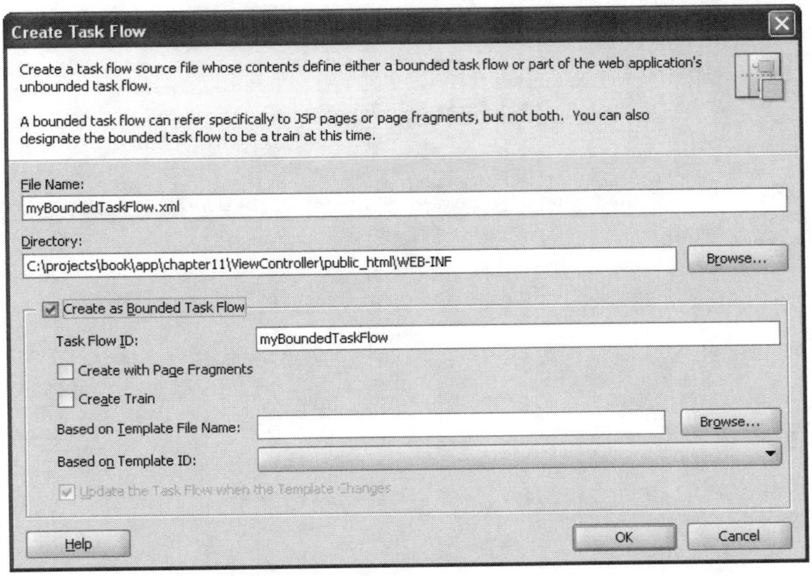

FIGURE 11-7. *Creating a bounded task flow*

The combination of the task flow file name and the task flow ID needs to be unique within the application. Although the JDeveloper design time does not expose it, it is possible to define multiple tasks flows within a particular XML definition file, hence the uniqueness of the combination of the ID and file name.

Once a bounded task flow is created, the editor opens and the flow can be constructed just like the unbounded task flow that we've been dealing with up until now. The first thing that you will notice, however, is that the first activity that you drop onto the diagram will gain a green halo. This indicator shows the default entry point or start of the flow. Only one activity within a particular flow can be marked as the default activity. To assign this status, you must select the required activity in the diagram and then select **Mark Activity | Default Activity** from the right-click menu. Notice that there is a corresponding **Unmark Activity** menu option; when a different activity is marked as the default, any previously selected activity will be automatically unmarked.

The default activity can also be set through the overview editor for the task flow where it is listed under the General category. Once a default activity is set, it will be encoded into the underlying task flow configuration XML file using the `<default-activity> . . . </ default-activity>` element.

Task Flow Parameters

One of the key reusability features of bounded task flows is the ability to parameterize them with a list of typed arguments. When a bounded task flow is started, values can be passed into the flow using expression language assigned to each parameter. From here, they are generally stored in the page flow scope.

Parameters are defined through the **Overview | Parameters** subtab of the task flow editor as shown in the following illustration.

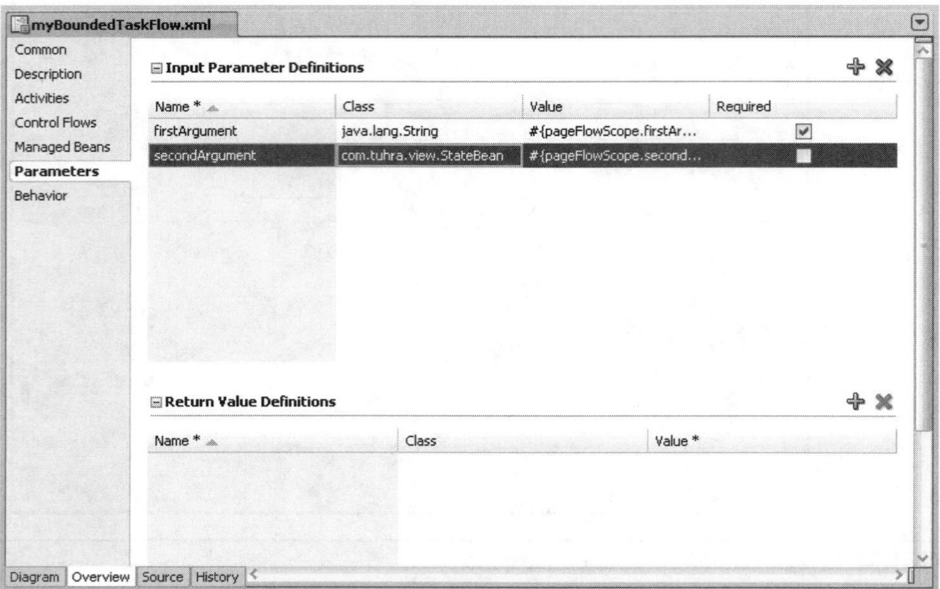

Name is the important attribute here, and of course, it defines the name of the parameter within the task flow's API. The value attribute of each parameter defines the place where the value of the parameter will be stored. If no storage location is supplied using this value attribute, then the name attribute is used as a pageFlow-scoped variable. Thus, in the preceding illustration, the value attributes are all superfluous, as they just follow this pattern. However, the availability of the value attribute does provide the availability to override this behavior explicitly if required.

Parameters can be marked as required and with a specific type, both of which help the developer of the task flow to make the API to the task flow more explicit. If, for example, a parameter marked as required is not populated when a task flow is called, then a runtime exception will be thrown. This exception can be captured by a nominated activity in the flow, as we cover later in this section.

Notice that parameters can also have a defined *converter* attribute in the Property Inspector. This attribute is identical in makeup and purpose to the converters we saw in relation to URL view activities, and the converter classes that you write for this purpose would implement the same `oracle.adf.controller.UrlParameterConverter` interface.

Passing Parameters into a Bounded Task Flow Earlier in the chapter we discussed the task flow call activity as the way that one task flow could call another. You can now see that parameters provide a way of passing some kind of context information into these called flows. If a called flow contains parameters, then the Property Inspector for the task flow call activity provides access to set the values as shown in Figure 11-8.

When the called task flow has parameters defined, these will be listed automatically in the Input Parameters *name* column as shown in Figure 11-8. The *value* property then needs to be set using expression language.

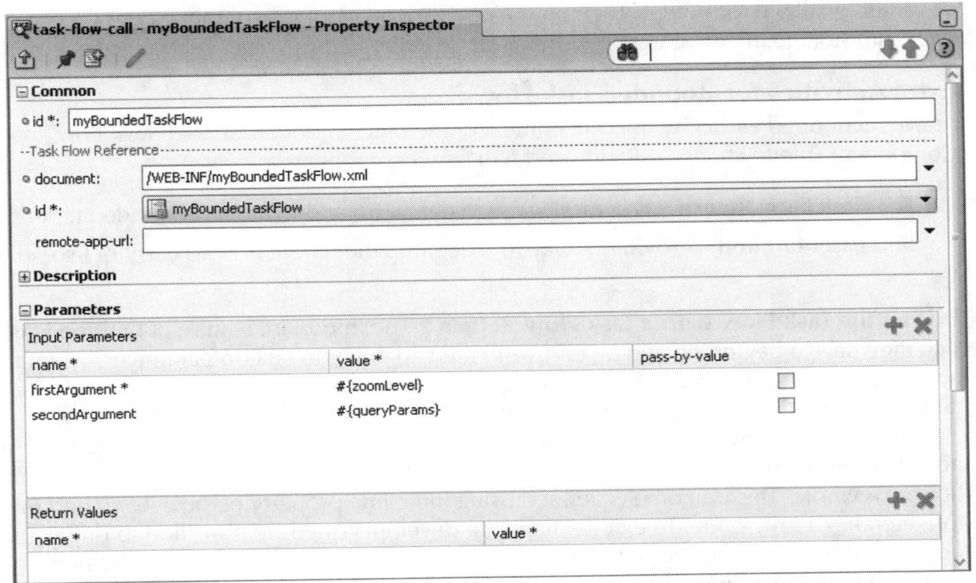

FIGURE 11-8. *Passing parameters to a task flow*

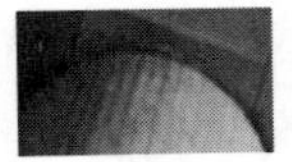

TIP
To pass a literal value such as the value 10, just wrap it with the EL designators—thus #{10} or if the value is a literal string #{'ten as text'}.

When a value is passed into a task flow as a parameter, if it refers to an object (as opposed to a scalar type), it is actually passed as a reference to that Java object. This means that the nested task flow has the ability to reach into the managed bean and change values, and those changed values will be visible to the parent when control is returned. This behavior can be changed by selecting the *pass-by-value* checkbox, which can be seen as the final column in Figure 11-8. Switching this feature on will cause the referenced bean to be cloned, and the copy will be passed to the nested flow. In this case any changes made to the input parameter will be thrown away when the child task flow has ended.

Scalar values or literals passed as parameters to a flow are always passed as copies, so this flag is ignored in those cases.

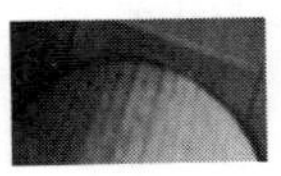

CAUTION
Although Strings are passed as references to the child task flow, they are immutable, so don't expect to be able to make a change to one of these and have that value sent back to the parent.

Returning Data from a Bounded Task Flow Not surprisingly, bounded task flows can also return data when they exit. The process is identical to the flow input parameters, with a set of

Return value definitions defined on the task flow definition itself that define the name and value of values available for output. Then on the task flow usage, these output values can be mapped back into storage in the parent flow. This is done in the Return Values section shown in Figure 11-8.

Extra Activities for Bounded Task Flows

As we mentioned earlier, within the context of the diagram for a bounded task flow, the Component Palette changes slightly and two new components appear:

- **Task Flow Return** Provides a way to define an endpoint for a bounded task flow.
- **Parent Action** Provides a way to reach into the parent flow to carry out some action.

Exiting the Task Flow with a Task Flow Return The important feature of bounded task flows is that they have a beginning and an end, with the capability to take in parameters when they start and return data as they exit. You can also associate code execution with the boundaries of the task flow, something that is covered in "Coding Around a Flow" later in the chapter.

To exit a bounded task flow, task flow return activities are used. One or more of these activities can be present in the task flow, each of which can represent a different outcome for the flow as a whole. This outcome is defined using the *name* property of the activity and must be set to a literal `String` value. To exit the flow, the developer needs to transition to one of these task flow return activities; control returns to the parent flow, with the outcome of the nested flow being determined by the outcome of the task flow return activity used to exit the flow.

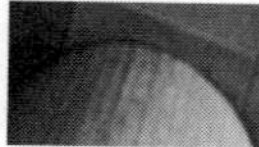

TIP
Task flow return activities have a gray halo around them in the same way that the default activity in a task flow has a green halo. The gray halo indicates that this is a possible exit point for the flow. URL view activities also have this halo.

Calling a Parent Action The parent action activity is specifically used when bounded task flows are used in the context of being embedded in a parent page as a region (we cover this in more detail in "Pages or Fragments?" a little later on). The purpose of the Parent Action is to provide a way for a nested task flow to communicate cleanly with the enclosing page by raising a navigation event. A use case for this might be that a nested task flow makes a change to some data that requires the parent page to explicitly re-query to refresh itself.

The Parent Action actually defines two parallel outcomes: the normal *outcome* property for the nested flow and the *parent-outcome,* which is the outcome that is sent to the enclosing page to process. Note that the navigation rule triggered by this parent outcome may cause the parent flow to replace the current view, thus destroying the nested task flow. However, if such a parent navigation does not occur, then the *outcome* property will drive the flow within the nested task flow in the normal way.

Exception Handler

When marking an activity as the default for a flow, you may have noticed the option to mark an activity as an *exception handler,* which is also available on the right-click menu. Doing so will overlay a red exclamation point over the activity as a visual indicator of this role. At runtime, if the framework encounters an unexpected exception the flow will redirect to this specified activity to handle the problem. Generally the activity used as an exception handler will be a view activity that can then display information about the error to help to diagnose the issue. Activities can be marked in this way in both bounded and unbounded task flows. When building task flows, it is a good idea to create a page or page fragment to handle unexpected errors using this capability, even if you never expect such a thing to happen.

Pages or Fragments?

Notice that Figure 11-7 shows a checkbox labeled *Create with Page Fragments* inside the Create as Bounded Task Flow area. This feature of the controller allows the developer to build flows that are not designed to step through whole pages of UI but rather to operate within a fixed area on a page rather like a portlet. Once a flow is marked as using fragments, any view activity that is created via the diagram will be correctly formatted and named with the .jsff extension. Page fragments can also be created through the New Gallery and then dragged onto the task flow diagram in the normal way to create view activities.

Consuming Fragment-Based Task Flows

A fragment-based flow cannot just be called from a URL; it must be embedded within a page. This is done by dragging and dropping the task flow from the Application Navigator onto the page in question. When this action is carried out, the drop menu will appear with two choices: Region or Dynamic Region. Selecting the first option (Region) will create two artifacts:

- A region component (`af:region`) in the page
- A taskFlow binding in the ADF binding metadata (pageDef file) for the page

The region component that is created will have its value attribute set to an expression that points to the created taskFlow binding in the parent page's data binding metadata file. This binding in the pageDef is analogous to the task flow call activity and contains the parameter mapping for the flow. When the drag-and-drop action takes place, a dialog pops up to gather the required value for any task flow parameters. These can also be set, after the fact, by navigating to the bindings editor for the parent page, locating the taskFlow binding in the executables section, and either locating the parameters in the Property Inspector or double clicking the binding to redisplay the parameter dialog.

Bounded flows used as regions can include a task flow return activity and end. In this case, the containing region will become empty as the flow ends. This could have the side effect of causing the page layout to shift around, as the space previously occupied by the task flow is now empty.

At design time, once a task flow is embedded into a region on the page, it will be represented by a grayed-out representation of the first activity, if that activity is a view activity. If the first activity in the flow is not a view activity (for example, if it is a router), then the message "This region cannot be rendered at design time" will be displayed.

Dynamic Regions We skipped over the second option that is offered when a task flow is dropped onto the page—Dynamic Region. With dynamic regions, rather than having the space on the page devoted to a single particular child task flow, several alternative task flows can exist and the decision can be made at runtime as to which one to display. When a flow is dropped as a dynamic region, a dialog will first pop up asking for a managed bean value and then prompt for the task flow parameters as normal. So, what's going on here? If you just follow through with all of the defaults and look at the results, you will see that three things have happened:

1. An `af:region` component is created in the page with a *value* property set to something like "#{bindings.tabletabflowdefinition1.regionModel}."
2. In the pageDef file for the parent page, a taskFlow binding is created, but rather than having a hard-coded reference to the page flow (such as /WEB-INF/bounded-flow-definition.xml#my-bounded-flow), it references an expression that uses the specified managed bean, such as ${regionManager.dynamicTaskFlowId}
3. The specified managed bean class will be created (`RegionManager` in this example), and the `getDynamicTaskFlowId()` method will be created automatically. At runtime, this method is called to return the ID of the required task flow. The following code listing shows the default contents for this method as generated when the table-tab-flow-definition task flow is dropped as a dynamic region. Notice that this generated method is just the starting point, and it's up to you to add the alternative flow IDs and the logic to decide which one to return to the binding container. Notice how the task flow that is required is defined using the unique combination of task flow file name and Task Flow ID.

```
public class RegionManager {
  private String taskFlowId
        = "/WEB-INF/bounded-flow-definition.xml#my-bounded-flow";
  //You would add the alternative flow names here...

  public RegionManager() {
  }

  public TaskFlowId getDynamicTaskFlowId() {
    //Add logic here to return one of the possible flows.
    return TaskFlowId.parse(taskFlowId);
  }
}
```

Introducing the ViewPort Using regions, you can see how a page can be constructed from various flows, all defined and running separately. This is in fact the normal way that Fusion-based applications are developed so as to provide maximum reuse and very dynamic pages. For the controller, these embedded regions introduce a large amount of complexity—each will be displaying different pieces of user interface, will be using different data bindings, and will have a life cycle that is separate from the enclosing page. To make matters worse, regions can be nested within regions, so the page can get very complex to manage. To help with this whole process, the controller introduced the concept of *ViewPorts*. The browser window is the top-level ViewPort, and then each nested region is its own ViewPort within that. The controller uses the ViewPorts to identify and manage these. Your main contact with ViewPorts will be when debugging your task flows, something that we cover at the end of this chapter.

More Options on Task Flow Creation

We've shown how the Create Task Flow dialog (Figure 11-7) can be used to create bounded and unbounded task flows and control whether whole pages or page fragments are used. There are two other options available from that dialog specifically for bounded task flows: trains and templates.

Trains

Trains are sequences of pages (or page fragments) that are executed in a known stepwise manner. The most common and familiar use of a train is in the creation of "wizard"-like user interfaces where the user is asked a series of simple questions to build up something more complex. The following illustration shows a typical wizard-style page and the specialized components used to provide navigation control.

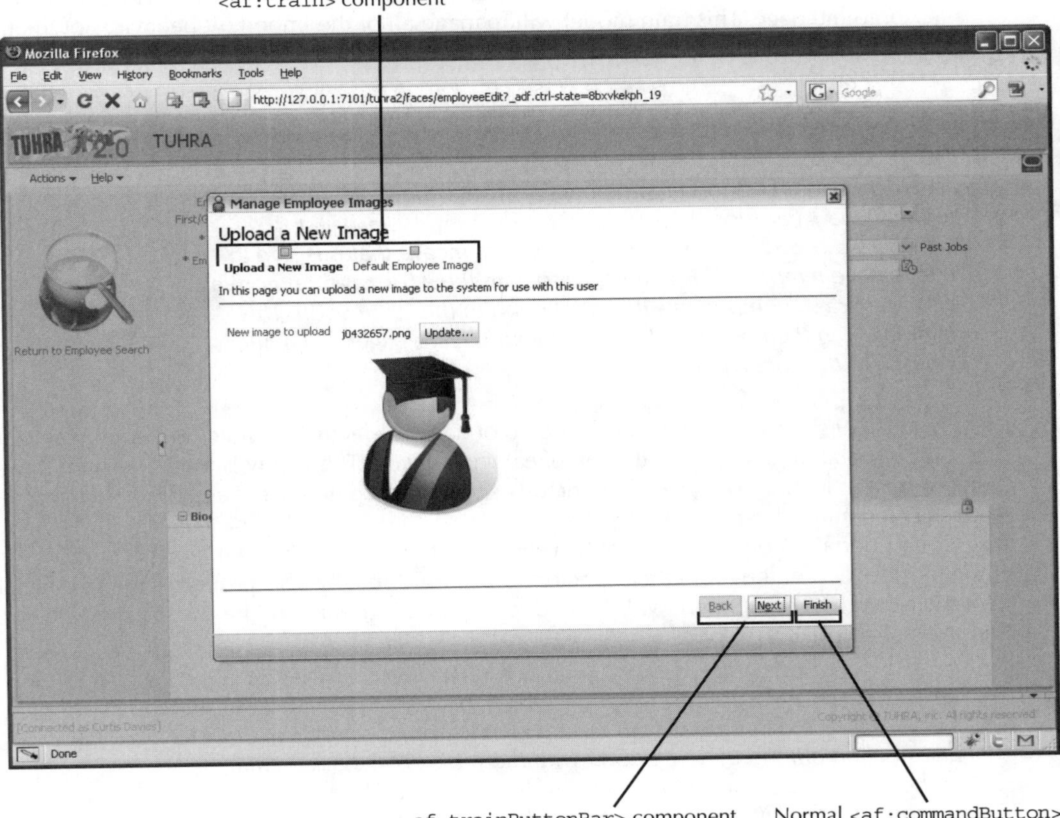

These control components, specifically the `af:train` component, allow the user to jump through all of the pages in the train flow. On the `af:train` control itself the user can click the icon or the label of any enabled train stop to navigate to it. However, the developer does have a lot of control over exactly which steps are available at any particular point in time using some of the properties, as we'll discuss shortly.

A task flow can be designated as a train by selecting the *Create Train* checkbox in the Create Task Flow dialog, or by taking an existing flow and in the overview editor Behavior tab, selecting the *Train* property checkbox there. Once a task flow is designated as a train, two things will happen:

- As View Activities are added to the flow, they will be linked with a dashed line. This represents the path and order of the steps (train stops) in the flow. This is shown in Figure 11-9. The default ordering is based upon the order in which the view activities are added to the task flow diagram; however, the train submenu on the right-click menu for the task flow can be used to change the order of views in the flow.
- At runtime, a model of the train will be available to automatically control the `af:trainButtonBar` and `af:train` components. If one of these components is added to any view that is part of a train flow, JDeveloper will recognize that there is a train model available and offer that as an option when the component is dropped onto the page. This train model will manage all of the important behaviors of the train for the developer, graying out buttons and train stops as required and doing the actual navigation.

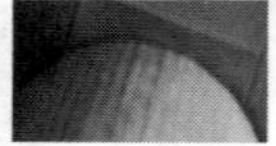

TIP
The expression used for a train model is always the same and set to the value `#{controllerContext.currentViewPort.taskFlowContext.trainModel}`. This means that it is safe to create page templates for trains that contain the `af:trainButtonBar` and `af:train` components that are bound to this expression. This template can then be reused for all of your wizard pages, no matter what train they are a part of.

Figure 11-9 shows a simple train made up of two view activities; note how each view activity has a representation of a train at the top of each page icon. The reality is that most train flows will need to be a little more complex than the one show here, so next we'll explore how more sophisticated trains can be created.

One important property to consider when using trains is the *display-name* property in the Train Stop section of the Property Inspector for the view activity. This property controls the label that the `af:train` component will use and render as a hyperlink for the user to navigate through the steps of a flow.

TIP
If you look at the task flow XML source, don't confuse the `<display-name>` child of the `<train-stop>` with the `<display-name>` child of the `<view>` tag. The former controls the labels used by the train component; the latter is ignored and only exists for compatibility with the metadata used by the faces-config.xml file.

Controlling Train Stop Availability With any complex train or wizard-type user interface, you need to be able to control how the user proceeds through the steps of the process. Often it will not make sense for the user to jump ahead to a particular page without making some intervening choices.

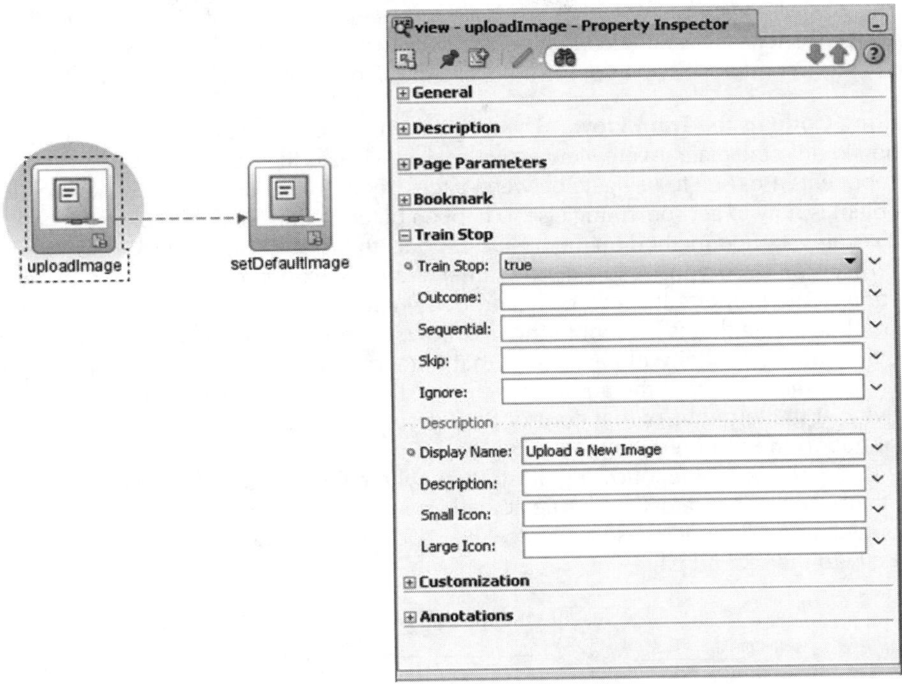

FIGURE 11-9. *A basic train showing train properties for a stop*

Likewise in some cases, based on user decisions, you might want to skip a page because it is not relevant. There are two properties available on each train stop to control this:

- **Sequential** is a Boolean property on the view that determines if the user can only access it from the preceding page (this is the true/default value) or jump to it directly. In most cases trains are sequential. From a particular train stop the user can jump back to any earlier stop.
- **Skip** is a Boolean property that allows steps in a train to be bypassed. If *skip* is set to true, then navigation using an `af:trainButtonBar` will skip over that view and access to it will be disabled in the `af:train` control itself.

When set to literal Boolean values, both *sequential* and *skip* are of limited use; their real power is revealed when they are configured to use expression language. When used with expressions, the value of those expressions can be dynamic. For example, you might want a train to be fully sequential when stepping through the creation of a new record, but when editing an existing record you want the user to be able to jump to any page in the process. By making the sequential property dynamic, the same train can be used for both purposes.

Finally notice that in the same Train Stop section of the Property Inspector for a view, there is the *train-stop* property itself. This property allows views to be defined that do not directly contribute to the train flow. Typically, all pages in the flow will be train stops, but perhaps the final summary page of the wizard is a special case that needs to be present but does not need to be accessed via the train components. This train-stop property can only have a literal Boolean value. If you need to make view conditionally part of the train, use the *skip* property with a suitable expression instead.

Calling Code in the Train Flow The only activities that get marked as train stops as they are dropped onto the diagram are view activities. Likewise, as the `af:train` and `af:trainButtonBar` components are used to navigate between pages, focus jumps directly from view to view. So a big problem is how to get something else to happen before a train stop is displayed. For example, how to execute a bound method on the business model to prepare some data for the page?

This is all accomplished using the rather strangely named *outcome* property in the Train Stop section of the Property Inspector. This property names a control flow case from a wildcard control flow rule that is present in the task flow. If a train view activity has this *outcome* property set, then the controller will navigate to that outcome rather than directly displaying the view. This gives the developer the ability to define a different activity type, such as a method call activity, at the terminus of that control flow case. Once that activity completes, the flow can continue to the required view activity.

This is shown in the following illustration, where the first activity in the train has an outcome of statusCheck. The statusCheck rule actually points to a router activity that will make a decision about what to do: in one case, execute some code and then continue to the first page, or jump directly to the second page.

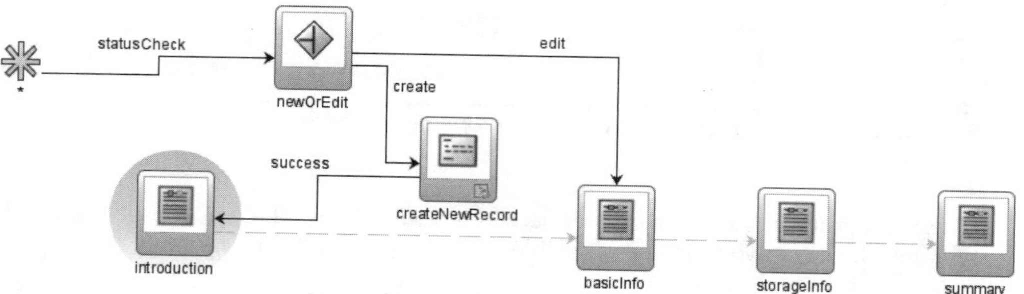

This capability makes it possible to meet any preconditions before navigating to a view.

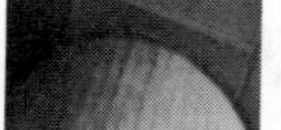

CAUTION

The outcome property makes it possible to execute code before navigating to a page; however, there is no simple mechanism for specifying code that should be executed on the way out of a page, nor is there any mechanism for attaching listeners or any extra code to the train components (`af:trainButtonBar`, `af:train`). Be aware of this restriction when defining the flow for your trains, and be aware that if a train stop is not sequential, the user may be able to bypass code validation that you place into methods called via the outcome property.

Bypassing the Train Model Just because a task flow is defined as a train, that does not mean that the only form of navigation through the activities is using the train components. You can revert to normal navigation control and components at any time. An example of where this might be relevant is on the last page of a wizard. Using the default train button bar, the Next and Previous buttons will be present and the Next button always grayed out. You might, quite reasonably, want to only display a Previous button and replace the Next button with a Finish button. This has to be done using normal button components and an extra navigation case to provide the "previous" navigation from the Previous button rather than the default rule implied by the dashed line. Overriding the train flow in this way is perfectly okay.

Branching in Trains The final topic to consider in relation to trains is the ability to branch to subflows. A certain amount of complexity can be introduced using the outcome property that was discussed earlier; however, more power is provided by the ability to define additional train-based task flows as stops in a train. To do this, subflows can be defined and dragged into the main train diagram. These task flow call activity–based train stops have the same properties as a normal view activity that is being used as a stop, for example, *outcome, sequential,* and *skip*. When a train steps into a subflow, as shown in the following illustration, the `af:train` component will display the stops from the current subflow, plus indicators to show the surrounding flow.

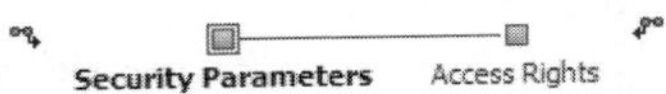

Subflows that are used as train stops must themselves be marked as trains and will require a task flow return activity with an associated outcome. When such a flow is dropped into the parent train, the outcome(s) needs to be manually wired to the next logical stop in the train. This manual wiring step provides the opportunity to jump to a variety of stops in the parent flow based on the returned outcome from the child train.

Task Flow Templates

Just like JSF-based pages, JDeveloper allows the developer to develop reusable templates for bounded task flows. Common uses for such templates would include defining common managed beans, parameters, exception handlers, or initializers and finalizers (see "Coding Around the Flow" later in this chapter). Unbounded task flows cannot use a template.

Just like page templates, any task flows that inherit from a task flow template can be permanently linked to the template to automatically inherit any updates. This is controlled by the check box labeled *Update the Task Flow when the Template Changes* in the Create Task Flow dialog (see Figure 11-7). This switch is enabled by default. If the reference is maintained, then any task flow that uses a template will contain a section similar to this:

```
<template-reference>
  <document>/WEB-INF/wizard-template.xml</document>
  <id>wizard-template</id>
</template-reference>
```

If the developer chooses not to maintain the template reference, then the information from the template is copied into the new task flow as if it had been manually entered.

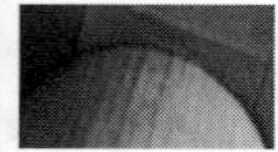

CAUTION

When using page templates for the user interface, JDeveloper will ghost in the template contents to help the developer to work in context. However, task flow templates do not have an equal degree of functionality in JDeveloper 11g. When using a task flow reference, none of the inherited artifacts are visible from any task flow that has consumed a template in the design-time environment. This has the potential for introducing errors and bugs with multiple definitions of the same object or control flow case. The JDeveloper Help and the ADF Developers Guide have a section on how collisions are resolved when things are defined both in the template and in the flow. Read this information about the feature carefully before using task flow templates.

Advanced Task Flows

So far, this chapter has discussed the basic features and mechanics of task flows. Next, we look at some of the more advanced features, specifically:

- Data control scope
- Transaction management
- Controlling re-entry behavior
- Adding code around task flows and debugging
- The ADF Controller coding APIs

Data Control Scope

So far, we've looked at the explicit transfer of data in and out of a task flow using parameters and return values. However, in the context of a Fusion application, a major source of data is, of course, the ADF data bindings. Although it is convenient to view task flows as black boxes with only limited, strictly defined, dependencies on their parents, things are rarely that simple. In some cases, a task flow may be strictly independent and have enough information passed into it through its parameters to display the required data. In other circumstances you might want the task flow to be contextual, that is, to display data that relates to some selection in the parent.

To address this requirement, task flows define an important property, *Data Control Scope,* which can be accessed through the Behavior tab of the overview editor for the flow. This property has two values, "isolated" and "shared":

- **Isolated** The ADF Controller creates a new data control instance for use in this task flow. When using ADF Business Components, this will results in a new application module instance being created and a separate connection to the database being used. The task flow therefore has no inheritance of the existing state of the application module being used by the parent.

- **Shared (default)** In this case, the data control instance (and therefore the application module instance) is shared with the parent flow. This implies that the same connection is being used, and all of the context from the parent, such as the current row in a particular view object instance, is known to the child task flow. This is the default mode for a task flow and the mode that is used if no explicit value is defined for the *Data Control Scope* property.

The capability to define task flow as isolated is a very powerful one, as you can essentially build a system that is engaged in multiple concurrent transactions in parallel. However, be aware of the cost of that decision with respect to memory requirements and connection pool sizes that could result if an application uses multiple isolated flows. Data controls are explained further in Chapter 13.

Transaction Management

Closely related to the issue of Data Control Scope is that of using a task flow to define a transaction boundary. For a bounded task flow, notice the *Transaction* property on the Behavior page of the task flow Overview. This property has four possible values:

- **Default (no value supplied)** ADF BC manages the transaction as required.
- **requires-existing-transaction** Indicates that the flow expects to be called from a parent flow that has already started a transaction. If the task flow is called without a suitable transaction open, a runtime exception will be thrown. This option is not relevant when using ADF BC as a service layer.
- **requires-transaction** Indicates that the flow must be called from a parent flow that already has an open transaction, or failing that, a new transaction should be started.
- **new-transaction** Causes the flow to start a new transaction.

When using ADF BC as a service layer, you generally don't have to worry about the management of transactions, and the default value is used; therefore, the subtleties of requires-transaction verses new-transaction can be ignored. However, the feature does provide a useful way of declaratively issuing a COMMIT or ROLLBACK to the database, saving the developer from having to explicitly bind these operations into the page or task flow.

To set this up, the task flow transaction behavior must be set to "requires-transaction" or "new-transaction". Once this is done, each task flow return activity can be marked to either automatically COMMIT or ROLLBACK. This option is set through the Behavior tab of the Property Inspector for the task flow return activity. Rollback can be a complete rollback, or you can have the framework roll back to an implicit save point that is created at the start of the task flow. Note that you can control whether this implicit save point is created or not from the task flow properties.

TIP
Setting up a transactional task flow with an initial save point can also help with managing the Back button in the browser. If the user enters a transactional task flow, makes some change, and then uses the Back button to back out and exit the flow, then the flow will automatically roll back to the implicit save point as the user crosses that boundary.

Save Points

The final related feature to transaction control is the save point restore activity. Although this feature refers to save points, these are different from the database save points implied by using the restore-to-savepoint feature on a transactional task flow. This alternative usage of the term save point refers to the ability that tasks flows exhibit to snapshot their current session state, using, for instance, pageFlowScope, and then restore that at a later point in time. This style of state management will rarely be used by a typical Fusion application, and the code required to do so is an advanced topic and beyond the scope of this book. Suffice to say, a save point restore activity is unrelated to the database save points used by the task flow transactional capabilities.

The Back Button

The use of the browser Back button was discussed briefly in relation to transactional task flows in the preceding section. In addition to this implicit rollback behavior, the developer has a degree of control over how the application should react to the Back button when such a navigation would take the user back into a flow that had been exited. This behavior is controlled by the *Task Flow Reentry* property on the task flow itself and augmented by the *Reentry* property on the task flow return activity. Using these properties, the programmer can declare that using the Back button to re-enter a task flow is not allowed; however, setting the properties in this way does not prevent the Back button from physically working. The user can still use the browser Back button (and the forbidden page displays); however, as soon as any action, such as pressing a button, is carried out, an `oracle.adf.controller.InvalidTaskFlowReentryException` exception is thrown. Catching this exception would be a good use for an exception handler activity, but be sure to define this activity on the parent page flow, as this is the context in which the exception will be raised.

The *Task Flow Reentry* property can be found on the Behavior tab of the Task Flow overview editor. It allows three explicit values:

- **reentry-allowed** Indicates that the flow should not try to detect this circumstance.
- **reentry-not-allowed** Indicates that the controller should throw the `InvalidTaskFlowReentryException` if the user Back-buttons (or bookmarks into the middle of) a flow.
- **reentry-outcome-dependent** Indicates that the decision about re-entry depends on the task flow return activity that was used to end the flow.

When reentry-outcome-dependent is selected as an option for the flow, then each of the task flow return activities in the flow will have to set its *Reentry* property to either "reentry-allowed" or "reentry-not-allowed." The effect of these settings is the same as the settings on the task flow as a whole, but the programmer now has more granularity.

An example of where this outcome dependent granularity might be useful is for a shopping cart. If the user has saved the contents of the cart for later, then it may be perfectly okay to Back-button to the cart and make additional changes. However, if the user has checked out, then the contents of the cart are no longer available and you don't want the user going back in to make changes to an order that has already been submitted.

Coding Around a Flow

We've see how code can be executed within a task flow using method call activities, but the framework also provides for two other sets of code that can be executed as a bounded task flow is entered and exited. The first set (initializers and finalizers) is part of the task flow definition itself, and additionally, listeners can be attached to a particular usage of a flow.

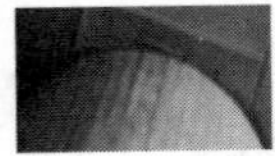

NOTE
In the case of both of these execution points, the code should not reference any ADF-bound data accessed through the bindings *expression root. Although the bindings object may be available on the request, the exact content is not guaranteed at the point in the life cycle at which these methods execute. If you need to carry out bound methods or access bound data, then do this in the formal flow using Method Call activities. Alternatively, pass the bound data into the page flow scope as part of the arguments to the task flow.*

Initializers and Finalizers

As a part of the task flow definition, EL Expressions can be used to define code that will be executed as the task flow starts up and as it ends. As the naming suggests, these initializer and finalizer methods fire as the very first and very last things that happen within the flow itself. What is more, these methods will always fire, even when the user navigates in and out of the task flow using the browser navigation buttons or the browser history. The finalizer is particularly useful when a bounded task flow is contained within a dynamic region on the page. If some external action in the page causes the contents of that dynamic region to be replaced, at least the finalizer will be executed, allowing the developer to clean up any work in progress that has now been aborted.

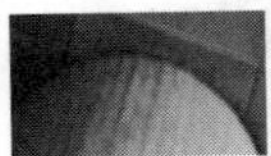

NOTE
There always seems to be an exception to phrases like "will always fire." In this case, note that the task flow finalizer currently does not fire if the user closes the browser window, although this restriction may be lifted in the future.

Initializers and finalizers are both defined through the Overview page of the task flow editor. The following output shows an initializer in use to provide some debugging information as the task flow is entered:

```
2008-05-27 07:48:43.171 Page Flow in Window: 1723699912_0
2008-05-27 07:48:43.171 Dumping pageFlowScope variables for:
2008-05-27 07:48:43.171 data.mainShellPageDef.tabletabflowdefinition1
2008-05-27 07:48:43.171     currentOwner=DDT
2008-05-27 07:48:43.171     currentTable=Worksheet
```

The corresponding XML in the configuration file for this would be the following:

```
<adfc-config xmlns="http://xmlns.oracle.com/adf/controller" version="1.2">
  <task-flow-definition id="table-tab-flow-definition">
    <default-activity>checkArgs</default-activity>
    <managed-bean>
      <managed-bean-name>taskFlowUtil</managed-bean-name>
      <managed-bean-class>
        com.tuhra.ddt.view.util.TaskFlowUtils
```

```
    </managed-bean-class>
    <managed-bean-scope>request</managed-bean-scope>
  </managed-bean>
  <initializer>#{taskFlowUtil.dumpTaskFlowState}</initializer>
  ...
```

In this case the method being used as an initializer is defined within the `com.tuhra.ddt.view.util.TaskFlowUtils` class, for reference, the `dumpTaskFlowState()` method is reproduced in the accompanying sidebar, "Dumping Out Page Flow Scope." There is no way to directly pass arguments to initializer or finalizer code, and any return value is ignored, so the basic signature of any method used in this way should be

```
public void methodName() {....}
```

Controlling Navigation with an Initializer Task flow initializers do not directly control the navigation within the flow; the default activity of the task flow is always the entry point for a bounded task flow (unless the Back button has been used). However, it is possible to control navigation indirectly by setting up a variable in the initializer that a router activity in the flow can then use to branch upon.

Dumping Out Page Flow Scope

The following routine is a really useful utility for your programming toolbox. In most task flows, pageFlowScope variables are used to pass arguments into the flow. This routine dumps out the contents of the pageFlowScope along with a little information about the unique identity of this *instance* of the task flow. The code currently prints the information to the console, although in a production system you would probably want to use a formal logging solution instead to control the destination for the output.

```
public void dumpTaskFlowState(){
  AdfFacesContext afctx = AdfFacesContext.getCurrentInstance();
  FacesContext ctx = FacesContext.getCurrentInstance();
  String windowName = afctx.getWindowIdProvider().getCurrentWindowId(ctx);
  Map flowScopeMap = afctx.getPageFlowScope();
  // Loop through the values in the map
  String viewp = ControllerState.getInstance().getCurrentViewPort().getClientId();
  System.out.println("Page Flow in Window: " + windowName);
  System.out.println("Dumping pageFlowScope variables for: " + viewp);
  Iterator iter = flowScopeMap.entrySet().iterator();
  while (iter.hasNext()){
    Map.Entry entry = (Map.Entry)iter.next();
    String mapKey = entry.getKey().toString();
    // Note value may be null - code expecting this!
    Object mapValue = entry.getValue();
    StringBuilder bldr = new StringBuilder("    ");
    bldr.append(mapKey);
    bldr.append("=");
    bldr.append((mapValue==null)?"<null>":mapValue.toString());

    System.out.println(bldr.toString())
  }
}
```

Task Flow Activity Listeners

Initializers and finalizers are part of the core definition for a task flow and will be used by every instance. However, it is also possible to define code that will wrap around a specific usage of a task flow, using Before and After listeners on a task flow call activity.

Comparing Listeners and Initializer/Finalizers The following table outlines the similarities and differences between these two coding points:

Feature	Initializer/Finalizer	Before / After Listeners
Method signature	`public void name()`	`public void name()`
Applies to	Bounded task flows	Bounded task flows
Defined	Within the task flow definition, shared by every instance	Within the parent task flow that calls this bounded task flow. Each set of listeners is unique to a particular task flow call activity
Number allowed	One initializer, one finalizer shared by every instance of the task flow	One Before and one After listener defined per usage of the task flow
Executes when a flow is re-entered/exited using the Back button or other browser navigation?	Yes	No

In a situation where a task flow has an initializer or finalizer and before or after listeners, the listeners are wrapped around the whole flow; that is, the Before listener will execute before the initializer and the After listener will execute after the finalizer.

Because listeners are defined in the surrounding parent flow, rather than in the calling flow, they can be used to store information in that context. For example, in an application where multiple copies of a bounded task flow are opened concurrently to view different customer accounts, such a set of listeners could be used to maintain an index of all of the account numbers that are open.

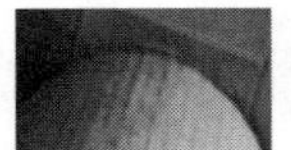

TIP

In this section we have looked at adding code around task flows; however, there is a lot of programming that the developer can do with ADF Controller APIs, which are beyond the scope of this book. If you are interested in that topic, we recommend that you read Oracle Fusion Developer Guide: Build Rich Internet Applications with Oracle ADF Business Components and ADF Faces *by Frank Nimphius and Lynn Munsinger (McGraw-Hill Professional, forthcoming), which has some more advanced use cases that exploit this ability.*

Debugging Task Flows

As a passive debugging technique, the state dumping initializer shown earlier is a useful tool, however, task flows also support interactive debugging. Within the task flow diagram, the right-click menu offers a Toggle Breakpoint option, allowing a debugging breakpoint to be set on an activity (the F5 key can also be used to set breakpoints). With breakpoints set on the diagram, running the application will suspend execution on the requested activities and the developer is able to examine all of the state, including the contents of the various state buckets.

When the debugger is active on a task flow node, several interesting panels will appear in the debugging section of the IDE.

ADF Structure Panel

As a peer to the debugger stack panel, the ADF Structure panel shown in Figure 11-10 shows a logical view of the task flows that are currently open and the views within them. This is particularly useful when dealing with complex pages consisting of a large number of nested flows and regions.

The nodes in the hierarchy displayed by Figure 11-10 can be selected with the mouse, and that will determine the contents of the ADF Data panel. Several different types of nodes are available to inspect:

- **ViewPorts** As we discussed in the section on regions, ADFc uses a concept of ViewPorts to define either the page as a whole or a region within a page that contains a running task flow.

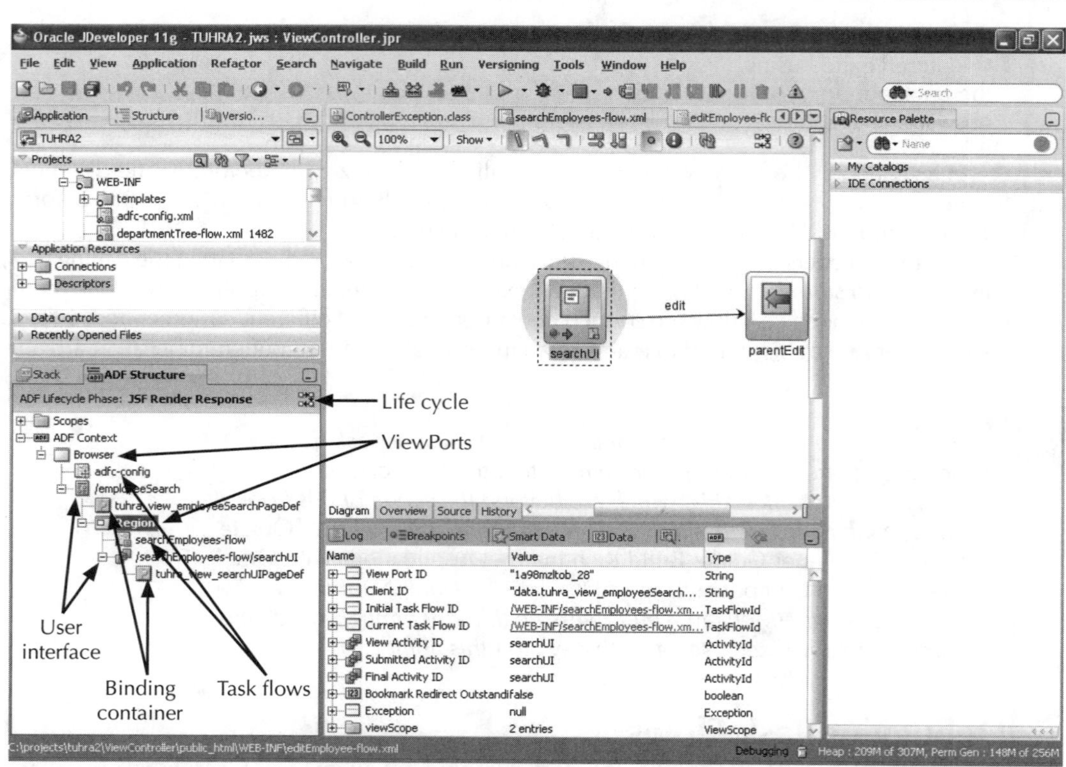

FIGURE 11-10. *ADF Structure window's Debug panel*

- **User Interface** The enclosing page and the UI defined by any nested page fragments that are currently active in the ViewPorts are visible here. You can drill into these and see the complete component tree that makes up the UI fragment, including all of the current property values for those components.
- **Binding Container** This is something that you will encounter in Chapter 13. Put simply, clicking one of these nodes will show you all of the ADF BC values that are in scope for a particular ViewPort.
- **Task Flows** These include both the top-level task flow that owns the page and any nested, bounded task flows being used within regions. Selecting one of these nodes will allow you to inspect all of the important state in the various scopes such as pageFlow and view scope for this ViewPort.

As you click each of these nodes in the ADF Structure panel, the ADF Data panel in the Debug area will display the relevant information.

Figure 11-10 also highlights the Lifecycle icon. Clicking this image will pop up this dialog, which allows the developer to set breakpoints at specific phases of the ADFc and JSF life cycles.

ADF Lifecycle Breakpoints
Toggle breakpoints before and after phases.
JSF Restore View
Initialize Context
Prepare Model
JSF Apply Request Values
JSF Process Validations
JSF Update Model Values
Validate Model Updates
JSF Invoke Application
Metadata Commit
Prepare Render
JSF Render Response

If you click the left-hand column before the Lifecycle phase name, the breakpoint will be set before the life cycle phase starts, and conversely setting the breakpoint in the right-hand column will set an after-phase breakpoint.

ADF Data Panel

As we mentioned, the ADF Data panel provides structured data views on the artifact types that the developer selects in the ADF Structure tree:

- **ViewPorts** The key information in this case is the ViewPort ID and the information about the task flow within the ViewPort (if the ViewPort is a region).

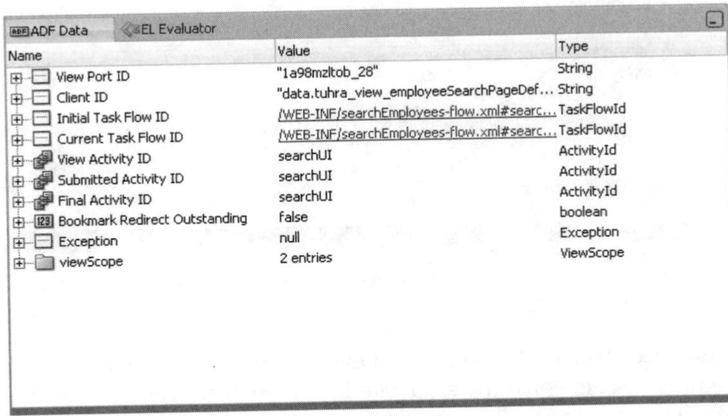

- **Task Flows** The whole hierarchy of task flows can be explored through the ADF Structure tree. Selecting a particular flow will provide a lot of information about that flow, including the name of the current activity, the transaction status, and the contents of the pageFlow scope.

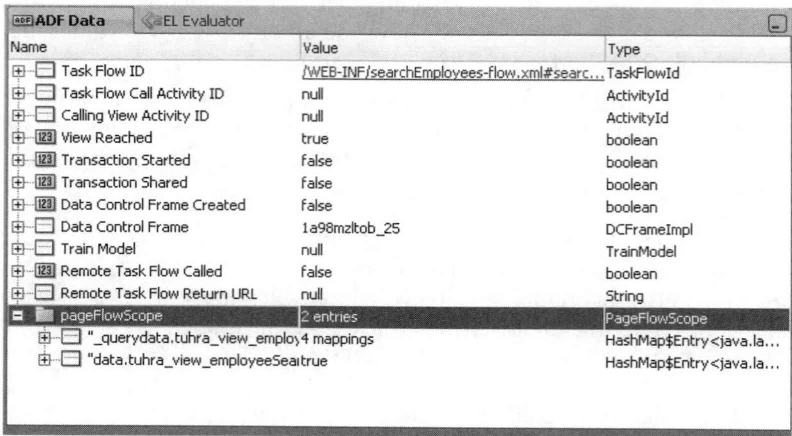

- **Views (pages and page fragments)** If a view is selected in the ADF Structure tree shown in Figure 11-10, the entire component hierarchy of that page or page fragment can be browsed in the ADF Data panel. This provides the ability to look at the values and properties of individual components.

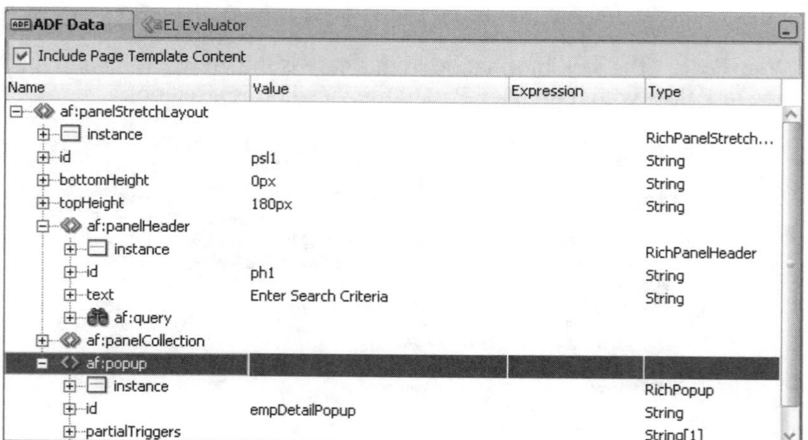

- **Binding Container** Nested within each view that has bound data, the ADF Structure tree provides access to the associated pageDef file. When one of these is selected, the ADF Data panel will allow the developer to explore the current binding container. In the following illustration both conventional data binding and region bindings are shown.

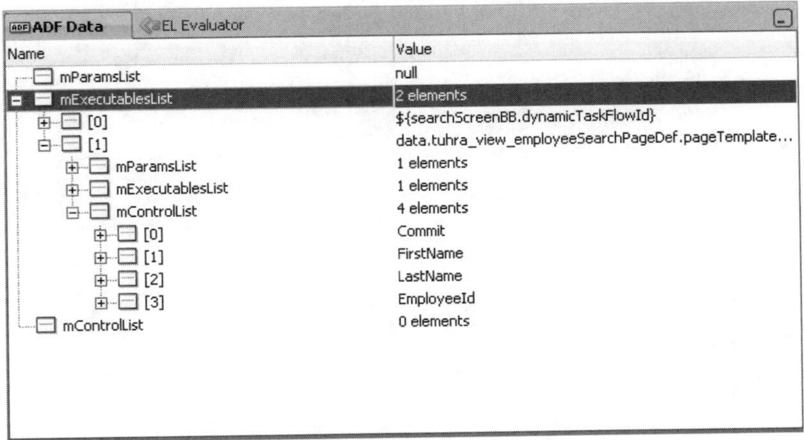

EL Evaluator

Finally we have the EL Evaluator panel. This panel allows the developer to enter, evaluate, and watch the values of Expression Language expressions. This capability is very powerful and useful when parts of a task flow or page formatting is dependent on such evaluated expressions.

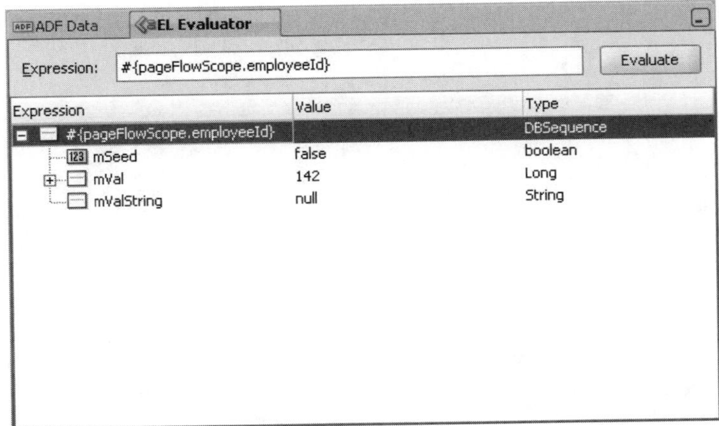

In the preceding illustration the value of a pageFlow scope variable called "employeeId" is being inspected and we can see that the current value is 142.

In this chapter we have covered at least the basic concepts and mechanics of task flows, to provide the Fusion programmer with a solid grounding. However, like many programming tasks, the way that a feature or API is used is often more interesting (and difficult) than the definition of the API itself. In Part V of this book we'll show how all of these task flow features come together to create a typical Fusion application.

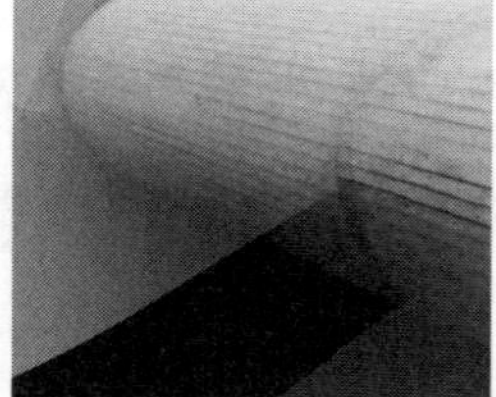

CHAPTER 12

ADF Faces Rich Client

The rich are different from you and me.
They have more money.

—F. Scott Fitzgerald (1896–1940), author,
and Mary McGuire Colum (1884–1957), critic

We didn't need dialogue.
We had faces.

—Norma Desmond, *Sunset Boulevard* (1950)

In Chapter 10, you built a basic JavaServer Faces (JSF) application using the Oracle JSF user interface library ADF Faces Rich Client. This chapter takes off where the ADF Faces RC introduction in Chapters 1 and 9 left off. It explains a lot more about the features of ADF Faces RC and demonstrates basic functionality and standard techniques for working with some of the ADF Faces RC components.

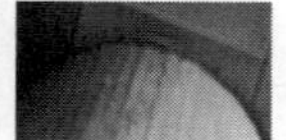

NOTE
*As mentioned earlier, whenever we refer to "ADF Faces" in this book, we are discussing the version available with JDeveloper 11*g *(ADF Faces RC). When we refer to the version of ADF Faces that premiered with JDeveloper 10*g*, we use the term "ADF Faces 10*g*," which was the source of Apache MyFaces Trinidad, available in JDeveloper 11*g*.*

The chapter focuses on answering the following questions:

- **What is ADF Faces and where did it come from?**
- **How does partial page rendering work?**
- **How can I achieve the perfect layout?**
- **What kinds of atomic components are available?**
- **How can I change the default ADF Faces appearance?**
- **How will I ever learn about all these components?**

As with any subject, the best way to learn is by doing, and you will receive plenty of experience working with ADF Faces components while building the application in Part V of this book. Therefore, the main objective of this chapter is to supply some background to give you a better basis for understanding what you are working with when building an application using ADF Faces. However, to further this background, you will be following some short, hands-on practices to get tastes of the features and components, which are introduced in this chapter.

What Is ADF Faces and Where Did It Come From?

ADF Faces is a JSF component set that provides a group of rich user interface controls for developing JSP pages with JSF components. ADF Faces is well integrated with JDeveloper, and the developer's experience using ADF Faces can be mostly declarative and visual. In addition, as mentioned before, ADF Faces is one of the technologies Oracle uses to build the Fusion Applications.

ADF Faces consists of class libraries and tag libraries of several categories. This chapter focuses on these two main categories that you will use to build JSF pages:

- **Atomic components**, which display a single object such as a text field with its prompt (`af:inputText`) or a pulldown (`af:selectOneChoice`).
- **Layout containers**, which surround atomic components and other layout containers and offer automatic layout features such as field alignment (`af:panelFormLayout`).

One of the last runtime processing steps for a JSF page is to pass the components through a *render kit,* a translation layer that converts the raw representation of the components into markup tags specific to the client display device.

HTML Render Kit

When the target client device is a web browser, ADF Faces uses the HTML render kit to form the component hierarchy into HTML tags that the web browser can display. Therefore for a web browser target device, an ADF Faces component such as `af:panelGroupLayout` will create an HTML table structure using tags such as `<table>` and `<tr>`. An ADF Faces text field component such as `af:inputText` will render as an HTML input tag, for example, `<input type="text" />`.

As a visual example of this translation, the first hands-on practice in this chapter creates the small form shown here in the JDeveloper visual editor:

The tag hierarchy that represents this form is shown next in the Structure window:

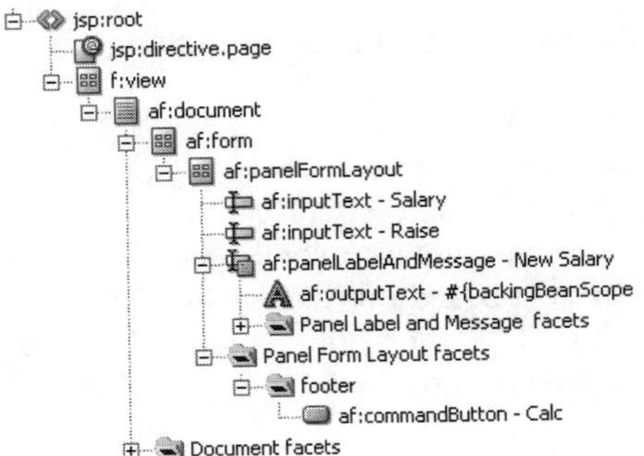

At runtime, the web page is created with standard HTML tags that would display in the JDeveloper visual editor as shown here. Notice the use of nested HTML table elements.

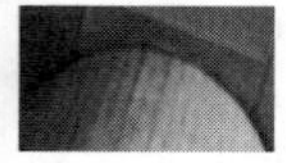

NOTE
As mentioned in Chapter 9, ADF Faces tags use the "af" prefix to refer to the tag library. The tags are represented with a friendlier name in the Component Palette. For example, the `af:inputText` tag is labeled as "Input Text" in the Component Palette. This book uses both types of names interchangeably.

A Very Brief History

Oracle E-Business Suite (EBS) applications (the predecessor to Oracle Fusion Applications) were developed early on using Oracle Forms. Although currently Oracle Forms applications are run in a web browser environment, Oracle saw the need for a lightweight, Java EE–oriented runtime environment and met the need in later versions of EBS with ADF UIX (formerly UIX or "User Interface XML"). *ADF UIX* is a framework consisting of components used to build user interfaces. UIX files are coded in XML (as the name implies), and the files run in a standard Java EE web client environment. UIX files are interpreted by the UIX Servlet process running in a standard Java EE web container. The servlet constructs an HTML page (for web browser clients) and that page returns to the client browser. JDeveloper 9*i* was the first release to offer development tools support for UIX; this support continued through JDeveloper 10*g*, release 2 (10.1.2).

After Oracle had released EBS applications that successfully used UIX, the industry adopted JSF technology as a Java EE standard. Oracle then rewrote the proprietary ADF UIX tag library to be completely compliant with the JSF standard and called this new framework ADF Faces (ADF Faces 10*g*). *ADF Faces,* therefore, is a JSF-compliant UI component set that is based on the JSF API. It is most commonly used to output HTML for web browsers, but it is capable of output to any type of display device, with native support for wireless devices. This multi-faced output style is defined in the JSF standards but is rarely implemented.

In JDeveloper 10*g*, Release 3 (10.1.3), tools support for ADF UIX was phased out in favor of support for ADF Faces 10*g*. JDeveloper 11*g* introduces ADF Faces Rich Client (ADF Faces RC, referred to in this book as just "ADF Faces") as a further evolution on and improvement of ADF Faces 10*g*.

Trinidad

Early in 2006, Oracle donated ADF Faces 10*g* to the open-source Apache MyFaces Project (myfaces.apache.org). Although Oracle continued to enhance and support ADF Faces for its customers, the larger Java community also contributed to the functionality of the donated version. The part of the MyFaces project based on ADF Faces 10*g* is called *Trinidad.* ADF Faces RC is a separate code base, which is at the moment maintained only by Oracle. The Trinidad library is also supported in JDeveloper 11*g*, and ADF Faces RC is built on top of it.

ADF Faces Is Better

Since "better" is a relative word, the first question is, "What is ADF Faces better than?" The short answer is that it is the latest step in an evolution, and therefore better than any of its predecessors (UIX, ADF UIX, and ADF Faces 10*g*). ADF Faces is arguably better than other JSF component sets because of its long-term evolution (few competing frameworks have such a long heritage) and its native features that make declarative and visual development of highly-functional user interfaces faster and easier. To further answer the question, it is helpful to know more about its features, which will be explored in this chapter and throughout the rest of this book. One such feature is partial page rendering.

How Does Partial Page Rendering Work?

Of all ADF features, partial page rendering (PPR) is one of the most powerful because it offers the developer a declarative way to create highly-interactive web pages. PPR uses JavaScript and XML to submit and update only some fields or data on a page. The concept behind PPR (and the use of JavaScript in general) is to achieve a more user-friendly interface by mitigating or completely removing the wait a user experiences when a full page is submitted to the server and rerendered after processing occurs.

You are no doubt familiar with web pages that rely on the full-page submit technique. You also may share the frustration that your experience with an application or website is interrupted by waiting for a server to return and redraw a web page. One of the tenets of Web 2.0 is that user interfaces are highly interactive and wait times as well as the ensuing frustrations are reduced.

PPR was one of the strengths of the early releases of ADF UIX and provided this high interactivity to Oracle EBS applications. Subsequently, the Java community evolved the core ideas behind PPR, and the technology that emerged is now called "Asynchronous JavaScript and XML" (AJAX, as discussed in the section "Asynchronous JavaScript and XML" in Chapter 4).

ADF Faces offers the PPR capability but works within the guidelines of the popular industry technology AJAX. Unlike typical AJAX development, where you need to write custom JavaScript code, define JavaScript events, and create custom Java servlet code to handle the requests, using PPR in ADF Faces is completely declarative. It could even be called "declarative AJAX."

You can think of PPR in simple terms as a process outside the normal page submit and full page rendering whereby a source component's change in value (or a user event such as a button click) triggers a target component to be rerendered. As the target component is rerendered, its property values are read and, in the case of EL expressions, reevaluated. The source component needs to be marked so that it automatically submits its value for processing; the target component needs to be marked so that it watches (listens) for a partial submit from one or more source components. You use the following properties to mark the source and target components:

- **AutoSubmit** Set this property to "true" on all source components that will initiate the partial page submission.
- **PartialTriggers** Set this property on the target component or components to listen for a change in the source component. The value of this property is a space-delimited list of IDs for the components that will trigger the PPR rerendering of the target component.

In addition, the *PartialSubmit* property of command components, such as `af:commandButton` and `af:commandLink`, declares whether that command component will initiate a PPR event. For example, you could declare a button and set its *PartialSubmit* property to "true" so that when the user clicks the button, any components declared with *AutoSubmit* as "true" will be rerendered. You can also use components called *listeners* to trigger partial submits on non-standard component actions, such as right-click, selection, or rollover.

You will use PPR extensively in building the application in Part V of this book, but you might want a taste of the concepts now. If so, follow these (abbreviated) steps in JDeveloper 11*g*.

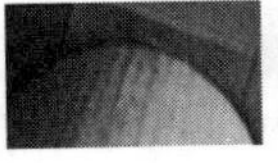

NOTE

As an additional reminder, you need to run ADF Faces RC applications in a compatible browser, for example, Internet Explorer 7.0 or later, Mozilla Firefox 2.0 or later, or Safari 3.0.

Hands-on Practice: Demonstrate Basic PPR

This hands-on practice shows how you can declare AJAX (PPR) functionality using the ADF Faces components. (As with all abbreviated practices, refer to earlier chapters such as Chapter 9 if you need help with a basic operation such as creating an application.) The application you will build is a three-field form with a Calc button and Salary, Raise, and New Salary fields. The New Salary field will automatically update when the value of the Salary or Raise field changes.

You will be building a form that appears as follows at runtime:

Salary 0
Raise 0
New Salary 0
Calc

For simplicity, this practice uses a backing bean (managed bean) to provide a source for binding the user interface fields.

1. If any applications are running, stop them as well as the Default Server (using the Terminate button).
2. Create an application called "ADFFacesTest" using the "Fusion Web Application (ADF)" application template. Specify an application prefix of "demo." This template will create two projects, although you will not use the Model project in this practice.

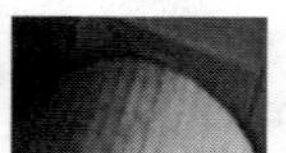

CAUTION
Remember to avoid typing the ending period or comma for property values we enclose inside quotes unless otherwise specified.

3. In the ViewController project, create a JSF page as an XML document with the name "testPPR.jspx." (Start this process from the New Gallery.) In the Page Implementation section of the Create JSF Page dialog, specify that the components will be exposed in a new managed bean.

   Additional Information: Automatically exposing UI components in a managed bean is something you will rarely do in a Fusion application, but we show it here to demonstrate how you can interact with managed beans using EL.
4. From the Component Palette, drop a Panel Form Layout component (from the Layout panel) onto the page.

   Additional Information: The `af:panelFormLayout` component provides automatic alignment for fields it contains. You will drop in some fields next.
5. Drop an Input Text component (Common Components) onto the `af:panelFormLayout` node in the Structure window. In the Property Inspector, set *Label* as "Salary" and *Value* as "0."

   Additional Information: The *Value* property supplies a default value that will be overridden by input from the user.
6. Drop another Input Text component onto the `af:panelFormLayout` and set *Label* as "Raise" and *Value* as "0."

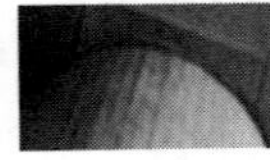

TIP
Dropping a component onto a layout container such as `af:panelFormLayout` *adds it under the other components within that container. You can reorder components within a container most easily using drag-and-drop operations in the Structure window.*

7. Drop an Output Text component onto the `af:panelFormLayout`.

   Additional Information: This read-only field will show the results of the calculation.

8. For the *Value* property, click the down arrow next to the field and select Expression Builder. Remove the existing expression. Enter or select nodes in the Expression Builder navigator to form the following expression (all on one line):

```
#{backingBeanScope.backing_testPPR.it1.value +
   backingBeanScope.backing_testPPR.it2.value}
```

   Additional Information: Open nodes under ADF Managed Beans\backingBeanScope to find the inputText ("it") items. The name of your backing bean and text item IDs may vary a bit. This expression adds the values of the two fields and assigns the value to the Output Text item after the page is submitted.

9. Now you need to add a label for the read-only field. Notice that the `af:panelFormLayout` container left aligns the `af:outputText` field with the existing fields, but `af:outputText` has no *Label* property so the line looks incomplete. Fortunately, there is an easy solution—the Panel Label and Message component.

10. On the `af:outputText` component in the visual editor or Structure window, select **Surround With** from the right-click menu. Select "Panel Label and Message" and click OK. Set *Label* for `af:panelLabelAndMessage` as "New Salary."

    Additional Information: This embeds the `af:outputText` component within the `af:PanelLabelAndMessage` component, which supplies the label. Now the fields and labels line up properly.

11. Drop a Button onto the footer facet of the `af:panelFormLayout`. Set *Text* as "Calc."

    Additional Information: This button will submit the values to the server (Model layer of code, which for this application is included with the ViewController code). The addition specified in the New Salary *Value* expression will fill in when the user clicks this button and the page is refreshed with updated values from the server. The Structure window should display the following nodes:

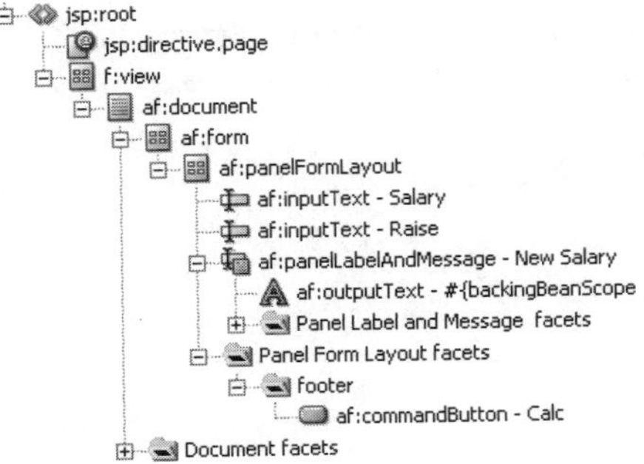

12. Run the page. Fill in Salary as 1000 and Raise as "200"; press TAB. The New Salary field value will not change. Click Calc. The New Salary field will display "1,200."

    Additional Information: This is the default behavior of a JSF page. No processing will occur unless the user actively submits the page, in this case, using a submit button. Now it is time to set up PPR so that the New Salary value will be refreshed automatically.

13. Close the browser.
14. On both Salary and Raise components, set *AutoSubmit* (Behavior section) as "true." This will trigger PPR when either of the component values change.
15. On the New Salary `af:panelLabelAndMessage` component, click the Edit selection in the pulldown to the right of *PartialTriggers* and move the names of the other two items to the *Selected* area as shown here:

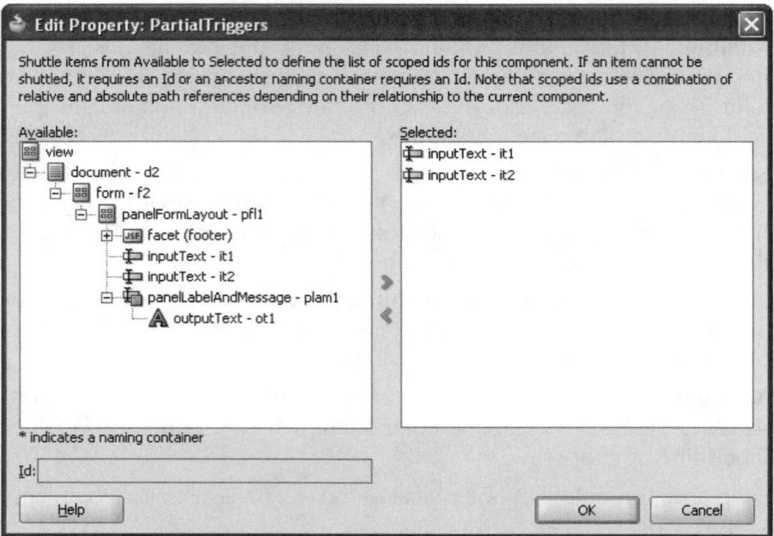

16. Click OK and the property will fill in with the names of the items separated by a space.
17. Click Save All. Run the page. Fill in Salary as "1000" and press TAB. The New Salary field will fill in with "1000." Fill in Raise as "200" and press TAB. The New Salary field will change to "1,200."

    Additional Information: You do not need to click Calc to cause the server to update the calculated field. PPR submits the values automatically when you navigate out of a changed field.

18. Close the browser. Stop the application.

What Did You Just Do? You created a JSF page containing input fields and a submit button. The page used a backing bean that provided access to values with Expression Language expressions. Without PPR, you needed to submit the page so that the entire page, including the calculated value, would refresh. You then set up PPR by verifying that the input fields were assigned ID values, setting *AutoSubmit* on the input fields, and setting *PartialTriggers* on the read-only field. With PPR declared in this way, when you changed a value in an input field and navigated out of the field, the calculation was performed and the read-only field value changed accordingly, without having to submit the entire page.

This practice also demonstrated several commonly used ADF Faces atomic components (`af:inputText` and `af:outputText`) and layout containers (`af:panelFormLayout` and `af:panelLabelAndMessage`).

CAUTION
If you use PPR to set the Rendered *property of a component to display or hide dynamically, you need to set the* Partial Triggers *property on a parent object such as an* `af:panelGroupLayout` *component that surrounds the component. Setting* Partial Triggers *on the component you are displaying or hiding will have no effect. This limitation applies only to the* Rendered *property.*

How Can I Achieve the Perfect Layout?

Success in laying out a page that uses ADF Faces components requires at least a modest comfort level with the concept of using layout containers. While you are in the process of attaining that comfort level, it helps to allocate some design time to planning how you will use the layout containers in your application. Several tools will help you achieve the layout you require.

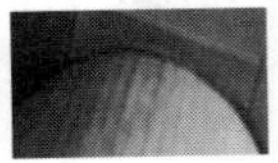

NOTE
The hands-on practices in Part V explore and demonstrate the use of templates and task flows that contain page fragments.

Facets

As mentioned in Chapter 9, layout containers offer *facets,* components into which you place other components. If the facet is responsible for a visual effect, at runtime, the facets maintain relative positioning of their contents. For example, the `af:panelFormLayout` layout container offers a footer facet that appears under all fields and is not bound by the alignment rules of the main area of the container. Facets is one tool you can use in achieving the perfect layout.

NOTE
Facets can contain only one component. However, the one component in a facet could be a layout container, which, in turn, can hold more than one component. JDeveloper leads by example in this case—if you drop a second component into a facet, instead of raising an error, JDeveloper will automatically add an `af:group` *container around the two components. An* `af:group` *container component is just used to group related components into a single unit but it offers no visual properties of its own.*

Knowledge of Layout Containers

The main tool you need to master for achieving the perfect layout is a knowledge of the layout containers. Fortunately, the list of layout containers is small at the moment as shown in the illustration on the right, from the Layout panel of the ADF Faces Component Palette page, where you can access most of the layout containers.

You will use many of these components in the hands-on practices in Part V of this book, but it is worthwhile previewing a few of them at this point.

Component Palette
ADF Faces
ADF Faces
Common Components
Layout
Decorative Box
Document
Inline Frame
Navigation Pane
Panel Accordion
Panel Border Layout
Panel Box
Panel Collection
Panel Dashboard
Panel Form Layout
Panel Group Layout
Panel Header
Panel List
Panel Splitter
Panel Stretch Layout
Panel Tabbed
Panel Window
Separator
Show Detail Header
Spacer
Toolbox
Operations

af:panelFormLayout As the PPR hands-on practice in this chapter demonstrated, this container allows you to lay out fields in columns without requiring any other embedded containers. The fields are left-aligned, and their prompts are right-aligned. All fields are stacked on top of one another, but you can specify the number of columns and rows for a columnar arrangement. This provides a familiar appearance for data entry needs. The fields are rendered down one column and then down the next column. This ordering implements a *tab order* (the order in which the cursor navigates fields when the TAB key is pressed) of down and across. (The section "Nesting Layout Containers" later in this chapter discusses tab order.) The PPR hands-on practice shows screenshots of the effect of this layout container on its child components.

af:panelHeaderLayout This container provides a title to denote a grouping of elements on the page. It offers properties for *Size* to set the height of the heading text, *MessageType* to automatically add an icon (information or warning, for example) to the left of the heading text, *Text* for the heading text, and others. Nesting components within this container will stack them vertically on the page as shown next. The *InlineStyle* property has been set to "border-color:Black; border-style:dotted; border-width:thin;" to make the edges of the container visible.

The Header Text Property
Field1
Pulldown1
Button1

TIP
Setting the background color as well as the border style of layout containers in this way is a useful debugging technique because it allows you to see the edges of each layout container.

af:panelGroupLayout This container lays out components in a single row (horizontal layout) or column (vertical layout). The *Layout* property sets the orientation by which components in the container will be arranged: horizontal, vertical, or scroll (vertical with scrollbars). The following illustration shows a `af:panelGroupLayout` component with a *Layout* of "horizontal" and under it, another with the same components but with a *Layout* of "vertical." As with the preceding illustration, *InlineStyle* defines a dotted line to show the edge of the containers.

TIP
`af:panelGroupLayout` works best when you explicitly assign a Layout *property value other than "default" rather than relying on the default.*

af:panelSplitter This container divides an area horizontally or vertically into two panels and optionally allows the user to move the dividing line between the panels to change the relative sizes of the panels. If the *Disabled* property is set to "true," the user will not be able to move the splitter bar. You drop components into the first and second facets in this container to assign them to one panel or the other. For example, if you define a horizontal splitter, the user can move the splitter bar (divider) between panels to the left or right to make the first panel narrower or wider. The following illustration shows this effect as the splitter bar is in motion (the mouse cursor is the double-headed arrow):

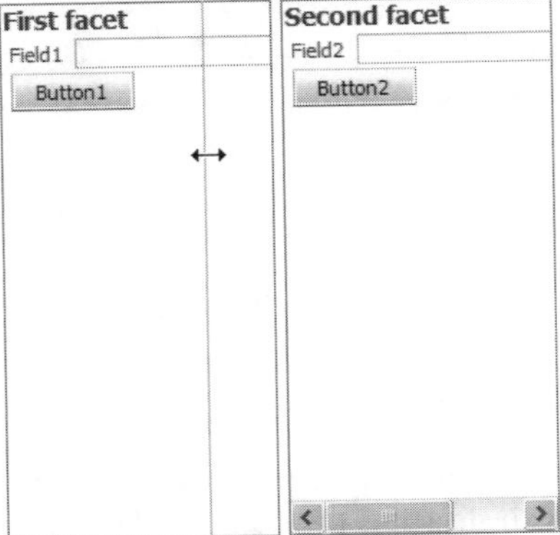

The user can click the arrow icon on the splitter bar (not shown when the splitter bar is in motion, as it is in the preceding illustration) to collapse the first panel completely. Notice that the components in this display are truncated. To help you solve layout issues such as this, JDeveloper offers a pulldown menu in the top-right corner of the component after selecting it in the visual editor as shown here:

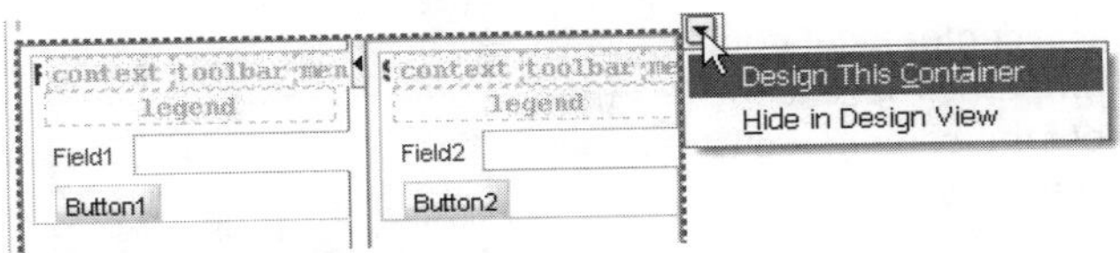

Selecting **Design This Container** opens an editor area that allows you to resize the component borders so that you could achieve a layout such as the following, where all components fit within the panels.

NOTE

This editor just sets InlineStyle and SplitterPositions, but it allows you to control the size visually instead of by experimenting with property values.

af:panelBorderLayout As explained in the "Facets" section in Chapter 9, this layout container provides facets such as top, bottom, start, and end. Components dropped into one of these facets will maintain their relative positions at runtime. You can use this layout container for pages that require a logo in the header area (top facet) and copyright and informational text in the footer area (bottom facet). The facets are easiest to see in the visual editor as shown here:

af:panelStretchLayout This container also offers facets for bottom, start, top, and end. It also provides a center facet, which stretches the contained component to fill the available width. You would use this container if another container cuts off the display of a layout container or atomic component. The following illustration shows this container with *StartWidth, EndWidth, TopWidth,* and *BottomWidth* properties set to "30." Each facet contains an `af:panelGroupLayout` component with a background color of "Silver" and dotted border to better display the facet areas. The center facet contains a button with no properties set except *Text* (the label). Notice how the center facet stretches the button to fill the available space.

The "Design This Container" editor described earlier allows you to set the size of the facets surrounding the center facet of the `af:panelStretchLayout` component as well its overall size.

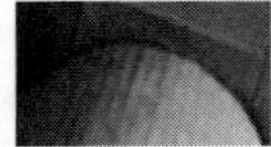

TIP
The `af:panelGroupLayout` component is only as large as its child components. Therefore, if you have trouble aligning components within this layout container, it could be because the `af:panelGroupLayout` component is not wide enough. Try surrounding it with an `af:panelStretchLayout` component, which will expand the `af:panelGroupLayout` component and align its child components properly.

As a short demonstration of layout container properties and alignment capabilities, open the PPR application you created earlier in the chapter. Navigate to the Property Inspector for the `af:panelFormLayout` component and set *MaxColumns* (in the Common region) as "2" and *Rows* as "2." Notice that the New Salary field moved into the second column because the tab (cursor navigation) order for an `af:panelFormLayout` layout container is across and down. The button retained its position at the bottom of the layout because it is placed in the footer facet.

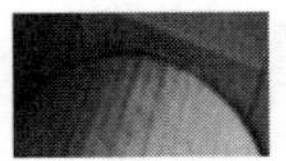

TIP
If you try to copy and paste components in the Structure window but JDeveloper copies and pastes property values or other components instead, click a window such as the Log window to hide the Property Inspector. Then try the copy and paste operation in the Structure window again.

On the Salary field, set the *Columns* property (Appearance region) as "10" to set the width of the field. Notice that the New Salary field retains its horizontal position as shown here:

This alignment occurs because the New Salary field is in the second column, which is sized according to the widest field in the first column (Raise).

Other Layout Containers

Although most of the layout containers are available in the Layout panel of the Component Palette displayed earlier, you will find some additional layout containers in the Common Components panel as in the following examples:

- **`af:form`** This container renders a submit form (in HTML, `<form>`) used to pass content to the server for processing. It is technically not a layout container because it does not provide layout characteristics, but it is a container that holds other components.
- **`af:menuBar`** This component provides an area into which you place pulldown menu components. This component is called "Panel Menu Bar" in the Component Palette.
- **`af:menu`** This component displays a pulldown menu and can be placed into a popup or menubar.

- **af:popup** This container has no visual aspect; it displays whatever you place in it on top of the page.
- **af:dialog** This component displays a window containing a border, one or more buttons, and a content area. This component must be placed inside an `af:popup` component.
- **af:toolbar** This component displays an area into which you place command components such as buttons. This component is usually placed inside another layout container—`af:toolbox` (in the Layout panel), which contains toolbars and menubars.
- **af:panelLabelAndMessage** As demonstrated in the PPR practice, this layout container supplies a label to its contents. For example, the `af:outputText` component does not have a *Label* property. If you want to use that component to display read-only data values in a form, you can surround the component with `af:panelLabelAndMessage` and set the layout container's *Label* property. Since you can place more than one component in a container, you could remove the labels on employee First Name and Last Name fields, surround those fields with `af:panelLabelAndMessage`, and fill in the container's Label as "Employee Name" as shown here:

  Employee Name | Harry | Houdini

  If the Employee Name structure is contained in an `af:panelFormLayout`, the container will treat it as a single field and apply the label and field layout alignments as shown next. The `af:panelFormLayout` is assigned a dotted border for visibility in this illustration.

  Employee Name | Harry | Houdini   City | New York
  Address | 278 W. 113th St.   State | NY

TIP

Set Simple *as "true" for `af:inputText` field components inside the `af:panelLabelAndMessage` container so that the field labels are not displayed. This setting also causes the fields to lay out horizontally as shown in the preceding illustration.*

Visual Component Guide

The JDeveloper help system contains a visual representation of ADF Faces container (as well as all other) components. Enter "enhanced tag doc" in the help search field and click the link with the same name in the search results. Alternatively, navigate in the Contents tree to Javadoc and Tag Library Reference\JDeveloper Tag Library Reference\Oracle ADF Faces Tag Library Overview.

Nesting Layout Containers

As with other tag languages, such as HTML, you can embed layout containers within layout containers to take advantage of more than one type of arrangement. This is a useful and necessary tool for achieving the perfect layout. For example, the next illustration shows an `af:panelGroupLayout` container (defined with *Layout* as "vertical") that surrounds three more `af:panelGroupLayout` components (defined with *Layout* as "horizontal"), each of which contains two `af:inputText` components. The *Columns* properties of the fields have been set differently to show the somewhat ragged alignment that will result.

WideField1 Field2
NarrowtField3 Field4
MediumField5 NarrowField6

TIP
Use the `af:spacer` component to add a fixed horizontal or vertical space between components. Enter values in the `af:spacer` properties "Width" and "Height" to designate a pixel width or height for the spacer, for example, "10px."

The tab order for an `af:panelGroupLayout` with Layout set to "horizontal" is across. The tab order for an `af:panelGroupLayout` set to "vertical" is down. Therefore, the preceding arrangement implements a tab order of across and down—within a inner horizontal `af:panelGroupLayout` component and between inner horizontal `af:panelGroupLayout` components. This type of layout provides an alternative to the `af:panelFormLayout` tab order of down and across. Techniques for implementing a tab order of across and down are explored in the following hands-on practice.

Hands-on Practice: Implement an Across and Down Tab Order

If you wanted to emulate the alignment characteristics of a `af:panelFormLayout` layout container in addition to implementing an across-and-down tab order, you could use these two alternative techniques:

I. Use spacers to align the fields

II. Use container properties to align the fields

This hands-on practice demonstrates both of these alternative techniques and mentions some of the benefits and drawbacks of each.

I. Use Spacers to Align the Fields

This technique consists of adding `af:spacer` components before and between fields to achieve the following layout:

WideField1 Field2
NarrowField3 Field4
MediumField5 NarrowField6

This arrangement looks similar to the arrangement of components within an `af:panelFormLayout` container. It has a more complicated setup (finding the widths required for each spacer takes experimentation) but allows you to provide a tab order that some users prefer.

1. In the ADFFacesTest application you used for the earlier hands-on practice, create a JSF page called tabOrder1.jspx. Specify that JDeveloper will not create a backing bean file.
2. Drop a Panel Group Layout component into the `af:form`. Set *Layout* to "vertical." Drop three more Panel Group Layout components on top of the first `af:panelGroupLayout` and set *Layout* for the three components to "horizontal." This will result in three rows inside the outer layout container.

3. In the first row, drag a Spacer component on top of the `af:panelGroupLayout` and set its *Width* property to "22"; then add an Input Text component and set *Columns* to "35"; add a Spacer and set its *Width* to "25"; and add a final Input Text and set *Columns* to "10." Repeat this process (using copy and paste if you want to) for the other two rows using the settings in the following table.

Row	Field (*Columns*) or Spacer (*Width*)
2	Spacer (11); Input Text (10); Spacer (150); Input Text (10)
3	Spacer (10); Input Text (20); Spacer (65); Input Text (5)

Additional Information: The Structure window should appear as follows (although the Structure window labels for your fields may be different at this point). Notice that the `af:spacer` nodes show the *Height* property (all defaulting to 10), not the *Width* property that you set. The *Columns* property represents character columns, not pixels.

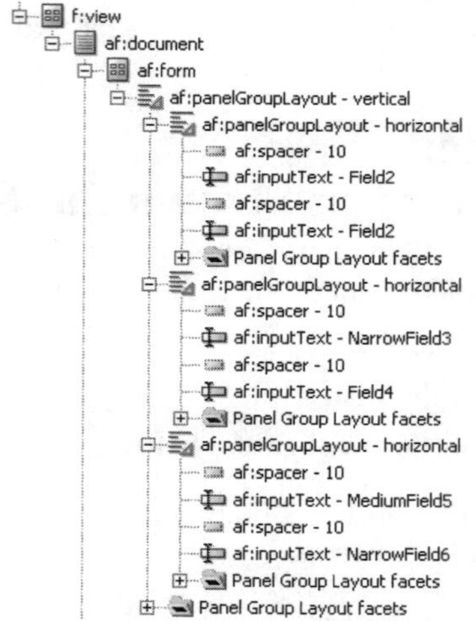

4. Set the field labels as shown in the preceding illustration. The layout editor will not show the final runtime alignment although the **Preview in Browser** right-click menu option will.

5. Run the file to test the field alignments. Proper alignment will depend upon the skin you are using (discussed in the section "Working with Skins" later on). If needed, so adjust the properties so the field alignment matches the earlier illustration. Resize the window width to test variations on the window size.

   Additional Information: Since the field labels are single words, the alignment will be maintained. If you change the labels to multiple words, they would wrap if the window width became too small; this would disrupt the field alignment. Since the field labels are used to maintain field alignment, if the field labels need to be changed dynamically based on the user's language, the work required for this technique becomes nearly unmanageable.

6. Close the browser.

What Did You Just Do? You set up nested layout containers with specific alignments to implement an across and down tab order. The problem with this layout arrangement is that it requires experimentation to find the correct size for the spacers. Another problem mentioned before is the dependency on the width of field labels, which may change based on the user's language and which are subject to wrapping if the window is narrowed sufficiently.

CAUTION
This alignment technique may not produce consistent results on all versions of all browsers. It is always a good idea to try your application with different browsers to verify the visual effects.

II. Use Container Properties to Align the Fields

An alternative technique for implementing an across and down tab order, but still maintaining the alignment of fields between rows, is to use multiple `af:panelFormLayout` components, each of which displays a single row. If you set each row's layout container with the same space allocated to the field width and label width, you can achieve the vertical alignment of fields, even if the fields and field labels are different widths. The following steps use this technique to create the layout shown in Figure 12-1.

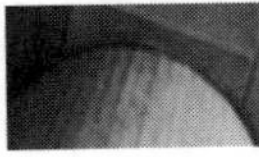

CAUTION
This is not a complete functional equivalent to the single `af:panelFormLayout` *solution. We explain the drawbacks of this technique after the hands-on practice.*

1. Create a JSF page called tabOrder2.jspx (no managed bean). You will be adding components to create the structure shown in the Structure window snippet here.

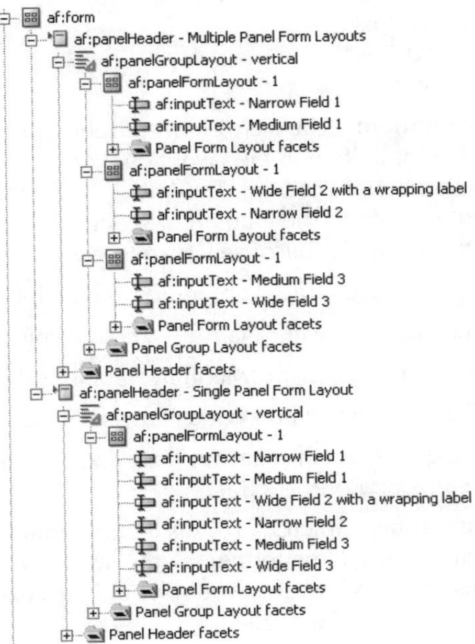

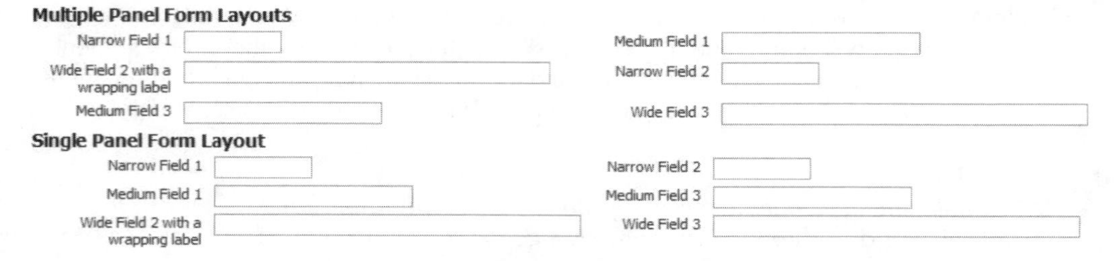

FIGURE 12-1. *af:panelFormLayout component tab order demonstration*

2. Drop a Panel Header on the page and set *Text* to "Multiple Panel Form Layouts."
3. Drop a Panel Group Layout into `af:panelHeader` and set *Layout* as "vertical." This component will supply the mechanism to stack rows of fields.
4. Drop a Panel Form Layout component onto the `af:panelGroupLayout` component and set *MaxColumns* as "2" and *Rows* as "1."
5. Select the `af:panelHeader` and copy it. Paste it onto the `af:form` component to create another region. Change *Text* of the copy to "Single Panel Form Layout."
6. In the Multiple Panel Form Layouts region, drop two Input Text components into the `af:panelFormLayout` component.
7. Copy the `af:panelFormLayout` component and paste on top of the `af:panelGroupLayout` component to create the second row of fields.
8. Repeat the preceding step to create the third row of fields.
9. Group the three `af:panelFormLayout` components and set the following properties:
   FieldWidth as "300px"
   LabelWidth as "100px"
   Inline Style as "width:800.0px;"

   Additional Information: The *FieldWidth* property designates how much space is available for each input item in the layout container. The *LabelWidth* property sets a fixed space for each input item's prompt. The *Inline Style* width sets the available space for the entire layout container. The amount of space allocated to each column is half of that (400 pixels in this example) because we are specifying two columns.
10. Change the `af:inputText` *Label* properties to match those shown in Figure 12-1.
11. Group the two components with "Narrow" labels (using CTRL-click) and set *Columns* as "10."
12. Group the two components with "Medium" labels and set *Columns* as "25."
13. Group the two components with "Wide" labels and set *Columns* as "50."
14. Under the the Single Panel Form Layout `af:panelGroupLayout`, set the `af:panelFormLayout` *Rows* as "3."

    Additional Information: *MaxColumns* is the important setting, but it is good practice to set *Rows* as well. Rows will be formed by the layout container placing the MaxColumns number of items on each line. If the number of items exceeds *MaxColumns* times *Rows*, the number of rows will be extended.

NOTE
Be sure the FieldWidth, LabelWidth *and* InlineStyle *properties are blank for the Single Panel Form Layout* `af:panelFormLayout` *component.*

15. Group all six fields from the three `af:panelFormLayout` components in the multiple panel region above and copy them, then paste them onto the `af:panelFormLayout` in the Single Panel Form Layout region. Compare your Structure window nodes with the illustration shown in Step 1.
16. Click Save All. Run the page.
17. Click in the first field and tab through the six fields in the top region to verify that the tab order is across and down.
18. Continue tabbing through the fields in the bottom region to verify that the tab order is down and across.
19. Resize the window width. Notice that the fields in the top region maintain their relative positions but they do not move based on the window width. The fields in the bottom region react to the window resizing and relocate so that more of the content is visible.
20. Close the browser. Stop the application.

What Did You Just Do? You created a tab across-and-down region and a tab down-and-across region each with six fields. The former layout technique uses multiple `af:panelGroupLayout` and `af:panelFormLayout` components to emulate the alignment effect of a single `af:panelFormLayout` component. The resulting layout is not as fragile as the technique demonstrated in the preceding practice and it does not require as much experimentation. However, it has some limitations: mainly that the container widths need to be set explicitly. This takes a small amount of calculation and experimentation. Also, if the user increases the browser font size or uses a different skin, the width of one of the fields may exceed the width allotted and one or more rows may lose their alignment with the other rows. A summary of the differences in features between the single `af:panelFormLayout` component technique and the multiple `af:panelFormLayout` technique appears in Table 12-1.

Feature	Single	Multiple
Tab order	Down and across	Across and down
Fields left-align and labels right-align	Yes	Yes
Width of the browser window determines width of the container	Yes	No
Width of a column within the container is based on the width of the widest field in that column	Yes	No
Calculations and experimentation are needed to assign widths	No	Yes
Technique is immune to the user increasing the browser font size	Yes	No

TABLE 12-1. *Comparison of Features for Single Panel Form Layout and Multiple Panel Form Layout Containers*

Should you decide to use this technique, you will need to experiment with setting the *FieldWidth* property (in pixels) to accommodate the widest field. Fields are sized in character columns, which does not translate to pixels, and this is why you need to experiment a bit. Remember that you need to multiply the sum of the largest field width plus a reasonable label width by the number of fields per line to reach the *InlineStyle* width for the `af:panelFormLayout` component. In other words, the formula to use (after finding the optimal field width and label width) follows (all widths use the unit pixels):

```
(FieldWidth + LabelWidth) = (Inline Style:Width / Number of Fields per Line)
```

Quick Start Layouts

One way to shortcut work with layout containers is to create the page using Quick Start Layouts. *Quick Start Layouts* are pre-built sets of layout containers that are designed for specific functionality. You access this feature from the Create JSF Page dialog (started from the New Gallery's JSF Page item). Selecting Click Start Layout in the dialog and then clicking Browse will open a dialog such as that shown in Figure 12-2.

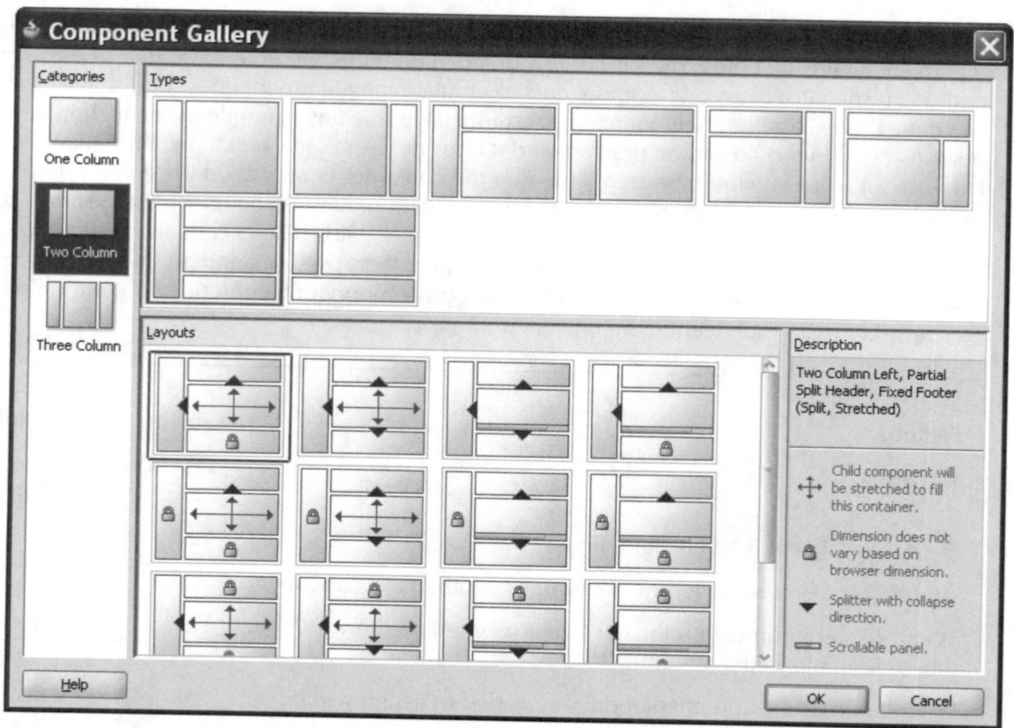

FIGURE 12-2. *Quick Start Layout Component Gallery window*

Selecting a category in the Categories panel and a type in the Types panel will display a number of options in the Layouts panel. Clicking a layout will display a short description about its layout. After selecting a layout, you click OK. JDeveloper will create the JSF page with a set of layout containers based on the layout you selected. For example, selecting "Two Column Left, Partial Split Header, Fixed Footer (Split, Stretched)" will preload the following structure onto the new JSF page:

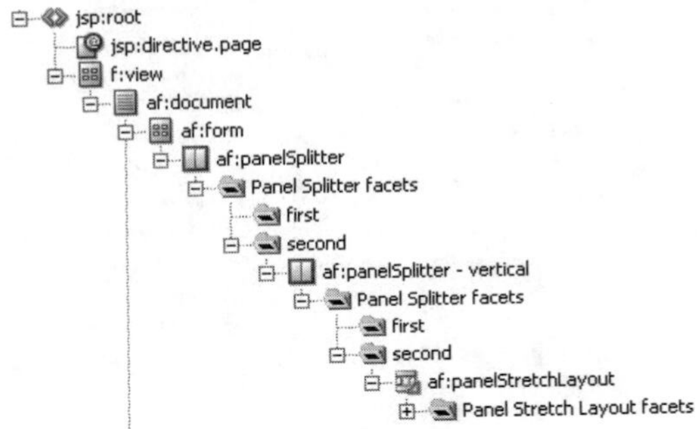

You then drop components into the pre-built layout containers.

Becoming familiar with this feature can save you some time in laying out the proper layout containers. If you study the resulting layout from a Quick Start Layout selection, you are likely to learn a bit about how to properly nest layout containers.

What Types of Atomic Components Are Available?

In addition to the layout container components, ADF Faces supplies a large number of atomic components that render as user interface elements such as input fields, selection lists, date and color pickers, menus, trees, tables, shuttle controls, and buttons. Figure 12-3 shows the Component Palette window with the Common Components panel (split into four columns to save space, although the Component Palette is actually a single column). Most of the components in this list are atomic components, although, as mentioned, some are layout containers.

Describing all of these components would not only take more pages than are allocated for this chapter, but it would also repeat a lot of good information available elsewhere, for example, the tag library visual overview mentioned in the earlier tip. However, it is useful to get a taste for the some of the components that you will use in the hands-on practices in Part V of this book. The visual representation of the components described is shown in Figure 12-4.

- **`af:inputText`** This component is a standard text item that includes a label (prompt) property. Another of its many properties is *Required*; if this property is set to "true," the framework will validate that a value is entered when the page is submitted. As shown in Figure 12-4, it will also display an asterisk ("*") before the label as a hint to the user that this field value is mandatory. If the user submits the page without a value, a message such as the following appears:

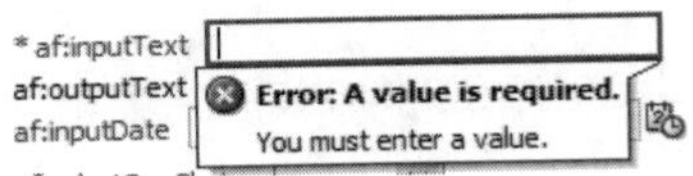

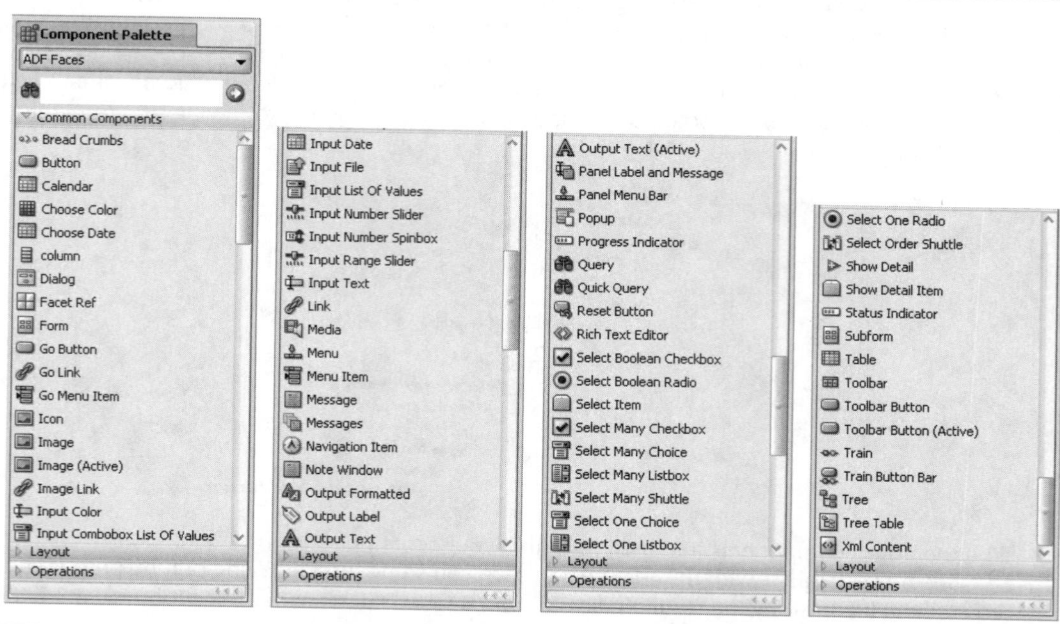

FIGURE 12-3. *ADF Faces Component Palette page, Common Components panel*

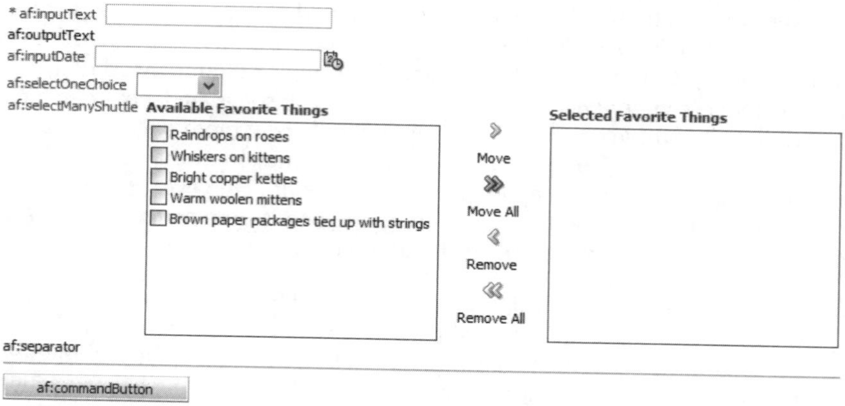

* af:inputText
af:outputText
af:inputDate
af:selectOneChoice
af:selectManyShuttle **Available Favorite Things**
Raindrops on roses
Whiskers on kittens
Bright copper kettles
Warm woolen mittens
Brown paper packages tied up with strings
Move
Move All
Remove
Remove All
Selected Favorite Things
af:separator
af:commandButton

FIGURE 12-4. *Some ADF Faces atomic components at runtime*

You can customize the message using the *RequiredMessageDetail* property. For example, suppose *RequiredMessageDetail* is set to "You must enter a value for {0}." The following will appear if the page is submitted. (The item label fills in for the "{0}" placeholder.)

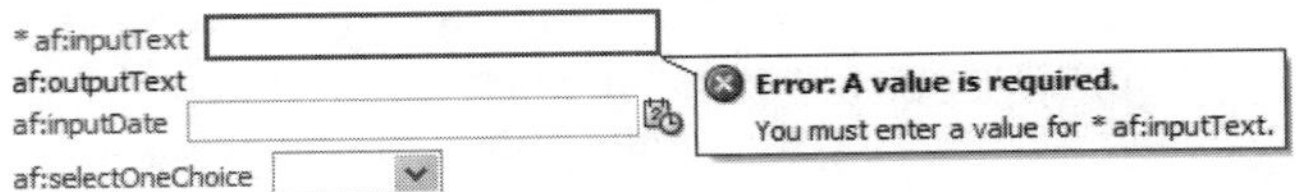

- **`af:outputText`** This component displays a read-only field and is handy for text that the user will never be able to edit. The component does not offer a *Label* property, but you can embed it inside an `af:panelLabelAndMessage` layout container and set the *Label* property of the layout container if needed. If you will allow users to enter data into the field conditionally (for example, based on the user's role or other values), use an `af:inputText` component instead and set that component's *Disabled* property conditionally.
- **`af:inputDate`** This component displays a text item with a graphical LOV button. When the user clicks this button, a calendar window will appear as in the illustration on the right. The user can select a date from this calendar window, and the selected date will be returned into the associated text item.
- **`af:selectOneChoice`** This component displays a standard pulldown item. After dropping an `af:selectOneChoice` component on the page, you will be prompted to define the source of the data in the pulldown. The hands-on practices later in this book demonstrate how to base the list on a database query, but you can also create a static list that will be embedded into the component tag as shown in this example:

```
<af:selectOneChoice label="af:selectOneChoice" id="soc1">
  <af:selectItem label="Choice1" value="1" id="si2"/>
  <af:selectItem label="Choice2" value="2" id="si1"/>
</af:selectOneChoice>
```

- **`af:selectManyShuttle`** This component displays a shuttle control—two text areas that allow the user to select more than one value for a single field. All headings, graphics buttons, and text areas are built into this component. Child components of this component define the values that appear in the available (left-hand) list.
- **`af:separator`** This component renders a horizontal line to divide a page horizontally. (The `af:separator` label in Figure 12-4 is an `af:outputText` item, not part of the `af:separator`.)
- **`af:commandButton`** This component displays an action button. When the user clicks this item, an event is triggered defined in the *Action* or *ActionListener* properties. For example, you define a navigation case from page1 to page2 in the faces-config.xml file and name the outcome "openPage2." You can then set the *Action* property for a button on page1 as "openPage2" so that when the user clicks the button, page2 will open.

Other Atomic Components

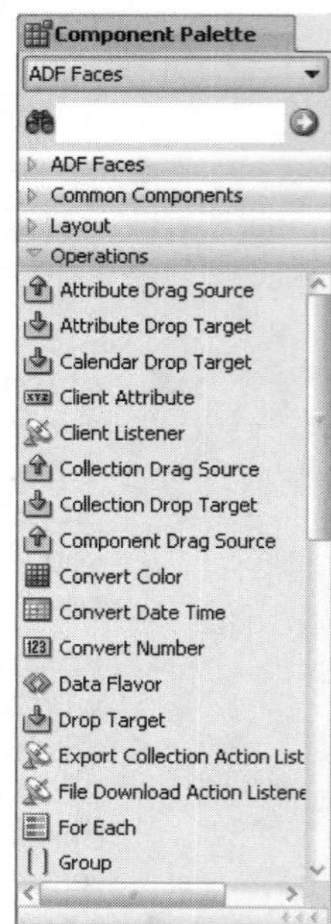

The most commonly used atomic components appear on the Common Components panel of the ADF Faces Component Palette (shown in Figure 12-3). The Component Palette also provides an Operations panel (shown on the right) that lists more atomic components, most of which are not visual in nature but are used in conjunction with other atomic components.

The online help system's visual tag library page contains links that navigate to the tag documentation for each component. Components are organized into three categories in this help page: converters, validators, and miscellaneous.

TIP
As mentioned, you can access the tag library help page using the Contents tree Designing and Developing Applications\Developing Oracle ADF Applications\Oracle ADF Faces Tag Library Overview node. This page shows and briefly describes the ADF Faces tags (over 130 at last count).

Converters

These components nest under data value components such as `af:inputText`. They transform the inherently string data type for HTML text fields to a number (`af:convertNumber`), date (`af:convertDateTime`), or color (`af:convertColor`, for red-green-blue value combinations). You use the *Pattern* property of the converter tag to specify the format mask.

Hands-on Practice: Test Converters As an example, try these steps in JDeveloper in the ADFFacesTest application:

1. Create a JSF page called "operationsDemo.jspx." In the Page Implementations area, specify that no managed bean will be created. Drop two Input Text items onto the page. Drop a Button under the second field (so that you can submit the page in a later step). Set the `af:commandButton` *Text* property as "Test." Run the page.
2. Enter a mixture of numbers and characters in the first field and tab to the second field. No validation occurs. Leave the browser open.
3. In JDeveloper, from the Operations panel, drop a Convert Number component on top of the first field in the Structure window. Repeat the drop operation for the second field.
4. With the second field's `af:convertNumber` node selected in the Structure window, set *Pattern* as "*###,###.##*" without quotes (the Java-style format mask for this converter). This format will be validated on the server when the value is submitted.

   Additional Information: The Javadoc for the `java.text.DecimalFormat` class contains details about the available number format mask characters.
5. Click Save All. Refresh the browser.
6. Enter alphabetic characters in the first field and press TAB. The field border will change to red, indicating a value error, and the hint will appear for the second field to indicate the proper format as shown next.

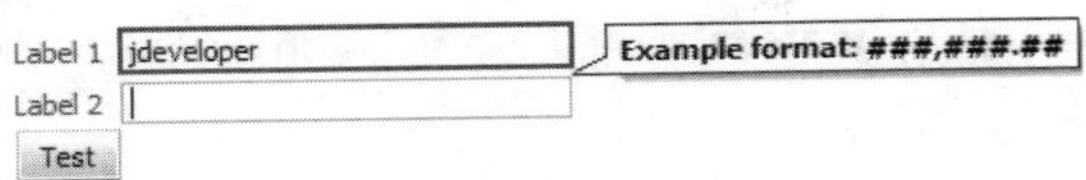

Additional Information: You can change this and other messages by setting properties on the converters and validators (explained in the following sections).

7. Enter alphabetic characters in the second field and click TAB. The cursor will move to the button, but the second field's border will not indicate a value error. Click Test. The cursor will move to the first field and the following error message will appear:

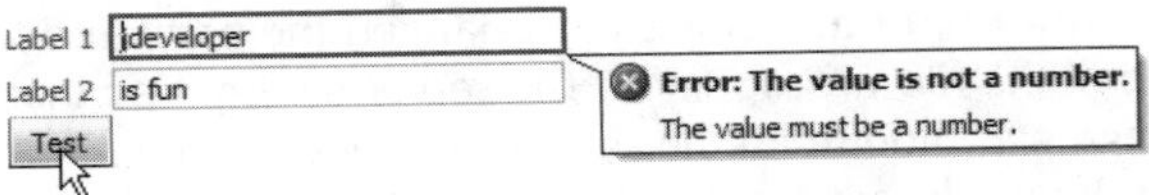

Additional Information: The validation for the second field occurs on the server side (after you submit the page) because the *Pattern* property is not supported on the client side.

8. Change the value in the first field to a number and click Test again. The following message will appear:

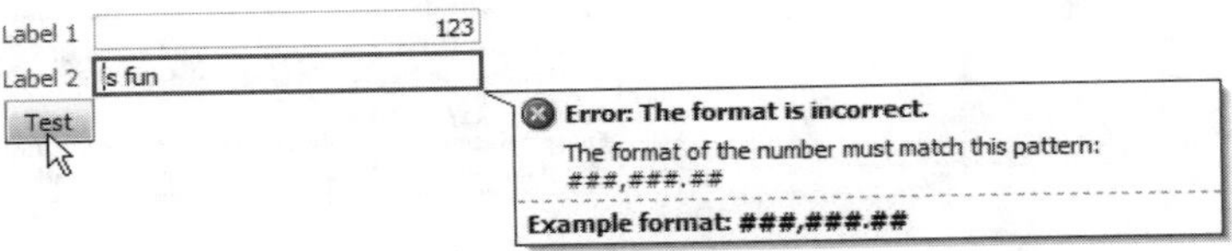

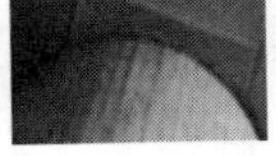

NOTE
Notice that the number value in the first field is right-aligned, whereas when you typed an alphabetic string, the value was left-aligned. This type of alignment is usually preferred so that stacked number fields can be more easily compared.

9. Change the second field's value to a number and click Test. The error state will be cleared and no messages will appear.
10. Close the browser.

TIP
Set the IntegerOnly *property of* `af:convertNumber` *to "true" if the value must be an integer. This property is validated on the client side.*

Validators

Validator components check component values for different aspects: range (`af:validateDateTimeRange`, `af:validateDoubleRange`, and `af:validateLongRange`); length (`af:validateByteLength` and `af:validateLength`); date characteristics (`af:validateDateRestriction`); and regular expression (`af:validateRegExp`).

Hands-on Practice: Test Validators Try these steps on the page you just used to test the number converter:

1. In the operationsDemo.jspx page, drop an Input Date component above the button. Drop a Validate Date Restriction (Operations) component on top of that component.
2. Set *InvalidDaysOfWeek* as "sat sun" and press ENTER. Click Save All.
3. In the Log window's Running tab, one of the messages in the last section will start with "Target URL." Click the HTTP link next to that label. The browser will reopen and the page will load. The new date field should be displayed.

   Additional Information: Since you changed the page and saved the changes, the timestamp of the file was updated. The server determined that the servlet already created for that page was older than the source JSP code and therefore recompiled it before running it. If you do not see the date field, stop the application and try this step again.
4. Move the cursor into the date field. A hint will appear indicating that a date other than Saturday and Sunday should be entered. Type in a Saturday or Sunday date and press TAB. A client-side error message such as the following should appear:

   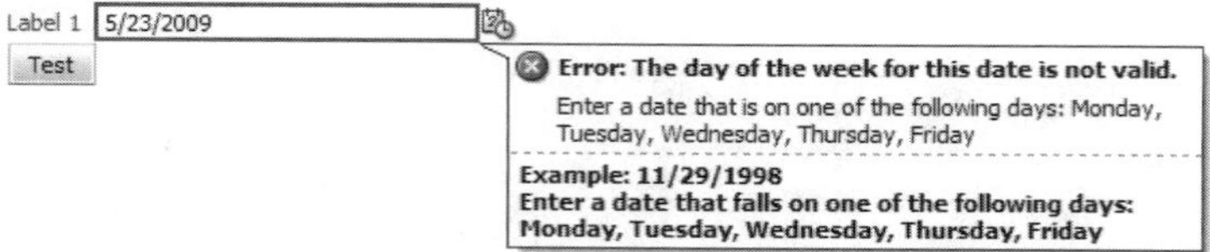

   Additional Information: Clear the value, and then click the calendar icon to the right of the field. The calendar (date picker) popup will appear. Selecting a Saturday or Sunday date from the calendar will cause the error message just displayed to appear without your having to press TAB.
5. Close the browser.

TIP

Another operations component, `af:validateRegExp`*, uses the power of regular expressions to validate the format of the value. It is useful for enforcing the format of string values, for example, Social Security Number, telephone number, or postal codes such as the six-digit codes used in Canada (for example, "K1S 4W7"). The* `af:validateLength` *component can help validate a postal code such as the base five-digit zip code in the United States that can be left-padded with zeros.*

Miscellaneous

This category of the Operations panel in the ADF Faces Component Palette page includes components with varied functionality, for example:

- **`af:forEach`** This component supplies iterative logic within the JSF page. It replaces the JSTL equivalent tag for ADF Faces work.

- **`af:pageTemplateDef`** This component serves as the root component in a page template. The Create JSF Page Template dialog creates a page containing this tag, but you can create templates manually if needed by dragging this tag from the Component Palette. You will use templates in the hands-on practice in Chapter 17.
- **`af:showPopupBehavior`** This component displays a popup (named in the *PopupId* property). You will use this tag when defining an About menu option in the Chapter 17 hands-on practice as well as in other chapters throughout Part V of this book.
- **Drag and drop components** When declaring drag-and-drop behavior, you use Operations tags such as `af:attributeDragSource`, `af:attributeDropTarget`, `af:clientAttribute`, `af:collectionDragSource`, `af:collectionDropTarget`, `af:componentDragSource`, and `af:dropTarget`. The next section steps through setting up drag-and-drop behavior in an ADF Faces application.

Hands-on Practice: Set Up Drag and Drop Behavior The Operations tab includes tags you can use to set up drag-and-drop actions in your application. This allows users to assign values to items based on values of other items. The following brief set of steps demonstrates how to use three drag-and-drop components.

1. Create a JSF page called dragDropDemo.jspx and for Page Implementation, specify that a managed bean will be created.
2. Drop in a Panel Group Layout. Into the `af:panelGroupLayout` component, drop the following components in this order, setting their properties as indicated:
   Input Text (*Label* as "Drag Source" and *Value* as "2000")
   Button (*Text* as "Submit")
   Separator
   Spacer (*Height* as "50")
   Input Text (*Label* as "Drop Target")

   Additional Information: The Submit button is required because the value you type into the Drag Source field must be submitted to the server so that it can be used to set the value of the drop target. The initial value of the Drag Source item ("2000") can be used right after the form starts because it is already set as the component value on the server side.

NOTE
The Common and the Appearance sections of the Property Inspector display the same Text *property.*

3. Run the page. Try dragging the Drag Source field. It will not move because you have not added drag-and-drop operations yet. Leave the browser open.
4. Drag an Attribute Drag Source from the Operations panel onto the Drag Source field. Set *Attribute* as value. Click OK.

   Additional Information: This `af:attributeDragSource` component defines the Input Item as the origin of a drag-and-drop operation.

5. Drag an Attribute Drop Target from the Operations panel onto the Drop Target field. Set *Attribute* as "value." This attribute specifies which property of the Drop Target field will be filled in by the drag-and-drop operation. Click OK.

   Additional Information: The `af:attributeDropTarget` component defines the destination for a drag-and-drop operation.

6. Click Save All. Refresh the browser. Grab the Drag Source field and drop it onto the Drop Target field as shown here:

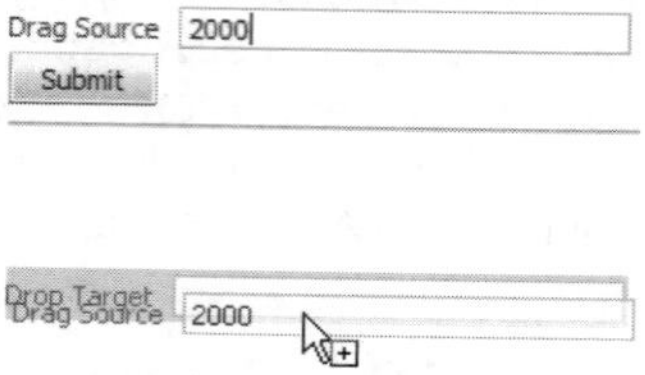

   Additional Information: The value will be copied to the Drop Target field.

7. Modify the Drag Source value and drop it onto the Drop Target again. The value will not change. Click Submit and try the drag-and-drop operation again. This time the value will change because the new value has been submitted to the server and has updated the component's value.

8. Close the browser.

Data Visualization Tools (DVT)

Another class of atomic components raises the bar on high interactivity—the *Data Visualization Tools (DVT)* tag library. DVT consists of the following component types you can use to display data visually:

- **Gantt chart** This component is used to track project work.
- **Gauge** This component displays minimum and maximum values for a data range and places a data point within that range.
- **Geographic map** This component displays a map and allows you to place data on the map. The user can use zoom and pan operations to access different views of the map.
- **Graph** This component allows you to represent the relations between sets of data in nearly any style, for example, area, bar, bubble, funnel, line, pareto (single-series bar graph), pie, radar, scatter/polar, and stock.
- **Hierarchy viewer** This DVT component displays parent-child relationships between data elements and allows the user to pan and zoom in the display. The data elements can support drill-down operations so that double clicking a node can open a window or dialog with more information.
- **Pivot table** This element displays an interactive spreadsheet that allows the user to drag and drop data to create summaries or sorts dynamically. This type of component is useful for multi-dimensional data or data used primarily for analysis.

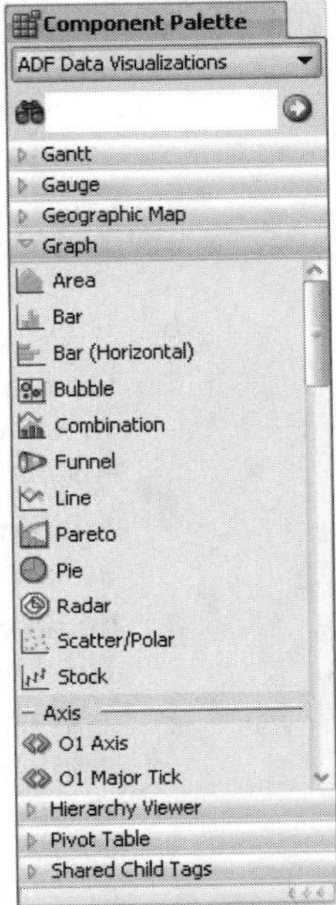

The illustration on the right shows the ADF Data Visualizations page of the Component Palette with the Graph panel partially expanded to show the major graph components. Each panel contains one or more major component and a number of child components that you place into the major component.

You will experience development with the hierarchy viewer component while building the application in the Part V hands-on practices, but to get an early taste, you can follow the steps in the next hands-on practice.

Hands-on Practice: Build a Bar Graph

In this practice, you will create a simple bar chart that shows the sum and average salaries in each department. You will modify several default properties to see how to work with the graph DVT component. In this practice, notice that when you drop a data collection from the Data Control panel, you will see options for several DVT style components as shown here:

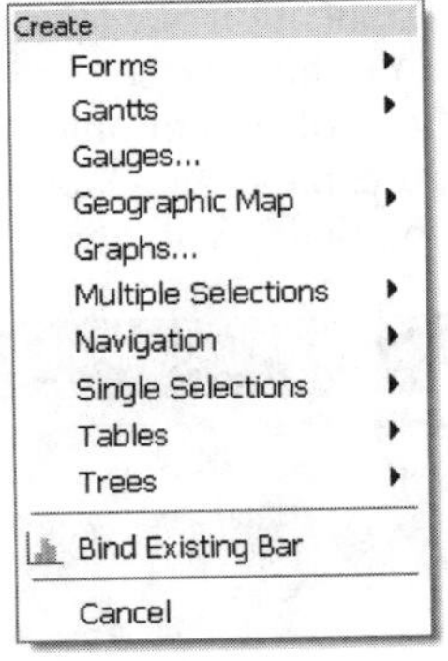

1. Create an application, called "DVTGraph" using the Fusion Web Application (ADF) template.
2. On the Model project node select **New** from the right-click menu. Double click the View Object item in the ADF Business Components category.
3. The Initialize Business Components Project dialog will appear. Create a connection or use an existing connection to the HR schema. Click OK.

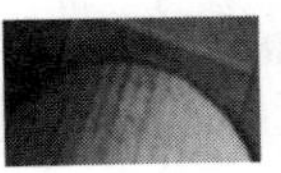

CAUTION
If you receive an error that the connection cannot be created, click Save All, restart JDeveloper, and continue from this point.

4. In the Create View Object Wizard, enter *Name* as "DepartmentSalary." Select "Read-only access through SQL query" and click Next.

5. Fill *Query Statement* as follows:

```
SELECT SUM(emp.salary) AS sum_salary,
       AVG(emp.salary) AS avg_salary,
       dept.department_id, dept.department_name
FROM   departments dept, employees emp
WHERE  dept.department_id = emp.department_id
GROUP BY dept.department_id, dept.department_name
```

6. Fill *Order By* as "department_name." Click Next, Next, and Finish.
7. On the demo.model node of the Model project select New Application Module. Fill in the wizard fields to create an application module called "HRService" and add an instance of DepartmentSalary to the data model.

   Additional Information: On the Step 2 page, move DepartmentSalary to the Data Model area and click Finish. Click Save All.
8. In the ViewController project node, create a JSF page called "deptSalaryGraph.jspx." For the Page Implementation section, specify that no managed bean will be created.
9. Find the Data Controls panel in the Application Navigator window. If the Application Navigator window does not appear, select it in the View menu. Drop DepartmentSalary1 from the Data Controls panel onto the page and select **Graphs**. (Select **View** | **Refresh** or collapse and expand the Data Controls panel if the Data Controls panel is empty.) The following dialog will appear:

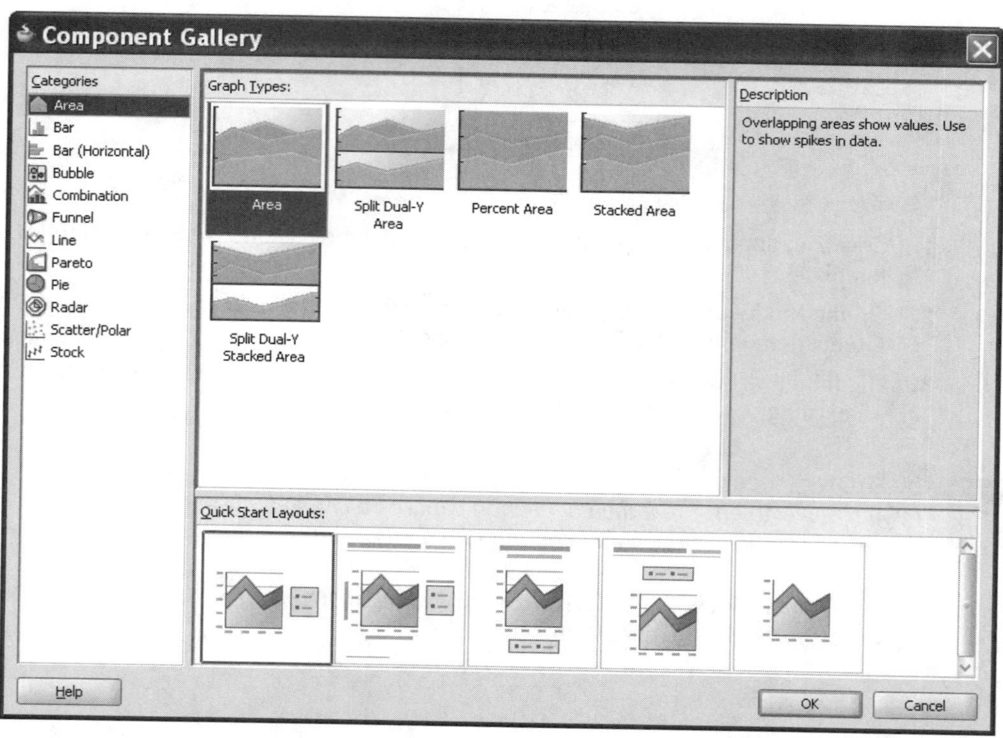

10. Select "Bar" in the *Categories* list and select "Bar" (the default) in *Graph Types*. Select the first selection in the *Quick Start Layouts* area (the default). Click OK.
11. Click the Add Attribute (green plus "+") button next to the *Bars* field and select "SumSalary." Click the same button and select "AvgSalary" to add that attribute to the *Bars* list. These two query columns will appear as bars in the graph.
12. In the Attribute Labels area, change the SumSalary label to "Total of All Salaries." Change the AvgSalary attribute label to "Average Salary."
13. Click Add Attribute next to the X-Axis field and select "DepartmentName." This declares that the department name will show as labels on the horizontal axis. The dialog should appear as follows:

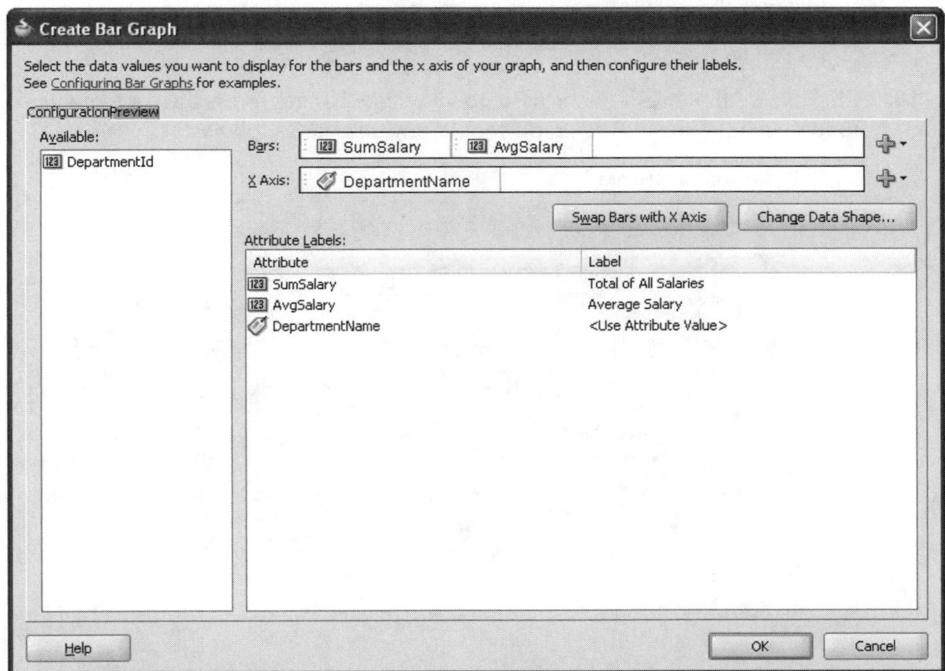

14. Click the Preview tab to see how the graph will appear. Click OK to dismiss the dialog.
15. Click Save All. Run the page. Move the mouse over a bar to view a popup with the data details.

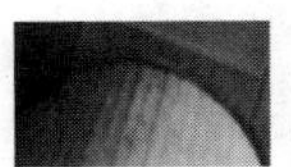

TIP
If you receive error messages in the server console (Log window) about lack of memory or other problems when running a page, save your work and exit JDeveloper. Then stop all java.exe processes (using Task Manager in a Windows environment), restart JDeveloper, and run the page again.

16. Leave the browser open and return to JDeveloper.

17. In the Design tab of the editor, click the graph component to select it. In the Property Inspector, Graph Data section, notice that the *Value* expression refers to a graphModel binding ("#{bindings.DepartmentSalary1.graphModel}"). Navigate to the Page Binding file (in the editor window, select **Go to Page Definition** from the right-click menu in the editor) and notice in the Source tab that the binding DepartmentSalary1 is defined as a graph binding (`<graph />`).

18. In the deptSalaryGraph.jspx editor, select the graph component again. In the Appearance section of the Property Inspector, change the following properties and notice the changes in the visual editor along the way:
    Style as "Southwest"
    Title as "Department Salaries"
    ImageHeight as "400"
    ImageWidth as "600"
    3D Effect to "true"

19. Click Save All. Refresh the browser to view the changes (press the SHIFT key while refreshing to force a full refresh). The graph should now appear as follows:

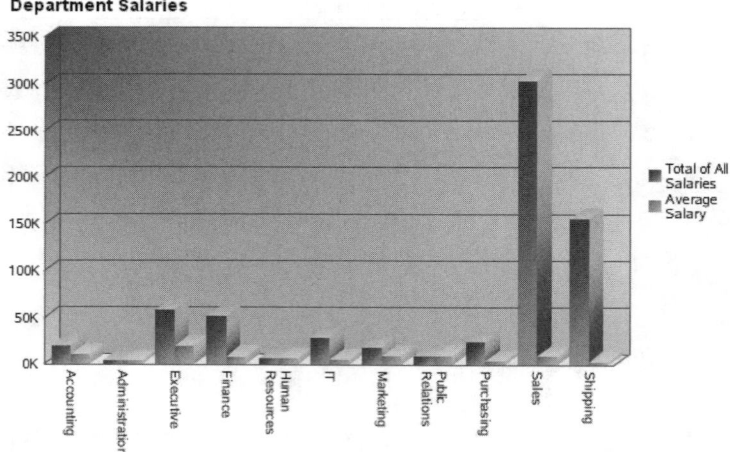

20. Close the browser. Stop the application.

What Did You Just Do? You sampled the development experience when working with a DVT component. You created a read-only view object as a SELECT statement to retrieve the total salaries for each department. You also created an application module to expose the view object to the View layer code. Then, you defined a bar graph based on the view object and changed some properties of that graph.

What Could You Do Next? To continue the experiment with the graph component, you can set up a master-detail drill-down feature using the following abbreviated steps. The effect will be that clicking a department bar in the graph will display a table of employee records for that department.

1. Create an entity object definition, Employees, based on the EMPLOYEES table and specify a default view object, EmployeeDetails. This will serve as the data source for the detail table.

2. Create a view link definition from DepartmentSalary (source) to EmployeeDetails (destination) based on DepartmentId. Open the HRService application module and add a detail instance of EmployeeDetails naming it "EmployeesInDepartment" as shown here.

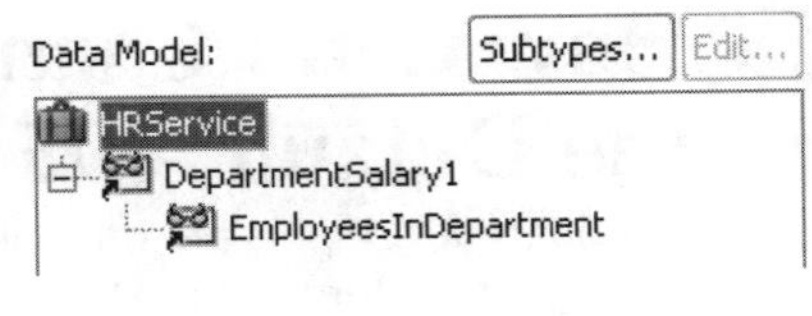

3. In the Application Navigator, refresh the Data Controls panel (**View** | **Refresh** after selecting a node). Select the deptGraphSalary.jspx document tab and drop the EmployeesInDepartment nested data collection on the `af:form` node of the Structure window. Select the **Tables** | **ADF Read-only Table** option. In the Edit Table Columns dialog, delete all but the EmployeeId, FirstName, LastName, Salary, and DepartmentId columns. Click OK.

   Additional Information: The DepartmentId column is included only for testing so that you can see that the same DepartmentId is retrieved for the click on a bar. You now need to set two properties to cause the table to refresh when a department bar is clicked.

4. Select the `af:table` node in the Structure window, and set *PartialTriggers* as "::barGraph1" (the bar graph).

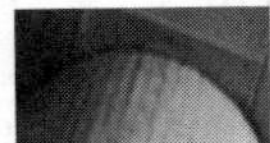

NOTE
The fully qualified name of a component refers to its relative path in the component hierarchy with each node delimited by a colon (":"). In this example, you need to refer to the ID of the top-level component "barGraph1" in a PartialTriggers *property, so refer to it as "::barGraph1." References to sibling components (components on the same level) do not need the path prefix.*

5. On the graph component, set *ClickListener* (Behavior section) to "#{bindings .DepartmentSalary1.graphModel.processClick}." (You may need to type in this value if the Expression Builder is not available for this property.) The method `processClick()` is automatically available to graphs.

6. Click Save All. Run the page. The employee table will appear under the graph. Click a bar in the graph and the employee table will refresh with the related employee records.

   Additional Information: The table appears truncated on the right side. The reason is that the table component does not automatically fill the available space. The solution is to surround the table with an `af:panelStretchLayout`, whose purpose is to cause its child components to fill the available space.

7. Leave the browser open and return to JDeveloper. In the Structure window, drop a Panel Stretch Layout component onto the `af:form` component so that it appears under the table. Then drag the existing `af:table` into that container's center facet. Click Save All and refresh the page. The table should better fill the screen.

8. Close the browser and stop the application.

TIP
Enclose objects that need to fill the available space in an `af:panelStretchLayout` *layout container.*

How Can I Change the Default ADF Faces Appearance?

Although developers are often impressed (regardless of whether they acknowledge it) with ADF Faces' rich features and extensive set of components, one of their first reactions (after being impressed) is to question how to change the appearance of the components. ADF Faces components are bound to a default set of Cascading Style Sheets (CSS) files and a resource bundle that defines an extensive set of selectors. These style sheets provide a consistent, well-designed, common look and feel to all components by default. This means that every `af:inputText` component that you use in an application will share the same visual characteristics.

The problem is that the default may not agree with the standards set up for your applications. The easiest way to solve this inconsistency is by changing your standards to match the ADF Faces defaults. This is the "WYSIWYG-IWYGIWYW" principle: What you see is what you get if what you get is what you want. That is, the default ADF Faces look-and-feel standards will serve you perfectly if your standards match the ADF Faces standards.

Naturally, that principle is easy to state, and although it seems a bit flippant, it is worth considering. However, many organizations do not have the freedom to change standards based on a technology choice. Fortunately, you have options; the first is to override the default CSS files using an ADF Faces feature called "skins"; the second is to make changes to the style properties for a specific component.

Working with Skins

An ADF skin offers a relatively easy way to make changes to the application. Instead of attaching CSS files to each page, ADF Faces defines a skin on an application level. An ADF Faces *skin* is a set of cascading style sheets containing selectors that define how each type of component will appear in an application. For example, a CSS selector is defined for the `af:inputText` component. Each time that component is rendered, it automatically uses that selector for its appearance. You do not need to apply the selector unless you want to override the default for a specific instance of a component.

Once a different skin is applied to the application, all components will then take on the characteristics defined in the new skin. Moreover, this change can be dynamic; that is, you can offer users the ability to change at runtime the skin that is being used to display the application. This ability has obvious benefits to users who are interested in specific color and font schemes for personal aesthetic reasons. It also has practical benefits for helping serve those who are visually disabled and whose interaction with the application could be easier with nonstandard fonts and colors.

You programmatically change from one skin to another by modifying a single application-level property. In the ADFFacesTest application you have used in this chapter, open trinidad-config.xml in the WEB-INF directory. You will see something like the following:

```
<?xml version="1.0" encoding="windows-1252"?>
<trinidad-config xmlns="http://myfaces.apache.org/trinidad/config">
  <skin-family>blafplus-rich</skin-family>
</trinidad-config>
```

The skin-family setting defines the skin. Change the "blafplus-rich" (or "fusion") skin family value to "simple," click Save All, and open a JSF page (for example, dragDropDemo.jspx) in the JDeveloper visual editor. (You may need to close the editor window and reopen the page for the changes to take effect.)

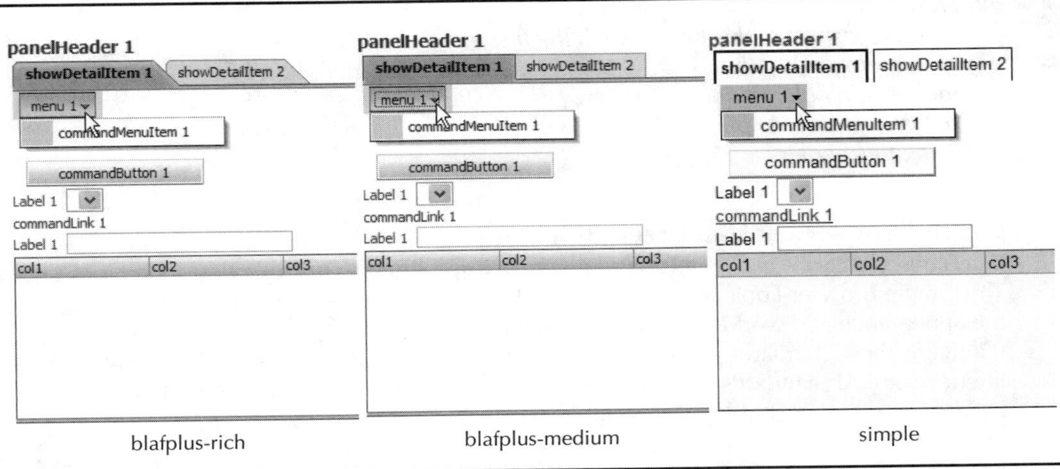

FIGURE 12-5. *Different skins applied to the same page*

ADF Faces ships with three skins; the default skin "blafplus-rich" is modeled using the Oracle Browser Look and Feel (BLAF) standards; the effect of applying this skin and the other two skins—blafplus-medium and simple—to a simple JSF page with various components is shown in Figure 12-5. No changes were made to the page between screen shots; only the skin was changed. You will notice the minor difference between the blafplus-rich skin and the blafplus-medium skin—only the tabs look different in this set of components. However, the difference between the simple skin and the blafplus-medium skin is much more dramatic.

If you want to try applying different skins and rerunning this same JSF page, drop components into a new JSF file called "skinsDemo.jspx" (no managed bean) so that they form the following arrangement in the Structure window. Nodes that are not expanded are empty. No properties were changed on any component after dropping them onto the page except the `af:spacer`, whose *Height* was set to "50." Remember that `af:menuBar` appears as "Panel Menu Bar."

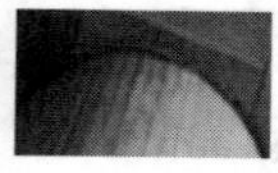

NOTE
The screenshots in this book match the first full production version of JDeveloper 11g (build 5407) but in later releases of ADF Faces, the default look-and-feel (skin) may change slightly. This small difference is not important to your work while learning JDeveloper using this book.

Oracle Browser Look and Feel (BLAF)

If you need to create a skin, it is helpful to take inspiration from a fully developed look and feel. The Oracle Browser Look and Feel (BLAF) is backed by an extensive set of standards for designing the appearance and workings of the user interface layer of an application. Oracle develops and maintains these standards primarily to support the Oracle EBS modules that present web browser interfaces. BLAF standards are exhaustively documented in hundreds of pages of public web files (www.oracle.com/technology/tech/blaf).

TIP
Even if you do not use BLAF standards, it is worthwhile using them for ideas about what type of look-and-feel standards to create and how the standards for different elements must complement each other.

Getting Started Defining Custom Skins

If you decide not to use the default ADF Faces skins, you can develop your own skin. The process is well documented in the JDeveloper help system. Enter "skins" in the help system search field and find the topic "Customizing the Appearance Using Styles and Skins." This topic will guide you through the steps you need to perform to create a custom skin. The first step is to prepare by reviewing details of the work, and to budget time for this work. Creating a skin entails working primarily with style sheets; the work is not difficult but can be time-consuming if you want to be thorough. Another preliminary step is defining a complete graphical design that you wish to implement. It will not be productive to make extensive changes to the design while coding the skin. Other major steps follow:

1. Starting with the simple skin, define property values for specially named CSS selectors (styles). This process will override the default look and feel that ADF Faces components use. Working with the CSS selectors will take the bulk of your skin development time.

TIP
You can extend an existing skin with your own skin, which means you can avoid writing an entire skin and, therefore, save time and effort.

2. Register the skin in a file called "trinidad-skins.xml" in the WEB-INF directory so that it is available to the *skin-family* property in the trinidad-config.xml file.
3. Activate the new skin by changing the skin-family property as described before.
4. Deploy the custom skin in a JAR file so that it can be more easily shared between applications.

Working with Component-Level Styles

A general development best practice is to take advantage of reuse and inheritance as much as possible so that maintenance and enhancements are easier; also, reuse theoretically means that you are taking advantage of pre-built and pre-tested code so fewer software defects should result. The ADF Faces use of skins falls into the category of reuse and inheritance because an application applies a consistent and tested appearance to each component.

However, there are always exceptions to any rule, so it is useful to know how to override the styles set by the skin you are using. It turns out that each ADF Faces visual component offers a number of properties that you can use to alter the default appearance of a component without having to modify a style sheet. You have used some of these already, so the following is intended as a refresher. As with other techniques, the hands-on practices in Part V of this book will use the manual overriding technique in many places to show the effects of various style settings.

TIP
If you find yourself overriding the same visual properties in the same way on most uses of the same component type, you need to consider making that change permanent in a skin.

Inline Styles

The *Inline Style* property appears in the Style section of the Property Inspector for most visible ADF Faces components (including layout containers). The property value can consist of a number of attributes and values delimited with semicolons (";"). JDeveloper provides an editor under the *Inline Style* property that allows you to enter values for the *Inline Style* properties. The values and property names are dynamically loaded from the editor into the *Inline Style* property as shown here:

Style
ContentStyle:
StyleClass:
InlineStyle: color:Fuchsia; font-family:'Courier New', Courier, monospace; font-size:xx-large;
Color: Fuchsia
Font: 'Courier New', Courier, monospace
Size: xx-large %
Italic:
Bold:
Horizontal Align:
Decoration:
Vertical Align: %

Modifying *Inline Style* properties uses the same techniques as other Property Inspector properties—a combination of typing values, selecting from a pulldown, interacting with a dedicated property editor (the Edit selection of the pulldown), or using the Expression Builder.

CAUTION

Although JDeveloper displays all Inline Style *properties for all visual components, not all of these properties are appropriate for all component types. Rather than issuing an error message if an inappropriate property is set, ADF Faces just ignores the property. For example, a border setting is not applicable to an anchor (*`<a>`*) tag.*

The properties in the Inline Style editor are divided into tabs for Text, Background, Box (for the area taken up by the component, most appropriate for layout containers), and Classification (for lists).

TIP

Be judicious when setting Inline Style *properties, especially for nested layout containers, because a setting on a parent layout component can affect child components. If a component is not being arranged the way you expect, it could be due to an* Inline Style *property setting on a parent component.*

Content Style

The *Content Style* property (shown in the preceding illustration) is available on components with data and other types of display such as `af:inputText`, `af:inputDate`, and `af:selectOneChoice`. For example, *Content Style* for the `af:inputText` component affects the way data in the field is displayed. If you set a *Content Style* width for an Input Text component, that width will override the *Columns* property of that field. The *Content Style* expression is the same format as the *Inline Style* expression.

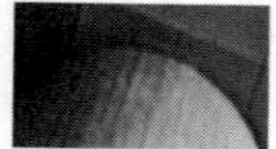

TIP

You can use the Inline Style *editor (tabbed property list in the Style section) to create an expression that you can cut and paste into the* Content Style *property. This editor makes it easy to create correctly formatted style expressions.*

Style Class

The *Style Class* property (also shown in the preceding illustration) allows you to assign one or more preexisting style sheet selectors to the component. Selecting Edit in this property's pulldown displays the Edit Property: StyleClass dialog shown here:

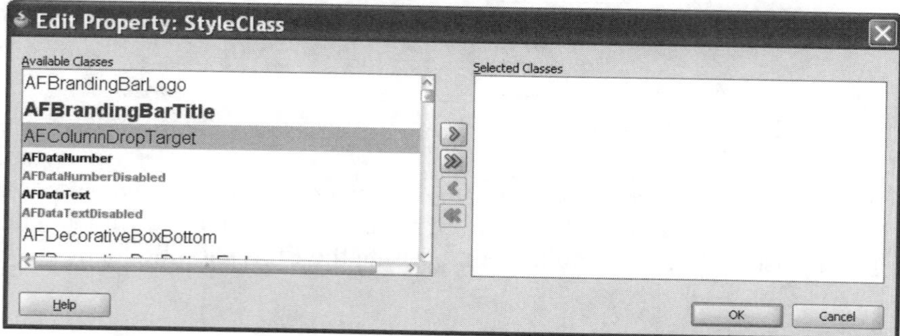

When you move one or more selector classes to the *Selected Classes* area and click OK, the property value will be populated with the selected names. Selecting more than one class will apply attributes from all classes to the component.

You can enable ADF component styles to appear in a *Style Class* property pulldown by selecting the *ADF Faces Extension* checkbox in the Preferences dialog (**Tools** | **Preferences**) CSS Editor page. Then, when you select an ADF Faces component, the *Style Class* property will display a pulldown from which you can choose a selector specific to that component as shown here:

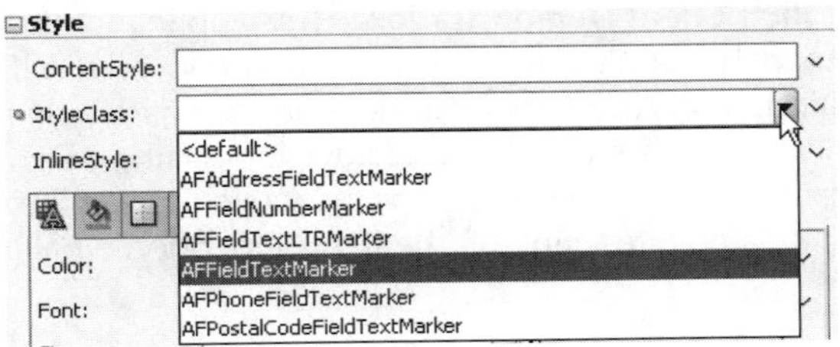

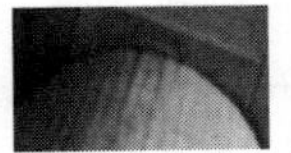

TIP
The ADF Faces Rich Client demonstration application (accessible and downloadable from www.oracle.com/technology/products/adf/adffaces) allows you to view all ADF Faces components and try out different settings for various properties. The Styles tab allows you to test run settings for Inline Style *and Style Class.*

How Will I Ever Learn about All These Components?

Now that you've gotten a taste for some of the commonly used components and features, you may be a feeling a bit overwhelmed because in addition to the ADF Faces techniques and components that this chapter discusses, you have gotten the sense that there are many more. Some of these additional subjects will be explained and demonstrated in the hands-on practices in subsequent chapters. After completing the study in this book, you will have a pretty good picture of the major components and methods you need to use for working with ADF Faces. However, we admit freely and without apology that this book does not completely discuss all ADF Faces subjects you will ever need to know to develop applications.

The key principle for further study is the same as always and is best expressed by Samuel Johnson (1820–1784) who said, "Knowledge is of two kinds: we know a subject ourselves, or we know where we can find information upon it." Here are several resources for finding the ADF Faces information you do not know yourself:

- **The JDeveloper Help Center** Mentioned several times in this chapter is a single topic you can access by searching for "enhanced tag doc." This topic shows all visual components and provides links to detailed information about each component. Since this source is the closest to your work in JDeveloper, it might also be your first resort.

- **The Fusion Developer's Guide for Oracle ADF** This document (over 1200 PDF pages) is available online and in downloadable PDF format at www.oracle.com/technology/products/jdev. It is also part of the JDeveloper help system. Look for it under the Contents tree node Designing and Developing Applications\Developing Oracle ADF Applications. The website version may be more up-to-date than the version in the JDeveloper help system.
- **OTN demos and white papers** Start looking for these documents from the JDeveloper home page on www.oracle.com/technology/products/jdev.
- **ADF Faces Rich Client Demonstration** This application is available online as well as in a downloadable application that you can run locally in JDeveloper 11*g*. It contains a demonstration of all ADF Faces components; a separate demo application exists for DVT components. It also contains tips and advice on using ADF Faces components. Access this application from the web page www.oracle.com/technology/products/adf/adffaces (or from a "Related Sites" link on the JDeveloper home page).

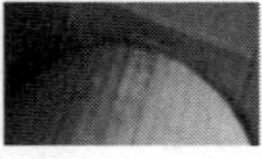

TIP

After you drop a component onto a page, press F1 to display the tag help page for that component. This reference page is helpful for learning more about the component because it explains the purpose of the tag as well as its properties. For layout containers, it also lists the supported facets.

PART IV

ADF Model

By copying, the ancient models should be perpetuated.

—Hsieh Ho (Xie Ho) (479–502),
Notes Concerning the Classification of Old Paintings, Sixth Principle

CHAPTER 13

ADF Model Basics

Now that we have all this useful information,
it would be nice to be able to do something with it.
(Actually, it can be emotionally fulfilling just to get information.
This is usually only true, however, if you have the social life of a kumquat.)

—UNIX Programmer's Manual

Now that we've discussed the basic technologies for defining business services and user interfaces (in Parts II and III, respectively), we now are ready to address the issue of gluing the two together. In traditional Java EE applications, this implies creating a large amount of Java code to carry out tasks such as managing the location of and connection to business services, obtaining collections of data, mapping that data into the UI layer, and so on. One major benefit of using ADF is that this task of binding the UI to the back-end business services is handled by the *ADF Model layer* (abbreviated in this book as *ADFm*).

In this chapter, we discuss the basics of the ADFm architecture and look at the ways to quickly create data-bound UI components and task flow activities using a JDeveloper design time tool called the "Data Controls panel" of the Application Navigator. Chapter 14 examines the binding architecture in more depth and explains how to edit bindings and implement relationships between UI controls and bindings beyond those that can be created using the Data Controls panel. Chapter 15 explains *executables*, ADFm components that perform actions during the page or activity life cycle, and explains how to work with ADFm from within managed beans.

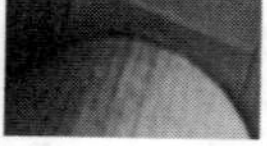

NOTE
This chapter relies heavily on concepts and techniques explained in Chapter 7. You should ensure that you are familiar with the material in that chapter before reading this one.

This chapter answers the following questions:

- **What is the ADF Model layer?**
- **How do you provide default or dynamic visual properties for UI controls?**
- **How do you create data-bound pages?**
- **How do you create data-bound activities?**
- **What files are involved in data binding?**

What Is the ADF Model Layer?

ADFm is an architectural layer that binds the UI of your application to the back-end business services. Before you can use the ADF Model layer effectively, it is important to understand the basics of its architecture. A single user session for an ADF application uses a single *binding context*, a container for all of the ADF Model layer components that the application needs. A binding context contains *data controls*, components that allow access to underlying business services, and *binding containers*, components that provide the data access needed for each page, page fragment, or task flow activity. You can see the architecture of the ADF Model layer

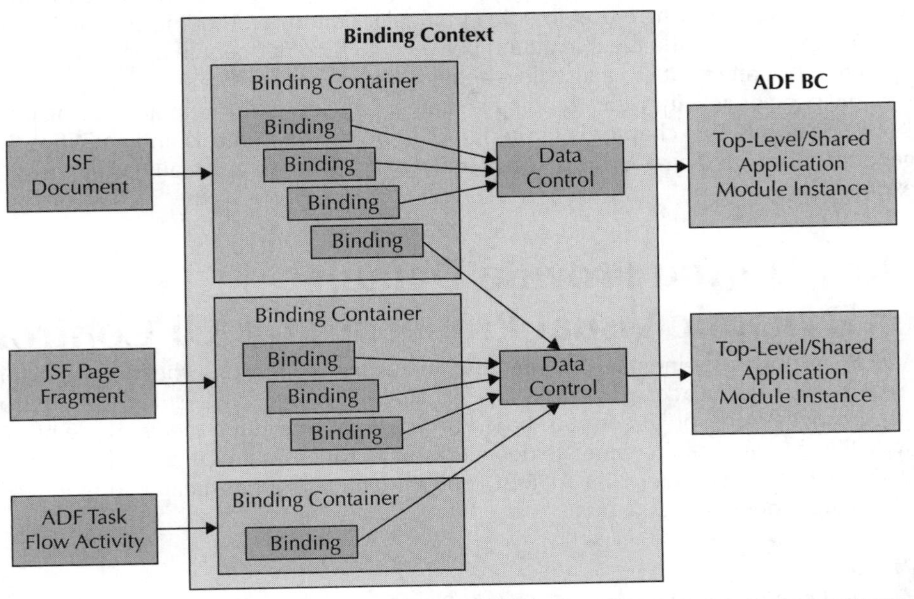

FIGURE 13-1. *ADF Model layer architecture with JSF, ADF Task Flow, and ADF BC*

in Figure 13-1. This figure shows a binding context interacting with view and controller components and ADF BC application module instances.

Data Controls

A *data control* is a Java object in the ADF Model layer that acts as an extra layer of code to abstract business services. Rather than reading data from or sending data to business services directly, the application sends all requests through data controls.

Without the use of data controls, ADF would need to use different APIs to communicate with ADF BC, web services, JPA, and other diverse business service technologies. Data controls provide a common API for ADF and convert calls to the common API into calls appropriate for each specific business services technology. As a result, JDeveloper provides a consistent view and controller development experience across various business service technologies.

In an ADF BC application, a data control corresponds to a single top-level application module instance. As discussed in Chapter 7, a top-level application module instance manages a particular database transaction (or rather, a serial set of database transactions interrupted by commit and rollback operations) and acts as a single point of contact between the data managed within that transaction and the rest of the application. The data control can go through the application module instance to access its data model, read and manipulate data, call custom service methods, and manage database transactions.

Binding Containers

A *binding container* is a Java object in the ADF Model layer that provides data access for a single page, page fragment, or activity in an ADF application. For example, a page allowing a user to browse through a department's employees would have its own binding container, as would a separate page allowing a user to edit a particular employee. Binding containers contain *bindings*, which provide the interaction between a UI component in a page or form, or a single operation or unit of data in a task flow activity, and a data control.

Any page or activity with a binding container can access that container using the EL expression `#{bindings}`. This chapter is limited to data-bound UI controls and activities that can be generated through drag-and-drop; Chapters 14 and 15 discuss manually using the `#{bindings}` expression.

How Do You Provide Default or Dynamic Visual Properties for UI Controls?

ADF BC is not a user-interface architecture; in Fusion applications, the job of providing the view layer is left to ADF Faces. However, in your ADF BC project, you can create *control hints*, or display suggestions for UI controls, based on your business components. These hints are exposed by ADFm and are used to generate default display properties for UI controls created from the Data Controls panel. Internally, ADF BC stores the hints in a translatable form in resource bundles within the Model project.

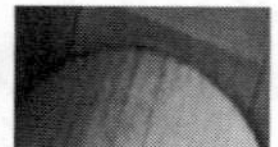

TIP
For the purposes of testing, the Oracle Business Component Browser (introduced in Chapter 18) also respects these UI hints when working with the objects.

Control Hints for Attributes

You can specify control hints on either view attributes or entity attributes using the Control Hints page of the Edit Attribute dialog, shown in Figure 13-2. (Accessing this dialog for entity attributes and view attributes is explained in Chapters 6 and 7.)

Types of Attribute Control Hints

The control hints you can specify for attributes are as follows:

- **Display Hint** Is a dropdown list allowing you to select "display" or "hide." This hint controls whether a control for the attribute will be displayed by default in generated forms and tables.
- **Label Text** Allows you to specify the default label for controls (in forms) or columns (in tables) for the attribute values. If you don't specify a label text, the attribute name is used as a label.
- **Tooltip Text** Specifies a default tooltip, or rollover popup, for controls for the attribute.
- **Format Type** Defines the general way in which the data should be formatted. The options available depend on the type of the attribute, and in the case of String attributes cannot be set at all. Most attribute types only allow for a single format type, but a few numeric types allow you to choose "Number" or "Currency" in this field.

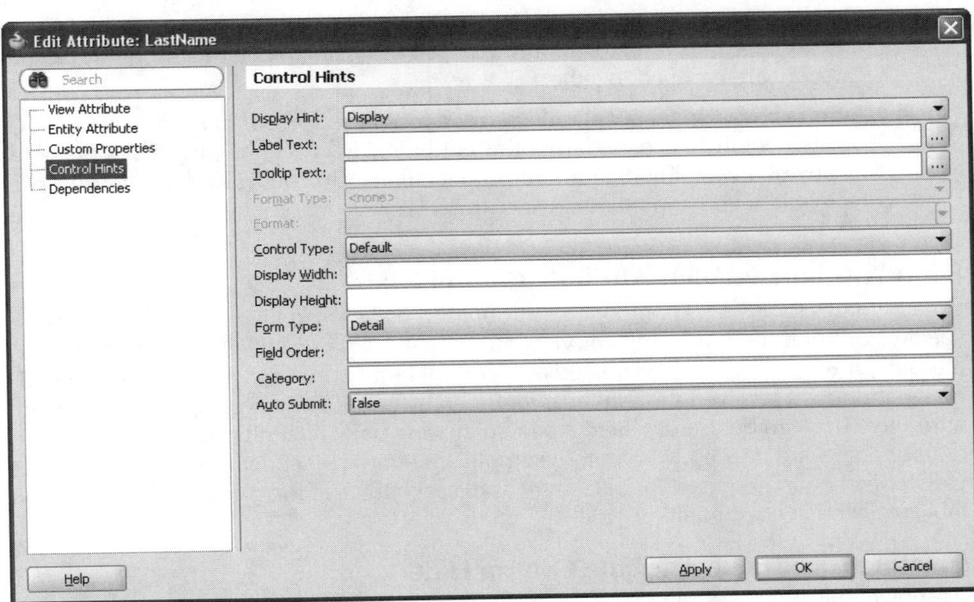

FIGURE 13-2. *The Control Hints page of the Edit Attribute dialog for a view object definition*

- **Format** Allows you to type in an Java-style format mask for your format, for example, "*yyyy-MM-dd*" as a typical date format.
- **Control Type** Allows you to select a default control type to use in forms and non-read-only tables. If you do not select a control hint, the default control type will be an `af:inputDate` component for Date attributes, and an `af:inputText` component for other non-LOV attributes (specifying default control types for LOV attributes is explained in the section "Control Hints for Lists of Values").
- **Display Width** Is for control types (such as `af:inputText`) that allow the specification of a width using the *columns* property, this specifies the default value of that attribute.
- **Display Height** Is not automatically used when the attribute is bound to a JSF component. However, you can manually bind, for example, the *rows* property of an `af:inputText` to a value that you store in this hint using the expression `#{bindings.<attribute_name>.hints.displayHeight}`, where "<attribute_name>" is the name of the attribute.
- **Form type** Is not used in ADF Faces applications.
- **Field Order** (This is only shown in the view attribute hints.) Allows you to specify an integer. Attributes with a specified "field order" will, by default be, displayed at the top of forms and the left end of tables (or table column groups), in ascending order according to this control hint. For attributes with no field order specified (which are always shown below or to the right of attributes with field order specified, if any), order will be according to attribute order in the view object definition.

- **Category** (This is only shown in the view attribute hints.) Is only used by the ADF read-only dynamic table (explained in the section "How Do You Create Data-Bound Pages?"). Categories correspond to column groups in such a table, and attributes that share a category are grouped together.
- **Auto Submit** In theory should be used to set the *autoSubmit* property of the UI component that is created from this attribute. However, the property is not actually set by any of the default drag-and-drop operations. That being said, just as with the Display Height hint you can manually use an EL expression to obtain the value of this hint.

Entity Attribute vs. View Attribute Control Hints

Data bindings to business components attributes are always to view attributes. However, you can specify control hints at the entity or view attribute level. If you specify a control hint on an entity attribute, it will, by default, be treated as a control hint for every view attribute mapped to that entity attribute. However, this will be overridden by control hints you specify directly on view attributes. This can be useful where a particular view object definition is used in a context where different hints are needed, where, for example, an entity object definition may be shared by a view object definition used for data entry and a second used for a list of values. Different screen labels may be needed in either case.

Creating Localizable Attribute Control Hints

As shown in Figure 13-2, the *Label text* and *Tooltip text* control hint fields have an expansion (". . .") button beside them. Clicking this button will display the Select Text Resource dialog, as shown here.

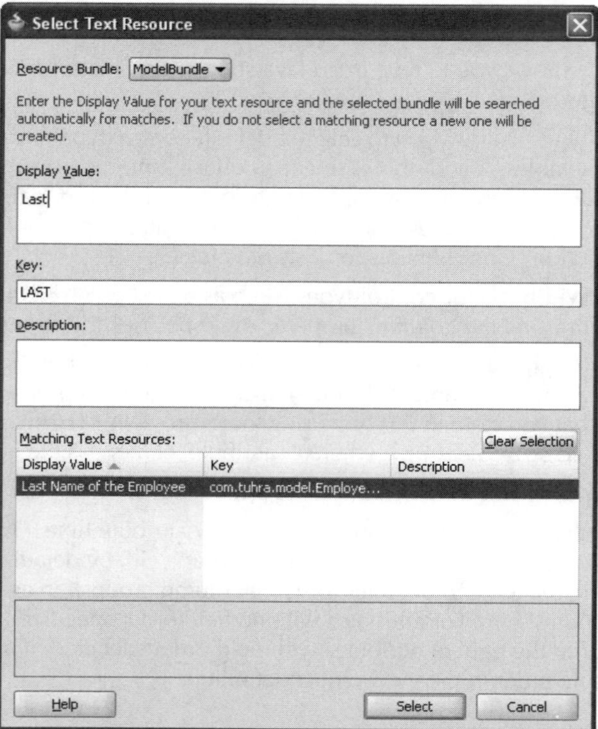

This dialog allows you to select an existing *text resource* (name/value pair stored in a resource bundle). In this case, the dialog has been used to search for an existing String beginning with the word "Last." This makes the process of reusing common strings much easier.

ADF BC stores the hints in a resource bundle that can be used both for translation purposes and also to allow the UI hints to be changed and polished without the business objects having to be touched. By default, a single shared property bundle called ModelBundle.properties is used for the project. This file is created in the root of the project directory. You can configure the way that the project handles resources and, for example, change from having a single global bundle to one bundle per entity object definition and view object definition. This configuration is done through the Resource Bundle node in the project properties as shown in the following illustration:

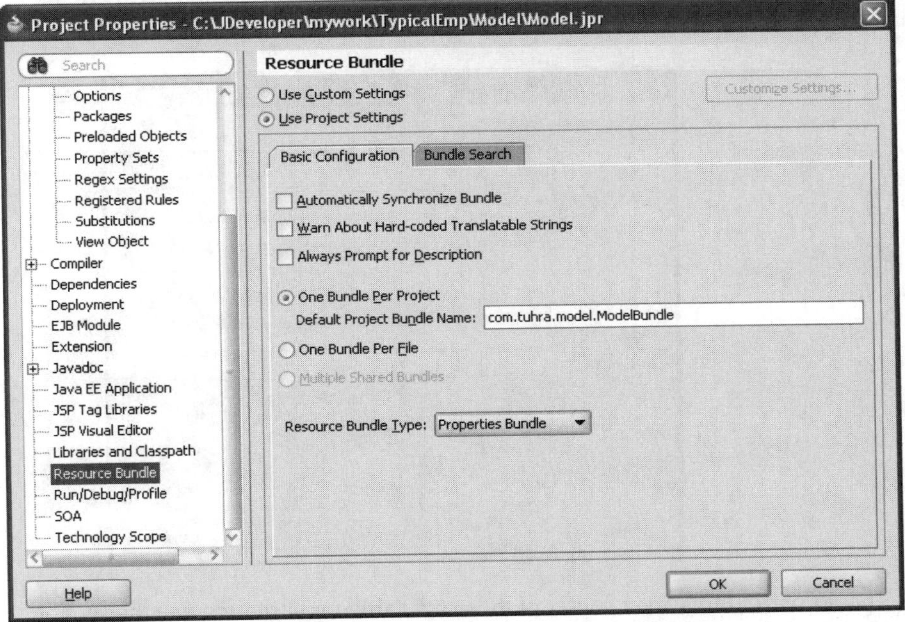

Property Sets

A *property set* (introduced in Chapter 5) allows you to abstract a set of control hints away from a particular attribute. For example, an HR application might have several different forms, all of which require entering an employee ID. These IDs correspond to columns in different tables, so there is no single view attribute, or even entity attribute, to which all these controls correspond. However, you might want all of these controls to use the label "Employee ID," the tooltip "The Employee ID is a two- or three-digit number," and a width of five. Rather than repeating these control hints for each employee ID attribute, you can instead create a property set that specifies these control hints, and attach the property set to each attribute that requires it. Attributes attached to property sets will, by default, use control hints from the property sets, although this can be overridden by either setting a particular control hint directly on the attribute or setting a particular control hint on an entity attribute on which the attribute is based.

Property sets are not particularly intuitive to use. The basic task of creating a property set is to just use the New Gallery. Once the property set is created, you need to use the Property Inspector for the property set object to set each of the relevant attributes. You then assign the property set to an entity or view attribute using the *Property Set* dropdown list on the attribute editor for either type of attribute. This list will display the names of all of the available property sets in the project.

Control Hints for Bind Variables

In many cases, a user needs to be able to directly enter bind-variable values. You can create control hints on bind variables to specify defaults for controls generated from them.

You specify control hints for bind variables on the "Control Hints" page of the Bind Variable dialog:

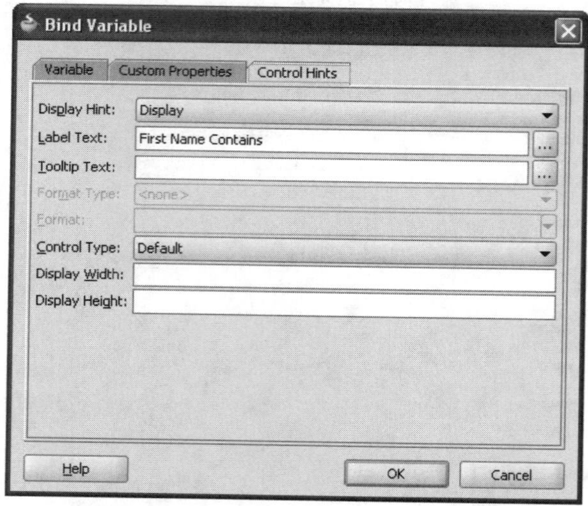

These control hints are a subset of those available for attributes; see the section "Control Hints for Attributes" for more details. You cannot use property sets with bind variables.

Control Hints for Lists of Values

As explained in the section "How Do You Create Data-Bound Pages?" users can select a value for an attribute based on a LOV using specialized controls such as dropdown lists and LOV popup windows.

There are two ways to specify control hints for such controls: You can set LOV control hints on a view object definition, which will be used by default by any attribute that uses a LOV from a view accessor to that definition or one of its instances. Alternatively, you can specify LOV control hints for particular LOV-based attributes; these will override any LOV control hints on the view object definitions they access.

To specify LOV hints at the view object definition level, select the List UI Hints page of a view object definition's editor. To do so at the LOV-based attribute level, select the UI Hints page of the List of Values dialog. These user interfaces are extremely similar; the UI Hints page of the List of Values dialog is shown next.

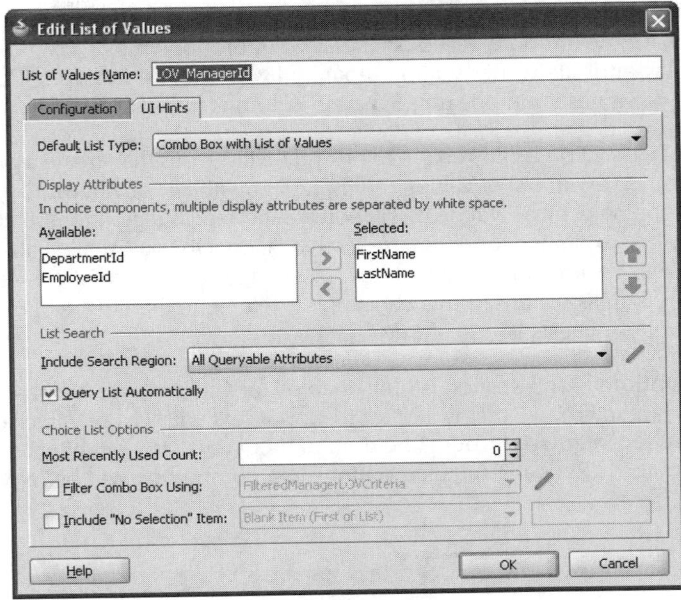

The "Default List Type" Dropdown The "Default List Type" dropdown allows you to select a default control type that users will use to select a list value. The available types are as follows:

- **Choice List** is a simple dropdown list from which the user can select a value.
- **Combo Box** is a control that, in addition to letting the user select a value from a dropdown list, also allows him or her to type a value in directly.
- **Combo Box with List of Values** is a combo box paired with a button. The button opens a popup dialog allowing the user to search for a row of the LOV, and browse through the results table, before selecting a particular row.
- **Input Text with List of Values** is an ordinary text field paired with a button that opens a popup LOV dialog.
- **List Box** is a fixed-size list box with a scrollbar. The user can select a single value from the list.
- **Radio Group** is a group of radio buttons, one for each row in the LOV.

In general, we recommend using a radio group, choice list, or combo box for relatively short lists of values, and using a combo box or input text with list of values for long lists of values.

Display Attributes A row from a LOV contains an attribute, the *list attribute*, whose value is used to populate the LOV-based attribute. However, the list attribute can be distinct from the LOV's *display attributes*, the attributes actually shown to the user in a dropdown, LOV dialog, list box, or radio button label set. For example, the JobId attribute of the AllEmployees view object definition is populated from the JobId attribute of the AllJobs view object definition. However, JobIds are just codes and so should not actually appear in the choice list from which the users select a job. Instead, the elements the user will see in the choice list are values of the JobTitle attribute of AllJobs.

The Display Attributes shuttle allows you to select one or more attributes that will appear in the UI control for the attribute based on the LOV. In dropdown lists, list boxes, or radio groups, multiple display attribute values will be separated with spaces. In popup LOV dialogs, multiple display attribute values will appear as separate columns in the LOV table.

List Search This section is only enabled for Choice List types that create a popup LOV window—namely, Combo Box with List of Values and Input Text with List of Values. They allow you to select a collection criteria object that will be used to create the search region for the LOV window. Collection criteria objects are explained further in the section "How Do You Create Data-Bound Pages?"

The Query List Automatically checkbox, if selected, will automatically search for LOV rows when the popup dialog opens. If this checkbox is left clear, the LOV will only be queried when the user explicitly requests it.

Choice List Options This section is only enabled for Choice List types that create a dropdown list, combo box, or radio group—that is, not for the Input Text with List of Values or List Box options.

The "Most Recently Used Count" field, in particular, is only enabled for Choice List types that create a combo box. Recently selected options in a combo box will be moved to the top of the list, as shown here:

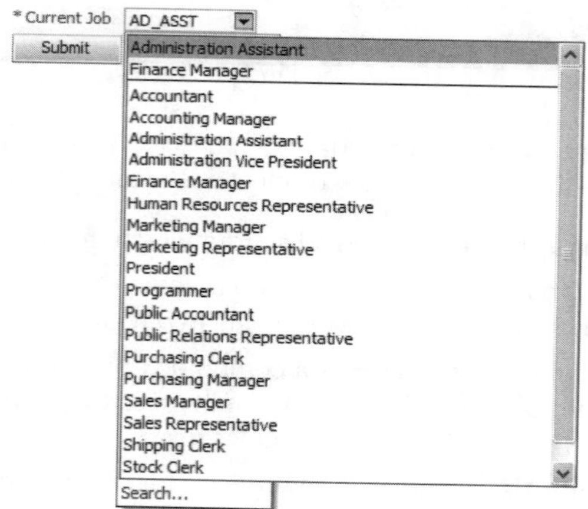

The value in this field indicates the maximum number of history items to display at the top of the list.

The "Include 'No Selection' Item" checkbox, if checked, will include a particular item in the list or radio group that will change the value of the LOV-based attribute to `null`. If you include a "No Selection" item, you can specify whether it should appear at the top or bottom of the list (or radio group), whether it should have a label, and, if so, what its label should be.

How Do You Create Data-Bound Pages?

The Data Controls panel of the Application Navigator provides the basic design-time user interface to ADFm. This panel exposes all of the data and public functions (operations) that the UI developer can use in an application's screens. Figure 13-3 shows the Data Controls panel structure from the TUHRA2 application:

- **Data control** The top-level nodes of the tree exposed in the panel are the data controls. In this case, the sole data control is TuhraServiceDataControl, the data control for a top-level instance of application module definition TuhraService.
- **Top-level collection** The Data Controls panel may expose data collections (sets of rows). When the data control represents an application module instance, each view object instance in the application module instance's data model will be represented as a data collection node; the top-level (nondetail) view object instances in the data model appear directly under the data control node in the tree. Some user interface components, such as table controls, trees, graphs, and charts, can be bound to a whole collection of data.
- **Nested collection** Where a master-detail relationship is implemented by a view link instance in the data model (or through other mechanisms in other business service technologies), the detail collection appears under the master collection in the Data Controls panel. In this case, the DepartmentTree collection represents the

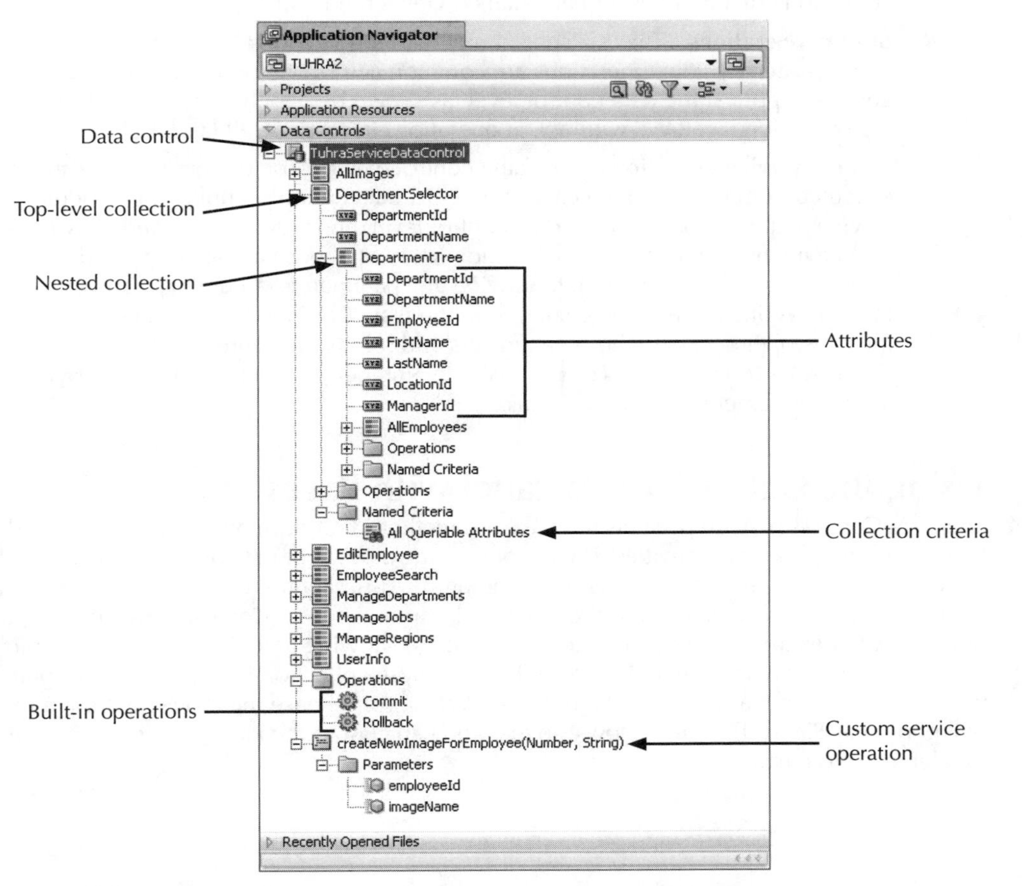

FIGURE 13-3. *The Data Controls panel of the Application Navigator*

DepartmentTree view object instance, accessed through a view link instance from the DepartmentSelector view object instance. The important feature here is that any nested collection (or attributes of that collection) will reveal data only within the context of, and coordinated with, the associated master row in the master collection.

- **Attribute** Individual data elements are exposed either at the top level of a data control or by expanding data collections. In the case of data controls for application module instances, there are no attributes at the top level of the data control, but there are attributes corresponding to each view attribute under the appropriate data collection. These can be dragged onto the page to bind the individual attributes to the user interface (UI).
- **Collection criteria** Every view object instance–based data collection always contains at least one "collection criteria" node, labeled "All Queriable Attributes." This represents a query-by-example search across all view attributes that are marked "Queriable" in the View Attribute page of the Attribute Editor for view attributes. In addition, data collections corresponding to view object instances with named view criteria have collection criteria nodes for each named view criteria object.
- **Built-in operations** This is a special method type provided by ADFm itself rather than being written by you. Operations are common across one or more types of data controls and may apply at the data control level (as shown here with Commit and Rollback) or at the collection level. We will look at operations in more detail later.
- **Custom service operations** Any data control may expose custom methods that can be executed from the UI. In the case of ADF BC data controls, application module–level service methods appear at the data control level, and view object– and view row–level service methods appear at the collection level. Methods can be bound in different ways: to provide a way to run them, to provide any parameters (arguments), and to gain access to their results. The method displayed in the Data Controls panel can be expanded to give the developer access to these parameters and results. In Figure 13-3, you can see that `createNewImageForEmployee()` takes a Number parameter called `employeeId`, and a String parameter called `imageName`.

Using the Data Controls Panel with Pages

The Data Controls panel represents the data and methods that developers can use, or bind to, in their pages and task flow activities. The act of creating a usage of data by a user interface element or activity is, therefore, referred to as data binding. The primary use of the Data Controls panel is to create bindings by dragging and dropping nodes from the Data Controls panel onto a page or activity. For example, if you need to create a page showing an editable table of Employee information, you would drag and drop the EditEmployee collection icon in the Data Controls panel onto the page, as shown in Figure 13-4. When you release the mouse button, a menu will pop up as Figure 13-4 also shows, so that you can choose the kind of user interface element (or elements) to create.

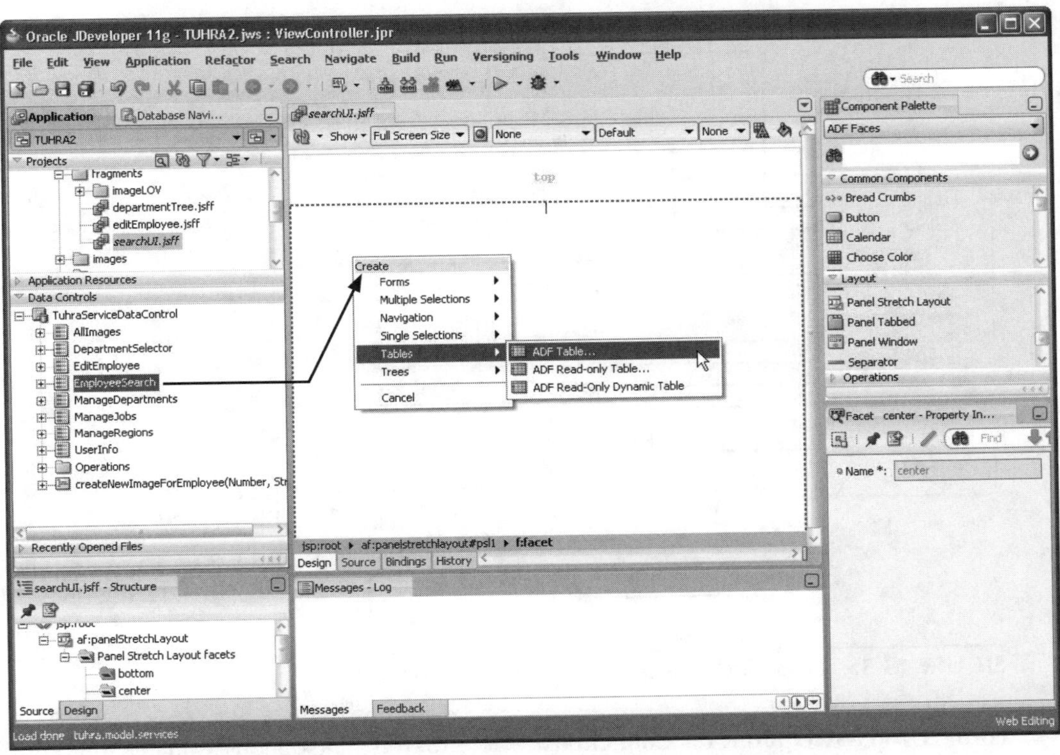

FIGURE 13-4. *Creating a table component*

The list of options displayed when the mouse button is released is dependent on the UI technology, whether the target is a page or task flow, and the type of object dragged from the panel (that is, a collection, an attribute, collection criteria, or an operation).

"Drop As" Options

In this section, we'll explore the various "drop as" UI options you can create using drag-and-drop from the Data Controls panel.

"Drop As" Options for Collections

Figure 13-5 shows the options available for collections when dropping onto a JSF page. The drop options for the collection are divided into twelve groups: Forms, Gantts, Gauges, Geographic Maps, Graphs, the Hierarchy Viewer, Master-Details, Multiple Selections, Navigation, Single Selections, Tables, and Trees.

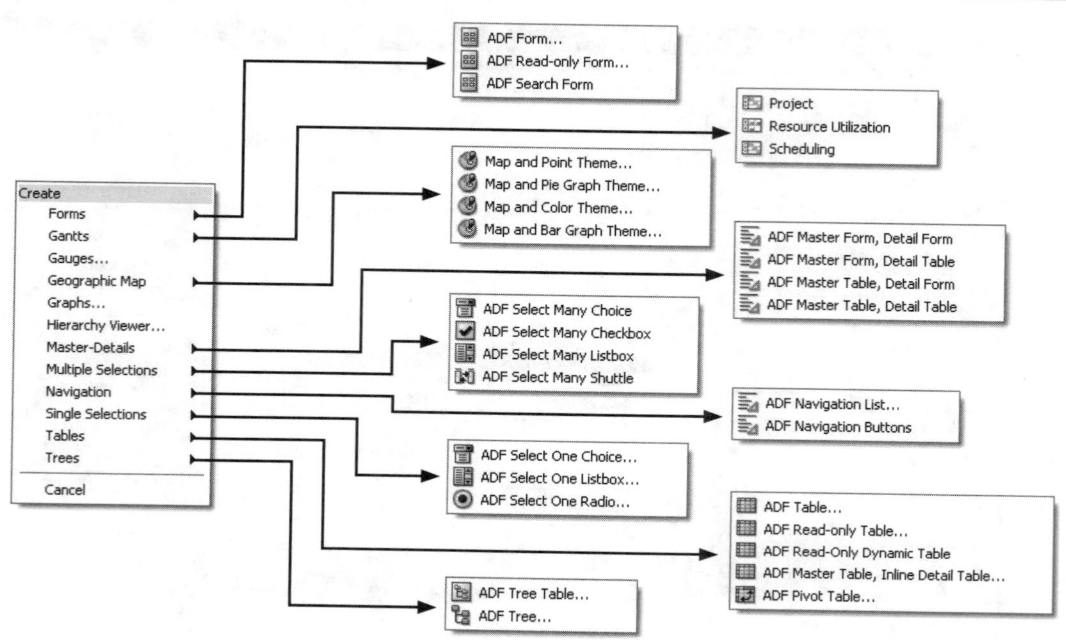

FIGURE 13-5. *Data binding a collection onto a JSF page*

Form "Drop As" Options for Collections Table 13-1 lists the options available for form layouts. In most cases, choosing one of the form options will display the Edit Form Fields dialog shown in Figure 13-6.

"Drop As" Option	Description
ADF Form	Dropping this form displays the Edit Form Fields dialog shown in Figure 13-6. Controls bound to the attributes of the collection are created, by default matching the attribute's "Control Type" control hint (or the LOV's "Control Type" control hint, for view attributes with LOVs) with properties matching the other control hints. The following illustration shows an ADF form created from the EditEmployee collection: Employee No. 174 First/Given Name Ellen * Last Name/Surname Abel Line Manager 149 * Current Job Sales Representative * Date Joined 5/11/1996

TABLE 13-1. *"Drop As" Form Options with ADF Faces*

"Drop As" Option	Description
	Fields created from ADF BC attributes marked as "mandatory" are displayed at runtime with an asterisk indicating a required value. The components are automatically aligned within an `af:panelForm` container component. JSF validators are also automatically defined for the fields to implement any validation defined in the model. If the user clicks the supplied Submit button, the controller will update the model but not commit any changes.
ADF Read-Only Form	Dropping this form on the page also displays the Edit Form Fields dialog. The only difference from the previous option is that the default components selected are ADF output text (`af:outputText`) rather than various input controls, and no validators or mandatory markers are created. Other properties (such as tips and labels) are still bound to the attribute's control hints. The following illustration shows an ADF read-only form created from the AllEmployees collection: Employee No. 174 First/Given Name Ellen Last Name/Surname Abel Line Manager 149 Current Job SA_REP Date Joined 5/11/1996
ADF Search Form	A search form provides a Query-by-Example (QBE) interface for a data collection. In general, we do not recommend using this component; query components (discussed in the section "'Drop As' Options for Collection Named Criteria") provide greater functionality.

TABLE 13-1. *"Drop As" Form Options with ADF Faces (continued)*

Each field in the source collection is listed, allowing you to add or delete fields or to change the field order using the buttons around the field list. The *Include Navigation Controls* checkbox adds navigation buttons used to scroll through the records. The *Include Submit Button* checkbox places a Submit button on the form. This button allows the user to apply any changes made in the screen to the Model layer. The navigation buttons can also be added later by individually binding the relevant operations or by dragging and dropping the collection again and selecting **Navigation | Navigation Buttons** in the appropriate style. The Submit button can also be added later by dropping in a normal CommandButton from the Component Palette.

In the list of fields displayed by the dialog shown in Figure 13-6, you can control how each field is represented in the generated form. The *Value Binding* column in the center lists the attributes that are available in the collection. The *Display Label* column controls the label for the field that is created to represent that attribute. If this is left to the default value of "<default>," the *Label Text* control hint or attribute name (if there is no control hint) defined for the underlying ADF BC entity or view attribute will be used at runtime. Alternatively, you can hard-code your own label value.

Gantt "Drop As" Options for Collections A *Gantt chart* is a graphical chart that displays, for a list of resources or tasks, bars representing periods of time, such as times during which particular

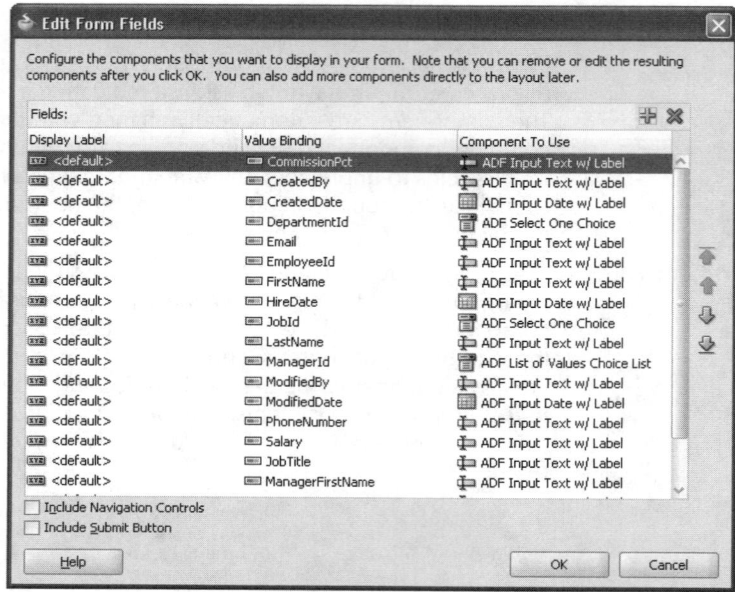

FIGURE 13-6. *The Edit Form Fields dialog*

resources are utilized, or times during which particular tasks are being executed. The vertical axis of the chart is the list of resources or tasks, and the horizontal axis is a calendar.

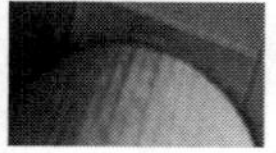

NOTE
Chapter 12 introduced the Data Visualization Tools components and provided a short hands-on practice for the graph component. You can find more information about these components in Chapter 24 ("Creating Databound ADF Data Visualization Components") of the Fusion Developer's Guide for Oracle ADF.

Gauge "Drop As" Options for Collections A *gauge* is a graphical way to display a single, numerical value. Optionally, gauges can also use visual properties like color to represent various ranges for the value, such as an "OK" range, a "Warning" range, and a "Critical" range. Again, gauges are covered in the JDeveloper documentation.

Geographic Map "Drop As" Options for Collections Geographic map–style "Drop As" options do not actually create maps (although if you drop one of these options onto a page that is not yet configured for a map, a dialog will appear allowing you to configure it as one before proceeding). Rather, they create various *themes*, or overlays of data, on maps supplied by an Oracle Application Server MapViewer service.

Graph "Drop As" Options for Collections ADF provides a wide range of graphs that you can use to display data, including bar graphs, line graphs, pie graphs, and many others.

Hierarchy Viewer "Drop As" Options for Collections ADF provides a very rich, tree-type navigator for viewing hierarchical relationships, called a "hierarchy viewer." You will create an ADF Hierarchy Viewer in Chapter 18.

Master-Detail "Drop As" Options for Collections When a collection that is a nested within another collection is dropped onto the page, four Master-Detail options will be available. Selecting one of these options is a shortcut for dropping an option for the master collection, followed by a second drop from the detail collection. The shortcut combinations available are as follows:

- ADF Master Table, Detail Form
- ADF Master Form, Detail Table
- ADF Master Form, Detail Form
- ADF Master Table, Detail Table

The forms and tables created using these options are identical to the read-only forms and read-only tables described in the sections "Form 'Drop As' Options for Collections" and "Table 'Drop As' Options for Collections."

Multiple Selection "Drop As" Options for Collections When you drop a collection onto a page, you have an option to create one of several components that allow the user to select multiple rows from a collection's result set. The component will pass an array of values for an attribute you choose. This form of binding is not declaratively handled when ADF BC is providing the data control, so you will need to process this array in code in a managed bean.

Table 13-2 lists the options available for these multiple selection form layouts. When these components are dropped, the Edit List Binding Editor, shown in Figure 13-7, pops up to gather the extra information needed to define the contents of the list options. List Bindings are described in more detail in Chapter 14, in the section "List Bindings."

"Drop As" Option	Description
ADF Select Many Choice	Dropping this component on a page creates an `af:selectManyChoice`, which renders a dropdown list with checkboxes beside each option. The user can expand the LOV and select one or more options, as shown here: 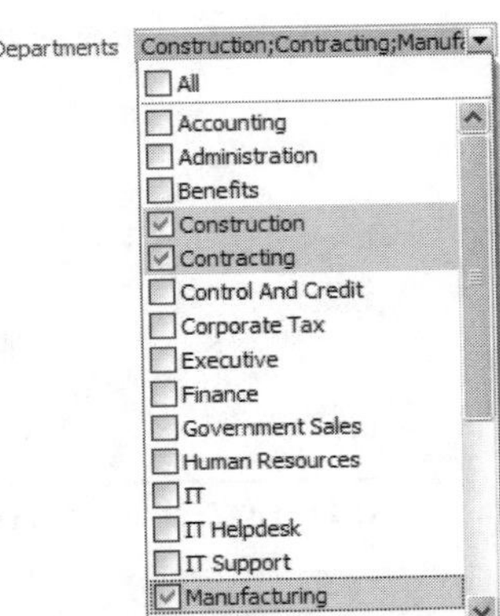

TABLE 13-2. *"Drop As" Multiple Selection Options with ADF Faces (continued)*

"Drop As" Option	Description
	The user can check the "All" box to automatically select every item in the list. The number of rows displayed (without scrolling) is under the control of the browser; because of this, the Select Many Choice component is only appropriate for collections with a small number of rows.
ADF Select Many Checkbox	Dropping this component on a page creates an `af:selectManyCheckbox`, which renders a set of checkboxes, one for each row in the collection. The user can select any combination of these checkboxes, as shown on the right. 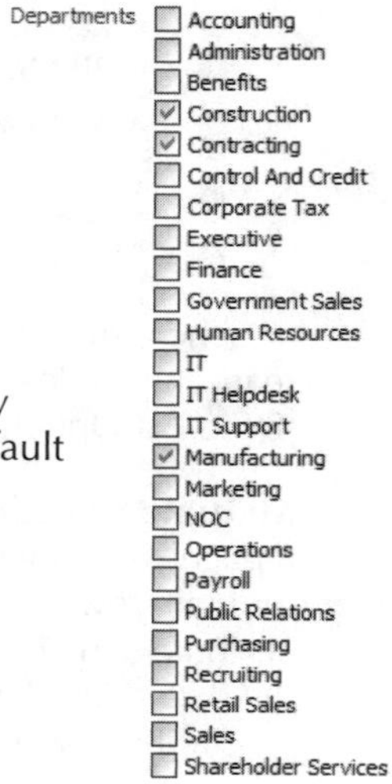 You can choose whether to lay out these checkboxes vertically or horizontally by setting the *Layout* property of the `af:selectManyCheckbox` (the default is vertical). We only recommend horizontal layout for very small collections that will not cause horizontal scrolling. Departments: Accounting, Administration, Benefits, Construction, Contracting, Control And Credit, Corporate Tax, Executive, Finance, Government Sales, Human Resources, IT, IT Helpdesk, IT Support, Manufacturing, Marketing, NOC, Operations, Payroll, Public Relations, Purchasing, Recruiting, Retail Sales, Sales, Shareholder Services
ADF Select Many Listbox	Dropping this component on a page creates an `af:selectManyListbox`, which renders a scrollable list of components, as shown here. 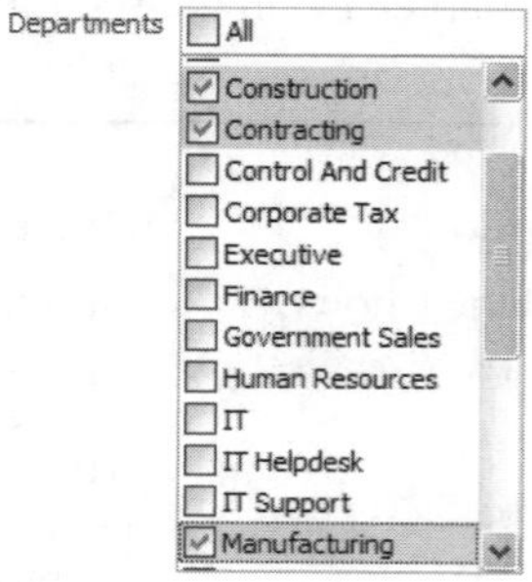 Departments: All, Construction, Contracting, Control And Credit, Corporate Tax, Executive, Finance, Government Sales, Human Resources, IT, IT Helpdesk, IT Support, Manufacturing You can control the size of the scrollable area by setting the *Size* property of the ADF Select Many Listbox. The value you select will be the maximum number of rows visible at once.

TABLE 13-2. *"Drop As" Multiple Selection Options with ADF Faces (continued)*

"Drop As" Option	Description
ADF Select Many Shuttle	Dropping this component on a page creates an `af:selectManyShuttle`, which renders a shuttle control (similar to the shuttle controls within the JDeveloper design time), as shown here. 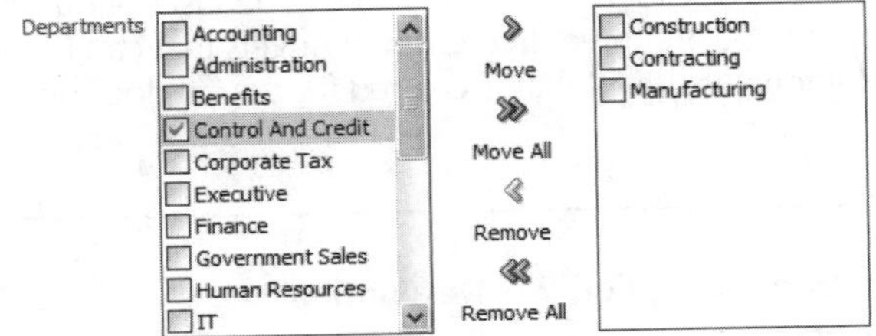 The user selects one or more items in the left-hand list and clicks the Move button to move them to the right-hand list, or clicks Move All to move all items in the left-hand list to the right-hand list. The user can also select one or more items in the right-hand list and click Remove to move them back to the left-hand list, or can click Remove All to move all items in the right-hand list to the left-hand list. When the form containing the component is submitted, items in the right-hand list are sent to the server.

TABLE 13-2. *"Drop As" Multiple Selection Options with ADF Faces (continued)*

FIGURE 13-7. *The Edit List Binding dialog for multiple selections*

Navigation "Drop As" Options for Collections We have already introduced the concept of navigational buttons. These buttons can be created using a checkbox in the Edit Form Fields dialog used to create forms from a collection. You can also create these buttons separately by dragging and dropping a data collection. Table 13-3 shows the types of navigational user interfaces that you can create by dragging and dropping a collection as a navigation type.

Single Selection "Drop As" Options for Collections The single selection options for a collection are effectively identical to the Navigation List option that we saw in Table 13-3. The only difference is that there are three different list widgets that can be used: Choice List, Select List, or Radio Group. Additionally, the UI that is created for the list does not contain the Panel Header.

"Drop As" Option	Description
ADF Navigation List	Dropping a navigation list will first pop up the Edit List Binding dialog to allow the selection of the attribute(s) for use as the list label, as shown in Figure 13-8. Then it will create an `af:panelGroup` containing a specialized dropdown list item, as shown in the illustration here. Department Name Accounting Details Accounting Administration Benefits Construction Contracting Control And Credit Corporate Tax Executive Finance Government Sales Human Resources IT IT Helpdesk IT Support Manufacturing Marketing NOC Operations Payroll Public Relations Purchasing Recruiting Retail Sales Sales Shareholder Services The list is bound to the rows in the collection in such a way that selecting a particular row in the list will set the row currency in the collection. This effectively "jumps" you to the selected record. This kind of navigation is best restricted to small collections of records; otherwise, the dropdown list will be too long. The panel group is labeled with a default header value of "Details." This can be changed by editing the properties of the embedded `af:panelHeader` that the drag-and-drop action creates. If you want to display detail fields after selecting a record in the dropdown list, you drop a form into the `af:panelHeader`. This will automatically show the row as it is selected from the navigation list.
ADF Navigation Buttons	This option will create and arrange buttons for the First, Previous, Next, and Last operations, as shown here:  These buttons are set up with expressions to automatically enable and disable the buttons. For example, when you are on the first record of the collection, the Previous and First buttons are disabled.

TABLE 13-3. *"Drop As" Navigation Options with ADF Faces*

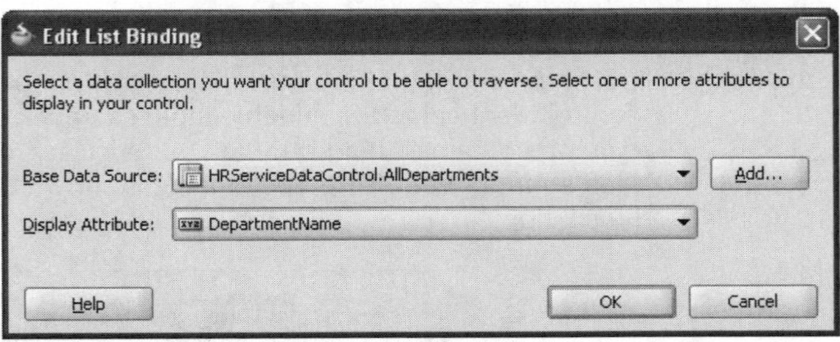

FIGURE 13-8. *The Edit List Binding dialog for navigation list selection*

Table "Drop As" Options for Collections You can drop various types of tabular layouts onto a page, in both writable and read-only alternatives. This ability to implement multi-row editing with no extra coding is one of the benefits of JSF. Table 13-4 shows the options available for tabular layouts when using the ADF libraries.

"Drop As" Option	Description
ADF Table	Dropping a data collection as "ADF Table . . ." displays an Edit Table Columns dialog as shown in Figure 13-9, with all fields designated as input fields by default. This will create an `af:table` component (see the sidebar "About af:table"), containing one `af:column` for each field and then an input component (as in the "ADF Form" "Drop As" option). The attribute label control hint (or the attribute name) is, by default, used as the column header, as shown on the right. The example table shown in this illustration was created with the sorting, filtering, and row selection options selected in the dialog.

DepartmentId	DepartmentName
10	Administrations
20	Marketing
30	Purchasing
40	Human Resources
50	Shipping
60	IT
70	Public Relations
80	Sales
90	Executive
100	Finance
110	Accounting
120	Treasury
130	Corporate Tax
140	Control And Credit
150	Shareholder Services

TABLE 13-4. *"Drop As" Table Options for Collections (continued)*

"Drop As" Option	Description
ADF Read-Only Table	Using the Edit Table Columns dialog, this option creates a table control identical to the editable table example, except that each column contains a read-only `af:outputText` component rather than an input field. This type of table is shown in the following illustration.

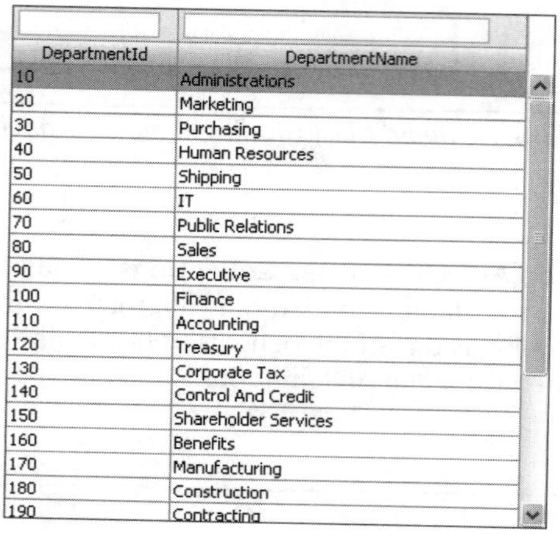

DepartmentId	DepartmentName
10	Administrations
20	Marketing
30	Purchasing
40	Human Resources
50	Shipping
60	IT
70	Public Relations
80	Sales
90	Executive
100	Finance
110	Accounting
120	Treasury
130	Corporate Tax
140	Control And Credit
150	Shareholder Services
160	Benefits
170	Manufacturing
180	Construction
190	Contracting

TIP
It is possible to have a table that contains a mixture of read-only fields and input fields. To define this effect, set the component types as required in the Edit Table Columns dialog.

"Drop As" Option	Description
ADF Read-Only Dynamic Table	The output from this option is identical to a read-only table, except that the columns in this option are not explicitly created in the page. Instead, an `af:forEach` loop is used to dynamically list the columns at runtime. This can be advantageous if you are building dynamic view object instances, because if the number of attributes in the data collection (or the actual data collection used) changes, the table will adjust automatically. Column labels will be determined dynamically at runtime from Label hints. The only way to not show a particular attribute in a dynamic table is to set its Display hint to "Hide."

TABLE 13-4. *"Drop As" Table Options for Collections (continued)*

"Drop As" Option	Description
ADF Pivot Table	Most tables use table rows to represent view rows, and table columns to represent attributes. An ADF Pivot table uses *cells* to represent view rows, and both table rows and table columns to represent possible attribute values. For example, consider a view object definition with this query:

```
SELECT DEPARTMENT_ID,
       JOB_ID,
       COUNT(EMPLOYEE_ID) NUM_EMPLOYEES
FROM EMPLOYEES
GROUP BY DEPARTMENT_ID, JOB_ID
```

In the following illustration, possible values of DepartmentId are represented as table rows, possible values of JobId are represented as table columns, and each view row matching the appropriate JobId and DepartmentId is represented as a cell, in which the view row's NumEmployees is displayed.

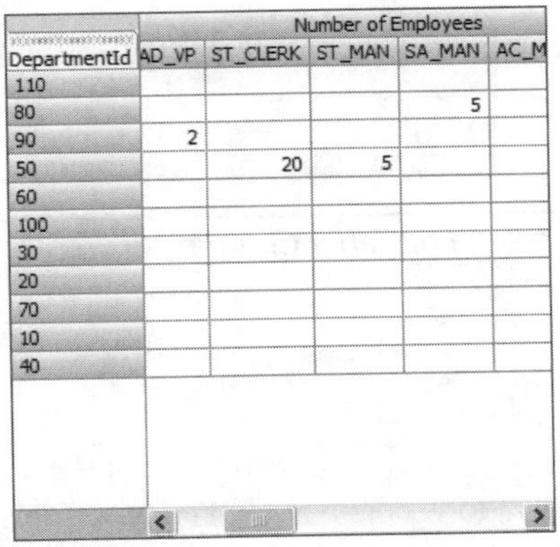

	Number of Employees				
DepartmentId	AD_VP	ST_CLERK	ST_MAN	SA_MAN	AC_M
110					
80				5	
90	2				
50		20	5		
60					
100					
30					
20					
70					
10					
40					

Developers can use pivot table rows or columns to represent multiple attributes, in which case possible *combinations* of attributes correspond to the rows or columns. At runtime, users can even change which attributes are represented where by dragging row or column headers to the opposite axis.

TABLE 13-4. *"Drop As" Table Options for Collections (continued)*

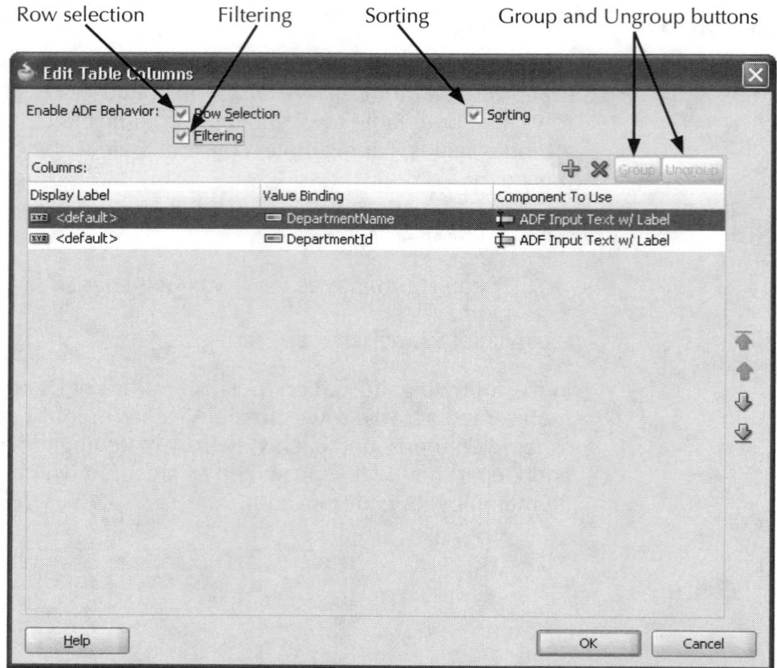

FIGURE 13-9. *Edit Table Columns dialog*

About af:table

All of the "Drop As" table options, with the exception of the pivot table, use the `af:table` component to generate a tabular layout. This component is quite powerful. It supports features such as sorting by column headers, lazy-loading of long tables, row selection, banding (shading or highlighting columns or rows at repeating intervals), and nested detail tables.

You bind a data collection to the `af:table` component. The individual attributes within the collection are then referenced using a variable that represents each row as it is processed (usually called "row"), which is defined using the `var` attribute of the `table` tag. For example, the value for Department Name in a table column is bound using the expression `#{row.DepartmentName}`.

The Edit Table Columns dialog, shown in Figure 13-9, is similar to the Edit Form Fields dialog, except that the navigation and Submit button check options are replaced by options to make the table sortable, enable record selection, and allow for filtering the table based on user-entered values for each column. The dialog also allows you to create column groups by selecting a set of columns and clicking the Group button. You can remove columns from the group by selecting them and clicking the Ungroup button.

Tree-Style "Drop As" Options for Collections ADF Faces includes some complex components that are capable of displaying master-detail relationships in a single component. If a collection contains such a relationship to another collection, such as employees within a department, then the tree-based components will be available. These components require you to define the relationship by filling in the tree binding information when you drop the control onto the page. This process is discussed in Chapter 14, in the section "Tree Bindings." Table 13-5 lists the tree options.

<table>
<tr><th>"Drop As" Option</th><th>Description</th></tr>
<tr><td>ADF Tree Table</td><td>
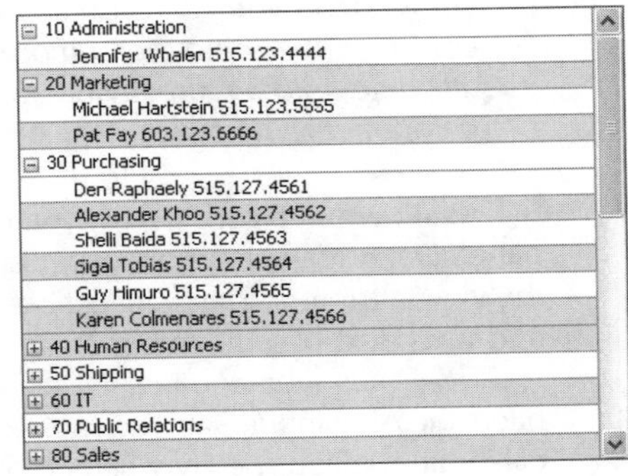

This option creates an `af:treeTable`, which represents hierarchical data in a table-like structure, as shown in this illustration.

The nodes in tree tables have a specialized right-click menu, allowing the user to zoom in on a node, expand the entire hierarchy below the node, or collapse the entire hierarchy below the node.

Tree-specific events—such as DisclosureEvent, an event that fires when the user expands a node in the tree—are supported by this control. This component is complex, and you will need to consult the ADF Faces documentation in the JDeveloper help system for the full list of attributes and events. The tree table is covered by Section 23.5, "Using Tree Tables to Display Master-Detail Objects," of the *Fusion Developer's Guide for Oracle ADF*.
</td></tr>
<tr><td>ADF Tree</td><td>
An ADF Tree provides a more conventional navigator or explorer tree control, as shown in the next illustration. Again, events are raised when the user clicks or expands a node.

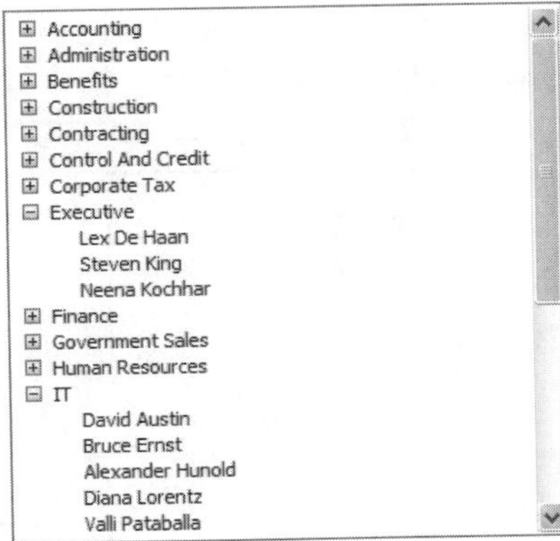

</td></tr>
</table>

TABLE 13-5. *"Drop As" Tree Options for Collections*

"Drop As" Options for Attributes

In many cases, it will not be enough to just drop a collection as a form or table onto the page. You can create UI controls individually by dragging and dropping the individual attributes from the expanded collection in the Data Controls panel. Although dragging and dropping a collection creates a group of components, when you drag and drop an attribute, you will usually create a single component.

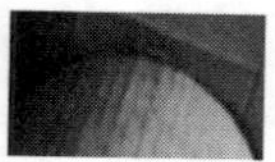

TIP

In addition to dropping an attribute into a container to create a component, you can drop an attribute onto a non-data-bound component to bind the component to the attribute, or drop an attribute onto an already data-bound component to change the component's binding.

As shown in Figure 13-10, you can create four classes of components from the Data Controls panel: Dates (date components), Lists of Values (list-based components using the LOV defined for the view attribute), Single Selections (list-based components using other sources of possible values), and Texts (text-based components).

The Dates submenu is only shown when the attribute being dropped is a date type. This submenu offers the ADF Input Date (`af:selectInputDate`) component, an input field with a built-in pop-up calendar. You can specify whether to label the date field or not.

The List of Values submenu is only shown when the attribute being dropped is based on a list of values. The ADF LOV Input (`af:inputListOfValues`) creates a text field with a search icon; clicking the icon brings up the LOV in a popup window. The popup window supports searching,

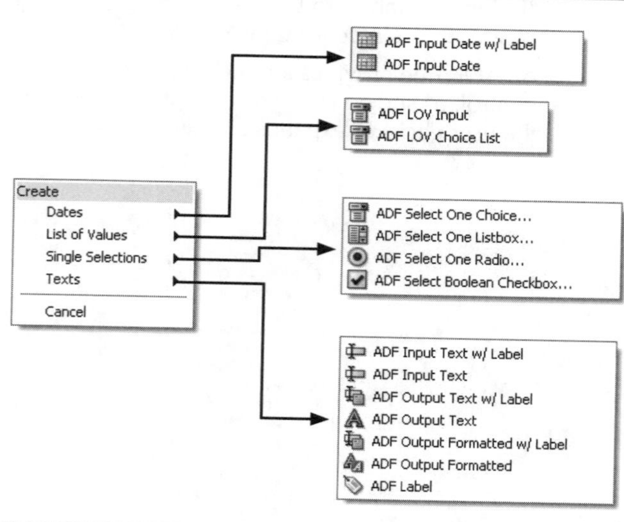

FIGURE 13-10. *Data binding an attribute onto a JSF page*

sorting, and range paging. This component is ideal for very long lists of values. The ADF LOV Choice List (`af:inputComboBoxListOfValues`) provides a combo box. Because it can be hard to find items in a long dropdown list, we recommend using the ADF LOV Choice List for relatively small lists of values.

With the Single Selections options, you need to do extra work after dropping the attribute to define the values to display, as well as the attribute to which the underlying value is bound. When these components are dropped, the List Binding Editor pops up to gather the extra information needed to define the contents of the list options. This dialog is described in more detail in Chapter 14, in the section "List Bindings."

The various components shown on the Texts menu are all self-explanatory. The Input Text and Output Text options come in two flavors: plain or with a label (labeled as "w/ Label" in the menu). Selecting the "w/ Label" version will set the relevant component property to be bound to the label UI hint defined in ADF BC.

"Drop As" Options for Collection Named Criteria

The list of collection criteria shown in the Data Controls panel is derived from the list of view criteria that are defined on the relevant view object definition. A default named criteria object called "All Queriable Attributes" is present for every view object instance and defines a default search operation where all of the view attributes are available for searching. Like a collection or an attribute, the criteria object can be dragged into the UI editor and bound to components. In this case several search-related UI constructions are offered as is shown on the right.

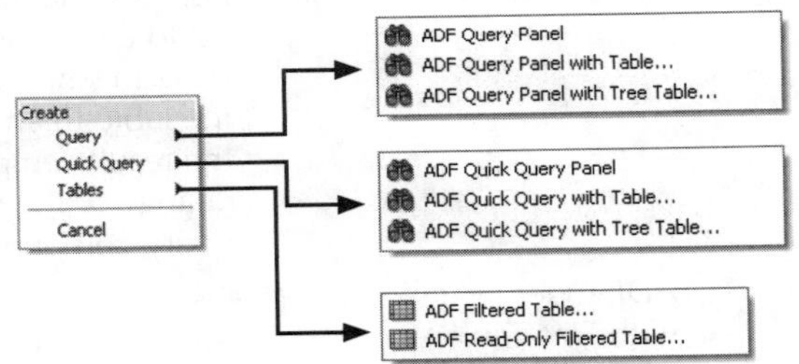

Table 13-6 discusses each of the options.

"Drop As" Option	Description
ADF Query Panel	The Query panel creates a classic query-by-example UI using the `af:query` component, as shown here.

TABLE 13-6. *"Drop As" Options for Named Criteria (continued)*

"Drop As" Option	Description
	This panel will, by default, show those fields defined in the underlying query criteria as queriable. You have control of various aspects of the query screen, such as the availability of the Advanced button through the properties of the `af:query` component itself. The labels for the fields are defined through the UI hints on the ADF BC entity and view object definitions. By default the whole query component is contained within a `af:panelHeader` component, but this is purely decorative and can be removed if not required.
ADF Query Panel with Table	Dropping as a query panel with table creates exactly the same query UI as the preceding option, but this time it also automatically creates a read-only table for the results of the query. This table is bound to the source collection (view object instance) for the query criteria. If you examine the component properties for the `af:query` component, you will note that its **resultComponentId** property is set to the ID of the table that was also created. If you move the table in some way that changes its ID, for example by enclosing the table in an `af:panelCollection`, then you must also change the resultComponentId on the `af:query` to correctly reflect the ID change or the results table will no longer be coordinated with the query component.
ADF Query Panel with Tree Table	Just like the Query Panel with Table option except that a tree table is created for the results instead.
ADF Quick Query Panel	Unlike the Query Panel, which shows all of the attributes associated with a view criterion, the Quick Query option shows a much simpler UI, using the `af:quickQuery` component, where only one query field is available, as shown here.  By changing the value in the selection list, the user can target the search field value to search that specific attribute. The quick query option is only available with the generic All Query Criteria named criteria that all view object instances will expose. So to create one, be sure to drag that named criterion onto the UI editor. The values displayed in the dropdown list of attributes are again inherited from the UI hints defined in ADF BC.
ADF Quick Query Panel with Table	As with the Query panel case, this associates a results table with the preceding `af:quickQuery` component.

TABLE 13-6. *"Drop As" Options for Named Criteria (continued)*

"Drop As" Option	Description
ADF Quick Query Panel with Tree Table	Again as before, this time with a Tree Table for the results.
ADF Filtered Table	When you drop a Named Criteria value as a filtered table, no `af:query` or `af:quickQuery` component is created. Instead, a results table is created with its column filters wired up to automatically filter the query results. Although the options for a filtered table are offered with any named criteria in the view object instance, it only really makes sense to do this in relation to the All Query Criteria, as the query is effectively controlled by the columns that you have available in the table.
ADF Filtered Read Only Table	As per the previous option but creating a read-only table.

TABLE 13-6. *"Drop As" Options for Named Criteria (continued)*

"Drop As" Options for Operations

Both built-in operations and service operations can be dragged onto JSF pages; the options this creates are shown in Figure 13-11.

The Methods menu (so-called for service operations; for built-in operations, this is labeled as the Operations menu) allows you to create command components that execute the operation.

The Parameters menu, which only appears for operations that accept parameters, has only one option—the ADF Parameter Form. Dragging this option onto a page creates an ADF Form (like the one described in the section "Form 'Drop As' Options for Collections"), except that instead of users entering attribute values, they instead enter parameter values for the operation. If the operation is subsequently executed (for example, by a method call activity), the values the user enters will be passed into it.

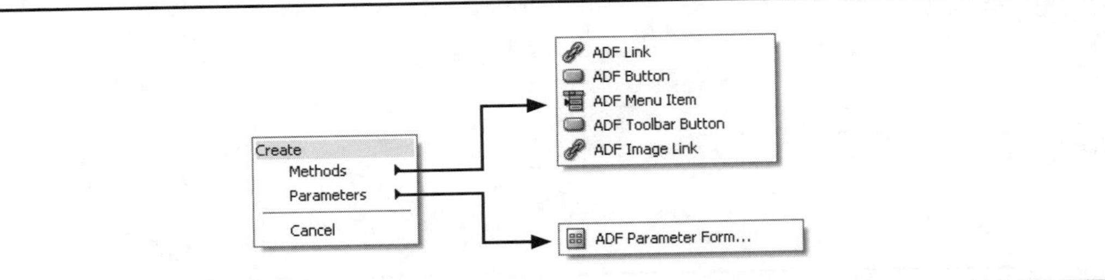

FIGURE 13-11. *Data binding an operation onto an ADF page*

Operation Node Subtrees in the Data Controls Panel Figure 13-12 shows the expanded nodes of three different kinds of operations. As it shows, different operations can take different numbers of parameters (including 0) and can have different return types (or no return value at all).

Dragging a parameter onto a form gives you a subset of the options (shown in Figure 13-10) you see when you drag an attribute onto a form. The Single Selections, Texts, and (if the parameter is a `Date`) Dates submenus are available for parameters. As with completely generated parameter forms, when the user enters a value into one of these controls and submits its form, that value will be used the next time the operation is executed (unless explicitly changed first).

Operations that return a simple value (such as a primitive or built-in domain) show that value as a node in the operation node subtree. An example is the `getDbSid()` operation shown in Figure 13-12. When you drag its return value onto a page, the same submenus are available as for

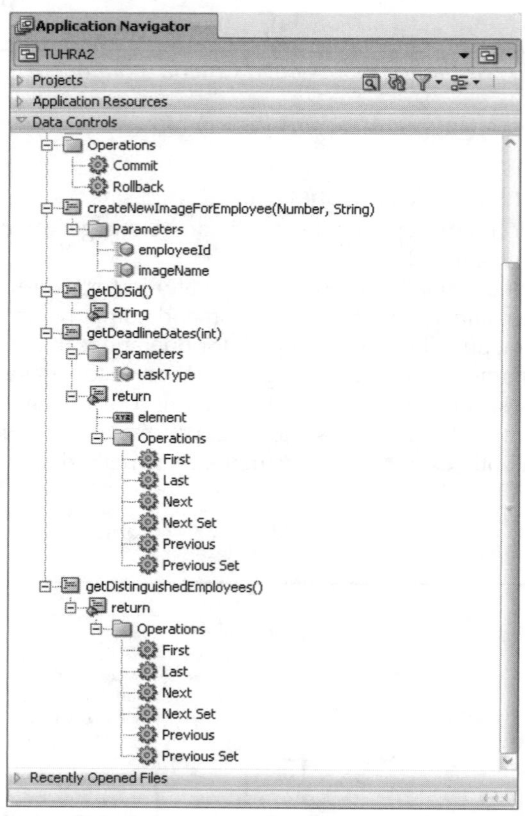

FIGURE 13-12. *Operation Node subtrees in the Data Controls panel*

a parameter of the same type. Note that before a return value for an operation will display on a page, the method must have been executed in some way within the current binding context (page).

Operations that return a `Collection` (or any of its subinterfaces, such as `List` or `Set`) have a subnode called "return." An example of this is the `getDeadlineDates(int)` operation shown in Figure 13-12. You can drag this node onto a JSF page, and you will be presented with a list of options that is a subset of the options (shown in Figure 13-5) for a collection. All submenus are available except the Master-Details, Multiple Selections, and Trees submenus.

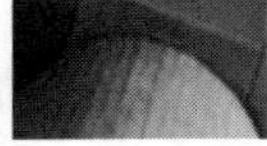

NOTE

A `Collection` return value is treated as having only a single attribute—the element of the collection. Therefore, if you drag a `Collection` return value as a form onto a page, the form will have only one input control; if you drag it as a table onto a page, the table will have only one column. To return structured data, return a `RowSet`, as explained later in this section.

Underneath the return node, there is an "element" node and a folder containing the six available navigation operations. Dragging the "element" node onto a page yields the same options as dragging a simple return value onto a page; the controls generated will display the value of the element for the current collection row. The navigation operations are self-explanatory, except for "Previous Set" and "Next Set," which are used to navigate forward and backward by range size. Range size is explained in Chapter 15, in the sidebar, "About Range Size."

Operations that return a `RowSet` (or any of its subinterfaces, such as `ViewObject`) also have a subnode called "return." An example of this is the `getDistinguishedEmployees()` operation shown in Figure 13-12. However, unlike the "return" node for `Collection` return values, dragging this "return" node onto a page always generates an ADF Read-Only Dynamic table. The table does not, in general, have just one column; instead, the number of columns is determined at runtime from the types of rows in the `RowSet`.

There is no "element" node under a `RowSet` return value, but there are the same six operations as are available for `Collection` return values.

How Do You Create Data-Bound Activities?

Dragging Data Controls panel nodes onto pages allows you to create components that allow users to see and/or change data, bind parameter values, and parameter values for operations; execute operations; and access operation results. Methods and operations can also be bound into Method Activities in a Task Flow.

Essentially, the process for doing this is identical to dragging such an operation onto a JSF page. Either the method or operation can be dropped directly onto the diagram, in which case a Method Activity is created for it, or it can be dropped onto an existing Method Activity as well.

When the method or operation is dropped, JDeveloper will pop up the Edit Action Binding dialog as shown here:

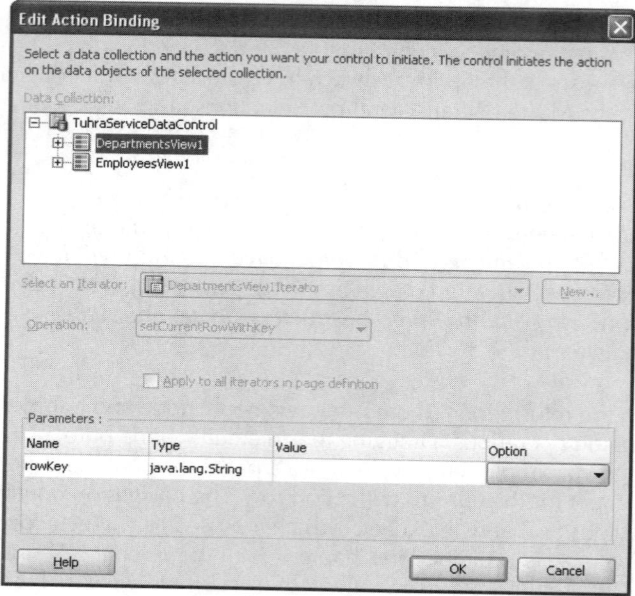

Notice now the parameters for the operation (if there are any) can be filled in on this screen. Generally you will set these parameters to EL values pointing to the data that you need to pass to the method.

What Files Are Involved in Data Binding?

So far, we've looked at the results of data binding within the design-time environment, but you might be wondering, what is actually going on here? How does the ADF Model actually work, and what files are used?

At a high level, the binding model is represented by a series of XML files, which we will examine shortly. At runtime, these XML files are translated by the framework into instances of lightweight Java classes (binding objects) that work with the framework to coordinate the requested business service with the UI.

- **Data control definition and collection definition files** These XML files, in the Model project, specify the details of the data controls ADFm should create at runtime. For many business services technologies, these data control definition and collection definition files must be explicitly generated by the developer, but for ADF BC, there is no special step to create these files. This is because application module and view object XML files act directly as data control definition and collection definition files, respectively.
- **Page definition files** These XML files, located by default in the `pageDefs` subpackage of the ViewController project's default package, each define a binding container. A page definition file contains and describes the bindings needed by the binding container. These files are further explained in Chapter 14.

- **Data binding registry** This file, located in the ViewController project's default package, is called DataBindings.cpx but is in fact an XML file. The file has a specialized editor, shown in Figure 13-13. The file contains three sorts of items:
  - **Page mappings** Each URL and task flow activity potentially requires a page definition usage. The data binding registry contains page mappings, which map URLs and activities to page definition usages.
  - **Page definition usages** Each page definition file may be used by one or more pages, fragments, templates, or activities. For each physical PageDef file, the data binding registry includes a page definition usage entry. Each page definition usage represents an individual binding container at runtime.
  - **Data control usages** Each data control definition may be used one or more times in the binding context. The data binding registry contains a data control usage for every data control in the binding context that must be created at runtime.

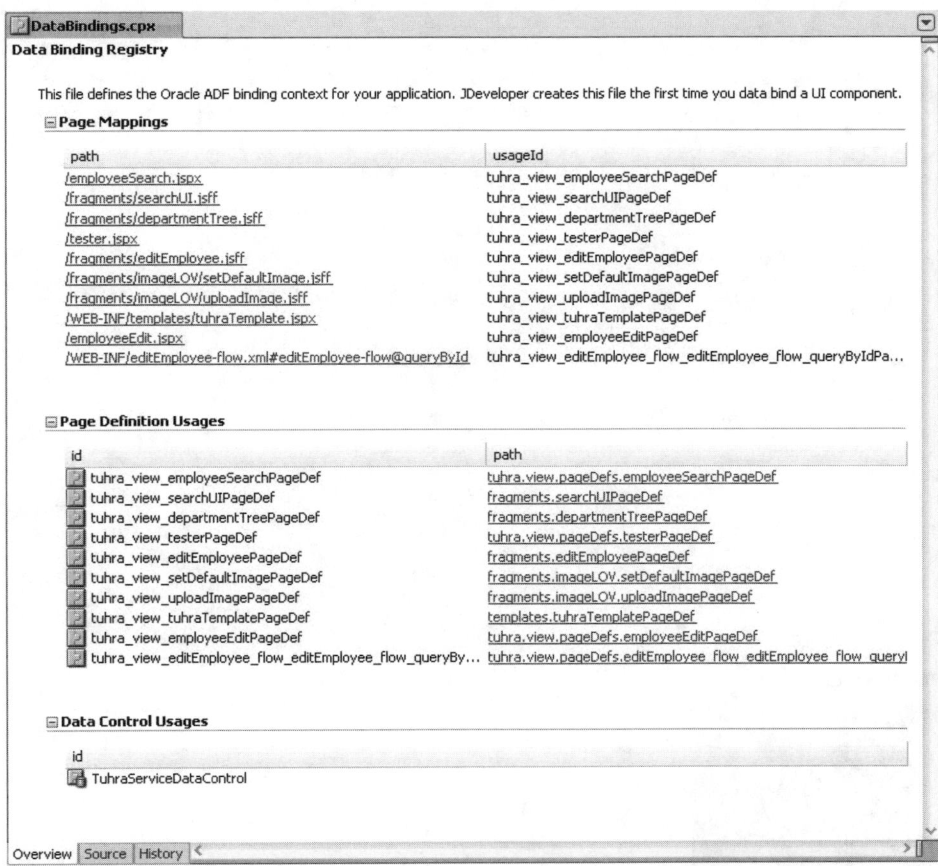

FIGURE 13-13. *The Data Binding Registry editor*

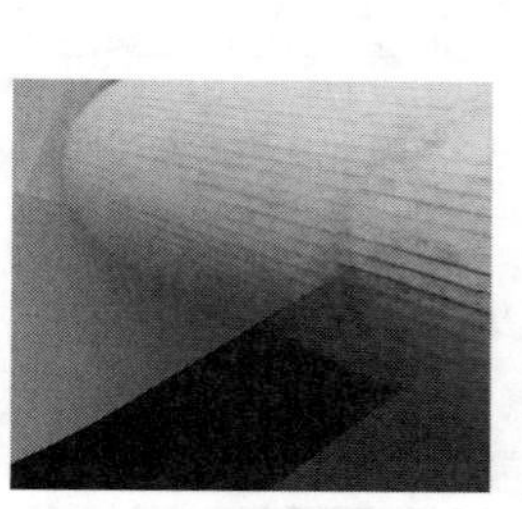

CHAPTER 14

ADF Advanced Bindings

Dig within.
Within is the wellspring of good;
and it is always ready to bubble up,
if you just dig.

—Marcus Aurelius (121–180),
Meditations, Book VII

In Chapter 13, we discussed the mechanics of binding data into the UI and files used in the process. In this chapter we'll spend some more time explaining the various types of bindings and how to edit them. This chapter is structured around the following questions:

- **How can I edit data bindings?**
- **What binding types are available?**
  - Attribute bindings
  - List bindings
  - List of values bindings
  - Tree bindings
  - Table bindings
  - Action bindings
  - Method bindings
  - Boolean bindings

CAUTION
If you are just starting out with ADF, you may find that the Chapters 14 and 15 are a little hard to absorb until you've had more exposure to using JDeveloper and the ADF framework. If this is the case, you might want to jump ahead to Part V of the book and spend a little time working with the software through the practices. Later, you can come back to these chapters and understand more about what you've really been doing. Before leaving this chapter, however, take a moment to read the section "Exploring the Binding Categories" in this chapter and the section "What Is an Iterator?" in Chapter 15.

Chapter 13 looked at the act of creating bindings through drag-and-drop actions into the visual editor. This action on the part of the developer does three things:

- **It creates the UI markup in the page source** to define the required components.
- **It writes information about the data bindings** that will be required to populate those components at runtime to the page definition file that services the page or page fragment.
- **It adds EL expressions to the new components on the page** that associates them with the bindings data defined in the page definition.

In this chapter you will become familiar with this page definition file, as it plays a key role in every ADF application. We will be referring to this file with its shortened name as used in the online documentation—*PageDef file* (or just *PageDef*). this chapter will also examine bindings in more detail and show how they can be changed after the drag-and-drop is done.

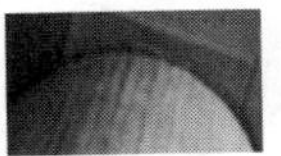

NOTE
Only data-bound pages or pages with embedded task flow regions have associated PageDef files.

As you become more familiar with ADF, you will find yourself spending more and more time in the PageDef file, or at least the graphical representation of it that is shown as one of the visual page editor views. Familiarity with manually creating and editing bindings is a vital skill for working successfully with the framework.

How Can I Edit Data Bindings?

To view and edit the bindings, you can either switch the page editor to the graphical bindings view using the visual editor Bindings tab or open up the underlying PageDef file from the Application Navigator. There are also a variety of shortcuts to navigate to the binding information, as follows:

- **Selecting Go To Page Definition** from the right-click menu on a page displays the underlying PageDef file.
- **Selecting Go To Binding** from the right-click menu on a bound item switches the page editor to the Bindings view tab and selects the relevant binding. The Property Inspector (or a double-click on the binding) displays the detail information on that binding.
- **Drilling from the Bindings TabView** can be done using the hyperlink shortcut on the Bindings tab in the main page editor which navigates to the underlying PageDef file. This is useful if you want to be able to edit the PageDef XML directly, rather than using the graphical view displayed on the Bindings tab.
- **Drilling from the DataBindings.cpx file** can be accomplished using the Overview tab of the DataBindings.cpx file (the data bindings registry file that maintains the master index of PageDef to page mappings introduced in Chapter 13). As shown in the following illustration, this tab shows all of the pages or UI fragments (under Page Mappings path)

and PageDefs (under Page Definition Usages path) as hyperlinks to allow drill-down into the relevant source files.

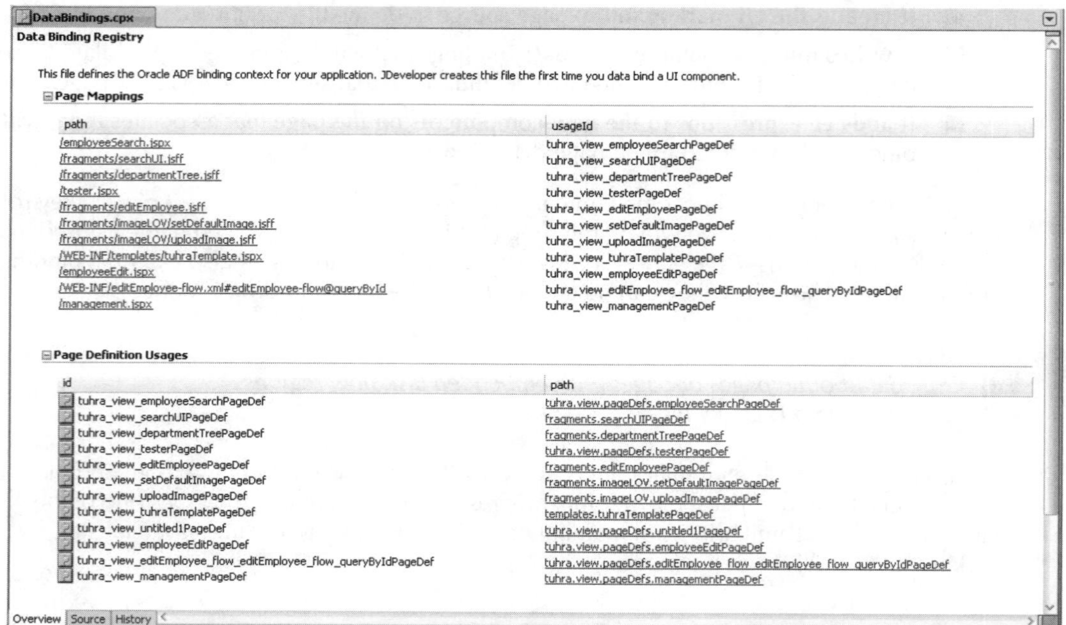

Cleaning Up Bindings

If a bound item is deleted from the Design view of the visual editor, JDeveloper will automatically remove the corresponding binding from the PageDef file. Deleting components from the Source view of the visual editor, however, will bypass the clean-up mechanism and will leave bindings orphaned in the PageDef file.

This behavior can be desirable. For example, to create a binding for programmatic purposes, it can be quicker to drag and drop the component onto the page and then delete the UI element, leaving the binding behind. If you take this approach, be sure to delete the component from the source view so that the automatic clean-up process is bypassed.

If you need to clean up bindings manually, open the Bindings editor of the page editor, select the required binding, and use the "Delete selected element" (red "x") button to delete it.

Exploring the Binding Categories

Getting to the PageDef file is the first step, but the important information is what to do once you get there and how to understand what it is telling you. You can think of binding types in two categories: generic bindings and data visualization bindings.

Generic Binding Types

The following generic binding types service standard user interface components such as InputText, OutputText, and SelectOneChoice.

- **Attribute bindings** More specifically called *attribute value bindings*, this binding type is used for a single attribute in a collection. When using ADF BC, a *collection* is essentially the contents of a view object—a result set of rows from the database. So an attribute binding is a binding to a particular attribute (column) in the result set. Implicitly, such a binding refers to the current row within that set of records, and the value of the attribute binding will change as the user navigates through the rowset.
- **List bindings** Also referred to as *list value bindings*, these are used to define the contents of data-bound list components, such as radio groups and dropdown lists.
- **NavigationList bindings** These are used to identify the current row in a row set and change the current record in a set.
- **ListOfValues binding** These provide a specialized binding for input fields with a popup list of values function that is very similar to the Oracle Forms LOV capability if you are familiar with that (see the sidebar "List of Values").
- **Tree bindings** These are one of the most common and yet complicated types of binding. They define sets of data, possibly defining master-detail relationships, used to populate both tables and hierarchical controls such as trees, tree-tables, or the hierarchy viewer component.
- **Table bindings** These are used to bind to a flat collection of data. They are used for lists that are looped through with the `af:forEach` and `af:iterator` components. Table bindings are no longer typically used for backing the `af:table` component, in a departure from the 10.1.3 release of ADF. As noted in the preceding item, the tree binding is now used for table controls, and the basic table binding now has a more limited role.
- **Action bindings** These are used to define the binding of standard operations, such as Commit, Next, and Last.
- **Method bindings** These are similar to action bindings but are used to bind custom code methods rather than standard operations.
- **Boolean bindings** Also called button bindings or Boolean value bindings, these are used to define a set of Boolean options. This binding is used for checkboxes in JSF pages.

List of Values

The significance of the term *list of values,* or *LOV*, may not immediately register. An LOV is very different from the kind of value list that you might see in a dropdown list. It provides the user with a popup window that displays possible choices in a tabular view. This UI provides the ability to interact with that list of data, including issuing searches against it and sorting the results set, before a value is selected to bring back to the field with the list attached. The LOV also exhibits some auto-complete and quick selection capabilities. List-of-Value bindings are discussed in detail, along with some screenshots, later in this chapter.

Data Visualization Binding Types

Another category of bindings is available to service the ADF Data Visualization Components, a set of charts and gauges that Chapter 12 touched on. Because of the complexity of these components, there is insufficient space to discuss them further in this chapter. However, what you learn about bindings here should be enough to help you reverse-engineer meaning from these specialized binding types as you encounter them. For your information the relevant bindings are

- **Graph binding** Defines the data used by the various chart types available through the ADF Data Visualization Components.
- **Gauge binding** Defines the data used by the various gauge and dial controls available through the ADF Data Visualization components.
- **PivotTable binding** Not surprisingly, this is used by the pivot table component and contains information about the rows, columns, and aggregations needed for the pivot.
- **Gantt binding** Defines the particular data structure needed to populate a Gantt chart, including the definition of tasks, subtasks, and the relationships between them. The Gantt chart is the cornerstone of scheduling and project management type user interfaces.
- **Map Theme binding** Defines the particular data structure needed to overlay data onto the GeoMap component in a location-aware way.

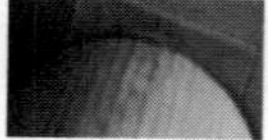

NOTE
An additional subset of bindings designed specifically for Swing applications are also available. These include slider and progressBar bindings. This book concentrates on the core Fusion web application technology stack that uses JSF and ADF Faces, so these binding types and Swing in general are not covered.

More Than Bindings

In addition to bindings, we need to discuss *executables,* which include taskFlow, searchRegion, and iterator. Iterators, in particular, are key to all of the bindings mentioned previously. The JDeveloper documentation refers in places to "iterator bindings," implying that they are just another binding type. Although this is strictly true (because they bind to a row set iterator in the underlying view object), iterators have a very different function from the other binding types. Iterators are covered in the section "What Is an Iterator?" in Chapter 15, but a brief introduction is included in the sidebar "About Iterators."

About Iterators

We haven't explained the concept of iterators yet. They are described more fully in the section "What Is an Iterator?" in Chapter 15. If you are familiar with Java, you will be familiar with the Iterator interface and the way that it can be used to step through a collection of data. If you are more familiar with SQL and PL/SQL, think of the iterator as an element used to navigate a row set, much as a cursor navigates a query result in PL/SQL.

What Binding Types Are Available?

Each of the binding types that has been introduced have various and specific behaviors so this section discusses each of the important bindings in detail.

FIGURE 14-1. *A form created from an ADF BC view object*

Attribute Bindings

Figure 14-1 shows a default screen created by dragging the default view object based on the HR schema Employees table onto the page and dropping it as an ADF Form. To make things a little more interesting here, some of the fields have various styles of list of values defined as hints in the business model and those are interpreted by the drag-and-drop operation to create specific UI components and some specialized bindings to go along with them. For now though we'll concentrate on the plain attribute bindings represented by fields such as First Name and Last Name in the form.

Each of the fields shown on the page has a matching binding in the PageDef file. Selecting **Go to Binding** from the right-click menu on one of the fields, such as *FirstName,* switches the page editor display to the Bindings panel as shown here:

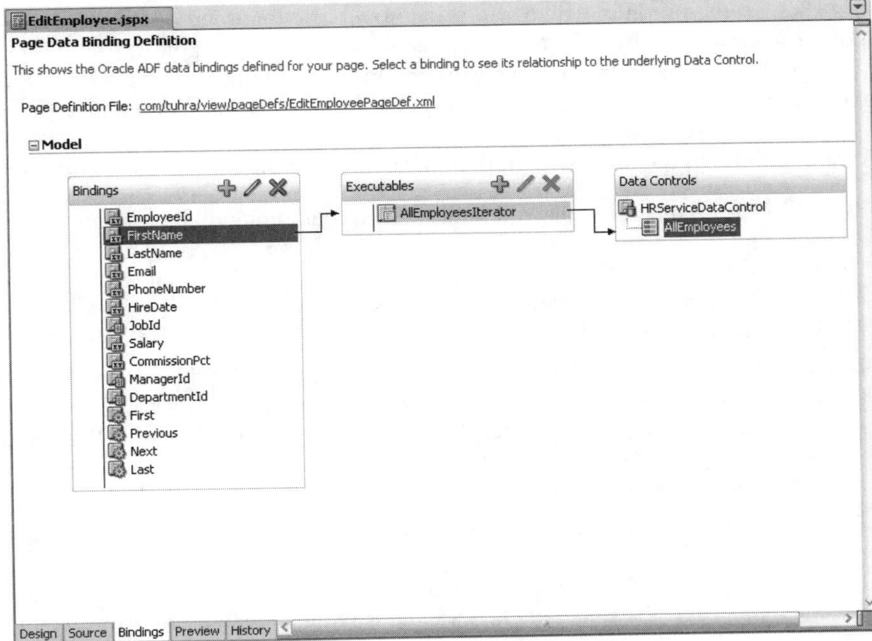

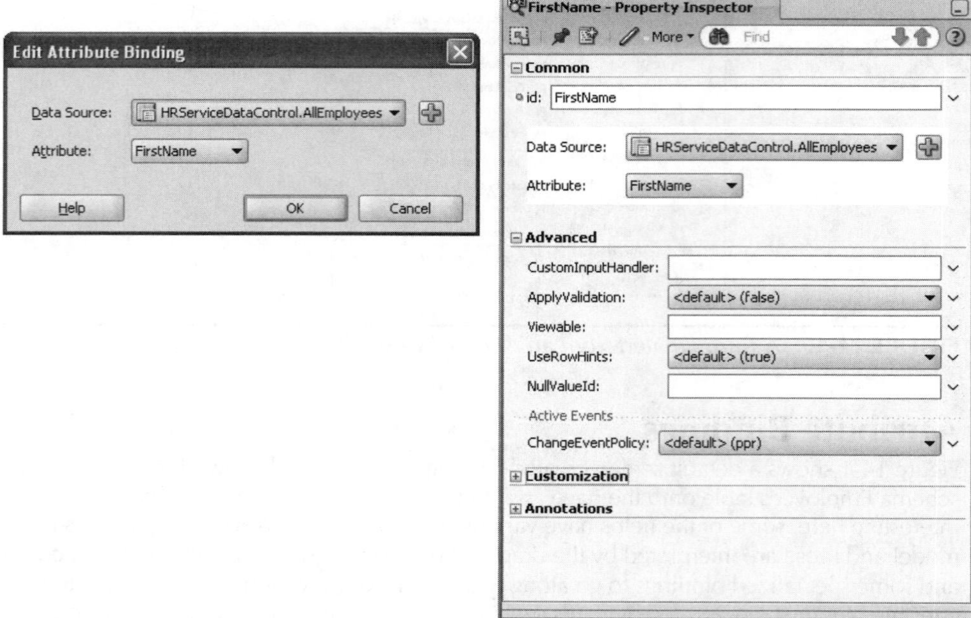

FIGURE 14-2. *Editing an Attribute Binding*

From here, the details of the binding can be examined in the Property Inspector, or by a double-click on the binding, which will bring up a basic mapping dialog. Figure 14-2 shows both of these views side by side. Notice how the contents of the Edit Attribute Binding dialog view mirror the General section of the Property Inspector. Either can be used to change the mapped attribute; however, the Property Inspector offers the ability to change the binding name as well as many advanced options.

Working through the properties in that Common section of the Property Inspector:

- **id** Defines the name by which this attribute binding will be referenced in the page. The segment "FirstName" in the expression `#{bindings.FirstName.inputValue}` refers to this ID property of the binding, not the actual mapped attribute from the view object. The inputValue in the preceding expression is a standard method exposed by any attribute binding to give access to the actual data pointed to by the binding.
- **Data Source** Is a dropdown list that indirectly specifies the iterator that this attribute is mapped from (see the sidebar "About Iterators" earlier in the chapter). The list will display all of the view object mappings that are currently available in this PageDef file. Click the Add (green plus "+") button to the right of the field to invoke a view of the Data Control list in the project to quickly map another view object if needed.

  The dropdown list for Data Source in the Property Inspector attempts to simplify things for the developer by just displaying the Data Control name and the view object instance name that the iterator represents, rather that showing the underlying iterator name. Thus, in Figure 14-2, the selected Data Source is HRServiceDataControl.AllEmployees, which, in the actual XML source for the binding, translates to the iterator "AllEmployeesIterator." If more than one iterator in the PageDef maps the same view object, then the dropdown here will display the actual iterator that is used for the mapping in parentheses after the name of the view object.

- **Attribute** Defines the attribute within the view object that the selected Data Source (iterator) points to. There is no requirement for the id and Attribute properties to match—any arbitrary name can be used for the ID; however, the value selected for Attribute must exist in the target collection. Therefore, the selection here uses a dropdown list that constrains the choices to the valid options.

If you edit a binding, for example, by changing the value in the *Attribute* list from "FirstName" to "LastName," the reference to the binding will not change on the page. The expression in the af:inputText component will still read `#{bindings.FirstName.inputValue}`. However, when the page runs, the "LastName" information will be displayed in the First Name field. This makes an important point: the name of the attribute used in the binding expression is an abstraction. Just because a field is bound to an expression containing the word "FirstName," that does not mean that the First Name value will be displayed; the value depends on the PageDef file entry.

Manually Creating an Attribute Binding

The bindings discussed so far were all created by drag-and-drop actions from the Data Controls panel. You can also create bindings manually, by editing the XML directly in the source view of the PageDef file editor, using menu options offered in the Structure window's right-click menus. An easier alternative for creating binding is to use the facilities of the Bindings pane of the visual editor (or the Overview pane of the PageDef editor, which shows the same view).

All binding types can be manually created from the Bindings tab by following these steps:

1. Open the page that needs the new binding and switch to the Bindings tab in the editor.
2. Click the "Create control binding" (green plus "+") button at the top of the list of bindings. Notice the pencil button, which can be used to edit an existing binding, and the red cross to delete an existing binding.

   A popup window then displays the various binding types that can be created.

If you follow these steps and choose "attributeValues" as the binding type, the Edit Attribute Binding dialog shown in Figure 14-2 displays.

When working with bindings it is always worth looking at the underlying XML markup so that you can see the cause and effect of making changes through the editor and the Property Inspector. Here is the XML for the FirstName attribute binding that has been illustrated:

```
<attributeValues id="FirstName" IterBinding="AllEmployeesIterator">
  <AttrNames>
    <Item Value="FirstName"/>
  </AttrNames>
</attributeValues>
```

Properties for the binding can be edited here directly in the XML, or the Property Inspector can be used for a more structured approach to the task.

Advanced Properties for Attribute Bindings

So far we've described the Common section of the Property Inspector for the binding; however, there are a number of options under the advanced section that need some explanation.

TIP
Not all of the properties displayed by every binding type in the advanced section are relevant. Some exist purely for backward compatibility, are used for test purposes, or have no effect on a particular binding subtype. Throughout this chapter we list the important and useful attributes.

- **CustomInputHandler** Is used to override the processing of new values defined by the user. The normal use for this is when using Oracle Multimedia (Intermedia) data types such as video and image, when the predefined `OrdDomainInputHandler` class will be used. Advanced developers can, however, develop their own handlers.
- **ApplyValidation** Is a Boolean flag (default = false) used to determine if the framework should process validations defined within the PageDef file. The framework allows the developer to add simple validations such as length, ranges, regular expressions, and so on to individual bindings. These validations are intended for use with back-end services that themselves have no declarative validation, such as a Web Service call. When using an ADF BC service layer, it is better to stick to defining the declarative validations on the entity objects, where they have more capabilities and are more reusable.

List Bindings

List bindings are a specialized subset of bindings used for populating lists, radio groups, and checkbox groups. In the form illustrated by Figure 14-1, the *JobId* and *DepartmentId* fields are both represented as dropdown lists and use a list binding. These components need to be bound to two pieces of information—the actual attribute in the underlying dataset that is being populated and the set of data that makes up the options. This set of data could be a static list of values, such as "Male" or "Female," or it could be fully dynamic and driven from a collection managed by a data control, for example, a list of departments coming from the database. Once a list is configured using a list binding, the framework will handle all of the runtime tasks of populating the list and managing the data type conversions if required, saving a lot of effort on the part of the programmer.

You can create a list binding by dragging and dropping a suitable attribute from the Data Controls panel. When you drop the attribute and choose a UI widget from the Single Selections submenu, the Edit List Binding dialog (shown in Figure 14-3) will appear.

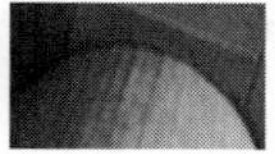

NOTE
If the underlying attribute already has a list of values defined in the data model, then dropping the attribute onto the visual page editor will not show the dialog from Figure 14-3. This is because JDeveloper already has all of the information that it needs to wire up the list correctly. This is discussed in the later section "Model-Driven Lists."

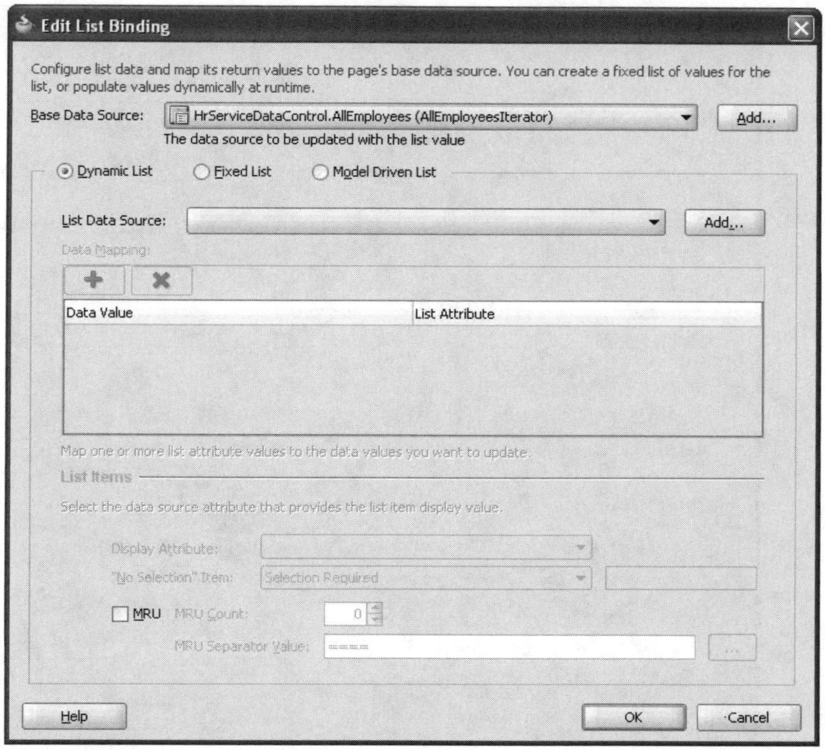

FIGURE 14-3. *The Edit List Binding dialog*

The Edit List Binding dialog shown in Figure 14-3 will automatically select the correct *Base Data Source* based on the attribute that was dragged from the Data Controls panel. So the important part of the dialog is the radio button group used to select the type of list to use. Note that this is the type of list binding, not the physical UI type of list (list-box, dropdown, radio-group, and so on). Any list binding can be used with all of these UI types. Let's examine the options for the subtypes of list bindings offered here. Each is selected using the relevant radio button in the group underneath the Base Data Source.

Dynamic Lists

With a dynamic list binding there is an explicit reference to the Data Source that provides the values for the list. This will generally map onto another ADF BC view object.

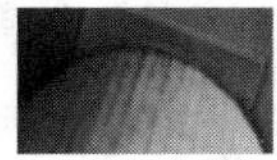

NOTE

As a best practice create separate view object instances to service your lists. These view objects can be read only and potentially could be shared across applications using the shared Application Module feature of ADF BC.

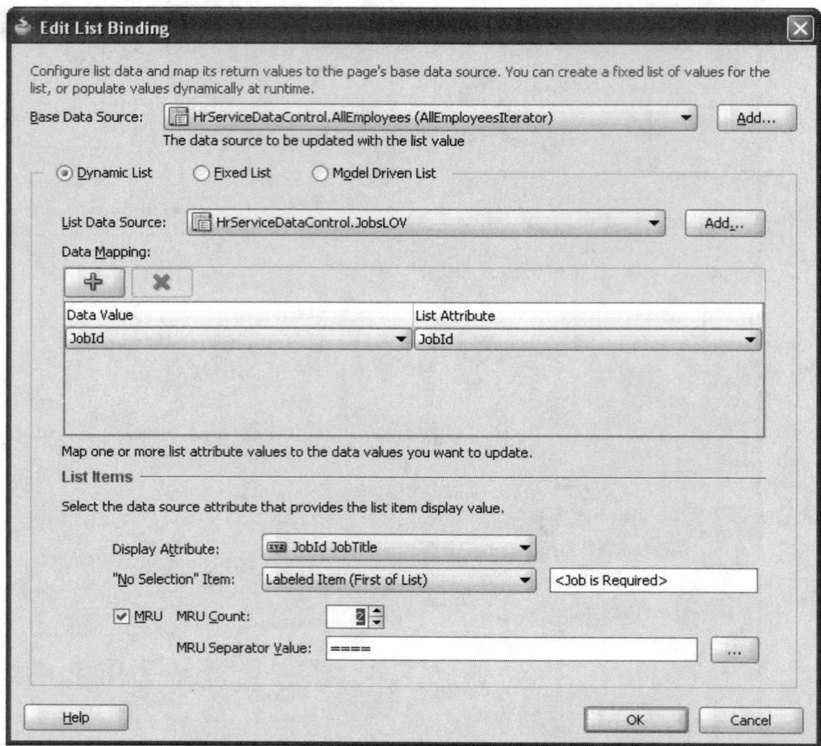

FIGURE 14-4. *Defining a dynamic list binding for JobId*

In Figure 14-4, the dynamic list binding has been created for the JobId attribute in the EMPLOYEES table.

To define a dynamic list, you carry out the following steps:

1. **Define the *Base Data Source*.** If the editor popped up after a drag-and-drop operation, this dropdown list will contain the correct data source already. If you are creating a binding manually, all existing iterators in the PageDef file will be listed in the data source format (ApplicationModuleName.ViewObjectInstanceName); you can also create a base data source using the Add button that is adjacent to this field. The base data source in a list binding is the target of the list—the iterator that holds the attribute for which you are setting the value using the list.
2. **Select the *Dynamic List*** option, as shown in Figure 14-4.
3. **Define the *List Data Source*** as the name of the iterator that will supply the data in the list. Again, you can use the Add button, which causes a dialog containing a list of all of the view object instances exposed through the data control to appear, so you can create an iterator if required.

4. **Map the key attribute(s) that define the relationship** between the list options and the value you are selecting. After you select both data sources, the lists labeled *Data Value* and *List Attribute* will be populated for you in the *Data Mapping* section of the dialog. Use these lists to define the relationship between the collections. The *Data Value* is the attribute that will be populated. The *List Attribute* is the attribute that will supply the value when the user selects from the list. The attribute you use will usually be the foreign key that links the table on which the page is based with the table that supplies values to the list, but a foreign key is not required. You can define more than one pair of attributes to populate more than one value on the page simultaneously.
5. **Define the value to display in the list.** The *Display Attribute* dropdown list allows you to specify one or more attributes from the list data source that will be used as the label for the list entries. In Figure 14-4, we are selecting JobId for the value attribute, but the list label *(Display Attribute)* will display the *JobId* followed by *JobTitle*. By default, the Display Attribute list allows the selection of a single attribute as the label; however, an option at the bottom of the list labeled as *Select Multiple* will bring up a second dialog, which will allow multiple attributes to be shuttled into the display list.
6. **Set up the "No selection" Item option.** Dropdown lists can display a blank item that can signify various values. The *No Selection Item* dropdown list allows you to declare how to handle this blank selection. Setting this property to "Selection Required" means that the populated list will have no blank item. Alternatively, you can allow nulls, either with an empty label ("Blank Item") or a custom label ("Labeled Item"), as is shown in Figure 14-4. In both cases, you can have this extra item appear at the start or at the end of the list. If you select "Labeled Item," the string that is entered in the dialog is stored in a message bundle file in the root source directory of the view project, for example `com.tuhra.view.ViewControllerBundle.properties`. This properties file is linked to the null value string in the list binding using a combination of the *NullValueId* attribute in the binding and a <ResourceBundle> element in the PageDef. By default, the property bundle that is used is always <project name>Bundle.properties, but by changing the <ResourceBundle> reference in the PageDef XML a different file can be used.

TIP
The value `ViewControllerBundle.properties` *is defined as a default value in the Resource Bundle category of the project properties and can be changed if required. You can also reuse this bundle to store your own resources for use elsewhere within the application, for example, for button labels and other boilerplate text.*

7. **Set the MRU options**. *MRU* stands for Most Recently Used, a feature where the list will remember the most common choices made by the user in the session and will display these first in the list to speed up selection. This quick list is separated from the full list by a separator string, in this case, a line of equal signs. With the MRU checkbox selected, the developer can customize this separator string in the *MRU Separator Value* field and also decide exactly how many selections should be remembered using the *MRU Count* spinbox. The string used for the separator is also stored in the same resource bundle that is used for the null list values. Once the MRU option is switched on, the framework takes care of managing that list at runtime.

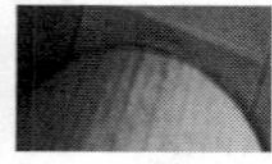

CAUTION
The MRU list remembers the most recent selections but does not detect if the contents of the list are changing dynamically. Thus, if the contents of the list change regularly, there may be MRU values that are not actually present in the current version of the list.

This definition will create a dropdown list for the employee JobId item on the page. The dropdown list will offer all Job IDs and Titles. When the user selects from the list, the Job ID will become the value for that item. Similarly, when the record is queried, the list will display the Job ID and Title information corresponding to the JobId value of the list item's attribute. The following code listing shows the XML in the PageDef file generated by the values selected for the binding in Figure 14-4:

```
<list id="JobId" IterBinding="AllEmployeesIterator"
      StaticList="false" ListIter="JobsLOVIterator"
      NullValueFlag="start" NullValueId="JobId_null"
      DTSupportsMRU="true"
      MRUCount="2" MRUId="mruId">
  <AttrNames>
    <Item Value="JobId"/>
  </AttrNames>
  <ListAttrNames>
    <Item Value="JobId"/>
  </ListAttrNames>
  <ListDisplayAttrNames>
    <Item Value="JobId"/>
    <Item Value="JobTitle"/>
  </ListDisplayAttrNames>
</list>
```

You can easily spot the mapping between the values selected in Figure 14-4 and the corresponding XML definition. Notice, for example, the *NullValueFlag* property and the *NullValueId* property. In this example, these properties specify that a null value is allowed on the list with the label for it appearing at the start of the list, and the NullValueId names the resource that contains the null value label (in the message bundle file). If you look at the bottom of the PageDef file, you'll also see that a reference to the message bundle file has been added:

```
<ResourceBundle>
  <PropertiesBundle xmlns="http://xmlns.oracle.com/adfm/resourcebundle"
                    PropertiesFile="com.tuhra.view.ViewControllerBundle"/>
</ResourceBundle>
```

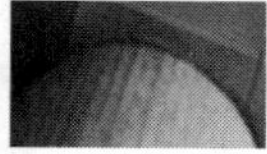

CAUTION
If you manually create a dynamic list binding in the PageDef file, be sure to set the "RangeSize" attribute of the iterator that is populating the list values to minus one (–1). This will ensure that all of the possible list items will appear in the list. Failure to do this will restrict your lists to a maximum of 25 entries, the default value of the "RangeSize" property. By default the framework will do all this for you if you create the iterators through the Edit List Binding dialog, but if you pick up an existing data source from the PageDef, it may not have the range set correctly.

Fixed Lists

In some circumstances, lists only require a set of static values. Fixed lists are defined through the same Edit List Binding dialog as dynamic lists. The following illustration shows such a definition:

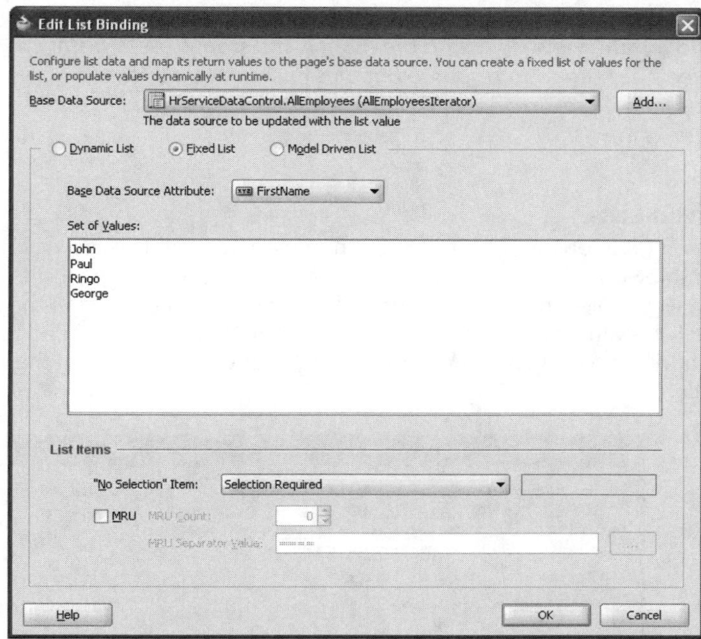

When defining a fixed list binding, the target data source is defined in the same way as for a dynamic list. The *Fixed List* option must be selected, and then the attribute within the target iterator that will take the selected value is defined. In this example, the *FirstName* attribute has been selected, and the values to display as options have been entered into the *Set of Values* field. As before, the list can be configured to display a null entry, or not, using the *"No Selection" Item* list.

Switching to the PageDef file, you can see that the list-binding definition is slightly different, indicating that this is a static list (using the *StaticList* attribute) and containing the literal values that will appear in the list.

```
<list id="FirstName" IterBinding="AllEmployeesIterator"
      DTSupportsMRU="true"
      StaticList="true">
  <AttrNames>
    <Item Value="FirstName"/>
  </AttrNames>
  <ValueList>
    <Item Value="John"/>
    <Item Value="Paul"/>
    <Item Value="Ringo"/>
    <Item Value="George"/>
  </ValueList>
</list>
```

TIP
As you can see in this listing, the values for the list items are hard-coded into the PageDef file. The strings are not translatable, and the value and label of each item is the same. If you need flexibility, such as multiple languages in a static list, you could use a dynamic list binding to a static view object on the model. The strings used in static view objects are stored in resource bundles and can be translated. Using this technique, you can also have separate values and labels for each entry in the list.

Model-Driven Lists

The final option for a lookup list binding is a model-driven list. This is a new feature for Release 11 of the ADF framework and provides a way for the information within a list to be defined centrally as part of the view object definition. With such a central definition, all of the information required to define the list is already known, so the only information that is needed for the binding is the name of the attribute to map and the name of the list of values defined in the view object definition, as is shown here:

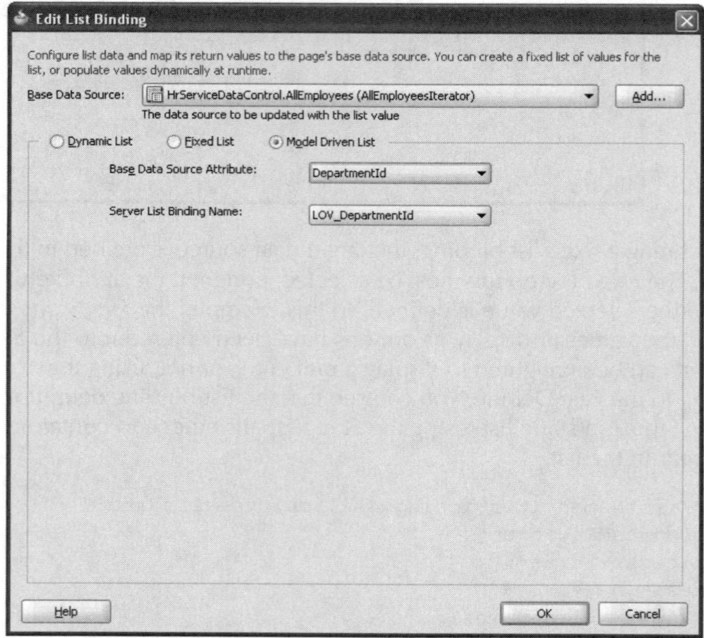

The corresponding XML markup for this type of binding is similarly quite simple:

```
<list id="DepartmentId"
      IterBinding="AllEmployeesIterator"
      StaticList="false"
      Uses="LOV_DepartmentId"
      DTSupportsMRU="true"/>
```

Within a Fusion application it makes sense to use this type of list binding as the default methodology for lists. The advantages of the approach are twofold: first the same list of values definition can be shared by multiple pieces of UI, and second, the view object that defines the list of valid values for the attribute does not have to be explicitly exposed through the application module data model. This makes the service interface (Application Module) simpler and cleaner.

List Binding Navigation Subtype

Although it is not offered as an option in the Edit List Binding dialog shown in Figure 14-3, there is a fourth subtype of list binding used for defining navigation lists. The navigation list subtype is historical and functionally identical to the newer navigation list binding. As such it is covered in the section "Navigation Lists" later in the chapter.

Creating a List Binding from the Binding Panel

As you would expect, it is possible to create a list binding directly from the binding editor (or the associated Structure window) as well as through drag-and-drop onto the visual page editor. The procedure is identical to the creation of an attribute binding except that the developer selects "list" from the *Generic Bindings* list in the Insert Item dialog. A selector dialog shown next then appears, and if the "Select one value list that updates a base data source" is selected, the Edit List Binding dialog from Figure 14-3 is then displayed. The binding process is then identical.

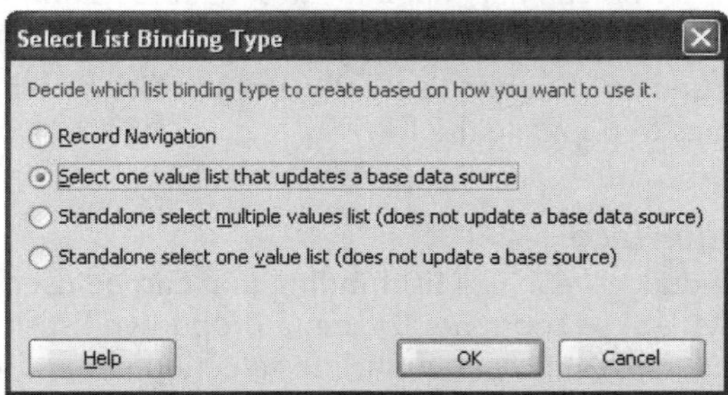

The other options offered by the Select List Binding Type dialog relate to more specialized versions of the list binding such as the Record Navigation List.

Advanced Property Inspector Options for List Bindings

When a list binding is selected in the Structure window or in the binding editor, the Property Inspector is synchronized to show its properties. Several of these attributes, such as *IterBinding,* are common with other binding types; however, the following are specific to the list binding type. You should be able to map these properties directly onto functions that we've examined already in this section:

- **ListOperMode** Defines the primary job of this list. The options here are "setAttribute," "navigation," and "multiSelect." An operating mode of "setAttribute" is used to indicate that this list is used for lookups (dynamic, fixed list, or model driven). A value of "navigation" indicates that the list should be used to change record currency (see "Navigation Lists" later in this chapter). The third option, "multiSelect," is not yet supported for web clients, so we don't discuss it further.

- **MRUId** Is used to map to the property in the PageDef resource bundle that defines the separator string for the list. Each list binding with an MRU will usually share the same ID so that the look and feel of the list is the same in every case. Typically, this will be the following string value in the resource bundle:

  ```
  mruId=\=\=\=\=
  ```

- **MRUCount** Defines how many entries should be displayed in the MRU section of the list. For usability, this value should set to 5 or less.
- **DTSupportsMRU** Is a flag used by the JDeveloper design time to indicate that MRU options should be displayed in the Edit List Binding dialog. MRU functionality is only supported by `af:selectOneChoice` components, and the DTSupportsMRU flag is automatically set to true for a binding that is created by drag-and-drop as that component type from the Data Controls Panel.
- **NullValueFlag** Indicates that this list supports an entry to represent a null value. The property can be set to "none" (default), "start," or "end." The start and end values determine where the null value entry should appear on the list. The actual label for the null value entry is defined by NullValueId.
- **NullValueId** Points to a resource in the PageDef's resource bundle that will be used to provide the translatable label for the null entry in the list.
- **StaticList** Is a Boolean flag that indicates that the list binding has a set of static values defined within the binding definition rather than needing an external list.
- **ListIter** Is used for dynamic lists and names the iterator that is being used to provide the range of values to populate the list.

Lists in the User Interface

The Edit List Binding dialog defines a list binding that can be used from several types of user interface components: `af:selectOneChoice` (a dropdown list style sometimes known as a "poplist," `af:selectOneListbox` (a multi-line selection item, also known as a "T-List"), and `af:selectOneRadio` (a radio group). As an example, here is the tag markup for a dropdown list:

```
<af:selectOneChoice
    value="#{bindings.JobId.inputValue}"
    label="#{bindings.JobId.label}">
  <f:selectItems
      value="#{bindings.JobId.items}"/>
</af:selectOneChoice>
```

And a radio group:

```
<af:selectOneRadio
    value="#{bindings.DepartmentId.inputValue}"
    label="#{bindings.DepartmentId.label}">
  <f:selectItems
      value="#{bindings.DepartmentId.items}"/>
</af:selectOneRadio>
```

These sets of markup are essentially identical, apart from the type of top-level component. The value that the component is bound to, and the set of options (the `f:selectItems` tag) are the same for both.

Navigation Lists

A navigation list binding (along with the corresponding navigation subtype of the list binding) is used less often than the other forms of list bindings and is really unrelated to them, except that it is displayed in a list-style UI component.

Rather than setting the value of a bound attribute, the navigation list binding is used to change the row currency within the view object collection. Selecting a value from a navigation list will navigate to that row. Since all rows in the collection appear in the list, navigation list bindings are most effectively used when the number of records in the collection is small.

Recall that the navigation list is one of the options offered when you drop a whole collection onto a page, as opposed to the single attribute that you would drop to create a value selection list. The following illustration shows the slightly different version of the Edit List Binding dialog that displays after dropping the collection as a navigation list:

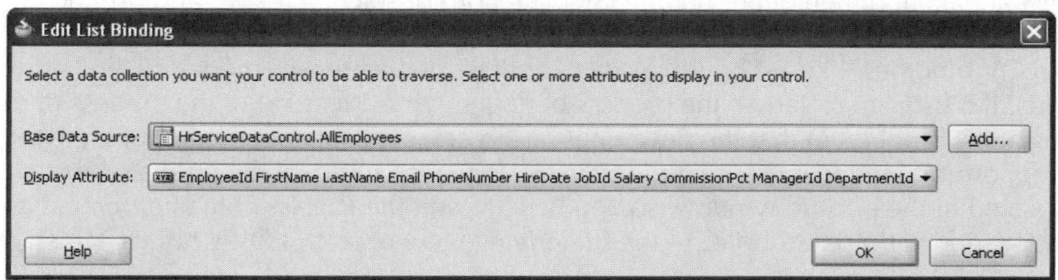

The *Base Data Source* list will be automatically wired up to the collection that was dropped. The *Display Attribute* list will list all of the attributes in the view object by default, but it can be used to change the label to a subset or even a single attribute if desired.

If you take a look at the XML created in the PageDef file, you will see the *AttrNames* element, which defines the attributes that will be used in the label of the list.

```
<navigationlist id="AllEmployees"
                IterBinding="AllEmployeesIterator"
                ListOperMode="navigation"
                ListIter="AllEmployeesIterator"
                DTSupportsMRU="false">
  <AttrNames>
    <Item Value="FirstName"/>
    <Item Value="LastName"/>
  </AttrNames>
</navigationlist>
```

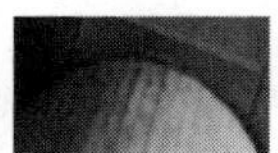

CAUTION
Just like dynamic list bindings, navigation list bindings are constrained by the default range size of the iterator. Of course, it may be a good idea to use an upper limit for the RangeSize *property for the navigation list, because showing a navigation list containing every row in a huge table is of minimal use.*

The XML shown here is the new form of the navigation list binding that uses the explicit *navigationList* element in the PageDef file. Older applications may use the secondary form of this binding, which is to use a conventional list binding, with the *ListOperMode* attribute set to "navigation." Functionally, both of these bindings are identical, although the newer navigation list binding should be used for clarity.

List of Values Bindings

To complete the review of list-related bindings, we need to describe the *listOfValues* binding. This binding type is a new feature in Release 11 of ADF and provides a much more powerful list searching capability than the simple drop-down and option-based lists that we have explained so far. They are created by dragging an attribute from the Data Controls panel and dropping it as one of the explicit list of values (LOV) types: ADF LOV input or ADF LOV Choice List. Figure 14-5 shows a list of values search window that these components make available in action.

As shown here, the modal LOV search window provides the user with the ability to search the relevant data and then either double click a record or select a record and use the OK button to bring a value back into the LOV UI field.

LOV bindings, like list bindings, can either be declarative or model driven (although not static). If a list is declarative, the process of defining it is identical to the process of defining a normal list binding, in that the developer has to create a Data Source to populate the list. There is no opportunity in the current binding dialog, however, to select the attributes that should be displayed in the pop-up window, so you need to edit the PageDef file after the fact to modify that list. Or specify those attributes in the underlying view object's LOV UI hints. When a LOV is

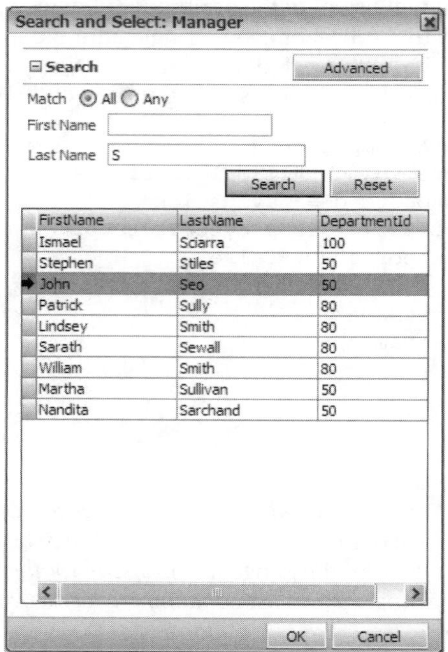

FIGURE 14-5. *LOV Selection window*

based on a declarative binding, it has no search capability and will just display the record set defined by the underlying view object as is shown in this illustration. Notice that the search region at the top of the dialog is not visible.

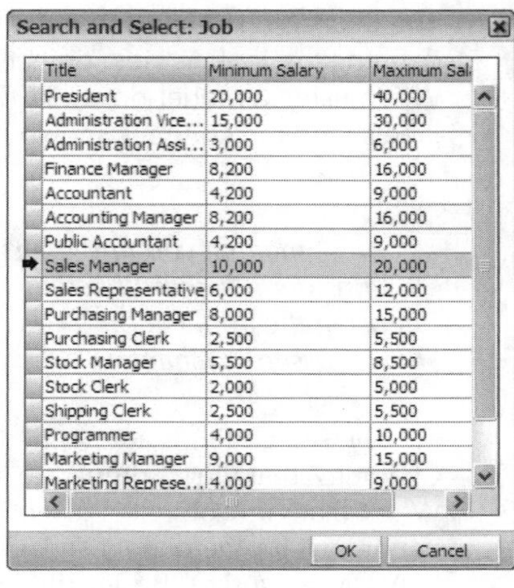

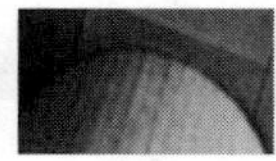

NOTE
All of the labels for search fields and column headings within the LOV window are derived from the underlying UI hints defined in the entity and view objects. There is no way to override these in the JSF page.

The underlying binding XML for the Job ID search is

```
<listOfValues id="JobId"
              StaticList="false"
              IterBinding="AllEmployeesIterator"
              DTSupportsMRU="false"
              ListIter="JobsLOVIterator">
  <AttrNames>
    <Item Value="JobId"/>
  </AttrNames>
  <ListAttrNames>
    <Item Value="JobId"/>
  </ListAttrNames>
  <ListDisplayAttrNames>
    <Item Value="JobTitle"/>
    <Item Value="MinSalary"/>
    <Item Value="MaxSalary"/>
  </ListDisplayAttrNames>
</listOfValues>
```

As you can see, the binding definition is very similar to the list bindings that we discussed previously. In this case, the *ListDisplayAttrNames* items have been manually edited through the PageDef file to remove the unwanted JobId field.

Model-Driven LOVs

The most common form of LOV is one that is driven off of the data model rather than the dynamic binding subtype shown for the JobId LOV in the preceding section. Using a declarative model-driven binding is slightly more complex to set up; however, it does provide several benefits:

1. Just as with model-driven list bindings, the same definition can be reused on multiple screens.
2. Search functionality becomes available in the LOV window. The searches can be predefined by the developer and even customized and saved by the end user.
3. The list can be configured to automatically query and display a quick selection list, rather than requiring the user to bring up the search popup every time.

A model-driven LOV has several moving parts, and it is useful to step through each of these to explain what the contribution to the whole is.

The Search List View Object Getting the functionality that you want with a LOV starts with defining the lookup view object definition that will provide the data set for the search window. When using a model-driven LOV component, all of the UI attributes, such as the search fields, the labels, and the columns shown in the results table, are derived from this view object definition.

TIP
Any time that you find yourself defining this kind of view object, consider if it should actually be shared among all of the sessions using the application by using the shared application module feature discussed in Chapter 7.

The search fields are defined by a view criteria definition on the LOV view object. Recall from Chapter 7 that view criteria are a way of creating precanned where clauses for a view object. When that view object is used for a LOV, a view criteria is selected to provide the default search conditions for the dialog. The following illustration shows the view criteria used for a manager LOV, "ManagerLOVBasicCriteria." These will be displayed in the LOV search dialog as two search fields, one for each bind variable defined for the view criteria.

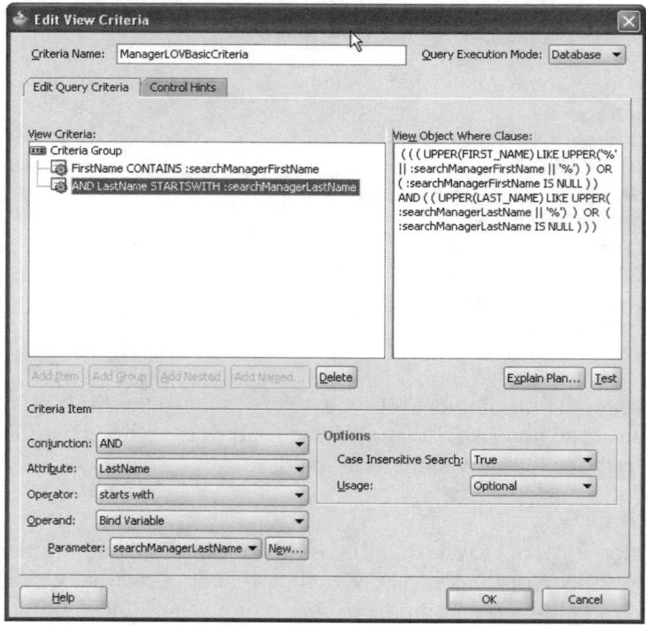

In this case, the criteria are fairly simple, but the available conjunctions and operators can be used to build complex queries if desired.

The *Control Hints* tab, shown next, on the same view criteria editing dialog is important in controlling exactly how the search area will appear in the final LOV.

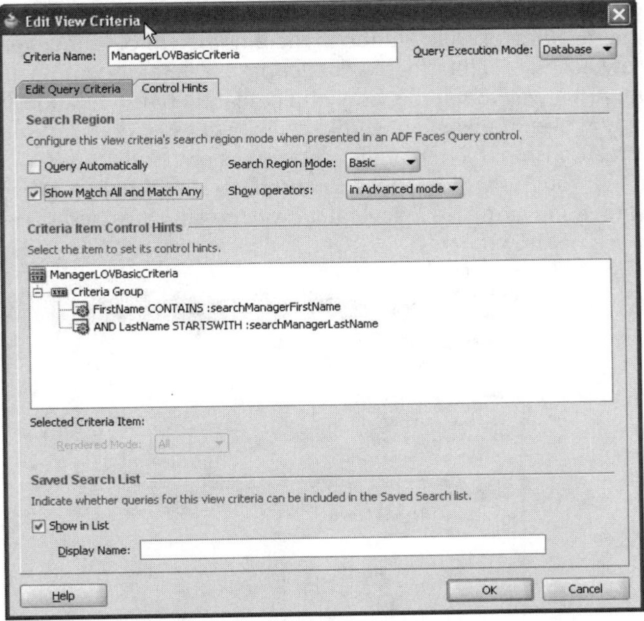

The options here, such as *Show Match All and Match Any* and *Search Region Mode,* directly correspond to options shown in the search area of Figure 14-5.

The LOV Definition on the Attribute With the underlying LOV view object defined, the next step is to wire it up to the required attribute in the data view object that needs the LOV functionality. Use the following steps to do this:

1. Select the attribute that needs the LOV in the view object editor and click the "Add list of values" (green plus "+") button in the List of Values section. This will invoke the List of Values dialog as shown here; notice the name LOV_ManagerId, which is auto-generated. This can be changed if required.

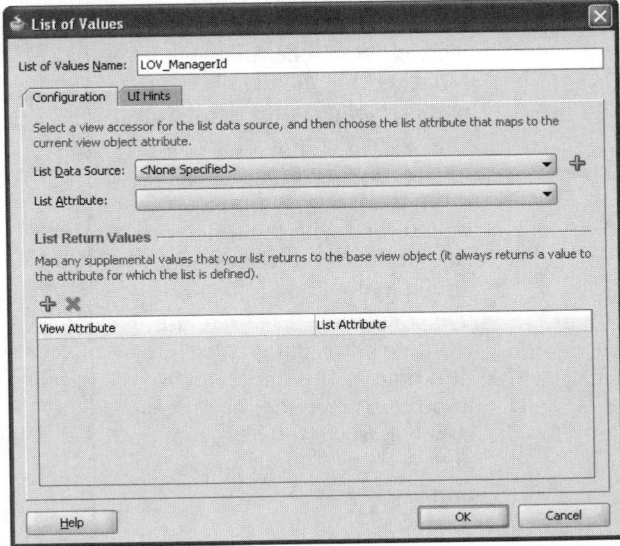

2. In the List of Values Editor a *List Data Source* needs to be defined. As you would expect, existing data sources are available in the list, or the "Create new view accessor" (green plus "+") button can

be used to add a new one. The meaning of Data Source is slightly different in this dialog from the meaning of Data Source in the binding editors shown earlier. In this case, it refers to a view accessor rather than a data control + iterator combination. A view accessor is really just a way to tell the view object that there is a relationship with another view object; however, unlike a view link, a view accessor does not specify the cardinality of that relationship. Note that view accessors can point to view objects that are made available through shared application modules. For the view object used to generate the form shown in Figure 14-1, several view accessors are used to define the various model-driven lists as shown here.

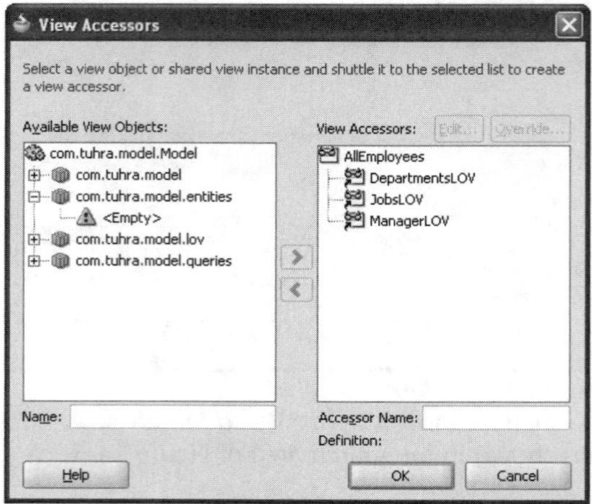

3. Once the view accessor to the LOV view object has been defined, the *List Attribute* value needs to be set to one of the available attributes in the LOV view object. In this example, we're building a LOV for selecting managers, so the EmployeeId is the value that needs to be selected from the LOV view object, to populate the ManagerId of the main view object. Notice in the screen shot shown here, that just like the Edit List Binding dialog, more than one attribute can be returned with the selection. Additional return values are added to the initial selection by clicking the "Create return attribute map" (green plus "+") button. This capability is important when the relationship between the base view object and the LOV uses a composite primary key.

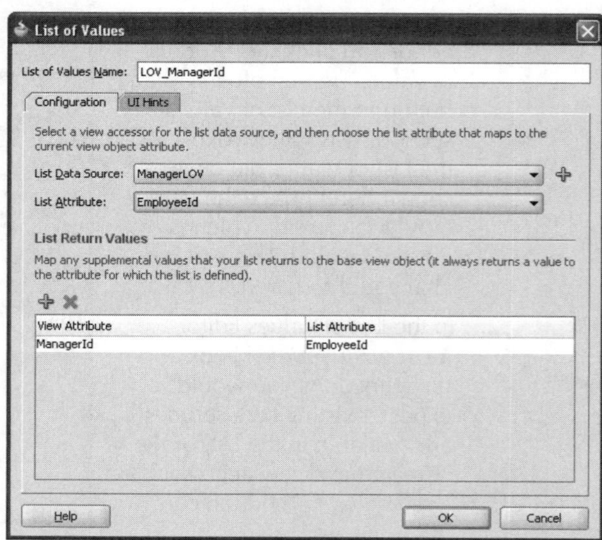

4. With the core data mapping between the base view object and the LOV view object complete, the next step is to set up the UI hints for the LOV. This is accomplished using the UI Hints tab on the List of Values Editor. The selections on this screen are fairly self-explanatory, with a shuttle control available to select the values that will appear in the selection table. The really important fields here are the *Include Search Region* field and the *Query List Automatically* checkbox.

   The *Include Search Region* dropdown provides two automatic choices, plus any of the custom view criteria that are defined on the LOV view object. The default choices are "< No Search >," which indicates that the LOV dialog should not provide a search area at all, and "All Queriable Attributes," which will create a search area with a field for every attribute in the LOV view object. Generally, if a search is used at all it is sensible to use a specific custom view criterion to define this rather than the supplied "All Queriable Attributes." This gives the developer much more control over the appearance and functionality of the search area in the LOV.

   Finally, as shown in the illustration that follows, the *Query List Automatically* option adds an important twist. The same option on the control hints of the view criterion defines that when the LOV window is displayed, the base query should already be executed to show the default list in the window. The option here in the LOV definition, however, has a very different effect. Specifically, when used with an `af:inputComboboxListOfValues` component it provides a quick list for user selection, before the whole search LOV is displayed. You can see an example of that in Figure 14-6.

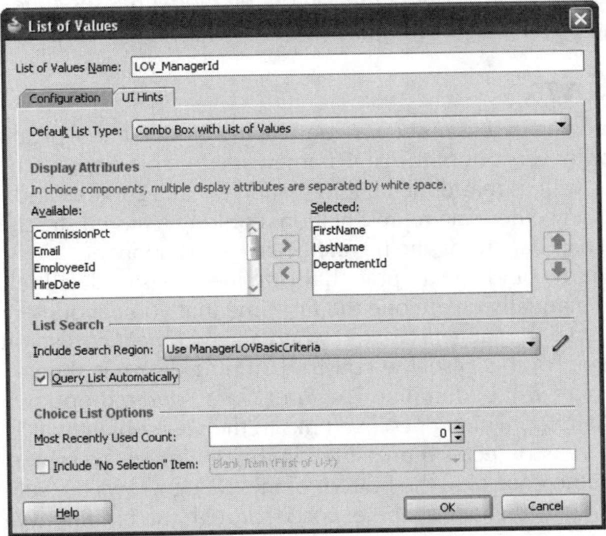

User Interfaces for List of Values Bindings

The LOV binding can be used with two specialized components that provide the infrastructure required to create the pop-up search window:

- **`af:inputListOfValues`** Displays a normal text input field with an associated search icon that is used to launch the LOV; it looks like this: * Job SH_CLERK

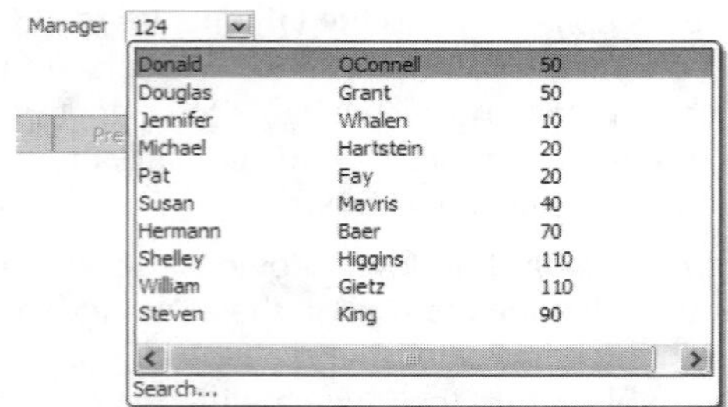

FIGURE 14-6. *The quick select list on a inputComboboxListOfValues*

- **`af:inputComboboxListOfValues`** Is a more sophisticated component that provides a different UI resembling a pull-down list for triggering the LOV as shown here: Manager 124

When this button is clicked, a quick select area appears. By default, this just contains a hyperlink labeled as "Search" as shown here. Clicking this will bring up the full LOV search dialog.

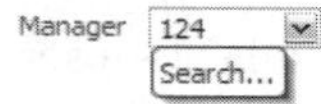

However, if the underlying LOV definition on the model has the *Query List Automatically* option set, then this quick select list will look something like Figure 14-6.

Tree Bindings

Tree bindings are one of the most common binding types that a typical application will use. In a big change from earlier versions of the ADF framework, tree bindings are now used to provide data for normal tables as well as master-detail information for tree controls and tree-tables. Tree bindings can also be used for any other data representation requiring a nested structure, for example, organizational chart data using the hierarchy viewer component.

Because the tree binding can potentially define a master-detail relationship, it is a little tricky to grasp how to manually create one the first time that you encounter it. For simplicity, start off by examining the binding that gets created when a view object collection is dropped as a read-only table onto a page. For this case, the Edit Tree Binding dialog is shown in Figure 14-7.

The basics here will be familiar. The *Root Data Source* dropdown allows the selection (or creation) of an iterator, which of course links to the view object that is being used to populate the table. The same view object is represented in the section of the screen labeled as *Tree Level Rules,* and then the shuttle control at the bottom of the dialog allows the selection and ordering of the view object attributes that should be exposed through the binding. We'll come back to the rules section later, but for a basic table that's all there is to it. If you examine the underlying PageDef XML data, it will look like this (line numbers added to aid explanation):

```
01:  <tree id="AllDepartments"
02:        IterBinding="AllDepartmentsIterator">
03:    <nodeDefinition DefName="com.tuhra.model.queries.AllDepartments">
04:      <AttrNames>
05:        <Item Value="DepartmentId"/>
```

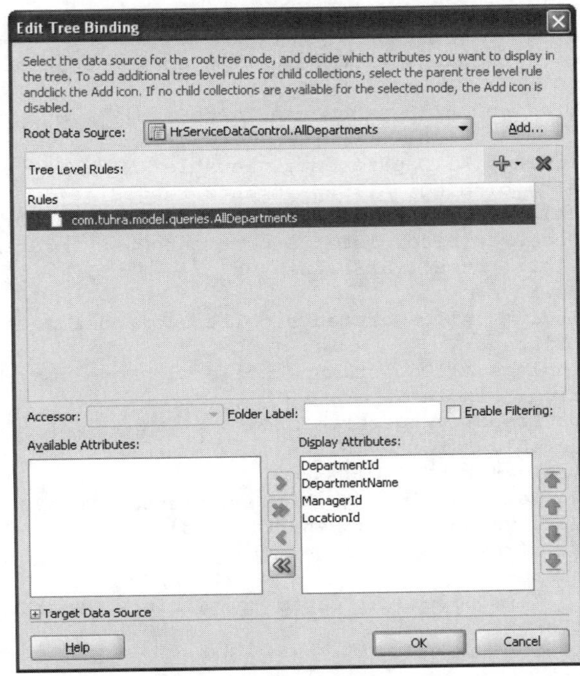

FIGURE 14-7. *Edit Tree Binding dialog*

```
06:          <Item Value="DepartmentName"/>
07:          <Item Value="ManagerId"/>
08:          <Item Value="LocationId"/>
09:        </AttrNames>
10:      </nodeDefinition>
11:    </tree>
```

- **Line 01** defines the ID of the binding. This will be used by to link the table component to the binding.
- **Line 02** defines the iterator for the collection.
- **Line 03** defines a node or level in the tree hierarchy. As this binding is used for a plain table, there is no master-detail relationship and so there is only one of these *nodeDefinition* elements. The nodeDefinition *defName* value defines the type of the node by linking back to the view object definition (`com.tuhra.model.queries.AllDepartments`). This tells the framework exactly what shape the data is. As you will see later, with master-detail tree bindings each node or level in the tree is likely to have a different shape and type.
- **Lines 04–10** list the attributes from the view object that are actually bound to the tree nodes. This list is initially defined by the choices that the developer made when working with the Edit Columns dialog that appeared when dropping the collection onto the page.

If you then examine the corresponding tags in the JSF page, the markup looks like this (some table columns have been omitted for brevity):

```
<af:table value="#{bindings.AllDepartments.collectionModel}"
      var="row"
      rows="#{bindings.AllDepartments.rangeSize}"
      emptyText=
          "#{bindings.AllDepartments.viewable?'No rows yet.':'Access Denied.'}"
      fetchSize="#{bindings.AllDepartments.rangeSize}"
      filterModel="#{bindings.AllDepartmentsQuery.queryDescriptor}"
      queryListener="#{bindings.AllDepartmentsQuery.processQuery}"
      filterVisible="true" varStatus="vs"
      selectedRowKeys=
          "#{bindings.AllDepartments.collectionModel.selectedRow}"
      selectionListener=
         " #{bindings.AllDepartments.collectionModel.makeCurrent}"
      rowSelection="single">
  <af:column sortProperty="DepartmentId"
           filterable="true"
           sortable="true"
           headerText="#{bindings.AllDepartments.hints.DepartmentId.label}">
    <af:outputText value="#{row.DepartmentId}">
      <af:convertNumber groupingUsed="false"
            pattern=
                 "#{bindings.AllDepartments.hints.DepartmentId.format}"/>
    </af:outputText>
  </af:column>
...
</af:table>
```

The *value* attribute of the `af:table` component points to the tree binding used to populate the table. Notice that the *collectionModel* attribute (`#{bindings.AllDepartments.collectionModel}`) of the tree binding is used to actually access the collection of data. There are other attributes of the binding that are used in the next few lines of the table definition and elsewhere. These are all documented in Table 14-1.

The second line in the definition defines the *var* attribute for the table tag and assigns it to the value "row." This *var* value is an alias by which the row in the table that is being processed can be referenced. Later on in the listing you can see this in action as the value of an `af:outputText` component is set to `#{row.DepartmentId}`, meaning "print the department ID of the row that is currently being processed by the table."

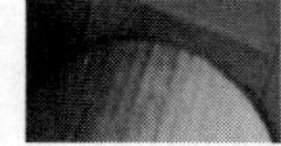

CAUTION
If you create an updatable table (as opposed to the read-only table used in this example), you will see an alternative notation used for the value of the input items, `#{row.bindings.DepartmentId.inputValue}`. Although these two notations are apparently synonymous for output purposes, when an input item is being used you should always use this longer notation to ensure correct operation.

Table 14-1 summarizes the important attributes and methods that are exposed to expression language by the tree binding. Many of the attributes are also shared by other binding types, and you will see them crop up in the code that you drag and drop.

Tree Binding Attribute	Use
collectionModel	This attribute adapts the tree binding to a form that any JSF table component can use. The object returned by the *collectionModel* attribute supports additional properties and methods—for example, `collectionModel.selectedRow`, which helps the table to mark the current record in the table, and `collectionModel.makeCurrent`, a method reference, which synchronizes the iterator with the selection that the user makes in the table UI.
rangeSize	This attribute indicates how many rows the table should display at once. It maps directly to the *RangeSize* attribute of the iterator that the table binding uses. Note that this does not actually control the number of rows displayed in the table.
rangeStart	Based on information provided by the iterator, this attribute will tell the table which record within the collection is currently at the top of the table.
viewable	If security is being used on the collection, this property of the table binding indicates if the user is actually able to view data from this collection. The expression that uses this attribute is a ternary expression; see the sidebar "What Is a Ternary Expression?" for more information.
queryDescriptor	Exposes a special data structure that the table control uses to filter columns.
processQuery	Provides a hook to a method to process the filter operation as the user enters a value in the filter fields.
hints	This is a very powerful attribute that provides direct access to all of the control hints and custom properties that are defined on the underlying View and Entity object definitions. It is being used in the code snippet in the accompanying text to retrieve the *Label* for the DepartmentId column using this expression: `#{bindings.AllDepartments.hints.DepartmentId.label}` It is also used here to retrieve formatting hints for numbers and dates.
Labels	The *labels* property of the tree binding is just a shorthand to get to the label of an attribute. It is a `java.util.Map` (a list indexed by the attribute name) of the labels on the underlying view object or Entity. The expression `#{bindings.AllDepartments.labels.DepartmentId}`, has exactly the same meaning as the hints example expression used in the text. It means to display the label of the attribute called *DepartmentId*. This label will be extracted from the control hint *Label Text*; on the view/entity object definition. If that UI hint is not set, the label will be the attribute name. Attribute bindings also support a *label* (singular) property, which provides the same information on a single attribute basis (as opposed to being a collection of labels).
rangeSet	Although not used in the accompanying example of a table, the *rangeSet* property of a tree binding is useful, so it deserves mention. This property is similar to the *collectionModel* property, but rather than adapting the table binding to a form acceptable to a JSF table control, it exposes the rows in the binding as an array that can be used inside `af:forEach` loops. The List object returned by this expression also exposes further attributes, which identify, among other things, the current row in the collection.

TABLE 14-1. *EL Reachable Expressions for a Table Binding*

What Is a Ternary Expression?

A *ternary expression* is a Java operator. It is also available for Expression Language constructs; it acts very much like the PL/SQL DECODE function. A ternary expression consists of three parts:

- **Evaluation** An expression, which evaluates to a Boolean.
- **True value** The value to return for the whole expression if the evaluation is true.
- **False value** The value to return for the whole expression if the evaluation is false.

The expression is written in the form: (evaluation)?(true value):(false value). Consider the following expression:

```
#{(1==2)? 'One does equal two':'One and two are different'}
```

This expression will print "One and two are different" because (1==2) evaluates to false. In JSF work, be careful with ternary expressions and null values. If the subject of the evaluation is null and you compare it to something other than null, the result will evaluate to false.

Tree Bindings with Hierarchical Data

Tree bindings, as used with a table, represent a single collection of rows from the same iterator. With tree components (`af:tree`, `af:treeTable`) the data sets are more complex. Figure 14-8 shows the Edit Tree Binding dialog for the master-detail relationship of Departments to Employees.

Notice here how the Rules section of the editor now shows AllEmployees nested beneath AllDepartments. Also, in comparison with Figure 14-7 notice that the AllDepartments root node has gained an "(<AllEmployees>)" suffix. This suffix indicates the name of the view link accessor in the AllDepartments view object that will be used to relate the employee data to the parent department. If the view object has a generated Java class, then this view link accessor may be exposed through a getter method, in which case it would be called something like `getAllEmployees()`, which returns a RowIterator. This iterator is used to populate the linked level or node within the tree.

Nesting is added to the binding by selecting a node in the rule list and pressing the "Add rule" (green plus "+") button. This displays a dropdown list that displays all of the available child view objects based on the view links defined for the parent. When the rule is created, the shuttle control at the bottom of the dialog is used to select the attributes for display in the tree. The tree populated by the binding in Figure 14-8 is shown in this illustration.

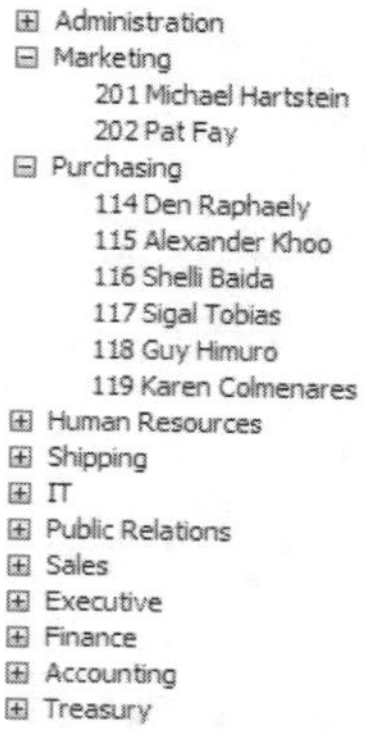

Notice how the Departments just use the department name as a node label in the tree and Employees have the ID, first name, and last name printed. For each rule, the appropriate attributes for that particular view object can be selected. Rules do not need to select the same number of attributes for display.

The binding XML, in this case, is a little more complex than the instance where the binding was being used for a simple table (line numbers added for the purposes of discussion).

```
01:  <tree id="AllDepartments"
02:        IterBinding="AllDepartmentsIterator">
03:    <nodeDefinition DefName="com.tuhra.model.queries.AllDepartments">
```

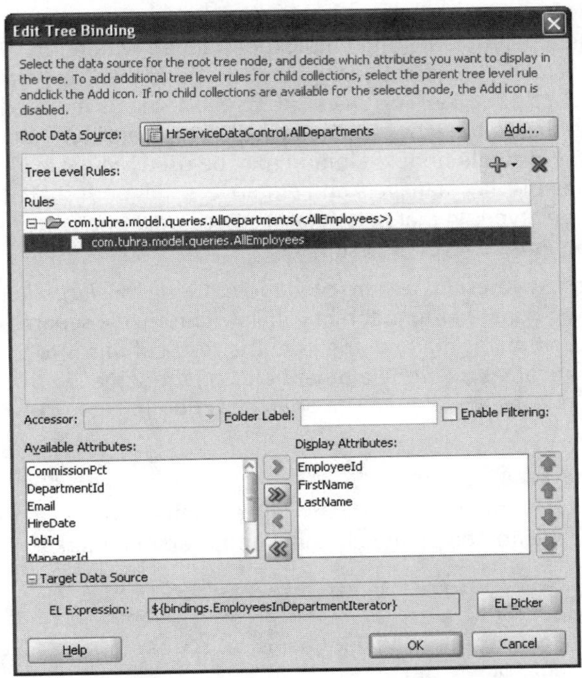

FIGURE 14-8. *Edit Tree Binding dialog for a master-detail binding*

```
04:      <AttrNames>
05:        <Item Value="DepartmentName"/>
06:      </AttrNames>
07:      <Accessors>
08:        <Item Value="AllEmployees"/>
09:      </Accessors>
10:    </nodeDefinition>
11:    <nodeDefinition DefName="com.tuhra.model.queries.AllEmployees"
12:                    TargetIterator=
                          "${bindings.EmployeesInDepartmentIterator}">
13:      <AttrNames>
14:        <Item Value="EmployeeId"/>
15:        <Item Value="FirstName"/>
16:        <Item Value="LastName"/>
17:      </AttrNames>
18:    </nodeDefinition>
19:  </tree>
```

- **Lines 07–09** define the view link accessor that will be used to traverse from the parent view object to its children.

- **Lines 11–17** define the second node type in the tree, "employee," and the selected attributes for it. It is important to notice that there is no direct relationship between the department parent node and employees defined within this XML. The way that the tree binding actually works is to examine the type of the RowIterator collection, for example `.tuhra.model.queries.AllEmployees`, that is returned by the accessor call and then map that to the types listed in the *defName* attribute (**line 11**) of the nodeDefinition. In this way, a single node definition may be used recursively in a tree binding, for example to display managers and employees that both share the same underlying AllEmployee type. In that particular instance only one nodeDefinition is required to service an infinite level of nesting.
- **Line 12** shows a useful feature of the rule. Using the *TargetIterator* attribute, you can ask the binding container to automatically synchronize a separate iterator on the page with the selection that is made in the tree. The result of this is to give the developer the ability to automatically synchronize other fields on the screen with the selection in the tree. This is also shown as the *Target Data Source* section in Figure 14-8.

Customizing the Tree Labels

A common question about the tree binding relates to the labels used for each branch and leaf. If you look at the tree definition created by drag-and-drop, the markup will look like this:

```
<af:tree value="#{bindings.AllDepartments.treeModel}"
         var="node"
         selectionListener="#{bindings.AllDepartments.treeModel.makeCurrent}"
         rowSelection="single">
  <f:facet name="nodeStamp">
    <af:outputText value="#{node}"/>
  </f:facet>
</af:tree>
```

The similarity to the table usage of the tree binding should be evident here, although notice that another attribute of the binding—*treeModel,* is used for the value of the control, and the selection listener is likewise provided by that object. Each row in the treeModel is referenced by the alias (var attribute) called node, and then this node value is printed out to create the branches and leaves of the tree. For each particular node, the value will be made up of each of the selected attributes for the corresponding rule, separated from the next with a space.

However, you can change the label of theses node. Sometimes, you will need access to data in the tree programmatically but not want to display that data in the label. For example, if the tree is used as a navigation device for selecting a department, the label of the tree node will only need to contain the department name, not the ID; however, the ID may need to be available in the binding definition for use in the drilldown.

It is important to understand that this node object encapsulates all of the attributes that you selected for display (as represented in the tree binding). This means that you can access those attributes explicitly using EL and define exactly what you want printed. For example, in the case of the departments and employees tree the following nodeStamp can be used to print just the last name and not the first name or ID for employee nodes.

Notice here how the EmployeeId attribute is tested for null using the EL operator *empty.* If it is null, the DepartmentName is used; otherwise, the LastName value is used:

```
<af:tree
       ...>
  <f:facet name="nodeStamp">
    <!-- af:group is used here because a facet can only have a single
         direct child -->
    <af:group>
      <!-- print Department for nonemployee records -->
      <af:outputText value="#{node.DepartmentName}"
                     rendered="#{empty node.EmployeeId}"/>
      <!-- EmployeeId only has a value on employee nodes -->
      <af:outputText value="#{node.LastName}"
                     rendered="#{!empty node.EmployeeId}"/>
    </af:group>
  </f:facet>
</af:tree>
```

Within the nodeStamp facet of the tree control, components other than simple outputText can be used. Typically this will include `af:image` components to add icons to the tree and even nonvisual components like `af:attributeDragSource` used to flag data as being used for drag-and-drop.

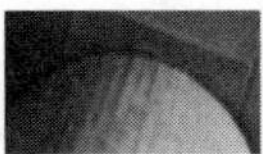

TIP
When grouping components within the nodeStamp facet of the tree, always use the `af:group` container, which has no visual aspect, rather than trying to use, say, an `af:panelGroupLayout` component. This latter layout container will cause problems in the alignment of the tree node data.

Adding Artificial Levels into the Tree

When using a tree to represent complex data sets, there is often a requirement to introduce grouping into the structure. For example, continuing with the departments and employees tree, what if you want to display both the manager for a department and the staff within it? An example of this is shown here.

Unfortunately it is not possible to achieve this nesting using the Edit Tree Binding dialog alone. For this more complex case, the PageDef file needs to be edited directly. Here's the XML definition of the tree binding used to create that illustration:

```
<tree id="AllDepartments"
      IterBinding="AllDepartmentsIterator">
  <nodeDefinition DefName="com.tuhra.model.queries.AllDepartments">
    <AttrNames>
      <Item Value="DepartmentName"/>
    </AttrNames>
    <Accessors>
      <Item Value="DepartmentalManager" Label="tree.manager.node.label"/>
      <Item Value="AllEmployees" Label="tree.staff.node.label"/>
    </Accessors>
  </nodeDefinition>
```

```
  <nodeDefinition DefName="com.tuhra.model.queries.AllEmployees">
    <AttrNames>
      <Item Value="FirstName"/>
      <Item Value="LastName"/>
        </AttrNames>
  </nodeDefinition>
</tree>
```

Notice that this definition is almost identical to the last one that we described. The only difference is that the `<Accessors>` element under the AllDepartments node definition now has two children, naming two different view link accessors. Each accessor also has a label value (for example, `tree.staff.node.label`, which is a lookup into the resource bundle defined inside the PageDef file). The AllEmployees node definition is shared by both the staff accessor and the manager accessor, as both ViewLinks return that same kind of object.

On a related subject, a particular rule on the tree can be filtered.

Node Filtering

The Edit Tree Binding dialog shown in Figure 14-7 displays an *Enable Filtering* checkbox. This is rarely used but is worth explaining. This option allows you to populate a particular level in the tree with more than one set of data, thus contradicting the previous statement that a rule defines a single level in the tree hierarchy. This data could be loaded from different child collections based on a discriminator column in the master collection, or it can be used to filter a single child collection by only displaying rows that match the entered criteria.

When *Enable Filtering* is selected, a dropdown list labeled as *Filter Attribute* is displayed, allowing you to select an attribute from the master and add a string value in the *Filter Value* field below, as shown here:

Accessor: Folder Label: Enable Filtering:
Filter Attribute: ManagerId
Filter Value: 101

At runtime, as this rule is processed, the indicated attribute will be compared with the fixed value and the node only displayed if they match.

TreeTable Binding

You may notice that you can also create another tree-related binding called a treeTable binding in the PageDef file. This binding type is not used. Tree bindings are used to populate the TreeTable component.

Table Bindings

Table bindings are no longer actually used for backing tables automatically, although they can be still used in that way. The most common use case for this style of binding is for stamping out a collection of data using one of the looping JSF components such as `af:forEach` or `af:iterator`. As table bindings are no longer used for any of the drag and drop operations from the Data Controls Panel, you will always have to create them manually from the binding editor.

Table bindings are similar to attribute bindings, except that a single binding encapsulates a set of attributes for display rather than just one attribute. When creating a table binding, you use the Create Table Binding dialog shown in Figure 14-9.

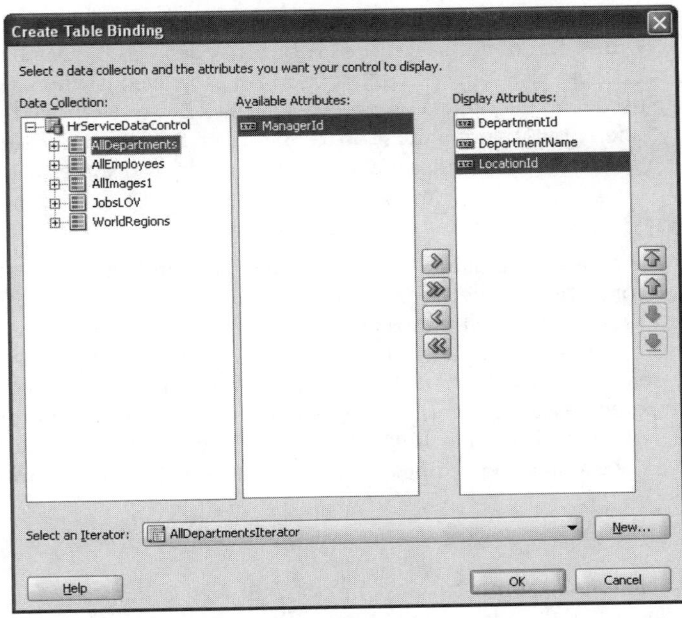

FIGURE 14-9. *Create Table Binding dialog*

Unlike some of the other binding editors, this editor still references iterators rather than data sources in its user interface. To create an iterator here, expand the *Data Collection* tree to the correct view object and then click the New button to the right of the *Select an Iterator* list. A further pop-up appears for the name of the new iterator to be set. Once an iterator is created or selected, the attributes of the underlying view object are displayed in the *Available Attributes* list and can be shuttled into the *Display Attributes* list and re-ordered if required.

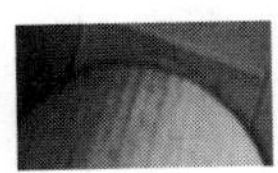

NOTE
Generally the ordering of attributes in a table binding has no effect. Code will refer to each attribute explicitly rather than to a pseudo-attribute such as node*, which is exposed by tree bindings.*

A typical table binding in XML form is straightforward. In the example shown in Figure 14-9, it looks like this:

```
<table id="AllDepartments"
       IterBinding="AllDepartmentsIterator">
  <AttrNames>
    <Item Value="DepartmentId"/>
    <Item Value="DepartmentName"/>
    <Item Value="LocationId"/>
  </AttrNames>
</table>
```

Using a Table Binding

It is possible to bind an `af:table` component to a table binding using the expression `#{bindings.[Table Binding Name].collectionModel}` as the value attribute—for example, `#{bindings.AllDepartments.collectionModel}` However, it's more common that a table binding will be used with a looping component such as `af:forEach`. In this case, the expression used is slightly different: `#{bindings.[Table Binding Name].rangeSet}`. Refer back to Table 14-1 for a more of the attributes that the table binding also shares with the tree binding.

Action Bindings

In addition to the data-bound fields shown in the JSF page in Figure 14-1, there are also a series of buttons used for navigating between records. Just like the fields, these buttons are bound and defined in the PageDef file. The buttons are bound to operations using an action binding.

Operations are data control items that perform an action on the data model. Available operations appear in the Data Controls Panel, and you can drop them onto the page as buttons or links (or, in some cases, as complete forms with input items and buttons). *Action bindings* connect the UI element (button or link) on the page (View layer) to the operation function in the model layer. These action bindings are defined in the PageDef file just like the data access binding types.

TIP

If you have an Oracle Forms background, the best way to think of operations is that they are like the Oracle Forms built-ins. Operations *are standard infrastructure functions that operate at the collection level (like the block level in triggers) or at the data control level (like Form-level triggers), as shown in this illustration.*

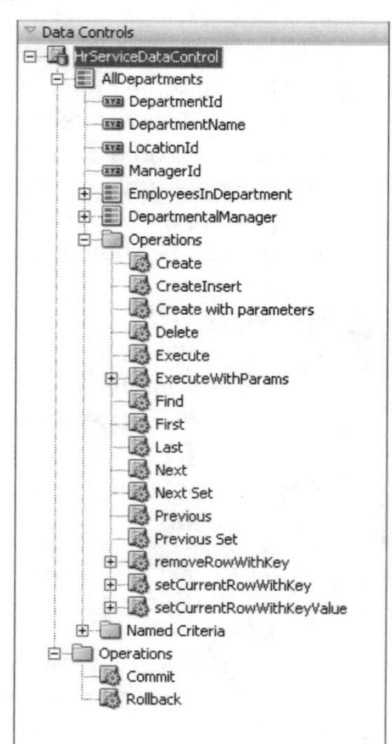

Available Operations

As mentioned in Chapter 13, operations are part of the abstraction provided by the ADFm layer, and different business services (data control types) will support a different subset of operations, depending on the capabilities of that service. With ADF BC–based data controls, a large set of operations are supported. At the other extreme, a data control that is based on a JavaBean may not support any operations.

Data Control–Level Operations The data control–level operations (shown in Table 14-2) are only exposed by ADF BC–based data controls and any other data controls that have the *supportsTransactions* property set to "true" in the DataControls.dcx file.

Operation	Description
Commit	This operation tells the data control to issue a database COMMIT to save changes in the transaction.
Rollback	This operation issues a database ROLLBACK to undo any changes posted after the last COMMIT. This operation also clears out the record caches in ADF Business Components and resets the iterators to the first record.

TABLE 14-2. *Data Control–Level Transactional Operations*

In the PageDef file, a data control–level action binding will look like this:

```
<action id="Commit"
        DataControl="HrServiceDataControl"
        InstanceName="HrServiceDataControl"
        RequiresUpdateModel="true"
        Action="commitTransaction"/>
```

The properties used in the action binding have the following meanings:

- **id** This property defines a name for the operation. This ID is used when binding the action into the UI. It matches the logical name of the operation by default, but it does not need to match.
- **InstanceName** This property is also set to the name of the data control for ADF BC work. It may or may not be present in the binding definition and can generally be ignored. It will only come into play if you are using nested application modules within your application.
- **DataControl** This property defines the data control that this operation acts on.
- **RequiresModelUpdate** This Boolean value indicates to the framework if any changes on the page should be applied to the Model layer before the operation executes.
- **Action** This keyword tells the framework what to do. Each operation has a unique text ID. For example, Commit is "commitTransaction," and Rollback is "rollbackTransaction." These identifiers are fixed within the framework.

NOTE
Earlier versions of the binding framework used numerical constants rather than meaningful text IDs for identifying the standard operations. For example, the Commit operation (commitTransaction) had a numerical value of 100. These values are still a valid way to identify actions, and you may encounter them in upgraded code.

Collection Operations Most operations are associated with a collection or, more strictly, are associated with an iterator. Table 14-3 lists the collection operations by text ID and the numerical codes associated with them.

Operation (Text ID)	Numerical Code	Description
Create createRow	41	This operation opens a slot for a new record in the collection. The new record is added to the collection after the page is submitted. Therefore, if the user abandons the page by navigating away, an empty record is not left orphaned. The new record opened by Create is inserted before the current record in the iterator.
CreateInsert createInsertRow	40	This operation is the same as Create, except that the new empty record is inserted into the collection as part of the operation. This means that even if the user never submits the page, the row will still be in the collection. See the sidebar "Create or CreateInsert" for details about how to decide between these operations.
Create with parameters createWithParams	42	Creates a row and initializes values at the same time see the later section "Defaulting Data During Record Creation."
Delete removeCurrentRow	30	This operation removes the current row from the collection. It is similar to the removeRowWithKey operation.
Execute iteratorExecute execute	2 1	This operation refreshes the current collection. This is like requerying the database, although it works with data in the mid-tier cache rather than data from the database. There are actually two forms of execute, which are discussed in "Scoped Action Bindings" later in this section.
ExecuteWithParams executeWithParams	95	This operation will be available if the source view object for a collection contains bind variable references. ExecuteWithParams combines the tasks of setting the bind variable values and refreshing the collection into one call.
Find find	3/1	This operation places the collection into 10.1.3 style Query-By-Example mode and is rendered obsolete by the newer `af:query` component. The Create and Delete operations take on overloaded meanings when in Find mode. They add and remove from the list of query criteria rather than adding and deleting rows.

TABLE 14-3. *Operations Available on a Collection*

Operation (Text ID)	Numerical Code	Description
First first	12	This operation repositions the current row, as defined by the iterator, to the initial record in the collection.
Last last	13	This operation repositions the current row to the final record in the collection.
Next next	10	Next moves the current row down one.
Next Set nextSet	14	This operation scrolls the current record location down a number of rows specified by the iterator's *RangeSize* property.
Previous previous	11	Previous moves the current row up one record.
Previous Set previousSet	15	This operation scrolls the current record location up by the number of rows specified by the iterator's *RangeSize* property.
removeRowWithKey removeRowWithKey	99	This operation deletes a specified row in the collection. This operation takes a parameter of the row identifier generated by ADFm and accessed through the binding attribute *rowKeyStr*. This attribute is available when iterating through a collection as a special attribute that is always present, rather like ROWNUM in a SQL Query. It is unlikely that you will need to use this operation in a JSF-based application, since JSF tables and trees manage row currency for you.
setCurrentRowWithKey setCurrentRowWithKey	96	Like removeRowWithKey, this operation takes a row identifier parameter and uses it to set the iterator currency (focus) onto a specific row. Again, you are unlikely to need this in JSF applications.
setCurrentRowWithKeyValue setCurrentRowWithKeyValue	98	This operation is a version of setCurrentRowWithKey that takes a parameter of the primary key value rather than the ADFm-generated key.
<custom methods> invokeMethod	999	Methods you create in the application module or view object Impl classes can appear in a similar way to operations and use this special ID.

TABLE 14-3. *Operations Available on a Collection (continued)*

Create or CreateInsert?

The two different create operations provided by ADF, Create and CreateInsert, can be a little confusing because they seem to accomplish the same task. The row created by the Create operation is managed as a temporary object by the framework. If the user abandons an input screen without submitting the new record, the row will simply disappear, leaving the programmer with no clean-up to do. CreateInsert, however, requires clean-up.

Although the Create behavior is generally more useful, there are still some circumstances where CreateInsert should be used. Typically, this will be when the side effects of entity object creation are desirable. For example, the create method on the entity object adds information defined as defaults for attributes such as dates and reference numbers. With CreateInsert, this default information will be visible to the user on the created (blank) record. If the Create operation is used, the defaults will not be set until after the user submits the new record.

An action binding for a collection-level operation has similar attributes to the data control-level operation bindings. The following code listing shows the binding of the First button shown in Figure 14-1:

```
<action id="First"
        IterBinding="AllEmployeesIterator"
        RequiresUpdateModel="true"
        Action="first"/>
```

The *id, Action,* and *RequiresUpdateModel* properties have the same meaning as the data control–level operations. In this case, the binding is associated with an iterator though the *IterBinding* property, rather than directly with a data control.

Defaulting Data During Record Creation A common use case for many applications is the requirement to create a new row in a view object and to initialize some of the attributes to a set of default values. In most cases, the developer should handle this using the capabilities of the underlying entity objects. However, in some circumstances, the data that needs to be defaulted in has to come from the UI layer and may not be directly discoverable by the ADF BC entities. There are two approaches to this scenario.

1. Create a custom method on the view object that takes in arguments from the UI layer, creates a new row in the view object, and then sets the relevant defaults. This method can then be bound to a page or a method activity in a task flow.
2. Use CreateWithParams to combine the creation and defaulting in a single call. Using this approach does require manual editing of the PageDef file to add the required attributes that need to be set. The following snippet shows such a definition where the DepartmentId attribute is defaulted to the literal value of 60, although this could also use expression language to define a more dynamic value.

```
<action id="CreateWithParams"
        IterBinding="AllEmployeesIterator"
        RequiresUpdateModel="true"
        Action="createWithParams">
```

```
        <NamedData NDName="DepartmentId"
                   NDType="java.lang.Integer"
                   NDValue="60"/>
    </action>
```

Both approaches work equally well. The custom method approach has the advantage of giving the developer more control over the creation process; on the other hand, CreateWithParams requires no extra code to implement the most common use cases.

Manually Creating Action Bindings

The most convenient way of creating an action binding is to drag and drop the operation from the Data Controls Panel onto the page. Like the other binding types, action bindings can be created from within the Bindings tab in the page editor or in the PageDef file using the "Create control binding" (green plus "+") button above the bindings list.

After selecting Action as the binding type, the following Create Action Binding dialog appears:

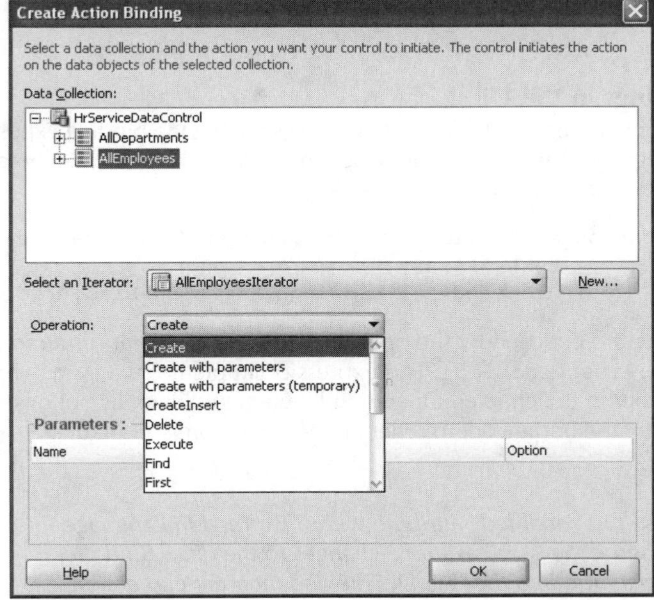

The Create Action Binding dialog shows the standard list of data collections at the top and offers a dropdown list of actions below. Selecting the top-level data control node will configure the *Operation* list to show the data control–level operations (Commit and Rollback), if they are available for the selected data control. When a collection/iterator is selected, the list reconfigures to display the valid operations for a collection.

Scoped Action Bindings If you scroll through the collection-level actions to the Execute and Find operations, you'll see the dialog reconfigure slightly. The *Apply to all iterators in page definition* checkbox becomes enabled. Execute and Find have special scopes of operation; the default level is *iterator level,* where the operation is associated explicitly with an iterator. The alternative, *binding container level,* operates at the page level and is switched on by selecting the checkbox. Clicking a button bound to the Execute operation scoped at the binding container level will refresh all collections on the page. If the button's operation were defined on the iterator level, only the bindings associated with the same iterator as the Execute action would be refreshed.

If you create both types of bindings (iterator and binding container) and compare them, you will see that the only difference is the ID of the action. Iterator-level Execute, for example, has an *Action* attribute of "iteratorExecute." The same operation bound at the binding container level has an *Action* attribute of "execute." So although these action bindings are considered two scopes or levels for the same operation, in reality, they are two separate operations. Table 14-3 shows both action codes when applicable. The lower-numbered code of any pair operates at the whole-page level.

NOTE
The term "binding container" is the formal name for the set of bindings on a page. All bindings defined within a PageDef file are within the same binding container. When building JSF user interfaces, there is generally a one-to-one relationship between a binding container and a page or page fragment.

Action Bindings in the UI

When we described tree and table bindings, you saw that the binding exposes extra features though Expression Language. The same is true of action bindings. For example, here is the markup for the First button shown in Figure 14-1:

```
<af:commandButton actionListener="#{bindings.First.execute}"
                  text="First"
                  disabled="#{!bindings.First.enabled}"/>
```

The first feature exposed by the operation is the enabled attribute in the expression `#{!bindings.First.enabled}`. This expression implements a framework behavior that we mentioned earlier in the chapter. Operation UI elements, such as buttons, are enabled or disabled automatically by the framework to reflect if the operation is available.

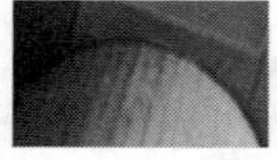

TIP
You can use this "enabled" attribute within Expression Language to understand if the user has made changes to the data. Bind the Commit operation into the PageDef file and then the expression `#{bindings.Commit.enabled}` can be used to detect if there are outstanding changes.

The second interesting property is shown in the *actionListener* property. An *actionListener* in JSF is code that will execute before the main *action* for a command item component. For example, consider the following code:

```
<af:commandButton actionListener="#{bindings.Commit.execute}"
                  action="Home"
                  text="Save and return"/>
```

The actionListener operation of a commit is processed, and then the navigation implied by the "Home" outcome takes place. The expression `#{bindings.[operation].execute}` is a

JSF method binding. Chapter 15's section "How Do I Write Code Using the ADF Model?" will look at how you can override or enhance these built-in operation calls.

Operations with Parameters

A subset of operations, of which the most important are executeWithParams and createWithParams, take arguments (parameters). The three operations named with "WithKey" suffixes (in Table 14-3) take a single argument value. ExecuteWithParams will take as many arguments as there are bind variables in the view object SQL statement and createWithParams takes as many arguments as it has attributes.

For operations with arguments, you can expand the operation's node in the Data Controls Panel to reveal a Parameters node. This node contains the arguments, except in the case of createWithParams, where the arguments are implicitly the same as the list of attributes.

Dropping an operation that takes arguments, such as executeWithParams, onto the page allows the creation of a parameter form as well as a command button or a command link.

As an example, let's take a look at the markup generated by dropping the executeWithParams operation for a view object with one bind variable. In this case, the view object is based on the DEPARTMENTS table and the bind variable is used to set the location value. Dropping this operation as a parameter form creates the following JSF tags:

```
<af:inputText value="#{bindings.location.inputValue}"
              label="#{bindings.location.hints.label}"
              required="#{bindings.location.hints.mandatory}"
              columns="#{bindings.location.hints.displayWidth}"
              maximumLength="#{bindings.location.hints.precision}"
              shortDesc="#{bindings.location.hints.tooltip}">
  <f:validator binding="#{bindings.location.validator}"/>
  <af:convertNumber groupingUsed="false"
              pattern="#{bindings.location.format}"/>
</af:inputText>
<af:commandButton actionListener="#{bindings.ExecuteWithParams.execute}"
              text="ExecuteWithParams"
              disabled="#{!bindings.ExecuteWithParams.enabled}"/>
```

Notice that the `af:inputText` uses a value binding to retrieve several of its UI attributes, such as the *label, columns* (width), and *required* attributes. All of the information powering these bindings is coming from the view object bind variable definition and its associated UI hints and data type information. That information is used here to configure the parameter form.

The input item used to enter the bind variable value has been bound to an attribute binding called "location" (in the PageDef file). To find out about this binding, on the field, select **Go To Binding** from the right-click menu and then double click the location binding. The Edit Attribute Binding dialog appears as follows:

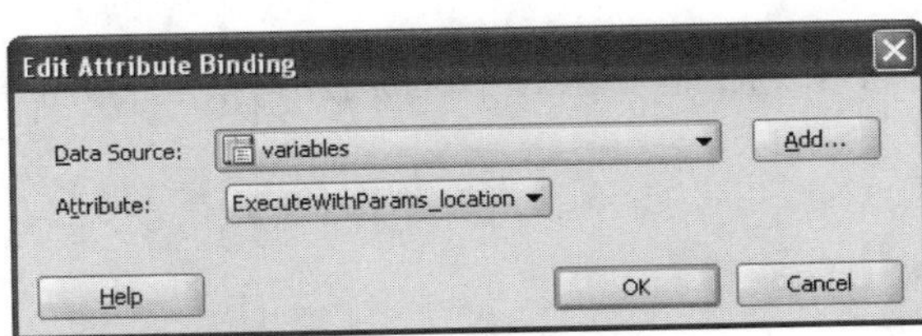

Notice that a Data Source (iterator) called "variables" is selected. The variable iterator is a special iterator that provides access to local variables defined in the PageDef file. In this case, the input field is bound to a variable called "ExecuteWithParams_location," using an attribute binding called "location."

The `af:commandButton` tag created by dropping the parameter form is identical to the examples described before. Its binding definition in the PageDef file, as shown in the following listing, should be relatively familiar:

```
<action id="ExecuteWithParams" IterBinding="DepartmentsInLocationIterator"
        RequiresUpdateModel="true" Action="executeWithParams">
  <NamedData NDName="location"
             NDType="oracle.jbo.domain.Number"
             NDValue="${bindings.ExecuteWithParams_location}"/>
</action>
```

You will see that the executeWithParams operation has an action ID of "executeWithParams" and that it is bound to the "DepartmentsInLocationIterator". In addition, you will see a child element of the action tag, the *NamedData* element.

NamedData is used to define arguments that the framework needs to pass to operations and methods that have arguments. This element has the following attributes:

- **NDName** This attribute is the name of the argument. It is important to assign a name if you need to programmatically set this value before calling the bound method.
- **NDType** This attribute identifies the datatype of the parameter, in this case the type is derived from the datatype set for the bind variable in the view object.
- **NDValue** This attribute is the value to pass to the parameter. This can be set to a literal value, or, as in this example, it can be set to an expression.

The ability to pass an expression to the parameter's value attribute is immensely powerful. The programmer can use any EL expression here, including conditional expressions using the ternary operator that we discussed earlier. In this case, the drag-and-drop operation has set up the expression as `${bindings.ExecuteWithParams_location}`. This expression binds the value of the ExecuteWithParams_location local variable as the argument to the operation call. Thus, you can see the relationship between the input field in the parameter form and the operation call. The input field sets the value of the local variable, and the operation passes that same value up to the model.

TIP

Expressions in the PageDef file can use either the dollar "$" or hash (pound) "#" symbol to mark the start of the expression. There is no functional difference between either notation, both forms are supported for compatibility with the forms of expression language that different UI technologies may use, specifically JSF and JSTL expressions.

Method Bindings

In principle, method bindings are virtually identical to the action bindings used to access operations. When a custom method is dropped into the UI as a parameter form, for example, input fields are created and bound to variables in the same way as for operations with parameters. The only difference between custom methods and operations is that custom methods may yield results. These results can then be bound into the page and treated just like any other normal attribute.

Editing Method Bindings

Custom methods are bound using a binding type called a *methodAction* binding. You can create a methodAction binding by dropping the method onto the page as a command button, command link, or parameter form in the normal way, or by using the binding editor. When manually creating or editing the binding from the binding screen, the parameters to the method can be set. The next illustration shows the Create Action Binding dialog for a method called `searchByLocation()`. In the example this method is exposed as a client method on the Department-based view object instance.

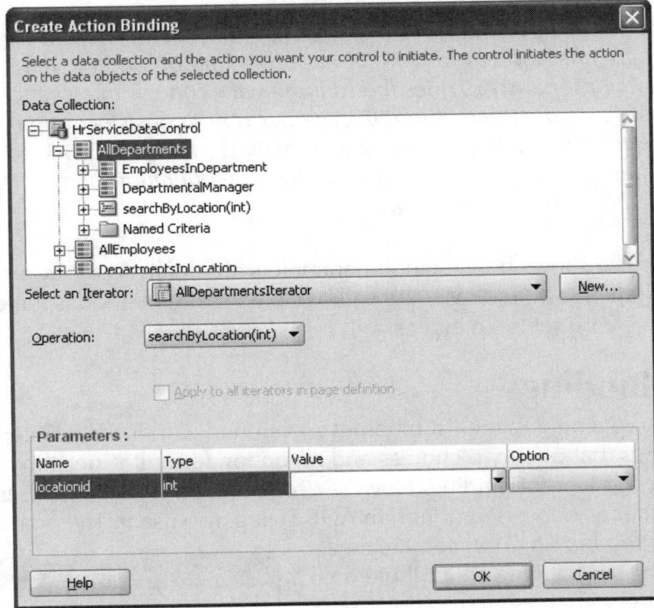

This method takes a single argument in this case (locationid), and the Create Action Binding dialog provides a place to set the value of the argument. The parameter can be set to a literal value or an expression. Clicking the *Value* field in the dialog causes a dropdown list to appear that gives access to the Expression Language dialog, allowing you to set an expression for the value.

The dropdown list labeled *Option* is only operational in Swing-based applications, so you can ignore it for JSF applications.

The XML for a method binding in the PageDef file looks similar to that of an operation binding:

```
<methodAction id="searchByLocation"
              IterBinding="AllDepartmentsIterator"
              RequiresUpdateModel="true"
              Action="invokeMethod"
              MethodName="searchByLocation"
              IsViewObjectMethod="true"
```

```
             DataControl="HrServiceDataControl"
             InstanceName="HrServiceDataControl.AllDepartments">
  <NamedData NDName="locationid"
            NDValue="10"
            NDType="int"/>
</methodAction>
```

In this case, the binding is to a method exposed by a view object instance, so there is additional information required to map that relationship. You can see that custom methods use the *Action* property in the same way that operation bindings do. However, custom methods always use the action ID of invokeMethod (numeric code "999") for that property. The framework interprets this as a call to the service.

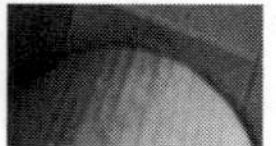

NOTE
If you reproduce this example, you may or may not see the IterBinding *property in the methodAction definition. In this kind of binding, the* InstanceName *property provides the runtime with enough information to locate and execute the method. JDeveloper is not consistent about adding iterator references for view object methods, and what you see in the binding will depend on what other binding operations have been carried out on the same page.*

This listing also shows how method parameters are defined as they are for operations—using *NamedData* elements. In this case, the value to pass to the method is a literal value ("10"), but it could alternatively be set to an expression.

Boolean Bindings

Finally, as a complement to the list bindings mentioned earlier, specialized bindings exist called *boolean bindings* that offer two choices and no option for null. Checkboxes are the usual UI component for this kind of binding. However, toggle buttons (which represent a Boolean value and display either as depressed or not) in ADF Swing also use it. Therefore, this binding is also known as a *button binding*. You can create a boolean binding by dragging an attribute onto the page and dropping it as a checkbox (ADF Select Boolean Checkbox). The Edit Boolean Binding dialog shown here, will display.

Edit Boolean Binding
Select a data collection and attribute you want your control to operate on. The value to return to the bound attribute is determined when the user changes the control's selection state. You must know what values the bound attribute takes in order to supply meaningful selection state values.
Base Data Source: HrServiceDataControl.AllEmployees Add...
Attribute: WorkingBasis
Selected State Value: FULL_TIME
Unselected State Value: PART_TIME
Help OK Cancel

The elements should be familiar. You can select a *Base Data Source* from the dropdown list (or create one with the Add button) to be a target of the binding. The collection will then automatically be selected. You can also select the target attribute within that collection (in the *Attribute* column). You need to type in the *Selected State Value* and *Unselected State Value* fields the values that the database expects for those states.

The following listing shows what a boolean binding looks like. For the sake of illustration we've added a transient attribute to the Employees view object to record the working status of an employee: full time or part time. As you can see, it's remarkably similar to a fixed list binding.

```
<button id="WorkingBasis"
        IterBinding="AllEmployeesIterator"
        DTSupportsMRU="false">
  <AttrNames>
    <Item Value="WorkingBasis"/>
  </AttrNames>
  <ValueList>
    <Item Value="FULL_TIME"/>
    <Item Value="PART_TIME"/>
  </ValueList>
</button>
```

In the ValueList element, the first child element represents the true (checked) value and the second represents the false (unchecked) value.

Boolean Bindings in a Table

One use case that is worth quickly discussing is where the developer wants to display an `af:selectBooleanCheckbox` within a table or tree. Earlier in the chapter you saw that the *nodeDefinition* within the tree binding is used to define all of the attributes that are available. As shown in this simple listing for a version of the employee table:

```
<nodeDefinition DefName="com.tuhra.model.queries.AllEmployees">
  <AttrNames>
    <Item Value="EmployeeId"/>
    <Item Value="FirstName"/>
    <Item Value="LastName"/>
    <Item Value="EmployeeWorkingBasis"/>
  </AttrNames>
</nodeDefinition>
```

As the definition stands each of the individual attributes within the node are treated exactly like standard attribute bindings. So what if you wanted to show the EmployeeWorkingBasis as a checkbox rather than the literal value? To do this you need to create the boolean binding manually in the binding editor as shown in the "WorkingBasis" listing. Then you link the Item definition to this new binding using the boolean binding ID using the *Binds* attribute. Here's what it would then look like:

```
<nodeDefinition DefName="com.tuhra.model.queries.AllEmployees">
  <AttrNames>
    <Item Value="EmployeeId"/>
    <Item Value="FirstName"/>
    <Item Value="LastName"/>
    <Item Value="EmployeeWorkingBasis" Binds="WorkingBasis"/>
  </AttrNames>
</nodeDefinition>
```

Now the EmployeeWorkingBasis attribute can be exposed using an `af:selectBooleanCheckbox` rather than being restricted to an `af:outputText` or `af:inputText`.

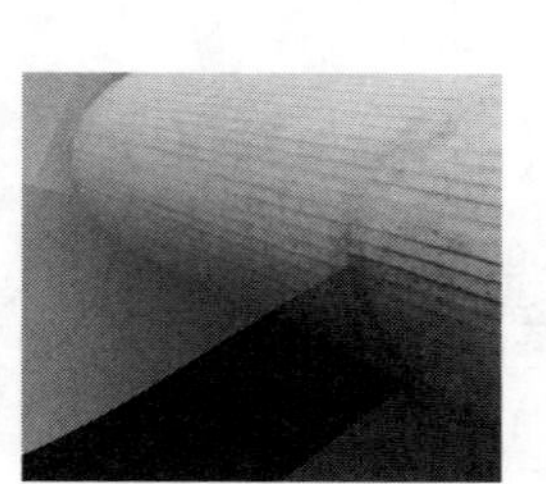

CHAPTER 15

ADF Bindings: Iterators, Executables, and Code

Real programmers can write assembly code in any language.

—Larry Wall (1954–), creator of the Perl language

In Chapter 14 we spent some time looking at the various binding types that ADF uses to provide data for the UI. In this second half of the binding topic we take a closer look at how the ADF Model (ADFm) handles bindings at runtime by answering the following questions:

- **What is an iterator?**
- **What are executables?**
- **How can I control execution in the ADF Model?**
- **How can I override and add to the ADF Model Life Cycle?**
- **What are parameters?**
- **What are contextual events?**
- **How can I write code using the ADF Model?**

Just like Chapter 14, this is an advanced chapter, and provided that you understand the basic concept of what an iterator is, you may want to skip over it and return after you have worked through the practices in Part V of the book.

What Is an Iterator?

As we mentioned in the preceding chapter, data access for attributes in a binding, as well as most operations and method bindings, requires iterators. You can think of an *iterator* as a current record pointer on a collection; for example, the expression `#{bindings.EmployeeId.inputValue}` actually evaluates to "the Employee ID of whatever record the Employees iterator is currently pointing to in the Employees." This link from EmployeeId to Employees Iterator is defined in the PageDef file, as you've seen in the preceding chapter.

In normal circumstances, a particular collection of records would maintain a single iterator to track the *row currency* (record marked as current) in the user interface. However, secondary iterators on the same collection are possible. A now-obsolete example of this is the old Find mode for a collection (this is now replaced by the new search component functionality). Find mode specifically uses one iterator, and therefore components associated with it, to be used for input to build up a Where clause for the view object, while the other tracks the result set of the view object.

The primary iterator for a collection is automatically created when binding data to the page in a drag-and-drop operation. The default name is made up of the name of the collection suffixed with the word "Iterator," for example, "AllEmployeesIterator." As you would expect, the name, however, is arbitrary and can be changed through the Property Inspector. Once an iterator is defined for a collection, any subsequent bindings to attributes, operations, or methods associated with that collection will reuse the same iterator.

Editing the Iterator

Iterators are defined in the PageDef file within the executables section before the bindings section. The sidebar "Why Are Iterators Called 'Executables?'" provides details about this designation.

Why Are Iterators Called "Executables?"

If the iterator is a current record pointer, why is it defined in a section called "executables" in the PageDef file?

The executables section defines work that is done when the PageDef file is loaded at runtime. The framework processes each entry in the order in which it appears in the PageDef file. In the case of the iterator, as ADFm processes the definition, it automatically fetches the collection data so that the iterator has something to work with. So, a side effect of executing (or refreshing) the iterator is to execute the query on the underlying view object (when using ADF BC) and put the contents of that query into the bindings object, ready for display on the page. The framework automatically manages fetching from the view object as the user scrolls through the data.

If more than one iterator is defined for a collection, only the first will invoke the side effect of executing the query on the view object.

To examine or edit an iterator, click the Bindings tab of the visual page editor or the associated PageDef file for the page and select the iterator within the executables section of the bindings. The Property Inspector will then show the relevant properties for the iterator. If you switch to the source view of the PageDef file, the code associated with this section looks like the following for AllEmployeesIterator (without the line numbers):

```
01: <executables>
02:   <iterator id="AllEmployeesIterator"
03:             RangeSize="25"
04:             Binds="AllEmployees"
05:             DataControl="HRServiceDataControl"/>
06: </executables>
```

- **Lines 01 and 06** mark the beginning and end of the executables section.
- **Line 02** defines the iterator and gives the iterator its identifier.
- **Line 03** declares how many rows should be pulled from the view object into the bindings at one time. The sidebar "About Range Size" explains this concept a bit more.
- **Line 04** defines the collection (view object instance) that this iterator works with.
- **Line 05** completes the definition by indicating which data control supplies the collection named in the *Binds* property (Line 04).

A single PageDef file may contain multiple iterator definitions, depending on the data sources required to service all of the bindings in the page.

TIP

You might expect that the RangeSize *property would control the number of rows displayed in a table based on the collection. In earlier versions of the framework, this was indeed the case. However, the rich table in ADF 11g actually will display as many rows as can fit into the available space physically allocated to the table component, so all the range size controls is the number of AJAX transactions that are required to populate the table as the user scrolls up and down.*

About Range Size

The *RangeSize* property defines the number of records to retrieve in the first request to the server, and the framework handles the fetching of extra batches as required. Twenty-five rows is the default value for the *RangeSize,* and this should be adjusted depending on the requirements of the application. *RangeSize* supports a magic value of minus 1 (–1), which declares that all rows will be retrieved in the first batch. This is useful for dropdown lists and other cases where all records need to be visible at once.

Controlling Iterator Execution

By default, an iterator will refresh when the user first enters the page or fragment. ADFm will then manage the collection when the user carries out actions such as scrolling through a table or inserting and deleting rows.

There are some circumstances, however, when you need to control exactly when (and if) an iterator is refreshed. For example, you call an application module method that recalculates the summary value in a record accessed through the iterator. You need to somehow refresh the iterator to display the updated value.

Iterator execution is controlled by the three optional iterator properties *Refresh, RefreshCondition,* and *RefreshAfter.* The section "How Can I Control Execution in the ADF Model?" later in this chapter looks at the purpose and settings of these properties.

The *ChangeEventPolicy* property, though, is worth a mention now. *ChangeEventPolicy* has three valid values:

- **none** With this setting the iterator, it is only refreshed according to its *refreshCondition* property.
- **push** Indicates that asynchronous data changes may occur in the model and the data will be automatically refreshed in response to this. This option is mostly used with the Business Activity Monitoring (BAM) data control, in combination with active components such as tables and charts.
- **ppr** Standing for Partial Page Refresh (introduced in Chapter 12), this value allows the framework to make the decision about when to manage the update of the iterator for the developer and automatically update the components bound to that iterator in the page. In earlier versions of the framework, the developer was responsible for the PPR settings on individual components and each component would be declaratively set up to pull data changes in response to some other component value change. With this new PPR setting on the iterator, much of this is handled automatically, the framework will work out that the current row of the iterator has changed, and, in cooperation with the ADF Faces Rich Client components, refresh all of the interested fields directly. This is the default setting for *ChangeEventPolicy*.

Types of Iterators

So far, we've explained the plain iterator used to manage a view object collection. If you manually create an iterator from the Structure window or the Bindings panel, you'll see four iterator types. These are described in Table 15-1.

Iterator Type	Description
accessorIterator	Accessor iterators give access to secondary (detail) sets of data, based on the selection in a master iterator. These iterators are not needed in ADF Business Components–based applications, since the view link mechanism handles master-detail coordination automatically.
Iterator	The plain iterator acts as the current record pointer for a collection (view object instance). This is the type you will normally use.
methodIterator	When a custom method that returns data is *bound to a page*, a method iterator provides access to the results of that method. It works just like a plain iterator and is created automatically if the return value of a custom method is dragged onto the page. Refreshing a method iterator will cause the associated method to be executed. Method iterators are used to access method call results, regardless whether the results returned are a collection or a single value. Because a method iterator acts just like a plain iterator, user interface elements such as tables and lists can be bound to the results returned from a method call. Like accessor iterators, method iterators are used frequently with service providers such as EJB, but you will encounter them in ADF BC–based applications if you use custom application module methods or view object methods.
variableIterator	The PageDef file supports the definition of local variables that are not bound to the business service, but rather are a convenient holder for temporary state. This iterator provides access to these variables. Unlike the other iterator types, the variableIterator only ever has one "row."

TABLE 15-1. *Iterator Types*

In most cases, you will only create iterators implicitly by dragging and dropping or by using one of the binding dialogs; in both cases, the correct type will be created for you.

What Are Executables?

Iterators are the most common executable elements within the binding layer, but, as you may have noticed while exploring the different iterator types, there are some additional artifacts to cover here.

invokeAction Executable

An *invokeAction* executable calls an existing action or method binding defined in the action bindings. The invokeAction executable is created using the "Add" (green plus "+") button in the Executables section of the Bindings panel, shown here:

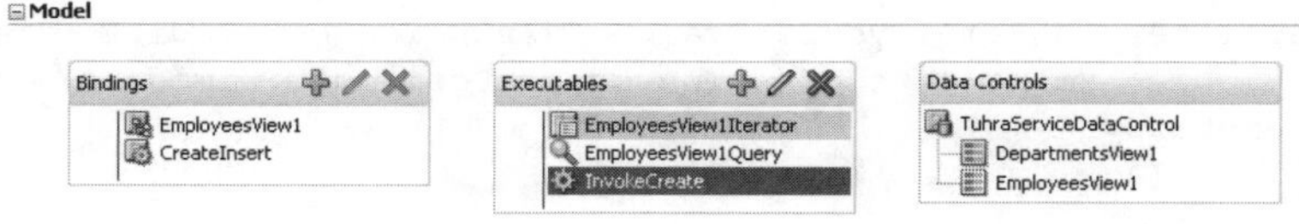

The invokeAction executable needs to be associated with an existing action (operation) or method binding in the PageDef file. For example, to create an insert form that creates a new record automatically, you would need to create a binding to the Create operation for the relevant iterator, and then create an invokeAction on that Create binding. When you create an invokeAction executable, the following Insert invokeAction dialog will appear; in this illustration, the *Binds* dropdown list shows all of the operations or methods that are already defined in the PageDef file. The *id* field can be set to any string value.

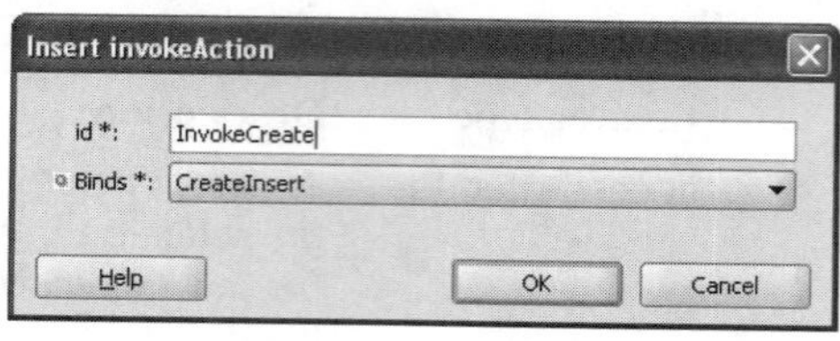

For clarity, adopt a naming convention that clearly identifies the purpose of the invokeAction executable. For example, call the invokeAction executable that calls Create "invokeCreate."

Once the invokeAction executable is created, be aware that it will automatically call the bound method as the page is refreshed. This can often lead to operations or methods being called more frequently than expected; however, we will explain how you can control this execution with more precision in the next section.

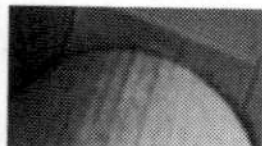

TIP
Although the invokeAction executable provides a way of invoking a bound method or operation as the page or page fragment is loaded, it is generally better to use an explicit call to a method activity in the task flow prior to the page or page fragment flow as a way of achieving this. This approach is much more explicit to maintain and makes it easier to control exactly when the required method or operation is executed.

taskFlow Executable

One of the important new features of ADF in Release 11 is the ADF Controller with its concept of task flows. As we discussed in Chapter 11, task flows can contain either whole pages or page fragments as view activities. When fragments are used, those task flows can be embedded into another page or fragment as a region. When a task flow is associated with the page in this way, an `af:region` component is used within the UI and that is coupled with a page binding in the executables section of the PageDef.

When a task flow is dragged into a page, the region component usage will look like this:

```
<af:region id="editEmployeeFlow"
           value="#{bindings.editEmployeeFlow.regionModel}"/>
```

Notice how the *value* of the region uses a binding expression to link to an associated taskFlow binding in the PageDef executables section:

```
<taskFlow id="editEmployeeFlow"
          taskFlowId="/WEB-INF/editEmployee-flow.xml#editEmployee-flow"
          xmlns="http://xmlns.oracle.com/adf/controller/binding">
  <parameters>
    <parameter id="employeeId" value="#{sessionScope.editEmployeeId}"
               xmlns="http://xmlns.oracle.com/adfm/uimodel"/>
  </parameters>
</taskFlow>
```

The main purpose of the executable binding, as you can see in this example, is as a place to define any parameter values that the task flow accepts. In this example, the parameter is called employeeId and is being set to the value of the session scope variable *editEmployeeId*.

Creating a taskFlow Executable

In most cases, you will create taskFlow executables as a side effect of a drag-and-drop operation as you associate a bounded task flow with a page. However, as you would expect, you can also create one manually using the "Add" button on the Executables section of the Bindings panel. Note that the taskFlow executable is not shown in the Generic Bindings category as is shown initially by the dialog; instead, you need to select the "ADF Task Flow Bindings" category from the drop-down list, as show here, and then taskFlow is the only option.

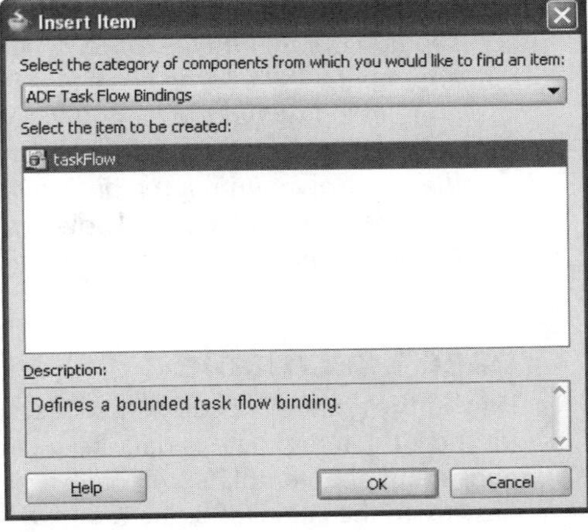

Once selected a simple dialog for entering an ID for the taskFlow executable and a reference to the actual task flow pops up. There are no lists or aids either here in this dialog or in the Property Inspector for the binding to help you to select the correct task flow ID reference, so start off by creating these bindings using drag-and-drop until you become familiar with the format of the PageDef metadata.

The taskFlowId property of the executable is usually assigned a literal string like "/WEB-INF/my-task-flow-definition.xml#my-task-flow-definition." However, you may also see it contains an expression such as `${tfManager.dynamicTaskFlowId}`. This latter usage is an example of a dynamic region, where the method `getDynamicTaskFlowId()` on a managed bean (tfManager in this case) is called to obtain the actual task flow that is required. Different task flows may be returned for different circumstances. You will see a dynamic region in use in the application that you will build in the next section of the book.

Parameters for the task flow are specified through the Property Inspector, or through a dialog that is invoked by a double-click on the executable binding as shown here:

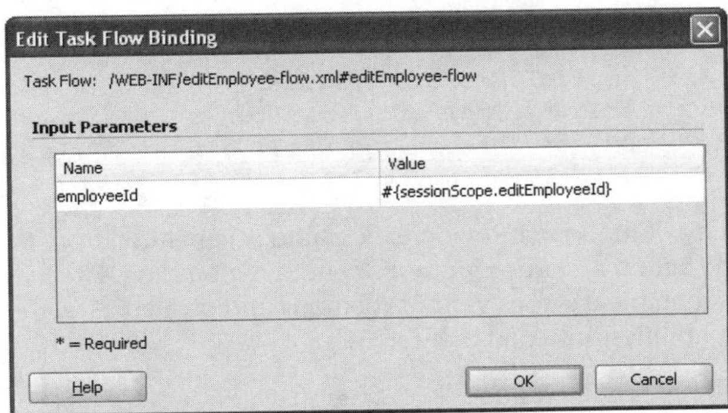

TIP

Parameters for the task flow can also be passed as a single Java Map containing name-value pairs rather than in addition to individual parameter elements nested inside the taskFlow binding. In this case the parametersMap *property of the taskFlow binding is used and should contain an EL expression that points to the relevant Map of arguments. If the same argument is passed as an explicit parameter and passed within the* parametersMap*, then the value in the latter takes precedence. The* parametersMap *feature is mainly used when the task flow within a region is dynamic and hence the number of parameters required is unknown or different between the candidate flows that might populate that region.*

page Executable

Page entries in the Executables section of the binding are related to any templates that are used for the UI. If a template is data-bound in some way and has its own PageDef file, then any page consuming that template will have a page executable entry in its PageDef. The page entry points directly to the PageDef of the template, allowing the framework to merge the two sets of binding information at runtime. These page executable bindings can be created manually using the Bindings panel; however, the only circumstances in which this would be required is when a template is being retrofitted into a page.

searchRegion Executable

The new search components (`af:query`, `af:quickQuery`) introduced with 11*g* depend on the searchRegion executable to operate. Like the taskFlow executable, the searchRegion is tightly coupled to some corresponding user interface elements, so manual creation of this kind of executable will be rare (although perfectly possible). If a search component is created on the page, the executable binding will be based on the view criteria that the developer selects when dragging from the Data Controls panel and, of course, the iterator for the view object being searched. The next code listing is an example based on the "All Queriable Attributes" named criteria of the AllDepartments view object. Notice how AllQueriableAttributes has a magic value of "__ImplicitViewCriteria__". Developer-created view criteria will use their defined name:

```
<searchRegion id="ImplicitViewCriteriaQuery"
              Criteria="__ImplicitViewCriteria__"
              Customizer="oracle.jbo.uicli.binding.JUSearchBindingCustomizer"
              Binds="AllDepartmentsIterator"/>
```

The *id* property of the searchRegion executable is generated from the view criteria name and is used to link the actual `af:query` component to the binding. Here you can see that the searchRegion executable exposes various methods and properties used to wire the UI component to the search capabilities provided by ADF BC:

```
<af:query id="implicitViewCriteriaQueryId"
          headerText="Search"
          disclosed="true"
          value="#{bindings.ImplicitViewCriteriaQuery.queryDescriptor}"
```

```
model="#{bindings.ImplicitViewCriteriaQuery.queryModel}"
queryListener="#{bindings.ImplicitViewCriteriaQuery.processQuery}"
queryOperationListener=
   "#{bindings.ImplicitViewCriteriaQuery.processQueryOperation}"/>
```

Properties Specific for the searchRegion

Most of the searchRegion properties are shared with the other executable types, with the exception of the following:

- **Criteria** Defines the name of the default view criteria for the search. As mentioned the implicit AllQueriableAttributes view criteria use a magic value of "__ImplicitViewCriteria__".
- **Customizer** Defines the class that controls how the query components and the searchBinding interact. For ADF BC–based applications the default JUSearchBindingCustomizer does everything that is required. Any customizer has to implement the `oracle.adf.model.binding.DCBindingCustomizerInterface` interface. You would only change this value if using a different data control type for which you had to develop your own search wiring.
- **DefaultQuickSearchAttrName** Is used specifically by the `af:quickQuery` component to define which attribute name is preselected in the dropdown list. If this value is not set, the first attribute in the view object is preselected. This attribute will allow you to set a preferred search attribute without having to alter the attribute order in the view object just for this purpose.
- **TrackQueryPerformed** Configures the searchRegion executable for how long it should remember that a search has actually been executed. This can be set to one of two values, the default "PageFlow" or "Page." This property is closely linked to a property that the executable exposes called *queryPerformed*. This property is made available through Expression Language (for example `#{bindings.ImplicitViewCriteriaQuery.queryPerformed}`) and is used to control the iterator associated with a search so that it only refreshes when the user has actually done a search. This is used to prevent an open query being executed by the iterator every time that the page is refreshed. The *TrackQueryPerformed* property on the searchRegion executable determines the granularity at which this flag should be reset. Imagine a scenario where a page has a set of tabs, one of those tabs contains a region containing a bounded task flow, and in that task flow is a search. By setting the *TrackQueryPerformed* value to "Page," the queried state will be remembered for the lifetime of the top-level page. So as the user switches between tabs, the search will not be continually re-run, even if you are using a dynamic region and switching the task flow containing the search in and out. Setting *TrackQueryPerformed* to "PageFlow" would cause the queried flag to be reset every time the task flow is restarted, so if that task flow is embedded in a dynamic region, there is the potential for unwanted queries.

shuttleRegion Executable

The shuttle executable is not yet used by JSF-based applications. It is, however, used in ADF Swing–based applications, where it is created when a shuttle control is bound.

How Can I Control Execution in the ADF Model?

In the last two chapters, we've been discussing the results of drag-and-drop operations and the core binding types. In this section, we'll dig into how the ADF Model can be controlled and extended. As a basis for this investigation, we'll look at how code can be executed as a page is loaded. This particular task touches on all of the key aspects of controlling ADFm.

We'll start by looking at how bound operations or methods can be called when the page loads. For example, the page may need to create a record when the user navigates to the page.

Another Look at Executables

Everything that we've discussed so far in this chapter has been based around creating bindings in association with user interface elements and the iterators and other executables to support that. One thing you may have noticed when you bind a collection onto a page is that the data appears as soon as you navigate to the page. So, although you've just been concerned about creating bound fields, somehow the collection has been populated by the framework automatically.

This automatic population is a default behavior of iterators. Recall that iterators are defined in a section of the PageDef file called executables. Anything defined in the executables section will be executed by the framework when the page is loaded. A little later, we'll describe how this process is controlled.

Controlling the Execution Order

By default, the elements defined in the executables section of the PageDef file will be processed from top to bottom in the order in which they appear in the file. This means that you can control the order of execution by reordering the elements. This can be done in the Bindings panel of the page or the PageDef by dragging the executable and dropping it elsewhere in the order. The Structure window can also be used for the same purpose. An example where execution order may be important would be where a custom method is used to set up some view criteria on a view object. For example, when drilling down into a detail page, a record key from the calling page has to be passed to a method that customizes the WHERE clause used by the called page. In this case, you obviously want to set up the query correctly before executing it.

Clearly, the simple ordering of the elements can provide an amount of control. However, the framework actually offers more flexibility than this. If you inspect an iterator or invokeAction definition, you'll see several properties within the Property Inspector with refresh in the name: *Refresh, RefreshCondition,* and *RefreshAfter.* By default, none of these properties will exist in the XML code, but the Property Inspector will show the default value of *refresh* as "deferred." The dropdown list for that property will show the following options:

- **always** This option will invoke the action or refresh the collection of data every time the page or page fragment is invoked. Page invocation occurs upon the initial navigation to the page or when the user submits the page using a command item.
- **deferred** This setting indicates that the executable should only be invoked if a binding that is associated with it is used in the UI. You use this mode to prevent the refresh of an iterator when regions of the page are dynamically hidden or displayed using the *rendered* property present on all JSF components. This is the default mode and ensures that only the required data is actually processed to populate a page.

- **ifNeeded** This value allows the framework to decide when to refresh the collection or execute the method. When using ADF BC as the service layer, the framework only refreshes the collection or method when it knows changes have been applied to the ADF Model. In earlier versions of the framework, this was the default value for the *refresh* property.
- **never** This option stops the framework from calling this executable. You would use this when you're explicitly managing execution from code. (The section "How Do I Write Code Using the ADF Model?" explains this subject further.)
- **prepareModel** This value provides more precise control over when in the life cycle the executable should be invoked. (We will provide an overview of the life cycle later.) An invokeAction executable with the *refresh* property set to "prepareModel" will be invoked before any changes posted by the user have been applied to the model.
- **prepareModelIfNeeded** This selection refreshes the executable only if the framework has detected that is required. If the refresh is required, then it takes place during the prepare model phase, just as the prepareModel option does.
- **RefreshAfter** Defines that this iterator is dependent on the execution of another, as defined by the actual *RefreshAfter* property that will name the iterator on which this executable depends.
- **renderModel** Like prepareModel, this option offers more precise control over when the executable is invoked. In this case, any changes made to the ADF Model by the user will have been applied before this invokeAction executable is called.
- **renderModelIfNeeded** This value also allows the framework to decide if execution is actually required, and if that is the case, executes during renderModel.

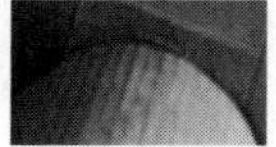

NOTE
The life cycle phases of prepareModel and renderModel are explained in more detail later in this chapter.

In most cases, when using ADF Business Components and ADF Faces, the default "deferred" is a sensible *refresh* property value for iterators.

However, with invokeAction executables, you should be more explicit about defining the phase in which the method or operation should be executed. The decision here comes down to whether the function you are calling needs access to any incoming changes that the user has just made on the screen. For example, an invokeAction executable is declared to execute an ExecuteWithParams operation. That operation passes the value of an "order ID" to populate a collection of order lines. If the user selects another order ID, refreshing the ExecuteWithParams in the prepareModel stage would pass the old ID to the ExecuteWithParams operation. Instead, if the invokeAction refresh were set to the renderModel stage, the ID selected by the user would be processed and applied; this new ID would then be used as the basis for the bind parameter (and the resulting query of order lines).

Refining Execution Further with *RefreshCondition*

The most powerful feature of a binding executable is the ability to conditionally control the execution. We've explained how both ordering, the *Refresh* property and the *RefreshAfter* property can be used to control when an executable is called or refreshed. *RefreshCondition* adds an "if" dimension to the refresh process.

In the earlier sections on action and method bindings, we discussed how expressions can be used to define arguments. Expressions can also be used to control execution using the *RefreshCondition* property. For example, here is a fragment of a PageDef that is created when an ADF Query Panel with Table is dropped onto the UI. This automatically assigns a *refreshCondition* property that ensures that the table is only populated once the user has entered some query.

```
<iterator id="AllDepartmentsIterator"
          Binds="AllDepartments"
          RangeSize="25"
          DataControl="HrServiceDataControl"
          RefreshCondition=
            "#{bindings.ImplicitViewCriteriaQuery.queryPerformed}"/>
```

The refresh condition in this case evaluates the *queryPerformed* property of the searchRegion binding, which returns a Boolean value. So in this example, if the search has not been triggered through the searchRegion, the *refreshCondition* will evaluate to "false" and the iterator will not be refreshed. This prevents the results table from needlessly doing an open query on the view object.

The conditions used in the expressions can refer to any bound data, or any valid EL for JSF. Therefore, information held in managed beans or cookies can be used to control execution.

Handling Postback One condition that deserves special mention is that of page postback. A *postback* is a request from one page to the same page. In a JSF page, all events are handled by posting back to the same page (view). Usually, you will want to carry out an operation when the user first enters the page but not repeat that operation every time a button or link is clicked. In JSF work, it is tricky to detect this situation, even though it is often essential to know, because JSF provides no simple expression that can be used from within the PageDef to distinguish the initial page display from a postback. However, ADF Faces does provide that information through the expression `adfFacesContext.initialRender`. This is often used as shown here:

```
<invokeAction id="ExecuteClearQuery"
              Binds="clearQueryCriteria"
              RefreshCondition="#{adfFacesContext.initialRender}"/>
```

This code declares that the custom method binding, "clearQueryCriteria", should only be called when `initialRender` is true, that is, when the page is initially loaded. However, there is one serious drawback with this particular expression: it is only effective in relation to whole pages and is not applicable for page fragments. Given that many ADF applications use a style of user interface that is assembled from page fragments running inside regions, this expression cannot be used to effectively control execution within those regions. For page fragments, the recommended approach, as mentioned earlier in this chapter, is to explicitly invoke the required code using a methodAction in the task flow that is hosting the page fragment.

How Can I Override and Add to the ADF Model Life Cycle?

We've shown how executables in the PageDef file can be used to automatically invoke operations and custom methods exposed by the business service. However, sometimes you need to carry out work that does not involve the ADF Model. An example of this is setting a cookie after a login to remember the name of the user who last logged in to the system. This can be achieved by using the extension mechanisms that ADFm supplies for creating a customized life cycle for the page.

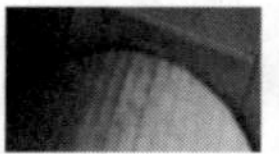

NOTE
The example given here is kept very basic to give an idea of the required code. However, the ability to override and customize the ADFm life cycle is extremely powerful, and you will use this ability more and more as you become more proficient at building ADF applications.

The ADFm Life Cycle

As we've seen with the various refresh values for an executable, preparing the bindings for a page proceeds through a fixed set of steps—the *ADFm life cycle*. This life cycle is an abstraction mechanism that allows the same sequence of events to take place no matter what UI technology is used. The ADFm life cycle corresponds quite closely to the JSF page life cycle, as shown in Figure 15-1. Figure 15-1 also shows how the ADFm life cycle methods map to the refresh options used by executables.

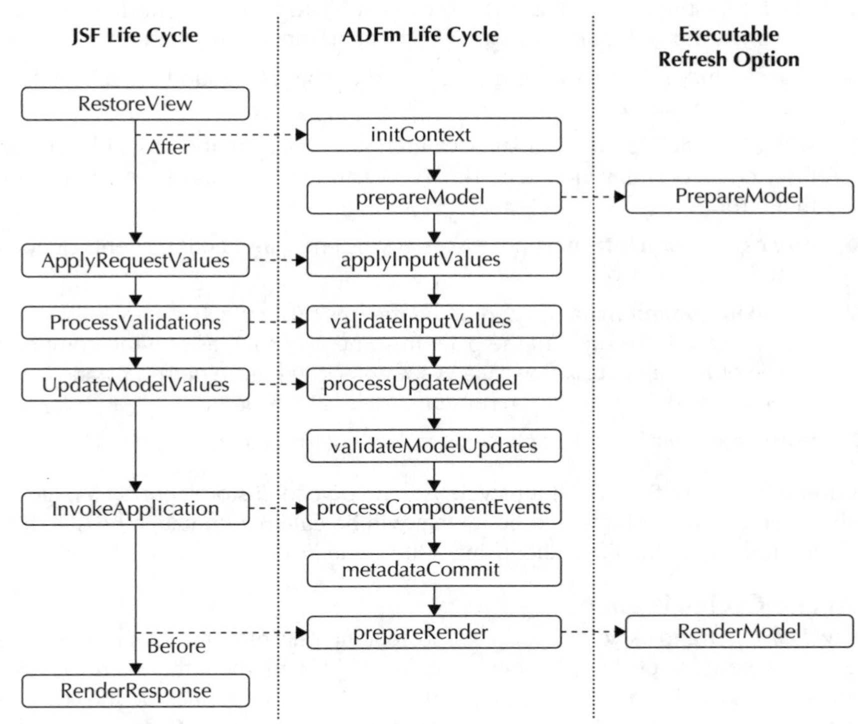

FIGURE 15-1. *The ADF Model life cycle in relation to the JSF life cycle and executable refresh options*

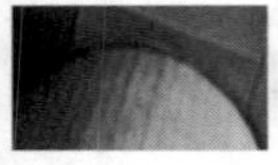

NOTE
Figure 15-1 shows the life cycle used specifically during a postback to a page. This life cycle is truncated when a page is initially loaded, because there are no changes to apply from user input. In this case, a shortened version of the ADFm life cycle also runs with the initContext, prepareModel, and prepareRender squeezed before the RenderResponse phase in the JSF life cycle.

In Figure 15-1, the ADFm life cycle is shown in the context of the JSF life cycle that we covered in Chapter 10. The dashed lines show at which point each of the ADFm life cycle methods is executed in relation to the JSF life cycle. Likewise, the Executable Refresh Option column shows the points which correspond to the *refresh* property values on executables (prepareModel, prepareRender) that we discussed earlier. The phases shown have the following functions:

- **initContext** sets up the life cycle, working out what PageDefs to load.
- **prepareModel** creates the bindings object and adds it to the HTTP request. Parameters are also evaluated at this point. (We explain parameters later in the chapter.)
- **applyInputValues** processes the values posted from the page and builds up an internal list of bindings to update and methods to execute as required.
- **validateInputValues** applies the client-side validators to the list of updates presented by the applyInputValues phase. These validators are defined as nested `f:validator` and `af:convertNumber` components within an input component.
- **processUpdateModel** sends the validated changes to bound objects to the model layer (ADF BC in this case).
- **validateModelUpdates** manages validation errors from the Model layer. For example, an inserted record may violate a primary key constraint. This phase will capture and report that error.
- **processComponentEvents** processes any listeners and action events queued up from the applyInputValues phase.
- **metadataCommit** manages part of the runtime customization capabilities of the framework. If the user has customized the page in some way such as moving components on the screen or adding in task flows via WebCenter, then those personalizations to the screen are saved away to the metadata repository (MDS) at this point.
- **prepareRender** is the last phase to execute before the page is displayed.

A useful feature of the ADFm life cycle is that you can customize it on a page-by-page basis. This allows you to add extra functionality that will be called automatically. ADFm offers two ways to add functionality to the life cycle: using a life cycle listener and using a custom page controller.

ADFm Life Cycle Listeners

A *life cycle listener* allows you to add code to specific phases of the ADFm life cycle without changing the basic life cycle. A life cycle listener must implement the interface `oracle.adf.controller.v2.lifecycle.PagePhaseListener`. This interface defines two methods—`beforePhase()` and `afterPhase()`—which the life cycle will automatically call before and after each phase, respectively. You can see from Figure 15-1 that you could define code to execute after the prepareRender phase. This code would look something like this:

```
public class CookieSettingListener implements PagePhaseListener
{
  public void beforePhase(PagePhaseEvent event) { }

  public void afterPhase(PagePhaseEvent event)
  {
    if (event.getPhaseId() == Lifecycle.PREPARE_RENDER_ID)
    {
      setCookie();
    }
  }
}
```

Our intention is to call the `setCookie()` method (implementation not shown) in the afterPhase handler for the prepareRender phase in the life cycle, that is, just before the page is displayed to the end user. In this example, no events fire in the beforePhase handler, so the implementation is empty. The standard life cycle process will still occur before the phase; this empty method just fulfills the requirement that methods defined in an interface must be implemented in the class built from the interface. Each of these methods can handle events from each phase of the life cycle. When the framework calls the methods in this class at the appropriate time in the life cycle, it passes in a `PagePhaseEvent` object that represents the phase of the life cycle. As shown in the sample code, this `PagePhaseEvent` object offers a `getPhaseId()` method that indicates the life cycle phase that called the method (in this example, prepareRender).

NOTE

If you attach a phase listener to a particular page life cycle, you may observe that there are more events than you would expect. You can use the `event.getDebugValue()` *method to get the name of the event being processed for reference. When you do so, you will see a series of events labeled with the prefix "jsf." These events directly correspond to the underlying JSF life cycle shown in Figure 15-1. Notice that there are no constants in the* `oracle.adf.controller.v2.lifecycle.Lifecycle` *class for these JSF life cycle events. For any listeners that you write, stick to the main ADFm life cycle events.*

The listener must be attached to the page life cycle so that the life cycle knows to raise the events. This attachment can occur in one of two places. The simplest place is to define the attachment in the PageDef file for the page that needs the customized life cycle. The top-level element of the PageDef file is the `<PageDefinition>` element. This element offers a *ControllerClass* property, in which you would indicate the custom listener class to use:

```
<PageDefinition
  xmlns="http://xmlns.oracle.com/adfm/uimodel"
  version="11.1.1.n.n"
  id="homePageDef"
  Package="com.tuhra.view.PageDefs"
  ControllerClass="com.tuhra.view.framework.CookieSettingListener">
```

You would add this reference to any PageDef files that need the same customization. If, however, it turns out that you need this listener for every page, it makes sense to register a global listener.

This is accomplished by defining a setting in the file *adf-settings.xml* in the ViewController project's src/META-INF directory:

```
<?xml version="1.0" encoding="windows-1252" ?>
<adf-config xmlns="http://xmlns.oracle.com/adf/config">
  <adfc-controller-config
          xmlns="http://xmlns.oracle.com/adf/controller/config">
    <lifecycle>
      <phase-listener>
        <listener-id>TUHRAPagePhaseListener</listener-id>
        <class>tuhra.view.framework.TUHRAPagePhaseListener</class>
      </phase-listener>
    </lifecycle>
  </adfc-controller-config>
</adf-config>
```

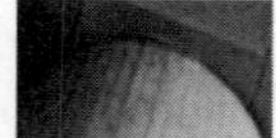

CAUTION
In the current release of JDeveloper 11g adf-settings.xml has limited design-time support, and so you will need to manually create the file as an XML file from the New Gallery. Some help is available in the ADF online documentation section: A5. Configuration in adf-settings .xml in the JDeveloper documentation set book Web User Interface Developer's Guide for Oracle Application Development Framework 11g *(available through the JDeveloper Help option).*

Using the adf-settings.xml mechanism, you can also register multiple listeners if required.

Custom ADFm Page Controller The listener approach just described is probably sufficient for most purposes. However, it is also possible to customize the ADFm life cycle by creating a custom page controller subclass from `oracle.adf.controller.v2.lifecycle.PageController`. A custom page controller that emulates the preceding life cycle listener example would look like this:

```
public class HomeSetup extends PageController
{
  public void prepareRender(LifecycleContext context)
  {
    super.prepareRender(context);
    setCookie();
  }
}
```

In this case, the subclass of the PageController only overrides one method—the `prepareRender()` method. The first line of `prepareRender()` calls the superclass' `prepareRender()` method so that the normal action for this phase occurs. Then, the custom code calls the cookie setting method (again implementation not shown). The `LifecycleContext` object that is passed into this method provides access to the HTTP request and response, which is usually enough external information for most purposes. As you might expect, if you want code to execute before the life cycle phase, you would place this code before the call to the superclass' method.

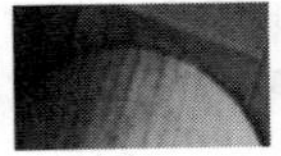

CAUTION
Be sure to include the call to the superclass code when you are replacing the life cycle phase. Otherwise, the normal life cycle code will not be called.

You can consult the Javadoc for that class for details about the methods and objects you will use when replacing the page controller. (Press ALT-SHIFT-MINUS to display the Go To Javadoc dialog, which will help you to locate the Javadoc.) In most cases, you will override the `prepareRender()` method if you want to execute code before the page renders.

You register a custom page controller using the same *ControllerClass* attribute in the PageDefinition element of the PageDef file. The framework will understand by the type of code if the class that you specify in this attribute is a listener (implementation of `PagePhaseListener`) or a custom page controller (subclass of `PageController`).

Customizing Error Handling

Finally, while we are on the subject of extending core parts of the ADFm framework, error handling is worth a mention. The binding layer has a mechanism for delivering error messages such as validation errors back to the page. In most circumstances this mechanism does a good job of taking the message defined in the business component layer and delivering it cleanly to the field that raised the error. Errors raised from the database, however, may have embedded ORA codes and need cleaning up in some fashion before presenting. To manage this process, developers have the ability to plug in a custom error handling class. This custom class needs to extend `oracle.adf.model.binding.DCErrrorHandlerImpl` and should implement the method `reportException(DCBindingContainer formBnd, Exception ex)`. This reportException method is called by the framework to turn an exception into a polished message for display.

A typical stub for a custom error handler class will look like the following code snippet. Note the two constructors for this class, which are required:

```
public class TuhraCustomErrors extends DCErrorHandlerImpl {
  public TuhraCustomErrors() {
    this(true);
  }

  public TuhraCustomErrors(boolean setToThrow) {
    super(setToThrow);
  }

  @Override
  public void reportException(DCBindingContainer formBnd, Exception ex) {
    //Errors can be suppressed here
    super.reportException(formBnd, ex);
  }
  public String getDisplayMessage(BindingContext ctx, Exception th) {
    String cleanMsg = super.getDisplayMessage(ctx,th);
    //Here each exception is stripped of any JBO codes by the superclass
    //and returned as a plain String. You can do further parsing
    //and change the message again here if required.
    return cleanMsg;
  }
}
```

Each exception that is raised and then processed by the framework and passed through the `reportException()` method in the custom error handler class. Here the developer can choose to suppress it if required, or, assuming that the message is desirable, it is cleaned up by the `getDisplayMessage()` method. The `getDisplayMessage()` method removes any framework chrome from the message and just returns the error string defined by the developer. If required, you can do some further work in this method to alter or clean up the message.

Configuring the Framework to Use a Custom Error Handler Once an error handler is defined, it is registered in the DataBindings.cpx file as an attribute called *ErrorHandlerClass* of the top-level `<Application>` element. This value can be set directly in the XML source view of the .cpx file, or by selecting the DataBindings node for the file in the Structure window and using the Property Inspector. Once set, the XML will look something like this:

```
<Application xmlns="http://xmlns.oracle.com/adfm/application"
             version="11.1.1.n.n"
             id="DataBindings"
             SeparateXMLFiles="false"
             Package="com.tuhra.view"
             ClientType="Generic"
             ErrorHandlerClass="com.tuhra.view.TuhraCustomErrors">
```

This error handler will then apply to the entire application. In the future, it is likely that the registration of the error handler will also be possible through the adf-settings.xml file so as to be consistent with the definition of custom life cycle.

What Are Parameters?

Parameters are another set of elements that can appear in the PageDef file. They provide a sort of public API for a PageDef. A common use case for these PageDef parameters is when a value needs to be passed to a method in the PageDef file as an argument. For example, a page that displays information for a given stock ticker symbol could define the stock symbol as a PageDef file parameter. The method binding would then refer to the PageDef parameter directly using the syntax `#{bindings.parameterName}`. Unlike variables, PageDef parameters can be accessed directly in EL without having to go through an attribute binding.

Populating PageDef Parameters

PageDef parameters have their own section at the top of the Bindings panel of the PageDef file. They are not shown in the normal Bindings panel that is shown as one of the editors for the page, so you will need to click the hyperlink in that panel to bring up the associated PageDef. As usual, pressing the Add (green plus "+") button in that section adds a new PageDef parameter to the list. Each PageDef parameter can be set to a hard-coded value or EL expression. A common approach is to map the value of the PageDef parameter to the EL expression, which will insert, for example, a URL parameter into the value. Here is an example:

```
<parameter id="status"
           value="${param.status}"/>
```

If the page was called with a URL, such as "http://tuhra.com/hr/mypage.jsp?status=open," the status parameter in the PageDef file would evaluate to "open."

URL parameters are coded into the URL created from a command link or command button using the `f:param` tag nested inside those items. Alternatively, these parameters may be defined in a hard-coded URL that identifies a resource external to an application. For example, you might generate an email as part of your application and require the user to click a link within the email to carry out some action. The combination of URL parameters and parameters within the PageDef file can then be used to set the data context correctly for the page being loaded.

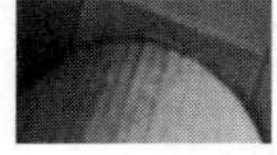

CAUTION
URL parameters are not a way to routinely pass context information around the application. JSF-managed beans and task flow parameters provide better ways to manage such tasks. Also consider the bookmarking capabilities of a ADFc View activity as discussed in Chapter 11.

Advanced PageDef Parameter Properties

Any expressions in PageDef parameters are usually evaluated every time the page is refreshed; however, three refresh possibilities are offered:

- **eachUse** The parameter EL is re-evaluated every time that it is referenced.
- **firstUse** The parameter EL is evaluated the first time that it is referenced, and then this cached value is used unchanged for any subsequent references.
- **inPrepareModel** The evaluation of the parameter EL is carried out at the start of the prepareModel phase and will be fixed at that value for the remainder of the life cycle. Thus this option is similar to *firstUse,* except that the time of evaluation is at the very start of the life cycle rather than at the point in time that the parameter is actually used (which may be later on).

Furthermore, extra control can be exercised over PageDef parameters. The *readonly* attribute is self-explanatory; the *option* attribute, however, is a little more involved. It has three possible values, which also mirror the options for task flow parameters, which are discussed in Chapter 11:

- **Final** Indicates that the PageDef parameter must be used as defined; essentially, it cannot be passed in to the binding container and is just used as a default value.
- **Optional** The PageDef parameter is not required to be passed in.
- **Required** The PageDef parameter must be passed to the binding container; an error will be raised if it is not supplied.

The reality is that 99 percent of the time developers will stick to the defaults here. Using these advanced options is really only going to be relevant if you are programmatically creating the binding container. Use task flows as a way of parameterizing pages in preference.

What Are Contextual Events?

Before we move on to cover programmatic interaction with the binding layer, there is one further advanced ADFm feature to discuss: contextual events. Contextual events provide a messaging mechanism between binding containers and can be useful in an application that uses multiple regions that need to be coordinated. In some circumstances this can be achieved using parameterized task flows and also the Task Flow Parent Action (refer to Chapter 11), or of course, when using a shared data control for the task flow context can be shared in that way. However, there are cases—where task flows are peers, for example—where messages need to be sent, and restarting the flows or sharing the data control is not an option. This is where contextual events fit in; they provide a publish and subscribe mechanism for binding containers to raise and listen for application-wide events.

A Worked Example of Contextual Events

For the purposes of illustration, we will work through a small example of contextual events to illustrate how they are used. The scenario we'll use is very simple, using the standard DEPARTMENTS and EMPLOYEES tables in a master-detail relationship from the HR schema. Imagine a page that contains a simple output text item and a task flow inside a region. The output text item is bound to a method on the Departments view object that calculates the sum of all of the employees within the currently selected department:

```
public Number departmentSalaryTotal(){
  Number totsal = new Number(0);
  //Get the current department
  DepartmentsViewRowImpl row = (DepartmentsViewRowImpl)this.getCurrentRow();

  //Get the associated list of employees in that department
  RowIterator rowSet = row.getEmployeesView();
  //loop through the employees in this department and add up SAL
  while (rowSet.hasNext()){
    EmployeesViewRowImpl empRow = (EmployeesViewRowImpl)rowSet.next();
    totsal = totsal.add(empRow.getSalary());
  }
  return totsal;
}
```

The task flow embedded in the page contains a tabular list of departments from which the user can select a particular department and then an edit form for editing employees within that department. The page looks like this illustration.

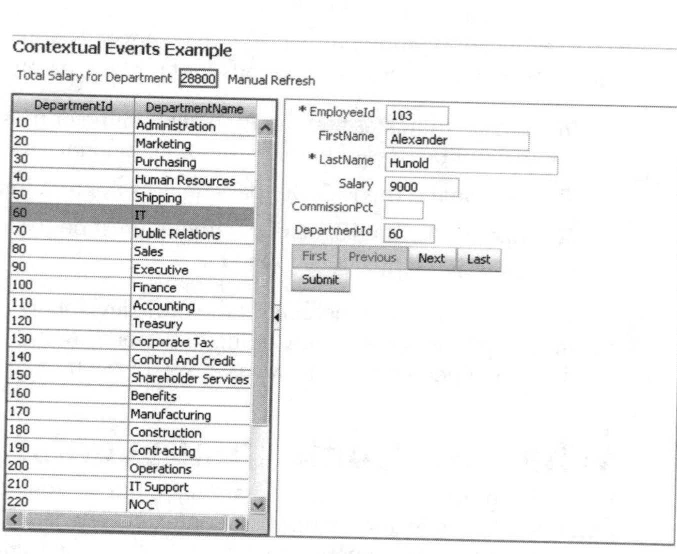

You can see from this scenario that there are two possible events that will require the salary sum field to be updated: The user may switch to a different department or, within a department, may change a salary for an employee and submit. The next section describes the simpler case of triggering an update when the Salary field is changed.

Event Producers

An *event producer* is a reference to a binding that will raise a contextual event. An example of this might be an action binding where you want to raise the event as well as carrying out the action, or an attribute binding where you want to raise an event when the value has been changed.

Registering an event producer is relatively simple, although all of the work has to be done by editing the PageDef XML directly or by using the combination of the Structure window and the Property Inspector. Here are the steps for raising an event when the Salary attribute value is changed:

1. **Open the producer's binding editor or PageDef file** Both views will give you access to create the event entries.
2. **Locate the attribute binding in the Structure window** In this case we want to raise the event when the Salary is changed.
3. **Insert a child for events** On the Salary attribute select **Insert inside Salary | Contextual Event | events** from the right-click menu.
4. **Insert the event** On the new events node, select **Insert inside events | event** from the right-click menu.
5. **Select the new event** Then define a name for the event, for example *salaryChangeEvent*. Notice at this stage that there is a second attribute shown in the Property Inspector for the event called *attribute*. This property is used to qualify the event so that it is only raised when that named attribute (for example DepartmentName) in the binding has been changed.

Using the Structure window with the preceding steps results in a binding definition something like this:

```
<attributeValues IterBinding="EmployeesView3Iterator" id="Salary">
  <events xmlns="http://xmlns.oracle.com/adfm/contextualEvent">
    <event name="salaryChangeEvent"/>
  </events>
  <AttrNames>
    <Item Value="Salary"/>
  </AttrNames>
</attributeValues>
```

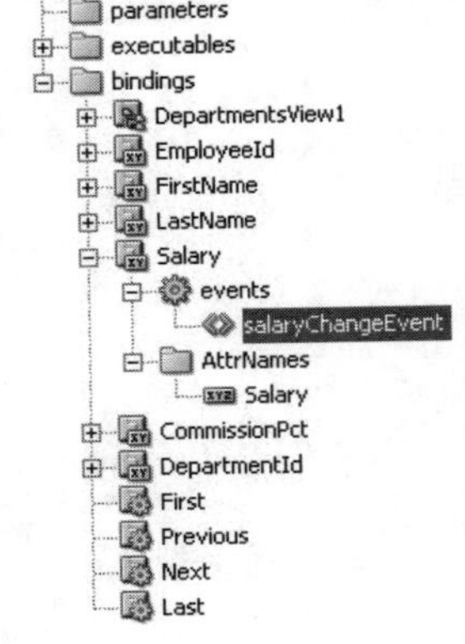

The Structure window will look like this screen shot.

If an event is associated with a method binding that has a return value, this value is automatically included in the event as a payload and will be accessible to consumers using the EL syntax `#{payload}`.

Event Consumers

An *event consumer* refers to an action binding or executable that you want to subscribe to and have react in some way to an incoming event.

Defining handlers, or consumers, for events is also accomplished from the PageDef file. Subscriptions are registered in the PageDef file of the View activity that wishes to consume the event. In this example you want the event to call the departmentSalaryTotal action binding in the main page.

1. **Open the consumer's binding editor or PageDef file** In this case, the consuming event is on the main page.

2. **Locate the root PageDef node in the Structure window** This will be labeled with the name of the PageDef, for example, mainPageDef.
3. **Open the Event Map editor** Use the right-click menu on the PageDef root node.
4. **Add an event** Use the "Add a New Event Entry" (green plus "+") button. This will display the Add New EventMap Entry dialog, which provides lists of all of the valid event producers and the events they raise, plus the valid consumer methods. Notice that using this dialog (shown here), you can choose consumer methods from either the page PageDef or the PageDef of any of the regions embedded within the page.

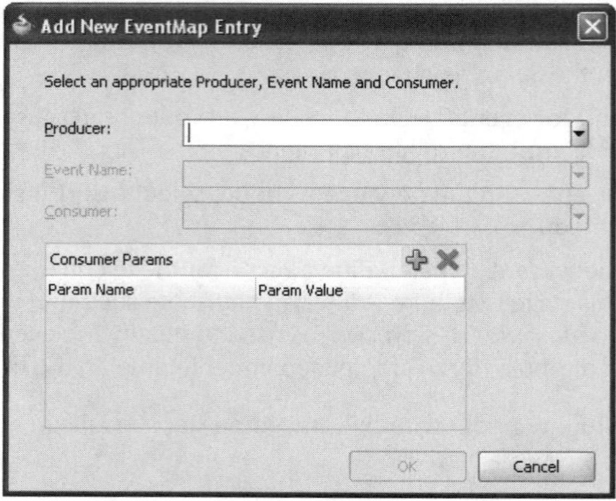

Once filled in, this dialog looks like this:

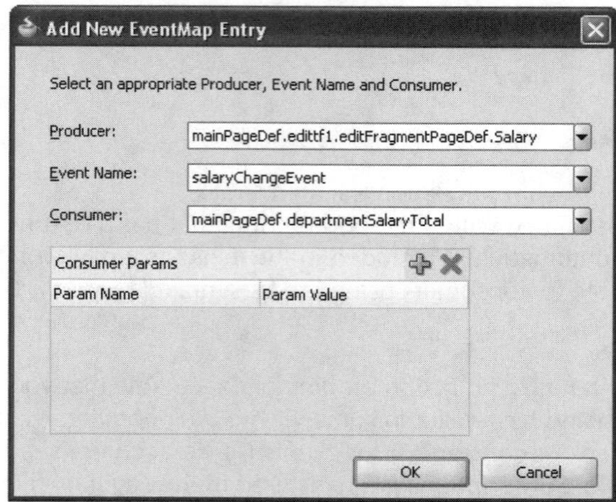

More Advanced Use of Contextual Events In this simple worked example you have just wired an attribute binding in one PageDef to an action binding in another. In most situations, however, the contextual event will need to execute UI layer code as well as bound methods. In order to achieve this, you need to create a Java class with a suitable method that manages the UI layer interaction. You then need to create a bean data control from this Java class and add an action binding to the bean data control in the consumer PageDef. You will then be able to subscribe this method to the event so that the contextual event mechanism can trigger it. For more information on this and other advanced features such as implementing your own event dispatchers, you can consult the JDeveloper online help. This topic is explained in section 27.6 ("Creating Contextual Events") of the *Fusion Developer's Guide for ADF.*

How Can I Write Code Using the ADF Model?

Much of what needs to be achieved in an ADF application can be handled declaratively through task flows, the various bindings, and use of Expression Language in those binding definitions, as we have already discussed. For example, conditionally executing a method exposed by an application module or carrying out a task in addition to a bound operation on a button click can all be handled without having to replace the default invocation mechanism. However, it is likely that you will need to write code that will interact with the bindings, either in the form of accessing bound data values or manually executing operations and methods. A example of this might be when you want to combine two or more data-bound method calls into a single button action.

Access to Data and Methods

When programming with JSF, it is possible to access any managed bean using Expression Language, both in the PageDef file and also from within the code. This maintains a loose coupling between the page, its associated code, and any ADF Model objects that it uses.

Therefore, you can use standard JSF Expression Language to access a bound data value using something like this in a page-backing bean (line numbers added):

```
01:  FacesContext ctx = FacesContext.getCurrentInstance();
02:  ELContext ectx =ctx.getELContext();
03:  Application app = ctx.getApplication();
04:  ExpressionFactory factory = app.getExpressionFactory();
05:  ValueExpression ve =
       factory.createValueExpression(ectx,
                                   "#{bindings.DepartmentName.inputValue}",
                                   java.lang.String);
06:  String dname = ve.getValue(ectx);
```

In JSF terms, this code translates an EL expression into an actual object that can be called from Java.

- **Line 01** obtains the `FacesContext` object.
- **Line 02** obtains the `ELContext` for JSF, which will be needed to help resolve the expression.
- **Line 03** obtains a reference to the JSF Application that is needed to locate the EL resolver factory.
- **Line 04** shows the `Application` object being used to obtain the current ExpressionFactory.

- **Line 05** uses the `ExpressionFactory` to parse the EL String `#{bindings.DepartmentName.inputValue}` to create a ValueExpression object. Note that the expected class of the resolved expression (in this case a String), is passed to this method. The Factory will attempt to coerce the value to this type and will throw an exception (`javax.faces.el.EvaluationException`) if unable to do so. If this argument is set to null, then the value will be returned as a plain Java object.
- **Line 06** calls `getValue()` on the ValueExpression to retrieve the actual value. This object also supports a `getType()` call if you need to check the class of the payload.

You have seen the expression `#{bindings.DepartmentName.inputValue}` already, in the expressions that JDeveloper generates for you when dragging and dropping from the Data Controls panel. These six lines of code are one of the programmatic ways to obtain the same data.

More Direct Access to the Bindings

When you implement a JSF page that contains ADF bindings and you double click a bound command button or command link to create some code, the Bind Action Property dialog will appear, as shown here.

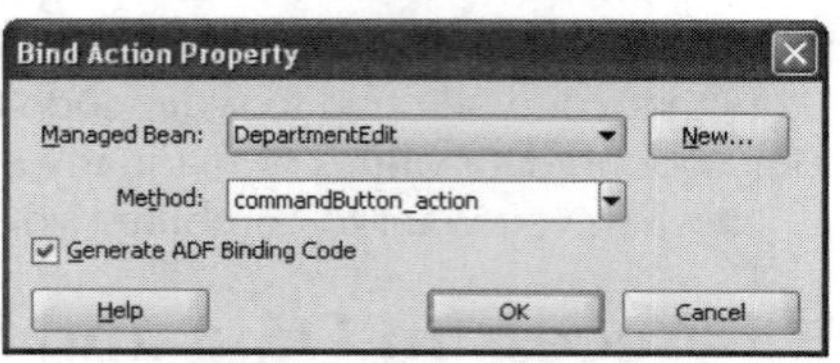

Selecting the *Generate ADF Binding Code* checkbox will set up shortcut access to your data bindings. The backing bean for the page will gain a new method, `getBindings()`. This generated `getBindings()` method contains code to programmatically obtain the binding container for use inside the bean. The end result is that you will now have access to the binding object directly in Java without having to use the expression-resolving facilities provided by the `ExpressionFactory` as shown in the preceding code example. However, the previous version holds true for any EL expression, not just bindings, so it is a useful code snippet to have in your toolbox.

Manually Defining the Bindings Object JDeveloper will only show the Bind Action Property dialog if you attempt to override an existing command component that is bound to a custom method or operation by double clicking the component in the visual editor or selecting **Create Method Binding for Action** from the right-click menu on the component.

In the cases where JDeveloper has not created a managed bean for you automatically, you may still want access to the binding context. In this situation, you need to use the following steps to manually configure the managed bean:

1. Add an Import the `oracle.binding.BindingContainer` interface into the bean.
2. Create a `getBindings()` method with a return type of `BindingContainer` and add the following code:

```
public BindingContainer getBindings() {
  return BindingContext.getCurrent().getCurrentBindingsEntry();
}
```

These steps are identical for any managed bean that needs to access bindings information. In most cases you would create this in a shared bean that all of your other managed beans will subclass.

Getting and Setting Attribute Values Using getBindings()

The following code uses the bindings object that was just created to access the department name:

```
AttributeBinding deptBinding=
  (AttributeBinding)getBindings().getControlBinding("DepartmentName");
String departmentName = (String)deptBinding.getInputValue();
```

This code is a little simpler than the code shown earlier, although with this code, we need to cast the `ControlBinding` returned by the `getControlBinding()` to an `AttributeBinding`.

This technique gives you access to all properties of the attribute binding, the most important of which is the underlying value, accessed from the `inputValue` attribute using the `getInputValue()` method.

You can similarly set the values of attributes using the `setInputValue()` method. Here is an example:

```
AttributeBinding deptBinding =
     (AttributeBinding)getBindings().getControlBinding("DepartmentName");
deptBinding.setInputValue("Special Projects");
```

Refreshing the UI When you change the value of a bound attribute in code, you are directly changing the Model layer. For output items, such as `af:outputText`, the new value that you've defined will be displayed (as you would expect) when the page or fragment is next rendered. However, for input items, you do not see the value when the page is next rendered, because JSF input components maintain their own version of the bound value and will continue to display that version. For input items to show the changed data immediately, you have to cause them to refresh from the model.

To cause this value refresh, you need to have a reference to the item in the page's backing bean so that you can call methods on the component. If you elected not to have JDeveloper create and manage a backing bean for you, you can create the required class file object and reference to it by selecting the component in the visual editor and clicking the arrow next to the *Binding* property in the Property Inspector. Clicking this arrow displays a dropdown list containing the option "Edit"; selecting this then displays a dialog, which allows you to select an existing managed bean to use as the backing bean or to create one if necessary. The dialog also allows you to specify a name for the component in that bean.

After you click OK in this dialog, JDeveloper will create a component variable in the page-backing bean using the name you have specified and of the appropriate type based on the selected component in the UI. It also generates getter and setter methods for that component, along with the binding reference in the JSF page to the component in the backing bean.

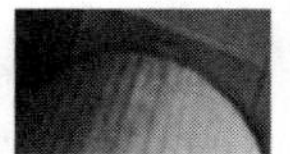

CAUTION
The binding *property supported by JSF components has nothing to do with the bindings object that we've been discussing in this chapter. Binding in this context means the binding of a component definition in the UI to a component reference in the page backing bean. This component reference can then be used to programmatically change the UI object. For example, you can set the* rendered *property from code to display or hide the component.*

Once you have created a reference to the object that represents the input field, you can call its `resetValue()` method to force it to refresh its internal state from the new model value. So to extend our earlier example with the DepartmentName:

```
AttributeBinding deptBinding =
     (AttributeBinding)getBindings().getControlBinding("DepartmentName");
deptBinding.setInputValue("Special Projects");
this.getDepartmentNameField().resetValue();
```

Accessing PageDef File Parameters

You can access parameters directly from the binding context in your managed beans obtained through the `getBindings()` method. The only twist here is that you need to cast the binding up to an `oracle.adf.model.DCBindingContainer` (see the sidebar "Which Binding Container Do I Use?"), which supports the `findParameter()` method. An example follows:

```
DCBindingContainer dcBindings = (DCBindingContainer)getBindings();
DCParameter param = dcBindings().findParameter("deptno");
String paramValue = (String)param.getValue();
```

Note that the exact return type of `param.getValue()` depends on what is stored in the parameter. Unlike when working with variables, you do not declare the type of parameters up front, so if you map an object into a parameter using EL, the type of the parameter will be the type of that object; it is your responsibility to cast the return from `getValue()` correctly.

> **Which Binding Container Do I Use?**
>
> When you are writing code using these binding classes, you may notice that the import insight feature displays two alternatives for many of the classes. For example, `oracle.adf.model.BindingContainer` and `oracle.binding.BindingContainer`.
>
> The classes in the `oracle.binding` package make up the generic data-binding APIs. The classes in the `oracle.adf.model` package extend the generic classes and add extra functionality to support some of the additional features found in ADF. In most cases, it is best to use the `oracle.binding.*` versions; if you need the extra functionality of the ADF-specific types, you can cast as required. The `oracle.binding.BindingContainer` is an interface, and DCBindingContainer is a concrete implementation of it. You would generally code to the interface unless you need a capability only found in the specific implementation, such as `findParameter()` in DCBindingContainer.

Executing Methods and Operations

Now that you have mastered basic access to get and set bound attributes, what about calling methods? This is similar, and it uses the same `getBindings()` method as a starting point. The method or operation is retrieved into an `OperationBinding` object using a lookup by name, and then its `execute()` method is called, as shown here for the First operation:

```
BindingContainer bindings = getBindings();
OperationBinding operationBinding =
```

```
    bindings.getOperationBinding("First");
Object result = operationBinding.execute();
```

When you choose to override a method call by double clicking a command item bound to a method, the previously shown code will be generated into the backing bean for you. Of course, a single command button could be coded to call multiple operations, looking each up by name and executing as required.

Method Results You will note in the example used to show how to execute an operation that the `execute()` call returns an `Object` type. If the method that you are calling returns a value, you will need to cast the object to the correct type. If the method or operation you are calling does not return a value, you can ignore this value.

Checking for Errors Once an operation binding has been executed, you can inspect the errors collection that it supports to see if any problems occurred. The code for this is identical for any operation binding and will generally take the form of an if statement to check for errors using the `isEmpty()` method of the List interface API:

```
if (!operationBinding.getErrors().isEmpty()) {
  //handle the error list here
  List<Throwable> errors = operationBinding.getErrors();
  for (Throwable error:errors){
    //Handle the error in some way
    System.out.println(error.getMessage());
  }
}
```

Note here how the error list contains `java.lang.Throwable` objects; you can consult the general Javadoc for the methods and attributes supported by this object type.

Setting Method Arguments In many cases, a method that is called programmatically will have its arguments set in the PageDef file, either as bindings to input fields or as EL expressions. However, in some cases, you will want to explicitly set the argument values from code.

You could, of course, add the data into the relevant PageDef file variables using the methods we just discussed, but there is a simpler way. The version of the `OperationBinding` within the `oracle.adf.model` package exposes a `getParamsMap()` method that returns a `java.util.Map`, allowing you to set the values of arguments using the `put()` method of the `Map` interface. Here is an example that sets an argument (`searchTerm`) on a method called `findDepartmentManagerId()`:

```
OperationBinding operationBinding =
    getBindings().getOperationBinding("findDepartmentManagerId");
Map params = operationBinding.getParamsMap();
params.put("searchTerm","Sales");
Number deptManager = operationBinding.execute();
```

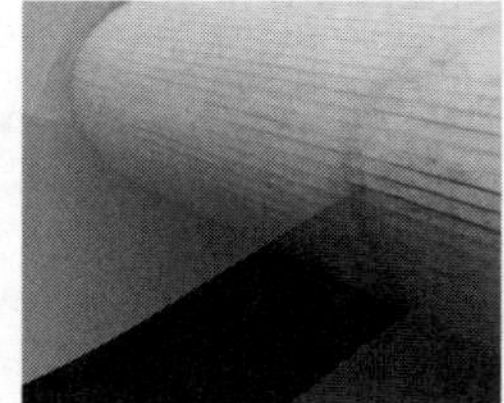

PART V

Developing the Sample Application

We learn by example and by direct experience
because there are real limits
to the adequacy of verbal instruction.

—Malcolm Gladwell (1963–)
Blink: The Power of Thinking Without Thinking

CHAPTER 16

Application Design Principles and Sample Application Overview

If you want to build a ship,
don't drum up people to collect wood
and don't assign them tasks and work,
but rather teach them to long for the endless immensity of the sea.

—Antoine de Saint-Exupéry (1900–1944)

This part of the book takes you out of all the theory and background of the preceding chapters into the useful practical work of building something with the Fusion framework. The quote at the head of this chapter is very apt in this case. We find much of our application design driven not by cold hard logic or a rigid design palette, but rather by the whims of our customers and users. Much of the skill that you will acquire as you become proficient with Fusion technologies will be the bending of the framework to your needs. Fortunately ADF is set up for this, and over the next few chapters we'll take you through creating a sample application that should put you in good stead for your own development work.

Chapters 16 through 22 build a simple application that interacts with the database called TUHRA. TUHRA is an acronym for "The Ultimate Human Resources Application," (pronounced "too-rah") and this is the second book that uses it as an example—therefore, we formally call this application "TUHRA2" although we refer to it in various places just as "THURA."

Although this is necessarily a small sample with only a handful of pages, we've packed a lot of key features into it. The application illustrates many of the key features and principles of Fusion application design.

TUHRA2 uses the familiar Oracle HR sample schema with a few twists to make the application a little more realistic. Chapter 16 discusses general design principles, team considerations and then specific design used for the TUHRA2 application. Chapter 17 covers the setup work that you'll need on the database and manages the creation of the initial workspace. Chapters 18-20 progressively add functionality to the application with search and edit screens. Chapter 21 then layers security onto the application and finally Chapter 22 explains how to deploy the completed application onto an application server.

For this part of the book it is very important that you follow the practices in order. Just like a real application some of the later stages of the practices end up having to revise design decisions made earlier on. The practices in Part V also assume that you have read the material that was introduced in the first four parts of the book and builds upon that knowledge, adding new concepts and techniques along the way.

The first chapter in this part of the book is all about the things you need to think about before launching into the development of an application. It is based around the following questions:

- **What is the design process for a Fusion application?**
- **What best practice should be adopted?**
- **What is the design of the sample application?**
- **What do I have to think about before starting?**

The chapter also includes a mini-practice on setting up your own application templates which you don't need to carry out in order to build the main THURA2 application, but which, nevertheless is an important exercise to go through.

What Is the Design Process for a Fusion Application?

The goal of system design is to outline details of system components that will fulfill requirements of the business. Business requirements are implemented in three different but integrated areas within an overall system design:

- **Database design** The data model determines what data structures (tables and views) you will need to create in the database. Some business rules and requirements derived from requirements analysis can be implemented as database design elements. For example, the system could require datatypes, sizes, and NOT NULL characteristics for specific columns. It could also require foreign key constraints. All of these would be implemented in the database.
- **Service design** As we discussed in Chapter 1, Fusion-based applications live in a world of service composition and orchestration. Part of the design of any application should begin with an examination of the high-level service interfaces. There is necessarily an overlap between this service design and the more UI-focused application design.
- **Application design** The functional process model helps form the application design. The application design consists of the user interface and back-end database (or application server) code to enforce business rules that implement the business requirements. Application design includes defining standard layout features that are common to all pages. It also includes *process flow*—the steps the user and system follow to complete a business function. These definitions translate to the elements available on the page as well as the functional responsibility of each page.

Design tools can assist with the process of capturing business requirements into service, database, and application definitions that you can use to build the application.

System Design Tools and the SDLC

The term "system design" evokes thoughts of a *system development life cycle (SDLC)*—a process by which system development is divided into phases, for example, Strategy, Analysis, Design, Development, and Deployment (Implementation). SDLCs guide the system through these phases in some order, such as sequential (known as a *waterfall approach*), iterative (as with Rapid Application Development, or RAD, approaches), or "middle out" (Development at the same time as analysis and design).

Various software tools can support the SDLC. In the past, *computer-aided software engineering (CASE)* software tools assisted the process by providing a repository for all information about the system's data and processes, and by generating some front-end and database code. Although JDeveloper contains a number of UML (Unified Modeling Language) diagramming tools that can be used for analysis and design, Oracle Designer currently still holds the niche as the full-system life cycle tool for the Oracle product line.

Oracle Designer

Oracle Designer, once categorized as a Computer Aided Software Engineering (CASE) tool, stores information about processes and data throughout an SDLC; it can generate application code in Oracle Forms, Oracle Reports, Web PL/SQL, and Visual Basic styles, as well as database DDL (Data Definition Language) code for any kind of Oracle database object, such as a table, view,

PL/SQL package, or sequence. Oracle Designer is still available, and Oracle still supports it. Oracle Designer still offers the most complete support for Oracle database objects.

Although Oracle Designer can store information and generate code for Java code stored in the database, it cannot generate front-end Java EE code or Business Tier code, such as ADF BC. Also, Oracle Designer does not support object-oriented analysis and design. So the main focus for the product in this context is purely from the perspective of the data architect.

Oracle SQLDeveloper and SQL Developer Data Modeler

At the time of writing, Oracle's SQL Developer tool is in the process of expanding out of its incumbent role as a visual development tool for the database into the design space. Modeling and repository capabilities are being added to a version of the SQL Developer tool to position it as a tool for data architects. Over the next year or so, as the road map is implemented, you might expect to see SQL Developer Data Modeler, or some derivative of it, largely replace Oracle Designer as the tool of choice for database design. One advantage that SQL Developer will offer over Oracle Designer in this particular niche is a more seamless interchange of information between it and JDeveloper.

Process Design and Orchestration Tools

Although we don't discuss the larger subject of service design and orchestration within this book, it is worth mentioning the Oracle Fusion Middleware tools available for this function. These include the following:

- **Business Process Architect** Oracle resells the ARIS Business Architect tool from IDS Scheer as part of the middleware Business Process Management suite(www.oracle.com/technologies/soa/bpa-suite.html). The ARIS tool provides a web-based user interface for architects to design business processes with formal methodologies. The tool also has the capability to generate BPEL processes out of these higher-level models.
- **BPM Studio** The Business Process Management Studio tool (www.oracle.com/technologies/bpm) is a desktop-based development environment designed for co-operative use by both business experts and developers. The tool visually creates processes using the Business Process Modeling Notation language, which is then executed using the engine provided as part of the BPM Suite. (The same engine is used to execute BPEL-based processes.) The BPM studio can also be used to generate the web user interfaces that are required as part of a process flow, although these are much more restrictive than the types of user interface that you will be building as part of a Fusion application.
- **BPEL** The visual design time for BPEL is contained within JDeveloper. Just like the BPMN language used by the BPM studio, BPEL is an XML syntax that is executed directly by the relevant engine in the middleware suite. BPEL is a lower-level language than BPMN, which affords developers more power and control over the business processes.

Unified Modeling Language Tools

Recently, many organizations have chosen newer *Unified Modeling Language (UML)* tools to assist with the SDLC phases. UML standardizes a symbolic syntax for diagramming system design in various ways; UML offers a richer symbol set and better support for object-oriented analysis and design than the traditional tools, such as those available in Oracle Designer.

JDeveloper's Diagrams As discussed in the section "Modeler and Diagrammers" in Chapter 2, JDeveloper offers the ability to create the following UML diagrams:

- **Activity Diagram** This modeling tool looks similar to the Process Modeler in Oracle Designer. It represents activities (processes) and the transitions (flows) between activities within partitions (swim lanes or organizational units). You cannot directly generate code from this diagram.
- **Class Diagram** This diagram can represent various domains of information, such as conceptual classes (not connected to code), Java classes and interfaces, EJBs (Enterprise JavaBeans), database objects, and business components. You can build this type of diagram from existing code (or database objects) and can also generate code in the form of Java class definitions from the diagram.
- **Sequence Diagram** This diagram shows the messages exchanged between classes. You do not generate code from this diagram.
- **Use Case Diagram** This diagram represents actors and their use cases (actions). It is used to represent details of how a system task (or process) is accomplished. You do not generate code from this diagram either.

In addition to these diagrams, JDeveloper contains several diagrams to assist in creating code: the *XML Schema Diagram*—for coding XML schemas, the *WSDL Modeler*—for visually creating Web Services Description Language files—and the *JSF Navigation* and *ADF Task Flow Diagrams*—for defining the navigation rules and navigation cases between JSF pages or fragments and coding the various faces configuration files.

The JDeveloper diagrams help greatly with the development phase of the system life cycle because they provide the ability to graphically represent the components in your system. However, they do not store information in a central repository, do not provide features for the Strategy and Analysis phases, and, except as noted, do not generate code.

Which Oracle Design Tool to Use

Currently, no one Oracle tool supports the complete system life cycle for a typical Fusion web project. If you want to stay with all Oracle development tools and feel that an SDLC tool is important, you can use Oracle Designer's Strategy and Analysis tools for the early stages of the system life cycle; then you can use JDeveloper's tools for the Design, Development, and Deployment stages. However, one can argue that the heyday of traditional model-driven development has passed or at least is at a low point in its cycle, and the currently popular design tools are aids to the application creation process rather than tools that accomplish the creation process.

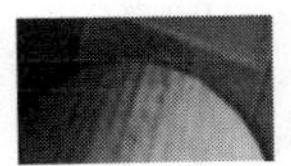

NOTE
As mentioned in the Introduction, this book focuses on the use of JDeveloper for web application development, and therefore bypasses the question of how to use Oracle Designer, and JDeveloper's diagramming tools within a full life system life cycle.

General Application Design Considerations

Application design consists of planning how to implement a user interface and other code to fulfill a set of business requirements. You need to consider several areas when designing an application's user interface.

Setting a Standard for Scrolling and Screen Resolution

The user's monitor size will affect the amount of content you can place on a page. Although it is best to place all content so that a user does not need to use the browser scrollbars to view parts of the screen, this is not always possible. A good guideline for web applications is to expect the user to use the vertical scrollbar but not the horizontal scrollbar. Scrolling to the right and left to see additional content is not a standard action for web applications because content is often grouped horizontally. That means, if the user is viewing a field, other fields with related information may be to the left or right and the user would not be able to see all related information at the same time. However, expecting the user to scroll the browser window up or down is reasonable and, in fact, common in web applications.

After setting the standard about avoiding horizontal scrolling, you can then set a standard on what monitor resolution size your application will support. This decision will affect the amount of content you can place horizontally on the page. These days, many applications standardize on support for a 1024 × 768 resolution, but it is always good to do some research to ensure that the majority of users can accommodate that standard. You need to publish whatever standard you choose for the minimum screen resolution so that users can be aware that anything under it could require horizontal scrolling.

When using the ADF Faces components, it is also important to understand how geometry is managed within them. Some container components such as `af:panelStretchLayout` and `af:decorativeBox` have the ability to automatically manage the size of their children. So for example, to make a table fill an area of a screen, you would put that table within a parent component that would perform this stretching for you, rather than setting the sizing on the table. We also recommend that any screen designs clearly specify what the expected screen behavior is as the user re-sizes the browser window. For example, which areas should stretch, which should scroll and which should remain fixed. There is no doubt that understanding and effectively using the geometry management features of the components is one of the most important factors in the UI design of Fusion applications. As you progress through the process of building the sample application over the remaining chapters, you'll see many of these factors come into play.

Achieving a Common Look and Feel

One of the steps in system design is creating a common look and feel for the user interface. A well-designed user interface is important from the standpoint of aesthetics. It is also a key to efficient use of the application. It, therefore, expresses both art and science. The page should be pleasant to look at with colors and graphics that do not distract from the functional purpose of the page.

Applications available on the Web are usually aimed at users who can teach themselves how the application function should be accomplished. Often, no formal training other than a help system is available for a web application. Clarity in the design allows users to quickly understand how to accomplish the intended business function. Consistency of this design means that the user needs to learn a particular interface design only once for the entire application. Therefore, to achieve user friendliness, the user interface and screen design should be clear and consistent.

NOTE
You may also need to plan your application for use by those who cannot see the screen or who cannot use a mouse. You will need to plan early in the application process if you want to use web component features such as access keys and alt text for these users. Fortunately the ADF Faces components have all of the base capabilities to support use of the application with screen readers and so forth. However, using the components alone is not enough; you still have to consider how those capabilities are used, and how usable the application as a whole is.

One factor to take into account in your design is also that of user expectation as to how a web user interface is used. The traditional model of interaction with web user interfaces was fairly simple, and user behavior was predictable because of this simplicity. This has led to the assumption that such web user interfaces are always simple enough for users to pick up and use with little or no help. Sadly, one of the downsides of the increased richness of the developer's palette is that it is entirely possible to create applications with increased complexity that may defeat the user's expectations. For example, ADF Faces supports a whole drag-and-drop framework for applications to use. Although such a capability is relatively normal within a desktop application, it is decidedly unusual for a web-based UI. When using some of these richer interactions, consider how the user can be trained or informed that these capabilities are present.

Reuse

One of the most effective ways to ensure that your application is consistently usable is to define strict UI standards for your developers to follow. However, the human element comes into play here, so rather than just relying on developers to follow documented standards, it is much more effective to enforce the standards in some way through one of the available reuse mechanisms: templates, declarative components, and task flows. All of these features have been introduced exactly for this purpose of maximizing reuse and minimizing the margin for error.

Page Templates The `af:template` tag, introduced in ADF 11*g*, allows the developer to define a shared template containing both defined areas of variable content (exposed as facets by the template) and also arguments or parameters that are passed to the template when it is evaluated and exposed through Expression Language. A common use for these template parameters is to pass information such as page titles—basically information that has to be different for each usage of the template by different pages, but that is not truly dynamic. The template mechanism in 11*g* has the primary benefit of allowing the template to contain binding information. At runtime the bindings used by the template are automatically combined with the bindings for the consuming page. This, then, solves the problem of integrating more dynamic content into the template body. One of the first things we do when creating the sample application in Chapter 17 is to define a basic template to control the overall look and feel of every page.

Declarative Components Templates save us from having to repeat common code across multiple pages to establish a unified look and feel. However, in many applications there is also the need for other forms of UI reuse, for example presenting a certain subset of data in a certain way. The canonical example of this would be an address record. Given the assumption that an application or suite of applications is using a common format for addresses, it would be useful to be able to expose that address in the user interface laid out in a common way. Declarative components provide just this capability. Just like templates, they can be parameterized to allow data to be passed in for display; however, unlike templates, declarative components have no bindings of their own, so any binding information has to be defined in the consuming page or page fragment.

Task Flows To complement declarative components, you use ADF task flows, which provide a very powerful reuse mechanism. Just like templates and declarative components, task flows can be parameterized, and as they can be constructed using page fragments, they can be used inline within a region on a page.

Recall from Chapter 11 that one of the attributes of a task flow is its ability to share the current binding context or create its own transaction. Both of these options have their place within your applications.

Approaching the User Interface Design

One approach to take when designing page flow for the user interface is to create a storyboard or sketch that shows the pages and action items (buttons or links) that will cause navigation to other pages. You use this sketch to communicate your design to users so that they can provide feedback before the application development is started. Also, this storyboard sketch guides you while developing the pages. A full user interface design will also include mockups of the screens so that you can prove the concepts.

This sketch can be drawn using any tool (software or manual). Although the JDeveloper JSF Navigation Diagrammer and Task Flow Diagrammers are intended as visual editors to assist in building the underlying configuration files used to define page flow, you can also use them to create an application page flow sketch. Navigation diagrams are not as descriptive as we would like for planning out the entire user interface flow, because they concentrate on the high-level artifacts of pages and page fragments. However, they can also contain documentation in the form of *notes* (boxes containing text), or *attachments* (dotted lines drawn from one attachment to another or from one page to an attachment). With smart use of notes and attachments, you can represent more detail defining how user interface elements should interact; these items will not become part of the code, so you can add any kind of documentation or note to them.

TIP

Although you can define page flow both within the faces-config .xml JSFNavigation Diagrammer and the adfc-config.xml Task Flow Diagrammer, things will get confusing if you attempt to use both. We recommend that you use task flows for everything and only use the faces-config.xml to define JSF configuration overrides.

The benefit of using the Task Flow Diagrammer for the page flow sketch is that drawing page and navigation case symbols on the diagram will create code in the task flow configuration files. This code can be used "as is" or refined later to define navigation. When you define a JSP or JSFF file for a page represented on the diagram, the yellow "undefined" triangle symbol will disappear. Details about the pages and the intention of the application follow.

NOTE

Since undefined pages on the diagram do not affect functionality of defined pages, you can wait until the end of the project to delete undefined pages from the diagram.

However, on the negative side, individual task flow diagrams generally only represent a subset of the application function. So, multiple task flow diagrams will need to be logically combined to represent the storyboard for the complete application.

Pages or Page Fragments? This last point leads us into the discussion about how task flows should be used to construct an application. Traditionally, web-based applications have been based around a page-centric design paradigm, that is, one function per page: query on one page, update on another, and so on. Task flows and specifically the capability of task flows to contain fragments rather than whole pages have changed all of this. Let's look at that concept and the effect it has on the UI design now.

Typical Fusion Page Design

Most Fusion-based applications, including the sample application that we demonstrate in this part of the book, are architected in a similar way. The application has very few whole pages, maybe only one whole page. Within this page, there will be various regions that will host dynamic content in the form of task flows that use page fragments. Most of the flow of the application, then, is within these various granular subflows. This model has several benefits:

- **Initial loading of ADF Faces applications is relatively expensive.** When a whole new page is sent down to the browser, it will include a large amount of extra material other than the page markup. This will include style sheets and a lot of JavaScript, which is used to make the components interactive. Such is the cost of this operation that you want to be able to keep it to a minimum.
- **By constraining dynamic content into regions, the user experience of navigation is much smoother and faster.** The only piece of the screen that needs to be updated is the child task flow in the region, and correspondingly less information has to be sent to the browser to accomplish this.
- **Task flows are intended to be reusable components.** By embracing task flows as a basic unit of work, reuse, both within and between applications, is encouraged. For example, the task flow for managing an address record can be easily reused across multiple Fusion applications, or if it is wrapped as a portlet, even outside of the Fusion world.
- **Functionality can be quickly tested in isolation from the larger page or process** by running the task flows in isolation. This helps to ensure that the task flows are truly behaving as expected and that your code does not have any hidden dependencies that are not handled by the parameters. This does raise the question about exactly how much external context you should allow to bleed through into a task flow. If a bounded task flow is reusing the existing data control context, then there will be some implicit relationship between the task flow and its container. Specifically, this will include the current transaction context, as you would expect, but also other contexts such as the current row in a particular view object instance. In some cases (such as a task flow to edit the current address) this bleed-through of row currency will be a useful thing. In other cases you might not want this, in which case the task flow will explicitly need to be linked with separate view object instances and explicitly set the row currency as desired using a method activity at the start of the flow.

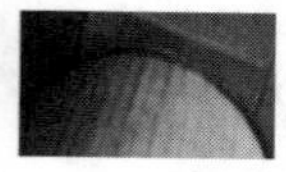

TIP

Task flows containing page fragments cannot be run in isolation. For testing purposes, you will need to drag the task flow as a region into a complete page created especially for that purpose. This test page can then be run to test the task flow contained within it. You will do this in the following practice chapters.

- **Task flows are the main unit of granularity defined by the ADF Security framework.** Most security will be applied at this level rather than to individual pages. If you choose not use task flows, you will not be able to exploit the ADF Security framework effectively and it will be much more difficult to secure your applications.

When to Use Unbounded Task Flows

We have explained that the common pattern for building your applications will be using only a small number of pages, each of which will contain dynamic data and flows defined by bounded task flows. So the question arises: exactly what defines your top-level pages which will appear in the adfc-config.xml diagram?

The decision point here is clear. The only things that should appear in the unbounded task flow are the entry points to your application. These will define pages (or flows) that you can reasonably expect the user to access via a URL or a bookmark. If you do not want users to navigate to a particular page out of context, then you should encapsulate it within a bounded task flow where the only entry point is known and controlled. For example, the unbounded task flow should never really contain a combination of a method activity setting some context and then navigating to a view in that same unbounded task flow. By definition, if the page that is navigated to as a secondary activity after the method executes is available in the unbounded task flow, then it is accessible via the URL and the user may bypass the preparatory method activity. If activities need to be executed in a specific order, then encapsulate them into a bounded task flow and expose the encapsulated process on the unbounded task flow.

Approaching ADF Business Components Design

An effective design method for the ADF BC layer is driving its design from the user interface screens as they are planned. View objects and view links should be developed to support the data requirements for each screen or fragment. In addition, entity objects are created to support the data needs of the view objects. This iterative approach needs constant monitoring to check for and consolidate any duplication, but the final design will fit the application requirements much more effectively than the alternate approach of generating default entity objects and view objects from the database schema and trying to force the user interface into using them.

When planning the view objects for a screen, take full advantage of the capability of the view objects to join entities. For example, view object definitions can be created which encapsulate the joins for reference data foreign key lookups. Such encapsulated lookups are much more efficient and simpler than trying to fetch the data separately.

Additionally, determine if a particular view object needs to be read-only. If a view object is always used only for populating dropdown lists or query-only screens, then marking it as read-only can save resources on the application server. You should also consider if that same view object is a candidate for a shared application module to further reduce the runtime resource usage.

Finally, look for opportunities to reuse objects. The view link, view criteria, and bind variable mechanisms discussed in Part II can be used to adapt a single view object for use in several different contexts, for example, to serve as a datasource for standalone data entry form and as part of a separate master-detail screen.

Implementing Business Rules and Validation

One of the most discussed areas of Java EE application design is where to locate application logic—we spent some time on this subject way back in Chapter 1. We have described how ADF Business Components provides places for both declarative and coded validation, and this will probably be the natural place for most of the logic. However, we also appreciate that a proven technique for implementing business rules is the *database-centric approach* that keeps as much of the business rule code in the database as possible, implemented through views and PL/SQL triggers. There are other approaches. The approach you use depends upon how much you want to rely on database code to enforce business rules and how important the customization capabilities of the framework are to you.

A Database-Centric Approach The authors have had success with the database-centric approach to business rules, which stores all business rules code in the database and calls this code from database triggers. That way, the application front-end layer can be changed more easily with less recoding. In addition, any application—past, present, or future—will pass through the same validation rules.

This is the idea behind the Table API that Oracle Designer generates. The Table API is a PL/SQL package of procedures that handle INSERT, UPDATE, DELETE, SELECT and LOCK operations for a table. A full set of table triggers ensures that access to the table (for INSERT, UPDATE, DELETE and LOCK) is allowed only by calling these procedures. By adding to this application fine-grained access control (also called virtual private database) policies to restrict access to specific rows of data, the table is effectively protected with a code layer that allows business rules code to be applied to any type of operation. If rules error messages from this layer are handled in a user-friendly way, this approach can, theoretically, serve any type of user interface layer.

A Modified Database-Centric Approach Using the database-centric approach, the application layer can, also theoretically, be devoid of business rules code. This situation is rarely completely practical, because some validations, such as datatype, format, and mandatory values, as well as JSF validators and converters, are most user-friendly when they occur immediately on the user interface level before the page is submitted to the application server and from there to the database. Therefore, you may opt for a modified database-centric approach where you repeat business rules, such as those just mentioned in the user interface layer. Validation in the UI layer has the advantage of providing more immediate feedback to users when they are in error. However, such code should always be used in addition to checks in the business and database layers, and should not be the only form of validation.

CAUTION
Always assume, however, that any validation in the user interface layer can be bypassed by alternative interfaces into the business service or by malicious users, so it should not be relied upon.

In addition, some business rules, such as field value comparisons and conditional logic based on cached data, can be easily handled on the application server side. Validation errors from this level of code would appear to the user faster than the corresponding errors coded in database triggers. In addition, enforcing these business rules on the application server level would not require database processing time or network messages to and from the database. In this case, the business rules code that implements these would also be duplicated in the application server layers (such as ADF BC code).

Duplicating business rules code in more than one layer does require extra coding as well as extra work in synchronizing the code that is duplicated between layers. Therefore, you need to seriously consider whether the benefits of this duplication—namely, saving database processing, saving network traffic, and providing friendlier feedback to users—are worthwhile.

Which Approach to Take? In addition to the database-centric approaches mentioned, you can select variations on coding all business rules in the application server and all business rules in the database. These variations would code a particular business rule in one place or the other.

The approach that you take will depend partially on your preference for Java or PL/SQL code; both types of code are valid, and both will be required at some level in each application. The important thing to remember, though, is that ultimate responsibility for the integrity of data must remain with the database. At the minimum, your approach should take full advantage of the relational integrity capability offered by database constraints (primary key, foreign key, and check) to ensure that data has a valid structure.

Designing Security

Most applications will need some security, even if it is just to determine the identity of a user. In the traditional Oracle world, this user information is generally gathered from the Oracle database account that connects the application to the database. However, for scalability reasons, Java enterprise applications do not generally work this way but use a shared database account to connect the application to the database.

The important thing about a security strategy is to think about it from the start. Base your thinking on application logical user roles rather than on specific user identities. As you lay out the user interface and the page flow, consider which pages or flows need to be restricted and which logical user roles are required. In some cases, you may need to hide regions of the page or make them read-only based on these roles, so plan out these requirements as you design the pages. Once the application is deployed, the logical application roles can be mapped to real users without your having to make changes to the application.

In principle there are two separate security mechanisms that you could use for your Fusion-based application: basic Java Enterprise Edition container security and ADF Security. Although these two approaches ultimately use the same credential stores for authentication and authorization, the ways in which they function can be a constraining factor in the overall system design.

- **Java EE Security** secures pages based on URL patterns. This means that in order for a security check to be applied, the URL must change during a navigation event. This further implies that applications should be architected around the concept of whole pages, not page fragments, and furthermore the JSF framework has to artificially ask the browser to redirect between page calls to ensure that the URL is changed so that the pattern matching can take place.
- **ADF Security** is based on task flows as a security unit. This allows much more granularity for security within a particular page, as the task flows in question may be using fragments and be running within a page region. Neither the owning page nor the URL has to change for security to be applied.

Given the typical UI architecture of Fusion applications as we discussed it earlier, ADF Security is a better choice for securing your applications. In Chapter 21 we look at how it can be applied to the sample TUHRA2 application.

What Best Practice Should Be Adopted?

Many of the core best practices in building out Fusion applications should, by now, be self-evident. We've discussed how the task flow mechanism points toward a very granular style of page assembly using fragments and regions. We've also discussed how the various reuse mechanisms such as templates and declarative components can be used to reduce the amount of repetition within our code. However, there are a few extra steps that you should take when starting out to ensure that things are a little easier down the line.

You will see these in use throughout the sample application discussed in the remainder of Part V of the book. This advice is intended to be a good starting point. As adoption of the ADF and Fusion Platform grows, the body of knowledge and best practices will evolve.

Use Framework Buffer Classes

Frameworks, such as ADF Business Components and the ADF Model, provide comprehensive framework extension points. You should use these capabilities to create *framework buffer classes*—Java classes that provide a layer between the framework implementation and any code that you write using that framework.

As an example, let's look at how this works for ADF Business Components. In "Entity Object Classes" from Chapter 6, we discussed how entity row definitions can be subclassed to add validation code. This is accomplished by choosing the *Generate Java File* option in the entity object properties, creating an *Impl* (implementation) subclass of the framework `EntityImpl` class, for example:

```
public class DepartmentsImpl extends EntityImpl
{
}
```

Your specific entity Impl class (`DepartmentsImpl`, in this case) should not directly extend the framework `EntityImpl` class but rather should extend a framework buffer class that you create that, in turn, extends the framework-supplied `EntityImpl`, as shown in the following illustration.

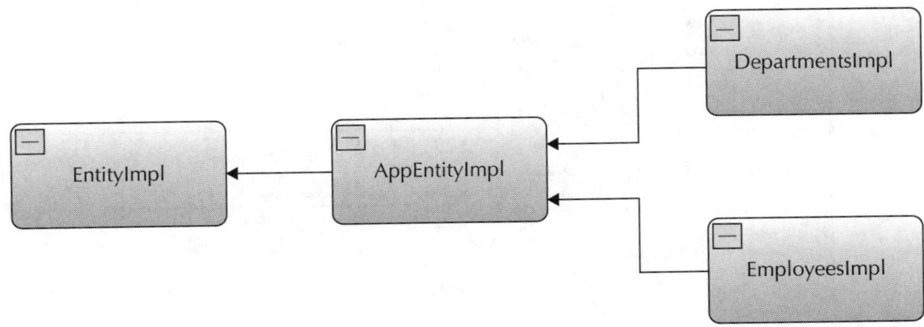

In this example, `DepartmentsImpl` and `EmployeesImpl` extend `AppEntityImpl`, which, in turn, extends the framework class, `EntityImpl`. The `AppEntityImpl` class does not initially need to contain any extra functionality; it just extends the `EntityImpl` class as follows:

```
public class AppEntityImpl extends EntityImpl
{
}
```

You would then change your code to extend the framework buffer class as follows:

```
public class DepartmentsImpl extends AppEntityImpl
{
}
```

Adding your own buffer classes between the application and the framework provides two benefits. First, as the application evolves, you will identify certain bits of reusable functionality or functionality that modifies the default way that the framework operates. These can be moved into the buffer class with a minimum of disruption and immediately become available to all your classes, since your classes will extend this framework buffer class. Second, the buffer class provides a good patching point. If you encounter a problem in the way that the base framework works, you can patch workarounds into the single buffer class, rather than having to make the change in every implementation.

Setting Up Framework Extensions

JDeveloper provides excellent support for layering in buffer classes with ADF Business Components. You can configure the IDE to automatically use your extension when creating new objects. You can define these buffer classes on a project-by-project basis (in the Project Properties screen) or from the Preferences dialog (**Tools | Preferences).** In the Preferences dialog, select Business Components\Base Classes in the preferences tree, and the following screen will display:

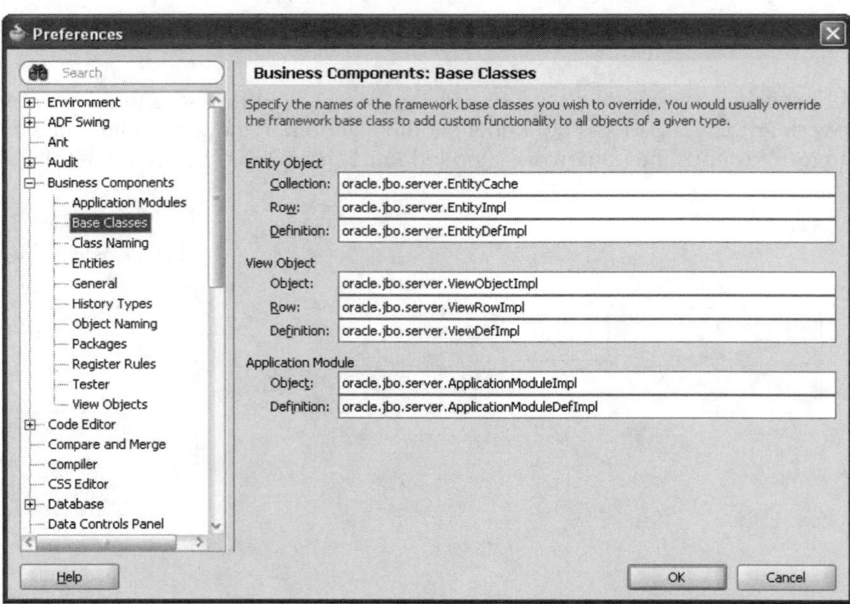

Each of the base classes shown in this dialog can be replaced with an application-specific subclass at the very start of the project build. For most applications, it will be sufficient to provide framework buffer classes for `EntityImpl`, `ViewObjectImpl`, `ViewRowImpl`, and `ApplicationModuleImpl` because they are the most commonly used extension points. When an ADF BC wizard creates a business component class, it will use the class of the appropriate type defined on this page as the superclass.

TIP
While you are looking at the base class configuration in the preferences, take a moment to examine all of the other settings you can override for the Business Components framework.

For other parts of the application that wire into the frameworks, such as backing beans for JSF pages, you will not be directly subclassing framework classes, but it is still useful to put a superclass in place that all your implementations subclass. This superclass will provide you with a place to put common functionality. In the sample application you will create just such a superclass and move various utility methods into it as you progress through the application development. Over the course of your first few ADF projects you will probably end up with a common backing bean superclass that you will then automatically use at the start of any new project.

Use Java Packaging

Java packages provide a mechanism for grouping objects together in a logical structure. In the context of ADF BC for example it is good practice to create your entity objects and view objects in separate packages within the model project to ease maintenance. This same principle can be extended to the ViewController project as well. Keep page backing beans, PageDef files, and other files partitioned into their own package structures.

Stick to JSF and Only JSF

In the design of the user interface, don't mix HTML markup with JSF components. Doing so can lead to unexpected results because of the different page-creation life cycles of JSF and normal JSP/HTML and problems with layouts, particularly stretching behavior. Using HTML markup in a JSF page will also make it harder to migrate the application to different user interface technologies that are evolving, such as Facelets, or to deploy to devices other than a standard web browser. Use the power of the JSF layout containers, rather than HTML or CSS, to position your components in a portable and consistent manner. It is important, therefore, to take the time to understand the layout capabilities of the various container components available.

Create a Custom Skin

Much like the concept behind framework buffer classes, a custom skin may be something that you never need to touch; however, it's useful to have it there just in case. One of the great improvements of skinning technology within ADF 11*g* is the ability to create skins that subclass the supplied Oracle skins rather than having to re-implement the whole thing.

As well as overriding the skinning behavior of an individual component at a global level, skins can also be used to create specialized versions of particular components, or even as a place to put custom styles for use in the *inlineStyle* property of components on your page.

In fact you should always use a skin for this rather than defining a custom style sheet for a particular page or introducing the style information directly into the component definition.

In the case of some of the more complex components such as `af:query`, it turns out that skinning is the only way to change aspects of the color and layout of the component. Although other than the general description in Chapter 12, we don't discuss details about skinning in this book, it is an extremely powerful feature of the component set as a whole and is a topic that advanced users of the framework will quickly need to become familiar with.

TIP

Skinning is a subject that is described in some depth in the accompanying volume to this book, Oracle Fusion Developer Guide: Building Rich Internet Applications with Oracle ADF Business Components and ADF Faces *(McGraw-Hill Professional, forthcoming).*

What Is the Design of the Sample Application?

As mentioned in the Introduction, the TUHRA2 application uses database objects installed in the demo HR schema in the Oracle database. The purpose of the application is to allow access to and modification of the data in the HR tables. The Security Administrator for the company assigns one of three application roles—user, admin, and manager—to each user (a process that is described in Chapter 21).

Users assigned the user role are allowed to search for any employee record but will not be able to edit any employee record but their own. Users assigned the manager role have the same access but are also able to edit or create any other employee record. Users assigned the admin role have the same access as managers but can also display the screens used to maintain reference data, such as job types.

Database Design

As mentioned, the application uses the basic HR schema available in all versions of the Oracle database; however, as part of Chapter 17 we will have you extend and augment that schema a little to add some extra twists to the data model. What we are attempting to do here is to more closely match many of the relational designs that we see in real life with awkward constructs to handle, such as many-to-many relationships. Figure 16-1 shows the JDeveloper database diagram for the revised schema.

The schema shown here depicts the following design features:

- **A hierarchy of tables** from REGIONS to COUNTRIES to LOCATIONS to DEPARTMENTS to EMPLOYEES. Each pair of tables represents a master-detail (parent-child) relationship.
- **An optional lookup relationship** between a single DEPARTMENTS record and the EMPLOYEES table to associate a manager with the department.
- **An optional self-referencing relationship** in EMPLOYEES to associate a manager record with an employee record.
- **A lookup table,** JOBS, that provides a job code for the EMPLOYEES and JOB_HISTORY tables.

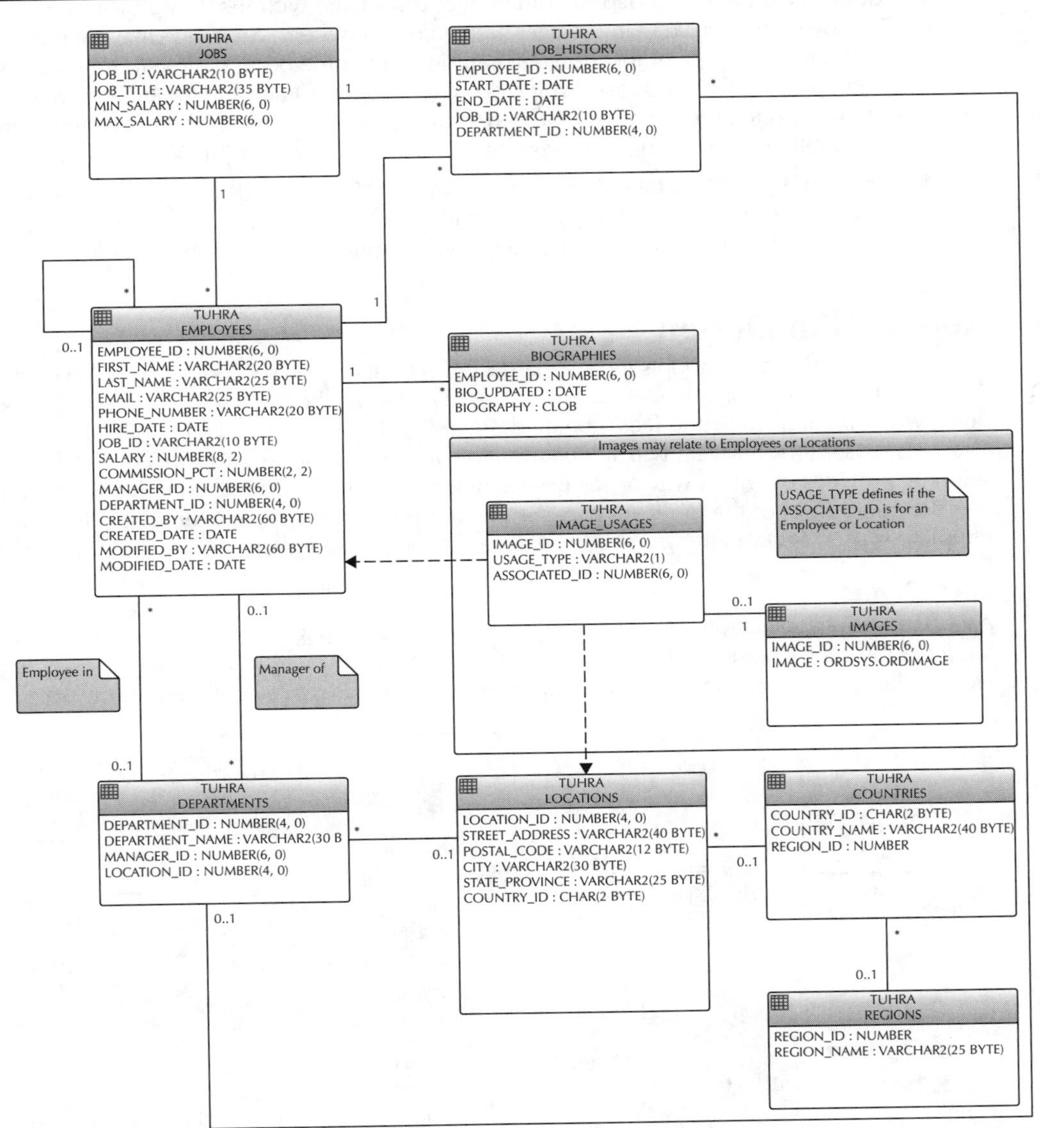

FIGURE 16-1. *THURA2 database design diagram showing the revised HR schema*

You will also make some small changes to the HR schema to add some additional points of interest:

- **Audit columns** are added to the EMPLOYEES table to record who last changed it and when.
- **A BIOGRAPHIES** table is added to hold historical information about the employees in a CLOB data type.

- **An IMAGES table** is added to hold images associated with both employees and locations. Employees may have many images associated with them. An image may be reused by multiple employees or locations. Because we want the book sample to be usable with the free Oracle XE database, which does not support Oracle Multimedia (formally Oracle *inter*Media) features, we have elected to only store the name of the image file in the table, rather than storing the image as a Binary Large Object (BLOB).
- **An IMAGE_USAGES table** is added to relate IMAGES and EMPLOYEES or IMAGES and LOCATIONS because employees or locations may have many images associated with them. In addition, an image may be reused by multiple employees or locations.

Application Design

The TUHRA2 application adopts the standard BLAF+ *Oracle Browser Look and Feel,* which is currently the default look and feel for Fusion applications. At the point in time when this book is being written, a new look and feel is being designed for the ADF Faces components, however, the Oracle Browser look and feel will still be available as the "blafplus-rich" skin. As noted previously, skinning provides us with a way of easily switching out the look and feel completely if desired.

The core layout of the top-level pages is defined by a common page template, and another template is used for formatting a subset of page fragments used by the employee editing screen.

Entry Points

As it stands, the application has only three entries in the main page flow (adfc-config.xml) file. These are the public entry points to the application. The following illustration shows a high-level logical view of the application, mapping out all of the functions that relate to each of its entry points:

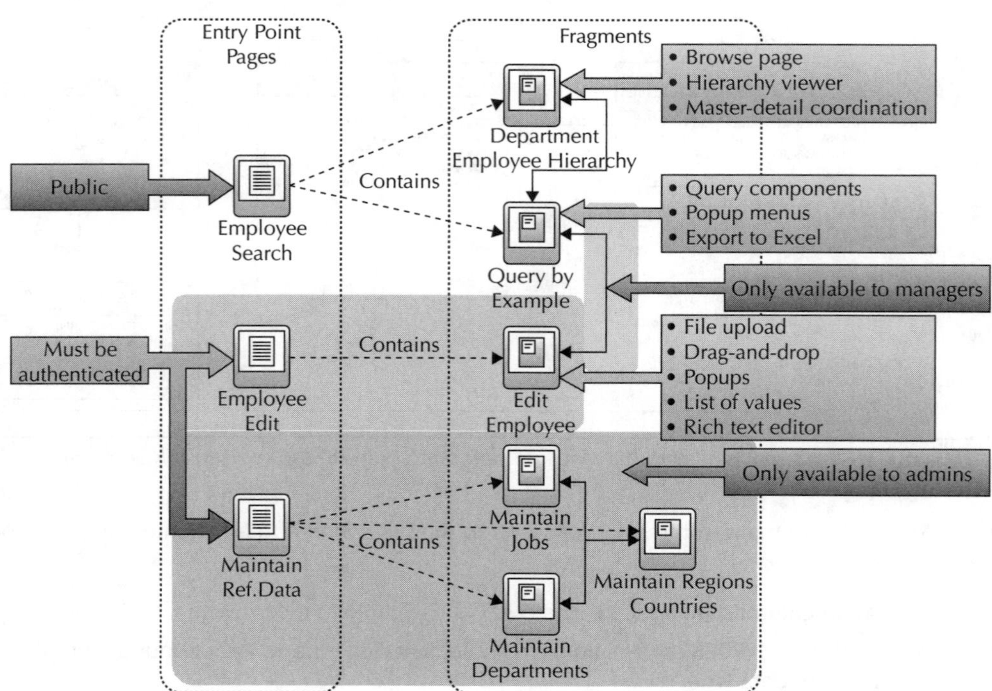

The actual implementation of these pages involves the use of nested task flows and page fragments.

Employee Search The search page shown here provides the user with the ability to perform both basic and complex searches for an employee in a highly customizable user interface. The search component that is being used can also be configured to allow customized search parameters to be saved. The screen also allows the search results to be exported to Excel.

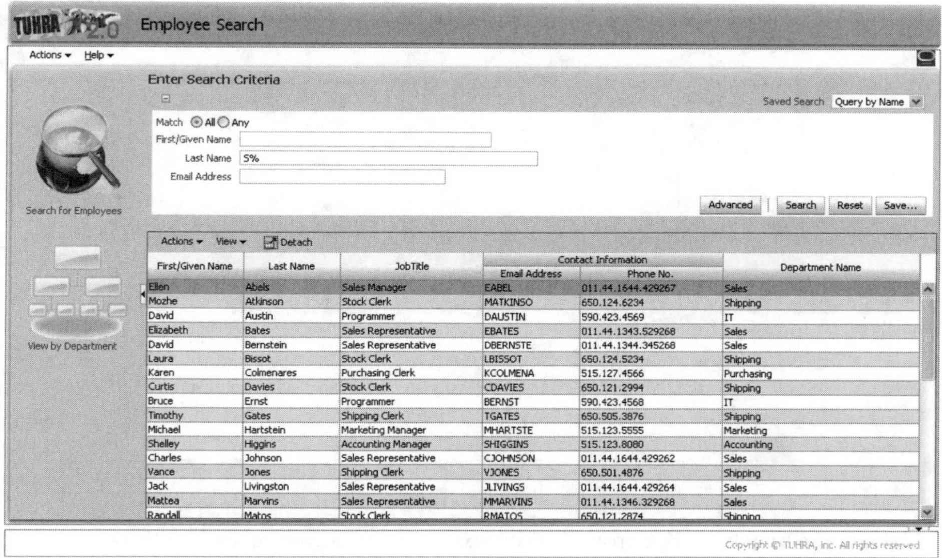

The search screen also gives access to another view of employee relationships, this time in the form of a hierarchical view of employees by department:

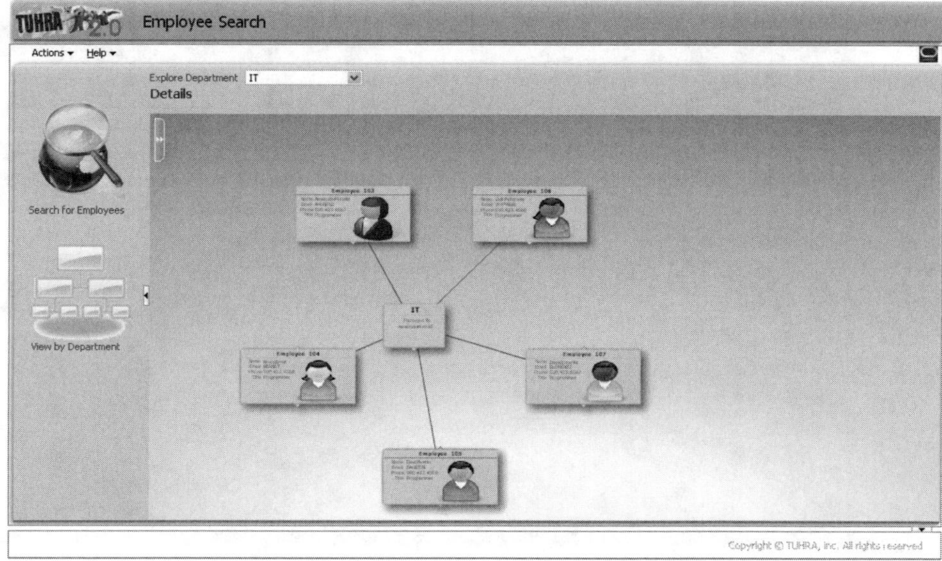

This second view is an example of where a region has been used to swap out one task flow with another inside a single page. Within this view the user can select different departments from the list box at the top of the screen and view the employees within that department.

Edit Employee The employee edit screen shown here is used to illustrate many of the key features of the framework with use of popups, lists of values, trains, file upload, and much more:

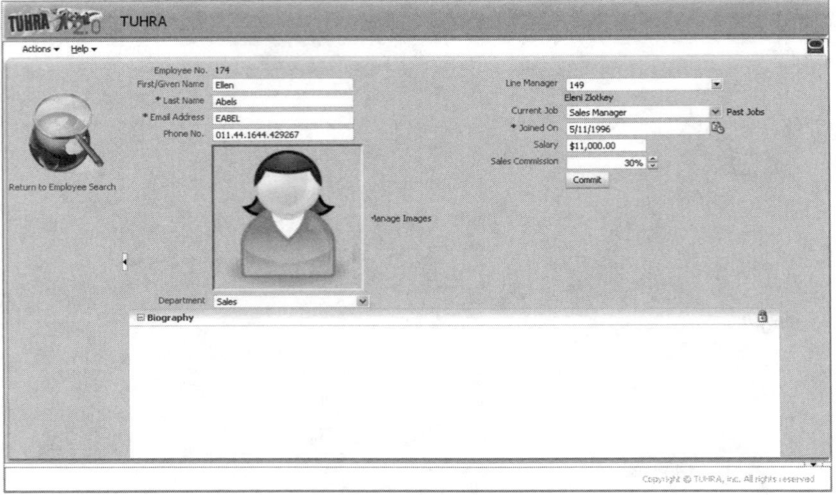

This page may be called from the context of an employee record on the search page, or it can be called directly from the URL, to edit an employee's own record.

Management Functions: Finally, the management screen provides access to some data maintenance tables using a tabbed interface:

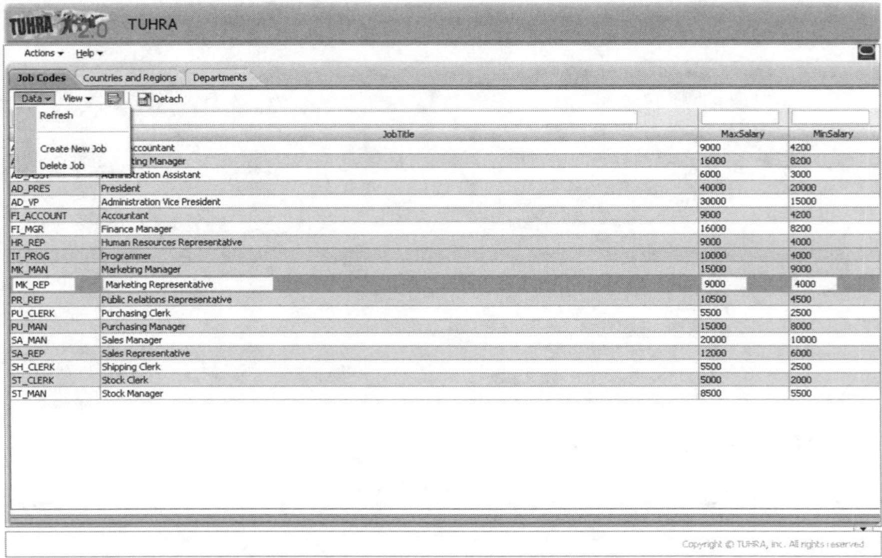

We do not walk you through the creation of this part of the application in the hands-on exercises, as it is just a repetition of the techniques that have already been covered in the creation of the previous pages. However, the complete application can be downloaded, for reference, from the websites mentioned in the Introduction under "Websites for Sample Files."

What Do I Have to Think about Before Starting?

In previous chapters we have discussed many of the physical interactions with the IDE and various pieces of technology within it. It is important to understand that the initial state of JDeveloper, as it is installed, is just a serving suggestion. It comes fully loaded with every feature needed to work with the middleware platform, many of which may not apply to what you are planning to do. Some aspects of the IDE, for example, how the windows are arranged, shortcut keys, code snippets, and code templates, will evolve as you become comfortable with the product. It is important to remember that you can change all of these things at any time.

However, from the start, for a particular application, use the Extensions page of the Preferences dialog (**Tools** | **Preferences**) to switch off the parts of the IDE that you do not need. This will improve memory use, load time and performance, particularly on actions like right mouse clicks in the IDE, when even a few tenths of a second saved is a good thing.

While you are deciding what extensions to have loaded, it is a good time to think about some specific aspects of day-to-day work with your code:

- Workspace application templates
- Source control
- Unit testing
- Auditing and code analysis

Application Templates

In Chapter 17 we explain and demonstrate the creation of templates for pages, but entire applications (as defined by a workspace) have templates that can be customized. When you create a workspace, from the New Gallery you are presented with the New Application dialog shown here:

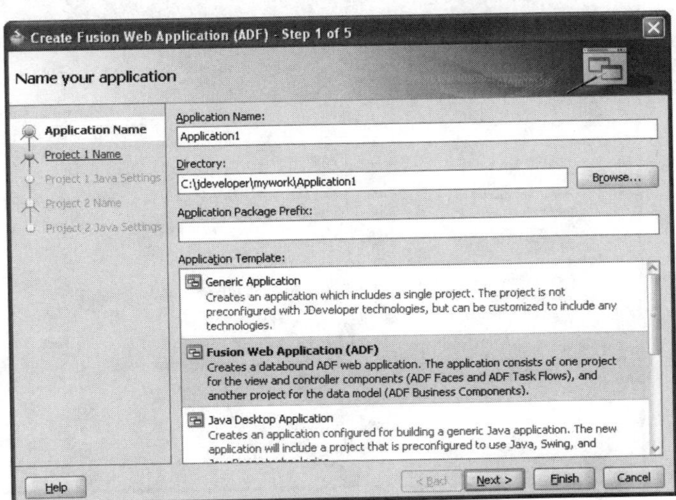

The key thing to understand here is that these templates are not a fixed list; you could and should adapt the existing ones or create your own. For example, you might want to define a default application template that includes a separate project for the database schema or documentation. As an example you can follow the steps here to copy and alter the default Fusion ADF application template.

Defining a Custom Application Template

An application template is composed of one or more project templates. In the case of the Fusion Application template, there are two project templates in use: ADF Model Project and ADF ViewController Project, as shown in the Create Fusion Web Application (ADF) dialog here:

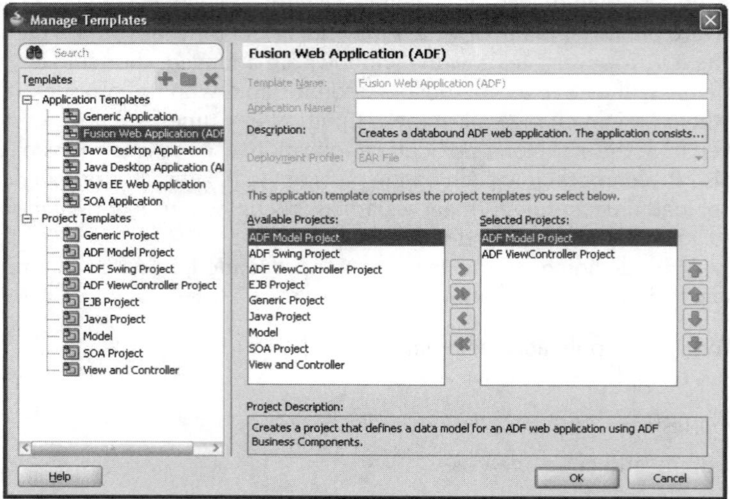

If you needed a third project template to hold information relating to the database for the application, after displaying the New Gallery, you would select General\Projects node as shown next and then double click Project Template:

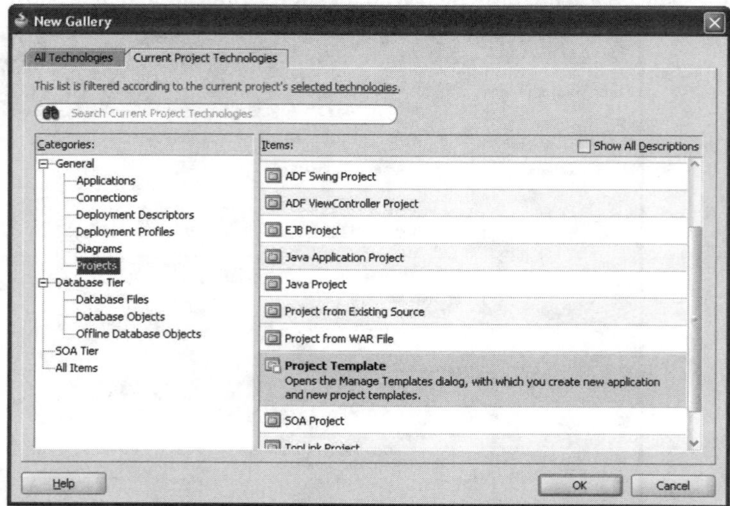

Select the Project Templates node and click the "Create a New Template" (green plus "+") button. A dialog will appear allowing you to name the new template and project (for example, "Database Schema Project" and "DatabaseSchema.jpr," respectively):

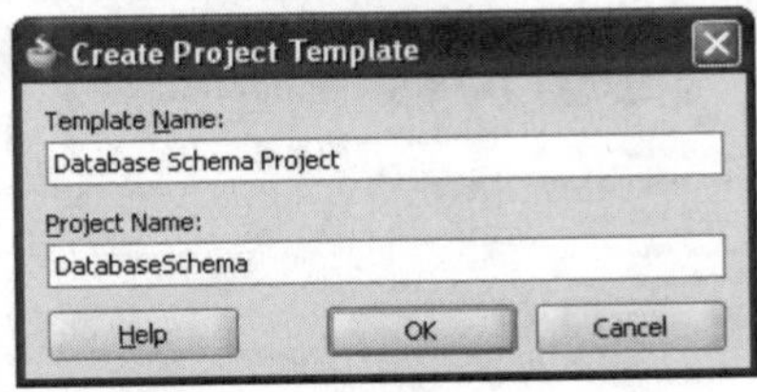

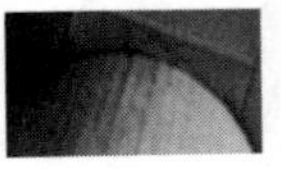

NOTE
The ".jpr" extension is added automatically to the Project name if you do not explicitly specify it.

After clicking OK, you can then shuttle the required libraries, in this case the Database (offline) library, into the template and set up the initial defaults such as the package suffix that will be appended to the value that the developer defines when using the template. In this case the *Default Package* "schema" is used, so if the developer enters a package root of *com.tuhra* when creating the application from the template, files in the project will use *com.tuhra.schema.*The completed dialog is shown in the following illustration:

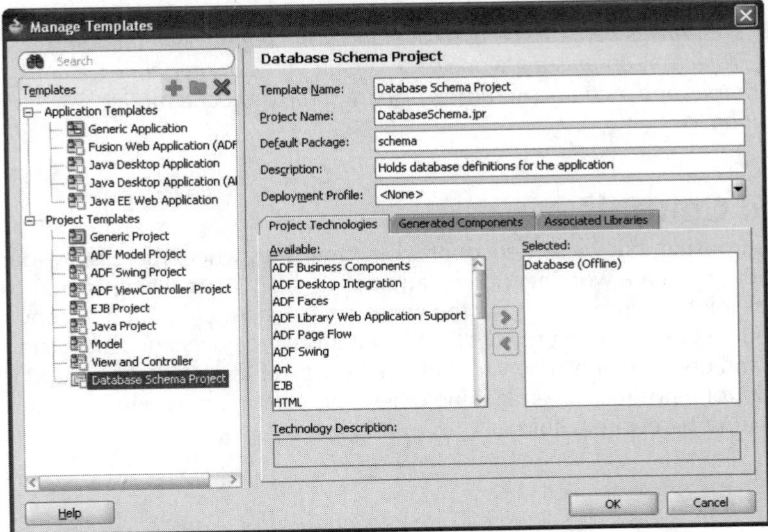

Finally, the new project template needs to be added to the application template. Since you can't change the shipped templates, you'll need to copy the Fusion Web Application (ADF) template to create a custom version. The same template management screen is used to create an application template in this case. The following illustration shows the settings used to create the TUHRA Fusion Template:

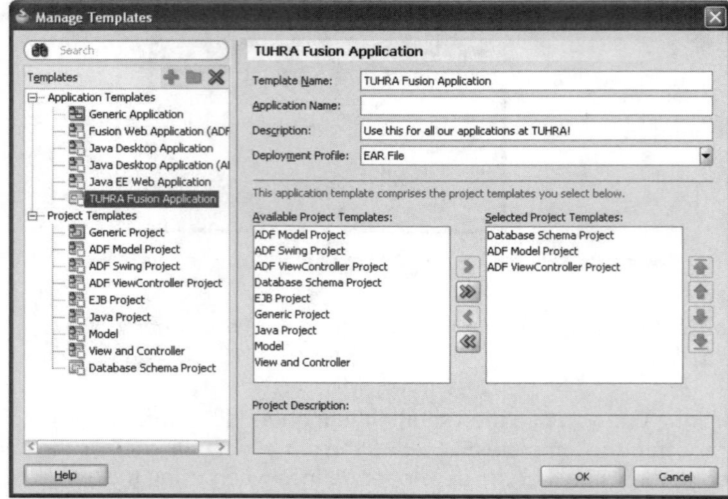

Now new applications can use this template and will have the DatabaseSchema project built in.

TIP
Project templates can also be used as standalone entities when adding extra projects to an existing workspace. Again you can predefine the libraries and technology scopes as part of the project template definition.

Source Control?

It seems surprising, but we still encounter customer sites where there is no source control system in use. Even if you are working individually or as a small team, using source control is something that makes a lot of sense, if only for the benefit of having more than one copy of the code. Open-source Source Control Management (SCM) systems like Subversion (subversion.tigris.org) are easy to install and use, and consume very little in the way of resources. It's a good idea to install your source control repository on a machine other than your main working machine, if you can, just to protect against hardware failure.

NOTE
The section "How Does Source Code Version Control Work in JDeveloper?" in Chapter 2 includes more information about setting up and using Subversion with JDeveloper.

Apart from the obvious benefit of having a complete audit trail in your code showing who changed what and when, having versions of the code in an SCM system also acts as a kind of super undo system. Occasionally developers do get things into a total mess, and the only option is to unwind to where you were yesterday and try again.

Source Control Strategies

Accepting that source control is a good idea, the question often comes up, how exactly should you work with it? Of course every team will have different circumstances and different dependencies, but let's consider a small Fusion project of the type that a team just starting out with the technology might undertake.

With any SCM system there are essentially two universal concepts: tagging and branching. *Tagging* is the process of defining a stripe across the repository at a certain point in time. It will do nothing to the structure of the repository but instead will mark a known point. Commonly teams will tag the code line as part of the nightly build process. Tags are useful primarily as a communication tool. For example, you want to have a QA team test your code, so you would tag it and export a copy for them to use. If any problems come up that you want to try and reproduce using exactly the same code as they received, then you can go back at any point in time by checking out that tag. If you're used to the Oracle database, think of this as being like a flashback query. Tags, on a SCM system such as Subversion, essentially cost nothing, so the rule here is to tag often. If you are using a build automation system such as Cruise Control (cruisecontrol.sourceforge.net), you can automatically tag the code after every good build.

Branching is a different concept from tagging. Normally when you work with an SCM system, you check code into the mainline or trunk. When you create a branch, you are creating a copy of the code at that point in time. Note that unlike a tag, which is just a marker or savepoint on the mainline, the branch has its own copy of the code. This code can be changed independently from the mainline and over time may diverge.

Why Would You Branch?

In a simple world, the only time that you would branch is when you release a version of the code. You want to be able to snapshot the code contained in that release so that you can continue to add new features for the next version on the mainline. You might ask "Well, why not just use a tag?" The problem here is that you may want to maintain the code for a release independently over time. Often the mainline will be in an unstable state, and if you want to make just a minor bug fix to an existing production version, you won't be able to do so. Generally when you find a critical bug in a production version, you would fix it in the mainline and then, if it really must be patched on the production system, backport the same fix into the branch you saved off. This ensures that the only changes going into the patch are the fixes you care about.

So apart from major product releases, what other reasons are there to branch the code? One common use of branches is to provide individual developers or teams with a private work area. For example, you may not allow a developer to check their work into the mainline until it has passed tests and been reviewed. However, you don't want to prevent them from having the benefits of an SCM system while they work. This can be addressed by the creation of private branches. The problem with private branches, though, is that the longer that the developer works on their own branch, the more it will diverge from the mainline, so the job of merging changes back into main will potentially be harder. If you can, avoid private branches for this reason.

In really large projects such as Oracle's Fusion Applications, the nature and size of the effort necessitates that all the teams work on different branches and then have to manage a complex dance to merge back into the mainline and refresh their branches with work from other teams. This kind of process needs a full-time, dedicated team just to manage the source control process and is probably overkill for most applications.

Golden Rules of SCM use

We've only had space to touch briefly on SCM as part of the development life cycle, but here are some simple rules to follow if it's a new area for you:

- **Use it.**
- **Use it.**
- **Use it.**
- **Assign a developer as the Source Control System owner.** Even if your team is not large enough to warrant a dedicated SCM team, you'll still need someone who understands the way that your SCM and automated build setup works. Assign one person and have that person be the gatekeeper of any key tasks such as branching.
- **Check in little and often.** The more granular your check-ins, the easier it is to work out the problem when something has gone wrong. Think in terms of one check-in per bug fix or at least one a day if you're developing something new. As a rule of thumb, if more than ten files have been changed or added, you should probably do a check-in.
- **Comment your check-ins** and use a unique identifier for each developer. This way, you can see exactly who changed what and why. This also makes it easier to resolve disputes when multiple changes to the same file have to be merged.
- **Identify hot files** and check these in as soon as a change is made. Within an ADF project there are certain files that a lot of the developers will be hitting, for example the DataBindings.cpx file and the adfc-config. You don't want those files to end up being different on the machines of separate developers, or it will lead to difficulties.
- **Assign an owner for hot files.** For these hot files assign someone to own them and communicate to the team when a change has been made. This way everyone can be told to pick up the new version, preventing conflicts. Hot files include ADFc task flow definitions and the web.xml descriptor, plus of course common framework superclasses that everyone depends on.
- **Automate your builds.** If you can, use a build automation system such as Cruise Control or Hudson (hudson.dev.java.net) to automate the basic tasks of compiling your code and testing it. This helps to identify build problems early on where one developer's code impacts others in unexpected ways.
- **Tag often,** ideally as part of your automated builds.
- **Branch as little as possible.** Fewer branches mean less merging to do.
- **Back up your SCM repository frequently;** there's a lot of useful information in there, don't lose it!

Local History

If you don't have an SCM system in place, JDeveloper still maintains a local history of changes that you make to files. However, this history is limited in its capabilities and will only show changes that have been made on this one copy of the application on the local system, rather than reflecting all of the changes made across the team. This local history cache is controlled through the **Tools** | **Preferences** dialog using the **Environment** | **Local History** option.

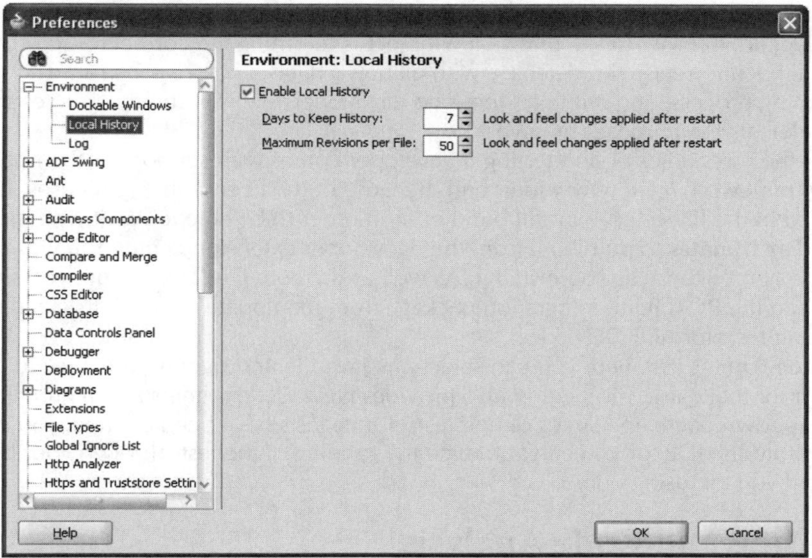

Unit Testing

Unit testing is one of the core principles of Agile programming, although there is much more to this style of development than just testing. The principle here is that every function within your code should have an accompanying test. Advocates propose that development should actually be test-driven—that is, the unit tests for a function should be written before the code, and then the code written to implement or pass the test. Such an approach involves much more investment on the part of the developer to think about the piece of code that they are writing. Done well, the code base for the tests alone will be of comparable size or greater than the code base that does useful work.

The reality is that this extreme programming view of test-driven development does not work especially well for a metadata-based framework like ADF. In ADF, much of the code that you write is actually XML metadata and is not expressed in a form that can be run from some command-line testing tool. The principle with unit testing is that you should test what you can, but don't get hung up on it. Some key candidates for testing are

- Application Module methods
- View Object methods
- View Object result sets
- Utility methods

Code that you would like to test, such as the action code associated with a button in the user interface, can be difficult to test in isolation, as it often has dependencies on the binding layer and the whole Servlet container.

Testing the user interface is a complete topic on its own, and beyond the scope of this book. If you are interested in this area, you should look at another open-source tool, called *Selenium* (selenium.seleniumhq.org). Selenium is used by the team that builds the ADF Faces components to test the components and so is proven to work well with the framework.

When writing the tests for the ADF BC layer, you have to consider how to make those tests reproducible. In order to test that a view object is returning the correct result set, for example, you will need to set up the database with a known dataset before each run. This can be a time-consuming process, and if it takes too long, developers will not run the unit tests very often, which defeats the purpose somewhat.

For the mechanics of unit testing, JDeveloper comes with support for the popular open-source testing framework *JUnit* (www.junit.org). Because of the license that JUnit uses, it cannot be included in the JDeveloper install bundle, so in order to be able to use it, you must use **Help | Check For Updates** to pull JUnit from the JDeveloper extension center. You will have to accept the separate JUnit license as you install it. As well as the core JUnit extension, you should also download the BC4J JUnit Integration package from the update center. This extension helps you build unit tests for ADF BC code.

Once JUnit is installed, you can select any Java file and right mouse click to create a skeleton unit test for that class. The plug-in also provides New Gallery items for creating fixtures (test setup and tear-down code) and suites of unit tests. Once tests have been defined, you can run them from within the IDE, or you can automate the running of the tests through your build management system if you are using one.

Auditing and Code Analysis

To finish up this section, we should review the general issues of code quality. Out of the box, JDeveloper comes with an audit mechanism, which will actually check your work as you go, providing you with various informational, warning, and error messages.

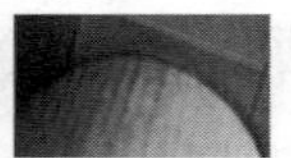

TIP
Problems flagged by the auditing mechanism are displayed in the right-hand margin when in code view for a particular file. Warnings are shown as an orange block and errors are shown in red. You can hover the mouse over the color block to see what the problem is. The information will also be posted at the top of the Structure window when the file is selected.

The built-in auditing capability within JDeveloper is extremely rich, and not all of the audit rules are activated by default. You can view and configure the whole mechanism through the **Tools | Preferences** dialog. It is possible to create your own audit profile by activating and combining those rules that you want to apply to your project. You can also create custom rules through the supplied export-import mechanism and the JDeveloper extension API, although this is not a trivial task.

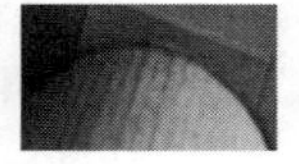

TIP
Audit is not just for Java code. The audit rules also include a large number of checks for your metadata, including JSF UIs. For example, you will be warned if component attributes such as shortDesc, *which are used by screen readers when processing a page, are missing. This helps you build accessible applications.*

As well as auditing concurrently as you work, you can also run audits from the **Build | Audit** menu option or even from a command line or build system using the *ojaudit* program, which you can find in the JDeveloper/bin directory.

The following illustration shows the result of running an audit on a version of TUHRA as it was being developed. Most of the warnings here are to do with the JavaDoc; however, the highlighted warning is an important one, as it points out an issue that may not surface as a bug until after the application is running in production in a cluster of application servers. In this case, if a session is migrated from one server to another as a failover happens, the contents of this managed bean uiState would not be copied—resulting in unpredictable behavior:

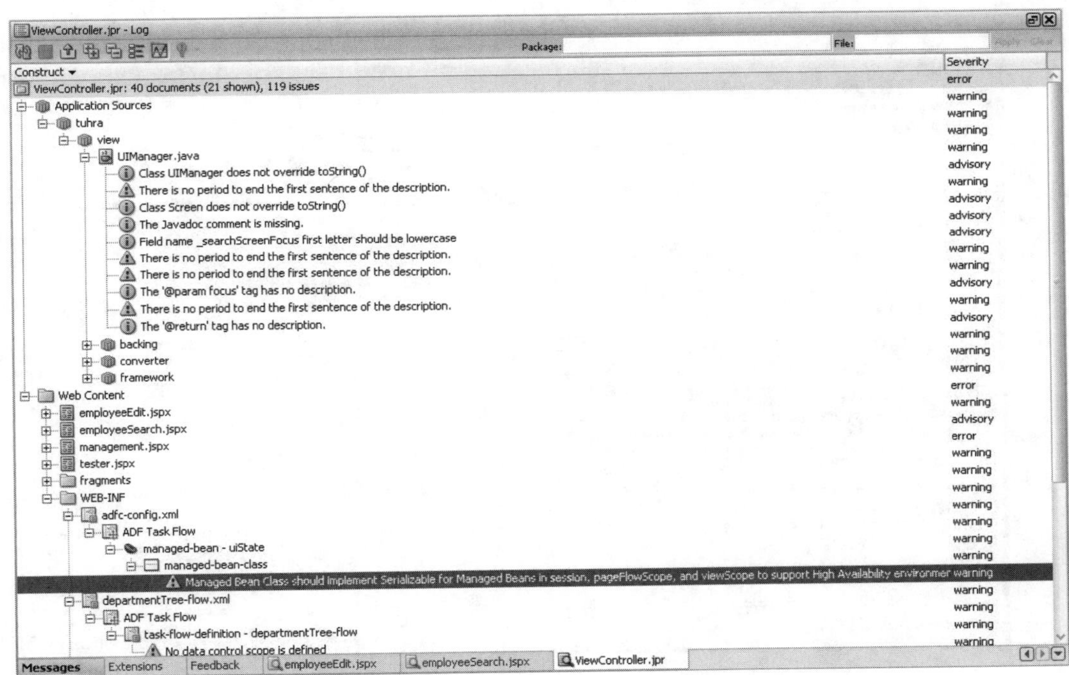

You can use the right mouse menu **About...** option to view a little more information about the error or warning, and double click to drill down to the file with the problem.

More Built-in Tools

The built-in audit capability provides a good baseline sanity check on your code, although it is not a substitute for testing. JDeveloper also provides CPU and memory profilers, which are accessible through the Run menu. Both of these tools actually run your application and then observe it and gather statistics. Using these tools, you can identify where your code is spending most of its time and allocating memory. You should be warned that your first experience of using these advanced tools should probably not be on an ADF project. When the framework is involved, you will be flooded with information relating to that and it will be hard to pick out your code. So for your first investigations, profile some of your unit test code where you are dealing with a much smaller set of classes.

FindBugs

Finally, we need to mention an open-source tool that can be a really useful addition to your armory—FindBugs (findbugs.sourceforge.net). *FindBugs* is a static analysis tool. It looks through your code in a different way from the audit capability that is built into JDeveloper, although often both techniques will highlight some of the same issues. In the following illustration you can see that FindBugs has noticed that there is a particular code path within the *EmployeeEditBean* where you have missed a check for null before referencing an object, in this case *lockedBinding*:

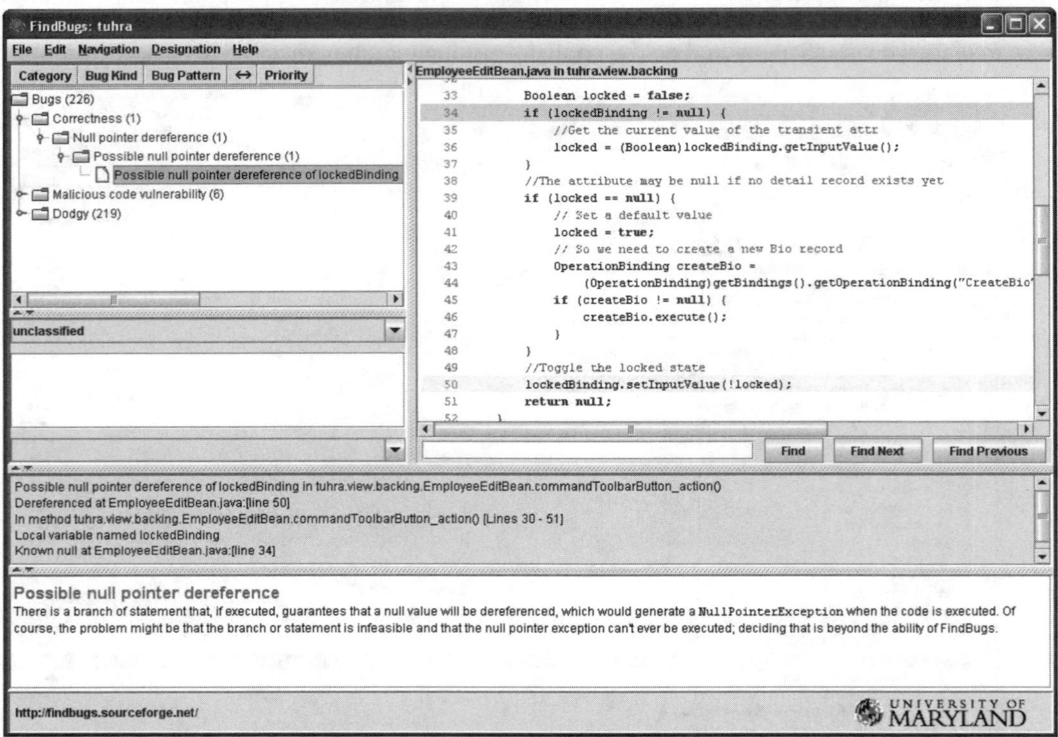

Notice that higher up in the same file the utility also reference the `lockedBinding` object, but in that case the code correctly places a guard condition around it to ensure that the object reference is not null. This is typical of the type of error that FindBugs can identify for you and how it can really help you to improve the quality of your code.

So, enough of all the theory and background—it's time to write some code.

CHAPTER 17

Sample Application: UI Patterns and Templates

Good design keeps the user happy,
the manufacturer in the black
and the aesthete unoffended.

—Raymond Loewy (1893–1986), industrial designer

In the design phase of an application, you will identify standards that will guide the development work. One category of standards to consider is the look and feel of the web pages in the application. Users will more easily understand your application and will therefore be more productive if all pages are designed to look and act the same. If UI consistency is properly implemented, users can learn the common features of one page and they will quickly understand all other pages in the application.

Standards for "common look and feel" are most often implemented by the use of templates. When discussing user interface development, the term *template* refers to a file that contains elements and functions that are common to many or all pages in the application. These common elements supply the consistent look and feel that helps the user understand the application. The common functions allow the user to perform operations such as logout and login on many pages. An additional benefit of template use is easier maintenance; changing common elements in a number of windows or pages is often as easy as modifying a common file that is used by all windows or pages.

JDeveloper 11*g* offers support for page templates on which you can base your JSF JSP files. The template contains content areas that you use for the components specific to the page such as a data input form or table specific to the screen function. It also contains common elements and functions (both visual and non-visual) such as commit actions, menus, title bars, and footer messages. When you run a page based on a template, the common elements and functions from the template are included onto the page; this means you do not need to copy these elements to each page.

The hands-on practice in this chapter shows how to define a JSF page template that will be used to supply common elements for the all pages in the application. Before setting up and testing the template, it shows how to prepare the application for work, including creating the application workspace, setting up project properties, and adding framework files.

Another preparation step for this practice application is to modify the standard HR schema to allow it to demonstrate some advanced principles in later chapters. The work in the hands-on practice is divided into the following phases:

I. Prepare the application workspace

II. Prepare the database

- Create a database diagram
- Modify the diagram
- Alter the database

III. Set up project defaults

- Create Model framework superclasses
- Set up ViewController properties
- Declare the application's skin

IV. Define a JSF page template

- Create the file
- Add boxes and panels
- Define a menu and popup
- Define the named content area of the template
- Test the template
- Fix the copyright text

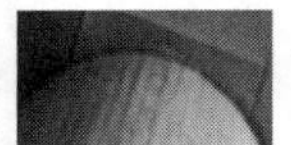

NOTE
As mentioned before, ADF Faces applications must be run in a compatible web browser: Internet Explorer version 7.0 or later; Mozilla Firefox 2.0 or later; or Safari 2.0 or later.

I. Prepare the Application Workspace

The first stage of any work in JDeveloper is to create the application (formerly called "application workspace"). As described in Chapter 3, an *application* is an organizational unit in JDeveloper that contains all projects required to fulfill a set of the business' needs. It is represented as a .jws file on disk. Each workspace contains one or more *projects,* which are represented as .jpr files and which encapsulate the actual coding of the application (except for some external files such as application security files as discussed in Chapter 22). The workspace has no real properties or attributes except for information about application deployment. The projects contained within it contain the source tree of code and metadata.

By convention, projects within an application are split along architectural lines. For instance, in a typical web application that uses the MVC architecture, the default application template creates two projects: one project called "Model," which will contain your application business logic (the Business Services layer primarily), and a second project called "ViewController," which will contain the user interface (View) and page flow (Controller) code. There is nothing to stop you from creating more projects to subdivide an application further, for example, for functional areas of the UI or for your database model, as we discussed in Chapter 16.

This phase of the practice sets up the application and a Model and ViewController project under it.

1. In the Application Navigator, select New Application in the application pulldown menu. The Create Generic Application dialog will appear as shown here:

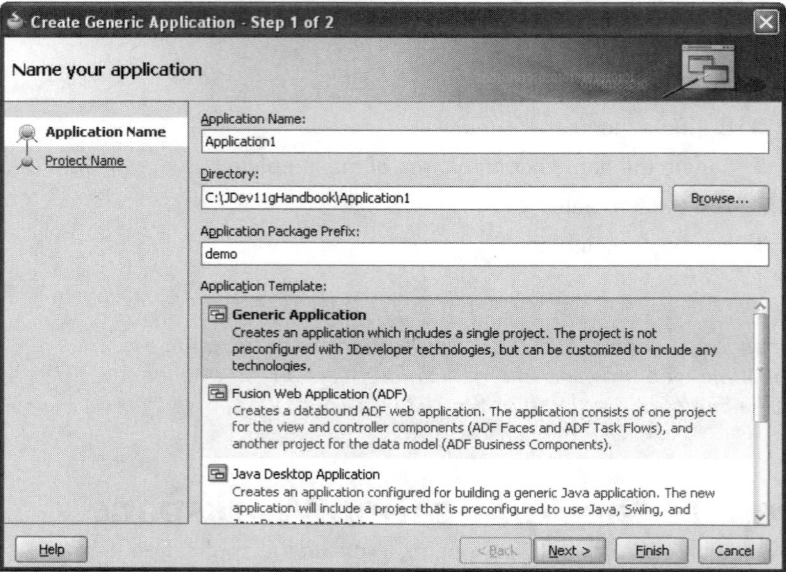

2. Enter the *Application Name* as "tuhra2." The *Directory* will default to a location such as C:\JDeveloper\mywork\<application name>, but you can change it if needed. Examples in this part of the book use "C:\JDev11gHandbook" as the root directory for all application directories, so this application directory would be "C:\JDev11gHandbook\tuhra2."

   Additional Information: This directory will contain the tuhra2.jws (application workspace) file and all project directories you include in the application. If you need to back up the application or store it in a source code control system such as Subversion, you will usually store the entire directory tree starting at the application level. This will ensure that all required files are included.

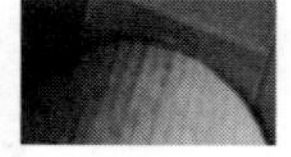

TIP
Remember that we comply with American typesetting standards, which place a sentence- or clause-ending punctuation mark inside the quotes. Do not type this punctuation mark into the value unless instructed to do so.

3. Set the *Application Package Prefix* as "tuhra" to specify the Java package (that corresponds to a file system folder) that will act as the root structure to contain all files you will deploy.

   Additional Information: The *Application Package Prefix* differs from the *Directory* designation you set in the preceding step because *Directory* is specific to the computer, which you are using for development whereas the *Application Package Prefix* is abstracted from the actual file system of any computer.

4. In the *Application Template* area, select "Fusion Web Application (ADF)."

   Additional Information: We discussed application templates and how to customize them in Chapter 16.

5. Click Next to display the "Name your project" page (for the Model project). You could alter the default to satisfy a specific application need, but in this case, the default will work.

6. Click Next to display the "Configure Java settings" page. Again, the defaults will work. Notice how the "model" suffix has been added to the tuhra package root that was specified at the start of the wizard.

7. Click Next and, on this page, click Finish to accept the default settings for the second (ViewController) project. The Application Overview window will appear in the editor window as shown in Figure 17-1.

   Additional Information: As described in Chapter 3, the *Application Overview window* summarizes the status of all elements in the application. Descriptions of the elements help you understand which types of files are needed. The objects are divided into panels that represent functional areas such as Java files and XML files. You can modify the scope of the display using the *Show* pulldown in the top window border. All panels contain controls for handling window operations (minimize and maximize) as well as a pulldown for filtering the objects displayed (shown as "Getting Started" in Figure 17-1) and a *New* pulldown for creating objects in that category. This view provides quick access to errors and to-do items within the application as well as other useful metrics such as audit warnings. You can view this overview at any time using the **Application** | **Show Overview** menu option.

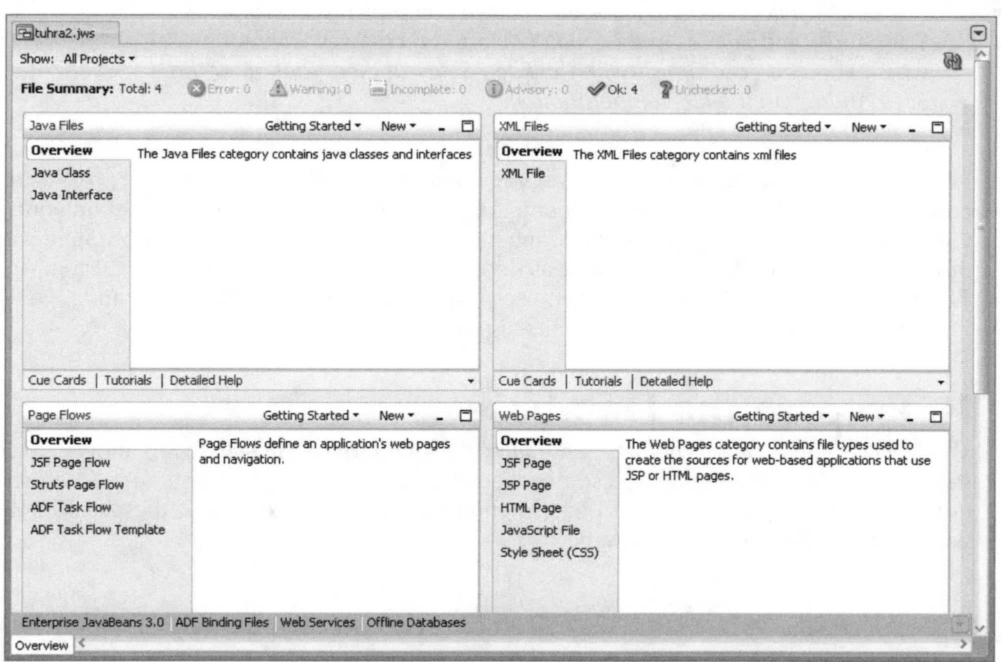

FIGURE 17-1. *Application Overview window*

8. You now need to create a project to hold scripts you will use to modify the database. In the application menu (the right-side pulldown above the toolbar) in the Application Navigator, select "New Project."

   Additional Information: The right-click menu in the Application Navigator will not show the New Project option, but it does have the more general New option, which, just like the CTRL-N keyboard shortcut, will invoke the New Gallery. From the New Gallery you can then select the Projects category.

9. Double click Generic Project to load the Create Generic Project dialog. In the Step 1 page, move "Database (Offline)" from the *Available* area to the *Selected* area.

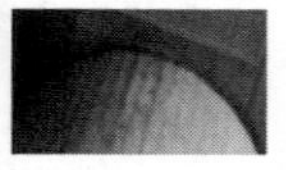

TIP
Double clicking an Available *item in any shuttle control will move it to the* Selected *area without a need to click the move (">") button. In addition, you can usually select more than one option using* CTRL*-click before clicking the move button.*

10. Fill in the Project Name as "DatabaseSchema" and click Finish. A DatabaseSchema project will appear in the navigator.
11. Click Save All.

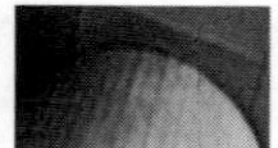

NOTE
Although JDeveloper automatically saves your work to temporary files, it is always a good idea to save after you've completed a unit of work. The hands-on practices in this book contain directives to Save All, which you can accomplish with the ***File | Save All*** *menu option or the Save All icon in the JDeveloper toolbar.*

What Did You Just Do? In this phase, you created the application and three projects that will contain all the files for it. This step is common to all work in JDeveloper. If you find yourself using the same application template and altering it in the same way for multiple new applications, it is time to create an application template as described in the section "Defining a Custom Application Template" in Chapter 16. Then you can use your custom application template and save the manual steps to alter the standard application template.

II. Prepare the Database

The TUHRA2 application requires some minor changes to the HR schema to allow automatic sequence number generation. It also needs several new tables to demonstrate the features of domains and image uploads. This phase demonstrates how to accomplish these tasks by starting with a JDeveloper database diagram.

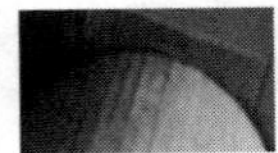

CAUTION
You are about to make changes to your default Oracle HR schema in the database. You might want to take a backup of the schema using ***Tools | Database Export*** *menu option from JDeveloper and then locate the scripts needed to re-create it in its original state. By default, the scripts to re-create the HR and other demo schemas can be found in the /demo/schema directory of your database install. The script you need is called mkplug.sql on an 11g and 10g R2 database. Alternatively, you can use scripts available on the websites mentioned in the "Websites for Sample Files" section of the Introduction.*

Create a Database Diagram

You can make modifications to the database using any tool with which you are comfortable. Sometimes, design changes are easier to understand if they are made in a visual tool, such as a diagram. JDeveloper supports this kind of visual design work for database objects as well as for Java-oriented objects. This section creates a diagram of the existing database objects and changes some of the default properties.

1. Select the DatabaseSchema project and press CTRL-N to display the New Gallery. Select the Database Tier\Database Objects category and double click Database Diagram.
2. Enter *Name* as "HR Schema Diagram." Leave the *Package* as "tuhra" and click OK. A blank diagram will open in the editor window.
3. The next steps create a database connection to the HR schema. The connection will allow you to drag and drop database objects onto the diagram as well as to connect ADF Business Components objects to the database for development and runtime purposes. Expand the Application Resources node of the navigator. On the Connections node, select **New Connection | Database** from the right-click menu to display the Create Database Connection dialog.
4. Fill in the Name as "HR_DB" and set the *Username* to "hr." Set *Password, Host Name, JDBC Port,* and *SID* as appropriate to your installation. Use the Test Connection button to check that the database is available. Fix any problems and click OK when all problems are cleared.

   Additional Information: New database installations usually leave the HR schema locked, so you will need to be sure the schema is unlocked and you will need the HR account password. The port for most Oracle installations is 1521. You will need to reset the default SID of "XE" if your Oracle installation is different. If you are running the Oracle database on your desktop machine, the *Host Name* will be "localhost."

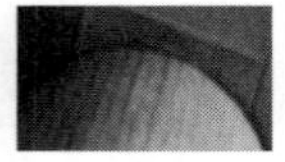

NOTE
*Database connections work differently in JDeveloper 10*g *and JDeveloper 11*g*. In JDeveloper 10*g*, the connection is global to the IDE, so everyone working on the application needs to create a connection with an identical name. In JDeveloper 11*g*, the connection is a resource (asset) of the application workspace. This means everyone working on the same application can use the same connection definition. JDeveloper 11*g *allows you to have global IDE connections for purposes such as ad hoc database queries that are outside an application. These global connections can be defined from the Database Navigator (***View | Database Navigator***) or the Resource Palette (CTRL-SHIFT-O). Once created, those global connections can also be dragged and dropped into a workspace to create an application resource connection with the same information.*

5. Expand the Connections\Database nodes to view the new HR_DB connection.
6. Expand the HR_DB and Tables nodes and multi-select (by holding down CTRL while clicking each selection) the tables COUNTRIES, DEPARTMENTS, EMPLOYEES, JOB_HISTORY, JOBS, LOCATIONS, and REGIONS. Drag and drop this group of tables onto the diagram. The Specify Location dialog will appear as shown here.

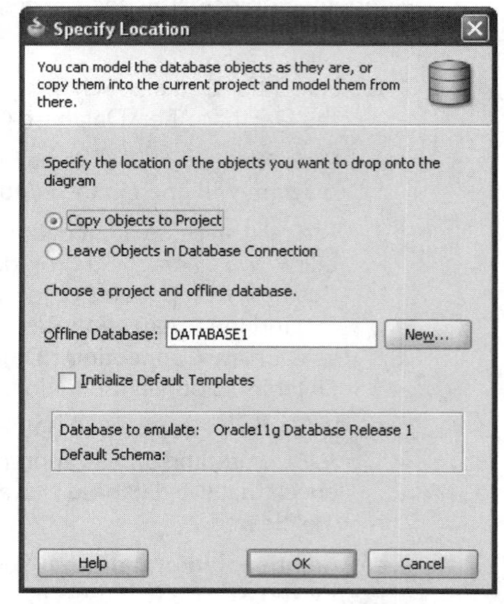

7. Leave the default selection for *Copy Objects to Project* and be sure *Initialize Default Templates* is deselected. Change *Offline Database* to "TUHRA." Click OK.

   Additional Information: Copying the objects to the project sets up definitions in the project that replicate the state of the objects when you performed the copy operation. This means you can work on the diagram objects without a database connection and without affecting objects in the database. The other option, *Leave Objects in Database Connection,* will not create local copies but will automatically synchronize the diagram with the state of objects in the online database.

   Selecting *Initialize Default Templates* causes JDeveloper to create additional features in objects you create in the diagram. For example, assume you had selected this checkbox when setting up the offline database name in the Specify Location dialog. If you then dragged a table object from the Component Palette to the diagram and changed its name, JDeveloper would create a default primary key column and primary key constraint for that new table. In this application, we want to create everything manually, so the TUHRA offline database does not use this feature.

8. Repeat steps 6 and 7 with the Sequences node objects. This will create diagram and offline database objects for three sequences: DEPARTMENTS_SEQ, EMPLOYEES_SEQ, and LOCATIONS_SEQ. Click a blank space in the diagram to deselect the sequences.

9. The sequence objects on the diagram use the same title bar color as the tables. To better distinguish the sequences, you can change the color of the objects in the diagram. Select **Select All This Type** from the right-click menu on DEPARTMENTS_SEQ. This will select all sequences.

10. Select **Visual Properties** from the right-click menu on one of the sequences. The Edit Visual Properties dialog will appear as follows:

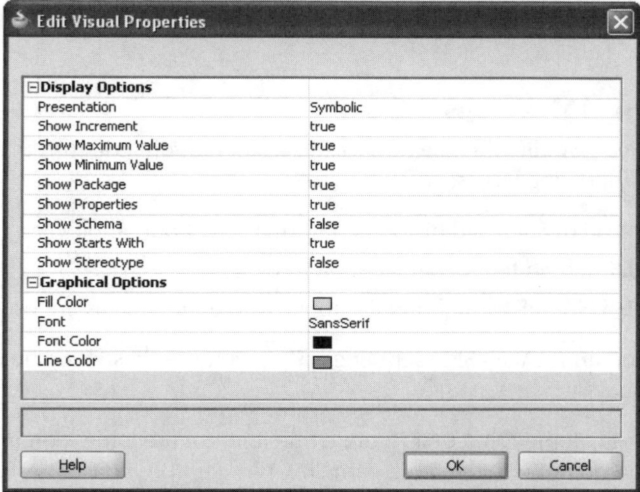

11. Click the color box next to the *Fill Color* property to display the color editor. Select the gray color in the second column of the first row of colors. Click OK. The title bars of all sequences will change to reflect the new color. (You can alternatively use the Property Inspector to set visual properties.)

TIP
You can change the default color for diagram objects by selecting ***Tools | Preferences*** *and selecting the Database page under the Diagrams node. For example, to change sequence objects to display with a different title bar color, select "Sequence" in the* Edit Preferences for *pulldown. On the Color\Font tab, select from the* Fill Color *pulldown and click OK.*

12. Spend a bit of time (five minutes at the most) modifying the layout on the diagram. Start by double clicking the editor tab labeled HR Schema Diagram to expand the diagram to fill the IDE window. Explore the right-click menu options for modifying the layout and for setting properties determining what will be displayed. For example, you can select a table and then set properties to hide the list of check constraints. Save the diagram when you are finished with the alterations.

TIP

Use the Zoom In and Zoom Out buttons in the toolbar, or hold the CTRL *key while using your mouse wheel, to assist in displaying a workable diagram size. Start layout modifications using the hierarchical pulldown (next to the zoom percentage pulldown) in the toolbar; for example, try "Hierarchical (Left to Right)" to show the master tables on the left with detail tables on the right. This pulldown is a powerful auto-layout tool that should result in a layout that is at least 90 percent of what you need. The exact percentage is based on your sense of aesthetics, but consider that it could be as much as 100 percent if your aesthetic matches (or can be flexible enough to be made to match) the layout of this tool.*

Modify the Diagram

In this section, you modify the diagram to add history (audit) columns to the EMPLOYEES table and to add the following tables:

- **BIOGRAPHIES** to hold historical information about employees
- **IMAGES** to hold the locations of pictures
- **IMAGE_USAGES** to store details about where the images are used

You will also add an IMAGE_SEQ sequence. Then you use these modifications in the diagram to alter the database.

1. Double click the EMPLOYEES table title (aim for the table icon in the top-left corner so that you do not edit the table name by mistake). The Edit Table dialog will appear.
2. On the Columns page, select the last column in the table and click the Add Column (green "+") button to add a column. Fill in *Name* as "CREATED_BY," *Type* as "VARCHAR2," *Size* as "30," and *Comment* as "The user who inserted this record." (including the period).

   Additional Information: Moving the cursor to another column or clicking a button will register the change in the column name. You do not need to dismiss the dialog using OK when making changes in the dialog.
3. Repeat the preceding step for the following columns:

Name	Type	Size	Comment
CREATED_DATE	DATE		The time and date when this record was inserted.
MODIFIED_BY	VARCHAR2	30	The user who last updated this record.
MODIFIED_DATE	DATE		The time and date when this record was last updated.

4. The new columns will appear at the end of the column list sorted by the order in which you created them. You can select columns and use the up and down arrow buttons to change the order if needed. Click OK. Click Save All.

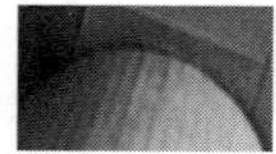

NOTE
You will set ADF BC to assign values to these history columns. The CREATED_BY and CREATED_DATE columns will be assigned when the record is created, so they should be set to NOT NULL. However, the table contains rows already, so you will run a script later on to update the existing rows and set up the NOT NULL constraints.

5. An employee owns one or no biographies, and the biography will be stored in the BIOGRAPHIES table. This table will have a zero-or-one relationship with EMPLOYEES. If the diagram window is maximized, double click the HR Schema Diagram editor tab to restore it. If the Component Palette is not currently visible, display it using **View | Component Palette** from the menu or CTRL-SHIFT-P.

6. Drag a Table from the Component Palette and drop it on the diagram. In the Specify Location dialog, select or leave selected "Application Project" and click OK. In the editable name box, fill in "BIOGRAPHIES" and press ENTER.

   Additional Information: Examine the table you just diagrammed. If JDeveloper automatically added a column, BIOGRAPHIES_ID, you did not deselect the *Initialize Default Templates* checkbox in the Select Location dialog in an earlier step. To correct this problem, delete the table on the diagram. Then, in the Application Navigator, expand the Offline Database Sources node. On the TUHRA node, select Properties from the right-click menu. The Edit Offline Database dialog will appear. On the Default Templates page, select an object type such as Functions and select the blank option in the *Name* field. Repeat this setting for each object type. Then follow this step again to create the table.

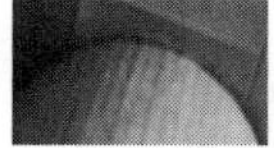

TIP
In the Edit Offline Database dialog we just described, you can select a template object type, and click Edit (pencil icon) to view and change the settings for the template that JDeveloper uses to create a diagram object of that type. Although you cannot modify the database version after it is created, instead of creating offline databases in the diagramming process, you can create them from the Offline Database Sources node (using the ***New*** *right-click menu option) and specify the database version in that process.*

7. Double click the table icon in the BIOGRAPHIES table to open the Edit Table dialog. Select the Comment node and fill in *Comment* as "A description of relevant history, accomplishments, and notable events for an employee." (including the period).

8. Select the Columns node in the navigator. Add columns with the following properties:

Name	Type	Size	Cannot be NULL	Comment
EMPLOYEE_ID	NUMBER	PRECISION: 6 SCALE: 0	Checked	Unique identifier for the biography text for an employee.

Name	Type	Size	Cannot be NULL	Comment
BIO_UPDATED_DATE	DATE		Checked	The date on which this biography was entered.
BIOGRAPHY	CLOB		Checked	Text that details relevant history, accomplishments, and notable events for the employee.

9. On the Primary Key page, move EMPLOYEE_ID to the *Selected Columns* area. Leave the default name. Click OK to dismiss the dialog.
10. Select Foreign Key in the Component Palette, click EMPLOYEES (the master table), and click BIOGRAPHIES (the detail table). Leave the default name. Select EMP_EMP_ID_PK as the referenced constraint and ensure that EMPLOYEE_ID appears in the *Local Column* and *Referenced Column on EMPLOYEES* fields. Ensure that *On Delete* is set to "RESTRICT." Click OK.
11. Using similar steps, add a table called IMAGES with a comment of "The location of a file containing a picture of the employee." (including the period) and the following columns:

Name	Type	Size	Cannot be NULL	Comment
IMAGE_ID	NUMBER	PRECISION: 6 SCALE: 0	Checked	The unique identifier for an image.
IMAGE	VARCHAR2	120	Checked	A file system path and file name for the graphic file. The path is relative to the project directory.

12. Define a primary key using IMAGE_ID is used as the primary key column. Click OK to dismiss the table dialog. Click Save All.
13. Using the same methods, add an IMAGE_USAGES table with a comment of "Information about where the image in the IMAGES table is utilized." (including the period) and with the following columns:

Name	Type	Size	Cannot be NULL	Default	Comment
IMAGE_ID	NUMBER	PRECISION: 6 SCALE: 0	Checked		The image referenced by this usage.

Name	Type	Size	Cannot be NULL	Default	Comment
USAGE_TYPE	VARCHAR2	1	Checked	'E'	What this image is associated with, for example, "E" means that this is an image for an employee.
ASSOCIATED_ID	NUMBER	PRECISION: 6 SCALE: 0	Checked		The unique ID value (for example, EMPLOYEE_ID) of the object with which the image is associated.
DEFAULT_IMAGE	VARCHAR2	1	Checked	'N'	"Y" if this image is the image used most often for the associated object. "N" otherwise.

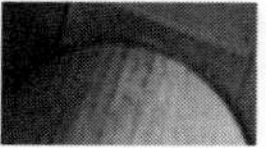

NOTE
Be sure to enter the default values using single quotes as shown.

14. Define a primary key consisting of three columns: IMAGE_ID, USAGE_TYPE, and ASSOCIATED_ID. Click OK to dismiss the table editor. Click Save All.
15. Select Foreign Key in the Component Palette, click IMAGES, and click IMAGE_USAGES. Leave the *Name* as the default. Ensure that IMAGE_ID appears in the *Local Column* and *Referenced Column on IMAGES* fields. Ensure that *On Delete* is set to "RESTRICT." Click OK.
16. Select Sequence in the Component Palette and drop it on the diagram. Fill in the name as IMAGES_SEQ. All sequence defaults will work as is, so you do not need to visit the Edit Sequence Database dialog, but you can double click the sequence icon in the IMAGES_SEQ title bar if you wish to review its properties. Click Cancel when you are finished viewing the properties.
17. Click on an empty space in the diagram and select **Visual Properties** from the right-click menu. Set the value of *Max Shape Width* as "300." Click OK.

    Additional Information: The visual properties of the diagrams in JDeveloper act within constraints defined for each diagram type. The automatic width adjustment, for example, will adjust the width up to the maximum allowed for that diagram type. Unfortunately, the default width of 200 is not quite wide enough for this schema, so you just increased the default for this particular diagram. You can also use the **Tools | Preferences** menu to change the defaults for any future diagrams that you create.
18. Group select the new tables and sequence. Select **Optimize Shape Size | Height and Width** from the right-click menu to show all of the content in the objects.
19. Select the new IMAGES_SEQ and set its color to gray as you did for the existing sequences.
20. Select a foreign key line and select **Select All This Type** from the right-click menu. With all foreign key lines selected in this way, select **Straighten Lines** from the right-click menu on a foreign key line. Move any lines that pass through table or sequence boxes. Click Save All.

TIP

*If you want to create a drawing point for an angled line, select **Line Style | Oblique** from the right-click menu on the line. You can then add points by holding the SHIFT key and clicking the line. You can delete a point by holding SHIFT and clicking the point.*

21. You can now create a script that will alter the database to match the diagram. On an open space in the diagram select **Synchronize with Database | Generate to | SQL script** from the right-click menu. The following dialog will appear:

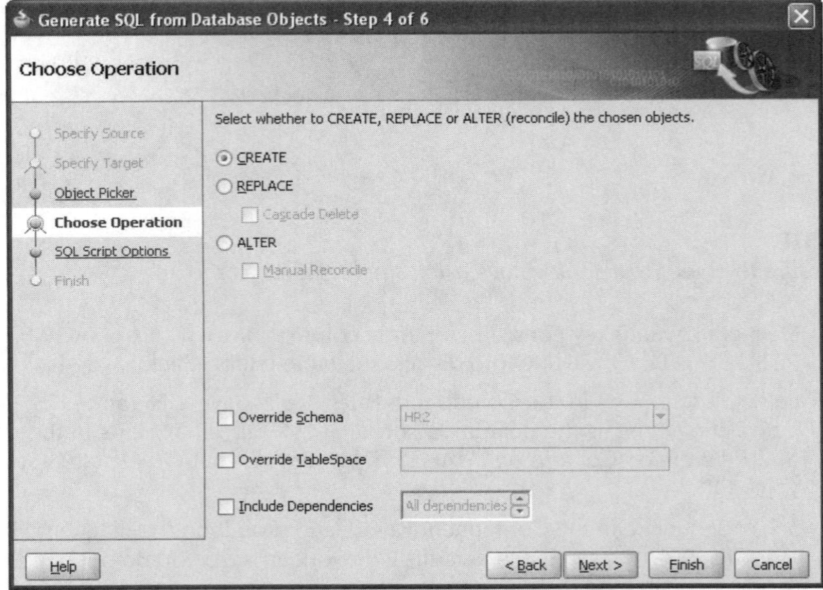

22. Select the *ALTER* radio button and the *Override Schema* checkbox. In the *Connections* pulldown look for an HR_DB connection. If it does not exist, click the "Create a new database connection" (green plus "+") button and fill in the properties, then dismiss the Create New Database Connection dialog. Be sure the schema name is "HR."
23. Click Next. If you receive a warning about generating 11*g* objects for a 10*g* Express database, click Yes. (You will not be creating anything that is Oracle 11*g*-specific.)
24. Enter the *SQL file Name* as "alter_hr_for_tuhra2.sql." Click Finish. The script will be generated and will appear in an editor window.

Alter the Database

The alter script you created will make changes to the database based on the modifications you made in the diagram. For this application, you also need to add some additional code to handle the automatically loaded column values. This section adds this code and then runs the script to make the changes to the database.

1. At the end of the script, add the following code to assign the history column values to EMPLOYEES and to set the created columns to NOT NULL:

```
UPDATE employees
SET created_by = 'HR',
    created_date = TO_DATE('01/01/1980 12:12','MM/DD/YYYY HH24:MI');

COMMIT;

ALTER TABLE employees
MODIFY (created_by CONSTRAINT emp_created_by_nn NOT NULL,
        created_date CONSTRAINT emp_created_date_nn NOT NULL);
```

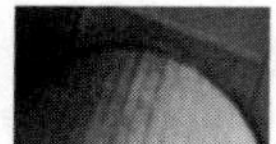

TIP
As mentioned, you can download a file containing code snippets for these practices from the websites mentioned in the "Websites for Sample Files" section of the Introduction.

2. At the end of the script, add the following code to create a trigger that will assign the sequence number for an employee when the record is created:

```
CREATE OR REPLACE TRIGGER employees_bi
   BEFORE INSERT
   ON employees
   FOR EACH ROW
BEGIN
   SELECT employees_seq.nextval
   INTO   :new.employee_id
   FROM   dual;
END;
/
```

3. Again, at the end of the script, add the following SQL to create the trigger that loads the IMAGES_SEQ value into IMAGE_ID during an INSERT:

```
CREATE OR REPLACE TRIGGER images_bi
   BEFORE INSERT
   ON images
   FOR EACH ROW
BEGIN
   SELECT images_seq.nextval
   INTO   :new.image_id
   FROM   dual;
END;
/
```

4. Click Save All.
5. In the top-right corner of the alter_hr_for_tuhra.sql editor window's toolbar, select HR_DB (tuhra2) from the pulldown to connect to the database.

6. Select **Run Script** from the right-click menu in the script (or click the Run Script button in the SQL Worksheet window).

   Additional Information: This script will alter the database with the changes you made in the diagram as well as the additional code for triggers and for setting the create history columns in EMPLOYEES to NOT NULL. You can view messages from the script in the Script Output tab at the bottom of the SQL Worksheet window.

7. Return to the diagram tab in the editor. Select **Synchronize with Database | Refresh from [HR_DB]** from the right-click menu. In the Confirm Offline Object Overwrite dialog, click Yes.
8. Visit the Edit Table dialog for EMPLOYEES to confirm that the NOT NULL constraints were added to CREATED_BY and CREATED_DATE. Click Cancel.
9. Click Save All. Close the editor windows.

What Did You Just Do? You just modified a database schema using the JDeveloper database diagram to visualize the changes and generate the Data Definition Language (DDL) script required to make the changes. You also ran the DDL script in the database.

In most development environments, you perform development work in a special development database instance separate from the production instance. When the application has been developed, you promote the changes made to the development database into the next level in your production process—usually a quality assurance or user acceptance test database instance—and test the application in that environment. Eventually, the application will go live and you will make changes to a production database. As you move through this promotion process, you can run the DDL script you created in this phase; it is part of the process and is stored with the application files.

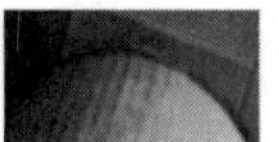

NOTE
It is important that any minor changes made outside of this script be captured so that the database alteration process can be complete.

III. Set Up Project Defaults

This phase creates the framework superclass files mentioned in Chapter 16. These files provide a central place for setting up and for changing the default behavior of all application module instances, entity object instances, and view object instances in the Model project. You will also set properties for the ViewController project that will modify how the application runs and where it looks for messages.

Create Model Framework Superclasses

This section adds framework superclasses to the Model project. You will add framework superclasses to the ViewController project in a later chapter. In most development situations you would actually want to share these same superclasses between all of your development projects and so would be creating them in a separate workspace and deploying them in a library for reuse in other applications. However, for simplicity here you will keep them in the Model project.

1. Select the Model project.

2. Press CTRL-N to display the New Gallery. Select the General\Java category and double click Java Class. The Create Java Class dialog will appear.
3. Fill in *Name* as "TuhraApplicationModuleImpl" and *Package* as "tuhra.model.framework."
4. Click the browse (magnifying glass) button next to the *Extends* field and type into the *Match Class Name* field "ApplicationModuleImpl." As you are typing, the classes matching this name will appear. Select the class with this name from the `oracle.jbo.server` package. Click OK.
5. Deselect *Constructors from Superclass* and click OK.
6. Select the tuhra.model.framework node in the Application Navigator

   Additional Information: Setting the navigator focus to the framework package before the next classes are created will indicate to JDeveloper which package you want the new classes to be created in, saving the work of re-entering the information each time.
7. Repeat steps 2–6 for the following classes:

New Class File	Extends
TuhraEntityImpl	EntityImpl
TuhraViewObjectImpl	ViewObjectImpl
TuhraViewRowImpl	ViewRowImpl

8. Double click the Model project to open its editor. Select the Business Components\Base Classes page and fill in the following settings to declare default superclasses for any objects you create in this project.

Field	Value
Entity Object: Row	tuhra.model.framework.TuhraEntityImpl
View Object: Object	tuhra.model.framework.TuhraViewObjectImpl
View Object: Row	tuhra.model.framework.TuhraViewRowImpl
Application Module: Object	tuhra.model.framework.TuhraApplicationModuleImpl

9. Select the Resource Bundle page and change *Default Project Bundle Name* to "tuhra.model.resources.ModelBundle."

   Additional Information: To simplify development, the book does not go out of its way to externalize labels and other strings into resource bundles, but this file can be used for any future strings that need to be stored in a resource bundle. Chapter 10 discusses and demonstrates resource bundles (message bundles).
10. Click OK (select Yes in the Confirm Change dialog). Click Save All.

Set Up ViewController Properties

In this section, you change properties for the ViewController project to set the context root (the runtime "directory") and web application name (to name the deployment file). You will also set some project properties that specify that runtime business components messages will appear in the console window.

1. Double click the ViewController project node to display its properties. On the Java EE Application page set *Java EE Web Application Name* as "tuhra2" *and Java EE Web Context Root* to "tuhra2."

   Additional Information: The *Java EE Web Application Name* will show in the application server (WebLogic Server) control. The *Java EE Web Context Root* is the directory name in the URL for the application.

2. Select the Resource Bundle page and change *Default Project Bundle Name* to "tuhra. view.resources.ViewControllerBundle."

   Additional Information: As with the Model project resources bundle, this file can store any strings that need to be moved from a component to the resource bundle.

3. You can now set an option to assist in debugging the ViewController project files. Select the Run/Debug/Profile page. Click Yes in the Confirm Change dialog. Click New and set *Name* as "FrameworkLogging" and *Copy Settings From* as "Default." Click OK.

4. With the FrameworkLogging run configuration selected, click Edit. Set *Java Options* as "-Djbo.debugoutput=console" (with an uppercase "D").

   Additional Information: This debugging switch sets up ADF BC to run in a mode that outputs information about all of the SQL statements that are sent to the database.

5. Click OK. Click OK. Click Save All.

Declare the Application's Skin

The TUHRA2 application as shown throughout the book uses the Oracle Browser Look and Feel (BLAF) as defined by the "blafplus-rich" skin (described in Chapter 12). If you are using a newer version of JDeveloper than the 11.1.1.1.0 release, you may find a different skin called "fusion" being used by default. In this section, you will ensure that the correct skin is being used.

1. In the ViewController project, expand the Web Content/WEB-INF node in the navigator and double click the trinidad-config.xml file to open it in the editor.

   Additional Information: The trinidad-config.xml controls several aspects of the behavior of the ADF Faces components including accessibility mode and debugging.

2. In the Structure window, select the `skin-family` node and ensure that the value is set to "blafplus-rich" rather than a value such as "fusion." The source code should read as follows:

   ```
   <skin-family>blafplus-rich</skin-family>
   ```

3. Click Save All if you made a change to the value.

What Did You Just Do? In this phase, you set up defaults for the Model project, in the form of framework superclasses that provide application-specific behavior to all business components in the application. You also set some default properties for the ViewController project for the context root and web application name. In addition, you set up a runtime configuration you can use to debug business components. Finally, you ensured that the correct skin was being used for the ADF Faces components.

IV. Define a JSF Page Template

This phase creates a UI template that will supply a common look and feel for the application pages. The basic layout for all pages will be a fixed title at the top of the page, a resizable copyright and message area at the bottom, and a stretchable pane for content in the middle. You will also add a menu bar with a Help About menu item that shows a popup dialog with information about the application. Figure 17-2 shows a page based on the template (with no content).

Create the File

This section creates a JSF page template that you will use as a basis for other pages in the application.

1. Select the ViewController project node and display the New Gallery (CTRL-N). In the Web Tier\JSF category double click JSF Page Template to display the Create JSF Page Template dialog.
2. Fill in *File Name* as "tuhraTemplate.jspx" and add to the *Directory* value after ". . . public_html" the value "\WEB-INF\templates." Leave the *Page Template Name* as "tuhraTemplate."

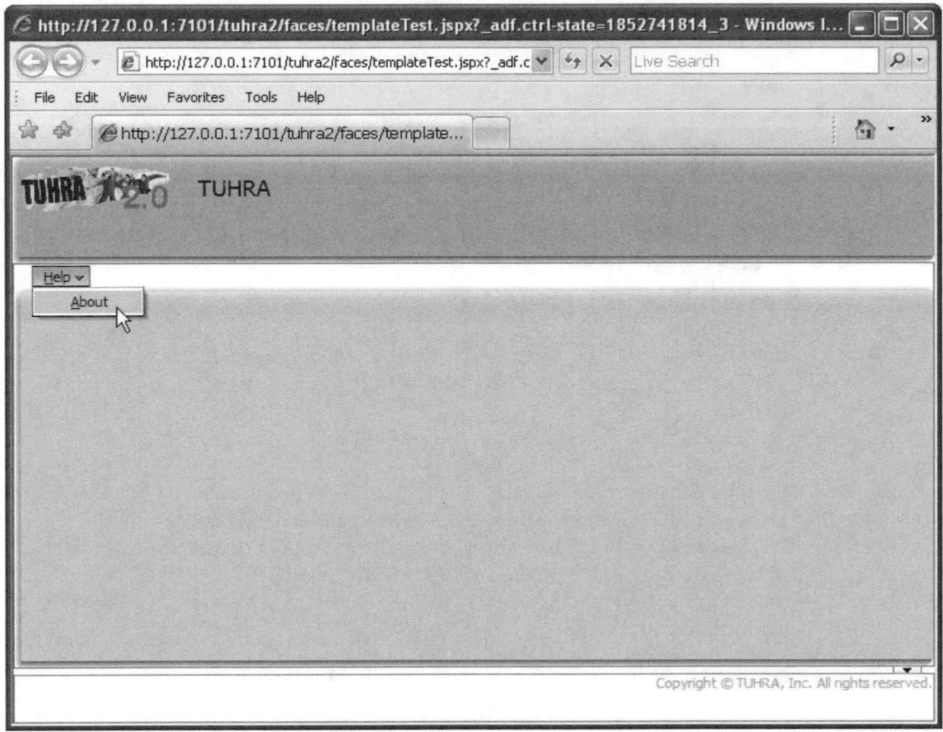

FIGURE 17-2. *A page based on the TUHRA template at runtime*

Additional Information: Any file stored in the WEB-INF directory (or subdirectory) of a web application cannot be directly run. This makes it a good place to store files such as templates; however, this is just a convention and you could put your templates anywhere under the HTML root (public_html).

3. Select the *Create Associated ADFm Page Definition* checkbox if it is not selected. You will add an ADF BC lookup to the template later and the page definition file will hold the binding for this lookup.
4. On the Facet Definitions tab, click the New (green plus "+") button to add a facet. Fill in *Name* as "content."

   Additional Information: This facet will be available for specific content for the pages you create from the template.
5. On the Attributes tab, click the New (green plus "+") button and fill in *Name* as "pageTitle." Leave *Type* as "java.lang.String" and fill in *Default Value* as "TUHRA."

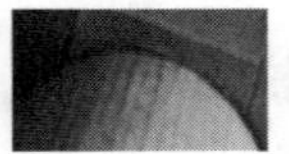

TIP
Before you close the Create dialog, select the Use a Quick Start Layout *checkbox (as described in Chapter 12) and click Browse to explore some of the default layouts that exist for templates and pages. In this example, you will be building the template from scratch, but for your own templates and pages, you will probably want to use this feature to save a little time. Cancel the dialog and deselect the* Use a Quick Start Layout *option when you are done.*

6. Be sure that *Use a Quick Start Layout* is deselected. Click OK. Click Save All.
7. The visual editor will open the new template file. Select the Source tab to view the code, if it is not already selected. You will see code like the following to represent the values you entered in the Create JSF Page Template dialog (surrounded by various `<jsp:>` tags that we have omitted to save space):

```
<af:pageTemplateDef var="attrs">
  <af:xmlContent>
    <component xmlns="http://xmlns.oracle.com/adf/faces/rich/component">
      <display-name>tuhraTemplate</display-name>
      <facet>
        <facet-name>content</facet-name>
      </facet>
      <attribute>
        <attribute-name>pageTitle</attribute-name>
        <attribute-class>java.lang.String</attribute-class>
        <default-value>TUHRA</default-value>
      </attribute>
    </component>
  </af:xmlContent>
</af:pageTemplateDef>
```

8. Switch to the Design tab of the editor. From the Component Palette ADF Faces page, scroll down in the Layout panel and find the Panel Stretch Layout component. Drop it into the template. The editor will display the facets of this component as shown next.

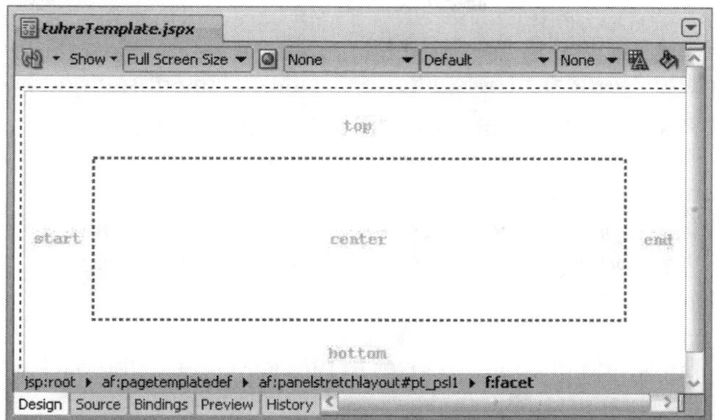

9. In this case you only care about the top and center facets, so you will hide the other facets. On the right-click menu for the `af:panelStretchLayout` node in the bottom breadcrumbs area of the visual editor (or in the Structure window), select **Facets – Panel Stretch Layout** and one at a time, uncheck the Bottom, Start, and End facets.

   Additional Information: You can alternatively delete the extraneous facets (for example, `<facet name="start"/>` in the source code).

10. In the sections that follow, we will refer to various image files for a icons, logos, and employee images. You can obtain these image files from the websites mentioned in the section "Websites for Sample Files" in the Introduction. All image files are contained within an archive file called tuhra2_application_images.zip. Alternatively, you can locate any other images that will work as a logo, help icon, and employee images.

11. Open a file system explorer (such as Windows Explorer) and navigate to <TUHRA_HOME>\ViewController\public_html (where "<TUHRA_HOME>" is the directory that holds the application workspace file, for example, "C:\JDev11gHandbook\tuhra2\").

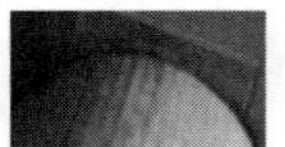

TIP
You can check the Application Properties for the location of your TUHRA_HOME directory or hold the mouse over any file in the navigator to view a tooltip with the file name and location.

12. Create a directory called "images" and copy the images including the TUHRA logo and help image files into it. These files will now be accessible in the application using a path relative to the public_html directory (for example, "/images/help.png").

Add Boxes and Panels

This section sets up the three main areas of the page: the top logo and title area, the middle content area, and the bottom message and copyright area.

1. In the tuhraTemplate.jspx file, select the `af:panelStretchLayout` component (using the Structure window or editor breadcrumbs bar) and in the Property Inspector set *TopHeight* to "50px" if it is not already "50px."

   Additional Information: This property defines the default height of the top facet of the layout, if it contains something. If the facet is empty, no space will be allocated.

2. From the Component Palette, drop a Panel Splitter into the center facet. It will appear as a horizontal split with a vertical bar. In the Property Inspector, change the *Orientation* property to "vertical." The splitter bar will become positioned horizontally.
3. Set the *PositionedFromEnd* property to true and *SplitterPosition* to "30."

NOTE
SplitterPosition *appears in both the Common and the Appearance sections of the Property Inspector. Changing one of these fields changes the other.*

4. You will now add decorative boxes to provide color to the backgrounds. Drop a Decorative Box component into the top facet of the `af:panelStretchLayout` container. Set *Theme* of the Decorative Box as "medium." The box background color will become a medium gray.
5. Hide the Top facet of the Decorative Box using the right-click menu method described before. (You can alternatively select the top facet in the Structure window and press DELETE.)
6. Drop another Decorative Box onto the first facet of the `af:panelSplitter` component; fill in *Theme* as "light," and hide the Top facet as before.

   Additional Information: At this point you should see three facets in the template: center, center, and second as shown here:

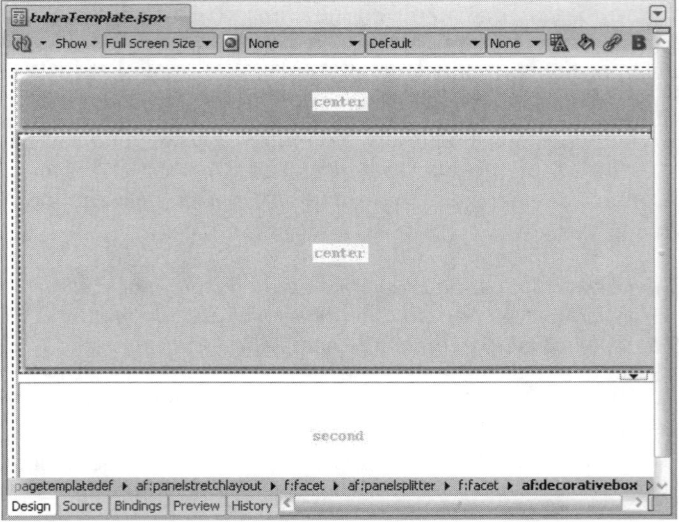

7. You can now add a logo. From the Common Components panel of the Component Palette, drop an Image into the topmost center facet. Select "tuhra.png" from the *Source* pulldown so the field contains "/images/tuhra.png." Fill in *ShortDesc* as "The Ultimate Human Resources Application 2.0 Website." Click OK.
8. In the Property Inspector for the `af:image` component, switch to the Style tab (or expand the Style area). Switch to the Box (third) tab within that section and set *Height* to "30" and select "px" (pixel) in the pulldown next to the *Height* field (scroll to the bottom to see it). The *InlineStyle* property will be set to the value "height:30.0px;" as is shown next.

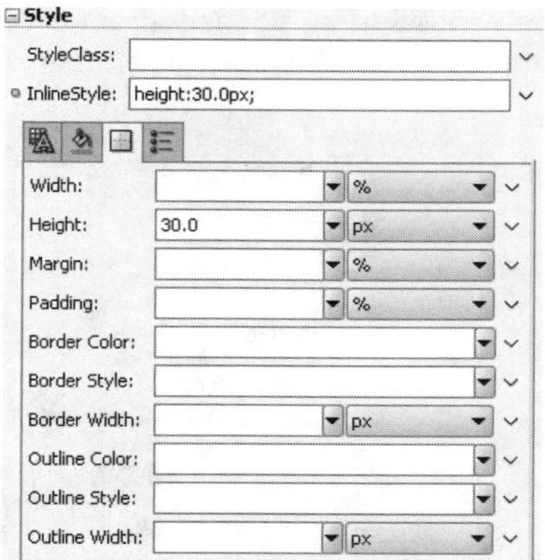

9. The logo will be a hyperlink to the TUHRA website. From the right-click menu on the image tag in the Structure window or visual editor, select **Surround With** and select Go Link (a component used for a hyperlink to specific URL). Set *Text* as a blank, *Destination* as "http://www.tuhra.com," and *TargetFrame* to "_blank" (including the initial underscore so that the link opens the website in a new window).

10. The title for the page will be assigned in the *pageTitle* attribute you set up for the template. Every page that uses the template can have a different title passed in via this template attribute. The *pageTitle* value will be assigned to an `af:outputText` component in the template.
A facet can contain only one object as a direct child, and in this case, the new `af:goLink` is already assigned as that child. However, you can wrap the `af:goLink` component in another layout container so that peer components can be added. Use the **Surround With** right-click menu option as before to add a Panel Group Layout component around the `af:goLink` component.

11. Set the *Layout* of the `af:panelGroupLayout` to "horizontal." This is an important setting, because if you leave the layout as the default the alignment will not work. Drop an Output Text component onto the `af:panelGroupLayout` container (in the Structure window) and set the *value* property to "#{attrs.pageTitle}" using the Expression Builder dialog as shown here.

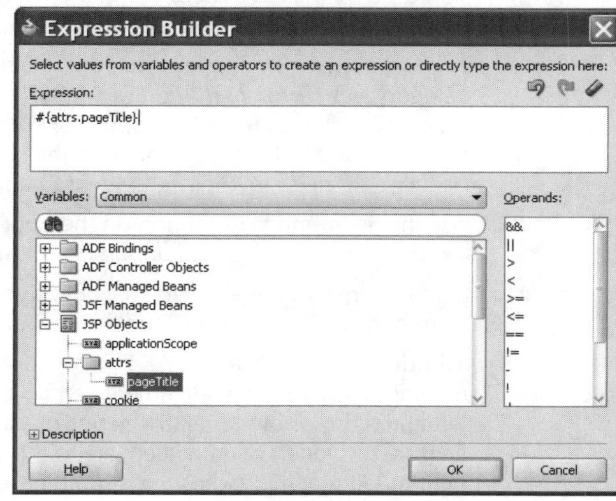

12. Ensure that the *Valign* property of the `af:panelGroupLayout` is set to "middle."

13. Using the Structure window, drag a Spacer (from the Layout panel of the Component Palette) between the `af:goLink` and `af:outputText` components as shown here:

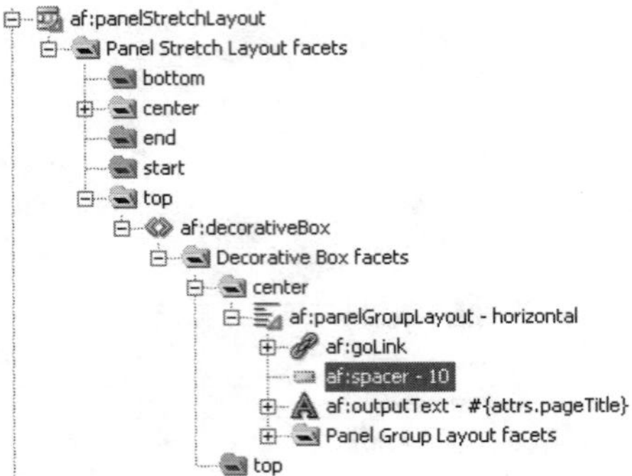

14. Select the `af:spacer` component and set the *Width* to "20."
15. Select the `af:outputText` component and in the *Style* property section, Text (first) tab set properties for *Color* as "Navy" and *Size* as "large."
16. Next you will add the copyright text in the bottom pane. This technique demonstrates how to achieve a relatively complex layout using the ADF Faces components. Drag an Output Formatted (not Output Text) component from the Component Palette and drop it into the second facet (of the `af:panelSplitter` layout container).
17. Fill in the *Value* property as "Copyright © TUHRA, Inc. All rights reserved." (including the period).

    Additional Information: The HTML entity "©" displays a copyright symbol.
18. Select the *StyleUsage* property (Style category) as "pageStamp" to set the font color.

    Additional Information: The pageStamp style is a predefined style within the default skin used by the ADF Faces components. It provides a color that harmonizes with the decorative box themes you applied earlier. The copyright symbol should appear.
19. The text appears on the left side, but it should appear on the right side. In the Style category, set *Horizontal Align* to "right." Note that this will align the text within the space allocated to the `af:outputFormatted` component, but it will not necessarily cause the text to be right-aligned to the screen as a whole. To make sure this alignment occurs, you need to enclose the text in a layout container.
20. Use the **Surround With** option on the right-click menu to enclose the `af:outputFormatted` component with an `af:panelGroupLayout` layout container.
21. On this surrounding `af:panelGroupLayout` component, set the *Halign* property (in the Common section) to "end" and the *Layout* property to "horizontal."

    Additional Information: ADF Faces supports applications that require bi-directional reading styles. As such, alignment can be expressed in two ways, either in terms of absolute left and right, or in the relative terms of start and end. In a left-to-right language such as English, the "end" value will equate to the right of the page. However, in a language with a right-to-left reading order such as Arabic, "end" will actually be on the left-hand edge of the page. The copyright text will still not appear correctly, but you will fix that later.

Define a Menu and Popup

In this section, you add a menu bar and menu item for a Help About selection. You also add a popup dialog that displays when the menu item is selected.

1. Select the Decorative Box in the first facet of the `af:panelSplitter` layout container (it contains the center facet). The top facet is hidden, but you can display it using the right-click menu option **Facets – Decorative Box | Top**.
2. Select the `af:decorativeBox` component and set *Top Height* to "26px" (26 pixels). You will see the facet become shorter in the visual editor.
3. Drop a Panel Menu Bar (Common Components panel) into the top facet. Drop a Menu (`af:menu`) onto the menu bar and set the property *TextAndAccessKey* (in the Appearance category) to "&Help."

   Additional Information: The visual editor will read the "&" and underline the following "H" to denote that the user can press ALT-H (in Internet Explorer or ALT-SHIFT-H in Firefox or Safari) to activate this menu.
4. Drop a Menu Item onto the `af:menu` component. Fill in *TextAndAccessKey* as "&About" and *Text* as "About." The former property displays the word "About" with an underlined "A"; the latter property is not displayed because *TextAndAccessKey* is filled in, but will help in finding this item in the Structure window.

   Additional Information: This menu item will display information about the application. Instead of having to code a special page for this display, you can use the ADF Faces popup component. You can define a popup anywhere in the JSP, but it will not display until it is activated by an action item.
5. Since the popup is associated with the menu bar, you will place it in the top facet after adding a container component to hold it and the menu bar inside the top facet; in this case, you will use `af:group` component (a basic, non-visual layout container with few properties). In the breadcrumb area at the bottom of the visual editor (or in the Structure window) select Surround With from the right-click menu on the `af:menubar` item. Select Group and click OK.
6. Select the `af:menuBar` breadcrumb or Structure window node and select **Insert Before Panel Menu Bar | ADF Faces** from the right-click menu. Select Popup and click OK. The popup will appear and the rest of the template will become disabled.

   Additional Information: The visual editor displays either the popup layout or the main page. To switch to the main page layout, select a component in the main page from the Structure window. To switch to the popup layout, select the popup or a component inside the popup from the Structure window. Take a moment to become familiar with switching the display from popup to main page. Be sure you are looking at the popup layout for the next step.
7. Fill in *Id* property as "aboutPopup." Drop a Dialog component into the popup. The `af:dialog` component shows an area with borders that looks like a window.
8. Fill in *Title* as "About TUHRA2." This text will appear in the top bar of the popup area. Select the *Type* property as "ok." This property defines the buttons that will appear in the dialog (just an "OK" button in this case).
9. Fill in *TitleIconSource* as "/images/help.png" to display a help image in the dialog's title bar.

10. Drop a Panel Group Layout component onto the `af:dialog` and set *Halign* to "center," *Valign* to "middle" (if it is not already set that way), and *Layout* to "vertical." The popup should appear as follows:

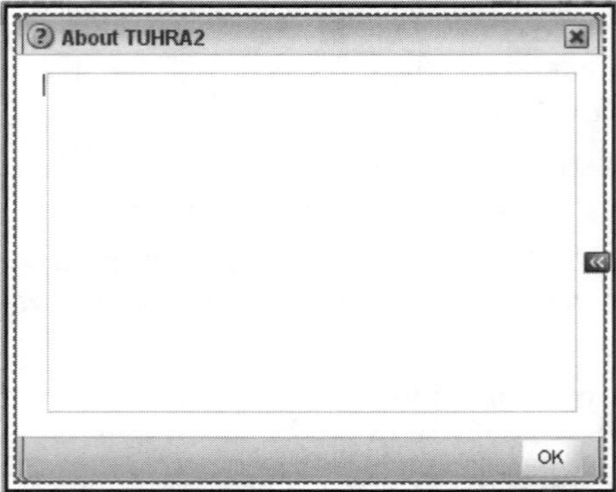

11. Drop three Output Text components into this `af:panelGroupLayout` component.

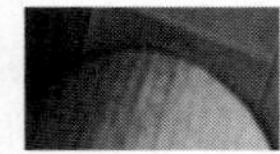

TIP
You may find it faster to copy the first `af:outputText` *component in the Structure window, select* `af:panelGroupLayout`*, and paste. Repeat this technique for the third component.*

12. Set the *Value* property for the first Output Text component to "The Ultimate Human Resources Application"; for the second component to "Copyright © 2006, 2009"; and for the third component to "Duncan Mills, Peter Koletzke, Avrom Roy-Faderman."
13. Select the second `af:outputText` item and set the *Escape* property (Behavior category) to "false" because the value contains an "&" entity that needs to be interpreted as HTML at runtime.

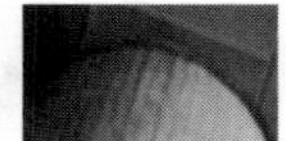

TIP
If the Property Inspector properties do not refresh after you select a component, click a different component then click the component you need again. If that still does not help, close and reopen the Property Inspector.

14. You can now link the Popup to the menu item. Select the "About" `af:commandMenuItem` in the Structure window. Drop a Show Popup Behavior component (from the Operations panel) onto it. Fill in *PopupId* as "aboutPopup" (the name of the popup you are displaying with the menu selection).

    Additional Information: Instead of typing in the *PopupId* property value, you can select Edit next to the field and select it from the navigator as shown next.

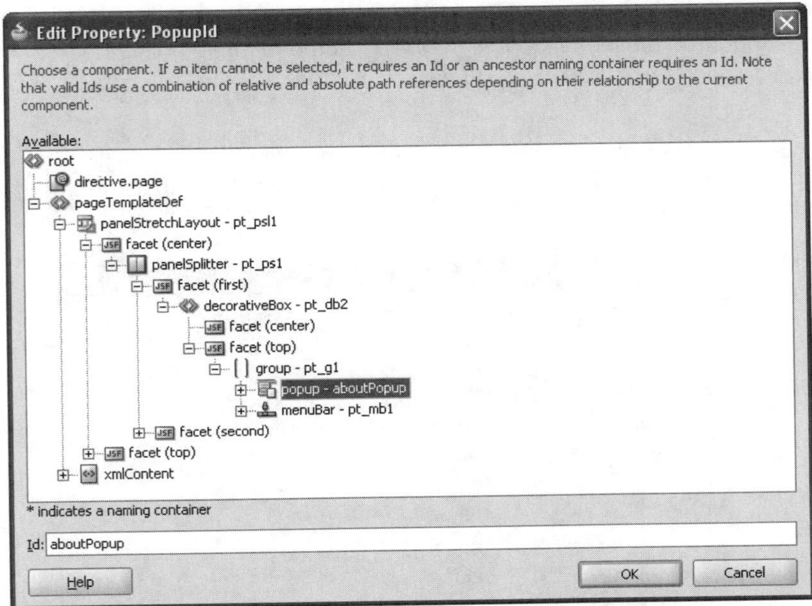

15. Select the *Trigger Type* as "action." This is the normal trigger type for this component; others are documented in the online reference. (Select the component and press F1 to load the help page for that component.)

Define the Named Content Area of the Template

In this section, you indicate where a page that uses the template will actually place its unique content.

1. You can use a Facet Ref component to indicate where the content area will be for a page based on a template. Drag a Facet Ref into the center facet of the `af:decorative` box within the `af:panelSplitter` layout container and select from the *Facet Name* pulldown "content" (the facet you defined when creating the template).

   Additional Information: As you will see in the next section, this facet will appear in the page that you create from the template. Your template can contain multiple named facets, each of which can be placed within the template definition in different areas.

2. Click OK. Click Save All. The template is now ready for use.

Test the Template

Since the template is merged into the page at runtime, any changes to its layout elements will affect all pages that use it. Therefore, you can make changes to the template at any stage of development. It is still a good idea to test the template and make refinements before you first use it. This section of the practice creates a sample JSF file that will allow you to test the menu and resizable panes in the template.

NOTE
You cannot run the template directly, so to test the runtime look and feel, you need to create a JSF test page.

1. Select ViewController and press CTRL-N. In the Web Tier\JSF category, double click JSF Page. The Create JSF Page dialog will appear as shown here (with the tuhraTemplate shown in the *Page Template* field):

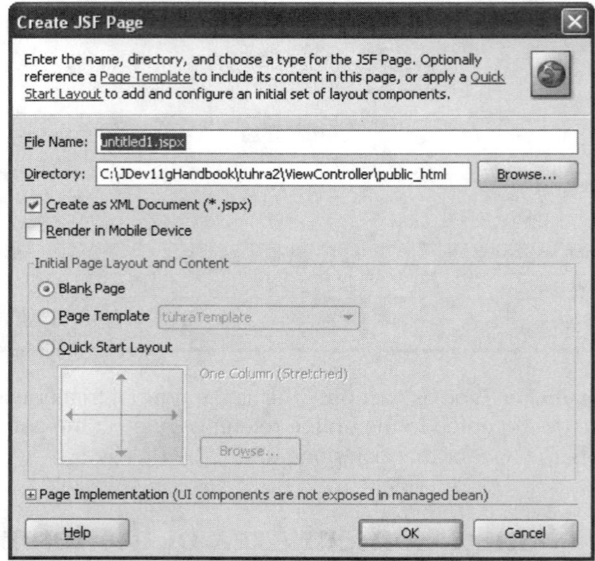

2. Fill in *File Name* as "templateTest" and select the *Page Template* "tuhraTemplate." Click OK to create the page.
3. The page will appear in the visual editor. Notice that the elements such as the TUHRA logo in the template are not selectable. (Selecting any of those elements makes an `af:pageTemplate` tag active.)
4. Click the Source tab. Other than the standard JSF structure tags, the only special tags are the following:

```
<af:pageTemplate viewId="/WEB-INF/templates/tuhraTemplate.jspx"
                 value="#{bindings.pageTemplateBinding}"
                 id="pt1">
  <f:facet name="content"/>
</af:pageTemplate>
```

Additional Information: The `af:pageTemplate` tag causes the template elements defined in tuhraTemplate.jspx to appear on the page, but you change them only by editing the template file. You will place all content inside the content facet, which is a child tag of the template reference tag.

5. Click the Design tab. Drop an Input Text item into the content facet. It will appear in the top-left corner of the center pane.
6. In the editor window, select **Run** from the right-click menu. The server will start up, and the page will appear in the browser.
7. Resize the width of the window and notice that the copyright text maintains its right justification. However, notice that the text is wrapped and that you may need to move the splitter bar up to see all of it. You'll fix that next.
8. Select **Help | About** from the page menu to display the popup dialog. Click the window close button or the OK button to close the About dialog.

Fix the Copyright Text

The copyright text was correctly aligned; however, it is wrapped onto multiple lines. One of the benefits of an HTML rendered layout is that text will move and flow as the browser is resized. However, this leads to an unwanted side effect on this page. You will fix that in this section.

1. Open the template file in the editor and locate the copyright `af:outputFormatted` component. To prevent the text from wrapping vertically, you need to control the width of the component. However, this component has no property to control the width. Instead, you need to control the amount of space available to the component.
2. With the `af:outputFormatted` component selected, select **Surround With** from the right-click menu, and enclose the output item with a Panel Group Layout.
3. Set the *Layout* for the `af:panelGroupLayout` layout container as "vertical."
4. Select the `af:outputFormatted` component in the Structure window again and select **Insert before `af:outputFormatted`** from the right-click menu and select **Spacer**.
5. Set the *Height* of the spacer to "8" and the *Width* to "230."

   Additional Information: By putting a fixed-width spacer inside of the `af:panelGroupLayout` layout container, you are forcing the layout container to be at least 230 pixels wide. Since the `af:outputFormatted` layout container is placed inside the same layout container, it now has room to display without having to wrap.

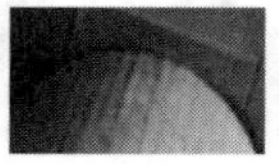

TIP

Sometimes it can be useful to see exactly how wide or high a layout container or other component is within the running screen. A simple way of accomplishing this is to temporarily change the inlineStyle *property for the component to "border-color:Red; border-style:dotted; border-width:2.0px;"—you will then see the outline of the component in the page.*

6. Save the template and re-run the test page. The copyright text will now appear on a single line as in the screenshot here:

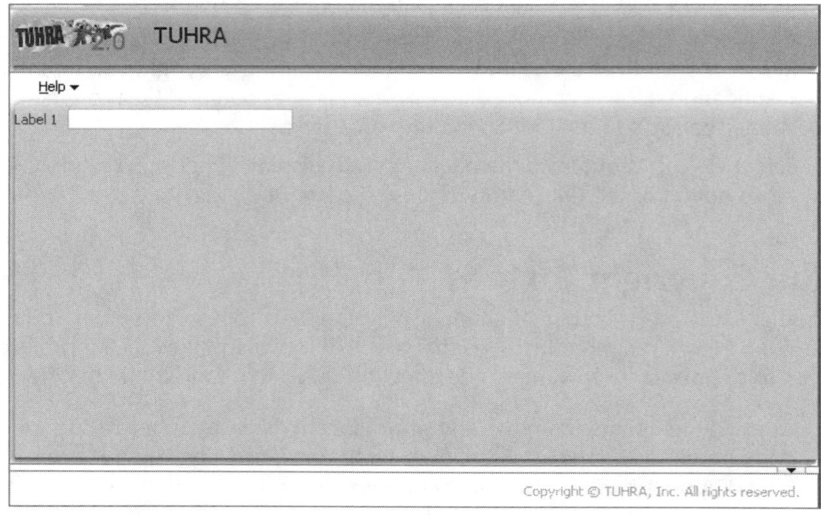

7. Close the browser and stop the tuhra2 application.

What Did You Just Do? You created a template that will provide common content to the pages of the application. The elements you added to the template will appear in all pages based on the template at runtime. The pages only include a reference to the template and the specific content needed for the page. You will use this template to create pages for this application. If you want to make a change to the template, you can use the templateTest.jspx page to test the changes. This file does not include data and is simpler and faster to run than the other pages in the application.

CHAPTER 18

Sample Application: Search Page

The search for truth is more precious than its possession.

—Albert Einstein (1879–1955),
The American Mathematical Monthly, v. 100, no. 3

Research is what I'm doing when I don't know what I'm doing.

—Wernher von Braun. (1912–1977)

his chapter uses the application workspace and template created in Chapter 17 to build a search page that allows the user to find an employee by entering query conditions or by browsing a department hierarchy viewer. Both of these functions are commonly used interface paradigms. Searching for a record or set of records based on query criteria is an essential part of nearly all Online Transaction Processing (OLTP) applications. The hierarchy or tree allows the user to navigate to a record or set of records that have a well-known parent-child relationship, for example, groups of employees who are organized into departments.

The hands-on practice in this chapter starts with the application you completed in Chapter 17. It sets up page fragments for both of these navigation interfaces and defines the capability to switch between them by clicking graphical icons in the left-hand pane. The practice steps through the following phases:

I. Prepare employee search business components
- Set up entity object definitions
- Create the employees view object definition
- Define named view criteria

II. Create the search page

III. Create the employee search area
- Define the search task flow and page fragment
- Refine the layout
- Add an export capability to the result set
- Add an employee details popup
- Add an in-process indicator

IV. Create the hierarchy viewer area
- Set up hierarchy node view object definitions
- Create the hierarchy task flow and page fragment
- Explore the page
- Refine the hierarchy viewer
- Improve the department node display
- Improve the employee node display
- Plug the hierarchy viewer into the page
- Write a UI manager to switch page fragments

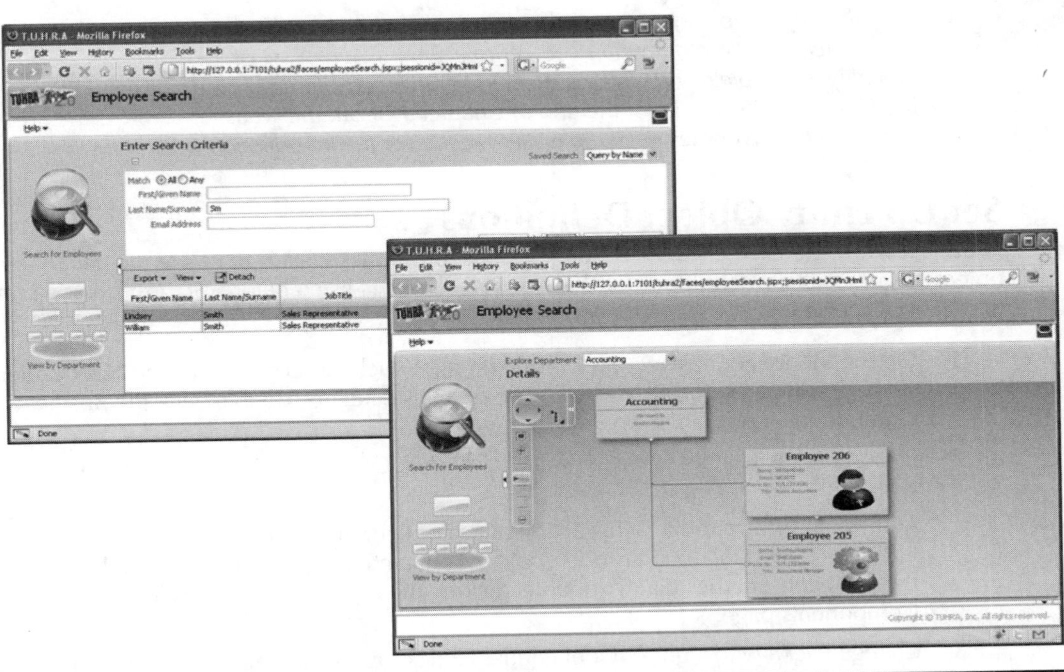

FIGURE 18-1. *Search page with employee search and hierarchy viewer areas*

Figure 18-1 shows the employee search in one page and the hierarchy viewer in another page.

I. Prepare Employee Search Business Components

The search page allows the user to find employee records. After finding a record, the user will be able to make changes to it using the edit page (described in Chapter 19). The information you need on the search page consists of the following elements:

- Details of the employee profile
- The name of the department
- The employee's job title

In addition, the departments hierarchy viewer will require these additional elements:

- Images
- Image usage by employees

Each of these elements represents a table: EMPLOYEES, DEPARTMENTS, JOBS, IMAGES, and IMAGE_USAGES, respectively. This phase sets up ADF BC objects for all of these tables.

TIP

When following the practices in this book, it is a good idea to back up the application directory when you get to a stage where a set of functionality is complete and working. Remember that you can download the application in its state as of the end of Chapter 17 from the website mentioned in the "Websites for Sample Files" section of the Introduction.

Set Up Entity Object Definitions

In this section, you use the Business Components from Tables wizard to create the default entity object and association definitions for the required elements listed before. Start this work in the tuhra2 application.

1. On the Model node, select New from the right-click menu to display the New Gallery. In the Business Tier\ADF Business Components category, double click the Business Components from Tables option.
2. Check that the Connection is "HR_DB" and click OK in the Initialize Business Components dialog.

   Additional Information: This action adds configuration information to associate the HR_DB connection to the Model project. You can change this information by displaying the project properties dialog (double clicking the Model node) and selecting the Business Components page.
3. Change *Package* to "tuhra.model.entities," click Query (assuming that *Auto-Query* is unchecked as is the default), and move DEPARTMENTS, EMPLOYEES, IMAGES, IMAGE_USAGES, and JOBS to the *Selected* area. Click Finish to dismiss the wizard and create the entity object definitions and associations.

   Additional Information: Bypassing the other pages of this wizard means that JDeveloper will only create entity object definitions to represent tables and associations to foreign key relationships between the selected tables.

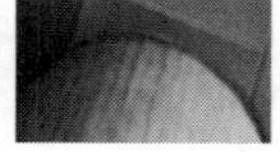

CAUTION

Use the Business Components from Tables wizard carefully because it can create more objects than you need. For example, you may not need the association created between Employees and Jobs, but this wizard will create one if you select both tables. These additional objects can, of course, be deleted after the fact to clean up the project, so it's mainly important to understand that the creation of extra definitions may take place when using this wizard. For the purposes of this hands-on practice, the wizard is controllable enough that no spurious definitions are created.

4. If it is not already open, expand the Model node.

   Additional Information: Expand the tuhra.model.entities node and notice that JDeveloper created entity object definitions for the selected tables and associations to represent the foreign key constraints between the selected tables. You should see something like this snippet on the right from the Application Navigator.

Model
Application Sources
tuhra.model
Model.jpx
tuhra.model.entities
Departments
DeptMgrFkAssoc
EmpDeptFkAssoc
EmpJobFkAssoc
Employees
EmpManagerFkAssoc
Images
ImageUsages
ImageUsagesImagesFkAssoc
Jobs
tuhra.model.framework

5. To verify that the framework superclass definition was applied, double click the Employees entity node. In the Source tab, you will see a *RowClass* attribute for the Entity element defined as "tuhra.model.framework.TuhraEntityImpl" to declare that your project-specific entity class will be used rather than `EntityImpl`.

6. You now need to set some properties on the Employees entity object definition. Click the Overview tab and click the Attributes tab. One at a time double click each attribute, set the following property values, and click OK (or use the Property Inspector):

Attribute	**Section: Property**	**Value**	**Notes (do not enter these)**
EmployeeId	Attribute: Type	DBSequence	This provides handling of the table trigger that assigns the primary key value.
CreatedBy	Attribute: History Column	Select the *History Column* checkbox and set the pulldown to "created by."	JDeveloper assigns default values to this and the next three attributes. These settings are alternatives to a table trigger assignment of the column values.
CreatedDate	Attribute: History Column	Select the *History Column* checkbox and set the pulldown to "created on."	Same
ModifiedBy	Attribute: History Column	Select the *History Column* checkbox and set the pulldown to "modified by."	Same
ModifiedDate	Attribute: History Column	Select the *History Column* checkbox and set the pulldown to "modified on."	Same

NOTE

The history column *feature provides values for columns that need to be automatically loaded with standard audit information. You can alternatively load these column values using a database table trigger. The history columns feature offers the benefit that the values are available on the screen without a need to set the "Update After" properties in the entity object definition. The table trigger offers the benefit that any application can write to the table without having to remember how to load the audit values. The best strategy will depend on which applications are actually accessing the table.*

7. Open the editor for the Images entity object definition and set the *Attribute: Type* of the ImageId attribute to "DBSequence."

   Additional Information: You have just set the `DBSequence` domain type for both the Images entity definition's ImageId and the Employees entity definitions EmployeeId because both of these entities will be used to create new records in the application. There is no need to define the same domain type for the Departments entity definition's DepartmentId because the TUHRA2 application will not be creating DEPARTMENTS records.

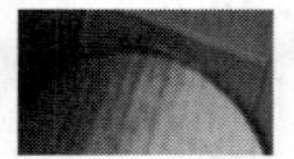

NOTE
As mentioned, we may include sentence- or clause-ending punctuation inside quotation marks for property or field values but you should not type in the end punctuation mark unless we instruct otherwise.

8. Click OK in the Edit Attribute dialog. Click Save All.

Create the Employees View Object Definition

The search page will query the EMPLOYEES table, so you need a view object definition to represent that table. This section defines this view object and assigns it some properties.

1. On the tuhra.model node, select New View Object from the right-click menu. Fill in *Package* as "tuhra.model.queries" and *Name* as "EmployeeSearch"; leave "Updatable access through entity objects" selected. Click Next.
2. Move Employees to the *Selected* area and leave *Updatable* selected. Also move Departments and Jobs to *Selected* and leave their defaults: *Updatable* unselected and *Reference* selected. The default *Association* properties will also suffice. Click Next.
3. In the attribute list move the following attributes to *Selected* (you can multi-select the attributes using CTRL-click before moving them to the *Selected* area):
   - Employees: EmployeeId
   - Employees: FirstName
   - Employees: LastName
   - Employees: Email
   - Employees: PhoneNumber
   - Departments: DepartmentName (this will also bring the DepartmentId across as well)
   - Jobs: JobTitle (again the key column JobId will be selected automatically too)
4. Click Next and then Next again. Fill in *Order By* as "Employees.LAST_NAME, Employees. FIRST_NAME" and click Finish. The EmployeeSearch view object definition will be created.
5. To test the view object definition, create an application module definition (on the tuhra .model node select **New Application Module** from the right-click menu). Fill in *Package* as "tuhra.model.services" and *Name* as "TuhraService" and click Next.

6. Select EmployeeSearch (under tuhra.model.queries) and change the *View Object Instance* field to "EmployeeSearch." Move it to the *Data Model* area. Click Finish.
7. Before testing the application module definition, it is a good idea to make two changes to the default configuration, which are helpful for web applications. (For more information refer to the Chapter 7 sections "Editing or Creating Configurations for Application Module Definitions" and "Locking.") On the TuhraService application module node, select **Configurations** from the right-click menu.
8. Be sure TuhraServiceLocal is selected and click Edit. In the Application Module tab change the connection type from the default value of "JDBC URL" to "JDBC Datasource." Leave the *Datasource Name* as the default value of "java:comp/env/jdbc/HR_DBDS."

   Additional Information: In earlier versions of ADF BC the Oracle Business Component Browser (ADF BC tester) would only work with a JDBC URL connection. In the 11*g* version, however, it understands JDBC datasources. This is a benefit because you will always want to use a JDBC *datasource* (which places the database connection information in the application server definition instead of in the application's files) when you finally deploy the application into a standalone server. So setting this at the outset is good practice.
9. Click the Properties tab and select *jbo.locking.mode*. Double click the "pessimistic" value next to the property to open the field editor and type "optimistic" over the value. Press ENTER.

   Additional Information: The text in this editor is small, and JDeveloper will not verify the spelling of the value. In addition, a typographical error may not cause a visible runtime error. Therefore, a good second step after changing a configuration property value is to double-check its spelling. Do so now.
10. Click OK. Click OK. Click Save All.
11. On the TuhraService application module definition node, select **Run** from the right-click menu (or press CTRL-F11). This will automatically run an instance of the application module with the "TuhraServiceLocal" configuration.
12. The Oracle Business Component Browser will appear. Double click the EmployeeSearch node to open the tester for the view object instance. Use the toolbar icons to scroll through records.

    Additional Information: Notice that the EmployeeId field is disabled—this is one of the features of the `DBSequence` domain that you assigned as the data type for that attribute. `DBSequence` only allows an attribute value to be changed when the record is still new (has not been sent to the database yet). Also, the DepartmentName, DepartmentId (from Departments), and Jobs fields are not updatable because their corresponding entity object usages in the EmployeeSearch view object definition are marked as reference only.
13. Close the tester window.

Define Named View Criteria

The application will offer a simple search screen where the user can search for employees by specifying values for FirstName, LastName, or Email attributes. You can easily define a default search screen that includes all of the attributes of the view object instance, but that presents too many options for a simple search. If you need a more focused search screen for fewer attributes, you can define *named view criteria*—declared sets of query conditions for specific attributes that you can define using bind variables (described more in the "Named View Criteria Objects" section of Chapter 7).

1. Open the EmployeeSearch view object definition's editor (double click its node or, if it is still open, click its tab in the editor) and click the Query tab. Click the "Create new view criteria" (green plus "+") button in the View Criteria section to display the Create View Criteria dialog.
2. Fill in Criteria Name as "BasicEmployeeSearchCriteria."
3. Click Add Item. A new node will be created in the Group hierarchy node. Select *Attribute* as "FirstName," the *Operator* as "Contains," and the Operand as "Bind Variable."
4. Click New (green "+") next to the *Parameter* pulldown, and in the Bind Variable dialog, enter the Name as "QueryFirstName." Leave the default *Type* as "String." Click OK.
5. In the Create View Criteria dialog, ensure that the *Ignore Case* checkbox is selected. The dialog will appear as follows:

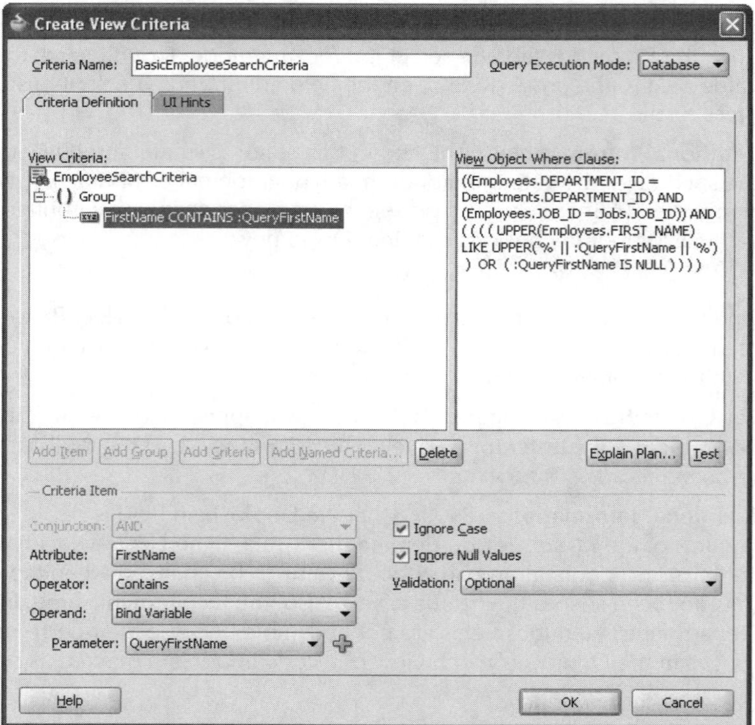

Additional Information: Notice that the settings you just made added a query predicate to the *View Object Where Clause* area.

6. Select the Group node. Repeat steps 3–5 for LastName using a *Conjunction* setting of "AND" and a bind variable of "QueryLastName."
7. Select the Group node. Repeat steps 3–5 for Email using a *Conjunction* setting of "AND" and a bind variable of "QueryEmail."

8. Click Test to check the query. Click OK in the notification dialog; click OK in the Create View Criteria dialog.
9. Click Save All.
10. Run the application module again to test this named view criteria. Open the EmployeeSearch page. Click the Specify View Criteria (binoculars) button in the toolbar.
11. Move BasicEmployeeSearchCriteria to *Selected* and click Find. A Bind Variables dialog will appear where you can select a bind variable and assign a value. Select LastName and enter *Value* as "Z." Click OK. The query should return only employees whose last names contain "Z."
12. Close the tester window.

What Did You Just Do? In this phase you set up ADF BC objects for the employee search and department edit page fragments. You also set up a named view criteria object that will present a subset of attributes to the user for querying purposes. Setting up the business services layer is generally the first major development step when developing an application with ADF. You then develop the View layer UI code that will allow the user to interact with data in the Business Services layer. As with any type of development, this process is iterative. That is, although you will make an attempt to be as complete as possible in the first stage of creating the Business Services layer, when working on View layer code, you will inevitably require a modification to the business services so you will return to that work.

This phase also showed how you can use the Oracle Business Component Browser to test the Business Services code you've created. Frequent use of this testing tool will help you ensure that the code in this data layer is solid before moving on to using the data layer in the UI code. This browser is also useful when troubleshooting problems in an application. If you can run the tester successfully, the problem is likely somewhere in the View or Controller layer. If the same problem occurs with and without the View and Controller layer code, you can be pretty sure that the problem is somewhere in the Business Services layer.

II. Create the Search Page

The Model objects are now complete enough to create a user interface. The strategy you will use is to create a JSP page based on the template with some simple elements. You will then create task flows and page fragments for the employee search and hierarchy viewer displays. You will also create code that switches the view between these two fragments when the user clicks the appropriate navigation icon in the left-hand pane.

This phase creates the search page with some title settings.

1. In the ViewController project follow the steps you used to create the templateTest.jspx page to test and create a JSF page in the public_html directory called "employeeSearch .jspx."

   Additional Information: Start the New Gallery from the Web Content node. Be sure you create an XML document (.jspx), use the tuhraTemplate, and under Page Implementation, leave the default selection of "Do Not Automatically Expose UI Components in a Managed Bean."

2. Select the `af:pageTemplate` in the Structure window (under `f:view\af:document\af:form`) and in the Property Inspector fill in *pageTitle* as "Employee Search." You will find the *pageTitle* property in the **Other** section of the Property Inspector.
3. Select `af:document` and fill in *Title* as "T.U.H.R.A." This property value will become the browser window title for all pages.
4. From the ADF Faces page of the Component Palette, drop a Panel Splitter (Layout panel) into the content facet. Set the *SplitterPosition* as "140" and ensure that the *Orientation* is set to "horizontal."

   Additional Information: The default value for the Orientation property of the `af:panelSplitter` is already "<default> horizontal" but setting the value explicitly has two benefits. First of all, developers can see exactly what you mean to do when you used the component and secondly, the Structure Window will show "af:panelSplitter - Horizontal, " making it easier to locate this component and relate it to what you see in the visual page editor.
5. Drop a Panel Group Layout component into the first facet of the splitter. Set *Layout* to "vertical."
6. Drop a Spacer into the `af:panelGroupLayout` and check that its *Height* is set to "10."
7. Drop a Link (Common Components panel) into the `af:panelGroupLayout`. Set the *Id* as "searchLink" and clear the *Text* property.

   Additional Information: JDeveloper will automatically generate IDs for all JSF components that you add to the page. However, sometimes it is a good idea to override the generated defaults with more meaningful names so that you can remember what this component is for.
8. Repeat the preceding step using an *Id* of "orgLink," dropping the new link after searchLink.
9. Drop a Panel Group Layout component into the first `af:commandLink` that is displayed in the Structure window. Select *Layout* as "vertical," and *Halign* as "center," and ensure that *Valign* is "middle."

   Additional Information: You will want to put both an image and some text within this link component, so the `af:panelGroupLayout` is needed to contain and align them.
10. Drag "search.png" from the images directory under the ViewController\Web Content node and drop it into the `af:panelGroupLayout` component in the visual editor. Specify that the component is an ADF Faces Image.
11. Set *ShortDesc* for the image as "Search for Employees." This text will appear as a tooltip (mouse rollover text). In the Style property category, Box (third) tab, set *Width* as "120.0px."
12. Drop an Output Label component on the `af:panelGroupLayout` in the Structure window. It will be automatically added after the `af:image`. Set *Value* as "Search for Employees" and *For* as "searchLink."

    Additional Information: The *For* property in this situation refers to the *Id* of the `af:commandLink` component. This helps screen reader software to understand that this is a textual description of the link.
13. You need another set of objects for the org chart link and image. The easiest way to repeat the effect of steps 9–13 is to copy to the clipboard the `af:panelGroupLayout` node under `af:commandLink` for the employee search image. Then select the second `af:commandLink` node and paste.

14. Change the `af:image` *Source* to "/images/orgchart.png," *ShortDesc* to "View by Department." Change the `af:outputLabel` *Value* to "View by Department" and *For* to "orgLink."

15. In the Structure window, expand the outer `af:panelGroupLayout` (under the first facet). Into its separator facet, drop a Spacer (Layout panel of the Component Palette) and set the spacer's *Height* to "20."

    Additional Information: Whatever you place within the separator facet of a `af:panelGroupLayout` will be repeated between every child component that is dropped into the layout container.

16. The `af:panelSplitter` nodes should appear in the Structure window as in this illustration:

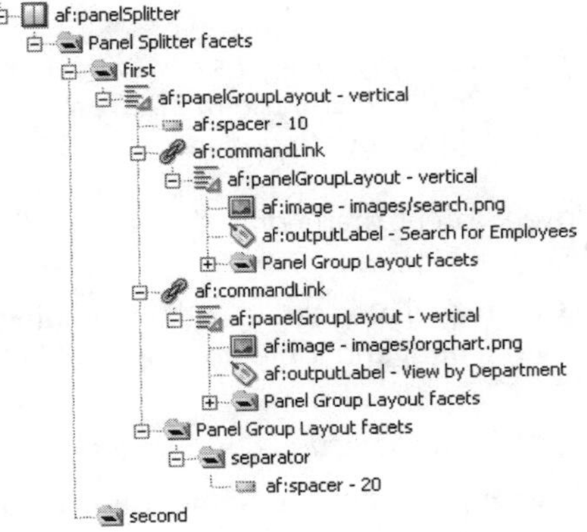

17. Adjust the components if they do not match using drag-and-drop operations. Click Save All.

What Did You Just Do? You just created a JSF page from the template. This page contains the navigational icon graphics in the left-hand pane and container components to hold the page fragments you will create next.

III. Create the Employee Search Area

Now you need to design the region that appears when the user clicks the top icon; this area will function as a basic Query-by-Example (QBE) search.

Define the Search Task Flow and Page Fragment

In this section, you diagram the task flow and create the page fragment from that task flow.

1. Select the ViewController project in the navigator. From the New Gallery, select an ADF Task Flow (Web Tier\JSF category) to display the Create Task Flow dialog. Specify File Name as "searchEmployees-flow.xml" and ensure that *Create with Page Fragments* is selected. Ensure that *Create as a Bounded Task Flow* is selected. Click OK.

2. Drop a View component from the Activities section of the Component Palette onto the diagram and change its name to "searchUI."

3. Double click searchUI to implement the task and add "\fragments" (including the backslash) to the directory name (leaving the rest intact) and click OK. The visual editor will appear.

   Additional Information: The page fragments you are creating here do not need to use the tuhraTemplate template, as they will be embedded within a page that uses that template.

4. In the Data Controls panel (located as a panel within the Application Navigator), expand the nodes TuhraServiceDataControl\EmployeeSearch\Named Criteria.

   Additional Information: Notice the "All Queriable Attributes" criteria that are available in the Data Controls panel hierarchy here. Every view object instance will have one of these, and as the name suggests, it would create a query form containing all of the attributes in the view object definition.

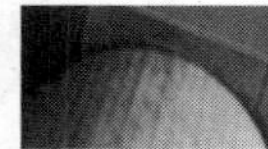

TIP
*If the Data Controls panel is empty or seems not to have reflected recent changes remember that you can use the **Refresh** option on the right-click menu to force JDeveloper to update it.*

5. Drag BasicEmployeeSearchCriteria onto the visual editor and select **Query** | **ADF Query Panel with Table**.
6. In the Edit Table Columns dialog, group-select (holding the CTRL key and selecting) the EmployeeId, DepartmentId, and JobId columns, and click the Delete (red "x") button to delete them.
7. Select the *Sorting* and *Row Selection* checkboxes.
8. Move the JobTitle to appear after LastName using the up arrow button.
9. Group select the Email and PhoneNumber columns and click Group. This will add a node above these two columns. Change the group label to "Contact Information" by clicking into it and typing. The dialog should appear as follows:

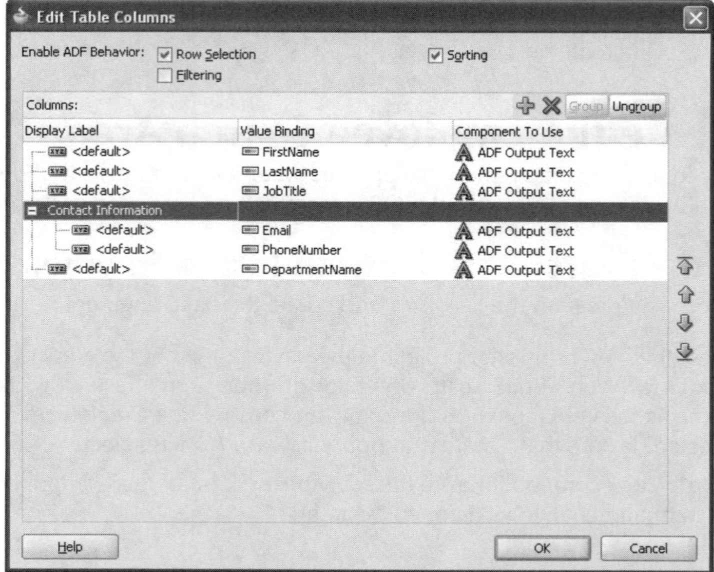

10. Click OK. Click Save All.
11. Click the document tab for employeeSearch.jspx to switch back to that page (or open it from the navigator). Select searchEmployees-flow under the Web Content \ Page Flows node in the Application Navigator. Drag it onto the second facet of the `af:panelSplitter` that you had previously added to that page, and select **Region** from the context menu. You will see a ghosted version of the search page fragment now appear, embedded within the employeeSearch page.
12. Click Save All.
13. Select **Run** from the right-click menu on the page to view the page. The browser should display a page like that shown in Figure 18-2. Try various searches using native search features like Match, Advanced, and Add Fields.
14. Close the browser.

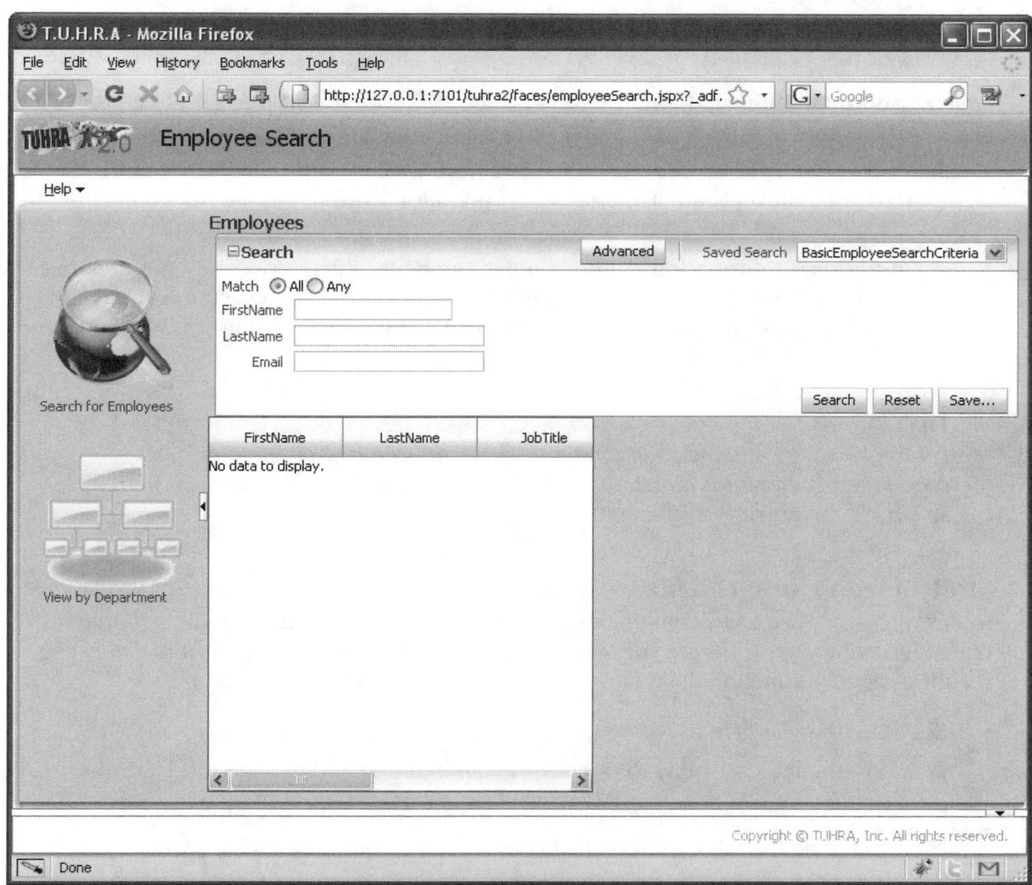

FIGURE 18-2. *Search employees page*

Refine the Layout

In this next section you will polish the user interface of the search screen and fix some UI problems that you may have noticed when running the application such as:

- The search component takes up lots of space and has a generic title of "Employees."
- The results table does not fill the entire width and height of the screen.
- The field labels show the attribute names, not user-friendly text.

The following sections will address these issues.

Compacting the Search Area

You can very easily change the default title and layout used for the search area that you created through drag-and-drop using these steps:

1. Click the searchUI.jsff tab of the editor to display the page fragment (or reopen the file if you had closed it).
2. Select the Employees heading and type "Enter Search Criteria" to replace it. This changes the *Text* property of the `af:panelHeader` component to a more meaningful title.

   Additional Information: If you have trouble with this in-place editing procedure, select the component and change the *Text* property using the Property Inspector.
3. Expand `af:panelHeader` in the Structure window and select `af:query`. Set *Id* as "basicEmployeeSearchCriteriaQuery" and *DisplayMode* (in the Appearance section) as "compact."

   Additional Information: The *compact mode* for the query component removes much of the extra chrome (decoration) for this component that you don't need on this screen. You also set the *Id* property for this component as that is something you will be referring to later in this practice.

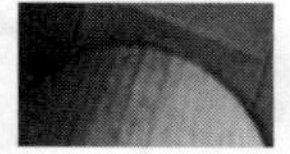

TIP
A long ID value is being used for clarity here; however, Oracle recommends that for optimal performance, component IDs should be seven characters or less in length.

Stretching the Results Table

In this next set of steps you will enclose the results table in a stretch layout container and panel collection component. The `af:panelCollection` container component is interesting because it adds a range of functionality to any table or tree that it encloses including:

- Providing a place to define table or tree specific menu choices
- Offering the capability to undock the table or tree and expand it up to full-screen mode
- Allowing the user to show, hide, and freeze table columns in the display
- Stretching the table or tree inside of it to use all of the available space

It is this latter geometry management behavior that is of the most interest here, but you will also add custom menu options to the `af:panelCollection` later on in the chapter.

1. Select the `af:table` component in the Structure window and select **Surround With** from the right-click menu. Select Panel Collection and click OK.
2. Select the *Id* of the `af:table` component as "basicEmployeeSearchCriteriaQueryResult."
3. The `af:query` component will by now be displaying an error (red "X" in the visual editor). Hold the mouse above the marker and you will see something like the following:

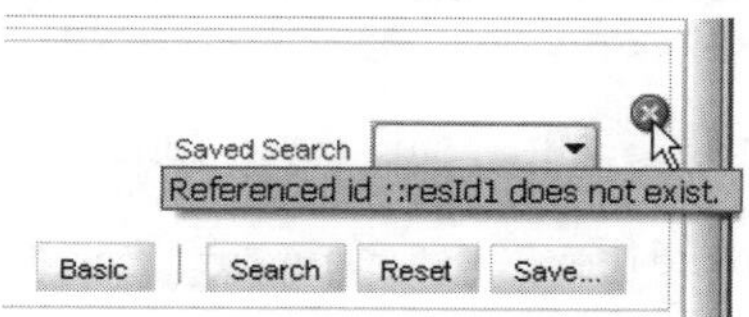

   Additional Information: The error indicator shows that the naming reference has been broken by the combination of adding the `af:panelCollection` component and changing the *Id* of the table.

4. Click the "X" indicator. The Property Inspector will outline the property containing the problem reference in the `af:query` component. In the Property Inspector select **Edit** from the pulldown next to the *ResultComponentId* field and navigate to the correct path ("::pc1:basicEmployeeSearchCriteriaQueryResult"). Click OK. The error state should be cleared.

   Additional Information: The "::" token denotes a path to the referenced component.

5. Click Save All.

   Additional Information: At this point, the results table still does not fill the width of the screen. This is because although the panel collection is now enclosing the table (and stretching it), the `af:panelCollection` itself is not being told to fill the available space. The solution for this problem is to add an `af:panelStretchLayout` component around the panel collection. It is easiest to modify existing layout containers like this in the Source tab of the editor window.

6. Click the Source tab in the editor for searchUI.jsff. Find the `af:panelGroupLayout` component under jsp:root. `af:panelGroupLayout` is the component that encloses everything within the page fragment.
7. Delete the tag "`<af:panelGroupLayout layout="vertical" ...>`" and type the following in its place:

```
<af:panelStretchLayout topHeight="180px" id="psl1">
  <f:facet name="top">
```

8. Close the facet component after the `af:panelHeader` that encloses the query component (before the `af:panelCollection` tag). If you just type "</" JDeveloper will autocomplete the closing tag to create `</f:facet>`.

   Additional Information: If JDeveloper does not autocomplete or adds a different closing tag, you have started typing in the wrong place.

9. Add a line after the `f:facet` closing and before the `af:panelCollection` tag and type the following code:

```
<f:facet name="center">
```

10. Close this facet after the `af:panelCollection` closing tag. Then change the closing `af:panelGroupLayout` tag (the second line from the bottom of the file) to "`af:panelStretchLayout`."

    Additional Information: The file should appear as in the following summary listing. (The line numbers are approximations and do not appear in the actual code.)

```
01: <?xml version='1.0' encoding='windows-1252'?>
02: <jsp:root xmls:jsp...
...
05:   <af:panelStretchLayout topHeight="180px" id="psl1">
06:     <f:facet name="top">
07:       <af:panelHeader text="Enter Search Criteria" id="ph1">
...
14:       </af:panelHeader>
15:     </f:facet>
16:     <f:facet name="center">
17:       <af:panelCollection id="pc1">
...
59:       </af:panelCollection>
60:     </f:facet>
61:   </af:panelStretchLayout>
61: </jsp:root>
```

11. Click Save All, then run employeeSearch.jspx. Click Search to show data in the results table. The table fills the allotted space properly now. You can also stretch columns to the right to verify that the full width of the lower pane is available. Leave the browser open.
12. Back in JDeveloper, in the searchUI.jsff tab, select `af:table` and set *ColumnStretching* as "last." This setting will cause the Department Name column to stretch to the right.

    Additional Information: You can see from this pulldown that the *ColumnStretching* property can be used to allocate any column, or add a blank one to expand and fill the spare space in the table. You can also set explicit widths on individual columns using the *Width* property of the `af:column` component.
13. Click Save All and then refresh the browser (or re-run the page if you had closed the browser) to see that this change caused the DepartmentName column to fill the remaining table width. Close the browser.

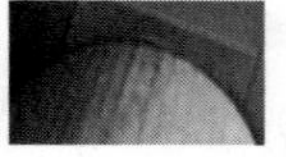

TIP
When making changes to a page where only the component tags have be altered and no data binding or ADF BC changes have been made, you will not actually have to re-run the application. Instead it will be sufficient to save the page file and then refresh the browser page to pick up the new version.

Setting UI Hints

You can set Model layer properties (UI Hints) to affect the UI layer. This section shows how to set properties on the view object definition, entity object definition, and view criteria levels. These labels will be inherited by both the search form and the table.

1. In the Model project, open the Employees entity object definition (double click Employees under the Model\Application Sources\tuhra.model.entities node).
2. In the Attributes tab of the Overview editor tab for the entity, select the FirstName attribute. In the Property Inspector UI Hints section (or tab), fill in *Label* as "First/Given Name" and Display Width as "50."
3. Repeat the preceding step for other attributes in the Employees entity object definition as noted here:

Attribute	**Label**	**Display Width**
LastName	Last Name/Surname	60
Email	Email Address	40
PhoneNumber	Phone No.	50

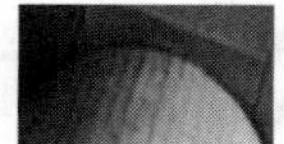

NOTE
By default the Display Width *property only affects the query fields, not the table columns, as the query fields are automatically wired to the entity UI hints whereas the table columns are not. The labels are connected using Expression Language to both the search fields and the column headers, so both parts of the screen automatically share the labels.*

4. In the Departments entity DepartmentName attribute, set the *Label* as "Department" and *Display Width* as "80."
5. In the Jobs entity *JobTitle* attribute, set the *Label* as "Job Title."
6. Open the editor for the EmployeeSearch view object definition (under `tuhra.model.queries`) and find the view criteria BasicEmployeeSearchCriteria (on the Query tab). Click the "Edit selected view criteria" (pencil) button and on the UI Hints tab, set the *Display Name* property to "Query by Name." Click OK.
7. In the searchUI.jsff Design tab, select `af:column` containing the Phone Number field in the table and set its *Width* (Appearance section) as "150." Set *Width* for the column containing Job Title to "150" as well.

TIP
Remember that you can use the search field in the Property Inspector to find fields that match a particular name.

8. Click Save All.
9. Run the employeeSearch.jspx to view the label and width changes.

   Additional Information: This time, because you have changed the ADF BC model by adding UI hints, you need to re-run the application rather than just saving and refreshing the browser.
10. Close the browser.

Add an Export Capability to the Result Set

In this section, you add functionality that allows the user to copy the search result data into an Excel file.

1. Click the Design tab for searchUI.jsff if it is not already displayed. Click the menus facet of the results table in the visual editor to expand the Structure window nodes. In the Structure window the menus facet of the `af:panelCollection` should be selected. Drop a Menu (not Menu Item) component from the Component Palette (Common Components panel) into the menus facet. Set *Text* as "Export."
2. Drop a Menu Item into the Export menu. Change *Text* to "Export to Excel."
3. Drop an Export Collection Action Listener from the components Operations panel inside of the "Export to Excel" menu item. Set the *ExportedId* as "basicEmployeeSearchCriteriaQueryResult" (the ID of the `af:table` component) and select *Type* as "excelHTML" (the only option). Click OK.
4. In the properties for the `af:exportCollectionActionListener` set the *Filename* as "SearchResults" and *Title* as "TUHRA Employee Search Results." If your browser is properly associated with Excel files, ADF Faces will automatically add the .xls extension to the file at runtime.
5. The export facility should only be available if a search has returned some results, so edit the `af:commandMenuItem` *Disabled* property (in the Behavior section) using the Expression Builder. Set the expression to "#{bindings.EmployeeSearch .estimatedRowCount < 1}."

   Additional Information: The estimatedRowCount will be zero if no data is retrieved or if the query has not been performed.

TIP
The Disabled *property is defined with a true/false dropdown list. To add a binding expression you will have to press the property menu (pulldown) icon to the right of the property in the Property Inspector. Select* ***Expression Builder*** *and then you will be able to enter (or construct) the binding expression.*

6. Finally you need to cause the menu item to update when a query is performed. Set the *PartialTriggers* property to "::basicEmployeeSearchCriteriaQuery" to define that the expression is evaluated when a change is made to the query component. (Use the field pulldown Edit functionality if needed, but remember that the query component is now contained within the top facet of the `af:panelStretchLayout`.)
7. Click Save All.
8. Run the employeeSearch.jspx page. The **Export** | **Export to Excel** menu item should be disabled before you run a query or if no rows are returned for specific query criteria.
9. Try querying some records. The **Export to Excel** menu option should be enabled. Try this option to test the export feature.

   Additional Information: Notice that the tab label is set to "TUHRA Employee Search Results"—the *Title* property of the `af:exportCollectionActionListener` component. The column headings in the spreadsheet also match those on the screen.

NOTE
This functionality requires that you have set up a browser association with Excel data. This type of association is made automatically when you install a program that handles Excel data. With Excel 2007 you may receive a warning that the file type does not match the contents. You can ignore this message.

10. Close the spreadsheet and the browser.

Add an Employee Details Popup

In this application the user will be able to see all of the employee details from a right-click menu option and from the pulldown menu. You will implement this functionality using a popup window wired into the results table.

1. In the searchUI.jsff editor, expand the Structure window and locate the `af:panelStretchLayout` component under jsp:root. The bottom facet of this component is not being used, so it can hold the popup object. Set *bottomHeight* "0px" on the `af:panelStretchLayout` so that it does not allocate screen space for the components.
2. Drop a Popup (Common Components panel) into the bottom facet of the `af:panelStretchLayout` component.
3. Drop a Dialog inside the `af:popup`. Set *Title* as "Employee Detail"; set Type as "ok."
4. If the popup is not shown in the visual editor yet, double click the `af:popup` component in the Structure window.
5. Drag and drop the EmployeeSearch view object instance from the Data Controls panel into the dialog as an ADF Read-only Form. Remove DepartmentId and JobId fields. Click OK to accept the Edit Form Fields dialog.
6. Now that the layout is complete, you can complete the wiring. Assign the `af:popup` *Id* a more meaningful value of "empDetailPopup" so that you easily can refer to it from another component.
7. In the Structure window, locate the `af:panelCollection` (under the center facet of the `af:panelStretchLayout`). Expand the Panel Collection facets node and drop a Menu Item component into the viewMenu facet. Set *Text* to "View Employee."

   Additional Information: Menu items added to this facet of the `af:panelCollection` are automatically inserted into the existing view menu that it provides.
8. Drop a Show Popup Behavior component (Operations panel) into the new `af:commandMenuItem` and set *PopupId* as "::empDetailPopup" to point to the new popup. Select *TriggerType* as "action." Leave the values for *Align* and *AlignId* as empty.

   Additional Information: If the *Align* property of the `af:showPopupBehavior` is not set, the popup will automatically be centered on the screen.
9. Now you will repeat part of this process for the right-click (context) menu. On the `af:table` component select **Facets – Table | Context Menu** from the right-click menu to display the contextMenu facet.

10. Drop a Popup component (Common Components panel) into the contextMenu facet (for the popup menu); set the *Id* to "contextMenu."
11. Drop a Menu component into the `af:popup` and a Menu Item into the `af:menu`. Set *Text* for the `af:commandMenuItem` as "View Employee."
12. To implement the popup behavior, drop a Show Popup Behavior (Operations panel) into the View Employee menu item and set its *PopupId* as ":::empDetailPopup" (the path to the popup). If you use the edit option in the *PopupId* to locate the popup, remember that you placed it in the "bottom" facet of the `af:panelStretchLayout`.
13. Click Save All.
14. Run the employeeSearch.jspx page. Click Search to populate the query results table. Select an employee record by clicking a row. Note the name. Now select **View | View Employee**. The popup dialog should display with the read-only form view of the employee data you noted. Click OK.
15. On another employee record, select **View Employee** from the right-click menu. You might expect that the popup dialog should appear with data for that employee. However, if you examine the employee details closely, you will find that the data matches the first record that you selected. The reason for this is that the popup data is not being refreshed. Click OK.
16. Leave the browser open. In the searchUI.jsff page fragment, find the `af:popup` in the bottom facet of `af:panelStretchLayout` and set *contentDelivery* to "lazyUncached."

    Additional Information: *contentDelivery* defines when data on the page are refreshed from the Model layer. The default value is "lazy," which means that the contents will be refreshed only when the popup first displays. The value "lazyUncached" signifies that the data should not be stored between displays; the values will be refreshed each time. Another value, "immediate," causes the popup to be loaded when the base page is loaded even before the popup is displayed.
17. Click Save All and refresh the browser. Test the popup and be sure it refreshes for each employee record.

    Additional Information: Also notice that you do not need to select the record before displaying the right-click menu. Pointing at a row and displaying the right-click menu is enough to change the context to that record.
18. Close the browser.

Add an In-Process Indicator

You may notice that when you run a search, nothing appears on the screen to indicate that processing is ongoing. This section shows how to add an indication to the user that some work is occurring.

1. Open the tuhraTemplate.jspx file (under ViewController\Web Content\WEB-INF\templates). In the editor, click the Source tab. Expand the nodes in the Structure window. Select the `af:group` node above the Menu Bar as shown next.

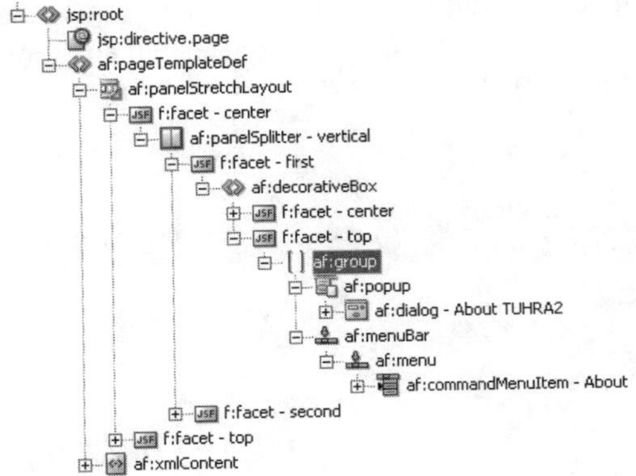

2. In the editor add an `af:panelStretchLayout` component and facet using the following two lines before the `af:group`:

```
<af:panelStretchLayout endWidth="20" id="pt_psl2">
  <f:facet name="center">
```

3. If the end tag facet appears, cut it. Find the closing `af:group` tag and add the following four lines after it:

```
  </f:facet>
  <f:facet name="end">
  </f:facet>
</af:panelStretchLayout>
```

Additional Information: These lines properly close the center facet (that now contains the `af:group` component) and create an empty "end" facet.

TIP
When the Source tab is in focus for a page or any other source file you can use the ***Reformat*** *option on the right-click menu to format the code according to the preferences defined for that file type. This will fix the tag indenting in the editor making it easier to read.*

4. Place the cursor between the open and close tags for the end facet tag and click Status Indicator in the Component Palette (Common Components panel). The Structure window will display nodes in this area as shown here.

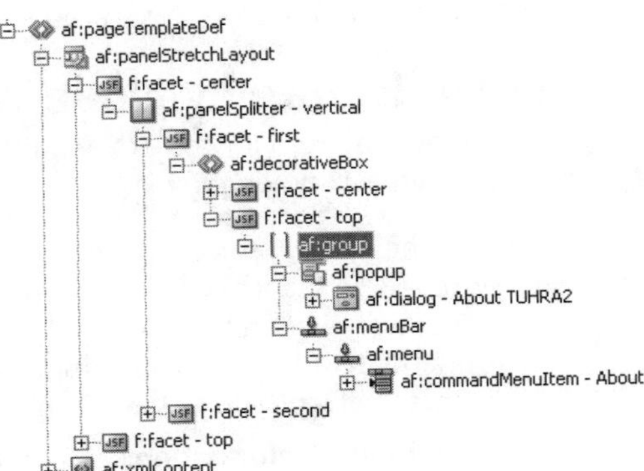

5. Click Save All. Run employeeSearch.jspx. Click Search and watch for the spinning "O" symbol in the top right-hand corner of the search area (above the Saved Search pulldown) as shown in the following screen snippet.
6. Close the browser.

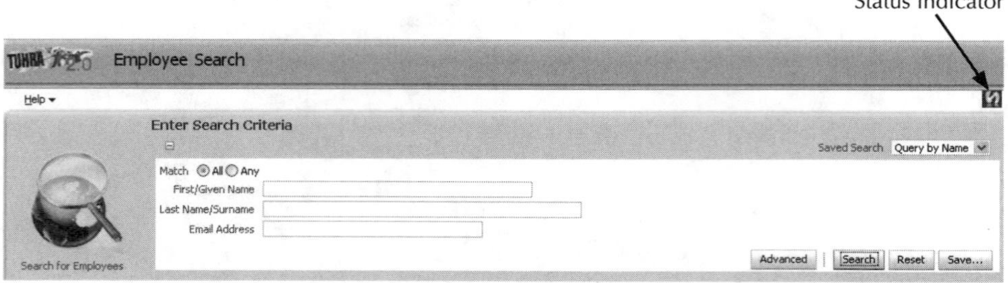

What Did You Just Do? In this phase, you created the task flow and corresponding page fragment to contain the elements of the employee search area. This area leverages standard search capabilities written into the ADF Faces components, for example, Any and All designators.

You also set up the table so that the user can export the result set to an Excel file. This is a very common user requirement and is easy to define in ADF Faces. This phase also gave you more practice with the ADF Faces container components such as `af:panelStretchLayout` and the ubiquitous `af:panelGroupLayout`.

What Could You Do Next? You could spend some time rearranging the fields in the search form. You could also add the employee image to the search results table by defining a column with an `af:image` component, which has a value based on a binding you need to add to the PageDef file for that page fragment. The next phase demonstrates how to add images to another view of the employees.

IV. Create the Hierarchy Viewer Area

The other function of the search page is to show a hierarchical view of the organization using the Data Visualization Tools (DVT) hierarchical viewer (HView) component. As shown in Figure 18-3, the department node will display the department name and manager name; the employee node will show the employee's name, profile information, and picture.

Set Up Hierarchy Node View Object Definitions

This display requires view object definitions for the two nodes in the hierarchy: departments (with manager names) and employees.

1. In the Model project create a view object definition named "AllDepartmentsWithManagers" based on usages of the Departments entity (not updatable) and the Employees entity (not updatable but reference) (so that the name of the department's manager can be shown). For clarity set the *Alias* of the Employees entity object usage to the value "Managers." Ensure that the DeptMgrFkAssoc.Employees association is selected for the Employees entity usage.

   Additional Information: Start the view object definition dialog using the **New View Object** selection on the right-click menu for the `tuhra.model.queries` node.

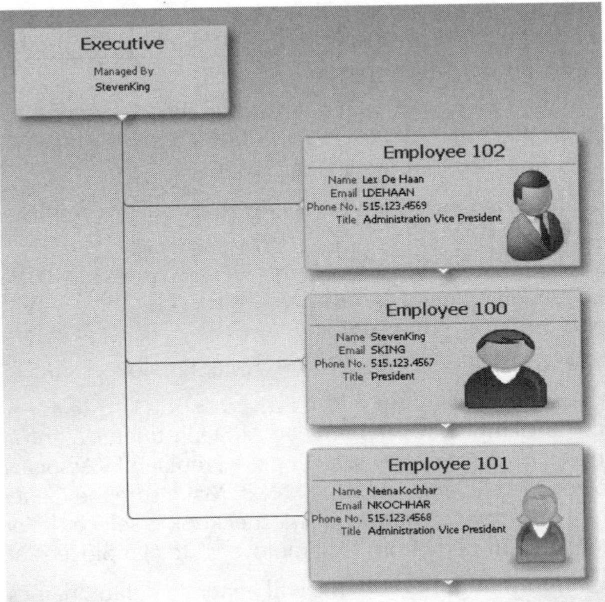

FIGURE 18-3. *Organization tree display*

2. When you reach the Attributes page of the Create View Object dialog, move the Managers attributes EmployeeId, FirstName, and LastName to the *Selected* area using the Add (">") button. Move all of the Departments attributes in the *Selected* area in the same way. Move the Departments attributes above the name attributes.

TIP
You can alternatively select the Departments node in the Available *list and click ">" to move all of its attributes to the* Selected *list.*

3. On the Query page, fill in *Order By* as "Departments.DEPARTMENT_NAME." Notice that the WHERE clause has been filled in based on the existing association between Departments and Managers (Employees); it is defined as an outer join because the value of MANAGER_ID in DEPARTMENTS is optional. Finish the Create View Object dialog.
4. Repeat the steps to create a view object definition for "AllEmployees" based on an updatable usage of the Employees entity object definition and reference usages of the Images, ImageUsages, and Jobs entity object definitions. Navigate to the Attributes page.
5. Move to the right the following attributes in this order: from Employees: EmployeeId, FirstName, LastName, Email, PhoneNumber, JobId; from ImageUsages: AssociatedId, DefaultImage, ImageId, UsageType; from Images: Image, ImageId; from Jobs: JobId, JobTitle.
6. Click Next. On the Attribute Settings page of the wizard select the JobId1 attribute (from Jobs) in the *Select Attribute:* pulldown and change the *Name* to "JobsJobId." Repeat for the ImageId1 attribute (from Images) setting the *Name* to "ImagesImageId."

Additional Information: It is always a good idea to provide more specific names for these duplicate key attributes so that it is clear to the developer which entity definition is the source of the attribute. Return to the Attributes page and be sure these two attributes reference the proper entity objects.

7. Navigate to the Query page of the wizard. In the *Where* property, change the default text to conditions that join EMPLOYEES with IMAGES though IMAGE_USAGES (using a usage type of "E"), and also join EMPLOYEES to JOBS.

   Additional Information: The following code will accomplish this task:

```
ImageUsages.IMAGE_ID = Images.IMAGE_ID(+)
AND ImageUsages.ASSOCIATED_ID(+) = Employees.EMPLOYEE_ID
AND ImageUsages.USAGE_TYPE(+) = 'E'
AND Employees.JOB_ID = Jobs.JOB_ID
```

8. Fill in *Order By* as "Employees.LAST_NAME, Employees.FIRST_NAME." Click Finish.

9. Create a view link definition in the `tuhra.model.queries` package called DepartmentsToEmployeesVL between AllDepartmentsWithManagers (source) and AllEmployees (destination) by selecting the EmpDeptFKAssoc association under each entity object and clicking Add. Click Next. Make sure the *Generate Accessor: In View Object: AllDepartmentsWithManagers* checkbox is selected. For clarity, change the default Accessor Name property from "AllEmployees" to "EmployeesInDepartment." Click Finish.

   Additional Information: ADF BC will generate default names for accessors based upon the names of the view object definitions involved. In this case, the default name would be misleading to a programmer using the accessor in Java code because the default name implies that all employees are accessible. The new name you have provided for the accessor provides a more accurate description of what the accessor will be doing.

10. Open the TuhraService application module definition; in the Data Model tab add an instance of the AllDepartmentsWithManagers view object definition to the data model and name this instance "DepartmentTree."

    Additional Information: Create this view object instance by selecting the AllDepartmentsWithManagers view object definition in the *Available* area, changing the *New View Instance* property to "DepartmentTree," and clicking the Add Instance (">") button.

11. Also in the data model, add an instance of AllEmployees as a child instance of AllDepartmentsWithManagers under DepartmentTree calling the view object instance "EmployeesByDepartment."

    Additional Information: To accomplish this step, select AllEmployees nested under AllDepartmentsWithManagers in the *Available View Objects* area. Then select DepartmentTree in the *Data Model* area, change the *New View Instance* name, and click Add Instance.

12. It is always a good idea to test all new view object definitions at the top level if possible. Therefore, also create an instance of the AllEmployees view object definition called "AllEmployeesTest" in the top level of the *Data Model* area. (Select TuhraService in the *Data Model* area before moving the view object definition.)

    Additional Information: This view object instance is only required for testing, and you will remove it afterward. The data model area of the application module definition editor should now appear as follows:

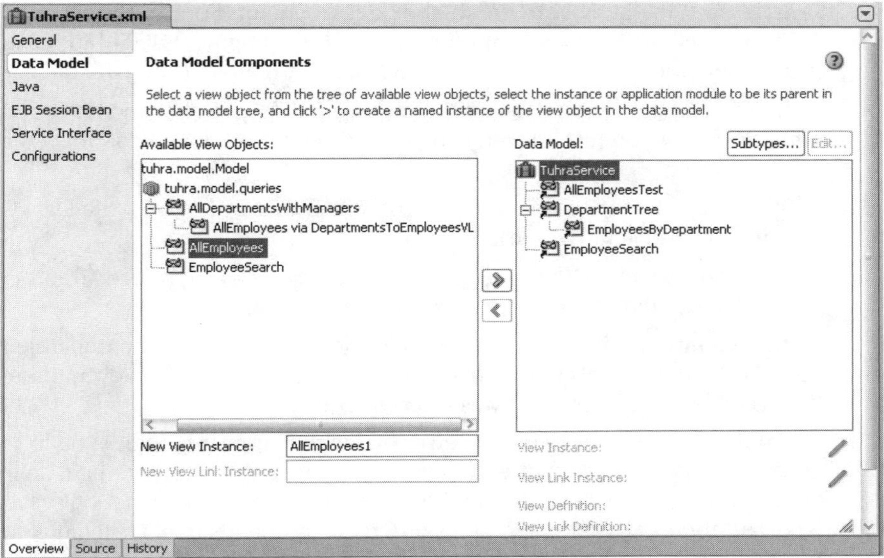

13. Select **Run** on the TuhraService application module definition node to run the Oracle Business Component Browser. Open the view link instance (DepartmentsToEmployeesVL1) to display the master-detail form. Scroll through records in the DepartmentTree (master) form to be sure the appropriate employees appear in the detail area.

NOTE
Some departments are not assigned any employees in the sample data.

14. Also open the AllEmployeesTest view object instance and scroll through its records to be sure the query is working properly. Close the components browser.

    Additional Information: As yet, all of the image attributes in this view object instance are empty. Later in the practice you will run a script to populate this information.

15. In the Data Model area, remove AllEmployeesTest (the top-level view object instance). The hierarchy viewer will use the employees view object instance that is a child of AllDepartmentsWithManagers.
16. Click Save All.

Create the Hierarchy Task Flow and Page Fragment

The Model layer is now set up for the hierarchy, so you can move over to the ViewController side. This section shows how to work with a DVT component, `dvt:hierarchyViewer`.

1. In the ViewController project, create an ADF bounded task flow called departmentTree-flow (in the WEB-INF directory). Like the searchEmployees-flow, this should use page fragments.
2. Drop a View component (Activities panel of the Component Palette) into the task flow editor and change the name to "departmentTree."

3. Double click the activity to create the page fragment. Specify the *Directory* as "<TUHRA_HOME>\ViewController\public_html\fragments." (Fill in the actual file system directory path for "<TUHRA_HOME>.") Create it as a blank page.
4. In the Data Controls panel, select **Refresh** from the right-click menu. The view object definitions that you just created should now appear (although you may need to expand some nodes).
5. Drag the DepartmentTree view object instance onto the page from the Data Controls panel, and drop it as a Hierarchy Viewer.
6. On the Component Gallery page, select *Hierarchy Viewer Types* as "Tree" and leave the default *Quick Start Layouts* selection (single page).

   Additional Information: The other *Quick Start Layouts* selection (multiple pages) defines zoom (drilldown) levels which this application does not use, however, these extra zoom levels can be defined manually as facets if required.
7. Click OK. The Create Hierarchy Viewer dialog will appear to allow you to specify the contents and zoom depth of each level of the hierarchy based on the data model. Select the DepartmentTree node, and in the Zoom 100% tab, ensure that only the following *Node Attributes* are included in this order: DepartmentName, FirstName, and LastName. All of these attributes can be defined as ADF Output Texts. Delete any other attributes.

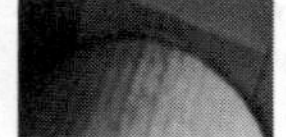

CAUTION
The hierarchy viewer is a complex component and the exact attributes and components that are created by default with a drag-and-drop operation from the Data Controls panel may vary depending on the release of JDeveloper that you are using.

8. Select the EmployeesInDepartment checkbox in the *Hierarchy* area. In the Zoom 100% tab, set up the attribute list as the following attributes in this order: EmployeeId, FirstName, LastName, Email, PhoneNumber, JobTitle, and Image, in that order. Click the New (green "+") button to add missing attributes. EmployeeId and Image should be defined as ADF Output Text, the other attributes should be defined as ADF OutputText w/Label. Click OK to create the hierarchy viewer.
9. Click Save All.

Explore the Page

The initial layout used by the department tree needs a bit of refinement. You are going to change the display so that it is a bit easier to read as in this illustration.

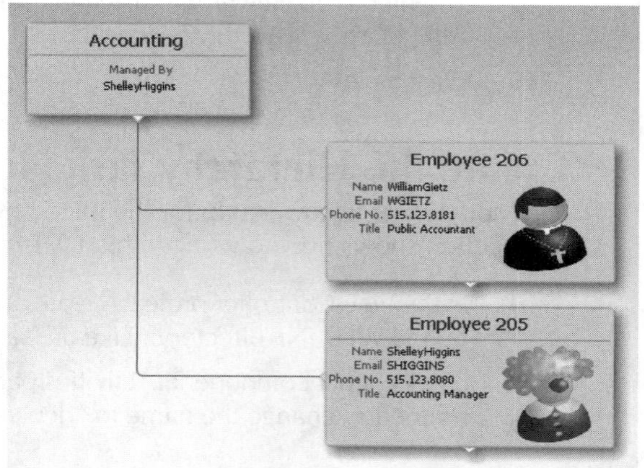

Before proceeding with that work, it is useful to explore the objects that were just created.

1. Click the Bindings tab of departmentTree.jsff to view the binding summary. On the binding DepartmentTree, select **Go to Declaration** from the right-click menu. The PageDef file will open.

2. Click the Source tab. Notice that the highlighted DepartmentTreeIterator executable is referenced by the following entry in the bindings section:

   ```
   <tree IterBinding="DepartmentTreeIterator" id="DepartmentTree">
   ```

   Additional Information: This code sets up a standard tree binding that points to the DepartmentTreeIterator iterator, which in turn queries the DepartmentTree view object instance.

3. Click the Source tab of the departmentTree.jsff file. Find the `dvt:hierarchyViewer` tag (around line 6).

   Additional Information: Notice that this element encloses a `dvt:node` component that refers to the view object instance (AllDepartmentsWithManagers) queried into that hierarchy node. It also encloses a second `dvt:node` component that refers to the query used in the next node level (AllEmployees). Each of these `dvt:node` elements contains a facet called "zoom100" for the 100% zoom properties you entered in the hierarchy dialog.

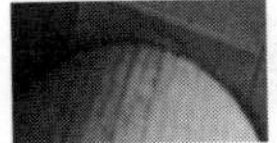

TIP
You can easily display line numbers in the editor by selecting ***Toggle Line Numbers*** *from the right-click menu on the editor left-hand gutter (margin).*

4. Examine the elements within the 100% facets. You will see familiar component tags for panel group layouts and output text items that show attribute values. The DVT components wrap these familiar components into a hierarchy display.

5. You can now run the hierarchy in this default form and compare it to the intended result. Since much of the layout is generated at runtime, it will be useful to run the page fragment within a page to test it. You can reuse the templateTest.jspx file you created in Chapter 17.

   Additional Information: If you do not have this file, complete the steps in the Chapter 17 section "Test the Template."

6. Open templateTest.jspx and remove the `af:inputText` item in the content facet. Drop the departmentTree-flow into the content facet and specify Region as the drop type.

7. Run templateTest.jspx. You will see a screen like that in Figure 18-4. Although you can use the pan and zoom tools in the control panel (accessed with the double arrow button on the top-left side of the screen), the data in the initial tree display is very small.

   Additional Information: The reason for this display is that the viewer needs to show all data in one screen. It would be better if you could restrict the diagram to one department at a time.

TIP
You may be able to use the mouse wheel to zoom in and out within the hierarchy viewer.

8. Close the browser.

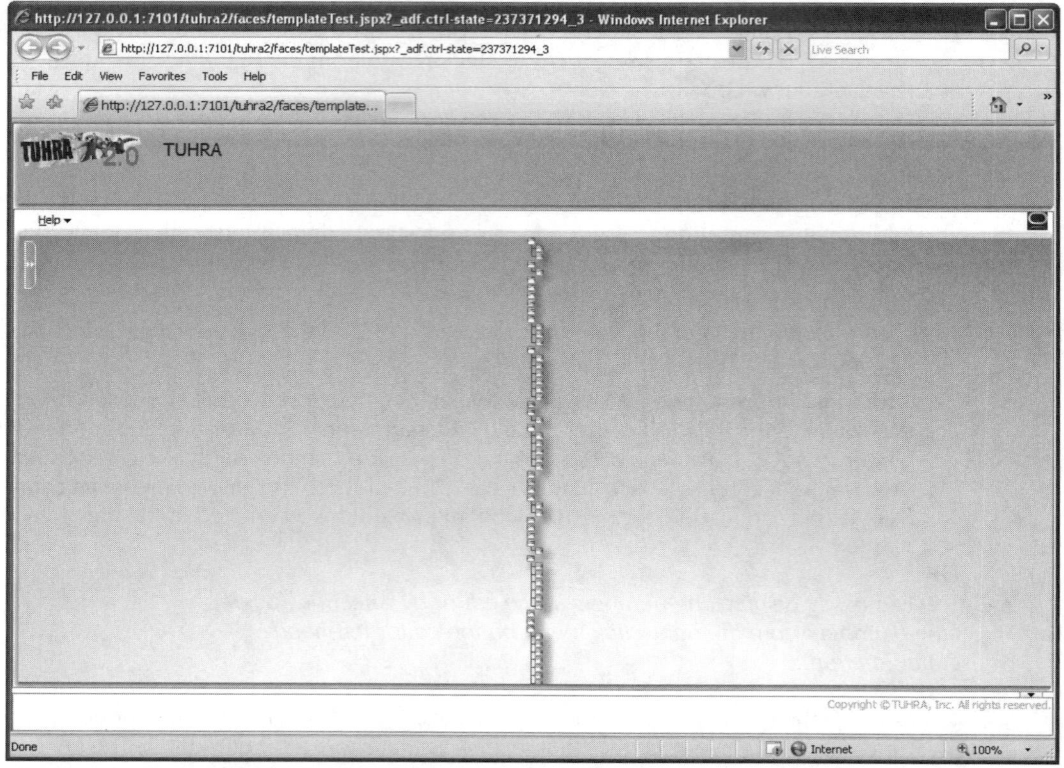

FIGURE 18-4. *Departments hierarchy viewer*

Refine the Hierarchy Viewer

As it stands, the hierarchy is showing too much information. Next, you will restrict the hierarchy viewer to only display data for one department at a time.

1. A view link can restrict the view to a single department without adding complexity to the query. Create a view object definition called DepartmentsList using the Departments entity definition. Specify attributes of DepartmentId and DepartmentName. Define an *Order By* of the department name ("Departments.DEPARTMENT_NAME").
2. Create a view link definition called "DepartmentSelectionVL" between DepartmentsList (source) and the AllDepartmentsWithManagers (destination) using the DepartmentId as a link. Specify *Cardinality* as "1-1." There is no need to worry about accessors in this case, so deselect all the accessor checkboxes.
3. Click Next and Finish. Edit the TuhraService application module definition and remove the DepartmentTree view object instance from the data model. (You need to remove EmployeesByDepartment first.)

4. Create an instance of the DepartmentsList view object definition with the name "DepartmentSelector"; then move the "AllDepartmentsWithManagers via DepartmentSelectionVL" view object definition and name the instance "DepartmentTree."

   Additional Information: Keeping the "DepartmentTree" name for this view object instance, you won't need to change the page bindings that have already been created.

5. Add the child object definition "AllEmployees via DepartmentsToEmployeesVL" under DepartmentTree, calling the view object instance "EmployeesByDepartment" (again preserving the name you used previously). The *Data Model* area will now appear as follows:

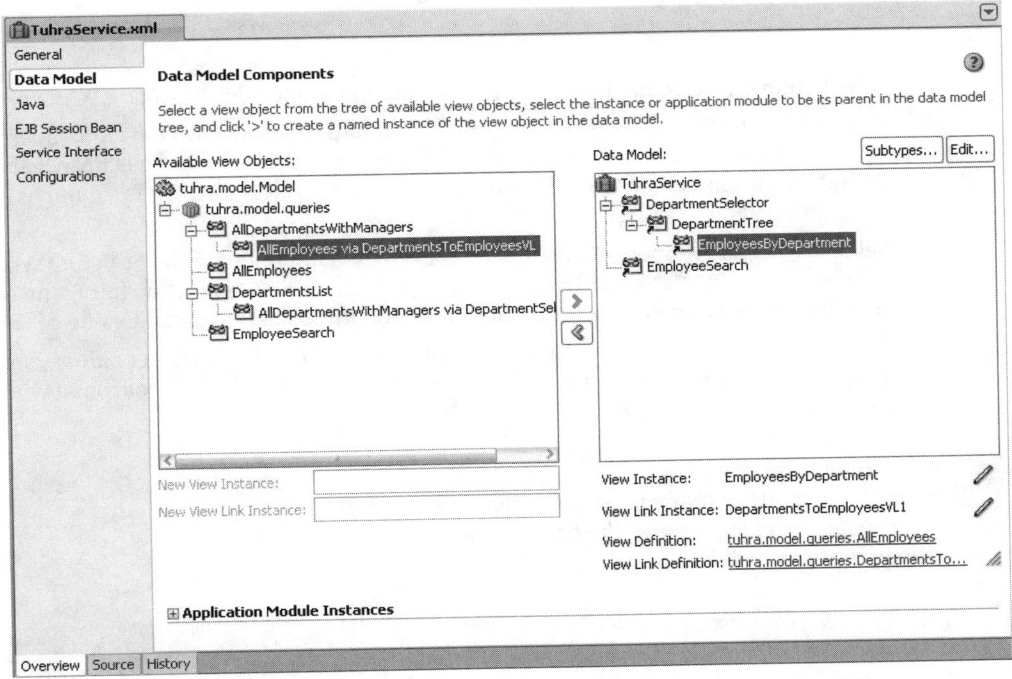

6. Open the Source tab of the departmentTree.jsff editor. Add the following lines of code before the `dvt:hierachyViewer` tag (which appears at around line 6):

```
<af:panelStretchLayout>
  <f:facet name="top">
  </f:facet>
  <f:facet name="center">
```

7. Under the closing `dvt:hiearchyViewer` tag (around line 93), add the following lines of code:

```
    </f:facet>
</af:panelStretchLayout>
```

Additional Information: This code surrounds the entire display with an `af:panelStretchLayout` container and moves all hierarchy components to a center facet. It also adds an empty top facet, which you will use in the next step. The Structure window will now show nodes like the following:

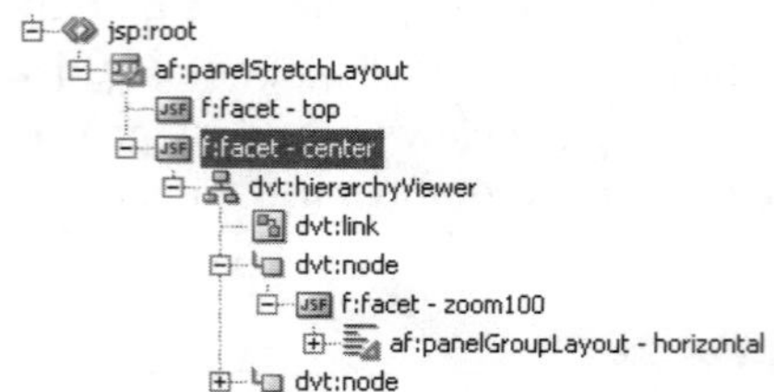

8. Select **Source** | **Reformat** from the right-click menu in the editor to fix the XML formatting.
9. Refresh the Data Controls panel and in the Structure Window drop the DepartmentSelector collection into the top facet of the new `af:panelStretchLayout`. Select **Navigation** | **ADF Navigation List**. In the Edit List Binding dialog, select *Display Attribute* as "DepartmentName." Click OK.
10. Select the `af:selectOneChoice` (the dropdown) component in the Structure window (under `af:panelStretchLayout`\top facet\`af:panelGroupLayout`), and set *Label* as "Explore Department." Check that the *Id* property is set to a default value of "nl1."
11. On the `dvt:hierarchyViewer` component (in the center facet), set *partialTriggers* property (Behavior section) as "::nl1" so that the hierarchy object is refreshed when the list changes. Click Save All.

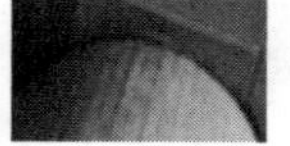

CAUTION
If the Property Inspector changes the partialTriggers *property to "[::nl1]" with square brackets, remove the brackets in the source code. This is a bug in the older versions of the product.*

12. Run templateTest.jspx. Select a department from the list, and the hierarchy view will only show that department with its employees. Try various selections from the pulldown. (Accounting, Executive, and IT departments, among others, should show employees.)
13. Zoom in using the control panel (accessed with the ">>" bar on the top-left side of the component), and you will see something like this for a department and employee node.
14. Close the browser.

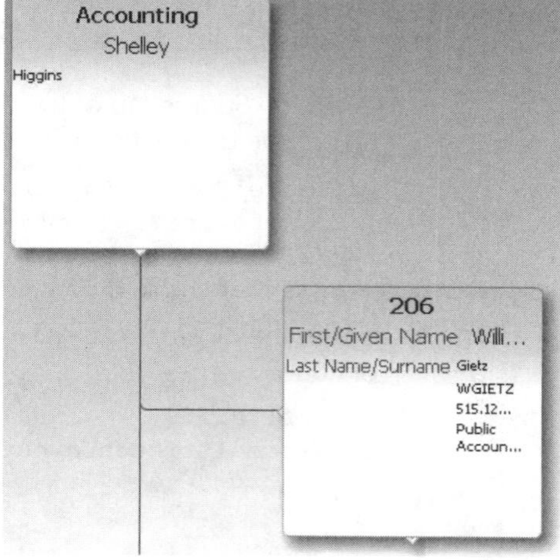

Improve the Department Node Display

To improve upon this display, the department name needs to be shown in boldface as a header and the full manager name should be displayed underneath on a single line.

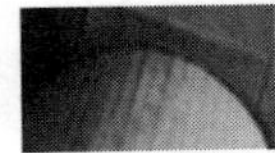

CAUTION

The following steps explain how to make these changes by modifying the code. Although we've explained it as clearly as possible, if something doesn't make complete sense along the way keep going and check your code against the code listing provided towards the end of this section. As we mentioned earlier in the chapter, the exact markup generated by the drag-and-drop operation for the `dvt:hierachyViewer` *may change from release to release, so if you find that your example is significantly differing from the instructions then just jump ahead and reconcile your code with the completed listing.*

1. In the Source tab for departmentTree.jsff, on the `dvt:node` component at the AllDepartmentsWithManagers level, change *Height* to "100" so that the department node box is shorter.
2. Locate the zoom100 facet for AllDepartmentsWithManagers (around line 26). The following steps refer to selecting code and changing properties in the Property Inspector.
3. Select the `af:panelGroupLayout` component directly under the zoom100 facet, and change *Valign* to "top" so the contents appear at the top of the hierarchy viewer box. Then add "background-color:#C0E4FD;border-color:#87CDFC;border-width:1;" to the end of the *InlineStyle* property to color the background of the boxes.

   Additional Information: Before adding the additional styles, add a semicolon to the end of the existing style string if one is not present.
4. Place the cursor inside the `af:outputText` tag for the DepartmentName attribute. In the Property Inspector, change the font-size value in the *InlineStyle* (Style section) to "18 px." The complete *inlineStyle* value in the code should read:

   ```
   inlineStyle="font-weight:bold;font-size:18px;color:#383A47;"
   ```

   Additional Information: The DepartmentName value will show in a bold, 18-point font. If a font-family setting also appears, you can leave it as is. The order of the properties in this listing is not critical. For example, font-size can appear after color.
5. In the Structure window, if the DepartmentName node appears below the LastName or FirstName nodes, drag it above those nodes. This may require dragging it out of an `af:panelFormLayout`. Also drag FirstName into the same container as LastName.
6. In the Source tab, drop a Spacer (Layout panel) after the DepartmentName field and change the height to "4." Drop a Separator after this and then another Spacer (unless a spacer already exists below the separator); set the second `af:spacer` height to "4" as well.

   Additional Information: You can alternatively drop these components into the page using the Structure window or visual editor.

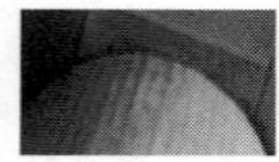

TIP
If you click a Component Palette component with the code editor active, JDeveloper will add it at the location of the cursor so you do not need to drag and drop. In this example, place the cursor after the `<af:outputText />` *tag and click the Spacer, Separator, and Spacer components in the Component Palette.*

7. Click the Design tab to look at the effect of these changes.
8. Drop a Panel Label and Message (Common Components panel) under the last spacer, and set *Label* as "#{empty node.LastName?'No Manager Assigned':'Managed By'}." This ternary expression will display "No Manager Assigned" if the LastName is NULL, which is the case in many of the records in the DEPARTMENTS table.
9. In the code editor remove any layouts such as `af:panelFormLayout` and `af:panelLabelAndMessage` that surround the FirstName and LastName fields (you may not have any of these layouts). Consolidate them into a single horizontal `af:panelGroupLayout` with a *Layout* set to "horizontal."

   Additional Information: One way to accomplish this task is to drop a Panel Group Layout component below the `af:panelLabelAndMessage` component. Then drag the `af:outputText` components for FirstName and LastName into the `af:panelGroupLayout`. You could alternatively group the fields together and use the **Surround With** right-click menu option.
10. Group the FirstName and LastName fields together and remove the *InlineStyle* value. If there is an empty `af:panelFormLayout` component, delete it. If an extra spacer appears at the end of this structure, delete it, too.
11. Check that the code under the zoom100 node appears as follows. Although the *inlineStyle* property spans three lines in the listing, it should appear on a single line in the code editor. The *Id* property values are not critical as long as IDs are unique on the page.

```
<af:panelGroupLayout inlineStyle=
                        "width:100%;height:100%;padding:3px;
                         background-color:#C0E4FD;border-color:#87CDFC;
                         border-width:1;"
                     layout="horizontal" valign="top" id="pgl1">
  <af:panelGroupLayout layout="vertical" halign="center"
                       inlineStyle="width:100%;" id="pgl2">
    <af:outputText value="#{node.DepartmentName}"
                   inlineStyle=
                        "font-weight:bold;font-size:18px;color:#383A47;"
                   id="ot6"/>
    <af:spacer width="10" height="4" id="s3"/>
    <af:separator id="s4"/>
    <af:spacer width="10" height="4" id="s5"/>
    <af:panelLabelAndMessage label=
               "#{empty node.LastName?'No Manager Assigned':'Managed By'}"
                             id="plam6"/>
    <af:panelGroupLayout layout="horizontal" id="pgl6">
       <af:outputText value="#{node.FirstName}" id="ot1"/>
       <af:outputText value="#{node.LastName}" id="ot2"/>
     </af:panelGroupLayout>
  </af:panelGroupLayout>
</af:panelGroupLayout>
```

12. Run templateTest.jspx. The department node box should now appear as follows:

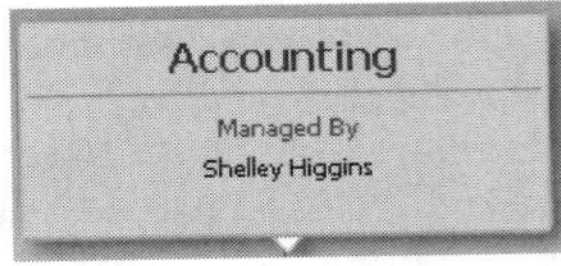

13. Switch to a department that is not assigned a manager (such as Benefits) to check the message. Close the browser.

Improve the Employee Node Display

You can now apply layout improvements to the employee node. You will be creating the following appearance:

The layout for employees is a little more complex than that for departments because the node display contains an image. The code to implement this display is shown in the next code listing. All code is within the zoom100 facet of the AllEmployees node. After following the first three steps in this section, you can follow the rest of the steps or use any other technique to make your code match this listing. (Although the *inlineStyle* property spans three lines in the listing, it should appear on a single line in the code editor. *Id* values do not have to be the same but should be unique.)

```
<af:panelGroupLayout inlineStyle=
                      "width:100%;height:100%;padding:3px;
                       background-color:#C0E4FD;border-color:#87CDFC;
                       border-width:1;"
                     layout="horizontal" valign="top" id="pgl3">
  <af:panelGroupLayout layout="vertical" halign="center"
                       inlineStyle="width:100%;" id="pgl4">
    <af:outputText value="Employee #{node.EmployeeId}" id="ot3"
                   inlineStyle=
                      "font-weight:bold;font-size:18px;color:#383A47;"/>
    <af:spacer width="10" height="4" id="s1"/>
    <af:separator id="s2"/>
    <af:spacer width="10" height="4" id="s6"/>
    <af:panelGroupLayout id="pgl7" layout="horizontal">
      <af:panelFormLayout id="pfl1">
        <af:panelLabelAndMessage label="Name" id="plam4">
          <af:outputText value="#{node.FirstName}" id="ot10"/>
          <af:outputText value="#{node.LastName}" id="ot7"/>
        </af:panelLabelAndMessage>
        <af:panelLabelAndMessage label="Email" id="plam2">
          <af:outputText value="#{node.Email}" id="ot8"/>
```

```
        </af:panelLabelAndMessage>
        <af:panelLabelAndMessage label="Phone No." id="plam5">
          <af:outputText value="#{node.PhoneNumber}" id="ot4"/>
        </af:panelLabelAndMessage>
        <af:panelLabelAndMessage label="Title" id="plam1">
          <af:outputText value="#{node.JobTitle}" id="ot9"/>
        </af:panelLabelAndMessage>
      </af:panelFormLayout>
      <af:image source="#{node.Image}"
                shortDesc="Picture of #{node.FirstName}  #{node.LastName}"
                id="i1" inlineStyle="width:144px;height:144px;"/>
    </af:panelGroupLayout>
  </af:panelGroupLayout>
</af:panelGroupLayout>
```

1. In the Structure window, select the `dvt:node` component for AllEmployees and set *Height* as "150" and *Width* as "300." This change modifies the size of the employee node box.
2. For the `af:panelGroupLayout` component directly under the zoom100 facet tag, change *Valign* to "top."
3. Add at the end of the *InlineStyle* property for the same `af:panelGroupLayout` component directly under the zoom100 facet, "background-color:#C0E4FD; border-color:#87CDFC; border-width:1;" to color the background of the boxes. Ensure that there is a semicolon between the existing style information and these extra values.
4. The remainder of the steps in this section demonstrate a technique for matching the code listing. If you want to try another method, you can make the code changes and skip to the last step for testing.
5. The best approach is to rebuild the node from scratch. Since you will need several container components around the display components, the changes are easiest to accomplish by moving the component tags into another editor, adding the container components, and pasting the component tags back into the containers. Expand the two outer `af:panelGroupLayout` components and select all nodes under them as shown here:

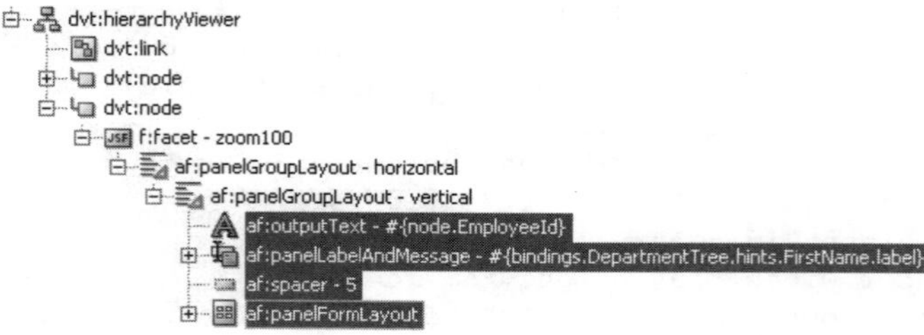

6. In the source code editor, cut (CTRL-X) those nodes and paste the code into a text editor outside of JDeveloper.
7. In JDeveloper, drop an Output Text component inside the inner `af:panelGroupLayout` component. Set *Value* as "Employee #{node.EmployeeId}" and *InlineStyle* to "font-weight: bold;font-size:18px;color:#383A47;" (including the semicolon).

8. Drop a Spacer after that and set the height to "4." Add a Separator, add another Spacer, and set the `af:spacer` *Height* as "4." This will create the same heading line as you created for the department node box.
9. Drop a Panel Group Layout and set *Layout* as "horizontal." Drop a Panel Form Layout inside that component.
10. In the editor holding the text you cut earlier, select each of the complete `af:panelLabelAndMessage` components (FirstName, LastName, Email, PhoneNumber and JobTitle) and their child tags and copy them into the new `af:panelFormLayout` (in the code editor).

    Additional Information: Depending on the version of JDeveloper you are using the FirstName `af:outputText` component may not be enclosed in an `af:panelLabelAndMessage`. This will not matter (see the next step).
11. In JDeveloper's code editor, combine FirstName and LastName `af:outputText` components under one `af:panelLabelAndMessage` component, deleting the empty `af:panelLabelAndMessage` that is left behind, if any. Change the *Label* of the `af:panelLabelAndMessage` to "Name."
12. Change the *Label* properties of the other `af:panelLabelAndMessage` components to "Email," "Phone No.," and "Title," respectively (instead of the EL expressions). This explicit setting is required because of a limitation of the components. Clear the *labelStyle* and *inlineStyle* property for all `af:panelLabelAndMessage` components in the employee node and `af:outputText` items within them.
13. Drop an `af:image` into the `af:panelGroupLayout` after the `af:panelFormLayout` component; this image will appear on the right side of the node box. Set the *Source* as "#{node.Image}," *ShortDesc as* "Picture of #{node.FirstName} #{node.LastName}," and *InlineStyle* as "width:144px;height:144px;" (again, including the semicolon).
14. Copy the script *import_employee_images.sql* from the authors' website (mentioned in the section "Websites for Sample Files" in the introduction) and place it in the <TUHRA_HOME>\DatabaseSchema\database\TUHRA directory. Open the script in JDeveloper and run it using the HR_DB connection. This script creates references to images in the /images directory and assigns them to associated IMAGE_USAGES records for each EMPLOYEE.
15. For departmentTree.jsff, look in the Errors node of the Structure window and resolve any errors (red circles) such as duplicate *Id* properties that resulted from dropping components whose IDs were used by code in the external text editor. You do not need to spend time clearing the warnings (yellow triangles).
16. Cross check your code with the listing at the start of this section. As before, the actual *Id* property values are not critical.
17. Click Save All. Run templateTest.jspx. The employee box should look something like this illustration.

18. Close the browser and stop the application.

Plug the Hierarchy Viewer into the Page

You have been testing changes to the departmentTree-flow in a separate page so far. Now that the functionality and appearance is refined and tested, you can integrate this fragment into the main search page. This section steps through that development process and also adds a mechanism for the user to switch between the criteria field search and the department tree browser using the images in the left-hand pane.

1. Open employeeSearch.jspx and delete the existing region in the second facet.
2. Now drop the searchEmployees-flow back into the same spot as before, but this time select **Dynamic Region**. The Choose Managed Bean for Dynamic Scope dialog will appear; the managed bean provides the logic that identifies the content for this region.
3. Click New (green "+") to add a managed bean. Set *Bean Name* as "searchScreenBB," *Class Name* as "SearchScreenBean," and *Package* as "tuhra.view.backing." Click OK. Click OK.
4. The Edit Task Flow Binding dialog will appear; neither the search form nor the hierarchy viewer task flows use parameters, so click OK.
5. Open the SearchScreenBean.java file (under `tuhra.view.backing`). Notice that this bean is very simple; it just provides a `getDynamicTaskFlowId()` method to derive the ID of the flow for the region based on the name.
6. Click Save All.
7. Open the bindings file for the employeeSearch.jspx page (on the Bindings tab of the jspx file, click the Page Definition File link). Click the Source tab and notice that it contains a single taskflow element, which uses EL to access `dynamicTaskFlowId` the result of the `getDynamicTaskFlowId()` method.

   Additional Information: For a one-off solution, you could add `if-else` logic into the `getDynamicTaskFlowId()` method to switch between flows, but it is better to create a generic UI manager class to handle task flow needs like this.

Write a UI Manager to Switch Page Fragments

It is a good idea to use a single managed bean to manage all the flags that configure the UI but that do not need to be stored in the database. In this case, the bean needs to store the region that is currently selected in the search page. In this section, you'll create a `UIManager` class to do this. It will be defined at a session-level scope and will contain a variable, `searchScreenFocus`, to store the selected region name.

1. In the ViewController project, create a Java class called "UIManager" in `tuhra.view` package. (In the New Gallery, select Java Class from the General\Java category and fill in *Name* and *Package*.)
2. Change the class to contain the following code (without the line number prefixes):

```
package tuhra.view;

/**
 * Class which manages persistent UI state
 * for the application.
 * Defined in the adfc-config.xml file as the
```

```
07:   * managed bean uiManager in session scope.
08:   */
09: public class UIManager implements Serializable{
10:   //This list could grow as we add more Pages / Screens
11:   public enum Screen {EMPLOYEE_SEARCH, DEPARTMENT_TREE}
12:
13:   //Store the current screen state
14:   private Screen _searchScreenFocus = Screen.EMPLOYEE_SEARCH;
15:
16:   /**
17:    * Set the searchScreenFocus flag from a text
18:    * version of the screen name
19:    * @param focus String matching the enumeration value
20:    */
21:   public void setSearchScreenFocus(String focus) {
22:     this._searchScreenFocus = Screen.valueOf(focus);
23:   }
24:
25:   /**
26:    * Set the searchScreenFocus flag from the enum value
27:    * @param focus
28:    */
29:   public void setSearchScreenFocus(UIManager.Screen focus){
30:     this._searchScreenFocus = focus;
31:   }
32:
33:   /**
34:    * Return the searchScreenFocus as the enum constant
35:    * @return
36:    */
37:   public UIManager.Screen getSearchScreenFocus() {
38:     return _searchScreenFocus;
39:   }
40: }
```

Additional Information: This code uses an `enum` (line 11) to define a group of constants; `enums`, which became available in JDK version 5.0, are more typesafe than conventional `int` (integer)–based constants. Also notice that the code contains an extra `setSearchScreenFocus()` method (line 21) that finds the `enum` from a string using `valueOf()` (line 22). This method allows you to set the focus by passing in the name (instead of the `enum`); this style of call is useful when you want to use `af:setActionListener` or `af:setPropertyListener` because they will not work directly with an `enum` argument.

3. Import the `java.io.Serializable` interface into the class.

   Additional Information: This will be stored in session state and as such may be migrated between nodes in an application server cluster. By using the `Serializable` interface you are telling the application server that it is alright to copy these UI settings between nodes on the cluster so that any of the servers can handle a request from a particular user of the application.

4. You now need to make this bean known to the runtime. Open adfc-config (under Page Flows in the Application Navigator). On the Overview tab, select Managed Beans and add a bean (using the green "+") and fill in *Name* as "uiState," *Class* as "tuhra.view .UIManager," and *Scope* as "session."
5. Click Save All.
6. Update SearchScreenBean.java to read as in the following code listing (without the line numbers).

```
package tuhra.view.backing;

import java.util.HashMap;
import oracle.adf.controller.TaskFlowId;
import tuhra.view.UIManager;

/**
 * Backing bean class for the main search screen used to
 * manage which view is shown on that screen.
 * Defined in the adfc-config.xml file as the managed bean
 * searchScreenBB in backingBean scope.
 * References the UI manager for a longer running state.
 * @see tuhra.view.UIManager
*/
public class SearchScreenBean {

  // The following Map and static block defines the mapping
  // between the focus flag held in the UIManager
  // and a particular pageflow definition to
  // swap into the region when that state is selected

  private static final HashMap<UIManager.Screen,String> _REGION_MAP;
  static {
    _REGION_MAP = new HashMap<UIManager.Screen,String>(2);
    _REGION_MAP.put(UIManager.Screen.EMPLOYEE_SEARCH,
              "/WEB-INF/searchEmployees-flow.xml#searchEmployees-flow");
    _REGION_MAP.put(UIManager.Screen.DEPARTMENT_TREE,
              "/WEB-INF/departmentTree-flow.xml#departmentTree-flow");
  }

  // Store a reference to the state holder (this will be injected)
  private UIManager _uiManager;

  public TaskFlowId getDynamicTaskFlowId(){
    return TaskFlowId.parse(
        _REGION_MAP.get(_uiManager.getSearchScreenFocus()));
  }

  /**
   * Used to inject the UI Manager during the creation of this bean
   * @see adfc-config.xml
   * @param _uiManager
   */
  public void setUiManager(UIManager _uiManager){
    this._uiManager = _uiManager;
  }
}
```

Additional Information: The `HashMap _REGION_MAP` is defined on line 22. It maps the screen focus to a particular region definition, which makes the actual selection of the region in the `getDynamicTaskFlowId()` method relatively simple. Since you have only two regions to swap, a `HashMap` is a bit of overkill (an `if-else` structure would suffice). However, if any more regions were needed, their names could be added to the `HashMap` static definition and `getDynamicTaskFlowId()` would remain the same.

7. Notice that you defined a `setUiManager()` method as part of the API for the `SearchScreenBean`. This is used to accept a reference to the UI manager that is being held in session scope.
8. To have JSF inject the UI manager value, switch back to the adfc-config.xml editor and locate the Managed Beans area on the Overview tab.

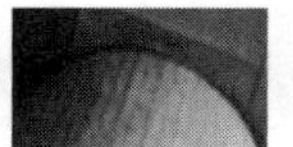

TIP
Be sure that the `SearchScreenBean` bean is set to a scope of "backingBean."

9. Select the searchScreenBB bean and then click Add (green "+") in the Managed Properties: searchScreenBB table. Set the managed property *Name* to "uiManager" (to match the `setUiManager()` method in the bean), the *Class* to tuhra.view.UIManager, and the *Value* to "#{uiState}."
10. Now that the logic to switch the screens is in place, you can define how the UI will activate the change in searchScreenFocus values. You could of course use a custom method in `SearchScreenBean`, but using a `af:setPropertyListener` is simpler. In the employeeSearch.jspx file, locate the `af:commandLink` that surrounds the "Search for Employees" image.
11. Drop into the `af:commandLink` a Set Property Listener (Operations panel). Set *From* as "#{'EMPLOYEE_SEARCH'}," *To* as "#{uiState.searchScreenFocus}," and *Type* as "action." Click OK.
12. Repeat the preceding step for the "View by Department" link. This time, fill in *From* as "#{'DEPARTMENT_TREE'}."

    Additional Information: Both of these `af:setPropertyListener` tags will call the `setSearchScreenFocus(String)` method to determine which region should be loaded next.
13. Click Save All.
14. Run employeeSearch.jspx. Click each navigation link on the left-hand pane to be sure you can switch between employee and departments task flow displays.

    Additional Information: You can make this code a bit more efficient. Currently, clicking the links refreshes the entire page in the process.
15. Exit the browser. In employeeSearch.jspx, check that the two `af:commandLink` components are assigned an *Id* property ("searchLink" and "orgLink").

    Additional Information: The *Id* properties must be set so that you can refer to them in the *partialTriggers* property.

16. On each of the two `af:commandLink` components, set *partialSubmit* to "true." This will activate a partial page refresh when the links are clicked.
17. On the `af:region` component (under the second facet), set the *partialTriggers* property on the `af:region` as "::searchLink ::orgLink" so that the region will refresh when those two components are activated.
18. Run employeeSearch.jspx. Now when you click the links, only the task flow region refreshes, not the entire page.

What Did You Just Do? In this phase, you completed the search page by adding another task flow and associated page fragment for the hierarchy viewer. You gained some experience with visual layout and code editing of a DVT component, `dvt:hierarchyViewer`. You also wrote a generalized Java class to manage the switching of page fragments into the base page.

CHAPTER 19

Sample Application: Edit Page

God has given you one face,
and you make yourself another.

—William Shakespeare (1564–1616) *Hamlet,* (II, 1, 1834)

If I could write the beauty of your eyes
And in fresh numbers number all your graces,
The age to come would say, "This poet lies;
Such heavenly touches ne'er touch'd earthly faces."

—William Shakespeare (1564–1616), *Sonnet XVII*

n this chapter, you will create a page fragment that allows the user to edit information about an employee. The practice builds on the results of the practice in Chapter 18 and demonstrates a number of techniques for working with ADF BC and ADF Faces.

The practice covers a lot of ground and demonstrates many concepts you need to know when building an edit screen. The practice steps through the following phases:

I. Set up the edit page and add LOVs
- Create the edit page fragment
- Add the department list of values
- Add the job list of values
- Add the manager list of values

II. Refine the Salary field
- Add validation to the Salary field
- Fix the salary validation and change the salary format

III. Refine the Commission field
- Add validation to the Commission field
- Change commission to a spin box
- Change the commission updatable property
- Clear the commission value for non-Sales employees

IV. Refine the image field and the layout
- Display the employee image
- Rearrange the layout and modify some labels
- Fix the forms and the field widths

V. Create a popup for job history
- Display the job history in a popup
- Update the job history

VI. Apply final refinements

- Define cascade delete functionality
- Add the biography
- Disable and enable the rich text editor
- Refactor the getBindings( ) method
- Display the manager name

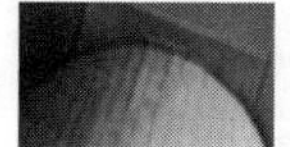

NOTE
As mentioned for other chapters, if you did not complete the hands-on practice in Chapter 18, you can use as a starting point application files available on the websites mentioned in the "Websites for Sample Files" section of the Introduction. You can use the end-of-Chapter-18 application files to start work in this chapter.

I. Set Up the Edit Page and Add LOVs

This phase creates the edit employee page fragment and sets up lists of values for the DepartmentId, JobId, and ManagerId fields. A *list of values (LOV)* offers a set of valid values from which the user selects. LOVs can appear as pulldowns or as popups where the user selects a value and the value is returned to the page. You usually supply data to the LOV using a read-only view object definition or a view object instance in a shared application module's data model. For simplicity, this practice uses view object definitions.

Create the Edit Page Fragment

This section adds a task flow and page fragment for the edit page starting with the application that you created in Chapters 17 and 18.

Just as in the search page, the main content of the edit page will be located in a task flow containing page fragments. Therefore, the first thing to do is to build a basic bounded task flow for the edit form.

1. In the ViewController project, create an ADF task flow from the New Gallery (Web Tier\JSF category) and call it "editEmployee-flow.xml." Be sure the *Create with Page Fragments* and *Create as Bounded Task Flow* checkboxes are selected and click OK.

   Additional Information: Notice that the new task flow appears twice in the navigator, under the directory that is specified in the dialog (WEB-INF by default) and in a separate node in the navigator called Page Flows. The *Page Flows* node is a virtual folder in the navigator that displays shortcuts to all of the task flows defined in the project. Opening the task flow from either place has the same effect.

2. In the Diagram page of the task flow, drop in a View activity from the Component Palette and name it "editEmployee." As this is the first activity you have added to this task flow, it is automatically marked as the default activity (denoted by a green halo).

3. Drop a Wildcard Control Flow Rule above editEmployee, leaving its name as the default value of "*" (matches any activity). Draw a Control Flow Case from the wildcard control flow rule to the editEmployee view and name it "refresh." The editEmployee-flow.xml diagram should appear as follows:

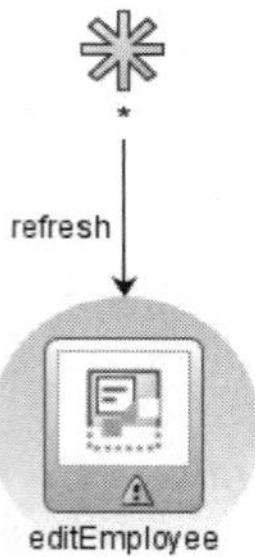

4. Next, you need to think about what to display on the page fragment. First of all, you need a view object instance to populate the data fields from the base EMPLOYEES table. You can reuse the AllEmployees view object definition in this context. In the Model project, open the TuhraService application module editor (under tuhra.model.services). In the Data Model page, name an AllEmployees instance as "EditEmployee" and move it to the *Selected* area as a top-level view object instance. The *Data Model* area should appear as follows:

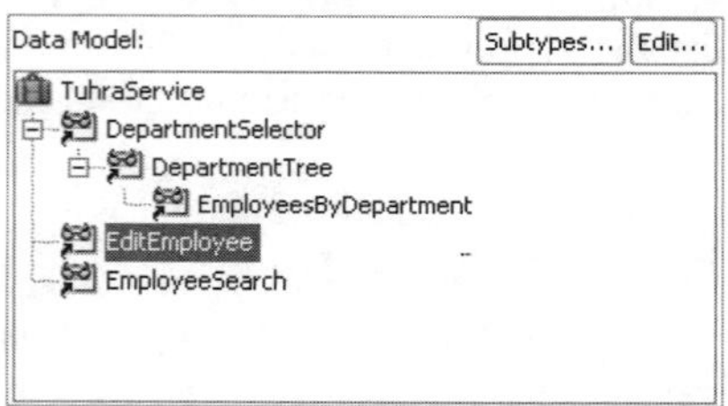

5. The edit UI also needs to display a little more information about the employee, such as their department, their compensation, and some audit information about when and by whom a record was created or changed. Edit the AllEmployees view object definition by double clicking that node in the tuhra.model.queries package of the Model project.

   Additional Information: As a developer, you will need to make the judgment about when to modify and reuse an existing view object definition and when you should just start over and create a specialized one. In this case it does not matter too much, as you are just adding a few extra attributes. However, in many cases you will want to create separate view object definitions to reduce the overhead of fetching more data than you really need. Alternatively, you could create a single view object definition with a declarative-mode query (explained in Chapter 7), which automatically defines the columns it fetches based on the UI requirements.

6. In the Overview tab of the view object editor, select the Attributes tab and click Add from Entity. From the Employees node in the *Available* pane, group select and shuttle the CommissionPct, CreatedBy, CreatedDate, DepartmentId, HireDate, ManagerId, ModifiedBy, ModifiedDate, and Salary attributes to the selected list. Click OK to close the Attributes dialog.

Additional Information: Because you are adding attributes to an existing View Object definition, this is a safe operation. If you need to remove attributes that are already in the definition, you need to exercise care that the attributes that you are about to remove are not referenced anywhere in existing bindings.

7. Click Save All.
8. In the editEmployee-flow, double click the editEmployee view activity and create a page fragment "editEmployee.jsff" in the fragments subdirectory under the ViewController project public-html directory (public_html\fragments\editEmployee.jsff). Leave the initial page layout as a blank page and specify that no managed bean will be created.
9. Refresh the Data Controls panel from the right-click menu, expand the nodes, and then drag and drop the new EditEmployee view object instance into the editEmployee.jsff page fragment as a Forms\ADF Form.
10. In the Edit Form Fields dialog, remove the following fields:
    - ImageId
    - AssociatedId
    - DefaultImage
    - ImagesImageId
    - UsageType
    - JobsJobId
    - JobTitle
11. Set the following attributes to be created as "ADF Output Text w/Label" components rather than the default components such as ADF Input Text w/Label or ADF Input Date w/Label:
    - EmployeeId
    - CreatedBy
    - CreatedDate
    - ModifiedBy
    - ModifiedDate
12. Set the Image attribute as an "ADF Output Text" component (without a label). You will change the type to an `af:image` later.
13. Notice that the attributes order in this dialog is dependent on the order in which the attributes were added to the view object. Reorder the attributes using the arrow buttons to match the following list (which we determined from a screen mockup in an earlier phase of the project):
    - EmployeeId
    - FirstName
    - LastName
    - Email
    - PhoneNumber
    - DepartmentId

- ManagerId
- JobId
- HireDate
- Salary
- CommissonPct
- Image
- CreatedBy
- CreatedDate
- ModifiedBy
- ModifiedDate

14. Select the *Include Navigation Controls* and *Include Submit Button* checkboxes. Check that the Edit Form Fields dialog looks like this:

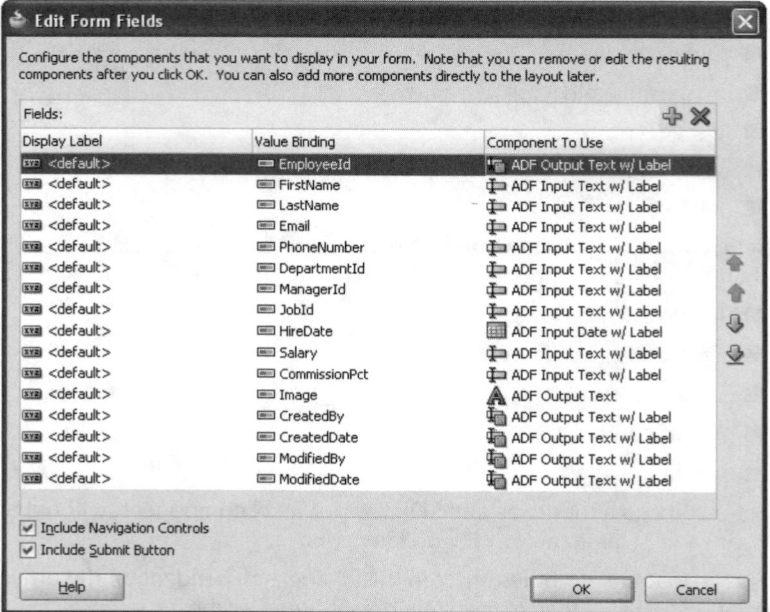

15. Click OK. At this point, you have a basic working data entry form. However, you need to make the interface a bit more user-friendly by adding LOVs for departments, jobs, and managers, and by improving the arrangement of fields. To see how the interface looks in its current state, open templateTest.jspx, remove the region from the content facet, and then drop the page flow (editEmployee-flow) into the content facet as a Region.
16. Run templateTest.jspx, and you should see something like the display in Figure 19-1.
17. Close the browser.

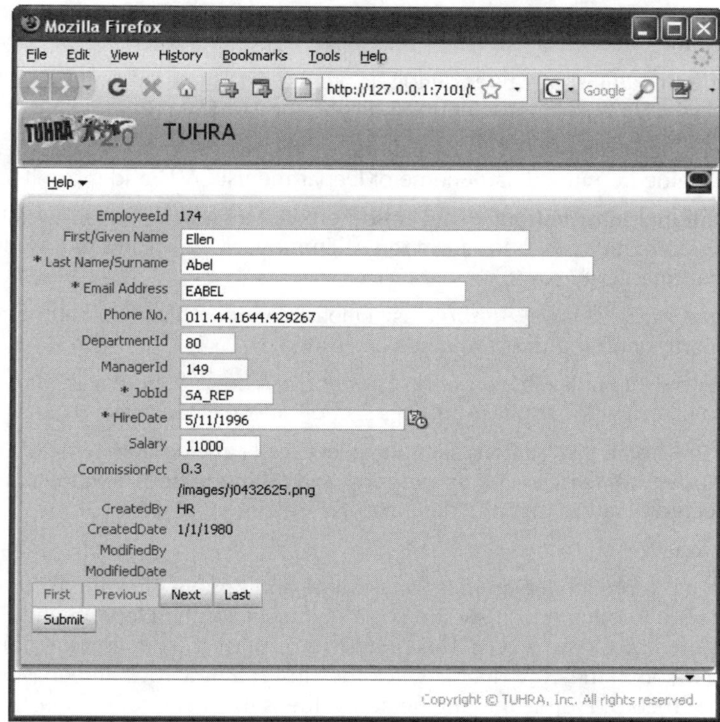

FIGURE 19-1. *Default form layout for the EditEmployee fields*

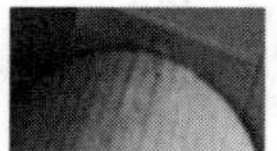

NOTE
Running the application will compile it. Before compiling, JDeveloper will, by default, save all modified files. You can change the automatic saving setting in the Preferences dialog's Compiler page although we recommend leaving it as is.

Add the Department List of Values

The department ID can be loaded from a simple pulldown because the list of departments is small. This section develops this pulldown.

1. In the Model project's tuhra.model.queries folder, create a view object definition called "DepartmentsLOV" based on a non-updatable usage of the Departments entity object definition.
2. In the Step 3 page, select the DepartmentId and DepartmentName attributes.
3. In the Step 5 page, fill in *Order By* as "Departments.DEPARTMENT_NAME" and click Finish.

4. Open the AllEmployees view object definition in the editor and click the Attributes tab. Select the DepartmentId attribute. Expand the "List of Values: DepartmentId" section and click the "Add list of values" (green plus "+") button to create an LOV.
5. In the Create List of Values dialog, leave the default name. Click the "Create new view accessor" (green plus "+") button next to the *List Data Source* field.
6. Select DepartmentsLOV in the left-hand side. Set *Name* as "DepartmentsLOVAccessor" (changing from the default name of DepartmentsLOV1) and move it to the right-hand side.

   Additional Information: This action creates a *view accessor,* which provides programmatic navigation from the AllEmployees view rows to the row sets containing DepartmentLOV rows.
7. Click OK. Set the *List Attribute* as "DepartmentId." This action automatically adds DepartmentId to the *List Return Values* area.
8. Click the UI Hints tab. Leave the *Default List Type* as "Choice List" (to specify a pulldown item) and, in the Display Attributes section, move "DepartmentName" to the *Selected* area.
9. In the Choice List Options section, select the "Labeled Item (First of List)" selection in the *Include "No Selection" Item* property and fill in the field next to it as "<No Department Selected>" rather than the default "<No Selection>." Click OK.
10. Click Save All.
11. Run the TuhraService application module and double click the EditEmployee view object instance to open it. You should see a pulldown for the DepartmentId column that is supplied by the new LOV. This pulldown displays the department name based on settings you made in the LOV dialog. Click the "Insert a new row" (green plus "+") button to add a record. Notice that the default value is the first one in the list—the blank label you specified. Close the Business Component Browser.
12. In the editEmployee.jsff page fragment file, delete the DepartmentId field (above the ManagerId field).
13. In the Data Controls panel, refresh the view from the right-click menu and expand the EditEmployee collection. Drag the DepartmentId attribute to the previous location of the DepartmentId field. Select **Single Selections | ADF Select One Choice**.

    Additional Information: You may find it easier to drop the DepartmentId attribute in the correct location if you use the Structure window.
14. Run templateTest.jspx. The DepartmentId pulldown should appear as seen next. (You will modify the width of the pulldown later.)

15. Close the browser.

Add the Job List of Values

In this section, you will create a pulldown LOV for JobId. Since it is the same type of item, the process is identical to the process for departments. Therefore, the following steps are somewhat abbreviated.

1. Create a view object definition called JobsLOV based on a non-updatable usage of the Jobs entity object definition (deselect the *Updatable* checkbox). Select the JobId and JobTitle attributes. Order by "Jobs.JOB_TITLE." Click Finish.

   Additional Information: Notice that you do not need LOV view object instances in the application module definition (TuhraService). This keeps the whole service interface and the data controls tree much simpler.

2. Select the JobId (not JobsJobId) attribute in the AllEmployees view object definition and define a list of values with a List Data Source (accessor) named "JobsLOVAccessor" using the new JobsLOV view object definition.
3. Specify JobId as the list attribute. On the UI Hints tab, ensure that the *Default List Type* is "Choice List" and move JobTitle to the *Selected* area for the Display Attributes section. Set the "No Selection" label as a "Labeled Item (First of List)" with the text "<Select a Job>." Click OK.
4. Click Save All.
5. Return to the editEmployee page fragment, refresh the Data Controls panel and replace the `af:inputText` component for JobId by dragging JobId from the EditEmployee collection and by selecting an ADF Select One Choice (in the **Single Selection** pulldown menu).
6. Run templateTest.jspx. The JobId field should appear as in this snippet from the browser:

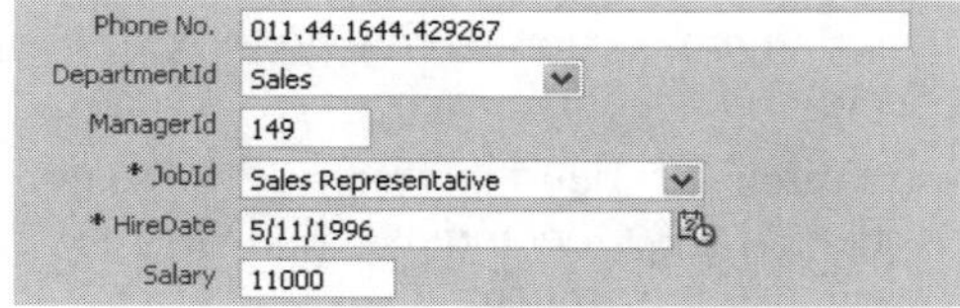

7. Close the browser.

Add the Manager List of Values

You want to allow the user to select the manager ID based on an LOV. The list of managers is too long (or you expect it to grow to be too long) for a pulldown. Therefore, you will create a popup LOV dialog to allow the user to search for a manager. In addition, the contents of this LOV will incorporate the following business rules:

- Employees cannot manage themselves.
- Employees can be managed only by other employees in the same department or in the Executive Department (ID of "90").

1. In the Model project, create a view object definition, in the tuhra.model.queries package, called "FilteredManagerLOV" and using the option "Updatable access through entity objects." Base this view object definition on a usage of the Employees entity object definition. Deselect the *Updatable* checkbox.
2. On the Attributes page, select the DepartmentId, EmployeeId, FirstName, and LastName attributes. On the Query page, define *Order By* as "Employees.FIRST_NAME,Employees .LAST_NAME." Click Finish.

3. Open the view object editor for FilteredManagerLOV if it is not open already and select the Query tab of the Overview editor.

   Additional Information: You need to add view criteria that filter the list based on two values: the EmployeeId of the current record (so that the current employee will not be displayed) and the DepartmentId of the current record (so only employees in that department or in Department 90 will be displayed).

4. In the Bind Variables section, click the "Create new bind variable" (green plus "+") button to add a bind variable. Fill in *Name* as "CurrentEmployeeId" and Type as "Number." Deselect the *Required* checkbox. Click OK.

NOTE
Be sure to define CurrentEmployeeId as non-required.

5. Repeat the preceding step to add another non-required `Number` bind variable called "CurrentDepartmentId."

6. In the View Criteria section, click "Create new view criteria" (green plus "+") button to display the Create View Criteria dialog.

7. Fill in *Criteria Name* as "FilteredManagerLOVCriteria" if it is not already present. Click Add Item to add a group and an initial item. Set *Validation* as "Required" and change values in the Criteria Item section to change the expression to "((EmployeeId <> :CurrentEmployeeId))."

   Additional Information: To build this expression, select *Attribute* as "EmployeeId," *Operator* as "Not equal to," *Operand* as "Bind Variable," and *Parameter* as "CurrentEmployeeId" as shown here:

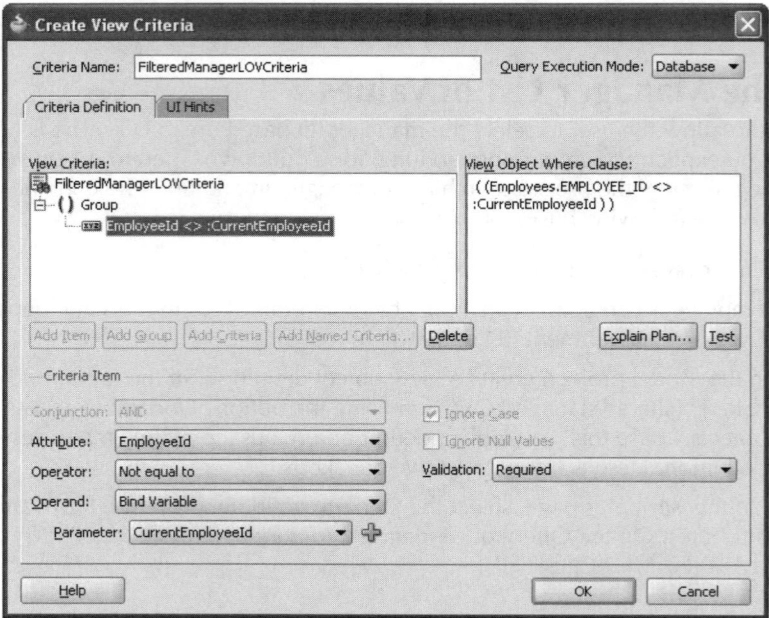

8. You have defined the expression for the first business rule. To define the second business rule, select the top-level node (FilteredManagerLOVCriteria) and click Add Group. This action adds an "Or Group" by default. With the new group node selected, set the *Conjunction* as "AND."
9. Click Add Item and define the expression "DepartmentId = 90" with a *Validation* of "Required." (*Operand* should be "Literal" in this case.)
10. Select the "AND Group" node and click Add Item again. Define the additional expression "DepartmentId = :CurrentDepartmentId" (a bind variable operand in this case). Change *Conjunction* to "OR" because the employee can be managed by any employee in the executive department or in the same department as that employee.

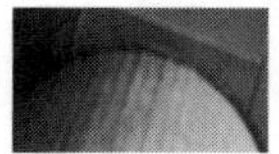

TIP

The Parameter list in this dialog only contains existing bind variables. You can add bind variables in this dialog by clicking the New (green plus "+") button in this dialog.

11. Set Validation to "Optional" because some employees are not assigned to departments. The Create View Criteria dialog should appear as follows:

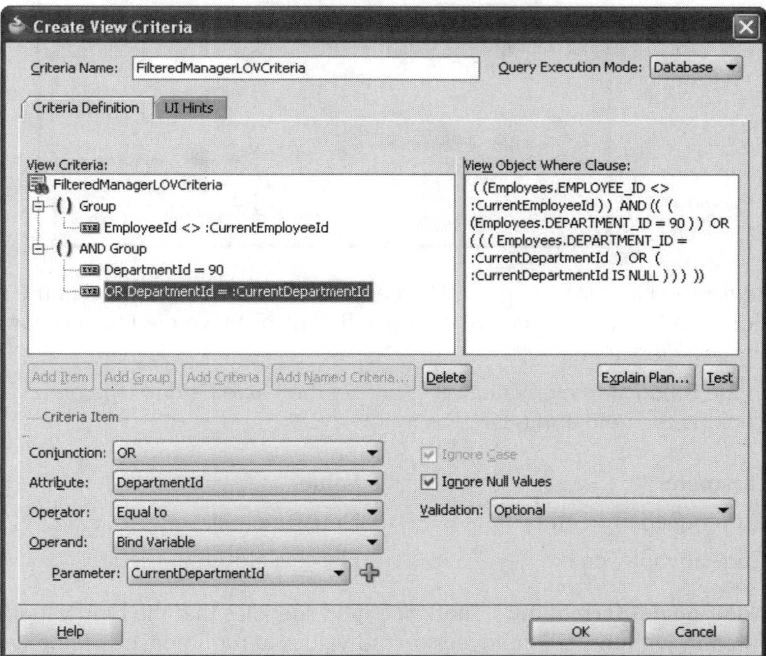

Additional Information: The declarations you enter in the Create View Criteria dialog are recorded as XML elements in the view object definition (XML) file. Therefore, it is useful to become familiar with entering view criteria using this dialog because apart from editing the view object definition source code, there is no other practical way to enter declarative criteria conditions. It is of course possible to define view objects in expert mode where you directly have to enter all of the SQL for a view object. However, we recommend that you restrict your use of expert mode view objects to a minimum, as they are harder to maintain in the long run. In addition, expert mode view objects cannot be customized after deployment.

12. Click OK. Open the AllEmployees view object editor and select the ManagerId attribute.
13. Create a list of values. Add a List Data Source item, and select "FilteredManagerLOV." Change the *Name* to "FilteredManagerLOVAccessor" and move it to the View *Accessors* area. The View Accessors dialog should now contain three accessors and look like this:

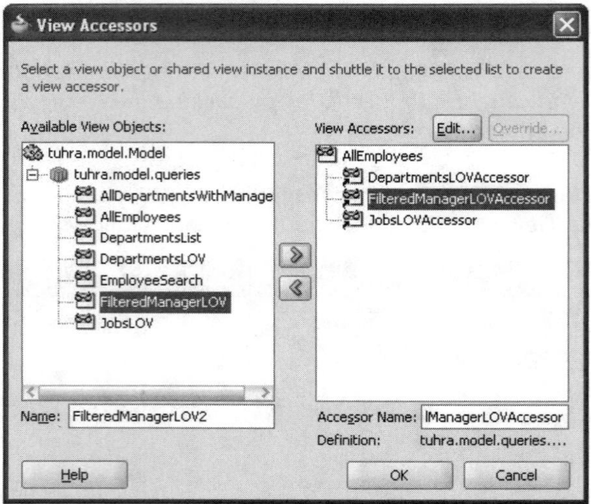

14. Select the FilteredManagerLOVAccessor in the right-hand pane of the shuttle and click Edit. The Edit View Accessor dialog will appear. Move the FilteredManagerLOVCriteria to the *Selected* area.
15. In the Bind Parameter Values section, set the *Value* field for the bind variables (by double clicking the field and typing) as follows:

Parameter	**Value**
CurrentDepartmentId	DepartmentId
CurrentEmployeeId	EmployeeId

Additional Information: The *Value* field specifies that the bind variable value will be filled in with the AllEmployees record values at runtime. The dialog will appear as shown in the following illustration.

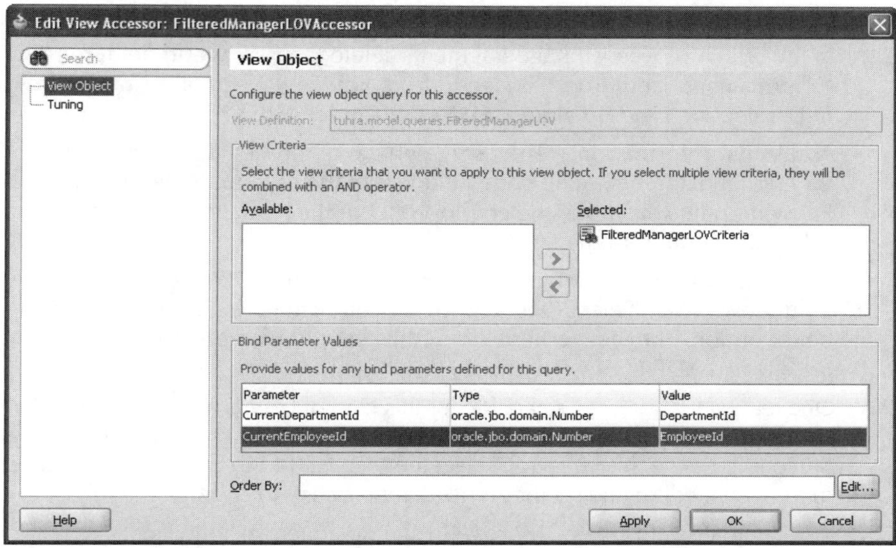

16. Click OK in the Edit View Accessor dialog. Click OK in the View Accessors dialog.
17. In the Create List of Values dialog, set the *List Attribute* to "EmployeeId." This action should set the *List Return Values* field for *View Attribute* as "ManagerId" and for *List Attribute* as "EmployeeId."
18. Click the UI Hints tab and set *Default List Type* as "Combo Box with List of Values." Move FirstName and LastName to the *Selected* area of the Display Attributes section.
19. In the List Search section, select the *Query List Automatically* checkbox so that the list will be displayed when the LOV appears. The UI Hints page should look like this:

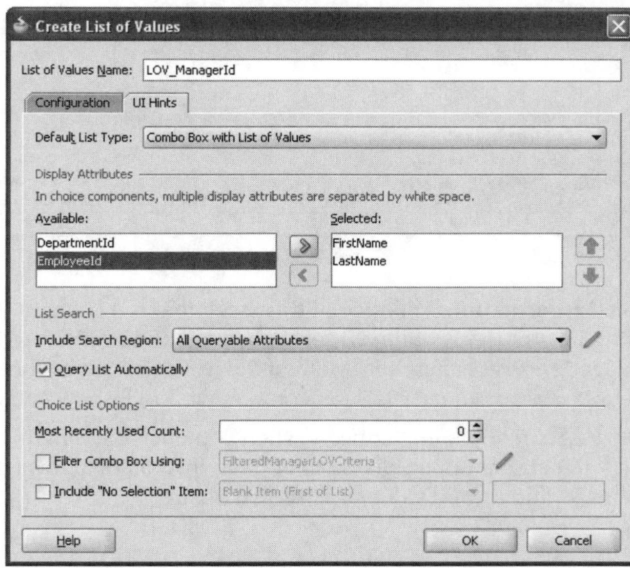

20. Click OK and click Save All.

21. In the editEmployee.jsff page fragment, delete the ManagerId field, refresh the Data Controls panel and drop ManagerId from EditEmployee collection to above the JobId field selecting **List Of Values | ADF LOV Choice List**.

    Additional Information: The user interface of the ADF LOV Choice List provides a traditional data-entry-style code field where the user can enter the code value if they know it (in this example, the employee ID of the manager); alternatively, the user can select the code from the LOV.

    If you know users are unlikely to know the employee ID and the list of values is short, a pulldown (ADF Select One Choice, as you defined for DepartmentId and JobId) is a better option. The view criteria filtered list would work the same for a pulldown as it does for an ADF LOV Choice List.

22. One feature that is useful to enable for this kind of LOV is automatic validation of the user's data entry. So if the user types in an invalid value into the field, the LOV will automatically launch. To define this behavior, select the ManagerId `af:inputComboboxListOfValues` in the visual editor and set the *AutoSubmit* property to "true."

23. Run templateTest.jspx; the ManagerId should appear as follows:

24. Check that you can type a value into the ManagerId field because it is a combobox. When you display the pulldown, you will see a list of valid manager choices as follows:

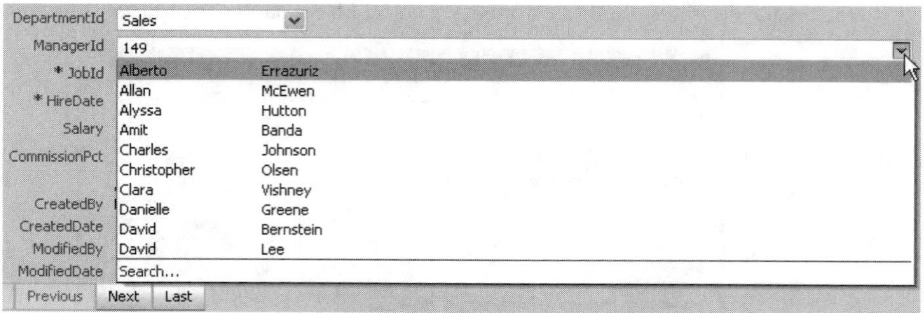

    Additional Information: Notice at this stage that the list area that appears in the preceding illustration is really wider than is needed to display only the names of the manager. This is because the width of the list is defined by the overall width of the `af:inputComboboxListOfValues` component. We'll show you how to fix this later on.

25. Look for the Search link that appears when you click the pulldown button. Selecting this link will cause a popup dialog to appear; this dialog allows the user to enter search conditions to find a valid value as is shown next.

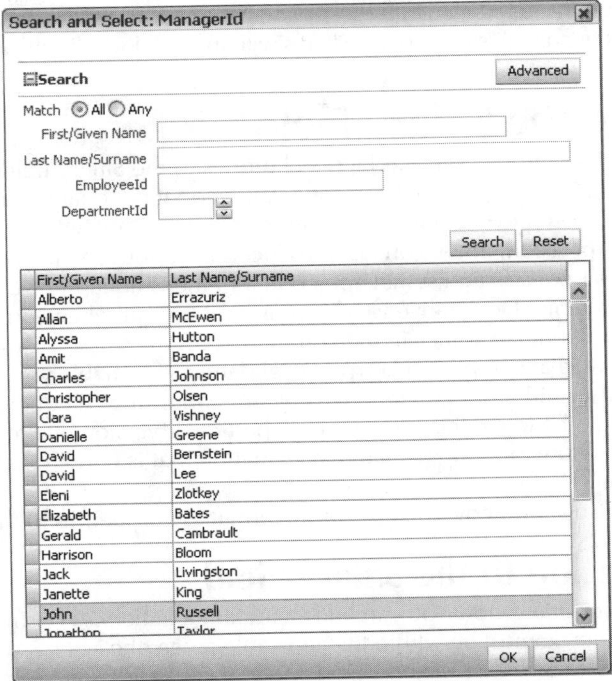

26. Dismiss the popup, type in an invalid manager ID (for example, 1000), and press TAB. The same search dialog will appear so that the user can find a valid manager. This feature that uses the LOV values to check the user input is sometimes called *LOV validation*.

27. Cancel the dialog. Close the browser.

What Did You Just Do? In this phase, you created the page fragment you will use to supply the user with employee record editing functionality. The work flowed in the same way as that in Chapter 18, which is typical when working with ADF: you first set up view object instances that contain attributes for the data entry fields; you then drop the view object collection or attributes from the data controls onto a JSF JSP page (in this case, a JSF page fragment). The drag-and-drop operation from the Data Controls panel creates data input elements that are prebound to the Model layer business services. In addition it sets up standard defaults for properties that you may need.

You then set up two different styles of LOVs for the fields that act as foreign keys to reference tables. Both styles contain lists of valid values queried from a table. The pulldown style uses the `af:selectOneChoice` component; in this page, you used this style for the DepartmentId and JobId attributes. The pulldown LOV displays a description that the user will recognize, and it stores the code value in the attribute. Pulldowns are good for lists that are small (for example, 50 or 60 choices). The advantage of this style is that the data domain consists of only valid options; therefore, you would not require additional validation on the UI side.

The other style of LOV you created in this phase was the combobox LOV, which also shows a pulldown list of values but also allows the user to type in the code value. The ADF Faces Rich Client component `af:inputComboboxListOfValues` also offers a selection that displays a search window. This window can be set up to appear if the user types in an invalid value (a value not in the list). Therefore, this component shares with the pulldown list the advantage of data validation.

II. Refine the Salary Field

This phase applies various user interface techniques to the Salary field to demonstrate how declarative validation can provide basic data validation functionality for values that the user types into fields. You can create declarative validation rules for many types of validation (comparison, range, regular expression, and so on, as introduced in various sections of Chapter 6) and use validation values from a fixed list that you code into the validation rule or from a dynamic list that is queried from a table. Declarative validation is a bit trickier when you need to use a dynamic value that is conditional to values in the current record.

Knowing how to accomplish this type of validation can enable you to define metadata for a requirement that would otherwise require programmatic code. The more you can define behavior through metadata, the less reliant you are on a particular version of a technology or language. This phase shows how to set up declarative validation that is conditionally based on values from the current record.

This phase also shows how to apply basic formatting properties to the Salary field.

Add Validation to the Salary Field

This section demonstrates how you can add validation to a field. A business rule states that the salary of the employee must be within the allowable range (the MIN_SALARY and MAX_SALARY values for that job in the JOBS table). This is one of those validation tasks that you would expect to have to write code to accomplish. However, in this case, you can define validation declaratively using a validation rule based on a view accessor (discussed in Chapters 6 and 7).

1. In the Model project, create a non-updatable view object definition called "SalaryValidator" based on a usage of the Jobs entity object definition.

   Additional Information: As a reminder, a non-updatable view object definition based on the usage of an entity object definition is defined by selecting "Updatable access through entity objects" on the Step 1 (Entity Objects) page, and then selecting an entity object on the Step 2 (Attributes) page and deselecting the *Updatable* checkbox.

2. Select all attributes and click Finish. In the view object editor for SalaryValidator, click the General tab, and expand the Tuning section. In the *Retrieve from the Database* section, select the "At Most One Row" radio button. You only need to retrieve one job record from the JOBS table to match the particular JobId in the employee record.

3. In the Query tab, Bind Variables section, add a bind variable called "JobIdToValidate." Specify the *Type* as "String" and set it as not required. Click OK.

4. Also on the Query tab, create view criteria that set JobId equal to the new bind variable, JobIdToValidate. Deselect *Ignore Case* and set *Validation* to "Required."

   Additional Information: Setting *Validation* to "Required" causes an exception to be thrown if a NULL value is passed in as the parameter. Deselecting *Ignore Case* eliminates uppercase conversions. Compare the value of *View Object Where Clause* value with *Ignore Case* checked and unchecked to see the difference. In this situation, the JobId is passed in from a valid list, so you do not need the uppercase conversion. Moreover, the query will be more efficient without the `UPPER()` function conversions.

5. The *View Object Where Clause* should contain "((Jobs.JOB_ID = :JobIdToValidate))." Click OK. Save All and close all the editor windows (using the right-click menu option on any editor tab).

6. Up to now, you have (hopefully) been creating view object definitions in the queries package. You might want to take time now to refactor the set of view objects into subpackages for main, lov, and validation. You can accomplish this task most easily by group selecting view objects (for example, those with an LOV suffix) and using the **Refactor | Move** option from the right-click menu. Here is a sample arrangement:

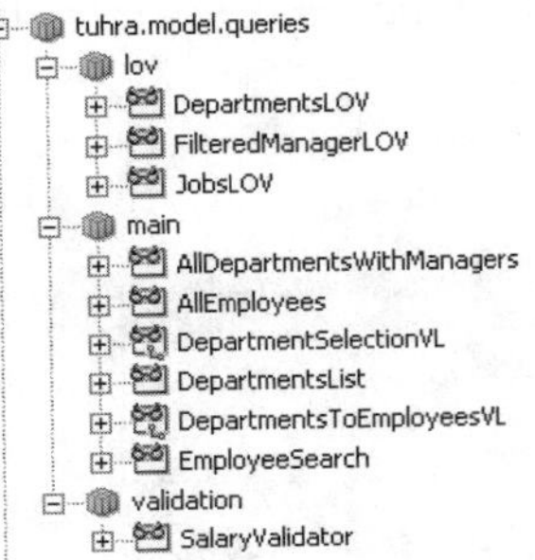

Additional Information: If spurious package nodes appear after refactoring, refresh the display or ignore them. They should disappear when you restart JDeveloper.

7. Next, you will create an accessor to the new validation view object from the JobId of the Employees record. Open the Employees entity object in the editor and click the View Accessors tab in the Overview tab of the editor.

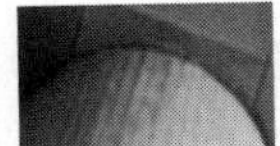

NOTE
Earlier, you created view accessors in the context of view objects, but you could alternatively have created them in the base entity object so that they would be shared with any view objects based on that entity object.

8. Create a view accessor called "SalaryValidatorAccessor" that points to the new SalaryValidator view object. (Do not click OK.)

9. Staying in the View Accessors dialog, select SalaryValidatorAccessor in the *View Accessors* area and click Edit. If you clicked OK before this step, click the "Edit selected View accessor" (pencil) button.

   Additional Information: As you may recall, the Edit View Accessor dialog allows you to select the view criteria for the view object to limit the results of the view object query (in this case, you will limit results to the JobId that matches the current employee record).

10. Move SalaryValidatorCriteria to the *Selected* area and in the Bind Parameter Values section, set the JobIdToValidate *Value* as "JobId."

    Additional Information: This setting declares that the query will use the JobId value in the current employee row to populate the bind variable (parameter); that bind variable will be used to query the JOBS table for the SalaryValidator view object. In this case, since the bind variable will contain a JobId value, only one row will be returned.

11. Click OK, and OK to dismiss both dialogs. Click the Validators tab and expand the Employees\Attributes\Salary node. You will see one validation rule already added by the entity object creation labeled as "Database Constraint – Precision : (8,2)."
12. Select the Salary node in this tree and click "Create new validator" (green plus "+"). The "Add Validation Rule for: Salary" dialog will appear.
13. You might be tempted to use the built-in range validation rule to check that the value of Salary is between the MinSalary and MaxSalary attributes. However, range validation rules can only be defined using literal values, not with values from a query. Select *Rule Type* as "Compare" (if it is not already selected), set *Operator* as "GreaterOrEqualTo," and set *Compare With* as "View Accessor Attribute."
14. The SalaryValidatorAccessor will appear in the *Select View Accessor Attribute* area. Expand this node and select MinSalary. The dialog will appear as follows:

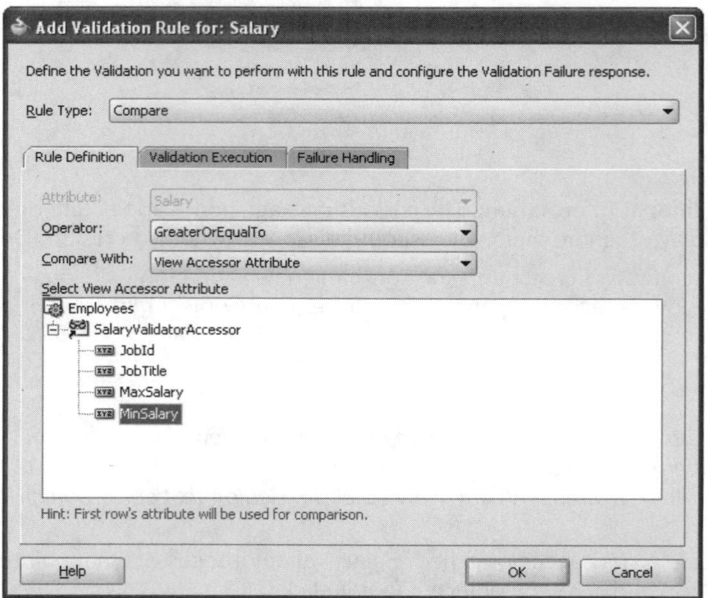

15. Click the Failure Handling tab and ensure that the *Error* radio button is selected.

    Additional Information: Notice the radio button *Informational Warning*. The ability to declare validation that raises only a warning (not a failure error) is a new feature with ADF 11*g*.
16. Fill in *Message Text* as follows (all on one line):

```
The defined salary of {empSalary} falls below the minimum of
{minSalary} defined for the {jobDescription} job.
```

    Additional Information: As you enter this text, the Token Message Exceptions section will be filled in to contain the message tokens in the text. *Message tokens* (or just "tokens") are placeholders delimited with curly brackets, which will be replaced by values at runtime.

17. You need to define the source of data for each token. You can declare the source to be a name of an attribute or a fully qualified expression that refers to a value. In the Token Message Expressions section, fill in the *Expressions* column as follows:

Message Token	**Expression**
empSalary	Salary
minSalary	SalaryValidatorAccessor.first().MinSalary
jobDescription	SalaryValidatorAccessor.first().JobTitle

Additional Information: These expressions are actually using the Groovy scripting language and the last two use the view object accessor (`SalaryValidatorAccessor`); for the first (and only) row in the JOBS table (`first()`) that matches the JobId of the current employee record, these expressions will reference the values of the MinSalary, and JobDescription attributes, respectively.

18. Click OK. Click Save All.

19. Run the application module and open the EditEmployee view object instance node. The first row in the EditEmployee collection should be Employee 174 (Ellen Abel) with a Job of "Sales Representative." Change the Salary value to 4000 and press TAB. The following error should appear: "The defined salary of 11000 falls below the minimum of 6000 defined for the Sales Representative job."

    Additional Information: That the message appears is correct, but the value of the "{empSalary}" is the value before you made the change (11000). This effect occurs because validation fires prior to setting the value of the Salary attribute. Since the validation stopped the value from being set, the old value is shown in the message. You need to access the value that failed the validation and you can use the special expression "newValue" to accomplish that access.

NOTE
In the Business Component Browser, the error message is prefixed with a string noting the Java exception type and the internal validation rule name. ADF Faces will remove this prefix at runtime so web application users will only see the message you have defined.

20. Dismiss the error dialog and close the Business Component Browser. Return to the Compare validation rule's Failure Handling tab and change the *Expression* for the empSalary token from "Salary" to "newValue." Run the application module and the error message should show something like, "The defined salary of 4000 falls below the minimum of 6000 defined for the Sales Representative job." Set the salary back to "11000."

21. Change the Job to "President," which has a minimum salary of 20000. The record is now invalid, but no error message is raised because the validation rule fires only for a change in salary. The next section demonstrates how to fix this problem.

22. Close the Business Component Browser.

Fix the Salary Validation and Change the Salary Format

You can use one of the following approaches to fix the problem that no validation error occurs when you change just the job value to cause an invalid combination of Job and MinSalary:

- Add a dependency, which would automatically force the Salary value to clear when the Job changes.
- Add the same validation to the JobId field as the salary field. (Chapter 6 explains more about cross-attribute validation and how to solve its potential problems.)
- Move the validation to the Entity level.

In this case it makes sense to move the validation to the Entity level.

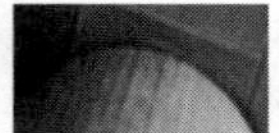

CAUTION
Since you know that all declarative property values are written into XML code, you might be tempted to edit the XML source code to move the code that defines the declarative validation rule. We very strongly urge you to resist this temptation because the XML definitions for these two validation rules are slightly different and because the editor automatically handles message bundle files for you. We predict that, if you give in to this temptation, you are likely to spend more time troubleshooting and debugging problems in the XML code than you would spend using the declarative property editors.

1. In the Employees entity object editor, click the Validators tab within the Overview editor and select the Entity node, which will currently be empty.
2. Click "Create new validator" (green plus "+") and recreate the Compare validation rule (as in the preceding section in steps 13-18). Select Salary as the attribute to validate and use "newValue" for the value of the empSalary token.
3. Remove the instance of the Compare validation rule on the Salary attribute (by selecting it and clicking the "Delete selected validator(s)" (red "x") button.
4. Run the application module again; opening the EditEmployee view object instance. For Ellen Abel, change Salary to "4000" and move the cursor to another field. No error message will result because the validation rule is defined on the Entity (row) level.
5. Navigate to the next record. The error message will now appear but it will contain something like "Entity [oracle.jbo.Key[174]]" rather than the entered salary value.

   Additional Information: This reference appears because the validation is on the entity level, so the Groovy expression "newValue" now refers to the whole row. You can refine the Groovy expression in the error message substitution variable to "newValue.Salary" to refer to the Salary value within the row.
6. Close the browser. Return to the validation rule editor and change the *Expression* for empSalary to "newValue.Salary."

7. Run the application module and change the salary to "4000." The correct error should appear when you try to navigate to another record. Restore the Salary field to "11000." Navigate to the next record to prove that the validation passes. Return to the Ellen Abel record.

8. Now it is time to test the validation when you change the Job value, remember that the minimum salary value directly relates to the JobId being passed in to the validating view object. On the Ellen Abel record, change the JobId to "President" and navigate to the next record. The error message does not appear.

   Additional Information: This problem occurs because the framework is optimized to trigger entity object validations only if a contributing attribute changes. In this case, the JobId is not defined as part of the validation, so just changing that does not force the validation event. Fortunately you can change this behavior.

9. Close the Business Component Browser. Edit the new entity level Compare validation rule and click the Validation Execution tab. Notice the Triggering Attributes section at the bottom. You can globally switch off the optimization effect by deselecting the "Execute only if one of the Selected Attributes has been changed" checkbox; in this case, you know that only JobId or Salary are triggering attributes, so just move JobId into the *Selected Attributes* list so that both are now listed. Click OK.

10. Run the application module to test that changing the Job to "President" and navigating to another record will raise the message. Close the Business Component Browser.

11. Now repeat the process to define an entity object–level Compare validation rule for the upper limit to Salary. This time use the "LessOrEqualTo" operator and the MaxSalary attribute from the SalaryValidatorAccessor object. Add JobId to the *Selected Attributes* in the *Triggering Attributes* section on the Validation Execution page.

12. On the Failure Handling page, define the error message as follows:

```
The defined salary of {empSalary} exceeds the maximum of {maxSalary}
defined for the {jobDescription} job.
```

13. Fill in the Expression column for the message tokens as follows:

Message Token	**Expression**
empSalary	newValue.Salary
maxSalary	SalaryValidatorAccessor.first().MaxSalary
jobDescription	SalaryValidatorAccessor.first().JobTitle

14. Click OK. Run the application module and test the upper limit for a record. (For example, "15000" for the Sales Representative job title held by Ellen Abel).

15. Close the Business Component Browser.

16. The final cleanup task is to change a label and format mask to clarify that Salary is a currency field. Open the editEmployee.jsff page fragment and locate the Salary field in the Structure window.

17. Expand the Salary field node in the Structure window and select the `af:convertNumber` tag. In the Property Inspector, set *Type* as "currency" and *Currency Code* as "USD."

18. Run the templateTest.jspx page and notice the currency formatting. Change Ellen Abel's Salary value to "4000" and click Next to cause the validation rule message to appear. You should see a validation error like the following:

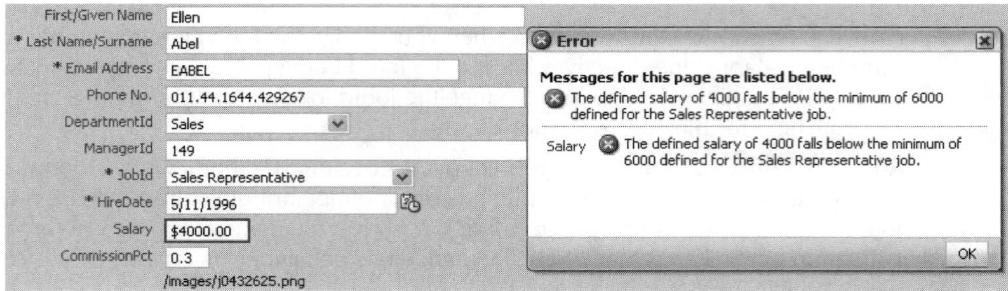

19. Close the browser.

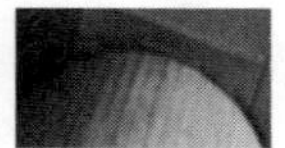

NOTE
If your application supports multiple currencies (U.S. dollars and UK pounds sterling, for example), instead of adding a formatter, you would instruct the user to enter the currency type in the value (and store the type in another column in the table). Alternatively, you could base the currency type label on an expression derived from the locale of the user.

What Did You Just Do? In this phase, you created declarative comparison validation rules to check the Salary field based on the minimum and maximum values for the job as listed in the JOBS table. This demonstrated the technique of defining declarative validation rules that rely on a value from another table based on the value in the current record. This technique required setting up a view object accessor to retrieve related records in another table and then defining the declarative validation to use that related data. This phase showed how to add dynamic values to error messages using message tokens that the framework substitutes with values at runtime.

You also defined currency formatting for the Salary field using the built-in currency type.

III. Refine the Commission Field

In this phase, you will add validation to the Commission field using a declarative range validation rule. The phase demonstrates how to add your own metadata to attributes using custom properties, and how to use those custom properties in messages as well as in component expressions. This phase also shows how to use the `af:inputNumberSpinBox` component to constrain values that the user enters. Then this phase explains how to set the *ReadOnly* property of an ADF Faces component dynamically and how to save and reset values using some Java code in a backing bean file.

Add Validation to the Commission Field

In this section, you will add a simple validation rule to restrict the commission value to between 0 percent and 50 percent. This section also shows how to set up and use custom properties for an entity object attribute. *Custom properties* offer a place where you can define attribute metadata that is specific to your application. You can refer to them in various locations programmatically or declaratively.

1. Navigate to the Employees entity object definition's editor and click the Validators tab in the Overview. Select the CommissionPct attribute and click the "Create new validator" (green plus "+") to create a validation rule.
2. Select the following properties:
   Rule Type as "Range"
   Operator as "Between"
   Minimum Value as "0"
   Maximum Value as "0.5"
3. Click the Failure Handling tab and fill in *Message Text* as "{commFld} must be less than or equal to 50%." (including the period).
4. In the Token Message Expressions section, set the *Expression* for commFld as "source.hints .CommissionPct.label."

   Additional Information: This setting will print the label UI hint for the attribute in the message rather than using the name of the attribute or a hard-coded value.
5. Click OK. On the Attributes tab, select CommissionPct and in the Property Inspector, set *Label* (UI Hints section) as "Sales Commission."
6. Click Save All.
7. Run the application module and open the EditEmployee node; you will see the Sales Commission label. Change the commission for Ellen Abel to "0.6" and press TAB; the error message should include the *Label* property value ("Sales Commission").

   Additional Information: Other attribute metadata is accessible in a similar way for messages (using Groovy expressions) and for setting properties of user interface components (using EL). For example, you could store the maximum percentage as a custom property of the CommissionPct attribute and then write a more complex validation rule that uses that custom property. In fact, that is a useful technique to show next.
8. Dismiss the error dialog. Close the Business Component Browser.
9. Double click the CommissionPct attribute to open the Edit Attribute dialog. Click the Custom Properties node. Enter *Name* as "MAX_ALLOWED_COMMISSION" and *Value* as "0.5." Click Add. The new property will display under the buttons as shown here:

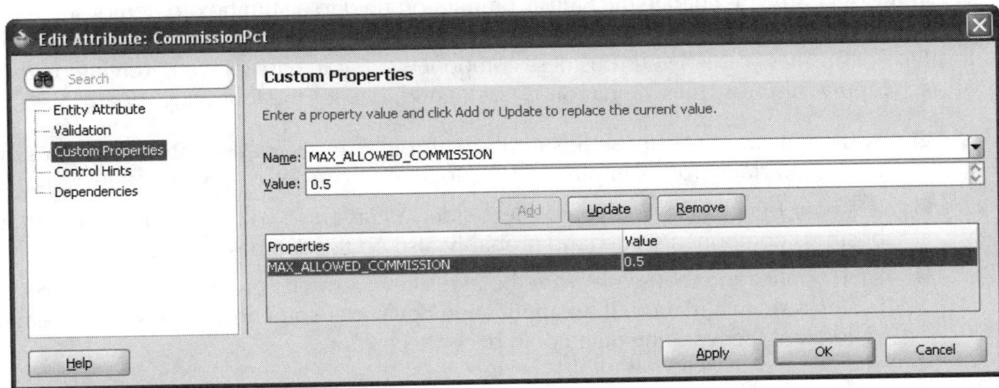

10. Click OK. Now open the CommissionPct Range validation rule (from the Validator tab) and click the Failure Handling tab. Change "50%" in the message to "{maxPercent}%." Set the *Expression* for the maxPercent token to the following Groovy expression. (Enter this all on one line.)

```
new java.lang.Float(
    source.hints.CommissionPct.MAX_ALLOWED_COMMISSION
    ).value * 100
```

    Additional Information: This is a slightly more complex Groovy expression that converts the String custom property to a float value and multiplies it by 100 to obtain a percentage for the error message.

11. Click OK. Click Yes in the confirmation dialog.
12. Run the application module and test the validation by entering a commission above 0.5 (50%). The message should display the custom property value.

    Additional Information: This technique of storing your own additional metadata with an attribute is really useful; for example, you might want to color certain fields differently or allow a user to customize certain fields. These custom properties on the attribute can be used to define the customizations centrally for all user interfaces. You can use custom properties with a common name (for example, "COLOR") on multiple attributes, and refer to these property names from user interface components; this allows the components to dynamically discover attribute metadata. The value of defining custom properties is discussed further at www.avromroyfaderman.com/2008/07/the-power-of-properties.

13. Close the browser.

Change Commission to a Spin Box

Now that you have enabled a rule on the Commission attribute to set minimum and maximum values, you have another idea: the spin box control (shown next on the Sales Commission field) allows you to define minimum and maximum values; if you change the item to a spin box, the component will not allow entry of values that are outside the minimum and maximum.

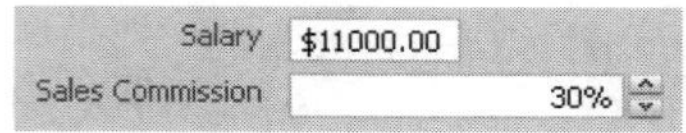

In this section, you change the Sales Commission field to a spin box to demonstrate how to change a component type and how the spin box works. Normally you would also want to enforce this type of business rule in your business components or database as well. Relying on the UI side alone to apply business rules validation is not a good idea for the following reasons:

- You might want to expose this attribute through another application that does not have a user interface (for example, a file upload application).
- It is easy for a hacker to bypass client-side validation so you must check the value on the business components side (and probably also on the database side).
- Each application that works with the attribute must write program code for the same business rule validation. If an application developer somehow forgets to implement this validation, the resulting data could become corrupt.

1. Open editEmployee.jsff in the editor. On the CommissionPct field, select **Convert** from the right-click menu. In the Convert Input Text dialog, select Input Number Spinbox and click OK. In the Confirm Convert dialog click OK after reviewing the contents (that the MaximumLength attribute will be removed).

   Additional Information: You just changed the `af:inputText` component to a `af:inputNumberSpinbox` component.

2. Select the new `af:inputNumberSpinBox` and in the Property Inspector set *Minimum* (in the Data section) to "0."

3. Use the Expression Builder on the *Maximum* property to set the value as "#{bindings .CommissionPct.hints.MAX_ALLOWED_COMMISSION}." This value refers to the custom property you set up in the preceding section.

4. Set *StepSize* (the increment used when the user clicks the up or down buttons on the spin box) to "0.01."

5. Expand the `af:inputNumberSpinbox` node in the Structure window and select the nested `af:convertNumber` component. Remove the *Pattern* value (Rules section) by selecting the Reset to Default option in the pulldown next to the field.

6. Change the *Type* of the converter to "percent."

7. Now run templateTest.jspx. The page will not load. The following error should appear in the server console (in the Log window), although you may need to scroll up a bit to see it: "Sales Commission java.lang.ClassCastException: java.lang.String cannot be cast to java.lang.Number."

   Additional Information: The problem is that a custom property like MAX_ALLOWED_ COMMISSION (that you set up to store the maximum commission value) is a String, and the *Maximum* property for the `af:InputNumberSpinbox` requires a Number.

8. Close the browser.

9. You can solve this problem in EL by causing an implicit conversion to a number. Change the bindings expression in the *Maximum* property to be prefixed with "0 + " as follows:

   ```
   #{0 + bindings.CommissionPct.hints.MAX_ALLOWED_COMMISSION}
   ```

   Additional Information: You might want to add a comment to the code here to explain that EL will interpret "+" as an addition (not a concatenation) operator and will treat both operands as numbers. Comments in a JSF file can be entered as XML comments, as in the following comment:

   ```
   <!-- the maximum property adds 0 to perform a Number type conversion -->
   ```

10. Run the page again. The spin box should constrain the value to between 0% and 50% inclusive.

11. Leave the browser open and return to JDeveloper.

Change the Commission Updatable Property

This section shows how to make Commission updatable only when the Department is set to "Sales" (department ID of "80"). This might seem to be a trivial problem that you could solve using Expression Language to set the *ReadOnly* property of the `af:inputNumberSpinbox` component. However, there are several twists, as the following steps demonstrate.

1. In the editEmployee.jsff page fragment file, navigate to the *ReadOnly* property (Behavior tab) of the `af:inputNumberSpinbox` and select Expression Builder from the property field pulldown. Set the value to "#{bindings.DepartmentId.inputValue != 80}" and click OK.

   Additional Information: By now, we think you know that this expression will return "false" if the value of the DepartmentId for the current record is not "80." Setting *ReadOnly* to "false" means that the field will be editable.

2. Click Save All. Refresh the browser and navigate to an employee like Ellen Abel who works in Sales. The Sales Commission spin box will be disabled, although the DepartmentId is "80" (Sales). The following steps show why this property value is ignored.

3. Do not close the browser. In JDeveloper, drop an Output Text component anywhere on the page fragment and set the *Value* property to "#{bindings.DepartmentId.inputValue}."

   Additional Information: This setting will display the value you are using in the expression. Displaying values in this way is a useful debugging technique.

4. Click Save All. Refresh the browser and you should see a value like "24," not "80," which you would expect for Sales.

   Additional Information: The inputValue used by a list binding is not the key value of the lookup; rather, it is an internal index value maintained by the list binding that refers to elements within the list. The list binding may actually be representing a compound primary key, but it still needs a single value to internally refer to the item in the list. The solution for this problem is to create a conventional attribute binding (in addition to the existing list binding) for DepartmentId so that you can derive the "real" value of the department.

5. Close the browser. In the page fragment editor, delete the `af:outputText` component you added for the preceding test.

6. Click the Bindings tab and in the Bindings section, click the "Create control binding" (green plus "+") button. Select "attributeValues" to indicate that you want to create an attribute binding and click OK.

7. Select Data Source as "TuhraServiceDataControl.EditEmployee" and select the DepartmentId attribute. Click OK. This will create a binding called "DepartmentId1."

   Additional Information: You now have a plain attribute binding (as opposed to a list binding) for which the inputValue will equal the real key for the Department ("80" for "Sales").

8. In the Property Inspector for the binding, change *Id* to "ComparableDepartmentId."

9. Click the Design tab and change the *ReadOnly* property of the CommissionPct field to the following:

   ```
   #{bindings.ComparableDepartmentId.inputValue != 80}
   ```

   Additional Information: You are now preforming the comparison with the real value of the department ID as exposed by the new attribute binding.

10. Run the test page; the "Loading" icon will stick and the page will not render. Now what?

11. Close the browser and return to JDeveloper. Something like the following error message will appear in the server console:

```
errorjava.lang.IllegalArgumentException: Cannot convert 80 of type
class oracle.jbo.domain.Number to class java.lang.Long
```

Additional Information: Is this another casting exception? The good news is that the value is correct this time (80 is displayed in the error message). However, the attribute binding for DepartmentId returns an oracle.jbo.domain.Number (the attribute type) and the Expression Language framework expects a java.lang.Long.

12. Display the Javadoc for oracle.jbo.domain.Number.

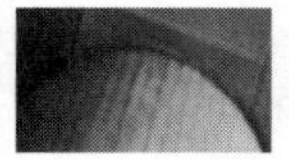

TIP
The easiest way to display Javadoc for a class that is not used in the current file is to press ALT-SHIFT-MINUS and type in the class name. In this case, type "Number" into the search field in the Go to Javadoc dialog that appears.

13. Find the `getValue()` method and notice that it returns a double and that it may be used to retrieve the value in EL. That sounds promising, so close the Javadoc window, change the EL expression for the Read Only property to the following:

```
#{bindings.ComparableDepartmentId.inputValue.value != 80}
```

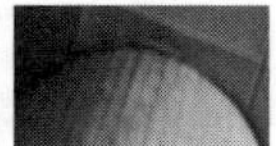

NOTE
You may recall that an EL reference to "value" runs the `getValue()` method on the object for which it is defined.

14. Run the test page. Now the Commission field will be writable only for Sales employees. Navigate through some records and notice that the field is disabled for non-Sales employees. (It appears to be hidden because no values appear for employees who are not in the Sales department.)
15. Navigate to Ellen Abel and change the department. The commission field is still enabled, even though the department is no longer Sales. If you navigate to the next employee and back to Ellen Abel, the field is correctly disabled. You need to use PPR to force a change after the pulldown value changes.
16. Leave the browser open and return to JDeveloper.
17. In the page fragment file, select the DepartmentId field and note the *Id* property value that JDeveloper assigned (for example, "soc1"); set *AutoSubmit* as "true" so that changes to the field will cause a partial page submit.
18. Set the CommissionPct *partialTriggers* property to the ID of the DepartmentId item ("soc1") so that the properties of this component will refresh when the DepartmentId changes.
19. Click Save All. Refresh the browser and change the department to and from Sales to be sure that the Commission field is disabled and enabled properly.
20. Close the browser and return to JDeveloper.

Clear the Commission Value for Non-Sales Employees

You may have already noticed this problem, although users would likely notice it if you did not: The act of disabling the Commission field will properly prevent the commission from being set when a new record is inserted, but it has a problem for updates of existing records that already have a commission set. For example, starting with an employee in Sales who does have a commission, moving that employee to a different department will disable the commission field but do nothing to remove the now invalid value (only employees in Sales can have commission set).

This section shows how a bit of Java code can solve this problem.

1. In the Model project, open the Employees entity object definition in the editor. Click the Java tab. Click the "Edit java options" (pencil) button and select the *Generate Entity Object Class* checkbox. Be sure the *Accessors* checkbox is selected (the default). Click OK.
2. An EmployeesImpl.java Java file containing getter and setter methods for each attribute will now appear under the Employees entity object definition node in the navigator. Double click it in the navigator to open it in the editor. Notice that it extends our framework class, `TuhraEntityImpl`.
3. Find the public `setDepartmentId()` method in the code (double click the method name in the Structure window to navigate to it).
4. Write code to change the Commission to null if the DepartmentId changes to something other than "Sales" ("80"). Sample code follows with brief explanations in the line comments. (The line numbers do not appear in the code.)

```
public void setDepartmentId(Number value) {
  // Define some variable names to make the code more readable
  final Number changeToDepartment = value;
  final Number sales = new Number(80);

  // First get the current value of the department  so we can
  // do something only if this value *was* Sales.
  Number changeFromDepartment = getDepartmentId();

  // Set the DepartmentId as usual.
  setAttributeInternal(DEPARTMENTID, value);

  // If changing from Sales to something else then
  // null out Commission. Check for null first to avoid an exception.
  if (!(changeFromDepartment == null)) {
    if (changeFromDepartment.equals(sales) &&
        !changeToDepartment.equals(sales)){
      setCommissionPct(null);
    }
  }
}
```

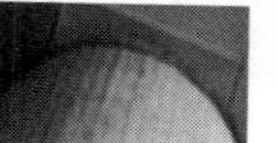

NOTE

Notice that the Sales department ID is written into the code. If this could change over time, or if other departments that require commissions could be added over time, you might want to query the commissionable departments from a view accessor instead of relying on values in the code.

5. Run the TuhraService application module and double click EditEmployee. Change the department of a Sales employee who has a commission. The Sales Commission value should be removed.

   Additional Information: There is another problem: if the user modifies the department by mistake and then wants to restore the commission value from the database, the user will need to reenter the value or requery the record. It would be nice to restore the previously saved Sales Commission value if the Department is restored to Sales. You could create a transient attribute in the entity object to store the original information that was queried from the database, and then restore that value if the department ID is restored to Sales. However, this is a pretty common requirement, so the framework offers a method, `getPostedAttribute()`, to serve this purpose.

NOTE
The `getPostedAttribute()` method provides functionality similar to the :OLD bind variable in an Oracle table trigger. For example, `getPostedAttribute(DEPARTMENTID)` will return the original database value in entity object code just as :OLD.DEPARTMENT_ID will return the same value in a row-level, update or delete trigger on the database table side.

6. Close the Business Component Browser.
7. Change the `if` structure (lines 15–18 in the preceding listing) as in the following code listing to handle the department changing to Sales.

```
if (!(changeFromDepartment == null)) {
  if (changeFromDepartment.equals(sales) &&
      !changeToDepartment.equals(sales)){
    setCommissionPct(null);
  }
  else {
    if (!changeFromDepartment.equals(sales) &&
             changeToDepartment.equals(sales)){
      Number originalCommission =
         (Number)this.getPostedAttribute(COMMISSIONPCT);
      if (originalCommission == null){
        originalCommission = new Number(0);
      }
      setCommissionPct(originalCommission);
    }
  }
}
```

   Additional Information: Notice that this helps the user by entering a Sales Commission default value of zero if the department is Sales; this allows the spin box to work correctly without the user having to type "0" to initialize it.

8. Run the application module and change the department of a Sales employee; the commission will disappear as before. Then change the department back to Sales and the Sales Commission value should be restored. Close the tester.

9. Another Sales Commission field enhancement is to display "N/A" for a non-Sales employee. This functionality can be implemented using a Switcher component and a ternary expression on the page. In the editEmployee.jsff editor, find the spin box component. Select **Go to Source** from the right-click menu on that component.

   Additional Information: The Source tab will be activated and the code block for the component selected.

10. Remove the nested `f:validator` subcomponent; it is not needed because the spin box prevents out of range data.

11. With the cursor in the spin box code block, the component node will be selected in the Structure window. In the Structure window, surround the spin box with an `af:panelLabelAndMessage` using the **Surround With** right-click menu option. Set the *Label* property to "#{bindings.CommissionPct.hints.label}" (to refer to the label UI hint); remove the *Label* property value from the spin box.

12. For the spin box component, set *Simple* (on the Appearance tab) as "true" to prevent the framework from displaying a default label for the spin box.

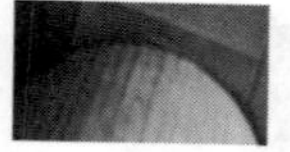

NOTE
Setting the "simple" property to "true" is useful when you embed one component such as an `af:inputText` inside another, such as `af:panelLabelAndMessage` or `af:table`. This setting suppresses the display of the nested component's label.

13. In the code editor, surround the spin box with a switcher so the code appears as follows:

```
<af:switcher defaultFacet="spinner" id="s1">
  <f:facet name="spinner">
    <af:inputNumberSpinbox ...
    </af:inputNumberSpinbox>
  </f:facet>
  <f:facet name="na">

  </f:facet>
</af:switcher>
```

   Additional Information: Enclose the full declaration of the spin box tag in place of the ellipses shown in this code listing. The empty "na" facet will contain the output text field containing "N/A." We are showing how to edit the code because the **Surround With** Structure window option does not contain this component or other components whose contents must be within a facet such as `af:panelStretchLayout`.

14. In the "na" facet, drop an Output Text component; set *Value* to "N/A."

15. In the Property Inspector for the switcher component, set *FacetName* to the following expression:

```
#{empty bindings.CommissionPct.inputValue?'na':'spinner'}
```

   Additional Information: *FacetName* specifies the displayed facet within the `af:switcher`. The EL declares that if the Sales Commission is null, display the na facet (containing the `af:outputText` item); otherwise, display the spinner facet (containing the `af:inputNumberSpinbox`). Remember that even if there is a problem with the data and a nonsalesperson has an amount in the Sales Commission field, the field will be read-only unless the employee is in Sales. Notice that you could also use the same expression to compare to department 80 in the switcher, but it is useful to see the EL *empty* operator, which evaluates if an attribute is null.

16. Check that the code appears as follows (although your Output Text *Id* property may vary:

```
<af:switcher defaultFacet="spinner"
    facetName="#{empty bindings.CommissionPct.inputValue?'na':'spinner'}"
    id="s1">
  <f:facet name="spinner">
    <af:inputNumberSpinbox ...
    </af:inputNumberSpinbox>
  </f:facet>
  <f:facet name="na">
    <af:outputText value="N/A" id="ot7"/>
  </f:facet>
</af:switcher>
```

17. Run the test page and you should see the field displayed as "N/A" for non-Sales employees or a spin box for Sales employees.
18. Close the browser.

What Did You Just Do? This phase showed how you could apply several useful techniques to the CommissionPct field: declarative validation for fixed maximum and minimum values, custom properties to store metadata specific to an attribute, the `af:inputNumberSpinBox` and `af:switcher` components, how to fix errors you might stumble upon with these frameworks, and entity code for setting and resetting the value of an attribute.

IV. Refine the Image Field and the Layout

You have added much functionality, validation, and user-friendliness to the form since you first dragged the collection onto the page. Now you can apply some other techniques to further enhance the screen. You will define the Image item to display the employee image instead of the image file name (as you did in Chapter 18). You will also set up some UI hints to make the field labels more user-friendly. Then you will set up multiple panels to display fields in a different number of columns. As we've mentioned, mastery of the various layout containers (panel components) is the secret to achieving the desired layout. This phase gives you some more practice with these layouts.

Display the Employee Image

In this section, you will set up an image item to display a picture of the employee. The steps in this section are similar to those in the preceding chapter where you added an image item to the hierarchy viewer.

1. In the editor, Design tab, for the editEmployee.jsff page fragment, on the `af:outputText` for the image field use **Go To Source** from the right-click menu to select the component in the Source view. Edit the existing definition to use an `af:image` component instead and change the *value* property to be the *source* property, retaining the binding that the existing *value* is using.

2. In the Property Inspector, or the code editor (your choice), set the following additional properties:
   ShortDesc as "Picture of #{bindings.FirstName.inputValue} #{bindings.LastName.inputValue}" (all on one line with a space between the expressions)
   InlineStyle as "border-style:inset; border-width:3px; border-color: rgb(181,231,255); height:180px; width:180px;" (again, all on one line but no spaces between lines)
3. Run the test page. Scroll through some records to be sure the image changes correctly.
4. Close the browser.

Rearrange the Layout and Modify Some Labels

The employee fields are still arranged in the default, single-column layout. In this section, you will split the information into multiple forms as a demonstration of how to align multiple, unrelated form layouts.

The idea is to show the employee ID in a one-column layout, the other profile fields in a two-column layout, the biography spanning the whole fragment, and finally the audit information in a separate four-column region at the bottom of the page as shown in Figure 19-2.

1. In the editEmployee page fragment, find the `af:panelFormLayout` under `jsp:root` in the Structure window. On the `af:panelFormLayout` node, select **Surround With** from the right-click menu and select Panel Group Layout. Click OK. Set *Layout* as "vertical" in the Property Inspector for the Panel Group Layout.
2. For the one column EmployeeId region, in the Structure window, drop a Panel Form Layout component above the existing `af:panelFormLayout`. Using the Structure window, drag the `af:panelLabelAndMessage` component for the EmployeeId attribute into the new `af:panelFormLayout` container.
3. Add an `af:panelHeader` after the second `af:panelFormLayout`. Set *Text* as "Audit Information" and *MessageType* as "info" (to add the "info" icon to the right-hand side of the heading).
4. Group select the CreatedBy, CreatedDate, ModifiedBy, and ModifiedDate fields, drag them into the `af:panelHeader`, and surround them with a Panel Form Layout (using the **Surround With** right-click menu option). Sort these audit fields so that CreatedDate is first, then CreatedBy, ModifiedDate, and ModifiedBy. The main containers and the fields you just set up should appear as shown to the right in the Structure window.

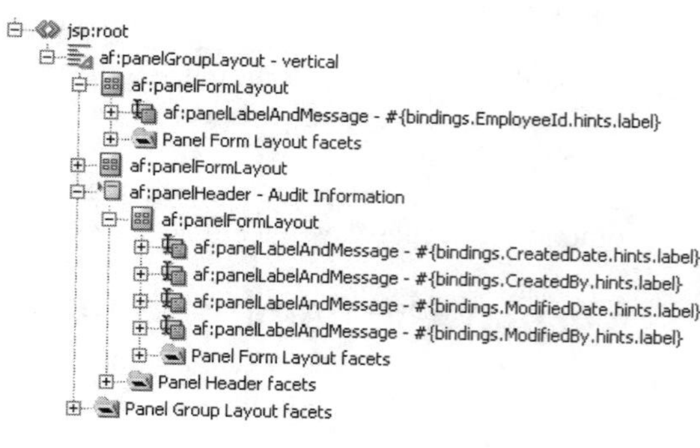

   Additional Information: In this illustration, the second `af:panelFormLayout` component is collapsed to save space. It includes all fields not in the other two layout containers.
5. In the Structure window, move the Image field under the Phone Number field.
6. In Property Inspector for the second `af:panelFormLayout`, set *MaxColumns* as "2" and *Rows* as "6."

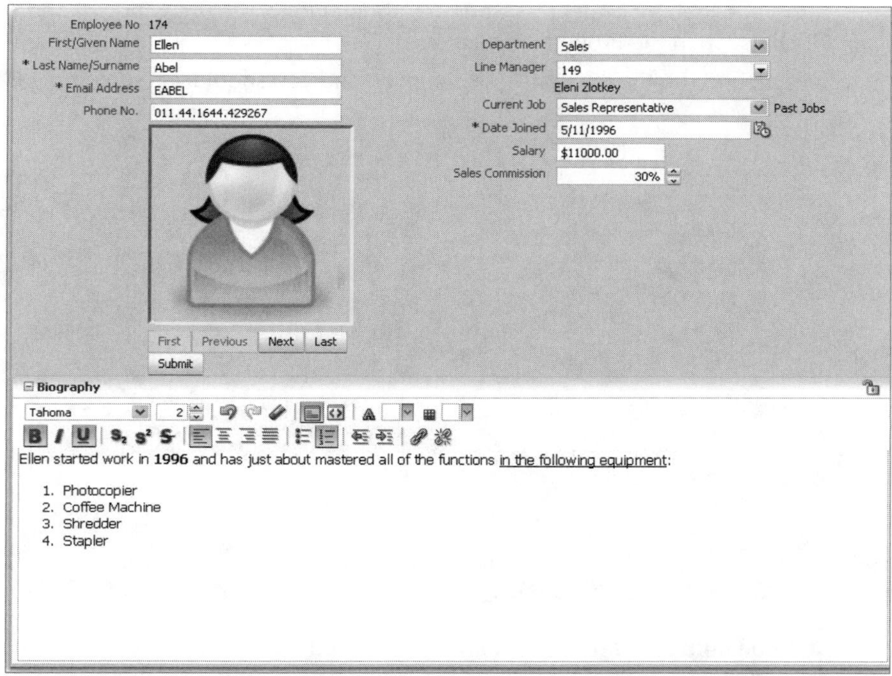

FIGURE 19-2. *Employee edit page*

7. In the Property Inspector for the third `af:panelFormLayout`, set *MaxColumns* as "4" and *Rows* as "1."

8. You set some of the UI Hint Label properties earlier, but some fields still require user-friendly prompts. In the Model project, open the Employees entity object definition's editor and set the label UI hints for the attributes as follows:

Attribute	Label
EmployeeId	Employee No.
HireDate	Date Joined
JobId	Current Job
ManagerId	Line Manager
DepartmentId	Department
CreatedBy	Record entered by
CreatedDate	Entry date
ModifiedBy	Record last changed by
ModifiedDate	Last change date

Additional Information: As a reminder, to set UI hints you select the attribute in the Attributes page (or under the Attributes node of the Structure window) and navigate to the UI Hints tab in the Property Inspector.

9. Save all and run the templateTest.jspx page and you should see something like this:

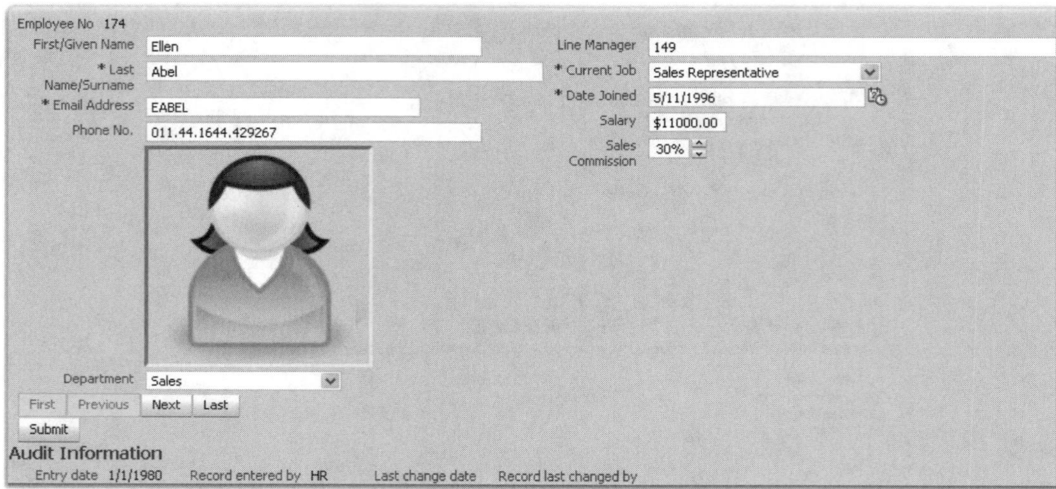

Additional Information: You may have noticed that the layout could still be improved; for example, the audit fields and the main fields do not line up because they are in different `af:panelFormLayout` containers. Also, the field widths are uneven, particularly the pulldowns.

10. Close the browser and return to JDeveloper.

Fix the Forms and the Field Widths

Now that you have set some layout properties in the Model layer and some in the View layer, you may be asking yourself, "Should the View layer or the Model layer be responsible for properties such as the field width and labels?" The sidebar, "Rule-of-Thumb for Setting Property Values," addresses this question.

Rule-of-Thumb for Setting Property Values

The question of whether to set UI-oriented property values on the Model (entity object or view object definition) level or the View (component) level arises often when developing with these frameworks. A useful rule-of-thumb is that property values that are likely to serve most purposes should be defined on the entity object definition level. That way, all view object definitions and UI components based on that entity object definition will inherit the properties. You can then specialize (override) those properties, if needed, in the view object definition level. The view object definition can serve many UI components, so a single view object definition setting can affect many places in the UI. The last place to override these properties is on the UI component level.

Applying the rule-of-thumb, you decide that the width properties should be set on the user interface level. You have already set the attribute width properties on the Employees entity object definition level. If you change those properties again, other screens will be affected. You have also used the AllEmployees view object definition elsewhere, so making changes at that level could affect other pages.

1. Open the editEmployee.jsff page fragment in the editor. For the FirstName field, set *columns* as "30." Repeat the setting for Last Name. For Email Address and Phone Number fields, set *columns* as "30."

   Additional Information: You may have noticed that all pulldown fields are different widths. The default width for a pulldown is based on the widest value in the list. However, you can use the *ContentStyle* property to override the default width and make all lists the same size. The JobId field happens to contain the widest values so that width will be used for the other fields.

TIP
We determined the values of these widths with a bit of experimentation. When you are responsible for this type of experimentation, remember that you can leave the browser open and the application running while you make changes in JDeveloper. To check the results, save in JDeveloper and refresh the browser.

2. In the Property Inspector for the ManagerId field, set *columns* as "31," which will emulate the width of the JobId field.
3. In the Property Inspector for JobId, set *ContentStyle* as "width:193px;." Job will now be the same width as Manager.

   Additional Information: The *ContentStyle* and *InlineStyle* for a component have different effects, depending on the component it is being set for. In the case of the `af:selectOneChoice` component, setting the width in the *InlineStyle* would change the width of the whole component including the label. Setting *ContentStyle,* however, just sets the width of the list part of the component.

   The value we have arrived at here, 193 px (pixels), is again based on trial and error and the default size at which the browser draws the fonts. If the user changes the font size in the browser, things may not quite line up.
4. Repeat the *ContentStyle* setting for DepartmentId. For Salary and CommissionPct (the spin box component under the `af:switcher` component), set *Columns* as "15."
5. It would also be nice to move the DepartmentId field to the right-hand column. It is currently positioned to the left because the `af:panelFormLayout` will fill in column order, not row order, and you only have 11 objects in the form. To do this, switch to the Structure window for the edit page fragment and drag a Panel Label And Message component from the Component Palette into the structure, after the `af:image` component. Clear out the *Label* property for this component. This component will act as a placeholder to move the other columns down (and across).

6. Run the test page. (Refreshing the browser is not sufficient here.) The fields should now look fairly neat as shown next.

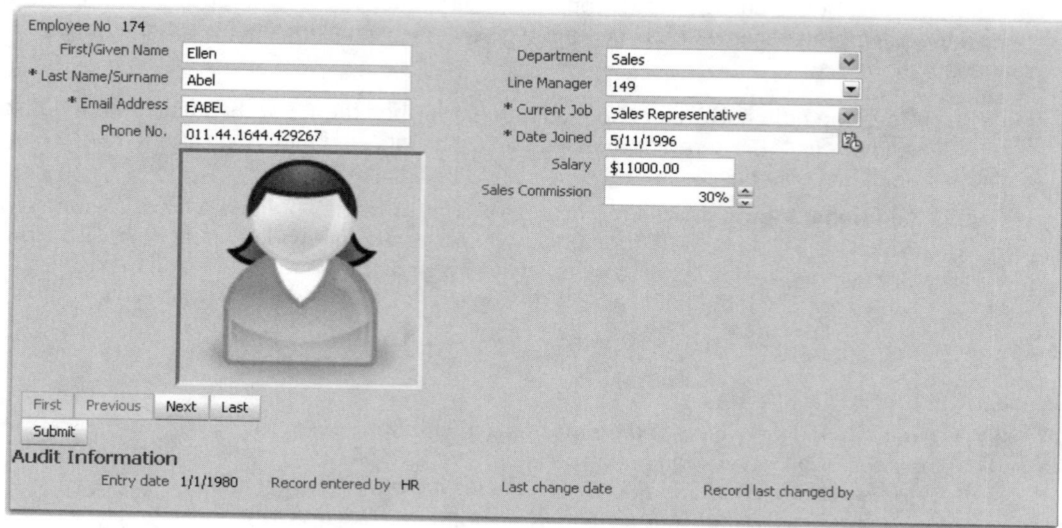

7. Notice that the EmployeeId prompt is outset from the fields immediately below it. This is caused by the field prompts being aligned differently across different `af:panelFormLayout` containers.
8. Do not close the browser. Select the first `af:panelFormLayout` that contains the employee ID field and set *LabelWidth* as "115."
9. Set *LabelWidth* to "115" for the other two `af:panelFormLayout` components as well.

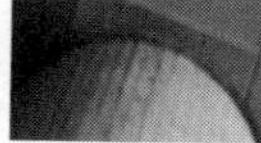

NOTE

You can also use the FieldWidth *property on the* `af:panelFormLayout` *component to help align multiple columns across forms. This is helpful when you are trying to line up two or more multi-column forms.*

10. Click Save All. Refresh in the browser. All left-hand column prompts should now align more closely as shown next.

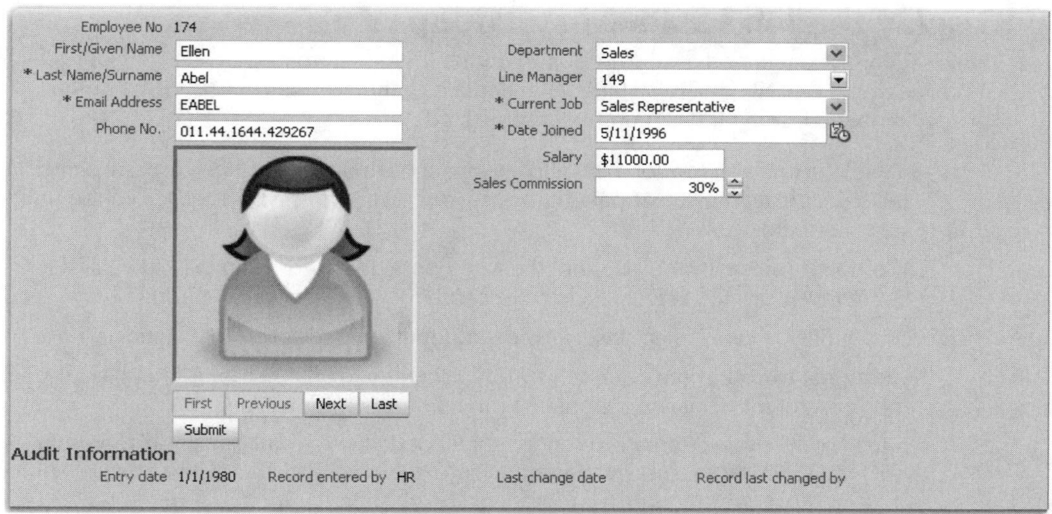

NOTE
If the alignment does not change, close the browser and rerun the page.

11. Close the browser.

What Did You Just Do? This phase gave you more practice with manipulating image items. The next chapter will demonstrate some more techniques for images, including uploading them. This phase also demonstrated how to change field labels using UI hints. Finally, it showed how to set up the `af:panelFormLayout` elements to define a page containing a one-column layout, a two-column layout, and a four-column layout. This gave you some experience using various container components to create this display.

V. Create a Popup for Job History

When an employee changes jobs, the user selects the new job and saves the record. A database trigger fires on update of DEPARTMENT_ID or JOB_ID and writes a record to the JOB_HISTORY table so that analysis can be performed on all jobs held by all employees over time. This phase shows how to define a popup using another ADF Faces component: `af:noteWindow`. The popup will be displayed when the user holds the mouse over certain text on the screen. You will spend some time modifying the properties of a standard ADF Faces `af:table` component to change the layout.

This phase also shows how to record the job history record using Model layer code. This piece of code demonstrates a number of concepts: how to retrieve data programmatically using an association, how to set up an object to hold information for a record in another table, and how to insert a record programmatically.

Display the Job History in a Popup

In this section, you will add a rollover popup on the JobId field to display the previous jobs for the employee from the JOB_HISTORY table. Since much of this section repeats tasks you have already completed, some instructions are abbreviated.

1. In the Structure window for the edit page fragment, find the top-level `af:panelGroupLayout` and select **Insert inside af:panelGroupLayout – vertical** | **ADF Faces** from the right-click menu; select Popup.

   Additional Information: Be sure the *Id* property is set (for example, "p1") and set *ContentDelivery* to "lazyUncached" because the user may scroll through many records.

2. On the new popup, select **Insert inside af:popup** and select a Note Window.

   Additional Information: A *note window* is a bit like a large tooltip that has no border and is useful for displaying supplemental read-only information.

3. In the Model project, create an entity object definition—JobHistory—to represent the JOB_HISTORY table; specify that the wizard generates a default view object definition (in the `tuhra.model.queries.main` package) called "AllJobHistory."

4. In the editor for AllJobHistory, add usages of the Departments and Jobs entity object definitions and using the Add from Entity button on the Attributes page add the JobTitle and DepartmentName attributes to display descriptions to the code values, JobId and DepartmentId, respectively.

5. Order the view rows by JobHistory.START_DATE with the most recent job first. (That is, click the Edit SQL Query (pencil) button in the Query page and fill in *Order By* as "JobHistory.START_DATE DESC.")

6. Create a view link definition called "EmployeeJobHistoryVL" in the `tuhra.model.queries.main` package. Define a relationship, with "1 to *" cardinality between AllEmployees (source) and AllJobHistory (destination).

   Additional Information: Some associations were automatically created when you created the JobHistory entity object. You should be able to find an association for the JobHistory to Employee relationship (JhistEmpFkAssoc) and use that as the basis for this view link.

7. In the TuhraService application module editor, add an instance of AllJobHistory with the name "EmployeeJobHistory" as a child of EditEmployee using an instance of this view link definition. The data model for the application module should now look like this:

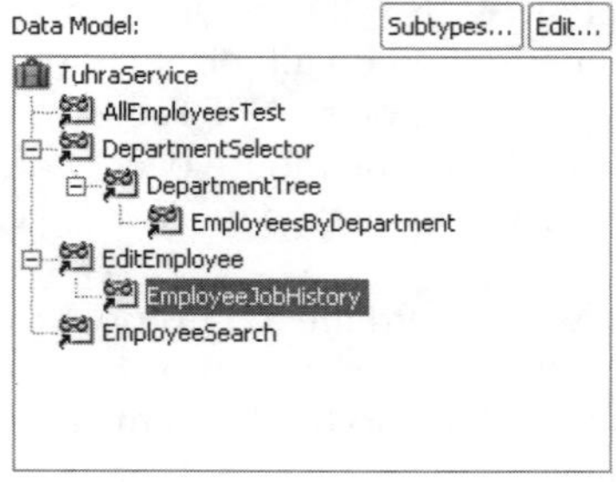

8. Run the application module and double click the EmployeeJobHistoryVL1 view link in the navigator of the test client. This will display the Employee record and any associated job history records. Scroll through the records until you find an employee with some job history (hint: Employee 101, Neena Kochhar, should have two previous jobs recorded.)
9. Close the Business Component Browser.
10. Activate the editEmployee.jsff page fragment editor window. Refresh the Data Controls panel and locate EmployeeJobHistory under the EditEmployee collection in the Data Controls panel. Drop it into the note window as an ADF Read-only Table (with all checkboxes unselected). Specify the following attributes (in this order):
    - StartDate
    - EndDate
    - JobTitle
    - DepartmentName
11. On the `af:table` component, set *emptyText* as "No job history." (Including the period.)
12. Finally, you need to provide a *gesture* (user action) to display the popup. In this case, you will add mouse-over text next to the Jobs pulldown. Click the JobId field in the Structure window. Surround the JobId field with a Panel Label and Message component. This container will allow you to maintain alignment within the form.
13. Move the *Label* property value from the Job pulldown (`af:selectOneChoice`) to the *Label* property of `af:panelLabelAndMessage`. (Be sure to remove the label from the Job pulldown.)
14. For the Job `af:selectOneChoice` component, set *simple* to "true" to prevent the component from displaying a default component label.
15. Be sure the Job `af:selectOneChoice` *id* property is set (for example, to "soc2") and set the `af:panelLabelAndMessage` *for* property as that ID value ("soc2"). This setting ensures that any error messages or help topics relating to the pulldown are displayed at the `af:panelLabelAndMessage` component level.
16. Inside `af:panelLabelAndMessage`, surround the Job `af:selectOneChoice` with a Panel Group Layout, and set the `af:panelGroupLayout` *Layout* property as "horizontal."
17. Drop a Spacer into the *separator* facet of the `af:panelGroupLayout` component. Set *Width* to "4."
18. Drop an Output Text component onto the `af:panelGroupLayout` component after `af:selectOneChoice`, and set *Value* as "Past Jobs." This component will display the text for the user to hover over.
19. Drop a Show Popup Behavior component (Operations panel) inside the new `af:outputText` item. Set the following properties:
    popupId as *id* of the popup (for example, "p1")
    TriggerType as "mouseOver"
    Align as "endBefore" to specify where the popup will appear
    AlignId to "soc2" (the *id* value of the JobId pulldown)

20. Notice that the *AlignId* value will be outlined in red, indicating an error. In the Structure window expand the Errors node at the top. You should see an error such as "Id soc2 referenced by alignId does not point to an ADF Faces component that sends a client component." To fix this error, select the JobId (`af:selectOneChoice`) component and set the *ClientComponent* property as "true." This signifies that the popup behavior can refer to this component ID; the error will disappear from the Structure window.

    Additional Information: The *ClientComponent* property forces the framework to create an object in the browser that can be referenced by JavaScript. You should only set this value to "true" when you need this capability. If the value is "false," ADF can optimize the way the component is created in the rendered HTML for the page, reducing the size of the page markup and increasing performance.

21. Now run the test page. Navigate to a record for an employee who has job history records. Employees with an ID of 101, 102, 114, 176, 200, or 201 have job history records (101, 176, and 200 have two history records each). Hold the mouse cursor above the Past Jobs label. You should see something like the following (for employee 101):

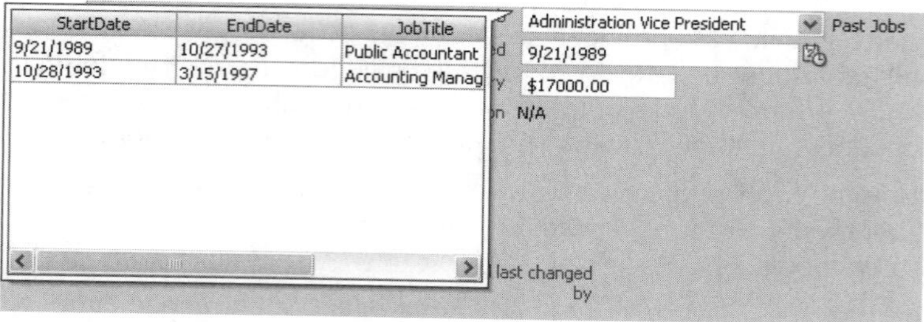

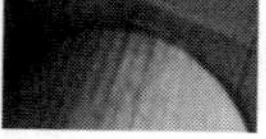

TIP

Leave the browser open with the page loaded so that after you make a change to components in the layout and save the file, you can test the change by refreshing the browser. This technique may not work in situations where you are changing Model layer code, controller files, or bindings files.

22. Notice that displaying the history using a table component wastes some space and requires scrolling to see the values. As an optional challenge, try to adapt the table component and note window to produce the following result:

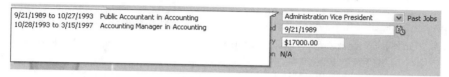

    Additional Information: The existing structure will work, but you will need to find formatting properties for the table and column components and add various items to remove the grid lines and banding and to stretch the table to the full width of the note window; to not display column headings; to combine the date fields; and to combine the job title and department name fields. The following hints may help you create this type of display:

- Use the table properties *HorizontalGridVisible* ("false"), *VerticalGridVisible* ("false"), *ColumnStretching* ("last"), and *InlineStyle* ("width:100%; height:100%; border-style:none;").
- Remove *HeaderText* from all columns.
- Set the size of the `af:noteWindow` component explicitly by setting *InlineStyle* as "width:400px;height:80px;."
- Add components and combine the date components in a single column to match the Structure window snippet shown on the right. The `af:spacer` *width* is "4" and the `af:column` *Width* and *MinimumWidth* are "130." (The "1" in the name of the `af:spacer` is the height, not the width.)

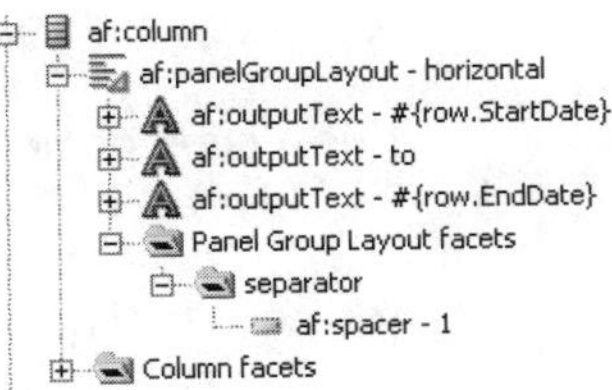

- Change the column's *Width* property if the data is truncated.

NOTE
ADF Faces requires all component ID properties to be unique within the same page.

- Combine the job title and department name fields in a similar way to the date fields. The Structure window snippet for this new column is shown on the right.

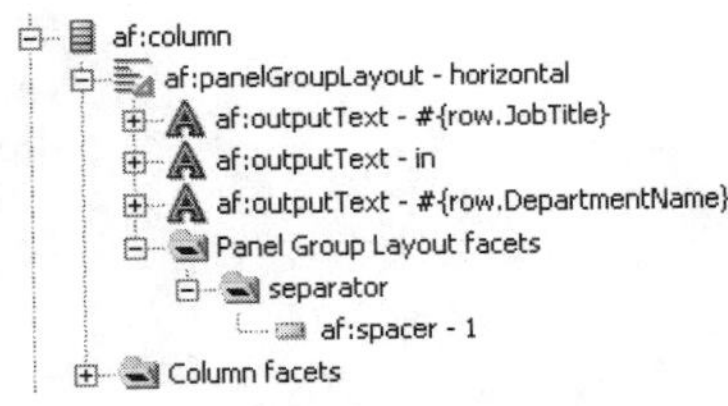

NOTE
Remember that the code for all practices in this book is available on the websites noted in the "Websites for Sample Files" section of the Introduction.

23. Close the browser and return to JDeveloper.

Update the Job History

Now that the job history is available on the page, it might be a good idea to actually load records into JOB_HISTORY as the user changes the job assigned to a particular employee. Of course, this kind of function could be carried out in a database trigger; in fact, the default HR schema contains an update trigger on employees (UPDATE_JOB_HISTORY) that records the job history.

However, if you examine the UPDATE_JOB_HISTORY trigger carefully, you will see that it calls a procedure that sets the start date of a job to the hire date of the employee; this logic works for the first job change: the starting date of the history record is the hire date and the ending date of the history record is the date on which the job was changed. It does not work for the second and subsequent job changes as shown in the following table. This table assumes the Hire Date for the employee is "01-JUN-1997"and the initial job for the employee is "FI_ACCOUNT." The value in the End Date column is the date on which the change was made (SYSDATE).

Job	Trigger-Assigned Start Date	Correct Start Date	End Date
FI_ACCOUNT	01-JUN-1997	01-JUN-1997	30-SEP-1997
AC_MGR	01-JUN-1997	30-SEP-1997	15-OCT-1997
PU_MAN	01-JUN-1997	15-OCT-1997	15-DEC-1997

This section demonstrates how to use some Java code in the Model layer to correct this logic. You would probably also correct the logic on the database trigger side to use the end date of the previous history record as the start date of the new history record.

You need to write code that inserts information into the JOB_HISTORY table only if the value of JOB_ID changes. The following data is required for the history record:

Column	Value
JOB_ID	The JOB_ID value of the employee row before the change was made (the "old job").
START_DATE	The day on which the employee changed to the old job. If this is the first job change, START_DATE will match the HIRE_DATE value of the EMPLOYEE record because the employee started the old job when she or he was hired. If this is a subsequent job change, START_DATE will match the END_DATE of the last job history record for that employee—the date the employee changed into the old job.
END_DATE	The day on which the employee left the old job; in other words, when the record changed. For simplicity, this practice assumes the employee record is updated with new job information on the same day as the job change occurred, in other words, today.
EMPLOYEE_ID	The ID of the employee record is copied to the history record to associate it with an employee.
DEPARTMENT_ID	The department ID of the employee record may be changed in the update, so you need to store the old value of the department ID.

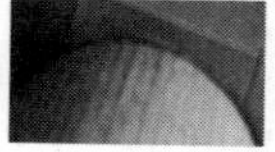

TIP
It might help to remember that the JOB_HISTORY table contains information about jobs the employee held before the job documented in the EMPLOYEE record.

1. Open a SQL Worksheet window (double click the HR_DB connection node in the Application Resources panel, Connection\Database node) and disable the existing trigger:

```
ALTER TRIGGER update_job_history DISABLE
```

2. Close the SQL worksheet; there is no need to save the contents when prompted.

3. In the Model project, open the Employees entity object definition's editor and navigate to the Java tab. Click the "Edit java options" (pencil) button to edit the Java classes for the entity object.

   Additional Information: You already created the `EmployeesImpl` class for this entity object to modify the behavior of the accessors.

4. In the Select Java Options dialog, select the *Data Manipulation Methods* checkbox (if it is not already selected) and click OK. This action generates methods such as `doDML()` that, as you may already know, submits inserts, updates, and deletes to the database.

5. Open EmployeesImpl.java and locate the `doDML()` method; this is a good method to use for job history functionality because it executes with insert, update, and delete operations to the table.

   Additional Information: Creating the JobHistory entity object definition automatically created some associations, one of which, JhistEmpFkAssoc, links the Employees to JobHistory. You can write code in `doDML()` that uses this association to navigate through the job history for that employee. The following steps add the code to this method in an incremental way so that you can understand the thought process used in building the code.

6. In the `doDML()` method, replace the existing contents with an `if` construct that detects an update operation. An example follows. (As usual, the line numbers should not appear in the code.)

```
01: if (operation == DML_UPDATE) {
02:   //Remember to do the update to Employees
03:   super.doDML(operation, e);
04: } else {
05:   super.doDML(operation, e);
06: }
```

   Additional Information: You only need to insert a record in the case of an Employees record update. Line 01 uses a built-in constant to check that the operation is an update. This code just defines a place to perform some processing only for an update operation (before line 03). In all operations, you want the framework functionality to work on the employee record, so both `if` and `else` sections contain super.doDML() (lines 03 and 05, respectively).

7. You want to define the creation of a JobHistory record only if the JobId has been changed. The database trigger already contains this type of code; in Java, you add the following code before line 02 in the preceding code listing.

```
String oldJobId = (String)getPostedAttribute(JOBID);
if (!getJobId().equals(oldJobId)) {
  //Do our code here
}
```

   Additional Information: You used `getPostedAttribute()` earlier to check the department ID for the commission field. Using this code, the old value of JobId is available as a local object (oldJobId).

8. Next you need the end date of the most recent job history entry for this employee. You can use the association JhistEmpFkAssoc to navigate the relevant job history records. Open the JobHistory entity object and select the Java tab. Generate the entity object class with accessors for use in subsequent code.

9. You will now define an iterator that will allow access to the JobHistory records. The framework automatically retrieves the rows based on the association. Return to EmployeesImpl.java and add the following lines inside the `if` structure, replacing the comment line "//Do our code here:"

```
//Get the set of JobHistory rows
RowSet pastJobs = (RowSet) this.getJobHistory();
```

Additional Information: The problem with the iterator collection is that you only need the latest row, but you cannot assume a specific order for the records returned by the query. You could write code to loop through all records and compare their dates, but that technique could be inefficient if the association leads to a large number of rows. The framework offers a more efficient method: you can define a view object to use as a proxy and to populate the association rows. That view object can be defined with a specific ORDER BY clause. You already have such a view object with the correct order by property—AllJobHistory.

10. Open the JhistEmpFkAssoc association. Select the Tuning tab and in the Custom View Objects section, click the "Edit accessors" (pencil) button to edit the view object selection. Select the *Use Custom View Object* checkbox on the Destination Entity Object (JobHistory) side of the dialog.

11. In the *Select Destination View Object* list, select the AllJobHistory view object.

Additional Information: This definition ensures that the first record retrieved from the association will be the most recent job history record for that employee (because the view object contains records ordered by START_DATE DESC). Naturally, the iterator may contain no rows if this is the first job change for the employee; in that situation, you will use the HireDate value from the current Employees record.

The Custom Views dialog will look like this:

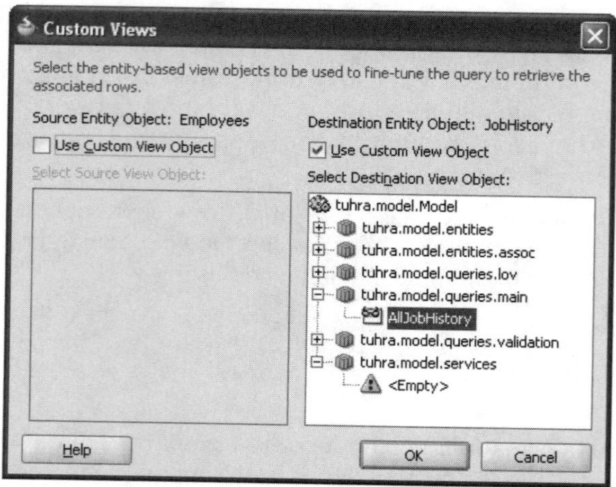

12. Click OK to close the dialog box. In the EmployeesImpl.java file, write code like the following to retrieve the first record from the iterator; place this code after the `pastJobs` declaration in the preceding code listing:

```
Date histStartDate;
if (pastJobs.hasNext()) {
  JobHistoryImpl row = (JobHistoryImpl)pastJobs.next();
  histStartDate = row.getEndDate();
} else {
  //No history rows - fall back to the hiredate
  histStartDate = getHireDate();
}
```

13. Now you have all the information required to construct a new history row. You need to add a call to `create()` for a new JobHistory record. You will then set the value for each attribute in that record. Lastly, you will call `insertRow()` for the JobHistory record.

Additional Information: The next code listing shows the entire contents of the `doDML()` method, including the additions just described (shown in boldface), which you will need to add in the code editor.

```
if (operation == DML_UPDATE)
{
  String oldJobId = (String)getPostedAttribute(JOBID);
  if (!getJobId().equals(oldJobId))
  {
    //Get the set of JobHistory rows
    RowIterator pastJobs = this.getJobHistory();
    Date histStartDate;
    if (pastJobs.hasNext())
    {
      JobHistoryImpl row = (JobHistoryImpl)pastJobs.next();
      histStartDate = row.getEndDate();
    } else
    {
      //No history rows - fall back to the hiredate
      histStartDate = getHireDate();
    }
    //You now have everything to create the JobHistory row
    JobHistoryImpl newRow = (JobHistoryImpl)pastJobs.createRow();
    newRow.setJobId(oldJobId);

    // the department may have been changed as part
    //of the same transaction so use the old version
    newRow.setDepartmentId((Number)getPostedAttribute(DEPARTMENTID));
    newRow.setStartDate(histStartDate);
    newRow.setEndDate(new Date(Date.getCurrentDate()));

    //And add the new row to the history rowset
    pastJobs.insertRow(newRow);
  }
  //Remember to do the update to Employees
  super.doDML(operation, e);
} else {
  super.doDML(operation, e);
}
```

NOTE
Notice that there is no need to set the EmployeeId value on the new Job History row because the association assigns the value automatically.

14. Run the application module and use the EmployeeJobHistoryVL1 page to update the job for one of the employee IDs mentioned before (employees with existing job history records, for example 101). Select **Database | Commit** and you will see a JOB_HISTORY record appear. Check that the history record has been added with the proper job and dates for that employee.

TIP
You can quickly navigate to a particular EmployeeId in the Business Component Browser by clicking the "Specify view criteria" (binoculars) button in the toolbar. Then just enter the ID, for example 101, into the EmployeeId field and click Find.

15. Try changing the job for the same employee again and selecting **Database | Commit**. You will receive an error message referring to the JHIST_DATE_INTERVAL constraint because the existing constraint specifies that the end date must be after the start date. (Click the Details button in the error message to view the full error.)

    Additional Information: Depending upon the business rules, this constraint may be accurate, but it is also within reason that the user could make a mistake, and the system should be able to handle this situation. In the latter situation, you could change the database constraint to be "end_date >= start_date" and also modify the primary key of the table (by adding a sequence-generated ID column, for example) because the current primary key (EMPLOYEE_ID, START_DATE) is not sufficient. Alternatively, you could adapt the `doDML()` code to update the existing history record if the iterator returned an end_date of today. (Database purists often frown on changing the values of history tables.)

16. Dismiss the error dialog. Close the Business Component Browser and click Save All.

What Did You Just Do? You practiced techniques for using an `af:noteWindow` in an ADF Faces RC popup that is activated by a mouseover event. You also practiced modifying the default table display so the popup took up less screen real estate. You also wrote code that creates a record in the JOB_HISTORY table.

One final note about the history record you created: although you tested submitting the record to the server (using the Submit button in the web browser page), you have not yet applied functionality to allow the user to commit the record (this will occur in the Chapter 20 hands-on practice). However, you can (and did) test the history functionality using the Business Component Browser, which offers a menu option to commit changes.

What Could You Do Next? As mentioned in Chapter 1, we feel that table triggers offer the surest means for universally applying business rules validation and application functionality (such as creating history records). However, there is value in duplicating some functionality on the middle tier, application side. Programming the job history insert on the application side offers access to cached data without additional queries that the database might require. Also, it can offer faster performance because no database message round-trip is required.

If you were to provide the job history functionality on both the database side (so that it is not possible for any application to miss this requirement) and the application side, you would write a bypass to the table trigger code into the application. For example, the application code could set a database package variable (or set a transient value in a database view column that is not saved to a table) indicating that the history record has been or will be inserted (by the application code). The table trigger would then not insert another history record.

CAUTION
You need to be careful that the package variable setting (for a table trigger bypass) is made in the same transaction as the employee update because ADF BC provides connection pooling where users share the same database session. The best bet would be to set the variable in `doDML()` before the commit occurs. Then reset the variable after the commit.

VI. Apply Final Refinements

The edit page is nearly complete, but you will apply several other techniques to further refine its functionality. You want to declare that deleting an employee record will automatically delete the job history records. You also want to set up a region in which the user can write a biography of the employee. Biographies will be written to the BIOGRAPHIES table that you created in Chapter 17.

You will use another ADF Faces RC component, `af:richTextEditor`, for the biography. The `af:richTextEditor` (Rich Text Editor) component allows the user to save formatting styles (such as boldface, italics, and bullets) as part of the text in an attribute. You will use some Java code to set a flag that stores whether the user may enter text into the Rich Text Editor component.

This phase also demonstrates how to move reusable code from a specific backing bean to a superclass backing bean that shares its functionality with other backing beans. Finally, in this phase, you will add a display of the manager name under the combobox for the ManagerId attribute. This display will be refreshed whenever the value of the ManagerId field changes.

Define Cascade Delete Functionality

The relationship between the EMPLOYEES table and JOB_HISTORY is stronger than a plain association—it is actually a *composition* because the JOB_HISTORY rows have no meaning without a parent EMPLOYEE row. This section runs through a short set of steps to define this relationship so that if the user issues a delete operation to the Employees entity object, all related JobHistory rows will also be deleted.

1. Open the editor for the JhistEmpFKAssoc association and select the Relationship tab in the Overview view of the editor.
2. Expand the Behavior section and select the *Composition Association* checkbox. Then select *Implement Cascade Delete*. The section "Compositions" in Chapter 6 explains these settings.
3. Run the application module. The easiest way to test the cascade delete is to first create an employee record: Last Name/Surname as "Smith," Email Address as "SMITH," Current Job as "Accountant," Department as "Accounting," and Date Joined as "2009-10-15." Commit this record (**Database | Commit**).

4. Change the Current Job value and commit again. A job history record will appear. Now click the "Delete the current row" in the employee toolbar (not the job history toolbar). Commit. This action will be allowed.
5. Close the Business Component Browser.

NOTE
The default HR schema implements delete restrict behavior (defined as "no action"), not cascade delete behavior, in the database. The database delete rule will not conflict with the application cascade delete because the application code will delete the detail records (JOB_HISTORY) before the master record (EMPLOYEES). This would not be possible without the cascade delete setting in the view link definition.

Add the Biography

In this section, you will add the capability to write a biography for each employee. An employee can be profiled with one or no biography. We have decided to implement this in a highly normalized way and store biographies in a separate table so that we can show you how to edit rich text using the ADF Faces component, Rich Text Editor. You have already created the BIOGRAPHIES table to hold this description.

1. Use the Refactor menu options to move the associations now in the `tuhra.model.entities` package into a new package: `tuhra.model.entities.assoc`.
2. In the Model project, create an entity object definition based on the BIOGRAPHIES table called Biographies. Place it in the entities package. Do not click Finish yet.

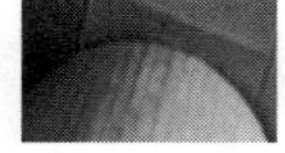

TIP
To save time in the Create Entity Object wizard, you can type in (or select using Browse) the Schema Object *field. The* Name *field above it will be filled in automatically.*

3. In the second page of the Create Entity Object Wizard, click New to add a nondatabase attribute called "Locked." You will use this transient attribute to control the UI and prevent accidental changes to the biography. Set the following properties:
   Type as "Boolean"
   (Default) *Value* as "true"
   Persistent unselected
4. Click OK. Move the Locked attribute so that it is third in the list (before the Biography attribute).
5. On the Step 3 page, set up the BioUpdatedDate attribute to be a history column with "modified on" as the type so that the framework will automatically manage the column value. Click Finish.

   Additional Information: JDeveloper will automatically generate an association between Employees and Biographies, BiographiesEmployeesFkAssoc, to represent the foreign key in the BIOGRAPHIES table.

6. Refactor the association to the assoc package.

   Additional Information: If a phantom node persists in the navigator, select another application and then reselect the tuhra2 application or ignore the node because it will clear when you reopen JDeveloper.

7. Open the editor for the association. In the Relationship tab, expand the Behavior section and select the *Composition Association* checkbox. Also select the *Implement Cascade Delete* and *Update Top Level History Columns* checkboxes.

   Additional Information: The latter setting ensures that the audit columns on the main employee record will also be changed when the Biographies detail record is updated.

8. Create an updatable view object definition in for Biographies called EmployeeBio (in tuhra.model.queries.main). Select all of the attributes. Click Finish.

9. Create a view link definition, EmployeeBioVL, in `tuhra.model.queries.main` with a relationship between AllEmployees (source) and EmployeeBio (destination) that is defined with a *Cardinality* of "1..0-1" and that uses the BiographiesEmployeesFkAssoc association. (Remember to click Add after selecting the association on both sides.)

10. In the application module definition, add an instance of the EmployeeBio view object definition (calling it 'EmployeeBio") as a child of EditEmployee via an instance of the new view link definition. Click Save All.

11. In the ViewController project, open the editor for the editEmployee page fragment. Drop an `af:panelBox` after the second `af:panelFormLayout`.

12. Set *Text* as "Biography" to specify the label.

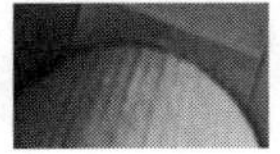

TIP
You can edit label properties by overtyping the text in the visual editor. Sometimes this technique is faster than opening the Property Inspector or locating and changing the property in the source code editor.

13. Set *InlineStyle* of the `af:panelBox` component to "width:800px;" to specify the size of the container.

14. Refresh the Data Control panel (**Refresh** from the right-click menu). Expand to the EditEmployee\EmployeeBio node, drag the Biography attribute into the `af:panelBox`, and specify the item type as **Texts | ADF Input Text** (no label). This component provides basic text editing, but using another component can provide richer editing capabilities.

15. Select **Convert** from the right-click menu on the `af:inputText` component and change the tag to an `af:richTextEditor`. In the Structure window, remove the nested validator tag, which is not a valid child of the `af:richTextEditor` component.

    Additional Information: This component allows the user to format the text with simple styles such as bold, italic, underline, different fonts and colors, bullets, numbered lists, indents, and so on.

16. Set *Rows* as "10" and *Columns* as "140" (both on the Appearance tab). Set *contentStyle* to "width:100%;" (remembering that *contentStyle* is best with a trailing semicolon, ";").

17. From the Data Controls panel, drag the Create operation for EmployeeBio into the `af:panelBox` component above `af:richTextEditor` and specify ADF Button. This button will assist in testing the functionality. Click Save All.

18. Run the test page. Click Create to add a biography record and enter some text into the rich text field. Try the formatting features of this component. Click Submit. An error message box will appear with a stack of messages. You should see a message about "Cannot convert … of type class java.lang.String to class oracle.jbo.domain.ClobDomain."

    Additional Information: This is a problem of using an ADF BC large object domain (such as `ClobDomain`) because the JSF components (Rich Text Editor) and the JSF runtime cannot automatically convert those types to types they can handle (like `String`). To work around this problem, you can build a basic converter. This will demonstrate a useful technique that can serve you in future work.

19. Close the browser.

20. Create a Java class in the ViewController project called "ClobConverter" and place it in the `tuhra.view.converter` package. Implement the `javax.faces.convert.Converter` interface. Click OK.

21. Notice that the following methods are required to implement this interface:

    - **`getAsObject()`** This method converts from the posted String type to another type (`ClobDomain` in this case).
    - **`getAsString()`** This method manages the conversion from the type (`ClobDomain` in this case) to a String so the value can be sent over HTTP.

22. Write `getAsObject()` as follows (you will need to import `oracle.jbo.domain.ClobDomain`):

```
public Object getAsObject(FacesContext facesContext,
                          UIComponent uIComponent,
                          String string) {
  return new ClobDomain(string);
}
```

23. Write `getAsString()` as follows:

```
public String getAsString(FacesContext facesContext,
                          UIComponent uIComponent,
                          Object object) {
  return ((ClobDomain)object).toString();
}
```

24. The next step is to register this converter in faces-config.xml. Open the faces-config.xml file (under WEB-INF) and click the Overview tab. Click the Converters tab.

25. Click the Add (green plus "+") button to add a converter; set *For-Class* as "oracle.jbo.domain.ClobDomain" and *Class* as "tuhra.view.converter.ClobConverter." Leave *ID* blank. This should fix the submit problem.

26. Next you will use the Locked attribute to enable and disable the rich text editor. Open the editor for the editEmployee page fragment and click the Bindings tab.

27. Select the Create operation binding and use the Property Inspector to change the *Id* to "CreateBio." This change will help later in locating the function in the source code.

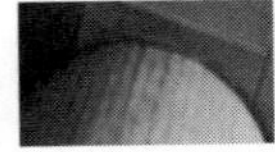

TIP
If the Property Inspector does not automatically load after you select an item, wait for a couple of seconds, then try clicking another tab in the Property Inspector and click the tab you are working with to refresh the properties.

28. Click the "Create control binding" (green plus "+") button in the Bindings area, and create an attributeValues binding for the Locked attribute (*Data Source* as "TuhraServiceDataControl.EmployeeBio). Click OK.
29. In the Design tab of the page, drag a Toolbar into the toolbar facet of the `af:panelBox`.
30. Drag a Toolbar Button into the Toolbar. Set *Icon* as the following expression (all on one line):

```
#{(empty bindings.Locked.inputValue || bindings.Locked.inputValue ) ?
'/images/locked.png': '/images/unlocked.png'}
```

Additional Information: The ternary expression returns a locked image file name to the *Icon* property if the value of the Locked attribute is null or true; otherwise, it returns the unlocked image file name.

31. Set *ShortDesc* as the following expression (all on one line):

```
#{(empty bindings.Locked.inputValue || bindings.Locked.inputValue ) ?
'Click to edit': 'Click to lock'}
```

32. Set the *id* property of the toolbar button as "lockIcon." Remove the label in the *Text* property.
33. For the `af:richTextEditor` component, set *PartialTriggers* as "lockIcon" so that it will refresh when the toolbar button is clicked.
34. Also for the `af:richTextEditor` component, set *ReadOnly* as "#{bindings.Locked .inputValue}." This setting specifies that the user will not be able to change the value in the field if Locked is "true." The code you create next will toggle Locked between true and false.

Disable and Enable the Rich Text Editor

The next step adds a bit of code to the button to toggle the Locked attribute value and to create a biography record, if necessary.

1. Create a Java class in the `tuhra.view.backing` package. Call the class "EmployeeEditBean."
2. Add the standard binding code to this new class (refer to Chapter 15 for an explanation), as in the following example:

```
import oracle.binding.BindingContainer;
import oracle.adf.model.BindingContext;
...
public BindingContainer getBindings() {
  return BindingContext.getCurrent().getCurrentBindingsEntry();
}
```

3. Open the editEmployee-flow task flow file and on the Overview tab, create a managed bean item called "employeeEditBB" using the new class (`tuhra.view.backing.EmployeeEditBean`); change the *Scope* to "view."
4. In the page fragment file, double click the lower right-hand corner of the toolbar button (or select **Create Method Binding for Action** from the right-click menu) and associate the action with the employeeEditBB bean. Use the default action name for the backing bean method—"lockIcon_action." Click OK.
5. Change the method code to the following:

```
public String lockIcon_action() {
  // Access the Locked attribute binding
  AttributeBinding lockedBinding =
    (AttributeBinding)getBindings().getControlBinding(
       "Locked");

  Boolean locked = false;
  if (lockedBinding != null) {
    //Get the current value of the transient attr
    locked = (Boolean)lockedBinding.getInputValue();
  }
  //The attribute may be null if no detail record exists yet
  if (locked == null) {
    // Set a default value
    locked = true;
    // Create a Biographies record
    OperationBinding createBio =
         getBindings().getOperationBinding("CreateBio");
    if (createBio != null) {
      createBio.execute();
    }
  }
  //Toggle the locked state
  lockedBinding.setInputValue(!locked);
  return null;
}
```

6. You will need to add the following imports:

```
import oracle.binding.AttributeBinding;
import oracle.binding.OperationBinding;
```

7. In the page fragment, ensure that the *action* property of the `af:commandToolbarButton` component explicitly includes the `viewScope` qualifier and reads as follows:

```
#{viewScope.employeeEditBB.lockIcon_action}
```

8. Delete the Create button. You don't need it anymore because the additional code will create a record.

9. Run the test page again. You should be able to click the lock button icon to toggle the state of the biography editor and to create a biography record. Also, click Submit after adding text to the editor to be sure the conversion error has been resolved.

   Additional Information: The Submit button submits the values to the server, but you have not written anything to save changes to the database yet. You will do that in Chapter 20. For now, you are testing whether the page mechanics work and values can be submitted to the server.

10. Close the browser.

Refactor the getBindings() Method

It is time to do a little refactoring. You just set up the employee edit managed bean to provide access to the bindings object. It seems like this might be a really useful function for many managed beans. In OO terms, the way to accomplish this would be to have all backing beans inherit from a common superclass. JDeveloper makes it easy to do this retroactively.

1. In the EmployeeEditBean.java editor, select **Refactor | Extract Superclass** from the right-click menu.
2. In the Extract Superclass dialog, set *Package Name* as "tuhra.view.framework" to match the pattern you set up in the Model project. Set *Class Name* as "TuhraBackingBean."
3. In the *Members to Extract* list, select the `getBindings()` checkbox. Select the *Replace Usages* checkbox. Click OK.
4. The newly created framework superclass will open. You will see the bindings code you created earlier.
5. Alter the declaration of the class to "public abstract class TuhraBackingBean," to indicate to anyone reading this code that this class is not designed to be used directly.
6. Add Javadoc to the backing bean to indicate that the purpose of this framework class is to access the bindings programmatically.

   Additional Information: You can click the cursor in the class name and select **Source | Add Javadoc Comments** from the right click menu to add a Javadoc block.

7. In the editor for EmployeeEditBean.java, notice that the bindings-related methods have been stripped out and the class now extends the framework class. Add the following import if it does not exist:

   ```
   import tuhra.view.framework.TuhraBackingBean;
   ```

8. You will now have some imports in the class that are not needed anymore (for example, FacesContext), so select **Organize Imports** from the right-click menu in the code editor to clean up the imports.
9. Click Save All. Run the test page again if you want to check that the refactoring worked.

Display the Manager Name

The LOV for the ManagerId field really needs to show the name of the manager as well as the Employee ID. This section implements this requirement. You can use this same technique to allow the user to input the name and use the AutoComplete capabilities of the LOV to select the correct ID.

1. In the Model project, edit the AllEmployees view object definition and move a second usage of the Employees entity object definition into the *Selected* area with *Alias* as "Manager." Be sure the *Association* is "EmpManagerFkAssoc.ManagerIdEmployees."
2. In the Attributes tab, click Add from Entity and move the FirstName and LastName attributes from the Manager usage. The EmployeeId of the Manager usage will be added automatically with an alias of "EmployeeId1."
3. Click OK. In the Attributes section, add the prefix "Manager" to the new FirstName, LastName, and EmployeeId attributes. Remove the "1" suffixes, if they appear.

   Additional Information: You can rename an attribute by selecting **Rename** from the right-click menu on the attribute name in the Attributes page.
4. Select the ManagerId attribute in the view object and edit the LOV_ManagerId list of values that you created before. In the *List Return Values* area add mappings for ManagerFirstName and ManagerLastName as shown here:

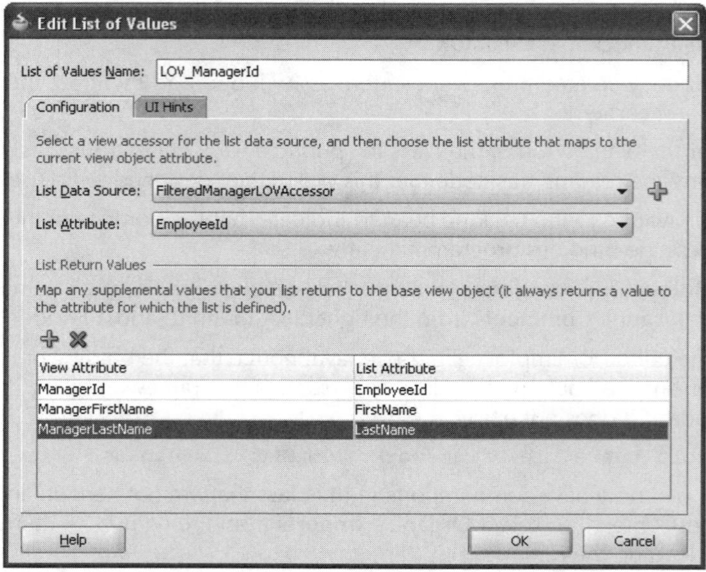

5. Click OK. Now run the application module to be sure you can see the manager names and ID at the bottom of the EditEmployee screen for the first employee and that they change correctly when you use the Manager LOV to change it.

6. If you scroll through records you may notice that you are now seeing multiple records for each employee (each with a different image). What is going on here is that the WHERE clause for the AllEmployees view object definition was reset when you added the extra usage of the Employees entity object definition. Therefore, you need to restore the custom parts of the WHERE clause that you added in Chapter 18. Close the Business Component Browser.

7. In JDeveloper, switch to the Query tab in the view object editor and click the "Edit SQL Query" (pencil) button to edit the Query. Change the *Where* property to read as follows:

```
ImageUsages.IMAGE_ID = Images.IMAGE_ID(+)
AND ImageUsages.ASSOCIATED_ID(+) = Employees.EMPLOYEE_ID
AND ImageUsages.USAGE_TYPE(+) = 'E'
AND Employees.JOB_ID = Jobs.JOB_ID
AND Employees.MANAGER_ID = Manager.EMPLOYEE_ID(+)
```

8. Test the application module again and be sure that scrolling through records works. Close the tester.

9. Edit the editEmployee page fragment and, using the Structure window, surround the ManagerId `af:inputComboboxListofValues` (combobox) with a Panel Label and Message component. Set *Label* as the value of the combobox *Label* property. For the combobox, remove *Label* value and set *Simple* to "true."

10. Set the *For* property of the `af:panelLabelAndMessage` to the ID of the ManagerId combobox.

11. Select the combobox and surround it again with a Panel Group Layout component; set the `af:panelGroupLayout` *Layout* to "vertical."

12. After the combobox in the `af:panelGroupLayout` component, insert an `af:outputText` component.

13. Refresh the Data Controls panel to include the changes you made in the Model project.

14. Click the Bindings tab of the editor and manually create attributeValues bindings based on the EditEmployee attributes ManagerFirstName and ManagerLastName.

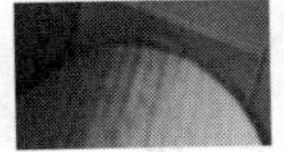

NOTE
If you do not see these attributes in the pulldown, cancel the dialog and refresh the Data Controls panel (again).

15. For the `af:outputText` item you added, use the Expression Builder for the *Value* property to create the following expression representing the full name of the manager:

```
#{bindings.ManagerFirstName} #{bindings.ManagerLastName}
```

16. The components for the ManagerId structure should appear as follows:

17. Run the test page and notice that the manager name is now printed as shown next. Make a change in the LOV and check that the selected name is also loaded into the output text field.

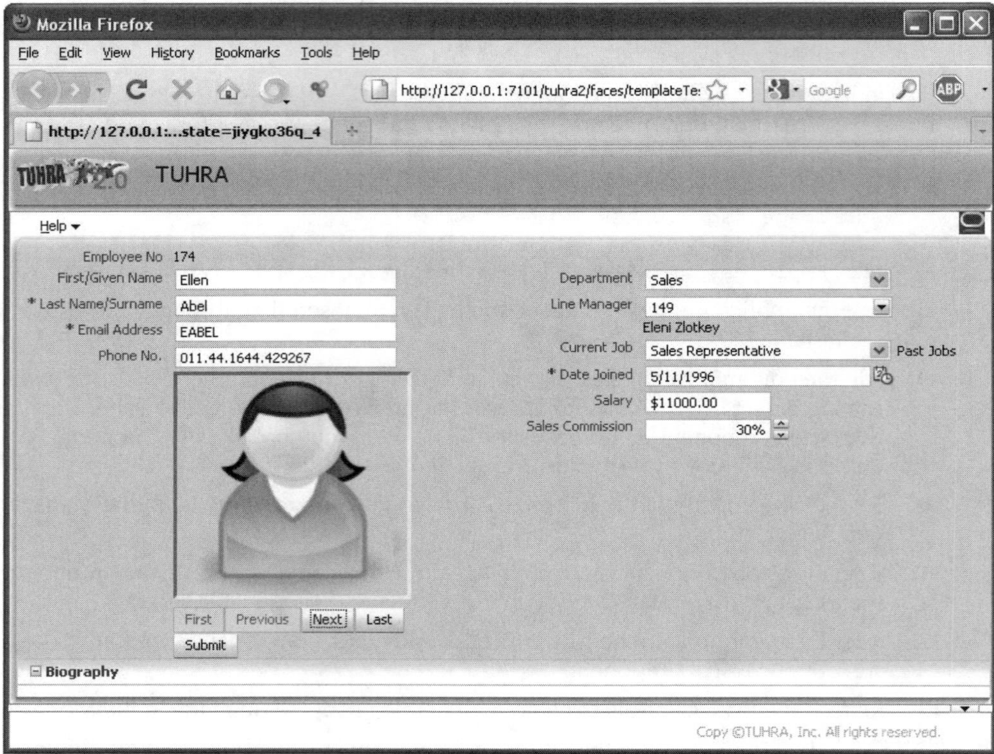

What Did You Just Do? In this phase, you enhanced the edit page fragment even more. You defined delete cascade functionality to delete the job history when an employee record is deleted. You also added an editor in which the user can record a biography for the employee. This technique demonstrated the functionality of the ADF Faces component, Rich Text Editor. You wrote some Java code to lock and unlock access to the item. You also practiced moving methods from a specific backing bean to a superclass backing bean. Finally, you added a display of the manager name to decode the manager ID.

CHAPTER 20

Sample Application: The Image LOV Dialog

You pays your money and you takes your choice.

—*Punch v. 10, no. 16* (1846)

his chapter uses the application workspace and template created in Chapters 17 and the search and edit pages built in Chapters 18–19 to build a user interface that allows the user to change and manipulate employee images. This functionality involves the commonly used interface paradigms of passing control and data to and from a modal popup window and of accomplishing a linear task by stepping through a train (a wizard-style user interface explained in the "Trains" section of Chapter 11).

NOTE
As with all chapters in this part of the book, you can download the files representing the application as it will be at the end of the preceding chapter from the websites mentioned in the section "Websites for Sample Files" in the Introduction.

The hands-on practice in this chapter sets up page fragments for the steps in the train and adds the capability to open the train in a modal popup and return data from the train to the primary application window. The practice steps through the following phases:

I. **Change how the business components handle image usages**
   - Create an entity hierarchy for image usages
   - Use the entity hierarchy in a view object definition

II. **Create the popup dialog**
   - Create a task flow for the dialog
   - Create a page template for the dialog
   - Create page fragments for the train stops
   - Wire the dialog to the edit page
   - Fix the popup behavior

III. **Implement the add image page**
   - Lay out the form components
   - Create a backing bean for the add image page
   - Use the Image component to preview the uploaded image
   - Create a service method to add an image
   - Fix association posting behavior
   - Create an upload listener to copy the file and call the service method

IV. **Implement the set default image page**
   - Lay out the form components
   - Create a backing bean for the set default image page

- Add drag-and-drop capabilities
- Create a service method to set the default image
- Implement a drop listener to call the service method
- Add commit functionality

V. Integrate the edit page with the rest of the application

- Create a link from the search page to the edit page
- Parameterize the Edit Employee task flow
- Restrict the EditEmployee view object instance's query using the parameters
- Pass parameters to the Edit Employee task flow

Figure 20-1 shows the edit page as it will appear at the end of this chapter. Figures 20-2 and 20-3 show pages of the modal train.

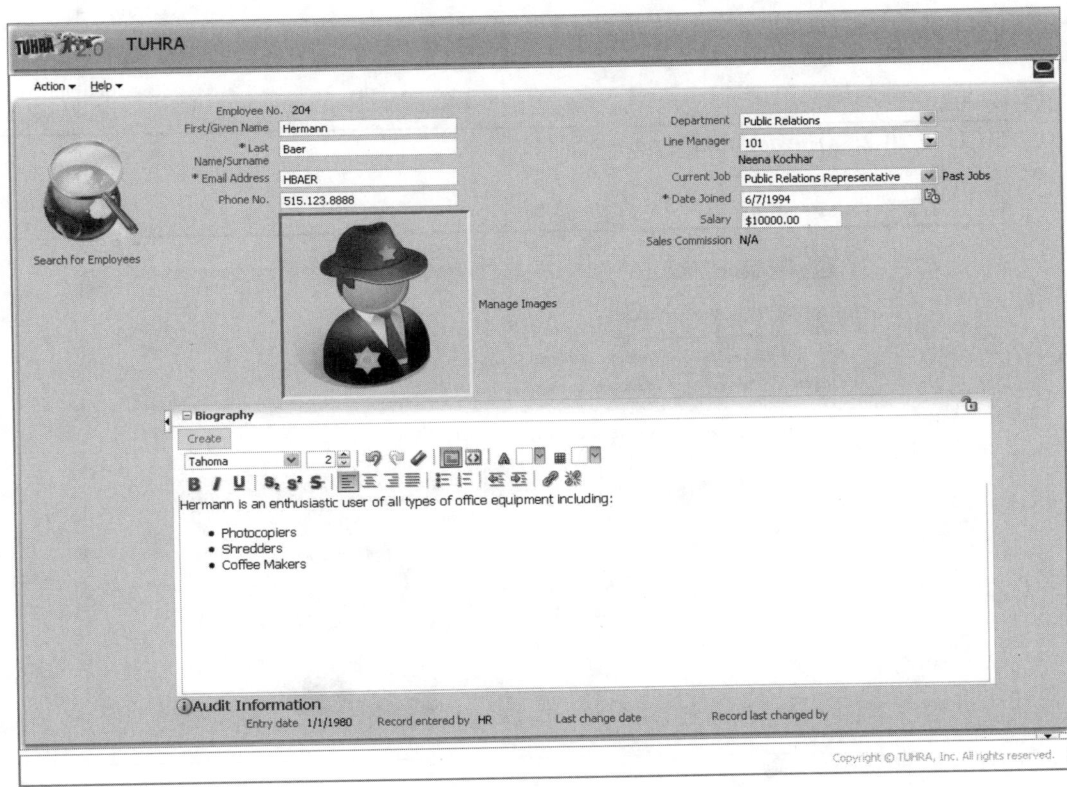

FIGURE 20-1. *The completed edit page*

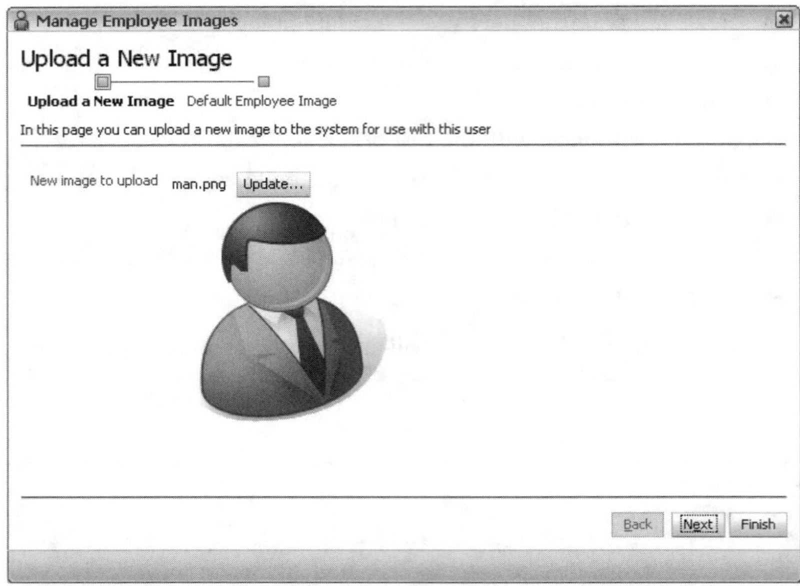

FIGURE 20-2. *The add image page*

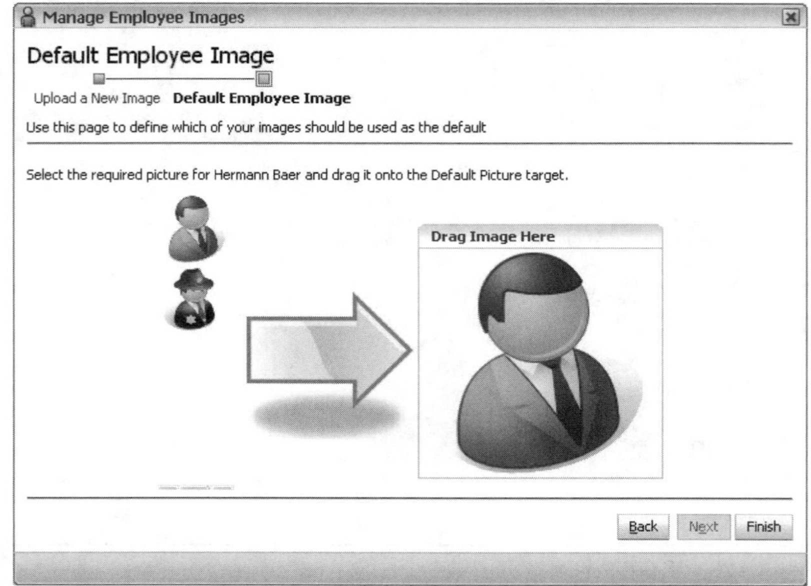

FIGURE 20-3. *The set default image page*

I. Change How the Business Components Handle Image Usages

Before creating the new user interface, pause to reconsider the way the application currently handles image usages. When the view object definition AllEmployees was originally created, it used the following WHERE clause:

```
WHERE ImageUsages.IMAGE_ID = Images.IMAGE_ID(+)
AND ImageUsages.ASSOCIATED_ID(+) = Employees.EMPLOYEE_ID
AND ImageUsages.USAGE_TYPE(+) = 'E'
AND Employees.JOB_ID = Jobs.JOB_ID
AND Employees.MANAGER_ID = Manager.EMPLOYEE_ID(+)
```

There are two issues with this WHERE clause:

- If an employee has more than one image, the query will return several rows for that employee.
- The `ImageUsages.ASSOCIATED_ID(+) = Employees.EMPLOYEE_ID AND ImageUsages.USAGE_TYPE(+) = 'E'` conditions needed to be manually added (and maintained if changes are made) to restrict image usages to those for employees.

In this phase, you will make the ImageUsages entity object definition polymorphic, with separate subtypes for employee and location image usages. Then you will change the way image usages are queried so as to solve the preceding two issues.

TIP
When following the practices in this book, in addition to relying on the sample files for this book mentioned before, we should reiterate that it is a good idea to back up the application directory when you get to a stage where a set of functionality is complete and working.

Create an Entity Hierarchy for Image Usages

In this section, you create two subtypes of the ImageUsages entity object definition: one for employee image usages, and one for location image usages. Then, you create an association between the Employees entity object definition and the employee subtype of ImageUsages.

1. In the Applications panel of the Navigator, under the "Model\Application Sources" node, expand the `tuhra.model.entities` package and edit the ImageUsages entity object definition.
2. On the Attributes page of the editor, select UsageType to give it focus in the Property Inspector.
3. Check the *Discriminator* checkbox in the *Type* section of the Property Inspector and Save.

   Additional Information: When you make the ImageUsages entity object polymorphic, marking this attribute as a Discriminator will allow you to use the attribute's value to determine which subtype of ImageUsages to instantiate.
4. Create an entity object definition in the `tuhra.model.entities` package.

5. On Step 1 of the wizard, fill in the following fields:
   Name as "EmployeeImageUsages"
   Extends Entity as "tuhra.model.entities.ImageUsages"
   Schema Object as "IMAGE_USAGES"

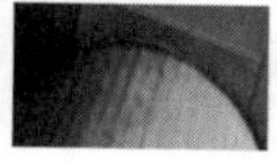

TIP
If you browse for the entity to extend, the schema object will be automatically filled in for you.

6. On Step 2 of the wizard, click Override to open the Inherited Attributes to Override dialog.
7. Shuttle UsageType to the *Selected* list and click OK to close the dialog.
8. On Step 3 of the wizard, set the *Default Value* field for UsageType to "E" and click Finish.

   Additional Information: This will cause rows with a USAGE_TYPE value of "E" to be encapsulated in instances of this entity object definition. Moreover, view object instances that use this entity object definition will at runtime restrict their query collections to return only rows with a USAGE_TYPE of "E."
9. Repeat Steps 4–8 to create an entity object definition named "LocationImageUsages," with a UsageType default value of "L."
10. Click Save All.
11. Create an association in the `tuhra.model.entities.assoc` package.
12. On Step 1 of the wizard, name the association "EmployeeImageUsagesAssoc."
13. On Step 2 of the wizard, specify that this is a "1 to *" association with the EmployeeId attribute of Employees as the source attribute and the AssociatedId attribute of EmployeeImageUsages as the destination attribute, as shown here:

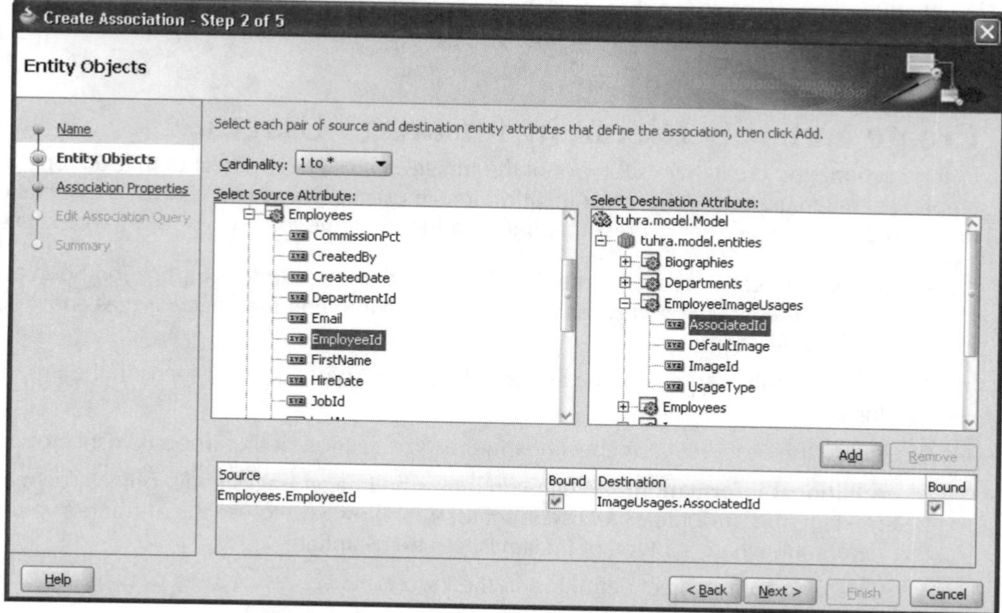

14. Finally, check the `tuhra.model.entities` package and delete any extra Image Usage associations that you find there. The only ones you want are those defined in the assoc package.

    Additional Information: In some cases, JDeveloper is trying to be a little too helpful and will automatically generate associations that in this case you no longer need—because you have more explicit relationships defined than the ones that can be deduced from the database alone.

15. Click Save All.

Use the Entity Hierarchy in a View Object Definition

In this section, you will change the AllEmployees view object definition to use the EmployeeImageUsages entity object definition, rather than the ImageUsages entity object definition. Then, you will modify the AllEmployees' query mode to the simple, easy-to-maintain declarative mode. Finally, you will change the way employee images are queried so that multiple images for a single employee will be handled gracefully.

1. Expand the `tuhra.model.queries.main` package and edit the AllEmployees view object definition.
2. On the Entity Objects page of the editor, remove the entity object usages of Images and ImageUsages.
3. Add a usage of EmployeeImageUsages, and confirm or set the following properties on it:
    Association as EmployeeImageUsagesAssoc.EmployeeImageUsages
    Source Usage as Employees
    Join Type as left outer join
4. Add a usage of Images, and confirm or set the following properties on it:
    Association as ImageUsagesImagesFkAssoc.Images
    Source Usage as EmployeeImageUsages
    Join Type as left outer join
5. On the Attributes page, click Add from Entity to open the Attributes dialog.
6. Add the Image attribute from the Images entity object definition.
7. Add the DefaultImage attribute from the EmployeeImageUsages entity object definition and click OK to close the Attributes dialog.
8. On the Query tab, check to see that the correct relationship has been generated in the SQL. Notice that there is no longer any reference to the UsageType in the WHERE clause, as this is now handled by the underlying polymorphic entity.

    Additional Information: The WHERE clause is getting relatively complex, and it will need to get more complex to solve the problem of employees with multiple image usages. Changing to declarative SQL mode will make the query easier to maintain by providing a structured form for the WHERE clause.

9. Click the Edit button to open the Edit Query: AllEmployees dialog.
10. Change the SQL Mode to "Declarative."

    Additional Information: The complete query listing disappears, as shown in Figure 20-4, because the SELECT and FROM clauses will be generated at runtime from the attributes and

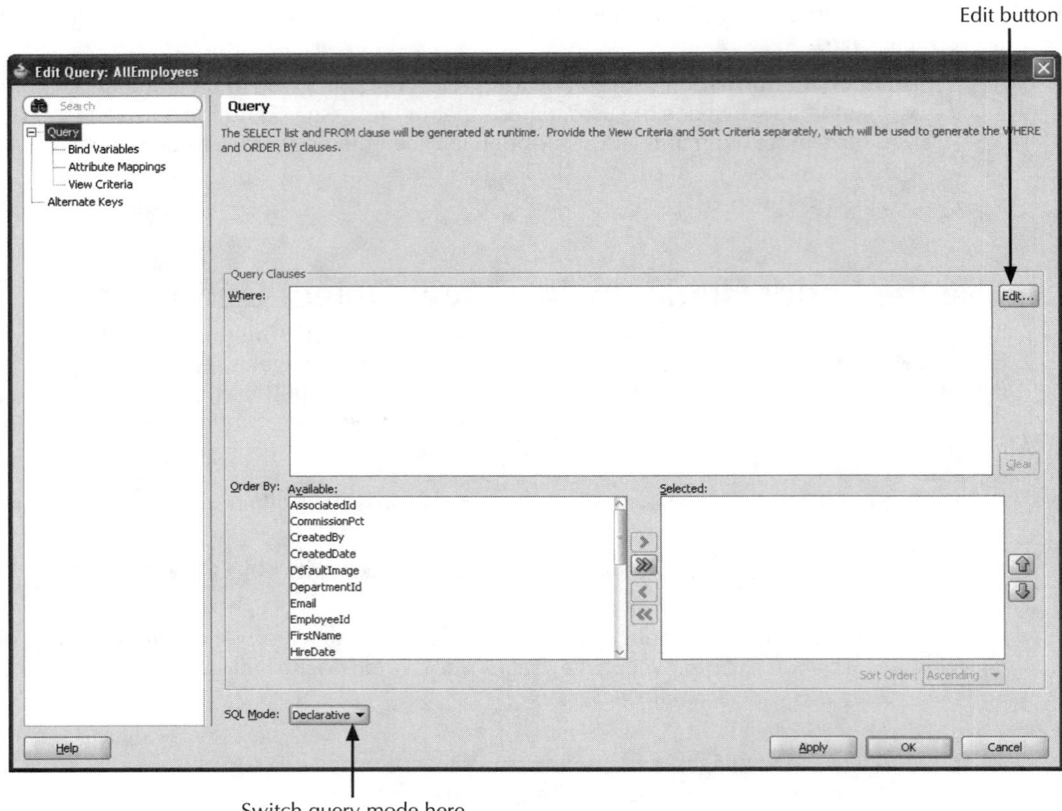

FIGURE 20-4. *The Edit Query dialog in declarative mode*

entity object usages at runtime, as will the portion of the WHERE clause that implements the associations between the entity usages. This allows you to restrict maintenance to custom portions of the WHERE clause and the order by clause, and to use a declarative interface to edit those.

11. Click the Edit button to open the Criteria Definition dialog.
12. Select AllEmployeesWhereCriteria and press Add Item.
13. Set the following properties on the new item:
    Attribute as "DefaultImage"
    Operator as "Equal To"
    Operand as "Literal"
    Value as "Y"
    Uncheck *Ignore Case*
    Validation as "Required"

Additional Information: The dialog should appear as shown here:

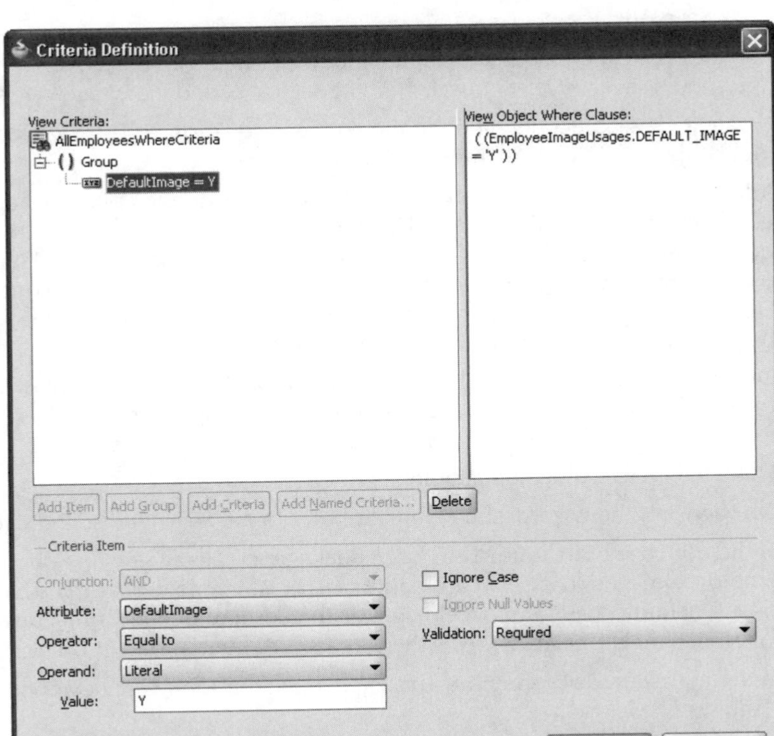

14. Select the Group node in the *View Criteria* tree, and click Add Item to create another item. Set the following properties on this item:
    Conjunction as "OR"
    Attribute as "DefaultImage"
    Operator as "Is blank"
    Uncheck *Ignore Case*
    Validation as "Required"

    Additional Information: "Is blank" is a generic way of testing for an empty value. On the Oracle database this will evaluate to "IS NULL"; however, on a different server it may cause different SQL specific to that server to be generated. This highlights an important feature of the declarative query mode: it adapts to the server being used rather than expecting a specific flavor of SQL.

    Additional Information: The view criteria object you have created restricts the query to return only rows containing the default image for the employee or no image at all, which supports employees with no images, thus preventing multiple employee images from translating into multiple AllEmployees rows.

15. Click OK to close the Criteria Definition dialog.

16. Shuttle the LastName and FirstName to the *Selected* list in the *Order By* clause.
17. Click Save All.
18. Run the application module tester and double click the EditEmployee view object instance. You should see the *DefaultImage* attribute set to "Y" and the *UsageType* set to "E."
19. Create a view object definition in the `tuhra.model.queries.main` package. Name this view object definition AllEmployeeImages.

    Additional Information: Previously, AllEmployees queried one row for every image an employee had (to a minimum of 1), which resulted in too many employee rows being queried. You have solved this problem by restricting the query of AllEmployees so that it only returns rows containing default images (or no image, for employees with no image). However, the user needs some way to access nondefault images for employees; you will use this view object definition to query these nondefault images.
20. On Page 2 of the wizard, add a usage of EmployeeImageUsages, followed by a usage of Images. Ensure that ImageUsagesImagesFkAssoc.Images is selected as the association end for the Images usage. Set the *Join Type* as "inner join."
21. Make the Images usage updatable.
22. On Page 3 of the wizard, shuttle all attributes to the Selected list and click Finish.
23. In the `tuhra.model.queries.main` package, create a view link definition, called EmployeeImagesVL. Use a cardinality of 1..*, AllEmployees as the source view object definition, AllEmployeeImages as the destination view object definition, and EmployeeImageUsagesAssoc as the source and destination attributes.
24. In the `tuhra.model.services` package, open the TuhraService application module definition.
25. On the Data Model page of the application module editor, add an instance of the AllEmployeeImages view object definition as a detail of EditEmployee in the *Data Model* list. Call the instance AllEmployeeImages as well.

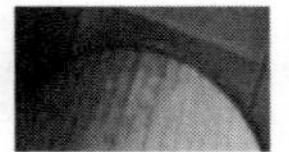

CAUTION
Be careful to add the instance as a detail of EditEmployee, not a detail of EmployeeSearch.

26. Click Save All.
27. Run TuhraService, and test EditEmployee and AllEmployeeImages instances to ensure that they are working properly.
28. In the ViewController project, run the templateTest page to ensure that the embedded edit screen still works correctly.

What Did You Just Do? You just created two subtypes for the ImageUsages entity object definition, which each handle a different type of image usage. Then, you changed the AllEmployees view object definition to use the EmployeeImageUsages subtype and to put it in declarative mode, fixing its behavior and improving its maintainability. Finally, you created a separate view object definition to handle employee images, since fixing the behavior of AllEmployeesView required you to limit its query to default images only.

II. Create the Popup Dialog

In this phase, you will create the dialog containing the train that allows the user to upload a new image and, optionally, choose a new default image for an employee.

Create a Task Flow for the Dialog

Since the dialog will contain a train of pages, it will require its own task flow definition, specialized to be a train.

1. In the ViewController project, create a new bounded ADF task flow, selecting the following options in the Create Task Flow dialog (and leaving all others as the default):
   File Name as "imageLOV-flow.xml"
   Create as Bounded Task Fow selected
   Create with Page Fragments selected
   Create Train selected
2. Select the "task-flow-definition - imageLOV-flow" node in the Structure pane.
3. In the Property Inspector, expand the Parameters panel and add an input parameter with the following values:
   name as "currentEmpId"
   class as "oracle.jbo.domain.Number"
   value as "#{pageFlowScope.currentEmpId}"
   required selected

   Additional Information: When this task flow is called from another task flow, that other task flow will be able to pass a `Number` value to this task flow as the parameter "currentEmpId." This task flow will then store that parameter in the location `#{pageFlowScope.currentEmpId}` so that its activities can access it.
4. Drop two view activities onto the task flow diagram view, naming them "addImage" and "setDefaultImage."

   Additional Information: Because this task flow is a train, JDeveloper automatically makes these view activities into train stops. It shows the order of the train with a dotted line, as shown here:

   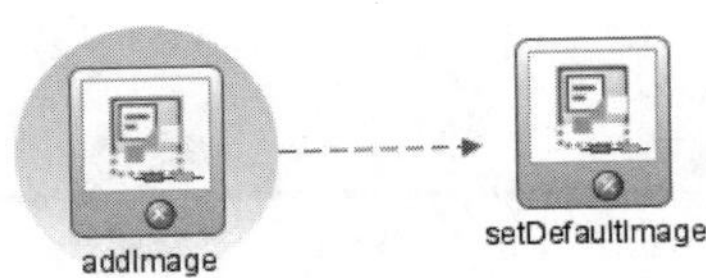

5. Add a task flow return activity onto the task flow. Name it "lovDone."
6. In the Property Inspector, set the name of lovDone's outcome to "refresh."

   Additional Information: When the task flow returns, the calling task flow will follow a control flow case called "refresh."
7. Add a wildcard control flow rule to the task flow.
8. Add a control flow case from the wildcard control flow rule to the task flow return activity. Name the case "finish."
9. Click Save All.

Create a Page Template for the Dialog

Train pages in the TUHRA application should have a consistent look and feel, but that supplied by the tuhraTemplate.jspx is not appropriate for a train page. In this section, you will create a separate template that supports the tasks required by the train.

1. In the WEB-INF/templates directory under the Web Content folder, create a JSF page template using the New Gallery (in the Web Tier \ JSF category). Set the following properties in the dialog, but do not yet click OK:
   File Name as "tuhraTrainTemplate.jspx"
   Directory as your "ViewController\public_html\WEB-INF\templates"
   Quickstart Layout as "One Column Header and Footer (Stretched), " as shown here:

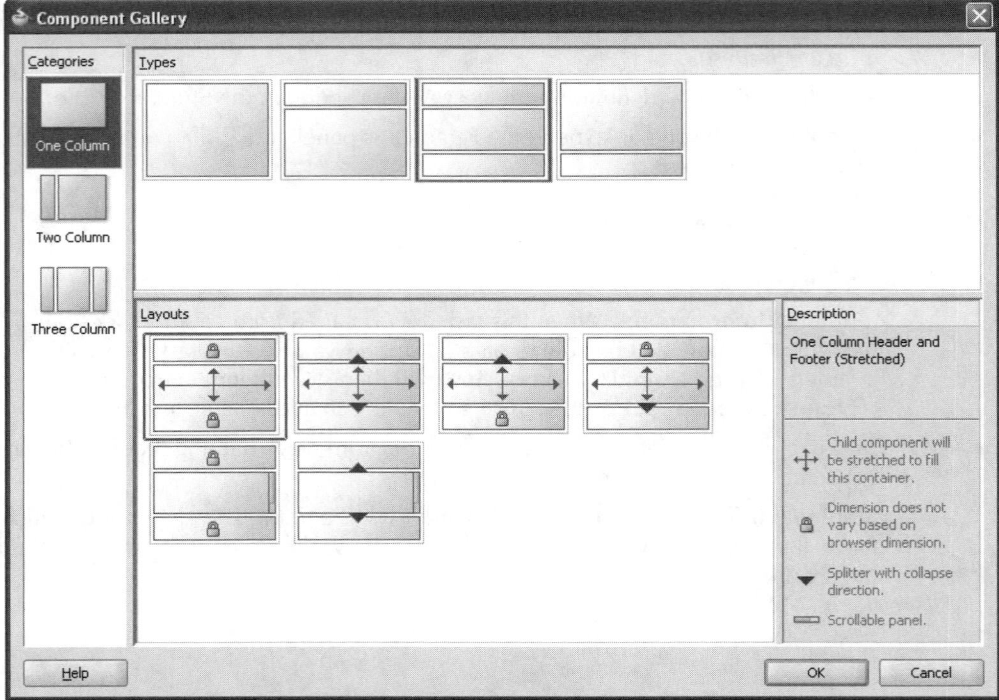

2. Add a facet definition named "trainContent," with the description "Train content goes here."
3. Add two attributes: pageUse and pageDescription. Both are of type String (the default). Mark both as required.
4. Click OK to create the template.
5. In the Structure pane, select the `af:panelStretchLayout` element.
6. In the Property Inspector, set the component's *inlineStyle* property to "height:450px; width:600px;".

7. Drag a panelGroupLayout onto the "top" facet of the `af:panelStretchLayout` in the visual editor.
8. Using the Property Inspector, set the *Layout* of the panelGroupLayout to "vertical."
9. Drop an Output Text into the panelGroupLayout, and set its *value* to "#{attrs.pageUse}."

   Additional Information: Since pageUse was declared as an attribute of the template, pages that use the template will provide it as an attribute in the template's XML tag. The expression `#{attrs.pageUse}` accesses the attribute value.
10. Set the outputText's *size* attribute in the style section to "large."
11. From the Common Components panel of the Component Palette, drop a Train after the output text.

    Additional Information: This component provides a visual indication of where the user is in the steps that make up the train process.
12. Set the *value* of the train to "#{controllerContext.currentViewPort.taskFlowContext.trainModel}."

    Additional Information: This expression returns the train model corresponding to the current train stop. It will allow the train component to display all the stops in the train, with the current stop highlighted.
13. Drop a Spacer after the train and set its *height* to 6.
14. Drop an Output Text after the spacer and set its *value* to "#{attrs.pageDescription}."
15. Drop a Separator component after the outputText to draw a horizontal line.
16. Drop another Panel Group Layout into the bottom facet of the Panel Stretch Layout, and set its *layout* to "vertical."
17. Drop a Separator into this Panel Group Layout.
18. Drop a Spacer after the Separator, and set its *height* to 6.
19. Drop a Panel Group Layout after the Spacer (creating nested `af:panelGroupLayout` components).
20. Set the following properties on the new Panel Group Layout:

    Halign as "end"
    Layout as "horizontal."
21. Drop a Train Button Bar into the new (inner) Panel Group Layout.

TIP
Remember that it may be easier to drop components onto the Structure pane than onto the visual editor.

22. Set the *value* of the Train Button Bar to "#{controllerContext.currentViewPort .taskFlowContext.trainModel}."

    Additional Information: This will create a button bar displaying Previous and Next buttons, as appropriate, for each train stop.
23. Drop a Button after the Train Button Bar.

24. Set the text of the button to "Finish" and its action to "finish."

    Additional Information: This action refers to the wildcard control flow case that leads to the lovDone task flow return. This will allow users to leave the popup dialog from either train stop.

25. Drop a Facet Ref into the "center" facet of the Panel Stretch Layout, and select the *Facet Name* "trainContent."

26. Click Save All.

Create Page Fragments for the Train Stops

In this section, you will create page fragments for each of the stops in the train.

1. Re-open the imageLOV-flow.xml task flow.
2. Select the addImage view activity and set its *Display Name* property, in the Description area of the Train Stop panel, to "Upload a New Image." Note that this is a different property than the ***Display Name*** property in the top-level Description panel.
3. Double click the view activity to open the Create New JSF Fragment dialog.
4. Append "\fragments\imageLOV" to the end of the Directory field. Do not change the rest of the path.
5. Select tuhraTrainTemplate from the Use Page Template pulldown, and click OK to generate the page.
6. In the Structure pane, note that there are two errors (and a warning) listed. The errors are the missing attributes that you specified in the page template's definition.
7. In the Structure pane, select the `af:pageTemplate` node.
8. Use the Property Inspector to set the following properties:

   pageDescription as "In this page you can upload a new image to the system for use with this user."

   pageUse as "Upload a New Image"
9. Re-open imageLOV-flow.xml.
10. Select the setDefaultImage view activity and set its *Display Name* property, in the Description area of the Train Stop panel, to "Default Employee Image."
11. Repeat steps 3–7 for the setDefaultImage view activity.
12. Use the Property Inspector to set the following properties on the `af:pageTemplate`:

    pageDescription as "Use this page to define which of your images should be used as the default."

    pageUse as "Default Employee Image"
13. Click Save All.

Wire the Dialog to the Edit Page

In this section, you will add a popup to the edit page that displays the dialog. Although the pages of the dialog are currently only stubs, this will allow you to test the task flow and template.

1. Open editEmployee.jsff (in the fragments folder in the Application Navigator).

2. In the Structure pane, find the `af:popup` component.

   Additional Information: This is the component, created in Chapter 19, that displays an employee's job history.

3. Drop another Popup directly after that component.
4. Set the *Id* of the popup to "imageLOV" and the *ContentDelivery* to "lazyUncached."
5. Drop a dialog inside the popup, and set the following properties on the dialog:
   Title as "Manage Employee Images"
   TitleIconSource as "/images/user.png"
   Type as "none"

   Additional Information: The train pages you have created for the image LOV already have a Finish button, so there is no need to have the additional OK and Cancel buttons that the Dialog component can supply. Therefore, the Type of the dialog is set to none.

6. Drag the imageLovFlow.xml task flow from the Application Navigator into the dialog, and drop it as a region into the `af:dialog`.
7. When the Edit Task Flow Binding dialog appears, set the *currentEmpId* input parameter to "#{bindings.EmployeeId.inputValue.sequenceNumber}" and click OK.

   Additional Information: This is the parameter you defined in imageLOV-flow, in the section "Create a Task Flow for the Dialog." The editEmployee page will pass the numeric value of EmployeeId into this parameter, which will store it on the page flow scope so that it can be accessed by activities and page fragments.

8. Select a non-popup node in the Structure window to return to the main view of editEmployee.jsff to switch focus back to the main part of the page.
9. Select the image.
10. As the popup LOV may be changing the default image of the employee, set the *partialTriggers* property for the image to point at the new popup using the value "imageLOV."

    Additional Information: This will refresh the image once the popup has been accessed.

11. Next, from the right-click menu on the image, select **Surround With** and surround the image with a Panel Label and Message.
12. In the Property Inspector, clear the *Label* property.
13. Drop a Link into the "end" facet of the Panel Label and Message.
14. Set the *Text* attribute of the link to "Manage Images."
15. Drop a Show Popup Behavior into the link.
16. Set the following properties on the Show Popup Behavior:
    PopupId as "imageLOV"
    TriggerType as "action"
17. Click Save All.
18. To test the popup functionality, run templateTest.jspx, which contains the editEmployee-flow task flow.
19. When the edit page opens, click Manage Images to open the popup dialog.

20. Try the Next and Previous buttons to see the pages of the train. They are still without content, but you can see the layout, as shown here for the set default image page:

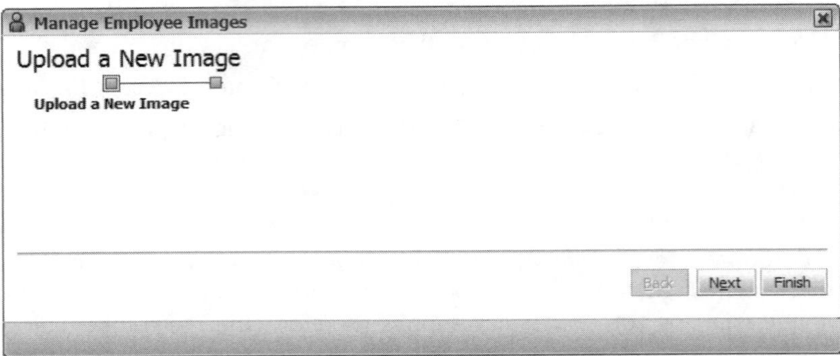

Notice how you're not seeing the whole of the header section. Because you based the train pages on a template, it is simple to go in and fix that.

21. Open the tuhraTrainTemplate file and select the top-level `af:panelStretchLayout` component in the Structure window. Change the *TopHeight* property to "100px."
22. Click Save All and rerun the test page. The dialog will now look like this:

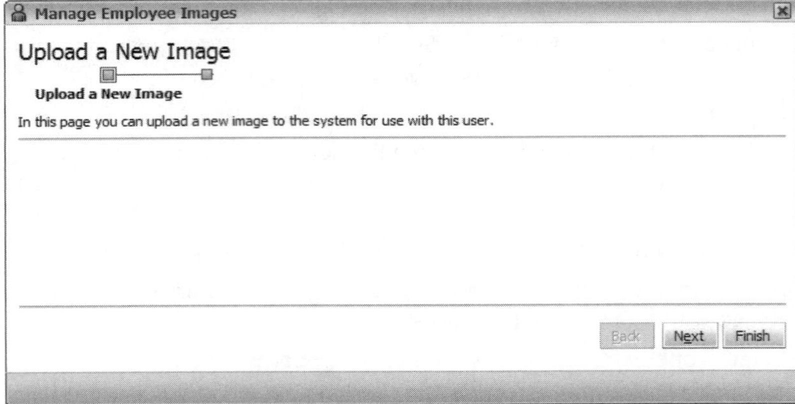

23. Press Finish in the popup and notice that although the content disappears, a small popup window is left behind that you have to close using the "x" button in the top right-hand corner. You will fix that problem next.
24. Close the browser.

Fix the Popup Behavior

The reason that the popup is not being closed when you finish the train is that all the Finish button does is to end the imageLOV-flow; the popup has no idea that it's no longer needed. To fix this behavior, you need to add a region listener to hide the popup when the task flow has completed.

This same section will also fix a problem that you have not seen yet, the fact that if you invoke the popup for the second time in the same session, it will appear as empty without showing the train.

1. Delete the `af:region` containing the imageLOV-flow from within the `af:dialog` inside the popup.
2. Drag and drop the imageLOV-flow task flow into the `af:dialog` again, but this time drop it as a Dynamic Region.
3. In the Choose Managed Bean for Dynamic Region dialog, choose "employeeEditBB" from the dropdown list and click OK.
4. The Edit Task Flow Binding dialog will appear as it did last time that you created a region from this flow. Create a parameter and set the *Name* to "currentEmpId" and the *Value* to "#{bindings.EmployeeId.inputValue.sequenceNumber}." Click OK.
5. Open the `EmployeeEditBean` class and add the following method (line numbers added for explanation):

```
01: public void navigationListener(
02:   RegionNavigationEvent regionNavigationEvent) {
03:   String newViewId = regionNavigationEvent.getNewViewId();
04:   if (newViewId == null) {
05:     RichRegion region = (RichRegion)regionNavigationEvent.getSource();
06:     RichPopup popup = findParentPopup(region);
07:     if (popup != null) {
08:       hidePopup(popup);
09:     }
10:   }
11: }
```

Additional Information: This method will contain syntax errors because it depends on classes that aren't yet imported and methods which aren't yet written. You will import the classes in the next step. This method goes through the following steps:

- **Lines 1–2** This listener is passed a RegionNavigationEvent event that provides information about the region that contains the task flow that is being ended.
- **Lines 3–4** Checks to see if this is the event raised comes from a Task Flow that is ended, and if that is the case, then the name of the region containing the flow is obtained.
- **Line 5** Retrieves the region holding the task flow.
- **Line 6** This call is to a method that you will create later in this section, `findParentPopup()`. You will implement this method to find the popup window, if any, containing the passed in component.
- **Line 8** This call is to a helper method, `hidePopup()`, which you will create shortly. This method will ensure that the popup is hidden when the request is completed.

TIP
This region navigation listener is generic enough to use in your own applications.

6. Use import assistance to import the following classes:
   - `oracle.adf.view.rich.event.RegionNavigationEvent`
   - `oracle.adf.view.rich.component.rich.fragment.RichRegion`
   - `oracle.adf.view.rich.component.rich.RichPopup`
7. Using code assistance on the remaining syntax errors, generate stubs for the `findParentPopup()` and `hidePopup()` methods.
8. Implement the `findParentPopup()` as follows, using import assistance to import `javax.faces.component.UIComponent` when you are done:

```
private RichPopup findParentPopup(UIComponent source) {
  UIComponent parent = source.getParent();
  while (parent != null && !(parent instanceof RichPopup)) {
    parent = parent.getParent();
  }
  return (RichPopup)parent;
}
```

   Additional Information: This method iteratively walks up the JSF component hierarchy to find the popup component (if any) that contains the parameter `source`.

9. Implement the `hidePopup()` method as follows:

```
01: private void hidePopup(RichPopup popup) {
02:   FacesContext context = FacesContext.getCurrentInstance();
03:   String popupId = popup.getClientId(context);
04:   Service.getRenderKitService(context,
05:     ExtendedRenderKitService.class).addScript(context,
06:       "var popup = AdfPage.PAGE.findComponent('" +
07:       popupId +
08:       "'); popup.hide();");
09: }
```

   Additional Information: This method will contain syntax errors because it depends on classes that aren't yet imported. The code steps through the following operations:

   - **Lines 2–3** retrieve the ID of the popup. An ID can be used to find a component and manipulate it on the server via Java, or, for components with Javascript objects generated on the client side, to manipulate the generated HTML on the client using the ADF Javascript API. Popup components always have client-side objects; to ensure generation of client side objects for other components, set the attribute value `clientComponent="true"` on the component. This comes with a significant performance cost, so do it only for components you need to manipulate through your own Javascript.
   - **Lines 4–8** add the following line to the generated page's Javascript code, in a location (outside of any method) which makes it execute immediately:

```
var popup = AdfPage.PAGE.findComponent('<component_id>'); popup.hide();
```

<component_id> is standing in for the component id retrieved in line 3. AdfPage and PAGE are Javascript objects created when ADF renders ADF faces pages; `findComponent()` is a Javascript function which returns a client-side object based on its component ID, and `hide()` is a Javascript function on client-side popup components.

10. Use import assistance to import the following classes:
    - `javax.faces.context.FacesContext`
    - `org.apache.myfaces.trinidad.util.Service`
    - `org.apache.myfaces.trinidad.render.ExtendedRenderKitService`
11. Open the editEmployee page fragment and locate the region used to host the imageLOV-flow. In the Other section of the Property Inspector, set the *RegionNavigationListener* property to the EL that evaluates to the listener code that you have just created, "#{viewScope.employeeEditBB.navigationListener}."
12. Click Save All and run the templateTest page. Click Manage Images and step through the steps and finally press the Finish button. Notice that the popup window now completely closes. However, click Manage Images again and notice that now the popup dialog is displayed empty. You will fix that next.

    Additional Information: A popup is always present in the page, and opening and closing it is really just showing and hiding it. So when the popup is displayed for the second time, it is just showing the current contents, and of course, you had just ended the task flow, so it is now empty.
13. Open the `EmployeeEditBean` class, and locate the member variable "taskFlowId." Use the **Refactor** | **Rename** option from the right-click menu to change the name of the variable to "_imageTaskFlowId."
14. Create one more member variable in the class as follows:

    ```
    private String _selectedTaskFlowId = "";
    ```

    Additional Information: One way to save resources in your application is to populate the region with a task flow only when it is visible. The selectedTaskFlowId variable will be used to hold the ID of the flow that is currently hosted within the dynamic region (either the imageLOV-flow or the empty flow). Notice that the selected flow is initially set to the null flow, represented by the default empty string.
15. Generate accessors (get and set) for the `_selectedTaskFlowId` variable using the right-click menu.
16. Generate a "get" accessor only for the `_imageTaskFlowId` variable.
17. Locate the `getDynamicTaskFlowId()` method in the class. This is the method that the dynamic region uses to decide which task flow to display. Now that you have two possible flows (imageLOV-flow and the null flow), you need to change this method to select the correct one. The value you will need is held in the `_selectedTaskFlowId` variable. Update the method to read as follows:

    ```
    public String getDynamicTaskFlowId() {
      return _selectedTaskFlowId;
    }
    ```

18. Next you need to indicate which flow should be selected as the user opens and closes the popup. Open the editEmployee fragment and locate the popup containing the region in the Structure window. Select **Insert inside af:popup | ADF Faces** from the right-click menu and select "Set Property Listener" in the Insert ADF Faces Item dialog.

19. The Insert Set Property Listener dialog will display. Set *From* to "#{viewScope.employeeEditBB .imageTaskFlowId}." Set *To* to "#{viewScope.employeeEditBB.selectedTaskFlowId}." Set *Type* to "popupFetch."

    Additional Information: When the popup is opened, you are copying the value for the imageLOV-flow into the selected flow for display in the region.

    The final step is to reset the region contents when the `af:popup` is closed; however, the popup close event is private to the browser and does not automatically call server-side code to allow you to reset the `_selectedTaskFlowId`, so next you will add a little JavaScript into the page to trigger the change of `_selectedTaskFlowId` on the server.

20. After the last `af:popup` tag in the editEmployee fragment add an `af:resource` component. Set the *Type* property to "javascript."

    Additional Information: The `af:resource` component allows you to embed both JavaScript and CSS into your pages, either in-line as we are showing here, or as a reference to an external .js or .css file. Although we are using in-line code for simplicity, in production applications we generally recommend externalizing resources to separate files.

21. Switch to the source code editor view for the page and add the following JavaScript inside the resource tag:

```
function popupClosedListener(event) {
  var source = event.getSource();
  var popupId = source.getClientId();

  var params = {};
  params['popupId'] = popupId;
  var type = "serverPopupClosed";
  var immediate = true;
  AdfCustomEvent.queue(source, type, params, immediate);
}
```

    Additional Information: This script uses the ADF JavaScript API to execute a custom server-side event called "serverPopupClosed." You will implement the handler for that event shortly. Specifying `true` as the last parameter to the method means that the custom event should trigger during the apply request values phase of the JSF lifecycle, just as specifying `immediate="true"` on a server-side component does.

22. Next, you need to wire the `popupClosedListener()` JavaScript method into the popup so that it is executed as the popup is closed. Select the second `af:popup` in the Structure window and select **Insert inside af:popup | ADF Faces** from the right-click menu. Then select "Client Listener" in the Insert ADF Faces Item dialog.

    Additional Information: The Client Listener component executes JavaScript methods in the browser. A Server Listener, which you will create next, executes a Java method on the server.

23. Set the *Method* property of the Client Listener to "popupClosedListener" and the *Type* to "popupClosed."

24. Repeat the insert process inside the af:popup, but this time insert an Server Listener. Set the Type to "serverPopupClosed" and click OK; then set the *method* as "#{viewScope .employeeEditBB.swapEmptyTaskFlow}." The markup for the entire popup containing the imageLOV-flow will now read:

```
<af:popup id="imageLOV" contentDelivery="lazyUncached"
          eventContext="launcher">
  <af:dialog id="d1" title="Manage Employee Images"
             titleIconSource="/images/user.png" type="none">
    <af:region value="#{bindings.dynamicRegion1.regionModel}"
               id="r1"
               regionNavigationListener=
                 "#{viewScope.employeeEditBB.navigationListener}"/>
  </af:dialog>
  <af:setPropertyListener from="#{viewScope.employeeEditBB.imageTaskFlowId}"
                          to="#{viewScope.employeeEditBB.selectedTaskFlowId}"
                          type="popupFetch"/>
  <af:clientListener method="popupClosedListener" type="popupClosed"/>
  <af:serverListener type="serverPopupClosed"
                     method="#{viewScope.employeeEditBB.swapEmptyTaskFlow}"/>
</af:popup>
```

25. Finally you need to implement the swapEmptyTaskFlow() method that the af:serverListener is calling. This method basically resets the value of the selectedTaskFlowId variable to the null value so that the popup is empty when it is not displayed. Reopen EmployeeEditBean and create the method as follows:

```
public void swapEmptyTaskFlow(ClientEvent event) {
  setSelectedTaskFlowId("");
  // If event delivery set to immediate="true",
  // short-circuit to renderResponse.
  // Forcing an empty taskflow releases the bindings and view port.
  Boolean immediate = (Boolean)event.getParameters().get("immediate");
  if (immediate != null && immediate) {
    FacesContext context = FacesContext.getCurrentInstance();
    context.renderResponse();
  }
}
```

26. Import oracle.adf.view.rich.render.ClientEvent using import assistance.

27. Click Save All and run the templateTest page. Click Manage Images to show the popup. You should now find that the Finish button works as expected and the LOV is also correctly displayed if you open it for a second time.

What Did You Just Do? You created a very basic prototype of the edit image functionality: A task flow train for image editing, a template for train stops, stubs of both of the train stops, and a popup dialog in which to run the task flow. You also spent some time integrating the task flow with the popup to ensure that the popup closes correctly and the contents are correctly reinitialized as you finish and restart the flow.

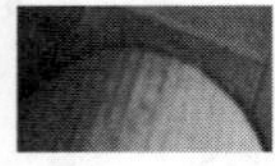

TIP
For a more comprehensive version of the generic code for managing region in popup behavior, we recommend that you read the white paper "Embedding Regions inside PopUp Windows" by David Giammona, which you can find on the Oracle Technology Network.

In the next sections, you will implement the train stops beyond the stub level.

III. Implement the Add Image Page

In this phase, you will add details and functionality to the first of your two train stops: the add image page, which allows the user to select an image file from their local machine, upload it to the server's file system, and create IMAGES and IMAGE_USAGES rows for it.

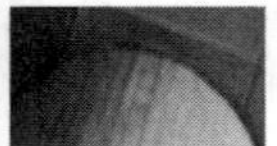

NOTE
In this application, the IMAGES table stores only an ID number and a relative path; the image file is stored on the application server's file system. This decision was made to allow the application to run on an Oracle XE database. In a production application using a full-featured Oracle database, we would not recommend storing data (such as employee images) in the application server's file system for reasons of reliability and scalability. Instead, we would recommend saving images to a more managed repository such as Oracle's content database product or an interMedia *datatype column in the database (Oracle XE does not support* interMedia *types).*

Lay Out the Form Components

In this section, you will lay out the UI components for the add image page, although many of them will not be functional until a later section.

1. Open the addImage.jsff page fragment (fragments\imageLOV) in the visual editor.
2. Drop a Panel Form Layout into the trainContent area of the page.
3. Drop an Input File component into the Panel Form Layout, and set the following properties on the component:
   Id as "upload"
   Label as "New image to upload"
   AutoSubmit as "true"

   Additional Information: This creates an input component into which a file name can be typed, or a Browse button used to open a file selection dialog to select a file name from the local (browser machine) file system. Because the *autoSubmit* attribute is true, as soon as a file is selected, or the field loses focus, the form data (including the contents of the file) will be sent to the server in a partial page request.
4. Drop an Image component after the Input File, specifying "Uploaded Image" as the ShortDesc in the Insert Image dialog. Leave the *Source* property empty for the moment.

5. In the Property Inspector, set the following properties on the Image:
   InlineStyle as "width:180px; height:180px;"
   PartialTriggers as "upload"

   Additional Information: By setting "upload" as a partial trigger, you ensure that the image will be refreshed after the Input File component (with id="upload") sends its partial page request.
6. Click Save All.

Create a Backing Bean for the Add Image Page

In this section, you will create a backing bean for the add image page. This bean will hold the uploaded file and will eventually execute the operation that will create the new AllEmployeeImages row for the new image.

1. Create a class in the `tuhra.view.backing` package, named `ImageUploadBean` and extending `tuhra.view.framework.TuhraBackingBean`.
2. Select **Source | Implement Interface** and make the class implement the `java.io.Serializable` interface.

   Additional Information: Classes for beans of scope longer than request or view need to implement `Serializable`, which is a marker interface that lets the JVM know that details of an instance of this class may be communicated or written to a stream in text form, allowing the content to be migrated between machines operating as a clustered application server. Because `Serializable` is a marker interface, implementing it does not require you to implement any methods.

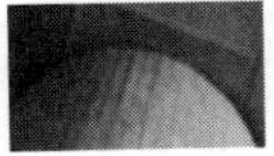

TIP
You can also specify interfaces in the Create Java Class dialog by adding them to the Option Attributes *list.*

3. Re-open imageLOV-flow.xml, and switch to the Overview tab in the editor. Within the Overview editor select the Managed Beans tab on the left-hand side and then use the Add (green "+") button to create a managed bean.
4. Specify the following properties in the table:
   Name as "imageUploadBB"
   Class as "tuhra.view.backing.ImageUploadBean"
   (searching for "ImageUploadBean" may be easier)
   Scope as "pageFlow"
5. Click Save All.

Use the Image Component to Preview the Uploaded Image

In this section, you will use the managed bean created in the preceding section to store the uploaded image, and you will wire the Image component created in the earlier section "Lay Out the Form Components" to the uploaded image.

1. Re-open the ImageUploadBean class in the source editor.

2. Add the following field declaration:

```
private String _uploadedImageName = "/images/uploadPlaceholder.png";
```

3. On the right-click menu for `_uploadedImageName`, select **Generate Accessors**.
4. When the Generate Accessors dialog opens, accept the defaults and click OK to create public getter and setter methods for the field.

   Additional Information: A public getter method allows the property to be accessed from a task flow activity or page; a public setter method allows the property's value to be injected through a managed property or changed from a task flow activity or page. This will override the default value of "/images/uploadPlaceholder.png."

5. Add the following field declaration:

```
private UploadedFile _uploadedImageFile;
```

6. Press ALT-ENTER to import the correct `UploadedFile` version (which is `org.apache.myfaces.trinidad.model.UploadedFile`).
7. Repeat steps 3–4 to create accessors for this field.
8. Re-open the addImage.jsff fragment and select the image.
9. In the Property Inspector, open the Expression Builder for the *Rendered* property, and set the expression to "#{! empty pageFlowScope.imageUploadBB.uploadedImageName}."
10. Similarly, set the image's *Source* property to "#{pageFlowScope.imageUploadBB.uploadedImageName}."

   Additional Information: The *Rendered* and *Source* values you entered will ensure that the image isn't displayed at all when the ImageUploadBB bean's `uploadedImageName` is null, and that, when it does show, it always displays the image at the relative path specified by `uploadedImageName`'s value.

11. Select the `af:inputFile` component in the Structure window.
12. In the Behavior panel of the Property Inspector, open the pulldown list to the right of the ValueChangeListener component and select Edit.
13. In the Edit Property dialog, select the imageUploadBB bean, and click New beside the Method pulldown to create a method in the bean's class. Name the method "fileUploadedListener," and click OK twice to close both open dialogs.

   Additional Information: This creates a method stub for the method `fileUploadedListener(ValueChangeEvent)`, which will be called (with a parameter describing the value change) whenever the value of the `af:inputFile` component changes (by the user selecting a new file to upload). You will implement this method in the section "Create an Upload Listener to Call the Service Method."

14. Open the `ImageUploadBean` class to ensure it looks like the following (except, possibly, for spacing and ordering of the fields, methods, constructor, and imports):

```
package tuhra.view.backing;

import java.io.Serializable;
import javax.faces.event.ValueChangeEvent;
import org.apache.myfaces.trinidad.model.UploadedFile;
import tuhra.view.framework.TuhraBackingBean;
```

```
public class ImageUploadBean extends TuhraBackingBean implements Serializable {

  private String _uploadedImageName = "/images/uploadPlaceholder.png";
  private UploadedFile _uploadedImageFile;

  public ImageUploadBean() {
  }

  public void setUploadedImageName(String _uploadedImageName) {
    this._uploadedImageName = _uploadedImageName;
  }

  public String getUploadedImageName() {
    return _uploadedImageName;
  }

  public void setUploadedImageFile(UploadedFile _uploadedImageFile) {
    this._uploadedImageFile = _uploadedImageFile;
  }

  public UploadedFile getUploadedImageFile() {
    return _uploadedImageFile;
  }

  public void fileUploadedListener(ValueChangeEvent valueChangeEvent) {
    // Add event code here...
  }
}
```

15. Make the class to ensure it compiles correctly.
16. Click Save All.

Create a Service Method to Add an Image

In this section, you will create an application module–level service method that will create a new image and image usage for a given employee number and image path.

1. In the `tuhra.model.services` package, double click the TuhraService application module definition to open it in an editor.
2. Select the Java tab, and click the "Edit java options" (pencil) button in the Java Classes section to open the Select Java Options dialog.
3. Select "Generate Application Module Class" and click OK to close the dialog.

   Additional Information: This generates an application module class, `TuhraServiceImpl`, for TuhraService. You will write the service method in this class.
4. In the `tuhra.model.queries.main` package, double click the AllEmployeeImages view object definition to open it in an editor.
5. Again select the Java tab, and click the Edit java options (pencil) button in the Java Classes section to open the Select Java Options dialog.
6. Select "Generate View Row Class," leave "Include accessors" selected, and click OK.

   Additional Information: This generates a view row class, `AllEmployeeImagesRowImpl`, for AllEmployeeImages. This class contains typesafe getters and setters on it that you can call from the service method to access and change attributes.

7. Repeat steps 4–6 for the AllEmployees view object definition.
8. Expand the TuhraService node, and double click `TuhraServiceImpl` to open it in a code editor.
9. Add the following method:

```
public void createNewImageForEmployee(Number employeeId,
                                      String imageName) {
  AllEmployeesRowImpl empRow = getEmpRow(employeeId);
  if (empRow != null) {
    createAndInsertImage(empRow, imageName);
    getAllEmployeeImages().setAssociationConsistent(true);
  }
}
```

Additional Information: This will be the service method, but most of it is not implemented yet (which is part of the reason you will see syntax errors highlighted). Most of the work is factored into two methods that aren't created yet: `getEmpRow()`, which returns an AllEmployees view row matching the passed-in employeeId, and `createAndInsertImage()`, which creates, initializes, and inserts an AllEmployeeImages view row. The call to `getAllEmployeeImages().setAssociationConsistent()` allows the newly created row to show up in the AllEmployeeImages view object instance. For more information, see the sidebar, "View Link Consistency."

View Link Consistency

View link consistency is a feature that allows view object instances with entity usages to immediately see rows based on new entity object instances as they get created. For example, suppose you create a row using EditEmployee. This would create an instance of the entity object definition Employees. View link consistency will allow that employee to appear as a row in EmployeeSearch (a different view object instance) without a database post and requery.

For simple view object definitions with only one updatable entity, this happens automatically unless you make manual changes to your application module. However, by default, view object definitions with multiple updatable entities do not have instances with view link consistency. This is because, if an instance of each entity usage is created, it may not be clear how many new view rows to base on them (one row with both, or two separate view rows, one with each).

However, in some cases, you are creating both entity object instances by creating a single view row appropriate to a particular view object instance. In that case, you can manually set view row consistency on the view object instance by passing a value of `true` to `ViewObjectImpl.setAssociationConsistent()`.

10. Use import assistance to import the `AllEmployeesRowImpl` class.
11. Add `oracle.jbo.domain.Number` manually to the import block of the class.

Additional Information: This is to ensure that the `Number` type of the first parameter is interpreted as `oracle.jbo.domain.Number` rather than `java.lang.Number`.

12. Click the red light bulb icon beside the call to `getEmpRow()`, and select "Create method getEmpRow" to generate a stub for that method.
13. Similarly, generate a stub for `createAndInsertImage()`.
14. Implement the `getEmpRow()` method as follows:

```
private AllEmployeesRowImpl getEmpRow(Number employeeId) {
  AllEmployeesRowImpl empRow = null;
  TuhraViewObjectImpl empRows = this.getEditEmployee();
  Key key = new Key(new Object[] {employeeId});
  Row[] hits = empRows.findByKey(key, 1);
  if (hits.length > 0) {
    empRow = (AllEmployeesRowImpl)hits[0];
  }
  return empRow;
}
```

Additional Information: This method creates a `Key` object based on the passed in employee ID (which forms the key for AllEmployees), and calls the method `findByKey()` to return an array of matching rows (in this case, because the key is complete, at most one row will match). It returns the matching row, if any, and returns null otherwise.

15. Using import assistance, import `oracle.jbo.Key` and `oracle.jbo.Row`.
16. Implement the `createAndInsertImage()` method as follows:

```
private void createAndInsertImage(AllEmployeesRowImpl empRow, String imageName) {
  RowSet empImages = (RowSet) empRow.getAllEmployeeImages();
  //Create an Image
  EntityDefImpl imageDef =
    EntityDefImpl.findDefObject("tuhra.model.entities.Images");
  ImagesImpl newImage =
    (ImagesImpl)imageDef.createInstance2(getDBTransaction(),null);
  newImage.setImage(imageName);

  //Initalize the values for, and then Create an Image Usage
  //in the context of the current Employee row
  NameValuePairs initializeUsage = new NameValuePairs();
  initializeUsage.setAttribute("ImageId", newImage.getImageId());
  initializeUsage.setAttribute("DefaultImage", "N");
  AllEmployeeImagesRowImpl newUsage =
    (AllEmployeeImagesRowImpl)empImages.createAndInitRow(initializeUsage);
}
```

Additional Information: This method retrieves the row set containing images that belong to the employee. Then, it creates a new image, setting its image (name) value in the process. Finally using the ID generated for the new image and a suitable value for the DefaultImage flag as initialization values, it creates a new usage row. The row iterator ensures that the foreign key attribute to AllEmployees is set correctly.

17. Use Import Assistance to import
    - `oracle.jbo.server.EntityDefImpl`
    - `oracle.jbo.NameValuePairs`
    - `oracle.jbo.RowSet`
    - `tuhra.model.queries.main.AllEmployeeImagesRowImpl`

18. The `ImagesImpl` class is still missing and needs to be generated. In the `tuhra.model.entities` package, double click the Images entity object definition to open it in an editor.
19. Again select the Java tab, and click the Edit java options (pencil) button in the Java Classes section to open the Select Java Options dialog.
20. Select "Generate Entity Object Class," leave "Accessors" selected in the *Include* section, and click OK.

    Additional Information: This generates an entity object class, `ImagesImpl`, which is needed by the `createAndInsert()` method in the application module class. In a later section, you will also need to add some code to this class to ensure that new images correctly propagate their primary key to any ImageUsages that use them.
21. Re-open `TuhraServiceImpl`, and use import assistance to import `tuhra.model.entities.ImagesImpl`.
22. Reopen the editor for TuhraService, and ensure that the Java page is displayed.
23. Click the "Edit application module client interface" (pencil) button beside the Client Interface section.

    Additional Information: This allows you to export methods, turning them into service methods that the client can use. For more information on service methods, see Chapter 8.
24. Shuttle "createNewImageForEmployee(Number,String):void" to the Selected list, and click OK to export the method.
25. Click Save All.
26. Run TuhraService to open an instance in the Business Component Browser.
27. In the Business Component Browser, double click the TuhraService top-level node to open it in a window, which will allow you to test its service method. The Business Components Browser screen will look like this:

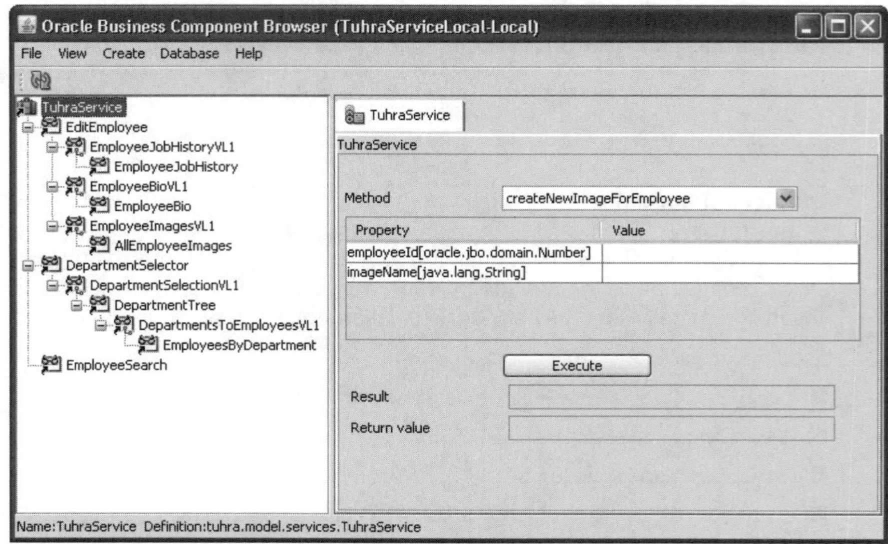

28. Enter the following parameters:
    oracle.jbo.domain.Number as "101" (the employeeID parameter)
    java.lang.String as "images/test.png" (the imageName parameter)
29. Click Execute to verify that the method executes correctly.
30. Still in the Business Component Browser, double click EmployeeImagesVL to open a master-detail view of AllEmployees and AllEmployeeImages.
31. Scroll the employees to employee number 101, and verify that the image and usage have been successfully inserted into the cache.
32. Close the Business Component Browser.

Fix Association Posting Behavior

If, rather than closing the Business Component Browser, you had attempted to commit your changes, you would have noticed a problem. The ImageId attribute of Images, which is of type `DBSequence`, holds a temporary (negative) value before posting. The ImageId attribute of EmployeesImageUsages is keyed to this value through the association ImageUsageImagesFkAssoc. If you had posted the Images row, the negative value for its ImageId attribute would have been replaced by the actual sequence value, causing it to become out of synch with the new EmployeesImageUsages row. You will fix this problem in this section.

1. Generate an entity object class, with accessors, for the ImageUsages entity object definition.
2. Open the `ImagesImpl` class (under the Images entity object definition) and select the **Source | Override Methods** menu option. Use the checkbox to override the `postChanges()` method.
3. Edit the `postChanges()` method to read as follows:

```
@Override
public void postChanges(TransactionEvent e) {
  /* Only references if Image is NEW */
  RowSet newImageUsagesBeforePost = null;
  if (getPostState() == STATUS_NEW) {
    // Store the rowset of imageUsages related
    // to this new image before calling super
    newImageUsagesBeforePost = (RowSet)getImageUsages();
  }
  super.postChanges(e);
  if (newImageUsagesBeforePost != null) {
    adjustImageUsages(newImageUsagesBeforePost);
  }
}
```

4. Use Import Assistance to import `oracle.jbo.RowSet`.
5. Implement the `adjustImageUsages()` method as follows:

```
private void adjustImageUsages(RowSet newImageUsagesBeforePost) {
  Number newFkValue = getImageId().getSequenceNumber();
  while (newImageUsagesBeforePost.hasNext()) {
    ImageUsagesImpl imageUsage =
```

```
        (ImageUsagesImpl) newImageUsagesBeforePost.next();
      imageUsage.setImageId(newFkValue);
    }
  }
```

Additional Information: This method will have syntax errors, which you will fix in the next step. It processes the row set of image usages that was stored away in the modified `postChanges()` method. This list of rows is then processed and the newly allocated DBSequence key assigned to the image is set as the ImageId in each ImageUsages row.

6. Manually add `oracle.jbo.domain.Number` to the import block.
7. Open the `ImageUsagesImpl` class and select the **Source | Override Methods** menu option. Use the checkbox to override the `postChanges()` method.
8. Implement the `postChanges()` method as follows:

```
@Override
public void postChanges(TransactionEvent e) {
  ImagesImpl image = getImages();
  if (STATUS_NEW == image.getPostState()) {
    image.postChanges(e);
  }
  super.postChanges(e);
}
```

Additional Information: If a particular ImageUsages entity object instance is associated with a new Images instance, this ensures that the Images instance is posted (and all its associated ImageUsages are updated) before the ImageUsages instance is posted.

Create an Upload Listener to Copy the File and Call the Service Method

In this section, you will create a method in a managed bean to process uploaded image information and call the service method to insert the appropriate database rows. You will configure this method to fire whenever the user requests a file upload on the add image page.

1. In the ViewController project, find addImage.jsff and open it in an editor.
2. Switch to the Bindings view in the editor.
3. In the Bindings area, click the "Create control binding" (green plus "+") button to open the Insert Item dialog.
4. Select methodAction and click OK.

   Additional Information: This will be a binding to the service method you created in the preceding section; it will allow the listener to invoke the service method.
5. The Create Action Binding dialog opens. Select TuhraServiceDataControl.

   Additional Information: Because the application module contains only one service method, the Operation will be prepopulated with that method. If you don't see the method, close the dialog, refresh the Data Controls panel, and then try again.
6. Click OK to create an operation binding, createNewImageForEmployee, bound to the service method.

7. Open `tuhra.view.backing.ImageUploadBean`.
8. Implement the `fileUploadedListener()` method as follows:

```
public void fileUploadedListener(ValueChangeEvent valueChangeEvent) {
  UploadedFile file = (UploadedFile)valueChangeEvent.getNewValue();
  if (file != null) {
    String fileName = file.getFilename();
    setUploadedImageName("/images/" + fileName);
    copyFileToImagesDir(file);
    insertRows();
  }
}
```

Additional Information: After retrieving the UploadedFile object from the event (that is, the user submitting a new file path for uploading), and setting the uploadedImageName field to match the relative path of the destination for the upload, this method calls two other methods that have not yet been defined, so all will show up as compile errors. `copyFileToImagesDir()` will actually handle the file upload, and `insertRows()` will call the service method to ensure that the new image and image usage rows are created.

9. Using code assistance, generate stubs for each of the nonexistent methods.

Additional Information: You can click the red light bulb in the margin to generate the methods.

10. Implement the `copyFileToImagesDir()` method as follows (not including line numbers):

```
01: private void copyFileToImagesDir(UploadedFile file) {
02:   ServletContext servletCtx = (ServletContext)
03:     FacesContext.getCurrentInstance().getExternalContext().getContext();
04:   String imageDirPath = servletCtx.getRealPath("/images");
05:   try {
06:     InputStream is = file.getInputStream();
07:     OutputStream os =
08:       new FileOutputStream(imageDirPath + "/" + file.getFilename());
09:     int readData;
10:     while ((readData = is.read()) != -1) {
11:       os.write(readData);
12:     }
13:     is.close();
14:     os.close();
15:   } catch (IOException ex) {
16:     ex.printStackTrace();
17:   }
18: }
```

Additional Information: This method will contain many syntax errors, because many of the classes aren't yet imported. You will import the classes in the next step. This method goes through the following steps:

- **Lines 1–4** Find the real directory on the server that corresponds to the relative path "/images." The file needs to be copied to that directory, so that the application, in the future, can access it through the relative path.

- **Line 6** Opens an input stream for the uploaded image, through which its contents can be read.
- **Lines 7–8** Open an output stream for the target location, through which the contents of the new copy can be written.
- **Lines 10–12** Copy the image data from the input stream to the output stream. Input streams are read in chunks (the size can be configured, but that is not necessary for these relatively small images). These chunks are positive integers that encode segments of data. When the last data has been read, the next call to `InputStream.read()` will return a value of –1; when that happens, the loop terminates. JDeveloper will warn you about this line, because assignments inside conditional tests (in this case, `readData = is.read()`) are usually mistakes; generally, the developer meant to type the equality operator == instead of the assignment operator. However, in this case, the loop is using a little-used feature of the assignment operator: in addition to assigning the value of the expression on the right to the variable on the left, it returns that value; so, when `is.read()` evaluates to –1, `readData = is.read()` also evaluates to –1.
- **Lines 13–14** Close the input stream and output stream, releasing the file resources.
- **Lines 15–17** Deal with I/O exceptions such as the target location not being writable. In this simple application, they print a stack trace of the exception to the console.

  In a more sophisticated application, you might include validation such as whether the target file already exists, whether the file to upload is really an image, and whether it falls within a certain size limit.

11. Use import assistance to import the following classes:
    - `javax.servlet.ServletContext`
    - `javax.faces.context.FacesContext`
    - `java.io.InputStream`
    - `java.io.OutputStream`
    - `java.io.FileOutputStream`
    - `java.io.IOException`
12. Implement the `insertRows()` method as follows (not including line numbers):

```
01: private void insertRows() {
02:   AdfFacesContext afctx = AdfFacesContext.getCurrentInstance();
03:   Map<String, Object> pfParams = afctx.getPageFlowScope();
04:   Number empId = (Number)pfParams.get("currentEmpId");
05:   OperationBinding insImage =
06:     getBindings().getOperationBinding("createNewImageForEmployee");
07:   Map args = insImage.getParamsMap();
08:   args.put("employeeId", empId);
09:   args.put("imageName", uploadedImageName);
10:   insImage.execute();
11: }
```

Additional Information: This method will also contain syntax errors due to missing imports (you will import the classes in the next step). The method goes through the following process:

- **Lines 2–3** Retrieve the page flow scope.
- **Line 4** Retrieves the value of the page flow–scoped variable "currentEmpId." In the section "Create a Task Flow for the Dialog," you set this variable to be the parameter passed into the page flow.
- **Lines 5–6** Retrieve the operation binding called "createNewImageForEmployee" from the binding context. In steps 3–6 of this section, you created that binding for the service method `createNewImageForEmployee()`.
- **Line 7** Gets the map that holds parameters for the operation binding.
- **Lines 8–9** Set the parameters for the operation binding.
- **Line 10** Executes the operation, creating the AllEmployeeImages view row.

13. Use import assistance to import the following classes:
    - `oracle.adf.view.rich.context.AdfFacesContext`
    - `java.util.Map`
    - `oracle.binding.OperationBinding`
14. Manually import `oracle.jbo.domain.Number`.
15. Open templateTest.jspx in an editor.
16. In the Structure window, find and select the `af:form` component.
17. Set the *UsesUpload* property to "true."

    Additional Information: For an upload component to work properly, the form containing it must have the attribute `usesUpload="true"`. Since the form is at the JSP page level, rather than the fragment level, to see the popup behavior from the test page requires that you set the value on the test page's form. When, later in this chapter, you hook the editEmployee fragment into the main application, you will need to repeat steps 15–17 for the correct application page.

    Before you can test the upload, you need to make a small configuration change to the application to make sure that the WebLogic application server allows you to upload the image into the running application.

18. In the ViewController project, open the New Gallery and create a WebLogic deployment descriptor (in the General \ Deployment Descriptors category).
19. In the Select Descriptor step of the Create WebLogic Deployment Descriptor Wizard select weblogic.xml as the descriptor type. Click Next.
20. Select 10.3 as the version of the descriptor and Finish the wizard.
21. The new weblogic.xml file will be created in the WEB-INF directory. Open it and switch to Source view. Replace the contents of the XML file with the following (note the xsi:schemaLocation entry should all be on one line):

```
<?xml version = '1.0' encoding = 'windows-1252'?>
<weblogic-web-app xmlns:xsi="http://www.w3.org/2001/XMLSchema-instance"
                  xsi:schemaLocation=
                        "http://www.bea.com/ns/weblogic/weblogic-web-app
http://www.bea.com/ns/weblogic/weblogic-web-app/1.0/weblogic-web-app.xsd"
                  xmlns="http://www.bea.com/ns/weblogic/weblogic-web-app">
  <container-descriptor>
```

```
    <show-archived-real-path-enabled>true</show-archived-real-path-enabled>
  </container-descriptor>
</weblogic-web-app>
```

Additional Information: The show-archived-real-path-enabled switch allows the call to `getRealPath("/images")` from the Servlet Context to return a suitable location for the image upload, even though the real image directory is packaged within a WAR file by the deploy process and is not directly writable. Without this switch, the call will return null and the upload will fail.

22. Run templateTest.jspx.
23. When the page appears, click "Manage Images."
24. When the train loads, click Browse, find an image file on your local drive, and click OK.

    Additional Information: The image is now uploaded and will display.
25. Close the browser.

What Did You Just Do? You implemented the functionality of the add image page, which included doing the following:

- Creating file upload functionality, including a listener that reacts when a file is uploaded
- Implementing an application module–level service method to create database rows to keep track of uploaded files
- Implementing functionality to keep the new ImageUsages and Images rows in synch during and after posting to the database
- Calling the service method from a managed bean

What Could You Do Next? The functionality you created in the section, "Fix Association Posting Behavior" will work to keep ImageUsages and Images in synch after posting, but it is not a general solution to the problem of how to post new entities in non-composition associations that involve DBSequence attributes. Chapter 6, in the section "The DBSequence Domain," contains a technique for doing this using a custom entity definition framework class. You could use the information there to implement a framework-level solution; if you do that, you will not need the code you added to `ImagesImpl` or `ImageUsagesImpl`. If you attempt this, remember that when you register a custom framework class after creating entity object definitions, you must "touch" each definition (such as by opening the Java Options dialog and immediately dismissing it by clicking "OK") so that they will use the new class.

IV. Implement the Set Default Image Page

In this phase, you will add details and functionality to the second train stop: the set default image page, which allows the user to select an image for the current employee and set it as the employee's default image.

Lay Out the Form Components

In this section, you will lay out the UI components for the set default image page, although many of them will not be functional until a later section.

1. Open the setDefaultImage.jsff page fragment in the visual editor.
2. Drop a Panel Group Layout into the trainContent area of the page, and set its *Layout* property to "vertical."
3. Drop an Output Formatted into the Panel Group Layout.
4. Set the following properties on the Output Formatted component:
   StyleUsage as "instruction"
   Value as "Select the required picture for #{bindings.FirstName.inputValue} #{bindings.LastName.inputValue} and drag it onto the Default Picture target."
5. In the Data Controls panel of the Application Navigator, drag TuhraServiceControl\EditEmployee\FirstName after the `af:outputFormatted` component and drop it as an ADF Output Text.
6. Delete the ADF Output Text you just created.

   Additional Information: Steps 5–6 represent a shortcut to creating a binding: Bindings are created as side-effects of dragging elements from the Data Controls panel onto a page to create a UI component. When the component is deleted, the binding remains if there is more than one reference to it in the page. In this case, the Output Formatted created in steps 3–4 refers to the binding with the expression `#{bindings.FirstName.inputValue}`.
7. Repeat steps 5–6 for the LastName attribute.
8. Drag a Spacer from the Component Palette to after the Output Formatted, and set its *Height* to "5."
9. Drop another Panel Group Layout after the spacer.
10. Set the following properties on the new (inner) Panel Group Layout:
    Layout as "horizontal"
    Halign as "center"
    InlineStyle as "height:260.0px;"
11. In the Data Controls panel, find the TuhraServiceDataControl\EditEmployee\AllEmployeeImages collection and drag it onto the inner Panel Group Layout. Drop it as an ADF Read-Only Table to open the Edit Table Columns dialog.
12. In the Edit Table Columns dialog, remove all columns except ImageId and Image and click OK to create the table.
13. Select the column containing ImageIds and delete it.

    Additional Information: Although you have deleted this column, it remains as an attribute in the underlying tree binding. This will allow you to access its value later, when you need to set the default image property.
14. Right click the remaining column and select **Go to Source**, to open the source editor with the column highlighted.
15. Find the `af:outputText` component inside the column, and change it to an `af:image` component like the following:

```
<af:image source="#{row.Image}"  id="availableImage"
          shortDesc="Available Image"
          inlineStyle="width:54px; height:54px;"/>
```

TIP
Even when you are working in a code editor, you can use the Property Inspector to edit or add attributes.

16. In the `af:column` surrounding the image, remove the *headerText* attribute, set the column *Width* to "60."
17. In the Structure window, select the `af:table`. Using the Property Inspector, set both the *HorizontalGridVisible* and *VerticalGridVisible* attributes to "false." In the inlineStyle set the *Width* to "60px," the *Height* to "250px," and the *Border Width* to "0px."
18. Return to the design view. The table should appear as follows:

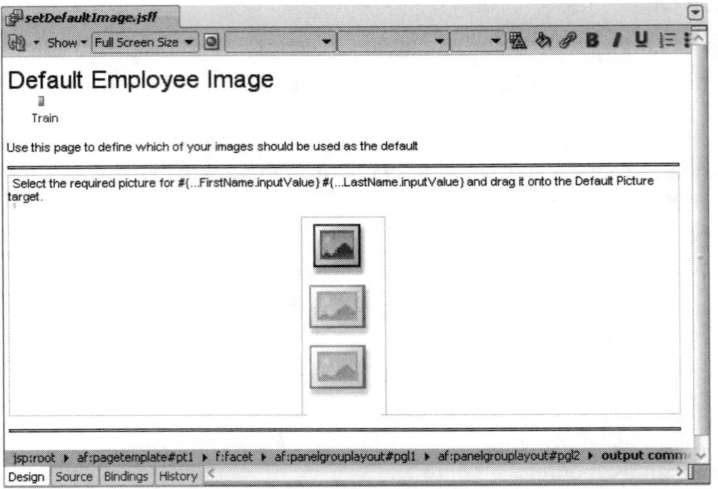

19. In the Structure window, on the `af:table` - t1 node, click **Insert after af:table - t1 | image** from the right-click menu.

    Additional Information: Because of the layout of the page, dragging an image component from the Component Palette into the correct position is difficult; this is an easier option.
20. Set the image's source as "/images/arrow.png"; you can leave the shortDesc attribute blank.
21. Drop a panel box after the new image, and set the following properties on the panel box:
    Text as "Drag Image Here"
    ShowDisclosure as "false"

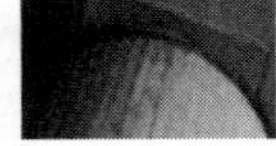

TIP
To ensure that the panel box is directly after the image and still inside the inner panel group, you may find it easier to drop the panel box into the Structure pane rather than the visual editor.

22. Drag an image into the panel box, leaving its source and short description blank for now.
23. Set the *Width* and *Height* properties of the picture to 180px, via the *inlineStyle* property
24. Click Save All.

Create a Backing Bean for the Set Default Image Page

In this section, you will create a backing bean for the set default image page. This bean will (in a later phase) hold the uploaded file and execute the operation that will create the new AllEmployeeImages row for the new image.

1. Create a class in the `tuhra.view.backing` package, named "DefaultImageSelectionBean" and extending `tuhra.view.framework.TuhraBackingBean`.
2. Make the class implement the `java.io.Serializable` interface.
3. Re-open imageLOV-flow.xml, and drag a managed bean from the Source Elements section of the Component Palette onto the task flow to open the Insert Managed Bean dialog.

   Additional Information: This technique is a shortcut to creating the same managed bean via the Overview panel of the editor.
4. Specify the following properties in the dialog:
   Managed Bean Name as "defaultImageSelectionBB"
   Managed Bean Class as "tuhra.view.backing.DefaultImageSelectionBean"
   Managed Bean Scope as "pageFlow"
5. Click Save All.

Add Drag-and-Drop Capabilities

In this section, you will use the managed bean created in the preceding section to store the path of the selected image, and will use this to enable drag-and-drop functionality.

1. Add a private `String` field to the class, as shown here:

   ```
   private String _selectedImage="/images/newDefaultPlaceholder.png";
   ```
2. Create public getter and setter methods for the field using **Generate Accessors** on the right-click menu.
3. Return to setDefaultImage.jsff.
4. Select the image inside the panel box, and set its *Source* property to "#{pageFlowScope .defaultImageSelectionBB.selectedImage}."

TIP
Using the Expression Builder may be easier than typing in the value.

5. From the Component Palette (Operations), drop a Collection Drag Source into the table. You may find this easiest if you drag onto the table in the Structure window.

   Additional Information: This specifies that the table is a potential source for drag-and-drop operations.
6. Set the following properties on the Collection Drag Source:
   Actions as "COPY"
   ModelName as "empImagesModel"

Additional Information: Setting the *actions* attribute to "COPY" ensures that, when the object is dropped, the event generated will have `DnDEvent.COPY` as its action, rather than prompting the user to choose an action (other possible actions include `DnDEvent.MOVE` and `DnDEvent.LINK`). The *modelName* attribute is referenced by the drop target; drop targets will only accept drops from drag sources with appropriate *modelName* values.

7. From the Component Palette, drop a Drop Target into the panel box (with the title Drag Image Here) to open the "Insert Drop Target" dialog.

   Additional Information: Any component containing a Drop Target will act as a target area for drag-and-drop, so this will make the entire panel box a target area. Notice that you only need to use an `af:dropTarget`, not an `af:collectionDropTarget`, as the target is a single component, not a collection-containing component such as a table.

8. Select Edit from the pulldown list beside the *DropListener* field in the Insert Drop Target dialog, to open the EditProperty: DropListener dialog.
9. Select defaultImageSelectionBB as the managed bean, and create a method, with "dragAndDropHandler" as the method name.

   Additional Information: This will create a method stub, `DefaultImageSelectionBean.dragAndDropHandler()`, which the application will call whenever an image is dropped onto the target area.

10. Click OK in each dialog, finishing by clicking OK in the Insert Drop Target dialog. The Insert Data Flavor dialog opens automatically.
11. Set the *FlavorClass* field to "org.apache.myfaces.trinidad.model.RowKeySet" and click OK.

    Additional Information: A RowKeySet represents one or more dragged rows (in this case, it will only be one row, because the table was not generated to support multiple row selection).

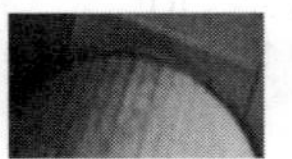

TIP
It may be easier to search for the class "RowKeySet" than to type the entire package-qualified name.

12. When the data flavor component is generated, use the Property Inspector to set its *Discriminant* property to "empImagesModel." The `af:dataFlavor` component can be found nested within the `af:dropTarget`.

    Additional Information: This property references the *modelName* attribute set in Step 6, ensuring that other drag sources cannot be dropped on this target.

13. Click Save All.

Create a Service Method to Set the Default Image

In this section, you will create a view row–level service method that will unset the current default image (if any) and set a new image as the default.

1. In the Model project, in the `tuhra.model.queries.main` package, expand the AllEmployees view object definition node, and open the `AllEmployeesRowImpl` class in an editor.

2. Add the following method:

```
01: public void defineDefaultImage(Number newDefaultImageId) {
02:   Number oldDefaultImageId =
03:     getImageId() == null ? null : getImageId().getSequenceNumber();
04:   if (newDefaultImageId != null &&
05:       !newDefaultImageId.equals(oldDefaultImageId)) {
06:     RowSet imageRows = (RowSet) getAllEmployeeImages();
07:     AllEmployeeImagesRowImpl oldDefaultImageRow =
08:       findImageUsagesRowByKey(imageRows, oldDefaultImageId);
09:     AllEmployeeImagesRowImpl newDefaultImageRow =
10:       findImageUsagesRowByKey(imageRows, newDefaultImageId);
11:     if (newDefaultImageRow != null) {
12:       newDefaultImageRow.setDefaultImage("Y");
13:       if (oldDefaultImageRow != null) {
14:         oldDefaultImageRow.setDefaultImage("N");
15:       }
16:       setEntity(3, newDefaultImageRow.getEmployeeImageUsages());
17:       setEntity(4, newDefaultImageRow.getImages());
18:     }
19:   }
20: }
```

Additional Information: Lines 8 and 10 will contain syntax errors, because they rely on a helper method you will create in the next step. The method executes the following steps:

- **Lines 2–3** determine the image ID of the current default image.
- **Lines 4–5** check whether a new default image has really been specified; if not, the method need do nothing.
- **Line 6** calls a view link accessor method to retrieve the AllEmployeeImages rows for this employee. For more information on view link accessor methods, see Chapter 7.
- **Lines 7–10** call a helper method that you will create in the next step. The method will find the old and new image rows (based on the old and new image IDs). The helper method will return null if the row is not found, that is, if the parameter is not an image ID for one of this employee's images.
- **Line 11** checks to ensure that the new default image ID really did correspond to an image for this employee.
- **Lines 12–14** set the newly selected image to be the default and, if there was an old default image, set it to not be the default.
- **Lines 16–17** set the EmployeesImageUsages and Images entity object usages of the AllEmployees view row to point at the new default ImageUsages and Images entity object instances. Although when AllEmployees' query was originally executed, the employee was joined to his or her default image, just marking a different image as default will not change the already-queried row. `AllEmployeeImagesRowImpl.getEmployeeImageUsages()` and `AllEmployeeImagesRowImpl.getImages()` retrieve the entity object instances from the AllEmployeeImages row, and `ViewRowImpl.setEntity()` sets the entity usage at the specified index to point to the entity object. (You can confirm that the EmployeesImageUsages usage is at index 3 and the Images usage is at index 4 by checking the automatically

generated methods `AllEmployeesRowImpl.getEmployeeImageUsages()` and `AllEmployeesRowImpl.getImages()`.)

3. Implement the `findImageUsagesRowByKey()` method as follows:

```
private AllEmployeeImagesRowImpl findImageUsagesRowByKey(RowSet imageRows,
                                                         Number imageId) {
  AllEmployeeImagesRowImpl retRow = null;
  Key key =
    new Key(new Object[] { getEmployeeId().getSequenceNumber(), imageId, "E" });
  Row[] hits = imageRows.findByKey(key, 1);
  if (hits.length > 0) {
    retRow = (AllEmployeeImagesRowImpl)hits[0];
  }
  return retRow;
}
```

CAUTION

The ordering of the elements in the array passed to the Key constructor assumes that the AssociatedId, ImageId, and UsageType attributes in the AllEmployeeImages view object definition are present in that order: with AssociatedId before ImageId, and ImageId before UsageType (they do not need to appear consecutively). Check and ensure this is the case; if not, either re-order the attributes in AllEmployeeImages to match this order, or re-order the elements in the array passed to the Key constructor to match the order that those attributes have in the view object definition.

Additional Information: This method uses the EmployeeId of the current employee, the supplied ImageId, and the discriminator "E" (for employee image usages) to find a particular image row by its key. The method will have syntax errors because of the unimported `Key` class; you will rectify this in the next step.

4. Use Import Assistance to import `oracle.jbo.Key`.
5. Open the AllEmployees view object definition in the editor.
6. Select the Java tab, and click the Edit button for the Client Row Interface panel to open the Edit Client Row Interface dialog.
7. Shuttle the `defineDefaultImage(Number):void` method from the Available list to the Selected list.
8. Click OK to close the dialog.
9. Click Save All.

Implement a Drop Listener to Call the Service Method

In this section, you will implement the drop listener created in the section "Add Drag-and-Drop Capabilities." This listener will analyze the drop event to discover the dragged image's ID and path, display the selected image in the drop target, and call the service method created in the preceding section to set the dropped image as the new default for the employee.

1. In the ViewController project, find setDefaultImage.jsff and open it in an editor.

2. Select the Bindings tab of the editor.
3. Click the "Create control binding" (green "+") button in the Bindings list to open the Insert Item dialog.
4. Select methodAction and click OK to open the Create Action Binding dialog.
5. Select "EditEmployeeIterator" from the *Select an Iterator* pulldown list.

   Additional Information: JDeveloper automatically selects the view row–level service method `defineDefaultImage(Number)` for the Operation list, because it is the only exported method on the AllEmployees view object definition, at either the view object or view row level.
6. Click OK to close the dialog.

   Additional Information: This creates an operation binding, defineDefaultImage, bound to the service method.
7. Open `tuhra.view.backing.DefaultImageSelectionBean`, and find the `dragAndDropHandler()` method.

   Additional Information: This method stub was created when you created the Drop Target component in the section "Add Drag-and-Drop Capabilities."
8. Implement the method as follows:

```
01: public DnDAction dragAndDropHandler(DropEvent dropEvent) {
02:   FacesCtrlHierNodeBinding draggedNode = findDraggedNode(dropEvent);
03:   if (draggedNode != null) {
04:     String imageName = (String)draggedNode.getAttribute("Image");
05:     Number imageId = (Number)draggedNode.getAttribute("ImageId");
06:     if (imageId != null) {
07:       _selectedImage = imageName;
08:       defineDefaultImage(imageId);
09:       return DnDAction.COPY;
10:     }
11:   }
12:   return DnDAction.NONE;
13: }
```

   Additional Information: As before, this method will contain syntax errors until you import classes and generate helper methods. The method executes the following steps:

   - **Line 2** Calls a helper method that you will implement in a later step, `findDraggedNode()`. This method will use information contained in the drop event to find the dragged row's node binding.
   - **Lines 4–5** Extract the image path and image ID from the node binding.
   - **Line 7** Sets the field selectedImage, which is used as the source of the image to be displayed in the drop target area, to be the extracted image path.
   - **Line 8** Calls a helper method that you will implement in a later step, `defineDefaultImage()`. This method will set parameters for and execute the defineDefaultImage operation binding.
9. Use import assistance to import `oracle.adfinternal.view.faces.model.binding.FacesCtrlHierNodeBinding`.
10. Manually import `oracle.jbo.domain.Number`.

11. Use code assistance to generate stubs for the helper methods.

12. Implement the `findDraggedNode()` method as follows:

```
01: private FacesCtrlHierNodeBinding findDraggedNode(DropEvent dropEvent) {
02:   FacesCtrlHierNodeBinding node = null;
03:   Transferable transferable = dropEvent.getTransferable();
04:   DataFlavor<RowKeySet> rowKeySetFlavor =
05:     DataFlavor.getDataFlavor(RowKeySet.class, "empImagesModel");
06:   RowKeySet rowKeySet = transferable.getData(rowKeySetFlavor);
07:   if (rowKeySet != null) {
08:     CollectionModel dragModel = transferable.getData(CollectionModel.class);
09:     if (dragModel != null) {
10:       Object currKey = rowKeySet.iterator().next();
11:       dragModel.setRowKey(currKey);
12:       node = (FacesCtrlHierNodeBinding)dragModel.getRowData();
13:     }
14:   }
15:   return node;
16: }
```

Additional Information: This method performs the following actions:

- **Line 3** Retrieves the drop event's `Transferable` object, which encapsulates the thing dropped.
- **Lines 4–6** Retrieve the `RowKeySet` (encapsulating the dragged row or rows) from the Transferable object. The `DataFlavor` must be specified to handle cases where multiple drag sources could be dropped on the drop target.
- **Line 8** Retrieves the underlying data (encapsulated as a `CollectionModel`) from the RowKeySet.
- **Lines 10–11** Advance the collection model to its first row. Since, in this case, only one row can be dragged and dropped, this is guaranteed to be the correct row.
- **Line 12** Extracts the first row from the `CollectionModel`.
- **Line 15** Returns the dragged row's data, or null if the data could not be found.

13. Use import assistance to import the following classes:

- `oracle.adf.view.rich.datatransfer.Transferable`
- `oracle.adf.view.rich.datatransfer.DataFlavor`
- `org.apache.myfaces.trinidad.model.RowKeySet`
- `org.apache.myfaces.trinidad.model.CollectionModel`

14. Implement the `defineDefaultImage()` method as follows:

```
private void defineDefaultImage(Number imageId) {
  OperationBinding setDefault =
    getBindings().getOperationBinding("defineDefaultImage");
  Map args = setDefault.getParamsMap();
  args.put("newDefaultImageId", imageId);
  setDefault.execute();
}
```

Additional Information: This method is very similar to the `insertRows()` method you created in step 12 of the section "Create an Upload Listener to Copy the File and Call the Service Method."

15. Import the appropriate classes, just as in step 13 of the section "Create an Upload Listener to Copy the File and Call the Service Method."
16. Click Save All.
17. Run templateTest.jspx.
18. When the browser opens, click Manage Images to open the popup.
19. On the "Upload a New Image" train stop, upload an image from your computer and click Next.
20. On the Edit Default Image page, drag the picture into the "Drag Image Here" area. The dialog should appear like Figure 20-3 as shown at the start of this chapter.

    Additional Information: If you uploaded a different image when you last run the application, you can see that it is not available in the source table; only the images added in the preceding step will show. This is because the new Image and ImageUsages rows were never committed to the database. You will enable committing to the database in the following section.
21. Click Finish.
22. Close the browser.

Add Commit Functionality

In this section, you will remove the navigation buttons from the editEmployee page and add a way of committing your changes to the database:

1. Re-open the editEmployee.jsff fragment in the design editor.
2. Find the Panel Form Layout footer facet containing both the submit button and the `af:panelGroupLayout` that contains the four navigation buttons, and delete it.

   Additional Information: This application will not allow navigation between employees directly on the editEmployees page, and there is no reason to submit the form without attempting to commit it to the database.
3. Open the tuhraTemplate.jspx template.
4. Drag a new Menu from the Component Palette onto the menu bar, and set its *Text* property to "Action."
5. In the Data Controls panel of the Application Navigator, expand TuhraServiceDataControl, and expand the Operations node beneath it.
6. Drag the Commit operation into the Action menu as an ADF menu item.
7. Set the following properties on the menu item:
   Text as "Save"
   Disabled as "<default> (false)" (use the "Reset to Default" option from the pulldown beside the property)
8. Click Save All.
9. Run templateTest.jspx. Continue through the train, adding an image and setting a default image, and click Finish. Note that all behavior is as expected.

What Did You Just Do? You implemented the functionality of the set default image page, which included doing the following:

- Creating drag-and-drop functionality, including a listener that reacts to the drop event
- Implementing a view row–level service method to manipulate the view row's detail rows
- Calling the service method from a managed bean
- Adding database commit functionality to the global template

What Could You Do Next? One possible next step would be to change the default drop target image so that, if the employee already had an existing default image, it would show the existing image. You could also enable single-selection in the table and turn the arrow on the page into an active component, where selecting a row and clicking the arrow would be equivalent to dragging the row onto the drop target.

V. Integrate the Edit Page with the Rest of the Application

The Edit page is now complete. In this phase, you will create a connection between the Employee Search page and the edit page, allowing users to edit employees they have found.

Create a Link from the Search Page to the Edit Page

In this section, you will create a JSF page to hold the Edit Employee fragment, and will implement the primary, unbounded control flow of the application.

1. Open the unbounded task flow adfc-config.xml.
2. Drag the page employeeSearch.jspx from the Application Navigator onto the task flow to create a view activity called "employeeSearch."
3. Drag a wildcard control-flow rule onto the diagram.
4. Create a control-flow case from that rule to the employeeSearch activity. Call this control-flow case "search."

   Additional Information: Specific control-flow cases between view activities will override the control-flow cases from a wildcard control flow rule, but this means that any action that does not trigger a specific control-flow case elsewhere will open the Employees Search page.
5. Drag a new view activity from the Component Palette onto the diagram, and name it employeeEdit.
6. Create a control-flow case from employeeSearch to employeeEdit, named "edit."
7. Double click the employeeEdit view activity to implement the page. Use tuhraTemplate as the page template.
8. In the Structure window, find and select the `af:form` component.

9. Set the component's *UsesUpload* property to "true."

   Additional Information: This is the same property as you set on the form inside templateTest.jspx in the section "Create an Upload Listener to Copy the File and Call the Service Method."

10. Open the employeeSearch.jspx page.
11. In the Structure pane, find and select the `af:panelSplitter` component.
12. Press CTRL-C to copy the component and its subtree.
13. Return to the employeeEdit.jspx page.
14. Select the "content" facet and press CTRL-V to paste the component and its subtree.
15. Select the command link containing the "Search" image and label, and set its *Action* property to "search."

    Additional Information: This action will fall back to the wildcard control flow rule and return the user to the Employee Search page.

16. Change the *value* property of the `af:outputLabel` that forms the label of the navigation icon so that it reads, "Return to Employee Search."
17. Select the command link containing the "View By Department" image and label, and delete it.
18. Delete the region in the right-hand pane of the splitter.
19. Drop editEmployee-flow into the "second" facet as a region.
20. Open the searchEmployees-flow task flow.
21. From the Component Palette, drop a Parent Action activity onto the diagram, and name it "parentEdit."

    Additional Information: This activity will allow an action in searchEmployees-flow to trigger navigation in the parent task flow, adfc-config.

22. Create a control flow case from searchUI to parentEdit, and name it "edit."
23. Set the *Parent Outcome* property of the parentEdit activity to "edit."

    Additional Information: This will cause adfc-config to follow the "edit" control flow case whenever searchEmployees-flow follows its own "edit" control flow case.

24. Open the searchUI.jsff page fragment.
25. Select the Export menu, and change its *Text* to "Actions."
26. Drop a Menu Item into the menu, and set the following properties on it:
    Text as "Edit Employee"
    Action as "edit"
27. Expand the `af:table` and its contextMenu facet. Find the `af:menu` inside the `af:popup` underneath it.
28. Drop a Menu Item into the `af:menu`, and set its properties as in Step 26.
29. Click Save All.
30. Re-open the adfc-config task flow, and run the employeeSearch activity.
31. When the browser opens, run a search with no criteria.

32. From David Austin's row, select **Edit Employee** from the right-click menu.

    Additional Information: The edit page opens, as expected. However, the selected employee is not David Austin, but the first employee in the query results, Ellen Abel. This is because currently, there is no way to pass information about which employee to edit from one task flow to the other.

33. Close the browser.

Parameterize the Edit Employee Task Flow

In order to specify a particular employee for the Edit Employee task flow to edit, you must parameterize the task flow to accept an employee ID. In this section, you will parameterize the task flow.

1. Open the editEmployee-flow task flow.
2. Select the Overview tab, and the Parameters tab within it.
3. Click the Add (green plus "+") button beside the Input Parameter Definitions panel to add a parameter.
4. Name the parameter "employeeId" and accept the default *Value* (the place this parameter will be stored, which is `#{pageFlowScope.employeeId}`.
5. Click the Diagram tab.
6. From the Component Palette, drop a Router activity onto the diagram to the left of the existing editEmployee View activity, and name it "checkForExplicitID."

   Additional Information: This router serves no direct purpose in the TUHRA application, because the application will always follow the same case from the router. It is presented as an example of how to add conditional routing to a task flow.

7. On the router, select **Mark Activity | Default Activity** from the right-click menu to make the router the starting activity of the task flow.
8. Reroute the "refresh" control flow case from the wildcard control flow rule so that it points to the router.
9. Create a control flow case from the router to the editEmployee view activity, and name it "currentUser."
10. Set the router's *Default Outcome* property to "currentUser."
11. Using the Property Inspector, add a case to the router, and set the following properties on it:
    Expression as "#{!empty pageFlowScope.employeeId}"
    Outcome as "byId"

    Additional Information: The expression will evaluate to true when an ID has been passed to the task flow, which is always the case when the task flow is called within the TUHRA application. The outcome refers to a control flow case that you will create shortly.

Restrict the EditEmployee View Object Instance's Query Using the Parameters

In this section, you will create a service method to restrict an instance of the AllEmployees view object definition to contain one employee only. The service method will accept a single parameter, the employee ID, that you will pass in through the task flow.

1. In the Model project, open the AllEmployees view object definition in an editor, and select the Query tab.
2. Click the "Create a new bind variable" (green plus "+") button beside the Bind Variables panel (you may have to scroll down the editor to see this section) to open the Bind Variable dialog.
3. Set the following properties in the dialog (leave the others as their defaults), and click OK:
   Name as "RestrictEmployeeId"
   Type as "Number"
   Required as unchecked
4. Click the "Create new view criteria" (green "+" button) beside the View Criteria panel to open the Create View Criteria dialog.
5. Name the view criteria object "EmployeeByIdCriteria."
6. Add an item, and set its properties as follows:
   Attribute as "EmployeeId"
   Operator as "Equal to"
   Operand as "Bind Variable"
   Parameter as "RestrictEmployeeId"
   Validation as "Required"
7. Click OK to create the view criteria object.
8. Run the TuhraService application module in the Model project to open the Business Component Browser.
9. When the Business Component Browser opens, double click EditEmployee to open it.
10. Click the Specify View Criteria (binoculars) button on the toolbar for the EditEmployee view object instance.
11. Shuttle EmployeeIdByCriteria from the Available list to the Selected list, and click Find.
12. When the Bind Variables dialog appears, set the value of the bind variable to 101 (the employee ID for Nina Kochhar) and click OK.

    Additional Information: Nina Kochhar's record is the only one displayed. The view criteria object, together with the bind variable, restricted the query to include only the employee with ID 101.
13. Close the Business Component Browser.
14. Click the Java tab in the AllEmployees editor, and click the "Edit java options" (pencil) button in the Java Classes section to open the Select Java Options dialog.
15. Select "Generate View Object Class: AllEmployeesImpl" and "Include bind variable accessors." Do not deselect any already-selected options.
16. Click OK to generate the view object class.
17. Open the newly created class, `AllEmployeesImpl`, in an editor.
18. Add the following static field to AllEmployeesImpl:

    ```
    private static final String EMPLOYEE_BY_ID_CRITERIA = "EmployeeByIdCriteria";
    ```

    Additional Information: "AllEmployeesWhereCriteria" is the name of the default view criteria object created from AllEmployees' declarative where clause. "EmployeeByIdCriteria" is the new named view criteria object you created.

19. Add the following method to AllEmployeesImpl:

```
public void queryEmployeeById(Number id) {
  if (id != null) {
    setApplyViewCriteriaName(EMPLOYEE_BY_ID_CRITERIA);
    setRestrictEmployeeId(id);
    executeQuery();
  }
}
```

    Additional Information: This method applies the named view criteria, sets the bind variable, and re-executes the query.

20. Return to the editor for the view object definition, and click the "Edit view client object interface" (pencil) button in the Client Interface section.
21. Expose the `queryEmployeeById(Number)` method and click OK.
22. In the View Controller project, return to the editEmployee-flow task flow.
23. In the Data Controls panel of the navigator, select **Refresh** from the right-click menu.
24. Expand TuhraServiceDataControl \ EditEmployee.
25. Drag the queryEmployeeById(Number) operation onto the editEmployee-flow diagram.
26. Set the value of the parameter to `#{pageFlowScope.employeeId}` and click OK.

    Additional Information: This creates an operation binding for the service method, and creates a method call activity that will execute it with a parameter taken from the page flow scope.

27. Create a control flow case named "byId" from the router to the method call.
28. Create a control flow case from the method call to the editEmployee view activity. Accept the default name of "queryEmployeeById."

    Additional Information: The method call activity will call a view-object level service method that will restrict the EditEmployee view object instance's query to only the employee requested.

29. Click Save All.
30. Open templateTest.jspx in the editor.
31. Delete the region, and re-drag editEmployee-flow onto the page as a region.

    Additional Information: Because you have added a parameter to editEmployee-flow, a dialog opens asking you to specify the parameter value.

32. Specify the parameter value as 101 (the ID for Nina Kochhar) and click OK.
33. Click Save All.
34. Run templateTest.jspx.

    Additional Information: When the browser opens, you can see that Nina Kochhar, rather than Ellen Abel, is the employee displayed.

Pass Parameters to the Edit Employee Task Flow

In this section, you will complete the link between the search and edit pages by passing the appropriate parameter value between the task flows.

1. Open the `tuhra.view.UIManager` Java class.
2. Introduce a new variable called `_editEmployeeId` and generate a getter and a setter for it.

   ```
   private long _editEmployeeId;
   ```
3. Re-open the searchUI.jsff page fragment in an editor.
4. Select the Actions menu. (Reminder you can find this inside the "menus" facet of the `af:panelCollection` surrounding the results table.)
5. In the Structure pane, expand the "af:menu - Actions" node and select the "af:commandMenuItem - Edit Employee" component.
6. Drag a Set Property Listener from the Component Palette onto the `af:commandMenuItem` to open the Insert Set Property Listener dialog.
7. Set the following properties for the listener, and click OK.
   From as "#{bindings.EmployeeId.inputValue.value}"
   To as "#{uiState.editEmployeeId}"
   Type as "action"

   Additional Information: The `af:setPropertyListener` is used here to copy the employee ID to a common known location that the region can read to pass the ID parameter.
8. Now open the bindings editor for the searchUI fragment and double click the EmployeeSearch tree binding. Shuttle the "EmployeeId" to the *Display Attributes* list to make it available in the binding context. Click OK and switch back to the Design view.
9. Repeat steps 4–5 for the "Edit Employee" menu item in the table's context menu. This time use the expression "#{row.EmployeeId.value}" as the *From* value.
10. Open the employeeEdit.jspx page in the editor.
11. Delete the region from the page. You will find this in the second facet of the panelSplitter.
12. Drag the editEmployee-flow task flow into the "second" facet as a region to open the Edit Task Flow Binding dialog.
13. Set the task flow parameter's value to `#{uiState.editEmployeeId}` and click OK.
14. Click Save All.
15. Run the employeeSearch.jspx page.
16. Search for employees, select an employee, and navigate to the edit page using either the context menu or the Actions menu.

    Additional Information: The correct employee is opened in the edit page.
17. Close the browser.

What Did You Just Do? You created navigation between the search and edit components of the application. This involved adding action components in the search page fragments and edit page and to navigate back and forth, parameterizing the editEmployee-flow task flow, and adding set property listeners to extract the parameter from context in the search page.

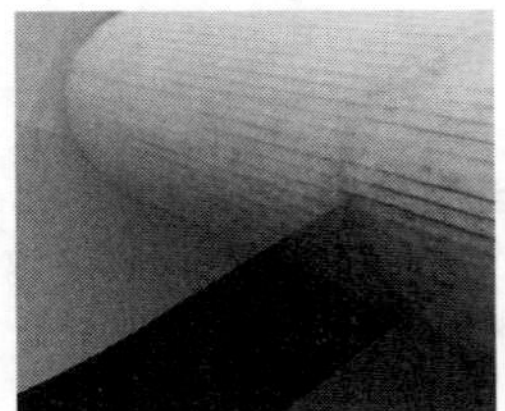

CHAPTER 21

Sample Application: Security

A white door in a hawthorn hedge– / Who lives through there?
A sorcerer? A wicked witch / With serpents in her hair? . . .
A queen with slippers made of ice? / I'd love to see.
A white door in a hawthorn hedge– / I wish I had a key.

—Richard Edwards (1949–), *The Door*

This chapter builds on the application you completed in Chapter 20 and implements authorization and authentication for the application. As shown in Figure 21-1, authorization for the TUHRA application is divided into four logical roles (represented by arrowed boxes): non-authenticated users (Public), the general user role (authenticated users without any specific privileges), the manager role, and the admin role. The application contains no hard-coded user names or group names; instead, these logical roles will be mapped to user and group names at runtime using WebLogic internal LDAP.

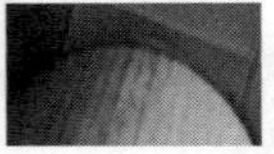

TIP
We recommend always implementing authorization for applications in terms of logical roles and using an identity store such as WebLogic internal LDAP or Oracle Internet Directory (OID) for runtime mapping of users to roles.

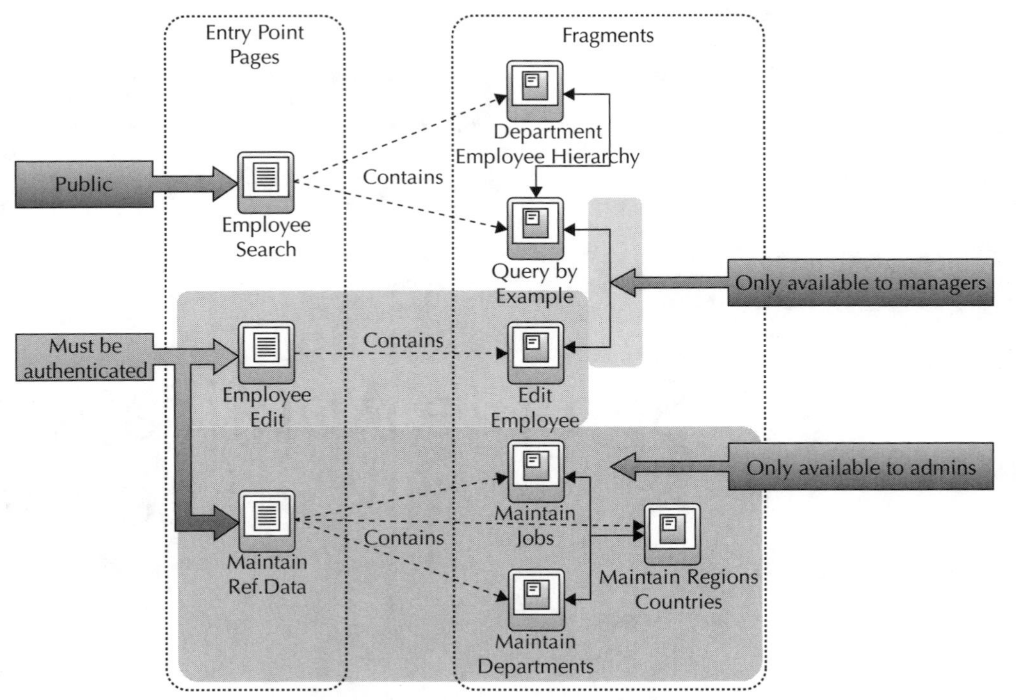

FIGURE 21-1. *Access in the TUHRA application*

The hands-on practice in this chapter sets up security for the sample application, creates a login page, and restricts access to task flows, data, and UI elements based on authorization status. The practice steps through the following phases:

I. Set up security for the application
- Enable ADF security
- Define application roles
- Define a credential store for testing
- Map application roles to credential store roles

II. Implement authorization
- Authorize access to pages
- Create basic management functionality
- Authorize access to task flows
- Authorize access to UI components

III. Implement custom login functionality
- Implement a managed bean to handle login
- Create the login popup
- Create menu options to log in and log out
- Implement a method to handle logout

IV. Access information about the logged-in user
- Create a view object definition to return user information
- Display user information
- Allow a user to edit his/her own records

NOTE
As mentioned throughout this part of the book, you can download a set of starting files for this chapter from the websites mentioned in the "Websites for Sample Files" section in the Introduction.

I. Set Up Security for the Application

Before you can implement the specifics of authorization for the application, you must perform some setup. In this phase, you will enable ADF security and prepare a simple, XML-based identity store for testing purposes.

Enable ADF Security

In this section, you will configure options for security in the TUHRA2 application.

1. With the TUHRA workspace open, select **Application | Secure | Configure ADF Security** to open the Configure ADF Security wizard.
2. On the first page, leave the default selection ("ADF Authentication and Authorization").

3. Click Next. On the "Select authentication type" page, select "Form-Based Authentication" and "Generate Default Pages."

   Additional Information: The various *Authentication Type* options correspond to different ways of authenticating the user:

   - **HTTP Basic Authentication** uses the browser's login functionality to send a user name and password in plain text across HTTP. This is not secure by modern standards but may be required to support certain very old browsers. However, given that ADF Faces only supports the more recent versions of the browsers, this option should never be used for an ADF page.
   - **HTTP Digest Authentication** uses the browser's login functionality to send a user name and encrypted password across HTTP. The server does not decrypt the sent password; rather, the server executes the encryption process on the user's real password and compares the results.
   - **HTTPS Client Authentication** issues an SSL certificate to the browser and requires it for future authentication.
   - **Form-Based Authentication** uses an HTML form, rather than browser functionality, to request user credentials. In a production environment, this type of authentication should only be used when the application is running in HTTPS mode.

   For more information about authentication types and their advantages and disadvantages, you can refer to books about application security, for example, *Core Security Patterns* by Christopher Steel, Ramesh Nagappan, and Ray Lai (Prentice Hall, 2005) and *Enterprise Java Security* by Marco Pistoia, Nataraj Nagaratnam, Larry Koved, and Anthony Nadalin (Addison-Wesley, 2004).

4. Click Next. On the "Enable automatic policy grants" page, leave the default (No Automatic Grants) and click Next.

   Additional Information: The other options automatically create a special testing role called "test-all," with access to all pages and task flows in the application. While this can be useful for testing, you will set up your own security roles in the next section, so it is not necessary to create the test-role now.

5. On the "Specify authenticated welcome" page, select *Redirect Upon Successful Authentication* and set the welcome page to "/employeeSearch.jspx."

   Additional Information: Upon successful authentication, this will send a browser redirect to reroute users to the search page.

6. Click Finish. When the Security Infrastructure Created dialog appears, click OK.

7. Click Save All.

   Additional Information: JDeveloper creates several files to implement security for the application:

   - **login.html** is the default login page created in step 3.
   - **error.html** is the default login error page created in step 3.
   - **jazn-data.xml** will store the security rules or permissions that you will create for the application, as well as providing a simple credential store for testing purposes. This file can be found in the Application Resources section of the Application Navigator, under Descriptors\META-INF.

JDeveloper also updates the following files, which already exist:

- **web.xml** Various security settings such as the selected authentication type and the name of the login and error pages have been added to this file. To view the changes, open the web.xml file and click the Security tab of the Overview editor.
- **weblogic.xml** Recall that you had already defined this file to control some of the WebLogic behavior with respect to handling files for the image upload. If you look at this file now, you will see that a new section called "security-role-assignment" has been created. This section is used to map users (also called "principals") to roles in WebLogic. In this case it is used to map a generic principal called "user" to the WebLogic role "valid-users."

  If you cross-reference with the web.xml file at this point, you will see the security role "valid-users" mentioned there as well; it has been automatically defined for you as a logical-application level role.
- **jps-config.xml** This file defines the high-level configuration of ADF Security. *JPS* in this context stands for "Java Platform Security." This file controls, among other things, where the credential store used for security is located. This file can be found in the Application Resources section of the Application Navigator, under Descriptors\META-INF.
- **adf-config.xml** This is the general ADF configuration file (do not confuse it with the unbounded task flow definition file adfc-config.xml). The changes made here just indicate to ADF that security is now enabled and handled by JPS. This file can be found in the Application Resources section of the Application Navigator, under Descriptors\ADF META-INF.

Define Application Roles

In this section, you will define the logical security roles for the application. As noted in the introduction to this chapter, these roles are distinct from users and groups in your credential store. They are mapped to the store at runtime, allowing for easy change of permissions.

1. In the Application Resources panel of the Navigator, open jazn-data.xml, and select the Overview tab if it is not already selected.
2. Click Custom Policies to open the Edit JPS Identity & Policy Store dialog. Select the Application Policy Store node.
3. Click the New button to create an application security policy. Accept the default name, "tuhra2."

   Additional Information: An application security policy is a collection of logical roles for an application and grants of portions of the application to these roles. In general, you will only have one application security policy per application.
4. In the tree, select the "Application Roles" node under tuhra2.
5. Click Add to open the Add Application Role dialog, and add a role named "user."
6. Repeat step 5 to add roles named "manager" and "admin."
7. Click OK to close the dialog.
8. Click Save All.

Define a Credential Store for Testing

In addition to storing logical roles for an application, jazn-data.xml can be used as a simple credential store, including actual users and/or groups. When an application is deployed in a production environment, we do not recommend using jazn-data.xml as a credential store; rather, the roles within your application should be mapped to roles provided by an external credential store (such as an LDAP server) using runtime mappings created in the application's Java EE container. However, we do recommend adding sample users and groups to jazn-data.xml for testing purposes within JDeveloper, and that is what you will do in this section.

1. In the editor for jazn-data.xml, click Users to re-open the Edit JPS Identity and Policy Store dialog, this time with the "Identity Store\jazn.com\Users" node preselected.

   Additional Information: jazn.com is the default *realm,* or identity namespace, used by Oracle.

2. Select the Roles node in the tree.

   Additional Information: Roles created on this panel are not logical application roles, but rather the equivalent of roles or groups in the credential store.

3. Click Add to display the New Role dialog.
4. Name the role "cs_admin" (for "credential store administrator role") and click OK.

   Additional Information: You could use identical role names for both the logical and credential store roles; however, you are using different role names here to help you to understand the mapping between the two.

5. Repeat steps 3–4 to create roles named "cs_manager" and "cs_user."
6. Select the "Users" node under jazn.com.
7. Click Add to create a user in the credential store.
8. Set the following properties on the user and click OK:
   Name as "TFOX"
   Credentials as "welcome2tuhra"

   Additional Information: WebLogic requires passwords of at least eight characters.

9. Repeat steps 7–8 to create users named "NKOCHHAR" and "CDAVIES," both with the password "welcome2tuhra."
10. Without leaving the dialog, select the Identity Store\jazn.com\Roles node again.
11. Select the Member Users tab.
12. Select the cs_admin role.
13. Shuttle TFOX to the *Selected* list.
14. Repeat steps 12–13 to add NKOCHHAR to the cs_manager role and CDAVIES to the cs_user role.
15. Click OK to close the dialog.
17. Click Save All.
18. Open the Source tab and examine the code.

Additional Information: The credential store is inside the `jazn-realm` element. A portion of the code is reproduced next. You may also see a `guid` element in your file, which is a unique global id for the user that WebLogic will automatically generate.

```
<jazn-realm default="jazn.com">
  <realm>
    <name>jazn.com</name>
    <users>
      <user>
        <name>TFOX</name>
        <credentials>{903}LJHErT4qy...WYKpkC0CpY=</credentials>
      </user>
    </users>
    <roles>
      <role>
        <name>cs_admin</name>
        <members>
          <member>
            <type>user</type>
            <name>TFOX</name>
          </member>
        </members>
      </role>
    </roles>
  </realm>
</jazn-realm>
```

Users, with their userid and encrypted credentials, are defined in `user` elements; roles are defined in `role` elements, with references to member users and member roles inside `member` elements.

Map Application Roles to Credential Store Roles

Now that you have created both application roles and a set of credential store roles for testing, you need to create a mapping between them. In a production application, the credential store is likely to be in a repository that is separate from the jazn-data.xml file, for example, the WebLogic LDAP repository or OID. However, for testing purposes, the same jazn-data.xml file can be used for storing both your credential store roles and application roles. Recall that you deliberately used different names for these so as to illustrate the mapping that is required.

1. Re-open the Overview tab in jazn-data.xml.
2. Click Application Roles.
3. Select the Member Roles tab.
4. Select the "user" role in the *Application Roles* list.
5. Shuttle all credential store roles to the *Selected* list.

   Additional Information: Any user with one of these roles in the credential store will automatically have the "user" application role.
6. Repeat steps 4–5 to make both cs_manager and cs_admin member roles of manager.
7. Repeat steps 4–5 to make cs_admin a member role of admin.

8. Click OK to close the dialog.
9. Click Save All.

What Did You Just Do? You set up the jazn-data.xml file to hold the following application metadata:

- **Application roles** Collections of application privileges
- **A sample credential store** Users and roles for testing purposes
- **Mappings** Mappings between application roles and roles in the credential store

II. Implement Authorization

When you first enable ADF security on an application, no users have any permissions on the application at all. In this phase, you will re-open access to various parts of the application based on user roles.

Authorize Access to Pages

In this section, you will open the search page to all users, including those who are not yet logged in, and will also open the edit page to all logged-in users.

1. Terminate the embedded WebLogic server (DefaultServer), if it's running.
2. Run the employeeSearch.jspx page.
3. When the default login page appears, enter the following information and click Submit:
   Username as "NKOCHHAR"
   Password as "welcome2tuhra"

   Additional Information: An HTTP 500 error is displayed:

   ```
   oracle.adf.controller.security.AuthorizationException: ADFC-0619:
   Authorization check failed: '/employeeSearch.jspx' 'VIEW'.
   ```

   This is because you have not yet granted permission on the page to the public or to any group of which NKOCHHAR is a member.
4. Close the browser and terminate the default server.

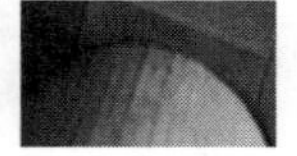

TIP
When developing and testing security, it is always a good idea to close the browser after every run. This is because, if the browser is not entirely shut down (including all windows and any other applications that share session cookies with the browser), it may still regard the session as authenticated. In addition, if you have changed the credential store or permissions, you will need to re-deploy the application (by stopping and restarting it in JDeveloper) to copy the new values across.

5. Re-open the Overview tab of jazn-data.xml, if it isn't already opened.
6. Select the Web Pages tab within the Overview page.

Additional Information: You can declaratively authorize access to application resources in two different ways: by authorizing access to a particular ADF page definition file (on this tab), or by authorizing access to a bounded task flow (on the "Task Flows" tab). Authorizing access to a particular ADF page definition file allows access to whatever resource—a page, page fragment, method call activity, or template—uses that page definition.

In general, the best practice is to authorize access to task flows rather than page definition files—this allows the same data-bound resource to be used in multiple task flows, with different authorization in each. However, this is not an option for resources embedded directly in the application's unbounded task flow, such as employeeSearch.jspx, so you must define the authorization at the page level in this case.

You will authorize resource access using the task flow method in the next section.

7. Select the employeeSearch page definition.
8. Click the "Add Application Role" (green plus "+") button in the *Granted To Roles* column.
9. In the Select Roles dialog, select anonymous-role as shown in Figure 21-2, and click OK.

   Additional Information: In addition to the three application roles you defined in the phase "Set Up Security for the Application," you will see two additional roles, anonymous-role and authenticated-role, as shown in Figure 21-2.

   These roles exist in any ADF Security-enabled application. Resources granted to anonymous-role can be accessed by any user, even a user who is not logged in. Resources granted to authenticated-role can be accessed by any logged-in user.

   Also, note that the right-most pane, as shown in Figure 21-3, contains a list entitled "actions"; for more information, see the sidebar "Authorized Actions."
10. Repeat steps 7–9 to grant access to employeeEdit.jspx to the "user" application role.
11. Click Save All.

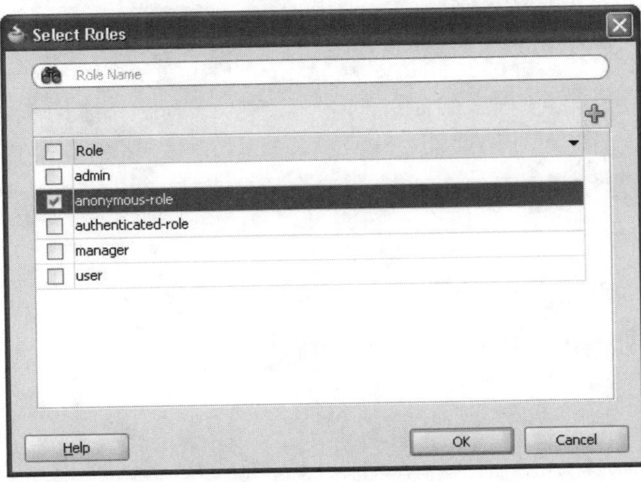

FIGURE 21-2. *Selecting the anonymous-role for the employeeSearch page*

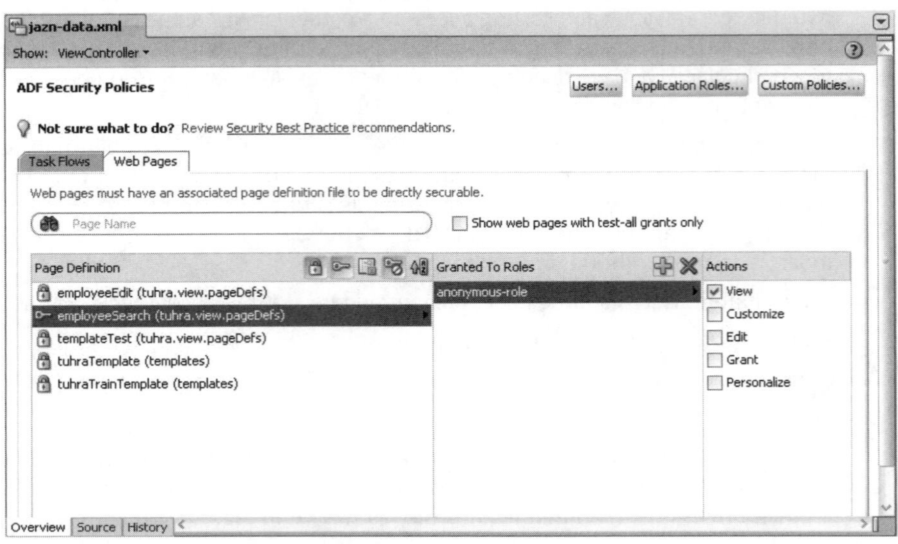

FIGURE 21-3. *The anonymous-role defined for the employeeSearch page*

12. Run employeeSearch.jspx.

Additional Information: When the browser opens, you will see the template, the panelSplitter, and the images, as shown here:

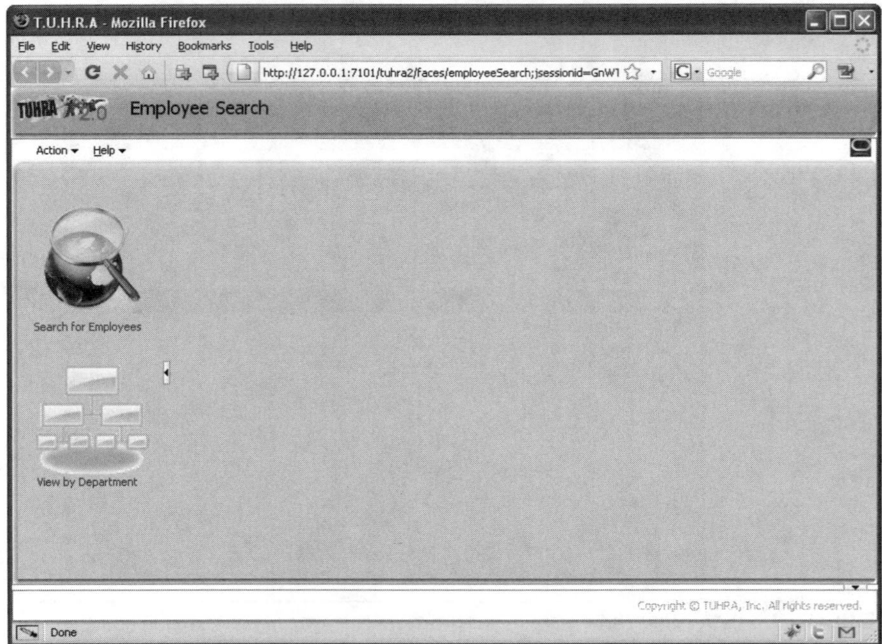

However, you will not see the expected fragment in the right-hand pane, because you have not yet authorized access to the bounded task flow searchEmployees-flow that should be running there. You will authorize access to searchEmployees-flow in the section "Authorize Access to Task Flows."

13. Close the browser and terminate the server.

Authorized Actions

When you specify that a particular application role is authorized to access a page definition or task flow, you can specify up to five actions that role is authorized to perform on the page or the contents of the task flow:

- **View** Selected by default, allows the role to access the page or task flow activities as designed by the developer. Note that this does not imply that the object is somehow read-only. The user can interact with the data on the page to make updates if the application allows that.
- **Customize** Allows the role to perform runtime customizations to the page, changing its contents for all viewers, as a portal administrator might do to a portal.
- **Edit** Allows the role to make changes to the page using Oracle Composer, and automatically grants the Customize and Personalize actions.
- **Grant** Allows the role to create authorizations for other roles to access the page or task flow at runtime.
- **Personalize** Allows the role to perform runtime personalization of the page, changing its contents for the logged-in user only, as a portal user might do to a user-customizable portal.

Runtime customization, editing, grants, and personalization are a feature exposed by applications using Oracle WebCenter capabilities and beyond the scope of this book.

Create Basic Management Functionality

In this section, you will create a page, management.jspx. A complete implementation of the management.jspx page is included in the sample application. However, because implementing the page uses no techniques not already covered in Chapters 17–20, you will leave the page blank for the purposes of this practice. You are creating this page so that, in the following section, you can see a technique for authorizing access to top-level pages other than by creating authorizations for their page definitions.

1. Create a bounded task flow, management-flow.xml, deselecting *Create with Page Fragments*.

   Additional Information: Unlike the other bounded task flows in the application, which contain fragments and are used inside regions, management-flow.xml will contain only a single, top-level page and will be accessed from the unbounded task flow via a control flow case.

2. Drag a view activity from the Component Palette onto the flow.
3. Name the activity "management."
4. Double-click the activity to open the Create JSF Page dialog.

5. Base the page on the tuhraTemplate template and click OK.
6. Return to the task flow and drag a task flow return from the Component Palette to the diagram, and name it "returnToSearch."
7. Create a control flow case named "search" from the management view activity to the task flow return activity.
8. Select the returnToSearch activity and set its *Outcome: Name* property to "search."

   Additional Information: When the task flow returns, it will follow the wildcard control flow case in the unbounded task flow to return to employeeSearch.jspx.
9. Click Save All.
10. Open the application's unbounded task flow, adfc-config.xml.
11. Drag management-flow from the Application Navigator onto the task flow diagram to create a task flow call activity.
12. Create a control flow case from the wildcard control flow rule to the task flow call activity, named "maintain."
13. Open employeeSearch.jspx in the editor.
14. Select the second command link *(View By Department)* in the "first" facet of the `af:panelSplitter`.
15. Using the Structure window, copy the link, and paste a copy immediately after it. The Structure window should look like the following:

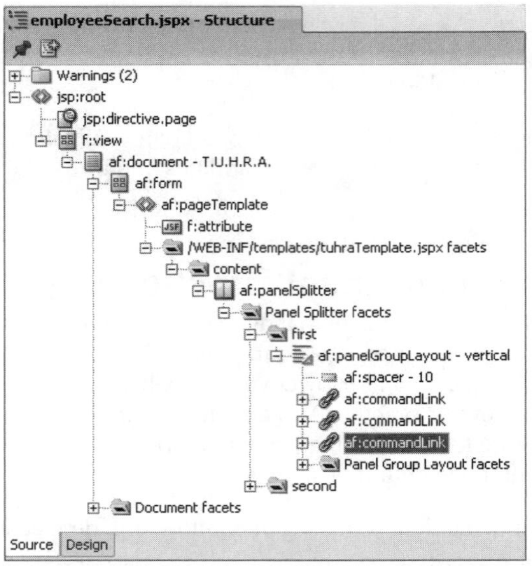

16. Set the following properties on the new command link:
    Id as "maintLink"
    Action as "maintain"
    PartialSubmit as "false"
17. Expand the link and `af:panelGroupLayout` inside it and select `af:image`.

18. Set the following properties on the image:
    Source as "images/maintain.png"
    ShortDesc as "Maintenance"
19. Select the `af:outputLabel`.
20. Set the following properties on `af:outputLabel`:
    For as "maintLink"
    Value as "Maintenance"
21. Delete the `af:setPropertyListener`.
22. Click Save All.

Authorize Access to Task Flows

Although you have granted access to the application's top-level pages, you also need to allow access to the task flows that run in regions of those pages. In addition, you need to allow access to the maintenance page you created in the previous section, which you can do by allowing access to its bounded task flow. In this section, you will implement authorization for the bounded task flows.

1. In the jazn-data.xml file's editor Overview tab, click the Task Flows tab.
2. Select searchEmployees-flow.
3. Click the Add Application Role (green "+") button, and authorize anonymous-role to access the task flow.
4. Repeat steps 2–3 to authorize anonymous-role to access the task flow departmentTree-flow.
5. Repeat steps 2–3 to authorize the "user" role to access editEmployee-flow and imageLOV-flow.
6. Repeat steps 2–3 to authorize the "admin" role to access management-flow.

   Additional Information: Instead of putting the management view activity directly in the application's unbounded task flow, in the preceding section you created a bounded task flow to hold it. This allows you to authorize access to everything inside the flow in one operation, rather than having to control access to each activity within the flow individually.
7. Click Save All.
8. Run employeeSearch.jspx.

   Additional Information: This time, the expected UI appears, because anonymous users are authorized to access both the page and the task flows running in the "second" facet of the panelSplitter.
9. Perform a search, select an employee in the results table, and select **Edit Employee** from the right click menu you created on the table in Chapter 20.

   Additional Information: The default login page appears. This is because, although employeeSearch access was granted to anonymous-role, employeeEdit access is restricted to the user role.
10. Log in with the credentials "CDAVIES"/"welcome2tuhra."

    Additional Information: The Edit Employee page appears, because CDAVIES has the "user" role, and that role has been authorized for the Edit Employee page and all of its internal task flows.

11. Click the "Return to Employee Search" link to return to the search page.
12. Click the Maintenance link.

    Additional Information: A page containing a 500 – Internal Server Error will appear. This is because CDAVIES does not have the "admin" application role, which is required for access to the management task flow.
13. Close the browser and terminate the server.
14. Repeat steps 8–12, this time logging in using the credentials "TFOX"/"welcome2tuhra."

    Additional Information: This time, when you click the Maintenance link, you will see the (empty except for the template components) Maintenance page. This is because TFOX has the required "admin" application role.
15. Close the browser and terminate the server.

Authorize Access to UI Components

When you attempted to access the Maintenance page when logged in as CDAVIES, you received an unfriendly error page. It would be better if the Maintenance link did not appear at all for users who did not have the required application role. In this section, you will hide that link from non-administrative users. You will also hide the command components that link to the Edit Employee page from anyone who is not a manager.

The reason you are hiding those components, instead of restricting access to the Edit Employee page to managers, is that users with only the "user" role will, eventually, need to use the Edit Employee page to edit their own record. You will implement this in the section "Allow a User to Edit His/Her Own Records." What an ordinary user will not be able to do is edit arbitrary records using command components on search results.

1. Re-open the employeeSearch.jspx page in an editor.
2. Select the maintLink command link.
3. Set the *Rendered* property of the link to "#{securityContext.taskflowViewable['/WEB-INF/management-flow.xml#management-flow']}."

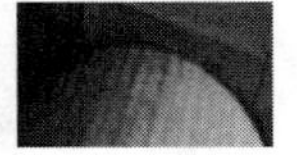

NOTE
You'll need to use the Expression Builder to set the property to a value other than "true," "false," or "default."

Additional Information: Here, securityContext is a JSF managed bean that ADF Security introduces at runtime to keep track of security information. Its *taskflowViewable* property is a `Map` from task flows to Boolean values, containing a value of `true` for task flows that the current authenticated user (or anonymous-role, for non-logged-in users) is allowed to access. The actual value that you test for in the taskflowViewable map is a compound value created from the name and location of the XML file containing the task flow—"/WEB-INF/management-flow.xml," followed by the name of the task flow in that file—" management-flow." These values are separated by "#."

You could use the much simpler `#{securityContext.userInRole['admin']}`, which evaluates to true if the current user is in the "admin" application role, but that effectively creates a duplicate reference to the "admin" role: The management-flow task flow is restricted to members of that role, and the role name would also be hard-coded in the page. If you were later to decide to change authorization for management-flow, you would have to change both of these references. By using the more complex EL expression, you will cause ADF to render the link for anyone authorized to access its destination, whatever role or roles that may translate into in the future.

4. Run employeeSearch.jspx.

   Additional Information: The Maintenance link is not displayed, since the user is not yet authenticated, and management-flow is not viewable by anonymous-role.

5. Edit an employee's record (to force a login), log in as CDAVIES, and return to the search page.

   Additional Information: The Maintenance link is still not displayed, since CDAVIES does not have the "admin" application role, which is required to view management-flow.

6. Close the browser.

7. Repeat steps 4–5, this time logging in as TFOX.

   Additional Information: This time, the Maintenance link is displayed.

8. Close the browser and terminate the server.

9. Open the searchUI.jsff page fragment in a visual editor.

10. In the Structure window, expand `af:panelStretchLayout` and its center facet to locate the `af:panelCollection` that surrounds the results table. In the menus facet of `af:panelCollection`, expand the Actions menu and select the Edit Employee command menu item.

11. Set the *Rendered* property on the item to "#{securityContext.userInRole['manager']}."

    Additional Information: This uses the alternative way of checking who the user is as we mentioned earlier—in this case, checking against an absolute role name rather than against a permission to do something. Best practice is generally to use the taskflowViewable approach, but here this is not possible, because members of only the "user" role can access the control flow; they just cannot access it from this menu.

12. Expand the `af:table` inside the `af:panelCollection` and locate `af:popup` inside the table contextMenu facet.

13. Select the **Edit Employee** menu item nested under the popup's menu.

14. Set the *Rendered* property on the item to "#{securityContext.userInRole['manager']}."

15. Click Save All and test employeeSearch.jspx. Notice now that all of the edit links have disappeared, and there is no way to make them appear. You will fix this problem in the following phase.

16. Close the browser and terminate the server.

What Did You Just Do? You implemented authorization for the application, exposing the search page to the public, restricting access to the Edit Employee page to authenticated users with the "user" role, and restricting access to the Management page to authenticated users with the "admin" role.

Then, you hid the UI components that link to the Edit Employee and Management pages from users not authorized to access those pages. Unfortunately, this has the effect of rendering the pages completely inaccessible. By default, ADF only displays a login page when a non-authenticated user tries to access a resource requiring authentication. Because you hid the links to these resources from non-authenticated users, there is now no way to trigger the display of the login page, so no way for the user to authenticate. You will fix this problem in the following phase by allowing any unauthenticated user to request authentication at any time.

III. Implement Custom Login Functionality

The default login form functionality provided by ADF is not appropriate for the TUHRA application. First, the default form does not have a look and feel consistent with the rest of the application. Also, and even more important, the default functionality does not provide any way for a user to trigger an authentication request, since all links to resources requiring authentication are hidden from users who are not already authenticated. In this phase, you will create a login popup that is better integrated into the application's appearance and can be accessed by any unauthenticated user on demand.

Implement a Managed Bean to Handle Login

In this section, you will create a managed bean that will handle login attempts in a manner consistent with application behavior. For example, it will provide an in-context message to a user upon failed login, rather than relying on browser behavior to handle authentication errors.

1. In the ViewController project, create a Java class, `tuhra.controller.LoginHandler`.
2. Create two private fields:

```
private String _username;
private String _password;
```

3. Generate or create public accessors for both fields.
4. Add the following method to the class:

```
public String performLogin() {
  byte[] pw = _password.getBytes();
  FacesContext ctx = FacesContext.getCurrentInstance();
  HttpServletRequest request =
    (HttpServletRequest)ctx.getExternalContext().getRequest();
  CallbackHandler handler = new SimpleCallbackHandler(_username, pw);
  try {
    Subject mySubject = Authentication.login(handler);
    ServletAuthentication.runAs(mySubject, request);
    String loginUrl = "/adfAuthentication?success_url=/faces" +
      ctx.getViewRoot().getViewId();
    HttpServletResponse response =
      (HttpServletResponse)ctx.getExternalContext().getResponse();
    sendForward(request, response, loginUrl);
  } catch (FailedLoginException fle) {
    FacesMessage msg = new FacesMessage(FacesMessage.SEVERITY_ERROR,
                                        "Incorrect Username or Password",
                                        "An incorrect Username or Password" +
                                        " was specified");
    ctx.addMessage(null, msg);
  } catch (LoginException le) {
    reportUnexpectedLoginError("LoginException", le);
  }
  return null;
}
```

Additional Information: This is the method that will be called as an action when a user attempts to log in. The method performs the following tasks:

- **Lines 04–05** get an object encapsulating the HTTP request from `FacesContext`.
- **Line 06** creates a `CallbackHandler`, which is an object that retrieves information for security operations. A `SimpleCallbackHandler` allows security operations to retrieve the user name and password that were passed to its constructor; other `CallbackHandler` implementations can obtain the user name and password from another source.
- **Line 08** creates a `Subject`, which is an object that encapsulates credentials, from the information provided by `CallbackHandler`.
- **Line 09** attempts to log in the user issuing the request using the credentials that are encapsulated by `Subject`.
- **Lines 10–11** construct a URL to which to forward the user. The `getViewId()` method returns the path, from the context root, to the currently rendered page. So, if the line executes when the user is on the employeeSearch.jspx page, `forwardURL` will be set to "/adfAuthentication?success_url=/faces/employeesSearch.jspx."
- **Lines 12–13** retrieve an object that encapsulates the HTTP response from `FacesContext`.
- **Line 14** calls a method, `sendForward()`, which you will implement later in this section to forward the user to the URL specified in Lines 11–12.
- **Lines 15–20** handles a `FailedLoginException`, which is the exception thrown when the credentials supplied are incorrect. The lines handle the exception by adding a new message to `FacesContext`.
- **Lines 21–22** handles a `LoginException`, which can be thrown by many different problems with a login, including not only incorrect credentials but also attempts to log in to a locked account or uses of an expired password. `FailedLoginException` is a subclass of `LoginException`, but since a `FailedLoginException` will be caught by Line 12, these lines will only be executed when there are login problems other than incorrect credentials. `reportUnexpectedLoginError()` is a method that you will implement later in this section to deal with miscellaneous problems with the login process.
- **Line 24** returns null so that the ADF controller will not attempt to follow a control flow case.

5. Import the following classes:
   - `javax.faces.context.FacesContext`
   - `javax.servlet.http.HttpServletRequest`
   - `javax.security.auth.callback.CallbackHandler`
   - `weblogic.security.SimpleCallbackHandler`
   - `javax.security.auth.Subject`
   - `weblogic.security.services.Authentication`
   - `weblogic.servlet.security.ServletAuthentication`

- `javax.servlet.http.HttpServletResponse`
- `javax.security.auth.login.FailedLoginException`
- `javax.faces.application.FacesMessage`
- `javax.security.auth.login.LoginException`

6. Implement the `sendForward()` method as follows:

```
01: private void sendForward(HttpServletRequest request,
02:                          HttpServletResponse response,
03:                          String loginUrl) {
04:   FacesContext ctx = FacesContext.getCurrentInstance();
05:   RequestDispatcher dispatcher = request
06:     .getRequestDispatcher(loginUrl);
07:   try {
08:     dispatcher.forward(request, response);
09:   } catch (ServletException se) {
10:     reportUnexpectedLoginError("ServletException", se);
11:   } catch (IOException ie) {
12:    reportUnexpectedLoginError("IOException", ie);
13:   }
14:   ctx.responseComplete();
15: }
```

Additional Information: This method performs the following actions:

- **Line 05–06** create a `RequestDispatcher`, which forwards a response to a particular URI.
- **Line 08** uses the `RequestDispatcher` to forward the current HTTP response to the URL specified by loginUrl.
- **Lines 09–10** handles a `ServletException`, which is thrown when the resource at the `RequestDispatcher`'s target URI throws an exception.
- **Lines 11–12** handles an `IOException`, which is thrown when the request cannot be read or the response cannot be written to.
- **Line 14** marks the HTTP response as complete so that the browser can finish rendering it.

7. Import the following classes:

- `javax.servlet.RequestDispatcher`
- `javax.servlet.ServletException`
- `java.io.IOException`

8. Implement the `reportUnexpectedLoginError()` method as follows:

```
private void reportUnexpectedLoginError(String errType, Exception e){
  FacesMessage msg =
    new FacesMessage(FacesMessage.SEVERITY_ERROR, "Unexpected Error During Login",
                     "Unexpected Error during Login (" + errType +
                     "), please consult logs for detail");
  FacesContext.getCurrentInstance().addMessage(null, msg);
  e.printStackTrace();
}
```

Additional Information: This method adds a summary error message to the `FacesContext`, and then prints the full stack trace of the exception to the console.

9. Select Make from the right-click menu in the editor to compile the file. Open adfc-config .xml and select the Overview tab.
10. Add a managed bean with the following properties:
    Name as "login"
    Class as "tuhra.controller.LoginHandler"
    Scope as "request"
11. Click Save All.

Create the Login Popup

In this section, you will create the custom login UI. This is not a separate page, but rather a popup that appears from within tuhraTemplate.

1. Open tuhraTemplate.jspx in a visual editor.
2. Select the Help menu defined in the menu bar for the page, and in the Structure window, select the `af:group` component containing the menu bar.
3. Drag a Popup into the group.
4. Set the Popup's *Id* to "pt_loginPopup."

   Additional Information: By convention, any object IDs assigned within a page template definition should be prefixed with "pt_." This reduces the possibility of experiencing a duplicate component name in a page that uses that template.
5. Drop a Panel Window into the Popup, and set the following properties on the Panel Window:
    Modal as "true"
    Title as "Log In to TUHRA"
    TitleIconSource as "/images/key.png"
6. Drop a Panel Form Layout into the window.
7. Drop an Input Text item into the Panel Form Layout, and set the following properties:
    Label as "User Name"
    Value as "#{login.username}"
8. Drop another Input Text item after the first (but not into the footer facet), and set the following properties:
    Label as "Password"
    Value as "#{login.password}"
    Secret as "true"
9. Drop a Panel Group Layout into the footer facet of the form, and set the following properties:
    Layout as "horizontal"
    Halign as "end"
10. Drop a Spacer into the separator facet of the Panel Group Layout, and set its *Width* to 4.

TIP
Use the Structure window, not the visual editor, to find the separator facet.

11. Drop a Button into the Panel Group Layout, and set the following properties:
    Text as "Log In"
    Action as "#{login.performLogin}"
12. Drop another Button into the Panel Group Layout, and set the following properties:
    Text as "Cancel"
    Immediate as "true"

    Additional Information: The popup should look like the following:

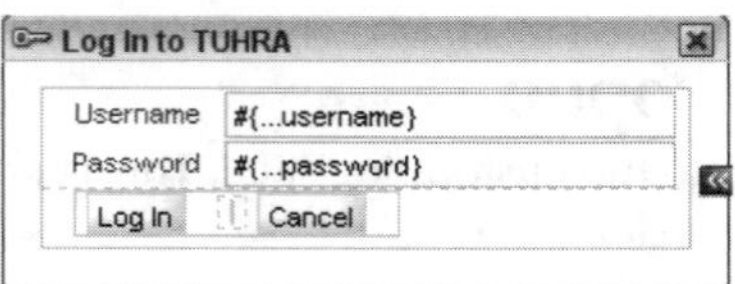

Create Menu Options to Log In and Log Out

In this section, you will create menu options to open the popup dialog and to log the user out.

1. In the Structure window, expand the `af:menuBar` that is a sibling of the popup.
2. Select **Insert inside af:menu - Action | Group** from the right-click menu on the Action menu component.
3. Still in the Structure window, drag the group so that it comes before the Save command menu item.
4. Drag a Menu Item into the `af:group`, and set the following properties on it:
    Text as "Log In"
    Rendered as "#{!securityContext.authenticated}"

    Additional Information: The *authenticated* property of the securityContext expression evaluates to true if the current user is authenticated; the Log In option will be rendered only if the user is not authenticated.
5. Drop a Show Popup Behavior into the Log In command menu item and set the following properties on it:
    PopupId as "pt_loginPopup"
    TriggerType as "action"
6. Drag another Menu Item into the group, and set the following properties on it:
    Text as "Log Out"
    Rendered as "#{securityContext.authenticated}"
7. Click Save All.
8. Run employeeSearch.jspx.
9. Expand the Action menu.

    Additional Information: The **Action | Log In** menu item is displayed, because the user is not yet logged in. The **Log Out** menu item is not displayed.
10. Select the Log In option to open the "Log In to TUHRA" popup.

11. Enter "TFOX"/"welcome2tuhra" and click Log In.

    Additional Information: The Maintenance link is now displayed, because TFOX has access to it.

12. Select **Action** | **Log Out** from the menu bar inside the TUHRA application.

    Additional Information: The Log Out menu item is displayed (and the Log In menu item is not) because the user is logged in. However, selecting the Log Out menu item does nothing. You will implement logout in the following section.

13. Close the browser and terminate the server.

Implement a Method to Handle Logout

In this section, you will implement a method to log the user out, and edit the Log Out menu item to call it.

1. Open the `LoginHandler` class in an editor.
2. Add the following method to the class:

```
public String performLogout() {
  FacesContext ctx = FacesContext.getCurrentInstance();
  HttpServletRequest request =
    (HttpServletRequest)ctx.getExternalContext().getRequest();
  HttpServletResponse response =
    (HttpServletResponse)ctx.getExternalContext().getResponse();
  String logoutUrl =
    "/adfAuthentication?logout=true&end_url=/faces/employeeSearch";
  sendForward(request, response, logoutUrl);
  return null;
}
```

   Additional Information: This method forwards the user to the URL specified in the `logoutUrl` variable. The adfAuthentication resource will log the user out (because of the logout parameter) and forward the user to /faces/employeeSearch (because of the end_url parameter).

3. Re-open tuhraTemplate.jspx.
4. Find and select the **Log Out** menu item.
5. Set the *Action* of the item to "#{login.performLogout}."
6. Click Save All.
7. Run employeeSearch.jspx, and retry the login and logout functionality.

   Additional Information: The Log Out menu item now logs the user out.

8. Close the browser and terminate the server.

What Did You Just Do? You created a managed bean with methods to log the user in and out. You also created a popup containing a login screen, which calls the login method, and menu items to bring up the popup for non-authenticated users and log authenticated users out.

IV. Access Information about the Logged-In User

The application already accesses certain information about the logged-in user—namely, whether the user has a particular role and whether the user is authorized to access a particular resource. In this phase, you will implement functionality that relies on other information about the user: displaying information about the user and allowing the user (even if not a manager) to edit his/her own records.

Create a View Object Definition to Return User Information

In this section, you will create a view object definition that retrieves information about the logged-in user, and add an instance of it to the data model.

1. In the Model project, in the `tuhra.model.queries.main` package, open the Create View Object wizard.
2. On the Name page, name the view object definition "UserInfo."
3. On the Entity Objects page, add a usage of the entity object definition Employees and deselect the *Updatable* checkbox.
4. On the Attributes page, select the following attributes:
   Email
   EmployeeId
   FirstName
   LastName
5. On the Query page, add the following WHERE clause:

   ```
   Employees.EMAIL = :AuthenticatedUserId
   ```

6. On the Bind Variables page, add a bind variable with the following properties and click Finish:
   Name as "AuthenticatedUserId"
   Type as "String"
   Value Type as "Expression"
   Value as "viewObject.DBTransaction.session.userPrincipalName"

   Additional Information: The value you specified is a Groovy expression, which calls the following methods on the view object and returns the result:

   ```
   geDBTransaction().getSession().getUserPrincipalName()
   ```

   This is the login ID (email) of the logged-in user.
7. Click Finish. In the editor for the UserInfo view object definition, in the General tab, expand the Tuning panel, and select "At Most One Row."

   Additional Information: This ensures that no more than one row will be fetched from the database, but also makes it clear that you as a developer only ever expect a single row to match.
8. Add an instance of this view object definition, also called "UserInfo," to TuhraService's data model.
9. Click Save All.

Display User Information

In this section, you will add information about the logged-in user to the application pages.

1. In the ViewController project, refresh the Data Controls panel and then open tuhraTemplate.jspx.
2. Select the Bindings tab.
3. Create attributeValues bindings for the FirstName and LastName attributes of UserInfo.
4. Return to the Design tab.
5. Select the copyright notice in the footer of the page, then in the Structure window, select the horizontal Panel Group Layout that contains the vertical Panel Group Layout above that text.
6. In the Source tab, surround this with a Panel Stretch Layout, placing `af:panelGroupLayout` into the center facet of `af:panelStretchLayout`.
7. Generate an appropriate unique ID (using the yellow lightbulb in the line gutter) for `af:panelStretchLayout` and set its *StartWidth* property to 200px. The relevant code should now look like this:

```
<af:panelStretchLayout id="pt_psl3" startWidth="200px">
  <f:facet name="center">
    <af:panelGroupLayout id="pt_pgl2" halign="end"
                         layout="horizontal">
      <af:panelGroupLayout id="pt_pgl4" layout="vertical">
        <af:spacer width="230" height="8" id="pt_s2"/>
        <af:outputFormatted
           value="Copyright &amp;copy; TUHRA, Inc. All rights reserved."
           id="pt_of1" styleUsage="pageStamp"
           inlineStyle="text-align:right;width:230.0em;"/>
      </af:panelGroupLayout>
    </af:panelGroupLayout>
  </f:facet>
</af:panelStretchLayout>
```

8. Add a start facet to the new Panel Stretch layout, drop a Panel Group Layout into the facet, and set the Panel Group Layout's *Layout* property to "vertical."
9. Drop a Spacer into the Panel Group Layout, and set the following properties:
   Height as 8
   Width as 200

TIP
*If you are finding it hard to work with the visual editor for manipulating components in the Panel Stretch Layout in the Structure window, then select **Design This Container** from the right-click menu. The visual page editor will then zoom in to that part of the screen.*

10. Drop another Panel Group Layout after the new spacer, still inside the vertical `af:panelGroupLayout` component, and set its *Layout* property to "horizontal."
11. Drop a Spacer inside this Panel Group Layout, and set its *Width* to "4."
12. Drop a Switcher after the Spacer, and set the following properties on it:
    FacetName as "#{securityContext.authenticated?'loggedon':'loggedoff'}"
    DefaultFacet as "loggedoff"

    Additional Information: Depending on whether the user is authenticated, the switcher will display one of two facets, "loggedon" or "loggedoff." If the call returns null, the switcher will display its default facet.
13. Select **Insert inside af:switcher | Facet** from the switcher's right-click menu.
14. Name the facet "loggedoff."
15. Drop an Output Formatted inside the facet, and set the following properties:
    Value as "[Not Connected]"
    StyleUsage as "pageStamp"
16. Repeat steps 12–14 to create a facet named "loggedon," with an Output Formatted with the *Value* "[Connected as #{bindings.FirstName.inputValue} #{bindings.LastName .inputValue}]." The Structure window at this point will look like this (under `jsp:root`):

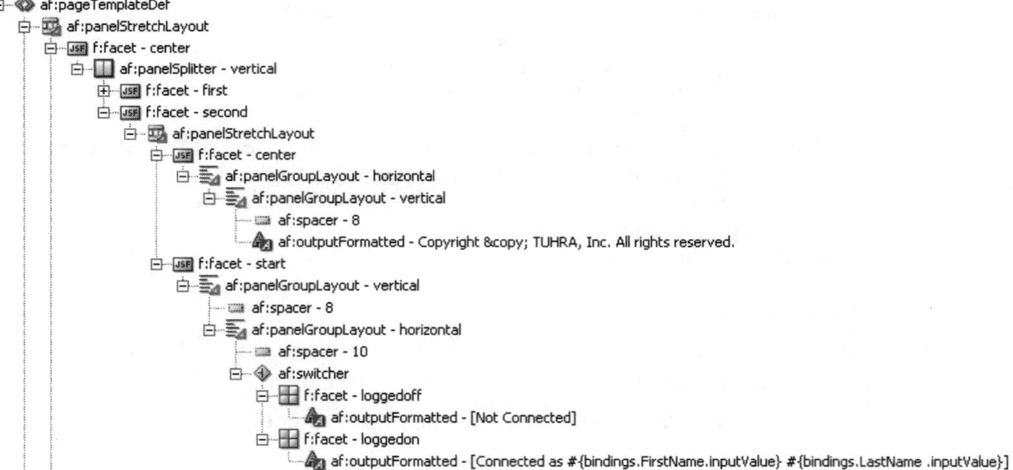

17. Click Save All.
18. Run employeeSearch.jspx.

    Additional Information: The text "[Not Connected]" should appear in the page footer, along with the copyright notice.
19. Log in as CDAVIES.

    Additional Information: The text "[Connected as Curtis Davies]" should appear in the page footer.
20. Close the browser and terminate the server.

Allow a User to Edit His/Her Own Records

In this section, you will add a menu item to the Action menu that will let users (even non-managers) edit their own information.

1. In tuhraTemplate.jspx, select the Action menu where you previously created the Log In and Log Out options.
2. Add a Menu Item to the `af:group` component inside the Action menu.
3. Set the following properties on the menu item:
   Text as "Edit My Information"
   Action as "edit"
   Disabled as "#{!securityContext.authenticated}"

   Additional Information: The "edit" control flow case points to editEmployee.jspx. By setting *Disabled* to `#{!securityContext.authenticated}`, rather than setting *Rendered* to `#{securityContext.authenticated}`, you gray out the item for non-authenticated users rather than hiding it entirely.
4. Select the Bindings tab.
5. Add an attributeValues binding for the EmployeeId attribute of UserInfo.
6. Reselect the Design tab.
7. Drop a Set Property Listener into the Edit My Information menu item and set the following properties:
   From as "#{bindings.EmployeeId.inputValue.value}"
   To as "#{uiState.editEmployeeId}"
   Type as "action"

   Additional Information: This sets the editEmployeeId that is used as a parameter to the editEmployee-flow task flow, to be the employee ID of the currently logged in user. That way, a user will always edit his or her own record if he or she open the Edit Employee page via this menu item (rather than from a search result as a manager).
8. Click Save All.
9. Run employeeSearch.jspx.
10. When the browser opens, expand the Action menu.

    Additional Information: The Edit My Information menu item appears but is disabled because you are not yet logged in.
11. Select **Action | Log In** and log in as CDAVIES.
12. Select **Action | Edit My Information**.

    Additional Information: The Edit Employee page opens to CDAVIES' record.
13. Close the browser.

What Did You Just Do? You added functionality to the application to display the logged in user's name and to allow the user (regardless of role) to access the Edit Employee page for his or her own record. The application is now complete, and in Chapter 22, you will deploy it.

What Could You Do Next? The Edit Employee page allows the user to edit too much information about him- or herself, including salary, hire date, and manager. You could set the *readOnly* attribute on these fields so that they can be edited only by a manager.

More ambitiously, you could change the way the link from search results to the edit page is implemented. Rather than allowing any manager to edit any employee, you could change the functionality such that a user can edit an employee from a search result only if one of the following is true:

- The user has the "admin" application role.
- The user is in the employee's management chain.

The latter would most likely involve creating a service method to determine if one employee is in another's management chain and passing the logged-in and selected employees' IDs as parameters to the method.

CHAPTER 22

Sample Application: Deployment

However beautiful the strategy,
you should occasionally look at the results.

—Winston Churchill (1874–1965)

This is not the end.
It is not even the beginning of the end.
But it is, perhaps, the end of the beginning.

—Winston Churchill (1874–1965),
Nov. 10, 1942, Mansion House

fter you create the code for your application and debug it, you need to install it in a testing or production environment. The term *deployment* refers to the process of copying and installing the necessary application and configuration files into a specific server environment.

During development, you should test your application in an environment that is as similar to the production environment as possible. Therefore, once development and unit testing of a phase of your application are complete, you will deploy the application to an environment that matches a production situation (for further testing). Your organization may also require other levels of testing (for user acceptance testing or volume testing) that may require additional preproduction deployments. After all testing is complete, you will deploy the application into the production environment.

In this final chapter for the sample application, you will deploy the completed application to a standalone Oracle WebLogic instance, a Java EE container used for running Java web applications; although this process does not employ a full application server, it very closely emulates the process used for deployment to a full application server environment. Although in many organizations it is not the responsibility of the developer to finally deploy applications into production, it is nevertheless an essential step in the testing of the application before you hand it over to those who will perform the deployment.

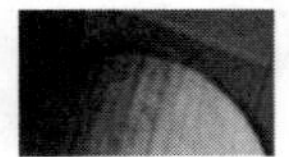

NOTE
As mentioned throughout this part of the book, if you did not complete the preceding chapter successfully, you can download a version of the application in its state at the end of the previous chapter from the websites mentioned in the "Websites for Sample Files" section in the Introduction.

For the purposes of this hands-on practice you will use the existing WebLogic software that is part of the JDeveloper installation and will proceed through the following steps:

I. Set up a standalone WebLogic server for testing

- Create and run a WebLogic domain
- Run the Oracle WebLogic Server Administration Console

II. Configure application-specific settings

- Define database connection information
- Set up users and groups

III. Deploy the application

- Deploy the application from JDeveloper
- Deploy and install the application from an EAR file

Deploying an application to a Java EE server requires collecting application files and supporting libraries into Java archive files (mentioned in Chapter 4), so before jumping into the hands-on practice, we need to start with a brief explanation of these files.

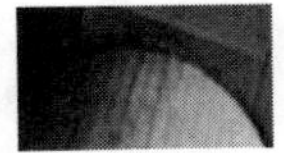

NOTE
Although ADF applications, in theory, are deployable to any Java EE–compliant server, the server must support JSF 1.2. Oracle WebLogic Server 10.3 and beyond fulfill this requirement. For the latest certification information contact Oracle support or refer to www.oracle.com/technology.

Java Archive Files

Java EE defines standards for file packages and locations as well as for standard configuration files expected by an application server that is Java EE–compliant. Using Java EE configuration and archive files, any Java EE–compliant server can find the proper files and process them in a standard way.

The first step in deploying an application is gathering together potentially thousands of application and library files that are located in various directories. Java EE defines standard *archive files,* single files that house more than one file and directory. Tools such as JDeveloper help you assemble the files into these archives. The next step in deployment is to copy the archive file to the proper directory on the server. The server then expands the archive file into individual files.

Each file contains one or more files in one or more directories. A single archive file can contain the equivalent of one or more file system directories (with nested subdirectories) and files. The JVM can access files inside an archive file in the same way as if they were located in a real file system directory. Any archive file can be viewed with an archive viewer (such as the Archive Viewer in JDeveloper) and manipulated with an archive file program (such as WinZip or 7-Zip). The Java archive files used for Java EE deployment are web application archive and enterprise application archive files. In addition, another archive, metadata application archive, is required for Metadata Services (MDS, discussed briefly in the Chapter 1 sidebar "The Importance of Metadata") customizations.

Web Application Archive (WAR) Also called "web archive," a *web application archive,* or *WAR,* file is an archive file that contains all files required for the application's runtime. The WAR file will contain all JSF files in your application with the directories set up in the ViewController project. The WAR file will also contain a number of files and directories inside a WEB-INF directory. These files are a combination of standard Java EE XML descriptor files (such as web.xml) and potentially library JAR files that support the application. The deployment process expands the WAR file into its component files and directories. A copy of the WAR file is kept in the project root directory. WAR files are named with a "war" extension.

TIP
ADF applications depend on many individual JAR files which are installed as shared resources on the target application server. These libraries of shared JAR files are referenced from a common location and are not packaged within the WAR file. A list of these shared JAR files and the libraries that they are included in is available in the Oracle Fusion Middleware Administrator's Guide 11g Release 1.

Enterprise Application Archive (EAR) Also called "enterprise archive," an *enterprise application archive*, or *EAR*, file is an archive file used for standard Java EE deployments. It provides a single archive that contains all other archive and other files needed for an entire enterprise (many applications). The EAR file can contain one or more WAR files, JAR files, and EJB JAR files, as well as several deployment descriptor files. EAR files are named with an "ear" extension.

Metadata Application Archive (MAR) The MAR file is an optional format that is not part of the Java EE standard and is specific to ADF based applications that contain metadata customizations. The MAR is essentially the same as an EAR file except that it contains all of the seeded MDS customizations for an application as well. The WebLogic container has special logic to correctly install applications in a MAR file and will both install the Java EE portion of the application and publish the MDS metadata to the metadata repository. In addition to WAR, EAR and MAR files, a deployment will likely include normal Java Archive (JAR) files, which contain supporting library code (and use a .jar file extension).

NOTE
Although some Java EE applications can be deployed as a simple WAR files without being embedded in an EAR, ADF applications will generally use the EAR or MAR files for deployment.

I. Set Up a Standalone WebLogic Server for Testing

Within your JDeveloper install, you already have all of the pieces required to set up a standalone WebLogic server for testing. When you run the TUHRA2 application from within JDeveloper, the IDE takes various shortcuts to speed up the runtime and so does not exactly emulate the final deployment environment with the Application Server. Therefore, this additional step to deploy to a standalone server is a valuable one because, if you've tested an EAR file by deploying it to a standalone server, the hand-off process for the final production environment will be smoother.

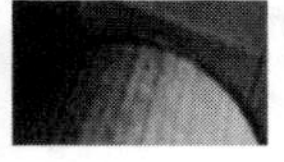

NOTE
You can read more information about the WebLogic Server in the online manual "Oracle Fusion Middleware Deploying Applications to Oracle WebLogic Server 11g Release 1 (10.3.1)," currently available at download.oracle.com/docs/cd/E12839_01/web.1111/e13702/toc.htm.

TIP
Links to specific on-line documents may change from time to time, however, you can always start from otn.oracle.com and click ***Documentation | Fusion Middleware*** *on the shortcuts menu bar to get to the very latest documentation on WebLogic.*

Create and Run a WebLogic Domain

When you set up a server environment in WebLogic, you need to create a *WebLogic domain,* one or more servers, all configured with a certain set of shared libraries. As shown in the following illustration: (a) a WebLogic Server (WLS) software installation on a single physical server machine may support multiple WLS domains configured for ADF, or (b) a single ADF WLS domain may be distributed across many physical servers, each having a WLS installation.

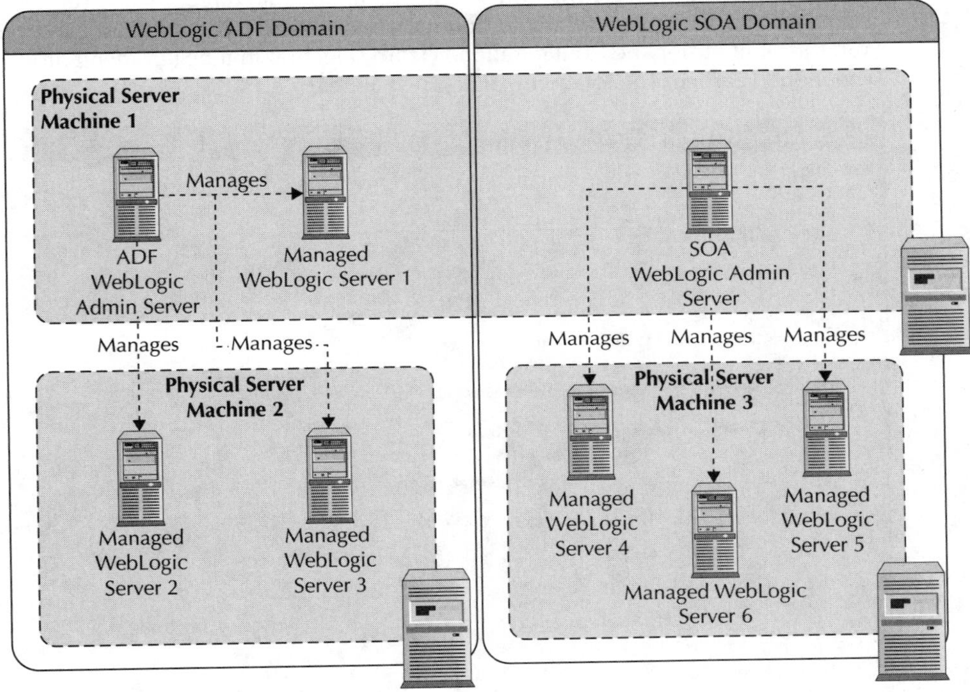

As a further twist, the architecture supports two kinds of servers: *administration servers,* used to control and monitor other servers but not intended to run applications, and *managed servers,* used to run applications. In a production domain there would generally be one administration server and many managed servers, to which applications would be deployed. For local testing purposes, it's fine to just create a single administration (admin) server and use that server for deployment.

This section starts with the final secured application that you created at the end of Chapter 21. The instructions in this section are based on the use of the command line rather than the Windows Start menu, although instead you can use the Windows Start menu options (in the **Start | Programs | Oracle Fusion Middleware 11.1.1.1.0 | WebLogic Server 11gR1 | Tools** program group). In all cases the scripts mentioned will have two versions, a ".cmd" version for Windows and a ".sh" version for Unix/Linux. Use the version that applies to your platform and the appropriate path separator in your commands (";" for Windows and ":" for Unix/Linux).

1. If JDeveloper is open, be sure to stop all server instances (default and application) using the Terminate (red box) button in the toolbar. (Stopping the default server will automatically stop any running application instances.)

2. Open a command shell (command-line) window and change (CD) to the directory into which you installed Oracle Fusion Middleware. In these examples, we use "FMW_HOME" to represent the directory into which you installed JDeveloper (for example, C:\Oracle\Middleware).

   Additional Information: In Windows, you can open a command-line window by selecting **Start** | **Run**, entering "CMD," and clicking OK.

3. Change to the <FMW_HOME>\jdeveloper\common\bin directory and run the config .cmd script. The Oracle WebLogic Configuration Wizard will start. (You can alternatively run this utility using the Configuration Wizard selection in the Start menu program group mentioned earlier.) The following dialog will appear:

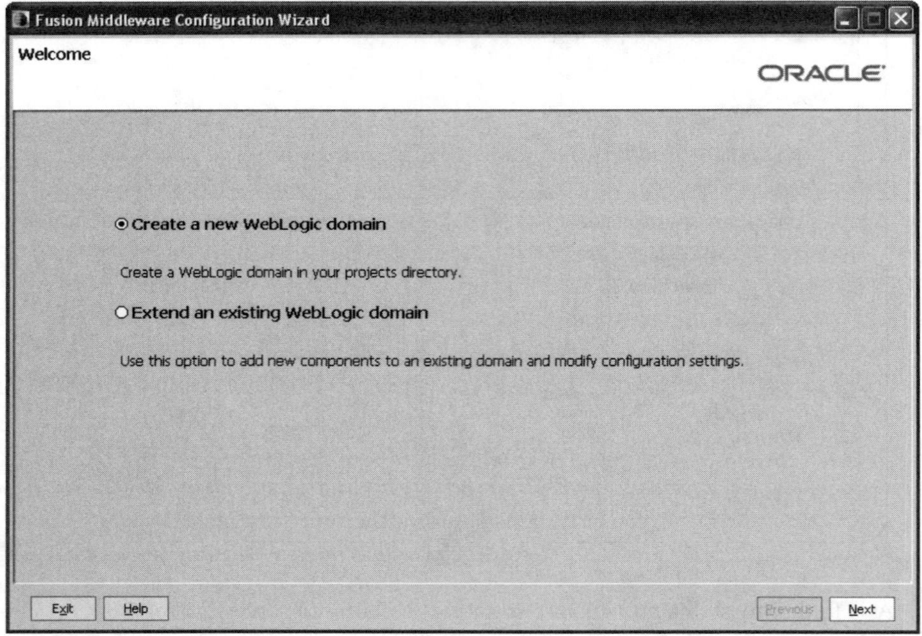

4. If no existing standalone domain exists, leave the *Create a new WebLogic domain* option selected and click Next.

5. The Select Domain Source page will appear with a list of possible products (libraries) to configure into the domain. Select the *Oracle JRF* checkbox and click Next.

   Additional Information: The Oracle JRF (Java Runtime Foundation) contains all of the shared JAR files used by ADF BC and ADFm; it also includes the ADF Faces components.

6. On the Specify Domain Name and Location page, set *Domain name* as "adf_test" and leave the *Domain location* as the default (for example, "<FMW_HOME>\user_projects\domains"). Click Next.

7. The Configure Administrator User and Password page will appear where you define the account used to manage the server. By convention the default user name used for the administrator is "weblogic," and that default will work. Set *User password* and *Confirm user password* to "weblogic1" (the password must contain a number). Click Next.

8. The Configure Server Start Mode and JDK page will appear. Ensure that the *WebLogic Domain Startup Mode* is set to "Development Mode," and accept the default for *JDK Selection,* which should be the same JDK version with which you are running JDeveloper (for example, "1.6.0_11"). Click Next.
9. The Select Optional Configuration page will appear. You will not need any of these options, so just click Next.
10. The Configuration Summary page will appear as follows. Review the settings. You can return to earlier pages using the Previous buttons.

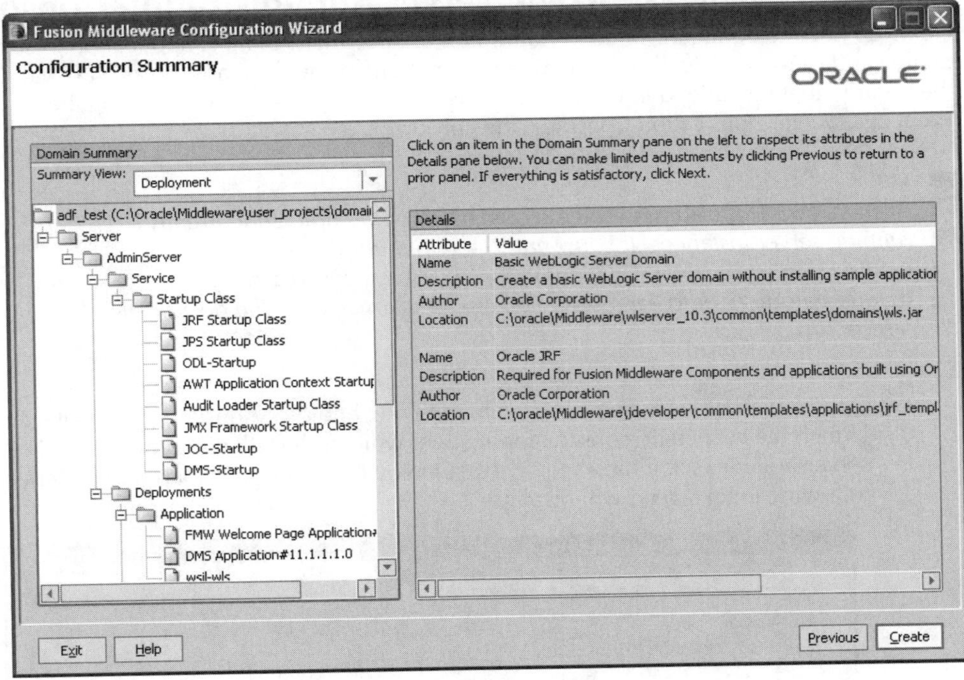

11. Once you have reviewed and confirmed the settings, click Create. The Creating Domain progress page will appear.
12. When the creation process completes, select the *Start Admin Server* checkbox in the lower-right corner of the dialog and click Done. The Configuration Wizard will exit, and another command-line window will open and display messages about the server startup. Wait for the message that ends with "<Server started in RUNNING mode>."

CAUTION
For now, leave the server command-line window open so that the server will continue to run. Closing this window will stop the server.

13. The original command-line window from which you started the Configuration Wizard will return to a command-line prompt. Close this window (but not the server window).

TIP

If you accidently close the server window, or forgot to start the server at the end of the Oracle WebLogic Configuration Wizard you can jump ahead to the sidebar "Starting the WebLogic Domain Server from the Command Line" for instructions on starting the server manually. This information will also help when you need to start the server outside of this hands-on practice.

Run the Oracle WebLogic Server Administration Console

Next you need to configure some key attributes to allow the TUHRA2 application to successfully deploy and run—specifically, connection information for the database and a list of valid users for the security that you added in Chapter 21. This configuration is performed using the Oracle WebLogic Server Application Console ("the console").

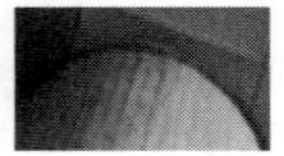

TIP

A single WebLogic admin server can be used for multiple concurrently running server instances. If you want to set up multiple servers, you would fill in some of the Configuration Wizard screens to assign a unique port number to each server on a physical machine. The default port is 7001.

1. Open a web browser and navigate to the URL: http://localhost:7001/console. This will launch the WebLogic console application, which is installed into every administration server. You will see a message saying "Deploying application for /console", then the following login screen will display.

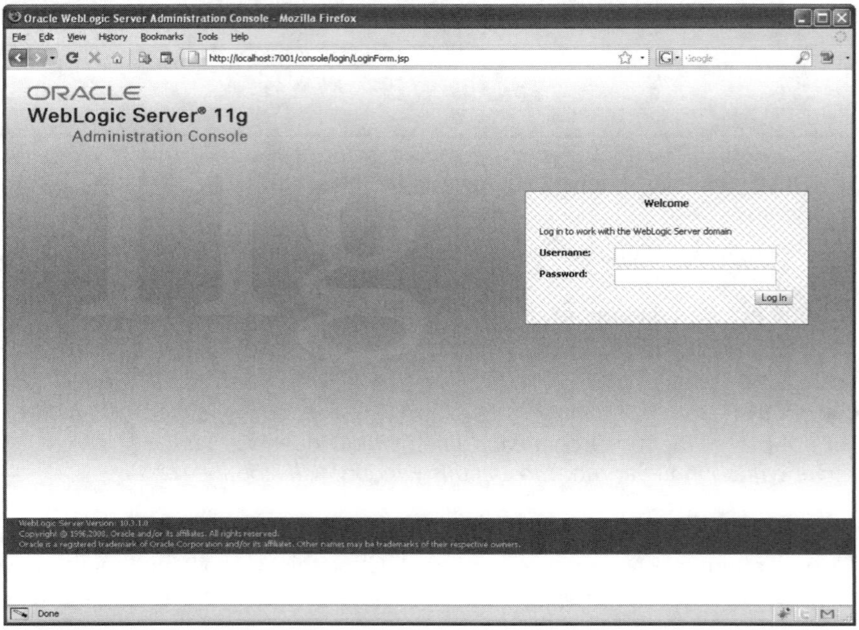

2. Log in to the console using the user name and password that you specified earlier (weblogic/weblogic1). The administration console page will then display as shown in Figure 22-1. Notice the domain name in the top right-hand corner ("Connected to") area.

What Did You Just Do? The configuration wizard that you ran in this phase creates a set of configuration files and scripts, which will start a WebLogic Server instance. This server is configured to use the default port: 7001, which is different from the port that is used when running within JDeveloper (port 7101), so you can safely use both the internal server and this new external testing server at the same time. The domain that you have created is set up with all of the libraries required to run an ADF application.

In this phase, you also ran the console, the tool you will use for the rest of the configuration tasks. Before you run the console, you need to start the server. The steps in this phase ran the server from the Configuration Wizard. The next time you need to start the server, you will be using the command line batch file or shell script (or shortcut) as described in the sidebar "Starting the WebLogic Domain Server from the Command Line."

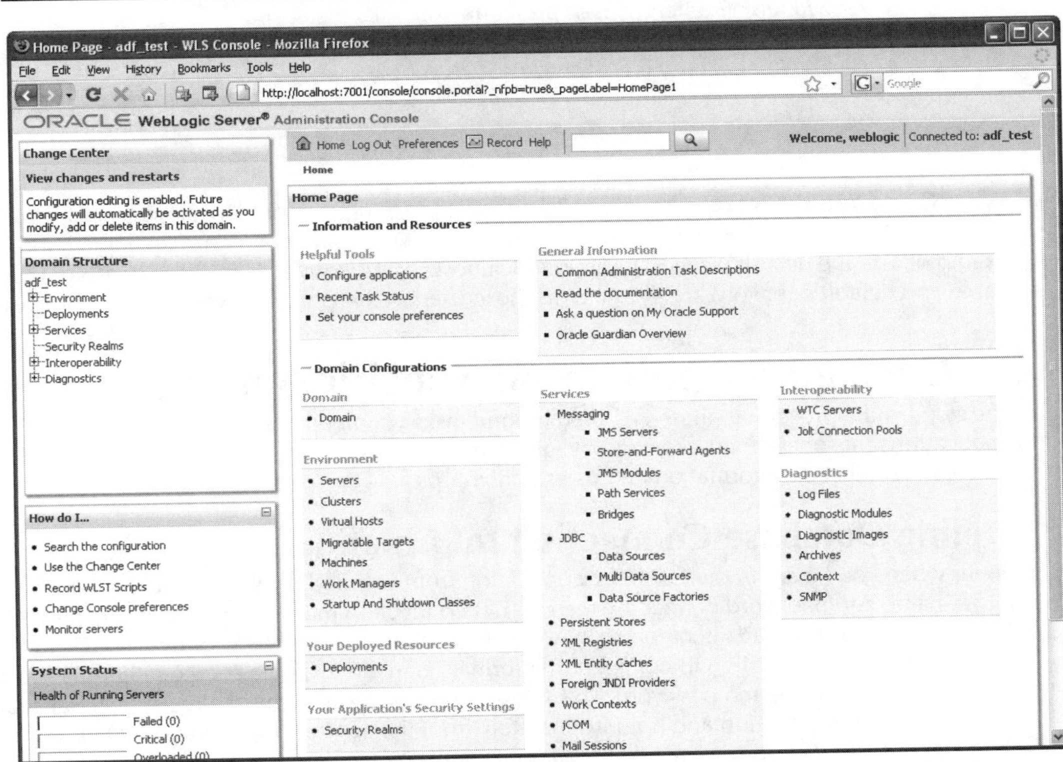

FIGURE 22-1. *Oracle WebLogic Server Administration Console for the adf_test domain*

Starting the WebLogic Domain Server from the Command Line

The last step of the Oracle WebLogic Configuration Wizard allowed you to start the server (domain). If you are not running the wizard, you can manually start up the server using the following steps. If the server is running and you want to try these steps, press CTRL-C, then enter "Y" at the prompt to stop the server, and then close the command-line window.

1. From a new command-line window, navigate to the FMW_HOME directory and then navigate to the user_projects\domains\adf_test. Notice that "adf_test" corresponds to the name and location of the domain that you created earlier.
2. At the command line, run the script startWebLogic.cmd (or .sh) script to start the server instance. As before, wait for the "Server started in RUNNING mode." message. Leave this window open. Reconnect to the console as described earlier.
3. To stop the server you can run the corresponding stopWeblogic.cmd (or .sh) script in the adf_test\bin directory rather than pressing CTRL-C in the server window.

TIP

As with any frequently used program, you will probably want to create a shortcut on your desktop for startWebLogic.cmd (Windows) or startWebLogic.sh (Unix or Linux).

What Could You Do Next? You can also access the administration console for the default server in JDeveloper. Once JDeveloper starts the default server (after you run an application, for example), use the default server URL (http://localhost:7101/console) to start the console. The user name and default password are the same as those used in this practice (weblogic / weblogic1).

II. Configure Application-Specific Settings

The steps in the preceding phase centered around tasks you need to complete regardless of the application. This phase focuses on tasks that are more specific to an application, for example, database connection information and users and groups.

Define Database Connection Information

So far when you have run the TUHRA2 application from within JDeveloper, you have been using a user name and password defined by the HR_DB connection that was created in Chapter 17. In Chapter 18, you made an alteration to the ADF BC configuration "TUHRAServiceLocal" to make the application use the HR_DB connection information in a JDBC data source rather than as a hard-coded user name and password. This *JDBC data source* mechanism allows you to abstract the connection information and hold it separately from the application definition. *Data sources* are a named connection resource that the application asks the Application Server for rather than holding the connection information directly. This feature allows the application to remain unchanged as it is moved from server to server, for example, test to production. In this section you will define this data source in the adf_test WebLogic domain.

1. Return to the WLS console (http://localhost:7001/console). In the Domain Structure (left-hand side) region expand the Services\JDBC node and click the Data Sources node. The screen will change to look like Figure 22-2.

   Additional Information: The Multi Data Sources node in the services section is used when configuring a data source to work with an Oracle Real Application Clusters (RAC) database. The "Data Source Factories" page is used only for backward compatibility.

2. Click New (above the Data Sources table) to launch the Create a New JDBC Data Sources wizard, which you will use to create a data source. On the first page of the wizard, set the values as follows:

Field	Value	Purpose
Name	TuhraDS	A name that identifies this resource in the console.
JNDI Name	jdbc/HR_DBDS	The name that is used to look up the connection. This value matches the value defined in the ADF BC configuration without the java:comp/env prefix.
Database Type	Oracle	This is the default; it assumes you're accessing an Oracle database.
Database Driver	Oracle's Driver (Thin) for Service Connections	The correct driver for a local XE or local Oracle 11*g* database installation. Do not select the "Thin XA" driver.

3. Click Next. On the next page leave all options as their defaults and click Next.

4. Fill in the fields on this page as in the following table to define the core connection information. The following values are based on a default Oracle XE database installed on the local machine; adapt these if you are using a different database type.

Field	Value	Purpose
Database Name	XE	The SID or service name of the database ("XE" for Oracle XE and "ORCL" for an 11*g* install, by default).
Host Name	localhost	This setting will loop back to your local machine; alternatively use the database machine's host name, if any.
Port	1521	The default port for an Oracle database.
Database User Name	hr	The schema owner as set up in Chapter 17.
Password	hr	Use the password for hr on your system.
Confirm Password	hr	The same as the password.

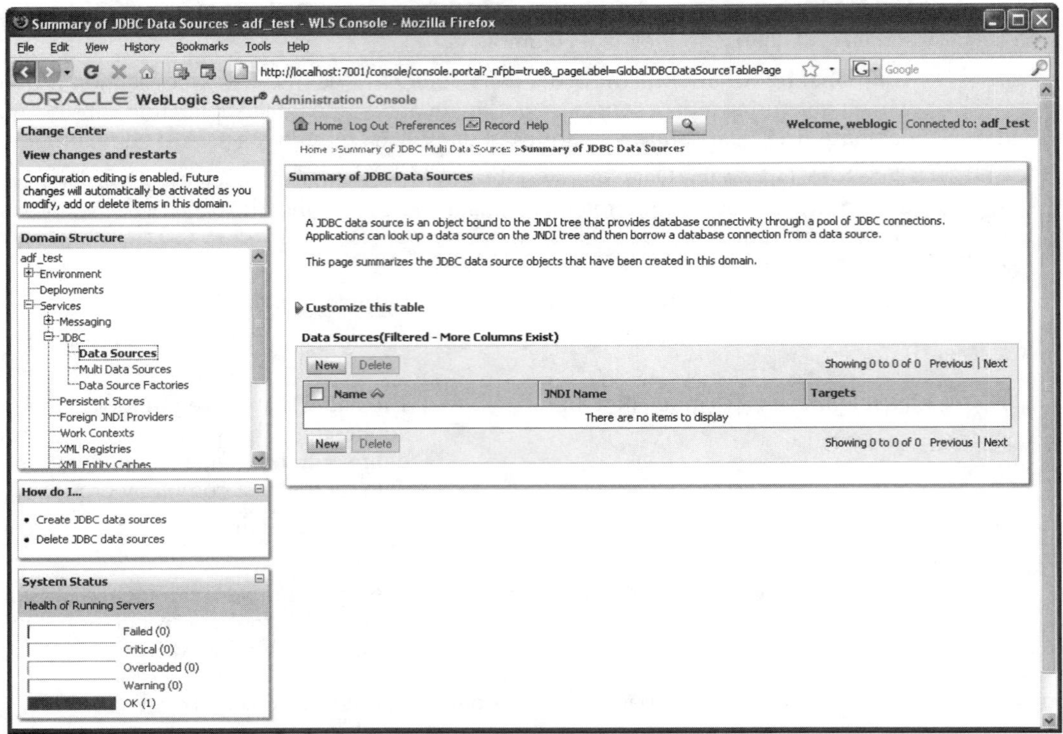

FIGURE 22-2. *Summary of JDBC Data Sources page of the console*

5. Click Next. The screen will change slightly adding fields at the bottom, one of which, *Test Table Name,* allows you to enter a sample SQL statement (one is entered by default) for testing purposes.

6. Be sure your database is started and click the Test Configuration button to check that the database is accessible. A green "Connection test succeeded" message will appear near the top of the screen if the connection is correctly defined and the database is reachable.

   Additional Information: If the connection fails, cross-check the settings on all pages with the settings in the preceding steps and with the HR_DB database connection information in JDeveloper.

7. Click Next to display the Select Targets page. At this point, you need to activate the data source for the administration server. Select the *AdminServer* checkbox.

   Additional Information: If you miss this step or need to deactivate the data source later, you can click the data source link after displaying the list of data sources, select the Targets tab, select (or deselect) the target server, and click Save.

8. Click Finish. The wizard will set up the data source and return you to the Data Sources list, which now contains TuhraDS.

Set Up Users and Groups

The next configuration task is to configure the WebLogic server's LDAP service for the users and roles that TUHRA2 needs. When you run the application from within the IDE, JDeveloper takes care of this for you, but running on a standalone server requires some setup steps.

1. In the WebLogic console's Domain Structure navigator area, click *Security Realms* to display a single predefined realm called "myrealm." Click myrealm.

NOTE
Remember that a realm in security is just a namespace. It does not matter that the realm you are using here is different from the one you used in Chapter 21 (jazn.com).

2. Click the Users and Groups tab in the "Settings for myrealm" page and click New to define each of the application users (CDAVIES, NKOCHHAR, and TFOX, all with passwords of "welcome2tuhra"). The screen should appear as in Figure 22-3.

   Additional Information: Feel free to add descriptions (as shown in Figure 22-3) and create extra users as well, as long as you assign them to the correct groups, as you will do for the main users in the next steps.

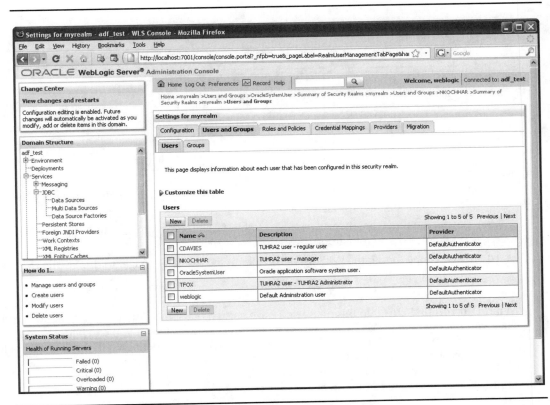

FIGURE 22-3. *Users and Groups tab of the Security Realm page*

3. Click the Groups subtab.
4. Click New on the Groups table to add a group called "cs_admin" that will represent the application's admin group. Provide a suitable description. Click OK.

   Additional Information: Naming the server group differently from the application's logical roles helps illustrate the kind of mapping that will often have to take place when using existing credential stores such as Oracle Internet Directory (OID). Each of the server's LDAP credential store groups will correspond to one of the local server groups you set up when testing security from within JDeveloper.
5. Repeat the preceding step to define groups for cs_manager and cs_user. Provide a suitable description for each group.
6. Click the Users subtab.
7. Click CDAVIES to display the "Settings for CDAVIES" page. Click the Groups subtab. Shuttle "cs_user" from *Available* to *Chosen*. The screen will contain the following areas:

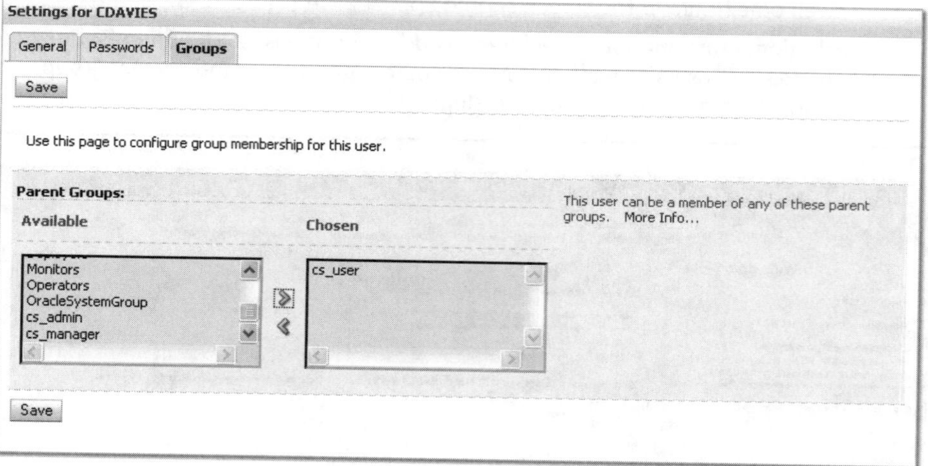

8. Click Save. Click the "Users and Groups" link in the breadcrumb area (above the title "Settings for myrealm").
9. Repeat the preceding two steps to assign NKOCHHAR to the cs_manager group and TFOX to the cs_admin group.
10. Click Home (under the WLS Server banner at the top of the page) to display the main console page.

What Did You Just Do? In this phase you have carried out some essential configuration work. First, you ran the Oracle WebLogic Server Application Console, where you can perform configuration and administrative tasks for the server instance. You defined a JDBC data source for the application to use for its database connections. Then you created a set of groups and test users in the internal LDAP server provided by Oracle WebLogic so that security in the deployed application can be tested. You also assigned users to groups.

III. Deploy the Application

Now that the server is set up, you can deploy the TUHRA2 application to it. This section will actually explain two alternative forms of deployment: deployment directly from JDeveloper, which you would use to test the deployment on a local WebLogic Server instance, and deployment using an EAR file, which is the technique that you or an administrator would usually use to roll out an application into a full application server environment.

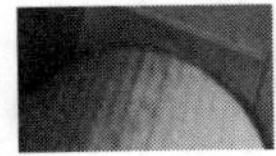

NOTE
If you have been using an earlier version of ADF security, you may be familiar with the concept of having to manually migrate security permissions from the application jazn-data.xml file into the application server. One of the big improvements you will see in this version of the framework is that this permission deployment is now handled by the direct deployment from JDeveloper.

Deploy the Application from JDeveloper

JDeveloper makes the process of deploying to either a local or a remote WebLogic server, a relatively easy, point-and-click task.

1. In JDeveloper, with the TUHRA2 application open in the Application Navigator (in its state as of the end of Chapter 21), display the project properties for the ViewController project (by double clicking the ViewController node). On the Java EE Application page, ensure that *Java EE Web Application Name* and *Java EE Web Context Root* are both set to "tuhra2."
2. Click OK.
3. Click the application menu for TUHRA2 shown in the following illustration:

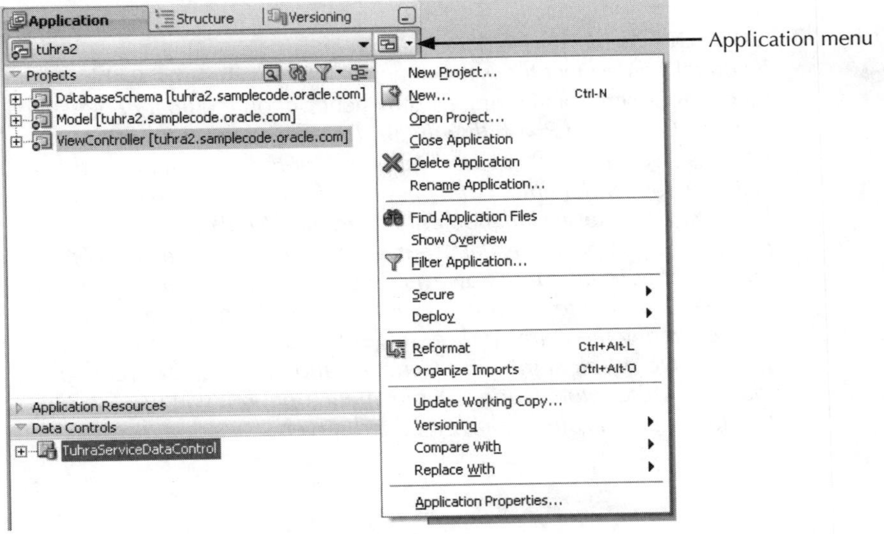

4. Select Application Properties (also available from **Application** | **Application Properties**), and in the Deployment page ensure that the *Application Policies* checkbox is selected and the *Auto Generate and Synchronize weblogic-jdbc.xml Descriptors During Deployment, Credentials,* and *Users* and *Groups* checkbox are unselected as shown here:

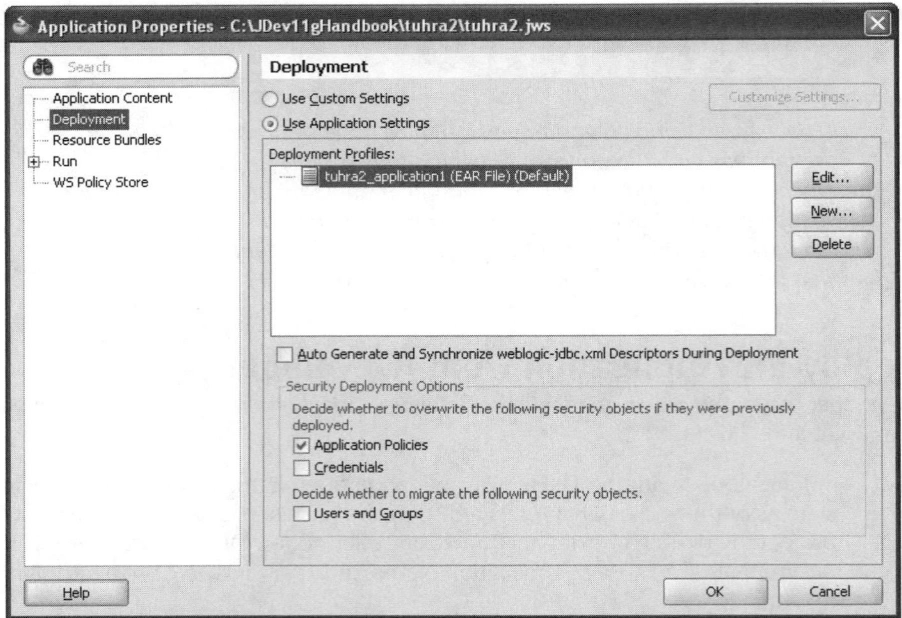

Additional Information: You have already explicitly defined the database connection, credentials, users, and groups on the server side and do not need to move those items.

CAUTION
If you fail to deselect the Auto Generate and Synchronize weblogic-jdbc.xml Descriptors During Deployment *option the final deployment from an EAR file in Phase III will fail. This is because this option embeds a separate data source definition for the application with the EAR file but cannot embed the password for it (the password has to be encrypted after installation onto the target WebLogic server). It is possible to complete this data source definition from the WebLogic console after installation; however, because you have already defined a global data source it is much simpler to avoid the whole problem by not generating the extra application level data source. Note, that you will need to re-select the Auto Generate and Synchronize weblogic-jdbc.xml Descriptors During Deployment option if you want to run the application again in the embedded server.*

5. Click OK to dismiss the dialog.
6. Be sure the WebLogic server is running from the preceding phase. If it is not, return to the sidebar "Starting the WebLogic Domain Server from the Command Line" in Phase I and start the server.
7. From the Application menu, select **Deploy | tuhra2_application1 | to | New Connection**. The Create Application Server Connection dialog will appear as shown here:

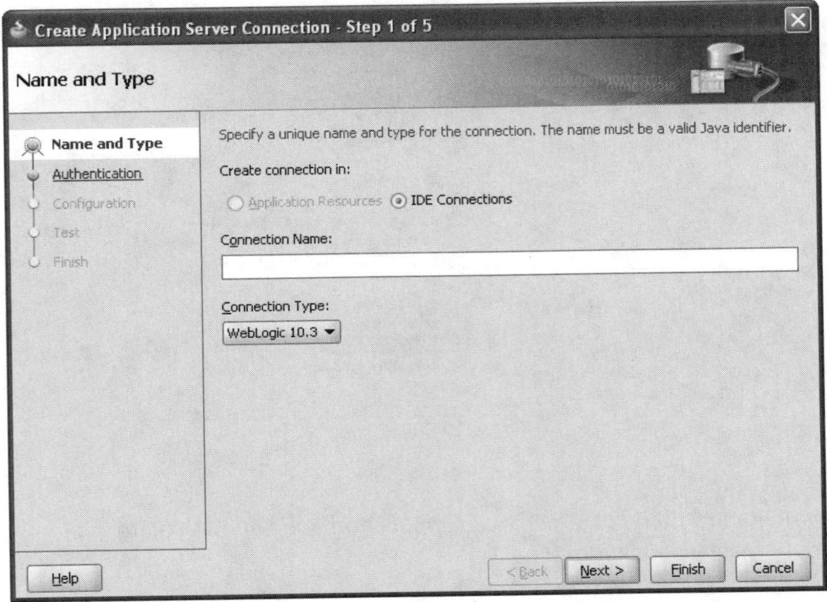

8. Set the *Connection Name* as "TestingServer." Leave the *Connection Type* as "WebLogic 10.3." Click Next.
9. On the Authentication page, provide the user name and password, which you used to log in to the WebLogic console for the adf_test domain (weblogic/weblogic1). Click Next.
10. On the Configuration page, leave all of the defaults except for setting the *WLS Domain* value to the name of your domain, "adf_test." Click Next.
11. Click Test Connection and wait for the test to complete. All of the tests should succeed. Click Finish.

    Additional Information: In the future, you will be able to select this connection from the Deploy menu option without having to step through this connection wizard.
12. The deployment will proceed, and you will see messages appear in the Log window.

TIP
If more than one server is defined for the domain that you are deploying to, an additional popup dialog allows you to select the target server.

13. When the process is complete, the Log window will display "Deployment finished."

14. Open the Application Server Navigator (**View** | **Application Server Navigator**). Expand the Application Servers\TestingServer\ deployments node to view all deployed applications as shown here with the TUHRA2 deployment highlighted:

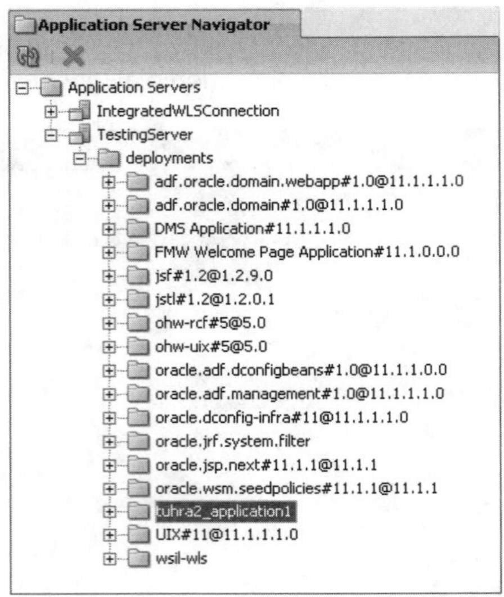

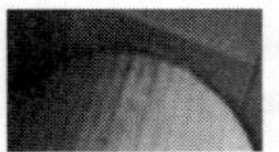

TIP
The right-click menu on a deployed application node allows you to undeploy the application.

15. Test the deployed application by opening a browser window and entering the URL http://localhost:7001/tuhra2/faces/employeeSearch into the browser location field.

    Additional Information: The Employee Search page will appear. Alternatively, you could test the login.html page (from Chapter 21) to confirm that the login works in this server arrangement.

16. Test various application functions and close the browser when you are finished testing.

Exploring the EAR File As mentioned earlier in this chapter, an EAR file is the standard deployment unit for Java EE applications; it contains all the bits of the application that have to be deployed except for the connection information and security setup, which are held in the server.

The EAR file created by this process was created, copied to the server, and deployed automatically by the JDeveloper deployment process. However, you can open and examine the contents of this file using the following steps:

1. In JDeveloper, look in the Deployment log window for a message about the EAR file that was created ("Wrote Enterprise Application Module to…"). Notice the file system location for the EAR file. Select **File** | **Open** and navigate to that deploy directory under TUHRA_HOME.

Additional Information: The deploy directory is parallel to the Model and ViewController directories. You will see two nodes for the one TUHRA2_application1.ear file. One node (displayed as a file icon) allows you to open the EAR as a file; the other node (displayed as a directory icon with a "?") allows you to look inside the EAR file and select one or more files.

TIP
You can copy the file system location from the Log window and paste it into the Open dialog instead of navigating through the file system.

2. Select the version of the EAR file that displays as a file (page with lines) icon and click Open. The list of EAR file contents should open in the Archive Viewer. The list of files in the EAR file is mostly configuration files and the WAR file, tuhra2_ViewController_webapp1.war.
3. Double click the WAR file to examine its contents. You should see familiar files as you browse this list, for example, Model project files that are required for the application, library JAR files, and ViewController files (JSF files and images).
4. You can open any of these files in an editor or viewer window by double clicking the file name. Close the Archive Viewer when you are finished browsing.

Deploy and Install the Application from an EAR file

Although the approach of deploying the application directly from JDeveloper will work successfully for both local and remote application servers, many organizations would prefer that their developers not directly update production servers. In these cases the developer will need to create an EAR file of the application to hand over to the administrator for deployment.

Most Java EE application servers (with exceptions such as Apache Tomcat, which is not a complete Java Enterprise Edition application server) understand how to automatically install an EAR file. The process of deployment directly from JDeveloper that we explained in the previous section is really just automating the process of packaging the EAR file, copying it to the target server machine, and triggering the installation. However, since most administrators will use manual deployment steps, we will run through that technique in this section. Although you've already created the EAR file as part of the JDeveloper deployment steps before, the following creates it again to demonstrate the steps. If you are in charge of deployment to the production application server, you can use these steps to practice the production deployment steps on a standalone local server.

1. Starting from the JDeveloper Application Navigator open the application menu, and select **Deploy | tuhra2_Application1 | to EAR File**. By default this will package the application into an EAR and copy it to the deploy subdirectory underneath the application directory root. You will see "Deployment finished" in the Log window when the process completes.

   Additional Information: You would then pass this EAR file to the application server administrator, who would deploy the application to the server, but the following steps demonstrate the process of deployment using the WebLogic console in your standalone WebLogic server.

2. Next, log in to the WebLogic console (http://localhost:7001/console) using the user name/password you set up (weblogic/weblogic1). From the Domain Structure tree on the left-hand side of the screen, click Deployments.
3. Browse the list of the deployed applications until you find tuhra2_application1 that you deployed from JDeveloper as shown here:

Deployments

Install | Update | Delete | Start | Stop — Showing 11 to 17 of 17 Previous | Next

	Name	State	Health	Type	Deployment Order
☐	oracle.dconfig-infra(11,11.1.1.1.0)	Active		Library	100
☐	oracle.jrf.system.filter	Active		Library	100
☐	oracle.jsp.next(11.1.1,11.1.1)	Active		Library	100
☐	oracle.wsm.seedpolicies(11.1.1,11.1.1)	Active		Library	100
☐	⊞ tuhra2_application1	Active	✔ OK	Enterprise Application	100
☐	UIX(11,11.1.1.1.0)	Active		Library	100
☐	⊞ wsil-wls	Active	✔ OK	Enterprise Application	150

Install | Update | Delete | Start | Stop — Showing 11 to 17 of 17 Previous | Next

4. Select the checkbox next to this deployment and click Delete to remove it.

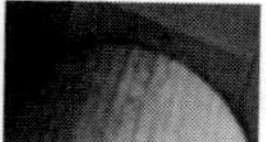

NOTE
This step just demonstrates how to remove a deployment, but it is not really necessary. You could choose instead to update the deployment.

5. Click the Install button in the *Deployments* table. This will launch the Install Application Assistant, the first screen of which will allow you to navigate to and select the EAR file for the application (tuhra2_application1.ear) from your local disk.
6. Find the file (as mentioned before, the name is provided at the end of the Log window messages in a line starting with "Wrote Enterprise Application Module to"). Select the radio button next to the file name and click Next.
7. On this page, leave the default option of "Install this deployment as an application" selected and click Next.
8. On this page, leave all of the options as default and click Finish. The "Summary of Deployments" page will display.
9. Scroll to the page containing tuhra2_application1 to confirm that the *State* is "Active" and *Health* is "OK."
10. Open a new browser session and connect to the application as before (http://localhost:7001/tuhra2/faces/employeeSearch). Test the application.
11. Close the browser and stop the server using the stopWeblogic script or by pressing CTRL-C and closing the server's command-line window.

What Did You Just Do? In the final section of this chapter, we showed how to deploy the application you developed into a standalone instance of WebLogic. In the process of doing this you used both automated deployment from JDeveloper as well as the more manual process using the console to deploy an EAR file. As mentioned, you would only need to deploy an application once, but this phase showed both methods to give you experience with the processes.

When deploying directly from JDeveloper, you also migrated the permissions used by ADF to secure bindings and task flows. The manual migration of these permissions is also discussed in some detail in the JDeveloper online help if you need to understand the steps in more detail.

This concludes the work to create a sample application that demonstrates many of the techniques you will use in real application development. Be sure to continue study of ADF Fusion web development concepts in the websites and reference materials we've mentioned throughout the book and stay tuned for future developments and enhancements to JDeveloper.

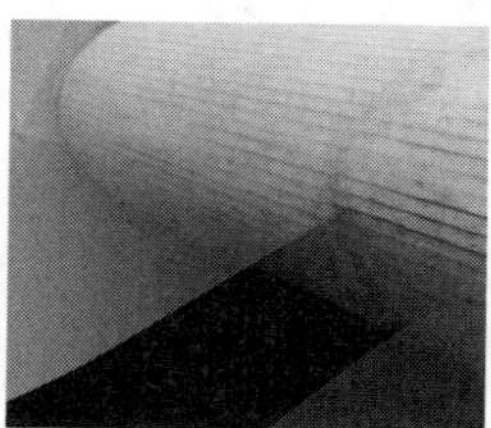

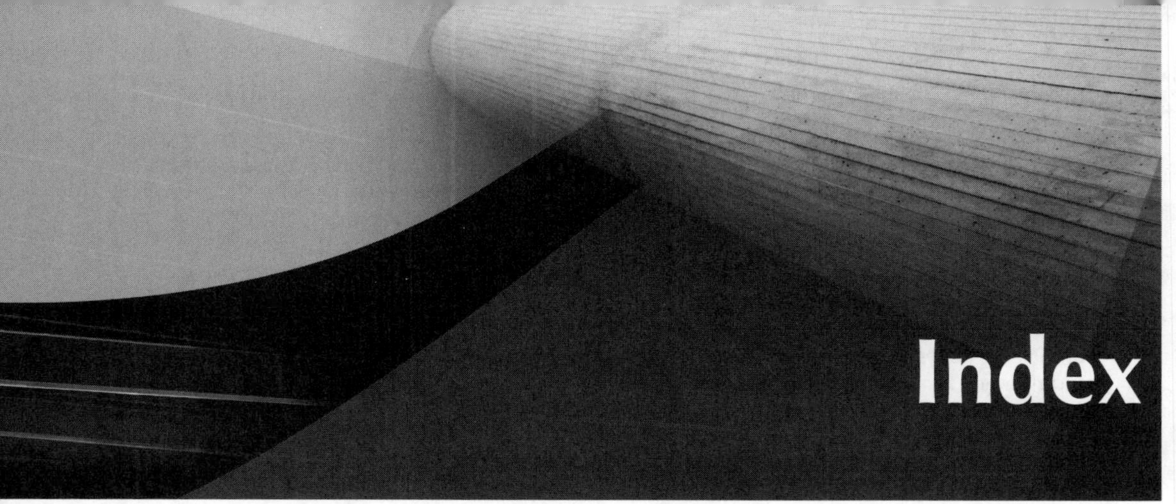

Symbols

A

B

C

D

E

F

G

H

I

J

K

L

N

O

Q

R

S

T

U

V

X

Z

Are You Oracle Certified?
Professional development and industry recognition are not the only benefits you gain from Oracle certifications. They also facilitate career growth, improve productivity, and enhance credibility. Hiring managers who want to distinguish among candidates for critical IT positions know that the Oracle Certification Program is one of the most highly valued benchmarks in the marketplace. Hundreds of thousands of Oracle certified technologists testify to the importance of this industry-recognized credential as the best way to get ahead—and stay there.
For details about the Oracle Certification Program, go to oracle.com/education/certification.
Oracle University — Learn technology from the source
ORACLE
UNIVERSITY

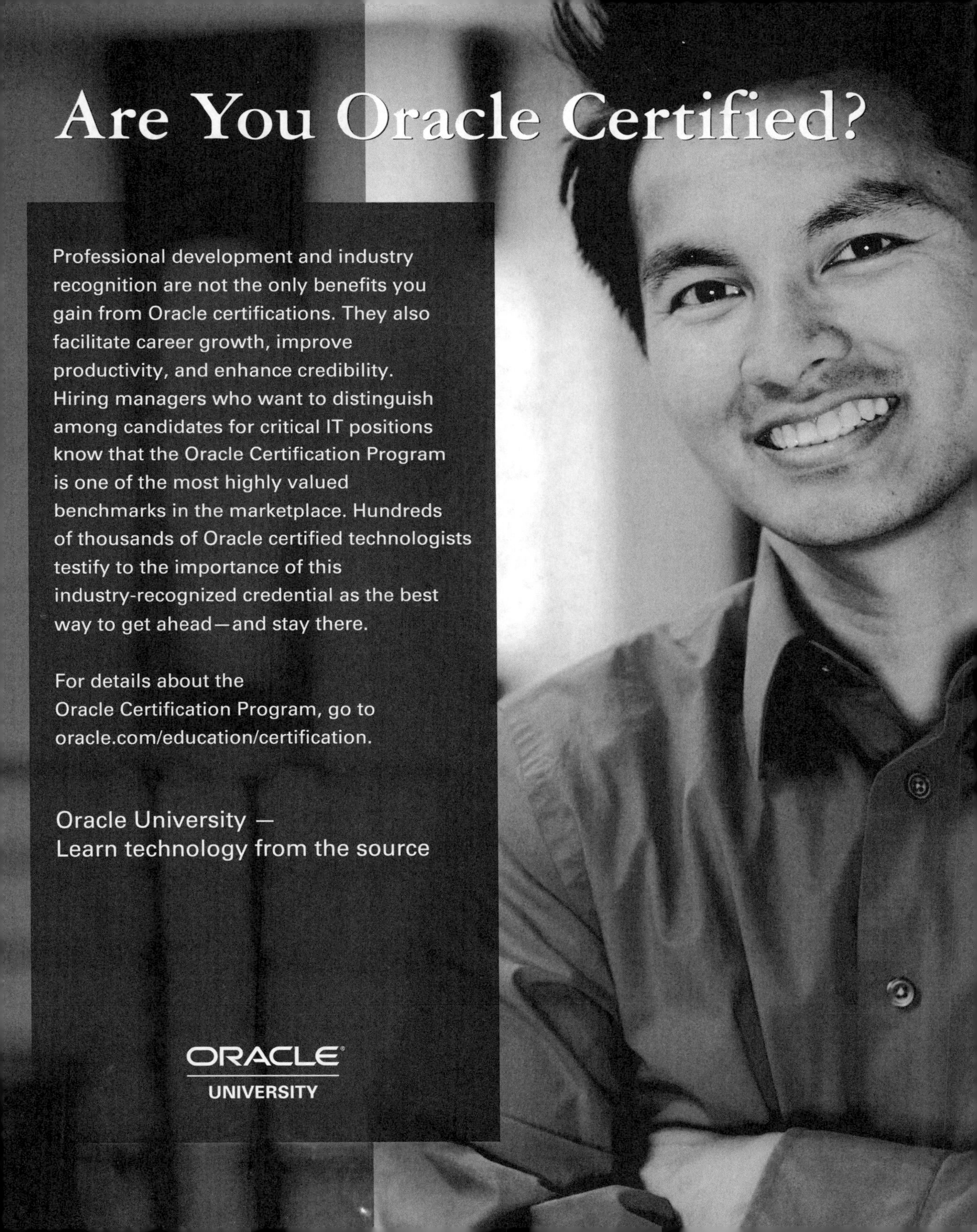

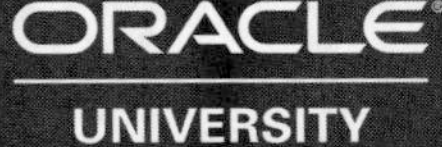

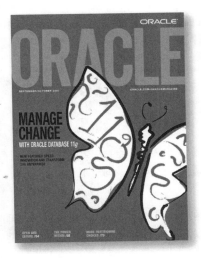

...nt your own FREE subscription?

...ve a free subscription to *Oracle Magazine*, you must fill out the entire card, sign it, and date ...omplete cards cannot be processed or acknowledged). You can also fax your application to +1.847.763.9638. **Or subscribe at our Web site at oracle.com/oraclemagazine**

O **Yes, please send me a FREE subscription *Oracle Magazine*.** O No.

O From time to time, Oracle Publishing allows our partners exclusive access to our e-mail addresses for special promotions and announcements. To be included in this program, please check this circle. If you do not wish to be included, you will only receive notices about your subscription via e-mail.

O Oracle Publishing allows sharing of our postal mailing list with selected third parties. If you prefer your mailing address not to be included in this program, please check this circle.

If at any time you would like to be removed from either mailing list, please contact Customer Service at +1.847.763.9635 or send an e-mail to oracle@halldata.com. If you opt in to the sharing of information, Oracle may also provide you with e-mail related to Oracle products, services, and events. If you want to completely unsubscribe from any e-mail communication from Oracle, please send an e-mail to: unsubscribe@oracle-mail.com with the following in the subject line: REMOVE [your e-mail address]. For complete information on Oracle Publishing's privacy practices, please visit oracle.com/html/privacy/html

X

signature (required) date

name title

company e-mail address

street/p.o. box

city/state/zip or postal code telephone

country fax

Would you like to receive your free subscription in digital format instead of print if it becomes available? O Yes O No

YOU MUST ANSWER ALL 10 QUESTIONS BELOW.

① WHAT IS THE PRIMARY BUSINESS ACTIVITY OF YOUR FIRM AT THIS LOCATION? (check one only)

- □ 01 Aerospace and Defense Manufacturing
- □ 02 Application Service Provider
- □ 03 Automotive Manufacturing
- □ 04 Chemicals
- □ 05 Media and Entertainment
- □ 06 Construction/Engineering
- □ 07 Consumer Sector/Consumer Packaged Goods
- □ 08 Education
- □ 09 Financial Services/Insurance
- □ 10 Health Care
- □ 11 High Technology Manufacturing, OEM
- □ 12 Industrial Manufacturing
- □ 13 Independent Software Vendor
- □ 14 Life Sciences (biotech, pharmaceuticals)
- □ 15 Natural Resources
- □ 16 Oil and Gas
- □ 17 Professional Services
- □ 18 Public Sector (government)
- □ 19 Research
- □ 20 Retail/Wholesale/Distribution
- □ 21 Systems Integrator, VAR/VAD
- □ 22 Telecommunications
- □ 23 Travel and Transportation
- □ 24 Utilities (electric, gas, sanitation, water)
- □ 98 Other Business and Services ________

② WHICH OF THE FOLLOWING BEST DESCRIBES YOUR PRIMARY JOB FUNCTION? (check one only)

CORPORATE MANAGEMENT/STAFF

- □ 01 Executive Management (President, Chair, CEO, CFO, Owner, Partner, Principal)
- □ 02 Finance/Administrative Management (VP/Director/ Manager/Controller, Purchasing, Administration)
- □ 03 Sales/Marketing Management (VP/Director/Manager)
- □ 04 Computer Systems/Operations Management (CIO/VP/Director/Manager MIS/IS/IT, Ops)

IS/IT STAFF

- □ 05 Application Development/Programming Management
- □ 06 Application Development/Programming Staff
- □ 07 Consulting
- □ 08 DBA/Systems Administrator
- □ 09 Education/Training
- □ 10 Technical Support Director/Manager
- □ 11 Other Technical Management/Staff
- □ 98 Other

③ WHAT IS YOUR CURRENT PRIMARY OPERATING PLATFORM (check all that apply)

- □ 01 Digital Equipment Corp UNIX/VAX/VMS
- □ 02 HP UNIX
- □ 03 IBM AIX
- □ 04 IBM UNIX
- □ 05 Linux (Red Hat)
- □ 06 Linux (SUSE)
- □ 07 Linux (Oracle Enterprise)
- □ 08 Linux (other)
- □ 09 Macintosh
- □ 10 MVS
- □ 11 Netware
- □ 12 Network Computing
- □ 13 SCO UNIX
- □ 14 Sun Solaris/SunOS
- □ 15 Windows
- □ 16 Other UNIX
- □ 98 Other
- 99 □ None of the Above

④ DO YOU EVALUATE, SPECIFY, RECOMMEND, OR AUTHORIZE THE PURCHASE OF ANY OF THE FOLLOWING? (check all that apply)

- □ 01 Hardware
- □ 02 Business Applications (ERP, CRM, etc.)
- □ 03 Application Development Tools
- □ 04 Database Products
- □ 05 Internet or Intranet Products
- □ 06 Other Software
- □ 07 Middleware Products
- 99 □ None of the Above

⑤ IN YOUR JOB, DO YOU USE OR PLAN TO PURCHASE ANY OF THE FOLLOWING PRODUCTS? (check all that apply)

SOFTWARE

- □ 01 CAD/CAE/CAM
- □ 02 Collaboration Software
- □ 03 Communications
- □ 04 Database Management
- □ 05 File Management
- □ 06 Finance
- □ 07 Java
- □ 08 Multimedia Authoring
- □ 09 Networking
- □ 10 Programming
- □ 11 Project Management
- □ 12 Scientific and Engineering
- □ 13 Systems Management
- □ 14 Workflow

HARDWARE

- □ 15 Macintosh
- □ 16 Mainframe
- □ 17 Massively Parallel Processing
- □ 18 Minicomputer
- □ 19 Intel x86(32)
- □ 20 Intel x86(64)
- □ 21 Network Computer
- □ 22 Symmetric Multiprocessing
- □ 23 Workstation Services

SERVICES

- □ 24 Consulting
- □ 25 Education/Training
- □ 26 Maintenance
- □ 27 Online Database
- □ 28 Support
- □ 29 Technology-Based Training
- □ 30 Other
- 99 □ None of the Above

⑥ WHAT IS YOUR COMPANY'S SIZE? (check one only)

- □ 01 More than 25,000 Employees
- □ 02 10,001 to 25,000 Employees
- □ 03 5,001 to 10,000 Employees
- □ 04 1,001 to 5,000 Employees
- □ 05 101 to 1,000 Employees
- □ 06 Fewer than 100 Employees

⑦ DURING THE NEXT 12 MONTHS, HOW MUCH DO YOU ANTICIPATE YOUR ORGANIZATION WILL SPEND ON COMPUTER HARDWARE, SOFTWARE, PERIPHERALS, AND SERVICES FOR YOUR LOCATION? (check one only)

- □ 01 Less than $10,000
- □ 02 $10,000 to $49,999
- □ 03 $50,000 to $99,999
- □ 04 $100,000 to $499,999
- □ 05 $500,000 to $999,999
- □ 06 $1,000,000 and Over

⑧ WHAT IS YOUR COMPANY'S YEARLY SALES REVENUE? (check one only)

- □ 01 $500, 000, 000 and above
- □ 02 $100, 000, 000 to $500, 000, 000
- □ 03 $50, 000, 000 to $100, 000, 000
- □ 04 $5, 000, 000 to $50, 000, 000
- □ 05 $1, 000, 000 to $5, 000, 000

⑨ WHAT LANGUAGES AND FRAMEWORKS DO YOU USE? (check all that apply)

- □ 01 Ajax
- □ 02 C
- □ 03 C++
- □ 04 C#
- □ 05 Hibernate
- □ 06 J++/J#
- □ 07 Java
- □ 08 JSP
- □ 09 .NET
- □ 10 Perl
- □ 11 PHP
- □ 12 PL/SQL
- □ 13 Python
- □ 14 Ruby/Rails
- □ 15 Spring
- □ 16 Struts
- □ 17 SQL
- □ 18 Visual Basic
- □ 98 Other

⑩ WHAT ORACLE PRODUCTS ARE IN USE AT YOUR SITE? (check all that apply)

ORACLE DATABASE

- □ 01 Oracle Database 11*g*
- □ 02 Oracle Database 10*g*
- □ 03 Oracle9*i* Database
- □ 04 Oracle Embedded Database (Oracle Lite, Times Ten, Berkeley DB)
- □ 05 Other Oracle Database Release

ORACLE FUSION MIDDLEWARE

- □ 06 Oracle Application Server
- □ 07 Oracle Portal
- □ 08 Oracle Enterprise Manager
- □ 09 Oracle BPEL Process Manager
- □ 10 Oracle Identity Management
- □ 11 Oracle SOA Suite
- □ 12 Oracle Data Hubs

ORACLE DEVELOPMENT TOOLS

- □ 13 Oracle JDeveloper
- □ 14 Oracle Forms
- □ 15 Oracle Reports
- □ 16 Oracle Designer
- □ 17 Oracle Discoverer
- □ 18 Oracle BI Beans
- □ 19 Oracle Warehouse Builder
- □ 20 Oracle WebCenter
- □ 21 Oracle Application Express

ORACLE APPLICATIONS

- □ 22 Oracle E-Business Suite
- □ 23 PeopleSoft Enterprise
- □ 24 JD Edwards EnterpriseOne
- □ 25 JD Edwards World
- □ 26 Oracle Fusion
- □ 27 Hyperion
- □ 28 Siebel CRM

ORACLE SERVICES

- □ 28 Oracle E-Business Suite On Demand
- □ 29 Oracle Technology On Demand
- □ 30 Siebel CRM On Demand
- □ 31 Oracle Consulting
- □ 32 Oracle Education
- □ 33 Oracle Support
- □ 98 Other
- 99 □ None of the Above